1 MONTH OF
FREE
READING

at
www.ForgottenBooks.com

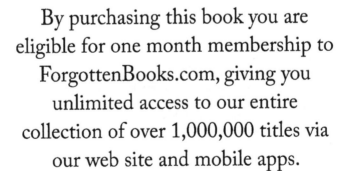

By purchasing this book you are eligible for one month membership to ForgottenBooks.com, giving you unlimited access to our entire collection of over 1,000,000 titles via our web site and mobile apps.

To claim your free month visit: www.forgottenbooks.com/free939767

ISBN 978-0-260-29587-3
PIBN 10939767

ENGLISH REVIEW.

VOL. XIII.

DECEMBER—JUNE.

LONDON:

FRANCIS & JOHN RIVINGTON,

ST. PAUL'S CHURCH YARD, & WATERLOO PLACE.

1850.

LONDON:

GILBERT & RIVINGTON, PRINTERS,

ST. JOHN'S SQUARE.

INDEX

OF

BOOKS REVIEWED.

. For remarkable Passages in the Criticisms, Extracts, Notices, and Intelligence, see the Index at the end of the Volume.

a

THE

ENGLISH REVIEW.

MARCH, 1850.

Art. I.—*Cabramatta and Woodleigh Farm. By Mrs.* VIDAL.
London: Rivingtons. 1850.

WE have our schools, our books, our various weapons of influence
for the high and low, for the rich and poor. Church literature,
whether sermons, biographies, tales, allegories, lie on the
polished surface of rosewood tables in drawing-rooms small and
great. Tracts, tales, allegories, also lie on the round deal table
or the deal shelf of poor men's homes. The matter of this
literature is suited to the class among which it finds its way.
We have books full of cottage life, or full of drawing-room life;
we describe cottagers and their habits, their mode of life, their
ways of speech, or homely expressions; we describe the manners
of the higher orders with like care, and in more delicate lines
paint their features, describe their defects, temptations, duties,
habits, character of mind. There are the " Margaret Percevals"
for the one, the " Susan Carters" for the other; the literary
ware is adapted to its market, and the literary manufactory
sends forth from the printer's loom cotton for the one class, satin
and velvet for the other. We are wisely issuing our literary bales
for these two classes in increasing numbers, and we may also hope
that we are sending forth better and heartier stuff.

So also is it with our schools; we have an abundant, an increasing supply of schools for the higher orders. From Eton to
Marlborough there is a sliding scale of expense, so that the
various grades of the higher orders may find something suited to
their means, while a warmer and more religious spirit begins to
leaven the system of education, such a school as Radley having
been expressly formed to give a more religious and churchlike
character to school life. We have, also, not an abundant, but a
fast increasing supply of schools for the poor; national schools,
containing from five hundred to fifty scholars, are dotted over the
land, and at a penny a week good education is supplied to the poor,
the clergy devoting themselves with increasing energy to the formation of the religious character of the children they teach.

And what we have said of literature or schools may be said of
all other ways or modes of acting on the minds of the rich or of
the poor; much has been done, more is doing, and much more is
about to be done by the Church for the spiritual elevation of both
these classes.

But one class has almost escaped all notice; we have walked

amid the cedars of the mountains; we have laboured in the flats
and levels at the bottom of the hills; but the half-way district, the
middle region of men, the middling classes, have but slightly at--
tracted the Church's toils.   We have left this important class
alone; we have let it increase amongst us without grappling with
it in any deep or searching way; its internal life is almost as
unknown as Central Africa; its internal codes, its principles, its
habits, its modes of thought, its temptations, its amusements, all
lie like an unexplored desert or a frozen sea.   The whole class of
tradesmen and shopkeepers with their maxims, their convention-
alities, their usages have been well-nigh untouched.   We look in
at the shop windows; we traffick across the counter; we receive,
as purchasers, studied civility; we look at the respectful outsides
of men; we hold mercantile converse; but here all communication ends: it is a mere buying or selling intercourse, a cold, stiff,
business-like interchange of words; our talk is of ribbons, or
grocery, or furniture, or plate, as it may be; it is mere shopping.
But what foot has got past all those bales of goods, those long
counters with busy customers on one side, and pale shopmen or
shopwomen on the other? What foot has pressed in to the shop
"parlour," or to the apprentices' room, or learnt the private life
of the principal, or the private manners of the apprentices?   Who
knows any thing, for instance, of the goings on, the recreations,
the leisure hours of the young men in the large drapers' shops
who are measuring tapes, or silks, or calico all the day?   The
clergy, if the truth be told, have but little knowledge on this
matter: and as they have little knowledge, they have little weight:
they feel their tradesmen to be difficult parishioners to deal with
or to know; and not unnaturally, though wrongly, they have
somewhat shrunk from diving deeper into the character of this
class, or from throwing themselves into their ways and working
themselves into any thing like real communion.   They pass into
drawing-rooms; they mix with the higher orders, because they
have come from them, and this is their natural position: it is true
that they are now acting upon the higher orders in a more ministerial way, and are obtaining a wholesome influence of a higher
kind; but their position by birth helps them in this matter; there
are many sympathies between them and the higher orders.   They
also find no difficulty in a free thorough intercourse with the poor
they lift up the latch of the cottage or of the houses in the bac
streets, and take their seat by the fireside, and are received w'
friendly courtesy; the intercourse on both sides is open, genu'
and unreserved, without artificial stiffness.   But with the tra
men it is different.   An occasional formal call, an occasi
admission into the parlour, in which hang the portraits of

tradesman and his wife, an occasional occupation of the bright mahogany arm-chair with its horse-hair bottom, is as much as many clergy can boast of; while the conversation is on both sides stiff, conventional, icy, and restrained. Neither party really knows each other; neither party talks freely; neither party thaws; and the visit ends with little fruit on either side.

We do not mean to say that the ice is not thick, and that it is not a difficult matter to thrust the wedge into the thick-grained material of that peculiar class, which, as it hangs between the high and low, just risen above the low and aspiring towards the high, wants the natural courtesy or freedom of the one, and the more easy and conscious refinement of the other; it is a class somewhat touchy, sensitive, afraid of not "doing the proper thing," oppressed with artificialities, afraid of losing dignity, profoundly versed in mysterious and peculiar laws of etiquette, the occupants of a middle territory which they tremblingly hold, ever fearful of aggression on either side, neither at the top of the ladder nor the bottom, suspended between earth and air, dreading to be pulled down by those beneath them or trodden down by those above them, the half-castes of our social system, too keenly alive to castes and grades, and ever suspicious of inroads on their position. But still, while many circumstances serve to make them a class difficult of access, hard intimately or closely to approach, yet enough has not been done to gain admittance among them, or to influence them for their good. With all these freezing points among them, there is heart and feeling, and many excellent traits and tendencies to be found beneath that crust of mannerism; there are sympathies that may be stirred, spiritual longings to be satisfied, when once the apparel, the artificial coating of the inner man of the heart can be unstarched. And it is now time to be stirring in this cause: past neglects must be remedied; the Church must no longer withhold herself from the tradesman class; we must not content ourselves with gazing at shop fronts; we must not creep round by the edges of the desert; but must plunge boldly into the interior life. We have lost time; we have lost ground already; large parts of London, of Manchester, of our commercial and manufacturing districts, have slipped out of our hands, and must be regained. We owe it to them to go among them, if our Church is to be the Church of all; and we may be sure that whatever class we may have neglected, therein we shall find the sharpest and strongest weapons that are formed against us.

Not only have the clergy failed as Pastors to obtain any real footing among those we speak of, of a decided kind, but other means of influence have been little used. Take our literature—

has this been adapted to the middling classes? Has it described
a tradesman's life? Has there been any thing between our
" Susan Carters" and our " Margaret Percevals," any midway
works bearing directly on the peculiar state of life of these classes,
showing intimate acquaintance with their peculiar features? Of
course there are many books which are of a general character,
which are not for this class or that, and which suit all alike. But
with the various modes of thought, tone, tendencies, pursuits,
influences, prejudices at work in each separate class, we want a
certain degree of what may be called class writing; and, as a
matter of fact, we *have* written for different classes, though we
have excepted this particular class. Of course we are speaking
generally throughout; there are some books for this class; there
are some clergy who have found their way into their interior life.

And yet we see the leisure of the whole trading masses begins
to be increased; the " Early Closing" movement is an important
one, which the Church must not forget or overlook; the whole
life is not given up to ribbons, and grocery, and soap; the streets
in the evening no longer glitter with the light of busy shops, a
glitter that was dearly bought, and that helped to burn out the
minds and bodies of the shopmen so ceaselessly employed.
Whether the time gained will be really gained rests much with
the Church: more time is not of itself a gain; it is a space that
may be filled with poisonous weeds or fair flowers; it may give
occasion to wildness and hurtful festivities, or to mental improvement sanctified by a religious spirit. Never was good literature
more wanted than among these freed apprentices and their masters;
there is a taste for literature rising up among them; but it is
not churchlike or even religious; as yet Chambers' books strew
" the parlour" table and reign supreme.

Again, what influence has the Church had in the schooling of
these classes? Clearly none: the " Commercial Schools" have
not been in Church hands; dissenting teachers, whose so-called
ministry makes no attempt to usurp hard work or pastoral duties,
often consume their days and eke out their incomes by taking
charge of tradesmen's children, whether in day schools or boarding-
schools. We have let these youths be trained up without any
efforts to mould them rightly, to gain a wholesome influence over
them in the earlier and more impressible stages of their life; we
have simply let them alone; their whole system of education ha
sprung from themselves; there has been no guiding hand, a
the " Dotheboys Halls," mere trading mercenary establishmer
have been the melancholy receptacles of youths, who
nothing high-minded, or generous, or self-devoted, or enthusia
in their guides or teachers. Where we have failed to direct

first runnings of the stream, we are not likely to make up afterwards for that neglect, and to obtain the rule of the full-grown tide ; if we have not a place in the sundry "academies" that stud the land, it is no wonder that we have not weight in the after scenes of middle-class life.

And what has been the result of all this backwardness in grappling with the middling classes? As might have been expected, no where has the Church such faint or feeble hold. We have the poor ; we have the rich ; but in the middle ground we have but little part. Here, consequently, lies the real strength of dissent : here it lives and thrives ; here are its best and most zealous sons ; serious tradesmen, in most cases, will be found to have joined the ranks of dissent. In some towns, or in some districts of towns, this may be true in a greater or less degree ; but, take England as a whole, there is less spirit and loyalty to the Church among the middling classes than in any other. From them the leading dissenting teachers spring ; by them are sustained the vast missions of the Wesleyan and other religious sects ; here is a large mass of wealth, here a large and increasing class, increasing in numbers, increasing in means, with ready money at their command, and few of the "calls" which belong to those who are owners of land, and who occupy a higher position. The vitals of dissent lie here—the churchmanship that is among them is cold, shallow, formal, getting little beyond an idea of the respectability of the Church ; better circumstances often bring tradesmen into the Church, simply because the rank to which they aspire is in it. All popular agitations against the Church rise from this class and mainly end with them ; they have been coldly cared for, and they return the coldness. We were eye-witnesses of the riots at Exeter some years since, and were struck by observing that the crowd, one rainy Sunday, all had umbrellas, a luxury not possessed by a mere mob, and an evidence of the component parts of that mob. Throughout that movement the poor could not be roused by the agitators ; it was a middle-class agitation ; we ourselves had sown to the wind, we reaped the whirlwind : we had done little for this class, and therefore they rebelled when Church authority was brought to bear upon them ; we had not won them, and therefore they were in no mood for a command. Go where we will, we find, on the whole, the same state of things —the Church does not really act upon the shop population, or at best acts in a languid way.

There are indeed signs of a change, some cheering symptoms of care towards this neglected class ; and the Church seems to be beginning at the beginning, that is, middle-class schools are rising up ; warm, earnest spirits are throwing themselves into this school movement, and we hail with deep joy the foundation of such true educational institutions as those at Harrow Weald and near Shoreham. Those who are there trained up with a warm and holy discipline, must be looked upon as a sort of missionaries, who will carry into their own homes the influences of the Church, and will draw towards us many hearts which are now estranged, and which only look on the outside of the Church in its character as an " Establishment." Through the young we shall spread heat and warmth into those of older age who coldly gaze at us from without, or profess but a cold and formal membership. It is impossible to over-rate the importance of such schools, and we must earnestly pray for an increased number of suchlike holy nurseries.

In literature our movements have been slower; and yet it will not do to let this sloth continue; in an intellectual age, the Church must send forth writers who shall study and meet the wants of *every* class. Every where must our books be pressed, adapted to every phase of our social system. We must have our popular literature leavened throughout with right principles, yet not thrusting them forward on every page; we must have a more direct and deeper teaching for those who begin to think more deeply. We must hasten to occupy the field over which Chambers has sent forth his armies of pale-faced, bloodless, and in this sense, symbolic books; we must have our opposing hosts of heartier works, and if there be leisure for reading among those large masses of apprentices, who now escape at an early hour from the close atmosphere and the monotonous occupations of their shop, that leisure needs to be seized upon, or else it will be given either to profitless, if not vicious literature, or to all manner of sensual excitements, to give some glitter to the fringe of a dull, wearisome, fagging day. It is an important work to direct the leisure of this younger portion of the middling classes into profitable or harmless channels. Many are at hand to ply them with wrong stimulants, to catch them as they hurry from the counter, to enlist them in wrong causes. There are fiery politicians waiting to set them on fire, to make them dissatisfied with their lot, to turn them against the higher classes, and to whisper dangerous and unsettling notions into their ears; while opportunities of speechifying are not wanting, and they begin to fancy themselves orators destined to work great changes in our social system. perhaps music becomes a snare, and tavern glee-clubs catch promising voice, and lead to the desecration of a gift which have exercised a purifying and elevating influence. In many and various are the snares which wait the enfranchised apprentices, as the shutters screen the scene of their labour the passers by; and it becomes the Church to decide w be done with that leisure which has been now achieved, and to supply good pursuits or guileless relaxations for those whose evenings are on their hands. At Leeds and at Exeter Christianized Mechanics' Institutes have been at work, and we trust with some success; at Exeter, a Church Music School has been the means of gathering many of the citizens together during winter nights, and we have there seen gentry, clergy, shopkeepers, bankers' clerks, a mixed company, really united by the associative principle which music undoubtedly contains. What more can be done to employ the leisure hours of those classes is a subject well worthy of anxious thought. We will content ourselves with recommending the establishment of *cheap* circulating libraries, in which a certain proportion of books, say a fourth or a fifth, shall bear a religious character.

In these remarks we have confined ourselves to town populations; we have not spoken of farmers, though this portion of the middling class deserves increased care and thought. That they have not been strongly acted upon by the Church is plain enough; that their education has been defective is proved at every confirmation; and the clergy, we suspect, have found them as a whole somewhat hard both intellectually and morally. The blame of this hardness does not entirely rest with themselves; the formation of their characters has been left to chance; no educational system has been at work on their behalf; and between the busier portions of the year their children have picked up where they could, in schools infinitely below the national schools, little learning, unleavened by any true religious principles. The fact of living in the country, where the influence of the Church is great, and where they are more constantly thrown with the clergy, has kept up an attachment to the Church which might now be ripened into a warmer feeling if the time is seized. But we must not disguise from ourselves that *time* is valuable; "coming events cast their shadows before;"—the jog-trot mode of farming is at an end; the farming schoolmaster is abroad; we are about to have the intellects of farmers sharpened by sheer necessity, and their wits brightened up; the new generation will be a different race from the old,—a race of keener, sharper men, who will not content themselves with stepping into their father's shoes, but will be shod more lightly; they will have to work harder and think more; the farming energy is roused, and there will be no dozing and dawdling over the work. It is well for us to see this and to meet it; the Church must look out and prepare herself for the change. She must provide good schools; she must win the mind of the agriculturists; the clergy must know the habits of the farmers, and we must have books adapted to their peculiar wants and needs.

And are we to forget the colonies? Here is a vast field for
which work must be done at home, Few of the higher orders go
out; the poor, and men of the middling classes with some little
capital, make up the main body of emigrants. And are we not
wanting a Colonial Literature? Should we not have our staff of
writers busily engaged in adapting their writings to colonial ways,
and endeavouring to raise colonial principles? Much must be
done for the colonies at home; much must be done for the middling classes, who there give the key to the morals of those
daughter lands; we should be able to put into the hands of the
colonial clergy large gifts of books, written by those who could
write with experience of Canadian and Australian life. The clergy
there are too busy to publish much, and their means suffer them
not to publish to any great extent. Their press must be here.
Of course this is only one way of influence, but it is an important
one.

Very vast is the work before the Church, even among one class,
the class among whom she has laboured least. The whole class
of tradesmen, small manufacturers, lesser merchants, with their
clerks, apprentices, shopmen, the farming class, the better class of
emigrants, all these claim earnest care and holy love. Much rests
upon the character which is given to this increasing body in the
next few years; it is a strong body, growing in intelligence, and
growing in weight. No thoughtful mind can contemplate their
progress without awe, even though the awe may be mixed with
hope. Our commercial and manufacturing towns, those busy hives
of English industry, hold within them strangely powerful elements
for good or evil; and if the good is to predominate, there needs
energy, earnestness, devotion, zeal, on the part of the Church,
greater than words can paint, and such as we must pray God to
give us. The next few years will be busy and momentous years indeed; the work of centuries seems to be crowded and concentrated
into a narrow space; life altogether seems more full of life; we
squeeze years into months; a high-pressure engine drives us on;
all brains are at work; schemes, projects, enterprises, questions,
are born and matured at once; every thing hurries on; we think
like lightning; as we see the river dashing, rushing on, we are
dizzy at the swiftness; we hardly dare think what is coming to
pass, or to what pitch of civilized maturity we are striding on.
Enough for us to know, as we thus look forward into the mist of
future time, that we must be on our watch-towers and pray; we
must be in our secret chambers as in our houses of prayer, ever
praying in these momentous times; we must also throw ourselves
among the poor; we must mix with the trading classes; we must
move amid the higher ranks; we must try to purify, to elevate, to
leaven with holy leaven every class, that great, mighty, majesti

England,—a nation of princes, the market of the world, the ruler of many lands,—may bow at the foot of the Cross, and hold fast the faith.

Having thus briefly freed our minds on a subject which only increases in interest the more it is considered, we must not lay down our pen without pausing for a moment to notice the works of one writer whose powers seem peculiarly adapted to deal with the middle and lower classes, and who, we hope, will devote her abilities to their cause; we allude to Mrs. Vidal, whose "Tales of the Bush" have been deservedly popular, and who has just issued another volume of much power and goodness; we allude to "Cabramatta and Woodleigh Farm." Here we have vivid, graphic descriptions of colonial life and colonial principles; while the volume closes with a longer tale adapted to an English farmer's household, and detailing the sins and troubles rising up in an ill-regulated nobleman's establishment. A strong religious tone is diffused through this and all Mrs. Vidal's works; while by seizing hold of the minute circumstances of daily life she gives finish and reality to the p cture she draws. We recommend her last volume with great confidence to our readers, and hope that her pen will be devoted to those classes whom she so thoroughly understands. We number her among those useful writers who do not carry us into the upper regions of life, but are bent on giving a higher tone and higher principles to those who are beneath her. With much heartiness we wish her success, and trust that her labours may bear goodly fruit.

Art. II.—1. *History and Present State of the Education Question; being a collection of Documents explanatory of the proceedings of the Committee of Privy Council on Education, from its
first appointment, in 1839, to the present time, and of the steps
taken for the defence of Church Education against the encroachments of the said Committee.* Printed for the Metropolitan
Church Union. London: Rivingtons. 1850.

2. *Report of the Sub-Committee on Education.* Adopted by the
General Committee of the London Union on Church Matters,
August 6, 1849.

3. *The Privy Council and the National Society. The question
concerning the Management of Church of England Schools stated
and examined.* By HENRY PARR HAMILTON, *M.A., F.R.S.,
late Fellow of Trinity College, Cambridge; Rector of Watt, and
Rural Dean.* London: J. W. Parker. 1850.

4. *A Bill to promote the Secular Education of the People in Eng-
land and Wales.* Proposed and brought in by Mr. William
Johnson Fox, Mr. Henry, and Mr. Osborne. Ordered by the
House of Commons to be printed, February 26, 1850.

5. *The Social Condition and the Education of the People in England and Europe; showing the results of the Primary Schools,
and of the Division of Landed Property, in Foreign Countries.*
By JOSEPH KAY, *M.A., of Trinity College, Cambridge, Barrister-
at-Law, and late Travelling Bachelor of the University of
Cambridge.* 2 vols. London: Longmans. 1850.

THE list of publications at the head of this article affords sufficient
proof that the Education question is not gone to sleep; and in
keeping our readers informed of its progress, we are happy to
have it in our power to announce to them the fact, that it is about
to be brought to the issue to which we ventured to predict a twelvemonth ago that it must ere long come, to wit, a consideration by
Parliament of the whole of the facts connected with the administration of the annual Education Grant by the Committee of Council
on Education. The chain of circumstances which has led to this
result, is detailed in the pamphlet (No. 1) published by the Me
tropolitan Church Union. Among its contents we recognize wit
pleasure our own two articles on the subject in the numbers o
March and September last—the former recapitulating the histor

of the struggle between the Church and the advocates of secular education down to the beginning of last session—the latter disclosing the pernicious scheme for an extensive education of the poorer classes under the exclusive control of the Committee of Council, of which the Kneller Hall establishment is the type and the centre. As a sequel to the history of the whole question, and in particular of the proceedings of the Committee of Council, sketched out in the former of these two articles, the pamphlet before us contains the close of the correspondence between the Committee of Council on Education, and the Committee of the National Society, commencing with the letter addressed by Mr. Kay Shuttleworth, in August, 1848, to the Archbishop of Canterbury, and concluding with the ultimatum of the Committee of Council of August, 1849, and the counter-ultimatum of the Committee of the National Society of December of the same year,—the sum of which is, that the National Society declines to recommend the management clauses, on the specific ground that the adoption of them is made compulsory on the part of the Committee of Council, and that the constraint thereby placed upon the founders of Church schools is at variance with the general principle of local freedom, which is one of the fundamental principles recognized from the very first by the National Society.

The latter part of this correspondence was conducted, on the part of the Committee of the National Society, under the influence of the strong Church feeling manifested at the Society's Annual Meeting, on the 6th of June of last year, a concise record of which, together with an account of the formation of the Education Committee of June the seventh, and of its proceedings up to the date of the great meeting at Willis's Rooms last month, is among the valuable collection of documents published by the Metropolitan Church Union. The Annual Meeting terminated, as our readers will remember, in the all but unanimous adoption of the resolution proposed by way of amendment by Archdeacon Manning, with the modification suggested by Mr. Denison. The resolution, in the form in which it was finally carried, was to the following effect:—

" That this meeting acknowledges the care and attention of the Committee in conducting the correspondence still pending with the Committee of Privy Council on Education, and regrets to find that a satisfactory conclusion has not yet been attained.

" Secondly, That while this meeting desires fully to co-operate with the State in promoting the education of the people, it is under the necessity of declaring, that no terms of co-operation can be satisfactory which shall not allow to the clergy and laity full freedom to constitute schools upon such principles and models as are both sanctioned and commended by the order and the practice of the Church of England; and, in particular, where they shall so desire it, to put the management of their schools solely in the clergyman of their parish and the bishop of the diocese."—*History and Present State of the Education Question,* p. 71.

A wish having been expressed at the close of the meeting that an adjourned general meeting of the Society should be held in November, by which time an answer from the Committee of Council to the communication about to be addressed to it by the Committee of the National Society, founded upon the resolution of the meeting, might be expected, it was ascertained that under the Charter of the Society there is no power to hold more than one general meeting annually, and that in the month of May or June. The members of the Society at large, finding themselves thus precluded from the possibility of consulting together on the important question then pending till after the lapse of a twelvemonth, arrangements were made on the following day, to remedy the inconvenience arising out of the limitation in the Society's Charter, by the appointment of a Committee which should watch the progress of the question, and should, in the event of any emergency arising, convene a public meeting of the friends of Church Education, or, in other words, though not formally, yet virtually, a meeting of the National Society. The Committee so appointed, to which a large addition of members was subsequently made, remained in a state of quiescence until after the publication of the ultimatum of the Committee of Council on Education, when it addressed to the Committee of the National Society a letter of inquiry which constitutes one of the most important documents in the whole case, and which will be found at p. 73 of the pamphlet of the Metropolitan Church Union. Being the first official intimation which the Committee of the National Society had of the existence of the Committee of June the seventh, the inquiries were very properly introduced by a paragraph which expressly disclaims all improper interference with the functions of the Committee of the National Society, and justifies the fact of its having been constituted, by the extraordinary emergency which had arisen. As it is important that the relative position of these two bodies should be clearly understood, we insert the passage in question from the letter of the Committee of June the seventh :—

"To obviate all misconceptions concerning the character and designs of the Committee in the name of which I write, let me premise that it recognizes the National Society as the accredited organ of the Church of England in the important matter of education; it gratefully acknowledges the long and valuable services of that Society; it regards its

President and Committee with feelings of unfeigned respect and attachment ; and it earnestly desires to maintain and advance, to the best of
its ability, the welfare and efficiency of ' The Incorporated National
Society for Promoting the Education of the Poor in the Principles of
the Established Church.'

" I am authorized to add, that under no *ordinary* circumstances
would the above Committee have been formed. But it is the deliberate
conviction of a very large and respectable portion of the National
Society, and of the National Church, that as far as regards education,
these are *no common times.*   The present is an unprecedented juncture,
—a very critical emergency."—*History and Present State of the Education Question,* pp. 73, 74.

To this expression of the feelings of a large body of the
Society's members, represented by the Committee of June the
seventh, the Committee of the National Society responded in the
following terms, in a letter addressed by the latter to Dr. Spry, the
chairman of the former Committee, in February last :

" The Committee are fully sensible of the zeal and energy displayed
in the cause of religious education by those gentlemen in whose name
you have addressed them, and will be at all times ready to co-operate
in carrying out any well-considered plan for extending its benefits,
with a strict adherence to the principles of the Church."

Such being the relative position of these two Committees, we
cannot but congratulate the Church on the happy expedient by
which the serious difficulty created by the National Society's
Charter has been avoided, and the Committee of the National
Society has been placed in a position to ascertain, in a manner
even more satisfactory in some respects than might possibly be
the case at formal general meetings of the members, the sense of
its constituents upon the great question in controversy between
the Church and the State.   The light in which that question is
viewed by those whom the Committee of June the seventh
represents, may be collected from the following passage of the
letter already referred to :—

" The Committee of Council on Education, a body of recent origin,
and consisting only of very few members, subject to political vicissitudes, professing in its corporate character no definite creed, but encouraging and endowing various and discordant religious opinions, con-
certing its measures privately, executing them silently and secretly, and
thus morally disqualified by its constitution and acts from exercising
any influence over the education of the people, yet, not satisfied with
the fiscal and distributive duties for which it was originally instituted,
is rapidly assuming the attitude, and engrossing the functions, of a
Legislative Board of Public Instruction, and, in a manner dangerous

alike to the Constitution and religion, is invading the rights, and usurping the office, both of Parliament and of the Church.

"The measures recently adopted, and now in course of execution, by the Committee of Council, appear to those in whose name I speak to demand an immediate and general effort of temperate but uncompromising resistance, on the part of the Clergy and Laity of the Church. We cannot refrain from expressing our persuasion, that, *unless* these measures of the Committee of Council are encountered and restrained, they will establish a latitudinarian system of popular instruction, similar to that of France and Germany, which has been recently eulogized by the Committee of Council as '*most closely suited to the wants and abilities of a large nation.*' (Minutes for 1848, p. 547.) *That* system has already produced in *those* countries the unhappy fruits of socialism in politics, and of scepticism in religion; and *if* the endeavours of the Committee of Council to propagate it in *England* are *not* counteracted, we believe that it will reduce *this* country to the condition of anarchy, confusion, and distress, in which those countries are plunged. It will also entail the forfeiture of the national blessings derived from the system of education administered by the Church of England, which, under Divine Providence, has long been the main source of the temporal and spiritual tranquillity and happiness of this kingdom."—*History and Present State of the Education Question*, p. 74.

The inquiries addressed by the Committee of June the seventh to the Committee of the National Society are four in number. The first of them relates to the Management Clauses, and is to the following effect :—

"Whether the Committee of the National Society will now continue to recommend the Management Clauses?—and whether, or no, it intends to join the Committee of Council in maintaining them, as now finally propounded and imposed by their Lordships on Church schools?"—*History and Present State of the Education Question*, p. 76.

The second inquiry has reference to the establishment of the Normal School at Kneller Hall. After setting forth the character of that institution, and its close resemblance to the plan reprobated by Parliament and the country in 1839, the transfer of the education of the pauper children of the country from the care of the Church, to the control of "a purely secular board, professing, in its official capacity, no definite form of religious belief," is pointed out as an infringement of the Society's charter :—

"The education of the children of the poor, and especially of the poorest classes, is, it may reasonably be supposed, an object of earnest solicitude to the National Society, and it was committed to its charge by the Crown, which, 'by and with the advice of the Privy Council' (Charter, p. 7), incorporated the Society in the year 1817, by royal

charter, in which it is recited, as a ground of incorporation (p. 7), that
the 'said society has been instituted principally for the purpose of
educating the *children of the poor* in the doctrine and discipline of the
Established Church, according to the Liturgy and Catechism.' Hence
it appears that the education of pauper children is entrusted to the
Society by the *Crown :* and the National Society, as the organ of the
Church, has still higher rights and graver responsibilities in *that* character."—*History and Present State of the Education Question*, p. 77.

This is followed by the inquiry—

"Whether the Committee of the National Society has been consulted
by the Committee of Council in framing the scheme for the establishment of Kneller Hall; whether its concurrence and co-operation in
that undertaking has been sought for; and, whether any steps have
been taken by the Committee of the National Society to remind the
Committee of Council of the authority with which the Society was invested, and of the purposes for which it was incorporated, with the
advice of the Privy Council, by the Crown ; and to call to its recollection the strong remonstrances and protests contained in the resolutions
moved by its late President, his Grace the Archbishop of Canterbury,
and ratified in a most striking manner by a vote of the House of
Lords ?"—*History and Present State of the Education Question*, pp.
77, 78.

The third inquiry relates to the inspection of Church schools,
and seeks to enlist the co-operation of the Committee of the
National Society, in substituting a uniform system of diocesan
inspection for the inspection of the Committee of Council; it
runs thus :—

"Whether the Committee of the National Society is disposed to
approve and promote an application to Parliament for a share of the
educational grant, to be applied to the uniform establishment and
efficient maintenance of diocesan inspection?"—*History and Present
State of the Education Question*, p. 78.

The fourth and last inquiry solicits the sanction of the National
Society's Committee to an effort to obtain the Parliamentary settlement of the question, upon a recapitulation of the whole case,
suggesting the following considerations :—

"Whether the members of the Church of England can any longer
acquiesce in the present position of National Education ? Can they be
satisfied that the functions of the Legislature and the Church should be
usurped and superseded by a ministerial department, and be centralized
in a small, new, and changeable board, subject to political influences,
and having no distinctive religion ? Can they be content to leave—
can they be justified in leaving—so important a matter, temporal and
spiritual, in the hands of a body so constituted as that committee is,

which (it is a melancholy duty to say), in the brief period of its ten years' existence, has given unequivocal proofs of an unscrupulous disregard for consistency and equity ; has assumed powers unknown to the laws, dangerous to the liberties, and alien to the constitution of the country ; has been continually making fresh aggressions, and putting forth new claims, capable of indefinite extension ; and has evinced an eager desire to grasp the entire management, secular and religious, of National Education ? Can they delay any longer to petition Parliament to consider whether 100,000*l.* of public money can be fitly entrusted *annually* to the management of that Committee ? Can they be willing to peril the interests, temporal and eternal, of the poorer classes of the community, which stand most in need of the guidance and control of sound religious education, especially in times of public excitement, and for whose benefit in particular the National Society was founded, and incorporated by royal authority, and who were specially committed to the teaching of the Church by her divine Head, when He declared that ' unto the poor the gospel is preached ?' "—*History and Present State of the Education Question,* pp. 79, 80.

The inquiry itself is thus conceived :—

" Is the Committee of the National Society willing and prepared to extend the sanction and approval of its venerable name to a general effort on the part of the Church towards extricating the sacred cause of education from the hands of the Committee of Council, and to promote an appeal to the Imperial Legislature with the view of establishing and consolidating National Education on a firm basis, such as may not be shaken by changes of time and fluctuations of party, but may have a public security for its consistency and permanence in the laws of the realm and the principles of the Constitution, and may leave the National Church free and unfettered to put forth her energies in educating her children according to her own principles and practice, and thus to labour in her proper vocation and ministry, so as most effectually to promote the safety of our national institutions and the spiritual and temporal welfare of all classes of society ?"—*History and Present State of the Education Question,* p. 80.

The Committee of the National Society being occupied in deliberating upon the answer to be given to the Committee of Council, no answer beyond an acknowledgment of its receipt reached the Committee of June the seventh, till on the eve of the meeting at Willis's Rooms, when an answer was returned to the first and second of the four inquiries before mentioned. In reply to the first, the Committee of the National Society refer to the letter addressed by them, on the 11th of December of last year, to the Committee of Council.   In reply to the second, it is stated that

" the scheme for the establishment of the Normal School at Kneller Hall was framed by the Committee of Council on Education without any communication with the Committee of the National Society, and carried into effect without concurrence or co-operation on their part."

With respect to the third and fourth heads of inquiry, the answer is of a more reserved character, the Committee pleading

" that the Society has never yet, as such, promoted an appeal to the Legislature, and that the question of doing so at this time is one of very grave importance, which the Committee is not at present prepared to determine."

At the same time, with a view to meet the wishes and difficulties of founders of Church schools, unwilling to adopt the Management Clauses, the Committee of the National Society express their readiness

" to accept any sums of money entrusted to them for the establishment and maintenance of those schools only, the promoters of which may decline to receive aid from the Committee of Council on Education, provided the Society's terms of union are observed in such schools."

As regards the last point, the necessity of a Parliamentary settlement of the whole question, it was the less necessary for the Committee of the National Society to give any direct sanction to such a step, as they had already in their last communication to the Committee of Council asserted their conviction that " the settlement of the terms on which the Parliamentary vote shall be distributed, must be left to the Legislature."

In pursuance of the determination expressed in the letter addressed to the Committee of the National Society by the Committee of June the seventh, the last-named body convened a meeting on the 7th of February last at Willis's Rooms, as the most efficient means of conveying to Government and to the Legislature, an adequate conception of the intensity of the feeling which prevails throughout the country in reference to the education question ; when the following resolutions were passed :—

" 1. That, in the opinion of this meeting, the present position and circumstances of National Education are of a critical nature, and such as to cause serious alarm, on grounds both civil and religious.

" 2. That the Committee of Council on Education, a body of recent origin, consisting of few members, subject to political changes, having, in their corporate capacity, no definite creed, but encouraging indiscriminately various and conflicting forms of belief,—is rapidly assuming the attitude, and engrossing the functions of a Legislative Board of Public Instruction, in a manner hitherto unknown to the laws of the land, and at variance with the principles of the Constitution ; thereby fully realizing the apprehensions which were expressed in Parliament in the year 1839, by eminent prelates and laymen of the Church, and which formed the subject of certain resolutions then moved by his Grace the late Archbishop of Canterbury, and carried in the House of Lords by an overwhelming majority.

" 3. That, notwithstanding that vote of the House of Lords in the year 1839, and in opposition to repeated remonstrances on the part of the National Society, the Committee of Council has been continually making fresh aggressions, particularly by the promulgation of arbitrary Minutes, and by the imposition of Management Clauses upon Church Schools, as indispensable conditions of public aid, and has thus impaired the energies and obstructed the operations of the Church in the discharge of her proper functions in educating the people.

" 4. That the system of popular instruction adopted by the Committee of Council, is avowedly formed on the model of that, which, in the opinion of this meeting, has led to most disastrous results in Germany and France; and that there is great reason to fear that, unless measures are promptly adopted to counteract the endeavours of the Committee of Council to propagate that system, it will in the end reduce *this* country to the condition of anarchy and confusion in which those nations have been recently plunged.

" 5. That the apprehensions of this meeting respecting the tendencies of the system adopted by the Committee of Council are considerably increased by the establishment of the Normal School at Kneller Hall, at the expenditure of more than 30,000l. of public money without previous Parliamentary sanction; and by the system of inspection exercised under the control of the Committee of Council, over the Union Schools of this country, which measures appear to this meeting to be fraught with danger to the religion of the people, and to have been effected in violation of the spirit of a previous understanding between the Committee of Council and the Church of England.

" 6. That, in the opinion of this meeting, it has now become necessary that an appeal should be made to the Imperial Parliament, with the view of removing the impediments created by the Committee of Council, which now preclude many Church Schools from receiving public money, voted by Parliament for Education, and contributed mainly by members of the Church; and of aiding the Church in putting forth her energies, free and unfettered, in educating the people according to her own principles, and thus most effectually promoting the peace and prosperity of the nation, and the temporal and spiritual interests of all classes of the community.

" 7. That an address to Her Most Gracious Majesty the Queen, and petitions to both Houses of Parliament, based upon the above resolutions, and now read to the meeting, be adopted."

The attendance at this meeting, and the unanimity which prevailed, with the exception of one or two parties, who foolishly attempted to obstruct the proceedings, but were very properly prevented from carrying their purpose into effect, amply justified the conveners of it; and the tone of angry abuse in which the members of the Committee of Council and its partisans have since assailed the meeting, and several of the principal speakers, both in Parliament and through the public press, proves at once how weak the case of the Committee of Council is, even in their own estimation, and to what extent they feel themselves to have been damaged by the meeting. The Lord President more particularly committed himself to a line of personal attack upon the veracity of the speakers, which happily furnishes the strongest possible argument for a Parliamentary inquiry into the whole subject. It is, we believe, certain that a motion for a Select Committee of Inquiry will be made in the House of Lords, immediately after Easter; and, considering the heavy grievances pleaded on the part of the Church, on the one hand, and on the other hand, the charges of exaggeration and wilful perversion of the truth publicly preferred against the promoters of the meeting by the Lord President, it is not easy to see how the Government can possibly refuse it, even if they were so inclined. Besides, the dissatisfaction which the schemes and proceedings of the Committee of Council have excited is so general, not only within the pale of the Church, but beyond it, that the Government can hardly be anxious to force their opponents into more aggressive movements, but will, in all probability, be glad to take temporary shelter under a Committee of Inquiry.

The importance of the manner in which that inquiry shall be conducted, and of the evidence that shall be tendered to the Committee, can hardly be overrated; and we take this opportunity of suggesting to the friends of Church education throughout the country, who may be able to furnish such evidence, that they should lose no time in placing themselves in communication with the Committee of June the seventh, stating the particulars of their respective grievances; in order that the case may be brought under the notice of the Parliamentary Committee of Inquiry in all its bearings, and fortified by all such facts as may serve to elucidate the pernicious operation of the Committee of Council. This it is the more imperative upon the friends of Church education to do, as no stone will be left unturned by the Committee of Council and its adherents, to elude the points on which the controversy turns, and to represent the opposition to the Committee of Council, as founded upon misconception and exaggeration. A specimen of the character of the defence which will be attempted, is already before us in the pamphlet of the Rev. Henry Parr Hamilton (No. 3, at the head of this article), which, as a masterpiece of special pleading, of false reasoning, and of deceptive assertion, is entitled to the highest praise, but which certainly has no pretension to be what it professes to be, a "Statement and Examination" of the "Question" in dispute.

The pamphlet literally swarms with misrepresentations and fallacies, which in themselves, perhaps, are scarcely worthy of notice, but which by their plausible character have so far succeeded in blinding the eyes of Churchmen to the real merits of the question, that a refutation of the more glaring and mischievous among them will not be out of place.

Mr. Hamilton sets out with an assertion which will not a little astonish those who are conversant with the history of this great controversy,—the assertion, namely, that the existence of a compact, restricting the conditions of participation in the Parliamentary grant with regard to Church schools to the right of inspection as settled in 1839-40, is "a gratuitous assumption." According to the construction put by Mr. Hamilton upon what took place in those memorable years, there was, indeed, some sort of agreement made at that period between the Government, represented by the Committee of Council, and the Church, represented by the Committee of the National Society, and by its President the Archbishop of Canterbury; but although it was right that the terms stipulated for in that compact should be acted upon, there was nothing to prevent the Committee of Council from imposing any other terms they pleased upon the Church, over and above the terms specified in that compact. It is hard to believe, and yet we are in common charity forced to suppose, that Mr. Hamilton is writing in total ignorance of all the transactions of the period referred to ; for the least knowledge of what then took place, would be sufficient to deter the boldest advocate from the line of defence which Mr. Hamilton has adopted.

An attempt had been made in 1839, of the like insidious character as all the proceedngs of the Committee of Council since the return of the Whigs to power, to supersede the Church in the education of the Poor, by the establishment of a so-called national system, centring in a Normal School, the plan of which, when laid before Parliament, was the signal for a great national resistance. In the House of Commons, though Ministers had a majority on other questions, on the education question it dwindled down to five, and upon a second division to two ; and in the House of Lords they had to contend against an adverse majority of 111, nearly two-thirds of the whole House voting for the Archbishop's resolutions. It was in this posture of affairs, when perseverance in their latitudinarian education scheme must have proved fatal to the continuance of the Whigs in power, that a negotiation was opened between the Archbishop of Canterbury and the Lord President of the Council, with a view to an adjustment of the terms on which the Education Grant should be administered by the then recently created Committee of Council. The result was the settlement of the terms of inspection, as set forth in the Order in Council of August 10th, 1840. The conclusion of this Concordat was formally announced in Parliament as the concession which had induced the Conservative party to withdraw in both Houses their opposition to the Committee of Council. There is a story current, on good authority, that the terms of this Concordat were reduced to writing; and that, when it had been assented to by the Archbishop on the part of the Church, the Lord President suggested, that such a document being of an unusual character, was somewhat informal, and that it would be better to record the understanding in the form of an Order in Council,—a suggestion which, as it seemed to turn upon a mere point of official etiquette, was assented to by the Archbishop. We give this anecdote, as it has reached us from a quarter likely to be well informed, merely as a curious incident in the history of these transactions, and not for the purpose of strengthening our position as regards the existence of a compact by which the terms of the grant to Church schools were limited to inspection as restricted in the Order of Council of August 10th, 1840. The Parliamentary history of that period, coupled with the order in question, furnishes conclusive evidence of the fact, that it was in consideration of this settlement of terms, and upon the faith of it, that no further Parliamentary opposition was made either to the existence of the Committee of Council on Education, or to the annual education grant. Yet Mr. Hamilton has the inconceivable hardihood to affirm, that it is "a gratuitous assumption" to represent the terms set forth in the Order in Council of August 10th, 1840, as "the *sole* condition of a Parliamentary grant." By way of supporting, contrary to an understanding which has continued for the last ten years, so preposterous a proposition, Mr. Hamilton charges those who "hazard this assertion," with confounding the Order in Council of August 10th, 1840, with the Order in Council of June 3rd, 1839; whereas, that very Order of Council of June 3rd, 1839, and specifically the clause relied on by Mr. Hamilton, which specifies the object of the right of inspection retained for the Committee of Council, viz. "to secure a conformity with such regulations as they may approve of for the management and discipline of all schools to which aid may be granted," is set forth as one of the chief *gravamina* in No. 3, of the Archbishop's resolutions carried on the 5th of July following, by that triumphant majority which forced the Government to give way, and to agree to the new rules for the administration of the grant in regard to Church schools, which are embodied in the Order in Council of August 10, 1840, and from which the obnoxious clause in question was purposely and necessarily omitted. The plea now set up by Mr. Hamilton, that the Committee of Council have a right to impose Management Clauses, or in fact any other conditions they please, and to treat the "compact" as a mere regulation touching the appointment of inspectors and the framing of their instructions, may be a correct representation of the *mala fides* of the Committee of Council; but it is a gross falsification of the real facts of the case. The Church said in effect to the State,—" I will consent to your inspection of my schools, on condition that your inspectors be appointed in a certain way, and that their instructions be framed in a certain way;" and the State accepted this as the understanding by which the future action of the Committee of Council in regard to the schools of the Church was to be regulated. To say after this, that it is open to the Committee of Council to interfere in other ways than by inspection, as, for example, by the imposition of Management Clauses,—to engraft upon the inspection a complicated machinery, tending to secularize the education of Church schools, such as is contained in the Minutes of August and December 1846,—and to take away from the Church altogether the education of her pauper children, subjecting them to the latitudinarian system of Kneller Hall,—is an insult to common sense, and an outrage upon common honesty. Bad indeed must be the cause which stands in need of such pleas for its defence !

This plea is the more remarkable, as the admission of its validity involves the admission of any future encroachments on the part of the Committee of Council, which may not have been foreseen and barred in express terms ; as in fact it converts every concession made by the Church into a step gained by the secular over the spiritual power, while no guarantee whatever is given to the latter against the adoption by the former of further measures of a still more obnoxious character. It is vain, therefore, for Mr. Hamilton to commend the Management Clauses to the Church for acceptance, on the ground that "they afford the strongest security against any apprehended interference on the part of the Privy Council;" that "they are binding on the Government no less than on the Church." This was precisely the ground on which the Church consented in 1840 to State inspection under certain restrictions ; it was supposed that those were the conditions on which the Church should receive her proper share of the Education grant, and that those conditions would be "binding on the Government no less than on the Church." They were indeed binding upon the Church, so as to subject her schools to State inspection, but they proved to be practically not binding upon the Committee of Council ; which, according to Mr. Hamilton's own showing, both has added, and, according to his view of the matter, is entitled to add, "new conditions." If the stipulations respecting the limits of State inspection, agreed upon in 1840, were no bar to the Committee of Council enacting, in August and December 1846, an entire system of inspection, without so much as consulting the authorities of the Church, what guarantee can the Management Clauses afford, that new regulations will not be pressed upon the schools hereafter by the Committee of Council, and that the Management Clauses will not act eventually, as the compact touching inspection has already done, as fetters upon the Church, rendering it more difficult for her to defend herself against the contemplated encroachment? The same arguments will apply in one case as in the other: it will still be open to Mr. Hamilton, or to any other advocate of the Committee of Council, to press upon the Church with the *in terrorem* argument, that any lasting misunderstanding between the Privy Council and the National Society, would be "detrimental to education and calamitous to the Church," and to endorse every call for a compromise of the Church's rights and of her principles in compliance with the demands of the Committee of Council, with the exclamation:—"Woe to us, if through unfounded jealousy or distrust of the civil power, we oppose any obstacles to it for the time to come!"

It is a great and a gratuitous assumption on the part of Mr. Hamilton,—which, however, is wilfully carried on through the whole of his pamphlet,—that those who object to the legislative powers over Church Education claimed and exercised by the Committee of Council, are insensible to the value of a cordial co-operation between the Church and the State in the education of the people. So far from being insensible to it, we should, on the contrary, say, that it is because they set a very high value upon that co-operation that the friends of true Church Education object to the arbitrary proceedings and the undefined powers of the Committee of Council, as having a constant tendency to disturb and to endanger that co-operation; and because they feel convinced that such co-operation can never be permanently secured, until it is settled upon a basis which, while it respects the just rights of the Church, shall, at the same time, be sanctioned by Parliament, and shall not leave it open to that variable body, the Committee of Council, to alter and modify the terms of that co-operation, from time to time, in accordance with the interests of the party in power, or with the crotchets of any individual, whether Lord President or Secretary, by whose influence the Committee of Council may be urged on to the adoption of untried, unpractical, and pernicious theories.

We deem it unnecessary to follow Mr. Hamilton into all the sophistical arguments by which he has attempted to show that the

Management Clauses, proposed by the Committee of Council, are not objectionable, because the point concerning the intrinsic merit of the clauses is gone by; the question has ceased to be one of details; it has, most fortunately so, as we cannot help thinking, become a question of principle, and of principle only; as such it must henceforth be argued, and upon the ground of principle it must be decided. We cannot, however, pass by unnoticed one remarkable fallacy which Mr. Hamilton has put forward, and on which he builds very generally throughout his argument. To hear him one would suppose that the Committee of Council had done nothing more than endeavoured to carry into effect the rules of the National Society, to secure their adoption in all schools aided by State grants, and to make provision for their being enforced.

"The clauses, if impartially examined, will be found to have for their great object to secure the efficiency of Church schools. They violate no engagement, direct or implied, with the Church. They give practical effect to the terms of union with the National Society. They involve no principle in the smallest degree at variance with them. They contain many provisions conducive to the efficiency of Church schools, which those terms confessedly want."—*The Privy Council and the National Society,* pp. 42, 43.

And again :—

"The very system of religious teaching approved by the rulers of the Church has been adopted by the Privy Council. The clergy have their appropriate duties and privileges secured to them. The Bishops have even a larger share of authority than was vested in them by the terms of union. The government of the school is purely local. It is confided entirely to Churchmen. This in sober truth is the grievance." *The Privy Council and the National Society,* p. 52.

In order to substantiate this novel position, Mr. Hamilton quotes with a great appearance of fairness and documentary exactness, the National Society's terms of union, and points out the various particulars adopted from them into the Management Clauses. But he quite overlooks, or tries to make his readers overlook, the important fact, that the National Society's terms of union contain the *minimum* of Church character, required by the Society in any school to which aid shall be given from its funds. By those terms of union, the National Society says in effect to the applicants for aid :—" If you want help from our funds, we shall require, *at least,* such and such guarantees for the Church character of your school;" but at the same time, the Society leaves it quite open to any founders of schools, to give to the schools founded by them, a far more stringent Church character. The most entire local freedom is carefully preserved, and nothing

is exacted but that without which the school would cease to be a
Church school altogether.   Now it is this *minimum* of a Church
character, which the Committee of Council have taken up, and
converted into the *maximum* of a Church character, which in their
scheme shall be permitted.   They say in effect :—" The smallest
guarantee which the National Society exacts from you, is the
largest which we will permit you to have," except in particular
and exceptional cases, where we cannot avoid giving a greater
preponderance to Church principles, but which we have taken
care so to define and to circumscribe, that our *maximum* shall
not be exceeded at your discretion.   The National Society says :
—" You may constitute your school as you please, provided you
comply with the following stipulations ;" the Committee of Council : "These are the stipulations which we will allow you to
make—neither more nor less—you shall not go one jot or tittle
beyond them."   And this is what Mr. Hamilton calls carrying
out the views and principles of the National Society !

But further ; when the National Society proposes a *minimum*
of Church character, and admits the utmost latitude beyond that
minimum, the National Society contemplates schools founded by
the Church, within her pale, by her sincerely attached members.   The whole movement emanates from the Church, and is
confined within her boundaries.   The relations between the
clergyman and the laity who co-operate with him, are, therefore,
as they may safely be, left to local adjustment, according to the
circumstances of each case—with this single provision, that the
clergyman, whose influence must necessarily preponderate, shall
be subject to be checked by his ecclesiastical superior, in the
event of his abusing the power naturally and inevitably devolving
upon him in a parochial school.   There is no ground for jealousy
on either side,—while the laity confide in the clergyman and his
bishop, the ecclesiastical authority treats the laity with equal confidence.   No hair-splitting adjustment of their mutual relation is
therefore thought of, because practically it is not required.

This state of things is altogether and most materially changed,
by the introduction of an extraneous, central State authority, such
as the Committee of Council is,—an authority deriving its origin
from a theory of education incompatible with the principles of the
Church, against which for some forty years the Church has been
forced to stand on her defence,—an authority which regards the
distinctive religious teaching of the Church as an impediment,
reluctantly endured, to the realization of its latitudinarian
schemes of what it terms "national" education.   When such a
State authority, central, identified with the political ministry,
with all the Government influence and large sums of money

annually voted by Parliament, at its disposal, with a large and
influential machinery reaching into the schoolroom, and swaying
the schoolmaster by the powerful incentives of ambition and of
gain, steps in and converts the *minimum* of Church character,
which the Church had fixed for herself, with the most perfect
liberty beyond it, into the *maximum* which this extraneous
authority prescribes to the Church, taking away all liberty beyond
it,—when this State authority does all in its power to convert
the relation of mutual confidence between the ecclesiastical
authority and the laity, into a relation of mutual jealousy, representing itself as the advocate and guardian of the rights of the
laity against the clergy, not without a strong and well-founded
suspicion of an intention to make use of that laity in furtherance
of its pet theory of secular and latitudinarian training, in opposition to the distinctive religious teaching of the Church,—
assuredly, in such a case, Churchmen, and more particularly the
Clergy, who are in an especial manner the guardians of the distinctive principles of the Church, are justified in looking narrowly
into the terms of the compulsory arrangement dictated to them
under such circumstances ; and it by no means follows, that
because they were perfectly satisfied with those terms while
they were only a matter of voluntary arrangement between the
members of the Church among themselves, they should acquiesce
in the same terms when forced upon them, as a matter of coercion,
by a State authority whose principles and aims they know to be
hostile to the distinctive principles of their Church.

Again, Mr. Hamilton insists, with much mis-placed emphasis,
upon the fact that the State proffers assistance for the foundation of
Church schools, as the price of compliance with its regulations,
arbitrarily and dictatorially imposed upon the Church; and, reverting
to the proceedings of the National Society, and to the conditions
annexed to its grants, as a precedent, argues as if the cases were
exactly parallel.   But, so far from the cases being parallel, there
is the greatest possible difference between them.   The National
Society derives its funds from the benevolence of voluntary contributors, who give their money in furtherance of certain principles ; and it is, therefore, perfectly just and right that the Committee, to whom the administration of these funds is entrusted,
should apply them in the manner and for the purposes intended
by the donors.   On the contrary, the funds administered by the
Committee of Council are funds levied from the people at large,
to which every individual is forced to contribute in the ratio of
his general liability to public imposts ; the funds are therefore
public funds, to be administered on principles of strict justice
and of an enlightened public policy.   If the State knew its

own interest, and its duty towards the Church, to whose teaching and influence it is indebted for its stability, the State would scarcely see it consistent with sound policy to spend any of those funds in aiding and abetting the inculcation of ideas adverse to the principles of the Church. But, if the State has so far lost its character, as to be unable or afraid to discriminate between truth and error, the least the State can do is to give to the Church her fair proportion of its funds, leaving her to use them in her own way, for the education of her children in her own principles. The State has no right to tempt the Church by the offer of money, or to try to coerce her by the threat to withhold it, to an abandonment of her principles; and, in whatever measure the State becomes incapable of holding or professing any faith in its corporate capacity, precisely in the same measure does it become manifestly disqualified to co-operate with the Church in the work of education. Common fairness, in fact, common justice and propriety, ought to restrain the State from all interference with the action of the Church in the internal regulation of her schools.

All this is so plain and obvious, that it is matter of just surprise how it could have been so entirely overlooked by a gentleman of Mr. Hamilton's acuteness of mind; it can be accounted for only by the supposition that he has entered upon the consideration of the question, not in the character of an inquirer, which his title-page bespeaks, but in that of a partisan—the partisan of a cause which it is not easy to see how a Churchman, much more a clergyman, can advocate consistently with his professed convictions, and, in the case of the latter, with his ordination engagements.

We regret that we have to drag forth into light yet another fallacy of which Mr. Hamilton is guilty; a fallacy so palpable and so ridiculous, that we should hardly have thought it worth while to notice it, but for the use which has been made of it in Parliament. The fallacy is thus set forth by Mr. Hamilton himself, in the opening of his argument:—

" The clauses were never intended to be imposed on Church schools already built, but only upon such as should thereafter be built with the aid of the Parliamentary grant. The adoption of the clauses, therefore, is not a necessary condition for receiving the benefits of the new Minutes. Even when the promoters of a school reject the clauses, and build it from their own resources alone, they are not on that account excluded from those benefits. This it is material to bear in mind. The rejection of the clauses entails the loss, not of a grant towards the support of the school, but merely of a grant towards its erection."—*The Privy Council and the National Society*, pp. 3, 4.

And again at the end, taking advantage of a loosely-worded

passage in the National Society's last letter to the Committee of Council, torn from its context, the fallacy is thus reproduced in a postscript:—

" There is some danger of this paragraph being misunderstood. From the terms in which it is expressed, it might be inferred that Church schools which rejected the management clauses would, for the time to come, be excluded from ' all share of the Parliamentary grant for education.' This would not be the case. The Parliamentary grant is now applied, not only to the building of schools, but also to their maintenance; and, as has been already remarked, ' the rejection of the clauses entails the loss, not of a grant towards the *support* of the school, but merely of a grant towards its *erection.*' Consequently, any Church school, if reported by the inspector to be efficiently conducted, will be admissible to the benefits of the Minutes of 1846, *notwithstanding that its trust-deeds may not have been constituted' on the model prescribed by their lordships.'*

" It is of great importance that there should exist no misconception with respect to the exact nature and extent of the loss incurred by a school, the promoters of which decline to accept a management clause. It cannot, therefore, be too often repeated, that the recent controversy had reference solely to a *building grant,* and did not in the slightest degree affect the claim of a school to a share of the Parliamentary grant towards its maintenance, *when built.*"—*The Privy Council and the National Society,* pp. 57, 58.

The uninitiated are led to suppose that there is here an enormous misrepresentation, and that in reality all Church schools get their share of the annual grant, with the exception of those whose founders are slightly mulcted of the amount of the building grant, for their obstinacy in refusing to accept the National Society's terms of union, when forwarded to them from the Council Office. But how in reality stands the case? The reason why founders of Church schools object to the management clauses is surely not, that they are afraid of the words on the parchment of their deeds. What they are afraid of, are the Government inspectors, with their machinery of inspection provided in the minutes of August and December, 1846, with their examination books and their rewards to masters and pupil-teachers,—the introduction into their schools of the bureaucracy of the Council Office, the spirit of which was exhibited with more ostentation than discretion by one of the inspectors, who, calling before him the pupil-teachers in a parochial girls' school, proceeded thus to charge them: " Now, girls, remember, that from this day forward you are Government officers !" It is the fear of this alien element intruding itself into the parochial school, and destroying its character, that causes founders of Church schools, who know what they are about, to decline the management clauses, which would bring them into perpetual bondage to the Committee of Council. Is it likely, then, that those who do so would afterwards apply to the Committee of Council for an annual grant, and thereby subject themselves to the operation of the very system which to eschew they deprived themselves of the benefit of the building grant? The very supposition is an absurdity. Whether the Lord President counted upon the credulity of Parliament, or whether, himself ignorant on the subject, he relied on the accuracy of Mr. Hamilton's representation, we cannot pretend to say. Certain it is, that when his lordship was brought to book by Lord Stanley, the fallacy exploded in the hands of the noble marquis, and his lordship had to make the somewhat lame confession, that, upon "searching the records," he found there was no case of an application for an annual grant from parties who had refused the building grant.

After this practical confutation, we may safely leave Mr. Hamilton alone in his ingenuity. Though the number of fallacious pleas and assertions which we noted in turning over the few pages of his pamphlet is "legion," we do not think it worth our own or our readers' while to devote to them more of our attention, considering that there are other and weightier matters still behind, which claim our notice—to wit, Mr. Fox's Education Bill, and Mr. Kay's volumes.

The simultaneous appearance of these two documents in the education case—the one in the House of Commons, the other in the warehouse of Messrs. Longman—seems to justify the surmise that there is some sort of connexion between them; a surmise which an investigation of their contents goes far to confirm. If Mr. Fox wished for a witness to testify from alleged experience to the excellency of his education scheme, he could not have put a better witness into the box than Mr. Kay; and, if Mr. Kay wished for a legislator to embody his theories in a bill, he could not have found a framer of enactments more to his mind than Mr. Fox. There is a coincidence between the "facts" of Mr. Kay's volumes and the "projects" of Mr. Fox's bill, which few will believe to be undesigned.

That Mr. Kay's volumes are written with consummate ability, it is needless to observe. It is not for the first time that he appears before the world as the literary advocate of the principles which his brother reduced to practice at the Council Office; and his worst enemies will not deny him the praise, such as it is, that he makes up in cleverness what he lacks in principle. The present work, though evidently written for the sole purpose of recommending the foreign secular education theory to the English

mind, takes professedly a much wider range, embracing in its
scope the whole social condition of the lower orders in foreign
countries. To follow Mr. Kay into the details of this portion of
his work would encroach too largely upon our space, and lead us
too far away from our immediate subject. We shall content ourselves with giving, in his own words, the upshot of the " observations " which he made in the course of his travels. It is this,—

" That the moral, intellectual, and social condition of the peasants
and operatives of those parts of Germany, Holland, Switzerland, and
France, where the poor have been educated, where the land has been
released from the feudal laws, and where the peasants have been
enabled to acquire, is very much higher, happier, and more satisfactory
than that of the peasants and operatives of England; and that, while
these latter are struggling in the deepest ignorance, pauperism, and
moral degradation, the former are steadily and progressively attaining a
condition, both socially and politically considered, of a higher, happier,
and more hopeful character."—*The Social Condition and Education of
the People in England and Europe, &c.*, vol. i. p. 7.

This Mr. Kay " does not hesitate to affirm," in spite of the
evidence which recent events have furnished of the deep demoralization, of the turbulence, of the licentiousness, and the savage
barbarism of the lower orders on the continent—in spite of the
fact, that the very countries which Mr. Kay instances (with the
exception of Holland) exhibit a condition in which political and
social restoration appears to be all but hopeless. But Mr. Kay
had a proposition to demonstrate, which is, that the state education of the continent produces the most desirable effects, while
the parochial education of England stands condemned by its fruits.
He was not, therefore, in a condition to take notice of such trifling
symptoms of the condition of the continental populations as the
revolutions of 1848, and the bayoneted peace of 1849. His
business was—and right well has he performed his task—to look
at the bright side of every thing abroad, and at the dark side here;
to take up the recollection of some favoured rural district abroad,
and to generalize his passing observations upon it—made in the
light and gladsome mood in which bachelors, and especially travelling bachelors, are wont to perform the pleasurable practice of
locomotion—into a general picture of the state of the country ;
and on the other hand, on his return, to seek out, during a November fog, and in a fit of November spleen, the darkest and most
unpromising corners of the land, and, grouping together in one
shocking *ensemble* all the wretchedness, the squalor, and immorality he could discover, to generalize that picture too, as a picture
of the condition of the lower classes in this country. It is by this

double process of positive and negative embellishment that Mr. Kay has succeeded in making out the striking contrast which his volumes present, between the condition of the people, moral, social, and intellectual, in Papal and infidel France and Germany, and in Protestant, religious England. So striking is that contrast, and so skilful are the pictures, that, but for the startling proofs of the real character of the lower orders on the continent, which recent events have furnished, we should have had little hope of persuading any one, or even of retaining our own conviction, that the lower classes abroad are not half as good, nor the lower classes in our own land half as bad, as they are both painted by Mr. Kay.

With regard to the former, we hold ourselves absolved from the necessity of making out a case against them; they have afforded sufficient opportunity of "knowing them by their fruits" to all who are not blinded by the most inveterate prejudice and the most unreasoning political partisanship. With regard to the latter, we have no wish whatever, as our readers will readily believe, to extenuate the grievous state of neglect in which, in too many instances, the poorer classes are left to pine; still less, to advocate the abandonment of their children to all the wretchedness and ignorance which they inherit from their parents. After making large deductions for the overdrawn pictures of vice and destitution which are to be found, not only in the volumes of Mr. Kay, but too often also in the reports of philanthropic societies, and in the communications of newspaper "commissioners," we are free to admit that there is a great deficiency of education in many parts of the country; but, so far from drawing from this fact the inference which Mr. Kay draws—that they are to be subjected to the process suggested by the educational theory of the Committee of Council,—on the contrary, we conclude that the State has grossly neglected its duty by not availing itself long ago of the eminent services of that greatest of all educational machineries that any country under the sun ever possessed, the Established Church of this country, and by sacrificing to the petty and rancorous jealousies of the sectarians the sound religious and intellectual training of the great mass of the population. We agree with him, that the children of our poor are left untaught and untended, abandoned to crimes and brutalizing influences to an extent which is perfectly disgraceful to a Christian country; and further, we agree with him that sectarianism is at the bottom of the mischief: the point on which we differ is this, that he reckons the Church among the sects, and fancies that a creedless State authority can do the work which belongs to the Church alone, and which the Church alone can perform in a satisfactory manner, in a manner conducive at once to individual happiness and to the national welfare. We have the more reason to complain of the unfairness of Mr. Kay's conclusions, as he is far from ignorant of the zeal and efficiency of the clergy in promoting the education of the poor. We gladly transcribe, in justice both to himself and to those to whose labours he bears witness, the following testimony from Mr. Kay's own pen:—

"The present system is bearing very unfairly, and very oppressively, upon many conscientious and benevolent clergymen in the remote and rural districts.

"The nation is entirely ignorant of the almost marvellous efforts which some of the clergy are making in the remote rural districts, to provide schools for the poor.

"Many poor clergymen, with not 150*l.* of annual income, are out of that small stipend supporting their schools and teachers themselves, wholly unaided either by the public or by their neighbours. How they can do it, God only knows; but that many of them, in all parts of the country, do effect this prodigy of self-denial, all the inspectors unanimously attest. These good men receive and expect no public praise as their reward. They are labouring, unheard of and unknown by their fellows, and are looking for their reward to heaven alone.

"But what a disgrace it is to us, as a nation, to impose such a burden upon any of our clergy! What a shame it is, that the small stipend of a religious and benevolent man should be made still smaller, by forcing him to pay what ought to be borne by the nation at large! And what a precarious means of support for these schools! It is not reasonable to expect, that each succeeding incumbent can or will be equally self-denying; and, when one fails to give the accustomed support, such a school must necessarily be closed."—*The Social Condition and Education of the People*, vol. ii. pp. 475, 476.

Yet, notwithstanding the practical knowledge which he evidently has of the anxiety of the clergy and of their praiseworthy exertions for the education of the people, Mr. Kay ceases not to reproach them as the great impediments to the extension of education. At one time he represents them as ignorant and incapable of superintending a school advantageously, from a want of the science of "pedagogy,"—at another time as peevish and tyrannical, likely to treat the schoolmaster with harshness and caprice, so as to require the protection of a State department of education with its staff of inspectors,—at another time unreasonably and causelessly jealous of State interference. The *animus* with which they are, as a body, regarded by Mr. Kay, shows itself at every turn ; he makes no scruple to lay the whole difficulty at their door, and to threaten them with the consequences :—

"I cannot imagine any thing more injurious to the clergy, more hostile to the influence they ought to possess over the people ; I cannot imagine any thing more certain to separate the people from them, than that it should be fancied for one moment, that they oppose Government interference (after sufficient guarantees have been offered them that it is not intended to take the direction and surveillance of the moral and religious education of the people out of their hands), merely from a vain desire to manage and direct the education of the people themselves, especially after they have given such proofs of their utter inability to raise a tithe of the funds necessary for such a purpose.   They are doubtless the fit and proper guardians of the religion and the morality of the country, and they are only performing their high duty, when they oppose any measure which may seem likely to undermine the religious and moral influence they ought to have ; but let them be most careful they do not demand more ; let them take care that they do not reject the assistance of Government, after having shown the country that they cannot raise one paltry half-million for the primary education of a nation of 16,000,000 souls.   Far from thwarting Government, it behoves them, *if* they can discern the signs of the times, to be the first to demand the co-operation of the State, and to confess their inability to carry on the education of the people without it, instead of appearing for one moment satisfied with, and still less venturing for one instant to vaunt, the miserably small progress that education has yet made."—*The Social Condition and Education of the People*, vol. ii. p. 512.

Again, he says :—

"As long as the State and the religious ministers exhibit so much distrust the one of the other, nothing can be done ; but that day will be advanced, when, after the turmoil of a fierce political strife, the people will create an educational system for themselves, and will reject the interference of the clergy altogether, having learned to associate their names with the idea of an unwillingness to advance their improvement ; and the consequence will be, that an educational system will be established void of all religion, thoroughly atheistical and revolutionary in its tendency, and which will completely overthrow all that influence, which it is most important, for the best interests of the people, that the clergy should have on the education of the nation."—*The Social Condition and Education of the People*, vol. ii. pp. 535, 536.

Such are the threats held up before the eyes of the clergy by Mr. Kay, who, we may be sure—good excellent man !—has not the least intention by his book to help to create the impression that the clergy are the great stumbling-blocks in the way of a more extensive system of popular education, and whose reverence for religious truth is thus forcibly attested by himself :—

"What are we doing?   Behold us, in 1850, with one of the most pauperised, demoralised, and worst educated people in Europe ; with the greatest accumulated masses in the world ; with one of the most rapidly increasing populations in the world ; behold us, in 1850, developing our productive powers, giving the most tremendous stimulus to our manufactures and our population—resolved to turn the North into one vast city—to collect there the labourers of the world, and to leave them without a religion! Not only are we fearfully careless of the best interest of our brethren, not only are we acting, as if we were ourselves convinced that our religion was a lie; but we are blind to the absolute necessities of the commonwealth. The very heathens would have laughed our policy to scorn. They all saw, that even if there were no God, it was necessary to invent one for the peace of mankind; they bound their people by religious formulas, wanting although these were of all true vitality; whilst we, in an age of the world when the intelligence of the multitude is advancing with giant strides, stand still, saying to one another, it is impossible to do any thing with our neighbours, for this party differs from one religious dogma we have started, and that party differs from another: each thus assuming for himself that perfection and that infallibility, which he scorns his neighbour for pretending to; whilst, alas! all are too ready to omit the inculcation of the weightier matters of the law—judgment, and justice, and mercy."—*The Social Condition and Education of the People,* vol. ii. pp. 507, 508.

Our readers will not fail to perceive that Mr. Kay is by no means insensible to the value of religious education. Quite the contrary. He wants religion in the school. But, unfortunately, none of the existing religions will do. The sects, of course, will not put up with the religion of the Church from which they have separated; and the Church herself has an old-fashioned attachment to "the faith once delivered to the Saints," and will not part with her "dogmas." What, then, is to be done, in such a dilemma? Obviously, to do as the heathen did, to "invent" a religion; that "general religion" of which Kneller Hall is to be the nursery, and the Lord President the Arch-Priest; unless, indeed, we might manage to make Popery the religion of our people,—a course for which Mr. Kay seems mightily inclined:—

" The very genius of the Protestant religion requires, more than any other ever did, that its members should be educated, in order that they should be influenced by it. The different religions of the old world and the Roman Catholic religion have retained their hold upon the mind of the multitude by striking and affecting ceremonies, and by means of the senses have established their empire over the spirit of mankind. But Protestantism has thrown aside almost all, and many forms of Protestantism have thrown aside all the ceremonies, which so strongly affected the mind of the unthinking people, and which so powerfully contributed, and in many countries at the present day still so very powerfully contribute, to excite a reverential and religious feeling among the ignorant; and we boast, that ours is not a religion merely of the feelings, but peculiarly one of the understanding. But do not Protestants perceive, that in order that an intellectual religion should affect the people, it is absolutely necessary, that their intellects should be fitted for the exercise, or that the religion will lose its hold upon them and be entirely neglected? What has contributed to the spread of many of the lowest kinds of dissent in this country? Simply because they have appealed to the *feelings* of the people. And so it will be, as long as we offer an intellectual and spiritual religion to a people incapable of reflection or of thought, and who cannot take any pleasure in a service, which to them appears cold, meaningless, and formal. In this way does the English Church contribute to the increase of the Ranters, the Mormonites, and all the wild and visionary enthusiasts, who have so great a hold upon the minds of the people in North Wales and in our manufacturing and mining districts, and who know right well, that a religion which appeals to the feelings and passions is the only one which can have any influence over an ignorant multitude. It is impossible for the intellectual and unimaginative Protestantism of the English Church ever to affect the masses, until the masses are sufficiently educated to dispense with all need of mental excitement, which they never will be able to do, until they can think. If, then, the Protestants of England are not willing to prepare the people for the reception of our pure and spiritual religion, and as there can be no doubt that some form of religion, even although erroneous, is better for mankind than the absence of all religion whatsoever, it surely would be better for us, if we had the ceremonial religion of the Romanists, with all its faults, capable, as it would be, of affecting and influencing an unthinking multitude, than the spiritual religion of the Protestants, requiring an educated mind for its reception, when the English Protestants have seemingly resolved they will not educate the people. Much better to have a faith for the people, although it be erroneous, than to have no faith at all."—*The Social Condition and Education of the People*, vol. ii. pp. 508—510.

Is it from such counsellors as these that our clergy are expected to receive instruction touching their duties, in regard to the religious instruction of the people? One who sees in a spiritual truth, in a doctrine of the faith, nothing but a dogma which might just as well be dispensed with,—who, upon the whole, is inclined to think superstition more efficacious in making men religious than the true faith and ordinance of God,—who is willing to put up with Popery or anythingarianism rather than allow the clergy of the Established Church to teach God's truth, in conformity with their ordination vows;—such an one it is that ventures to lecture the clergy on their responsibilities, and to threaten them with extermination, if they continue to obstruct "national" education upon Mr. Kay's principle, by their pertinacious adherence to the faith of the Church Catholic.

With regard to the plans which Mr. Kay proposes, they are sufficiently extensive, as well as sufficiently un-Christian and un-English.

" Whenever we do resolve to undertake the education of the country, it will be necessary for Government so to increase its force of inspectors, as to obtain information of the exact condition of the means for education in every parish throughout the kingdom. The state of the different parishes should then be ranged under the following heads :—

" 1. Parishes, which are already supplied with sufficient school-room.

" 2. Parishes, which have some school-room, but require more, and are able to provide what is wanted.

" 3. Parishes, which have some school-room, but require more, and are unable to provide what is wanted.

" 4. Parishes, which have no school-room, but which are able to provide sufficient.

" 5. Parishes, which have no school-room, and are not able to provide any.

" Now, as I have already shown, and as the reports of the inspectors still more clearly show, there is no hope of any thing being done in very many parishes capable of great local efforts, unless Government requires it of them. As several of the inspectors show, over great tracts of country, there does not at present exist a single school. It is evident, therefore, that the present voluntary system cannot, with all our efforts, provide the country with schools, and that, if we are to have them, *Government must interfere, and oblige each parish, as far as it is able, and assist it when unable, to provide itself with sufficient school-room for its population.*

" In each parish, all tenants of houses, whose rent amounts say to at least 10*l.* per annum, might be made liable to a certain rate, to be apportioned according to the wants of the parish and the number of the householders who are liable to the rate. Each of these householders might have a vote in the election of a committee of eight or ten members, for the administration of the educational expenditure of the parish. Of this committee, the clergy and the dissenting ministers ought to be, as in all European countries, ex-officio members.

" Before this committee, when elected, the inspector for the district should lay an account of the exact state of education in the parish, showing the quantity of school-room required for the population ; where the required school or schools should be situated, so as best to suit the convenience of the poor of the parish ; and also how many houses for teachers should be provided. The committee might then deliberate, whether it would supply the wants of the parish by mixed schools for the different religious sects, or by separate schools for each sect, and whether it would at once provide for all the schools required, or by the imposition of separate rates in separate years. At these deliberations the clergy, the dissenting ministers, and the inspectors, should be entitled to assist the latter, by affording all necessary information as to the exact wants of the district.

" I am firmly of opinion, that were the Government to oblige each parish to provide itself with sufficient school-room, and to leave it to the option of the several parishes whether they would support separate or mixed schools, that there would be little difficulty. Wherever any one party was decidedly too small to establish a school for itself, it would concur in the arrangement for a mixed school. It is when Government endeavours itself to decide upon it, that all parties are alarmed, and begin to suspect ulterior designs, and to fear the effects of a scheme over which they have had no control. All that Government should do, *is to oblige each parish, as far as it is able, to supply itself with sufficient school-room,* and to leave to its own decision the *manner* in which this should be done. I am confirmed in my opinion that mixed schools would not be objected to, if the establishing of them were left to the inhabitants of the different parishes, by the experience I have had in the north, where I have frequently found schools, expressly intended for the Church, filled partly with the children of dissenters, who did not object in the least to their children remaining, even during the religious lessons given in the school. But whenever a power from without endeavours to force mixed schools upon a locality, then the clergy and the dissenting ministers, and many of the parents, begin to be alarmed. Of course Government ought to require, when a school was established for two sects, and the schoolmaster was chosen from the most numerous sect, that the children should either attend the religious lessons given in the school, or should receive daily religious instruction from one of the ministers of their own sect.

" In those cases where the committee could not agree to provide a mixed school, and where the minority was too small to support a school for themselves, the majority should be obliged and empowered to levy the rate and build the school, on condition that the minority should be allowed to send their children to the secular instruction, and remove them during the religious instruction given in the school. We should soon find, that the minority would not object to their children attending the secular instruction given at the school, and receiving their religious instruction from their own minister. Many parishes, moreover, would require *several* schools, and in these cases the committee could easily arrange, if desired, that the schools should be appropriated to the different sects, according to their respective numbers.

" Where a parish was not capable of doing more than it had already done, or of making any but very inefficient efforts, Government ought to be prepared to give the necessary assistance, instead of confining its grants, as at present, to those parishes alone, which are able to raise a considerable part of the necessary funds. But in the poorest parishes, where several schools were required, the householders ought to be consulted, whether they wish to have *separate* or *mixed* schools.

" These parish committees might be called on to meet at certain periods, to examine the state of the school-buildings, and to provide, by the levying of a small rate on the householders, for all the repairs required for all the schools and schoolmasters' houses in the parish; and when the population was increased so much, as to require another school, for the building of another school in the parish. The inspectors of the district would inform them of the exact wants of the parish.

It would be also wise to give these parish committees the power of re-
quiring the attendance of all the children at school between certain ages,
and of enforcing that attendance, whenever they saw fit to do so.

" In many districts, the parochial authorities would not object to
put this regulation into force, while Government will be wholly unable
for some time to enforce a general regulation of this kind.   The people
would not object to it, if it issued from themselves, although they
would call it unwarrantable interference on the part of Government.
And although, doubtless, very many districts would not consent to
enforce such a regulation for some years to come, yet it would be a
great gain to the country, if the inspectors could induce any of the
towns or parishes to make such a regulation."— *The Social Condition*
and Education of the People, vol. ii. pp. 515—519.

For the purpose of carrying out this extensive scheme, Mr.
Kay proposes the establishment of a number of normal schools—
he estimates it at forty-one for England and Wales—in which
proper masters should be trained, and placed under the power
and patronage of the Government :—

" In the case of all schools at present established, directed by trustees, school societies, religious congregations, or private individuals, I
would, of course, leave the selection of the teachers in the hands of the
persons in whom it is now vested, reserving for Government, however,
the right of examining by means of its inspectors the persons chosen,
and the power of annulling the election, if the candidate was found upon
examination to be unfitted for the exercise of his important duties.   In
the case of schools erected by the parochial authorities, the teachers
should be always chosen, if the school was intended for only one sect,
from that sect, by its school committee, and if for several sects, by the
minister and members of the school committee, who belonged to the
most numerous sect in the parish, subject, however, in every case to
the approval of Government.   When we have a sufficient number of
normal colleges, of course no person should be permitted to be a candidate for the situation of teacher, but one, who had been educated in
such a college, and who had obtained a certificate from its director and
professors of high moral character, and of satisfactory intellectual
attainments.

" It is very important that Government should have the right of examining every candidate for the situation of a schoolmaster, and the
power of rejecting him, if found upon examination unworthy of the
situation."— *The Social Condition and Education of the People,* vol. ii.
pp. 520, 521.

And further still :—

" The reports of the inspectors prove only too plainly, that the country can have no security against the negligence or ignorance of local
authorities, until Government has the *surveillance*—I do not say the

direction, but the mere *surveillance*—of all the primary schools in the country, and a veto on the appointment *and dismissal* of all the teachers in the country. It is what all foreign countries, where education has made any progress, have granted their government, and it is what our Government must have sooner or later."—*The Social Condition and Education of the People*, vol. ii. p. 524.

Since Mr. Kay appeals so confidently to the example of foreign countries, in which those teachers are under the immediate control of the civil government, he will not, we feel sure, consider it unfair that we should insert, as a set-off to his recommendation, a charge delivered recently to a body of schoolmasters at Heidelberg by the town magistrate, which will go further than any thing we could say, to illustrate the practical meaning of Mr. Kay's theory.

"I address myself to you, the professional teachers of schools. I must tell you that you have thoroughly agitated the country, and left nothing undone that could undermine the ground on which we stand. In this task you have spared neither zeal nor labour. The fruits of your exertions are visible to all. The generation you have trained is completely ruined; that which you are training is without hope or trust, and almost incurably corrupted. It has lost all feeling of right, of aversion to what is wrong, all respect for authority, all idea of Divine and human ordinances, all attachment to the Church and creed of their forefathers; and there is no prospect of its condition becoming better. This is for the most part your work, because you have made your schools the centres of sedition; because, instead of training the scholars intrusted to you to be good citizens and Christians, you have made of them revolutionary, discontented, and wretched men, fallen away from God and His ordinances. And yet the rising generation is still intrusted to you! If you have remaining in you one spark of Christian feeling, you cannot surely ruin these children also by training them to rebellion, seeing that your activity in the past has only brought our poor native land and the people to the verge of destruction. If this lust of sedition again seizes you, then I beg you will remember the oath you have to-day taken, and the God to whom you have raised your hands with the promise to live as true and faithful subjects of your Sovereign."

Our readers are now in possession of the principle upon which the bill introduced into the House of Commons by the *quondam* Socinian preacher, Mr. William Johnson Fox, is founded. The principle is not new, it was broached seven years ago by Lord John Russell in the resolutions which he attempted to engraft upon Sir James Graham's Factory Education Bill[1]; and it is not surprising, therefore, that a measure founded upon it should have met with so hearty a welcome at his lordship's hands. We confess

---

[1] See English Review, vol. xi. pp. 116, 117.

that we share in some degree the satisfaction expressed by the noble Premier. It saves a world of argument to have the cloven foot displayed at once. The scheme of Mr. Fox is briefly this. Inspectors appointed by the Committee of Privy Council on Education are to overrun the country, and (Clause II.) to make full and detailed reports to the Committee of Privy Council on Education, of the state of secular education in each parish of their respective districts, and of the adequacy of the existing provisions of each parish to afford secular education for the wants of the entire population thereof; in which reports " regard shall be had *to the effect of any exclusion from instruction*, whether arising from the expense of schooling, *from peculiar or special religious teaching adopted in any school*, or from any other cause whatsoever." The course of proceeding to be adopted in the event of the education being found inadequate *ex gr.* from the exclusion of a few dissenting children from a Church school, is thus stated in Clause III.

" That whenever it shall appear from any such report of the inspectors of schools that the existing provisions for education in any parish are insufficient for the wants of the entire population of such parish, the Committee of Privy Council for Education shall, by a letter signed by their secretary, addressed and sent to the overseers of such parish, direct the overseers to summon a meeting of the inhabitants, within a time to be named in such letter, who shall elect not less than [*five*] nor more than [*fifteen*] of the inhabitants of such parish to form the educational committee for such parish ; and thereupon the election of such educational committee, and the names of the members thereof, shall be forthwith certified to the Committee of Council on Education by the said overseers ; and such educational committee shall remain in office for *twelve* calendar months from the day of election ; and fifteen days at least before the expiration of such *twelve* calendar months the said overseers shall summon a meeting of the inhabitants, who shall elect a like educational committee for the year then next succeeding the expiration of the said *twelve* calendar months, and so on from time to time for every succeeding year ; and after every such election the said overseers shall forthwith certify the names of the members of the educational committee so elected to the Committee of Council on Education."

Clause IV. provides—

" That the first elected educational committee of any parish shall forthwith propose a plan to supply the deficiency of the existing provisions for secular education in such parish, for the approval of the Committee of Council on Education, and on being approved by the said Committee of Council the same shall be carried into execution by the educational committee ; and such educational committee shall appoint a clerk, secretary, treasurer, or other officer, with such reasonable compensation as they may think fit, to assist in executing the plan so approved as aforesaid."

The nature of the instruction to be afforded in such schools may be further collected from the provisions of Clause V.

" That in every parish where such deficiency as aforesaid shall be reported, one or more free school or schools shall be established under the provisions of this act, which shall be under the management of the educational committee of such parish, who shall appoint the schoolmaster and mistress ; and in all schools established under this act (except the infant, evening, adult, and other schools hereinafter mentioned), provision shall be made for affording gratuitously sufficient instruction which shall be secular only, to all the children of each parish between the ages of *seven* and *thirteen* years ; and every schoolmaster and mistress shall be allowed a net yearly salary of not less than *one hundred pounds* for every fifty pupils who shall attend the free school of such master or mistress for one year : provided always, that the same course of secular education shall be afforded to all the pupils attending any such free school as aforesaid ; and all such pupils shall be free from all charges and payments whatever : provided also, that the master and mistress of every free school shall allow to each pupil sufficient time for receiving religious instruction, under the direction of the parents of such pupils : provided also, that each pupil of any free school, on completing his education, shall, upon receiving from the master or mistress of such school a certificate of approval, be entitled to books of the value of *fifty shillings*, to be selected by the said master or mistress, and one of such books shall be a copy of the Holy Scriptures ; and such certificate of approval shall relate to and certify approval of the continuous and regular attendance of such pupil at school, as well as his acquirements and good conduct."

The expenses of the school are to be defrayed by means of a school rate ; and in the event of any locality not proceeding to execute the orders of the Committee of Council, it is provided, in Clause XIII.,

" That in case no educational committee as aforesaid shall be elected in any parish, in pursuance of the direction of the said Committee of Council, or if no such plan as aforesaid shall be proposed by such Educational Committee, or, being proposed, shall not obtain the sanction and approval of the said Committee of Council, it shall be lawful for the said Committee of Council to undertake to supply the deficiency of provision for secular education by the establishment of a free school or schools under this act, and to exercise the powers hereby given to the Educational Committee of such parishes."

Comment upon such an enactment as this is wholly unnecessary. It is a measure of a directly revolutionary character, which, if carried into effect, could not fail to subvert every institution in the country. There is, of course, no fear whatever of its being carried; Mr. Fox himself has no hope, Lord John Russell no idea, of its becoming law. It is introduced, significantly, *in terrorem*, with a view to coerce the clergy into co-operation with the Committee of Council, upon the principle expounded by Mr. Hamilton, who, in strange inconsistency with his assertion, that the Committee of Council desire nothing more than to give efficiency to the system of the Church, thus discloses the real object which the Committee of Council are driving at :—

" It is quite certain that the Church is incompetent to sustain, much less to extend, her present educational system without the assistance of the State. It is just as certain that the State would be unable to carry out the scheme embodied in the Minutes of 1846, without the co-operation of the Church. Their joint action, as regards Church schools, is essential to success. But, to derive from this educational alliance all the benefits which it is capable of yielding, two conditions are indispensable: that the State refrain from all interference with the religious teaching of the Church; and that the Church throw open her schools, with the fullest recognition of the rights of conscience, to the children of Nonconformists. The State has fulfilled the first of these conditions —it remains for the Church to fulfil the second. By so doing, she would give up, or compromise, none of her distinctive doctrines. She would only be exercising that forbearance towards the religious scruples of those without her pale, which sound policy recommends and which Christian charity enjoins. She would only be carrying into effect a principle, which she has herself already recognised, which other religious communions have adopted, and which the Legislature has formally sanctioned. She would thus be enabled, without the smallest sacrifice of her own tenets, to remove one of the chief obstacles to the general education of the people."—*The Privy Council and the National Society*, pp. 53, 54.

Whether the Church is prepared to make the sacrifice of principle here recommended, may well be doubted. At present there is no appearance of it. Mr. Hamilton may try to wheedle her ; the Marquis of Lansdowne and Lord John Russell may frown and scold ; and Mr. Fox may try to overawe the Church with his Socinian Bill. None of these things will move the Clergy and the sound portion of the laity of the Church. They will bide their time ; they will continue to remonstrate ; they will carry their grievance to Parliament ; and they will not rest until the Legislature shall have dealt out to them at least even-handed justice. That justice cannot be withheld much longer ; the days of the Committee of Council, or, at all events, the days of its exorbitant and irresponsible power, are numbered. The struggle is drawing to a close, and the Church has the victory all but within her grasp. The rising generation will, in the blessings of a sound religious education, reap the fruit of stedfast adherence on the part of the Church to principles which the change of times and the fickleness of men cannot affect. And when England shall, through the influence of a faithful and laborious Clergy, be once more blessed with a religious population, it will be recorded by some future historian for the admiration of posterity, that there was once a Minister of the British Crown who suffered the prejudices and the necessities of party to prevail so far over every better principle of action and every rule of wisdom, as to place himself in an attitude of hostility against the Clergy of the Established Church, and to hail with malicious pleasure the abortive Education Bill of Mr. William Johnson Fox.

ART. III.—*The History of England during the Thirty Years'
Peace*, 1816—1846. *By* HARRIET MARTINEAU. London :
Charles Knight, 90, Fleet Street. 1849.

A FEW years ago, when the mania for universal suffrage had
arisen to a great height, we remember that a gentleman, at a
conservative dinner, said, "that, for his part, all he wanted was
universal suffrage to give England a more conservative parliament
than ever." His hearers seemed astonished ; but he repeated the
sentiment, and, looking round to a large gallery filled with ladies,
he explained himself by saying, "that, as all women were conservative, if every woman had a vote, he should have one-half of
the human race with him, and at least a tolerable proportion of
the other." Now, if this assertion were true, we are sorry to find
at least one exception to the rule in an eminent writer of our own
time. Women are generally opposed to theory and rash speculation on political subjects, but Miss Martineau is an exception to
the rule ; her book is a valuable addition to our modern information, and it is well put together, but the moral is bad ; her great
object is to inculcate what she calls progress, and what we call
democratic principles. This she does sometimes temperately
enough, but in the flippant style usual in her class of political
economists, and with the self-satisfied assumption of her own
superior knowledge, so that we sometimes feel inclined to exclaim
with the patriarch of old, "Doubtless ye are the people, and
wisdom shall die with you." As the thirty years which elapsed
from the battle of Waterloo to 1846 are to us the most important
period of history, the book will probably be widely circulated ; our
object therefore is, if possible, to counteract the moral tendency
of the work, and to show that, with considerable semblance of
reason, there is abundant room for detecting fallacies. Miss
Martineau, like the rest of her school of popular writers, is one
who deals in words rather than ideas—"Reform," "social progress," "rotten boroughs," "noble character of the people,"
"great measures," "patriotic ministers," "liberal and enlightened
statesmen,"—these and several other such terms are, in our view,
the English translation of "Liberty, Equality, and Fraternity,"
from the French. They mean really nothing but social disorder ;
but they catch the ear of the unwary, and lead them into serious
practical errors.

Let us examine the real principles of the British constitution, and see what it is that the nation ought to desire. There may be too much liberty; social equality is an utter impossibility; and political franchises may be a curse, and not a blessing. As we are thus contradicting much of the spirit of the age, we must begin by defining our terms, which popular writers seldom do, and we shall here cite the highest authorities we can find. " Liberty," says De Lolme, " consists in the power given by the State, that every man shall be able to enjoy the proceeds of his own industry, while, at the same time, he is taught to respect the proceeds of the industry of others." The latter part of this definition is sometimes overlooked.

In speaking of the different kinds of government, Aristotle [1] says, " The object of a monarchy is security; the object of an oligarchy is wealth; and the object of a democracy is liberty." Now the constitution of England was evidently intended to combine the three advantages, as the three elements are combined in her government. Modern politicians, however, endeavour to throw all the weight into the democratic scale; and by this means, in the endeavour to increase liberty, which was fully enjoyed before, they diminish the elements which provide for the security and prosperity of the nation.

Before Reform the three elements existed in the English government; the House of Commons, having the control of the supplies, was the most powerful of the three estates, or rather it was a combination of all three. The king's ministers sat, as a matter of course, for the government boroughs; or, if they could obtain more popular seats, the subordinates filled them up, and thus the Crown was represented in the Commons. The nobility also had a certain number of nomination seats, and thus the Lower House became the arena [2] on which the three powers tried their strength. The king has not for a long time exercised his right of veto; and under the old system this was fair, because he had at first nominated his advisers, and, if they were not able to command a majority, it became his duty to try a more popular administration. His real power consisted in the fact, that he had the deliberate power of choice of measures, and then asking the nation to support them, first by appointing his ministry, and, secondly, by a dissolution of parliament. This power William the Fourth ceded to his subjects. The Reform Bill became an act for perpetuating a Whig ministry in England; and, as in former reigns Whigs in office became Tories, so now, when in office, Tories are obliged to

---

[1] Rhet. 1. 8.

[2] Our readers will be surprised to learn that this idea is taken from one of the early numbers of the " Edinburgh Review," by the late Lord Jeffrey, where the old constitution is admirably explained and defended; but Radicals of the early part of the century might well pass for Tories at present.

turn Whigs. The reason is plain, the people now send the prime minister to the king, and not the king to the people; the cabinet no longer govern by desire of the Crown, subject to the control of popular opinion; but they are the creatures of popular opinion as represented in the House of Commons, and uncontrolled by the regal power. Instead, therefore, of an hereditary and constitutional monarch, we have an elective prime minister, and just in proportion to the destruction of the monarchical element the security of the constitution is lost. This, we can show, has been done in two ways. First as to property—Land is the most valuable property in England, because it produces food, and is least liable to waste. It binds the rich and the poor together in the relation of patron and client more firmly than any other species of property. The manufacturer dismisses his operatives at a week's notice; a fall in the market obliges him to do so, clothes being not so necessary as food: when the nation is poor, less goods are consumed. But as there is but one harvest in the year, and food cannot be dispensed with, the tenant must hold by the year, and his produce must find a sale. His labour is, therefore, the most important to the State, and his interests are most closely identified with his master. The proprietor of land has an influence, a respectability, a power of improvement and usefulness which no other owner of property can claim; the great object, therefore, of the industrious is to invest their proceeds in land,—

> " Est aliquid quocunque loco, quocunque recessu,
> Unius sese dominum fecisse lacertæ."

Now it happened in the year 1838, at a public dinner at Manchester, that certain democratic capitalists chose to express a wish that the landlords of England should divide their property with them. These landlords had agreed before to pay eight hundred millions to carry on the wars, which secured to England the carrying trade of the world, and introduced a new aristocracy of wealth. To enable the land to meet its engagements, protection had been established, and the manufacturers thought that, by laying this aside, and having food untaxed, they could diminish wages and increase their own production. Hence the cry for free trade, and the origin of the Anti-Corn-Law League. We are not here arguing on principles of political economy—we are merely stating a fact. Landlords had possession of certain emoluments by certain laws, and the League wished to take possession of them. The principle was modified communism; you have property, we have numbers, therefore you must divide. Now how was this transfer effected? By the power of the democracy. Large sums (we believe about a million) were subscribed; tons' weights of tracts were circulated; the farmers were told that the proposed

changes could not affect them, as it was merely a question of rent,
and could only damage their landlords. New freeholds were
created in equally balanced counties, which a Radical might obtain
for about 19*l*. (This scheme Miss Martineau praises, while she
finds fault with the Chandos clause for giving weight to the landlords.) The effect has been that the democratic party have
carried their point, and transferred a large portion of the property of their neighbours to themselves; at least, they thought
they had done so, though they may be mistaken. In our opinion
they will find it a mistake. God's rule of the world is to encourage every man to improve his own position, but it is also his
rule to make men dependent on each other; when, therefore, a
class of men agree to raise themselves by pulling down a neighbour,
they often find that their own downfal is involved in the injury
which they intended for others. If the agricultural interest cannot afford to buy, the manufacturing interest may not be able
to sell. All property is, of course, liable to fluctuation, but
no class of men have a right to create or increase this fluctuation by legislative enactment. So also it has happened in the
case of the clergy. Their property (called a tenth, but really
not a twentieth) was some years ago commuted for a sum
varying according to the average prices of corn. Now any Act of
Parliament intended to lower these averages is so much against
their income, and so much added to the insecurity of property
and of national faith. This is a branch of the subject on which
we may naturally be expected to offer something more than
a transient allusion, affecting, as it does, most seriously the
interests of many of our readers. The clergy have before them
the prospect of a very large diminution in their means. They
must look, we fear, in the course of a few years to the annihilation of one-third of their incomes. The Church has been despoiled of more than 1,000,000*l*. per annum of her income, by the
abolition of the Corn-Laws! So much is in the course of being
abstracted from the means of maintaining the education of the
poor, and of dispensing alms to the distressed and afflicted.
Each year the incomes of the clergy will be smaller than in the
preceding year; and the power, consequently, of aiding in those
charitable and religious objects which have hitherto been extensively, and in many cases almost exclusively, supported by the
clergy, will be more and.more limited. We must extract the
following statements, which have appeared already in the public
prints; the former of which, by Mr. Willich, will show how
things have been, and the other how they are to be. Mr.
Willich's statement is this:—

"*To the Editor of the Evening Mail.*

"Sir,—As your agricultural as well as clerical readers may feel anxious to know the result of the corn averages for the seven years to Christmas last, published in the 'London Gazette' of this evening, viz.—

Wheat............	6*s*.	$7\frac{1}{2}$*d*.	per Imperial bushel.
Barley............	4	$1\frac{1}{4}$	ditto,
Oats..............	2	$8\frac{1}{2}$	ditto.

"I beg to state for their information, that each 100*l*. of rent-charge will, for the year 1850, amount to 98*l*. 16*s*. 10*d*., or about one and one-third per cent. lower than last year.

"The following statement from my Annual Tithe Commutation Tables will show the worth of 100*l*. of rent-charge for each year since the passing of the Tithe Commutation Act, viz. :—

For the year	1837..............	£98	13	$9\frac{3}{4}$
"	1838..............	97	7	11
"	1839..............	95	7	9
"	1840..............	98	15	$9\frac{1}{2}$
"	1841..............	102	12	$5\frac{1}{4}$
"	1842..............	105	8	$2\frac{3}{4}$
"	1843..............	105	12	$2\frac{1}{4}$
"	1844..............	104	3	$5\frac{1}{4}$
"	1845..............	103	17	$11\frac{1}{2}$
"	1846..............	102	17	$8\frac{3}{4}$
"	1847..............	99	18	$10\frac{1}{4}$
"	1848..............	102	1	0
"	1849..............	100	3	$7\frac{3}{4}$
"	1850..............	98	16	10
		£1415	17	$6\frac{3}{4}$
	14)			
General average for 14 years....		£101	2	8

"I am, Sir, yours obediently, "CHARLES M. WILLICH."

We have now to present another view of the question contained in a very sensible and useful letter from the Rev. J. F. Francklin, who has, most properly, brought before his clerical brethren the effects of recent legislation on the interests of the Church. We cite this letter *in extenso*, because it contains statements on matters of fact which are well worthy of attention, and because its tone is perfectly unexceptionable.

"*To the Clergy and Tithe-Owners.*

"Gentlemen,—It may possibly appear somewhat presumptuous that so humble an individual as myself should venture to address so large and influential a class as those who (whether they be clergy or laymen) possess such considerable property as the tithe-rent-charge of this kingdom most unquestionably represents; but I trust I shall be pardoned for thus stepping forward, when it is considered that the revenues of the Church are now, openly and avowedly, threatened with spoliation by the great leader of free trade, Mr. Cobden. And, although I could have much desired some other and more influential person had taken the matter in hand; yet, since from some cause or other which it is not my province to determine, all have alike at present shrunk from the task, I deem it a duty which I owe to all connected with ecclesiastical affairs, to lay before them the present and future prospects of the property of the tithe-owner.

"By a letter lately addressed by myself to Mr. Cobden, upon the subject of the tithe-rent-charge, I elicited from that gentleman, in reply, the acknowledgment that the revenues of the Church will be eventually reduced, by the operation of free trade, to the extent of upwards of £30 per cent. per annum.

"And I am consequently of opinion that, with this threatened injury before us, if no higher and nobler motive should influence the tithe-owner to aid and assist the agricultural interest, yet the principle of self-preservation should induce a body of men, confessedly one of the most powerful in the kingdom, to stand forward and uphold the rights and privileges of a class at once the most peaceful and simple, yet by far the most numerous in the British empire.

"Why, indeed, should the owners and tillers of the soil be unfairly burdened?—and why should the clergy in particular be unjustly deprived of their revenues? Is it that they are considered 'dumb dogs who cannot bark?' or, 'labourers who are unworthy of their hire?' If so, it is time that they be replaced by other and better men. But I deny the fact. I believe never was the Established Church so well and efficiently administered as at the present—never were the clergy more zealous and active than at this period.

"Consequently, as we have divine authority for saying, 'They who wait at the altar shall be partakers with the altar,' and that, 'it is ordained that they who preach the gospel shall live of the gospel,' I maintain that it is both unjust and inexpedient that the clergy should be mulcted of nearly one-third of their apportioned wages for the questionable benefit of a class of the community who, for the most part, are as turbulent and disaffected to the Government of the country as the agricultural population are loyal and peaceable.

"It may be doubted by some of my brother tithe-owners whether such an injury as I have described will be ever really inflicted upon their property; and consequently, for their information, I have subjoined a table of the next seven years' average of the tithe commutation, which will determine their incomes year by year, should wheat range no lower than 40s. per quarter, barley 21s., and oats 19s., viz. :—

		£	s.	d.
£100 in	1850	£98	16	10
"	1851	97	0	8
"	1852	93	14	10
"	1853	90	7	0
"	1854	86	7	8
"	1855	77	14	10
"	1856	75	7	5

"The slightest fall below this standard will cause a depreciation in the general averages to the amount which I have before stated, viz., to 230 per cent. per annum.

"Having called the attention of the tithe-owners to the foregoing fact, I will say no more at present than, should they delay too long in coming forward and co-operating together with the landed interest to redress the great and grievous wrong inflicted upon the agriculturists, they will incur a serious responsibility, for they may rest assured that the battle now to be fought is not simply (as it is pretended) for free trade in corn, but

"'Pro aris et focis!'"

"'For God, for the Queen, and the country!'"

"And believe me, gentlemen, with every sentiment of respect,

"Your very humble and faithful servant,

"JOHN FAIRFAX FRANCKLIN.

"*West Newton, 26th Feb.* 1850."

Mr. Francklin might have carried his statement further, and might have shown that, for several years after 1856, the incomes of the clergy will probably descend at the rate of two, three, and four per cent. annually, independently of the loss in the value of their glebe lands, which takes effect *at once.*

We are borne out by these lamentable facts in stating that the Church of England has, by recent legislation, been deprived of a full THIRD of her property. She does not lose it at once; but gradually, it is true; still the fact is as we have stated it. And we regret to remember that, during the debates in the House of Lords on the subject, the probability of such a result was urged distinctly and emphatically upon the representatives of the Church in that august assembly, as a reason why *they* at least should pause before they gave their support to a measure which threatened to impoverish their clergy. That appeal, however, was made in vain. The imagined necessity of supporting the political views of the Government of the day, and of the leaders of influential political parties, outweighed the claims of a clergy whose prospects and position were extremely imperilled; and so large a majority of the Episcopal bench voted for Sir Robert Peel, that the measure may be said to have been carried by them. The speeches of the Bishops of Oxford and of St. David's will long be remembered; nor can it be forgotten that the former reverend prelate volunteered to answer on behalf of the clergy of England, for their willingness to consent to any reduction in their incomes that might be called for under the proposed Bill. The cause of the Church in Parliament was advocated by lay peers, who urged on prelates of the Church the unfairness of leaving the clergy to suffer from the reduction in the corn averages, while they themselves were, from the nature of their property, liable to no such reductions. The majority of the Episcopal body may have acted very wisely and properly, in their own view, in voting as they did; but we fear that many persons have been convinced by this and similar instances, in which the interests of governments and political parties have been considered in the FIRST place, to feel doubtful whether the Church derives great practical benefits from the presence of its bishops in the House of Lords. And it can scarcely be expected that those whose incomes were sacrificed, without scruple, for the purpose of retaining Sir Robert Peel in power, and carrying his measures, should, in all cases, feel the same kind of anxiety to maintain the incomes of the hierarchy on their present scale, if reduction should hereafter be called for, as they might have felt, had the claims of gratitude for fidelity to the Church's interests been superadded to those of personal respect, or of official connexion. The too great subserviency to the Government of the day, manifested on that and other previous occasions, more especially on the Maynooth Bill, will, we hope, be atoned for by greater fidelity hereafter. But to return to our leading subject. The attack on landed property was successful, because, since reform, the landed interest is comparatively weak. The English boroughs return 323 members, which is nearly half the whole House of 658. The household interest, taking in Scotland and Ireland, has therefore the power of the empire in its hands. But let us suppose a case. If it were desirable to a certain number of capitalists to carry any measure, to annihilate the House of Lords, to repudiate the national debt, or establish the Pope at St. Paul's, we doubt not means could be found under the present system to accomplish it. First, large sums of money must be collected, then the intentions of the House of Commons must be sounded; perhaps from twenty to fifty members might vote in a minority on the first division, and the proposition be rejected with laughter. After a while, however, some might turn a serious attention to the business, and a party would be formed. As Whig and Tory are nearly equally balanced, the new party, like the Leaguers, would be respected as giving weight to one or the other; so that a ministry would find it necessary to flatter them in order to preserve its existence. When a general election comes, then the monied party have their real weight; there are in every town numbers who notoriously sell their votes; these, say 200 each, in 200 boroughs, would be enough to turn a scale and unseat a ministry; so that there is nothing to prevent the worst portion of the electors being the real rulers of England. Of course this may seem to be an extreme case, but it is what the League have actually done; they have turned a scale tin he House of Com-

mons by means of money and agitation, and so gained their own
ends in an attack upon property, in opposition to the Lords, and
without hindrance from the Crown.   Mr. Cobden, like Jugurtha,
seemed to consider the State as set up for sale, and that contested
elections were his market; he brought his money and his freeholders to bear upon the council of the State and public opinion,
and he was able to carry his point.   It is unreasonable to complain of purchased seats, nomination boroughs, and corrupt
electors, under the old system, when the most active reformers
carry out the same principle to a greater extent.

There is nothing new in this connexion of democracy and insecurity; history teaches us that they have always gone together.
The Athenians never allowed a fellow citizen to grow rich; if he
were beyond his neighbours, they taxed him with an order to fit
out "two galleys and a tender," or compelled him to provide the
expense of a theatrical exhibition.   The free citizen must either
submit, or point out another citizen who was richer than himself.
If the second denied the fact, he could be obliged to exchange
property with the first.   All this was done on democratic principles; here is one who has property, but the people have votes, and
the good of the majority is the supreme advantage.   So far had
this system proceeded, that one of the comic poets represents a
citizen as telling his friend, that he was determined to eat and
drink as fast as he could, as he never considered his property secure until he had swallowed it.

But our opponents will reply, "Democracy certainly injures the
security of the rich, but it adds to the security of the poor—see
what cheap bread can do."   Now this, also, we deny: the poor
man may have no property to lose, but he has his employment;
and, what is more valuable than either, he has his life; and the
abrogation of the royal functions has been attended with want of
security for life as well as for property.   It is a rule of our constitution that "the king can do no wrong:" now one meaning of
this is, that he has a right to act on an emergency without being
responsible afterwards.   In war, for instance, the constitution
gives the king immense powers, only limited by the necessity of
asking supplies from the Commons.   This sovereignty is intended
for the security of all, and in less civilized times it was often
necessary to use it, and to anticipate or repel force by force.
There are, however, other calamities equally destructive as war.
The loss of the potato crop in Ireland in 1846 left three or four
millions of her Majesty's poorest subjects without their expected
food, and whole provinces were likely to be in a state of utter
destitution.   Here, then, was an emergency: the Romans would
have created a dictator; and the old constitution of England had
provided a remedy—the king ought to act.   The king, being

placed above responsibility, represents the whole body of his subjects, and would naturally act for the interest of all. He can have the advice of all classes and creeds, and of both sides of the house, while a prime minister cannot be advised by his political opponents. George the Third was one who knew his own place, and would have acted on it. He could, with the advice of the best political economists of the day, have obtained the best information, and taken the most strenuous measures. Supposing the proposal had cost one or two millions, if the king had raised the money, and by this means saved the nation from famine, the Commons must have granted the supply when called on; or, if not, an appeal to the people to support the king would have given him any Parliament he pleased, and the only danger would have been that over-popularity might make him too absolute. When George the Third once found his cabinet refractory, he threatened to send for thirteen respectable gentlemen to supply their places, and then, said he, " I shall ask my people whether they choose to be governed by you or by me."

But how stood the case in 1846? In a reformed Parliament, our elected king, Lord John Russell, must first be returned by the London merchants before he can direct the councils of the nation; he, therefore, represents but a small section of the community, and, of course, having no government borough to fall back upon, he speaks the sentiments of his constituents. He talks of not interfering with mercantile speculation— that demand will produce adequate supply, that sound principles of political economy tell us we must not force a market lest we discourage regular merchants, and that in the end there will always be enough. Sir Robert Peel acted much more wisely (he represented a private borough)—he ordered certain supplies in a quiet way, which provided against the partial failure of 1845. It is an axiom with us, that a minister can never be a king in the proper acceptation of the word. It is part of his business to answer questions, he is subject to misrepresentation in parliament, and in the newspapers; so that, when an emergency arises, the time for action is often lost in consultation, or sounding the disposition of the House. Thus the unity of the executive, one of our great constitutional advantages, is lost.

A joint-stock company, a religious society, or a charitable institution, always flourishes or retrogrades in proportion to the acts and ability of the secretary. The working man, who can have the whole subject in his mind, who can bring matters properly before the committee, and both advise them and carry out their plans, is the real king of the society. Though he must be restrained by public opinion, yet it is his duty to give a proper

tone to that opinion, and, when he has ascertained it, to carry out
the views of his friends in the best way. If, however, a society
should determine that their secretary shall have no power, that he
shall be changed every year, and if they are afraid that he will do
too much, we should soon find the exertions of the society crippled,
and their objects unsteadily carried out. Security, then, depending on the power of the Crown to meet an emergency, and to
prevent one subject, or class of subjects, from encroaching on the
rights of another, has been very much diminished. As we have
not yet attained to universal suffrage or the ballot, we have not
ventured upon repudiation or open confiscation; but, while we have
approached more closely to the ultra-democratic principle, we
have fallen under some of the losses attendant on it.

The passing of the Reform Bill, by which these changes were
effected, is one of the most interesting passages in Miss Martineau's history; the popular cry, the sudden dissolution of Parliament by the unexpected arrival of William IV. during a
debate on the 22nd of April, 1831, while the peers were in the
act of preparing a remonstrance against it; "the waverers" in the
House of Lords; the question, first, "What will the Lords do?"
and, afterwards, "What must be done with the Lords?" and,
finally, the advice of Lord Grey to the king to create peers in
order to pass the Bill;—all these are matters which Miss Martineau relates with the greatest zest. For our part, we confess,
we look back upon these events as among the most unfortunate
which ever befell the nation. De Lolme's motto, "Ponderibus
librata suis," no longer applies to the British Constitution; two
estates of the realm combined to destroy the weight of the third,
or rather the king was induced by a desire of popularity to throw
away the trust committed to him for the good of his subjects.
This the peers foresaw; and the Duke of Wellington asked the
question, "But, my lords, How is the king's government to be
carried on?" Nearly twenty years' experience enables us to
answer the question; it is not carried on: a new form of government is introduced, new kings are elected and dethroned in
each succeeding Parliament, and while the people glory in
their imaginary rights they have really gained nothing in liberty,
while they have lost much in the security and value of their
property.

Louis Philippe went a step further than William IV.: one of
his first acts was to create peers to destroy the hereditary peerage; and the event has shown that his unconstitutional act has
destroyed his throne, while an unconstitutional threat has weakened the Crown of England. The royal prerogative of creating
peers now merges in the prime minister, thus giving a subject a

fearful degree of power. He may at any time use the king's name to annihilate the power of the Upper House, if the Commons have so decreed. Miss Martineau relates, with the greatest satisfaction, O'Connell's agitation for an elective house of peers ; the various motions for the expulsion of the bishops ; and Mr. Hume's modest proposition that the lords should only be allowed to delay the progress of a measure for one session, and that the royal assent should be given to a bill as soon as it had passed the Commons a second time. (See vol. ii. p. 258, &c.)

Miss Martineau confesses that reform is a failure. On this subject she writes thus :—

" There were men among the working classes, sound-headed and sound-hearted, wanting nothing but a wider social knowledge and experience to make them fit and safe guides for their order (some few of them not deficient even in these), who saw that the Reform Bill was, if not a failure in itself, a failure in regard to the popular expectation from it. If it was not all that its framers meant it to be, they must give a supplement."

We have, then, an extract from Carlyle's " Chartism," in which he shows that, in a reformed Parliament, the same questions and struggles go on as before :—

" What ministry should be in office, game laws, Irish affairs, usury laws, African blacks," &c., &c.

He is surprised that the real representatives of the people cannot remedy the evils under which the people suffer ; and this Miss Martineau adds in conclusion :—

" These men wanted a strong, steady-going progression ; and they would have therefore neither the pomp and prancings of Toryism, nor the incapacity of Whiggism. They were Radical Reformers."—Vol. ii. p. 264.

The fallacy here, that any body of representatives can effect impossibilities ; the extreme folly of expecting a redress of natural evils by the force of legislation ; the mistake that better members must be found by universal suffrage than by representation of interests, are too clear to require refutation. France has universal suffrage ; but are the people more secure, more religious, more wealthy, or more content ?

But the cry is still with Miss Martineau and her admirers, " Give us progress and equal rights, extend the franchise, let no man be unrepresented, but let every one who pays taxes (or who does not) have a voice in their disposal." Now we say, Represent every class in the community ; but the indiscriminate extension of the franchise may be a curse and not a blessing : it is the very means by which classes are not represented, as other interests are swal-

lowed up in numbers.   The difference, says De Lolme, between a
popular government (like Athens) and a representative one is,
that "a popular government places the power in the hands of
those who cause the disorder; a representative government places
it in the hands of those who feel the disorder."   Now the extension of the franchise, as in great towns, often puts the power into
the hands of the popular man, the man who talks loudest and gives
the most trouble; and thus, as in the case of the Anti-Corn-Law
League, members were returned to Parliament to legislate on the
very commotion which they themselves had created.   Here the
franchise, instead of serving the State or the holder, only serves
the orator who makes a tool of the elector for his own purpose.
The householder is taught for the time to consider himself a great
man, and he is led into drunkenness, bribery, perjury, and every
species of demoralization, if it will only secure the return of the
aspirant to parliamentary honours.   This is, of course, only an
abuse, and is no argument against the lawful use of the privilege.
True; but what we want to show is, that extension of suffrage is
not the way to reform a nation : it has its crying evils as well as
its advantages.

Besides, at this moment, the Whigs are endeavouring to force
thousands into the strife of political controversy, who have hitherto
shrunk from it, and repudiated the boon.   The Irish tenant farmers
have been so unwilling to register, that many of them have refused
leases, and the Irish constituencies have greatly fallen away.   A
bill is now before Parliament to make the poor-rate the test of
the franchise, and to register each occupier, valued at 8*l.*, without
consulting him; thus forcing the unfortunate tenant to vote either
against the landlord or the priest; or rather giving the Roman
Catholic priests the power, on the day of election, of driving them
to the poll like a flock of sheep [3].   Of all the arrangements ever
proposed for a starving and disorganized country, this seems to be
the most monstrous.   It has never even been asked for, and would
be deeply regretted by the unfortunate men to whom the privilege
is given, and does much more harm than a sweeping measure of
the kind in England.   At present Ireland is quite incapable of
understanding her own interests.   English radicals and manufacturers saw, or thought they saw, a benefit in repealing the corn-
laws; but the Irish tenant farmers only did what the priests de-

[3] Mr. Bright, seeing this difficulty, lately proposed the ballot as a remedy.   To
this we answer by a quotation from Mitford's "Greece," which disposes of the subject
very concisely.   "Alcibiades, being asked if he could not trust his country, replied,
' Yes, for every thing else : but, in a trial for life, not my mother ; lest, by mistake, she put a black bean for a white one.'   Whatever authority there be for this
anecdote, it contains a very just reproof of the Athenian mode of giving judgment
on life and death by a secret ballot, which, without preventing corruption, admits
mistake, excludes responsibility, and covers shame."   (Vol. iii. p. 459.)

sired them. The landed interest presented a barrier between the
Roman Catholic Church and the rule of the country, and this
they were determined, at all hazards, to pull down. They, therefore,
told the freeholders that it was a religious question; the people
believed (like all Roman Catholics) that they must obey their
spiritual superior in all spiritual matters, and, when their landlords
reasoned with them on the destruction they were bringing upon
their own trade, the answer was, " Give us a big loaf and high
wages." Ireland, therefore, has no right to complain of the late
changes in the price of corn; she herself voted against protection,
more than half the Irish members sided with the Whigs, and if
the Irish constituencies chose to throw away their own market
for the benefit of foreigners, and at the teaching of the Pope, they
have no one to blame but themselves and their advisers. Where
the blame really lies is upon those who create constituencies unqualified to understand their own interests, and who, in the
endeavour to destroy the undue influence of the nobility in electing representatives, have given greater power to those who have
less interest in the general welfare.

To prove our assertion, we need only take the example of the
proposer of the Irish Franchise Bill, now before Parliament, by
which he intends to raise the number of voters in a tenfold ratio.
Sir William Somerville, the chief secretary for Ireland, has, for
the last two or three Parliaments, represented the town of Drogheda, with a constituency of about 700. As he is one of those
politicians who would govern Ireland through the priests, and as
he resides close to the town which he represents, we should suppose him well qualified to express the opinions of his constituents,
except that, unfortunately, he happens to be a gentleman. When
the present Government came into office, he was appointed chief
secretary,—a position which gives him the management of the local
administration at Dublin Castle, and also the best patronage in
the kingdom. Here, then, were abundant places for needy constituents, and we should have expected to have heard of Drogheda
men or their sons in all the small places under the Crown. The
police, the excise, the government stores would naturally have
opened for the sons and brothers of the secretary's constituents.
We cannot blame a minister for thus playing into the hands of
those who support him; he owes his political existence, not to
the Crown, but to the electors of a borough; and, therefore, they
must be his first object. Now, to carry out the views of those
who are represented, a voice in the Government is worth twenty
votes in the House, and we might have thought Sir William's
supporters would have been satisfied; but it was not so. As
soon as Parliament was dissolved, one of his friends waited on
him, and told him he must have a certain number of places, with

certain salaries annexed, or Sir William must expect to lose his seat. Here is again the fatal mistake of reform: the powers of the executive are left at the mercy of the rabble ; the acceptance of office vacates a seat, and, if the new minister be turned out of his former place, the Crown has no power to provide him with another. Inefficient officers are thus often appointed because their seats are secure. Sir William Somerville, as an honest man, could not swallow the pledge, a violent opposition was got up in favour of a stranger unknown in the town before, and the chief secretary was only returned by a majority of two. He would have lost his seat, as the Conservative party intended not to vote ; but a few gentlemen took pity on him, and came forward to support him within half an hour of the close of the poll. We should have thought such an election would have been a lesson to the Irish secretary, but we fear no experience will teach a Whig to forego a little temporary popularity.

As to the second species of government, an aristocracy, whose end is wealth, there has been some loss occasioned by reform, but not to the same degree as in the destruction of the power of the Crown. The Reform Bill left great weight with the aristocracy ; but this was because, in the very nature of things, wealth and knowledge must confer power. The division of the counties and the Chandos clause (at which Miss Martineau is very angry) gave a counterbalance to the small tenures in towns, and the counties now return the aristocratic members instead of the boroughs. This leaves matters pretty much as they were ; but one element which favours wealth has been omitted, we mean corporate representation. For this, numerical suffrage has been substituted. Corporations were originally intended to encourage and protect industry; serving an apprenticeship was a very common title to freedom : thus corporate interests, particular trades (ship-builders, cotton-spinners, wool-staplers, &c., according to the different manufactures of the towns), were supposed to be represented in the legislature. Corporations certainly had fallen into the hands of individuals; these were generally rich proprietors who spent money on the improvement of the town, and expected the corporation to lend them parliamentary influence in return. Jobs were often thus managed, but we believe the reformed corporations understand jobbing quite as well; the new electors are quite as open to bribery, and in many places municipal taxation is increased. Though reform has done its part to take away the representation of interests, there are still certain interests which force themselves into the House. The East India Company, for instance, are obliged to have some of their directors in Parliament, and instead of the old plan they buy a few hundred electors *in some* corrupt borough, where the inhabitants are anxious to

get up a contest. It is remarkable that the two members for
Old Sarum twenty years ago were two of the great bankers of
Calcutta ; so that the most rotten borough in England actually
represented the monied interests of India, and perhaps twenty or
thirty millions of his majesty's subjects.

Parliament is not the real place of representation ; the true
representation is in the cabinet. Here trade, India, the colonies,
foreign relations, the government at home and in Ireland, are all
efficiently represented by men who really understand their subjects ; and this is the real ground on which all great questions are
decided. We have heard a very high character of the respectability and dignity of the American senate. Now this assembly
(their upper house) are neither more nor less than the representatives of the States in their corporate capacity. Each local
government sends two senators to Congress ; and these men,
though a weak body as compared with the house of representatives, yet seem to command the respect of the better class of their
countrymen, which the popular assembly certainly does not. The
outcry against rotten boroughs arose from the fact that a single
individual, like the Duke of Newcastle, could send six or eight
members to the House of Commons, and that therefore he could
carry certain points with the Government for his own private
benefit ; he was a monopolist—he could sell the freedom of England, and had too much power for a free and enlightened country.

Now we ask, Were not O'Connell and Cobden quite as extensive
borough-mongers as any great lord before reform ? The only
difference between them and the former monopolist is, that the
one served themselves openly and avowedly ; and the others did so
in the name of the people, whom they kept in agitation in order
to retain their influence. If we might propose a new species of
reform, we should say that the best measure would be to disfran-
chise all boroughs where corruption is proved, and then give the
members to the old and respectable corporations. We mean the
East India Company, the Bank of England, the Colleges of
Physicians and Surgeons. Afterwards the railway interests
might be incorporated for the purposes of the franchise. These
great bodies must be heard in Parliament : and the only question
is, whether they shall be heard unfairly by buying corrupt electors ;
or whether they shall have a legal and honest right given them
to that which they already possess. We have but three corporations now remaining in possession of the franchise ; and these
afford the six best and most respectable seats in the House—we
mean the three Universities. This is the only instance where old
privilege was spared, and where local and numerical suffrage did
not supersede intelligence and qualification. We do not see why
knowledge of medicine and surgery should not be as good a title

to the franchise as a degree in arts; the medical profession is now in the greatest difficulties for want of proper legislation, on subjects which few but professional men can understand.   We believe that the possession of Bank Stock or East Indian securities (both requiring regulation by law) will give quite as good an interest in the welfare of the State as a ten-pound household which requires no such legal protection.   Wherever, then, the householders disqualify themselves (as many do at least once in seven years), let another qualification be sought; there will still be boroughs enough left to represent the class of householders, and several great interests will be brought into direct consideration which are now only indirectly or unfairly represented.   As the third object in government is liberty, and as this is the great benefit to be expected from democracy, let us consider whether, in our evident losses on the other two points, we have gained an equivalent in the third.   Before reform we believe England was perfectly free.   The king could not interfere with private rights; and, if Parliament did so, they always awarded compensation. The inherent weakness of the ancient democracy was such, that at Rome and Sparta the people were obliged to create a class of magistrates for their own protection, who became in the end the greatest tyrants.   The Tribunes, and the Ephori, being protected personally by law, soon abused their power, and became corrupt in the exercise of their trust.   Now, as the British Constitution gives us each of the great features of the ancient republics, we also have our protecting magistrates chosen for the people, and not by them : we mean the judges.   They are officially independent, though personally responsible.   A judge can be prosecuted for an assault (if such a thing could happen) though he can administer the law to rich and poor alike, and the whole power of the State is bound to support his decision.   This great bulwark of constitutional liberty existed long before reform, and when a reformed House of Commons attempted to interfere with it, the whole democracy of England, with Sir Robert Peel at its head, was defeated by Lord Denman, on the question of breach of privilege.   This steady execution of the law is the real safeguard of our liberties, and we should wish to be informed upon the point as to what greater degree of liberty honest men require than the English enjoyed before the year 1832.

De Lolme's definition of liberty, quoted above, includes the fact, that every one must respect the rights of his neighbour; and in this sense the effect of all the late democratic movements has been to diminish liberty.   When at Paris, in 1848, an English lady saw her coachman shot on her carriage, because he was an Englishman; the only answer she received from the police was, " Madam, have you not seen the proclamation ?   It is the will of the people that no foreign servants be employed." When, at the same period, a gentleman was removing his property to London, he was only allowed to take a small portion of his plate, for the will of the people did not allow property to be removed from France.

Liberty does not consist in the power of insulting our neighbours, or wearing our hats in public places, or abusing others anonymously through the medium of the press. Where each man can enjoy his property and his rights, he is truly free. Americans consider it a violation of freedom when they are not allowed to beat their own niggers; and Frenchmen left us a lasting burlesque on liberty when they cut down the trees which ornamented the Boulevards of Paris, and planted them to wither under tri-coloured garlands. A few foolish fellows might be seen dancing round them, and crying, "Vive la république!" but this affords a striking exemplification of those who seek for a mistaken liberty by destroying our constitution. The tree has made progress certainly; but its beauty, usefulness, and stability are gone, and the old fabric of the British Constitution which sheltered our fathers is exchanged for temporary excitement. The radical press, the great enemy of true liberty, calumniating every thing good and virtuous at a penny a line, are the interest who really gain by the commotion. The newspaper editor, whose stock in trade consists in a few unmeaning phrases, is either to be the public instructor, or a member of a provisional government; and thus, while a phantom is pursued, the reality is lost.

Every nation must be led by somebody. The question is, Shall it be by the king or a minister? by the Duke of Wellington or by Fergus O'Connor? From the latter alternative, and the evils of the French revolution, nothing saved us but the providence of God, who gave firmness to the Duke of Wellington and good sense to the citizens of London. The natural step from the licentiousness of a mob is to a military despotism, and the extreme of liberty ends in its total loss. A few interested persons, like the orators of Athens, or the revolutionary writers of the present day, get up a disturbance in order to profit by it themselves. They enjoy the excitement, and gratify their jealousy against their superiors. The freedom of opinion and the liberty of the press are watchwords which sound well, when in reality the liberty claimed is only the privilege of injuring others. We must recollect, that while the democracy of Athens has left us the orations of Demosthenes and the comedies of Aristophanes, the benefit has been reaped by the rest of the world, while the citizens lived in continual fear of each other, and the ballot of the model republic condemned Socrates to die.

It is hardly fair to an author to close a review without, at least, a specimen of the style of the book, and we select a striking passage. It will give our readers a true idea of her talents as a writer, which are considerable; and her feelings as a politician, which are unfair. The advocate of progress cannot help sneering at those who desire to uphold the institutions of the country, while the striking scene which we have chosen gives great scope for description. It is the death and funeral of the Duke of York.

" The Duke of York was the first who was withdrawn. The Lord Chancellor saw much of him for some weeks before his death; and the chancellor's opinion was, that his thoughts were almost exclusively occupied by the Catholic question, and the dread in regard to that question of the ascendancy of Mr. Canning. In Lord Eldon's own opinion, his existence was essential to the effectual counteraction of Mr. Canning's influence, and to his displacement from the councils of the king. 'His death,' declares Lord Eldon, 'must affect every man's political situation, perhaps nobody's more than my own; it may ·shorten, it may prolong my stay in office.' Of course, Mr. Canning himself must have known, as well as other people, the importance of the life that had gone, the significance of the death that had arrived. It must have been with a singular mixture of feelings, that a man of his patriotism and power of will, and of his magnanimity and sensibility, must have bent over the vault in St. George's Chapel, into whose darkness, amidst the blaze of torches, the body of his arch-enemy was descending. It was then and there that he took his own death,— perhaps at the moment when he was thinking how quiet in that resting-place at the goal of every human career, where the small and the great lie down together, and 'princes and counsellors of the earth,' like his foe and himself, are quiet, and sleep after their warfare. If those who attended the funeral could have seen their own position, between the past and the future, as we see it now, it would have so absorbed all their thoughts, that the body might have been lowered into its vault unseen, and the funeral anthems have been unheard. A more singular assemblage than the doomed group about the mouth of that vault has seldom been seen. In virtue of our survivorship, we can observe them now, each one with his fate hovering over his uncovered head. He who was next to be lowered into that vault was not there. He was in his palace, weak in health and spirits,—relieved, and yet perplexed, that the course of government was simplified by the removal of his remonstrant brother, whose plea of nearness to the throne—now so solemnly set aside—had made his interference at once irksome and difficult to disregard. There would be no more interference now, no more painful audiences, no more letters brought in with that familiar superscription. The way was clear now; but to what? Liverpool and Canning must settle that. If they felt that the Catholic question must be settled, they must show how it was to be done, and they must do it. Liverpool and Canning! By that day twelvemonth how was it with them? Lord *Liverpool* was not at Windsor that night. He laid down his care-worn head to rest, unaware that but a few more days of life (as he considered life) remained to him. The body breathed for some months, but in a few days after this the mind was dead. As for Canning,—his heart and his mind were full as his noble brow shone in the torch-light. He well knew that it was not only his chief personal enemy who was here laid low, but the only insurmountable barrier to his policy! He saw an open course before him, or one which he himself could clear. He saw the foul fiend Revolution descend into that vault, to be sealed down in it with that coffin. He saw beyond that torch-lit chapel a vision of Ireland tranquillized; and the hope rose within him that he might achieve a peace at home, the sound peace of freedom—as blessed as the peace which he had spread over the world abroad. And all the time the chill and damps of that chapel, dim amidst the yellow glare with the night fog of January, were poisoning his vitals and shortening his allowance of life to a mere span. Beside him stood his friend and comrade Huskisson. They were born in the same spring; they were neither of them to know another moment of health, after this chilly night service; and their deaths were to be not far apart. What remained for both were the bitter last drops of the cup of life; sickness, toil, perplexity, some humiliation, and infinite anguish. Here, if they had known their future, they would have laid down all self-regards, all ambition, all hope and mirth, all thoughts of finished work and a serene old age, and have gone forth to do and suffer the last stage of their service, before drooping into their untimely rest. These two had made no professions of grief about the death of the prince: they did not vaunt their feelings; yet here they were, sad and solemn; while beside them stood one whose woes about the loss of his royal friend, and about the irreparable loss to the empire, were paraded before all men's eyes, and dinned into the ears of all who would listen. Here stood Lord Chancellor Eldon, beside the open grave in which he declared that the hopes of his country were being buried. Was he lost in grief? his ready tears in fuller flow than ever? his soul absorbed in patriotic meditation? 'Lord Eldon recollecting'—what? that he might catch cold—stood upon his hat, to avoid the chill from the flags: and ' his precaution was completely successful.' "

(We think the old gentleman was quite right to take care of his health, whatever opinion Liberals may have formed.)

" If it had but occurred to Canning to stand upon his hat! but he was thinking of other things. There were others for whom death was in waiting; and some for whom great labours and deeds were preparing in life: the troublesome opponent of ministers, Mr. Tierney, who was to be found dead in his study before the next royal funeral; and Lord Graves, who was to die by his own hand under the provocation of royal vice or levity. And what tasks lay before those who were to live and work! Among the six dukes who bore the pall, was he who was to succeed to the highest military office now thus vacated: and Wellington himself, no doubt, thought this night that he was of one mind in the great political questions of the day with the prince whose pall he bore.

No doubt he believed that he should, in his proper place, do what he could to exclude the Catholics, and to keep the conscience of the sovereign fixed upon the coronation oath, and his duty to Protestantism :—in his proper place, we say, because the duke spurned the idea of a military chief, like himself, taking civil office, and openly declared, with indignation at an unfounded rumour, that he should be mad if he dreamed of the premiership. Yet, before this royal vault should again be opened, Wellington was to be premier, and use his office to repeal the disabilities of the Catholics. Truly, pledges and prophecies are dangerous things for statesmen to meddle with in times of transition : and it would seem to be a main feature in the mission of the honest and resolute Wellington, honest and resolute beyond all cavil, to prove the presumption of pledges and prophecies in times of transition. Then there was Peel, with the same work before him, and much more of which he had not yet begun to dream ; and with the fate before him of losing his best beloved honour, the representation of his university, and gaining several others, any one of which would suffice to make an immortality. And there was Hardinge, the friend of both the deceased and the incoming commander-in-chief, who was to signalize his age in the history of India by his administration and achievements both in peace and war. And there was, as chief mourner, he who was to be our next king, and in whose reign was to occur that vital renovation of our representative system, which will be to thoughtful students a thousand years hence what Magna Charta is to us. What a group was here collected within the curtain of the future, seeing nothing but the vault at their feet and the banners of the past waving above their heads, and wherever they thought they saw their way into coming time, seeing wrongly, mistaking their own fancy painting on the curtain for the discernment of that which was behind it. And behind that veil agents were at work unheard ; death at his grave-digging, and the people with their demands and acclamations, and the trumpet-voice of conviction summoning prejudice to surrender. But what they saw not we as survivors see ; and what they heard not we hear ; for now that curtain of futurity is hung up over our heads as banners of the past ; and the summons of death, and of the popular will and of individual conscience, are still audible to us, not in their first stunning crash, but as funeral echoes to which those banners float."—Vol. i. p. 430.

Of course any recognition of God's over-ruling Providence, that " by Him kings reign and princes decree justice," that it is the God of heaven and earth, " who stilleth the noise of the waves and the madness of the people," but sometimes allows progress as the punishment of presumption, are all antiquated prejudices which modern liberalism altogether disclaims. To Miss Martineau the people are a God, their will is the supreme law, and death is the eternal sleep which is to close the scene upon the great and good. So solemn an occasion as the funeral of an expectant king, we have no doubt, called up very different feelings from those above described ; and, if it did not, it is only another proof of the utter vanity of all worldly ambition, and the misery of those who in this world only have hope. As Miss Martineau's two quarto volumes are large and expensive, they carry the best antidote to their own evil. The book is not likely to have much circulation among the less-educated classes, and we hope that a little attentive consideration will enable her readers to take what is really valuable, because it is true, and leave what is dangerous, because it disguises revolution under specious expressions.

We would respectfully ask Miss Martineau what she means by progress? Is she an advocate for communism, anarchy, and repudiation? if not, what is it that she desires, and where are we to stop? Of course she wishes to remove the bishops from the House of Lords: does she wish to include the whole house in a schedule of disfranchisement? She wishes for all religions to be on an equality, destroying of course the property of the Established Church: does she propose to respect the property of the laity, including the Funds and copyright? She is anxious for education without bigotry: does she propose to exclude the Bible and religion from our schools? She wishes for an extension of the franchise (this is popular and seems to mean something): is she an advocate for universal suffrage? and, if so, are women to have votes in the new commonwealth? She does not approve of their admission to the gallery of the House of Commons, though she wishes to see them organized in clubs and literary societies. In short, we call for a definition of her favourite term "Progress," we want to know whither we are going. If England could see, as we have endeavoured to show, that under a democracy property is insecure, a reaction must at once take place; but we fear things must go farther before this is clearly seen. For our own part, we feel that progress has gone too far already, and that many of its advocates, like the Tories who advocated reform, or the farmers who shouted for cheap bread, do not know what they are asking for. We wish we could see an agitation in England to restore the legitimate power of the Crown, as upon it depends much of our social liberty, and where we have diminished it we have lost the constitutional element for the protection of the nation against sudden emergencies, and for the security of property at home.

Art. IV.—1. *The Doctrine of the Church of England, as to the Effects of Baptism in the Case of Infants. With an Appendix, containing the Baptismal Services of Luther and the Nuremburg and Cologne Liturgies.* By WILLIAM GOODE, *M.A., F.S.A., Rector of Allhallows the Great and Less, London. Second Edition.* Hatchards : London.

2. *The Doctrine of Holy Baptism, with Remarks on the Rev. W. Goode's "Effects of Infant Baptism."* By ROBERT ISAAC WILBERFORCE, *A.M., Archdeacon of the East Riding.* London: Murray.

3. *The Argument of Dr. Bayford in behalf of the Rev. G. C. Gorham, in the Arches Court of Canterbury.* London: Seeleys.

4. *Church Matters in* MDCCCL. *No. 1. Trial of Doctrine.* By *the* Rev. JOHN KEBLE, *M.A., Vicar of Hursley.* Oxford and London : J. H. Parker.

5. *A First Letter on the present position of the High Church Party in the Church of England.* By *the* Rev. WILLIAM MASKELL, *Vicar of St. Mary Church. The Royal Supremacy and the authority of the Judicial Committee of the Privy Council.* London : Pickering.

6. *Bishop Jewell on the Sacraments of Holy Baptism and the Lord's Supper.* London : Rivingtons.

7. *Baptismal Regeneration, &c.* By the Rev. G. TOWNSEND, *D.D., &c.* London: Rivingtons.

8. *The Opponents of Baptismal Regeneration Solemnly Warned, &c.* By the Rev. W. B. BARTER. London: Rivingtons.

9. *A Scriptural View of the Rites of Baptism.* By JEREMIAH JACKSON, *M.A., Rector of Elm with Emneth.* London: J. W. Parker.

10. *The Doctrine of Holy Baptism Explained.* By the Rev. C. E. DOUGLAS, *B.A., Curate of Brighton.* Brighton : King.

11. *Suggestions to Minds Perplexed by the Gorham Case. A Sermon.* By the Rev. W. SEWELL, *B.D., &c.*

THE decision of the Committee of Privy Council having been given in the Gorham case, we feel more at liberty to speak freely and fully on the various topics connected with this serious subject, than we did in the course of the legal investigations which have issued so far in the decision of the judicial Committee of Council. We hope that we shall be enabled to speak on the question with the calmness which its deep importance requires, though it may be difficult to preserve the tone of mind in which it ought to be approached, in the midst of the extreme excitement which it has not unnaturally created; and which is united with an evidently unsettled state of opinion in some cases, and with habits of bold action and decision on partial consideration of questions, which the controversies of late years have, unfortunately, tended to foster; and also with a tendency to extreme and overstrained views on some points, in which men easily deviate into error, and in which the course of truth is marked by no such broad and striking features that " he who runs may read."

The case is, indeed, one of no ordinary difficulty; and though we have the fullest and most unshaken confidence that the truth will in the end be vindicated; and that the course of those who hold the truth in the many difficult and complex questions before us, will become more plain than it may seem to them at present, when, confessedly, matters are in a state of great complexity; yet we must, undoubtedly, look in great anxiety at the course which may be taken by some members of the Church; and, although we are aware that our suggestions are not likely to receive much attention in the quarters referred to, we would yet entreat on behalf of the Church of England, that if, indeed, there be that filial attachment to her, which has been ere now in some degree professed, and which is undoubtedly due to the Church which has administered to us the sacrament of regeneration—if there be any remaining loyalty to the Church of England, and the love once borne to her has not turned into gall and bitterness, under the influence of disappointment and fear—that she should not now be condemned, and delivered unto Satan as one that is faithless to her Redeemer's cause—that the desertion of her wayward children may not add to her affliction—and that no heart fail for fear lest the cause of Catholic and Apostolic truth be overcome, or believe that it *is* to be overcome in the Church of England.

Why should the Church of England be now regarded with a different feeling from what she was a year ago? Were there not many persons within her communion then, who taught unsound doctrine on the point of baptismal regeneration? Have there not been various persons—nay, clergymen—who broadly and openly denied regeneration in any sense in Baptism? And have not those persons been permitted to remain in possession of benefices? Have not even Bishops been uncertain on that doctrine? And yet have they not remained in their sees? It is a simple fact, that for many years there have been large numbers of clergy, who have denied the doctrine of the Church of England in this matter, and have, in various and contradictory ways, attempted to explain her formularies in accordance with their views, or have sought for their alteration. Well—it may be, that the question ought to have been long ago brought to the test of some ecclesiastical tribunal, and that the defenders of the Church's doctrine ought not to have satisfied themselves as they did with mere controversy; but still they may well be excused for the course they took. They, perhaps, were of opinion that controversy, in so very plain a matter, in which their own cause was so triumphant in point of argument, was sufficient. They trusted to the force of truth; the heads of the Church did not deem it necessary to interfere; and others were unwilling to take the movement out of their hands.

We do not mean to deny that the decision of the Committee of Council gives the sanction of the temporal power, as far as it goes, to the continuance of teaching at variance with the formularies of the Church. The temporal power declares, that in *its* judgment the difference is not such in this case as to prevent both parties holding office in the Church of England. The temporal power decides *in its own favour*, the presentee to the vacant living being presented by a functionary of the temporal power; and it naturally opens the doors as wide as it possibly can to admit those whom it may nominate to the possession of the temporalities which it bestows.

We do not see what the Church of England has *now* done to alter her position. From whatever cause, there has been for some time a division on certain points, especially on the question of regeneration. We are far from saying or thinking that truth is exclusively on one side of the question, in the various matters under discussion. We think that there have been faults in both directions; that the one party has disputed the teaching of the Church on regeneration, and that some on the other side have not adequately received her teaching on election and final perseverance. But we certainly do not see how it is possible, consistently with justice, to affirm that the Church of England has spoken in the late decision of the Committee of Council, and affirmed that she sanctions contradictory doctrines. We know it is easy for malice to misrepresent her position, or for excited feeling to misapprehend it; but the only real change in her position is, that it is now ascertained that the present Court, to which the State devolves its supreme power in Church matters, has decided that the doctrines which have been so long taught with impunity in the Church shall still be taught with impunity; that the plain and evident meaning of the formularies of the Church, and the evident intentions of the compilers, shall still be perverted by the evasions and subtleties by which men have hitherto been enabled to continue to teach doctrines contrary to them.

The formularies of the Church remain as they were a year

since, when it was affirmed, by all who upheld the doctrine of baptismal regeneration, that they distinctly taught that doctrine. Are those formularies changed, or is their meaning now different from what it then was? The Committee of Council has, from whatever motives or reasons, placed a wrong interpretation on those formularies, and has in its action frustrated the effort to maintain the evident doctrine of those formularies. But all that results from the matter is this, that the Church has not at this moment the power of expelling false doctrine on the point referred to, by any appeal to the Committee of Privy Council. It remains however to be seen what course she must pursue for the maintenance of the truth which is enshrined in her formularies. The present is only one item in the series of difficulties which are continually and increasingly presenting themselves in the present relations of the Church with the temporal power. The Church of England is now involved in great difficulties, having before her the difficult task of managing the controversy within herself on the very important questions involved in the predestinarian doctrine, and at the same time of defending herself from the aggressions, or rather from the abuse of power (originally granted under different circumstances), which must be expected from the State. We are placed in circumstances, as a Church, in which party spirit is greatly to be deprecated; in which angry feelings should be, as far as possible, removed; and in which sound heads and sound hearts, firm faith, patience, and courageous perseverance, are eminently requisite, not merely to maintain one particular doctrine from being denied, but to retain the deposit of the faith in all points, and to obtain such reasonable securities as shall enable the Church to go on her way undisturbed by the attempts of worldly men to render her the tool and agent of their earthly ends, and to induce her to cease from her office of proclaiming the truth of God. We deeply regret the existence of that party spirit, which precludes co-operation for common objects. The Church cannot without such co-operation remain in her present position in the country.

In offering the preceding remarks, we have been addressing ourselves chiefly to those who may have been, in some degree, disturbed and confused by the recent decision in the Gorham case, but who have been always really attached to the Church of England, and are not disposed in a captious spirit to avail themselves of every possible circumstance to throw discredit on their spiritual mother. We are anxious to retain such faithful members of the Church—men of sincerity, of piety, and of Christian zeal; but we must confess that we do not think the Church would lose any thing by the secession of some of her members, whose usefulness is marred by conceit and arrogance, and whose first thought in any difficulty is to suggest disloyal feelings towards the Church of England. Such men we cannot recognize as friends or allies in the cause of the Church. Their co-operation always causes embarrassment, and their desertion is deferred to the moment when it is calculated to do most harm. The Church has certainly no reason to wish for their continuance in her communion, in their actual frame of mind. If they leave us, we shall lament it for their sakes, but not for the sake of the Church of England. They may go out from us, but they are not of us.

In proceeding to the consideration of the principal points of the Gorham case, we shall, in the first place, consider the ground taken by Mr. Gorham, and the various arguments employed to support it; and, subsequently, pass to the judgment lately delivered, and its bearing upon the Church of England.

The doctrine maintained by Mr. Gorham is doubtless familiar to our readers generally. He admits that regeneration takes place sometimes in infancy. But he asserts that the baptismal offices must always be understood as expressing the judgment of charity when they speak of regeneration as conferred in baptism. He argues that, as regeneration does not always accompany the rite in adults, so it does not always in the case of infants —that it always supposes an act of prevenient grace. Thus, then, he denies that all infants are regenerated in baptism; and, though he does not himself openly assert the doctrine, yet it is really meant by the distinction, that regenerating grace is only bestowed on the elect, because regenerating grace is supposed to be indefectible, and to involve in all cases final perseverance. It is this doctrine which is really at the root of the controversy, so far, at least, as to explain the earnestness with which it is carried on; for modern Calvinists and Evangelicals generally hold that regenerating grace can never be lost.

The line of argument in support of Mr. Gorham's position consists very much in an attempt to prove that such doctrine as his has always been held without censure in the Church, and that it was involved in the tenets of those who drew up our Articles and other formularies.

The whole question in debate appears to resolve itself into one point—namely, whether the grace of God once given can ever be lost. This doctrine of the indefectibility of grace simply, is a different one from that of the indefectibility of grace in the elect. It may be held that grace given to the elect is irresistible and indefectible, and yet it need not necessarily be held that grace can *never* be given except to the elect. To prove that large numbers of persons in the Church have held the doctrines of the particular election, the irresistible and indefectible grace, and the final perseverance of the saints, and personal assurance, is not to prove that they believed grace of all kinds restricted to the elect, or that they believed it impossible to fall finally from a state of grace. So that any amount of proof which may be brought to show that our divines at or after the Reformation held what are called Calvinistic doctrines, are absolutely worthless as regards the present discussion, unless they are shown distinctly to have taught, not merely *that grace in the elect is indefectible*, but that *grace is never received except by the elect.*

Bearing this in mind, let us approach Mr. Goode's proofs, and endeavour to ascertain their bearing on the question.

Mr. Goode examines, in his third chapter, "the school of theology to which our Reformers and early divines belonged" (p. 38.); and he then speaks in the following terms :—

" It may be useful, therefore, if, before I proceed further, I endeavour to throw some light upon the question, what was the prevailing bias of the theology of our reformers and early divines, especially respecting the Church, predestination, and some kindred topics. . . . . I would premise, however, that while I adduce the following testimonies, as showing the *prevailing* bias of the theology of our Church at the time spoken of, I by no means wish to imply that the articles and formularies of our Church were formed upon a Procrustean principle of reducing the views of all to the *precise* standard of that prevailing bias. Our reformers were men of far too much Christian charity to adopt such a principle. But the object which I have in view is simply this, to prove, by shewing the general tone and character of the theology of our early divines of the reformed school, what modern school among us approaches the nearest to their standard, and consequently to *the intended meaning of the formularies they drew up.* My conviction is, that I might take *much higher* *ground* than this ; but with this I am contented. And, though the discussion has only a general bearing upon the subject more immediately before us, yet its indirect evidence respecting it will be admitted, by all those who know how much any one's doctrine upon the point in question may be judged by the system of theology to which he is attached, to be of very great force. In fact, if it shall appear (and I believe it to be undeniable) that their doctrine was, in the most important points, what is now called ' Calvinistic,' there is, or ought to be, an *end* to the controversy as to the interpretation they intended to give to our formularies, both as it respects baptism and several other points."—pp. 38, 39.

A long extract then follows, taken from the " Institution of a Christian Man," published in 1537, and in the composition of which Archbishop Cranmer took a part. This extract, or rather series of extracts, shows that the compilers believed in the " appropriating character of true faith ;" *i. e.* the believer was taught to profess his belief that the gospel, with its promises, applied not merely to the world in general, but to himself in particular. It is also clear that the authors of this work held the doctrine of election and predestination to eternal life; that they believed the elect would never fall away finally; and that they considered them to constitute the real and living members of the Church, all others being regarded as only apparently and outwardly members of it. This is all very true, but we do not see that it advances Mr. Goode nearer to his point. With the exception of the doctrine of appropriating faith, there is nothing in the above which the Church of Rome itself does not say—nothing more than even Arminians have said; and, certainly, nothing more than the Seventeenth Article has said. There is no assertion that grace is given only to the elect. We are perfectly ready to accept, as consistent with the faith, the statements which Mr. Goode has quoted. They do not in any degree militate against the belief in baptismal grace, or furnish any evidence of a set of doctrines opposed to such belief. The tenet of appropriating faith was first put forward by the Lutherans. It is prominently stated in the confession of Augsburg, and the defence written by Melancthon, and confirmed several years before Calvin wrote his " Institutes :" and yet the doctrine of baptismal regeneration is taught by the very same work. We extract the following passages in illustration of this. First from the Confession of Augsburg :—

" De Justificatione.

" Item docent, quod homines non possint justificari coram Deo propriis viribus, meritis, aut operibus, sed gratis justificentur propter Christum per fidem, *cum credunt se in gratiam recipi et peccata remitti propter Christum,* qui sua morte pro nostris peccatis satisfecit."

And the " Defence" remarks as follows :—

" *Hæc igitur fides specialis qua credit unusquisque sibi remitti peccata* propter Christum, et Deum placatum et propitium esse propter Christum, consequitur remissionem peccatorum, et justificat nos." — Apologia Confess. August. Art. ii.

This special or appropriating faith was therefore the tenet of the Lutherans. And yet they also held that baptism is necessary to salvation, and condemned the anabaptists, who affirmed that infants might be saved without baptism.

" De Baptismo docent, quod sit necessarium ad salutem, quodque per baptismum offeratur *gratia* Dei, et quod pueri sint baptizandi, qui per baptismum oblati Deo recipiantur in *gratiam Dei,* et fiant filii Dei. . . . Damnant anabaptistas, qui improbant baptismum puerorum, et affirmant infantes sine baptismo et extra Ecclesiam Dei salvos fieri."— Art. ix.

In the remarks on this in Melancthon's " Defence," it is declared that "God gives the Holy Spirit" to infants who receive baptism; and in neither case is any exception made, but the grace is supposed to be given in all cases to baptized infants. It is, however, superfluous to enter into proofs of the Lutheran doctrines ; for it is generally admitted, that they combined the tenet of appropriating faith with that of baptismal regeneration. Therefore no such expressions as Mr. Goode has quoted from the earlier Reformation-formularies of the English Church are of the slightest value, as a proof that they held the Calvinistic tenets as to the restriction of grace to the elect.

Again, Mr. Goode depends on passages in these writings, and in some of Cranmer's works, in which it is asserted that the elect will persevere to the end. He underlines passages in which Cranmer speaks of " *the elect*, in whom finally no fault shall be, but they shall perpetually continue and endure ;"—that " *the elect shall not wilfully and obstinately withstand God's calling*," and other similar passages ; and he remarks on these various passages that they show plainly that Cranmer's views, and those taught by public authority in the " Institution," comprehended the following points :—" (1.) That election is wholly and entirely of God's free and sovereign mercy, and that such as are elected continue Christ's disciples to the end. (2.) That true Christian faith is enjoyed by such only, and is indefectible. (3.) That true Christian faith is an appropriating faith. (4.) That those who ultimately perish, never were members of the true Catholic Church or mystical body of Christ." (pp. 48—52.) And we are invited to believe that all this is Calvinism, and therefore that it is incredible that the Reformers could have believed that regeneration was conferred on all infants in baptism. We suppose, on the same grounds, the Seventeenth Article is Calvinistic—purely Calvinistic. If the assertion of the doctrine of election and predestination—if the assertion of the final perseverance of the elect is Calvinistic, the Seventeenth Article is very explicit on these points ; and it is wholly superfluous to go back to Cranmer and the preceding formularies of the Church of England. Mr. Goode might have saved himself a great deal of trouble by simply citing the Seventeenth Article. Let us quote it, and see what it states :—

" XVII. *Of Predestination and Election.*

" Predestination to life is the everlasting purpose of God, whereby (before the foundations of the world were laid) he hath constantly decreed, by his counsel, secret to us, to deliver from curse and damnation those whom he hath chosen in Christ out of mankind, and to bring them by Christ to everlasting salvation, as vessels made to honour. Wherefore, they which be endued with so excellent a benefit of God, be called according to God's purpose by his Spirit working in

due season : they through grace obey the calling: they be justified
freely : they be made sons of God by adoption : they be made like the
image of his only begotten Son Jesus Christ : they walk religiously in
good works, *and at length, by God's mercy, they attain to everlasting
life.*"

Now really this does seem to speak quite as plainly and distinctly of the election and final perseverance of the saints as well
can be expressed. But is this Calvinism? If it be so, we can
only say that the Church of Rome and the disciples of Arminius
are Calvinists. There is nothing in the above except what has
been admitted in common by Calvinists, Arminians, and Jesuits.
We will just quote from Mosheim an account of the tenets of
the disciples of Arminius. They held

"That God, from all eternity, determined to bestow salvation on
those whom he foresaw would *persevere unto the end in their faith* in
Christ Jesus ;"

And

"That true faith cannot proceed from the exercise of our natural
faculties and powers, nor from the force and operation of free-will ;
since man, in consequence of his natural corruption, is incapable of
thinking or doing any good thing ; and that therefore it is necessary to
his conversion and salvation, that he be regenerated and renewed by the
operation of the Holy Ghost, which is the gift of God, through Jesus
Christ."—*Cant.* xvii. sect. ii. part ii. c. 3.

Here, of course, we have a doctrine of election and final
perseverance. And now let us turn in another direction :—

"Predestination is ordinarily taken in the good sense as the election
and appointing of some to grace and to glory ; which predestination is
entitled in the Scriptures, 'Calling according to the purpose of God,
love, separation, election, preparation, fore-ordaining,' &c. . . . Predestination is defined by St. Augustine as . . 'the fore-knowledge and
preparation of God's benefits, by which those who are delivered are
most surely delivered.' . . . 'A real predestination by God must
be admitted. This belief of the Church is demonstrated by so many
testimonies of Scripture, that it is marvellous that it can be doubted by
Christians.' Matt. xxv. 34 ; Luke xii. 32 ; Rom. viii. 30 ; Ephes. i.
4, 5. 'That this is the faith of the Church, which cannot be denied
without error, St. Augustine affirms several times, who wrote also expressly against the Semipelagians two books, one on the Predestination
of the Saints, the other on the Gift of Perseverance.' . . . 'The orthodox all unite in professing that predestination to grace is altogether
gratuitous, and this is the capital doctrine of faith, in the defence of
which St. Augustine was engaged for twenty years against the Pelagians and Semipelagians.' 'Amongst supernatural benefits, there are
three principal effects of predestination, namely, calling, justification,
and glorification.' 'Predestination is certain and unalterable.' 'The'

number of the predestinated is certain and determined.' 'The reprobation of some is so clearly expressed in Holy Scripture, that there is
no need of any long proof to demonstrate it. The texts of Scripture
quoted above, and especially that of Matthew xxv. 'Go ye cursed into
everlasting fire prepared for the devil and his angels,' are amply sufficient. And the reason is evident, first, because God possesses the
fore-knowledge that the wickedness of some will not come to an end,
and has prepared a punishment which will never end, and this is
reprobation ; secondly, because it pertains to the Providence of a
supreme being, an universal agent, who foresees all things, to permit
for the manifestation of his glory certain intellectual creatures freely to
depart from the end of their being."

We suppose there are many persons who might look on this as
all very sound Calvinism ; and, if Mr. Goode had quoted such language from Cranmer and the other reformers, he would have
argued that persons who thus unequivocally taught the doctrines
of personal election, final perseverance, and even the reprobation
of individuals, could not possibly have held the doctrine of baptismal grace. He would have argued that the question was quite
settled by such statements—that it would be quite impossible
that such persons could ever hold that the grace of regeneration
was given in baptism except to the elect. And yet, to show the
fallacy of such reasoning, it is only necessary to state that the
above passage consists of a series of extracts from one of the
theological treatises of Dr. Tournely, one of the leading divines of
the Church of Rome [1].

To return, then, to the point immediately before us, it is evidently most fallacious to assume, as Mr. Goode has done, that the
Reformers and others who held, what are frequently called " Calvinistic" doctrines by those who are not well versed in the controversy, must necessarily have believed that grace is only given
to the saints who are predestinated to eternal life ; and, consequently, that regeneration is not in all cases bestowed on infants
in baptism.

It is of little consequence to the argument then, whether Peter
Martyr and others, in the reign of Edward VI., held the " prevailing system" on " the points of election, predestination, and
final perseverance." (p. 55.) All this has nothing to do with
the question. Romanists held these doctrines as well as the Reformers. Mr. Goode quotes from Peter Martyr the following
passage :—

" From a misunderstanding of the *holy fathers* [what does Mr. Goode
think of such an expression ?] there has sometimes risen that error, that

---

[1] Vide "Prælectiones Theologicæ de Deo et Divinis Attributis quasin Scholis
Sorbonicis habuit *Honoratus Tournely*, Sacræ Facultatis Parisiensis Doctor, Socius
Sorbonicus," &c.—Tom. ii. *passim.*

our good works are in some manner the cause of our predestination ; namely, that God foreseeing that his people will embrace his offered grace, and make a good use of his gifts, does, for this cause, predestine and predetermine them to salvation."—p. 58.

This doctrine has been denied by many even in the Church of Rome, so that it is really of no use to produce language of this kind. Mr. Goode quotes copiously similar passages from Bucer (p. 61, &c.); from Becon (p. 68, 69) ; and from Traheron (p. 70, 71). In a letter written by the latter in 1552, he states that many of the clergy agreed with Calvin in his view that God not only foresaw, but foreordained, the fall of Adam and the ruin of his posterity. We have already seen that those who held that God pre-ordained that punishment of the reprobate, have not denied the grace of the Sacraments, but most strongly upheld it. Therefore, this opinion, extreme as it is, has nothing to say to the question before us. It is perfectly useless to quote passages, as Mr. Goode does (p. 73), from the "Short Catechism" of Edward VI., comprising the doctrine of election. Of course the Seventeenth Article teaches that doctrine. The "Reformatio Legum" teaches the same doctrine (p. 74); but what has this to do with the question? And again, the testimony of Bradford and his controversy with his fellow-prisoners, who held the doctrine of free will (p. 75, &c.), is really altogether beside the question. It only proves that Bradford held the doctrine of predestination, and that he considered his fellow-prisoners to hold Pelagian errors on the subject of free will. It shows that Bishop Ferrar, Rowland Taylor, and Philpot, subscribed their names to a document in which the doctrine of election, predestination, and final perseverance, was clearly taught. But it does not in any way teach that these confessors of the truth held that grace was never given except to the elect—that grace is in all cases indefectible. Mr. Goode endeavours to account for Cranmer, Latimer, and Ridley, not "setting their hands" to the document in question ; but we really think it is of little consequence to the matter in hand, whether they did or not. If they had done so, it would not advance Mr. Goode towards his conclusion.

But, in fact, at this point Mr. Goode makes an admission which appears to us at once completely subversive of his whole line of argument. In a note, at p. 81, he speaks thus :—

"Dr. Laurence says, ' The doctrine which seems to have been a principal point of controversy between the Predestinarian and Anti-Predestinarian party, and to have proved most offensive to the latter, was that which is usually called *the indefectibility of grace.*' (p. xl.) Now, if instead of the phrase ' the indefectibility of grace,' which (though it has certainly often been used by divines) is ambiguous, and likely to mislead, inasmuch as it is very generally granted that every kind of grace is not indefectible, we insert the phrase *the indefectibility of true Christian faith and justification*, Cranmer was clearly, from the passages given above, a supporter of the doctrine."

This is really a very striking passage as bearing on the case before us. Here is Mr. Goode expending great research and pains to produce authorities from the Reformation writers, to show that very many of them held the doctrines of election, predestination, final perseverance, &c. But what does he let out incidentally in this note! " IT IS VERY GENERALLY GRANTED THAT EVERY KIND OF GRACE IS NOT INDEFECTIBLE !" Granted by whom! By Mr. Goode and those who think with him—by the Reformers too—by those who hold such " Calvinistic" doctrines as the above. So, then, it appears that those who hold such doctrines, " generally grant" that " every kind of grace is not indefectible." They can, therefore, have no kind of difficulty in admitting that *grace is given in baptism*, though many fall from that grace afterwards. And, therefore, Cranmer, Becon, Bradford, Philpot, the authors of the " Institution," the " Reformatio Legum," the " Short Catechism," and the " Seventeenth Article" may, every one of them, have taken the expressions of the baptismal service simply and straightforwardly as declaring that the grace of God is given to all baptized infants, though some of them fall from grace afterwards. The moment it can be shown, as Mr. Goode has here done, that the *literal meaning* of the baptismal service is perfectly consistent with the general tenets of all who can have been supposed to have had any share in its composition, or any influence on it, the whole matter is settled. All those writers—nay, all their opponents in the Church of Rome, would have granted that " indefectible grace"—or such grace as is connected with final perseverance, is not given to all infants in baptism ; but they might and did hold that the gift of grace was not always connected with final perseverance, and, therefore, that infants are regenerated by grace in baptism, though some of them afterwards " fall from grace," as the article distinctly teaches that some do.

We must now return to Mr. Goode's arguments. He next quotes (p. 83) a passage from Archdeacon Philpot, conveying the doctrine of election and predestination ; and another passage, (p. 84), in which he states, in his examination before Queen Mary's Commissioners in 1555, that the Romanists were not able to answer Calvin's " Institutes," and he acknowledged the Church of Geneva to be orthodox, and held that the doctrine of the Church of England in King Edward's days was, as well as that of Geneva, " according" to " the doctrine that the apostles did preach." Mr. Goode remarks that this passage is " conclusive upon the question at issue." How it can be so we are at a loss to see,

when Mr. Goode himself says it " is generally admitted that all
grace is not indefectible," and when the identity of doctrine, of
which Philpot speaks, plainly refers chiefly to the testimony borne
by Geneva and England against Romanism.   The concurrence
which was expressed with Calvin's views by such men as Philpot
and others should not be interpreted as conveying any evidence
of an absolute agreement with that eminent writer in all respects.
Some of his tenets were extreme, and he himself, as is well
known, relaxed his system so far as to adopt ultimately the sub-
lapsarian doctrine.   But Mr. Goode's own pages furnish ample
evidence that all who hold what he calls Calvinistic tenets do not
adopt every part of the tenets of Calvin, or follow out the Calvinistic theory into all its details.   He himself speaks (p. 70) of
"an extreme statement of Calvin as to God's predetermination
of the evil actions of men,"—and quotes a passage from Traheron
in which the supralapsarian doctrine is stated.   And in p. 85 he
observes, that " the general view of doctrine which prevailed
among our old divines is encumbered in the writings of some of
the Reformers, and of those that succeeded them at the latter
part of the sixteenth century, with notions and phrases of *dangerous and unscriptural character* ; as, for instance, that " Christ
died only for the elect, that *the predestination of God, and not sin,
is the cause of man's condemnation*," &c.   This latter tenet is,
decidedly, one of the tenets of Calvin ; and yet " against these
notions," says Mr. Goode, " it is, of course, not difficult to find
passages in the writings of our Reformers."   So that it is plain
that approbation of Calvin, and agreement with him and with
others, in holding the doctrines of predestination, election, and
final perseverance, affords no proof of concurrence with him in all
points of his system, or in all the adjuncts to or deductions
from it.

In p. 86, Mr. Goode proceeds to inquire into the tone of
theological doctrine current amongst the divines of the English
Church at the accession, and during the reign of Elizabeth ; and
he begins by quoting from writers who speak of the Calvinistic
tendencies of the divines of that period.   Be it so.   We cannot
see that Mr. Goode is any nearer to his point.   He lays hold of
these statements of anti-Calvinistic writers, and he makes the
following deduction :—

" If their views were what are called ' Calvinistic ' (which is clearly
admitted in the above passages), are we to suppose that the formularies
they *voluntarily* established are opposed to their views ? Is it credible,
is it within the bounds of reason to suppose, that those who had the remodelling of our formularies on the accession of Queen Elizabeth,
should establish such a doctrine as they themselves could not honestly
subscribe, or even such as did not *favour* their views? The question

so completely answers itself, that it would be absurd to propose it, but for the fact, that men prepossessed by the prejudices of habit and education, and judging from the circumstance that almost the whole of the wealth and power of the National Church have long been in the hands of divines of contrary views, venture to assert that our formularies are opposed to, and inconsistent with the maintenance of such doctrines."—p. 87.

We fully admit the improbability that the Elizabethan divines should have established formularies contradictory to, or inconsistent with, their own faith. There can be no question of this. But we should infer from this, that they did not hold the doctrine of " the indefectibility of grace ; " because that doctrine is plainly rejected in the Articles, and because Mr. Goode himself admits that, in a certain sense, it is generally denied. And proceeding another step we should infer further, that they *did* hold the doctrine of baptismal grace, of regeneration in baptism, as given to all baptized infants, because it is too plainly expressed in the formularies for any fair-minded man to avoid seeing it there. If they had doubted baptismal grace, they could not have established such formularies as they did : and their Calvinism, whatever it was, was plainly such as to be reconcileable with the doctrine of baptismal regeneration. Such is our inference from the alleged and undeniable fact that Calvinistic views prevailed largely amongst the Elizabethan divines. Those divines were more extreme in some instances than Mr. Goode himself. It was, doubtless, the tendency to over speculation on the awful and profound subjects involved in the controversies on predestination, that led to a reaction in the shape of Arminianism, which, we believe, led some astray from the plain doctrines of the Church of England—of the Western Church in former ages—and of Scripture itself on these points. But, we have no reason to believe, that the compilers or revisers of our formularies ever taught such tenets as are inconsistent with a belief in the gift of baptismal grace to all infants who are baptized.

In testimony of the Calvinistic character of the Elizabethan divines, Mr. Goode first quotes Nowell's catechism (pp. 88, 89) ; and undoubtedly that formulary teaches the doctrine of predestination. That is all which bears on the point before us. The next extracts are from the " Bishops' Bible " (p. 92). They teach the same doctrine as the Seventeenth Article does. After this we have an extract from a letter of Bishop Jewell to Peter Martyr, in which he declares that he entirely agreed with him in doctrine, and did not differ " by a nail's breadth." We know what such expressions mean when we remember Mr. Goode's own admission of differences between our Reformers and the extreme statements of some Calvinists. Jewell, however, evidently was not thinking of the point of baptismal regeneration, or else did not consider the foreign Reformers to deny it, for he himself plainly teaches the doctrine. The writings of Bullinger are referred to, and Mr. Goode informs us (p. 94), that Jewell, in a letter to that divine, declares the agreement between the doctrine of the Church of England and the Helvetic Confession drawn up by Bullinger in 1566. This is, of course, to be understood with some reserve; but the fact is, that the Helvetic Confession there referred to is a very judicious and moderate work on the Calvinistic controversy. There is a great deal in it which we should cordially rejoice to see admitted by many members of the Church of England.

On the point of baptismal regeneration, there is nothing therein inconsistent with the plain language of our baptismal formularies. It recognizes in sacraments not only an outward sign, but an inward grace given with the sign. It says that sacraments are " symbola mystica, vel ritus sancti aut sacræ actiones, a Deo ipso institutæ, constantes verbo suo, signis, et *rebus significatis* .... quibus promissiones suas obsignat, *et quod ipse nobis internis præstat,* externis repræsentat," &c. And " in Baptism," it says, " signum est elementum aquæ, ablutioque illa visibilis, quæ fit per ministrum. Res autem significata est *regeneratio* vel ablutio a peccatis." It declares that the water of baptism is to be called regeneration, or the laver of renovation. It disapproves of the doctrine of those who speak of the sacraments as common signs, not sanctified and " efficacious signs" (Confessio Helvetica, cap. xix). " To be baptized in the name of Christ is," according to this expression, " to be inscribed, initiated, and received into the covenant and family, and so into the inheritance of the children of God, yea, to be called by the name of God, that is, to be called a son of God; to be cleansed from the pollution of sin, and to be gifted with the various graces of God unto a new and innocent life." " All these things are sealed to us by baptism; for we are inwardly *regenerated,* purified, and renewed of God by the Holy Spirit; but outwardly we receive the sealing of these exceeding great gifts, in the water." " We condemn the anabaptists, who deny that the new-born infants of the faithful should be baptized. For, according to the doctrine of the gospel, of such is the kingdom of God, and they are included in the covenant of God. Why therefore should not the sign of the covenant of God be given to them? Why should not they be initiated by holy baptism, who are the possession and in the Church of God?" (Confess. Helvetica, cap. xx.) Most certainly there is nothing in this confession which militates against the plain and simple statements of the baptismal offices of our Church. It teaches that all the infants of Christians are in covenant with God, and members of his Church, even before baptism. So that none of them are excluded from his grace, and hence it is argued that they ought to receive the outward sign of grace. The language used would seem to imply that they are born in a state of salvation, or else are placed fully in such a state in baptism. Calvin himself distinctly teaches the same doctrine. He defends the baptism of infants on the ground that they are within the covenant; and that, therefore, when a child has been baptized and dies shortly, the parents may feel assured that it is saved.

We must offer one or two remarks on this view of the subject. If it be held that the infants of all Christians are within the covenant, it must be also held that all Christians themselves are within the covenant. So that grace is not limited to the elect; and consequently grace is not always indefectible. Baptismal grace, therefore, may be received by many, who will afterwards lose it finally. If it be replied to this, that Bullinger and Calvin only meant that the children of the *elect* are in the covenant, and that they only ought to be baptized; the immediate answer is, that they taught that the children of *all* Christians ought to be baptized; and that they did not restrict baptism to the children of the elect. If, therefore, the Elizabethan divines were admirers of Bullinger and Calvin, we do not see what possible difficulty they could have in declaring every child regenerate who had received baptism. They must have held that there was some covenant distinct from election and predestination—some covenant, and some union with God, which did not imply final perseverance; some grace of the Holy Spirit which might be lost. The doctrine of Calvin and Bullinger is here rather inconsistent with itself, and with other tenets held by Calvin, at least; but we think it leads to a view of grace being given irrespective of election, which is just as inconsistent with modern Calvinistic teaching, as the doctrine of baptismal regeneration itself.

Mr. Goode takes much pains to prove the agreement of the doctrines of our Elizabethan divines with foreign reformed communions (p. 95, &c.); and that the Church did not differ from the Puritans in doctrine. We do not see how all this, in any degree, affects the question. Granted that many of our divines held a good deal of Calvinism, it still does not follow that they doubted baptismal grace. As to the quotations from Parker, Whitgift, Bancroft, Rogers, Abbott, Sandys, Hutton, Matthew, and sundry other bishops; and from Martyr, Holland, Robert Abbott, Prideaux, Calfhill, Bunfield, Whitaker, Cartwright, Playfere, Davenant, Hooker, and the condemnation of Barrett (pp. 98—119), we cannot see how they bear on the question. They all

teach such points as election, and final perseverance; but not
one of them denies that grace is given except to the elect.
Consequently, all these persons may have held that baptismal grace
is given to all infants who are baptized.

One passage from Playfere's Sermons we must dwell upon for
a moment. It suggests a difficulty in the doctrine of predestination and election, and solves it thus :—

> " It is nothing but a slander which the Church of Rome casteth upon
> us, that forsooth we should teach a man, whose person is justified by
> faith in Christ, committing some foul act, is never a whit the worse for
> it. Nay, our doctrine is this, that such an one hath hurt himself two
> ways. In respect to his own guiltiness, and in respect of God's righteous-
> ness. For the first, though God for his part do not break off the pur-
> pose of adoption and adjudge him to wrath, and therefore he is not
> guilty of condemnation for sin, yet he is simply guilty of sin, and
> hath grievously wounded his own conscience. For the second, though
> God again hath pardoned all the sins of his elect, even those that are to
> come, by his decree, by his promise, by the value and price of his
> Son's merits, yet absolutely and actually He doth not apply this
> pardon to the apprehension and feeling of the sinner's faith, till he
> recover himself, and renew his repentance."—p. 109.

Thus, then, it is admitted, that the elect of God may fall into
sin, and be guilty simply of sin, and thus hurt himself, and be in
need of God's pardon. If, then, the elect and the justified are
capable of falling into sin and of requiring God's pardon, there is
no more difficulty in supposing that the reprobate, or those who
will finally perish, may nevertheless receive the grace of God, and
thus be made acceptable to Him, or be justified for a time. There is
no more inconsistency in supposing the reprobate justified in baptism,
than in supposing the elect subject to God's displeasure for sin.

We now come to the Lambeth Articles, which were drawn up
in 1595, and which certainly teach several doctrines connected
with predestination, in a very forcible manner. They forsake
Calvin however in the doctrine of reprobation, and they only assert that "*saving grace* is not given to all men, by which they
may be saved if they will" (p. 120); but they do not assert that
"grace" is given only to the elect, and that it is always indefectible. Therefore, they are not inconsistent with the doctrine
of the baptismal regeneration of infants. There is a most essential difference between asserting that " grace" is given only to the
elect, and that "*saving* grace" is only given to the elect. The
former would be the position of the modern Calvinists so called,
and includes a denial of the baptismal regeneration of infants, except in certain cases. The latter, which was the position of the
authors of the Lambeth Articles, is not opposed to the doctrine

of grace being given to all infants in baptism. Those authors doubtless held that all baptized infants receive grace in baptism, though saving grace, *i. e.* such grace as is connected with final perseverance in a state of grace, was only given to the predestinated. Archbishop Whitgift, it appears, declared that the doctrine of the Lambeth Articles was "agreeable to the Articles of Religion established by authority;" and that it had been "uniformly professed in the Church of England." And from these statements Mr. Goode argues thus :—

" The value and force of the testimony I leave the reader to appreciate. He may also, I suppose, easily determine the question, whether, in the face of these proceedings, within a few years of the establishment of our standard of doctrine, and of the affirmations here made of such doctrine having been *the uniform doctrine* of our Church, it can be maintained, not merely that these propositions go *beyond* the express statements of our Articles (which is a totally different question), but that the statements of the two are *opposed* to each other."—pp. 121, 122.

From what has been said, it is evident that the Lambeth Articles do not contradict the doctrine of the gift of God's grace in baptism to all infants. So that the above argument is fallacious.

We pass on to some extracts from Bishop Overall's writings, and certain remarks made on them. In the controversy which arose on the subject of Arminianism early in the seventeenth century, Overall compiled a paper containing his judgment on the points in controversy. In this paper he takes a middle course between the contending parties. We are not concerned with his views, except so far as they bear directly on the point before us. Overall, then, is a marked instance of what we have been pointing out; namely, that the acknowledgment of election, predestination, and final perseverance, is perfectly reconcilable with the belief that grace is given in baptism even to those infants who are not amongst the elect. He holds " the more common opinion of the Church since Augustine"—that God gives " common and sufficient grace in the means divinely ordained" to all; but " a special grace, more efficacious and abundant," to the elect only. Now we have seen that even Mr. Goode himself grants that it is " generally granted" by the Reformers " that every kind of grace is not indefectible ; " *i. e.*, of course, that there are different kinds of grace. He also says, immediately after the passages we are considering, " That there is a species of faith from which men may fall away, all admit" (p. 133). Thus, then, Overall merely draws a distinction which he was authorized to do by general consent. That is to say, he distinguishes between grace given to all Christians, and grace given to the elect; though he unites with this the ne-tion of a more efficacious or powerful grace in the one case than in the other, which was a peculiar opinion. In the distinction generally, however, abstracted from this peculiarity, there is nothing but what all Calvinists in these ages admitted.

We must here extract a passage from Mr. Goode's pages :—

" The difference, then, between the view of Overall (following Augustine) and that of the great body of our Reformation divines, on the subject of final perseverance seem only this, that the latter held, that those once made members of Christ, and partakers of true faith and repentance, never fall away, while the former held that some to whom these blessings are vouchsafed do fall away, but that to certain individuals, elected by God to salvation, God of his free mercy vouchsafes to superadd a measure of grace that ensures perseverance.

" In what way Augustine's doctrine smooths the difficulties of the subject, I cannot understand. It appears to me that the doctrine—that spiritual regeneration and its accompanying graces and gifts are generally given, but that none but those upon whom the gift of final perseverance is bestowed will be saved, and that that gift is bestowed only upon the elect,—is equally difficult of reception with the doctrine that spiritual regeneration and its accompanying blessings are given only to the elect, and that those to whom they are given have also the gift of final perseverance. The exclusion of those who are not among the elect is as complete in the former system as in the latter ; and the only difference between the two systems is as to the amount of spiritual gifts bestowed upon those whom God has not appointed to salvation. This seems to me a question of no very material moment. . . . . Augustine, no doubt, speaks of all baptized in infancy as spiritually regenerated." —p. 135.

At the commencement of this passage Mr. Goode makes an assumption, which he has not attempted to establish by proof, that there was a difference between the views of Augustine and those of the Reformation divines on the subject of final perseverance ; and that this difference referred to the gift of regeneration, which the one supposed universally bestowed on Christians, and the other restricted to the elect. None of Mr. Goode's quotations and proofs so far have pointed at such a difference as is here alleged to exist. His pages are full of extracts from the writings of the Reformers and of subsequent writers who held what are called " Calvinistic " opinions ; and no authority so frequently is referred to in these passages as St. Augustine. It is indeed well known that the authority of St. Augustine was deeply reverenced by the Reformers generally. Nevertheless, it is singular that Mr. Goode should not have been able to produce any passages in which the Reformers express dissent from St. Augustine's views on this point. They, of course, all knew perfectly well that St.

Augustine combined a belief in baptismal regeneration with the doctrine of election, predestination, and final perseverance; yet Mr. Goode does not show that they differed from his doctrine. We are therefore entitled to assume that they *agreed* with him in this respect; and that they took the expressions of the baptismal offices in their natural sense. Mr. Goode himself distinctly proves that there could not have been any difficulty on their part in receiving the doctrine of baptismal regeneration, as applicable in a certain sense to all; for he remarks, that the only difference between the two systems [that of Calvinism and the doctrine of St. Augustine] " is as to the *amount* of spiritual gifts bestowed upon those whom God has not appointed to salvation;" and he thinks this is " a question of no very material moment." So that the adherents of Calvinism could not have had any reluctance to admit that grace is given to all infants in baptism.

This appears to us perfectly conclusive of the question. It is in vain for Mr. Goode, after this, to contend that, because the Reformers or Elizabethan divines held Calvinistic tenets, they could not have received the baptismal formularies in their simple direct meaning, but must have understood them to mean what they plainly do *not* mean—namely, that grace and regeneration is only given to the elect, and not to all children lawfully baptized. These subterfuges were unknown to the Reformers and the Elizabethan divines. If they had held the views of Mr. Goode, and of modern dissenters, they could not possibly have compiled offices which so distinctly retain the teaching of St. Augustine on regeneration. What dissenter or Calvinist in the present day would compose offices like our baptismal offices!

We must quote another passage for the purpose of noticing an assumption like that which we have just shown to be unfounded:—

" Those who confound the Predestinarian system that prevailed amongst the reformed with that of St. Augustine, suppose that that system had no bearing upon the views of the Reformers as to the effects of baptism; whereas, in truth, it had a very material influence upon them. Our Reformers, as a body, held that the elect only are made partakers of those spiritual gifts that are essential to regeneration, and that final perseverance was always connected with these gifts. I am not, of course, denying that some among the Reformers themselves may have held precisely St. Augustine's view; but the evidence already adduced shows that the prevalent opinion was in favour of what is *now* commonly called the *Calvinistic* view."—p. 136.

From the preceding survey of Mr. Goode's evidence, as to the tone of theology prevalent at the period of the Reformation, and

subsequently, it is clear that he has not so far adduced the
slightest ground for his assertion, that the Reformers held that
" the elect only are made partakers of the spiritual gifts essential
to regeneration." We repeat that the assertion is made without
proof. For we have shown that the assertion of the doctrines of
appropriating faith, final perseverance, election, and indefectible
faith, which he has shown to have been frequent, does not include
necessarily any denial of baptismal grace.

We have some further proofs of the Calvinistic character of
English theology during the reign of Elizabeth (pp. 136—142).
Admitting that Calvinism (in reference to the Predestinarian
controversy) had then great influence in the Church, we must
decline to admit the ultra and overstrained statements of the
" British Critic," as possessing the slightest value or weight on
such a subject. The object of the " British Critic," in the article
quoted by Mr. Goode, was to show the propriety of a development of the Church of England in a Romish direction ; and it
therefore dwelt as strongly as possible on the alteration which
took place in consequence of the Arminian principles superseding
the Calvinistic in the seventeenth century ; but we think that no
true Churchman will recognize in the statements of the " British
Critic," in its Romanizing days, any authority in questions affecting the doctrines of the Church of England.

We next come to Mr. Goode's argument, founded on the
doctrine of the confessions of faith of the foreign Reformers. The
connexion which existed between the English and the foreign Reformers is referred to, with a view to identify the opinions of the
former with the latter. Without doubt this argument is to a certain extent a good one. That is, we may infer that there was a
general agreement when it was acknowledged on both sides ; but
we have no right to strain such expressions so far as to suppose
them to infer an agreement in *all* points of doctrine, more especially on the *amount* of grace given in baptism, which Mr. Goode
himself holds to be a matter of no great moment, as we have seen.

In proceeding with our task, we must offer one or two explanatory remarks. In maintaining that an inward and spiritual
grace is given in the sacraments, it is rightly conceded, and indeed affirmed, that *faith* is necessary to the reception of that
grace. In saying this, however, it is not of course meant to deny
that infants who cannot exhibit faith themselves, are capable of
receiving baptismal grace. So that, while in general we affirm
that faith is necessary to receive the grace of the sacraments, we
make an exception in the case of infants. Looking at the statements of Holy Scripture on the subject of holy baptism, it is
perfectly correct to say that repentance and faith are the condi-

tions of baptism; that regeneration, which is united to justification, or *is* justification in a certain aspect, is given only to believers in Jesus Christ. Nay, it is not unsound in doctrine, though it may be incorrect in expression, to use regeneration as equivalent to justification, and to speak of a person as regenerated when he is justified, and therefore to use that term of regeneration at times for something distinct from baptismal grace. Such language as this is quite consistent with a belief that all baptized infants receive baptismal grace, and are in *some sense* justified. Those who so speak may sometimes omit to specify the exception to the general rule of faith, as a prerequisite to the effectual reception of the sacraments; but we are not therefore to conclude that they do not recognize any such exception.

But we may also say, that in a certain sense the benefits of baptism are only given to the elect. The justification which is imparted to believers in that sacrament is, in the highest and most emphatic sense, only given to those who will persevere to the end. The justification of those who will fall finally from grace is of course temporary; nor can they be equally the subjects of God's favour with the elect. So that it is true, in a certain sense, that the elect are the subjects of baptismal grace: they alone are so in the highest sense of all—they alone are perfectly so. Others are imperfectly and transiently justified, regenerated, and adopted. They are rejected as regards their life generally; they are accepted in particular actions or points of that life: whereas the elect, on the other hand, are accepted on the whole, and displeasing in the particular sinful actions which they commit. The justification of the elect is certainly a different thing from that of the non-elect. It cannot be affirmed that the latter are *ever* regarded by God in all respects with the same favour as the former are. And therefore the adoption and acceptance in baptism of those who are not elect is in reality different from that of the elect. Grace is not given with the same effects to all alike.

These remarks will suffice to set aside the greater part of Mr. Goode's proofs. It is perfectly beside the question to produce extracts in which it is taught that the benefits of baptism are restricted to believers—that faith is an essential prerequisite—or that the elect only are regenerated in baptism. Such quotations may be well calculated to impose on the unwary reader, but they have really nothing to say to the question. It does not follow that these writers denied regeneration or its equivalent to be given to all infants in baptism.

Mr. Goode quotes several passages from the Helvetic Confession drawn up by Bullinger, on which we have already offered

some remarks, and, amongst the rest, one in which it is said
that

" To be baptized in the name of Christ is to be invited, initiated, and
received into the covenant and family, and so into the inheritance of the
sons of God : moreover, to be now called by the name of God, that is, to
be entitled a son of God, to be cleansed likewise from the pollution of
our sins, and to be endued with the manifold grace of God, that we may
lead a new and innocent life," &c.—p. 145.

In order to explain this strong and clear language, Mr. Goode
quotes some other parts of the same confession, in which the
benefits of baptism are connected with the salvation of the
" elect," and " regeneration" is spoken of as the result of " faith "
(pp. 146, 147). It will appear, from our preceding remarks, that
such passages as this do not in the least degree diminish the force
of so striking a testimony to baptismal regeneration, as that of
the Helvetic Confession.

Mr. Goode quotes such expressions, not only from the Helvetic, but from the Belgic Confession, and from the Catechism of
Heidelberg, with the object of shewing that the bishop of Exeter
was mistaken in quoting the strong language of these formularies
on baptismal grace, in favour of the view, that all infants are
regenerated in baptism. But it is most fallacious to argue as
Mr. Goode has done, applying to the case of infant baptism expressions which were not written with any view to that exceptional
case, and which refer solely to baptism where faith and repentance
are the necessary preliminaries. It is also very fallacious to quote
passages in which regeneration is used for justification, and
affirmed to apply to the elect only, as if this implied any assertion
that baptismal grace in every sense and degree is given to the
elect only. It is in vain that such quotations are made to invali-
date such passages as the following, which Mr. Goode himself
produces from the Heidelberg Catechism.

" Q. 69. In what way are you admonished and confirmed in baptism,
that you are a partaker of that new sacrifice of Christ ?
" A. Because Christ has commanded the external laver of water, with
this promise annexed, that I am not less certainly washed by his blood
and spirit from the pollutions of the soul, that is, from all my sins, than
I am cleansed externally by water, by which the pollutions of the body
are said to be washed away.
" Q. Where has Christ promised that He will as certainly cleanse us
by his blood and spirit, as we are cleansed by the water of baptism ?
" A. In the institution of baptism, in these words : ' Go and teach
all nations,' &c. (Matt. xxviii. 19.) ' He that believeth, and is baptized,' &c. (Mark xvi. 16.) This promise is repeated when Scripture

calls baptism the laver of regeneration (Titus iii. 5), and the washing away of sins (Acts xxii. 16).''—p. 148.

Mr. Goode's answer to this explicit testimony is, that the author was a well known *Calvinist* (p. 149), the inference being, we suppose, that he must have meant that baptismal grace was only given to the elect. We have already seen the fallacy of any such inference ; nor does Mr. Goode mend the matter by quoting passages from other works of the author of the Heidelberg Catechism, in which he maintains that faith, justification, and regeneration are the effect of " election ;" that the reprobate are never members of the *invisible* Church—the company of saints—that the regenerate can never finally fall away (p. 150). He is here using the term regeneration in connexion with final perseverance in the case of the elect. He does not seem to employ the *term* " regeneration " to designate the grace given in baptism, but " remission of sins," " renewal," and " cleansing," which describe what we mean by regeneration. So that there is no sort of reason to assume that he supposes the baptismal graces to be restricted absolutely to the elect, and that others have no part in them in any sense or degree.

" Regeneration " is, in fact, frequently used in the reformed confessions, such as the French, the Bohemian, &c., as equivalent to justification, and as obtained by faith. Baptismal grace is not unfrequently described under different names, or terms, as in the case above referred to. In the Bohemian confession " sanctification, renewal, or regeneration," is spoken of as the same thing.

We must pass over several very striking testimonies to the doctrine of baptismal grace which Mr. Goode quotes from Calvin, Beza, and others, with a view to explain them away, as he has endeavoured to explain away our offices. What has been already said is a sufficient answer to his arguments, that because men held Calvinistic doctrines in many points, they could not possibly hold that grace was given to all infants in baptism.

We must next follow Mr. Goode into his examination of the doctrines of Bucer and Peter Martyr on the subject of infant baptism. Mr. Goode attaches very great weight to their testimony, as showing the views of Cranmer and other of the English Reformers who thought highly of them. The first quotation which is produced from the records of a conference between Luther and the Reformed school at Wittenburg, in 1536, commences with a declaration of Luther's, that infants ought to be baptized, " and that baptism is truly efficacious and confers the adoption of the sons of God "—in other words—*regeneration.* The reply of Bucer on behalf of the reformed is, that although they do not hold (with

Luther and his disciples) that infants have *faith*, yet *they believe in baptismal grace.*

" Moreover that baptism is held sacred by us, and that we teach concerning it, *not as of some naked sign*, but as *the true cause of regeneration*, which (regeneration) is, through the power of God and the ministry of the minister, *supplied to us with the water*. . . . . For that *we simply believe and teach*, that TRUE REGENERATION AND TRUE ADOPTION INTO THE SONS OF GOD *are communicated to infants in baptism*, and that the Holy Spirit works in them according to the measure and proportion given to them, as we read of St. John, that he was filled with the Holy Ghost from his mother's womb. . . . . But that where there is any foundation in Scripture for what some affirm, that infants when they are baptized *understand the words of the gospel, and actually believe them*, and thus are saved,—whence this can be proved from the sacred writings, we are unable as yet to see."—p. 163.

With this declaration Luther was satisfied. (p. 164.) And indeed he well might beso, for although his own notion, with regard to infants being possessed of faith, was not adopted, still the great point was admitted—that infants ought to be baptized, and that they receive regeneration and adoption in baptism. Nothing can be more clear and explicit than the statement of the Reformers on this point. Luther himself subsequently stated (p. 164) that infants ought to be baptized because "they belong to the Church."

Mr. Goode observes on the passage, that both Luther and Bucer " held that infants ought to be baptized *because* they were faithful, that is, in the sense of having the principle of faith implanted in them by the mercy of God. . . . The possession of this gift of faith, however, by infants was, of course (as Luther speaks in his Catechism, and as we shall find Bucer stating), a matter of charitable hope." (pp. 164, 165.) We must demur to this statement. Bucer and the Reformed did not receive the notion of any real faith existing in infants. They *did not rest* the lawfulness of baptism on the assumption of such faith existing; and Luther himself did not require them to receive the view, from whence it is evident that he did not think it necessary. There is nothing in the passage about any "charitable hope." All infants are declared to be regenerated in baptism. In fact this testimony of the Lutherans and Reformed is a very strong confirmation of the doctrine of baptismal regeneration. We should be happy to see Mr. Goode and Mr. Gorham, and their disciples, employing such language as the Lutherans and Reformers did on this occasion. What would Bucer and Luther have thought of those who declaim against the " soul-destroying" error of baptismal regeneration, and teach that baptism is a mere sign or seal, and that regeneration is to be looked for at another time, and not in baptism! We can have no doubt that such persons would have been regarded as "heretics" by Luther and the Reformed: they would have been classed with the anabaptists.

But Mr. Goode endeavours to explain away this very strong testimony to baptismal regeneration, by quoting a long passage from Bucer's writings, in which he contends that the sacraments are only beneficial; that their graces can *only reach* them who partake of them worthily and with faith. He argues against Luther and his adherents, who maintained that the body and blood of Christ is received by *all* who partake of the elements of bread and wine, no matter whether they have faith or no. He contends that doctrine of this kind is calculated to have bad moral effects. He asserts that faith is a necessary condition to the reception of sacramental grace, whether in baptism or in the Eucharist. And surely he is right in so saying. He teaches here nothing except what the Articles of the Church of England, at least, declare; but then he is not speaking of *infant* baptism, because he and his colleagues expressly stated in the passage quoted above, that infants do not possess faith—at least, such faith as is necessary in all cases where it is possible. All, therefore, that he says about faith being a necessary requisite to the right reception of baptism we admit, while we affirm with him that infants have not faith, and yet are regenerated and adopted in baptism.

Mr. Goode goes on to produce several passages from Bucer's writings, in which baptismal grace and regeneration are most strongly affirmed (pp. 168, 169). We accept these testimonies with pleasure, and are thankful to Mr. Goode for producing them. They are exactly the same kind of expressions as the Church of England uses. Well may Mr. Goode say that "Bucer had no hesitation in using the strongest language as to the benefit of baptism, when enunciating in general terms its nature and effects" (p. 170). But we draw a very different inference from that which Mr. Goode implies in saying that these passages show us with what views the Reformers used language, on several points, which "from its ambiguity and capability of diverse interpretations, has been since their time the cause of so much contention in the Church." Mr. Goode means that their language asserting *baptismal regeneration* is ambiguous, and that it must be interpreted by their statements as to the necessity of faith as a prerequisite for receiving the benefit of regeneration. We hold, on the contrary, that such language as he has quoted gives *unambiguous and clear* evidence of belief in baptismal regeneration, while the assertion of the necessity of *faith* is really ambiguous and liable to mistake, for it is not *meant* to extend to the case of infants, though the exception is not expressly made.   It is plain, from the passage he has himself quoted from the "conferences," that whenever the "Reformed" speak of the necessity of *faith* in order to obtain baptismal regeneration, they must be understood to except the case of infants, who are regenerated without the actual possession of faith.   And indeed it is grossly inconsistent in any one to maintain, *absolutely and without exception,* that faith is a prerequisite for receiving regeneration in baptism, and yet to admit, as Mr. Goode and Mr. Gorham and their friends do, that regeneration is ever actually given in baptism to infants; for infants have no faith.   If faith in the case of infants be requisite to regeneration, they are never regenerated ; and thus the formularies of the Church of England and of all the Reformation, and the admissions of Mr. Gorham himself, are flatly contradicted. To interpret the assertions of the Reformers as to the necessity of faith, as applying to infant baptism, is to make a clean sweep not only of the doctrine of baptismal regeneration, but of the practice of infant baptism, and of the practice and doctrine of the Church of England—so that it is *absolutely essential* for Mr. Goode himself to understand all such language as he has quoted on this point, as *not extending to infant baptism.*

Mr. Goode follows up this extract from Bucer, by another, which comprises a strong and explicit statement of the doctrine of election and predestination.   In this passage Bucer asserts that "those who can at any time fall away from Christ never were Christ's ;" that "the reprobate never were known to Christ ;" that "those to whom it has once been given, like Him, can never perish ;" that though "infants are destitute of faith," yet "with elect infants the Spirit of the Lord is present," &c. (p. 170-171).   All this passage refers to the gift of such grace as God foresees will be efficacious for its end—such grace as is combined with final perseverance and liberation from sin.   It does not refer to grace in general, or imply any denial that grace, which shall not in all cases be joined with final perseverance, is given to infants in baptism.   There is no reference to baptism or the sacraments generally in this passage : it refers simply to election and final perseverance ; and it must be understood with the distinctions which the doctrine of the sacrament requires, and which even Mr. Goode and Mr. Gorham do not deny, for Mr. Goode himself does not assert that all grace is *indefectible ;* nor does he consider the question, as to the amount of grace given in baptism, to be a very important one.   We do not see any thing in the doctrine of Bucer, as stated by Mr. Goode, which is inconsistent with the clear and explicit declaration of himself and the other Reformers, that regeneration is given to infants in baptism.

The next quotations are from Peter Martyr; and the object is to show that, while he held the divinity chair at Oxford, and approved the English formularies, he understood and taught that the benefit of baptism is restricted to the predestinate, though the sacrament is administered to all. In this passage Martyr is arguing against the anabaptists, who contended that baptism ought not to be administered to infants, "because we know nothing concerning the spirit, or faith, or election of these little ones." Martyr asserts that some infants are elect, and others not so; and he restricts the spiritual benefit of the sacraments to the elect; but teaches that baptism should be administered to all infants, because we cannot distinguish who *are* elect. This passage, like many others adduced by Mr. Goode, refers to the grace of baptism as united with final perseverance; as the gift of grace in the high and peculiar sense in which it belongs to the elect only. Martyr does not deny that grace is given in a certain sense to many who are not elect: at least there is nothing in the passages quoted by Mr. Goode to lead us to suppose that he would have denied that all infants receive regenerating grace, in some degree, in baptism. There is nothing in these passages to lead to the inference that the baptismal grace which Martyr so strongly *asserted* in a passage, also produced by Mr. Goode (p. 175), was not given generally to infants, though only effectual, finally, in the case of the elect. We see nothing in the language of Martyr inconsistent with a belief that all infants are regenerated, and made children of God in baptism; though, in some cases, that state of grace is only temporary and transient; in others, permanent.

The doctrine of election necessitates a distinction between the relation of those who are elect, and those who are not so, to God, at all times. The elect may fall into sin, and become subject to God's wrath, and yet it is the wrath of a Father who thinketh upon mercy. The reprobate may have a temporary faith, and may be temporarily and partially justified, but their acceptance with God is never the *same kind* of acceptance which is extended to those who are the chosen children of God. But still this should not prevent any one from believing that the grace of God in general may be extended to all children in baptism.

The examination of Mr. Goode's argument would demand far more space than we can afford for its discussion. We trust, however, that what has been already said will, in some degree, suffice to point out the fallacies in which it abounds. We think that he has been led to overlook, in the urgency of his advocacy, the real meaning and bearing of much that he has collected to establish his point. We can very readily understand that his reasoning and authorities may, to very many persons, appear perfectly conclusive. His work is one which, from the absence of necessary distinctions, the very intricate, delicate, and profound questions on which it treats, is calculated to mislead men of the most educated intelligence. The discussion of topics on which the wisest and the best of men have often been at variance, and on which human language is most imperfect and liable to mistake, is difficult under all circumstances, but more especially in the heat of controversy ; and we would extend to others the same fair construction which we are desirous to claim for ourselves. It is deeply to be regretted that controversies on such subjects should continue to disturb the Church. We know that there are great differences of opinion amongst those who admit the teaching of the Church of England, yet they are scarcely greater than those which exist in the Church of Rome on the same sort of questions. It is, therefore, a matter for deep regret that some way cannot be found for arriving at some arrangement which shall define the limits within which freedom of opinion is permissible, and which shall repress the violence of controversy.

Though we fear we are trespassing at too great length on the reader's attention, the importance of the subject-matter will plead our excuse for proceeding with our examination of Mr. Goode's series of arguments.

The next authorities which he quotes in favour of his views are the formularies issued by authority in the reign of King Henry VIII. The very decided language of these formularies, in connecting regenerating grace with baptism, is admitted by Mr. Goode to have been common both to these and to the "majority of the most distinguished continental Reformers" (p. 190.) Baptism is, according to them all, "a rite divinely appointed as the instrument, in the use of which a certain spiritual blessing is conveyed by God to the recipient." (Ibid.) The mode in which he explains such language is this—

" It is palpably a misinterpretation of this language to infer from it, that this sacrament is represented thereby as having this effect upon *all* who partake of it ; because such general statements refer to the case of *adults* as well as *infants ;* and in the former case, it is admitted even in these documents, that faith and repentance are necessary to a salutary reception of this sacrament. Therefore some similar qualifications may have been held necessary in the latter case. . . . To interpret these words as meaning that *all* infants are *alike* the objects of the divine mercy, is a gratuitous and unwarranted assumption, and, I may add, a

misrepresentation founded upon a forgetfulness of the doctrinal views
of many of the authors of such statements."—pp. 190, 191.

If it be argued or maintained, as it is in this passage, that
repentance and faith on the part of infants are requisite to the
salutary reception of baptism, we really do not see how it is
possible to avoid the anabaptist inference, that baptism is useless
to infants; for, whatever may have been thought by some persons
about infants themselves possessing faith, there is no proof for
such a view in Holy Scripture, and certainly none from reason
and experience. The natural and obvious inference from the
statements connecting regeneration with baptism in the case of
infants as well as adults, is that the writers referred to in general
did not think it necessary expressly to except the case of infants
when they spoke of repentance and faith as requisite for the
effective reception of the grace of baptism, because they must
have supposed that every one could make that exception, which
was dictated by obvious necessity and common sense. We pass
over various passages from Lancelot Ridley, who followed Luther's
doctrine as to the existence of faith in infants, and from the
formularies in the reign of Henry VIII., which assert the
necessity of faith for the effectual reception of the sacraments
(much as our own Articles do), and state the doctrine of election,
and the efficacy of the sacraments only to the elect (p. 191—207).
All this is merely the repetition of positions which have been
already examined, and will be readily understood as indicating no
doubt of the gift of regenerating grace to all baptized infants, in
some sense. It may not, and does not imply, that " *all* infants
are *alike* the objects of the divine mercy" (p. 191); but it is not
inconsistent with the doctrine that all *are* objects of the divine
mercy, which is openly stated.

We next proceed to the testimonies quoted from our leading
Reformers and divines during the reigns of Edward VI. and his
successors. The first quotations (from the Catechism of 1553)
only speak of faith being a requisite condition of adult baptism
(p. 210). In Cranmer's Catechism a distinction is made in the
subjects of baptism, *some* only being supposed to be " born again "
(p. 213). This will, of course, be admitted in the case of adults,
some of whom may be baptized without faith and repentance. We
also find the Church identified with those who " believe in the
gospel, and are saved "—a position which has nothing to do with
the matter before us. Mr. Goode admits that in Cranmer's works
it is easy to find statements connecting *regeneration* with *baptism*
(p. 215); but he quotes various passages in which the necessity
of faith is asserted, obviously referring to the case of adult bap-

tism, or else assuming, as Luther did, that all infants *have* faith (pp. 216, 217).

The arguments which Mr. Goode employs (pp. 217, 218) with a view to establish the necessity of certain conditions to the reception of baptismal grace in the case of infants, are deserving of attention. He urges that we have no right to affirm that general statements of regeneration taking place in baptism are to be understood conditionally in the case of adults, but " be understood as ap' lving universally in the case of infants." The latter assertion h.,.ttempts to raise a prejudice against as a reproduction of the Romish doctrine of *opus operatum*—" that the sacraments confer grace on all who do not oppose the obstacle of mental sin " —" without any good and deserving motive,"—which has obviously no application to the case of infants, who, as Mr. Goode himself admits, are within the covenant of grace, and cannot need the conditions of repentance and faith, as Calvin himself argues in reply to the anabaptists. If Mr. Goode means to assert that the same conditions as in the case of adults are requisite in infant baptism, he is condemned by Calvin, and he holds the anabaptist tenets. If these conditions are not requisite, his argument is worth nothing.

Mr. Goode says :—

" I have thought it right to make these remarks at the very outset of our review of the statements of our early divines on the subject of this work, in order that the reader may bear in mind throughout, that the assertion—that the sacraments confer grace upon all not putting a bar in the way, and consequently that the general statements of our divines as to the effects of baptism, though to be understood with limitations in the case of adults, are to be considered as applicable in their full force to *all* infants—is wholly unwarranted, and directly opposed to the doctrine of our most learned divines of the school of Reformers."—p. 220.

We must deny that the doctrine of *opus operatum* applies to the case of infant baptism. The expressions of " not putting a bar in the way," and having no " good and deserving motive," &c., refer to the case of persons who are capable of interposing obstacles, such as committing actual sin, and possessing a dead faith : they do not properly refer to infants who are simply in a state of unconsciousness in reference to spiritual things. So that *opus operatum* seems a doctrine which refers evidently to adults ; and Mr. Goode must greatly mistake his adversaries' argument in making them infer the partial operation of the doctrine of *opus operatum* in the case of adults, but its total and unconditional application in the case of infants. The truth is, that the tenet of *opus operatum* is not held by such persons as applicable to adults, and if it be ever applied to the case of infants, which we are not aware that it is, the application seems mistaken; though the doctrine of the regeneration of all baptized infants is certain.

Nor can we admit, as a fair representation of the view opposed to Mr. Goode's, that the general statements of our divines are necessarily to be understood as applicable in their full force to all infants; for this statement, thus nakedly made, might imply that we meant to assert that God looks exactly in the same point of view on the elect and the non-elect; or that we mean to .. ny the doctrines of election and predestination, while asserting the doctrine of baptismal grace. Whether all infants receive regenerating grace in the same degree, or with the same effects and results, we need not pretend to determine; but that God does actually regenerate all infants in baptism, and make them his children by adoption, in a certain sense, is plainly and manifestly the doctrine of the Church of England and of the whole Catholic Church; and no other teaching ought to be permitted.

It does not follow that, because general statements as to the effects of baptism are to be understood conditionally in the case of adults, they must therefore be so understood in the case of infants (p. 220). Nothing could be more unreasonable than such an inference; in fact, it goes to the length of declaring that regeneration is *never* given to infants, because they are incapable of supplying the conditions which are prescribed by the Word of God in the case of adults. It may here be remarked, that any of the Reformers who suppose faith to be a necessary condition even in infant baptism, supposed faith to be given to all infants baptized. Mr. Goode argues, that "when we find the Church specifically demanding a promise of future faith and repentance to be exercised by the child when grown up, and giving baptism to none likely to reach that age without that promise being made, we reasonably infer, that she, *at least*, limits the baptismal blessing to those who, as adults, fulfil that promise" (p. 220).

We have no right to make such an inference as this, because the Church believes that the promise *actually* made by others is sufficient to authorize her to administer baptism, consisting of an outward sign and an inward grace. It is the promise itself, and not the future *performance* of that promise, which the Church accepts as a condition. The case of baptism in case of sickness shows that the Church does not consider such promise as *necessary* in the case of infants. In fact, if it were not made at all, the obligation to renounce sin, and to live in faith and holiness, which is the substance of the baptismal promise, is strictly binding on all persons baptized. Baptism is the admission to the privileges of the Christian covenant; it is the rite appointed by Christ,

Himself for the initiation of new members into his family; and
the conditions of existence in that state are abstinence from sin,
and a walk of faith and of sanctification. This obligation is
incumbent on all who hope for salvation; it is involved as a
matter of necessity in the acceptance of baptism, without any
express promise to that effect. If renunciations and professions
are made either by adults previous to baptism, or by sponsors
for infants, it is as a safeguard against the evil of an unconditional
admission to baptism, or for the purpose of reminding Christians
of the duties which they have undertaken, or are to undertake,
as Christians.

The Church of England distinctly teaches, that infants baptized privately, *without any promises*, are "fully and sufficiently
baptized;" and of such she declares that they are now, "by the
laver of regeneration in baptism, received into the number of the
children of God, and heirs of everlasting life." Therefore it is
most fallacious to argue that she considers the grace of baptism
to be given only in contemplation of the future fulfilment of the
promises made at baptism by sponsors.

We must offer some remarks on a passage which immediately
succeeds that on which we have been commenting. It is as
follows:—

" No doubt infants are so far interested in their parents' faith, that
they may be reckoned by us, as infants, as being acceptable in the eye
of God (the Apostle calling them holy); and, if they die in infancy,
are partakers, as such, of the full baptismal blessing. Nor need we,
I think, be anxious to deny that, in the case of infants, there may
always be bestowed the pardon of original sin. And when the term
regeneration is applied in this sense, by those who speak of the universal regeneration of infants in baptism, and the distinction is preserved
between this infantine regeneration, and that regeneration of heart
which is necessary for the salvation of an adult, then (whether or not
we agree in the view taken) it seems very unnecessary to raise a
further controversy. But that spiritual regeneration of the heart, of
which Scripture speaks, and which sanctifies the adult, is a gift, not
conferred by God in consequence of the parents' faith, but according to
his own good pleasure."—p. 221.

If this really be the view taken by those who think with Mr.
Goode generally, we should not be without hope of some kind of
arrangement of the controversies at present existing on this
most important subject. The difference, as thus stated by Mr.
Goode, is, in some degree, a verbal difference. We allude to the
use of the term regeneration, as applied by him to designate the
change of heart by which adults enter into a state of justification,
from which they have fallen through the temptations of the

world, the flesh, and the devil. There is no authority in our
formularies to speak of this change of heart, as regeneration; but
at the same time we would not say that false *doctrine* is connected
with the use of the term for this process. Though there is no
authority in Scripture for such a use of the term, there are not
wanting instances of its use in this sense in the early writers, and
in some of our modern divines. Therefore, while we think such
a use of the term is not to be recommended, we would not condemn those who thus employ it.

And again—the regeneration of infants and their reception of
baptismal graces does not imply the *same* change of heart which,
in the case of an adult, is the preparation for baptism, and which
is completed by baptismal grace. As infants have no actual sins
to repent of, their regeneration is not exactly a regeneration in
the same sense as that of adults; and in asserting that they
obtain remission of their sins, and a new birth in baptism, through
the sanctifying influences of the Spirit of God, it cannot be meant
to deny that the necessity of subsequent change of heart and conversion to God is, in most cases, absolutely requisite. Mr. Goode
does not deny, that grace and the gift of regeneration to infants is
extended to them all in baptism; and, if so, we really think, that
those who think with him ought to have no difficulty in accepting
the baptismal services in their plain and simple meaning, which
supposes regeneration and grace to be given to infants in all
cases: and, if this were fairly and consistently done, we think
there would be very little objection to the mere use of the term as
an equivalent for conversion in the case of adults. The great evil
of which all members of the Church of England have to complain
is, that the "doctrine of baptismal regeneration," which is distinctly taught in all our formularies, and which has always, even
from the beginning, been taught in the Church, and which the
whole body of the Reformers held, should be denied, and rejected,
and denounced. While the formularies of the Church of England
remain what they are, a denial of the doctrine that infants are
regenerated in baptism is a positive censure of the Church of
England. It is to accuse her of teaching erroneous doctrine—
nay, as it is sometimes called—"soul-destroying error."

Mr. Goode, and those who think with him, do not object to the
doctrine that *all* infants *are regenerated* in baptism. Why, then,
should they undertake to prove that the Reformers did not hold
this view, or that they held regeneration to be confined strictly to
the elect! We really think, that such admissions as this are
fatal to the whole argument of Mr. Goode's book. They show
that the force of evidence is so strong, that he is *obliged* to admit,
in the first place, the doctrine of baptismal regeneration in some

sense, in order to bring his teaching in any degree into accordance with that of the author he quotes; and then he proceeds to overthrow this doctrine by quotations which plainly have reference only to the case of adult baptism, or which refer to the doctrine of election and its concomitants without connexion with baptism.

To follow Mr. Goode further through the mass of quotations which he has accumulated for this purpose would be impossible within our necessary limits. We have merely indicated the key to the explanation of these quotations. We have scarcely seen any which appear in any degree to support the theory proposed by him in the case of *infants*. The fact is, that, notwithstanding all Mr. Goode's efforts to produce authorities in support of his view, his work affords throughout the most clear and unequivocal testimony to the doctrine of the Church generally, and of the Reformation in particular, in favour of baptismal regeneration. We are met continually by quotations of the strongest kind asserting that regeneration is given in baptism—that it is the undoubted spiritual grace of that sacrament. Passages of this kind are continually produced or referred to, as among the writings of the Reformers, and the reformed confessions, and our later divines, expressing the doctrine of regeneration in baptism *as strongly as it is taught in our own formularies.* Mr. Goode's testimony is uniform as to his sense of the clearness and strength with which that doctrine *is* taught in our formularies. This is all extremely valuable in its way; we can only regret that Mr. Gorham and Mr. Goode attempt, without any reason, to narrow the spiritual benefit of baptism to a selected few, when they themselves admit that, in a certain sense, they are applicable to all.

No one pretends to say that grace is given to all in baptism, so that it cannot be lost. No one can have a right to say, that grace is given to the elect and the reprobate with exactly the same results; or that they are both regarded at any time as equal in God's sight. No one has a right to deny that a real change of life, including a new heart and sincere repentance for past sin, is not for the most part necessary to those adults who have received baptism in infancy. No one can pretend that *such* a change takes place in infancy. Yet, on the other hand, no member of the Church of England has a right to deny that grace is given to all, except the impenitent and unbelieving, in baptism, and that this grace is rightly called regeneration. No member of the Church of England can consistently deny that those who have received grace may fall from it. The Articles declare this fall possible, and describe recovery from it as *only possible* also. Therefore, the wicked may fall, finally, from the grace of regeneration received in baptism.

That parties should be permitted to go on denying the plain and obvious teaching of the Church of England, and yet professing to be her members, is a serious evil; an evil which cannot be permitted, consistently with the security of the Church. We should regret to see any attempt to narrow the limits of those fair and reasonable differences of opinion which have existed for many ages in the Church on the subject of predestination, and the connected mysteries of God's Providence; but liberty ought not to be permitted to degenerate into licence, or members of the Church of England be allowed to continue in the open inculcation of tenets directly opposed to the formularies of the Church. The Bishop of Exeter has, in our opinion, acted with wisdom, as well as with firmness and moral courage, in endeavouring to prevent the inculcation of doctrines opposed to those of the Church of England in reference to baptism; and, although his praiseworthy and Christian zeal has been unsuccessful in the immediate object of preventing a clergyman of unsound doctrine from officiating in his diocese, we yet believe that great real good has been done: for it is not right that the state of things which we have had so long to lament should continue permanently; and it is plain that the proceedings in the case of Gorham must lead to ulterior consequences, which cannot fail to be of great moment, and which will, we hope, lead to the adoption of some measures by ecclesiastical authority, which, in declaring the truth, and in defining the limits within which private opinion may be exercised, may protect the faith of the English Church from the assaults of misguided men, and establish a greater degree of harmony amongst persons of different views than now prevails.

We have dwelt, perhaps, too long on Mr. Goode's view of baptism, and we now turn with pleasure to Archdeacon Wilberforce's able and effective reply. The archdeacon has demonstrated in this work the possibility of combining a belief in baptismal regeneration with views on predestination and election which would be generally considered as "Calvinistic;" and he has thus very satisfactorily met the argument so extensively employed by Mr. Goode and his friends, that the Reformers and their successors, as being more or less Calvinistic, could not have understood that regeneration was given to all infants in baptism. We regard the archdeacon's work as most triumphant in its argument on this head, and in its refutation generally of the attempts to connect the authority of English writers with Mr. Gorham's views. We are not so certain that we are able to concur in the archdeacon's definition of regeneration, which he has not supported by authorities, as far as we have observed. "A new birth unto righteousness," as it is described in the Catechism, does not convey to our minds precisely the same idea as that of "*Christ taking up his dwelling in man*" (p. 28). The doctrine may be sound, but it strikes us as rather novel in its statement. Passing this over, however, and also some obscurity of language, we must acknowledge the great value of the archdeacon's work, and thank him for so seasonable a contribution to the cause of truth.

We must place before our readers some statement of the archdeacon's views on certain important points. And first, as to the amount and cause of the actual difference on the subject of baptism :—

" The opposition to baptismal regeneration on the part of earnest men seems to have arisen mainly from a fear lest it should do away with the necessity, or detract from the importance, of conversion. I will not enter into controversy, says Mr. Scott, with persons who believe that those who have neglected their baptismal vows ' do still need that great and radical change on which the Scriptures insist.' And even Mr. Goode allows that, ' when the distinction is preserved between this infantine regeneration and that regeneration of heart which is necessary for the salvation of an adult, then (whether or not we agree in the view taken) it seems very unnecessary to raise a further controversy.' Now, had these and other writers always kept this truth before them, a large part of the distrust and hostility which the subject has excited might probably have been avoided. Their feeling plainly was, that the importance of a change of character had not been duly remembered; that regeneration had too often been spoken of as a mere technical, official process; and thus has man's salvation been rested only on his external profession, and not on any real alteration of the heart. Against such an error it was impossible to protest too strongly. But unfortunately, in their earnestness to resist falsehood, men have sometimes sacrificed truth; they have supposed it impossible to exalt regeneration, unless at the same time they disparaged baptism. Thus does Mr. Scott refer, as though it were an admitted truth, to the opinion that, if our Lord's statement respecting the new birth, in the third chapter of St. John, ' relate to baptism, or what necessarily or inseparably accompanies baptism, then it means nothing to us who have received baptism.' Yet no words can possibly be more opposed to the opinions of those who believe in the efficacy of baptismal grace. This misdirection in the efforts of those who desired to vindicate the importance of regeneration has involved a corresponding reaction on the part of some who were jealous for the honour of holy baptism. Insomuch that it was supposed, at one time, that a man could not have a due appreciation of the one if he was disposed to do hearty justice to the other."

We are glad to have Archdeacon Wilberforce's authority in confirmation of our own view, that if persons holding Mr. Gorham's views would consistently and honestly adhere to the distinction here made between infantine regeneration and the " regeneration of heart " in an adult, the controversy would be much diminished. We think that one party might tolerate the other in the incorrect theological use of the term regeneration, if the other on their part would fairly and consistently admit that there is such a thing as infantine regeneration, which places infants in a state of grace, and which is not restricted to the elect. It is one of the greatest evils of the recent decision, that persons will now be encouraged to deny baptismal regeneration wholly, as Mr. Gorham is permitted to deny it partially.

We must pause for a moment on an assertion of the archdeacon's at p. 119, that " Christian education is based entirely upon a belief in baptismal grace." We have heard this position laid down by the Rev. G. A. Denison in a recent speech, and by others ; and we do not feel satisfied of its correctness. The archdeacon assumes that, in order to conduct a Christian education, we must believe that our children have received a measure of grace. This may be supposed, without necessarily assuming that it has been given by baptismal regeneration, we think. We can conceive a Christian education where baptism has not yet been received. We have sometimes to teach children who have never been baptized. It is therefore plain that a Christian education may be conducted without assuming that regenerating grace *has* been received. We are of opinion, that belief in the Lord Jesus Christ, and in Him crucified, is the foundation on which Christian education is to be based—" Other foundation can no man lay."

We now turn to some valuable remarks of Archdeacon Wilberforce on the possibility of combining a belief in the doctrine of predestination with the doctrine of baptismal regeneration. The following remarks on St. Augustine are worthy of attention :—

" What can be more decisive than such passages as the following ? ' We say that the Holy Spirit dwells in baptized infants, although they know it not. For they are ignorant of it, although it is in them, as they are ignorant of their own mind. For it lies in them, as yet unable to be used, like some buried spark, to be quickened by increasing years. Or again, ' It is matter of the utmost wonder, that to some of His sons, whom He has regenerated in Christ, to whom He has given faith, hope, and charity, God does not give perseverance.' We need not to be surprised, therefore, at finding that he speaks of the blessing of election as conferred through the ministration of baptism. And his example illustrates the rule, by which it may be decided whether those who profess agreement with Calvin are really able to accord with the English Church. For it is indifferent whether the charge which has been brought against St. Augustin be well grounded or no, seeing that his error, if it existed,. was only one of philosophy, and did not affect his religious faith. For, by affirming the reality of baptismal grace, he maintained the great truth of our Lord's mediation. And this is a test of universal applicability. Are there any, whose minds dwell exclusively on the beauty and harmony of the divine decrees, whose habit is to refer every thing to God's purpose, but whose language does not do justice to the importance of human responsibility ?—still, if the error be only one of philosophy; if it does not lead them to detract from the reality of the mediation of Christ; if they admit that sacramental system through which the Incarnate Son has made his humanity the channel of heavenly gifts; they may be bad reasoners, but sound Christians. But, if their theory induces them to deny the reality of those gifts which are bestowed through sacraments on the members of Christ—if they will not recognise the blessings of that renewed nature, whereby the second Adam restores what was corrupted by the first (of all which the regeneration of infants has been shown to be the test)—how can they hold the great truth of our Lord's mediation, or believe those assertions of the Prayer Book, to which they are required to assent ?"

We must also quote an extract from Bishop Bethell to the same effect :—

" The ancient predestinarians never questioned the certainty of regeneration in baptism, because this doctrine was consistent with their theory. For, though they maintained that only the elect or predestinate are endued with the gift of perseverance to the end, and will be finally saved, yet they believed that God bestows at His pleasure every other kind and measure of grace on those persons, from whom He withholds this special grace of perseverance. They therefore held, in common with the rest of the Church, that the forgiveness of sin, and the gift of the Holy Ghost, are generally bestowed in baptism," &c. " This was Augustin's doctrine," &c.—*Bishop Bethell on Regeneration*, cap. ix. p. 140.

Such facts as these show how futile it is to quote passages from writers containing predestinarian views, and then assume that all such persons must have denied baptismal regeneration; and they prove also that, consistently with holding that doctrine in its integrity, there may be differences of opinion on the question of predestination; and that the believers of baptismal regeneration exact no rigid and impracticable uniformity of opinion on points which are fairly open to inquiry, and on which Christians always have been divided in opinion.

Having noticed some of the principal works on either side of this controversy, it is not our purpose to enter into further details on this branch of the subject, but to proceed at once to the recent decision in this very anxious case, its bearings upon the position of Churchmen, and the course which should be pursued by those who are faithful members of the Church of England. The recent inquiry before the Committee of Privy Council must have left a very painful impression, we should think, on the minds of all who saw theological questions of the most profound and intricate description argued before six laymen (one of whom was a Presbyterian), in order to determine whether a *bishop* were right or wrong in supposing that certain tenets were opposed to those of the Church of England. The obvious want of qualification in several of the judges to decide on a question which involved theological points of the most refined character was most painful and humiliating to the Church. Although this court has declared in its judgment that it " has no jurisdiction or authority to settle matters of faith, or to determine what ought, in any particular, to be the doctrine of the Church of England," still the fact remains, that it has decided, and has the power, by law, of virtually deciding questions of doctrine, by determining whether certain tenets are or are not in accordance with those of the Church of England. The effect of the judgment is to hold out an encouragement to persons maintaining one class of doctrines, and proportionably to cause dissatisfaction to others, who thus see a legal recognition given to tenets which they hold to be untrue in themselves and contradictory to those of the Church of England. Every one feels that a doctrinal decision has, in reality, been made by a court which disclaims its power to settle matters of faith. We hold that the occurrence of any such decision, by a court constituted like the Committee of Privy Council, is an extreme evil in itself, as calculated to supply arguments to the enemies of the Church. Romanists and Dissenters will treat it as an additional proof of what they are always urging, that the Church of England's faith is decided by the State—that the Church is nothing more than the creature of the legislature—and is, therefore, not a genuine or true Church. Many of our own members are greatly scandalized at such a tribunal for the decision of doctrinal questions. There is no security even that the members of the court should be believers, or members of the Church. It may comprise sectarians, as it has on the late occasion. The members are not persons who, from their profession, can be expected to have any such knowledge of theology as would enable them to decide intricate questions.

On all these grounds the present arrangements (created by Act of Parliament some years since) appear to be most objectionable, and dangerous, not only to the peace of the Church, but to the due enforcement and maintenance of its doctrines. A tribunal ought either to be constituted which would possess undoubted authority and qualifications to determine questions affecting the doctrines of the Church, or else all such questions should be remitted to the decision of the Church itself in Convocation, or of judges appointed by it. As long as a court, which may include heretics and unbelievers of all kinds, is possessed of the power of putting its own interpretation on the doctrines of the Church of England, and of deciding whether a clergyman shall or shall not teach in the Church, so long will the strongest distrust, uneasiness, and alarm be felt, and a state of things fostered which may lead to results of the most dangerous character to the Church. It would be a great evil if large numbers of pious, zealous, and influential men were driven, in their despair at such a state of things, to go over to Rome. We know, of course, that there are troublesome and unsettled men on both sides of the question, whose loss would not be severely felt; but the evil would be great in all respects, if any considerable secession of men of a better description should occur. We should regret to see Rome thus strengthened; and it must be remembered that, although the judgment has gone in one direction now, it does not follow that all decisions would be in the same direction. For instance, it might happen that the Committee of Council would see no sufficient reason to exclude a person holding Socinian or Sabellian tenets from officiating as a minister of the Church. No one who knows the craft and ingenuity with which such tenets may be put forward and maintained can doubt, we think, that the Committee of Council might easily be induced to decide in their favour. The same might be said of Pelagian and ultra-Arminian doctrines; so that, in truth, all members of the Church have reason to look with apprehension at what may be the future working of the tribunal in question.

We do not purpose to enter on an examination of the particular reasons on which the judgment professes to be based—*Valeant quantum.* The hypothetical meaning attached to some of our services is extended to the baptism of infants, without considering the difference of the cases; and the language of divines on the subject of baptism generally is applied without distinction to the case of infant baptism. The argument, on the whole, scarcely requires an answer, and we refrain from taking up space by attempting it. Our concern is rather with the bearing of the case on the Church of England and the cause of truth. There are a great number of questions and opinions afloat at present in consequence of this judgment, which indicate in some cases an unsettled state of mind, and in others an undue excitement and want of discrimination.

Mr. Maskell, vicar of St. Mary Church, and author of several elaborate works on the "Mediæval Rituals of the Church," and on some other subjects, has published a pamphlet which we have perused with more pain than surprise. We have already remarked in this author at various times an overstrained reliance on the truth of mediæval doctrines, and we must add, a too great confidence in the possession of abilities and learning, which has occasionally led to a positiveness of tone, and a somewhat arrogant criticism, which we have long observed with deep regret. The pamphlet which he has now produced is not only offensive in its title, "The Present Position of the *High-Church Party*," but it is decidedly disloyal in its tone. It is in fact a strong attack upon the Church of England, ascribing to her, on the strength of certain Acts of Parliament, the most Erastian doctrines possible. As Mr. Maskell regards such doctrines as heretical, his secession would seem to follow as a matter of course. He takes exactly the ground which all Romanists and Dissenters do in assailing the Church. To refute his statements would be quite superfluous : it has been already done by many of our leading divines in controversy with Romanism ; and for an able and satisfactory reply we refer to the Rev. W. J. Irons' " Present Crisis of the Church of England."

The earnest and vigorous publications of Messrs. Bennett and Dodsworth on this question evince the great excitement which it has created, and the difficulties which it has raised in many minds. We have not space to enter on an examination of their contents ; but we must pause for a little on one publication which possesses peculiar claims on attention. The publication to which we refer is a tract, by the Rev. J. Keble, entitled, " Church Matters in 1850." We offer no apology for the following extract :—

" Our consciences, then, are quite clear of any obligation by this engagement to receive the doctrinal decisions of the Privy Council as part of the doctrine of the Church. No number nor amount of them can make the Church of England formally heretical, nor bind us to withdraw from her ministrations. It is not, perhaps, often that men taking a pledge can be quite so sure that they take it according to the meaning of him who imposes it, as we may be sure, that in thus construing the Oath of Supremacy we are just doing what our rulers, from Henry and Elizabeth downwards, have directed us to do.

" What, then, is our condition ? It is little to say that it is extremely anomalous and imperfect ; that we are, practically, without a court of final appeal in doctrinal causes. We might bear that, as the whole Church has now for centuries borne with her sad divisions and perplexities, because, in the workings of God's inscrutable providence her court of final appeal—a true Œcumenical Council—has been long denied her. Such a defect does not destroy the Being of the Church Universal—she goes on in her several branches, under appeal to such authority, and ready to submit to it, when it shall please Him to grant it : so neither does the like calamitous deficiency destroy the *Being* of the particular Church of England. But it very seriously affects her *well-being :* more especially now that it comes before us, not merely as a restraint, but as a positive interference and intrusion on the part of an alien power. For,

" 1. If we seriously believe that our Lord and Saviour delivered the faith once for all to the saints,—intrusted them with it, as with a precious deposit, which they are not at liberty to make over to others,—then we must believe that it is a great and grievous sin in any church or any clergyman voluntarily to part with that deposit, or any portion of it, into the keeping of aliens, or of any whom He never called to such trust : a great and grievous sin in all ; greater and more grievous, in proportion as a man's office comes nearer to that of the holy apostles, to whom and to their successors the treasure was at first committed. Now, we seem in our ignorance to have come very near indeed to that sin ; and, being wakened up, we find ourselves on the absolute edge of it. If we go on at all to accept or connive at the claim of the Privy Council to settle controversies of faith, what do we but render ourselves actual and wilful partakers in that sin?

" 2. Apart from all such solemn considerations, and regarding the Church simply as we might any other society, what a strange, unsettled condition of things, both in doctrine and discipline, have we to look forward to, if this anomaly is to continue! It was bad enough, when we thought we had an appellate court, namely, Convocation, only that for reasons prudential and charitable we abstained from pressing to have it called into action. Now it will be ten times worse : for those who believe the Church's divine commission will hardly, if ever, think it right to recognise the Privy Council court as fit to overrule the courts of the Church : if they are wronged elsewhere, they will be precluded from appeal ; and from defence, if any appeal against them : so that it will necessarily be a partial and one-sided court. The consciousness of its being at hand will of course greatly embolden the propagators of new doctrine among us, and dispirit the defenders of the old. And the scorn is inexpressible which it will bring—nay, which it has already brought—on the English Church ; as also the scandal to those who are weak, on the side both of Dissenters and of Roman Catholics.

" 3. All this, observe, holds equally true, whether the decision in the present case be according to the Nicene Creed or no. But, if it be adverse, see what presently follows ; even granting, what needs to be distinctly proved, that a bishop or archbishop, acting on that decision, would not involve in direct heresy both himself and all in communion with him. The Church indeed will continue as it was (for, even if the court were as legitimate as it is irregular, a judicial decision would not overthrow what is beyond all question synodically decreed) ; the

Church, and the position of each clergyman in it, will continue in theory just what they were, but in practice all will be confusion. There is no need to put cases in detail : every one will understand at once the kind of difficulties which must and will arise between bishops and priests, dignitaries and inferior clergy, incumbents and curates, visitors and teachers of schools, pastors and parishioners, academical governors and students ; in ordination, in institution, in licensing of curates, in catechising, in examinations, in testimonials. There is not an ecclesiastical relation but will be greatly disturbed : from time to time real conflicts will occur, which, if carried out consistently with the decision now supposed, must end in depriving the English Church of the ministry of some, more or fewer, of those who most earnestly desire to help in her labours : some, worn out, will retire from work altogether, many, zealous, but so far unstable, will be driven to forsake and renounce her."

We certainly look on the constitution of the Court of Appeal in Church matters as most strangely defective. If the supremacy of the Crown is permitted to extend in any degree to questions affecting doctrine, the very least that can be expected is, that the members of the court, or some of them at all events, should be competent, from profession and study, to exercise a sound judgment in such questions. This is not now provided for. The Episcopate is wholly excluded. It seems to us that the Bishop of London's proposal would be a vast improvement on such a court. In fact, considering that it is a State Court, for the revision of Church decisions, it seems that the Bishop's proposal is as fair a one as can be ; and, though some men see objections in it at first, we think it will finally be approved by all who recognize in the State any power of examining decisions on mixed questions.

And now to touch a painful branch of the subject—we allude to the overstrained excitement caused by the decision, and the disloyal language towards the Church of England, and the avowed doubts which have been heard in so many quarters. In truth, we are most deeply humiliated at much of what we see and hear. Alas ! have Church principles degenerated from their natural healthy, honest, and confiding tone, into a peevish and irritable mood, in which real evils are magnified into extravagant dimensions, and principles are overborne and forgotten ! We should have no uneasiness, if men would take time to consider the real state of things. But it is, in truth, mortifying to the deepest degree, to see the faith of Churchmen so very fragile, and so open to temptations. A difficulty with some men immediately leads to the most unworthily desponding thoughts, or induces them to give up the contest in utter hopelessness. Such faint hearts

are not really faithful ; they are overthrown by the slightest wind
of temptation.

But we trust, as we have ever done, that the influence of such
an unhealthy and morbid state of feeling is not very widely spread.
We are sure that the mass of the parochial Clergy—the real
strength of the Church—are robust in faith, and prepared to
struggle in the cause of the Church of England. Their love of
that Church is not shaken by any injuries she may suffer from
the State, nor do they willingly impute to *her* the unchristian
doings of statesmen or of parliaments. If her faith is imperilled,
they will stand by her in the contest, for the protection of that faith.

There was a time when the Church's faith was, for nearly a
century, endangered on the most vital point of all,—the divinity
of the Son of God. The temporal power first sided with the
orthodox faith, then attempted to force a latitudinarian compromise upon the Church, and persecuted all those who refused to
acquiesce in it. In those times the orthodox faith was condemned,
not merely by Emperors and State officials, but by many synods
of Bishops. It was not merely heterodox *priests* who were then
established by the temporal power, with the aid of subservient
bishops, in parochial benefices ; but the bishops themselves, in
numberless cases, were either actual heretics, or else acted as
heretics directed. Not merely were heretics ordained and placed
in the episcopal office, but large numbers of orthodox bishops
were deposed and driven from their sees by synods and the State,
and heretics were placed in their stead. The bishops of the whole
Church, on one occasion, with but a few exceptions, subscribed
by compulsion to what was heretical, and "the world was astonished to find itself Arian." The first bishop of the Church—
Liberius of Rome—fell ; and the orthodox faith was visibly
maintained only by Athanasius, and a small number of expelled
and persecuted bishops.

And yet do we ever find, throughout that long and terrible
struggle, that the orthodox ever dreamt of quitting the Church !
Never. They might have joined another communion. There
was one ready at hand. The Novatians were orthodox in their
doctrine, and maintained generally the catholic system. But it
never occurred to Athanasius, or to the other confessors in the
cause of Christian truth, to leave the Church under the influence
of heresy, even when heresy seemed most triumphant, and to
relinquish the struggle by retiring into communion with the
Novatians. They felt that they had to contend even to death for
the truth of Jesus Christ, and never to relinquish the struggle to
rescue the souls of their brethren and children in the faith from
the poisonous and fatal errors of Arianism. It was the strong
principles of faith in God's blessing on his own cause, and love

for the souls of Christians, that bore them through the deepest
discouragements and most unexpected reverses, in steadfast endurance, until the clouds which so long had hung over the Church's
faith were dispersed, and heresy was finally and utterly discom-
fited. That struggle lasted from the reign of Constantine to the
time of Theodosius.

In the subsequent controversies on the Monothelite doctrine,
the leading bishops of the Oriental Church and the Eastern
Emperors, upheld for a long time the heterodox view. Yet no
one ever dreamt of forsaking the Church, because it was not
possible at once to get rid of false doctrine. During the controversies on Images, the sees were filled by prelates who held contradictory views, and the one party regarded the other as heretical.
There were counter decisions on the point by councils calling
themselves Œcumenical, and attended by hundreds of bishops.
Yet no one thought of forsaking the Church. Nay—to come
nearer to our own times—Cranmer and Ridley never dreamt of
relinquishing the communion of the Church, even when Romanism
was in the ascendant; and neither did Bonner and Gardiner,
when they saw bishoprics filled by those whom they regarded as
heretics. Each held fast to his position, with the hope of finally
succeeding in establishing the faith which he believed to be
catholic.

Any one who looks at the facts of ecclesiastical history will
see at once that controversies on so difficult and important a
subject as that of baptism, in its connexion with predestination,
are not to be settled in a day. We attribute the *extent* of
division which exists on this subject altogether to the absence of
any fitting tribunal for the decision of doctrinal questions. Had the
Convocation been permitted to exercise its legal and constitutional rights,—had not the temporal government, by its influence
on the heads of the Church, silenced the voice of the Church, in
the hope of managing it more easily,—the baptismal controversy
would have been set at rest half a century ago. We can conceive
nothing more really dangerous to the Church than a chronic
disease like that of the dispute on regeneration, and kindred
topics; and, great as might have been the risks of bringing such
questions before any synod, we yet think that far less evil would
have ensued, under any event, than has arisen from the virtual
permission given for so long a series of years to inculcate tenets
wholly subversive of the doctrines of the English Church. We
are persuaded that Convocation would never have made any
decision that would not have been both moderate and orthodox;
and, although the difficulty of the case is now vastly increased by
the suppression of all but the executive authority of the Church
for so many years, we are of opinion that a resort to the Convo-

cation would still, on the whole, be the best remedy for the evils around us.

We cannot think that any one, except, perhaps, Mr. Gorham himself, can be satisfied at the present state of things. ·It can be no real satisfaction to those partisans who have been in the habit of denouncing baptismal regeneration as "a soul-destroying error," and as "contrary to the truth as it is in Jesus," to have it declared by the judicial Committee of Privy Council, and admitted by Mr. Gorham's advocates, that the advocates of this detested doctrine may lawfully act as ministers of the Church of England. On the other hand, it creates universal uneasiness amongst the believers in baptismal regeneration to find a judgment given, which favours the deniers of that doctrine to a certain extent. The controversy will not be in any degree closed by such a decision as has been given,—a decision which bears with it the recognition of its own incompetence and nullity, as regards any authority to decide on matters of faith. The decision will only add to the flame of controversy; it will only suffice to embitter feelings, and will lead to further and stronger struggles.

We deem such a state of things as is likely to ensue, and to be long continued, as fraught with consequences of the most grave importance in every point of view, — consequences which we would earnestly but most respectfully press upon the consideration of the Episcopate, and of all those members of the Clergy whose position and character gives them weight and influence. We are anxious to regard the matter in such a point of view as may appeal to the minds of men of all parties and schools, who are capable of exercising a dispassionate judgment on the question, and who look beyond the excitement of the present controversy to the general interests of the Church of England.

And, in the first place, to speak of the interests of truth itself, as stated and expressed in the authorised formularies of the English Church, we think that every fair-minded and intelligent observer must feel that, amidst the controversies so long carried on, there has been much said which is really and truly inconsistent with the belief of the Church of England, and with sound doctrine. Exaggerated, false, and scandalous doctrines have been broached, and the minds of the people have been disturbed in various directions; in many instances a spirit of hostility has been engendered against the formularies of the Church; pious men have been induced to forsake her in consequence; and belief has become widely unsettled on the important point of regeneration.

And, in the next place, to speak of the evils hence arising to the Church. We must, in the first place, speak of the incalculable harm of division in itself, the diminution of Christian charity

and benevolence, the impediments which are offered to co-operation in religious undertakings, the many bad effects which arise
from divided courses of action.   We are too much accustomed to
such things, but still the suffering and the evil caused by them
are very great.   It is a lamentable fact that in too many places
the clergy are separated by an impassable line, and hold no
intercourse.   In some places, members of the same communion
look on each other as heretics, and entertain more charitable
feelings towards members of different communions.   We need
not speak of the moral tendencies and effects of such a state of
things.   Divisions like these tend to diminish the growth of
Christian holiness: they are opposed to the best interests of piety
and devotion; they are deeply injurious to the efficiency of the,
Church.   Nothing can be more deplorable than either the existence of differences which can in any degree justify the hostile
feelings which exist, or the great violence of parties, if the
differences between them do not authorize such extreme courses.
In either case the Church is in a very unsatisfactory state.

But now, to take another view of the question.   Is it safe, for
the general interests of the Church, regarded in its capacity of the
national Established Church, that the present controversies should
be permitted to become permanent?   We think there can be
very little doubt on this subject.   Be it remembered that the
Church of England is no longer in such a position of ascendancy,
that she can afford to act exactly as if she were in the political
position she occupied a century ago.   We have lost the exclusive
position we then occupied.   We are surrounded by powerful and
vigilant enemies, who have forced their way into political power
and influence, in spite of all the opposition we could make.   Romanism and Dissent confront us in Parliament; and what is still
worse, if possible, is the spirit of latitudinarian indifference, the
spirit of heartless godlessness, of irreligious cupidity, of revolutionary innovation, which *exists* in the Legislature, and is ready to combine with any allies for the destruction of existing institutions.   To
believe that these circumstances do not deeply affect the Church,
and throw a shadow over her prospects, is, we think, impossible.
Now then, we do say with confidence, that the continuance of so
extensive a division in the Church as exists, is most highly perilous
to our general interest at present.   We cannot help feeling alarm
at the prospect of its further continuance without check.   Were
the Church any thing like a united body, did it possess the power
of joining even for the promotion of its most vital interests and
securities, we should feel little apprehension; but to permit
it much longer to be a divided body, before a host of enemies, an
unscrupulous Parliament, and an impoverished and discontented

nation,—to present it in this point of view, while it is still
showing so many signs of resistance to the will of leading parties,
would, we think, be a fearful risk. It may not be possible to
escape from this position, but we are convinced that no efforts
ought to be spared for the purpose of endeavouring to escape
from it. The Church is weakened by her divisions, at the very
time when her strength requires to be concentrated, as far as
possible, to maintain her position.

Our readers will do us the justice of admitting, that it has ever
been our effort to promote harmony and mutual forbearance among
Churchmen. We have never promoted party-spirit, or attempted
to pass sentences of condemnation on " Evangelicals." But we
are convinced that a great change has come upon the Church.

We are of opinion that the time has arrived in which the risks,
whatever they may be, of a doctrinal decision by the authority of
the collective Church of England, are far less than those to be apprehended from leaving controversy to continue. Every one must feel
anxious—most deeply anxious at such a prospect. But we think
there is now no alternative. If prelates pass judgment on the
question in their individual capacity, it may be apprehended that
the division and excitement will only be continually augmenting,
because we have no reason to expect such unanimity as might
amount to a combined judgment of the whole. Independently of
this, we think that subjects of so intricate and anxious a character
should not be left to individual judgment, but should be settled
after lengthened consideration, conference, and study. The condemnation of Tractarian doctrines here furnishes no sufficient precedent : it does not at all follow that there would be either so
united a judgment, or so unequal a division of parties as there
was in that case. Something more authoritative is now requisite.
Something which shall be distinctly recognized as the voice of the
Church of England herself.

We think that Convocation is *the* tribunal which alone would
supply the authority needed. We should, ourselves, have no objection to see the question submitted to the episcopate alone ; but
we do not think such a measure would give satisfaction. There are
three objections to such a plan. (1.) The episcopate is considered
by many as too much under the influence of Government to decide
freely. (2.) It is not the recognized and ordinary synod which
has acted since the Reformation. (3.) The anxiety which exists
would induce dissatisfaction, if the clergy by their representatives
were *excluded* from the decision of questions in which they have
hitherto been permitted to take part by the law of the land.
We, therefore, look on Convocation as the only synod that could
be safely employed.

With reference to the constitution of Convocation we are ready
to admit that it might possibly be more perfect in theory; but
we must remember that it remains in the same state as it has
done for six hundred years—in the same state as when it authorized our present formularies. It comprises in one house the
episcopate of the Church, and in the other a certain number of
the second order of the clergy holding important offices in the
Church, and the elected representatives of the whole body of the
clergy. The authority of such a body is as great as any synod of
the English Church could possess.

With reference to the qualifications of the members of Convocation to discuss and examine the questions now disturbing the
Church, we think there is no reason to entertain any doubt. In
the first place, the great body of its members hold their places *ex
officio*, and therefore cannot be returned under any temporary
excitement. In the next place, the present representatives of the
clergy were returned when there was no contemplation of the
decision of any such question by Convocation, and therefore they
are to be supposed to represent the general mind of the clergy.
Very possibly, in some instances, abler men might have been
chosen if it had been expected that Convocation was to act; but
we think the great advantage is, that the present members of
Convocation were not chosen at a contested election.

And now, as regards the theological attainments of the members of Convocation, we see no reason to doubt that, as a body,
they are sufficiently qualified. Supposing that some of their
members are not much versed in such questions, still it must be
remarked, that the ancient synods contained many bishops who
were not very learned, but rather the reverse. And besides this,
we hold that no question such as is now disturbing the Church,
could or ought to be decided until after a very lengthened inquiry. The congregation appointed at Rome to examine the
works of Jansenius, and the complicated doctrines connected,
were two years in making their inquiries; and we think that any
decision in the present case, in order to be satisfactory, and to
have weight, ought to be based on extensive examination, and
long and dispassionate inquiry. If any of the members of Convocation are not prepared at once, and without further inquiry,
to pronounce their decision on the very complicated and difficult
questions in debate, they could at least prepare themselves for
giving an opinion by careful study. We must express our own
opinion, that to pronounce a really sound judgment, taking in the
subject in its various relations, is no easy task, even to men of
learning and intelligence.

It has always been the practice, in synods of the Church, to

submit questions to the fullest examination, before any resolution
is come to; and if this course were pursued in the present instance, we do not think there would be any danger either of an
unworthy compromise of truth, or of any decision which would·
drive large numbers of persons from the Church's communion.

The Convocation includes amongst its members many representatives of each side of the question, and many others whose
views are not before the public. We think it must be regarded
therefore as an impartial tribunal, while it possesses the supreme
authority in the Church of England. A body which includes the
hierarchy in one house (without whose consent no measure could
pass), and which includes in the other house all the presbyters
of the Church, whose station, age, and mode of appointment afford
reasonable grounds for expecting moderation, and a regard to
practical results, is, we think, most unlikely to wish to come to
any decision which would have the effect of rending the Church
asunder; and we will express a strong conviction, that though
there *are* differences of the most striking kind in the Church, and
more differences than are tolerable, yet the differences existing
between the *greater* numbers on each side, are not such as to forbid mutual forbearance in regard to those points, or to render the
task of a synod altogether a hopeless one.

We have been anxious to dwell on such practical considerations
as the above, with a view to show that there would not be so
much difficulty as many persons might be inclined to anticipate
from any meeting of Convocation. We will advance further, to
state the mode of proceeding which might be calculated to obviate
the further inconveniences which might be anticipated, and to
afford a prospect of a satisfactory solution of our present difficulties.

It would be desirable, we think, that the Convocation of the
province of York should be transferred by the Queen's writ or
letters patent, and by the metropolitan, to London, and united to
the Convocation of the province of Canterbury, and that the
united Convocation should be declared by its own first act and by
the Sovereign to be a national synod of the Church of England.

The subject-matter for consideration would be " the differences
within the Church on the subject of baptismal regeneration,
with a view to the termination of controversies, and a settlement
of the doctrine of the Church on those points." This subject
would be placed before the Convocation by some authority, either
that of the State alone, or of the State at the request of the
Bishops, or some of them. The first step to be taken, before
entering into any discussions or controversies, should, we think,
be the appointment of a joint committee of the two houses of

Convocation, to regulate the *mode of proceeding* in both houses, and to examine *the state of the controversies* in the Church— that is, to ascertain what views and statements are, and have been, put forward, which seem to merit attention. The object of this inquiry would be, to ascertain and place before Convocation, in some authentic form, an exposition of the statements and modes of speaking, which appear to be censurable or prejudicial to the peace of the Church. We should think that the result of such an inquiry would disclose many statements which would meet with general disapproval ; and the repression of extreme, erroneous, and rash statements on both sides, would, we think, tend, as much as any thing else, to the restoration of sufficient unity in the Church.

But this alone would be insufficient, unless it were accompanied by a statement of the positive doctrine of the Church of England in the matter of baptismal regeneration. And here, it may be imagined, would be the signal for a violent contest and struggle in Convocation itself. We do not think this need be the case, if the proceedings are regulated in a certain way. We think, that *viva voce* discussion, except perhaps by advocates, as before an Ecclesiastical Court, or by selected Divines, should be avoided on many accounts. Various scandals might be created, in the present state of the public press, and the authority and dignity of the synod might be diminished, were hasty words permitted to escape any one. The total alteration of the circumstances and habits of the times, and the facilities for criticism of a certain kind professed by the lowest classes, renders it, in our view, essential that the proceedings of synods should be conducted, as much as possible, on paper. The mode of proceeding, which seems to us as desirable, is this : a committee of each house should be elected, and should be united in one body, for the purpose of preparing a very few questions on the doctrine of baptism, calculated to elicit the judgment of the members of Convocation, as to the doctrine of the Church of England on the point. These questions, when prepared, should be considered by both houses, and if deemed insufficient or obscure in any point, should be amended. When the questions were finally agreed on, they should be submitted on paper to every member of Convocation, to be answered on paper within assigned limits, and within a certain number of months. Sufficient space should be allowed for full consideration of the subject.

When the answers had been all received, the Convocation should meet again, and the questions having been read separately, the answers to each should be read *seriatim*. In this way the judgment of the synod as to the doctrine of the Church would be solemnly and effectively delivered, without risk of any scandal.

And the proceedings would take the form which was usual in ancient synods.

The next step would be, to appoint a committee of both houses for the purpose of drawing up a judgment or decision stating the doctrine of the Church of England. In this judgment we should think that if the positive declarations of the Church of England in her various formularies—declarations, the plainness and stringency of which is admitted by all parties—were adhered to as far as possible, without going beyond her own expressions, the truth would be secured on all sides, and general satisfaction would be felt. On the other hand, we think that to this positive declaration should be annexed some general declaration, that it was not the purpose of the Church to enforce a uniformity of opinion on certain mysterious and difficult doctrines connected with the Divine predestination. And this ought to be followed up by the condemnation of certain modes of speaking calculated to bring contempt on the sacrament and to promote division, requiring all clergy to abstain from such language in future on penalty of suspension.

This decision should be submitted to each house of Convocation in a private session or general committee, and, after having received the necessary emendations, should be finally passed in a public session.

It appears to us, that such a mode of proceeding as we have attempted to sketch, would afford a fair prospect of arriving at a safe and satisfactory conclusion, and of allaying the great excitement and divisions which now exist, and which will continue to increase, if some mode be not taken to set them at rest. The Church of England is extremely endangered by the continuance of the present divisions. These angry disputes ought to be put an end to. We think it very possible, that some ultra and extreme men on either side might fall away from the Church if any decision were made. But we think such a risk indefinitely less than that of leaving the present controversy to rage in the Church unchecked. The loss of a certain number of individuals would be nothing in comparison with the permanent weakness of the whole Church. We cannot believe that any decision of Convocation would really narrow the legitimate limits of private opinion in the Church of England, or thoughtlessly and inconsiderately define more than the Church herself has already defined. We shall not have the slightest apprehension of the result, if there be a sufficient degree of inquiry and of deliberation. We feel assured that the effect would be to leave diversities of opinion, while it ensured uniformity in belief, and compelled moderation of language.

We now come to consider the course which should be pursued

by the advocates of sound doctrine in the present circumstances. To permit the decision of the Committee of Privy Council to pass without remark and protest, would be as inexpedient and wrong, as it would be impossible. The strong and too excited feelings of men must find some immediate vent; and we see no evil in 'protests, as affording a relief to the exigencies of many minds. Such protests, however, are of a transitory character, and have no consequences of a practical nature. They may serve for a particular crisis, but they are not calculated to make any permanent impression, or to lead to the final settlement of the question. The right step to be taken is, we think, to call for the decision of the controversies on the subject of regeneration by the Convocation of the Church of England. We should recommend men to direct their attention to this single point; and to press it in every possible way, by petitions and memorials to the Crown, archbishops, and bishops, pointing out the urgent necessity for some authoritative decision, with a view to remove the great evils of a controversy which has so long been permitted to weaken and divide the Church.

Need we add to this, that there is another remedy which is to be resorted to by all faithful members of the Church? Reliance on the Divine protection, with continual prayer for guidance amidst the great dangers and difficulties of the present time, are, we hope, the habitual resources of many amongst us; and to the sanctifying, tranquillizing, and enlightening influences thence resulting, we look with greater hope than to any contrivances of mere human wisdom. In such a spirit of firm reliance, combined with a spirit of genuine and enlarged charity, we feel hopeful that Churchmen will face the difficulties of their position; and, remote alike from a spirit of latitudinarian compromise, or of sectarian dogmatism, will stedfastly seek for the establishment of the truth, and the removal of the scandals which now abound. To remain apathetic and inactive in the present grave circumstances, would be injurious at once to the truth of Christian doctrine, and to the best interests of the Church of England. An effort to obtain the settlement of most dangerous and exciting controversies, cannot be justly regarded as any improper disturbance of the Church. It is, on the contrary, the act of true peace-makers. It was not the act of disturbers of the Church, or of agitators, to lay before the Apostolic council at Jerusalem the controversies in reference to the obligation of the law. Need we despair of a similar conclusion in giving peace to the Church now, if the same spirit of moderation and of inquiry be pursued which guided the synod at Jerusalem? Whether so great a blessing be in store for us we cannot foretel, but we heartily pray that it may be so.

. In the mean time, we are not likely to see any intermission of controversy on the subject of this article. In truth, the question is one which is of no transient interest: it has been troubling the Church for the last thirty or forty years; and it directly affects the doctrines of the Gospel. In proportion as religious zeal and earnestness increase, more anxiety is felt on the subject. We are now only at the commencement of troubles which have no visible termination but in ruin, unless they be arrested in time. Those troubles cannot be stayed by force, by attempts at intimidation, or by such bungling and ill-contrived schemes of accommodation between opposing parties, as would give no satisfaction to either. The only mode in which they can be settled is by an attempt to settle them, not merely on grounds of policy, or with a view to conciliation, but under a sense of duty to truth, and to the God of truth. If the case be treated in this spirit of faith, the Divine blessing may be reasonably expected, and thus alone will peace be obtained.

At present there can be no peace: a judgment has been given which leaves the whole case in more complexity than ever. We hear each day of solemn protests against the measure; and those protests deeply affect the public mind. The Rev. George Denison has the distinction of leading the way in the remarkable documents which follow.

" Protest A.

" In the name of the most Holy Trinity.—Amen.

" Whereas the Universal Church alone possesses, by the commission and command of its Divine Founder, the power of defining in matter of doctrine; and, subject to the same, the Church of England alone possesses, within its sphere, the power of interpreting and declaring the intention of such definitions as the Universal Church has framed;—

" And whereas a power to interpret formularies of the Church by a final judicial sentence, the Synods of the Church not being, in practice, admitted to declare the doctrine of the Church, becomes in effect a power to declare and make such interpretations binding upon the Church;—

" And whereas by the suit of Gorham *v.* the Bishop of Exeter, as well as by the case of Escott *v.* Mastin, in the year 1842, it appears that the Crown, through a Court constituted by Act of Parliament alone, claims and exercises a power to confirm, reserve, or vary, by a final judicial sentence, the decisions and interpretations of the Courts of the Church in matters of doctrine;—

" And whereas in the present state of the law nothing hinders but that an interpretation which shall have been judged to be unsound by the Courts of the Church may be finally declared to be sound by the said *Judicial Committee*; or, that a person who shall have been judged to be unfit for cure of souls by the spiritual tribunal may be declared to be fit for cure of souls by the civil power ;—

" And whereas the existence of such state of the law cannot be reconciled with the Divine constitution and office of the Church, and is contrary to the law of Christ ;—

" And whereas the exercise of power in such matters, under such state of the law, endangers the public maintenance of the faith of Christ ;—

" And whereas the existence of such a state of things is a grievance of conscience ;—

" And whereas no judgment pronounced by the Judicial Committee of Privy Council, in respect of matters of doctrine, can be accepted by the Church ;—

" I, George Anthony Denison, Clerk, M.A., Vicar of East Brent, in the county of Somerset, and diocese of Bath and Wells, do hereby enter my solemn protest against the state of the law which empowers the Judicial Committee of the Privy Council to take cognizance of matters of doctrine, and against the exercise of that power by the said Judicial Committee in each particular case ; and I do hereby pledge myself to use all lawful means within my reach to prevent the continuance of such state of the law, and of the power claimed and exercised under the same.

(Signed)   " GEORGE ANTHONY DENISON.
" East Brent, 4th Sunday in Lent, March 10, 1850.

" Read in the vestry of the parish church of East Brent, in the presence of the churchwardens and other witnesses, and copies delivered to the churchwardens, and transmitted to the Bishop, Sunday, March 10, 1850.

" PROTEST B.   •

" In the name of the most Holy Trinity.—Amen.

" I. Whereas the Church of England is a branch of the One Catholic and Apostolic Church, and in virtue thereof holds, absolutely and exclusively, all the doctrines of the Catholic faith ;—

" II. And whereas George Cornelius Gorham, Clerk, B.D., Priest of the Church of England, has formally denied the Catholic faith in respect of the holy sacrament of baptism ;—

" And whereas the Judicial Committee of the Privy Council has, in the case of Gorham v. Bishop of Exeter, reversed the judgment of the Church Court, and has pronounced, by final sentence, the said George Cornelius Gorham to be fit to be instituted by the Bishop to a benefice with cure of souls ;—

·   " And whereas this sentence is necessarily false ;—

" And whereas such sentence gives public legal sanction to the teaching of false doctrine, and therein and thereby has a great and manifest tendency to lead into error of doctrine, or to encourage to persevere in error of doctrine, or to plunge finally into heresy, all such as are tempted, in one degree or another, to deny the faith of Christ in respect of the holy sacrament of baptism ;—

" And whereas such sentence does injury and dishonour to Christ and to His Holy Church ;—

" And whereas all, who with a full knowledge of the intent, meaning, and purpose of such sentence, are, or shall be, concerned in promulging or executing it, and all who, with a like knowledge, shall approve of, or acquiesce in it, are or will be involved in heresy ;—

" And whereas it has become necessary—in consequence of such sentence—that the Church of England should free herself from any participation in the guilt thereof by proceeding, *without delay*, to make some further formal declaration in respect of the Holy Sacrament of Baptism ;—

" I, George Anthony Denison, Clerk, M.A., Vicar of East Brent, in the county of Somerset, and diocese of Bath and Wells, do hereby enter my solemn protest against the said sentence of the Judicial Committee of the Privy Council, and do warn all the Christian people of this parish to beware of allowing themselves to be moved or influenced thereby in the least degree ; and I do also hereby pledge myself to use all lawful means within my reach to assist in obtaining, without delay, some further formal declaration, by a lawful Synod of the Church of England as to what is, and what is not, the doctrine of the Church of England in respect of the Holy Sacrament of Baptism.

(Signed)   " GEORGE ANTHONY DENISON.

" East Brent, 4th Sunday in Lent, March 10, 1850.

" Read in the vestry of the parish church of East Brent, in the presence of the churchwardens and other witnesses, and copies delivered to the churchwardens, and transmitted to the Bishop, Sunday, March 10, 1850."

We must confess that our first impulse in perusing the above documents was to regret the course taken by Mr. Denison, and to regard his statements as overstrained and violent. But more attentive consideration has induced us to alter our opinion, both as regards the sentiments expressed and the mode of expression. This protest was not intended merely to express the author's own private sentiments, or to relieve his own feelings. It was invested with every degree of formality; evidently for the purpose of meeting the imperative demand for such protests arising from the unsettled state of mind of various Churchmen, who deemed the Church of England in danger of becoming heretical in the matter of baptism, if no protest against the decision of the Committee of Council were made. His protest appears throughout to consider the evil and danger in the present case to arise from the suppression of the synods of the Church, which gives to the decisions of the Committee of Council a weight they ought not to possess ; and he denies to that Committee only the power which it repudiates itself—the decision of controversies of faith. On the whole, the more we examine Mr. Denison's protests, the more we are satisfied *of their propriety* in all respects ; and the insults of the " Times," and the threats of Government, will only tend to raise Mr. Denison's influence, and increase the widely-extended sympathy which he possesses. In his contrast to the principles of the " Times," Mr. Denison appears in the light of a champion of ecclesiastical liberties; and we intreat him as such to act with the caution and deliberation, as well as the resolution which such a position imperatively demands.

We do not feel altogether satisfied with some parts of the following protest, subscribed, as it is, with names which must command general respect :—

RESOLUTIONS.

" 1. That whatever, at the present time, be the force of the sentence delivered on appeal in the case of Gorham *v.* the Bishop of Exeter, the Church of England will eventually be bound by the said sentence, unless it shall openly and expressly reject the erroneous doctrine sanctioned thereby.

" 2. That the remission of original sin to all infants in and by the grace of Baptism is an essential part of the Article ' One Baptism for the remission of sins.'

" 3. That—to omit other questions raised by the said sentence—such sentence, while it does not deny the liberty of holding that Article in the sense heretofore received, does equally sanction the assertion that original sin is a bar to the right reception of Baptism, and is not remitted except when God bestows regeneration beforehand by an act of prevenient grace, (whereof Holy Scripture and the Church are wholly silent,) thereby rendering the benefits of Holy Baptism altogether uncertain and precarious.

" 4. That to admit the lawfulness of holding an exposition of an Article of the Creed, contradictory of the essential meaning of that Article, is, in truth and in fact, to abandon that Article.

" 5. That, inasmuch as the Faith is one, and rests upon one principle of authority, the conscious, deliberate, and wilful abandonment of the essential meaning of an Article of the Creed, destroys the Divine Foundation upon which alone the entire Faith is propounded by the Church.

" 6. That any portion of the Church which does so abandon the essential meaning of an Article of the Creed forfeits, not only the Catholic doctrine in that Article, but also the office and authority to witness and teach as a Member of the Universal Church.

" 7. That, by such conscious, wilful, and deliberate act, such portion of the Church becomes formally separated from the Catholic body, and can no longer assure to its members the grace of the sacraments and the remission of sins.

" 8. That all measures consistent with the present legal position of the Church ought to be taken without delay, to obtain an authoritative declaration by the Church of the doctrine of holy baptism, impugned by the recent sentence: as, for instance, by praying licence for the Church

in Convocation to declare that doctrine: or by obtaining an Act of
Parliament, to give legal effect to the decisions of the collective episcopate on this and all other matters purely spiritual.

"9. That, failing such measures, all efforts must be made to obtain
from the said episcopate, acting only in its spiritual character, a re-
affirmation of the doctrine of holy baptism, impugned by the said
sentence.

" H. E. MANNING, M.A., Archdeacon of Chichester.
ROBERT J. WILBERFORCE, M.A., Archdeacon of the East Riding.
THOMAS THORP, B.D., Archdeacon of Bristol.
W. H. MILL, D.D., Regius Professor of Hebrew, Cambridge.
E. B. PUSEY, D.D., Regius Professor of Hebrew, Oxford.
JOHN KEBLE, M.A., Vicar of Hursley.
W. DODSWORTH, M.A., Perpetual Curate of Christ Church, St.
Pancras.
W. J. E. BENNETT, M.A., Perpetual Curate of St. Paul's,
Knightsbridge.
HENRY W. WILBERFORCE, M.A., Vicar of East Farleigh.
JOHN C. TALBOT, M.A., Barrister-at-Law.
RICHARD CAVENDISH, M.A.
EDWARD BADELEY, M.A., Barrister-at-Law.
JAMES R. HOPE, D.C.L., Barrister-at-Law."

If this protest be intended for general adoption, it appears to us
that it is not so drawn up as to obtain the assent of very many
who strongly object to the recent decision. It is very true that
to deny an article of the Creed is heresy. Still we should not
have thought it expedient in the present temper of men's minds
to contemplate, so distinctly as this document does, the abandonment of an article of the Creed by the Church of England. We
do not like this tone. We should prefer to see men declaring,
indeed, the evils of the judgment that has passed, and its dangers,
but looking in a more hopeful spirit to the remedy of these evils.
Perhaps our criticism is too captious; but we look with anxiety
at a document signed with such names. It is, indeed, one of the
most important documents that has come before us for years;
and we have no doubt that it will have the greatest weight.
Associations of Churchmen in all parts of the country are also
joining in protesting against the recent decision; and the daily
increase of publications on the subject shows the intense and
lively interest of all classes; and the controversy on which we have
now entered bids fair to endure for years to come with equal or
increasing strength. Shall this be so? Shall we be left to waste
our strength by incessant quarrelling? or will any attempt be
made to settle our controversies by authority? It is, in our view,
the only remaining hope for the Church.

Art. V.—*The Life of Torquato Tasso. By the Rev.* R. Milman. 2 vols. London: Colburn. 1850.

There are few things which strike a reflecting mind more keenly than the ignorance of man. It was said by one of the wisest of our species, that in proportion as his actual knowledge increased, so did his perception of his own want of knowledge; so that the more he knew, the less he seemed to know; and the utmost triumph of his knowledge was to know that he knew nothing.

How little do we know of the mighty universe which we inhabit: of the higher heaven we have but a faint and feeble glimmering; of the lower depth but a flickering far-off reflection. And how many bright worlds are careering around us in the appointed orbits which they have trod since the day in which they were created— worlds which we see and wonder at, and whose speechless voices we hear—yet of which we know nothing. And if, leaving heaven and hell and the celestial system, we look upon the things nearer home, still the same thought strikes us—we know nothing. The sun, which under the Divine Will gives life and light to every earthly formation, remains an unknown wonder—a marvel unintelligible; the moon, which for countless ages has tracked our course through æther, the humble though beautiful attendant of mother earth, what know we of her life? her destiny? save as concerns a portion of her office to our parent. Nearer still,—we see the clouds arise, we hear the winds blow, yet the clouds arise without our knowledge, and the wind bloweth where it listeth, and we cannot tell whence it cometh nor whither it goeth. We can calculate, speculate, divide, construct, theorize, and dream, yet to any being really acquainted with the truths of nature, our thoughts must appear lighter than vanity itself. Take a nearer view still —look at the fowls of the air and the beasts of the earth, the trees of the forest and the herbs of the field, and all those forms animate or inanimate, whose home is in the depths of the ocean or the bowels of the earth. How little do we really *know* of them; we observe phenomena, and dot them down and arrange them, and draw our wise conclusions from them; yet it may safely be said, that the smallest living creature, nay, the meanest herb, contains more that we do not know than the round world contains of what we do.

And nearer still,—how little do we know of the real history of the globe which we inhabit; the history of those living creatures

of our own species who have been born, and grown up, and died
since the days when the earth was divided amongst the children
of Noah.   How often do we find reliques of nations and empires
of whom nothing but the name remains, and scarcely that.   And
even in the histories of those states which have been recorded,
how many outward facts are in dispute, how many inward agencies
of mighty influence are entirely misapprehended and misappre-
ciated, if not utterly unknown !   Why ! in our own recollection
there have been disputes as to which of the contending armies deserved the honour of gaining a victory.   Nay, even in biography,
which confining itself to a more simple, and therefore a more easily
cognizable subject, should, one would *à priori* think, be free from
such doubts and difficulties—mistakes prevail, and disputes arise,
till the very ground upon which our hero stands, shakes under
him, and, like some eastern genie, changing from hour to hour,
he either vanishes altogether, or assumes a form totally different
from that which was familiar to our original impressions.

And thus, whilst the founders of mighty empires are now worshipped as demi-gods, and anon deprived altogether of a personal
being ; whilst statesmen are one day lauded as patriots, and before night hooted as traitors ; whilst one generation calls the
victor a hero, and a succeeding one styles him a brigand—the
race of poets shares the common lot.

From disputing the birthplace, the era, and the fortunes of the
greatest of poets, we have come to doubt of his existence ; not
WE individually, but we collectively ; the men of this generation.
No ! forbid it taste, forbid it justice, forbid it common sense, that
WE should, for the veriest fractional part of the millessimal portion
of a second, doubt the reality of Homer's being.   He who does so
can have no soul for poetry, no perception of unity, no power of
appreciating the masterpiece of man.   What Scott beautifully
said on another subject may well be applied to such a sceptic :—

> " If such there breathe, go mark him well,
>   For him no minstrel raptures swell."

In sober truth, and without irreverence, we avow it, that the
spirit which cannot see unity and design in the Iliad, is more or
less the same as that which ignores them in the universe.   Let
critics of this description confine themselves to works within their
sphere—a fresh edition, for instance, of the " Critica Nova Zea-
landica Futura," " Mother Hubbard," is suited to their comprehension—*Ne sutor ultra crepidam.*

And now that we have got on the theme, we would willingly
throw down the gauntlet for a few more of the injured sons of
song ; especially our own great Shakspeare, whose life, and prin-

ciples, and mighty genius, and consummate art, have been assailed by pigmies, small, wicked, and mischievous, whose effusions satisfactorily prove that they ought never to have been allowed the use of a copy-book.

And whither does all this tend! It tends to this, that the great and sweet poet, Torquato Tasso, is not exempt from the common destiny of men and of poets, and that the universal ignorance of which we have spoken is further exemplified in the conflicting accounts of his life and sorrows which have come down to us.

The author of the life of Tasso, which stands at the head of this article, is not the Dean of St. Paul's, as from the subject of the work the reader might be led to imagine, but his nephew, the Rev. R. Milman, Vicar of Chaddleworth, in the county of Berks.

" In hazarding," says he, " a new biography of Tasso, my object has been to represent his character, sometimes unjustly depreciated, in its true colours: to narrate the vicissitudes and trials he underwent, to trace their effect upon his mind, to show the good purposes to which they were secretly and mercifully directed ; and thus to exhibit one of those rare examples, when great genius and a vivid imagination, meeting with disappointment and oppression, are still not hardened into misanthropy and selfishness, but, on the contrary, improved and chastened in the ordeal through which they pass.

" At the same time, the changing and restless course of Tasso's history, leading us from country to country, and city to city, conducting into various and most opposite scenes, hurrying to and fro from one extreme of life to the other, calling up before us in animated characters the school, the college, the court, the prison, the monastery, the palace, the amusement, shows, studies, spectacles, devotions, tyrannies, through which, as through an intricate labyrinth, we with difficulty follow the clue of his fortunes, will present us, I trust, with a lively delineation of Italian manners and feelings, in the latter half of the famous sixteenth century."—vol. i. pp. 1, 2.

" If this history" (Mr. Milman thus concludes his introduction) "·shall warn any youth of the dangers which attend a vivid imagination, and the indulgence of its glittering day-dreams; of the sad consequences often entailed upon one sin ; of the use and excellence of habits of perseverance ; of the gracious end and purposes of disappointment and affliction; of the value of early devotion, often, even when lost amidst sin and vanity for a season, re-appearing in the earnestness and depth of sincere repentance, and bearing, if late, yet blessed and abundant fruit, my labours will be a source to me of the deepest thankfulness." —vol. i. p. 10.

Pleasingly and ably has the biographer performed his task, though there are here and there blunders and blemishes which we shall at once point out, in the hope that they will be rectified in a

second edition.   In reading the work rapidly through, two mistakes caught our attention ; the first occurs at p. 132 of the first
volume, where he says that " Tasso reached Ferrara to enter the
service of Ippolito, the second cardinal then living of the d'Este
family." Tasso's patron, however, as Mr. Milman himself informs
us frequently, both before and afterwards, was the Cardinal Luigi
d'Este.

This is scarcely more than an error of transcription.   The
second mistake is less excusable ; it regards the date of " a remarkable memorial, intended apparently as a will."

" The date," says Mr. Milman, " 1573 is certainly a mistake for
1570, and from the will it appears that the remains of Bernardo had
been transferred, from St. Egidio in Mantua, to the Church of St. Paul
in Ferrara, through the interest, doubtless, of the Cardinal d'Este."—
vol. i. p. 165.

Previously, we had been informed that

" Bernardo's malady rapidly increased after his son's arrival ; and on
the 4th of September he died, to the deep grief of Torquato, and the
great regret of the Duke of Mantua, his patron.   By that prince's
order, his body was transferred to Mantua, and buried in the Church of
St. Egidio in that city, under a marble monument, with the simple
inscription

OSSA BERNARDI TASSI.

This, however, did not long remain : it fell among the sepulchres which
were removed or broken down, when Pope Gregory XIII. published
an order for the demolition of all tombs much elevated above the
pavement, judging that they interfered with the reverence due to the
altar.   Bernardo's bones were next transferred to the churchyard, and
there interred for awhile without any mark of distinction."—vol. i.
pp. 155, 156.

Now it happens that Gregory XIII. did not become Pope till
1572, and it consequently follows that whatever zeal and expedition he exercised in demolishing the tombs in question, he
could not have effected it more than two years before he commenced it.   Even retrospective acts can only affect the present
and the future ; and the most determined advocates of the papal
prerogative will scarcely extend its efficacy so far.   So after all,
it turns out that Tasso is *right*, and his biographer *wrong*.   It is
easy to see how the mistake has arisen.   The memorandum
begins thus :—

" Because life is uncertain, if it pleases God to dispose otherwise of
me in my journey to France, I pray the Signor Ercole Rondinelli to
take care of some of my effects," &c.

Now Tasso did go into France in 1570, and not in 1573. Therefore &c. Q. E. D., says Mr. Milman. But here, like many other skilful reasoners, he falls the victim to a fallacy. Tasso does not write after a journey to France and state that he had completed it; but he writes under the impression that he is just about to undertake one. All, therefore, that is proved by the date in question is, that in 1573 the poet had serious thoughts of making a journey to France, (probably in company with Cardinal Luigi,) a journey which never took place, and that in the apparently near prospect of this event he wrote the will.

It will be seen, that neither of these errors affect in any degree the plot, so to speak, nor do they interfere with the conduct of the biography, or the moral which the writer carefully draws throughout; still they are errors, and as such should be excided.

With regard to blemishes, such as faults of style or diction, the following does not read well (vol. i. p. 157): "The nuptials were honoured with a fine canzone by Tasso, who was rewarded with several favours and gifts by the two spouses." We do not at least think, that had Tasso written his canzone in English, he would have spoken of "the two spouses;" we have heard of spouse, and spousey too, but the plurals are not euphonious. The singular even is used rather too frequently by this author, as in vol. i. p. 130, vol. ii. p. 226; and in vol. ii. p. 91, we have "THE TWO SPOUSES" again.

There are also many paragraphs which would acquire either strength or elegance by being slightly pruned; and in the 115th page of the second volume he has volunteered the following droll translation of the famous πολλὰ τὰ δεινά of Sophocles:

"Many a thing hath craft and skill,
But man is craftier, wiser still;
And wondrous cures does he devise,
For strange, resistless maladies."

It is easy to see that it was not Tasso himself, but only his biographer who manufactured these lines.

Notwithstanding, however, these little peccadilloes, the work before us is one which we can most warmly recommend to our readers. We have derived very great pleasure from perusing it ourselves, and doubt not but that they would do the same. The style, though often careless, is always pleasant; frequently rich in beauty, and sometimes even sublime. The varied scenes of Tasso's eventful career are vividly brought before the eye; the characters of his friends and enemies, his companions and patrons, his rivals and protectors, are clearly depicted. The course of his life, the culture of his mind, the growth of his intellect, are carefully pourtrayed. The vast and beautiful magnificence of his noble genius is finely exhibited. The yet more wonderful history of his inner life is traced with a master's hand; we seem whilst following the author to walk beside the sufferer, and receive a vivid yet mystical impression, such as might be produced on the mind by painting set to music; that is to say paintings of various scenes in the hero's life, illustrated by the most touching and appropriate music; now breathing ardent hope, now muttering anxious fear, now rising into passion, now dying into melancholy—now expressing the craft and malice of his enemies—now whispering the unuttered secret of his life—now exerting all its deepest power to tell the gloomy horrors of the hospital of Santa Anna; and then suddenly rushing into light to celebrate the advent of his ideal guests.

The whole story is one in every way of the deepest interest, and Mr. Milman is entirely absorbed in his subject. The catastrophe (to use a technical term for want of a better) surpasses almost any thing in real life, except perhaps the coronation of the skeleton of Inez de Castro.

Tasso was sprung from a very ancient and very noble family, many branches of which had acquired considerable wealth by superintending the imperial posts; the system of which was either invented or revived by an ancestor of the house. The eldest branch of the family, that from which the poet's father sprung, was settled at Bergamo.

"Bernardo Tasso, though he had more than a full share of the hereditary capacity for literature, for business, and for war, by no means participated in the hereditary prosperity of his relatives; and the ill fortune which attended him, settled more heavily on his son Torquato. He was left an orphan very young by the death of his father Gabriel, with the burden of two little sisters, Laura and Bordelisia."—i. 18.

After various changes of fortune, in the year 1531 he was appointed his chief secretary, by Ferrante Sanseverino, Prince of Salerno, the first nobleman in the kingdom of Naples, celebrated for his magnanimity and valour, no less than for his patronage of literature and the arts. In his service Bernardo remained for three-and-twenty years, enjoying his regard and esteem with scarcely any interruption. For many years this connexion proved a source of happiness and prosperity to him, which he shared with a beautiful wife, to whom he was tenderly attached. At length, however, one of those reverses so common at that period—and still so common in every land where the strong hand of tyranny has not altogether destroyed the spirit of those whom it desires to crush,—befel this excellent and patriotic noble, and Bernardo was driven into exile in company with his patron. His son Torquato joined him, whilst yet a child, and the wandering life which he was compelled to lead must have tended greatly to increase that restlessness of disposition which caused him, in after life, so much suffering. But we are forestalling.

It was in one of the loveliest spots of the loveliest region of the earth, that the earliest years of the future poet were spent.

"Sorrento is situated in the Bay of Naples, to the south-west of that city, at the base of that spur of the Appennines which projects between the Gulfs of Naples and Salerno. ' It is so pleasant and delightful,' says Bernardo, ' that the poets feigned it to be the dwelling of the Sirens. This allegory alone would demonstrate its beauty. Its delights, however, are not those which entangle the mind in vice and luxury, but such as tend to the health and pleasure of mind and body together.' ' A most sweet abode is it,' says Manso, ' especially for the Muses ; for the verdure of the leaves, the shade of the trees, the continual fanning of soft airs, the freshness of the clear waters which spring in the retiring valleys and hanging hills, the fertility of the opening plains, the serenity of the sky, the tranquillity of the sea, where the fishes, and the birds, and the savoury fruits, appear to rival one another in abundance and variety, when thus appealing in one harmony to the eye and to the mind, frame indeed a great and marvellous garden, such as poets have assigned to Falerina, Alcina, or Armida. A narrow plain spreads out towards the north, rich and fruitful to a proverb, containing corn-fields and vineyards, interspersed with stately clumps of pines and other trees. The mountain of Santa Agata shuts this round, sloping rapidly in one part down to the very walls. The town itself, besides a cluster of houses round the cathedral, is chiefly a succession of villas, running along the bay, on steep, precipitous rocks of considerable height. The edifices are bosomed in groves of myrtles and oranges, where the perfume of the flowers and the songs of the nightingales are said to be sweeter than any where else in Italy. Chesnut and ilex woods rise behind, clothing the bases and sides of the mountainous amphitheatre with dense and deep foliage. Streams sparkle here and there through the shade, some gliding in the valleys, some tumbling down the hills ; the former appearing as if lingering amid the charms of the fair land, the latter as if hastening towards the lovely sea, which reflects the impending cliff in its deep sheltered calm. Hollowed along their base are natural grottoes and baths, true caves of the nymphs, some square and some round, and some paved with red, some with yellow, others with silver sand, but all translucent and sparkling, and contrasting marvellously with the deep blue waters outside.

"Amongst these villas, and overhanging the bay, next to the Church of San Francesco, still stands the house of Tasso. For here Bernardo, as he tells us, 'recalled to his studies, his mind, which had so long been wandering on from one affair to another, as a bird from branch to branch;' and here, on the eve of St. Gregory, the 11th of

March, A.D. 1544, when the sun was in its highest meridian, Torquato was born."—Vol. i. pp. 28—31.

It was indeed a fitting cradle for the genius of a poet, especially of such a poet as Tasso, in whose writings, as in a mirror, we may trace the hues and forms of his native land. Truly, an Italian has not half the credit in being a poet, which of right belongs to the children of less fortunate climes. He must have something not merely unpoetical but absolutely antipoetical in his nature, who is not warmed into inspiration by the glories of a southern sky and all that it covers. There is no wonder that France has no poets—she would have had them in plenty had the Counts of Thoulouse gained the ascendancy instead of their northern rivals. The wonder is when a man like Crabbe starts up a poet, in such a county as Suffolk. He must have had a superabundance of the celestial fire, who could feel his soul kindle amongst uninteresting flats, vast forests of turnips, lifeless streams, and mighty flocks, not of Heliconian swans, but East Anglian geese ; and perhaps the want of charm with which this truly great poet is frequently charged, and not always unjustly, may arise in some measure from those early influences through which even a Homer or a Shakspeare could not have passed scatheless.

At any rate, our opinion will scarcely be called in question when we refer the exquisite grace and rich loveliness, it is a bold expression but a just one, so conspicuous in the writings of Tasso, not only to the natural gifts of the poet however great, nor to his industry however unwearied, but also in some degree to the effect of that scenery in which his earlier years were spent.

It is rather the habit of the day to speak slightingly of the " Jerusalem " and its author, and the celebrated saying of Boileau, who rebukes those that prefer—

> " Le *clinquant* du Tasse à tout l'or de Virgile,"

has passed almost into a proverb. And yet if we examine the question fairly, we shall find many grounds for admiring the poet of the Crusaders, and not a few for depreciating the exaggerated praise bestowed on the earlier Italian bard. Whatever be the comparative merits of the two minstrels, and we are not about to discuss them at present ; to neither of them can be accorded that degree, or even that kind of praise which belongs to the author of the first—the only epic. The two Italians are first-rate second-class poets ; but it is a mere puerility to claim any thing higher for either of them. And yet what exquisite pleasure are their works, or certain portions of them, calculated to confer on those who are capable of appreciating them. Take up the " Jerusalem " and read a page at random any where, and you cannot avoid being charmed with the melody of the numbers, the richness of the diction, the exquisite grace and delicacy and elegance of the thought and the expression. Nor are these the only merits of Tasso: he has the fire and the sublimity of the poet, as well as the skill and taste of the artist; and if, as is perhaps the case, he has injured his renown by bending his genius too strictly and too constantly to his art; it is a fault which now-a-days is of so rare occurrence, that we could almost admire him for it, when we witness the unwarrantable carelessness and insufferable presumption, which is so often evinced by those who deem themselves the gifted children of song.

Tasso then lived as a child at Sorrento, Salerno, and Naples, giving wonderful promises of his future renown, such as every nurse records concerning her own foster children, though they are not preserved, except when their after fulfilment makes them more interesting as well as credible.

" During these fruitless expeditions of his father," (says Mr. Milman after describing Bernardo's wanderings,) " Torquato had been fulfilling in his childhood the marvellous promises of his infancy. After his mother had brought him to Naples, his education was superintended by his tutor Don Angeluzzo, under whom, when he was six years old, he had already mastered the rudiments of Latin. At this time the Jesuits, whose society had lately been established by Paul III., after much debate and hesitation, opened at Naples, as was their custom every where, a small church with schools for different classes of children attached to it, in a street near the Palazzo de' Gambacorti, and therefore convenient for young Tasso's attendance. For young children their system was admirably adapted, however narrow and mind-repressing afterwards. Under their tuition Torquato's progress was astonishing. His ardour and diligence were almost incredible. He never let the day surprise him in bed. Often he rose up while it was yet deep night. His mother had even to provide torches for him, that he might arrive at the very early hour when the fathers commenced instruction. He began his attendance at this school A.D. 1551, directly after it was opened. During the three years that he remained in it he became a good Latin scholar, made some proficiency in Greek, and acquired such readiness in speaking and writing, both in prose and verse, that at ten years old he publicly recited some of his compositions to the amazement of those who heard him. Here also, by his mother's watchfulness, and the care of his teachers, his mind seems to have been imbued with that strong religious tone, which, though choked for a season under the temptations of youth, and ambition, and the love of glory, still never, as it appears, was altogether fruitless, and which afterwards, under God's blessing, became his support in the overwhelming afflictions through which he passed, was his one stay in the restlessness and despondency which those afflictions naturally left behind, and being purified, and if we may dare

say so, perfected through suffering, brought him repose and quiet at his
end, and a happy departure after his many miseries. Writing, many
years afterwards, to Jacopo Buoncompagno, General of the Church, to
ask for his intercession with the Duke of Ferrara, in his letter from the
hospital of Santa Anna, he recalls the first communion to which he was
taken by his teachers, and describes it as having made an ineffaceable
impression upon his mind. He was, he tells us, at the time scarcely
nine years old in reality, but so forward, both in body and mind, as to
be equal to a boy of twelve or thirteen. Without fully understanding
the mystery, he yet participated, he assures us, with the deepest devotion and joy ; 'and remembering,' he adds, 'my sensations at the time,
I now feel confident, that I then received into this earthly body of mine
the Son of God, who deigned to show in me the marvels of his working,
because He beheld me receive them, *i. e.* the elements, into a dwelling-
place, yet uncontaminated, simple, and pure.' "—Vol. i. pp. 58—61.

This deep sense of religion is one of the most striking and
interesting features in the character and history of Tasso. The
biographies of really great poets have not, alas ! often this attraction. It is, indeed, painful to think how generally men have
abused the highest and holiest gifts of their Maker—how little
has been given to the service of God, and how much to that of
the devil—how few of the sons of song have left behind them any
proof that their souls were blessed with Christian faith, their
spirits cheered by Christian hope, or their bosoms warmed with
Christian love. In Tasso, however, despite the errors of his
youth, and the sorrows of his manhood, we see the blessed leaven
working on till it at length leavens the whole lump.

And now Bernardo being unable to reunite himself to his wife
and children, and finding his loneliness insupportable, determined
that Torquato, at least, should join him at Rome, with his tutor
Don Angeluzzo. After dismissing her young son with much
affection and regret, Porzia, such was the name of Bernardo's
wife, retired with her daughter into a convent. The mother and
son never met again—but in after years the sister gave refuge to
her brother, when fleeing from his merciless persecutors. Arrived at Rome, Torquato recommenced his studies with the same
diligence which had before characterized him, and which he retained throughout all his wanderings and all his woes.

The following anecdote is very characteristic. The circumstance took place whilst Bernardo and his son were at Rome :—

" Provoked at last by the dealings of the Pope with the King of
France, Philip II., who had succeeded his father, Charles, on the throne
of Spain, reluctantly commanded the Duke of Alva to advance from the
Neapolitan dominions against Rome. He forthwith occupied the
greater part of the papal territories, south of the city, and spread his

forces over the Campagna, so that his light horse made inroads up to the very gates. . . . . With that adventurous spirit, which was reckoned, as we have noticed, hereditary in the Tassi, young Torquato, at the age of twelve years and a half, hearing that a Giambatista Manso was left in command of the army during some absence of the Duke of Alva, and imagining him to be his godfather, an advocate of the same name, resolved to seek an interview with him, with a notion, perhaps, of inquiring about his property. He stole away by himself, and in secret. As he approached Anagni, the head-quarters of the Spanish troops, he met a squadron of their cavalry, under the Marquis of Santa Agata, who, struck by his youth, beauty, and courage, brought him, at his request, to Manso. Torquato immediately perceived his mistake, and was alarmed when he saw a stranger, and remembered his participation in his father's condemnation. The warriors, however, only admired his spirit, and avowing their old friendship for his unfortunate parent, conducted him back to the neighbourhood of the city."—Vol. i. pp. 70—72.

We can bestow short space upon the period which intervened between Torquato's departure from Rome and his arrival at Ferrara, the scene of his glory and his grief. In that interval he had laboured incessantly at his studies. At seventeen he had entered the university of Padua, and attempted, according to his father's earnest wish, to study for the law. At the end, nevertheless, of the first year, he produced an epic poem, "the Rinaldo." The hero is the famous paladin, cousin of Orlando, so well known to the readers of Boiardo and Ariosto. His love and marriage with Clarice, daughter of Ivon, king of Gascony, and the adventures through which he passes in achieving this object, are the theme of the poem. "There is much polish and elegance in his verse: the stanzas in 'ottava rima' are sonorous and well rounded. . . . It may justify the assertion of Menage, quoted by Serassi, that as the Odyssey is called by Longinus the production of age, but of the age of Homer, so the "Rinaldo" is the production of youth, but that youth, Tasso's."

The college life of Tasso is strikingly pourtrayed, and gives us an interesting picture of that life as it then existed in the Italian universities. Of the many distinguished men who resorted to Padua,

"Some were public lecturers. Some were private teachers. Others had no definite appointment, but opened their apartments to all industrious scholars, where the subjects of their studies were discussed with much freedom, and both masters and disciples met and contested with one another the palm of wit and eloquence. The distinguished citizens joined in these assemblies, or gave entertainments themselves, where the same discussions were renewed. The students also were of all classes, and yet mingled in these reunions on terms of equality and liberty. Opinions were started, passages or sentences from ancient or modern authors, new discoveries in science or art, compositions in prose and verse, were submitted to the criticisms of the assembled company. The most celebrated champions undertook opposite sides in the arguments. Poems were read, canto after canto, or stanza after stanza, as they were written ; improvements in the past, suggestions for the future, were freely offered, attentively discussed, and thankfully received.

"The lecturers and professors, as of old in Athens, in gardens of Academus or the Stoic porch, and afterwards in early Christian times, when the Basils and Gregories resorted to that city, contested, with the keenest rivalry and jealousy, who should attract the most numerous and most renowned disciples. If the antagonist parties met in the streets, they could not refrain from open and violent disputes ; sometimes they came to blows ; daggers even were drawn, and blood shed." —Vol. i. pp. 93—95.

One of these quarrels induced Tasso to migrate to Bologna. Here he was received with open arms, and commenced writing his " Jerusalem ;" but being injuriously treated, on the charge of having written a squib—a charge totally devoid of proof—he returned once more to Padua. It would have been well for him had he remained there and followed a purely literary career ; it would have been better still had he adopted the course which his father pointed out—that of the law. But the imagination of the young poet was dazzled by the fatal splendour of the courtier life, and he at length succeeded in attaching himself to the Cardinal Luigi d'Este — fatal success. Alas ! how often does Heaven grant us the object of our passionate desire, not in love, but in anger ; or, if not in anger, in that stern love which would teach us by experience the folly as well as the sin of attempting to struggle with the wise decrees of an all-merciful Providence.

"Torquato therefore, full of youthful hope, and an ardent thirst for distinction — his vivid imagination glowing with the brightest daydreams—bade a tender farewell to his college companions and friends, especially his beloved host, Scipio Gonzaga, and departed amidst the general regret of the whole university ; and, revisiting first his father at Mantua, where he fell ill, but speedily recovered, arrived towards the end of October, A.D. 1565, at the court of Ferrara, ordained to be the scene of his unrivalled success, and then of his unrivalled oppression and affliction.

"Tasso was twenty years of age when he reached Ferrara, but appeared older than he really was. He was very tall, of strong and active frame, of stately carriage, a little short-sighted, and with a slight hesitation in his speech, but of that grave and melancholy beauty which is said to be most attractive in men. He excelled in all warlike and knightly exercises. He had mastered all the learning of the times, and

though somewhat addicted to taciturnity and gloominess, and occasionally very absent, could, when he pleased, throw the greatest brilliancy
and charm, both of manner and eloquence, over his carriage and conversation in society. Add noble birth, a name already blazoned over the
whole of Italy, the highest reputation for honour as well as genius at
that early age, and the expectation of a yet more glorious future, and
such a character stands before us as could scarcely fail of attracting the
favour and affection of his patrons, and all the distinguished personages
of the Ferrarese court, and of awakening dangerous envy and jealousy
in the hearts of those courtiers whom he eclipsed, and perhaps more
dangerous attachment in the breast of those of the other sex, into whose
intimate society he was thrown."—Vol. i. pp. 117—120.

Alfonso II., son of Ercole II., by Renée of France, was at this
time Duke of Ferrara. Having privately made away with his first
wife, Lucrezia de Medici, he was now about to espouse Barbara,
Archduchess of Austria. The account which Mr. Milman gives
of the preparations for this bridal, and the pageants which accompanied it, is very graphic and vivid. Leonora was prevented from
joining in these festivities by indisposition, and Tasso's first introduction was therefore to her sister Lucrezia, afterwards Princess
of Urbino, who always retained a sincere friendship for him :—

"On Leonora's recovery, Tasso was introduced to her. He had admired her portrait before ; and now, as he testifies in one of his most
celebrated canzoni, 'On this, the first day, that the beauteous serene of
her countenance met his eyes, and he beheld love walk there, if reverence and wonder had not turned his heart into stone, he would have
perished with a double death !'"

It has been disputed whether Tasso really loved the princess as
a man, or merely admired her as a poet. And, again, whether,
supposing him to have really loved her, his passion was returned.
To us the question admits of no doubt whatever. Tasso did love
Leonora with all the deep intensity of his powerful and sensitive
heart, and the princess not only returned his passion, but perhaps
gave only too strong proofs of her attachment. It was the discovery
of this secret, though carefully concealed by Tasso, which insti-
gated Alfonso to pursue that diabolical system of vengeance by
which he well-nigh produced the madness of which he accused
his victim. It was the strength of this passion which recalled
Tasso into the power of his relentless enemy when he had regained
his liberty. It was the reciprocation of this attachment which
brought Leonora to the grave, whilst her lover was wasting away
in a madhouse. It was the undying recollection of this love, together with a consciousness of guilt, which rendered Tasso so
anxious, up to the very last, to obtain the forgiveness of Alfonso.

Alas! that such things should be! that the noblest of earthly feelings should become the source of sorrow and the occasion of sin.

It is strange, now, in looking back at the picture which lies before us, to consider how the relative position of the parties in the drama is changed. Tasso, though noble amongst the noble by his high and ancient lineage, and the great qualities which frequently seen in his ancestors were eclipsed by his own, was at an immeasurable distance from Leonora d'Este.

And now! her very name only lives in that of her admirer. The proud and vindictive Alfonso would have been long ago forgotten but for his inspired victim. Time has vindicated the intrinsic superiority of the homeless wanderer. The mighty of his day, whether friends or foes, are now but his attendants. Nature, inverted by the living, has exerted her prerogatives over the dead.

For a time Tasso's brightest hopes were realized in the court of Ferrara. All was *couleur de rose.* The duke honoured him, the princesses made him their constant companion, and whilst proceeding with his greater works, especially his "Jerusalem," he found time to exercise his skill in composing a variety of smaller poems upon every event connected with either the princesses or the court. The number of these sonnets and canzoni, and their ease and appropriateness, appear almost incredible. Indeed his tongue was never silent, his pen never still; and until his brilliant success called forth the jealousy of his associates he was universally popular.

We will not follow him through the various scenes of fame and splendour now spread in his path, nor accompany him in his journey to France, and the various excursions which he made after his return to Italy. It was now that he obtained the object of his anxious wishes, an appointment in the court and service of the Duke of Ferrara. The absence of the duke in the early part of 1573, on a visit to Rome, giving him more than ordinary leisure, he finished in two months his long-meditated "Aminta," universally considered the perfection of the pastoral drama; and each month as it rolled by saw the "Jerusalem" advancing nearer and nearer towards completion. The labour which he bestowed on his great work, the eagerness with which he sought, and the humility with which he adopted the corrections and suggestions of the literati of his time seems almost beyond belief. The anxiety with which the whole literary world awaited the appearance of the great poem is something which we can scarcely comprehend. The day however of his prosperity was drawing rapidly to a close— fear and doubt and suspicion gathered around him—warnings were given and unheeded—advice proffered and disregarded—he felt himself suspected, but he would not fly—the walls of his prison-house were slowly but surely closing around him—every day his enemies became more numerous, more powerful, and more anxious for his destruction, and he read his fate in the altered look and manner, and tone of voice of his patron. During one of his excursions his room had been ransacked, his locks broken open, his papers examined and seized. And whilst every day showed darker signs of the gathering tempest, powerful princes vied with each other in soliciting his presence at their courts. But warnings, advice, danger, ambition were all in vain; the ill-fated poet felt a viewless chain which bound him to the court of Alfonso; he would not, he could not leave the presence of Leonora.

We pass over the change in Alfonso's conduct, the machinations of Tasso's rivals; his dread of the Inquisition, that terrible tribunal which was frequently used as an instrument of secular as well as religious tyranny; his fears of poison and assassination; his suspicions almost amounting to certainty, that the proud and jealous and malignant and unscrupulous d'Este had discovered the secret; the arts by which the duke endeavoured to entangle him; the steps which led to his ruin, and avail ourselves of the language in which Mr. Milman has described the awful consummation :—

"There is a room in Venice containing a curious and fearful collection. There are the rack, the horse, the boot, the wheel, the cord, the strangling chair, arm-screws and thumb-screws, and many other contrivances for stretching or compressing, dislocating or crushing, the poor human body and its several members. There are other more ingenious, and almost more terrible, because more treacherous instruments; boxes, and vessels, and bottles, once full of strange and subtle, rapid or slow poisons; scent-boxes from which leaped a knife to gash the fair cheek, or split the beautiful nostrils, or otherwise mutilate the lovely face, as it bent over them to inhale the perfume; jewel-cases, from which some long, sharp needle should start, or some pungent mixture, or detonating powder should be suddenly cast to extinguish the bright eye, hastening to inspect her wedding ornaments, or her lover's offering; necklaces which should contract round the white neck; bracelets which should run into the snowy arm; helmets, breastplates, gauntlets, secret pistols which should perform the same offices to the warriors of the age; implements of dreadful ingenuity, which conjure up dark scenes of horrible cruelty and subtle remorseless vengeance, not to speak of other guilt, too often acted in that time and country.

"Amidst these ingenious, but abominable treasures of tyranny, whether royal, oligarchical, or democratical, I doubt if Alfonso could have selected a more subtle and tremendous instrument of torture and revenge, than that which he chose for the punishment of Tasso. He resolved to accuse him of madness ; to wring from him first, if possible, an acknowledgment of his offence, and, if that failed, a confession of madness ; thus saving his honour in all points, he would have him at his mercy, to deal with him as he pleased.   He appears, however, first of all to have done all he could to drive him really out of his senses.

" Long harassing insults and vexations, amidst simulated kindness ; alarms about his poem, first lest it should be published without his knowledge, then lest it should be burned ; delays and excuses in grant- ing him justice upon the assassins who attacked him ; attempts to set him at enmity with his best friends ; interception of correspondence ; • corruption of all his servants ; violent entry into his rooms, false keys forged for his desks ; investigation of papers, so ruinous if known ; dim threats of the dreadful accusation of heresy, and fears of the Inquisition ; rumours of danger to his person or his life, hints that the fatal know- ledge had been gained ; all these were employed to work upon his mind—if we add a dependant condition ; love which could not be uttered ; the irresolution produced by the contest between terror and affection, between his attachment and the exhortation of his friends ; a high spirit, a frank and confiding, but melancholy disposition, liable to occasional fits of abstraction, though hitherto always esteemed, even remarkably courteous and grave ; a vivid imagination, a great dislike of solitude, an eager, even inordinate desire of renown ; if we thus put together the means employed to work on Tasso's mind, and the character of the mind on which they were exerted, it would not be very wonderful if they had succeeded, certainly they were well adapted to their object. Still nothing has hitherto transpired ; Tasso seems restored to favour ; the duke has spoken kindly ; he finds that he cannot drive Tasso into any open transgression ; he seems inclined to disappoint his enemies, to advance him in his favour.   All of a sudden the blow falls !

" One evening, in the chambers and presence of the Duchess of Urbino, Tasso is arrested by the duke's order on a strange charge of having seized and raised a knife against one of his attendants, in a fit of frenzy.   Not a word, not a suspicion of madness had been whis- pered before, but now it is given out that Tasso is a maniac ; and, under the pretence of preventing further mischief, Alfonso commands, with many expressions of compassion, that he shall be shut up for the moment in some rooms looking on the court-yard of the palace." —Vol. i. pp. 255—260.

Hence he obtained a partial release in answer to his earnest entreaties, being allowed to return to his own apartments under the strictest surveillance.   Soon however he had to undergo a still severer trial, for the duke desired that he would accompany him to his country palace of Belguardo ; and—

" There in the gorgeous apartments, or the pleasant gardens, where he had so often read and sung, and feasted with the great and gay, and with the objects of his admiration and affection, Tasso was submitted to a kind of moral torture. ' With rough harshness, and with unwonted arts and acts and words' (they are his own expressions), Alfonso endeavoured to 'wring from him some reason of anger against him.' What threats, what promises, what crafty hints, what enticements and persecutions the duke employed, the marble walls and sculptured pillars, or the flowing waters and waving groves were alone conscious. We may imagine him now kind, now furious, now stern, now smiling, now solemnly recounting his favours, and Tasso's ingratitude, now making light of the business, and smiling to entrap him into some unwary acknowledgment.

"Now he might speak as if he knew nothing, now as if he knew all that occurred, now he might invite confession as a friend, now command it as a sovereign. When his 'unwonted arts' failed, he might grow more open in his displeasure: he might alarm him with renewed fears of the Inquisition, or the rack, or death; now he might assail him by suggestions of punishment impending over the object of his attachment. When Tasso continued resolute in his silence, he might inform him of, perhaps show him, the condemning papers, the wanton verses, and demand with angry sarcasms for whom they were intended. Whatsoever the mental torture was, to which Tasso was submitted for more than a week, we must conclude that it could not overcome his determination to make no revelation.

"Then the grievous sentence was past on him, that he must be a madman for the rest of his days. This declaration also he was required to confirm, by his own acknowledgment of its truth, and by his subsequent conduct, and by submitting to the confinement necessary for such unfortunates, and to the medical treatment calculated for their recovery.

"When this racking examination was concluded, still with words of simulated friendship and pity, Alfonso gave directions that Tasso should be carried back to Ferrara, and confined in the convent of St. Francesco, with two friars to keep watch on him continually; and 'because' (said the Duke's missive) 'he is used to utter every thing in confession, and to break out into a mountain of frenzies, so that he is far worse than ever, the superior is to choose for his keepers, persons fit to admonish him of his madness.' Tasso was shut up according to these orders, and at first exclaimed that he would become himself a monk; a not unusual way in that age of escaping the merciless persecutions of the powerful. This, however, was not the duke's aim. His mind seems to have been made up. Tasso was to be a maniac. Accordingly, as such, he was committed to the convent."—vol. i. pp. 263—266.

He contrived, however, soon to make his escape from this confinement, and arrived safely at the house of his sister Lucrezia, who dwelt at Sorrento. Here he passed in calm seclusion some of the happiest days of his life. The respite was, however, but of short duration. Like the storm-tossed sailor, who reaches some lovely island under a southern sky, and, after sharing its delights for a brief season, leaves them, perhaps for ever, to buffet once

more with wind and wave, Torquato, heedless of the destruction
that yawned upon him, resigned the sweet peace of his sister's
home for the court of Ferrara. *A letter from Leonora recalled
him*, and he departed, " thinking it more noble to put his life into
the duke's hands than to deny Leonora's wishes."

> "A few words of formal courtesy were at first vouchsafed to him,
> but in a day or two his persecutions recommenced. Studied insults
> were offered him by the courtiers. No apartments were provided for
> him, nor any means of subsistence assigned to him. His papers were
> detained by some man of rank, who refused him their possession in
> terms of contempt. He applied to the duke, but could obtain no
> answer. He was forbidden to speak to him. He supplicated in dumb
> show. He used signs and gestures of entreaty and submission, and
> was answered only with signs and gestures of scorn. Explanations,
> even words, were refused to him.
> "He turned to the princesses; he could not win a reply. Soon the
> doors were shut in his face, with every mark of insolence, even by the
> grooms and porters of the palace."—Vol. i. pp. 177, 178.

Once more he fled, and, after meeting with many strange adventures and much unkindness, reached Turin, where he was
treated with the greatest hospitality, courtesy, and respect. Yet,
though cherished, courted, honoured by the sovereign and his
attendants, by princes, nobles, and people, he still feels the power
of the irresistible attraction : he still finds it impossible to live
but in Ferrara : he still prefers every danger in the neighbourhood of Leonora to every delight in separation from her; and,
though urged by his host to remain, and warned by his friends to
desist, the attraction is too strong, the impulse too powerful, and
he returns to one of the darkest dooms that ever was the lot of
man.

He chose for the season of his return to Ferrara that of
Alfonso's nuptials with his third wife, Margherita Gonzaga,
daughter of the Duke of Mantua. On his arrival he found himself treated with as cruel neglect, as insolent inhumanity as
before. And the entry of the bride brought him neither consolation nor relief.

> " The revel, the feast, the tourney, the harmonious concert, the mag-
> nificent spectacle, the gorgeous pageant, fill the city, as at Tasso's first
> coming, with melody and splendour. But Tasso, deceived, insulted,
> trampled on, scoffed at as mad, wandered to and fro alone, houseless,
> disconsolate, and trembling, amid the glittering tumult, groaning and
> repenting that he had ever left Turin, where he was so kindly and
> honourably treated. The studied impertinences and insults of the
> courtiers and servants were renewed with greater licence than ever.

All shunned, or mocked, or reviled him. None comforted, none sheltered him.

"Not one of the promises made to him were fulfilled. Every thing was done, which subtlety or malignity could devise, to irritate him. For a month he bore the brunt of this miserable persecution, and wrestled hard against this cold torrent of contumely. Worn out at last with the continual struggle, stung to the quick in his tenderest point, his reputation, and provoked by some more cruel insult than usual, his patience exhausted, and his indignation aroused, he broke out into vehement reproaches against the duke and his court, lamenting his long thankless service, retracting the praises which he had poured upon them, and complaining of the treachery and false promises which had beguiled him. His words were carefully conveyed to the duke.

"The long sought opportunity was come. Without delay Tasso is apprehended by Alfonso's order, though with many expressions of concern and pity, calculated to enforce the impression of his madness which the duke had so long laboured to establish. He is declared a confirmed maniac, and as such, committed to the hospital of Santa Anna, an establishment for patients, and especially for lunatics, of the lowest class of society. In a wretched cell of this building, solitary, helpless, destitute, with the threatening voices of the keepers, the hissing of the lash, the clanking of chains, with the shrieks of the frantic, the gibbering laughter of idiots, the yells and howls of maniacs, ringing continually in his ears, and reminding him without ceasing that he had become one of them, Tasso lay for many days overwhelmed and stupefied. He aroused himself, he looked around, he began to discern and comprehend his misery. But he awakened at the same time to exert himself."—Vol. i. pp. 306—308.

"He had loved renown, society, the sweet face of nature, the praise of men, the affection of women. He had been delicate in his food, particular in his dress, fastidious in his person. He had a dread, we have seen, as many imaginative persons have, of confinement, of scorn, of solitude. The cell in which he was shut up, was narrow, and dim, and unfurnished. There was no prospect from it. His only objects of view were the blank, damp walls around him, and 'the gate shut ever in his face.'

"No one at first was admitted to visit him. He was never allowed to move forth, even to the holy rites of religion. Of the physicians for body and soul, so often spoken of before, nothing was now heard. The sad, terrible sounds of a madhouse were continually breaking in upon him. Person, dress, food, were now disordered and foul. The chaplain of the hospital was not permitted to attend him. The prior, a man otherwise of high character, and a friend of Ariosto, we must conclude by the direction of higher authorities, treated him with the greatest inhumanity. The rough attendants of such an asylum behaved to him with insolence and contumely; even more fearful treatment seems to have been dealt out to him, so grievous, that he who published Tasso's account, has left blanks in the worst particulars."—Vol. i. pp. 317, 318.

" He had, however, writing materials. And surely by a very great exertion of courage, and with a resolution and energy, wonderful in such circumstances, he was able to use them, and, at times, very diligently. Even in that cell, that gloom and solitude, surrounded and harassed by the fearful noises of his abode, under that awful impending apprehension of never coming forth any more, he commands himself to write such poetry as has not often been surpassed or equalled, to frame supplications in prose and verse to persecutors and friends, scholars and prelates, princes and princesses, emperors and imperial counsellors; to compose philosophical dialogues of the most regular and elaborate nature."—Vol. i. pp. 320, 321.

But even this was not all. The seclusion of a prison, the tortures of a madhouse were not the only afflictions of the ill-fated one. It seemed as if on his doomed head were to be showered all the evils which it was capable of receiving. For whilst he was thus immured in base, and miserable, and, as it it seemed, hopeless captivity, two fresh calamities befel him. The Princess Leonora, who had sickened from the moment of his incarceration, grew worse and worse, till at length, after an illness of several months' duration, she expired. And the "Jerusalem," by which he had hoped to command both fame and competence, was piratically published, and then scurrilously attacked. But enough of the madhouse, and its tale of woe ; for all further particulars of his trials and consolations there we must refer to the ample materials contained in the volumes before us. We cannot however leave this painful subject without paying a just tribute of praise to the poet Guarini. The rival of Tasso in the time of his liberty, he endeavoured to serve him in every possible manner during his captivity ; he joined in the various attempts made to liberate him ; he published Tasso's works under his direction, he did every thing that he could to advance his interest and alleviate his distress.

And now at length the continual applications made to Alfonso on Tasso's behalf produced their effect, and the vindictive d'Este permitted the Duke of Mantua to take him to his court. But freedom came too late for earthly happiness to be its result ; Tasso had become restless, fearful, melancholy, and he wandered from one end of Italy to another, now caressed, and now cruelly neglected, till at length he was discovered by his cousin Alexander, in a public hospital at Bergamo, founded by his own family, in which he had taken refuge to avoid the necessity of begging in the streets.

The contrasts exhibited in this period of his eventful life are as striking as we can well conceive. We see him in one city honoured by the highest nobles, in another denied admittance by the menials of his oldest friends ; at one time resting in the hospitable seclusion of a monastery, at another domesticated at the lordly castle of some passionate admirer. During this period it was that he performed the pilgrimage to Loretto which he had vowed in his captivity.

"The city was full of inns and hostelries, and as was usual with places of pilgrimage, was rather noted for its noise and immorality ; for often the votaries, after the appointed penitences and ceremonies were fulfilled, made up for the self-denial and toil of the journey by indulgence in all kinds of gaiety and revelling. It was in general a strange scene of mingled solemnity and frivolity, devotion and dissipation.

"Tasso, however, was sincere in his penitence, and thoroughly in earnest in his pilgrimage. Fearful as it is to perceive how much the Blessed Virgin is regarded, even by such a man, as the object of confidence, the fountain of grace, the great trust and consolation of the afflicted, it is impossible to help feeling the deep resolution and seriousness with which he implores her all-powerful intercession, and the devotedness and reality with which he henceforth consecrates his energies and life to the service of religion. Neither in him do we perceive what is too often discernible as an accompaniment of the former opinion, that awful view of the Saviour as only a severe and terrible Judge, who must not be approached or appealed to directly, and to soften whose rigorous and unbending justice, the soft prayers and tears, not to say commands, of the Virgin Mother are needed. In other verses, and other writings of his life, he turns his gaze, and pours out his soul, whither the Scriptures and the early Church direct our whole trust. With apparently the most fervent contrition, faith, and love, he seeks the mediation, and cleaves to the atonement of Him who took our nature into His, that He might fulfil those offices toward us, and that we might be able, and have confidence to come unto Himself. One hopes that this faith will be accepted, and for it the other misbelief forgiven."—Vol. ii. pp. 156—158.

The narrative of this portion of Tasso's life, together with the incidental descriptions of men, and manners, and scenery, will amply repay a careful perusal. The episode concerning the holy house of Loretto is excellently told. But we shall pass over these interesting subjects untouched, and proceed to the conclusion.

The tide of Tasso's fortunes was at length decidedly turning. At Naples, success of every kind attended him, and thence, summoned apparently by the new pope, Clement VIII., he started for Rome, the great robber-chief, Marco Sciarra, withdrew his victorious bands to give him free passage, and he reached the imperial city in safety. It was here that he had suffered, perhaps more than any where else, since his liberation, neglect, poverty, insult ; but now, all was changed.

"He was received into the house of the Aldobrandini, the pope's nephews, on conditions most agreeable to his disposition, that he should be exempt from all attendance and service, and have full leisure for philosophy and poetry."—Vol. ii. p. 242.

" I know not," says Mr. Milman, " if any dwelling in hall, bower, or palace, in the stateliest and most famous cities, is so adapted to poetical imaginings, as the woods and the hills, ' where inspiration breathes around.' If any such is to be found it certainly would be an apartment in the Vatican. . . . . Here he dwelt favoured by the pope himself, honoured and beloved by his two nephews, especially the Cardinal Cintio, who admitted him freely and fully to all the honours of their society and table. All the ' sacred college ' vied in showing him attention. The nobles and princes of Rome, the Gaetani, Orsini, Colonnas, the haughtiest barons in existence, were equally anxious to entertain him. The prelates immediately attached to the court befriended him in every way. The scholars and authors among them, sought eagerly the privilege of his society and conversation."—Vol. ii. pp. 248—250.

His health, however, rendered feeble by all that he had gone through, was gradually declining ; and in the summer months he retired once more to Naples with the consent of the Aldobrandini. Here he employed himself in his " Mondo Creato," and various other works ; and in his lawsuit with the Prince of Avellino, who had obtained unjust possession of his mother's fortune. Hence he was recalled to Rome, which he seems well-nigh to have forgotten, by the pope and the senate, who, at the instance of Cardinal Cintio, resolved to grant him " a triumph, and the laurel crown in the Capitol, the highest reward of poetic merit, and of which Tasso, in previous days, had professed some desire."

" He was conscious of his approaching dissolution, and declared to Manso, before he departed, that although he went by his advice, he yet felt sure that he should not be in time to receive that honour, his coronation, namely, which he persuaded him to seek. Then, having embraced his friend with much tenderness, as if never expecting to see him any more, he started about the first of November. . . . . At some little distance from the gates of Rome he was met by the household of the two cardinal nephews, and by a great part of the pope's own suite, and by many prelates, and ministers, and noblemen, and conducted by them in grand state as if in prelude to his intended triumph to the Vatican palace, where he was immediately admitted to salute Cintio and Pietro. . . . . The following morning he was solemnly introduced into the pope's presence, who received him most kindly and graciously, and after many commendations of his virtue and merit, said to him, ' We have destined for you the laurel crown, that it may henceforth remain as much honoured by your wearing it, as it has heretofore conferred honour on those who have worn it.'

" Tasso kissed the pope's feet according to custom, and returned thanks with much humility for his kind expressions, and for the honour

proposed; showing, however, no symptoms of pride or of gladness at
the announcement, as if ever foreseeing his approaching decease, and at
last freed from the 'fatal garment,' which had so long cleft to him, the
love of the vain distinctions of the world.

"A continuance of stormy weather prevented the immediate execution of the ceremony. Tasso made all the delays he could, and it was
put off till the spring should offer a bright day and clear sunshine, to
adorn and illuminate the arrangements.

"Meanwhile the city was resounding with preparations. The Vatican, whence the procession was to start, the streets through which it
was to pass, the Capitol, where the pope was to set the crown with his
own hand upon the poet's forehead, were all to be magnificently
adorned for the occasion. Prelates, princes, nobles, professors, and
students were thronging from all quarters into the city to witness the
triumph. All the bards of Italy were inditing pæans for the occasion
with universal emulation. But there was no glow on the pallid, calm
cheek of the poet."—Vol. ii. pp. 264, 265.

We would gladly transcribe the next chapter, the last, *in extenso*. The matter is so very striking, the manner so very appropriate, the different parts form such an harmonious whole, that
we sincerely regret our inability to do so. The opening, describing
Tasso's oak, the view from the garden of the Hieronomite monastery of St. Onofrio, and the thoughts which the place and scene
naturally call up, is as eloquent and beautiful a piece of writing as
any with which we are acquainted, and forms a fine prelude to
the sad burden of the remainder—the death of Tasso:—

"It was a haunt," says Mr. Milman, speaking of St. Onofrio,
"suited to the decline of life, the glow of whose sunset rested now upon
Tasso; for the tide of his fortunes seemed now to be changing; all
things began to wear with him an aspect of prosperity. Honours and
renown seemed exhausting themselves for his advancement. Those
deemed highest and greatest upon earth vied in doing him reverence.
Independence also and comfort, so long vainly yearned for, were on the
point of pouring in upon him. The pope assigned him a regular pen-
sion of 200 scudi. The Prince of Avellino agreed to pay him an an-
nuity of 200 ducats, and a considerable sum at once, in addition: thus
raising him immediately to competence and ease. The papal nephews
and the whole court were anxious to show him every possible kindness.
. . . . He was only in his fifty-second year, when all things looked
thus smilingly upon him; and now the month of April, A.D. 1595,
the time of his coronation, was just come, and all things were in readiness for its splendid celebration.

"At this moment his prophetic forebodings were fulfilled. He had
eaten some sweetcakes or macaroons, which had been presented to him
on his journey from Naples, and had felt sickly, and in pain, ever afterwards. And now his illness increased upon him. He perceived that
his days were numbered, and his end imminent."—Vol. ii. pp. 273—275.

The Cardinal Cintio, to whom he applied for leave to depart, immediately granted him permission to do so, and conveyed him in his own carriage to the convent of St. Onofrio, the spot which he had chosen. The rain was falling heavily as the fathers saw the princely vehicle toil up the steep ascent which led to their gates, and at once divining that no common event could bring it there under such circumstances, they hastened forth to meet it. They received their guest with the utmost tenderness of affection, and shed tears when he told them that he was come to die among them. "They conducted him to one of their best apartments, and used every possible means to restore and revive him, and every possible argument to encourage him. His illness, however, was beyond the reach of medicine, and his expectation of death firm and continual." He wrote at this time a most touching and edifying letter to his friend Costantini, and showed every sign of fervent and genuine piety :—

- "On the 10th of April he grew worse; fever ensued; and the physicians began to despair of his recovery. The tidings spread over the city, and diffused an universal gloom. On the seventh day of the fever Cesalpini, the pope's physician, and an old friend of Tasso's, announced to him that there was no chance of his recovery. Tasso embraced him with a tranquil countenance, and thanked him with fervour for the announcement; and then immediately raising his eyes, and keeping them fixed on heaven, with yet greater earnestness and affection, he gave humble thanks to the merciful God, who was pleased at last, after so many and violent tempests, to bring him thus to the desired harbour. . . . . From the hour of that announcement of his death, and that heavenward thanksgiving, to translate Manso's words, 'he spoke no more of any thing relating to this life, or to his fame after death, but turning altogether toward heavenly glories, thought of nothing save preparing himself for that high eternal flight which he hoped soon to make. . . . And disburdening himself of every worldly weight by the strength of holy Sacraments, which he would receive in the Church below his apartments, where he had himself carried the morning following his death-stroke, in despite of his weakness. He there received the penitential absolution from the hands of the priest, and afterward the holy host from the altar. He was carried back to his bed in the arms of the brethren."—Vol. ii. pp. 277—280.

He then, at the suggestion of the prior, made his will; and, at his especial request, directed that his body should be buried in the church of the convent. It is a relic far more precious as well as genuine than many of those preserved on the European continent, whether we consider the literary renown or the Christian sanctity of the distinguished guest. His writings he left to Cintio; a small picture of himself to Manso, his faithful generous friend; and a silver crucifix, the gift of Clement VIII., to the convent.—

"Then Torquato," says Mr. Milman, still quoting the words of Manso, "all intent on the perilous journey he was about to undertake, lay the seven following days, that is, till the fourteenth day of his attack, continually communing with his Saviour; and so abstracted from earthly things, and so sensible of heavenly things, that all the by-standers, of whom there were many every day, felt consolation and compunction together. This was especially the case with his confessor, who, after his death, declared to many friends, that for many years before his death, he had never discovered in him any trace of deadly sin.

"When he had reached the fourteenth day of his illness, and the last but one of his life, feeling himself growing weaker every hour, and perceiving that he was on the point of dissolution, he desired to strengthen himself once more with the Viaticum of the holiest body of our Lord Jesus Christ. As he was unable to rise from his bed, it was brought to him by the prior. On his entering the room, he, beholding it, cried out with a loud voice, 'Expectans Expectavi Dominum;' and then, devoutly receiving it, united himself with Him, with such affection and humility, that the company present, as they looked wondering on, could not help seeing in his manner an earnest of future blessedness. . . . . In the meanwhile, Cardinal Cintio, informed by the physicians that Torquato had only a few hours of life remaining, proceeded toward him, and conveyed him in the name of the pope his solemn benediction, which is in general only bestowed in such a way, on cardinals, or people of the highest importance. . . . . . . After this, (i.e. the car-dinal's departure,) no one was admitted except his confessor, and some fathers of approved learning and sanctity, who sang psalms alternately one with another, Torquato joining in at times, as far as his failing breath allowed. So he remained all the night, and till noon the following day, the 25th of April, St. Mark the Evangelist's feast,—when, feeling himself giving way altogether,—with his crucifix closely embraced, he began to chant the words, 'In manus tuas Domine' (Into Thy hands, O Lord); but not having sufficient strength to finish the verse, he ended the short but glorious career of his mortal life, to enter, as we ought to hope, on the other immortal career of eternal glory in the heavenly Jerusalem."—Vol. ii. pp. 282—287.

As we have been unable to transcribe the whole account of Tasso's death, as it is given by Milman from Manso, we have, for the most part, selected such portions as exhibit that religion which was essential to him as a sincere Christian, rather than those which illustrate that superstition which was incidental to him as a devout Romanist. Such descriptions have their lessons, if we would learn them aright; they bring before us painfully the errors of our fallen sister, and show how, for the most part, those errors darken

the mind of the holiest of her children ; and yet, at the same time,
they prove that even in the midst of errors, when faith is keen and
love is true, the Father of love vouchsafes to take to Himself,
and clothe with His blessing, those who seek Him earnestly and
humbly.

But there is one scene more—

"The honours which had been lost to him in his life were paid to him
after his death. . . . . The body, ... was arrayed in a splendid
gown, the laurel which had been prepared was wreathed round the head,
and thus laid on a stately bier.   Tasso was borne, from the monastery
where he died, through the Borgo, and the piazza of St. Peter's, and
back to the church of St. Onofrio, with a grand display of candles, followed by a great number of various monastic brethren, by all the
courtiers of the papal palace, by the household of the two cardinal
nephews, by the professors of theology and philosophy, and by a crowd
of nobles and scholars.   All thronged to see for the last time, the
man who had conferred such distinction on the age, and who concentrated on himself so many different kinds of renown.   Painters and
sculptors trode upon each other, in their anxiety to catch a clear
impression of the celebrated lineaments, which had attracted such high
affections, and been wasted and withered by such unrivalled affliction,
in order to commit them to the canvas or the marble with as much
accuracy as possible."—Vol. ii. pp. 288, 289.

Having thus traced, though briefly, the career of Tasso from
his cradle to his grave, we cannot conclude this article more
appropriately, and we trust more usefully, than by the paragraph
with which Mr. Milman concludes his life.

"When he was asked by some young Sorrentines what was most
needful for students, he replied, ' Perseverance ;'—and what next ?—
' Perseverance !'—and what in the third place ?—' Perseverance !'—
His own rule, it is much like Cicero's, seems to have carried him not
only to the summit of literary renown, but to have formed in him the
grace of constancy, which afterwards, as he said in Santa Anna, was
' his one only rock of refuge.'   And this, indeed, is one great use of early
application, too often overlooked, that it forms the habits of resolution,
energy, and constancy, not for study only, but for higher uses.   Only
let it be blessed with that, which, his biographer tells us, was the light
of Tasso's later years, continual meditation on the incarnation and passion of the Saviour, the contemplation of His cross, and the charity
which flows from it.   These will sanctify and settle upon a sure foundation that fortitude, which, without them, is in truth but stubbornness,
and must shatter itself at last against the decrees of God.   These will
transform it into the image of His infinite patience, on whose Atoning
Sacrifice it rests."

Art. VI. — *Œdipus, King of Thebes; translated from the "Œdipus Tyrannus"* of Sophocles, *by Sir* Francis Hastings Doyle. J. H. Parker, 377, Strand.

The translator of Greek tragedy has, assuredly, no light task. His resources for acting on the minds of his public are out of all proportion less than those which were at the command of the Greek poet. He undertakes to convey to the solitary and in-different modern reader by mere written words, and through the veil of a foreign language, the effect of dramatic works which were produced under a concentration of favouring circumstances such as the world has never again seen. The drama of the Athe-nians was delivered in the spoken words of a most beautiful language, aided by all the appliances of the scenic art, in a vast theatre, under the bright sun of Greece, open to all the exhila-rating influences of nature; above all, before an audience who combined a correct taste with a high enthusiasm, to whom these performances were at once their most valued enjoyment, and an important religious duty, and who saw in them the highest development of their national life.

That such a concourse of favouring circumstances should have stimulated genius to the noblest efforts, is what might be naturally expected, and the high excellence of the Greek drama has been proclaimed by the critics of all ages and countries. Yet it can hardly be thought that the modern reader, even when he is capable of reading the Greek drama in the original, should peruse these works with the same feelings with which they were at first beheld. It ought not to surprise us if we feel some little dis-appointment in the perusal of works produced under circumstances so widely different, if we cannot always sympathize with the enthusiasm of the ancients for poems so inadequately presented to us. And if this is apt to be the case even with the scholar, how difficult must be the task of the translator, who has to make his author felt through all the difficulties which attend the attempt to render ancient ideas in modern language. But whatever may be the difficulties of presenting the Greek drama in an English dress, they have not been sufficient to deter translators, at least, from the tragedies of the writer with whom we are most particu-

larly concerned, Sophocles. Of his tragedies there are three
translations in English verse, those of Franklin, Potter, and Dale.
The first author, who dedicated his work to George the Third when
Prince of Wales, tells us that Sophocles "seems purposely to have
waited for the present happy opportunity of making his first
appearance among us, under the patronage of his Royal Highness;" "a circumstance" which, he is of opinion, must make
Sophocles an ample recompense for the neglect with which he was
till then regarded. However fortunate Sophocles may have been in
his patron, he can hardly be said to have been very much so in his
translator, which he would perhaps have thought of at least equal
importance. Franklin has little regard for exactness, and still less
poetical vigour; he writes like a man who thought more of his
patron than of his subject; he shows little anxiety to do justice
to his author, and little power to do so, had he entertained such a
feeling. -
    Potter is, indeed, far superior to Franklin; his versification is
grave and dignified, and his powers far more on a level with the
subject. Yet he seems to have written with little enthusiasm
for his task, and to have been little penetrated with the spirit of
antiquity; he is, on the whole, flat and heavy, and, in the most
trying parts, the choruses, he allows himself great licence in
paring and clipping whatever was difficult to handle.
    Dale, who tells us that he was "invited and encouraged by a
highly respectable list of subscribers," assigns, as the principal
motive of his translation, that he desired "to render the diversified metres of the original by measures as nearly corresponding
as the genius of our language will permit." Yet his version is
much better than might be expected from so odd an introduction;
it is regular, correct, and accurate, and if it does not rise high,
neither does it fall very low. But he is cold and tame, and shows
little poetical taste or vigour.
    Nor indeed could any very favourable result be reasonably
expected from the translators of that school. The taste of the
eighteenth century, however exact it may have been, was certainly
very narrow. The age which could accept the brilliant *mis-
translation* of Pope as a version of the Iliad of Homer, which
abused the gen us of Dryden in the attempt to cut down Shakspeare; and in which Johnson, in his great collection of English
poetry, left out Spenser and Chaucer to insert Blackmore and
Pomfret, can little pretend to any but the most contracted and conventional views of poetry. In truth, during the prevalence among
us of what may be called the French taste, every thing which did
not fall in with the preconceived notions of the critics, formed
upon a very slight knowledge of the ancients, and a much more

accurate one of their French imitators, was thought to be hope-lessly barbarous. In our own time criticism has acquired a more healthy tone ; the principles and rules of taste have been enlarged, and the circle of our literary pleasures is become wider. We are not now satisfied with a translation which does not truly represent the sense and spirit of the original.

But this the translator cannot convey to the reader, unless the latter is prepared to judge of the work before him by other rules than those to which, by the perusal of modern works, he has become habituated.

We must expect much in the works of antiquity which does not chime in with our ideas, and while we enjoy that inheritance which the great men of old have left for foreign nations and for other ages, if we persist in judging them by our preconceived notions of taste, we shall hardly escape some feelings of dis-appointment, perhaps even of disgust.

The thoughts and feelings of the Greeks were not as ours, and half the value of their great works, a most important part of the history of the human mind, would be lost, did we try to force them into an unnatural congruity with our own conventional ideas and feelings. In truth, the ancients and the moderns look upon the drama from very different points of view, and try its merits by very different tests.

We value dramatic poetry chiefly for its expression of human passions, and if this be done in a poetical manner, our highest standard of excellence is attained. But with the Greeks it was far otherwise. Their drama was part of their national worship, and this was assuredly no mere hypocritical fiction, but really felt and acted upon by the most serious and religious part of the community. When in the inevitable decline of the primitive state of feelings in Athens, Euripides made human passions predominant in his tragedies, it was regarded as a serious offence against pro-priety by those who desired to uphold the old manners. Strange as it may appear to our notions, the Greek tragedies were, and were intended to be, *sermons*. The poets were the preachers of the ancients [1]. It has been often remarked how close was the connexion between the poetry and religion of the Greeks, and doubtless there were poets not altogether unworthy of their high calling, who had a real reverence for a deity, however imperfectly known, and a sincere desire to benefit their fellow-men. The religion of the early Greeks, while it enforced much of morality, by no means enjoined either a pure or a perfect code of duties, its

[1] It might, perhaps, be said, that Sophocles and Pindar were orthodox preachers ; Æschylus, an heretical ; and Euripides, a free-thinking one.

chief basis was terror, the dread of unknown powers greater than man, whose will was revealed only to the initiated, and its great aim was to procure their favour or to propitiate their wrath by mysterious ceremonies. And the early tragedy, as a part of religious worship, was intended to strengthen and deepen these feelings, and to impress on the people the necessity of the accustomed rites, and the danger of neglecting to give due honour to the gods. The aim and tendency of Greek tragedy was to subdue the mind by striking it with a sense of the instability of all human things, and of the irresistible force of "that unknown combination of infinite power which men call fortune;" and thus, by the exhibition of terrible catastrophes, to show forth the might of the gods and the nothingness of man. Nor was this lesson without its value, strange and confused as were the notions of the ancients with respect to the character of their gods and the moral relations of actions, they were surely far better than a cold insensibility to the one, or a presumptuous denial of the other. It was quite in accordance with these feelings that Aristotle should lay so great, and, as it seems to us, so disproportionate a stress upon the plot of a tragedy. It was the "περιπετεία," the revolution in human affairs, which was to make manifest the power of the gods; and it was by the completeness of this that the effect of the tragedy was measured.

And we shall find this character strongly marked in the two great dramatists Æschylus and Sophocles, who represent the ideal of the Athenian tragedy, for Euripides, as we have seen, belongs to another school.

Of the seven plays of Æschylus which have come down to us, in one, "The Prometheus," the personages are altogether supernatural. In the trilogy of "Agamemnon," the characters act under the directions, or by the inspiration, of divinities whether good or evil; and in the "Furies," these deities are themselves the chief actors. In the "Suppliants," the interest turns upon an important point of the national religion. In the "Seven against Thebes," the gods interfere to punish the impious vaunts of the besiegers. In the "Persians," alone, the actors and the action are purely human, and even in this we find the ghost of Darius, while the whole play was no doubt understood to be an offering of thanksgiving to the gods who had delivered Greece.

Of the seven remaining plays of Sophocles nearly the same may be said. The hero of the "Trachiniæ" is a god; in the "Ajax" and "Philoctetes" the gods interfere in person; the subject of the "Electra," the expiation of the murder of Agamemnon, is the same with that of one play of the Æschylean trilogy, and of the trilogy of Sophocles; the two others, besides the one now under consideration, are most intimately connected with the Greek worship. The subject of the " Œdipus at Colonos" is the purification of Œdipus from the guilt of his involuntary crimes, and of the " Antigone," the due performance of the funeral rites of the heroine's brother, which were thought necessary to ensure the repose of his soul. Hence the rigid severity, and, to modern taste, the nakedness and hardness of the early Greek drama, both in construction and ornament. The human element was kept strictly subordinate, the will of the gods was to be the main spring of the plot ; little of the variety, which arises from the play of human passions, was allowed ; and even poetical ornaments were sparingly used, except in the choruses, which were often direct hymns to gods. Too much decoration would have been inconsistent with the main object of the writer—to subdue the mind by the terrors of the unseen world. And this severity the audience might well endure, for they were fascinated by superstitious fear, and during the action of a tragedy, their minds filled with the horror of the coming calamity, were little at leisure to attend to mere idle ornament—

" They heard the wheels of an avenging god
    Groan heavily along the distant road."

In the " Antigone " of Sophocles the heroine, though actually betrothed to Hæmon, while she bewails the terrible fate to which she is doomed, is allowed to make no allusion whatever to her lover. She laments, indeed, that she is to die without marriage, and without offspring, for to desire them was a part of the religious feelings of the ancient world ; but any intrusion of merely personal feelings would have seemed to the poet to detract from the purity of her martyrdom.

The theory of Schlegel, that the subject of Greek tragedy is the struggle of the human will against destiny, is little borne out by the facts. It would, in truth, be much more applicable to the Homeric poems, in which far more play is allowed to the passions and will of man ; who is often represented as contending with the gods themselves. In the early tragedy (of which only we are speaking), men are little more than passive instruments in the hands of the divinities. In the most terrible passage of Æschylus, Clytemnestra exclaims that she has indeed slain the King of Mycene, but that she is not now the wife of Agamemnon, but the avenging fiend of the house of Tantalus. In the same play Cassandra, prescient of approaching death, rushes into the slaughter-house, driven by the impulse of the god who has doomed her to destruction. This is not to represent the struggle of the human will against destiny as the main spring of the action, but rather to annihilate it altogether. In truth, the Homeric poems treated the old legends in a poetical and romantic, the tragedies in a religious and sacerdotal sense; the tendency of the former is to inspirit and fortify the mind; of the latter, to terrify and subdue it. It is the difference between enthusiasm and superstition.

With the Greeks, as afterwards in Christendom, the drama sprang from religious ceremonies; the worship of Bacchus produced the first, as the mystery plays of the middle ages did the second. But the Greek drama rose up at once to its full stature: its character was stamped at first. Our own grew by degrees, and its great works were composed when the religious element was no longer predominant. Hence the type and tendencies of the two are altogether different. And this may be seen most easily where the Greek and English tragedians have to traverse common ground; where their subjects are very similar, their mode of treatment is yet entirely distinct.

The situations of Clytemnestra and of Lady Macbeth have much in common; in both the leading feature is a fierce and resolute daring, an intensity of passion and crime, which tramples on all the charities and duties of life, which is deaf to every suggestion of fear or pity. But, in the work of the English dramatist, we are called on to admire or to detest the strength of the human will, and the perverseness of the human heart; we are admitted to the workings of human passions, and we behold their punishment in the obscure visitings of nightly remorse. Nothing of this came within the plan of the Greek tragedian; there is no preparation of the mind, no self-hardening of the heart of Clytemnestra for the deed of death that she is to do. The invocation of Lady Macbeth to the mysterious powers of nature to close up in her "the access and passage of remorse," has, in the Greek murderess, been already accomplished by the dark agencies of evil which pursue the accursed house of Atreus. She is possessed by a fury, and she moves on to her purpose with the remorseless and undeviating energy of some senseless engine. We have heard the characters contrasted to the disadvantage of Æschylus, but with little reason. Each poet chooses those sources of effect which are most proper to the end which he has in view; he strikes at his audience where they are most sensitive; and while Shakspeare far surpasses his predecessor in skill and variety, his subject could not admit of his attaining the terrible grandeur of conception in which Æschylus has surpassed all men. And the same differences will be found on comparing Hamlet with those Greek tragedies which embrace a subject of the same nature. The situation of Hamlet is the same as that of Orestes—both are supernaturally commissioned to avenge great crimes upon their nearest relatives—but how different is the treatment of this common theme. In "Hamlet," the chief interest is concentrated upon the mind and character of Hamlet himself. In the cruel position in which he is placed, the poet has been careful to bestow on him that precise character and frame of mind which is most adapted to afford the dramatic effects of opposing passions, and to throw light on the pathology of the human heart, by exhibiting it in so strange and trying a situation. Hence the ultra-philosophic, reflective, and vacillating character of Hamlet. Having to express the struggle of man against circumstances which overpower him, the poet has chosen that character in which the internal conflict of the human will against an irresistible destiny is most strongly manifested. No other character would have exhibited with equal force and propriety the workings of the human heart under the pressure of inextricable difficulties, which form the proper subject of the play.

Both Æschylus and Sophocles, in their extant works, have treated the retributive slaughter of Clytemnestra, but in neither does Orestes possess any character or excite any interest. The struggles of the heart and conscience in his dreadful position, which seem so natural and obvious a dramatic topic, appear to be little thought of, and he slays his mother without reluctance or remorse; for he is the inspired avenger of blood, the mere instrument of the Divine justice; and though he is afterwards to suffer terrible punishment for his violation of the ties of blood, he cannot be supposed to resist for one moment the inexorable will of the gods.

Both in "Macbeth" and "Hamlet" the machinery of the plot is set in motion by supernatural agency, but in neither does it exclude the free workings of the human spirit. The witches in "Macbeth," the ghost in "Hamlet," act by and through the human personages; they incite indeed, but do not compel; the free will of man is not annihilated. Macbeth is tempted, indeed, by the powers of darkness, but is under no necessity to yield to their unholy suggestions; and Hamlet long questions and doubts whether he shall obey the admonitions of his father's spirit. We have already seen how differently the supernatural element is treated in the Greek tragedy,—how it absorbs the human will, and becomes the main spring of the whole drama.

So far did this view of the subject lead the dramatists, that even the most natural feelings of the heart are personified into divinities. The natural remorse of Orestes is embodied in the furies who pursue the slayer of his mother; and he is tormented, not by his own thoughts, but by the personal interference of those mysterious goddesses.

It is sufficiently evident that such a school of poetry could not endure very long. As knowledge and science advanced, the old religion fell into discredit; pious men were scandalized at the strange and immoral actions which the poets attributed to the gods; the sceptics laughed more or less openly at the whole popular system; the blind and unreasoning faith of a primitive people was to be found no where. All the extravagancies of the old legends, no longer softened by the mists of early and inveterate prejudice, became glaringly obvious. The audience began to look out for improbabilities, and to demand variety. The poet thought more of himself, and less of his subject. In the tragedies of Euripides we may clearly discover this downward tendency. Euripides may be said to have made the Muse of Tragedy descend from her buskin, as Æschylus to have mounted her upon it. He gave much more room than his predecessors for the play of human passions, and was esteemed the most tragic, that is, the most pathetic, of the tragedians. Feeling the want of variety in the old tragedy, he no longer confined his choruses to the subject of the action. They became odes, in which any subject might be introduced in the most arbitrary manner. On the other hand, it is sufficiently evident, from the jokes of Aristophanes, that he was reproached by his contemporaries with having lowered the tone of tragedy by the undignified costume and language with which he delighted to represent his heroes; and his immoral sentiments and free-thinking subtleties were frequent subjects of blame. And in truth, the attempt to treat the wild legends of early times in a sceptical or rationalising spirit, could hardly be very successful. The incongruity between the subject and the mode of handling it, could scarcely be got over by any ingenuity; and it seems to have been a nearly universal tradition among the Greek critics, that the ideal of tragedy was to be found in Sophocles.

It may not be impossible to trace in the criticism of Aristotle the conflict of two very different schools of dramatic art. On the whole, he decidedly prefers the school of Sophocles to that of Euripides. He professes to regard the tragedy which we are now examining as a model of excellence. He is of opinion that the Chorus ought to form one of the persons of the drama, and he exacts an ideal excellence of character from the personages of tragedy which clearly is inconsistent with the exigencies of what we may call the natural school. On the other hand, he is evidently offended by the improbability of the legends from which the tragedies were framed. Such stories, he says, ought not to be put upon the stage at all. The licence of improbable fiction which may be indulged to the epic, cannot be allowed to the dramatic poet. The celebrated sentence, "that the office and end of tragedy is to purify the passions by pity and terror," belongs to an age of quite different feelings from those out of which the early tragedy arose. The doctrine that tragedy was to teach had survived the teaching. But in truth the philosopher, if his meaning was that tragedy should give a didactic instruction in morals, demanded of dramatic art, what it was altogether unable to give, except by the entire sacrifice of its peculiar characteristics.

To the taste of the sceptical Horace, the direct and personal interference of the deities, so common in the old tragedy, no doubt appeared strangely incongruous and unsuitable; and we may easily trace in his advice, that the gods should only appear on extraordinary occasions; a lurking feeling that it would be better to dispense with their presence altogether, and keep them entirely out of the action.

Still less was such a school of poetry susceptible of being imitated by other nations, and in other languages. It is indeed very remarkable, in the history of letters, that such frequent and obstinate attempts should have been made to imitate the Greek tragedy, when it is in truth, of all the great- works of antiquity, that which least admits of a successful imitation. The feelings which gave life and warmth and vigour to the old dramatists, were necessarily wanting to their modern successors. Those grim old legends were strangely unsuited to an audience who, instead of accepting them with a pious awe, were on the watch for incidents to criticise, and were offended at improbabilities. The French dramatists were altogether unable to treat the Greek subjects with the simplicity which properly belonged to them; and they conceived it absolutely necessary to introduce a pair of lovers to utter the cold exaggerations of the conventional passion of their stage. Even Racine, when he took for his subject the sacrifice of Iphigenia, has perverted the story in the strangest manner, by sacrificing another princess in the place of Iphigenia; and is afraid to have recourse to the miraculous substitution of a hind for the princess, lest it should seem too improbable. Yet surely in dealing with the legendary traditions of ancient Greece, a greater or less amount of improbability in the supernatural machinery, where almost every thing is supernatural, can be of little moment.

Nor was the form of the ancient tragedy, so tenaciously retained, favourable to the development of the modern. The simplicity of construction which confined the action of the piece nearly to one point of time, though it allowed space for the catastrophe of the Greek tragedy, could hardly give room enough for the greater variety of action and of sentiment of a modern play. The workings of the human heart, the development of human character, can seldom be adequately exhibited within such narrow limits. Straightened by the limits of their subject, the French and Italian tragedians have sought refuge in impertinent love scenes, or in frigid and interminable declarations. A French critic says, with much justice, " nos pièces en cinq actes, denuées de chœurs, ne peuvent être conduites jusqu'au dernier acte sans des secours étrangers au sujet."

The strong sense and masculine taste of Alfieri rejected the exaggerated sentimentality of the French school; but the difficulties of the subject were too great; he was driven to take refuge in the dreary deserts of declamation, where it requires no small patience to follow him.

It is not, perhaps, too much to say, that it was the severe self-restraint, which a rigid and religious view of their art imposed upon the early Greek tragedians, that gave rise to that chastened tone of feeling, and that rigid abstinence from unnecessary ornament, which so strongly marks what we call the classical school of literature. Nor was this voluntary rejection of beauty without its compensation ; as in the early and religious styles of the imitative arts, whether in Egypt, Greece, or Italy, art may well have gained as much in dignity and intensity of expression, as it lost in variety. The tree that is trained and clipped, may bear a finer fruit than that which grows in the wild luxuriance of nature. The hard and stiff forms of early art, often affect the mind more forcibly than a more lively and natural manner could do, and the serenity of repose is no less congenial and salutary to the human mind than the search for novelty. Coleridge tells us that in his youth, of the Greek tragedians, he most admired Æschylus ; as a man, Euripides ; but in his old age, Sophocles.

Of all the Greek tragedians, it is Sophocles who the oftenest appeals to the sentiments, and enforces the duties of the national religion ; and this tendency is peculiarly prominent in the play before us.

The plan is very simple, and the incidents few. But fairly to understand it—to enter into the feelings and motives of the personages, we must again request the reader to carry back his thoughts over three-and-twenty centuries, and to endeavour, as far as may be, to look at the play in the light in which it was originally intended to be viewed.

It was one of the most deeply-rooted religious feelings of antiquity, derived perhaps in part from the traditions of an older and purer faith, that homicide polluted the land where it had taken place ; the blood of the slain was held to cry out from the

ground, and to call aloud for vengeance. These evil consequences might be averted, and the anger of the spirits of the
dead appeased by proper sacrifices and expiations which were
directed by the priests or the oracles; but where they were
neglected, the elements were thought to be cursed—the blood-
stained earth refused her increase—the air was tainted with
death—the cattle perished, and the land became a prey to famine
and pestilence[*].

The unexpiated slaughter of Laius has afflicted Thebes with
disease and death; and an embassy, headed by Creon, has been
sent to Delphi, to consult the oracle on the causes and cure of
these calamities. The play opens as the Chorus headed by the
High Priest comes to supplicate Œdipus to assist in discovering
the source of their calamities; at this moment Creon returns,
and declares the response of the oracle, that the slayer of Laius
must be either put to death or exiled. The Chorus sing a hymn to
Apollo, and Œdipus solemnly imprecates a curse on the unknown
regicide; he is to be excommunicated, deprived of fire and water,
and thrust forth from the society of his fellow-men.

As the oracle has not declared who the slayer of Laius is, the
aged and blind Tiresias is sent for, and interrogated by Œdipus.
He at first refuses to answer; but when the king charges him as
an accomplice in the deed, he loses temper, "genus irritabile
vatum," and declares that the regicide is the monarch himself.
Œdipus breaks out into fury, asserting that the accusation has
been forged by the prophet and Creon; and even the Chorus hint
their doubts as to the accuracy of the oracle.

An altercation between Œdipus and Creon ensues, and brings
out Jocasta, who laughs at all prophets and prophesyings; but
in doing so she explains to Œdipus, what he is strangely enough
supposed never to have yet heard, the circumstances of the death
of Laius. Œdipus begins to fear that he is himself the devoted
author of the fatal deed. There is but one survivor of the
slaughter, a herdsman, and he is sent for. The Chorus utter a
train of general moral and pious sentiments, and the result seems
to be doubtful.

But the catastrophe is imminent; a messenger now arrives from
Corinth, with the news that Polybus, the supposed father of
Œdipus, is dead. The oracle had foretold that Œdipus should
kill his father, and Œdipus and Jocasta exult over the futility of
divination. In the alienation of her mind, Jocasta encourages

[*] The salutary and harmonizing influences of such an opinion are sufficiently
manifest: it might well be wished that such a superstition could become popular
in Tipperary.

Œdipus in the terrible line,

> " Yet what a light breaks from thy father's tomb[3]!"

The interest is now wound up to the highest point, and the catastrophe comes down at once like an avalanche.   The messenger
explains to Œdipus that he is not the son of Polybus, but was
given to him by the herdsman of Laius, with his feet pierced.
The dreadful truth now glares before the eyes of Jocasta.   It is
very characteristic of the spirit of the old Greek tragedy, that she
is kept on the stage to hear this tremendous revelation, uttering no
word or exclamation; mute, as if thunderstruck with the tidings
of Divine wrath.

The herdsman is the man who has been already sent for as the
survivor of the attendants of Laius.   Jocasta attempts in broken
sentences to hinder his coming; she fails, and departs to hang herself, the mode of suicide commonly attributed to the ancient
heroines.   The herdsman is brought in, is forced to answer by
threats of torture; he reveals the whole truth, and Œdipus, declaring himself unworthy to see the light, rushes off to put out
his eyes.   A magnificent chorus bewails the instability of human
things.   The action of the play ends here, but it is prolonged by
a description of the manner in which Œdipus puts out his eyes,
with which Corneille is very reasonably disgusted; by the lamentations of Œdipus, than which silence were better; by a scene certainly of great pathos, in which he bewails the fate of his daughters;
and by another altercation between him and Creon, of which the
author seems to have been more fond than was necessary[4].

The faults of the plot are obvious, and have been often remarked.
Nothing can well be more absurd, than that Œdipus should not
know the reason of his own name, or that he should have gone
into exile, because ignorant of what it seems every one else knew,
that Polybus was not his father, except perhaps that he should
reign for many years at Thebes, and be unacquainted with the manner of his predecessor's death. But the dramatic interest is wrought
up and sustained with extraordinary skill and energy; the plot is
evolved, and the situations constructed with great care and
wonderful power, and the catastrophe comes down at last with
terrible weight and force.   Above all, with reference to its main
end, to uphold the religion of the times, the play is worked out
with wonderful skill.   It enforces throughout that favourite topic
of the ancient moralists, the instability of human affairs, and

---

[3] It would be mere pusillanimity in a reviewer not to observe that this line is
far finer in the English than in the original.

[4] Some snarling scholiast has said, from the frequency of scenes of this kind in
Sophocles, that that tragedian must have kept a dog to assist him in writing his
tragedies.

that moral which it so naturally suggests, that "pride goeth before destruction, and a haughty spirit before a fall." The poet carefully contrasts the overbearing conduct and language of Œdipus, the levity of Jocasta, and the presumptuous incredulity which both exhibited towards the oracle, with the terrible calamities into which they are so soon plunged. The very message that lulls Œdipus into fancied security, by the intelligence that his supposed father is dead at Corinth, causes the revelation of the tremendous truth.

The footsteps of advancing destiny seem to sound like the tread of the statue in the awful music of Mozart, audible to all but the victim ; the thunder-cloud of Divine wrath hangs low over the head of the devoted Œdipus; the thunder growls, but his ears are charmed and he cannot hear it ; he sees the fatal truth only by the flash of the thunderbolt that strikes him helpless and blasted to the earth. The oracles and their fulfilment are the main spring of the action ; the catastrophe is foretold by one oracle, it is brought about by another, which directs that the slayer of Laius shall be sought out and punished ; and it is aggravated by the obstinacy of Œdipus, who rejects the advice of the prophet Tiresias. And to estimate the effects of this on the audience, we must reflect that these things were by them believed to be true in the main ; that they thought them to be true accounts of real persons, and that the oracles were still reverenced as the divinely-inspired guides and directors of human life, the instructors of kings and nations.

And even that which most shocks modern feelings, that the terrible misfortunes of Œdipus should be undeserved, helps to point the main moral, that the ways of the deity are unsearchable and past finding out ; and that there is no security for man, not even in a clear conscience, against the worst of human calamities.

The fame of the tragedy of Œdipus has attracted many imitators ; the story has been given by the poet who passes under the name of Seneca ; and it has been presented both to a French and an English audience, under the great names of Corneille and Dryden. Yet neither of the great modern poets has achieved any success in the attempt ; their rivalry with the Athenian has only betrayed their inferiority ; and their attempts to improve upon their original, have only served to make their failure more conspicuous. As might be supposed, the imitations all depart more or less from the simplicity of the original. Seneca has ornamented the play with the ghost of Laius, who is evoked by the foul and cruel rites of a vulgar necromancy, a profanation to which the spirit of a god-descended hero would never have been exposed in the age of Sophocles.

The subject of the play has afforded ample scope for those cold atrocities in which that author, with the taste of a true Roman, seems to have delighted, while the perpetual succession of unnatural conceits contrasts most unfavourably with the dignified simplicity of the Greek original.

Corneille, who appears to have valued himself not a little upon his alterations of this play, and who tells us that no other of his tragedies is composed with equal art, has invented what he is pleased to call "l'heureux épisode" of the loves of Theseus and Dirce, who ring the changes upon all the variations of the conventional gallantry of the French romantic drama, and, in fact, throw Œdipus himself very much into the shade. Dryden (who was assisted by Lee in his Œdipus), while he has severely blamed Corneille for his episode, and has expressed so high an opinion of the Greek author, that he even assures the audience in his prologue, that if they do not approve his tragedy they must be content to be universally stigmatized as barbarians, has by no means made his practice conformable to his precepts; and the tragedy which he has presented to his English hearers bears little resemblance to that of Sophocles. He has made, indeed, a much stranger medley than Corneille. For while he has suppressed Theseus and Dirce, he has invented an Adrastus and Eurydice, who are altogether as extravagant as their predecessors. He calls up the ghost of Laius with invocations which are evidently borrowed from the witches in "Macbeth." He has converted Creon into a feeble imitation of Richard the Third; while the play ends with a general massacre, which sweeps away all the pr nc pa personages, and leaves hardly enough to bury the dead. i i l

But the calamities of Œdipus were not yet terminated. About the year 1820, a *production* on the subject of Œdipus was placed in the hands of a "Mr. J. Saville Faucit," author of the "Lazar's Grave," "Scripture Concurrence," "Justice," "The Miller's Maid," &c. This production was the occasion of an operation "which it is but justice to add was very unwillingly *undertook*," and which, after the space of ten days, had for its result, "Œdipus, a Musical Drama; compiled, selected, and adapted from the translations from the Greek of Sophocles, by Dryden, Lee, Corneille, and J. Maurice, Esq." The drama in question is, for the most part, taken from Dryden's play; but in spite of the short period allowed for its composition, the author found time to adorn it with some most curious and original ornaments. Œdipus enters upon the stage, like Marlowe's Tamerlane, in a triumphal car, drawn by captured Argives, with which people he has been at war. Œdipus suddenly bethinks himself of inquiring into the cause of the quarrel, and asks Adrastus, the vanquished sovereign, "Why were we foes?" "'Cause we were kings," replies Adrastus; and upon this very satisfactory explanation, they are struck with a vehement admiration of each other's virtues, swear eternal friendship; and Œdipus having successfully driven into Thebes, and having apparently no further occasion for the services of his draft Argives, suddenly promotes Adrastus from his post as near wheeler, to the more pleasant and less laborious one of his son-in-law, by giving him the hand of his daughter Eurydice. This wonderful performance is announced in the dedication as an attempt to revive the Greek Drama! We sincerely hope that the attempt will not be renewed, and that the much-vexed ghost of Œdipus may be at length suffered to rest in peace, and be no more raised up to minister to the unhallowed purposes of modern playwrights.

To the tragedy before us the voice of antiquity has always assigned the highest rank. Sophocles has been commonly regarded as the most perfect of the Greek tragedians, and this has been generally esteemed as his greatest work. Aristotle, in the treatise which goes under the name of the "Poetics," appears to consider it as almost a model tragedy; and though he bases this judgment upon very narrow and technical grounds, we may feel sure that he would never have hazarded so decided an opinion, had not the play been conceived and executed in a tone of thought altogether suitable to the feelings of antiquity. It was pitched in the right key for the audience to whom it was addressed. And yet to our feelings it seems strangely dry and hard, exhibiting little character or play of passion,—improbable in its story, odious in its plot, and shocking in its catastrophe.

It is evident that in such a work the modern reader must at first find much to disappoint him; he misses much that he is accustomed to look for, and many of the sources of interest which it contains are to him shut up. It is only by some attention and thought, that he will attain to a full conception of the dignity and austere beauty which pervades and informs the whole.

And yet there are few greater services which can be rendered to literature in our own time, than to make such poetry acceptable to us. The study of the severe models of antiquity is, above all things, adapted to correct the false taste, the love of glare and glitter, the vagueness of purpose, the looseness of expression, and the idle or false sentimentality which have so much overrun the literature of the present age. But in proportion as the object is desirable, it is difficult; and the more such a work is useful, the less is it likely to meet favour. It requires some courage, as well as much skill to present to an English public the Greek tragedy as the Greeks made it; and to introduce to an audience of this fantastical century the Attic Muse in the native simplicity of her country's costume—

"Great is the glory, for the strife is hard."

And this Sir Francis Doyle has dared to do; he has given us a real translation of his author, not, as has been too much the fashion in dealing with the classics (however sanctioned by the great names of Pope and Dryden), another poem upon the same subject. While his original poems show sufficiently that he wants neither power of invention nor facility of expression, he has, with a most praiseworthy abstinence, refrained from introducing any thing of his own; he has scrupulously left his original as he found it. It is in truth hard to say, whether it is more difficult to find an idea of the original which has been left unexpressed in the translation, or a new one which has been introduced without warrant. The difficulty of so representing an ancient author, under all the exigencies of versification, is hardly to be estimated; it requires an expenditure of time and thought which few men would give at all to a literary undertaking, and fewer still would bestow upon the work of another[5].

The power of compression shown in the translation is truly remarkable, and ought to redeem the English language from a charge often brought against it—of want of conciseness. The translation does not contain an hundred lines more than the original; and, allowing for the greater length of the Greek line, probably no greater number of syllables.

The following citations may not unfairly represent our translator's method of rendering the most characteristic and most difficult parts of the play, the choruses. (See pp. 10, 11, and 51, v. 195 to 212, and 1245 to 1266.)

> " Wives too, and greyhair'd mothers, round
> The high-raised shrine, in suppliant guise
>   From every side have wended ;
>   Over these bitter agonies
> They lengthen out their mournful cries,
> Whilst the loud Pæan's sparkling sound,
> With sounds of wail is blended.
> Wherefore Jove's golden daughter hear us,
> Send smiling help to cheer us ;

---

[5] In this merit of merits in a translator,—close and accurate rendering,—Sir Francis has had a noble precedent in that great work, one of the most valuable presents that could have been made to the English reader, Wright's admirable translation of Dante.

And Ares, the death-spirit dire,
Who now, not arm'd for war, but still
With savage shoutings bent to kill,
Raves round us, a consuming fire,
Him, exiled from my country, force,
Re-rushing on his rapid course,
To turn him back again, and flee
To the great chamber of the sea,
Or where, around Barbaric shores,
The swell of Thracian surges roars."

———

" Man, child of dust, your little life I deem
No better than a baseless dream,
For who of human birth has looked on bliss
More stedfast to the eye than this;
A something that may seem to shine,
And in its seeming straight decline ?—
Thy fate, lost Œdipus, is strong to show
That none are blessed here below.
Thy arrowy flight, too fortunate its aim,
Soared up, the pride of life to claim,
And that oracular grim thing of prey,
The virgin Sphinx, God gave thee power to slay.
When on thy native land in that dark hour
Death smote, like an imperial tower
For refuge and defence thou stood'st alone,
So that we placed thee on a throne,
And raised thee up to high renown,
Lord of this mighty Theban town.—
But who, from all we hear, more wretched now,
High heart of Œdipus, than thou?
Who by sad change of lot is forced to dwell
With griefs and agonies more fell ! "

Of his vigour in dialogue let the following serve as an example, as a not infelicitous instance of the combination of the stateliness of Greek tragedy, with the liveliness of expression required in the drama by the countrymen of Shakspeare. (See p. 58, v. 1458 to 1467[*].)

" Having myself denounced against myself
Such a contaminating curse, how could I
Confront it here with an unshrinking eye ?
No, were there any power of crushing up

[*] We cannot but think that the second line would be improved by omitting " how."

The fountain-head of sound within mine ears,
I would not rest till this afflicted frame
Were clean walled out from nature; so I might
Live without sight, and hearing nothing; for
. To keep all senses dead to pain were best."

The following quotation, from a speech of Œdipus, may also
be given as a specimen of grave and vigorous versification. (See
p. 13, v. 268 to 277.)

" Yea! in the self-same curse, if to my knowledge
An inmate of my halls this man should be,
I bind myself to suffer every ill
I have invoked on him; and as for you,
What I have said I charge you to fulfil
For my sake, for the god's, and for this land
Now withered up in godless desolation;
Nay, though no deity had urged the guest,
When that a king of his great race was slain,
It were not right to leave it unaton'd."

Of the two difficulties between which every translator of poetry
finds himself pressed, of failing to give the sense of his original on
one side, or of expressing himself in a harsh and unidiomatic
manner on the other, our author certainly falls most frequently
into the latter, and his dialogue is often open to the charge of
stiffness.   Yet this is undoubtedly the less fault of the two, and
it must be remembered that the dialogue of the ancient tragedies
was more laboured and stately than that in use on our stage.
The heroes of Greek tragedy could scarcely speak like ordinary
mortals, nor would the spirit of the original be fairly conveyed,
unless the language were somewhat more stately than the English
dramatic taste will easily endure.   Yet the language has not
always been brought to the flexibility, which, always desirable, is
especially so for dialogue.   In English blank verse, the ear wanting the accustomed stimulus of rhyme, makes the reader exceedingly intolerant of any flatness or want of vigour either in sense
or sound.   Milton is always especially careful so to modify his
verses that the pauses may give the necessary variety, by not
coinciding with the ends of the lines; and, perhaps, something of
the same kind may be discerned in the frequent breakings of the
lines in the dialogues of Shakspeare.   In the " Œdipus Tyrannus"
the dialogue is so often inevitably divided into single lines, that
the difficulty is probably not altogether surmountable.
: In the first chorus (v. 170) the oracle is besought to " declare
the same;" a phraseology which appears to recal the legal, rather

than the poetical studies of the learned translator, and is surely more appropriate to an indictment than to an ode. This expression " the same," seems indeed to be rather a favourite with our translator, it occurs three times as the termination of a line (see v. 390 and 1030), not, we think, without a certain flatness of effect.

These faults are no doubt trifling, but the labour of correcting them is also trifling, and a minute perfection in a work of art is assuredly no trifle. We may hope to see these things amended in a future edition.

One mistake in the meaning may be noticed; the translation runs vv. 1187-8—

> " faithful among the first,
> To Laius, that is for a shepherd swain ;"

which sounds as if a shepherd, by some law of nature, was necessarily less honest than other men. In truth, πιστός signifies *trusted* as well as *trustworthy ;* and the meaning is, that the shepherd in question was as much in the confidence of his master, as a man of his rank was likely to be, and this explains why he was charged with the important task of exposing Œdipus.

It is assuredly no light task to give an adequate and satisfactory rendering of one of the great authors of antiquity, difficult to be done at all, and almost, if not quite impossible, to be done without occasional stiffness and hardness. As it is one of the most useful and arduous, so it is one of the most meritorious of literary achievements; while it exacts more labour than original composition, it bestows less fame; nor would the necessary labour be given from any meaner motive than that pure love and disinterested devotion for art, which is at once the incentive, the test, and the reward of genius.

While the translation before us is certainly not exempt from faults of diction, though it sometimes wants grace, and still oftener ease, it may be truly said of it that it is a real translation ; that there is scarcely an idea of the original which is not rendered, and that it fully and faithfully conveys to the English reader the mind and the sentiments of one of the great and most famous works of antiquity. This Sir Francis Doyle has done ; and he who has done this has done much.

The form in which the present publication appears, is not undeserving of notice. It is one of the objects of the translator that the benefits of his work, as introducing the reader to a very important part of classical literature, should be extended as widely as possible, and should serve to lift up some portion of the veil which shrouds the ancient world from the eyes of that large portion of the reading public, whose early studies have not rendered them familiar with the languages of antiquity. Hence the present translation is published as cheaply as possible, and sold at the price of a shilling; a mode of publication which deprives the translator of all chance of pecuniary remuneration,—a piece of literary disinterestedness not very common in our day, when peers publish private letters, and illustrious statesmen discount their own posthumous memoirs. And we may venture to anticipate, not without some ground of confidence, that such hopes may not be altogether disappointed.

However remote from the habits and feelings engendered by modern literature may be those of Greek tragedy, we may yet expect that real poetry, easily accessible to the multitude, will never be wholly lost upon them. The frippery of affected ornament dies away with the fashion which has produced it. The simplicity of nature is eternal. The natural flower may be outshone in the drawing-room by the more gaudy hues of its artificial imitator, but it has its roots in the all-nourishing earth; it is fed with the dew of heaven from above, and it will flourish and give delight to men long ages after its flaring competitor shall be swept into the dust of oblivion.

Whether or not such a popularizing among us of the austere muse of Greek tragedy be possible, it is surely much to be desired. Of the advantages of classical literature, two are perhaps the chief,—that it serves as a standard of taste, and that it helps powerfully to enlarge the mind. Upon the first point we have already had occasion to touch. With respect to the second and more important point, it may here be sufficient to observe that there is no other secular study, which for its effect in opening the mental vision, in freeing us from the narrowing effect of the prejudices of our particular age and country, can be compared with that of the authors of Greece and Rome; for they instruct us by the most forcible teaching, that of example—that human nature has been always the same; that in the ages the most remote from ours, with very different, and, in some respects, very savage manners, and with a most vicious religion, there was yet virtue and goodness, kind feelings and high honour; they teach us wisdom, and its best consequence, charity.

And they teach us no less the highest political lessons, where human nature is likely to err, where they have erred, and where we are most apt to do the same. Their wrecks ought to be our beacons. And of this teaching, not the least powerful when gradual and insensible, the multitude stand even more in need than their richer fellow-citizens. Limited to the observation of few objects, their views are narrow; with little opportunity of elevated enjoyment, their tastes are gross; and whatever may tend to enlarge the one, or to purify the other, is matter of no mean importance. The literature which is current among a people can never have a light effect upon their tastes, their morals, or their happiness.

Nor is it only to the mere English reader that such a translation is of use. It may be made hardly less beneficial to the student. The inevitable habits and tendencies of all institutions for education go to concentrate attention upon the words rather than upon the meaning of authors; to lead the student to banquet upon the husk, and neglect the kernel; and to value a poet more for his difficulties than his beauties. We have ourselves known a passage from Æschylus set for translation to candidates for honours, which, from notorious corruption, was absolute nonsense. It will be in the recollection of most of our readers that Byron professed himself unable to enjoy Horace, so disgusted had he been by "that dull dry lesson, forced down word by word." And, doubtless, numbers must have felt the same, and been precluded from all taste for classical literature; shut out from many important sources, both of enjoyment and of improvement, by that exclusive attention to words into which all philological studies are so apt to degenerate. It is, no doubt, in the first place, necessary that an author should be understood; but this necessity is too apt to lead men, as in other pursuits, to take the means for the end, and to limit scholarship to a mere knowledge of the meaning of words, till, to use the metaphor of Bacon, they become money when they should have been counters.

It is obvious enough that such an exclusive course of study has a strong tendency to cramp and narrow the faculties. Nor is this all, the concentration of attention upon the dead languages is apt to cause a neglect of our own, the habit of *construing* of which Arnold lamented the substitution for *translation*, accustoms the ear and the taste to the strangest and most barbarous English. It is but a bad substitute, if while we learn to read good Greek, we learn also to write and speak bad English. Those strange productions, which in University language, are commonly termed *cribs*, literal translations of the classical authors into English prose, and which make a very important part of the ordinary University studies, can hardly fail to exercise an unfavourable effect, both upon the purity and geniality of style of those who are much accustomed to them. Let us hope that a version like the present, at once close enough to assist in the interpretation of the author, and elegant enough to afford a standard of taste, may help to lead to a better practice in this very important matter. The interpretation of a classical author ought to be as much a lesson in English as in Greek or Latin.

Sir Francis Doyle gives us some promise that the present work may be only the first of a series of translations of the plays of Sophocles. We cannot conclude without the expression of a wish that this intention may not be without fruit. As the translator goes on, his work will become lighter, practice will beget facility, and the language of dramatic dialogue flow more easily from his pen. Many of the succeeding plays of Sophocles abound more in variety of situation and in passages of poetical beauty, than the one before us, and are more likely to arrest the attention and please the taste of a modern audience; and as the labour becomes lighter, the reward will be more sure and in more full measure.

We hope that the intended work may go on, and that it may remain as an enduring monument to the fame at once of the Greek and the English poet.

Art. VII.—1. *The Church, the Crown, and the State. Two Sermons. By the Rev.* W. J. E. Bennett, *M.A.* Cleaver: London.

2. *The Things of Cæsar and the Things of God. A Discourse by* W. Dodsworth, *M.A., Perpetual Curate of Christ Church, St. Pancras.* Masters: London.

3. *The Reformers of the Anglican Church, and Mr. Macaulay's History of England. Second Edition. By* E. C. Harrington, *M.A., Chancellor of the Cathedral Church of Exeter.* London: Rivingtons.

4. *Addresses of the London Church Union.* Rivingtons.

5. *Rules of the London, Bristol, Metropolitan, Leicester, Leamington, Yeovil, Dorset, Plymouth, Gloucester, Church Unions.*

6. *The Present Crisis of the Church of England. Illustrated by a brief Inquiry as to the Royal Supremacy, &c. By* W. J. Irons, *B.D., Vicar of Brompton.* London: Masters.

There is scarcely, perhaps, in the whole circle of secondary doctrines connected with Christianity, one that has furnished more room for controversy, and led to more serious divisions than the question of the relation of the temporal Government to religion. In the present day the Church of England stands almost alone, in ascribing to the State any authority over the Church. Such authority is disclaimed and resisted by the Church of Rome. It is equally resisted and denounced by Dissenters, as involving an anti-Christian usurpation on the one side, and a sacrifice of the Church's rights on the other. The modern schools of politics which date from the French Revolution, unite in declaring that the State has nothing to do with religion. In our own days we have seen the disruption of the Established Presbyterian system of Scotland on this question. In Ireland we have seen the Romish bishops and clergy again and again refuse the golden bait by which political parties have sought to place limits on their freedom, and to render them the agents of political parties. In France we have seen the Church engaged in a long and strenuous resistance to the State, and gradually winning its way to liberty. In Prussia we have seen the State divesting itself of power over the various religious confessions and restoring them to freedom. The cause of dissension in all these cases has been the same. The State has gradually lost, or has long been entirely devoid of any substantial agreement of objects and principles with the

Church. It has not exercised its power for the good of the Church, but simply for its own good, without caring whether the Church suffers or not in the process.

Nor have there been wanting amongst the members of the Church of England instances of persons who have entertained opinions adverse to the exercise of any power by the State in ecclesiastical matters. The non-juring writers generally took very strong ground on this subject; and the doctrines of Leslie, and Dodwell, and Johnson, and many other able men who held the same views, have not been without adherents at any time in the English Church. The doctrines, however, of the independence of the Church on the temporal power, were not for a long time regarded with favour in the Church of England. Until the present generation, the supremacy of the Crown was generally looked on as a sacred and distinctive tenet of the Church of England, which every orthodox Churchman was bound to defend most vigorously, and to look with pious horror on every one who dreamt of the separation of Church and State. And so matters continued during the reigns of the Georges. The regal supremacy was then as much prized and as jealously guarded by Churchmen as it had ever been. The ground commonly taken against the agitation of the Romish claims for political power was its inconsistency with the king's supremacy. The union of Church and State was all but an article of faith.

Now, however, matters are changed. The Church is greatly divided on the question of its union with the State. Resistance is manifested in many ways to State measures. Jealousy is shown of State interference. State patronage is not so much valued, and the royal supremacy is treated without much ceremony. The Church and State are no longer on good terms, though they are allied. There is dissension between the two parties—the one trying to hold its grasp as well as it can over a subject that is getting every day more restive, and the other becoming each day more irritated and uneasy under an authority which has become burdensome.

And how has all this come to pass? Is "Puseyism" the evil spirit that has made the Church no longer the acquiescent and easily-managed body that it was? Perhaps it *has* done something in this way; and yet "Puseyism" did not cause Mr. Baptist Noel to forsake the Church, nor can it exclusively bear the responsibility of the change which has come over us.

It is the State itself which has *altered its position* in regard to the Church, and has, therefore, wrought a change in the mind of the Church. During the reigns of the Georges, the Sovereign, the Ministers, the Lords and the Commons were all Churchmen.

No Dissenter or Romanist was admitted into the Royal Councils, or could legislate for or against the Church. The State may have employed its Church patronage without reference to the true interests of religion; but it was firm and resolute in its support of the Church. Within the last thirty years, however, all this is changed. Dissenters, Romanists, Socinians, are admissible to all the offices of the State: they are eligible to Parliament; they are ministers of state and privy-councillors. The sovereign power has gradually fallen into the hands of the ministers of the Crown, who are virtually appointed and dismissed by a House of Commons, which includes sectarians of all kinds, and radical enemies of the Church. And, accordingly, what has been the result? In the first place, the Church of Ireland has been ruined by the suppression of half its episcopal sees; by the introduction of poor laws, by which its property is taxed twice as heavily as that of the laity; by the confiscation of a quarter of its revenues in the times of the Reform Bill, and a third of the remainder by the Corn Law Bill; by the withdrawal of Government aid from its educational establishments, and the institution of rival establishments, with a view to satisfy Romanists and Dissenters; by the abuse of the Crown patronage to compel the Church to support an educational system to which it objects; by the foundation of colleges for Romanists and dissenters, in opposition to the established University; by the endowment of Maynooth, and the augmentation thus given to the means and influence of Romanism; by the further endowment of Presbyterianism, and the establishment of sectarian ministers as authorized to celebrate marriages; by the recognition of the titles and authority of Romish ecclesiastics, and the avowed wish in all ways to conciliate and aid them; by the discouragement of all persons and parties favourable to the continuance of the ascendancy of the Church, or the preservation of her rights or revenues. We think there can be little doubt that the State has changed its position in regard to the Church in Ireland.

But all, perhaps, has remained as before in the *English* Church. We can hardly say this on a survey of the facts of the case. True, the progress of events has been gradual here as it has been in Ireland, yet it is not less evident or alarming. Dissent, long ago, obtained its full share of Parliamentary grants for education. Those grants are now made to Romish, and Wesleyan Methodist schools as much as to Church schools. Romish bishops are salaried in the colonies, and placed on a level with our own, or even above them. Aid is refused to schools of an exclusively and strictly Church character. The Church is first limited by the Tithe Commutation Act to a certain extent of property, so that she can derive no benefit from future improvements in value; and this Act has scarcely come into operation, till, by the alteration in the Corn Laws, *one-third of her income is swept away!* Men of unsound theological tenets, tinged with the latitudinarian philosophy of the day, are promoted to her bishoprics, and other influential positions. The Crown patronage may be exercised by persons who attend sectarian worship. The Church is refused any further aid from pub c funds; and her own property is taken out of her hands ánd dealt with by Parliament. Her universities are deprived of their exclusive privileges, as far as possible, and an opposite system encouraged. She is refused the organization of a hierarchy adequate to her wants, while she sees Romanism freely, and without check, developing itself.

And besides the evils which have actually taken effect, the Church has, on many occasions, been in great perils. The Church rates have often been nearly extinguished. The subversion of her laws of marriage has been nearly successful. The most dangerous plans of latitudinarian education have been only just escaped. Ours has been a troubled and anxious existence for the last twenty years, continually on the verge of fearful evils; and in the struggle we have already lost annual income to the amount of more than a million. Events, too, have brought out in strong relief the fact that the State, latitudinarian or unbelieving as it now is, has the power of influencing the *doctrinal* teaching of the Church by its appointments to benefices; and that it is evidently inclined to do so; and, further, that it can nominate who it pleases to act on the tribunal for the judgment of Church causes which involve doctrinal questions.

On a survey of what has been going on for the last twenty years, we think no one can wonder that the feelings of the Church of England towards the State should be somewhat changed. The spirit of legislation as regards the Church has totally altered. A great transition is in progress. It cannot be a matter of indifference to the Church whether those who enact laws are friendly to her, or otherwise. She cannot look upon a State exclusively attached to her, and a State which includes all her opponents, in exactly the same point of view. Hence it is perfectly natural, that the supremacy which was cherished at one time, should be regarded with different feelings at another.

It would be a great mistake to suppose that " Puseyism," as it is called, has been the only cause of change in the Church's views of the State supremacy. It might with more justice be said, that the Church has been driven by the exigencies of her position to inquire into first principles, and to look for the rules and the precedents which are to guide her in the painful trials to which she is exposed from the alienation of the State. It is the State which has broken the alliance, not the Church.

Deeply painful, however, as is much of what we have witnessed, in the evidence it affords of a total change on the part of the State towards the Church, still we must be careful, lest, in adapting our maxims to the altered circumstances in which we are placed, we should so state the question as to cast undeserved blame upon the Church of England in former ages, or contradict and deny those principles which she has sanctioned in her formularies. On this account we think the doctrines of the Non-jurors, in the relations of Church and State, are not adapted to the present day, though they are more so than those of many of our writers in the sixteenth and seventeenth centuries, which ascribe powers to the State which the State itself has ceased to assert. The only safe and reasonable ground to take seems to us to be this:—that the formularies of the Church of England were composed in contemplation of a different state of things from that which now exists, and that the Church assumed as a necessary condition in her notion of temporal sovereignty—its Christianity, and its reality—but that it has now lost both these conditions.

The temporal sovereignty has lost its Christianity, as it was understood by the Church, because, though the *person* of the Sovereign remains Christian, the sovereign *power* is exercised by a body which is not Christian, and by its nominees. The Parliament is no longer Christian in the sense of the Church, because it includes members holding every possible variety of religious error, and even many infidels. The ministry are the nominees of this Parliament, and really derive power from it; and the *powers* of the Sovereign are exercised by the ministry. The Sovereign is therefore only personally Christian; *officially* he is not so in the sense of the Church.

The hypothesis on which the Church bases her recognition of the regal supremacy, is no longer in existence. The Thirty-seventh Article—" Of the civil magistrates"—speaks only of the prerogative " which we see to have been given always to all GODLY Princes in Holy Scriptures by God Himself." David and Solomon, Hezekiah, Jehu and Josiah, were indeed godly in their dealings with religion and their subjects; but that power was used in contradiction to God's commands, when it was employed by ungodly kings in introducing idolatries into the Temple, and combining the worship of the true God with that of the gods of the heathen, and other actions subversive of true religion. Therefore, if the Article refers only to the power given to godly princes, we cannot in justice assume that it is meant to apply in the same way to an "ungodly" sovereignty. The example of a David or

a Josiah is not parallel to that of a Jeroboam or an Ahab.   The
Church which might gladly recognize a supremacy in a Constantine, a Theodosius, an Edward, or an Elizabeth, would not feel
that the same Divine sanction was given to the supremacy of a
Constantius, a Julian, a Valens, or a Cromwell.   We are not
saying that the Church may not and does not recognize a supremacy sometimes even in infidel sovereignties; but it is a very
different thing from that which is recognized in godly and Christian sovereignties.   In England, at present, we subscribe to views
which the State has repudiated.   We declare the Sovereign to
be supreme in all causes and over all persons—all estates and
degrees.   But the Sovereigns of England have abandoned that
power.   They do not *claim* to be supreme over all persons and in
all causes.   They sanction the *Papal* supremacy over one portion
of the people, and another portion they allow to reject all supremacy but their own.   They do not "punish with the civil sword
the evil-doers," as the godly kings in Scripture did; but permit
idolatries and heresies to flourish unchecked, and even encouraged.
If, therefore, we still declare that the Sovereign is supreme in
religious matters over all the people, we can only mean that he is
so in the abstract, and by God's ordinance, in order to promote
God's glory; but that he is no longer so in fact and reality, in
the full meaning of the Church.   The supremacy, *in its present
state*, has no support from our formularies, or from the Scriptures.
It is the mere exercise of certain legal prerogatives given by Act
of Parliament.   With mere prerogative we are in no way concerned as a matter of principle.   The Parliament may increase
or diminish the prerogative of the executive power, but this is a
mere matter of State arrangement, and is based on fitness, expediency, or justice; not on the law of God and religious considerations.   The temporal power has long since foregone all
claims founded on *religious* considerations; and yet the Church
of England bases the supremacy which she acknowledges, and
which, as understood by her, has become a theory and a tradition,
on Scripture and God's will only.
   Our reply then to those who blame our writers at the Reformation or subsequently, or who even censure the Articles and
formularies of the Church of England, as recognizing an ecclesiastical supremacy in the Sovereign, is, that it was conceded only
on the supposition that the prince was "godly," *i. e.* a sincere
adherent of the true faith, and that his power was given and was
to be used for the welfare of God's Church and the promotion of
God's glory.   The temporal power, in those times, took precisely
the same view, and was extremely busy in regulating and reforming religious matters, and repressing evil-doers of all kinds.   The

"civil sword" was active against heretics. And this was just what Josiah and such godly kings did under the old Covenant.

The Canons of 1604 declare that—

> "Whosoever shall affirm that the King's Majesty hath not the same authority in causes ecclesiastical that the *godly* kings had among the Jews, and *Christian* emperors of the primitive Church, or impeach any part of his regal supremacy in the said causes restored to the Crown, and by the laws of the realm herein established, let him be excommunicated *ipso facto,* and not restored, but only by the Archbishop, after his repentance and public revocation of these his wicked errors."

It is evident that the Church supposed in this canon that the Crown of England would always be "Christian" and "godly," and would never tolerate or encourage schism and heresy by legal enactments. The Sovereigns of England are still Christian in their personal capacity; but the fact is, that if they were to cease to be of the communion of the Church, or to become dissenters, Romanists, or open unbelievers, the mere *letter* of the canon and Articles, detached from their spirit, might be quoted to prove that God had given to unbelievers or idolatrous princes the government of His Church. And no matter how grossly and monstrously the legal powers of the State were abused—even if they were employed in the most manifest contradiction to the doctrines and belief of the Church—even if they were employed for the purpose of encouraging Romanism, or infidelity, or rationalism, or Unitarianism in the Church, and introducing by legal process any amount of heresy into her, the State and its ministers would still appeal at *law* to the letter of the Articles, and the canons, and the statutes of the realm, passed when the realm was governed by orthodox princes.

Opinions, however, cannot be tied down in the present day to exactly such an interpretation of the supremacy of the Crown, as may be most in accordance with the views of politicians. The mind of the Church of England will venture to think for itself, and will look at the facts of the case, notwithstanding the dicta of ministers, lawyers, and journals. The sovereign power in England is personally irresponsible and infallible in the eye of the law, and should be so in the eyes of all Churchmen; but the exercise of the prerogatives of the Crown is in the hands of responsible ministers; the power of the Crown is *only exercised through ministers* now; and it is this which has ceased to be "godly" or "Christian" in the sense of the Church of England. It is out of the question to succeed any longer in blinding the public mind to the gradual revolution which has taken place in the relations of the State to

the Church.   There is *some* difference between the state of things
in 1550 and in 1850.

We readily admit that Henry VIII., and one or two of his
successors, exaggerated the notion of the regal supremacy, and
that some of our prelates and divines have occasionally put forward
opinions, or consented to acts of royal power, which have, to say
the least, been questionable.   But setting aside these, as matters
of no great importance, we cordially and fully sympathize with the
feelings of those who were ready to concur in what were in some
degree irregularities, in associating themselves with the laudable
intentions of "Christian" and "godly" sovereigns; of sovereigns,
who were more than shadows of kingly power, but who wielded
in their own persons the authority of the State—of sovereigns,
earnest in their protection and purification of the Church, and
in their efforts to reduce all the nation into obedience to the true
faith.

How widely changed is the sovereign power in England now !
Time has been the greatest innovator of all.   Names have lost
their meaning.   The "supremacy of the *Crown*" is in reality a
"misnomer."   It no longer means the supremacy of the head of
the State, but the supremacy of an oligarchy of ministers called
to their office by the House of Commons.   Hence it must be
expected that ministers and legislators should be most anxious to
maintain what they call the "supremacy of the *Crown*," which
really means *their own supremacy.*

It is a truth which we think no right thinking person can dispute, that if GOD has ever authorized Jewish and Christian
princes to exercise jurisdiction and control over the Church, it
has been simply for the promotion of His glory, and His designs
for the salvation of men.   It has not been for the purpose
of augmenting the power of the State, or for any material or
earthly objects.   Princes have been authorized by God to co-
operate thus with their earthly means and power in promoting
His kingdom upon earth, with that express object.

There are many persons, to whom the statement of such opinions will seem strange and unreasonable, and we fear that all
who look on the question in this point of view, and act on that
view in any degree, must be prepared to hear themselves described
as disloyal, turbulent, and mischievous men—as disturbers of the
Church, and as inconsistent in remaining in her communion.
We think that the increasing exigencies of the times, and the
increasing manifestations of the State's real character, will render
faithful men more and more indifferent to such accusations, and
more and more resolved in their opinions and course of action.
We are placed in circumstances of extreme difficulty.   The letter

of institutions and formularies, in opposition to their real meaning
and spirit, is against us. An unbelieving State has taken the
place of a Christian one. The Church is, in the face of this state
of things, divided to such an extent, that whatever is taken up by
one party is sure to be opposed by the other, or looked on with
jealousy. The State has, therefore, fearful odds in its favour, in
the contest to remodel the Church on its own principles of indifference. There is, however, one, and only one, *ultimate* remedy left. It may be impossible to induce the Church *generally*
to unite in demanding, or the State to yield, any alteration and
adaptation of its relations and powers to the exigencies of the
nineteenth century. We may ask in vain for Convocation; we
may appeal in vain even to the heads of our Church. Caution
on the one hand, and love of power on the other, may attempt to
quash all our demands. We may be told to remain satisfied with
the institutions of the sixteenth century, pervaded by the spirit
and principles of the nineteenth, and to fold our hands in resignation to the will of God. We may be told to refrain from seeking what our rulers are unwilling to grant, and to remain as we
are, in order to avoid greater risks and dangers. To these injunctions and exhortations we *dare* not yield acquiescence. We
cannot, and ought not, to remain in peace, while the inheritance
of the Lord is defiled, and the greatest interests of the Church—
its most vital truths, and its spiritual efficiency—are endangered
in so many ways. What then is our remedy? It consists in
PERSEVERANCE. If the claims of the Church are not conceded—
if the strong arm of power is raised to crush attempts at Reform
which are as essential now as they were in the sixteenth century,
then we do not say, "Leave the Church." On the contrary, we
say, "Remain firmly in the Church, to struggle for her through
evil report and good report, as faithful soldiers of JESUS CHRIST.
Remain in her—hold your ground—quit you like men. Let no
extravagance disgrace you; let no disloyalty to the Church find
a place in your hearts. Pay the most perfect respect to constituted authorities; but never rest until you have gained a sufficient Reform of the existing relations of Church and State. If
others will not join you, go on without them; and you will find
that weariness and indifference will, in the course of years, concede to you those claims, for the sake of peace, which never will
be yielded as a matter of justice."

The really faithful members of the Church have, we think,
only this course before them. They must not allow themselves
to be irritated or dispirited; but they must be indefatigably persevering. They must act in the mode which is taken by a minority in the House of Commons, determined to carry their point;

and they will in all probability carry it, if they persevere so earnestly and so long as to become a real trouble to the State. A trifling or intermittent opposition will be disregarded: it is only a vigorous, a diversified, a never-ceasing activity that is likely to prevail. That movement must be strictly a " Church of England" one, or it will be powerless.

And this brings us to a subject on which we have been for some time inclined to speak—a subject of daily increasing importance. We allude to the formation of " Church Unions," and the line of policy which they should pursue.

The institution of " Church Unions" began about two years since, with a view to enlist the *combined* exertions of Churchmen for the attainment of certain objects, on the desirableness of which all Churchmen are agreed, or at least Churchmen of all parties. We refer to such measures as an increase in the number of bishops, with due provision for the appointment of persons well qualified for that sacred office, the extension of the Church; the restoration of an Ecclesiastical legislature in place of Parliamentary legislation in Church matters; and the revival of Church discipline. The hope of the founders of these societies was, that the unexceptionableness of their objects would have enlisted the general co-operation of Churchmen of all shades of opinion. That hope, however, has been imperfectly realized; for the Evangelical party has, to a considerable extent, stood aloof, and declined to unite in the movement. We must confess· that, with the knowledge of the original object of Church Unions fully before us, we have lamented the partial character of the movement—its being left so much to men of one class of views in the Church—to those with whom we generally agree. We have observed, from time to time, with regret, that the leading Church Union established at Bristol has appeared to have forgotten the simple general objects prominently put forth at its foundation, and has occupied itself almost exclusively with the important question of National Education. We have also felt much regret at the resolutions which have been published occasionally, with the signatures of the able and energetic secretaries of the Bristol Union, on a variety of subjects which were certainly very far from being of that class on which Churchmen are agreed. We could not see the advantage of expressing opinions on the conduct of bishops, or on other disputed questions; and it seemed that a course was being taken which was calculated to defeat entirely the object of union and co-operation with which such societies were formed originally. We must confess that we have often lamented a course which seemed to be frustrating all the hopes which we had conceived from the institution of those societies. It seemed that if only one part of the Church engaged in the effort to obtain sufficient securities from the State, there could be no hope of success, humanly speaking, considering the powers arrayed against us.

But in fact, whatever may be the cause, the Evangelical section of the Church appears to be at present completely under the influence of the State; and it would, most probably, have been impossible, under any circumstances, to have secured their co-operation. We are inclined to think that no amount of prudence and forbearance would have enlisted them in the cause of ecclesiastical freedom. They are, apparently, satisfied at the present prospects of the Church, and possibly look to the exaltation of their own views under the influence of Government patronage; and to a depression of opinions, which they reject, under the discouragement of the State and of the chief heads of the Church. They remain quiescent at all events, and, perhaps, they may even pass from this state of quiescence to one of actual support of Government in its contest with the Church.

The hope of the co-operation of the Evangelical party in the Church's cause must, therefore, be relinquished with regret; and if there had not been sufficient indications already that they were resolved to stand aloof from any movement such as that of the Church Unions, the state of things connected with the recent decision by the Committee of Council in the Gorham case, shows that it would be now hopeless to attempt any combination of parties. The extreme pressure of these times would compel any association to take some side in the controversy.

Since circumstances have taken this direction, so different from what had been originally contemplated, it remains to make the best of them. It is, in our opinion, a matter of imperative duty in Churchmen to *combine* in the present times for counsel and mutual encouragement. In the midst of the increasing dangers of the Church—dangers affecting her temporal position, and the permanence of her institutions, and laws, and doctrines—it is no longer possible to remain passive, or to go on contented with the system of defence or management which has permitted so many dangerous innovations already. The Church is without defenders in the House of Commons. We have many assailants and reformers of a certain kind there; but we see no body of men who take up our cause and seek to advance it. We have many friends, but they are very quiet and retiring friends, who are led by other parties, and who look to their political connexions before they look to the cause of the Church of England. We have no Montalembert. The same may be said of the House of Lords. There are many excellent bishops and peers; but we have no set of men there endeavouring systematically to push forward the cause of the Church. Nor can it be expected, perhaps, that it should be much otherwise in the House of Lords. In saying this, however, we would not be understood to be insensible of the efforts of some excellent prelates to obtain benefits for the Church. More especially would we acknowledge with gratitude the recent exertions of the Lord Bishop of London to obtain an improvement in the constitution of the appellate tribunal for the decision of causes involving doctrine; the speeches of the Lord Bishop of Chichester and other peers on the education question; and the well-judged efforts of the Earl of Powis, the Bishop of Salisbury, and others, prelates and peers, in reference to the Ecclesiastical Commission Bill. In all this there is much to gratify and encourage; and, could the single point of the re-establishment of Convocation be carried, there could be no further necessity for any voluntary combination of Churchmen; but, until either there is a decided, active, and influential Church interest in the House of Lords or Commons, or until Convocation is *free to act*, we think that it is imperatively necessary that some kind of organization should exist amongst Churchmen.

Undoubtedly there are and will be evils in any such organization. Most happy should we be to see its necessity superseded by the organization of a satisfactory Church party in Parliament, or by the immediate restoration of Convocation with full and unshackled powers of deliberation; but nothing less than one or other of these events, including in the former case the avowed object of obtaining the restoration of the constitutional legislature of the Church, would, in our opinion, justify Churchmen, in respect of their duties to the Church and to its Divine Head, in retiring from the united struggle for religious liberty and security.

We now have the Church Unions as a means of co-operation amongst Churchmen. It is true that they do not represent all parts of the Church. They do, however, represent a very large part, probably the majority. We still trust and hope, and, as far as we may, entreat that the Church Unions will abstain, *as far as possible*, from any language or proceedings calculated to offend and irritate the Evangelical party; because it should be considered that future events may possibly in some degree change their attitude of neutrality into one of co-operation, and the door should be left open as far as possible; and the contest in itself *is not for the purpose of exalting or depressing any party in the Church; but for the purpose of restoring the rights of the Church.* But their co-operation is, we trust, not essential to the success of the Church's cause.

The contest on the subject of education, which has been so perseveringly kept up, is a sufficient proof of what may be effected by zeal and union. Great effects have followed from the agitation of the question so far. The Committee of Council have given way on many points, and every one sees that education will receive a most serious check, unless means be taken to satisfy the Church. We trust that this struggle will be persisted in, with the temper, energy, and firmness which have hitherto characterized it. The evident irritation of the President of the Council on a recent occasion, intimates sufficiently the pressure brought to bear upon the Government. Let that pressure be continued without abatement or respite, and they will give way at length, wearied out.

To this struggle will now be added, we presume, a call for *Convocation*, to settle the baptismal controversy which has arisen, and to act as the permanent legislature of the Church. And in this, we think, there is so much that appeals to the common sense and feeling of all attached members of the Church of England, that it is likely gradually to command general support. The protection of the Church's faith is of quite as much importance and interest as the education question. A Parliament containing Dissenters, Romanists, Quakers, Socinians, and Infidels, is obviously not the proper legislature for Church questions. Every one must acknowledge this, and see that the Repeal of the Test and Corporation Acts, and Roman Catholic Emancipation, have totally changed the character of that body. Independently of which, the call for Convocation appeals to our natural desires for *religious liberty*, and is directed to the recovery of *constitutional rights* long withheld. It is a demand not unsuited to the spirit of the age, appealing on intelligible grounds to the sense of natural justice as well as of religion. We, therefore, anticipate extensive and vigorous support being given to the demand for the liberty of Convocation. This will bring another pressure on Government; and the jealousy with which all its measures will be watched, and, when necessary, opposed and resisted, will at length, if persevered in, bring it to make terms with the Church.

Although, therefore, we deeply regret the quarrelling, dissension, agitation, disturbance, and irritation which now exists, and which must continue to exist and to increase, we regard it as a necessary evil. It all arises simply from the alteration of the State from a " Church of England" character, to indifference in religion; and the want of a fair revision, by the Legislature, of the relations between Church and State, which ought to have followed immediately on the repeal of the Test and Corporation Acts and Roman Catholic Emancipation.

Having thus stated our views on the existing relations of Church and State, and the necessity of considerable alterations,

we must produce a few extracts from the publications mentioned
at the head of this article, with a view to show the questions
which have been stirred up by the operation of the existing state
of things.   We must first quote the following striking passages
from Mr. Dodsworth's publication :—

" If then these things be so, it seems plain, beyond all possibility of
contradiction, that what is now transacting in the highest place in this
kingdom, and to which so much attention is now justly directed, is an
invasion of the Church's office.   It is the civil power interfering in a
matter which does not belong to it, taking cognizance of a matter altogether out of its province ; it is giving unto Cæsar the things which are
God's.   For what are the facts of the case ?   Here is a temporal or
civil court sitting in judgment, with power to confirm or reverse a decision, on matters of doctrine, in the courts of the Church.   I am aware
of what is here said by some, that it is a question of facts rather than of
doctrine ; that the question is not so much what is the doctrine of the
Church of England, as the fitness of the person supposing himself to be
aggrieved to minister at her altars.   It may be replied, that in such a
case it is impossible to separate between facts and doctrines ; that in
deciding upon one the decision must virtually include the other.   For,
since the fitness of the person in question depends upon the accordance
or non-accordance of his doctrines with the doctrines of the Church, it
is impossible to decide upon that fitness without first deciding what the
doctrine of the Church is.

" Others have maintained that it is a matter of property, because the
possession of a living is involved in it.   But this it plainly is not, as
well for other reasons as this, that a temporal court exists in which the
question of property may be rightly settled.

" Others, again, have said that this decision will settle no law of the
Church, but only the interpretation of the law : to which it may be replied, he who finally interprets the law in effect makes it ; for the force
of law obviously depends upon its application.   And this remark most
especially applies where, as in the present case, the Church has no legislative synod to correct the decisions of its law.

" But, without insisting upon these points, I must say that it is too
grave and great a matter to be put aside upon any mere theory, however true.   It is really and practically, in the common-sense view
of a people, themselves pre-eminently practical, an inquiry into doctrine.

" The matter practically to be decided is, whether the doctrine of
baptismal regeneration is the *authoritative* doctrine of the Church of
England : whether it may be taught, not as the private opinion of this
person or that, as the authoritative doctrine of the Church, that our
children are made in baptism the children of God : whether the Church
teaches us to regard them as partakers of spiritual grace, or leaves us to
affirm it, to deny it, or doubt it as we please.   It is indeed, my

brethren, a most vital doctrine that is called in question; one which lies at the foundation of all Christian teaching, and must influence it at every step. And I am heartily glad that this is so: I mean that it is a question of such great moment, and not any smaller matter that is in dispute, because it affords a better hope that the grievous wrongfulness of the proceeding may be clearly seen. For let me ask any fair man of plain common sense, is this a matter suitable to be brought before a temporal court? Is this a matter, right or wrong as the decision may be, in which the Church ought to sit quietly by, and see the State step in and decide for her? A temporal court sitting by temporal authority to decide for us whether we may teach what we believe Christ has enjoined upon us to teach! to decide for us whether or not we are bound to tell you that you lie under the blessing or the burden of the gift of heavenly life!

"Were we to acquiesce in such a state of things, how should we be put to shame by other religious bodies, less blessed and less responsible than ourselves; by bodies to which we have been fain to refuse the name of Church. We have recently seen what sacrifice multitudes of zealous men in the Presbyterian establishment of Scotland were ready to make, and did make, under a supposed invasion of spiritual rights immeasurably less important than this. Whatever might be the merits of their cause, who can but honour the manly stand which they made for what they deemed to be the prerogative of Christ, and of the sacred rights of conscience? And does not every dissenting body in the land assert its right to judge of its own doctrines? Would the Wesleyans, or Independents, or Baptists, or any other sect, endure that the civil power should change one jot or tittle of their peculiar tenets? Nay, is not their dissent for the most part grounded upon their refusal to allow the Church itself to dictate to them in such matters? and can it be a right thing to demand on the part of the State, can it be endurable on the part of the Church, (that body which we must maintain has an exclusive title to spiritual power,) that this intrusion should be made into things sacred, and this violence done to conscience? Can it be intended by the people of this great nation to inflict upon us, nay, and still more upon themselves, so great wrong—to subject us to such a plain and palpable injustice? This surely cannot be. The injury could not be intentional. People have not known of its existence. If the Church be recognized in any sense, or to any extent, as the teacher of the people, it could scarcely be intended thus to degrade her in the eyes of her children; nay, and to rob her of that sacred deposit of the faith, and of the office of being sole keeper of the faith, which she cannot part with without unfaithfulness to Him Who intrusted her with it.

"There is indeed in this case a feature of aggravation, which, though I cannot admit that it enters as an element into the subject of our complaint, may illustrate the magnitude of the evil. I have spoken of the court to which this sacred matter of Christian doctrine is referred, merely as a temporal court, that is, a court sitting by authority only of the temporal power. And on this, I repeat, I would found the strength of the objection to it. This would remain in all its strength, even if all its members were bound under solemn obligations and duties to the Church as her own members. But it must not be overlooked, that according to the existing constitution of this country the members actually sitting to decide such questions may all be dissenters, of any faith, or no faith at all. So, to put a case, and not a very extreme case, it may be on some future occasion that the doctrine of our Lord's true divinity may come to be questioned in the same way that baptismal regeneration now is; and it might be that every member of the court who is to decide it might himself be an unbeliever in the doctrine. Thus a court composed of Socinians would sit to decide whether the Church holds the true doctrine of our Lord's divine nature! Why, surely it only requires that such a serious grievance, involving such fatal results, should be known, in order to be appreciated. Who can defend it? What pious Christian can think of it without horror?"—pp. 12—16.

The subject here more immediately under discussion is one which requires a few remarks. We allude to the constitution and office of the Judicial Committee of Privy Council. We believe that every one feels that the Committee of Council is not a proper tribunal for the decision of doctrinal questions. In the recent decision in the case of Gorham, the Committee itself disclaims any such power; and in truth, with the highest respect for that Committee, it would be perfectly absurd to suppose it invested with any power of the kind. That a body which includes distinguished personages who are not in communion with the Church of England, should be invested with the power of deciding what her doctrines are, would be monstrous. That Lords Brougham and Campbell, Sir Stephen Lushington, &c., should be invested with the power of deciding, without the Bishops of the Church of England, and in opposition to the Bishops if they liked it, what shall and shall not be taught by clergy of the Church, would be really absurd. To give to a certain set of lawyers the power of deciding the faith of the Church of England, would be as reasonable as that system which gives to Messrs. Cobden, Bright, Fox, and O'Connell the power of deciding on her discipline and morality. But, while we say this, we are not prepared to deny that the temporal power may fairly, and legitimately, under certain conditions, take cognizance in its courts of causes which have passed before the Church tribunals. It must be remembered that there are certain temporal rights connected with the occupation of benefices, which have always been admitted to furnish some reason for the interference of the temporal power, in case of appeal from the proceedings of the spiritual power. It has not merely been the custom in England to admit such appeal, which is continually made to the Court of Queen's Bench, and without any objection, as far as we have observed; but the very same practice prevails, and has for ages prevailed in every country of Christendom. In all Roman Catholic countries, just as much as in England, appeals are made to temporal courts from spiritual, that is, in fact, to the Crown. So that the supremacy of the Crown or the State (whatever be the form of government) is more or less admitted or enforced, in practice, in all parts of the world. We think, however, that it is perfectly obvious that such appeal must be to the temporal power, not as invested by God with the power of deciding grave questions of controversy in the Church, but for the purpose of correcting manifest excesses in the action of the Spiritual Courts; such excesses as argue a plain want of justice, or an evident partiality; or an infringement on ordinary rights and liberties. The principle of an appeal so guarded will, we think, be conceded by every one, not only as fair in itself, but as consistent with the practice of Christian Churches and States from the period when the State became Christian.

Nay, there is even a higher power than this in Christian states; for we maintain, that ecclesiastical history shows throughout, that Christian princes have interfered in general controversies on matters of faith; and have often acted most effectively and with the approbation of all good Churchmen, for the suppression of heresy and schisms. Need we refer to the General Councils which were convened by Christian princes, and confirmed by their laws? Constantine the Great received appeals from the decrees of Synods, and commanded causes to be reheard by Bishops, thus exercising, without dispute, a supreme power in Ecclesiastical causes. But in all these cases, the temporal power never arrogated *to itself* the decision of controversies in matters of faith or general discipline. It availed itself always of the constituted authorities in the Church.—It recognized in them the commission given by Jesus Christ to teach the Gospel. It did not take on itself the office of teaching in the Church; and we are borne out by the Thirty-seventh Article, in saying, that such is not the office of Christian sovereigns.

Where matters of form, or regularity of proceeding, or moral conduct of individuals, or other points not affecting the faith, morality, or discipline of the Church, as a body, are in question, the State is competent to receive appeals from Church tribunals, and to decide them in its ordinary courts, constituted as it may deem most advisable for the ends of justice. The Judicial Committee of Council appears to us very well calculated to exercise the powers of the State in all such matters, and we should be satisfied with any similar tribunal to which the State might devolve its power in these causes. The language of St. Paul, (1 Cor. vi.

2—5,) appears to render it a matter of indifference who may judge in minor matters of difference between man and man.

But the case is widely different when the cause refers to the doctrines of the Gospel—when it relates to the teaching of doctrine, *viz.* the general belief, discipline, or morality of the Church. Here we have in the Scriptures the precedent of the Assembly of the Apostles, Elders, and Brethren at Jerusalem, (Acts xv.) to guide us. Such matters are of vital importance, and are not to be submitted to the ordinary tribunals. The Committee of Council, or any similar body consisting merely of State functionaries, or persons skilled in the law of the land, is evidently unfitted to decide here. The aid of the Church itself must be invoked, *i. e.* the State is bound to call in and avail itself of the judgment of the Bishops of the Church ; and this is, we think, fairly provided for by the Bill of the Bishop of London now before Parliament. It is difficult to speak positively on such questions without full consideration. We think that, if such a tribunal is to be established, it would be *desirable* that the subject should be discussed in Convocation. But, at the same time, we are not prepared to say, that the consent of Convocation is necessary to give validity to the acts of such a tribunal as the Bishop of London proposes. The State is bound, in justice, and in prudence too, not to attempt to decide questions involving doctrine, without the Bishops of the Church, or a sufficient proportion of them *fairly* chosen. But if the tribunal proposed by the Bishop of London were conceded, we are really of opinion, that the Church ought to be contented with the arrangement, as far as the exercise of the temporal power in such a court is concerned.

Having premised these remarks, we have to notice some resolutions proposed at a meeting of an influential Church Union, previously to the decision on the Gorham case. They are as follows :—

" Resolved—

" 1. That by the suit of Gorham *v.* the Bishop of Exeter, now pending by appeal in the Judicial Committee of the Privy Council, as well as by the case of Mastin *v.* Escott, in the year 1842, it appears that the State exercises a power to confirm, reverse, or vary, by a final judicial sentence, the decisions and interpretations of the courts of the Church in matters of doctrine.

" 2. That a power to interpret the formularies of the Church by a final and definitive judgment (the Synod of the Church not being, in practice, admitted to declare the doctrine of the Church irrespective of such sentence,) becomes, in effect, a power to declare and to make such interpretations binding on the Church.

" 3. That while the fullest confidence may be placed in the integrity and legal ability of the Judges in the case now pending, nevertheless no judgment can be pronounced by them either one way or the other, without affirming the false principle on which, in reference to spiritual matters, the tribunal itself is constituted.

"4. That whereas, the Universal Church alone possesses, by the commission and command of its Divine Founder, the power of defining in matter of doctrine; and, subject to the same, particular Churches alone possess, within their sphere, the power of interpreting and declaring, by final judicial sentence, the intention of such definitions as the Universal Church has framed, it appears that the power claimed and exercised by the State, through the Judicial Committee, in taking cognizance of doctrinal questions, is contrary to the law of CHRIST.

" 5. That in the present state of the law nothing hinders but that an interpretation of doctrine judged to be unsound by the Courts of the Church may be finally declared sound by the Judicial Committee; or that a person who shall have been judged to be unfit for cure of souls by the spiritual tribunal may be declared fit for cure of souls by the civil power.

" 6. That the existence of such a state of the law cannot be reconciled with the Divine constitution and office of the Church.

" 7. That the exercise of power in such matters under such state of the law endangers the public maintenance of the Faith of CHRIST.

" 8. That the existence of such a state of things constitutes a grievance of conscience.

" 9. That for the redress of such grievance the following steps are necessary:—

" (1.) That the Church in Convocation or Synod deliberate for the special purpose of devising A PROPER TRIBUNAL for determining all questions of doctrine, and other matters purely spiritual; whether they arise directly in the way of ordinary trial and appeal, or incidentally in proceedings before the temporal courts.

" (2.) That an Act of Parliament be passed for the purpose of making the judgment or the certificate of such tribunal binding on the temporal courts of these realms.

" (3.) That the Acts of Parliament relating to the Privy Council be so amended as to exempt questions of doctrine and other matters purely spiritual from the cognizance of the Privy Council."

It will be observed here, that the objection raised to the Committee of Council is founded on the suppression of the constitutional legislature of the Church, which gives to the Supreme Executive *Court* an *authority* in matters of doctrine that it ought not to possess. It is not, we apprehend, that the compilers of the above resolutions mean to deny the propriety of the State, through its constituted tribunals, taking cognizance of Church causes; but what is objected to is, that the State is permitted *virtually* in this way to declare the faith of the Church, because the Church cannot herself speak at all. This is the real evil and danger of our present position. When the Church assented to the regal supremacy in such causes, it was never contemplated that the State would suppress the voice of the Church, and by an arbitrary exercise of power, reduce her Convocations to silence for an hundred and thirty years. It was never supposed that the State would thus deprive the Church of those religious liberties which the law and constitution give her. The State has, we think, no *moral right* to call for the recognition of those powers conferred on it by law, until the Church has been restored to the exercise—the full and unfettered exercise of *her* rights. Let the Church have her Convocation to which she has a legal and constitutional right, of which she has too long been deprived; and then it will not be of much consequence as to the particular shape which the State gives to its supreme tribunal. The Church in Convocation will watch over her own faith.

We have perused in the "Guardian" some letters from Messrs. Allies and Henry Wilberforce on the subject of the authority of the Committee of Council. Mr. Allies says:—

" In the question of Church and State now raised by the Gorham case, a clear view of first principles is so very important, that I venture to address to you a few lines on what appears to me a radical mistake, affecting the whole question, which is contained in your leading article of last Wednesday.

" You observe, 'It now appears, by the matter-of-fact issue of things, what that Court of Appeal, to which the Church assented at the Reformation, really was. It was a *bona fide* Church Court; not a State Court. It was a Court of ecclesiastics, *appointed indeed by the Crown*, but which, when met, dictated to the Crown; the Crown not professing to judge itself upon doctrine, but accepting the decisions of the ecclesiastics.'

" Neither does the Crown profess to judge itself upon the law of the land, but accepts the decisions of the Courts of Chancery, of Queen's Bench, of Exchequer, of Common Pleas. Yet are they no less State Courts. Nay, there was a time when the judges of those Courts were ecclesiastics; yet they were no less State Courts then.

" I assert, then, as a proposition self-evident, when stated, to every Churchman, but likewise borne witness to by the principles, the acts, and the position of the Church for eighteen hundred years, that the whole question, whether any particular Court be a Church Court or a State Court, depends upon this one point, *whence it receives its jurisdiction*.

" For instance, the Court of the Dean of Arches is a Spiritual Court, for it receives its jurisdiction from the Archbishop of Canterbury. It matters nothing that the judge is a layman.

" The Court of the Judicial Committee of the Privy Council is a

State Court, because it derives its jurisdiction from the civil power. That the judges actually sitting in it are laymen, matters nothing. If the civil power had commissioned, instead of six laymen, as many bishops, or the whole bench of bishops, to sit as judges, the Court would have been no less a State Court, for the bishops would have sat as commissioners of the civil power, and not in virtue of their inherent right as successors of the Apostles.

" On the other hand, if the Church in synod had commissioned the present six judges of the Privy Council, or any others, to void the question touching Mr. Gorham, it would have been a Church Court.

" So little does the fact, whether the judges are ecclesiastics, matter *in principle*, that if the Church were to appoint six infidels, were such a thing morally possible, their jurisdiction would be valid.

" Accordingly, the Court of Delegates, appointed by the 28th Henry VIII., was a State Court, for it derived its jurisdiction from the civil and not from the spiritual power. No doubt, the appointment of ecclesiastics did then, and would again, disguise the evil, and the Church is more plainly insulted by the nomination of laymen ; but the *principle* is the same.

"The whole question, therefore, at issue between the Church and the State resolves itself into this,—*Where is the source of spiritual jurisdiction ?*

" Let us make it an A B case, discarding the remotest appearance of personalities.

" Surely, then, the source of spiritual jurisdiction all over the earth, whether in England, or France, or Germany, or Russia, or the United States, or Turkey, does not lie in the civil power. Our Lord has not given the keys of the kingdom of heaven to any authority of this world; neither to absolute nor to constitutional monarchs ; neither to parliaments nor to democracies ; nor to any power compounded of them, or derived from them. Whether the civil authority in a State is exercised by the one or the many, neither the one nor the many have any right to spiritual jurisdiction."

Mr. Wilberforce argues in the following way :—

" 1. The Bishop of London's measure does not touch the pending Gorham case, but leaves the State to settle that and the questions which it raises, without regard to the fact that they have already been settled by the Church.

" 2. For the future, it provides that a new Court shall be constituted by purely state and political authority (for the mention of Convocation is merely the expression of a wish, not a practical proposal), the members of which shall be six Bishops, four theologians, and some lawyers, and that the Court thus constituted shall decide future doctrinal appeals from the Court of the Archbishop.

" I observe, then—

" 1. Any Court established merely by Parliamentary authority is a

secular and State Court, though its members may undoubtedly be
ecclesiastics.   The personal fitness of a judge is one question, the
authority by which he sits another.   The Committee of Council are (in
theological questions) personally unqualified to judge, and also un-
authorised by the Church to so.   The members of the proposed Court,
however they may be held to be personally qualified, will have no
higher authority than the Committee of Council.   The one is, the other
will be, a Court sitting by the authority of an Act of Parliament, and in
the name of the Queen, i. e. a secular Court.

"2. The personal fitness of the proposed judges is not secured by
the Church, but conceded by the State.   Queen Elizabeth appointed as
Chancellor a mere courtier, Hatton, and Charles II. a political intriguer,
Shaftesbury.   If the Queen should issue an order in Council binding
herself and her successors to appoint none but ' barristers of five years'
standing,' the Court of Chancery would not be less a Queen's Court.
At the present moment the good sense of English statesmen is revolted
by an arrangement which has set Lords Langdale and Campbell to
decide upon the doctrine of baptism ; and they propose, in future, to
remedy this absurdity by authorising men whom they believe to be
personally competent to the task, to decide in the name and in behalf
of the State what shall be the doctrine of the Church of England.   This
is all.

"I have hitherto argued on the supposition that the proposed Court
is all that could be desired if it were authorised by the Church ; although,
if established by the State, as seems to be intended, it will have no
authority at all in matters sacred.   But I think it may be easily shown
that, if the assent of the Church were asked for its establishment, that
assent ought to be refused.

"Not to mention several other grave objections, both to the principle
and details of the bill; the only authority which, by the laws of the
Church, could be superior to that of the Archbishop's Court is the
synod of the Provincial Bishops.   For this strictly ecclesiastical body
the proposed plan would substitute a court of six Bishops, three lay
judges, and four professors.   Thus, not merely is a fourth part of the
Provincial Synod invested with the authority of the whole, but that
part is made a minority in the Court.   The plan is wholly uncatholic.
But a more serious objection is, that the Gorham case, with all its
momentous issues, is left to be decided again by the State, after the
Church has determined it."

Now it will be observed that, in both these passages, the objection raised to the Committee of Council, or to any proposed
tribunal to be appointed by the temporal power, is that it is a
temporal tribunal, deriving its jurisdiction from the State; and
that the position is laid down, that the spiritual power alone has
any right to decide in any spiritual causes.   Now we cannot go to
this length, which is, in our opinion, inconsistent with the general

practice of the Church. We cannot deny to the temporal power the right of interfering, *in a proper way*, with Church questions. We deny that it has the right by itself of deciding controversies of faith; but we maintain that the most Christian sovereign might, with strict propriety, and consistently with Catholic principles, do justice in cases of appeal, even on doctrinal matters, with the advice and judgment of Bishops fairly and honestly chosen; and we think there could be no practical evils worth mentioning in *such* a temporal court, provided the Church were free to legislate and to decide in matters of doctrine. We must be careful lest, in our natural repugnance to the decision of controversies by a secular tribunal, we should take up positions which are untenable. We must be careful not to give our enemies any advantage, by permitting them to wield the authority of canon, and statute, and precedent, against the *principle* we maintain. The following remarks, extracted from Mr. Irons' able, sound, and most timely pub cat on, in which he satisfactorily shows the real meaning and intëntion of the Church in acknowledging the supremacy of the Crown, will be perused with interest in connexion with this matter :—

" There must, however, be owned to be most serious defects, not only in such a tribunal of appeal as this which is proposed, but in all our Church acts, if we persist in trying to go on, on the *present* theory of the union of Church and State. I am not insensible of the fact, that the ecclesiastical system of England is intimately interwoven with our whole social fabric,—that is in truth, with the most advanced form of civilization which the world has yet seen. It can be no light matter to intermeddle with—it must be done with conscience and caution, but not at hazard: but it cannot remain where it is; and, if we are not alive to this, it will soon become an absurdity.

" Let any one look, for instance, at the canons of the Church; or again, at the fact, that the existence of non-conformity is ignored at one time (as by the law of church-rates, and the forced administration of Church rites to Dissenters); at another time recognized by every kind of legislation. Or, once more, let any one contemplate the fact, that statesmen are hoping to raise, and educate, and keep in order a people, by means of a Church whom they degrade and suspect, and treat as if destitute of conscience, and ask, can this state of things endure? . . . What remedy can be hoped for, for our whole position, until the Church herself shall meet and act in synod?

" For myself, I am free to confess that the overthrow, political or religious, of the Church of England seems to me, when I try to realize it (after I have just risen from the perusal of some revolutionary speech), as the greatest calamity that can befall civilization and Christianity. . . . If such a convulsion is to be saved, it can only be by a thoughtful and voluntary modification of our relations with the State.

o 2

The recent reckless defiance of the conscience of the Church, the infatuated oppression of us by the State, has forced on a crisis, which a different treatment by a wise and religious government might have long avoided. •

"I suppose every one can see that it is only a question of time, whether the bishops continue in parliament; whether the remains of the royal supremacy be swept away; whether church-rates be abolished; and the like. Woe unto England, if, before these things come to pass, we have not FREEDOM FOR THE CHURCH in synod to manage her doctrines, her ministers, and her property for herself, like all other religious bodies."—pp. 53, 54.

To attempt any longer to go on maintaining unreformed a system of relations between Church and State, which is each year stimulating the Church to greater and more violent struggles, and which is therefore enabling her enemies, through her weakness, continually to gain more and more upon her, is real infatuation. There *must* be a reform in the relations of Church and State,— such a reform as shall preserve the supremacy of the Crown with the modifications and safeguards which the legislation of 1828 and 1829 render essential. For that reform we must never cease to struggle; and we believe that it is not far distant. Let no one despair of success; because a cause, founded on plain and *obvious justice* and *common sense*, cannot fail in this day, if urged with unceasing perseverance.

Art. VIII.—1. *A Speech delivered in the House of Commons on Thursday, May 3, 1849, on the Motion for the Second Reading of Mr. Stuart Wortley's Bill for Altering the Law of Marriage.* By ROUNDELL PALMER, Q.C., M.A., *late Fellow of Magdalen College, Oxford, M.P. for Plymouth.* Oxford: J. H. Parker.

2. *An Examination of the Scriptural Grounds on which the Prohibition against Marriage with a Deceased Wife's Sister is based.* By JOHN DARLING, M.A., *Barrister at Law.* London: Rivingtons.

3. *A Summary of the Chief Arguments for and against Marriage with a Deceased Wife's Sister.* London: Houlston and Stoneman.

ALTHOUGH Mr. Stuart Wortley has succeeded this year in pressing forward his measure for the alteration of the Marriage Laws at so early a period of the session, that a very great advantage has been gained by the advocates of that measure, we avail ourselves of the earliest opportunity to record a distinct and energetic protest against an alteration which is calculated to have the most dangerous effects on public morality, and which would place the law of the land in opposition to that which the Church of England believes to be the law of God. Mr. Wortley has endeavoured, to a certain extent, to remove the objections against the measure, as directly interfering with the discipline of the Church of England. We shall hereafter see what value there is in the concession made by the present measure. But we must first advance objections of a more general nature to the proposal.

We have, on a former occasion, stated the grounds on which we entirely concur with those who hold that the marriage of a widower with his deceased wife's sister is forbidden by God's law. In this doctrine it is needless to say, that we are only following the belief of the Church of England herself, since, in the ninety-ninth canon of 1604, she declares as follows :—

"No one shall marry within the degrees *prohibited by the laws of God*, and expressed in a table set forth, *by authority*, in the year of our Lord God 1563. And all marriages so made and contracted shall be adjudged *incestuous* and unlawful, and consequently shall be dissolved, *as void from the beginning*, and the parties so married shall by course of law be *separated.* And the aforesaid table shall be in every Church publicly set up and fixed at the charge of the parish."

Now, it may be very easy for the advocates of Mr. Wortley's Bill to say, that this canon is not legally binding on the laity, and that the Church of England may have been in error in making such statements; but the question is—Has not the Church of England, in the above canon, declared in the most unequivocal manner her belief, that the marriages forbidden by the table of prohibited degrees are " prohibited by the laws of God," and are " incestuous," and "void from the beginning?" And, with this declaration patent to all the world, how can the Church of England consent that such marriages should be contracted, or, if contracted, in any way sanctioned, or recognized, or allowed? Can she consent to have any part in what she has declared " incestuous?" Would not any, the very slightest sanction or permission on her part to contract such marriages, or to continue in them, be made, and justly made, an immediate ground of attack upon her, as most grossly inconsistent, or most utterly unprincipled?

We have hitherto, in respect of the Marriage Law, acted on those moral principles which have subsisted even from the earliest ages in the Church, were re-asserted by Archbishops Cranmer, Parker, and all the English Reformers in opposition to Papal laxity and corruption; were continued, as they had always been, in our ecclesiastical laws; were fenced round by repeated Acts of Parliament made at the time of the Reformation; and have continued in full and uninterrupted force and obligation to the present moment.

We are now called on to reverse the laws of the Church and State—not in some matter of mere human regulation, not in some matter of mere external discipline, of changeable rites and ceremonies; but on a point in which GOD's LAW is at stake—on a point in which the judgment of the Church of England, on a great point of Christian *morality*, is in question.

We must here be permitted to refer to the able arguments of Mr. Roundell Palmer, member for Plymouth, in his speech last year on Mr. Wortley's Bill. The Scriptural argument is thus treated:—

" Now first, to introduce this argument, let us look at the table of prohibited degrees. That table contains *thirty* degrees in all, within which marriage is prohibited; with only *two* of which the right honourable member for Bute now proposes to interfere. Of those thirty degrees, *only fourteen are prohibited in express terms in the Book of Leviticus;* the intermarriages of father and daughter, uncle and niece, and others more remote, both in consanguinity and in affinity, are among those not in terms forbidden; and there are, therefore, *not less than sixteen degrees, a majority of the whole table, including several of near consanguinity*, which must be abandoned, if those who support the prohibitions are not permitted to argue from something more than the naked, dry letter of Scripture,—if they are not allowed to collect one prohibition from another, to construct a consistent system upon the principles indicated by the instances given in Scripture, and to look to the general tenor and effect of the whole passage of Scripture in which the prohibitions are found. I would ask the House to approach this argument, not in the spirit of sophistry,—

'I cannot find it; 'tis not in the bond;'

but in the spirit of those who wish *bonâ fide* to look to the law of God, fairly to collect its meaning, and to submit themselves to it fully and implicitly. Before referring to any authorities, I will deal with the text; and the House will judge whether the argument, on these principles, is not at least sufficiently probable to make them pause before they depart from a rule of interpretation which has been recognized in the legislation of all Christendom down to the present time.

The first point to be considered is, whether the Levitical prohibitions are applicable as a rule for Christians, or only for the Jews. The right honourable gentleman does not (as I understand) dispute that they are generally binding upon Christians as part of the moral law; his Bill, certainly, does not propose so extensive an alteration of the law as would follow from a denial of this principle, though it is denied by some of his witnesses, and by some of his advocates in this House. As the prohibitions themselves stand in the Book of Leviticus, this point would seem to be free from doubt, because they are introduced by a preamble referring to the practices of heathen nations, which the Jews were not to follow; and the instances of prohibited marriage, together with a few other practices of a different kind, having been enumerated, all these things are spoken of as abominations and defilements, and causes of penal judgments, not in the Jews, but in the Gentile nations who were not subject to the peculiar Jewish law. Assuming, then, that the prohibitions are moral, and of general application, what are they? They begin with a general principle thus laid down :—' None of you shall approach to any that is near of kin to him :' and the question is, where that principle is to be limited? A number of cases are enumerated, some of consanguinity, some of affinity, showing that affinity is here clearly included in the notion of kindred; and among the enumerated cases there is an express general prohibition of marriage with a brother's wife. The enumerated cases do not exhaust more than half the instances which the common reason of mankind perceives to fall within the same principle; the common reason of mankind requires the application under such circumstances of these principles, that the more remote includes the nearer, that equal implies equal, and that the rule laid down as to a man shall govern the converse case of a woman, where the degree of propinquity is exactly the same, and nothing but the sex is different. On these principles of interpretation our table of prohibited degrees is founded; and marriage with a wife's

sister is held to be prohibited, because it is the exact converse of the
marriage, expressly prohibited, with a husband's brother.   But the argument from the text of Scripture does not stop here.   In the 17th
verse of the chapter, a man is expressly forbidden to marry 'a woman
and her daughter,' or to take 'her son's daughter or her daughter's
daughter;' because '*they are her near kinswomen; it is wickedness.*'
It is wickedness, therefore, to marry the *near kinswoman* of a wife ;
and, for that reason only, marriages with a wife's mother, daughter, or
grandaughter (none of which marriages the right honourable gentleman
proposes to legalise), are forbidden.   But is not a wife's sister her near
kinswoman ?   Does not the common sense of mankind answer that
question ?   Or, if it must be strictly proved that a sister is a near kinswoman in the sense of this passage, look at the 12th and 13th verses,
where marriage with a father's sister, or a mother's sister, is prohibited,
'*because she is thy father's*' (or, 'thy mother's') '*near kinswoman.*'
If the father's sister is the father's near kinswoman, the wife's sister is
the near kinswoman of the wife ; and, if it be 'wickedness' to marry
the wife's near kinswoman (as the 17th verse expressly says it is), how
can it be otherwise than wickedness to marry the wife's sister ?"

The favourite text of the advocates of this measure is thus
satisfactorily disposed of :—

"If the passage had ended here, I cannot think any logical reasoner,
or any serious Christian, could have entertained a moment's doubt that
the prohibitions of this chapter extend to the case of a deceased wife's
sister.   But it is said that the next verse (the 18th) is in these terms :—
'Neither shalt thou take a wife to her sister, to vex her, beside the
other, in her lifetime ;' and the argument is, that in this verse the prohibition of marriage with a wife's sister is limited to the wife's lifetime,
and that permission to marry a wife's sister after her death is, therefore,
implied.   I pause for a moment to notice the very unfair way in which
it has been continually represented, that the argument *for* the prohibition rests upon this verse.   The fact is precisely the contrary :—it is
upon this verse, and upon this translation of it, and upon this inference
from the verse so translated, that the argument *against* the prohibition
entirely and exclusively rests.   Take this verse away, and, as I have already shown, this prohibition must of necessity be inferred from the unambiguous language of the previous verses.   Before, therefore, we suffer
that conclusion to be shaken by any inference from this 18th verse, as it
stands translated in the text of our English Bibles, it is not immaterial to
inquire whether that translation is certainly correct and free from doubt.
When the argument from that verse was lately insisted upon before the
Court of Queen's Bench, by parties who then sought to persuade that
Court that marriage with a deceased wife's sister was not prohibited by the
existing law, Lord Chief Justice Denman made these pertinent observations :—'If I am to be the judge to pass a judgment upon the meaning
of the Scriptures, am I bound by any particular translation of them?
That is one of the stumbling-blocks at the very threshold of such an

inquiry, and we have witnessed the effect of it upon the present occasion. Six different interpretations have been put upon the text of Scripture, as it presents itself to us in the Old Testament.'

" Six different interpretations had been put upon that 18th verse in the discussion before the court of law. I do not, however propose to detain the House by referring to more than one of them; and I refer to that, because it is an interpretation resting, not on any private or conjectural criticism, but on the authority of the translators of the English Bible themselves. Those translators have themselves told us in the margin, that there is room for doubting the accuracy of the version which they have adopted in the text; they have warned us not to rely upon inferences drawn merely from that translation, by telling us in the margin that the verse may with equal propriety be rendered, ' *Thou shalt not take one wife to another*, to vex her, in her lifetime.' Adopt that reading, and the verse ceases to bear upon the question now before the House: it refers to the subject of polygamy, and not of incest; and is a prohibition of polygamy under circumstances which tend to the vexation or infraction of the rights of the first wife. That this is the real meaning of the verse was the opinion of Schleusner and of other very considerable Hebrew scholars; and the verse so rendered would correspond in sense with another precept which we find in the book of Exodus, concerning a maid-servant married by her master or her master's son: ' If he take him another wife, her food, her raiment, and her duty of marriage, shall he not diminish.' The form of expression with which the verse is introduced, and the great preponderance of arguments from probability, appear also to favour this sense; for the reading even in the received text is not, 'Thou shalt not take *her sister to thy wife*,' but, ' Thou shalt not *take a wife* to her sister;' and if polygamy were allowed in all other cases, and marriage with a wife's sister were allowed after her death, it would be difficult to conceive any consistent and satisfactory reason why, among these moral precepts of universal obligation, a marriage with two sisters at once, like that of the patriarch Jacob, should be specially forbidden. Without, therefore, troubling the House with any philological disquisition, I think I have at least stated sufficient ground for the conclusion that a prohibition, clearly and certainly collected from the first seventeen verses of this chapter, cannot safely or reasonably be set aside in favour of an inference drawn from the letter of the 18th verse as it stands translated in the text of the English Bible, but which inference cannot be drawn either from the letter or the spirit of the same verse as it is translated in the margin—an inference which the translators themselves did not draw, because they unquestionably held the Levitical prohibitions to be correctly expounded by the table of prohibited degrees."

It were the merest and most shallow sophistry to compare alterations which time or legislation has introduced into the laws of the Church, on minor points of ceremony and order, with such a question as is now before us. Until the Church of England has declared in Convocation that she has altered her views on the *religious obligation* of the table of prohibited degrees, it is a most extreme injury to that Church to attempt any alteration in the law. The effect of an alteration, such as is now proposed, would be to place the laws of the land and the laws of the Church in direct collision. The State would say, on the one hand, to the people of England, that they are fully at liberty to contract certain marriages,—that they incur no risk either from God's or man's laws in so doing. The Church, on the contrary, would teach in every parish church throughout the kingdom, that these very marriages were forbidden by God's law. She would be bound to suspend and depose those of her clergy who celebrated such marriages. She would be obliged to refuse to admit persons guilty of them to the sacrament ; she would be obliged to consider these unions unhallowed and null, even while they were valid by the laws of the land. She would be obliged to take all measures to separate the guilty parties, under penalty of excommunication, while the laws of the land would forbid such persons to cease their cohabitation, and would compel them by force to continue in their unhallowed union.

There can be no doubt of what the present law of the Church of England is in these respects. Even if the statutes on the subject were all repealed to-morrow, her own laws and canons would suffice to punish severely any clergyman officiating at such marriages, would dissolve such marriages on penalty of excommunication, and would require communion to be refused to those guilty of them. This is the undoubted state of things in the Church of England, irrespective of any statutes whatever. If therefore the Church of England is to retain her laws and rights inviolate in this matter, as the advocates of the measure pretend, no such marriages can possibly take place by the aid of her clergy, or be recognized in any way. Her courts must dissolve them when formed, and she must in every way condemn them. Is the Church of England to be at liberty to do this still! If she is *not* at liberty to do it, her laws are grossly interfered with. She is told that she may *continue* to regard these marriages as "incestuous," and yet she is to be tied up from putting an end to them. She is to be compelled to recognize as valid, marriages which she believes to be contrary to God's law ; and—monstrous inconsistency !— by the very Act which so far acknowledges her belief and her laws, that it expressly abstains from sheltering her clergy from the punishment due to them, if they take part in performing such marriages ! Now, we would really put it to the ingenious compilers of this Bill, whether they mean to say, that actions which the Church forbids the clergy to take part in as "incestuous" can possibly, with any shadow of consistency, be permitted to the laity. Are the laity at full liberty to commit incest, while the clergy are to be punished for taking any part in sanctioning it? If the clergy deserve punishment for sanctioning incest, what would the Church *herself* deserve for administering the sacraments to her members guilty of incest, or permitting them to remain in her communion, unless they repent and abstain from their sin? If the courts of the Church are to be interfered with, as this Bill proposes to do, so as to prevent any proceedings to be taken against persons guilty of contracting such incestuous marriages, what is it but to say, that the Church shall take no steps for the purpose of removing sin and scandal from her own communion,— that she shall extend her favour to persons guilty of a gross sin, as if they were innocent? We know that the corrective discipline of the Church has fallen too much into disuse, and that this very circumstance has been one of the commonest arguments against her in the mouths of Dissenters of all kinds; but what new force such an argument must acquire, if almost the only remaining point in which discipline is still in force, and in which some check is interposed to the tide of licentiousness and passion, is forcibly and deliberately broken through by Act of Parliament, overriding and bearing down the religious principles of the Church of England, and at the very moment too that it recognizes the force of those principles!

If the author of this Bill assume the ground that such marriages are perfectly allowable by God's law, and that the Church of England is not in any way committed against them, why do they still leave the clergy subject to penalties for performing marriages which they themselves acknowledge to be perfectly innocent and Christian? If the object be to avoid any interference with the doctrine and discipline of the Church of England, why are that doctrine and discipline interfered with as regards the *laity?* To say that there is no interference by the present Bill would be most untrue. There is a gross and palpable interference with the Ecclesiastical Courts, and with the ninety-ninth canon. The Church is tied up from vindicating her principles of morality, and is compelled to recognize incestuous marriages. We are not certain, indeed, whether Clergy themselves would not be at liberty to *contract* such marriages, though they could not celebrate them! At all events, we should be placed in the ridiculously inconsistent position of seeing prosecutions of clergy going on for performing incestuous marriages, which, when performed, we were bound to admit and recognize as perfectly proper and legal. We should be seeing clergy refusing the holy sacrament to persons who were joined in lawful wedlock, on the ground that they were living in incest. Every conscientious clergyman would be placed in this most painful position. He would appear to be acting most tyrannically, and yet he would only be doing his duty. He would be liable to be taxed with disobedience to the laws of the land, when he was acting most righteously.

Mr. Wortley might just as reasonably call on the Church of England at once to license fornication. We affirm that fornication is a sin of inferior guilt to incest. We maintain that adultery is not a greater sin. If the Church of England is to be *required by law* to abstain from all attempts to remove incest from her communion, then we say that, *à fortiori*, she might be required to permit fornication amongst her members, and, *à pari*, adultery. Shall fornication and adultery be unlicensed, when incest is licensed? There seems no adequate reason why this latter sin should be taken up with such special favour, and patronized by the law of the land, while other and lesser sins, of the same genus, are left unprotected.

But to pass on to another branch of the subject. It is admitted that it is desirable to keep up *some* restrictions on marriage. In short, Mr. Wortley and the present advocates of the Bill are quite willing that the law should remain as it is in all respects but one. The opulent and titled personages, for whose relief this measure is pushed forwards, have no views of an *extensive* nature. They are not radical reformers. They do not go to the root of the question, and determine how many of the degrees are prohibited by merely human authority, and attempt to obtain general liberty for *all* who are restrained from the gratification of their wishes. Far from it. Our Reformers, in the present case, have no such large and philanthropic views. Their exertions—their money—their petitions—their solicitors, are all employed for a definite and limited purpose—*the legitimizing of their own bastard issue!* There is a species of *paternal* interest, and of anxiety for family *honour* and respectability in this, that is excessively amusing. Certain men have illegitimate children; they wish to make them cease to be bastards—it is a slur upon them. They subscribe for the purpose, and a Bill is brought into Parliament, which conceals their actual object under an attempt at general legislation. " The feeling of the country is against it." No matter. " The Church denounces it." No matter. " The laws of Church and State, from the earliest ages and the Reformation itself, are against it." No matter. There is money enough to push it on again and again; and by perseverance, it is hoped, it may succeed. We really think the history of the present Bill is without parallel in the annals of English legislation. A more grossly partial, selfish, and corrupt proceeding we never yet heard of.

Such as it is, however, it does not profess to interfere, beyond the selfish objects of its promoters, with the table of prohibited degrees. That table they wish to remain in force. We all wish so too. We are not yet prepared to see mothers and sons, brothers and sisters, joined in wedlock; so that every one would wish to keep up the table of prohibited degrees. But, if this measure should pass, we cannot see any reason why the alteration should stop there. Precisely the same arguments may be hereafter brought forward in other cases. Persons may contract marriages within other prohibited degrees in large numbers. They are likely to do so if a breach is now made in the table of degrees. It may then be alleged that it is a grievance to have their children illegitimate. Money may, and undoubtedly *will*, be subscribed, and precisely the same kind of agitation will be again attempted. To break through the table in one point is to set the public mind fermenting on the subject of marriage regulations, and no one can tell where inquiry might lead men. It might lead to a great variety of questions, most dangerous to morality and most injurious to domestic peace.

There is another view of the question which is, perhaps, not the least important, in its bearing upon the Church, and the State too. A large portion of the Church is extremely dissatisfied at the present relations of Church and State. It has been deeply disgusted by ecclesiastical appointments, injurious, in its opinion, to the Church's faith. It has been recently offended by the decision of a temporal court on matters of very important doctrine. It has witnessed, with the highest dissatisfaction and distrust, the attempts of the Committee of Council to interfere in the regulation of Church schools, and more than suspects the intention of the State to press an infidel system of education. In the midst of all the ferment and excitement caused by these circumstances, this Bill of Mr. Wortley proposes to subvert the doctrine which the Church of England has always hitherto held on the subject of marriage. It proposes further to narrow and fetter her liberties. It proposes to tie up her hands from punishing vice and immorality. And it does all this in the face of the *admitted* hostility of the great mass of the clergy. Very well— what will be the effect? Let this Bill pass, and it will only add double vigour to the agitation which prevails. It will be another item in the catalogue of wrongs done to the Church by the State. It will be only another argument—and a potent and affecting one—in the hands of those who claim liberty for the

Church, and demand, as a matter of right, that the ecclesiastical legislation of the Church of England shall be released from the unconstitutional and arbitrary power which has so long shackled and silenced it. We know not whether the Government wish to give power to the agitation which has for some time existed in the Church. If they do so, they cannot, we firmly believe, take a more effectual way than by supporting Mr. Wortley's Bill. Measures of this kind will work their own cure before long.

We protest, on behalf of the Church, against the passing of this, or of *any further measures whatever* affecting the Church, without the consent of that Church in Convocation. We claim this, as a matter of common justice and constitutional right. The protest of Churchmen on this and similar subjects may be disregarded; it may be thrust aside; it may be treated with contempt. But it will be henceforward repeated again and again; and each blow that is aimed against the Church will only nerve the resolution of men, in the struggle for her liberation from a position of danger and difficulty. Her perplexities all arise from her relations to the State. Could these be adjusted, in accordance with the altered character of the State legislature, all would be quiet again.

We trust that, amidst the great pressure of other novel and more immediately exciting causes of alarm, Churchmen will not permit this bill of Mr. Wortley's to proceed on its course without offering every opposition to it in their power. We hope that petitions against it will not be overlooked; but that as many as possible will be immediately sent to both Houses. It is really a great hardship that people will not let the Church alone. If they go on meddling with it, they will yet repent their folly. They are rousing a spirit which will give them plenty to do. The Church of England has hitherto been passive generally, but a long series of injuries and outrages is beginning to work its effect at length. In that catalogue the present Bill is not the least item : its peculiarly obnoxious nature—its encouragement of vice—its *reward* of perjury, incest, and disobedience to the laws of the land—and its gross selfishness—constitute altogether so odious a compound, that a violation of the rights of the Church and of the laws of God could never have come in a more offensive shape. If the Bill passes, it will have other effects and consequences besides those on public morals; and with this suggestion, respectfully addressed to the various parties interested, we conclude for the present.

NOTICES OF RECENT PUBLICATIONS,

ETC.

---

1. Poems. 2. Reverberations. 3. The Heiress in her Minority. 4. Practical Remarks on the Reformation of Cathedral Music. 5. The Vegetarian Messenger. 6. Woodward's Sermons. 7. De Havillard's History of Ancient and Modern Rome. 8. Babington's Oration of Hyperides against Demosthenes. 9. Wilson's Plain Sermons on the Sacraments and Services of the Church of England. 10. Landon's Ecclesiastical Dictionary. 11. Maskell's Sermons. 12. Doctor Johnson : his religious Life and Death. 13. Thompson's Original Ballads. 14. The City of God. 15. Sermons of the late Rev. John Hamilton Forsyth. By the Rev. E. Wilson. 16. The Words from the Cross. By Rev. W. H. Anderdon. 17. Letters on Secession to Rome. By Rev. J. L. Ross.

I.—1. *Poems.* By ARTHUR H. CLOUGH.

2. *The Bothie of Toper-Na-Fuosich. A Long Vacation Pastoral.* By ARTHUR HUGH CLOUGH. London : Chapman and Hall.

3. *The Strayed Reveller and other Poems.* By A. London : B. Fellowes. 1849.

EVERY age has its own mannerisms of thought and expression, in art, and in literature, and more especially in poetry. Where there is much original genius, this mannerism is not wont to appear offensive. There is a good deal of it even in the Elizabethan age : it offends us in " Beaumont and Fletcher," and in " Massinger ;" it is sometimes tedious in " Ben Jonson ;" but it is scarcely perceptible in Shakspeare. In our own days, a certain *transcendental* school has arisen, both in prose and poetry, which has succeeded in gaining no little of the public attention, and which really counts men and women of genius among its chiefs : these are Tennyson, Browning, and Mrs. Browning, late Miss Barrett ; further we may add, Carlyle, though we are unwilling to name this mischievous yet brilliant word-monger in such good company. But most of our young poets and poetesses, for some time past, have emulated the three first-named in their various ways. True, we have still a hearty, honest, genial Anglo-Saxon in Martin Farquhar Tupper, and other " originals " in " Helen Lowe," and Miss Drury, but the general current has set of late in the transcendental direction we have intimated : and here are two fresh authors, who may be said to be " rowing in the same boat," and struggling with the same rapids. Yet, it would be unfair to confound the pensive but Christian mysticism of Tennyson and of Mrs. Browning, or the dramatic earnestness of that lady's husband, to whom we so recently devoted an article, with the hopeless despondency and vague dreaming of the poets we are now about to treat of. Poets they are, with all their faults and weaknesses; and this is a great word:—and yet, in some sort, poets at second hand; frequently, nay, constantly reminding us of their models and prototypes, or at least of *those*, whom they have so long and so ardently admired, that they unconsciously reflect them in almost all their " inspirations." The " Pastoral Long Vacation," indeed, forms an exception to this rule, and is more like Goethe's " Herrman and Dorothea," than any other poem we are acquainted with; though even here there are some unnatural passages, which read like *bad* bits of " Browning" *at second hand.* Such is the very strained imagery, concerning the " two bridges and the great keystone" (see p. 41), which, from the vile taste of the age, has probably been pronounced and considered by far the finest thing in the whole poem. However, there is some feeling, some humour, some taste, and a good deal of common sense, in this whimsical production. The concluding letter from " Hobbes," respecting marriage, has great merit: we cite a few lines, which appear to us right worthy of note:—

> " Rachel we found, as we fled from the daughters of Heth by the desert;
> Rachel we met at the well; we came, we saw, we kiss'd her;
> Rachel we serve for long years,—that seem a few days only,
> E'en for the love we have to her,—and win her at last of Laban.
> Is it not *Rachel* we take in our joy from the hand of her father?
> Is it not *Rachel* we lead in the mystical veil from the altar?
> *Rachel we dream of at night: in the morning, behold, it is Leah.*
> Happy and wise who consents to redouble his service to Laban;
> So, fulfilling his week, he may add to the elder the younger;
> Not repudiates Leah, but wins him the Rachel unto her."

" Which things are an allegory," indeed, but a very beautiful allegory, and one which we may safely leave to the application of our readers. But dismissing this said " Bothie of Toper-Na-Fuosich" from our consideration, as a whim, but a whim which only genius could indulge in, we approach the " minor poems" of this same writer, " Arthur Clough," with some little anxiety to discover the real mind of the poet, yet with a good hope that all our doubts may be satisfactorily cleared away. Alas! this hope is not realized; on the contrary, we soon discover that Mr. Clough is professedly in search of a religion, and of an object in life; and as mere Byronism is altogether out of fashion, and nobody affects the miserable, that we know of, nowadays, for the sake of admiration, we have only to commiserate our author's mental darkness. His poem, however (p. 23), headed " When Israel came out of Egypt," is (as *we* understand it), though it is intentionally obscure, one of the most painful, and, we may add, the most *blasphemous*, we ever remember to have glanced at. Schiller's " Resignation," or " Gods of Greece," was Christian compared to this! The poet starts with deprecating all existing revelation: he says,—

> " ' Lo, here is God, and there is God!'
> Believe it not, O man!—
> In such vain sort to this and that
> The ancient heathen ran.
>
> Though old Religion shake her head
> And say in bitter grief,
> ' The day behold, at first foretold,
> Of Atheist unbelief,'—
>
> Take better part, with manly heart!
> Thine adult spirit can:
> Receive it not! believe it not!
> Believe it *not*, O man!' "

This is pretty cool, we think, for an Oxford Tutor. Indeed, we are rather disposed to wonder these poems should not have shared in the holocaust to which the " Nemesis" of Mr. Froude was recently devoted. There is much more in the same strain: we cannot follow this lengthened war-note of audacious misbelief or rather unbelief through all its " changes." Our author informs us, however, that our present scientific knowledge impels us to the conclusion, that " there is no God: "—

> " Earth goes by chemic forces; heaven's
> A ' Mécanique Céleste;'
> And heart and mind of human kind
> A watch-work as the rest!' "

The poet proceeds to inquire whether *this* is a true " voice;" and he certainly *appears* to answer this question in the affirmative. However, he bids us *hope* that some *prophet* may arise, who, from Atheism's self, will hew out *a new religion:* in other words, Mr. Clough swells the modern outcry for the individual anti-Christ, which Carlyle, and Emerson, and " George Sand," and many others have raised before him. There are some more utterances, headed " Blank misgivings of a Creature moving about in worlds not realized," which are utterly joyless and hopeless and lifeless: they remind us much, not in matter, but in style, of the blank

verse of Browning's " Paracelsus."   Such is the somewhat mysterious fragment." (p. 44.)

> " —Roused by importunate knocks,
> I rose, I turn'd the key, and let them in.
> First one, anon another, and at length
> In troops they came ; *for how could I, who once*
> *Had let one in, nor look'd him in the face,*
> *Show scruples as again ?*   So in they came,
> A noisy band of revellers,—vain hopes,
> Wild fancies, fitful joys ; and there they sit
> In my heart's holy place, and through the night
> Carouse, to leave it when the cold grey dawn
> Gleams from the East, to tell me that the time
> For watching and for thought bestow'd is gone."

This, both in matter and expression, seems an obvious reminiscence of some of the speeches of the Sage of " Wurzburg."   At
times, Mr. Clough's mannerism is decidedly offensive ; for instance,
a vile imitation, or at least reflection of Tennyson's worst peculiarities, may be observed in the morbid and silly effusion (p. 52.),
headed " Natura Naturans."   We have rarely met with any thing
more grotesquely out of place, than the ὁ θεὸς μετά σοῦ, which Mr.
Clough has given us, as the refrain to his " Farewell, my High-
land lassie ! "   Such a manifest incongruity is startling.   Can
he have been led astray by the remembrance of Byron's appropriate and poetical " Zoe mou, sas agapo ? "—We suppose so.
The lines abusing " Duty" (p. 39, 40) are very clever, but still
more wicked.   Mr. Clough, do you feel no compunction of conscience for having given such mischievous rhymes to the world ?
But we suspect you are not much troubled with this said com-
modity of conscience.   Before we part, however, from this author,
let us quote his first and best poem, which reminds us of
Tennyson's mighty " Vision of Sin," and which is altogether
Tennysonian in scope and treatment, though it has much merit
of its own.

> " The human spirits saw I on a day,
>   Sitting, and looking each a different way :
>   And, hardly talking, subtly questioning,
>   Another spirit went around the ring
>   To each and each : and as he ceased his say,
>   Each after each, I heard them singly sing,
> Some querulously loud, some softly, sadly low,
>   ' We know not,—what avails to know ?'
>   ' We know not,—wherefore need we know ?'
>   This answer gave they still unto his suing,
>   ' We know not : let us do as we are doing.'

'Dost thou not know that these things only seem?'—
'I know not: let me dream my dream.'
'Are dust and ashes fit to make a treasure?'—
'I know not, let me take my pleasure.'
'What shall avail the knowledge thou hast sought?'—
'I know not: let me think my thought.'
'What is the end of strife?'—
'I know not: let me live my life.'
'How many days, or ere thou mean'st to move?'—
'I know not: let me love my love.'
'Were not things old once new?'—
'I know not: let me do as others do.'
And when the rest were overpast,
'I know not: I will do my duty!' said the last."

'Thy duty do?' rejoin'd the voice:
'Ah, do it, do it, and rejoice:
But shalt thou then, when all is done,
Enjoy a love, embrace a beauty,
Like *these*, that may be seen and won
In life, whose course will then be run;
Or wilt thou be where there is none?'
'I know not: I will do my duty.'"

And taking up the word, around, above, below,
Some querulously high, some softly, sadly low,
'We know not,' sang they all, 'nor ever need we know.'
'We know not,' sang they; 'what avails to know?'
Whereat the questioning spirit, some short space,
Though unabash'd, stood quiet in his place.
But as the echoing chorus died away,
And to their dreams the rest return'd apace,
By the one spirit I saw him kneeling low,
And in a silvery whisper heard him say,
'Truly, thou know'st not, and thou need'st not know,
Hope only, hope thou, and believe alway;
I also knew not, and I need not know:
Only with questionings pass I to and fro,
Perplexing those that sleep, and in their folly
Imbreeding doubt and sceptic melancholy,
Till that, their dreams deserting, they with me
Come all to this true ignorance, and thee.'"

A still more helpless, cheerless doubter is "A.," author of the "Strayed Reveller, and other Poems," whom, for the sake of his father's memory, we forbear to name more particularly. Yet, not surprised are we, such teaching should have led to such results: by the fruit we know the seed. Any thing more darkly melancholy, more painfully sombre, than the last poem in the volume, entitled " Resignation," and addressed to " Fausta," we never remember to have seen.   The poet, in the very heyday of his youthful spring, arrives at the conclusion, that all life, whether for ourselves or others' sakes, is vanity.   He says (p. 125) : —

> " Blame thou not, therefore, him, who dares
> Judge vain beforehand human cares ;
> Whose natural insight can discern
> What through experience others learn :
> Who needs not love and power, to know
> Love transient, power an unreal show :
> Who treads at ease life's uncheer'd ways :—
> Him blame not, Fausta, rather praise.

>   *   *   *

> " Enough, we live :—and if a life,
> With large results so little rife,
> Though bearable, seem hardly worth
> *This pomp of worlds*, this pain of birth ;
> Yet, Fausta,—the mute turf we tread,
> The solemn hills around us spread,
> This stream that falls incessantly,
> The strange-scrawl'd rocks, the lonely sky,—
> If I might lend their life a voice,
> *Seem to bear rather than rejoice.*
> And even *could* the intemperate prayer
> Man iterates, while these forbear,
> For movement, for an ampler sphere,
> *Pierce Fate's impenetrable ear,—*
> Not milder is the general lot,
> Because *our* spirits have forgot,
> In action's dizzying eddy whirl'd,
> The something that infects the world."

This melancholy is deep indeed.   The very first longer poem in the volume, " Mycerinus," is a kind of apotheosis of despair ; it looks as if suggested by a father's fate.   At the same time, it seems almost a profession of atheism !   " Emerson," we learn from the sonnet on p. 52, is one of " A.'s" great teachers : a " god of his idolatry."   Poor worshipper, with such a god !—The reminiscences of Tennyson and Browning are manifold also in this volume.   Thus " A Modern Sappho" (p. 64) is a rather confused imitation, or reminiscence, of one of Browning's " Dramatic Romances," entitled " The Laboratory ; " and a very mystical affair, called " The New Sirens, a Palisode," is more Tennysonian than Tennyson himself.   Even the most beautiful poem in the volume, " The Forsaken Merman," reminds us of Tennyson, but

not unpleasantly : it is far superior to *that* poet's " Merman " or
" Mermaid ;" and, perhaps, equal to any of his lyrical creations.
There is a musical cadence in the rhythm almost unrivalled. The
same merit will be discovered in the somewhat aimless, yet
lyrically beautiful poem, which gives its name to the volume.

Altogether, of these two new poets, " A." is, we think, the
superior, being at once the more earnest and the more poetical ;
but each has real claims. " A's" singing is like the musical
wind wailing through the forest tops on the high mountains far
away. " Clough " resembles rather the monotonous heaving of
the sea against a rock-bound shore. Both are very *sad ;* and
neither Oxford nor Cambridge need rejoice in their children.

ii—1. *Reverberations.* London : John Chapman, Strand. 1849.

2. *Reverberations.* Part II. London. 1849.

CHARLES SWAIN, the reciter of these strains, is possibly known to
many of our readers as the frequent occupier of the Poet's corner
in country newspapers, and a ladies' album-filler after the most
approved fashion. Here he appears in quite a new character
(anonymously by the way), as an Emersonian prophet, a transcendental philosopher, a sublime " anythingarian ;" and, to tell the
plain truth, he has written a vast amount of wordy twaddle in
conformity with his new vocation, and said some few, some *very*
few, good things. It is singular how this style of writing palls
upon one : how inconceivably tiresome it grows, as soon as we
discover that the gigantic mountain is bringing forth a mouse.
Yet there is much good feeling and honest endeavour in these
metrical talkifications. The first three are by far the best ;
" Balder," " Thor," and " Believe in God." " Balder " *seems* to be
suggestive of something very wonderful, if we could only discover
it, and is apt to inspire the general reader with a certain amount
of *awe.* True, it has no great meaning ; or, if it has any meaning, it is a very bad one.

> " But the Fates relent not ; strong Endeavour,
> Courage, noble Feeling, are in vain ;
> For the Beautiful has gone for ever :
> Vain are Courage, Genius, strong Endeavour :
> Never comes the Beautiful again."

" Lillibullero !" say we. By the by, none of these transcendental gentlemen understand the simplest elements of *punctuation :*
we are compelled to *stop* their effusions, before we can yield them
admission to our pages. " Thor " is less poetical, and altogether
less striking, yet is not devoid of a certain mystical effect.

"Believe in God" is an almost noble strain: it was by this, which we have seen quoted with its author's name, that we were enabled to fix the authorship of "Reverberations." Here Mr. Swain seems to have been frightened by Socialism into something like a Christian mood, though he still makes very bold with God's truth, and talks of "The hero of our race" in a strain "by no means to be commended." Still this, if not a poem (it is scarcely *artistic* enough to deserve that appellation), is at all events a manly cheerful utterance, one to which we are glad to award its meed of praise. But O! the dreary strains that follow, the big-mouthed oracular warnings, and lessons, and voices! all the old Socinian commonplace of Channing and his crew, given to us, as some wonderful revelation of novelty! And "Part II." is worse again: still more wordy, more prosaic, more tame, more preten-tious (if possible), more twaddling! Here and there we catch a momentary gleam of sunshine, light reflected from "Tennyson" for the most part: thus "the Lady Alva's Web" *seems* to have something in it, reminds us for a moment of other and better things, (a strange intermixture of the lady-witch in "Thalaba" and Alford's "Lady Alice,") and after all it turns out to be the old dull story. There is next to no "poetry" in these effusions: "Reverberations" they are, no doubt,—faint and hollow echoes of the worthless optimism of the age, shadows of a shade, the commonplace of "the worser half" of the nineteenth century, transmuted into rhymes, almost as dreary, and apparently as interminable, as those of "De Lamartine" himself. Better the honest confession of his own imbecility and weakness, and that of all his school, with which poor Carlyle favours us, than this wordy twaddle about intellectual glory and moral splendour: better despair itself than this futile inanity and childish self-con-fidence. We scarcely meant to be so severe, but it is better the plain truth should be spoken. These "Reverberations" are "nought."

III.—*The Heiress in her Minority; or, the Progress of Cha-racter. By the Author of "Bertha's Journal."* 2 vols. Murray.

SEVERAL years have elapsed since the publication of "Bertha's Journal;" the great popularity of which has justly induced the authoress to offer another work for the benefit and amusement of the present generation. "The Minority of an Heiress" will be found as useful as it is interesting to all who seek acquaintance with the phenomena of nature, the gems of history, and the curi-osities of art; a large variety of these are here brought together, framed in an agreeable picture of domestic life, and accompanied

by many moral and just observations. The reader must not here
expect any romantic adventures, the interest chiefly consisting in
the history of a young girl of quick, intelligent powers, and ardent disposition, who, being suddenly thrown into a situation of
great trust, power, and difficulty, is gradually taught the means
of disciplining her character, and the realities of daily life, by her
own good sense and the affectionately wise forbearance of her
friends. The want of incident in the story will not be perceived
by the many who like to acquire facts without the trouble of
seeking them for themselves. The religious information is conducted much in the same way. There is a great deal of useful
knowledge conveyed in didactic conversations, interspersed with
many moral and a few practical reflections. If, on the one hand,
it is not very spiritual teaching; on the other, it is not sentimental.

Many pages are also devoted to the progression of taste in
manners and in literature, past and present. In this department
especially much of the interest is destroyed by the multiplicity of
subjects brought together into a few consecutive pages, which
precludes the possibility of working out any *one* idea, and frequently renders the conversations flat. Nor is it true to nature;
for in real life, even where we do but lay a passing touch on a
subject, yet each is dwelt on sufficiently to bear its quantum of
interest, expressed or understood, enough to make social intercourse a *reality* of feeling and intelligence, and not a painted
canvass of imitative superficiality.

It is ever tiresome to find fault: let us rather indulge ourselves in pointing out the more peculiar merits of this work, on
which, it is evident, much labour and care have been bestowed.
Among other merits, it has that of self-evident truth in the pour-
traying of the Irish character; and we would much recommend
those chapters where the heiress, Evelyn O'Brien, comes into
personal contact with her tenantry. We must forbear quoting
any of these scenes, as we had wished to do—to be understood,
they must be read with the context—and there they will be
found really interesting in connexion with the histories of the
poor families on her estate, and with the mistakes and misunder-
standings which arise from Evelyn's eagerness to do good, and her
ignorance of the means of doing it. We heartily wish that a few
more of the Irish proprietors were as well fitted to guide and assist their poor neighbours as this youthful heiress; indeed, there
are few, though older and apparently wiser, at this time in Ireland, who might not learn from this book the principles and practice derived from the experience of a calm-judging and right-
feeling mind, balanced by a thorough knowledge of the Irish

character and the history of the nation; without which no arguments can prevail, nor advice assist, among a misguided and bigoted, but affectionate and fiery people.

We quote one little anecdote, recounting the judicious efforts of two ladies to benefit their poor neighbours by encouraging their own industry :—

"Some young ladies, who went to reside near the sea-side in another part of Ireland, found that, among numerous applications for charity, the greatest number were from the families of fishermen. On inquiring into the cause of their poverty, it was found that some had bad worn-out nets, nearly good for nothing; and, having large families to support, they were too poor to buy new ones, so that even in the most favourable weather they could earn but little; the old fishermen too, no longer able to take their part in their daily calling, and having no employment by which they could support themselves, were a burden on those to whom they belonged, and the consequent distress was at times severe. These young ladies, not having much experience, sent to a neighbouring sea-port for several nets, on which they laid out a good deal of money; but the person they employed to procure them bought half-worn nets, which soon became bad. In a short time the poor fishermen had to complain again that half their time was spent in mending them; so these excellent and now more prudent ladies thought of a better scheme—one which would ensure good nets, and give employment to three different sets of people.

" ' Pray tell it then exactly,' said Evelyn; 'perhaps in some way I might imitate them.'

" ' They bought raw hemp—I mean, not spun—and employed the poor women in their neighbourhood to spin it into strong yarn, fit for the sort of twine of which fishing-nets are made; it was then twisted into twine of two or three strands, according to the kind required; but they had some trouble before the women learned to do all this in the proper way. When it was all rightly prepared, the old fishermen were employed to make it into nets, which they all knew how to do. I have frequently seen them netting with a very coarse needle filled with twine, and using their thumb, to form the stitch, instead of. a netting-pin. At length the new nets were made, and the young ladies sold them at a very moderate price to those who wanted them, receiving the payment in small instalments.'

" 'Sold them!' exclaimed Evelyn; ' oh, how shabby and paltry !'

" 'Stop, my dear; do not judge too quickly. One good *take* of fish with the new nets would have enabled the fishermen to pay the full price at once; but they only paid it by instalments, which was, you will allow, a very great relief to such poor people: and, as to selling them, I assure you that experience has shown that the poor value much more what they pay for than what they receive as charity, and take care of it accordingly.'

" 'Well; and how has the business gone on ?'

"'Exceedingly well. The nets, being made of good homespun hemp, are remarkably strong, and their excellence is so well known now, that all the neighbouring fishermen are glad to buy them at their full price, so there is a constant, well-established manufacture and traffic going on: the women spin, the old men net and support themselves, the fishermen buy, and, no longer deceived by unsound nets, have their excellent fish always ready for their customers. Thus, you see, those young ladies, by combining their charity with prudence, have the delightful and lasting gratification of having preserved numbers of industrious people from distress by ensuring to them the means of pursuing their healthy and honest vocations. They are amply repaid by those feelings for their risk and exertions, which were known only to a few friends, ultimately costing them but little, and all effected without the smallest ostentation.'"—Vol. i. pp. 423—425.

There is, in chapters xxx. and xxxii., a pleasant account of the effect on the social intercourse of the country-people of the rebellion of 1798, of the anxieties and excitement among the gentry in the disaffected parts, and some amusing anecdotes of their ingenuity in defending themselves. We must quote one little *ruse de guerre* :—

"'I must first tell you that my father was a clergyman, and resided at a small village not many miles from the place where that action was fought. All the military quartered there and in the neighbourhood were called out early on that morning, as well as the yeomanry corps, led by their captain, who was the principal person in the village, and a magistrate. Many of the inhabitants followed, well armed, to join, with their loyal though perhaps unskilful bravery, in defence of their property and of the common cause. Much depended on the issue of this battle ; if the rebels were victorious, they would probably march direct to that little village, to seize upon a large store of arms and ammunition deposited there. But, Evelyn, while all the able-bodied men were thus marched off, what was to become of these stores, which would have been an easy prey to any straggling parties of the enemy? In the centre of the village, which stood on a hill, four high roads met, and there a field-piece had been placed ; a few old men established themselves round it as a guard, and they were headed by the vicar, my dear father, the most mild and peaceful of men! My sister, who was then a child, enjoyed the novelty of the scene, though catching a little of the general alarm; and you would be amused at the vivacity with which she describes the singular group assembled under our venerable father as a garrison for the village. In order to give a martial appearance to his little regiments of ancients, when seen from the neighbouring hills, all the old caps, red jackets, and waistcoats of the militia and yeomanry, and even the women's red petticoats, were put in requisition ; and such was the effect of this skilful stratagem, that some of the flying parties from the battle, who

were approaching, were seen to pause, and then to cross over into
another line of road. On these occasions, swords and muskets, and even
polished spits and pokers, were made gleam in the sun whenever my
father gave the signal, by brandishing his long bright telescope.'"—
Vol. i. p. 243.

Most of our English readers will probably be interested in an
account of the formation of the bogs, which occupy so large a portion of the country, and are in themselves so curious and interesting, and about which some very singular discoveries have lately
been made :—

"As their path skirted it for some way, Evelyn's attention was directed by her father to the variations of the soils, which were marked by
the different wild plants. On the most solid part of the bog heath
grew in profusion, with sometimes a few furze-bushes intermixed;
while on the damp edges of the path were sedge-grass and rushes; the
beautiful pingucula showing here and there in purple tufts. He then
pointed to many wet patches, where bright green moss appeared thickly
spread over the surface, and, gathering a specimen of it, gave it to Mabel
to put in her botanical case.

"'That soft green mossy place looks very different from this on
which we are walking,' said Evelyn.

"'Yes: but they are both called bog,' said Mr. Desmond. 'The
name is given indiscriminately to very different kinds of substances; it
always implies, however, something loose and infirm, a soft earthy substance: it is an Irish word which signifies shaky or trembling. In
that mossy part the water is pent up near the surface, and renders it so
soft, that if you attempted to walk there you would sink. On the other
hand, those parts that have been either naturally or artificially drained
become, as you see, more dry and solid; and in that state bog may
more justly be termed peat.'

"'You told me, papa, that bog is said to be formed of decayed trees
and other vegetable substances,' said Evelyn.

"'Yes, that seems to be the general impression,' he replied, 'and
with good reason, I think; for it is well known that formerly extensive
woods stood in the very places now occupied by bogs, both in this country
and Great Britain, as well as on the Continent; indeed, I have heard of
some instances where the trees that formerly stood there are still remembered by old people: and in many of our bogs the stems and roots
of large trees are found at a great depth beneath the surface, which
seems to confirm that opinion.'

"'But what threw down the trees, papa?'

"'Some one of the many accidental causes by which nature seems to
work—a deposit of sand, washed down from the hills, may have formed
a barrier or dam across the stream which conveyed it; fallen leaves,
broken twigs, and fresh materials from the higher grounds, increase the
barrier; and large pools of stagnant water being thus formed, the soil
in which the trees stand becomes soft and loose, the roots gradually

decay, and at length, easily yielding to the force of the winds, the trees themselves fall, adding immediate weight and solidity to the mass.'

" ' It seems extraordinary,' said Mr. Stanley, ' that there should have been formerly such extensive forests in a country where nothing but bog now appears.'

" ' Yes,' but you remember Spenser says—

" ' Of woods and forests which therein abound,'

replied Mr. Desmond. ' The face of the country has indeed changed ; but observe, I do not confine the formation of bog to the fall of forests only, for many shallow bogs are to be found on the steep sides of our mountains, where it is not probable that thick woods ever stood, and where it is not possible that pools and stagnant waters could have ever existed. The humidity of our climate encourages the rapid growth of several plants, which I shall presently have an opportunity of showing you, and which seems to be an essential part of all bogs. But in the mean time I wish to mention a fact worth your observation. It is— that pieces of the bark of trees are often found, undecayed, in the sub-stance of the peat ; their structure and fibrous appearance being so distinct in the inner rind, that the very species of tree to which they belonged can be easily distinguished . . . . and I will add, that the peculiar character of each bog may be traced, by observing the remains of the different plants of which it was chiefly composed.'

" ' I wish you would show me an instance,' said Mr. Stanley.

" ' Most willingly,' Mr. Desmond replied, leading them towards a party of men who were cutting a drain. ' In the first place,' ' said he, ' you may observe the evident remains of heath in some places ; but now, compare those scraps to which I point with my stick, with the thick tufts of soft green moss that I showed you on the wet, impassable bog. Mabel, have you the specimen I gave you ?'

" ' Yes, papa, here it is ; and here are also specimens that Gerald and I gathered of the conferva and the pretty little water ranunculus.'

" ' Oh ! as to that ranunculus aquatica, it contributes as much as any plant to the formation of bog. Growing very rapidly, it will in one summer spread over the whole surface of the water in which it is found, and, its stems being all matted together, it drops in winter to the bot-tom. The following summer a new layer spreads over the surface, and then subsides in the same manner, and so on year after year ; so that this plant alone in a very few years, by accumulating from the bottom, decaying, and becoming mixed up with earthy particles, almost forms a bog in itself. The same may be said of this conferva, so common in water. But the sphagnum, the most abundant of all the plants which tend to produce bog, and which flourishes equally in damp ground or in water, and in every region, assists in the formation of bog more than any other plant, in consequence of its peculiar habits. Some mosses grow only in shady places, others prevail in meadows, and the various aquatic plants require different soils ; while the sphagnum is found every where.'

" ' I should like to know that peculiar habit of the sphagnum to which you allude,' said Mr. Stanley.

" ' It is this:—its seed-vessel has no foot-stalk, like that which you may have observed in all other mosses, where the pretty little cups, supported on slender threads, scatter their seeds around ; but, in the sphagnum, the seed-vessel continues always close to the tuft of leaves in which it was formed ; the seeds vegetate among those leaves, and thus spread a new bed over its last year's withered layer. The young plants, in due course, produce their seed and wither in their turn ; and the same process thus continually taking place, layer upon layer is formed, which, acting like a wet sponge, presses down the old layers by its weight, and forms, at length, a compact mass of decaying vegetable matter.' . . . .

" ' I have heard of your bog-oak and bog-wood, which are, I suppose, the same thing,' said Mr. Stanley.

" ' No,' replied Mr. Desmond ; ' the pine, of which more is found than of any other tree, is usually termed bog-wood ; and it is a curious circumstance, that it retains so much of its resinous nature as to make it an admirable fire-wood. It is indeed a treasure to the poor in the neighbourhood of those bogs where it is found ; for, while the turf supplies fuel, the bog-wood gives so good a light, that splinters of it are an excellent substitute for candles. But this wood has another valuable property ; the tanning process it receives, during its long immersion in the bog, shields it from decay, and it becomes therefore a favourite material with the poor for the rafters of their houses, and still more for their gate-posts. You know common gate-posts, though ever so well painted, decay at the surface of the ground ; whereas posts of bog-wood defy alike both drought and moisture.'

" ' You said in the bogs where the pine is found. Is it not found in all bogs, papa ?' Evelyn asked.

" ' No, my dear ; it is a curious fact that neither pine nor yew are ever found in the same place with oak. The oak is always in black bogs ; the pine and yew in red bogs.'

" ' I suppose,' said Mr. Stanley, ' that, being formed chiefly of oak, the bog becomes black from the effect of that acid which exists in oak, and produces ink when combined with iron.'

" ' Very probably,' replied Mr. Desmond. ' There is certainly a great difference between various bogs, which I attribute to the preponderance of one or other tree or plant in their formation.'

" ' The finding of that bog-timber is, of course, a mere chance,' said Mr. Stanley.

" ' The manner of discovering it is remarkable,' said Mr. Desmond. ' As the dew never lies on those places beneath which trees are buried, a man goes out early in the morning before the dew evaporates, taking with him a long slender spear. Thrusting this down wherever the absence of dew indicates timber, he discovers, by the touch of the spear, whether it be decayed or sound; if sound, he marks the spot, and at his leisure proceeds to dig up his prize ; and in doing so he may some-

times happen to discover other curious remains of former times.'"—
Vol. i. pp. 111—117.

We wish that we had room for a chapter on the by-gone
Knighthood of Ireland, which would interest all our readers ; and
for several chapters on Irish antiquities, such as the Phœnician
remains, vol. i. p. 51,—the yet unaccounted-for peculiarity of
Ireland, her Round Towers, p. 79,—the numerous *raths* and
cromleachs, pillars, and circles of stones, pp. 280 and 298, 303 ;
concerning all of which there is a great deal that is excellent in
learning and research, adapted not only to the understandings of
the young people to whom the book is chiefly addressed, but containing instruction for many older heads.

We have not time to point out to our readers more of the
many pleasing and instructive portions of these volumes ; but
such passages will not be difficult to find ; and we are satisfied
that no one can peruse them without feeling present interest, and
deriving lasting improvement.

iv.—*Practical Remarks on the Reformation of Cathedral Music.*
London : Rivingtons.   1849.

THIS is a *brochure* not more seasonable than earnest and practical :
written, too, by one manifestly master of his subject.

It is notorious that " a dislike to cathedral service" is harboured
by many persons, of whom it can no more be predicated that they
labour under a distaste for music, than that they are indevout or
generally under the influence of Puritan prejudices.   To what,
then, is this to be ascribed ?—to "cathedral service," in its essence
or its accident ? Such persons complain of distraction. To what is
this due ?—to anything that of necessity belongs to choral service, or
to certain modern innovations upon it, certain " indecent levities"
(to use Bishop Gibson's expression) which have so generally crept
into its performance, that people suppose them (and what wonder ?)
to be essential characteristics of that glorious arrangement which
was published under direction of Cranmer, who in this, as in other
matters, aimed, in opposition to Romish corruptions, to restore us
to the simplicity and solemnity of the primitive worship ?   It is
needless to indicate which side of this alternative the author es-
pouses.   Accordingly, the object of his work is to " state plainly
the grounds of uneasiness" felt by such persons as we have spoken
of, " so far as they can be definitely assigned and ascertained ; so
that, if possible, practicable, and really desirable, they may be
removed."

The following is an enumeration of " the points in detail which have been most commonly and urgently spoken of as deserving, at least, of investigation :"—

" I.—The practical exclusion of the congregation from their privilege of joining in the Psalms and Responses of Divine Worship, and the practical assumption by the choir of the office of substitute for, instead of leader of, the people.

" Which is brought about by—

" 1. The adoption of the theory that the choir *ought* to be the representative of the people.

" 2. The arrangement of the harmonies, so that the melody is in the treble part only.

" 3. The high pitch often adopted for the melody.

"4. The want of due care in the recitation of the words by the choir.

" 5. The use of airy ' chants.'

" 6. The substitution of services for chants for the Canticles.

" II.—The adoption of a sing-song whine, or lugubrious drone, in the minister's recitation.

" III.—The introduction of a secular, in the place of a sacred, style of music.   Including under this head—

" 1. Anthems.—In particular,

"*a.* The adoption of the music of Mozart, Haydn, and their followers, for anthems, especially their mass music from the modern use of the Church of Rome in some places.

" *b.* The use of choruses, &c., from semi-operatic oratorios.

" *c.* The use of (so-called) anthems of a school utterly wanting in the characteristics of solemnity and sublimity.

" 2. Chants and services :—

"*a.* The substitution of airy sing-song chants for sober chants of recitation.

" *b.* The substitution of services in the place of plain chants for the Canticles ; and the use of services unfit for the purpose they are intended to subserve.

" 3. Voluntaries.—The use of secular exhibitional voluntaries."— pp. 13, 14.

In considering the first of the six causes assigned to the first head, the author is at issue with a great authority on such matters, the Rev. J. Jebb in his book on the Choral Service ; with whom, however, he seems to agree in most respects. We must own to a coincidence of view with this writer, both in regard of general concurrence and the particular exception—if such be Mr. Jebb's theory ; but we have not his admirable work at hand to refer to. However, by whomsoever broached, we feel it to be our duty energetically to protest against any such theory as that "the choir *ought* to represent the congregation, as far as the audible portion of the service is concerned." In the words of the writer before us :—

" It is gravely objectionable. For while it is undoubtedly true that in most cathedrals the choir does, at this time, practically represent the congregation (for the latter are—unwillingly and of compulsion, as we believe—too generally silent); we are yet wholly at a loss to discover any justification of this practice in the formularies of the Church, or in any authoritative document whatever; and certainly we are aware of no elements of advantage of any kind which appertain to it.

" On the contrary, we are persuaded that it is opposed both to the usage of the Church previously to Romanist innovation, and to the view and intention of our reformed Church, as distinctly inferrible from her rubrics and canons; fully as much as it is opposed to common sense, and devoid to the perception of, we think we may say, most persons, of devotional and edifying effect."—p. 15.

Silence on the part of the congregation has, in effect, come to be the rule, not, alas! the exception; and this, whether in cathedrals or in parish churches which affect a choral service. Unfortunately it cannot be said that *these* are the *only* churches in which the congregation fail to take their due share in the service. It is too much the case in those where no such excuse can be alleged. There of course we must seek for other causes. We must remember the coldness and formalism of the bygone century. We must trace in it the congregational development of that spirit, which in the minister has resulted in the pompous preaching of the prayers, and the *via-media* kneeling-box between the clerk and pulpit. But, be this as it may, the congregational silence in "places where they sing," is undoubtedly owing to several of the causes assigned above. For that of which we have already spoken, three remedies are suggested in the pamphlet before us. The one approved, as " most practicable, profitable, and in accordance with the intention of the Church," is, that the congregational chanting " should consist of the predominant melody or plain chant by the congregation in unisons (or octaves rather), and, if desired, the subordinate accompaniment of the choral harmony by the choir or organ." Our own opinion, based upon the experience of several years in congregations of various characters, is, both that this accompaniment must be kept decidedly " subordinate;" and that,—whatever we may be able to accomplish after a while—it is vain to expect, in the present state of knowledge of Church music, congregations to do their part, so long as Psalms, Canticles, and Preces are sung in full harmony. They must be chanted in unison, else we get confused. And that this, whatever musicians may tell us about the effect of consecutive octaves, was what our Reformers intended, Mr. Dyce has shown good cause for believing.

We cannot follow the writer through all his "Remarks," but we would call special attention to the "fourth cause" of the matter complained of, viz.—"*the want of due care in chanting by the choir.*" Gabbling over the recitative portions, so as to allow time neither for the just pronunciation of syllables, nor for attention to stops; stopping on the last word, and drawling out the inflected notes :—these are amongst the commonest as well as most vicious faults of choirs. We entirely and heartily concur in the following sentiments :—

> "Constant attention to the sense, to the rhythmical, grammatical, and rhetorical pauses; continued practice and instruction by an intelligent and painstaking precentor; above all, a due regard to the awful nature of the service in which they are engaged, reciting or chanting it as if they both understood and felt it: these only can succeed in producing the desired result; these only can impress it upon the congregation that the service is not merely formal and exhibitional; these only can make the choir to lead the congregation, and these only can induce the latter to follow as the choir lead."—p. 29.

Several pages are devoted to a disquisition on the uses of the words *say, read, sing,* in the Rubrics, Acts of Uniformity, Injunctions, &c.; the modern sense differing from that originally attached to them; whereas "it is evident that they are not only not used invariably as opposed to each other, but were often applied indifferently, and sometimes convertibly, in speaking of the same thing." And in the older service-books "we find precisely the same kind of application of *dico, lego, canto,* and *cano.* The solution of all difficulty on this point," the writer continues, "will be found in the fact, that previously to, and at the time of the Reformation, there was an established mode of performing *each* particular part of the service; and that the musical notation adopted by Cranmer and Merbecke was adapted and reformed from them. There was one kind of plain song for reading or reciting prayers, which was upon one sustained tone throughout; another for reading Scripture, which was similarly upon one tone, but with inflections, or 'accents,' corresponding to the grammatical stops; a third kind, for such parts of the offices as were chanted antiphonally; another for anthems, &c.; and, lastly, one for metrical hymns." He presently continues :—

> "The inference, then, which we draw from the diverse application of the word *dico* is, that it was used in the Latin Service as a general term applied indifferently to denote the performance of any whatever portion of the Service, according to the accustomed method which belonged to it. And, similarly, the corresponding word *say* was adopted in the English as a general term, applied to denote the performance of any whatever

particular portion of the Service, according to that accustomed, *but reformed*, method which was arranged to belong to it. And this, without any reference to whether *distinctively* that mode of performance might not with propriety be denominated saying, or reading, or reciting, or chanting, or singing. So the Rubric—' The Order for Morning and Evening Prayer, daily to be *said and used* throughout the Year,'—is the general Rubric under which are many directions for particular portions of the Service to be '*sung or said*.' As under *dico* we find the particular expressions 'dicere cum nota,' 'dicere sine nota,' &c. . . . . . We conclude, therefore, that the word *sing* may be applied without necessarily signifying any elaborate degree of singing, &c. . . . . . On the other hand, that there is nothing in the use of the word *say* to prohibit the continued use of the plain chant arranged by Cranmer and Merbecke." —pp. 32—37.

We could with pleasure cite much more from this pamphlet, did our space perm t. We must, however, content ourselves with recommending it to the attentive consideration of all interested in the subject—a subject most closely connected with the glory of God and the edification of man.

v.—*The Vegetarian Messenger; a Quarterly Magazine, designed to aid in the extensive diffusion of true principles in relation to the food of man; advocating total abstinence from the flesh of animals, and the adoption of Vegetarian habits of Diet, as prescribed by the nature of the human constitution, and consequently most conducive to the full development and healthful exercise of the physical, intellectual, and moral powers.* Manchester: Abel Heywood. London: William Horsell. Part I.

STARK nonsense from beginning to end, making assertions which are untrue, and recommending a course which, when long persevered in, has been proved pernicious. As a specimen of the style of argument, it may be mentioned, that they tell us that "most obstinate scurvy has often been cured by vegetable diet:" and *therefore*, they would have us infer, vegetable diet must be wholesome for those who are not attacked with scurvy ! Why not set the example of living upon sarsaparilla and senna ? delightful meal—sarsaparilla pudding ! refreshing beverage—senna beer !

Infinite Wisdom said to the Apostle, "Peter, kill and eat ;" words which, we apprehend, must outweigh all vegetarian newspapers, even in these days of religious fanaticism. We recommend the proprietors of this magazine to remove their press to Nauvoo or California.

VI.—*Sermons preached in St. Stephen's Chapel, Dublin. By*
FRANCIS B. WOODWARD, *M.A., Chaplain.* London : Rivingtons.

THESE discourses were evidently addressed to a highly intelligent
and educated congregation, fitted to enter into the merits of
theological argument. We have seldom met such clearly reasoned discourses as those before us. Their style is simple and
unaffected, terse and logical, abounding in divisions, and the argument goes right a-head to the point to be proved. Of what is
generally understood by eloquence and oratory, there is none to
be found. Clear, vigorous good sense, acute observation, pointed
remarks, and (though last not least) sound doctrine, constitute the
characteristic merits of Mr. Woodward's volume. All that we
have read of it we have read with pleasure and interest. It is
really refreshing to meet with such writing as this :—

" I. First then, with regard to the doctrine of God's inward working :
' it is God which worketh in you both to will and to do of his good
pleasure.'
" I shall commence with two general observations.
" 1. God's inward working is not inconsistent with our freedom.
What God works in us is to *will*, and, as a consequence of willing, to
do ; but the willing and doing are *our own*. We are not mere machines,
or passive instruments in God's hands. A machine or instrument can
have no *will*. In short, to *will*, and in consequence, *to do*, is to be free ;
and, therefore, God's working in us to will and to do, so far from being
incompatible with our freedom, is, in fact, working in us to exercise our
freedom. *How* this can be we know not,—perhaps no created intelligence can understand it, but it is manifest that what I have stated is
the case. If the essence of freedom consist in *willing*, and in consequence of willing, *doing*, it is, I say, manifest that God's working in us
to will and to do does not nullify or encroach upon our freedom : He
worketh in us, as I have said, to exercise our freedom.
" 2. The other general observation I have to make is this : God's
working in us to *do* is dependent on, or rather, resolves itself into, His
working in us to *will*. Doing is, in fact, the will in action. What we
call moral strength, whereby we act, is nothing but the steadiness of
the will up to the moment of acting. If the will continue firm, the
action is done ; while, if the action be not done, it is because the resolution has given way. This is quite manifest, because we can do nothing
contrary to our own will. In a popular sense, indeed, people are said
sometimes to do things against their will : but this means, against their
general inclination ; not against their will at the moment of action. In
this, the strict sense, the thing is impossible ; for before we do any thing,
however we dislike it, we must first resolve to do it. But if this be so,
if our actions must obey the mandates of the will, then the difference

between the man who does what he resolves on, and the man who does
not, is simply, that the one continues unshaken in his resolve up to the
decisive moment of action ; while the other has vacillated and changed
his purpose ; the one has had a stedfast will, the other an unstedfast
one.   The moral strength, then, exhibited in the one case, and wanting
in the other, consists simply in this stedfastness of will carried on into,
and resulting in, the action resolved on.   Whatever, therefore, gives
this stedfastness,—that is, whatever keeps the will firm and unbending
up to the decisive point,—this communicates moral strength ; and,
therefore, God, in thus sustaining the *will*, worketh in us to do of His
good pleasure."—pp. 3, 4.

Mr. Woodward's volume is, very distinctly, an assertion of definite and practical views of Christianity, in opposition to that
vague and monotonous assertion of the doctrine of justification
by faith, which virtually sets aside, as unchristian, the necessity
of sanctification.

VII.—*An Outline of the History of Ancient and Modern Rome, com-
prising an Account of Italy from its most remote antiquity to the
Present Time, and embodying the History of Christianity from its
earliest date.   In Question and Answer.   By* Mrs. CHARLES
DE HAVILLAND.   Second Edition.   London : Houlston and
Stoneman.

A VAST amount of really valuable information is condensed in this
work, especially in that portion of it which treats of the Modern
(that is, the comparatively Modern) History of Rome, from the
date of the fall of the Roman Empire.   The authoress is a strong
and *unrelenting* adversary of Romanism and the Church of Rome ;
but in such days as the present even this excess of zeal seems
pardonable, when contrasted with the predilections of certain of
our Church's children.   On the whole, we should conceive that
the "Outline" before us was likely to be exceedingly popular
with "stout Protestants ;" so much so, indeed, as to sell its
thousands, perhaps, tens of thousands, in course of time.   We do
not like the preface as well as the body of the work ; it is carelessly written in parts, and should be revised, if not altogether
removed from the next edition.

VIII.—ΥΠΕΡΙΔΗΣ ΚΑΤΑ ΔΗΜΟΣΘΕΝΟΥΣ.   *The Oration of
Hyperides against Demosthenes, respecting the Treasure of Har-
palus, &c.   By* CHURCHILL BABINGTON, *M.A., Fellow of St.
John's College, Cambridge.*   London : J. W. Parker ; Cambridge : Deighton ; Oxford : Parker.

THE recovery of the Oration of Hyperides against Demosthenes

is amongst the most interesting literary events of the present
age. This long-lost work has turned up at last, where one
would not exactly have expected to meet it. It has tumbled out of
some mummy-case in Egypt, and has luckily fallen into the hands
of persons who were able to appreciate its value. We have the
following very interesting account of the discovery :—

" With respect to the discovery of the MS., our information on this
point is derived from N. C. Harris, Esq., of Alexandria. In a paper
entitled *Description of a Greek MS. found at Thebes*, which was read
before the Royal Society of Literature (Jan. 13, 1848), and has since
been printed in their transactions (vol. iii. new series), Mr. Harris says,
' When inquiring at Thebes last summer for Tahidic fragments, some
broken Greek papyri were shown to me for sale, and I purchased
them. One of them is remarkable, and will prove to be of great interest
to the lovers of classical literature.' "

It appears that Mr. Harris purchased the fragments of the
papyrus containing the Oration of Hyperides from a dealer of
antiquities at Thebes, in Upper Egypt, in 1847. He subsequently
endeavoured to discover the spot from which the MS. was taken
by the Arab excavators, but ineffectually. The minutes of the
Royal Society of Literature observe, that this MS. is unique
among the contents of the Theban tombs, and it suggests the
probability that the present discovery may be followed hereafter
by the discovery of other portions of the lost writings of antiquity,
inasmuch as it appears to have been customary for philosophers
and literary men to flock from Greece and Rome to the banks of
the Nile, and writings were sometimes buried with the dead.

We have a very accurate account of this curious relic, which
appears to have been written on a long roll of papyrus, in successive pages with margins, the length of the whole page being
about twelve inches and a half. There are no capital letters,
contractions, stops, breathings, accents, or other marks in the
whole. As to the age of this manuscript, it is difficult to speak
with certainty. The form of the characters resembles those in
the oldest manuscripts we possess, such as the Codex Cottonianus
and the Codex Alexandrinus, both of which are supposed to be
as old as the fifth century. The Codex Frederico Augustanus,
which is of the fourth century, agrees still better with it. The
Codex Bankesianus of Homer, discovered in Upper Egypt, and
supposed to be of the *third* century, resembles it even more. A
papyrus found at Herculaneum, and which cannot be therefore
of later date than the first century, is very like our MS ; and
even a papyrus referred to the third century *before* Christ, cor-
responds to a great extent with it. On the whole, Mr. Babington

leaves the reader to form his own opinion. He states that there
is nothing to lead us to the belief that it was written later than
the Christian era, though it was probably later than the time
of Hyperides. He leaves the reader to judge whether it may
not be as old as the third century before Christ. Might it
be allowed to hazard a passing conjecture that it may possibly
have been buried in the tomb of Hyperides himself—that the
Grecian orator may have passed his last days at Thebes? We
have not time to examine whether such a notion is tenable; but
these strange discoveries set the imagination roving. Mr. Babington has executed his work with the greatest possible care,
and with great judgment, as far as we can see. We think a man
who has been engaged in such a work as this is really a subject
for envy. The fac-similes are beautifully finished.

IX.—*Plain Sermons on the Holy Sacraments and Services of the
Church of England. By the Rev.* BENJAMIN WILSON, *B.A.*
London: Rivingtons.

THESE Sermons are sound in doctrine, and earnest, simple, and
affectionate in tone. They are more like what is suited to the
common people than any discourses we have seen for a long time.
The preacher has studied to be intelligible, and he has succeeded.
On the whole, we think this a really good volume of sermons for
an uneducated congregation, and one which requires to be taught
the first elements of Churchmanship.

X. — *A New General Ecclesiastical Dictionary. By the Rev.*
EDWARD H. LANDON, *M.A., Author of a Manual of Councils.
Vol. I.* London: Rivingtons.

IF this work should be continued with the care, accuracy, and
research which characterizes the volume before us, we confidently say, that a more valuable work on theological topics will
not exist in the English language. Mr. Landon has begun
admirably, and he is supplying a want which is most extensively
felt. It will be a great benefit to the Church to be relieved from
the necessity of referring continually to Ferraris, and other works
composed by persons of different communions, and whose teaching
must be more or less unsound. The volume before us contains an
immense variety of information, and, in all cases, *references to
authorities* are appended. A more unpretending and more useful
volume we do not remember to have seen.

xi. — *Sermons preached in the Parish Church of St. Mary Church, in the Diocese of Exeter.* By the Rev. W. MASKELL, *Vicar.* London: Pickering.

THESE sermons are written with vigour and clearness; but we cannot recommend them to our readers as judicious or unexceptionable in tone or in doctrine. The Sermon on the Eucharist we think contains many questionable positions. We do not think it right to call the Sacrament "adorable:" there is no authority for such a term in our formularies; and we wonder to find the author assuming the duty of paying external worship to the Sacrament.

xii.—*Doctor Johnson: his Religious Life and his Death.* By the Author of "Dr. Hookwell." London: Bentley.

THIS is an interesting book, as indeed any collection of Johnson's opinions must be, though it does not tell us much that we did not already know. It seems very well executed on the whole. We cannot, however, sympathize with the author in his objections to Convocation, or his comfortable assurance that "the State has g ven you much discipline, especially of late, through Acts of Parliament!" We presume the author is speaking ironically. In this point the comment departs sadly from the text; for Dr. Johnson had very strong opinions on the subject of Convocation :—

"Boswell once said to him, as an instance of the strange opinions some persons would ascribe to him, 'David Hume told me, you said that you would stand before a battery of cannon to restore the Convocation to its full powers!' With a determined look he thundered forth, 'And would I not, sir? Shall the Presbyterian *Kirk* of Scotland have its General Assembly, and the Church of England be denied its Convocation.' "—p. 139.

And Johnson was perfectly right. If he thought Convocation necessary then, how much more necessary would he think it now, when Presbyterians and Dissenters are interfering in every way with the doctrine and discipline of the Church of England.

xiii—*Original Ballads. By Living Authors.* MDCCCL. *Edited by the Rev.* HENRY THOMPSON, *M.A. Cantab.* London: Masters.

THERE is a great deal of very beautiful poetry in this elegant volume, which will, we are sure, gain a permanent place in our literature. We must quote the following spirited lines on " The

Battle of Drageshan, in the Greek war of Freedom," by the Rev. J. M. Neale :—

" In the deep grey of the morning, when Bulgarian cocks are shrill,
Our Hydriote scout, on panting steed, came pricking o'er the hill;
And 'Mount!' he cried, 'each horseman! each footman bend the
    lance!
The circumcised battalions are in full and quick advance!
I heard the morning call to prayer of that unholy law,
And the dark Vizier is there himself, and Ibrahim Pasha;
So let your sins be shriven well, and let your hearts be right;—
There's many an one, I trow, shall sleep in Paradise to-night.'"

And this description of the battle :—

" Ay! here they come; the crescent gleams above their mid-most fight,
By them that fell at Marathon! It is a gallant sight!
Now, lance to breast, and gun to cheek, and sabre gleaming free,
And the prayers of them that died for Greece, and good Saint Dimitri!
Ho! men of Joannina! draw bridle and keep rank!
Count Capo d'Istria to the left;—they seek to turn our flank!
Look to your priming, cannoneers!—be calm and play the men;
Depress your pieces to the brook, and when they cross it—THEN!"

                                                          pp. 209-10.

This is real poetry; and there is much of the same kind of thing in the volume.

XIV.—*The City of God. A vision of the Past, the Present, and the Future, being a symbolical history of the Church of all ages, and especially as depicted in some of the scenes of the Apocalypse.* London : J. W. Parker.

THIS work consists of two parts, the first being an allegorical representation of the Church, entering into many details, and ingeniously enough wrought out. In the second the reader is supposed to be placed in the presence of one who wrote the symbolical history of the Church, and who becomes its interpreter. On the whole, it seems well executed, as far as we can see.

XV.—*Sermons of the late Rev.* JOHN HAMILTON FORSYTH, *M.A. Curate of Weston-Super-Mare, Somerset, and afterwards Minister of Dowry Chapel, Clifton. With a Memoir of the Author. By the Rev.* EDWARD WILSON, *M.A., &c.* London : Hatchards.

WE are really at a loss to understand the publication of this volume, or at least the long Memoir prefixed to it. We have no doubt Mr. Forsyth was a good man, but there seems to have been

nothing in his history or character calling for the Memoir. We
trust there are thousands of such men in the Church, and it would
be rather odd if every good clergyman were to have the honour
not merely of a marble monument, but of a book. The sermons
are moderately evangelical.

XVI.—*The Words from the Cross; a Series of Lent Sermons.
By* W. H. ANDERDON, *M.A., Vicar of St. Margaret's, Leicester. Second Edition, revised.* London : Pickering.

THESE discourses come nearer to what we think the ideal of
Christian Sermons, than almost any that we have seen. Earnestness in promoting God's glory and man's salvation is their great
characteristic. The preacher has no theories to establish. His
natural power of eloquence—the eloquence of feeling and of a cultivated mind—is laid aside as an object of display, and as it were
forgotten, in the earnestness of his application to the souls of his
hearers. It is a spirit of devotion which cannot fail to draw down
a blessing on the hearers and the preacher. Were this powerful
and faithful preaching of the Gospel universal—the days of primitive Christianity would be revived. The man who could preach
thus, would be instant "in season and out of season" in the sublime work of his ministry.

XVII.—*Letters on Secession to Rome: addressed to a late Member
of the Church. By the Rev.* JOHN LOCKHART ROSS, *M.A., &c.*
Part I. Edinburgh: Lendrum.

THIS work consists of some letters written to a friend, with a
view to induce him not to secede from the Church to Romanism.
The author's persuasions were, it appears, ineffectual ; but he has
shown considerable zeal and research in his volume.

NOTE.

We have just received and perused the Bishop of Exeter's " Letter to the Archbishop of Canterbury." As these sheets are passing through the press, we have
only time to express our sense of the high value and importance of the noble and
Christian protest which the Bishop has here recorded. The portion of the letter to
which we would direct especial attention is, pp. 48—52, in which it is demonstrated,
that Mr. Gorham distinctly *denies that Regeneration* IS EVER GIVEN IN INFANT BAP-
TISM. It is *this* doctrine which the Committee of Council, and the Archbishops of
Canterbury and York, have virtually sanctioned by the recent decision. Can matters rest here ?

The pressure of important matter in this Number obliges us to defer the notice
of several other works.

ERRATUM.

In our last No. (p. 265, l. 18.) Dr. Pusey was, through some unaccountable slip
of the pen, identified with those who have deified the Virgin Mary. It is well
known, that Dr. Pusey is a decided *opponent* of such errors.

Foreign and Colonial Intelligence.

AUSTRALIA.—*Church Discipline.*—At the ordination of the Bishop of Sydney, on Trinity Sunday last, the admission of one of the Deacons, the Rev. F. T. C. Russell, of St. Mark's Chapel, Sydney, was objected to on the ground of his having slandered his brethren in the ministry, and insulted the Bishop. The objection was raised on the day before the ordination, and on being subsequently cited into the Consistorial Court, he was sentenced to three months' suspension, and inhibited from performing any diaconal office until he shall have made satisfactory acknowledgment of his fault to the Bishop.

AUSTRIA.—*Church Government by Martial Law.*—In these days, in which Church government assumes all manner of aspects, the following specimen of Church government, as practised in Hungary by Field-Marshal Haynau, will not be uninteresting. In a circular, dated from head-quarters at Pesth, February 10th, and addressed to the military commanders of the different districts, the Field-Marshal, commander-in-chief of the army in Hungary, thus expresses the *quasi*-episcopal solicitude with which he attends to the " care of all the Churches."

" Wishing to remedy the melancholy condition to which the Protestant Church in Hungary has been reduced by some of her prelates, who have abused their official position for the furtherance of party purposes, and excited the people to rebellion, as likewise to secure to the congregations of that communion the exercise of their constitutional rights, even during the state of siege, under the limitations incident to that state, I have, after consultation with the commissioner-plenipotentiary for civil affairs, seen fit to decree as follows :—1. The functions of general inspector and district inspector among the Protestants, of the Augustan confession, and those of curator among the Protestants of the Helvetic confession, are to be considered as extinguished. 2. As the election of superintendents to fill the vacancies which have been created, according to the usual custom of election by the congregation, is, during the state of siege, inadmissible, and as, at the same time, men must be found, by whose means the Protestant clergy and laity may be contained within the bounds of law, and the further disorganization of the Church prevented, I shall appoint to the several offices of superintendents trustworthy men and men of character, who are temporarily to administer the ecclesiastical government, under the name of Administrators of the Diocese, in concert with the senior clergy of the diocese, whom they are to consult, and with a few men selected by themselves from among the laity. 3. The superintendents or their administrators will, during the continuance of the state of siege, perform, along with their own, the functions of the former district inspectors and curators, and will, accordingly, transmit their petitions and suggestions to the superior authority, through the military commanders of the respective districts; and in order to preserve a proper account of the Church and school funds, hitherto administered by the general and district conventions, the said superintendents or their administrators will, after consultation with the senior clergy and with their lay assessors, make their report on the future administration of the said funds through the commander of their military district.   4. At all the consultations which take place of the district conventions, a military president, to be appointed upon petition by the military commander of the district, must be present. 5. As the incomes of the Protestant clergy are generally scanty, and the temporary rulers of the Church are to be enabled to devote themselves fully to their important calling, I shall obtain for them an allowance from the treasury for the time of their continuance in office.   6. The newly appointed administrators will be supported in the exercise of their functions by all the civil and military authorities.   From the moment of their entering upon those functions, the functions of the superintendents to whose districts they are appointed are at an end.   7. The superintendents who are thus deposed from their office will continue to exercise their functions in the ordinary cure of souls, provided always that any further steps to be taken against them on account of their political conduct are hereby reserved.   8. A more suitable arrangement of the limits of the former superintendents' districts, with reference to the division of the country into military districts, and the appointment of the official residences of the temporary administrators, is a subject of urgent importance.   The superintendents and administrators will find, on the part of the Government, a readiness of co-operation with regard to these, or any other arrangements which have for their object to connect the Protestant Church more intimately with the State, and to ameliorate its condition.   9. In accordance with these principles, which are to be notified in due course to the superintendents, inspectors, and curators, whom it may concern, I hereby nominate the following administrators :"—here follow the names of the dioceses or superintendents' districts, and the names of the persons substituted in the places of the cashiered ecclesiastics ; after which the mandate thus continues : " I expect of those men who are to be forthwith apprized of their nominations, and called upon to enter upon their functions, that they will, with judgment and zeal, perform their duties in a manner corresponding with the benevolent intentions of the Government, and calculated to promote the moral and religious well-being of the churches placed under their charge, whereunto they are to pledge themselves by a solemn vow to the commanders of their respective districts; and I shall expect to receive without delay reports as to the steps which have been taken in the matter.

        "(Signed)   HAYNAU, Field-Marshal."

Fancy, some fine morning, Field-Marshal the Duke of Wellington issuing orders from the Horse Guards, deposing refractory bishops and archdeacons, appointing others to take their places, and exacting from them the oath of canonical obedience; ordering diocesan synods and visitations to be held, in presence of an aide-de-camp, and the whole government of the Church to be carried on through the intervention and with the concurrence of the military commanders of the respective districts. The precedent seems really a tempting one, and might be more effectual in settling disputed points, than either application for a *mandamus* in the Queen's Bench, or appeals to the Judicial Committee of Privy Council. At all events, we thought the precedent too piquant, not to be brought under the notice of our readers.

Religious Statistics of Hungary.—Of the population of Hungary, more than 3,000,000 are Roman Catholics; more than 2,000,000 in Hungary and Transylvania profess the Reformed (Calvinistic) faith; a very small number adhere to the Augustan (Lutheran) confession; upwards of 44,000 are Socinians and Unitarians; and several thousands belong to the German Catholic Church. Of the Croats, two-thirds are Roman Catholics, and one-third German Catholics.

CANADA.—*Church Statistics.*—The following statistics are taken from a retrospect of the state of the Church in Canada, during the year 1849 :—

Clergy in the diocese of Toronto, 1st January, 1849 130

    Deaths during the year 5
    Superannuated   " 1
    Left the diocese " .... 3——— 9

                                           121

Ordained within the diocese during the year 14
Received from other dioceses .... 3———17

Clergy in the diocese of Toronto, 31st December, 1849 138

    Settled incumbents or missions 110
    Travelling missionaries 8
    Indian missionaries, having no other charge 7
    Garrison chaplain, having no other charge............ 1
    Assistant ministers.............................. 12

                                           138

Settled clergy have been established in the following places :—Pickering, Seymour, Marysburgh, Malahide, Owen Sound, Elora.

Rural Deans.—The Bishop of Toronto issued Commissions, on the last day of the year, to ten of his clergy to act as rural deans for the following districts :—the Home district; the districts of Simcoe; Gore and Wellington; Niagara; London, Huron, and Western; Brock and Talbot; Midland; Victoria and Prince Edward; Bathurst and Dalhousie; Johnstown, Eastern, and Ottawa.

CAPE.—*Proposed College at Cape Town.*—Bishop Gray has issued an appeal for assistance from the mother country, to aid him in his intention of establishing a collegiate institution in the vicinity of Cape Town, where he has already purchased a house, with about fifty acres of land for the purpose. The bishop's plan embraces the following objects :—

1. To erect collegiate buildings, capable of affording accommodation for fifty pupils, together with suitable rooms for the principal and other officers of the college, and, if possible, to build the chapel, library, and hall, with due regard to ecclesiastical and architectural beauty.

2. To provide an endowment for the principal, and a foundation for the maintenance of fellows, and of poor and deserving scholars.

The college is intended to embrace an upper and a lower department; pupils to be received into the lower department at the age of ten years, and to remain till the age of eighteen; the upper department to receive students at the age of seventeen or eighteen, if found duly qualified on examination. The education given to be such as to fit the pupils for secular employments and professions, as well as for the ministry of the Church.

It is proposed that the college should be governed by a body of statutes similar to those by which our ancient institutions in the mother country are ruled. The bishop will be visitor. There will be a principal, and, it is hoped, at no time fewer than three fellows and tutors, of whom one will be vice-principal. The principal will be appointed by the bishop: the other offices in the college will be filled up by the society itself, subject to the approval of the bishop, as soon as it is sufficiently matured to supply duly qualified candidates for them. In the meantime, the appointments to these offices also will rest with the bishop. The Rev. H. M. White, M.A., Fellow and late Tutor of New College, Oxford, will be the first Principal; the Rev. H. Badnall, B.A., Fellow of University College, Durham, Vice-Principal; T. B. Sykes, B. A., and H. Herbert, both of Worcester College, Oxford, Fellows and Tutors. The two gentlemen last named are to be admitted to Holy Orders next Christmas.

Suggestions for Missionary Proceedings in the Colony.—One of the Missionaries, who have recently gone out to the Cape, has sent home an interesting journal (extracts from which appear in the *Colonial Church Chronicle*) and has appended to it the following valuable suggestions, as to the best course of conducting the missionary work in the Colony :—

" 1st. Whether it would not be advisable, instead of bringing men out from England, to ordain as Deacons certain 'elder' men of good report and honest conversation, if such be found, in destitute districts, who might offer the prayers of the congregation, and baptize, and perform such other functions as belong to the Deacon, without calling on them to quit their worldly employ, by which they get their bread.

" 2nd. Whether it would not be best to restrict Deacons from preaching, as a general rule, and, instead thereof, to limit them to the public reading of certain specified works.

" 3rd. Whether an order of unpreaching ministers would not tend to call people's minds back to a right regard for Liturgical Offices and Sacraments, which is now lost sight of in the feverish desire of listening to sermons. Also, whether the restricting Deacons from preaching would not give greater opportunities of preparing for Priest's Orders, to those whom it might be advisable afterwards to admit to that degree.

" 4th. Whether it might not be well to have one such Deacon attached to each Priest, where the population around him could furnish one such according to his choice.

" 5th. Whether a certain amount of ecclesiastical discipline in such men, (such as joining in the daily prayer, the observance of all holidays prescribed in the Prayer-book, and the like,) would not supply the place of much learning.

" 6th. Whether it would not be best to sanction and recommend that Divine Service should be held in the open air in places where there is want of church accommodation, and especially where there is a great amount of coloured population professing Christianity, but quite unable, from want of *free* room, to join in the worship of the Church.

" 7th. Whether it would not be well to recommend, in certain places, some division of the service on Sundays, in reference to catechising in the afternoon, and certain other exigencies.

" 8th. How far it is advisable to relax or alter the canon respecting sponsors. Should not parents be admitted?

" 9th. Whether it would not be well to exact, from those seeking Priest's Orders, the thorough digestion of some work bearing on Missions, and the principles and rules to be acted on in Missionary work.

" 10th. Whether some plan might not be adopted to promote the sale and reading of Church books among the members of the Church in the Colony, by means of an itinerant vendor, with a stock recommended by the Bishop."

FRANCE.—*The New Law on Education.*—After a severe and protracted conflict between the Conservative party and the Socialists, the new Education law of the French Republic has been passed by the Assembly. Several of its provisions provoked violent opposition on the part of the Romish bishops, among whom the Bishop of Langres took the lead; and although in all probability the French Episcopate will deem it prudent to acquiesce in the law as finally settled, yet no less than sixty-two different remonstrances against it have been transmitted to the Bishop of Langres by his colleagues. Being publicly challenged as to the nature of these declarations, the bishop himself has however declared, that they are not in the nature of protests. The bishop himself, who is a member of the Assembly, forbore to vote on the occasion. The following is an abstract of the law as it now stands.

It consists of 85 Articles, arranged under four titles:—
1. Of the authorities by whom education is governed; 2. Of primary instruction; 3. Of secondary instruction; 4. General provisions.

Art. 1. Establishes a superior council of Public Instruction, consisting of the following members:—The Minister of Public Instruction, who is president of this council; four archbishops or bishops, chosen by their colleagues; one minister of the Reformed Church, chosen by the consistories; one minister of the Church of the Augsburg Confession, chosen by the consistories; a member of the Central Israelitish consistory, chosen by his colleagues; three councillors of State, chosen by their colleagues; three members of the Council of Cassation, chosen by their colleagues; three members of the Institute, chosen at a general assembly of the Institute; eight members nominated by the President of the Republic in council, selected from among the former members of the council of the University, the general or superior inspectors, the rectors and professors of the faculties, which eight members form a permanent section of the council; and three members belonging to the category of free instruction, nominated by the President of the Republic, upon the proposition of the Minister of Public Instruction.

Art. 2. The members of the permanent section are appointed for life, removeable only by the President of the Republic in council, on the proposition of the Minister of Public Instruction. They alone receive a salary.

Art. 3. The other members of the council hold office for six years, but are re-eligible.

Art. 4. The superior council is to hold at least four annual meetings, but may be specially summoned at any time by the Minister of Public Instruction.

Art. 5. The superior council *may* be consulted by the minister upon projects of law relative to public instruction, and on any question connected with the subject which he may see fit to submit to them. The minister is *bound* to take their advice upon all regulations touching examinations, superintendence, inspection, and any other matter connected with public educational establishments; also upon the assistance and countenance to be given to free establishments for secondary education; upon the books to be introduced in public schools, and upon those which are to be prohibited in free schools, as being opposed to morality, the constitution, and the laws. The superior council is moreover the final court of appeal in cases falling under the jurisdiction of the academical councils. Lastly, the council is to present to the minister annually a report on the general state of education.

Art. 6. The permanent section of the Superior Council is charged with the preparation of all administrative measures, and may be consulted by the minister in reference to promotions and other points connected with the government of the *personnel* of education. It also makes an annual report to the Council.

Art. 7—10. Provide for the establishment of an "Academy" in every department; to be governed by a rector, inspectors, and an academic council. The rectors may be chosen indifferently from the body connected with public, or from the body connected with free, i. e. private instruction. They must be licentiates, and must have filled a higher post in some educational establishment for ten years at least. The Academic Council is composed as follows;—

The rector, who is president *ex officio;* an inspector of the academy, a teacher, or an inspector of primary schools, appointed by the minister; the prefect or his deputy ; the bishop or his deputy ; an ecclesiastic appointed by the bishop; a minister of one of the two Protestant Churches, appointed by the minister of public instruction, in those departments where there is a legally constituted Protestant Church ; a delegate of the Israelitish consistory, in those departments where such a consistory is established ; the *procureur-général* of the Court of Appeal, in towns where there is such a court, and in the other towns a *procureur* of the Republic at the tribunal of the first instance ; a member of the Court of Appeal or the tribunal of the first instance, chosen by the court or tribunal ; four members chosen by the council-general of the department, two of whom must be chosen from its own body. The deans of the faculties to be called in for consultation, but without a vote, on questions touching their respective faculties.

Art. 11. Modifies the foregoing arrangement for the department of the Seine, adapting it to the peculiar position of the capital.

Art. 12—16. Regulate the functions of the academic council, the elected members of which are chosen for three years. These bear generally upon the government of all the public schools, with a limited power of control over free, or private, establishments; subject, of course, to the orders of the superior council. Annual reports are to be made by the academic councils, and transmitted to the minister, for the information of the superior council.

Art. 17. Declares that the law recognizes two kinds of primary or secondary schools :—1. Schools founded or supported by the *commune,* the department, or the State, called *public schools.* 2. Schools founded or supported by individuals, or by associations, called *free schools.*

Art. 18. Provides for the inspection of the schools by the following functionaries, all of whom have a right of inspection :—1. General and superior (state) inspectors. 2. The rectors and inspectors of the academies, in their respective departments. 3. Inspectors of primary instruction. 4. The cantonal delegates, the *maire* and the *curé,* the (Protestant) pastor, and the delegate of the Israelitish consistory, as regards primary instruction. The ministers of the different denominations are only to inspect the schools of their own communion, or, in mixed schools, only the scholars of their own communion.

Art. 19—22. Provide for the appointment of the inspectors, by the minister of public instruction, with the advice of the Superior Council, and for the functions of the inspectors. In free or private establishments the inspection is limited to the questions of morals and health, and bears upon instruction only so far as to see that nothing is taught which is contrary to morals, the Constitution, or the laws. The refusal to submit to inspection is punishable as a misdemeanor, and if repeated, may entail the closing of the school.

Art. 23. Determines the branches of primary instruction :—they are, moral and religious instruction, reading, writing, the elements of the French language, the first rules of arithmetic, with a knowledge of weights and measures; it may extend to the higher rules of arithmetic, to the rudiments of history and geography, of physical science and natural history; and to elementary instruction in agriculture, industry, sanatory knowledge, land surveying, drawing, singing, and gymnastics.

Art. 24. Provides that the instruction is to be given gratuitously to all the children whose families are unable to pay for it.

Art. 25, 26. Treat of the qualifications of the schoolmaster, among which is a certificate of capacity: ministers of the different denominations, while not interdicted by their own communions, are *ipso facto* qualified.

Art. 27—30. Regulate the formalities to be observed in the opening of a private or free school, the conditions on which the establishment of such free schools is to be sanctioned by the authorities, and the jurisdiction to be exercised over the masters of free schools by the Academic Council.

Art. 31—35. Treat of the qualifications, the appointment, the duties, and position of communal schoolmasters; express provision is made for the admissibility of members of religious orders to the office of communal schoolmaster.

Art. 36—41. Treat of communal schools, prescribing the establishment of sufficient schools in every *commune*, the circumstances under which separate schools for the different religious denominations, or else mixed schools are to be established, and regulate generally the management of communal schools.

Art. 42—47. Define the functions of the cantonal delegates, and other authorities charged with the government and supervision of primary instruction, and regulate the granting of certificates.

Art. 48—52. Contain the necessary modifications of the foregoing provisions, when applied to girls' schools and their governesses.

Art. 53. Regulates the establishment of *pensionnats* or boarding schools in connexion with primary instruction.

Art. 54—56. Regulate the establishment of adult and apprentice schools.

Art. 57—59. Treat of infant schools.

Art. 60—70. Regulate all private institutions for secondary instruction, among which ecclesiastical colleges are included. The provisions refer to the formalities to be complied with before opening an institution, to the qualifications of the master and of the teachers, to the State inspection, and the jurisdiction over all the institutions of the Academic Council, and, by appeal, of the Superior Council of Instruction. In determining the qualifications of the teachers, a species of academic jury of men skilled *in pari materiá*, is brought into play, by which candidates are to be examined for their certificates. An exception from the regulations for opening an establishment of education is made in favour of ministers of any religion recognized by the State, who are permitted to educate, in their families, youths not exceeeding four in number, without coming under the operation of the law. With regard to ecclesiastical colleges the law sanctions those already existing, subjecting them, however, to State inspection ; but no new ones are to be established without previous authority having been obtained from the Government.

Art. 71—76. Provide for the establishment of public colleges. The municipalities of the towns where it is proposed to establish them, are required to comply with certain conditions, upon which the State, through the Superior Council of Instruction, gives its sanction, and in some cases pecuniary aid.

Art. 77—85. Are of a general character, harmonizing the provisions of this enactment with the general state of the law.

Projected Popish University.—The Provincial Council of Avignon having determined to establish a " Catholic University," has applied to the Pope for his sanction to the project, to be signified by a Papal brief.

A Jewish Professor of Philosophy.—An angry controversy has taken place in consequence of the Bishop of Luçon having put the *lycée* of Napoléon Vendée in his diocese under an interdict, on the ground of a Jew being appointed to it as Professor of Philosophy. The Episcopal Act to this effect has been violently attacked by the Liberal press.

Provincial Councils.—Among the decrees of the recent Provincial Council of Avignon, is one expressing the desire of the Council to have the Immaculate Conception of the Virgin declared an article of the faith, while another places the province under the special protection of " The Sacred Heart of Jesus." The Pope in his reply to a letter submitting the acts of the Council of Paris for his confirmation, thus expresses himself on the subject of these Councils—" Although from circumstances we have not yet received the documents, we are sure they will soon reach us, for we have ordered that they shall be forwarded to us with the greatest diligence. But in the mean time we feel desirous to congratulate you warmly, venerable brothers, on your admirable sentiments of religion and duty towards your pastoral charge, and the warm solicitude you have shown for the welfare of your dioceses ; you have hastened, with the most praiseworthy zeal, and faithful to the wise prescription of the Holy Canons, according to our own wishes, to celebrate this council, in order to state in concert, in these hard and difficult times, what before God you have thought best calculated to excite and increase our Most Holy Religion amongst the people, and to keep up in them piety and purity of manners, and maintain ecclesiastical discipline. It is not certainly without true and profound consolation that we have learnt by your letter the desire which you have to re-establish in your own dioceses the Roman liturgy, already, to our great satisfaction, again put in use in several dioceses of France : and the determination which you feel, to apply with common accord all your care to remove, when circumstances will permit it, according to the rules of wisdom and prudence, the obstacles which have hitherto prevented you from bringing this affair to the desired end."

Clerical Conference.—The Archbishop of Paris has addressed to his clergy a pastoral letter accompanying three ordinances relating to ecclesiastical matters. The first establishes for five years severe examinations for young priests on the principal points of ecclesiastical knowledge; the second prescribes certain modifications in the diocesan conferences established at Paris by his predecessor; and the third orders for the diocese of Paris conferences for the examination of cases of conscience, as is practised at Rome. They are to be held every two months under the presidency of the archbishop, and are to be composed of all the priests of the diocese. The first of these conferences commenced on February 8, in the church of the Madeleine.

The Abbé Chantome.—The Abbé Chantome, of whose principles we gave a brief account in our last [1], having been cited before the "officiality" of the Bishop of Langres, to whose diocese he belongs, pleaded exemption, by virtue of a papal brief, from the jurisdiction of his ordinary. The court, however, overruled his plea, and the Abbé has since been suspended by a formal sentence from all his ecclesiastical functions.

GERMANY.—*Revived Church feeling.*—At a recent Assembly of Lutheran Clergy and laity held at Marburg, it was proposed by the Director of the gymnasium or college, that the ancient hours of prayer should be revived, and that in the morning, at noon, and in the evening, the bell should be tolled as of old, to give the signal for prayer, when every body at home, in the fields, and in the streets should stop and make a short pause for repeating a paternoster with the creed and the doxology, according to ancient practice. It was further suggested that at those times the church should be open, and the minister in his place to pray with such as might come to join with him. Not only was this not opposed, but it was added by one of the parties present, that the schoolmaster should bring his pupils to church regularly at those hours —a proposal which met with all but universal approbation. A decided movement for the revival of religion is likewise taking place among the clergy in the kingdom of Wurtemberg, a large number of whom have formed themselves into unions, with a central committee, for the purpose of providing a proper organization, with a view to united action upon questions affecting the Church and clergy.

Romish Home Mission.—At a general meeting, recently held, of the "Catholic Association" for Germany, it was resolved to found, under the name of the "Association of St. Boniface," a Romish Home Mission, whose operations are to be directed upon the Protestant parts of Germany, and those districts where Protestants and Roman Catholics are intermixed. Missions for reviving the religious feelings of the population in the Roman Catholic Districts have also been organized;

---

[1] English Review, vol. xii. p. 480.

and a wonderful account is given by the popish prints of the success of one of these missions in the Duchy of Baden, where Romanism had fallen greatly into decay. At the town of Seckingen, on the borders of the Black Forest, illustrious for the tomb of St. Fridolin, it is stated that thirty-two priests went on hearing confession for the space of twelve days from four o'clock in the morning till nine at night, the result of which was a conflux of communicants from a distance of ten, twenty, and thirty leagues round, to the number of 11,000. Similar accounts are given of a mission of this kind at Munster.

The Friends of Light.—This body of rationalists who, during the revolution, attempted to regain a regular footing in the established Churches, have been compelled to re-form their separatist ranks. Among others, Pastor Uhlich, at Magdeburg, who was deposed from his office as a clergyman of the Established Church of Prussia, in the autumn of 1847, and, thereupon, solemnly renounced all connexion with the Evangelic Church, but who, in the summer of 1848, during the revolutionary period, got himself re-elected by his former congregation of St. Catharine's, has been informed, that his election cannot be recognized, as he does not come within the qualifications of a candidate for the ministerial office according to the ecclesiastical law of Prussia. The coryphæus of the " Church of the Friends of Light," or "the Free Congregation," has therefore been compelled to fall back upon the reconstruction of his separatist body, resuming the position which he occupied before the revolution. He has since published, in a periodical which he conducts, the following graphic sketch of a portion of his followers : " We are perfectly aware that frivolity is not wanting in our ranks. Those who do not take a deep and serious view of life, are apt to catch at every new manifestation. Change is pleasurable to them, novelty attracts them. More especially, they delight in boldly opposing prejudices of all sorts, and they gratify their egotism by announcing loudly, that they have thrown off a yoke under which thousands are still bending their necks. We shall therefore find people in our ranks who are well aware what they do not want, but scarcely know what it is they want.—Unscrupulousness may also be met with in our ranks. Those who quarrel with any limit set to the indulgence of their appetites, are sometimes led to think that the "free congregation" is the very communion for them. Wherefore they join with the rest in protesting against priestcraft, but, in their hearts, their protest is aimed at the moral order established by God for the government of the world, which they find inconvenient. Unpromising members, certainly, of any congregation !—We have abolished all surplice fees. Our contributions as members of the congregation, are purely voluntary gifts of love, offered by every one according to his ability. This may have induced many to join us who have long grudgingly discharged their fees. A questionable motive this, no doubt, for joining the Free Church, especially if it be the only one.—Besides, it is to be considered, that in pulling down old things, we may, perchance, overthrow much that might have been left to stand. It is impossible to fell a tree in the forest, without damaging and breaking down some of the surrounding trees. Many an old and obsolete doctrine may, in some hearts, be so identified with eternal verities and principles, that the one cannot be rooted out, without eradicating the other with it. In getting rid of the Triune God, we may lose sight of God altogether; and, with the Godhead of Jesus, a moral ideal may vanish, which hitherto has supplied the soul with firmness and strength." This protest of Uhlich against the use which he apprehends may be made of his congregation, as a place of refuge for all spiritual uncleanness and lawlessness, is remarkable not only for its extreme candour in acknowledging the fact that such a spirit as that described by him is abroad among the rationalists of Germany, and for its boldness in rebuking that spirit; but for the distinctness with which it enunciates the form and substance of his unbelief,—the doctrine of the Holy Trinity and of the Divinity of the Lord Jesus being pronounced "old and obsolete;" pure Deism being substituted for belief in the former; and for belief in the latter, a reliance on the moral effect upon the heart and mind of a "moral ideal," to which the name of Jesus is attached.

The same undisguised openness in the denial of the Christian faith characterizes a "profession of principles" recently put forth by the "Free Congregation" at Halle, on the express ground that the declaration of its principles, which the "Free Congregation" made on its first institution, is no longer satisfactory. This "profession of principles" is as follows:—

" 1. The belief of the Church in revelation having succumbed to the spirit of progress, and the whole doctrine and organization of the Church having thereby become powerless, we have united together in a new communion, in order to cherish in ourselves spiritual and moral life in accordance with the progress of the age, and to spread the same beyond our own communion in the world at large.

" 2. We profess *humanism,* the religion of humanity, (Humanismus, die Religion der Menschlichkeit,) whose foundation, centre, and aim is the being and the welfare of man ; we have taken our stand upon the basis of free science and of fraternity. ˙

" 3. In true human culture and in the union of all upon this basis alone, we see deliverance for mankind from this present distress, and the groundwork of a new life.

" 4. The means which, according to our power, we employ for the attainment of these objects are :—Addresses for the development of our principles, as well upon all the various topics of life and science— discussions on the same subjects—promotion of self-tuition by the formation of libraries,—singing, music, and art generally—the education of the young—social meetings—diffusion of our views by word and writing.

" 5. We proceed herein upon the principle that the word is free, and that there is to be a reciprocity of instruction and of quickening. Every.

member is morally bound to promote both these objects to the best of his ability. Where existing abilities are insufficient, means must be used to attract the necessary abilities from without.

" 6. The necessary funds are procured by self-taxation. Every ordinary member pays a contribution, to be fixed by himself, with reference to his own means, and the wants of the congregation, which contribution may be increased or diminished by himself under a change of circumstances.

" 7. The right to order the affairs of the congregation, reposes in the body at large, which may exercise that right as it shall see fit, either by taking the sense of the majority, or by delegating its powers to individuals.

" 8. Every man or woman being eighteen years old, is admissible as an ordinary member, every person under that age, as an extraordinary member. The ordinary members alone have a vote, and are bound to pay a contribution. Admission to ordinary membership is given, after previous notice to the governing body, upon profession of these principles by subscription ; admission to extraordinary membership is given upon the declaration of parents or of others filling their place. The right of withdrawing is at all times free. The communion requires of all its members an honest and moral life, and active participation in its labours.

" 9. We invite all who are of the same mind with us,—who, as in duty bound, desire to promote the universal ascendancy of truth and justice,—to join our communion."

In transcribing this novel confession of faith, we cannot forbear calling particular attention to the enumeration of the means to be employed, under the fourth head ; being the identical means which are at this moment put forward by certain parties in this country, both in the legislature, and in the public at large, as the means of elevating the social condition of the people. There is not the same plain-spoken candour in avowing the end ; but, that the end is the same, the similarity of the means too clearly evinces. So striking is the parallel, that it requires only to be pointed out in order to carry conviction to the mind.

The German Catholics.—The infidel character of the body styling itself the " German Catholic Church " is becoming more and more manifest ; and the consequence is, that the established Protestant communions, which at one time seemed disposed to hold out the right hand of fellowship to those separatists from the rival Church of Rome, refuse to connect themselves with them, or in any way to recognise them. In Bavaria the Supreme Consistory of the Protestant Church has issued a rescript, with regard to the position which the German Catholic congregations are to occupy in relation to the Protestant Churches, of which the following is the substance :—

" 1. Forasmuch as the so-called Free or German Catholic congregations in Bavaria do not, according to their published confessions of faith, acknowledge the revealed Word of God as the only rule and standard in matters of faith ; and forasmuch as they reject the chief doctrines of the Christian Church based upon Holy Scripture, and frequently allege that their ideas of God, of man, and of the world, are altogether different from those of the existing Churches, for which reason also they declare themselves to be separated from the existing Churches, it follows that the Evangelic Protestant Church in Bavaria cannot hold communion with them.

" 2. The said congregations administer holy baptism, not in the name of the Triune God, according to the rule of all Christian Churches, founded upon Christ's own command ; they pledge the child to be baptized to no profession of faith, and generally they regard baptism, not as a reception into the communion of the Christian Church, but only as a reception into its outward society ; consequently that act of theirs cannot be acknowledged as Christian baptism ; but proper baptism must be administered to those who, having been formerly baptized in any of the said congregations, wish subsequently to join the Evangelic Church." The remaining parts of the decree declare the members of " free" or German Catholic congregations inadmissible as sponsors, and regulate the solemnization of mixed marriages and the settlement of property in such cases.

The provisions of this rescript have been abundantly justified since, by the Committee empowered to make preparations for the approaching General Synod of the German Catholic Church, to be held at Frankfort in May next. After considerable discussion, it was agreed that both the " Free Protestants," that is, the Rationalistic Separatists from the Lutheran and Calvinistic communions, and the " Free Jews," that is to say, the Jews who have exchanged their Judaism for rationalistic unbelief, shall be invited to attend the Council of the " German Catholic Church." The Council to be held will therefore be, in fact, a formal synod of unbelievers ; the first event of its kind that has taken place since the promulgation of the Gospel,—when apostate members of Christian and Jewish Communions will meet together for the express purpose of constituting a Church on the basis of the rejection of all revelation.

The Irvingite Sect.—The Irvingite Sect is extending itself rapidly in Germany, and absorbing, naturally enough, whatever there is left of deep piety and religious sympathy among the shaking and tottering national Churches. One of the most notable conquests which the Sect has as yet made, is the " conversion" of Dr. Heinrich Thiersch, professor of divinity at Marburg, and, though not actually ordained in the Lutheran Communion, yet in progress towards ordination, being what is technically termed an " examined Candidate *cum veniâ concionandi.*" In a letter which he has recently addressed to his ecclesiastical superior, the Lutheran Superintendent of the province of Upper Hessia, he draws the following picture of the present state of religion in Germany. " The revolution of 1848 has shown to what extent the destruction of the ancient faith, and of its fruit, a primitive, holy, and reverent temper, had proceeded, and how little is required to shake to its very foundation the spiritual and moral character of our people. Experience has proved that, generally speaking, the voice of the most mischievous self-constituted leaders, and the influence of equally mischievous unions formed under their auspices, were far more powerful than the authority of the Christian Clergy. Not one of the real and deeply seated evils is remedied ; the means which the Church has at her disposal for promoting Christian discipline, righteousness, and godliness, have proved more than ever inadequate. This is the case not only in our German fatherland ; it is the state of all the nations of Christendom. The antichristian principle has become one of the great powers of the world, nay, the greatest power of the age. Hence it is probable, that we are actually in the very midst of that time of terrible perplexity, for which, according to the prophecies of Holy Scripture, there is no other solution than the coming of Christ for the redemption of one, and the judgment of the other part of Christendom." After this sketch of the disorganized state of Christendom, Dr. Thiersch goes on to argue that, all the ordinary resources of the Church and of Christian civilization being exhausted, those that are to be healed can be healed only by some extraordinary interposition of God, by a manifestation of divine power, far more potent than any the world has yet witnessed. Thus, by a semi-theological, semi-philosophical train of reasoning, Dr. Thiersch arrives at the conclusion, that Irvingism is the very thing which the world wants at this moment, and thereupon professes himself to be a convert to this new revelation." After years of examination, after personal inspection, after a thorough acquaintance with the whole matter, he "bears witness" that God has made a beginning for the renovation of the Church, by the restoration of the necessary offices in all their purity and completeness, even of the Apostolate itself. For this conviction he declares himself ready to make any sacrifice. At the same time he maintains that the ministry which for the comfort and support of His children God is now raising up afresh, does not rise in opposition against those already invested with the office, but recognizes them in the hope of a reciprocal acknowledgment on the ground of the fruits of its labours. The name Irvingism he carefully eschews, setting forth his sect, in accordance with its pretensions in this country, as a new phasis of the Church.

The conversion of Professor Thiersch dates back as far as the year 1847. As soon as he had himself arrived at a definite conclusion, he submitted all he had heard to his ecclesiastical superior. Not having been ordained as yet in the Evangelic Church of Germany, he considered himself entitled to seek ordination, where it appeared to him "most legitimate and most salutary" to obtain it. He paid a visit to England, and is said to have been ordained as "Evangelist" for Hessia. In the course of last year, he began to hold meetings for public worship with his co-religionists. He resigned his post as professor, not on account of the change which had taken place in his religious views, but because he thought himself bound to devote more time to his new calling. "I do not find it easy," he says, in the concluding part of the letter before quoted, "to give up a profession for which I have been educated,

and to which I have devoted ten years of my life.   But, however great
my fondness for the office of academic teaching, I cannot conceal from
myself how impossible it is to do any good to the Church, by a system
of instruction which treats the most important thing of all—the doing
the commandments of Christ—as a matter of secondary importance,
which does not make religion its ground-work, but only admits its existence in a manner utterly nugatory, and therefore builds all upon sand.
Neither do I intend the steps which I have now taken to be considered
as a separation from the Evangelic Church, or as a display of ingratitude towards her.   I and all those who are embarked in the same course
with me are anxious to preserve a feeling of gratitude towards our
mother Church, although we have found something higher than it,
namely, the work of Apostolic reformation, in which we find all the
verities of the Evangelic Church, and rich treasures besides."

The reply of the Superintendent to this notification, while treating Dr. Thiersch personally with all tenderness and respect, contains
a decisive condemnation of Irvingism, and of the course pursued
with regard to it by Dr. Thiersch, whose assurance that he intended
no separation from the Evangelic Church, he declares to be irreconcilable with the other contents of his letter, and with the position
which he announces himself to have assumed.   The Superintendent
complains particularly that the new communion which Dr. Thiersch
has joined, and which claims to be a higher and more comprehensive
communion in which the Evangelic Church is to be absorbed,
should fail to present to the Churches which it approaches with
such lofty claims, a formal, definite, and public confession of
faith, leaving the members of other communions to find out, as best
they may, wherein its distinctive character consists.   With regard to
the ordination which Dr. Thiersch declared himself to have obtained,
where he thought it most "legitimate and salutary" to do so, the Superintendent remarks that the Evangelic Church having an ordination of her
own, which she deems sufficient and in all respects valid, cannot recognize within her pale another ordination by superiors placed beyond
her pale, and laying claim to a higher authority.   And as Dr. Thiersch
proposes still to recognize the authority of the Evangelic Church, and
of his own superiors in it, the Superintendent inquires officially, what
functions and what obligations Dr. Thiersch has undertaken by virtue
of his ordination in another communion?   And further he inquires,
whether his undertaking such functions and obligations, and receiving
such ordination, setting aside the rule and order of the Evangelic
Church in regard to the ordination and appointment of ministers, can be
consistent with the prior obedience due from him to the Church for whose
orders he was a candidate, whose licence to preach the Gospel he had obtained, and to which he was bound by the obligation of an oath?   Ad-
verting to the superiority ascribed by Dr. Thiersch to the new communion
which he had joined, and to his apparent assumption of the right, by
virtue of his ordination in it, to minister the Word and Sacraments, not
only in that communion itself, but in the Evangelic Church also, as

being a subordinate body, the Superintendent distinctly refuses to recognize such a claim. "It is impossible," he says, "for an Evangelic Church to acknowledge a Church authority by the side of, or, properly speaking, above the existing and duly ordained government of the Church; a ministry by the side of, or, more accurately viewed, above the regularly called ministers of the Word; an altar, if not against, at least beside, or rather above, the existing altar, at which we believe that we find the promised blessing in accordance with the divine ordinance. Being in possession of the rich treasures of the Divine Word, to the pure and unadulterated declaration of which she binds her ministers; in possession of the Holy Sacraments, which she administers agreeably to the divine institution; in possession of all the means of grace, of which she stands in need for the service of her Lord, she will ever gratefully acknowledge any assistance rendered her by word or by writing for the confirmation of her members; but she cannot permit her members to form separate communions, to introduce a form, and to order seasons, of worship distinct from her own, including the performance of ministerial offices, and more especially the administration of the Holy Sacraments." Such irregular and unauthorized proceedings the Superintendent declares to be wholly incompatible with the order and discipline of the Evangelic Church, and intimates that Dr. Thiersch ought to know as much, without requiring to have it pointed out to him. In conclusion, the Superintendent calls upon Dr. Thiersch to consider whether the position he has assumed is compatible with that which he still claims to occupy; and, since they are incompatible, to make his option between the two, and either openly to renounce the communion of the Evangelic Church, or else to submit himself to her rule and order.

Death of Prince Hohenlohe.—Prince Alexander Von Hohenlohe, Provost of Greatwardein, whose pretended miracles excited so much attention some years ago, died at Vöslau, on the 14th November last, in the fifty-fourth year of his age.

ITALY.—*The Jesuits.*—Father Roothan, General of the Jesuits, has joined the Pope at Portici. Throughout the kingdom of Naples the members of the Order are taking possession again of their houses and other property.

NEWFOUNDLAND.—*Church Education.*—The Church is experiencing similar treatment from the Government in Newfoundland, respecting its schools, as at home. The legislative grant for education has been given among the Dissenters almost unconditionally, while the Church has been unable to obtain any share of it, on account of the terms insisted upon for its acceptance. The Bishop is laudably exerting himself to remove this injustice.

SPAIN.—*Poverty of the Romish Church.*—A petition, addressed to the Queen of Spain by nineteen incumbents of the Archdiocese of Toledo, states that out of the last four years' stipend, two and a half years' are in arrear; that in 1849 not a maravedi was bestowed either upon the stipends of the clergy or the support of the churches. They announce the impending cessation of public worship for the want of supplies, and complain that the church presents in her ornaments as beggarly an appearance as the clergy in their gras.

SWITZERLAND.—*Statistics of the Romish Church.*—There are, according to a recent account in the Roman Catholic part of Switzerland, 2500 secular priests, and 1500 regulars in priests' orders, being at the rate of one priest to each 250 inhabitants. The number of nuns in the Swiss convents is stated at 1000. Their property is estimated as follows :—convents, twenty millions of Swiss francs ; other foundations, five and a half millions ; endowments of parish churches, near thirty millions.

UNITED STATES.—*Bishop De Lancey on Religious Training.*—The Charge delivered by Dr. De Lancey to the clergy of the diocese of Western New York, at the opening of the Convention in Trinity Church, Geneva, in the course of last autumn, and since published, furnishes an impartial and most valuable testimony to the great principle of Church Education. The Bishop distinguishes two systems in the process of religious education—the system of excitement, and the system of training. The former supposes the baptized individual to be incapable of religious or spiritual action, until he is, at some period of life, early or late, awakened, impressed and changed by the Holy Spirit ; with a view to whose action upon him it is necessary that human means should be used to arrest, disturb, and excite his mind on the subject of his salvation. The latter—the system of training—supposes the individual to be capable of religious exercises from the earliest period of intelligence, not by nature, but in virtue of imparted grace pledged by covenant to him ; by means of which, as he is empowered for moral action, so moral action is required, and may be acceptably rendered by him. Hence he is to be taught religious duties which he is to perform ; he is to be taught religious doctrine which he is to believe ; he is to be swayed by religious motives to which he is accessible ; he is to be led to moral obedience which he can render ; he is to share in Christian ordinances which are profitable to him. He is to be trained in knowledge, holiness, virtue, graces, spiritual duties, doctrines, ordinances, and in acts of faith, holiness, and grace that may attest his conformity to the will of God, and secure through Christ, as its meritorious origin, his everlasting salvation. Of these two systems the latter is that which the Bishop points out as the Church system, to be carried out in parochial schools :—

"By parochial or church schools, we mean the identification of religion as the Church holds it, with education ; educating our children as children of the Church, in schools of the Church ; providing each large parish, if possible, with a school of its own, where the children connected with it may be taught by competent religious teachers connected with the Church, who will make religion, as the Church holds it, not only the basis of all instruction, but the pervading principle and influence running through all its parts and progress, imbuing the mind with the knowledge of it, warming the heart with the love of it, and moulding the intellect and habits to its devotions, worship, doctrines, liturgy, and usages.

"Some, you know, hold that religion and education should stand apart from each other. Others teach, that morality only should be allied with education. Others, again, that only a general and abstract view of religion should be associated with education. Others, again, put forth their views in the form that education is to be unchurched. 'Education without a church' is the principle claimed and avowed to be the right principle.

"In opposition to such views, the true theory of the Bible and the Church is, that religion is the foundation of a sound education; that the God who gave the mind should govern the mind; that the expansion and training of the intellect should ever be according to, and in association with, His laws, influence, and grace; that to mould the intellectual habits without reference to the Deity and His laws, His institutions, and His Spirit, is in direct hostility to man's true interest, duty, and responsibility; and hence, that over the union of religion with education we are bound to pronounce the solemn declaration, 'what God hath joined together let no man put asunder.'

"Now this can only be carried out by Church schools and Church colleges, which shall unite, avowedly, religious instruction with literary instruction; which shall connect Church worship, Church doctrines, Church usages, Church feelings, Church principles, with the daily business of education; which shall daily present the great and glorious God before the mind, humble it on the knee of confession to Him, raise it in supplication to His throne, inspirit it by the melody of praise to Him, and send it forth in the feeling of utter dependence on His infinite mercy for existence, faculties, and knowledge; for redemption, grace, and glory, through the mediation of His blessed Son, and the power of His Holy Spirit.

"The Parochial School system keeps constantly before the eyes of both children and parents, the authority to which both are responsible. In its practical exhibition it is presented to view in some such form as this: The children assembled for receiving instruction begin by calling upon God in prayer, and singing to his praise. Those prayers and hymns are from the Prayer Book; the very services, in part, in which they are accustomed to unite on the Lord's Day in the sanctuary with their parents and friends. Sunday is thus carried into the school. They see that religion is not merely for the Lord's Day, or for the Church, but is something for every day; that it mingles with their learning and their business; that God is to be served, thought of, worshipped, obeyed, and loved in the school, as well as elsewhere.

"A reference to God's will is intermingled with all their learning. His doctrines are inculcated; duties to Him are enforced; the worship of Him is practised. Dependence on His Spirit for strength, on His blessed Son for pardon, on His Holy Word for light and guidance, is constantly presented to the mind. The holy warnings, the earnest counsels, the warm appeals, the affectionate interest of a Divine Saviour, are brought to their view. In the principles, the grounds, the usages, the doctrine, the ministry which God has established, they are instructed by the Minister himself. In the nature, character, and claims of the holy and spiritual kingdom which Christ established, and taught his disciples to pray for in the daily petition, 'Thy kingdom come,' they are instructed why we adhere to its constitution as Christ gave it to us, why its Liturgy was adopted, how it conforms to Holy Scripture, and has for ages edified His members, in what relation they stand to the Church, how and why it should never be deserted, or discountenanced, or shunned.

In conclusion the Bishop argues that "the training system is the system of common sense, the system of analogy, the system of the Gospel, the true system ;" and after illustrating the first two propositions by remarks of a general nature, proceeds to demonstrate that "the training system is the system of the Church." This the Bishop does by reference to the sponsorial promises and the baptismal office ; to the Catechism, with the rubrics attached to it ; to the provision made for the confirmation of baptized children ; and to the Office for Confirmation, with its rubrics ; to the exhortation and prayers in the Communion Service, and to the twenty-eighth Canon of the General Convention :—

" ' It shall be the duty of ministers to prepare young persons and others for the holy ordinance of Confirmation.

" 'The ministers of this Church who have charge of parishes orcures, shall not only be diligent in instructing the children in the catechism, but shall also, by stated catechetical lectures and instruction, be diligent in informing the youth, and others, in the doctrines, constitution, and liturgy of the Church.'"

Planting of the Church in California.—Movement towards a Reformation in the Romish Church in South America.—The following extracts from a letter addressed by the Rev. Thos. Mines, an American Missionary in California, to a friend in New York, dated San Francisco, November 1st, 1849, give a graphic description of the state of religion in the gold country :—

" My first invitation to officiate as a clergyman was the Sunday we spent at sea, between New York and Chagres, on the ' Crescent City.' About a hundred persons assembled on Saturday evening, and, appointing a committee from all the companies on board, invited me to officiate the following day. I agreed to do so, but the day was the roughest we experienced on the trip, and thwarted our intentions. The attempt, however, was not lost. The formality of the proceeding, and the universal support it received, at an *impromptu* meeting, indicated that there were elements *en route* for California that gave good men good cause to hope. At Panama, I officiated regularly, gave the Holy Communion to some thirty persons on Easter Day, and held services appropriate to Passion Week . . . . I am quite confident that prudent measures would throw beauty and life again into the Church of New

Granada. See what has been done in Chili, in the international reformation of the Romish Church. The Church of Chili is, if accounts I have heard be true, far advanced in the path of Reformation. A Bishop is appointed; the Pope refuses to confirm the choice;—the nomination is renewed, in the form of a demand,—the Pope issues a Bull ordering the consecration, declaring that ' We have *proprio motu* appointed the said A. B.,' &c. :—the Bull is sent back, demanding the erasure of the *proprio motu*, as the nomination had been by the Church and government of Chili—and the Pope yielded. In Yucatan, as a military officer informed me, the papal authority was at that moment, for causes he did not know, disavowed and interrupted. In fact, the Romish Church in some of these countries has touched bottom, and I am sure her reformation might be effected. You will be surprised to hear that, since leaving home, the curate and several inhabitants of a certain place urged me much to accept the use of their church and perform our service. No explanation that I was not a Romanist, would be allowed. Officiate and preach I must. Only my engagements to leave the place the same day prevented my complying. I told them in answer to their questions, I was a ' Christian—a Catholic,'—' Apostolic' too—not a Romanist—holding to no Pope—no prayers to saints —no masses or propitiatory sacrifices by Priests for the living and the dead—no auricular confession—no Purgatory, &c., &c.; but believed in the commemorative sacrifice—showed my Prayer-book—and was almost forced by them to exhibit our faith in its forms of worship. A Baptist, Methodist, and Presbyterian minister were present, and joined in the importunity—and I have since almost regretted that I did not do violence to all my plans, and accept the invitation. . . . . We must have a man at Panama, Christian, Catholic, and Apostolic—acknowledging a priesthood and an altar—him they will hear.

" On the vessel from Panama to this port, I found our services numerously attended, and well sustained. At sea they are impressive, and possess a charm that cannot be counterfeited. This is found to be the case on board our men-of-war. Methodists, Presbyterians, all on board men-of-war, with scarcely an exception, use our forms; and any thing else appears incongruous with the majesty and the glory of the sea. Our congregation on board increased up to the very last Sunday, when the entire ship-full appeared to be present.

" On my arrival here, not being well enough to enter on the task, I waited till the 22nd of July, when, after Divine service (conducted by the Rev. Mr. Fitch, of Staten Island, who had officiated here a few Sundays, and myself), I stated distinctly the plan on which I had set out—the parochial—that and nothing else ; and said, that if the congregation to which I might be attached was not organized here, independently of all missionary agency, I should go to some other point. Resolutions were adopted, and the 29th of July appointed for the election of wardens and vestrymen. Subsequently I was elected rector of the parish, the name of which is the Church of the Holy Trinity. At our last communion but one we had twenty-eight communicants, and at our last thirty-six. I have already baptized two adults, and admitted five new communicants to the Church, the whirl in which we live seeming to lead certain thoughtful minds to seek something fixed and satisfied in the provisions of our holy faith. As soon as we could, we purchased a lot for six thousand dollars (for which we were soon afterwards offered ten) on an eminence commanding a view scarcely possible to be excelled. It is a lot, called here a fifty *vara* lot, nearly 140 feet square, large enough for church, rectory, Trinity-school (which we have in view), and other purposes. In the mean time, the rents of the unoccupied ground alone will, we suppose, more than half support the Church. Knowing that any building we could possibly now erect would not give satisfaction even a year hence, we have contracted for a temporary place of worship, twenty-five feet by fifty, of wood, and very plain, which will yet cost us (the building alone) eight thousand dollars. The church for posterity we hope to begin in a year or two. I am happy to say that we are likely to have this whole property from the beginning free from incumbrance and all debt. The new building is oblong—four windows in each side, two in the end—prayers, litany, and sermons on the chancel steps, just outside the chancel railing. Such a church in New York would perhaps have not cost over a thousand dollars. If churches could be brought out here by our clergy, or sent out here by some good layman, say five or six churches, with a view to a profit of 100 per cent. (which to a good Churchman ought to be sufficient), I guarantee their purchase here upon the spot. Our church will be sanded and blocked outside, and, if we can make it, for ever free. We have determined not in any case to sell pews, even if, for building rectory, school-house, &c., we deem it proper for a year or two to rent a part of them. Next Sunday we expect, by God's blessing, to offer up praise in the new sanctuary.

"On the 14th of September, I undertook, against many remonstrances, on account of prevalent sickness, a journey into the interior, and every where was welcomed as a messenger of rest to the weary. At Sacramento city, about 130 miles distant, on the Sacramento river, I officiated on the 16th of September, and at three successive meetings of the congregation or parish, which goes by the name of 'Grace Church,' and includes plans for a 'Grace Church Academy.' Messrs. Cornwall and Lee gave us on the spot a lot of land, valued then at 2000 dollars. This parish is now waiting for a clergyman. Only yesterday one of the wardens was here begging me to make, if possible, some arrangements for providing them the Church's services, which Mr. Fitch will be able partially to do.

"On the Sunday following I officiated, for large and interesting congregations, at a place called Vernon, one of the future cities, at the junction of Feather River and the Sacramento—a very eligible site, in direct communication with vast mining districts. Mr. Schoolcraft presented me a lot for a church in this place, and Mr. Crosby (a member of our late California State Convention) gave us another adjoining the former, the two together being 100 feet front, and 100 feet deep, shaded by magnificent trees, and in the very best place. These gentlemen gave me a *carte blanche* to choose what lot I pleased. The agent of Captain Sutter has promised me, in glebes, an endowment of fifty acres each, for the churches of Vernon and Sacramento city.

"At San Jose, which I visited two weeks ago, I received the donation of a fifty vara lot (140 feet square), the gift of James F. Reed, for the use of an Episcopal parish, ten minutes from the State-house and public square (the late Convention having made this the seat of Government). It is important to have the Church here at once, and, if we are to have a Church University in this country, the valley of St. Jose is undoubtedly the place. . . . .

"Wherever I go, I hear but one expression of feeling, that California need not draw upon the mites and stinted offerings to our Missionary Board. The feeling is: 'We can take care of ourselves; let our starving missionaries nearer home be paid their dues, and be kept from starving; at the high rates and prices in California, the little the Missionary Society could do for us here would be only an incumbrance, and no relief.' But if our Society are determined on real 'missionary' work in California, here are thousands and tens of thousands of Indians immersed in heathenism, who are docile and open to receive the white man's religion. At Vernon, some thirty or forty Indians gathered around us, observing intently our religious rites. I visited their camp, having been attracted to it by the howlings and wailings the night before, and which were in commemoration of some of their dead. . . . .

"The Indians in this country are stupid, and lack entirely the animation and intelligent fire of the aborigines toward the east. They are also darker, and approach decidedly to the features of the negro, though their hair is straight and long. The Missionary Society will find them perfectly tractable, harmless, and docile, and I doubt not Christianity would advance rapidly among them.

"The last few Sundays we have had the Crown Prince of the Sandwich Islands, and his cousin, at our church. They have attended regularly, joined in the services, and seemed much interested. It would be premature to anticipate the future on this subject, but I hear that the present king desires to have our Church represented in the islands, and that it will meet with favour, and will probably have the royal attendance. I have taken the necessary means to ascertain the true state of the case. Our Church will save the Sandwich Islands from the Romanists;—from much that I hear, perhaps nothing else can, as the old missionary influence and hold upon the people is represented as of doubtful duration."

Consecration of the Bishop of Indiana.—On Sunday, Dec. 16, the Right Rev. Dr. Chase, Bishop of Illinois, and Presiding Bishop of the House of Bishops of the United States, assisted by the Bishops of Kentucky, Ohio, and Missouri, and Dr. Kemper, Missionary Bishop, consecrated the Rev. George Upfold, D.D., Bishop elect for the diocese of Indiana.

New Diocese of Texas.—A new diocese has been organized in the state of Texas. The primary Convention was held in Christ Church, in the city of Matagorda, on Monday, the first day of January, 1849, for the purpose of considering the propriety of organizing the Church of the said state into a diocese, when, among others, the following resolutions were adopted :—

. " That the clergy and laity of said Church, living in Texas, are hereby united and formed into a diocese, to be styled and known as the Protestant Episcopal Church in the state of Texas, and to be in union with the General Convention of said Church when admitted to a representation therein.

" That we place the diocese of Texas under the full episcopal charge and authority of the Right Rev. G. W. Freeman, D.D., Missionary Bishop of the Protestant Episcopal Church, appointed to exercise episcopal functions in the states of Arkansas and Texas, and in the Indian territory south of 36 1-2 deg. parallel of latitude.

" That, inasmuch as the exigencies of the Church in Texas require organization, and it is still too feeble to support a bishop, that the Board of Missions be, and hereby are, respectfully requested to continue to us the aid hitherto extended.

" That the deputies to the General Convention be authorized and requested to apply for the admission of this diocese to representation in that body."

Statistics of the Romish Church.—According to the data furnished by the Roman Catholics themselves, they have in the United States three Archbishops, 24 Bishops, 1081 Priests, and 1073 churches, or, including California and New Mexico, 1141 Priests, and 1133 churches. The Roman Catholic population is computed at 1,523,350 souls.

A Transatlantic Cardinal.—According to an announcement in the last message of the President of Mexico, Pius IX. has signified his desire to confer the dignity of Cardinal upon some Mexican Bishop, who will be the first Cardinal on the American continent.

Novel Practice of Anti-Pædobaptists.—It appears that, among the Baptists in Baltimore, a practice is growing up of " blessing " children, in imitation of the Saviour. The ceremony is performed either in the public congregation, or in private in the family circle ; and the services consist of a prayer, and admonitions addressed to the parents. " If," says a letter in the *Christian Intelligencer,* from a Baptist at Baltimore, " this custom were introduced into our Churches generally, it might perhaps modify or abrogate the present mode of infant baptism among our Pædobaptist brethren." The practice is recommended by the Baltimore Baptists to their Baptist brethren throughout the Union.

THE

ENGLISH REVIEW.

JUNE, 1850.

ART. I.—*The Voyage and Shipwreck of St. Paul: with Dissertations on the Sources of the Writings of St. Luke, and the Ships and Navigation of the Ancients.* By JAMES SMITH, Esq., *of Jordan Hill, F.R.S., &c.* London: Longmans. 1848.

THE investigation announced in the title of Mr. Smith's work is one which requires a combination of qualities and capacities which are seldom found in the possession of a single individual. Classical scholarship, of no mean calibre or contracted span; antiquarian knowledge, stretching from the days of Pericles to the dawn of modern civilization; seamanship, both scientific and experimental; a familiar acquaintance with the lands and seas, the winds and waves of the Eastern Mediterranean,—all these requisites, together with patient industry and clear judgment, are needed. Nor is it too much to say, that all these are eminently possessed by Mr. Smith; and that all of them have been employed in considering the Voyage and Shipwreck of St. Paul, and in elucidating the hitherto obscure subject of the Ships and Navigation of the Ancients. The concluding Dissertation on the Sources of the Writings of St. Luke contains important matter and valuable suggestions; but the author has, we think, in more than one instance, arrived at conclusions which are not borne out by the arguments adduced to establish them.

Amongst the many false theories which a perverse ingenuity has broached and maintained, in defiance of a clear matter-of-fact, there is perhaps none more astonishing than that which represents the shipwreck of St. Paul as having taken place on the obscure island of Meleda, situated on the Illyrian side of the Gulf of Venice, instead of the well-known island of Malta, or Melita.

"Tradition," says Mr. Smith, "from time immemorial, has pointed out a bay in the island of Malta as the scene of St. Paul's shipwreck. It has never been known by any other name than 'Cala di S. Paolo,' or St. Paul's Bay. There is no mode of perpetuating the memory of events more effectual than that of naming places after them; but, although we can scarcely have a stronger case of traditional evidence than the present, in the following inquiry I attach no weight to it whatever. I do not even assume the authenticity of the narrative of the voyage and shipwreck contained in the Acts of the Apostles, but scrutinize St. Luke's account of the voyage precisely as I would those of Baffin or Middleton, or of any ancient voyage of doubtful authority, or involving points on which controversies have been raised! A searching comparison of the narrative with the localities where the events so circumstantially related are said to have taken place, with the aids which recent advances in our knowledge of the geography and the navigation of the eastern part of the Mediterranean supply, accounts for every transaction—clears up every difficulty, and exhibits an agreement so perfect in all its parts as to admit but of one explanation, namely, that it is a narrative of real events, written by one personally engaged in them, and that the tradition respecting the locality is true." —p. vj.

Untenable as is the hypothesis that the Melita of St. Paul was the Meleda of the Venetian gulf, the investigation of the subject has been hitherto much obstructed by the want of information respecting the various localities in dispute, and the great ignorance which has prevailed up to the present time, regarding the vessels of the ancients, and their method of navigating them. Recent observations have, however, taught us much concerning the winds and currents of the Levant ; recent surveys have furnished us with a correct outline of the coast of Crete. " At Malta, where we require to know not only the outline and peculiar features of the coast, but the soundings and peculiar nature of the bottom, we have Captain Smyth's chart of the island, and, above all, his plan of St. Paul's Bay, to a scale of 8 — 6 inches to the mile :"—A careful and judicious examination of all that ancient writers and ancient remains tell, either directly or inferentially, of the nautical science of the ancients, with constant reference to the accounts of early voyagers and the practice of Levantine sailors, has enabled Mr. Smith to clear up most of the difficulties existing with regard to the ships and navigation of the age of the Cæsars. And all these advantages have been increased and rendered more effective by a personal examination of the Cala di S. Paolo.

" A winter's residence in Malta (says our author) afforded me ample opportunities for a personal examination of the localities. In the ships of war stationed there, I could consult with skilful and scientific seamen, familiar with the navigation of the Levant, an advantage I did not fail to avail myself of ; and, as it is my intention to put my reader in possession of my authorities, I have never scrupled to name them. In the Knights' Library I had access to an extensive collection of works, printed and manuscript, on the controversy as to the scene of the shipwreck, on the hydrography of the Mediterranean, and on local and classical antiquities. The following summer I spent on the Continent, and devoted my time almost exclusively to the investigation, with the advantages which the Museums of Naples, Florence, Lausanne, and Paris afforded. Since my return, I have continued it, with the advantages our own country possesses; particularly in the libraries and medal-rooms of the British Museum and Records of the Admiralty, and with a private library which I may term rich in early sea voyages."—p. xii.

Speaking of his own researches and qualifications for the task which he has undertaken, he adds,—

" I have, in the first place, endeavoured to identify the locality of a shipwreck which took place eighteen centuries ago. An attempt to do this would be of little value unless the geological changes to which sea-coasts are liable, which may or must have occurred in the interval, are taken into account. Now it so happens that this is a department of geology which I have been engaged many years in investigating."

After speaking of the importance in this investigation of " some practical knowledge of navigation and seamanship," Mr. Smith proceeds :—

" My knowledge of these subjects is only that of an amateur; yet a yacht sailor, of more than thirty years' standing, can scarcely fail to have acquired some skill in those principles of nautical science which are common to all times. . . . I find, at all events, the knowledge I have thus acquired enables me to consult my nautical friends with advantage."

In addition to this, we are told that

" Nautical antiquities have long been a favourite study [with Mr. Smith]; and not a little practical experience in planning, building, and altering vessels, has given me definite notions both of external form and internal capabilities; whilst the opportunity of testing my con-clusions by experiment, and the success of those I have made, give me confidence in their accuracy."

Mr. Smith has also derived much information " from the pic-tures and marbles exhumed at Herculaneum and Pompeii," and especially from the discovery of the inventories of the Athenian fleet, which were excavated at the Piræus in 1834.

With such advantages, and others which we have been obliged to pass over in silence, Mr. Smith has undertaken the investigation in question. We have been thus particular in detailing these advantages that our readers may feel at once assured that the author deserves a hearing : we now propose to join him in accom-panying St. Paul and St. Luke on their memorable voyage.

Mr. Smith commences his Essay by some observations on the character and style of St. Luke. He points out various inci-dental touches which bear witness to his Antiochian origin, his medical profession, his classical education, and his intimate ac-quaintance with naval affairs; the acquaintance however, as he shows, not of a sailor, but of a landsman who had been a good

deal at sea.   He compares his account of the voyage with those
of modern naval surgeons, and hazards the conjecture that
St. Luke may, in the earlier part of his life, have sailed as medical attendant in some large vessel.   The minute exactness of
nautical phraseology, combined with the feelings and notions of a
landsman; are curiously worked out by Mr. Smith.

But let us weigh anchor, and set sail ourselves, or we shall
never arrive at the end of our voyage.

St. Paul, having been intrusted by Festus to a Roman centurion, by name Julius, set sail from Cæsarea in a vessel belongiug
to Adramyttium, bound to the sea-ports on the western coast of
Asia Minor.   They reached Sidon, a distance of sixty-seven
miles, on the next day.   The wind was, therefore, probably west ;
the prevailing wind in those seas.   Hence they had intended to
strike right across to the Lycian extremity of the great Pamphy-
lian Bay—the Chelidonian Promontory.   Being prevented by the
prevalence of the westerly winds from making this straight course,
they were compelled to steer in a northerly direction, slightly inclining to the west ; and thus, under the lee of Cyprus, which
they left on the left hand, enter the Cilician Sea, and, striking
across it, avail themselves of the shelter of the continental coast
and the assistance of the land breezes and westerly current.   It
has been conjectured that the Apostle sailed to the south and
west instead of the east of Cyprus ; but that this notion is erroneous is clear from St. Luke's statement of his crossing the
Cilician Sea, which, supposing them to have steered north-west
under the pressure of a north or north-east wind, they could not
have entered : in fact, such a course was that which they desired
to make, but from which they were prevented by adverse winds.
Mr. Smith brings several passages from modern navigators, who,
under similar circumstances, notice the prevalence of westerly
winds, and cites examples of vessels which were compelled to take
the same course as that indicated by St. Luke.

" Favoured, as they probably were by the land breeze and currents,
they arrive without any recorded incident at Myra of Lycia, then a
flourishing sea-port, now a desolate waste.   The stupendous magnitude
of its theatre attests the extent of its former population ; the splendour
of its tombs, its wealth."—p. 30.

" The voyage has hitherto been prosperous, and the object which the
party had in view in proceeding to 'the places in Asia[1],' is attained.
At the first of them which lay in their way, the centurion found a ship
of Alexandria, loaded, as we afterwards learn, with wheat, bound for

---

[1] The " *Asia* " mentioned by St. Luke, in Acts xxvii. 2, is the Roman province
of which Ephesus was the capital.   It is marked in Greek by the article, ἡ 'Ασία,
as in Acts ii. 9 ; xx. 16 ; xxvii. 2, and many other places.

Italy, in which he embarked his charge. Egypt was at this time one of the granaries of Rome, and the corn which was sent from thence to Italy, was conveyed in ships of very great size. From the dimensions given of one of them by Lucian, they appear to have been quite as large as the largest class of merchant ships of modern times. We need not be surprised, therefore, at the number of souls which we afterwards find were embarked in this one, or that another ship of the same class could after the shipwreck convey them to Italy, in addition to her own crew."—p. 32.

It seems probable that the same westerly wind which prevented St. Paul's vessel from striking across from Sidon to Asia, had induced the Alexandrian to steer for Myra, which lies almost due north from Alexandria, as she could not take the direct course from Egypt to Italy.

"In this ship of Alexandria in which the centurion and his party embarked, they proceeded on their voyage. Their progress, after leaving Myra, was extremely slow ; for we are told that it was many days before they were 'come over against Cnidus,' that is before they reached the entrance of the Ægean Sea. As the distance between the two places is not more than 130 geographical miles, which they could easily have accomplished with a fair wind in one day, they must either have met with calms or contrary winds. I infer that the delay was caused by unfavourable winds, from the expression μόλις, which is translated in our authorized version 'scarce,' producing the impression that the ship had scarcely reached Cnidus, when the winds became contrary ; but which ought to be rendered 'with difficulty,' expressing the difficulty which ships experience in contending with adverse winds. The same word occurs in the following verse, where it is translated 'hardly,' where there can be no doubt as to its meaning . . . . I am satisfied, therefore, that the words in the original 'βραδυπλοοῦντες καὶ μόλις γενόμενοι,' 'sailing slowly and with difficulty, were come,' &c., express the delays which a ship experiences in working to windward."—p. 35.

There can be no doubt that Mr. Smith's interpretation of μόλες is the right one, and that the seventh verse may be rendered freely—*And after sailing slowly for some days, and having with difficulty arrived off Cnidus, as the wind would not allow us to pursue our right course* [which lay straight through the Ægean at about west by south], *we sailed under the lee of Crete by Cape Salmone*—i. e. they made for Cape Salmone, and thence sailed under the lee of Crete. In the next verse the αὐτήν refers, not to the promontory of Salmone, but to the island of Crete ; and the whole verse may be rendered—*And beating up against the wind, we coasted the island until we arrived at a place called Fair Havens, near to which was the city Lasea.*

" The question now occurs, What was the direction of the wind which produced the effects recorded in the narrative?" It must have been a wind which would not permit the vessel to shape her course west and by south—which would allow her to go without any difficulty from Cnidus to Salmone—and which would admit of her slowly bearing up from Myra to Cnidus, and from Salmone to Fair Havens.

Now if a wind can be found fulfilling all these conditions—if that wind be commonly prevalent in the Levant towards the close of summer—if under the pressure of this wind vessels do now actually take the same course under the same circumstances; then we shall be justified in assuming that we have found the wind which we are in search of. Now all these conditions are fulfilled by the north-west, " which cannot be more than two points, and is probably not more than one from the true direction. The wind, therefore, would in common language have been termed north-west."

" This," says Mr. Smith, after carefully working the problem out, " is precisely the wind which might have been expected in those seas towards the end of summer. We learn from the sailing directions for the Mediterranean, that throughout the whole of that sea, ' but mostly in the eastern half, including the Adriatic and Archipelago, the north-west winds prevail in the summer months . . . . the summer etesiæ come from the north-west,' (p. 197,) which agrees with Aristotle's account of these winds. According to Pliny they begin in August, and blow for forty days.

" With north-west winds the ship could work up from Myra to Cnidus; because, until she reached that point she had the advantage of a weather shore . . . . &c. At Cnidus that advantage ceased; and unless she had put into that harbour, and waited for a fair wind, her only course was to run under the lee of Crete, κατα Σαλμώνην, in the direction of Salmone, which is the eastern extremity of that island. After passing this point, the difficulty they experienced in navigating to the westward along the coast of Asia would recur; but as the south side of Crete is also a weather shore, with north-west winds, they would be able to work up as far as Cape Matala. Here the land bends suddenly to the north, and the advantages of a weather shore cease, and their only resource was to make for a harbour. Now, Fair Havens is the harbour nearest to Cape Matala, the furthest point to which an ancient ship would have attained with north-westerly winds."—p. 37.

Those commentators who dispute this view of the question, are compelled to place Fair Havens on the north of Crete—its situation has, however, been ascertained beyond all doubt. Besides other evidence, Pococke says:—

" In searching for Lebena, further to the west, I found out a place which I thought to be of greater importance, because mentioned in Holy Scripture, and also honoured by the presence of St. Paul, that is, the Fair Havens, near unto the city of Lasea; for there is another small bay, about two leagues to the east of Matala, which is now called by the Greeks Good or Fair Havens (Λιμέονες Καλούς)."—p. 44.

The character of this place is not that of a harbour; it consists of two adjacent bays, slightly varying in their aspect, and each furnishing a good roadstead.

"Here we learn," continues Mr. Smith, "they were detained till navigation had become dangerous, in consequence of the advanced state of the season. The fast, supposed to be that of the expiation, which took place about the period of the autumnal equinox, was now passed. It would appear that all hope of completing the voyage during the present season was abandoned, and it became a question whether they should winter at Fair Havens, or move the vessel to Port Phenicè, a harbour on the same side of Crete, about forty miles further to the westward."—p. 46.

St. Paul assisted at the consultation which was held on this occasion, and warned them of the dangers which they would incur, should they attempt to make Port Phenicè— where it is to be however observed that the phrase ἀλλὰ καὶ τῶν ψυχῶν ἡμῶν—should not have been rendered "but also of our lives"—but, "but also of our persons"—such being frequently the sense of ψυχή, and agreeing both with the context and sequel. The centurion, not being aware of the mysterious and unerring source of St. Paul's warning, preferred naturally the opinion of the ship's officers to that of his prisoner.

And since the roadstead [of the Fair Havens] was badly situated for wintering in, the majority were for departing thence also, if they could by any possibility make their way across to Phenicè so as to winter there—an haven of Crete having the same aspect as Libs and Caurus.

"Although they never reached this harbour, it becomes matter of importance to ascertain its position; because, unless we do so, we can draw no sound inferences respecting the ship's place when she encountered the gale, a point which it is of importance to determine. Phenicè no longer retains its name. . . . . Lutro, Sphakia, and Franco Castello, places on the south coast of Crete, have each been supposed to be Port Phenicè. For our present purpose of ascertaining the ship's course, it is not very material which of them is meant; I am, however, satisfied that it is the harbour of Lutro.

"This harbour, however, looks to the east. I have already shown that the words of St. Luke in the original (proceeds Mr. Smith) are generally supposed to indicate a harbour open in the opposite direction;

unless, therefore, we get over this difficulty, we must give up the idea that Lutro is meant. The question as to the import of the passage must depend on the meaning we affix to the preposition "κατά," in connexion with the winds; I apprehend it means "*in the same direction as*" (in Latin, secundum). If I am right, βλέποντα κατὰ Λίβα does not mean, as is generally supposed, that it is open to the point *from* which that wind (Libs) blows, but to the point *towards* which it blows, that is, it is not open to the south-west, but to the north-east.

"Herodotus speaks of a vessel being driven κατὰ κῦμα καὶ ἄνεμον: now, it is quite clear that, in this sense, a ship driven κατὰ Λίβα must be driven to the north-east. There is a passage in Arrian still more apposite to the point. In his Periplus of the Euxine he tells us that, when navigating the south coast of that sea, towards the east, he observed, during a calm, a cloud suddenly arise, 'driven before the east wind,' ἐξεῤῥάγη κατ' εὖρον. Here there can be no mistake; the cloud must have been driven to the west. When St. Luke, therefore, describes the harbour of Phenicè as looking κατὰ Λίβα καὶ κατὰ Χῶρον, I understand that it looks to the north-east, which is the point towards which Libs blows, and to the south-east, that *to* which Caurus blows. Now, this is exactly the description of Lutro, which looks, or is opened to, the east; but having an island in front, which shelters it, it has two entrances, one looking to the north-east, which is κατὰ Λίβα, and the other to the south-east, κατὰ Χῶρον."—p. 50.

Mr. Smith carefully verifies the position of this place, which lies on the south side of the Cretan Isthmus, in the Bay of Messara, due north of Clauda, the present Gozo.

The vessel did not remain long at Fair Havens after it had been decided that she should try to make Port Phenicè; for soon a gentle breeze arose from the south; and, supposing that they had obtained their purpose, loosing thence, they kept close in shore until they had rounded Cape Matala.

"A ship, which could not lie nearer to the wind than seven points, would just weather that point, which bears west by south from the entrance of Fair Havens. . . . From the anchorage at Fair Havens to Cape Matala the distance is four or five miles, and from thence to Port Phenicè the distance is thirty-four miles: and, as the bearing of the course is west-north-west, the south wind was as favourable as could be desired, being two points abaft the beam. They had every prospect, therefore, of reaching their destination in a few hours. Their course lay across the great southern bight to the west of Cape Matala. They had not proceeded far (οὐ πολύ), however, when a sudden change in the weather took place . . . the ship was caught (συναρπασθέντος) in a typhoon[2] (ἄνεμος τυφωνικός), which blew with such violence, that

[2] Bloomfield has exhibited even more than his usual inconclusive prosiness in investigating the derivation of "τυφωνικός." For ourselves, we entertain no doubt whatever on the subject. Typho was the Egyptian devil; and although, in the

they could not face it, but were forced, in the first instance, to scud before it, for such is the evident meaning of the expression ἐπιδόντες ἐφερόμεθα, 'yielding to it we were borne along by it.' "—p. 57.

The next point to be ascertained is, what was the direction in which the typhoon, or typhonic, gale [a] blew. And here, again, we are enabled to arrive at a definite conclusion by considering the various conditions required, and indicating the only wind which fulfils them—which fulfils them all.

What wind would blow a vessel, which scudded before it, from the western side of Cape Matala to the south side of Gozo? What wind would drive a vessel, if she did not alter her course, from the south side of Gozo to the shore of the African Tripoli? What wind is there which is in the habit of suddenly arising in the Levant, accompanied by all the characteristics of a typhoon, when the prevailing westerly gales have been for a brief interval superseded by a "gentle south?"

To each of these questions the answer is the same, namely, "east-north-east!" And, such being the case, it matters little whether we read, as the appellation of the gale in question, EΥ'ΡΟΚΛΥ'ΔΩΝ, which Bloomfield renders "*east-souser*," or EΥ'ΡΥΚΛΥ'ΔΩΝ, which may be rendered "*broad-souser*," or EΥ'ΡΑΚΥ'ΛΩΝ, which may be translated "EAST-*nordest*," or EΥ'ΡΙΚΛΙ'ΔΩΝ, which has not yet been interpreted; it matters little, we repeat, whether we mingle wind with wave, or compound Latin with Greek, to produce a becoming title for the typhoon in question. The thing is the same, by whatever name we call it; the wind blows from the same quarter, under whatever title it is spoken of.

It is evident that the mariners lost no time in striking sail, and that they must have scudded under bare poles till they arrived off Clauda (Gozo). Taking advantage of the comparative stillness of the water close to this island, they took in the boat, and undergirded the vessel.

" Upon reaching it (Clauda) they availed themselves of the smooth water under its lee to prepare the ship to resist the fury of the storm.

time of the Cæsars, " ἄνεμος τυφωνικός " had become a technical term, it was, originally, nothing more than a nautical colloquialism, equivalent to "a devil of a gale."

[a] "The term *typhonic*, by which it is described, indicates that it was accompanied by some of the phenomena which might be expected in such a case, namely, the agitation and whirling motion of the clouds, caused by the meeting of the opposite currents of air when the change took place, and probably, also, of the sea, raising it in columns of spray. Pliny, in describing the effects of sudden blasts, says, that they cause a vortex, which is called "typhoon ;" and Gellius, in his account of a storm at sea, notices " frequent whirlwinds," " . . . and the dreaded appearances in the clouds which they call typhoons."—p. 60.

Their first care was to secure the boat by hoisting it on board. This had not been done at first, because the weather was moderate, and the distance they had to go short.   Under such circumstances, it is not usual to hoist the boats on board, but it had now become necessary. In running down upon Clauda it could not be done, on account of the ship's way through the water.   To enable them to do it, the ship must have been rounded to, with her head to the wind, and her sails, if she had any at the time, trimmed, so that she had no headway or progressive movement: in this position she would drift broadside to leeward. I conclude that they passed round the east end of the island; not only because it was nearest, but because there are dangers at the opposite end.   In this case the ship would be brought to on the starboard tack, —that is, with the right side to windward.   This must be kept in mind, because it throws light upon a subsequent passage."—p. 65.

The boat was probably full of water, which increased the difficulty, mentioned by St. Luke, of getting it on board.   The object of undergirding the vessel was to support and tighten her planks, so that they might exclude the water, and resist the waves.   The practice, now uncommon, was so general in ancient times, that scarcely a vessel ever left a harbour on a long voyage without laying in a stock of undergirths (ὑποζώματα).   We make a few short extracts on the subject of these articles from Mr. Smith's dissertation on the ships of the ancients.

" In the first place," says he, after clearing away various mistakes of less intelligent writers, " they were external, as the name implied, ' under zones.'   Plato, in his legend of the vision of Eros, compares the most distant starry zone to the hypozomata of galleys, binding the whole together.   It is probable that ships were occasionally undergirded with wooden planks; but this could only be done in harbour.   In the Louvre there is a statue of a marine goddess standing upon a galley, upon the sides of which planks are seen placed vertically.   Polybius talks of ships being ' undergirded' before putting to sea, evidently meaning that they were to be repaired in a temporary manner; but this can have no reference to the ' helps,' which were carried with the ships for the purpose of being applied at sea, when required, which were necessarily flexible.   Isidore of Seville mentions ' the mitra' as a *cable*, by which a ship is bound round the middle.   Hesychius says, also, that they were ' cables binding ships round the middle.' " —p. 174.

" It would appear from the Attic tables, that the hypozomata formed a regular part of the gear of every ship, and that they were laid up in the magazines."—p. 177.

It appears needless to add, that the *helps*, or *hypozomata*, were bound round the middle of the vessel, at right angles to the length: they must not be confounded (as they are by Bökh and others) with the *tormentum*, a contrivance occasionally made use of in the *naves longæ*, or *vessels of war*.

" Ropes were occasionally applied in a longitudinal as well as a transverse direction, to prevent ships from straining. ' The tormentum is a cable in *long* ships, which is extended from stem to stern, in order to bind them together.' . . . . The 'naves longæ,' from the weight of the rostra and towers at the extremity, and from their great length, must have been extremely apt to ' hog,' or fall down at each end ; but as the stem and stern posts rose above the rest of the vessel, a simple way of preventing this would be, to pass a rope round them and heave a strain upon it, by twisting the parts together, as was done in the military engines called tormenta; and Isidore's etymology of the name—' tormenta, à tortu dicta,' seems to confirm this."—p. 176.

In modern times the practice of undergirding has not unfrequently been resorted to, in cases where circumstances have rendered it advisable. Falconer, in his Marine Dictionary, gives an account of the mode in which it is effected :

" To frap a ship (*ceintrer un vaisseau*) is to pass four or five turns of a large cable-laid rope round the hull or frame of a ship, to support her in a great storm, or otherwise, when it is apprehended that she is not strong enough to resist the violent effort of the sea. . . . It would not be difficult to multiply instances where this mode of strengthening ships has been put in practice in modern times. I content myself with the latest I can find. Captain (now Sir George) Back, on his perilous return from his Arctic voyage in 1837, was forced, in consequence of the shattered and leaky condition of his ship, to undergird her. It was thus done :—' a length of the stream chain-cable was passed under the bottom of the ship, four feet before the mizen-mast, hove tight by the capstan, and finally immovably fixed to six ring-bolts on the quarterdeck. The effect was at once manifested by a great diminution in the working of the parts already mentioned, and, in a less agreeable way, by impeding her rate of sailing: a trifling consideration, however, when compared with the benefit received.' "—p. 66.

Mr. Smith adds in a foot note—

" The ' Albion,' 74, encountered a hurricane on her voyage from India, and was under the necessity of frapping her hull together, to prevent her sinking. *United Service Magazine, May,* 1846. The ' Queen' came home from Jamaica frapped, or undergirded; and the ' Blenheim,' in which Sir Thomas Troubridge was lost, left India frapped."

After having taken these preliminary measures, St. Luke goes on to say :—"φοβούμενοί τε μὴ εἰς τὴν Σύρτιν ἐκπέσωσι, χαλάσαντες τὸ σκεῦος, οὕτως ἐφέροντο."
Upon this Mr. Smith very justly remarks :—

" It is not easy to imagine a more erroneous translation than that of
our authorized version : ' Fearing lest they should fall into the quick-
sands, strake sail, and so were driven.' (ver. 17.) It is, in fact, equivalent to saying, that, fearing a certain danger, they deprived themselves
of the only possible means of avoiding it. . . . Under the circumstances
in which they were now placed, they had but one course to pursue in
order to avoid the apprehended danger, which was, to turn the ship's
head off shore, and to set such sail as the violence of the gale would
permit them to carry. As they did avoid the danger, we may be certain, notwithstanding the silence of the historian, that this was the
course which was adopted. I have already assigned my reasons for
supposing that the ship must have been brought to on the starboard
tack, under Clauda, for it was only on this tack that it was possible to
avoid being driven on the African coast ; when, therefore, they had
taken every precaution against foundering which prudence and skilful
seamanship could dictate, all that was required was, to fill their storm-
sail, probably already set, and to stand on."—pp. 67, 68.

The expression which the authorized version renders " *strake
sail*," Mr. Smith renders, " *lowered the gear.*" With some diffi-
dence we beg to propose a third suggestion—" having spread the
customary sail." This, though at first sight preposterous, will,
we think, when closely examined, turn out to be the right rendering of the contested expression. Let us go back a few verses.
The vessel which bore the Apostle and Evangelist was crossing
from Cape Matala to Port Phœnix, with a gentle breeze from the
south, when suddenly she was caught in a typhoon which rose
from the ε. ν. ε. The gale was of that tremendous character
well known in those latitudes at that season. The vessel was
totally unable to make head against it. She was seized by it, we
are told, and the sailors, without any choice, yielded to its fury,
and scudded before it, till they came under the lee of Clauda[4].
Now it appears to us not improbable that, under such circumstances, they would, when first caught in the typhoon, lower every
thing that they could lay hands on, to prevent their being swamped
head foremost. Mr. Smith has shown what must have been the
direction of the ship's head when, after the boat was in, and the
vessel undergirded, she had passed Clauda (Gozo), and was again
exposed to the full fury of the hurricane. It was now that the
danger of being driven into the Syrtis, and the mode of escaping
that danger, at once presented themselves.

[4] In a note, occurring at p. 61, Mr. Smith observes, " ὑποδραμόντες," " *running*
in under the lee of." St. Luke exhibits here, as on every other occasion, the most
perfect command of nautical terms, and gives the utmost precision to his language,
by selecting the most appropriate : they ran before the wind to leeward of Clauda,
hence it is ὑποδραμόντες : they sailed with a side wind to leeward of Cyprus and
Crete, hence it is ὑπεπλεύσαμεν.

"*And fearing lest they should fall into the Syrtis, having spread their sail, they were thus borne along.*"

In defence of this interpretation we have to advance, 1. The antecedent probability that they had no sail whatever set at the time when they reached Clauda. 2ndly. The fact that Σκεῦος does not unfrequently stand for " the sail and its appurtenances." 3rdly. That in the Septuagint version of Isaiah xxxiii. 23, they could not spread the sail, is rendered by ΧΑΛΑ΄Ω΄. When we recollect the Alexandrian origin of that translation, and the fact that St. Luke was sailing on board an Alexandrian vessel, this will have some weight—to say nothing of the general influence of the style of that version, on all the writers of the New Testament.

We proceed again in Mr. Smith's words:—

" We are thus forced to the conclusion, when we are told that they were thus borne along, οὕτως ἐφέροντο that it was not only with the ship undergirded, and made snug, but that she had stormsails set, and was on the starboard tack, which was the only course by which she could avoid falling into the Syrtis. With this notice concludes the first eventful day.

" On the following day (τῇ ἑξῆς, ver. 18) the gale continuing unabated, they lightened the ship. Every step hitherto taken indicates skilful seamanship. In an old French work on maritime law, I find every one of these precautions pointed out as proper to be taken by able mariners under similar circumstances. . . .

" On the third day they threw overboard ' the tackling of the ship' (ver. 19). From the expression ' with our own hands,' αὐτόχειρες, I suppose the mainyard is meant; an immense spar, probably as long as the ship, and which would require the united efforts of passengers and crew to launch overboard. The relief which a ship would experience by this, would be of the same kind as in a modern ship, when the guns are thrown overboard.

" A dreary interval of eleven days succeeds ; the gale continues with unabated fury (σφοδρῶς δὲ χειμαζομένων); neither sun nor stars can be observed ; and at length we are told that ' all hope of being saved was taken away.' But why was all hope taken away ? An ancient ship, without a compass, and without celestial observation, had no means of keeping a reckoning. This was, no doubt, a situation of danger, but not one of despair, for she might have been driven into safety. The true explanation, I apprehend, is this : their exertions to subdue the leak had been unavailing ; they could not tell which way to make for the nearest land, in order to run their ship ashore, the only resource for a sinking ship ; but unless they did make the land they must founder at sea."—pp. 72—74.

⁵ " 'Ἐῤῥάγησαν τὰ σχοινία σου, ὅτι οὐκ ἐνίσχυσαν· " ὁ ἱστός σου ἔκλινεν, οὐ χαλάσει τὰ ἱστία, οὐκ ἀρεῖ σημεῖον ἕως οὐ παραδοθῇ εἰς προνομήν· τοίνυν πολλοὶ χωλοὶ προνομὴν ποιήσουσι, κ.τ.λ.

Hope, however, now dawned upon them from the Source of hope. He who had before warned them of the perils which they were now suffering, is at length commissioned to announce their speedy deliverance; for *when there was much lack of food, Paul stood forth in the midst of them*, and related to them the words of an angel, who had appeared to him in a vision on a previous night.

The lack of food was occasioned not by the failure of provisions, for they were of course victualled for a long voyage, and the vessel was laden with corn; nor is it likely to have arisen from work and anxiety, leaving them neither the time nor the desire to eat; but it was the natural effect of the storm and its consequences: "Although the connexion between heavy gales and 'much abstinence,' is by no means obvious, yet we find it is one of the most frequent concomitants. The impossibility of cooking, or the destruction of provisions from leakage, are the principal causes which produce it." Mr. Smith illustrates this by the cases of Breydenbach dean of Mentz, John Newton vicar of Olney, and that of the Guipuscoa mentioned in Anson's voyage.

"At length, on the fourteenth night of their being ' driven through' (διαφερομένων) the sea of Adria,⁶ towards midnight the seamen suspected (ὑπενόουν) that land was near (προσάγειν αὐτοῖς), literally, was nearing them."—p. 78.

As they were in utter darkness, this suspicion has been generally attributed to some information conveyed to them either by the sense of smell or by that of hearing. As however the shore was to leeward, they could not have received any scent from it, they must therefore have heard the breakers on a rocky coast. Nor is it impossible that the foam might render itself visible to the practised eye of the sailor even when the night appeared pitch dark.

"If we assume that St. Paul's Bay, in Malta, is the actual scene of the shipwreck, we can have no difficulty in explaining what these indications must have been. No ship can enter it from the east, without passing within a quarter of a mile of the point of Koura; but, before reaching it, the land is too low, and too far from the track of a ship driven from the eastward, to be seen in a dark night. When she does come within this distance, it is impossible to avoid observing the breakers; for, with north-easterly gales, the sea breaks upon it with such violence, that Captain Smyth, in his view of the headland, has made the breakers its distinctive character. By a singular chance," says Mr. Smith, " I can establish an important link in the chain of

⁶ As the use of the word *Adria* is the chief ground for the untenable conjecture, that the Melita of St. Luke is the Illyrian Meleda, Mr. Smith has carefully proved that the term at that time included the expanse lying between Crete and Malta.

evidence respecting the identity of this locality, namely, that the distance at which the breakers could be seen here, is about a quarter of a mile, and that they are seen at this distance when the land itself is not seen.

"On one of those rare occasions when there was no ground swell, and a boat could land on the point of Koura, I landed with my friend, the Rev. Mr. Robertson, of Saline, and was engaged in demonstrating to him, upon the spot, how rigidly every one of the conditions required to make it agree with the narrative was here fulfilled. To the east lay the low and receding shores of Malta, no where ' approaching' within a mile of the track of a ship coming from Clauda, and which, therefore, could not be seen on a night such as that described in the narrative. In the opposite direction the shore, begirt with mural precipices (τραχεῖς τόπους), where a ship would be dashed to pieces, but with ' creeks with shores,' into which she might be thrust; and on the rocks where we stood, not more than twenty feet above the surface of the sea, and totally destitute of vegetation, lay huge fragments of rock, forcibly torn up by the waves, and lodged at least twelve feet above the level of a tideless sea, affording no doubtful evidence of what must have been the force of the breakers in a gale from the Greco-Levante, E.N.E. (Euro-aquilo), the point to which it is most exposed."—p. 80.

For fourteen days the vessel has been rushing through the foaming waters under the pressure of the unabated gale. Her crew and passengers are chilled by the cold, wet with the waves that have of late frequently broken over her side; they are weary from labour and sleeplessness; they are weak from lack of food; the fury of the storm has been clad in additional terrors by the denseness of the atmosphere, and the darkness of the sky; and now, at the dead of night, her death-note seems to be sounded by the voice of the ravenous surges lashing the murderous shore.

"Such indications are the usual harbingers of destruction. Here they call forth a display of presence of mind, promptitude, and seamanship, which could not be surpassed in the present day, and by which, under Providence, the lives of all on board were saved.

"However appalling the alarm of breakers may be to a ship unexpectedly falling in with the land on an unknown coast, and in a dark and stormy night, it afforded, in the present case, a chance, at least, of safety. The hope which was taken away is restored. They can now adopt the last resource for a sinking ship, and run her ashore; but to do so before it was day would have been to have rushed on certain destruction. They must bring the ship, if it be possible, to anchor, and hold on till daybreak, when they may, perhaps, discover some ' creek with a shore,' into which they may be able ' to thrust the ship.'"

Having thus followed the course of St. Luke's narrative, from the moment of his first embarkation to the eve of the shipwreck,

we are now called upon to consider the last disputed question,
viz., whether the spot to which Maltese tradition points as the
scene of that catastrophe be really so or not. Mr. Smith proves,
to our entire satisfaction, that it is so, by showing the number of
conditions required to identify the spot, and their exact fulfilment
in St. Paul's Bay. We must again let him speak for himself.

" The first circumstance mentioned is, that, at midnight, the shipmen
suspected the vicinity of land, evidently without seeing it. The ship
was driving from Clauda ; her previous track must have been at such
a distance from the land, and the land itself must be so low, as to prevent its being seen. Now, upon laying down the track of a ship driving
in that direction to St. Paul's Bay, on Captain Smyth's Chart of Malta,
I find that the land, which in that part of the island is very low, no
where approaches within a mile of it, but that it is impossible to enter
the bay without passing within a quarter of a mile of a low rocky point,
which juts out and forms its eastern entrance (the point of Koura).
When the ' Lively ' frigate unexpectedly fell in with this very point,
the quartermaster on the look out, who first observed it, states, in his
evidence at the court-martial, that, at the distance of a quarter of a
mile, the land could not be seen, but that he saw the surf on the shore.
Here, then, we establish the explanation of a hitherto unexplained
passage.of Scripture by a competent witness. Till the ship arrived at
the entrance of the bay, they could not be aware of the vicinity of
land ; when they did come to it, they could not avoid being aware of
it. When they did so they sounded, and found twenty fathoms. But
a ship coming from the eastward must, immediately after passing the
point, pass over this depth. It is quite true that every ship, in approaching the land, must pass over twenty fathoms and fifteen fathoms.
But here, not only must the twenty fathoms depth be close to the spot
where they had the indications of land, but it must bear east by south
from the fifteen fathoms depth, and at such a distance as would allow of
preparation for anchoring, with four anchors from the stern ; for we are
not to suppose that ships from sea, unexpectedly falling in with land,
can be prepared to anchor in an unusual manner on the instant. Now,
about half an hour farther, estimating the ship's rate of progression by
the time which had been hitherto consumed, we find the depth to be
fifteen fathoms. Here we are told ' that, fearing lest they should have
fallen upon rocks, they cast four anchors out of the stern.' This implies
that there were rocks to leeward, on which, if they had not anchored,
they must have fallen ; but the fifteen fathom depth is, as nearly as
possible, a quarter of a mile from the shore, which is here girt with
mural precipices, and upon which the sea must have been breaking
with great violence. Upon the former alarm the ship weathered the
point ; here it was impossible. From the position of the ship's head,
the breakers must have been seen over the lee bow. Their only chance
of safety, therefore, was to anchor ; but to do so successfully in a gale
of wind, on a lee shore, requires not only time for preparation, but

holding ground of extraordinary tenacity. In St. Paul's Bay the anchorage is thus described in the sailing directions :—

"' The harbour of St. Paul is open to easterly and north-east winds. It is, notwithstanding, safe for small ships, the ground generally being very good ; and
while the cables hold there is no danger, *as the anchors will never start.'*—p. 161."
—p. 92.

Mr. Smith then proceeds to show, which he does most satisfactorily, that the anchoring by the stern, instead of the prow,
was not a practice peculiar to any particular class of ancient
vessels, but an expedient which they adopted to meet the circumstances of the case ; inasmuch as, in the first place, it is far easier
to arrest a ship's way by the stern than by the bow ; and,
secondly, the position of the ship thus anchored afforded greater
facilities for running her ashore next day, which was the captain's
ulterior object.

" It is proper, however, to observe, (proceeds Mr. Smith,) that from
the very necessity of the case, the ancient navigators were forced to
depend much more upon their ground-tackle than the moderns. Ships
constructed and rigged like theirs, could not, when caught in a gale,
work off a lee shore, they must of necessity anchor ; hence they must
have been very amply provided with anchors and cables, and habituated
to the use of them in every possible contingency. I may also add,
that, as both ends of their ships were alike, there was nothing in their
form to prevent this mode of anchoring from being put in practice."—
p. 93.

We now come to one of those numberless passages which show
the immense research and minute practical examination which
Mr. Smith has employed in the elucidation of his subject.

" There is still one difficulty to be obviated, which I am indebted to
a naval friend for starting. Upon pointing out to Captain McLean,
R.N., whose authority I have already cited, the advantageous position
in which it placed the ship for the purpose of running her ashore, he
replied, ' Very true ; but were the ships of the ancients fitted to anchor
by the stern, had they hawse-holes aft ? because, if they had, we are
only coming back to old practices.'
" This is the difficulty of a seaman, who immediately thinks of how
the thing is to be done. I must admit myself too much of a landsman to
have thought of it ; otherwise I should have been able to have answered
it, which I was not at the time: for I had copied from the ' Antichita
di Ercolano,' the figure of the ship in the picture of Theseus deserting
Ariadne, which contains details, showing, not only that they were so
fitted, but the manner in which it was done ; and that, too, in a ship so
strictly contemporaneous with that of St. Paul, that there is nothing
impossible in the supposition, that the artist had taken his subject from
that very ship on loosing from the pier of Puteoli. A hawser is seen

towing astern, it passes through the rudder-port, and within board it is seen coiled round an upright beam or capstan, in front of the break of the poop-deck."—p. 94.

It is probable that the rudders were lifted out of the water, and secured by lashings, a measure which, under the circumstances of the case, would be as difficult as it was important. "We are not expressly told that this precaution was taken, but we learn indirectly that it was: perhaps also the mainmast was cut away."

"The advantages," observes Mr. Smith, "of being anchored in this manner are, that by cutting away the anchors (τὰς ἀγκύρας περιελόντες), loosing the bands of the rudders (ἀνέντες τὰς ζευκτηρίας τῶν πηδαλίων), and hoisting the artemon (ἐπάραντες τὸν ἀρτέμονα), all which could be, as they were in effect, done simultaneously, the ship was immediately under command, and could be directed with precision to any part of the shore, which offered a prospect of safety. Whereas, if anchored in the usual mode, she might have taken the ' wrong cast,' or drifted on the rocks, before she was under command."—p. 96.

The interval which now succeeded was one of intense anxiety; but the most laboured description of the situation and feelings of those concerned, cannot surpass in force and graphic truth the simple words of St. Luke, when he tells us that after taking these precautions they " wished for the day."

"When the day broke they did not know the land; but it had certain peculiarities, and unless we can show that the shore to the west of the ship's supposed position possesses the same peculiarities, it will not agree with that mentioned in the text. The first of these is ' rocky places' (τραχεῖς τόπους), the fear of falling upon which at night had caused them to come to anchor. Now the shore here is skirted with precipices, against which the ship must have been dashed to pieces, had she not been anchored. The next is ' a creek with a sandy beach' (κόλπον ἔχοντα αἰγιαλόν); and the third is a place of two seas (τόπον διθάλασσον). It will be seen how perfectly these features still distinguish the coast."

After identifying these circumstances with that happy ingenuity and lucid accuracy which distinguish his work throughout, Mr. Smith goes on to another equally striking point.

"Selmoon Island," says he, " which separates the bay from the sea on the outside, is formed by a long rocky ridge, separated from the mainland by a channel of not more than a hundred yards in length. Near this channel, which a glance at the chart will show, must be where a ship from the eastward would be driven: they ran the ship ashore (ἐπώκειλαν τὴν ναῦν); the fore part stuck fast (ἐρείσασα), and remained entire, but the stern was dashed to pieces by the force of the waves. This is a remarkable circumstance, which but for the peculiar nature of the bottom of St. Paul's Bay, it would be difficult to account for. The rocks of Malta disintegrate into extremely small particles of sand and clay, which when acted upon by the currents, or surface agitation, form a deposit of tenacious clay; but in still water where these causes do not exist, mud is formed; but it is only in the creeks where there are no currents, and at such a depth as to be undisturbed by the waves, that the mud occurs. In Captain Smyth's chart of the bay, the nearest soundings to the mud indicate a depth of about three fathoms, which is about what a large ship would draw. A ship, therefore, impelled by the force of a gale into a creek with a bottom such as that laid down in the chart, would strike a bottom of mud, graduating into tenacious clay, into which the fore part would fix itself, and be held fast, whilst the stern was exposed to the fury of the waves."— p. 104.

This very interesting chapter entitled THE SHIPWRECK, concludes with some appropriate illustrations of the circumstances and sufferings of the voyage, extracted from two modern accounts of vessels similarly circumstanced: " that of a crazy ship, undergirded and struggling with a gale, namely, Captain Back's; the other, of a ship caught in a typhoon, namely, the Indian Company's ship ' Bridgewater.' " In the last chapter, headed " THE VOYAGE FROM MELITA TO ITALY," the few objections still remaining are combatted and fully answered, and the crew and passengers safely landed at their destination.

Thus have we followed minutely the course of St. Luke's narrative as explained and illustrated by his able commentator—and we can safely say that we have never taken a more pleasant voyage or found a more intelligent and delightful companion.

We have already quoted at some length from the dissertation on the ships of the ancients. We will only therefore express our entire concurrence in Mr. Smith's carefully established opinion, that the *artemon* was the foresail, and extract a passage in which he sums up his view, of the mode in which the rowers were arranged in an ancient trireme.

" The thalamite I suppose to have sat on the deck, not far from the side of the vessel; and to have rowed in an oar-port little higher than the deck, and probably little more than two feet above the water; and the distance between two successive oar-ports of the same tier I suppose to have been about three feet six inches. About fourteen inches nearer the stern, and about fourteen inches higher than the oar-port of a thalamite, was the oar-port of a zygite, who sat on a bench, or stool, placed upon the deck, on the inner side of the thalamite, about fourteen inches in front of his seat, and whose oar worked in the angle made by the body and legs of the thalamite. Immediately over the heads of the thalamites a platform extended from the side of the vessel, probably not extending so far inwards as the zygites, but reaching to their shoulders; and this platform projected a short distance over the side of the vessel. On this platform the thranites sat and rowed: their oar-ports were arranged along the outer edge of the platform; each oar-port being about fourteen inches nearer the stern than the nearest oar-port of a zygite, and fourteen inches nearer the bow than the nearest oar-port of a thalamite; being about three feet higher from the water than the oar-ports of the thalamites, and one foot nine inches higher than the oar-ports of the zygites. The highest oar-port was, therefore, probably not more than five feet above the water; a height not too great for the use of the oars mentioned in the Attic Tables, viz., nine, or nine and ahalf cubits, or about eleven feet."

In the Dissertation on the Sources of the Writings of St. Luke, Mr. Smith has laboured, and we think successfully, to prove that the Gospel of St. Mark is an apostolically authorized translation from a memoir written many years before, by St. Peter, in the Aramäic or Syro-Chaldee dialect. The only difficulty which Mr. Smith meets with in the way of this conclusion—a difficulty which will, we think, vanish upon a more careful investigation—is, that Eusebius quotes a passage from Papias, which our author gives thus:—" Καὶ ταῦτα ὁ πρεσβύτερος ἔλεγε,—Μάρκος μὲν ἑρμενευτὴς Πέτρου, καὶ ὅσα ἐμνημόνευσεν ἀκριβῶς ἔγραψεν;" and which he renders—" The Presbyter (John) said this: Mark was the translator of Peter, and he wrote accurately the things which he remembered." We, however, entertain no doubt but that Peter is the subject of ἐμνημόνευσεν, and Mark of ἔγραψεν: nor should we hesitate to render ἐμνημόνευσεν, *recorded*—" Mark *wrote* what Peter *recorded*." The sense is still clearer as it stands in the text of the Cambridge edition (the best, we believe) of Eusebius—"Μάρκος μὲν ἑρμηνευτὴς Πέτρου γενόμενος, ὅσα ἐμνημόνευσεν ἀκριβῶς ἔγραψεν,—which we should give thus: " Mark being[7] the translator (or interpreter) of Peter, wrote accurately whatsoever *he* (Peter) recorded."

We cannot leave this Essay without transcribing a passage which has greatly interested us, in that it satisfactorily explains a circumstance in our Lord's history which has been made a handle of by the foes of our holy religion. We give it *in extenso*. The incident referred to occurs in the narrative of " the sick of the palsy :" St. Matthew ix, St. Mark ii, and St. Luke v.

" It is long since the incident of the entrance by the roof has been made a handle of by those whose object it was to discredit the writings

---

[7] γενόμενος, literally, " *having been*," or " *having become*."

of the Evangelists. It is right that such objections should be stated as broadly as possible, in order that they may be answered. I take Strauss's statement of them, as embracing them all. He says,—

"'In the description of the scene, in which the paralytic (Matt. ix. 1, ff. parall.) is brought to Jesus, there is a remarkable gradation in the three accounts. Matthew says simply, that, as Jesus, after an excursion to the opposite shore, returned to Capernaum, there was brought to him a paralytic, stretched upon a bed. Luke describes particularly, how Jesus, surrounded by a great multitude, chiefly Pharisees and Scribes, taught and healed in a certain house, and how the bearers, because, on account of the press, they could not reach Jesus, let the sick man down to Him through the roof. If we call to mind the structure of Oriental houses, which had a flat roof, to which an opening led from the upper story ; and if we add to this the rabbinical manner of speaking, in which the *via per portam* was opposed to the *via per tectum*, as a no less ordinary way for reaching the ὑπερῷον, upper story or chamber, we cannot, under the expression καθεῖναι διὰ τῶν κεράμων, understand any thing else than that the bearers, who, either by means of stairs, leading directly thither from the street, or from the roof of a neighbouring house, gained access to the roof of the house in which Jesus was, let down the sick man, with his bed, apparently by cords, through the opening already existing in the roof. Mark, who, while with Matthew he places the scene at Capernaum, agrees with Luke in the description of the great crowd, and the consequent ascent to the roof, goes yet further than Luke, not only in determining the number of the bearers to be four, but also in making them, regardless of the opening already existing, uncover the roof, and let down the man through an aperture newly broken.

"'If we ask here, also, in which direction, upwards or downwards, the climax may most probably have been formed, the narrative of St. Mark, which stands at the summit, has so many difficulties, that it can scarcely be regarded as nearest the truth ; for not only have opponents asked, How could the roof be broken open without injury to those beneath ! but Olshausen himself admits that the disturbance of the roof, covered with tiles, partakes of the extravagant. To avoid this, many expositors suppose that Jesus taught either in the inner court, or in the open air in front of the house, and that the bearers only broke down a part of the parapet, in order to let down the sick man more conveniently. But both the phrase, διὰ τῶν κεράμων, in Luke, and the expression in Mark, render this conception of the thing impossible ; since here neither can στέγη mean parapet, nor ἀποστεγάζω the breaking of the parapet, while ἐξορύττω can only mean the breaking of a hole. Thus, the disturbance of the roof subsists ; but this is further rendered improbable, on the ground that it was altogether superfluous, inasmuch as there was a door in every roof. Hence help has been sought in the supposition, that the bearers indeed used the door previously there, but because this was too narrow for the bed of the patient, they widened it, by the removal of the surrounding tiles. Still, however, there remains the danger to those below ; and the words imply an opening actually made, not widened. But dangerous and superfluous as such a proceeding would be in reality, it is easy to explain how Mark, wishing to elaborate the narrative of St. Luke, might be led to add such a feature.'—vol. ii. p. 311.

" It is quite true that there is no difficulty in entering Eastern houses by the roof. How, then, was it necessary in this case to break open the roof ? How came St. Luke to mention 'tiling,' seeing the roofs of Eastern houses are flat, and covered with cement ? And how could the roof be broken open without endangering the inmates of the house ? The answer to these questions will be best furnished by an examination of the peculiarities of the structure of the roofs of the houses of the East.

" Dr. Shaw, in his Travels in Barbary, has produced an array of authorities, from ancient writers, to show that the preposition διά does not necessarily mean 'through;' that στέγη might mean, the awning of the open court (impluvium), which was merely drawn aside, and the man lowered over the wall.   This is evading the difficulty rather than answering it: and the word ἐξορύξαντες, in St. Mark's account, implies violence; especially when we find that it is super-added to ἀπεστέγασαν, uncovered, or unroofed.   Neither can I understand how a person upon the roof can be lowered *by* the tiling, although it is quite intelligible that he should be lowered *through* it when broken open.

" The answer to these difficulties I apprehend to be this.—The roof is itself flat; but the opening in it is necessarily covered by a secondary roof, to keep out the rain ; just as the entrance from the deck to the cabin of a ship is covered by a secondary roof called ' the companion.' Now these secondary roofs are frequently sloping, and covered with tiles ; and it will easily be understood why it might be necessary to remove such a roof from the horizontal opening, or trap-door, in order to allow a person in a horizontal position, in a couch, to pass through it.   The removal of a few tiles would probably not occupy many minutes,—the replacing them not many hours : hence St. Matthew left the circum- stance unnoticed, as unimportant; whilst St. Luke, by adding ' through the tiling,' explained it.   It is sufficiently obvious that such a process could not injure those below."—pp. 274—277.

We have already entered so fully into Mr. Smith's merits, that we have nothing to add, save the hope that this may not prove his last work,—and the wish (alas ! how vain !) that all those who un- dertake to write upon equally important subjects would bring to the task as much knowledge, as much patience, as much good taste, and as much good sense.

ART. II.—1. *Report of the Case of the Right Rev. R. D. Hampden, D.D., Lord Bishop Elect of Hereford, in Hereford Cathedral, the Ecclesiastical Courts, and the Queen's Bench.* By RICHARD JEBB, *Esq., M.A., of Lincoln's Inn, Barrister-at-Law.* London: Benning and Co., 43, Fleet-street. 1849.

2. *The Ecclesiastical Law.* By RICHARD BURN, *LL.D.* By ROBERT PHILLIMORE, *D.C.L., Advocate in Doctors' Commons, &c.* London: Sweet; V. and R. Stevens, and G. S. Norton.

THE course of events around us renders it essential to enter on the examination of questions, which, in times of more quiet and security, might have been safely left at rest. It has been the will of Providence to alter very widely the character of the State in England from what it formerly was; and this alteration, brought about by circumstances over which the Church could not exercise control, and which have certainly led to this result without her free will and consent, has exercised, and threatens to exercise, a most dangerous influence on the Church herself. As long as the State was united in faith to the Church, as long as all offices in the State were restricted to those who declared themselves members of the Church, the union of Church and State was a reality, as far, at least, as theory went; but when the legislation of the last twenty-two years has removed all that ancient system by which the State was united in faith to the Church, and ministers, judges, peers, members of Parliament, and officials of all kinds, may now be of any creed, the State has wholly changed the position in which she formerly stood to the Church. The State, until the reign of George IV., was a "Church of England" State. It is now a State without any creed: it has, as a State, no distinctive belief: and yet, notwithstanding this complete revolution in the character of the State, it still retains precisely the same powers and influence over the Church of England which it did previously.

It may be the opinion of some persons, that the State *ought* to possess the same powers over the Church which she now does, and even increased powers. We are not about to discuss this question; but we presume that every one must feel, that, looking at the case merely as a question of *fact*, the State, which exercises precisely the same influence over the Church that she has done for three centuries, has ceased, within the last twenty-two years, to be what she had always before been, *of the same faith as the Church of England.*

We ought, perhaps, to apologize for claiming any faith for the Church of England. There are, we know, many persons, of creeds differing from that of the Church, or of no creed at all, who are in the habit of asserting or assuming, that the members of the Church of England have no distinctive belief; that their creed has been prescribed by Acts of Parliament; and that they are bound to alter their views as Parliament shall dictate. Of course such assertions are either simply offensive and insulting, or else made for controversial purposes. But, without attempting any reply to misrepresentations, which are sufficiently obvious, and easily to be refuted, the plain fact is, that members of the Church of England *have* a positive belief, hold certain doctrines, and are as warmly and strongly attached to them as the members of any other religious communion are to their peculiar tenets. There may be latitudinarians in the Church of England as there are in other communions. There may be men who care little about any religion: there may be men who are secretly dissatisfied with some doctrine of the Church, and wish to evade or subvert it. But, notwithstanding this, the Church of England is a body holding a certain creed, and firmly and resolutely attached to it; so that very many of its members would adhere to the doctrine of the Church, at all hazards, and, if necessary, in opposition to the mandates of the temporal powers. In so doing, they would merely act on the principle of the right of conscience, which every other denomination of professing Christians in the empire has acted on, and which the Legislature has recognized in the amplest manner in their case.

The case, then, is as we have stated it. A large body of Christians—the *largest* communion in the empire, holding certain distinctive religious tenets—is now under the influence and authority of a State, which has ceased to hold those tenets, and which has no settled creed at all, a State composed of members of all sects, who can agree on no one point in religion. A State thus negative in its religion now exercises the full authority over the Church of England, which the Church agreed to entrust to the State only on the condition or assumption of the peculiar religious character of the State. A State which has no positive religion has, by law, not merely the nomination of bishops, but the *absolute* and *arbitrary* power of nominating whom it pleases to that office in the Church, on which the efficiency, the sanctity, the discipline, and the doctrine of the Church mainly depend.

Now, we are very far, indeed, from any sympathy with those who have, in various past ages, assailed the Church of England,

and the Crown of England, on this question. Doubtless the appointment of bishops by the Crown of England was treated as a great infringement on all sound principle, by those who had persuaded themselves that all episcopal power emanated from the Pope, and that the appointment must therefore come from him. And Dissenters, too, had their objections, not only to episcopacy in general, but to the interference of the State in the appointment of bishops. The arguments of these opponents of the Church and the State were ably and satisfactorily met by the divines of the English Church in the sixteenth and seventeenth centuries; and we cordially admit the force of their arguments on behalf of the order of things under which they found themselves. There were plenty of instances of Christian princes nominating to bishoprics, to be found in history. There could not be any objection on principle to such nominations. Nay, the whole history of the Roman communion, even to the present day, shows Roman Catholic princes in the full exercise of the right of appointing bishops in their States. Indeed cases may be pointed out, in which the see of Rome has consented that sovereigns not of its own creed should have the right of nominating to Romish sees in their States; and Russia and Prussia are existing instances. In such cases as these, however, the appointment to episcopal sees is regulated by special concordat, or agreements between the ecclesiastical and temporal powers.

We are very far from denying, in general, that the appointment to episcopal sees may not be lawfully and rightly vested in the hands of the temporal rulers. We contend, on the contrary, that it may very fitly be given to them, and that the laws of England, in the position of the country in former times, were perfectly defensible as regarded episcopal appointments.

But while this is maintained, it must be remembered that there *is* a view of the subject directly contrary to that of Dissenters and members of the Church of Rome, and which not merely asserts the lawfulness of State appointments to episcopal sees, but claims it as a matter of positive right and indispensable necessity. To such thinkers, appointment by the Crown is a notion which they cannot disengage from the idea of a bishop; or, the power of the Crown under all circumstances to nominate to episcopal sees is held as a fundamental principle of right, a prerogative which is so inseparably annexed to the Crown, that it cannot, in the nature of things, be divided from it. Those to whom we allude are as absolute and as unreasonable dogmatists in their way, as the highest advocates of the papal claims in theirs.

But, after all, the right of the Crown to every one of its prerogatives must be open to discussion in the present day. Those who claim for the Crown the absolute right of appointing bishops, must be prepared to prove the justice of that claim, or they will imperil the power they maintain; for, in the present day, nothing that is incapable of defence on rational grounds can long maintain its place.

When we come to consider the actual ground, then, on which the right of the Crown to nominate to episcopal sees is established by jurists, we find it resolve itself into the privilege arising from the assumed *foundation* of all the sees of England and Wales by the sovereigns.

The following extract from the speech of the Attorney-General, in the case of Dr. Hampden in the Queen's Bench, traces briefly the steps by which the State acquired the power of nominating to bishoprics. We shall take the liberty of offering occasional comments on it.

"My Lords, I find this matter [of canonical elections] sufficiently explained in a book to which my learned friend referred, but in a passage which he did not notice, in his motion, in the first instance. In 'Ayliffe's Paragon,' p. 126, we read, 'When cities were first converted to Christianity, the bishops were elected *per clerum et populum;* for it was then thought convenient that the laity, as well as the clergy, should be considered in the election of their bishops, and that both laity and clergy should concur in the nomination of them; because he who was to have the inspection of them all, might come in by a general consent.'" —*Case of Dr. Hampden*, p. 124.

The Attorney-General here admits, on the authority of Ayliffe, that elections of bishops were, in the first instance, *free;* that the clergy and laity elected their own bishops; that the State had nothing to do with the matter. This is, indeed, indisputable. No one ever dreamt in those days of giving the nomination of bishops to sovereigns who were not Christian. The reason, too, assigned for elections by the clergy and laity then, applies at all times: the bishop has still the inspection of clergy and laity, and the "convenience," therefore, of their taking part in elections of bishops, is sufficiently manifest. But to proceed:

"But as the number of Christians afterwards very much increased, this was found to be very inconvenient; for tumults were raised, and sometimes murders committed at such popular elections; and particularly, at one time, no less than three hundred persons were killed at such an election. To prevent the like disorders; the Emperors, being then Christians, reserved the election of bishops to themselves; but in some measure conformable to the old way, that is to say, upon a bishop's death, the chapter sent a ring and pastoral staff to the emperor, which he delivered to the person whom he appointed to be Bishop of the place."

We believe there is truth, to a certain extent, in the statement here made, that the Christian emperors and other sovereigns made the divisions and disputes which sometimes arose at elections, a pretext for interfering in the appointment of bishops, and gradually taking to themselves the nomination. Yet we do not see why the mere fact of disputes or disturbances in elections, should have led to the substitution of nomination for election. There have been many serious riots in elections for Parliament, and much blood has been shed at times in such elections; and yet the Crown has never claimed the right of nominating the representatives of the people. We cannot see, therefore, why the mere fact of occasional disturbances at elections, ought to have been a sufficient ground for Christian emperors to "reserve" to themselves the privilege of nominating bishops, thus, in fact, depriving the clergy and laity of the Church of their original rights. The equitable course would have been, to make such regulations as would be sufficient for preserving peace and good order in elections of bishops. The right of the emperors was, then, according to Ayliffe's statement, admitted by the Attorney-General, founded in usurpation of the rights of the Christian clergy and laity.

"And though the Pope, or Bishop of Rome, who in process of time got to be the head of the Church, was well enough pleased to see the clergy grow rich, yet he was not satisfied that they should have any dependence on princes; and therefore he pretended that they took money for their nomination of bishops, or (at least) charged their revenues with pensions; and thereupon the canons in cathedral churches came to have choice of their bishops, which, by an encroachment of the Papacy, were usually confirmed at Rome."

It is not our business to defend the proceedings of the Popes in this matter, or to investigate their motives. Most persons, however, will be inclined to believe, that if the Popes have shown a disposition at times to encroach, and to derive pecuniary advantages from the Church, the State has been just as liable to the same imputation. The emperors who could extinguish the freedom of elections on pretence of occasional disturbances, were not likely to be very scrupulous in their use of the power thus attained. It was doubtless employed then, as it is now, for purposes of State policy.

"But princes had still some power in these elections; for we find in the Saxon times that all ecclesiastical dignities were conferred in Parliament."

It is not our intention here to correct any historical inaccuracies. We will therefore only remark, that if " ecclesiastical dignities " were sometimes " conferred in Parliament," it does not follow that they were conferred by the Crown alone.   In fact, the only claim here made is, that princes had " SOME powers " in elections of bishops, which may be safely admitted.

" And this appears by Ingulphus, Abbot of Crowland, in the reign of William the Conqueror, who tells that *a multis annis retro-actis nulla erat canonica prælatorum electio ;* because they were donative by the delivery of the ring and pastoral staff as aforesaid."

The sovereigns, in those ages, frequently restored the temporalities of sees, after the election had taken place ; and they did so in the way here stated, which was considered by the greater part of the Church to be unlawful ; so that a bishop thus appointed, was irregularly appointed in their opinion.   There can however be no doubt, that the sovereigns of England *did* give investiture by pastoral staff and ring, and thus showed that they had " some " power in disposing of bishoprics.   This donation did not necessarily interfere with the freedom of elections, which were generally held *previously* to the royal " donation " of the bishopric.

" Hildebrand, who was Pope in the reign of the Conqueror, was the first that opposed this way of making bishops here ; and for that purpose he called a council of 110 bishops, and excommunicated the Emperor Henry IV., and all prelates that received investiture at his hands, or by any layman, *per traditionem annuli et baculi.* But, notwithstanding that excommunication, Lanfranc was made Archbishop of Canterbury at the same time, and by the same means, according to Malmesbury ; but the Saxon Annals in Bennet College Library are, that he was chosen by the senior monks of Christ Church, together with the laity and clergy of England, in the King's great council."

The appointment of Lanfranc shows exactly what we have said, that the royal donation of bishoprics, or investiture by ring and pastoral staff, was quite consistent with elections.   Here we have a case, in which the election took place first, and was followed by the investiture.   It may be observed, in order to avoid mistakes, that Lanfranc was made Archbishop of Canterbury *before* Hildebrand was made Pope.

" Howbeit, Anselm did not scruple to accept the bishopric by the delivery of the ring and pastoral staff at the hands of William Rufus, though never chosen by the monks of Canterbury : and this was the man who afterwards contested this matter with Henry I. in a most extraordinary manner.   For that king, being forbidden by the Pope to dispose of bishoprics as his predecessors had, by the delivery of the ring and staff, and he, not regarding that prohibition, but insisting on his prerogative, the Archbishop refused to consecrate those bishops whom the King had appointed: at which he was so much incensed, that he commanded the Archbishop to obey the ancient customs of the kings his predecessors, under pain of being banished the kingdom. This contest grew so high, that the Pope sent two bishops to acquaint the King, that he would connive at this matter so long as he acted the part of a good prince in other offices; whereupon the King commanded the Archbishop to do homage, and to consecrate those bishops whom he had made. But this being only a feigned message, to keep fair with the King, and the Archbishop having received a private letter to the contrary, the Archbishop still disobeyed the King. And at length, after several heats, the King yielded up the point, reserving only the ceremony of homage from the bishops, in respect of the temporalities, to himself: whereunto Anselm consented, provided it was done before consecration. And then the Archbishop consecrated those bishops whom the King had appointed, and promised that no person elected to be a prelate should be refused consecration, because of the homage he had done to the King."

This statement represents one side of the question. However, it establishes this instructive fact, that the Crown, in the time of King Henry I., was obliged to relinquish privileges and prerogatives which it had become possessed of, whether rightly or wrongly; and the right of the Church to a considerable influence in the election of bishops was distinctly admitted.

" And then a passage proceeds to state, as your lordships know, that, in the result of that controversy between the Pope and the Crown, King John granted a charter, that bishops should be elected by canonical election; reserving to himself the power of veto, and the power of receiving the profits during the vacancy of the see. ' Now, to add more solemnity to this matter, and that canonical elections might not seem usurpations on the King's prerogatives, in appointing whom he pleased to vacant sees, King John, by his Charter *de communi Baronum consensu*, granted that bishops should be canonically elected, provided leave was first asked of him, and his assent required after such election, and that he might have the temporalities during any vacancy. So they were then chosen by the dean and chapter, or by prior and convents: but yet the King retained this ancient prerogative of recommending the person to them; and, that he might influence the election, he usually sent for the dean and chapter, or some of their number commissioned by the rest, who met in his royal chapel, or in some church near it, and there chose the person he had recommended.' "

If such were the state of the case,—and we are not disposed to deny its truth to a certain extent,—the only inference, we think, that could be fairly drawn is, that the sovereigns of England employed every expedient in their power for subverting free elections, while the law of the land, and their own promises, strictly pledged them to grant free elections. To call chapters into the royal presence, and to recommend them to elect certain persons, was really to interfere with those liberties which the law of the land guaranteed. A similar course of proceeding in reference to the election of a member of parliament would be understood as a gross violation of the liberties of the people.

And yet these sovereigns, who thus interfered with elections which the law declared to be free, had no scruple in remonstrating against the Popes, when they reserved the appointment to bishoprics to themselves, and in claiming the right of *free elections* for the Churches of England! Edward III. in 1373, according to Walsingham, took this tone, in a communication with the Pope; and the same writer adds, that the Parliament of England at the same time passed an act that cathedral churches should enjoy the right of free elections, and that the King should not in future interfere with them, by opposing the persons elected by them, and endeavouring to prevent their confirmation. But we must proceed to the Attorney-General's further remarks.

" It appears therefore, my Lords, from that general statement, that the bishops having originally been elected by the people and the clergy; their election having afterwards been limited to the clergy, by reason of the increase of electors; and having then been taken by the Crown; a conflict arose between the Crown and the Pope; the Pope desiring, and in fact insisting upon the right of confirmation, and in that confirmation being, I presume, according to the doctrine of their Church, infallible."

We really beg pardon—but we must relax into a smile at this worthy lawyer's mode of dealing with the facts of ecclesiastical history. There is a curious jumble of chronology in the foregoing. The speaker leaps from the third to the twelfth century —then back again to the sixth or seventh, then forward to the thirteenth and fourteenth; imagining himself all the time to be proceeding on in regular chronological order; and the self-satisfied air of the concluding remark, is really admirable. We certainly never heard before of infallibility attaching to Papal confirmations of bishops—such a claim being generally understood to refer to the decision of questions of doctrine and morals in controversy. But to proceed:

" Ultimately it was compromised by the Charter of King John, granting that bishops shall be canonically elected, he reserving to himself the power of appointing or nominating the person to be elected, and influencing at that time, by his presence, the election that was to take place."

This is a most unfair representation, wholly unwarranted by

the authority quoted. That authority says nothing of any *such* reservation. It simply states that by his Charter King John granted canonical elections "provided leave was asked of him, and *his assent required after such election*"—which implies that he did not reserve any power of recommending persons to be elected; for if he had, his assent to the election could not have been necessary, and especially if the elections were to be conducted in his presence. It is said indeed that "the king retained this ancient prerogative of recommending," &c.; but it is not said that he retained it by any formal reservation. The Charter in fact excluded it, but the King nevertheless assumed it, and thus violated the Charter.

We now come to a statement of the only ground of public right (except merely that of royal prerogative) which we remember to have seen urged as a foundation for the power of the Crown in appointing to bishoprics. It is thus stated:

"Your Lordships will find the same matter shortly stated in the 'First Institute,' chap. 11, fol. 134 *a*. '*Episcopus*, a bishop, is regularly the king's immediate officer to the king's court of justice in causes ecclesiastical, and all the bishoprics in England are of the king's foundation, and the king is patron of them all; and at the first they were donative, and so it appears by our books, and by acts of parliament, and by history, and that was *per traditionem annuli et pastoralis baculi*, *i. e.* the crosier. And King Henry the First, being persuaded by the Bishops of Rome to make them elective by their chapter or convent, refused it. But King John by his Charter acknowledging the custom and right of the Crown in former times, yet granted *de communi consensu Baronum*, that they should be eligible, which after was confirmed by divers acts of parliament.'"

We here find the patronage of the sees of England claimed for the Crown on the ground of its foundation of the bishoprics. This is a clear ground of right as far as it extends. If it can be established it infers the right of the English sovereigns under certain conditions to appoint bishops, though not with any absolute and arbitrary authority, irrespective of the Church's consent.

We purpose to examine this alleged claim in the first instance, reserving the question of mere prerogative for after consideration.

Now, on this claim of foundation, two questions arise. In the first place, How far were all episcopal sees in England exclusively founded by the Crown? And, secondly, If they were founded by the Crown, did such a fact imply necessarily the right of patronage in the Crown? We purpose to answer these questions successively.

With reference to the former question, we must refer somewhat to history; and omitting, as regards the English Church, the earlier and more fabulous portion of her history, we will commence with the period of Gregory the Great, when the sees of Canterbury and York were founded, and the Anglo-Saxon Church commenced.

CANTERBURY.—We shall take the see of Canterbury in the first place. It appears, from Venerable Bede, that this see was founded by authority of Gregory the Great, Bishop of Rome, and that the English sovereigns had nothing to do with its foundation.

Venerable Bede (i. 23), having described the mission of certain monks by Pope Gregory for the purpose of effecting the conversion of England, adds that, while on their journey, they became fearful of undertaking the enterprise before them, and sent back to Pope Gregory, Augustine, whom *he* had appointed to be ordained bishop, "*quem eis episcopum ordinandum si ab Anglis susciperentur disposuerat.*" We next find (i. 25) Augustine in the character of abbot, accompanied by his monks, landing in Kent, and received favourably by King Ethelbert, who, after his baptism (c. 26), granted to the Abbot and monks a residence in Canterbury, and various possessions, "*Nec distulit, quin etiam ipsis doctoribus suis locum sedis eorum gradui congruum in Duroverni Metropoli sua donaret, simul et necessarias in diversis speciebus possessiones conferret.*"

This endowment was given to the monks in common. There is not the slightest mention of any endowment of a bishopric, or a foundation of one, by the royal authority.

The very next passage (c. 27) states, that, in the mean time, that is, even *before this endowment had been made by the Crown,* Augustine was consecrated *Archbishop to the nation* of the Angli by Ætherius, Archbishop of Arles, *according to the directions of Pope Gregory:* "*Interea vir Domini Augustinus venit Arelas, et ab Archiepiscopo ejusdem civitatis Ætherio, juxta quod jussa sancti patris Gregorii acceperant, Archiepiscopus genti Anglorum ordinatus est.*" There is not a single word as to the foundation of the see by the King. Augustine was made bishop simply by the authority of Pope Gregory.

Shortly afterwards (c. 29) we find Gregory sending to Augustine the pall, and giving him direction to ordain twelve bishops, to be subject to his authority; the Bishop of London to be ever after consecrated by his own synod, and to receive the pall; and also to consecrate as Bishop of York, to be metropolitan over twelve bishops, *whomsoever he may judge fit:* "*ita ut per loca singula duodecim episcopos ordines, qui tuæ subjiciant ditioni . . . Ad Eburacam vero civitatem te volumus episcopum mittere, quem ipse judicaveris ordinare; ita duntaxat, ut si eadem civitas cum fini-*

timis locis verbum Dei receperit, ipse quoque duodecim episcopos ordinet, et metropolitani honore perfruatur."

It is obvious from this, that the whole power of constituting bishoprics in those times was in the ecclesiastical authority, and not in the temporal. And this, perhaps, will be sufficient to show that the Crown has no claim to be considered as the sole founder of the see of Canterbury.

YORK.—The first Archbishop of York was Paulinus, who was appointed and ordained Bishop by Justus, Archbishop of Canterbury (Bede, ii. 9), according to the directions of Pope Gregory, and accompanied the daughter of the King of Kent, who was espoused to Edwin, King of Northumberland. The appointment of this Bishop for the kingdom of Northumberland, was thus the act of the ecclesiastical power. The King was afterwards converted to Christianity, and he then gave to Paulinus the seat of his bishopric at York. "*In qua etiam civitate ipse doctori atque antistiti suo Paulino sedem episcopatus donavit.*" That is to say, he recognised the episcopal authority of Paulinus in his dominions, and erected a church to be the seat of his episcopate. Such appears to be the meaning of the passage when compared with similar passages in Bede (see ii. 3).

LONDON and ROCHESTER.—Of the foundation of the sees of London and Rochester, we read as follows. In 604 (Bede, ii. 3), Augustine ordained Mellitus Bishop of London, in which city King Ethelbert built a church as a place for the episcopal see; and Justus was also ordained by Augustine as Bishop of Rochester, where a church was erected by the same prince; and many gifts were made to the bishops of both churches by the King *and the Archbishop.* In the case of these sees, the Crown was certainly not the *sole* founder, to say the least.

The see of DUNWICH, in East-Anglia, was founded in 631, where Bishop Felix, who had been born and ordained in Burgundy, having expressed to Honorius, Archbishop of Canterbury, his wish to preach in East-Anglia, was commissioned by him, and subsequently received the seat of his episcopate in the city of Dumnoc or Dunwich (Bede, ii. 15). There is not any evidence that the sovereign was the sole founder of this see, or indeed that he founded it at all. Felix, as we learn from the context, promoted the wishes of Sigebert, King of East-Anglia, in preaching Christianity; but there is no evidence that the latter was the founder of the see of Dumnoc.

In the foundation of the see of LINDISFARNE, A.D. 635, the co-operation of the ecclesiastical with the temporal power in the foundation of the episcopate is clear. It is stated by Bede, that Oswald, King of Northumberland, desiring that his people should be converted to Christianity, applied to the Scots, requesting "that a bishop might be sent to him," and accordingly Aidan was immediately commissioned, to whom the King, at his own request, gave the island of Lindisfarne as the place of his episcopal see (Bede, iii. 3).

Another see was founded in 635 through the efforts of Birinus, who was consecrated bishop by desire of Pope Honorius, and came into England to preach amongst the heathen. This bishop having converted and baptized the King of Wessex, was granted by him the city of DORCHESTER, to establish his episcopal see there : "*Donaverunt autem ambo reges eidem episcopo civitatem quæ vocatur Dorcia, ad faciendum inibi sedem episcopalem.*" (Bede, iii. 7.) The only circumstance here mentioned, appears to amount simply to the endowment of the see by the Sovereign. There is not the slightest reason to suppose that any thing further was done by the Sovereign, or that he alone pretended to establish the bishopric.

The bishopric of WINCHESTER seems to have been founded in a somewhat irregular way about A.D. 664, when Coinwald, King of Wessex, being dissatisfied with a bishop named Agilbert, whom he had requested to exercise his ministry amongst his people, divided the province into two dioceses, and gave to a bishop named Vini, who had been consecrated in France, an episcopal see at Winchester (Bede, iii. 7).

The next case we meet is the bishopric of the MERCIANS. Penda, son of Peada, King of Mercia, A.D. 653, having embraced the Christian religion, at the court of Northumberland, brought away with him four presbyters to preach to his people, one of whom was ordained by Finan, Bishop of Lindisfarne, as Bishop for the Mercians and Middle-Angli (Bede, iii. 21). There is no allusion to any foundation of a see by the sovereigns.

The bishopric of the EAST-SAXONS arose in this way. Sigebert, King of Essex, having received the Christian faith about A.D. 653, requested of the King of Northumberland Christian teachers for his people. He sent two presbyters, who preached with great success among the East-Saxons. After some time, Cedd, one of these presbyters, went to visit and confer with Finan, Bishop of Lindisfarne, by whom, assisted by two other bishops, he was ordained Bishop of the East-Saxons : "*Fecit eum episcopum in gentem Orientalium Saxonum, vocatis ad se in ministerium ordinationis aliis duobus episcopis*" (Bede, iii. 22). There is not the slightest evidence that the King had any thing to do with the matter. But we are told that Cedd, having received the rank of the episcopate, returned back again to his province, and fulfilled his ministry as bishop.

The bishoprics of HEXHAM and of LINCOLN were established by Theodore, Archbishop of Canterbury, in A.D. 678, when he deprived Wilfrid of his see of York, and divided it into three bishoprics (Bede, iv. 12). There is no mention of any act of the King in erecting these new sees.

The bishopric of SELSEY (afterward of Chichester) was established in 681 by Wilfrid, the deprived Bishop of York, who preached the Gospel in Sussex, and was granted the estate of Selsey, where he established a monastery and an episcopal see (Bede, iv. 13).

At a subsequent period, A.D. 909, the three bishoprics of WELLS, BODMIN, and CREDITON were established, the King *and the bishops* having divided the previously existing sees, and their regulation was confirmed by the Pope. (See Guil. Malms. p. 47, an. 904, cited by Thomassin, Benef. i. 58.)

The bishopric of Lincoln was divided, and the see of ELY erected, by Anselm, Archbishop of Canterbury, with consent of the King, and by authority of the Pope (Eadmer, Hist. Nov. cited by Thomassin).

In short there is not an instance, as far as we can see, in English history of the foundation of any see merely by the authority of the State, until the reign of King Henry VIII.—when the six new sees of Gloucester, Chester, Bristol, Westminster, Oxford, and Peterborough, of which only four are now remaining, were established by the Crown under the authority of an act of Parliament, and without the intervention of the spiritual power.

It is observable however, that the fact of such an act of Parliament is a sufficient proof that the Crown is not of itself competent to found bishoprics, and the same principle is established by the subsequent practice up to the present time, for whatever bishoprics have been founded, have not been founded by the Crown, but under the powers given by act of Parliament. From this we may infer that the Crown is not to be held the sole founder of bishoprics ; and if it be alleged that the Crown's prerogative has been narrowed and limited in this respect, and that Parliament now gives power to the Crown, which the Crown originally exercised by its own right, it follows that the prerogative of the Crown has been already limited in this respect, and therefore there is no reason why it shall not be limited further, if good reason for so doing can be shown.

To revert to our subject—The bishoprics founded since the time of Henry VIII. have been founded under act of Parliament, and not merely by the Crown. And none of these sees have been endowed by the Crown. The see of Ripon was endowed by the.

ecclesiastical commissioners under authority of an act of Parliament. The colonial bishoprics have not been in any case, we believe, endowed by the Crown. Some receive salaries from the public funds, others are supported by endowments; but in no case has the Crown been the sole founder or the endower of these sees. As far as regards the colonial sees and the see of Ripon, the Crown cannot put forward any claim, as the founder, to the perpetual right of presentation.

With reference to the ancient bishoprics the case is somewhat different. They were for the most part, though not exclusively, endowed by the Crown, and in *this* sense the Crown may be considered their founder. There is another sense in which the term may be taken, as implying the *sole and exclusive* establishment of bishoprics by some authoritative act. This was never the case in England. The *Church* in all cases exercised her authority in the establishment of bishoprics, and the Crown confirmed this authority, gave it legal support, and supplied endowments to maintain the bishops independently of voluntary contributions. The way in which bishoprics were in all cases established in the earlier ages of the Anglo-Saxon Church was this:—The ecclesiastical authorities ordained a Missionary bishop for a certain heathen or unconverted country, or else a prince made a request to the ecclesiastical authorities to ordain a bishop for his people. The bishop thus sent forth, if he were received by the monarch and the people, obtained from the sovereign and nobles grants of lands and other property towards the support of himself and his successors, and perhaps had a church built for him. Such was the whole process in founding sees in ancient times.

We have now considered briefly one branch of the question, namely, In what sense the Crown is to be considered as the founder of all episcopal sees. We are now to examine the further question, How far does the qualification of "Founder" give to the Crown the *right* of nominating to episcopal sees?

Now, in the first place, we are not to discuss the question, How far it may or may not be expedient, and fair, and fitting, to give to founders the patronage of sees endowed by them. We are simply considering it as a question of *right;* and looking at it in this point of view, we cannot see any necessity that founders should always possess the right of patronage. We have seen two sees endowed by a private individual, and yet patronage was not reserved. Patronage appears to be in all cases regulated by *agreement*, and limited at the discretion of the Legislature. The right of perpetual patronage is not secured by any Act of Parliament to all persons who may endow churches; and yet, if the principle as applied to the Crown is a matter of right, it must be equally so in the case of private individuals. As, then, the Legislature does not recognise any such principle in the case of individuals, neither can it in the case of the Crown.

The right of patronage of churches can only be acquired by *covenant* between the parties concerned. It is very possible that the Church might not in all cases wish to receive endowments coupled with the condition of granting the power of nomination. On the other hand, persons endowing might not wish to acquire for themselves or their successors the privilege of nominating. So that, in all cases, the right of patronage must depend on some covenant expressed or implied between the Church and the party concerned.

Now, if such a covenant can be shown to have been expressed or implied in the foundation of English sees; if it can be shown that the sovereigns of England, in granting endowments to the bishoprics, stipulated for the right of perpetual patronage, we are ready to concede that the Crown's right of patronage rests on the basis of its having founded those sees. But for evidence of any such covenant we may look in vain. There is not a tittle of evidence in favour of it. Let it be produced, if there be any evidence in existence. We challenge its production.

We are well aware that there is no such evidence. It is not necessary for us here to enter into the argument on the other side, or to prove that the whole history of the Church shows that no such covenant could have existed, *because it was never acted on.* We will here merely say, again, that the right of the Crown to appoint to bishoprics, depends wholly on covenant with the Church, and that no such covenant can be produced.

It is needless to say that the Crown never could have possessed *in itself* any absolute power of making bishops, because it cannot *consecrate* a bishop. For *that* act it must go to the Church. No Christian sovereign ever did, or could pretend, that he possessed the power of consecrating a bishop; and, until the time of Henry VIII., no law ever gave the prince the power of compelling bishops, under penalty of premunire, to consecrate. It is undeniable that the Statute of Premunire was, for the first time, in the reign of Henry VIII., applied to compel bishops to consecrate royal nominees to sees. At all previous times there was no law compelling consecrations, though the kings of England have sometimes, in virtue of their prerogative, deprived bishops of their temporalities, and banished them for not consecrating such bishops as they had appointed. Still, whether the Church authorities were required by fine, confiscation, or exile, or by the penalties of premunire, to consecrate the king's nominees, the truth is still undeniable, that without such consecration a bishop cannot be made, and that the Crown does not possess the power of consecrating, and *must* come to the Church to send forth and ordain bishops. Such is the *principle* even of the present law ; and as this principle was in full and unfettered operation for centuries after the foundation of the English bishoprics, it follows necessarily, that the Crown in those ages could not have possessed any absolute power of appointing bishops, inasmuch as the Church authorities possessed the power of rejecting the royal nominees, when there were any such persons.

We have said designedly "when there *were* any such persons," because, as we shall presently see, there were almost no royal nominees to bishoprics for a long series of years. The early history of the English Church in the pages of Venerable Bede show that nominations and elections to bishoprics were not the office of the Crown, but of the Church, *notwithstanding* the endowment of many of the sees by the Crown ; and this fact is an argument to prove, that, so far from there being any covenant or stipulation with the Church that the Crown should nominate to vacant sees, there was rather a stipulation the other way, that the *Church* should have the nomination. The facts of the case go to prove the latter claim rather than the former, though we would not be understood as affirming that there was any covenant at all, for we believe there was none.

Let us now consider the actual mode of appointment of the early bishops of the English sees, as recorded in the pages of Venerable Bede.

CANTERBURY.—The first Archbishop of Canterbury was appointed by Pope Gregory the Great. Bede (i. 23) states, that Pope Gregory, in sending his mission to England, had appointed Augustine to be made bishop if the mission proved successful: "Augustinum, *quem eis episcopum ordinandum, si ab Anglis susciperentur, disposuerat.*" And, accordingly, the mission having been favourably received, we next read (i. 27) that Augustine was consecrated, according to the directions of Pope Gregory: "Interea vir Domini Augustinus venit Arelas, et ab Archiepiscopo ejusdem civitatis Ætherio, juxta quod *jussa sancti patris Gregorii acceperant,* Archiepiscopus genti Anglorum ordinatus est." The King had no part in this appointment or ordination.

After this first appointment to the see of Canterbury by Pope Gregory, the archbishops were nominated by their predecessors, or by the bishops of England. The Crown did not appoint: there is no trace of such a right. The letters of Pope Gregory to Augustine give to the latter and his successors, and to the Metropolitan of York when ordained by Augustine, the power of making bishops. These letters assume throughout that the power of constituting bishops was in the Church. Thus, in reply to a question of Augustine, Gregory says, "he wishes Augustine to ordain bishops in such sort, that they be not remote from each other." "*Fraternitatem tuam ita volumus episcopos ordinare, ut ipsi sibi episcopi longo intervallo minime disjungantur*" (Bede, i. 27). Not a word is said about any other power but that of the archbishop. Again, Pope Gregory gives to Augustine the pallium, that he may ordain twelve bishops, directing that the bishop of London, in future, be ordained by a provincial synod, and that Augustine should *send* a bishop to York, who, if received, shall also ordain twelve bishops (Bede, i. 29). Not a word, again, about the Crown's right of nomination; the whole appointment being supposed to rest with the archbishop and bishops.

The second archbishop of Canterbury, Laurentius, was appointed by Augustine during his lifetime, and succeeded on his death: "*Successit Augustino in Episcopatum Laurentius, quem ipse idcirco adhuc vivens ordinaverat*" (Bede, ii. 4).

Of Mellitus and Justus the third and fourth archbishops of Canterbury we only read in Venerable Bede, that they successively became archbishops (ii. 7, 8). There is no allusion to any royal appointments or interference of any kind. They had both been ordained by Augustine, and succeeded him apparently in the order of consecration, by mutual agreement and choice.

Honorius, the fifth archbishop of Canterbury, is said by Bede to have been "effectus," or, as some editions say, "electus," after Justus: "*Honorius pro illo est in præsulatum effectus*" [or *electus*], Bede, ii. 18; and was ordained by Paulinus Archbishop of York. There is no allusion to any royal interference.

Deusdedit, the sixth archbishop, was *elected*: "*Cessante episcopatu per annum et sex menses, electus est archiepiscopus Cathedræ Doruvernensis sextus Deusdedit de gente Occidentalium Saxonum: quem ordinaturus venit illuc Ithamar, Antistes Ecclesiæ Hrofensis*" (Bede, iii. 20). No allusion is made to any rights of the Crown.

On the death of Deusdedit, Oswy king of Northumberland and Egbert king of Kent, having no bishop in their dominions of Roman ordination, and being desirous of having that ordination in preference to the British or Scottish succession, which they regarded as schismatical, chose, "*with the election and consent of the holy Church*" of England, one of the clergy of Canterbury named Wighard, and sent him to be consecrated bishop by the Pope, in order that he might ordain Catholic bishops throughout England: "*Adsumpserunt cum electione et consensu sanctæ ecclesiæ gentis Anglorum virum bonum, et aptum episcopatu presbytorum nomine Vighardum, de clero Deusdedit Episcopi, et hunc antistitem ordinandum Romam miserunt*" (Bede, iii. 29). Here we must observe, that not only the king of Kent in whose dominions the archbishopric of Canterbury was, but also the king of Northumberland, who could have no pretence to appoint to the see of Canterbury on the plea of *foundation*, took part in this application ; and, in fact, it appears to have been made in the name of *Oswy*, for the Pope's reply is only directed to him ; thus ignoring any claim on the part of the Crown of Kent to appoint to the see of Canterbury. And further—the nomination was only made " with the *election* and *consent*" of the Church of England. And further—these English kings *petitioned the Pope to send them a bishop of his own choice*, as appears from his reply to Oswy (Bede, iii. 29) ; and accordingly, Wighard having died at Rome, the *Pope* chose and consecrated Theodore of Tarsus the seventh archbishop of Canterbury, who was received with the utmost respect and obedience by the sovereigns and people of England (Bede, iv. 1). So much for the royal powers of nominating to the see of Canterbury in those times !

We now come to Bertwald the eighth archbishop, who was *elected* to the see ; and there is no mention of any royal nomination—" *qui electus est quidem in episcopatum anno Dominicæ incarnationis sexcentesimo nonagesimo secundo* " (Bede, v. 8).

Tatwin is the latest archbishop of Canterbury mentioned by Bede, and of him it is merely said that he was made archbishop, and consecrated by certain bishops—" *pro quo anno eodem factus est archiepiscopus vocabulo Tatuini* " (Bede, v. 23). Here there is no allusion to any royal nomination.

The result then, as regards the see of Canterbury, is, that from the year 595 when that bishopric was founded, and when it was endowed by King Ethelbert, down to 731 when Tatwin was appointed archbishop, the Crown's alleged right of nomination had never taken effect. The archbishops were either appointed by the Popes, by the archbishops and bishops, or elected by the clergy. There is not a trace of any royal nomination. And hence we infer that the endowment of the see of Canterbury by the Crown of England could not have been accompanied by any covenant with the Church, or any arrangement of any kind, by which the Crown was to exercise a right of nomination ; for it is incredible that this right should have remained unexercised for such a length of time, if it had existed at all. It would be in vain to argue here, that the Crown had voluntarily abstained from exercising its rights, for the question is whether it ever had *any* rights. That it had none—that the endowment of the see of Canterbury was given under the supposition, and with the full understanding that the Church was to nominate her own bishops, according to the rules originally in force in all Churches, is, we think, so very manifest, that we cannot imagine on what grounds it is possible for the Crown to claim the right of nominating archbishops of Canterbury, as derived from the foundation of the see.

YORK.—In the next place we come to consider the right of the Crown to appoint to the archiepiscopal see of York.

The first archbishop of York, Paulinus, was *appointed*, and consecrated bishop by Justus, archbishop of Canterbury, in 625, according to the directions of Pope Gregory (Bede, i. 29 ; ii. 9).

Paulinus being obliged to retire from the kingdom of Northumberland by wars and commotions, he had no immediate successor at York. But the diocese afterwards became subject to Aidan, bishop of Lindisfarne, who was appointed and ordained bishop by the Scottish Church, at the request of King Oswald, who sent to them to desire the aid of a Christian bishop (Bede, iii. 3). The next bishop of Northumberland, Finanus, was also appointed and consecrated at Iona (Bede, iii. 17—25). Colman, the following bishop, was appointed in a similar way (Bede, iii. 25). On his departure, after the conference of Whitby A.D. 664, in which the Roman rules were adopted, he left Tuda as bishop in his place, who had been consecrated in Ireland : "*Suscepit pro illo pontificatum Nordanhymbrorum famulus Christi Tuda*" (Bede, iii. 26).

On the death of Tuda, the king of Northumberland, having adopted the Roman rules, and therefore being prevented from sending to Iona for another bishop for his people, chose Wilfrid a presbyter, and sent him to France to be ordained bishop of York. Here occurs clearly, and for the first time, in 664, an instance of royal nomination.

Of the appointment of the next bishop of York, Bosa, who was consecrated by Archbishop Theodore after Wilfrid had been deposed, no particulars are stated (Bede, iv. 12), nor do we see any evidence as to the mode of appointment of the next bishop, John (Bede, v. 3). Wilfrid II. was ordained by John in 718 prior to his own relinquishment of the see ; but it is not clearly stated whether the nomination was by Wilfrid himself, or by the sovereign, or by the clergy (Bede, v. 6) ; yet the language of Bede seems rather to favour the first supposition : "*Cum præ majore senectute minus episcopatui administrando sufficeret, ordinato in Episcopatum Eboracensis Ecclesiæ Vilfrido presbytero suo, secessit ad monasterium præfatum*" (Bede, v. 6).

As regards the bishops of York, then, we arrive at the following result. We find the first nominated by the Archbishop of Canterbury ; the second, third, fourth, and fifth, nominated by the monks of Iona, at the petition of the Crown ; the sixth nominated by the Crown ; the seventh and eighth not specified. It is quite clear that in this case also, there was no covenant at the erection of an episcopal see in the kingdom of Northumberland, that the Crown should have the patronage of it.

LONDON.—Mellitus was ordained by Augustine A.D. 604 to preach to the East-Saxons, whose chief city was London. This province having received the Christian faith, Mellitus was its bishop (Bede, ii. 3). But after some years he was compelled to leave the province, the inhabitants reverting to heathenism.

The next bishop of the East-Saxons was Chedd, who, having preached at the request of the King, was subsequently ordained bishop of the East-Saxons by Finan, bishop of Lindisfarne, and it is clear, from the language of Bede, that it was done without even consulting the king (Bede, iii. 22).

The next bishop, Erconwald, was *appointed* by the archbishop of Canterbury: *"Tunc etiam Orientalibus-Saxonibus, quibus eo tempore præfuerunt Sebbi et Sigheri, quorum supra meminimus, Earconvaldum constituit Episcopum in civitate Lundinia"* [*sc.* Theodorus] (Bede, iv. 6). Of his successor Waldhere's appointment, nothing is stated (Bede, xv. 11); and little more than the names of the succeeding bishops is known.

The only three cases in which we have clear evidence as to the mode of appointment exclude the royal patronage. Two bishops were appointed by archbishops of Canterbury, the third by the bishop of Lindisfarne.

DURHAM.—Of the bishops of Lindisfarne, the predecessors of the bishops of Durham, we have already spoken under the see of York. It there appears that Aidan, Finan, Colman, Tuda, were successively bishops of Lindisfarne by election and consecration of the Scottish bishops and monks of Iona. The next bishop of Lindisfarne was ordained by Theodore, archbishop of Canterbury, and no mention is made of any royal appointment (Bede, iv. 12). But in the appointment of the succeeding bishop, Cuthbert, we have a very plain proof that the Crown had then no power of nomination. Bede states that "a great synod having met in the presence of King Egfrid, near the river Alne, in which Archbishop Theodore presided, Cuthbert was *elected* to the bishopric of Lindisfarne, with perfect unanimity and general consent:" "*Uno animo omniumque consensu ad Episcopatum Ecclesiæ Lindisfarnensis eligeretur*" (Bede, iv. 28). This appears to be sufficiently conclusive: it took place in 684.

Of the ordination of Eadburt, the next bishop, we only know that there is no allusion to any interference of the Crown (Bede, iv. 29); and the same may be said of the succeeding bishops.

WINCHESTER. — The first bishop of the West-Saxons was Birinus, who, by direction of Pope Honorius, was consecrated a bishop by Asterius, bishop of Genoa, and preached the gospel amongst the West-Saxons, where he was favourably received (Bede, iii. 7).

Agilbert, a French bishop, on his return from Ireland to France, was requested by the king of Wessex to become bishop, to which he acceded; and in this case we have an instance of the interference of the Crown (Bede, iii. 7). This prince, however, appears to have had notions on the royal authority unusual in that age, for he divided the bishopric without consulting Agilbert, and established Vini, whom he had caused to be ordained in France, as bishop of Winchester (Bede, iii. 7). But Vini also was expelled by this prince ere long.

The next bishop, Leutherius, nephew of Agilbert, was "received honourably by the people and the king, and *they* requested Theodore, then archbishop of Canterbury, to consecrate him as their bishop" (Bede, iii. 7). This is not consistent with the notion of a sole nomination by the Crown; and it probably explains the preceding statements. Of Hæddi, the next bishop, we only read that he was consecrated at London by Archbishop Theodore (Bede, iv. 12), and nothing is stated regarding the consecration of his successor.

We shall not weary the reader or ourselves by entering any further on the details of the appointment of the first bishops of sees in England. We think, however, that from what has been said in reference to the five principal sees, it is evident that for about 140 years after the foundation of the Anglo-Saxon Church, the episcopal sees were not "donative" by the Crown, either by "pastoral staff and ring," or in any other way. The Crown often *asked* for bishops, *received* bishops, and occasionally nominated bishops (though, even in this case, we have reason to believe that it was always with consent of the laity and clergy); but it never conferred bishoprics by mere right of patronage. No particular rule was laid down as to the appointment of bishops. They were constituted in different ways. So that it is perfectly incredible that there could have been any compact or agreement between the Crown and the Church, that, in return for endowments, the State should hold the patronage of episcopal sees. With reference to parish churches, the case is quite different. In the foundation of parish churches, there was a distinct understanding, from the time of Archbishop Theodore, that the patronage of churches should be vested in those who built and endowed them. But the Crown cannot show any such agreement or compact with regard to bishoprics, as it can with regard to parish churches.

Having thus far examined the questions, how far the Crown is the founder of the English sees, and how far the foundation of sees, if established, proves the right of nominating bishops, next proceed to consider the ground on which many persons be disposed to rest the *right* of the Crown to the patron of bishoprics,—the alleged sacredness and inviolability of royal prerogative. We trust we do not yield to others in obedience to the royal prerogative. At the same time, if we ar opinion that the prerogative may in some point require limitat and that it is capable of limitation by the law of the land; we t that we are taking no ground except that which has been peatedly taken by the English nation and its representative Parliament.

The royal prerogative has been *frequently* restricted in p times. James I. and Charles I. attempted to do without P liaments, as our recent sovereigns have attempted to do with Convocations; but the royal prerogative has been restrained that point. Elizabeth and her successors erected the S Chamber; but the large prerogatives extending to Church matte and included in that jurisdiction, have been abolished by P liament. In the Coventry Act, the Parliament deprived Crown of the power of pardoning certain persons. By the To ration Act, and the repeal of the Test and Corporation Ac and the Emancipation Act of 1829, and the Maynooth Bill, a the Charitable Bequests Bill, the Crown's supremacy over persons in the empire was annulled; and spiritual jurisdictic not derived from the Crown, but from the Pope, and from varic sects, were recognised as legal. By the Scotch Act of Unic the Crown is excluded from the power of making peers of Sc land; by the Irish Act of Union, its power of creating peers limited. By the Cathedral Bill the Crown patronage was reduce and many benefices in its gift were suppressed. But, what is s more to the point, the royal prerogative, in appointing to bisho rics, had been for more than three hundred years extinguish by law, until it was revived and augmented by King Henry VI

Perhaps there never were sovereigns who had higher notio of their prerogatives in the appointment of bishops than Willia Rufus, Henry I., and Henry II. The contest between the fir two and Archbishop Anselm places this matter in the cleare point of view. Banishment from the kingdom, withdrawal fro communion with the Pope, and every other species of threat, a even violence, were resorted to, in order to compel Anselm acquiesce in the royal claim of granting investiture of bishopri by ring and pastoral staff, which Rufus and Henry I. declared be their prerogative, and that of their predecessors. The bisho took part with the Crown; and it was earnestly hoped that Ansel would resign his see on finding himself involved in opposition the royal prerogative. This, however, he declined to do; and, being supported by the Church authorities out of England, and especially by the Pope, the issue of the contest, which continued for *twelve* years (from 1095 to 1107), was, that a compromise was effected between the Crown and the Church, by which it was enacted, " That, for the future, none shall be invested by the king, or by any lay patron, in any bishopric or abbey, by delivery of a pastoral staff and ring ; and none who is *elected* to any prelacy shall be denied consecration on account of the homage that he does to the king."

It may be here remarked, that it was during the existence of this compromise that the sees of Carlisle and Ely were founded, so that the Crown could not claim the right of granting investiture to bishops of those sees.

Thomas à Becket was *elected* by the monks of Canterbury and the bishops, and, after his death, Roger was *elected* archbishop. Richard, prior of Dover, was next *elected* by the monks and bishops, and approved by the king. Archbishop Baldwin was *elected* by the monks of Canterbury. On his death, A.D. 1191, a letter was sent by King Richard I. to the monks of Canterbury, recommending William, archbishop of Monreale in Sicily, and commanding them to receive him as archbishop. The monks of Canterbury, after due deliberation, *elected* Reginald, bishop of Bath, and installed him as archbishop. Hubert, the next archbishop, was *elected* by the monks of Canterbury, and approved by the bishops of England.

After the death of Archbishop Hubert, the monks, being jealous of any interference with the election of archbishops by the bishops of England, suddenly assembled, and having elected their sub-prior Reginald, sent him to Rome to obtain the approbation of the Pope. Reginald, having broken the oath of secrecy they had imposed on him, they then asked the king's leave to make an election, and elected John Gray, bishop of Norwich, archbishop, who was placed in possession of the temporalities by the king. The bishops protested against both elections, as they claimed a share in the election. The Pope, after examining the case, pronounced the right of election to be vested in the monks only, and then annulled both elections as irregular. After which he caused fourteen monks of Canterbury, then at Rome, to elect Stephen Langton, who was at once consecrated archbishop by the Pope, A.D. 1207.

Throughout all these proceedings, it is quite clear that the Crown did not possess the right of nominating the archbishops.

King John was obliged ultimately to acknowledge Stephen Langton as archbishop; and, in 1214, he was further obliged to confirm to the Church the full liberty of electing her own bishops, abbots, and deans, only on condition that the royal licence should be obtained to hold each election, that the Crown should enjoy the custody of the temporalities during the vacancy of the see, and that homage should be done for those temporalities. This restoration of the liberties of the Church was confirmed by the first article of Magna Charta, granted to the barons of England, in 1215, by King John, and which constituted the fundamental law of England. The words of the Charter for the freedom of elections are very remarkable : "John, &c. . . . we have conceded, appointed, and by this our present Charter confirmed, that, henceforth, in all and singular churches and monasteries, cathedral and conventual, of all our kingdom of England, the elections of all prelates whatsoever, both greater and lesser, *be free* in perpetuity, saving to us and our heirs the guardianship of vacant churches and monasteries which belong to us. We also promise that we will neither impede, or permit to be impeded by ours, nor will procure, but that in singular and all the churches and monasteries aforesaid, when they become vacant, the electors may freely set over the prelacy whomsoever they will as pastor ; licence of election, however, being first sought from us and our heirs, which we will not refuse or defer. And if perchance (which God forbid) we should refuse or defer, the electors may, nevertheless, proceed to make a canonical election, and our assent be likewise required after the election, which we likewise will not refuse, unless we should have proposed, and lawfully proved, that there is some reason for which we ought not to consent." The original will be found in " Dr. Hampden's Case," p. 125. The confirmation of this Charter in Magna Charta is in these terms : " John, &c. . . . have granted to God, and by this our present Charter have confirmed for us, and *our heirs for ever:* First, that the English Church shall be free, and shall have her whole rights and her liberties inviolate ; and I will this to be observed in such a manner, that it may appear from thence that *the freedom of elections*, which was reputed most necessary to the English Church, which we granted, and by our Charter confirmed, and obtained the confirmation of it from Pope Innocent III. before the rupture between us and our barons, *was of our own free-will.* Which Charter we shall observe ; and we will it to be observed, with good faith, *by our heirs for ever.*"

There can be no doubt that the royal prerogative was diminished by this, and by very many other enactments in Magna Charta. The sovereigns of England had arrogated rights which the nation deemed inconsistent with its liberty ; and the encroachments on the liberties of the Church in elections were only parallel to the general course of infringements on laws and customs. In Magna Charta the prerogative of the Crown was restricted, by fixing the rate of reliefs of the heirs of the military tenants of the Crown; by declaring the liberties of the cities and boroughs; by enacting that freemen should not be punished except by judgment of their peers, or by the law of the land; that justice should not be sold; that none should be made judges except persons acquainted with the law; that the legal tribunals should not follow the Court, but be stationary; that amercements should only be by peers, or be reasonable; that the right of pre-emption should be restricted. In these, and other points, as well as by the declaration of the absolute freedom of ecclesiastical elections, the royal prerogative was materially limited and restricted.

If the mere fact that the Crown possesses a certain prerogative, is a sufficient reason to prevent absolutely any interference with that prerogative by the law, we must be prepared to condemn Magna Charta in all its most essential features. We must be prepared to condemn the whole subsequent legislation of England down to the present day, which has always been based on Magna Charta, and has confirmed it by more acts than can be now enumerated. And, in fine, such a principle would be inconsistent with the legislation of England since the Reformation, which has, as we have already shown, repeatedly limited or diminished the royal prerogative in various respects, and especially in respect to the Church. That the royal prerogative ought not to be diminished without some good reason, we readily admit; but that the royal prerogative should be upheld unlimited, even if sufficient *reason* should exist for its limitation in some point, is a doctrine altogether inconsistent with the English law and constitution.

We proceed to quote a few of the statutes in which the ecclesiastical liberties recognised in Magna Charta were afterwards confirmed, referring to Mr. Stephens's very useful work, "The Statutes relating to the Ecclesiastical and Eleemosynary Institutions."

" Stat. 9 Hen. III. c. 1, A.D. 1225.—' A Confirmation of Liberties.' "

" First, we have granted to God, and by this our present Charter have confirmed, for us and for our heirs for ever, that the Church of England shall be free, and shall have all her whole rights and liberties inviolable."

" Stat. 9 Edward II., St. i. c. 14, A.D. 1315.—' There shall be free elections of dignities of the Church.' "

" Also, if any dignity be vacant, when election is to be made, it is moved that the electors may freely make their election without fear of any power temporal, and that all prayers and oppressions shall in this

behalf cease." *The answer.* "They shall be made free according to
the form of statutes and ordinances."

"Stat. 14 Edward III., St. i. c. 1, A.D. 1340.—'A Confirmation of
Liberties.' "

" First, that holy Church have her liberties in quietness, without interruption or disturbance."

"Stat. 25 Edwardi III., St. iii. c. 1, A.D. 1350.—'All privileges
granted to the clergy confirmed.' "

" First, that all the privileges and franchises granted heretofore to the
said clergy be confirmed and holden in all points."

We now come to a very important statute—the Statute of
Provisors, passed in 1350, in consequence of the usurpations of
the Popes, who pretended to dispose of the bishoprics and other
prelacies of England, setting altogether aside the Church's right
of free election.   By the Statute of Provisors it was represented
that the prelacies of England had been founded by the kings *and
nobles* of England; that great evils resulted from the Papal usurpation of the appointment to such prelacies; that therefore, it
was enacted *that all elections to prelacies should be free* according
to law; and that if the Pope presented, in disturbance of such
free elections, the king ought to have the collation for that term,
because the conditions made when free elections were granted
were not kept, and consequently the former rights of the Crown
ought to revive.   We shall quote a few passages.

" Whereas the holy Church of England was founded in the estate of
prelacy within the realm of England, by the said grandfather and his
progenitors, and the earls, barons, and other nobles of his said realm,
and their ancestors, to inform them and the people of the law of God,
&c. . . . . and certain possessions, as well in fees, lands, rents, as in
advowsons, which do extend to a great value, were assigned by the said
founders to the prelates and other people of the holy Church of the said
realm to sustain the same charge, &c. . . . .

" The Bishop of Rome, accroching to him, the seigniories of such possessions and benefices, doth give and grant the same benefices to aliens,
which did never dwell in England, and to cardinals, &c. . . .

" Our Lord the King, seeing the mischiefs and damages before mentioned . . . willing to ordain a remedy for the great damages and mischiefs which have happened and daily do happen to the Church of
England by the said cause; by the assent of all the great men and the
commonalty of the said realm, to the honour of God, and profit of the
said Church of England, and of all his realm, hath ordered and established, *that the free elections* of archbishops, bishops, and all other
dignities and benefices elective in England, shall hold from henceforth
in the manner as they were granted by the king's progenitors, and the
ancestors of other lords, founders of the said dignities and other benefices . . . and in case that reservation, collation, or provision be

made by the court of Rome, of any archbishopric, bishopric, dignity, or other benefice, in disturbance of the free elections, collations, or presentations aforenamed, that at the same time of the voidance, that such reservations, collations, and provisions ought to take effect, our Lord the King and his heirs shall have and enjoy for the same time the collations to the archbishoprics and other dignities elective, which be of his advowry, such as his progenitors had before that free election was granted, since that the election was first granted by the king's progenitors upon a certain form and condition, as to demand license of the king to choose, and after the election to have his royal assent, and not in other manner; which conditions not kept, the thing ought by reason to resort to his first nature."

This act is clearly intended to maintain the right of free elections heretofore conceded by the kings of England, though it claims for the Crown the patronage of the prelacies, in case the conditions made in granting these free elections are not observed. Accordingly we afterwards find the *liberties* of the Church again confirmed.

"Stat. 50 Edwardi III. c. 1, A.D. 1376.—'A Confirmation of the Liberties of the Church.'"

"First, it is ordained and established, that holy Church have all her liberties and franchises in quietness, without impeachment or other disturbance."

"Stat. 1 Richardi II. c. 1, A.D. 1377.—'A Confirmation of the Liberties of the Church, and of all statutes not repealed.'"

"Stat. 13 Richardi II., St. ii. c. 2, A.D. 1389.—'A Confirmation of the Statute of Provisors, &c.'"

"Item, whereas the noble King Edward . . . did ordain and establish that the free elections of archbishoprics, bishoprics, and all other dignities and benefices elective in England, should hold from henceforth and the manner as they were granted by his progenitors, and by the ancestors of other lords founders . . . . our Lord the King that now is hath ordained and established," &c. (confirming such elections.)

"Stat. 1 Henrici IV. c. 1, A.D. 1399.—'A Confirmation of the Liberties of the Church, &c.'"

"Stat. 4 Henrici IV. c. 3, A.D. 1402.—'A Confirmation of the Liberties of the Church and Clergy.'"

"Stat. 3 Henrici V., St. ii. c. 1, A.D. 1415.—'A Confirmation of the Liberties of the Church.'"

"Stat. 2 Henrici VI. c. 1, A.D. 1423.—'A Confirmation of the Liberties of the Church.'"

This series of statutes will show sufficiently what the law of England was till the reign of King Henry VIII., A.D. 1533, when the present laws were enacted, and the existing prerogative of the Crown was created.

The state of the case in general then is this. The Crown of England had originally no prerogative of appointing bishops in England. That right was vested in the bishops, clergy, and Church at large. In process of time the Crown acquired, partly by usurpation, the power of interfering in elections, and sometimes even directly nominated to sees. The power of investiture which seems to have arisen at the Conquest, was lost again about A.D. 1107, when it relinquished that power.

It subsequently, in 1214, restored the original rights of the Church in the amplest manner, by conceding free elections, without any interference on the part of the Crown or its ministers.

And this remained the law of the land up to the time of Henry VIII., during ages when the Crown of England was surrounded with glory such as has since perhaps hardly fallen to its lot. In the reign of Henry VIII. the liberty of election guaranteed by so many successive monarchs and Parliaments of England, was extinguished; and the Crown was given the absolute prerogative of nominating to bishoprics, and compelling consecration, which it had never before possessed.

This shows, altogether, that the prerogative of the Crown may *vary* in different ages according to circumstances; and that it may be augmented or diminished by the law of the land. The conclusion, therefore, to which we here arrive is, that it would be very unreasonable to contend that the Crown must necessarily retain the absolute right of nomination to bishoprics, because it now possesses it.

In the preceding pages it has been admitted, that the sovereigns of England exercised a greater or less influence in the appointment of bishops, at various times before the reign of King Henry VIII., though such interference did not take place till after the foundation of the English bishoprics, and was at length suppressed by law for several centuries. It is, however, carefully to be observed, that even where the sovereigns of England *did* interfere in the appointment of bishops, it was not to the exclusion of the regular electors. The Norman sovereigns took part in the election of their archbishops, but the clergy and the bishops *also* took part; and the consecration then remained, which was not compellable by any law, except the exercise of the royal prerogative in banishing those who refused, and confiscating their temporalities. The exercise of this power required great caution in the face of public opinion, and of an ecclesiastical superior so vigilant and so fearless as the Pope. So that the kings of England in those ages, could only succeed in their interference with episcopal nominations, by persuasion and other means of influence over the electors; but they possessed no absolute power themselves.

There was a continual struggle on the part of the Crown to get its own creatures appointed to bishoprics; but it not unfrequently failed in the attempt, and if it lost temper, defeat was sure to follow.

And there is another important feature which should not be lost sight of. The sovereigns who thus interfered in episcopal elections were always of the same faith as the Church itself, and could not in any case be suspected of wishing to promote heresy, or to subvert the faith of the Church. They acted as the principal laymen of the Church, and it was not unreasonable that they should have more or less influence in the appointment of bishops. The sovereign certainly could not be excluded from taking a share in ecclesiastical appointments, when the rest of the laity, clergy, and bishops, all had their parts. The union of Church and State was as perfect in those days, as it has ever been since the Reformation; and infinitely more perfect than it is now.

It is not our purpose to discuss at length the legislation of Henry VIII. on the subject of nomination to bishoprics. There are points in that legislation which appear to be conceived in an arbitrary spirit. The infliction of the penalty of premunire, for instance, on the dean and chapter, for refusing to elect the royal nominee, while, at the same time, the Crown is given the remedy of nominating by letters patent, appears to be a gratuitous piece of severity. But, without entering further into details, we will only say, that, considering the position in which the Church was placed at *that* time; considering that the liberty of election so long supported by the statute law of England, had been infringed by papal reservations, papal confirmations, and royal influence; considering the moral power which the Papacy exercised, and the difficulty of rescuing the elections of the Church of England from the grasp of the Papacy, and restoring them to the rightful hands; considering all this, it is very probable that the nomination of bishops may not have been ill-placed in the hands of the Crown at *that* time. The Reformation could not probably have been carried out, unless this change had been made; and it was doubtless this probability which reconciled the Church generally to the assumption of this power by Henry VIII. and his successors. The royal supremacy and prerogative became one of the chief points of contest between the Reformation and its opponents; and the irregularities or excesses which marked some of its acts or pretensions, were forgotten in the main principle which was connected with them. The sovereign of England was the leader of the anti-papal movement; and it was this, which raised the royal power and prerogative to so great a height, that they almost extinguished the liberties of the people for a time, and two successful rebellions took place before the royal prerogative was reduced to more moderate dimensions. The "Protestant cause" was the bulwark of the Crown of England for nearly three hundred years: on that cause its prerogative gained ground, its popularity became very great, and the loyalty of the people was almost boundless; but that "Protestant" feeling has gradually decayed. It has died out of the higher classes. It has been discouraged by the State. It has no hold over the masses of the community. It is virtually extinct: and with it the Crown has lost a firm supporter of its Church prerogatives.

We are simply stating *facts* here, not expressing any opinions. The absolute and arbitrary prerogative of the Crown in State matters was put an end to in the seventeenth century; but in Church matters it has continued unaltered to the nineteenth. And it has been the re-action against Romanism, which has sustained that branch of the royal prerogative. Churchmen were very zealous in maintaining the royal supremacy and the royal power against all opponents, because the royal supremacy was the great political safeguard of the Church against the Papacy and against dissent. The State would not tolerate Romanism, because it was inconsistent with the dignity and rights of the Crown of England. Nonconformity was a high crime and misdemeanour against that authority. The one and the other were acts of rebellion against the State. Both absolutely denied the right of the Crown to interfere with their religious opinions and rites, and laughed to scorn the royal supremacy.

The Crown, on the other hand, was firmly united to the Church. It filled the office of head of the Church; had the right of exercising the most extensive jurisdiction over it; could appoint commissioners to expel heretics and schismatics; was held by the Church to possess the sword for the purpose of restraining all evil-doers; acted on this power, by punishing all Nonconformists, and employing none but Churchmen; was most anxious to appoint orthodox, learned, and zealous bishops and deans: *did*, in fact, appoint men of this character. Can it be a matter of surprise that the Church, thus effectively aided and supported by the Crown, should be zealous on behalf of the royal prerogative! Whatever defects there might be in the theory of the law, they were overlooked in its practice, which was so beneficial to the Church.

We are here reminded of a subject which ought, perhaps, to have been alluded to before, but which we may as well speak of at present, though it will cause a slight digression from our argument. We refer to the Crown's prerogative in appointing to *deaneries*. How and why is it that the Crown appoints to deaneries! Deaneries were not originally, as far as we remember, ever conferred by investiture. They are amongst those prelacies, to which the right of free election was conceded by King John. They remained free by law till the time of Henry VIII., and we believe that they *continued* free up to within the last ten years, *as far as the law was concerned.* The present dean of Exeter was *elected* by the chapter of Exeter in opposition to the royal nominee; and the case coming before the courts of law, it was determined that he was *lawfully* elected, and that the Crown had no right to appoint. Now, we apprehend, that the deaneries of the old foundation, *i. e.* those founded prior to the time of Henry VIII., were all in the same position. These deaneries are, we believe, as follows:—York, London, Bangor, Wells, Chichester, Exeter, Hereford, Lichfield, Lincoln, Llandaff, Salisbury, St. Asaph, St. David's. No Act of Parliament transferred the right of nominating to these deaneries to the Crown; and yet the Crown's Letter missive was always deferentially attended to by these chapters. At length the chapter of Exeter acted on its legal rights, and the result was, that, in the next Ecclesiastical Bill, the Crown contrived to get a clause inserted, giving to it the patronage of all these deaneries for the future; and this without protest or objection from the Church! It is plain that there could have been no "Church unions" when so great a usurpation took place. Indeed, the legislation of the last fifty years on Church subjects gives evidence of the same want of vigilance on the part of the Church.

And how did the Crown acquire the right to nominate to the deaneries of the *new* foundation? It obtained an Act of Parliament suppressing all monasteries. Several of the cathedral chapters were monastic. They were therefore suppressed along with the other monasteries. The Crown founded them again as chapters of prebendaries, and reserved the right of presentation in the charters of foundation.

Now this was, we contend, a very unfair mode of proceeding. These cathedrals had been founded by the Crown and the nobles of England originally, without any reservation of patronage. They included secular clergy as well as monks, till the time of Dunstan. The secular clergy were then expelled. Still the law gave to the Crown no power of nominating their superiors. It expressly prohibited any such attempts from the time of King John. Henry VIII., in altering the constitution of these cathedrals, and restoring the secular clergy to the exclusion of the monks, had no more right, morally, to seize the patronage, than had his predecessors in the time of Dunstan, when the form of the chapters was altered. He was not *really* the founder of these chapters, i.e. he did not grant to them endowments out of the Crown lands, but merely gave back to them that which the chapters had always possessed, and which could only have been confiscated in their case, in the intention of restoring it again. In this way, however, the law of the land, as regarded the free elections of deans, was set aside; while the influence of the Crown prevailed over the law in the ca-e even of all the deaneries of the old foundation. The whole case furnishes an additional evidence of the disposition of the Crown to grasp powers which are not given to it by law.

We certainly think that the Crown has no moral right to appoint to the deaneries of the new foundation; and if it had, the course of proceeding by which the right of free election has been usurped from the *old* chapters, appears sufficient to annul any moral claims arising from the foundation of the new deaneries.

After this digression on deaneries, we now revert to the leading subject.

We have remarked, then, that the Church acquiesced, and, on the whole, rightly acquiesced, in the somewhat exorbitant power of the Crown in respect to the appointment of bishops given to Henry VIII., because that power was most laudably and beneficially exercised, with a clear and manifest view to the welfare of the Church, and always under the control of public opinion.

With William III., however, a new policy came in. The royal prerogative was constrained to yield to the acknowledgment and toleration of dissent, thereby relinquishing the claim to supremacy over all the nation in points of faith. The episcopal appointments immediately began to partake of the latitudinarian character of the State policy, and thus commenced the "High Church" and "Low Church" divisions, of which the former asserts the rights of the Church, and the latter subjects them to the State's policy. The object of the State was to break down the former, and by the persevering exercise of patronage, combined with the remains of the Protestant feeling in its favour, it succeeded to a great extent. There was much danger to faith when men like Hoadly were appointed to bishoprics; but the power of the Church was greatly weakened by the secession of the nonjurors, whose cause was eminently unpopular; and men were not prepared at that crisis to examine the rights of the Crown, or to unite in any claim for justice. The law and practice of two centuries, approved by so many eminent divines of the Church, possessed so much authority, that it could only be expected that men would by slow degrees, and very reluctantly, open their eyes to the real state of things.

Thus matters proceeded, appointments to bishoprics and other inferior prelacies (we use the old language on this subject) had gradually ceased to be made, except on political considerations, with an occasional exception ; when, in 1828 and 1829, the State at length proclaimed the admission to political power, and to all its offices, of persons of all creeds and denominations : and thus relinquished at once its union in faith with the Church of England. Not satisfied with tolerating all religious sects, it extends to them the same favour and encouragement which it extends to the Church ; and limits itself, at the very utmost, even in theory, to protect the Church from positive and direct injury by them.

Nor is this merely a matter in which theory and principle have been altered, but the actual working of the State has proved increasingly, that from the year 1828, the State is no longer a " Church of England " State. It is needless now to go into details on this, or to remind the reader of facts which have shown each year a steady progress of principles and of enactments, dangerous to the Church, subversive of her rights, prejudicial to her interests, insulting in their tone, contrary to her discipline, and perilous to her faith. Can any one, possessed of common sense and ordinary penetration, look on the position of the Church in England and in Ireland, as it has been altered by the legislation of twenty-two years, and not see that the State is no longer a " Church of England " State ?

This is really no mere matter of theory, no conjuring up of imaginary evils · the facts are too plain. In every possible way the Church has suffered. In England she has experienced a blow, the effects of which will not be seen for some years : nearly half her property has been swept away by the repeal of the Corn-Laws. This is merely one instance.

The conclusion, then, to which our argument comes is this. The Church is bound to consider the altered character of the State, as bearing on the security of her most essential principles and of the faith entrusted to her ; and she can no longer remain satisfied with the state of the law, which gives to the Crown the *absolute* power of nominating to bishoprics and deaneries, without consulting the opinions and wishes of the Church.

From what has been said, it appears that originally the Crown possessed no right of nominating to bishoprics and deaneries ; that it afterwards acquired influence in the elections, without ever being absolute and uncontrolled ; that it afterwards was obliged for centuries to recognise the most ample and unlimited freedom of election ; and that all this took place, even while the Crown possessed vast power, which it has since lost, and while it and all its subjects were in the most entire agreement with the Church's faith. We have seen that the present law, by which all the old freedom of election was destroyed, was enacted at a time when the Crown was still in harmony with the Church (at least, when the *Church of England* holds that it was so), and that ever since, up to 1828, the power of the Crown has been in " Church of England " hands.

We know not in whose hands the nomination of bishops is now placed. We only know that it is *not* in the sovereign of the country. It has long ceased to be so, except in theory. It has descended to the ministers, and they are under the influence of other members of the legislature. So that it is impossible to say by which of the religious denominations included in Parliament, the appointment of bishops may be most influenced ; or how far it may be intended to promote this or that line of policy, or this or that view of religion. In short, the appointment of bishops is now so circumstanced, that there is no kind of security for the appointment of bishops who are sound in the faith.

The latitudinarian views prevalent amongst statesmen and politicians,—the general spirit of the age,—the character of recent appointments in the Church,—and the principles avowed by the Government, and by many other influential persons, on occasion of an opposition being offered to the appointment of a bishop of questionable faith,—are all signs of what is before us. In a few years we may have our episcopal bench filled with open latitudinarians, or concealed heretics ; with men whose only claim consists in their having assailed the principles on which all faith rests. We may have the advocate of Erastianism in its most offensive forms,—we may have the advocate of German infidelity, —we may have the philosophizing divine, who saps and undermines the creeds and formularies of the Church, and finds in them nothing but bigotry and false philosophy,—selected on account of their demerits, and consecrated by an obedient episcopate under the terrors of the law of premunire, to carry out the design of " liberalizing the Church," by subverting its distinctive principles.

Is it not manifest that, in exact proportion to the unfitness of any person to be a bishop, as regards his religious views, is his popularity with the more influential portion of the political world! If any clergyman be supposed unsound in his faith, or if he have assailed the faith of the English Church, his appointment as a bishop is acceptable in the highest degree to the more active and influential spirit of the age. If such appointment be viewed with alarm by the Church of England as tending to endanger her faith, the State, and all its influential members, feel themselves bound to trample down all opposition, and to assert the *absolute* right of the temporal power to appoint whom it pleases to be bishops, without any check or control.

We see the course of events very plainly before us. The Church is justly dissatisfied at several of the proceedings of the State, and is evidently looking with increasing jealousy and watchfulness on what is going on.

She is becoming awake to her real position, and a considerable number of her members are resolved to exert themselves for the purpose of maintaining her faith, wherever they consider it endangered. The State is embarrassed in its policy by this course of proceeding. It was never very well inclined to "High Church" men, and it now *hates* them. It will employ its rights of patronage to put them down: it will promote persons who will carry out its own latitudinarian and semi-infidel views. It will discourage, insult, and forcibly bear down all that part of the Church which adheres firmly to its faith, and is prepared to oppose all attempts to tamper with it. Hence it is clear that appointments of the most exceptionable characters are likely to occur. "Evangelicalism" is the least evil to be apprehended.

And yet, with the full perception of this before us—do we recommend Churchmen to retire from the contest, and to leave the interests of their religion to the care of a State which has ceased to possess any distinctive religion? There can be but one answer. There is no choice here. The Church has, before now, prevailed, when there were greater odds against her, and when she was just as much divided as she is now. She has entered on the task of obtaining securities for her faith, and from that task she cannot retire without withdrawing from the cause of GOD.

The claim, then, which the Church has a right to urge is, for some sufficient security, that the appointment of bishops and of deans shall be restricted to men who possess some merit to recommend them, and who are of sound faith; and who are judged by the Church, after due inquiry, to possess such qualifications.

Although the State has ceased to be of the same faith as the Church, still all that it seems strictly necessary to have is, the *absolute* power of veto on State appointments, either on the ground of want of sufficient merit, or of unsatisfactory religious opinions. That power of rejection ought to be placed in some body representing the Church only, and not under the influence of the State. The power of objecting at the confirmation of bishops appears to us insufficient to meet what is wanted. It would not, we think, secure us against the appointment of *secret* heretics and unbelievers, whose unsoundness might be *suspected* only, and who might yet be appointed with a distinct understanding of their principles by the State. It would not secure us from the decision of complaisant archbishops, unwilling to offend the Government and to take an unpopular course. It would compel strict legal proof for every thing. It would put the candidate merely on the defensive, and would not elicit from him any positive declaration or profession of faith, which might be very necessary in some cases. If the archiepiscopal confirmation could be modified so as to avoid these objections; if it could become, as it was originally, a confirmation by a provincial synod of bishops; if it included an examination and profession of faith; if it guarded, even in some degree, against Crown influence on the bishops themselves, by the addition of freely elected clergy; then we might see sufficient security in an archiepiscopal confirmation. But otherwise we should prefer some body, elected in part by the bishops and representing them, and in part by the parochial clergy of the diocese, and invested with the fullest power of veto, until some person was found mutually satisfactory both to State and Church. We think that this might precede any formal appointment by letter missive or patent, so as to leave the law as it now stands, each person being proposed by the Crown to the Church for approbation, before actual appointment is made.

Very possibly some of our readers may be disposed to see difficulties in the way of this arrangement. We do not propose it as the most desirable plan; and, in truth, there are various plans which might be adopted, and with as much advantage to the Church. The details of any arrangement would however be easily arranged. The real difficulty which is before us, is the resolution of the State to keep all the patronage it can, and without permitting the slightest interference from others. This must be expected; and if any resistance be offered, or any opportunity be given to the State for striking a blow, there can be no doubt that it will be done with hearty good will. We think, however, that the claims of the Church should be made *boldly;* and while we have above suggested what might possibly be accepted by the Church *if offered by the State,* we are not disposed to recommend so moderate a claim in the first instance. The Church should, we think, seek for the restoration of *the freedom of elections* as recognised by the ancient laws of England, and reiterate her claims in the face of every opposition that may be raised. We would have her *claim* the amplest liberty, though she might possibly accept, *by compromise,* a *somewhat less* measure of it. We maintain that she has a perfect moral right to free election, and we should not think it wise to demand *less* than her rights.

We shall, however, have a desperate opposition to the restoration of those rights.

We believe that neither William Rufus nor Henry I. were one whit more resolved to keep their Church patronage than are the ministers of the present day. But we believe, that as powerful kings have been forced ere now to give up their prerogative to pertinacious opposition, so ministers may be obliged, by a steady and unceasing course of agitation, keeping within the limits of the law, to come to terms at last. The two last appointments to deaneries are additional proofs offered by Government of their uneasiness at the opposition offered by the sounder part of the Church to their measures. Facts like this prove, that it is no insignificant movement which the Church is now making.

In conclusion, we have to meet an objection which some persons may raise to the discussion of the rights of the Crown in this respect. It may be said that the canons of 1603 require all the clergy to observe and cause to be observed all laws made for restoring to the Crown the ancient jurisdiction over the Church; and that they denounce excommunication against those who impeach any part of the royal supremacy in ecclesiastical causes restored to the Crown; and hence it may be argued, that it is forbidden to seek for any alteration in the laws on this subject. But such an interpretation as this would be evidently mistaken, for the Church could never have intended to prevent the State from making alterations in the laws, should it be necessary so to do. The State, in fact, has taken from the Crown the power of erecting a court of ecclesiastical commission for the trial of heresy; and to place such an interpretation on the canons, would be to condemn the State for so doing, and to infringe on its liberties. It could only be the intention of the canon to maintain obedience *according to the laws*—to the laws actually in force—and not to preclude the State from further legislation on the subject, or to prevent the clergy and laity from seeking improvements in the law by the legislature, whenever they may be deemed necessary.

ART. III.—1. *Democracy and its Mission.* By M. GUIZOT. 1848.

2. *The Causes of the Success of the English Revolution,* 1640—
   1688. *By* M. GUIZOT. 1850.

3. *The Revolution in France, a warning to England.* 1848.

IN our last number we asked a question of our Radical cotemporaries, What is meant by progress? They tell us continually
" to move on," and they must not be surprised if we ask them
where we are going. " Lord John Russell is a man behind his
times," says a popular writer; "he cannot keep pace with the
intelligence of the day: he does not understand the rights and
liberties of a great and intelligent people. *We,* who understand
matters, are in advance of the times. We can anticipate popular
improvement." Now all this sounds well, and catches the ear of the
unwary. Progress there certainly is, and a progress which we cannot arrest,—it is the greatest progress of all, which some of our
cotemporaries altogether overlook, the progress of man to eternity.
Man is but a short time here, his time of probation is diminishing
every day, and he is advancing rapidly to death and judgment.
This is the personal progress which all must make, whether they
will or no, and in comparison of this all political or intellectual
progress is of no value. But there is also a social progress or
growth in society, and here the advances of modern days have
tended in a great degree to break down the ancient distinctions
of rank; but legitimate progress, while it tends to bring mankind to a level, does so, not by injuring one for the benefit of
many, but by serving all, though perhaps in different degrees.
Let us consider the effects of the great modern innovator upon
ancient usage, the steam-engine. In old times the nobleman set
out on his journey with four long-tailed black horses, and reached
his destination, after a remarkably quick journey of six miles an
hour for two or three consecutive days. The peasant was then
obliged to make the same journey on foot, and might expect to
reach his destination after a week's fatigue, occasionally relieving
himself by a few troublesome miles in a stage waggon; he
might naturally have looked with envy upon the owner of a handsome equipage as it passed him upon the road, and he might have
felt what a vast difference there is between the poor and the
rich. Now, however, prince, peer, and peasant meet on the

same platform. The same train, impelled by the same giant force, hurries each to his destination with equal speed. The same tunnel opens for all, and the same terminus receives them together. The nobleman leaves his first class carriage, congratulating himself upon the easiness of his journey ; he never objects to the fact, that his humble dependent has received a similar accommodation, and a slight salute upon the platform is a sufficient recognition of the difference of rank. Now this is real progress. All parties are gainers, the poor man perhaps in a tenfold degree beyond the prince, but still the prince has gained enough to make him feel grateful to the inventor, and to lead him to say what a wonderful advantage is afforded by the successful application of science. Now we should consider ourselves as behind our times, if we were to prefer the heavy travelling carriage of the last century to a modern first class, merely because a third class carriage can be attached to the same engine. We should as little wish to throw our fellow-subjects back upon stage waggons, as we should desire to avail ourselves of the accommodation of a fast coach, which could actually reach York in four days. Our modern advocates of progress would break the nobleman's carriage without providing a better mode of travelling, and because they themselves could only afford to pay the fare of a stage cart, would object to their neighbour having money to ensure him a better conveyance.

" It is unfair," says the luxurious socialist, Eugene Sue, " for any man to have superfluities while his neighbour is in want of necessaries." The nobleman must, therefore, on this principle, descend from his carriage because his neighbour is obliged to walk.

Again, men are behind their times when they do not act up to what they see to be real improvements. We have heard of a club of country farmers who every year subscribed for a prize to be given at a ploughing match. The prize was won for three years by the holder of the only iron plough, which was then new to them. Instead of introducing iron ploughs, to compete with the man in advance of his times, they passed a resolution that no iron plough should be allowed to enter the lists, and that the prize should be confined to the wooden ones of the old fashion. Here the love of old fashions clearly marred the benefit intended by the institution ; whatever is done best should be imitated ; the object of a farming society, on Lord Bacon's principles, is not to display the skill of a good workman with bad instruments, but to have the work done in the best possible style. He who increases his crop is a benefactor to all, and he who points out the best way of doing it, promotes legitimate progress. A Radical would be disposed to break the iron plough, because it interfered with the rights of the people ; that one man should be better off than his neighbours, a Socialist would seize upon the overplus of the crop provided by superior workmanship ; a high Tory might oppose it as an innovation upon established custom, but we could not sympathize with any of these. Let us by all means have progress where all are to gain, and let the husbandman that laboureth be first partaker of the fruits. Let us however return to the question, whither does the progress of radicalism tend! The answer is to infidelity, insecurity, and tyranny. Perhaps the best exposition of radical theories is to be found in the writings of Rousseau ; he has carried out his opinions to their full length, and honestly explained them ; and his works have had a most decided influence over France ever since their first publication. His idea is that the will of man is supreme ; he objects to a representative government because no man can fetter his own will: when he has elected his representative, he has delegated his powers to him, but as his will may change immediately after, his nominee ceases properly to represent him.

" ' The will,' says Rousseau, ' does not admit of being represented, it is the same, or it is different, there is no medium.' Since man's will is the sole legitimate source of his power over himself, how can he delegate that power to another ? can he cause his will to reside away from him ? He would then create not a representative but a master. All representation then is deceitful, and all power based on representation is tyrannical ; for liberty consists in the sovereignty over ourselves, and man is only free in so far as he obeys no other will than his own.

" The consequence is unavoidable, Rousseau was wrong but in one respect, he did not carry his argument far enough, had he carried it to its full extent, he must have declared the unlawfulness of every durable law and of all permanent power. What does it signify if a law received my sanction yesterday, if to-day my will has changed ? Can I only exercise my will once ? Does my will exhaust its authority by a single act ? and as this is the sole master that I am bound to obey, must I submit for the rest of my life to the slavery of obeying those laws from which the master who made them commands me to liberate myself ?

" Such is the tendency of this principle in its full extent. Rousseau either did not perceive or durst not look upon it. It is destructive of all government, nay, more, of all society ; it does not permit a man to contract any engagements nor bind himself to any law, and carries the seeds of dissolution even into the bosom of each individual, since he can no more bind himself to himself than to another ; for his by-gone will, that is his will which has had its exercise, possesses no more authority over him than the will of any other person. Rousseau indeed observes, ' It is absurd that the will should fetter itself with chains for the future.' "—*Democracy*, p. 33.

It is clear that if the will of man is to be his only rule, and that will may change; if all men are equal, and that equality such that no man or number of men can bind an individual, we come at once to savage life, or rather to the life of the wild beasts; for all savage tribes recognise some authority. Rousseau, though he preferred savage life, saw, that as mankind had attained to a degree of civilization, he could not expect them at once to adopt the habits of Nebuchadnezzar; he therefore attempts to lead us to the system of small and independent states. In these, if we understand him aright, every citizen should be free to live as he pleases, and each should have a voice in the deliberations of the commonwealth. We see this system tried in the States of Greece; but we find at once that it leads to the loss of liberty by some, and to the practice of oppression by others. Lycurgus found Sparta in this state: he saw that physical force must prevail in the end, he therefore enacted a code of laws which should make the Spartans the strongest soldiers in Greece. To this object he sacrificed the lives of the infirm, the honesty of the men, and the modesty of the women. The Lacedemonians had the pre-eminence in foreign wars, but at home their domestic system was a tissue of miserable barbarity. Their youths and maidens suffered alike:

Θεινόμεναι βουπλῆγι ὑπ' ἀνδροφόνοιο Λυκούργου.

But while Lycurgus provided that Sparta should be able to assert her own freedom, he had no idea of extending the blessings of liberty to any other state. Whatever may have been his patriotism, philanthropy never entered into the number of his virtues. Sparta might prosper, but all her neighbours must be in subjection. The city of Helos had quite as good a right to freedom as Sparta; but, being weaker for war, its inhabitants were reduced to the vilest slavery. The degradation of the Helots is proverbial, and the stronger city soon trampled on the weaker. Thus it must always be where there is no ultimate appeal to recognised authority; where physical force alone is to prevail; and where the will of fallen man is to be the dominant power.

Radicals of the present day appeal to what they call moral force. They assert that public opinion and the decision of the majority are to rule. But this is only because, at present, physical force is against them. The army, with its overwhelming power of military engines, is, they know, an insuperable barrier against any attempt at insurrection; but the moment these are withdrawn, we shall see what progress our radical neighbours will make, and how soon they will call for the law which arises from the will of the most powerful. One feature in modern progress is, to cry down the army and navy of England, to talk of their great expense, and the advantages of peaceful negotiation; but we believe that these very attempts to depreciate the strength of the executive government are only symptoms of what our reformers really desire; and that, if the physical restraints were removed, they would be quite ready to cry out for the rights of gunpowder and barricades.

Moral force, in the radical sense of the word, is a mere change of name. It substitutes the will of the majority for the rule of one, or of a regular government. Now a majority can never be said really to govern, public opinion may elect a leader, but this is all; the leader then assumes the place which the majority has given him, and thus, if he be unjust or tyrannical, the will of the majority is represented by him; but even if we can suppose that a majority could govern a country without delegating their authority, there is nothing to prevent them becoming quite as tyrannical as any individual. On this point M. Guizot says—

"Let then the sovereignty of the number renounce these vain subterfuges, and let it consent to stand forth such as it is in reality, the absolute power of the majority over the minority; in other words, a tyranny."—*Democracy*, p. 47.

The object of the pamphlet, third on our list, is to assert this principle, the right of numbers to rule; to show that reform has made the middle classes our rulers, instead of the aristocracy, and that a new measure ought to transfer this sovereignty to the people. The author thus writes:—

"What is termed civilization is the advance, not of the human race, but of certain portions of it. A constant element of all civilization has been the subservience of the majority to the minority. In the despotism of the East, the slavery of the ancient European republics, the serfdom of feudal Europe, the artisan and peasant system of the present day, we find this element ever present—the very foundation of the social scheme. The great majority of the human race are but servants, bound over under heavy penalties (of actual coercion, or the fear of starvation) to do the will of the remaining few. And so burdened are they by the requisitions of this will, that no time is left them for ministering to any but their mere animal wants. Now there is nothing in human nature to countenance this arrangement. The prince is not more, the peasant is not less than man. What then but a violation of nature is the difference of their lots? if the prince have right done him by society, it cannot be but the peasant have foul wrong. Nor can any assertion of the contrary avail, as long as it is true that human nature is one.

"Now so long as society upholds the principle that any class of men is worthy of more respect than human nature itself, misery, uneasiness, danger must be the consequences; for nature is stronger than human institutions, and will prevail. The problem, therefore, for future civilization to solve is, how can man be made what nature points out he should be ? We must no longer rest satisfied with raising barriers to protect one class against the inroads of another. This is but giving strength to wrong. Wherever a class thus acts on the defensive, it is conscious of the possession of exclusive privileges. These indeed are what constitute it a class ; but no man, or set of men, has a right to the possession of exclusive privileges. The common rights of humanity, as they are the highest that can be enjoyed, so they are the only rights that can be enjoyed without injustice and oppression."—*Preface to the Revolution in France, a Warning to the Aristocracy and Middle Classes of England.*

Now all these theories of progress from Rousseau to the present day arise from two false assumptions, the natural equality and the perfectibility of man. The Scripture plainly asserts that men must labour, and denies that they are naturally equal. When there were but two of the human race, Eve was put in subjection to Adam ; and out of the first two in the second generation, God Himself asserts the natural superiority of Cain to Abel—"Unto thee shall be his desire, and thou shalt rule over him." Cain forfeited his birthright by his sin, and Seth was appointed to supersede him, but still in each case the inferiority of one party is plain. The idea of social equality has no doubt been countenanced by Christianity, its advocates have found arguments in its favour, from the fact that religion teaches us that in one sense all are equal—we mean, as before God. All lines from any points on this earth to a fixed star are considered equal and parallel, because the distance is immense, but the astronomer, who would tell us that for this reason Exeter and New York are equidistant from London, would only be considered as a fool. So while Christianity brings all men to a level, as sinners equally responsible, and equally requiring pardon, it also teaches that God has placed one man above another, and that the powers that be are ordained of God. But let democrats reason as they will upon the equality of man, it is a point to which they can never practically attain, because it is contrary to the ordinance of God. Let us try an extreme case. Perhaps the triumph of equality is to be found in a Parisian club of Socialists. These gentlemen deny the right of their neighbours to hold property, and assert the rights of labour, that each ouvrier has a right to work as he will, and be supported at the public expense ; yet we see them constantly disobeying the precept of their founder, and fettering the freedom of their own will. They enter into a solemn engagement to vote for the candidate whom the majority shall sanction, "even if the name of Louis Philippe himself should issue from the urn ;" now to gain a majority there must be influence, and influence with numbers is one great test of superiority. It is perhaps the first step to royalty. If all the members of the club be equal to-day, before a week has passed, one or two leaders must arise among them, and these are obliged to give way one by one until the club has elected a dictator. The member who has the most influence thus becomes the king for the time being, and those who are foremost in denying the rights of kings, are obliged to find a leader among themselves.

Again, modern theorists evidently hold the perfectibility of man, that he can make such progress that he shall always improve.

> "But what is man in his own proud esteem?
> Hear him himself the poet and the theme :
> A monarch clothed with majesty and awe ;
> His mind his kingdom, and his will his law ;
> Grace in his mien, and glory in his eyes ;
> Supreme on earth, and worthy of the skies ;
> Strength in his heart, dominion in his nod,
> And, thunderbolts excepted, quite a god."
>
> *Cowper.*

Now, these assertions are clearly the voice of infidelity to which modern progress must lead; they amount to a denial of the fall of man, or, in other words, they maintain that he is able, by his own power, to regain a state of perfection. "Educate the masses of the people, 'give them intelligence,' let them understand their own interests, and they will soon give you a government which will demonstrate the perfectibility of man." Now, let us suppose that our Socialist club are so well educated, that every man has a perfect knowledge of his own interest (this he never can have, but let us suppose it possible); there are 1000 persons who have really ten different interests and objects. The bricklayer, the carpenter, and the currier would each fortify the town in his own way, and according to his own trade, but, in order to make a trial of strength, the club will naturally divide into two parties; here 400 take one side, and 600 the other; 400 might be found to vote for Guizot, because they think he has good sense, while 600 would support Lamartine, because he tells them the Republic is one and indivisible. Must, then, the 400 submit to the 600! Rousseau would say not, for the will cannot be submitted to others. They must, therefore, form two clubs or two nations; but, at the next meeting, the carpenters, after outvoting the curriers, may probably split from the bricklayers. Must there then be a new division, upon every new question?

Against all these absurdities of the absolute rights of the will and the perfectibility of man, M. Guizot puts forward one or two simple arguments: that children are in subjection to their parents, and that even in savage life the children, as soon as they can use their reason, have a voice in the movements of their father,—in other words, while the will is under control, expression of opinion is allowable, and must have weight; that idiots and lunatics must be restrained, because they are incapable of understanding what is right. Truth, therefore, and reason must be our guides, and not the mere unfettered will of any man or body of men, who have as little knowledge on many subjects as children. He then puts forward the true principles of social agreement, which alone can give permanence to any society.

"1. Permanent unity of social opinion represented by Government.

"2. Respect for public authorities.

"3. Subordination of individual inclinations to the law.

"4. Partition of rights according to capacity.

"5. Universal guarantee of liberty to every grade of persons; the supremacy of the Government being rigidly secured, for the affairs of the community are above all others, and can only be conducted by those who occupy a lofty position in the social scale. Such are the maxims of good sense, and the fundamental principles of social order.

"Let a community be democratic or aristocratic, be its form of government monarchical or republican, it matters but little. These principles are not the less necessary, for they result, not from this or that condition of society, not from this or that form of government, but from the nature of man himself and all human relations; so that, wherever they degenerate, not only government, but society itself, becomes tottering and degraded."—*Democracy,* p. 60.

After studying, as we have done, the writings of Lamartine, it is most agreeable to find good sense in a Frenchman of the nineteenth century. The man who exalts the Revolution of 1789 into "a gospel of social rights," who imagines that by over-throwing existing institutions society is to be regenerated, and to burst forth into some imaginary effulgence which is to en-lighten and renew the face of the world, such a one may think himself an eloquent writer, but we should be inclined to treat him as M. Guizot would a dangerous lunatic: we should wish to see his will put under some restraint. No man could better know or describe the horrors of the guillotine, yet this is the man who led France into the Revolution of 1848.

England was once tempted in the same way, but England was a Protestant country, scriptural light was widely diffused, and though truth was obscured by the dark clouds of Puritanism, still scriptural light was there, and prevailed in the end. M. Guizot, in his short pamphlet on the English revolution, has taken up the points of history with admirable skill. He has led us through the mazes of the great Rebellion, the Commonwealth, and the Restoration, as one who sees clearly cause and effect. He has evidently before his mind the Revolution in France, with its frightful ebullitions of democratic tyranny, and the awful effects of the unrestrained passions of a multitude. England in 1649 passed through a revolution, but it was guided by mistaken views of true religion: there was still the fear of God and the recognition of his service, and Englishmen sought rather to defend their ancient rights, than to acquire some new and untried system of political perfection.

"The English Reformers, especially those who aimed only at political reform, did not think a revolution necessary. The whole past history of their country, its laws, traditions, and precedents, were dear and sacred in their eyes; they found in them the justification of their claims, as well as the sanction of their principles. It was in the name of the Great Charter, and of all those statutes by which, through the course of four centuries, it had been confirmed, that they demanded their liberties: for four centuries not a generation of men had dwelt upon the soil of England, without uttering the name and beholding the presence of Parliament. The great barons and the people, the country gentlemen and the burgesses, met together in 1640, not to dispute with each other claims to new acquisitions, but to regain in concert their common inheritance; they met to recover their ancient and positive rights, not to pursue the boundless combinations and hopes suggested by the imagination of man. . . . Providence also granted them an especial favour; they were not doomed at the outset to commit the dangerous wrong of attacking spontaneously, and without a clear and urgent necessity, a mild and inoffensive ruler. Charles I., full of haughty pretensions, though devoid of elevated ambition, and moved rather by the desire of not derogating in the eyes of the kings, his peers, than by that of ruling with a strong hand over his people, twice attempted to introduce into the country the maxims and practice of absolute monarchy. The first time, in presence of Parliament, at the instigation of a vain and frivolous favourite, whose presumptuous incapacity shocked the good sense and wounded the self-respect of the humblest citizen. The second time, by dispensing with Parliament altogether, and ruling alone by the hand of a minister, able and energetic, ambitious and imperious, though not without greatness of mind, devoted to his master, by whom he was imperfectly understood and ill-supported, and aware too late that kings are not to be saved solely by incurring ruin, however nobly, in their service.—*English Revolution*, pp. 4, 5.

Thus the Revolution began with religion and the assertion of political rights; but when it had arisen to its height, and the king had actually suffered death, a re-action was beginning: the good sense of the English nation showed them that they had gone too far. England, under the fear of worse consequences, for a while supported Oliver Cromwell as a dictator, and as forming the strongest government; but he felt his own want of hereditary right, or, in other words, the common consent of public opinion to support his rule. On this subject M. Guizot says,

"When the House of Commons, now absolute sovereign of the country, nominated the republican Council of State, twenty-two, out of its forty-one members, positively refused to take the oath which contained an approval of the king's sentence. The republican regicides, with Cromwell at their head, were compelled to accept as colleagues men whom nothing could induce to pass for their accomplices.

"The resistance which the new form of government encountered was at first merely passive, but it was almost universal.

"Six out of the twelve judges absolutely refused to continue the exercise of their functions, and the six others only consented to sit, on condition that they should continue to administer justice according to the ancient laws of the country. To these terms the republican Parliament acceded.

"Orders had been given that the Republic should be proclaimed in the City of London. The lord mayor refused; he was superseded, and thrown into prison. But though a new lord mayor was chosen, three months passed away before the proclamation was attempted; and when at length it was read, several aldermen absented themselves from the ceremony, which, in spite of the presence of troops, was interrupted by popular insult. The common council of the City was re-organized; several of the members elected refused to serve, and it was necessary that a smaller number than that appointed by law should be empowered to act. The Government was on the point of being driven to abolish the franchises of the City.

When the Mint was ordered to coin republican money, the master declared he would have nothing to do with it, and threw up his office. Civil functionaries and beneficed clergymen were required to take an oath of fidelity to the Republic; and though it was rendered as simple and as inoffensive as possible, thousands gave up their places or their livings rather than comply. More than a year after the establishment of the Republic, the Assembly of the Presbyterian Clergy, held in London, formally declared that it was not lawful to take it. In the Universities of Oxford and Cambridge it was made compulsory; upon which, the most eminent members of those learned corporations resigned their offices.

The order issued to efface and destroy the insignia of royalty on all the public edifices throughout England, was scarcely any where executed. It was reiterated several times, with no better success; and the Republic, which had been established for more than two years, was compelled to repeat the same injunction all over the country, and to render the parishes responsible for its execution.

"Lastly,—it was not till nearly two years after the king's death that the republican Parliament dared to pass a formal vote, declaring that the authors, judges, and executors of that act had done their duty;

approving the whole proceeding, and ordering it to be entered on the journals of Parliament.

" Never did a people vanquished by a revolutionary faction, and enduring its defeat without open insurrection, more distinctly refuse to recognize the authority of its conquerors.

" The passive resistance of the country to the republican Government was soon succeeded by the attacks of declared enemies." — *English Revolution*, p. 20.

Here we have, no doubt, a very true picture : England first resisting tyranny under royalty, and then refusing to acknowledge the usurper. There were, however, advocates of progress in those days as well as in the present. These were the destroyers of all government, who could not rest satisfied with the republic of Sidney and Milton, but declared themselves levellers and communists. Four insurrections of sectarian soldiers rapidly succeeded each other ; and men who had something to lose began to fear for their property. The natural step from anarchy is to tyranny : and this Cromwell effectually established by dissolving the Long Parliament. M. Guizot thus continues :—

" The Republic had been established in the name of liberty ; but under the rule of the Parliament, liberty had been a vain name, covering the tyranny of a faction. After the expulsion of the Parliament, the Republic became in its turn an empty word, preserved like one of those falsehoods which still serve a purpose, though they have ceased to deceive ; and the despotism of one man constituted for five years the Government of England."—*English Revolution*, p. 35.

For a while the talents of Cromwell kept the army together, but after his death the Commonwealth, or rather the dictatorship, fell to pieces by its own inherent weakness, and all parties, including Richard Cromwell, rejoiced in the restoration of Charles II.

The great value of M. Guizot's pamphlet is, that it gives an opportunity of comparing France and England. England broke out into rebellion, and passed from anarchy and tyranny to her former constitution. France passed through two revolutions, and still continues to make progress. We extract two passages from " The Times " to show the nature of a Parisian election in 1850, and what the English House of Commons is likely to be, if the advocates of progress could only obtain their ends.

" The first name on the list was that of our old friend citizen Cabet, of Icarian celebrity, whose experimental knowledge of Socialist principles is undoubted, since he dispatched a cargo of his fraternal associates to perish in the wilds of Texas, and found means to plunder a still larger class of dupes of all they possessed. No man certainly has done more than M. Cabet to demonstrate that 'property is theft.' In spite, however, of this auspicious commencement, the chances of Cabet wore away with the night. A more formidable competitor followed in the second place, in the person of Jean Daniel, *alias* Henry, a private in the 23rd Regiment of the Line, whose qualifications were thus pithily described by his supporters:—'Daniel was born on the 24*th of February*, 1825, in the Finisterre.' [We suspect that the remarkable coincidence of the birth-day of this mute inglorious Hampden with the anniversary of the last 'glorious' revolution, was his most powerful claim to public sympathy.] 'He never knew his parents; as a shepherd, a shoemaker, and a soldier, he is a self-taught man; and for four years *has never once been punished!*' And thereby, oh! invincible force of democracy, this shepherd, shoemaker, and soldier, was very nearly chosen to be the representative of the mighty city of Paris!"

"The well-known Abbé Chatel turned the Scriptures into ridicule, and observed that 'the Christian religion had made a grievous mistake in setting bounds to the gratification of the passions.' He advocated, in gross terms, the full and unrestrained gratification of all human appetites, and maintained that in the most sensual materialism was placed the supreme felicity of man. He designated the Saviour of the world in terms not to be hinted at. In fact, of the Abbé Chatel's speech, which was enthusiastically applauded, the less that is said the better. His doctrines were, he maintained, indispensable to the perfection of the republican form of government. Another made an open profession of Atheism. 'I know no God,' he cried, 'except the sun, and him because he is visible.' The chairman qualified the declaration by adding, that no doubt he spoke of the sun as the '*commis* of another still more powerful.' He spoke of the men who have fled from the justice of their own country, and are now in a foreign land, and of the transported insurgents of June as 'martyrs.'

"Another speaker maintained that the soil belonged only to the people (the Socialists), and that the poor were the slaves and serfs of the rich.

"The claims of a person described as 'a distinguished artist,' were rejected at the same meeting, from no other reason than that it was believed he was a proprietor.

"Another candidate founded his claim to public favour on the fact of his having shed much blood, and having been for years a conspirator against every form of Government."

Now to us it is as plain as any mathematical demonstration, that tyranny must be the result of such proceedings, because insecurity is the predominant feature of all such governments. When a ruler begins to wear armour under his clothes, like Oliver Cromwell, or to fear the sentence of another faction, like Robespierre, he must become a tyrant in his own defence; he must sacrifice the lives of others for the protection of his own.

This is the real secret of the cruelty of the French Revolution; each party only held office by the will of the people, and their uncertain tenure obliged them to destroy their competitors, for they knew that if they did not, they themselves must be the victims. The title of Queen Victoria to the throne of England is universally acknowledged; not only her life, but her office is guaranteed to her by law under all circumstances; she can therefore afford to be merciful to a rival; in other words, if a traitor denies her right, she may pardon him without danger to herself. When Smith O'Brien and the other Irish rebels were convicted of high treason, his friends endeavoured to intimidate the Government and to urge them upon the score of weakness, and the pressure of public opinion. Now this was a course exactly opposite to the right one—revenge could be no gratification to those in office, and it is to be presumed that the cabinet would naturally lean to the side of mercy; but if the ministry had supposed that the throne of England was in danger, or if they had had private information that the rebellion were likely to break out again, or if they had thought that the institutions and property of the country were seriously threatened, their duty would have been to allow the law to take its course.

We read with horror of the cruelty of Tiberius and Caligula, but it must in a great degree be attributed to the position in which they were placed. They were not kings by inheritance or by the laws of their country, they were merely generals—"imperator" only signifies the commander of an army. They were surrounded with dangerous rivals, and obliged to put them out of their way. Like Waldemar Fitzurse, in "Ivanhoe," they felt to their opponents that "there is no prison like what the sexton makes," that a banished rival may return with increased popularity, and thus self-defence and necessity always became the tyrant's plea. The insecurity of the French democratic rulers, and the fears of the Roman Emperors, gave rise to two new crimes unknown to the law in countries where the government is secure: these were *incivism* and *majestas*. Thousands perished in the French Revolution for the supposed crime of disliking the new form of government, and hundreds suffered under the Roman Empire under the accusation of assaulting the majesty of the Republic. The real meaning of these words is opposition to those invested with temporary power: their fears magnify a rash word into treason, and their influence at the moment enables them to identify themselves with the State. The dictator says, "Here are persons whom I fear; if I do not kill them, they will kill me."

In the history of the Roman empire a change of administration usually involved the execution of the late ministers; in revolutionary France it always did. Now there must be changes in public opinion and in administrations; but where there is a constitutional and hereditary king, acknowledged *jure divino*, there is always a rallying point for honest and loyal subjects. We may lawfully prefer Lord John Russell or Sir Robert Peel, and we may properly endeavour to substitute the one for the other, but the Crown itself is inviolable; and while the advisers of the Crown are responsible to the nation, the penalty is not the loss of life, but of office. If it were the fashion (as in Paris in 1796) to behead a prime minister as soon as he could no longer command a majority, he would be bound, in self-protection, to get rid of his opponents; but when the penalty imposed on ill-success only amounts to a change of his side in the House of Commons, he can afford to treat his political enemies with the lenity which he himself expects. Louis Napoleon is not so; he sees under his feet the volcano of a Socialist mob, ready to burst forth in a moment; from these he knows that he can expect no mercy. He may probably hold his place for some time, as there is still some sense left in France, and some property to be protected. The upper and middle classes cling to him as a refuge against the tyranny of the *forçats* and *sans culottes;* but this is all. He has no acknowledged right, the votes which placed him in office can displace him again; and unless he could follow his uncle's example, and declare himself emperor, he is not likely to find any real stability for his government. Napoleon, like Cromwell, was a military despot, but his talents and his army gave him vast power; he was a usurper, but his great support was, that one tyrant is preferable to many. Perhaps such a government is the best for France; for if something of the kind does not arise, and God does not interpose to save the nation from itself, we do not see how France can avoid the conclusion to which its progress is bringing it,—that property is robbery, and Christianity has had its day.

Art. IV.—*The Royal Supremacy not an Arbitrary Authority, but Limited by the Laws of the Church, of which Kings are Members. By the Rev.* E. B. Pusey, *D.D., Regius Professor of Hebrew, &c.* Oxford: J. H. Parker.

THE subject of the Royal, or, rather, the *State* supremacy, is one which has assumed recently new bearings in reference to the Church. Time was, and that not long since, when the words "Church" and "King," in their combination, conveyed to the Churchman's mind something for which he could have been willing to lay down his life. It reminded him of a State, sanctified and blessed by faith—of sovereigns, who were "the nursing fathers" and "the nursing mothers" of the Church—of a Church knit by ties of gratitude to monarchs, who felt the care of the faith their first and highest duty; and in her fidelity sharing the persecution, the exile, and the restoration of that sacred monarchy. When we looked back on those times, our hearts might well burn within us, and we might endeavour to persuade ourselves that such things were not wholly lost, that our country still retained the same essential characteristics, though outward forms were changing around us. We could not, and we would not, for many years, open our eyes to the progress of events; and perhaps we should have gone on for ever defending the supremacy of the Crown against all classes of opponents—Dissenters, Romanists, and others—had not the State itself, by its own course of action, brought conviction to our minds, that the supremacy of 1850 is, indeed, a very different thing from that of 1550; that the dominion has, in truth, passed from the Edwards and the Elizabeths to the Parliaments of the nineteenth century, and to *their* ministers.

Our submission to the "powers that be," our loyalty to the Crown, our desire to maintain the existing order of things, our averseness to agitation and change, have not gained for the Church of England the consideration which is extended to every sect in the country, however petty and insignificant. Our wishes have been disregarded on all occasions. Our petitions have been again and again rejected, and with contempt. If we have sought for years for an increase in the Episcopate—if the justice of the claim has been conceded so far, and so strongly supported, that even the Government has come forward and proposed to accede to our wishes in some imperfect degree—we are doomed to see the utter disappointment of our expectations. But we will not go through the painful survey of all the thousand acts of the State, each year becoming more and more pointed, intelligible, and manifest to the most ordinary comprehension, and demonstrating that the union between Church and State, founded on a community of principle and of interest, has become the *servitude* of the Church to an alienated power, which no longer shares her religion, or desires her spiritual welfare.

Let it not be alleged, in answer to this, that Parliament busies itself in enacting laws about our revenues and our duties, our cathedrals and our ecclesiastical commissions, our residence and our pluralities. Yes, Parliament is very busy at times in such matters; and we have Horsmans, and Halls, and Cobdens, and Bernal Osbornes, and Humes, who are very ready and willing to interfere in our affairs on all occasions. But we cannot recognize in these movements any thing that demands our gratitude. *Reform* is busy in every direction where Parliament can have any pretext for intermeddling. It is the *fashion* of the day: and far be it from us to deny that it is largely needed. But it *is* the fashion of the day; and every politician who seeks pre-eminence must be known as a reformer. And the Church is, according to the doctrine most fashionable in Parliament, a department of the public service, an establishment of the State, an establishment which owes its faith and its discipline, its temporalities and its spiritualities, to the State. And therefore they hold that all its affairs and concerns are matters of State cognizance, and are within the limits to which reform, conducted in the usual way, by Acts of Parliament and commissions, and the other apparatus of State machinery, is applicable. And each interference of the kind is a source of satisfaction to the enemies of the Church in Parliament and in the State generally, because it is an additional assertion of the principle of absolute *power* over the temporalities and spiritualities of the Church, which is the first step to the overthrow of both.

It may be very well for persons to talk of the desirableness of augmenting the income of the poorer livings at the expense of the bishoprics, or of the wealthier livings, and so forth: but it is very possible to talk thus, and yet to desire the overthrow of the Church altogether. It is still easier to talk thus, by way of being in the fashion, and gaining the credit of a reformer of State institutions, and yet to resist all real reform of the Church; all such reform as would not merely put a clergyman in each parish, but would animate that clergyman to the discharge of his duty, and aid him in the care of his people, by restoring the apostolical spirit, and taking the Church as far away as possible from the carnal spirit, and the earthly objects of all mere State establishments.

These pretended *Church* reformers, when do they ever look beyond the division and sharing of temporalities, and the material facts of income, pluralities, and parsonage-houses ; to the *faith* of the Church; its discipline; the discipline not merely of the clergy, but of all its members ; the *morality* which it is to inculcate, not only by precept and example, but by discouragement and censure of evil ?   When do they dream of allowing the Church to deliberate and to act for the removal of the vast moral evils around us! When do they think of ensuring the appointment of holy and God-fearing men to our bishoprics and other high offices ? When do they seek to promote the more diligent supervision of the Church by an increased number of overseers ?   No ; they can consent to meddle with our temporalities : the worst enemies of the Church are willing to do so, and even by so doing to add to the apparent strength of the Church in some districts.   But they will neither themselves seek really to improve the Church in more essential points, nor will they let the Church herself act, if they can help it.

We speak thus merely by way of reply to those who might remind us of such Acts as the Cathedral Bill, or Sir Robert Peel's Bill, as indicating an anxiety on the part of the State for the welfare of the Church.   We do not deny that some part of the State feels favourably to the Church, but we have yet to hear of any acts that show such a feeling on the part of the State itself, as a whole.   We point to a few simple and conclusive facts, which refute any such notion.   Ten bishoprics have been suppressed ; two-thirds of the income of the clergy in Ireland has been taken from them ; one-half the income of the English clergy is in the process of annihilation ; our universities are invaded ; our parochial education is placed under the absolute and arbitrary control of the State ; and our faith is interfered with by the State tribunals.

The Church has been, comparatively speaking, passive amidst the events of the last twenty-two years ; but her peaceful attitude, the absence of agitation which has long marked her course, have not induced her opponents to imitate her example.   Every thing like "agitation" on behalf of the Church has uniformly been frowned on by the State, and by those ecclesiastical functionaries who are under State influence, or who represent State authority.   We have been taught to depend on the heads of the Church, and on the ministers, or on some political party, for every thing.   And what has been the result ?   If the Church is quiet, her enemies are not so ; they are always seeking their objects, they are always resisting Church objects, and they are generally successful. The State listens to *them* with respect and deference: to the Church, its tone is contemptuous, and its proceedings arbitrary and tyrannical. The moderation and loyalty of the Church cannot obtain for it the terms which are conceded to the obstinate demands of sectarians, who have had no scruple in disobeying the laws.

We have thus far been contending that the union of Church and State has become an essentially different relation from what it formerly was, since the State has relinquished its creed. We have been arguing that a creedless State is a very different thing from a " Church of England " State. But what is our inference from this? Do we hence infer that no kind of concord, alliance, or harmony may subsist between the Church of England and the creedless State of England? We should be far from laying down such a principle as this. There seems no reason why the State of England should not be in alliance with the Church, though it does not hold the faith of the Church. The relations of the Prussian and Russian Governments to the Roman Churches in their states; the relations of the Greek Government (which is Romish) to the Greek Church; the relations of the French and Belgian states, which are creedless, like ours, to the Gallican and Belgic Churches; all are instances of States being connected with Churches where there is no religious union, no union in faith. So that there is no *impossibility* in such an alliance taking place, under certain conditions, satisfactory to both parties concerned. The Church of Rome willingly enters into such relations with sovereigns not of its communion; and we need not be more scrupulous, provided the advantages and securities in our case are equal.

There is, however, a very great difference between our case and that of the continental Churches referred to. In those cases the sovereign of the State holds relation to the Church of his State in virtue of a *concordat* or treaty with the Papal See, as an independent power, and as the *recognized head of the Church*. The appointment of bishops, the endowment of sees, parishes, seminaries, &c., are matters agreed upon by the Pope and the sovereign. So that in all cases there is an actual treaty and alliance of the State with the Church as an independent power. Certain benefits are conferred by the State, and, in return for these, certain privileges are given by the Church; and both may be resumed.

And, again, the State in all those cases where concordats have been entered into, is a Monarchy or a State possessed of a vigorous central power, which refrains itself, and causes others to refrain, from meddling with the internal concerns of the Church. The internal concerns of the Church in such cases as we refer to, are regulated by the bishops, or the Pope. If synods are not often held, the current of legislation and spiritual regulation is always going on by ordinances of the congregations at Rome, and new papal bulls and decrees. The State does not take the internal affairs of the Church under its cognizance, or interfere with them at all. If it goes beyond its limits, and usurps what belongs to the Church only, it is met not merely by the protests of the Church thus injured, but by the protests and censure of the Papacy, and of all the rest of the Roman communion; and the maintainer of Church liberties is sure of sympathy and support in every other country, if not in his own.

Many of the continental sovereigns possess, by modern or ancient concordats, the right of nominating bishops in their dominions; but the Pope has the right of rejecting Crown nominees, and refusing to permit their consecration. So completely established is the power of the Papacy in respect to the confirmation and appointment of bishops, that, in case of non-recognition of a government by the Pope, or of any dispute, bishoprics sometimes remain vacant for years, and even the whole episcopate of a country sometimes seems almost on the verge of extinction.

Now this shows how fully an alliance or union between Church and State, which is quite sufficient for all State and Church purposes respectively, is consistent with the acknowledgment of independence in the Church on certain po nts. Even in Spain, Portugal, Austria, and other Roman Catholic governments, the appointment of bishops is subject to the papal consent, so that in all cases the Church has some real control over the State, some power of self-protection.

As to the Russian Church, it is much in the position in which the Church of England was from the time of the Reformation to that of William III. The State is *absolute* in Church matters, but the State is rigidly and earnestly *orthodox;* its great object is to promote the Church's extension, to bring all its subjects within the pale of the Church. Therefore, on the whole, it does all that is possible to promote the efficiency of the Church, just as our Elizabeth, James, and Charles did.

The Russian State assumes the great powers in Church matters which the Greek emperors in the later ages acquired. We do not think that the assumption of such power by any State, or its concession by any Church, is to be desired: it may, under some circumstances, however, be very *tolerable;* and those circumstances applied, we think, in the case of the Church of England after the Reformation, as they now do in Russia.

In considering the present state of the connexion between Church and State in England, it is, of course, necessary to bear in mind, that, whatever those relations might have been as recognized and approved on principle by the Church in her Articles and Canons, the whole state of the case is altered, by the State ceasing to possess a Creed, or coming to include persons of all religions. The idea of the State conceived by the Church in the sixteenth century, as a religious and godly State, is practically extinct; the head of the State alone retaining the Christian character, but without any political power annexed to it.

But there is another point, also, well deserving of examination by *Churchmen*. What does the *Church of England* really ascribe, in point of principle, to the State? Does it recognize in a Christian State, as of right, any absolute power in Church matters? Or is its view such as is calculated, if acted on, to maintain a fair and reasonable degree of liberty for the Church, while it holds that Christian States have duties and powers in reference to religion?

We hold that the Church of England is not in any degree tied to acknowledge such a supremacy as now exists by *law*, as one that has any claim to her support, either on the grounds of Scripture or of ancient practice. The Church of England recognizes a very different species of supremacy: it believes in the supremacy of a *Christian* Sovereign. Let us briefly survey its declarations:—

"Art. XXXVII. *Of the Civil Magistrates.*—The Queen's Majesty hath the chief power in this realm of England, and other her dominions, unto whom the chief government of all estates of this realm, whether they be ecclesiastical or civil, in all causes doth appertain, and is not, nor ought to be, subject to any foreign jurisdiction."

This portion of the Article makes an assertion relative to the Crown, which was strictly borne out by *fact* when the Articles were composed. The Crown then *had* the chief government *in reality*, as it now has nominally. The chief government has now fallen into other hands, and the Crown is divested of power. The Church of England, therefore, did not contemplate the *present* state of the Crown, when she expressed thus firmly and decidedly her views of the Crown's power in relation to ecclesiastical affairs. Her declaration referred to a state of things widely different from the present; nor is her Article, which recognizes the chief government of the Crown, to be strained into a recognition of the chief government of the *House of Commons*, and the *ministers* really appointed by it. No power is referred to but the Crown, as possessed of its old constitutional powers, now lost.

"Where we attribute to the Queen's Majesty the chief government, by which titles we understand the minds of some slanderous folks to be offended, we give not to our princes the ministering, either of God's word or of the sacraments, the which thing the injunctions also lately set forth by Elizabeth our queen do most plainly testify, but that only prerogative which we see to have been given always to all godly princes in Holy Scripture by God Himself; that is, that they should rule all states and degrees committed to their charge by God, whether they be ecclesiastical or temporal, and restrain with the civil sword the stubborn and evil-doers."

It will be here observed, that the Church is speaking of a sovereign who is not only a real sovereign, possessed of power, but who represents the "*godly* princes" mentioned in Holy Scripture. In short, the Church here sets out on the notion of a "Church of England" prince, whose powers are not exercised by a House of Commons, but by himself. She refers to such princes as David, Solomon, Asa, Jehoshaphat, Hezekiah, Josiah, who were all worshippers of the true God, and exercised the royal power for the maintenance of the true faith against idolatry, and "restrained with the civil sword" the worshippers of false gods, the heretics and schismatics of their days. The Church here distinctly supposes a sovereign who does not tolerate or patronize false religion, but who acts on the powers at that time *claimed* by the Crown (and regularly exercised), of *punishing* by the civil sword all who dissented from the faith and worship of the Church of England; or restraining them by civil penalties. The Church of England could not have any other notion of a sovereign power but this; for the whole law of the land, up to the time of William III., went on the assumption that it was the duty of the sovereign to use the civil sword for the suppression of all religions contrary to that of the Church of England. Nor was there any State in Europe that had ever acted on the principle of toleration.

Hence we may reasonably infer that in this article, the Church of England, in ascribing the supreme government of the Church to the sovereign, supposed a sovereign who was possessed of sovereign *power*, who was also "godly" in her sense, and whose "godliness" included as an essential element the non-toleration of all doctrines different from those of the Church of England. The Constitution has put an end to such a sovereignty as the Church of England contemplated in her Articles and Prayer Book, so that our subscription in the present day supposes a state of things in the State that has been long obsolete; and in declaring by subscription to the Articles that the Queen is supreme governor, and that she possesses the power of restraining evil-doers given to godly kings in the Bible, and of ruling all states and degrees, we must understand ourselves as rather declaring that the Queen *was* supreme, and *did* possess such powers in the sixteenth century, than that she does so in fact in the nineteenth. We can only say now, that the sovereign *possesses* those powers IN THEORY, not in fact; and that the Church, which supposes them to be possessed in fact, does not mean to pronounce any thing about a state of things in which they are merely possessed in theory. We maintain that the language of the XXXVIIth Article, though it may, in its mere technical and *legal* construction, apply to the present state of things, does not *really* apply to it at all; and that it would be a slavish adherence to the letter, divorced from the spirit, to uphold this or any similar declarations of the Church of England in the sixteenth or seventeenth centuries as applicable to a totally different state of things in the nineteenth.

The first Article in the thirty-sixth Canon again refers to a state of things which has been put an end to by the law.

"That the King's Majesty, under God, is the *only* supreme governor of this realm, and of all other His Highness's dominions and countries, as well in all spiritual or ecclesiastical things or causes, as temporal; and that no foreign prince, person, prelate, state, or potentate hath, or ought to have, any jurisdiction, power, superiority, pre-eminence, or authority, ecclesiastical or spiritual, within His Majesty's said realms, dominions, or countries."

This Article contemplates a state of things very different indeed from what now exists. It asserts the sole supremacy of the sovereign in *all* spiritual or ecclesiastical *things* or causes. But the law has put an end to this sole supremacy; for the supremacy of the Wesleyan Conference is now recognized as the sole authority over Methodists; the supremacy of the Pope is allowed in the case of the Romanists; and every other sect has its own supreme authority. The Crown has *ceased* to be supreme over Dissenters and sectarians generally, and is therefore no longer the "*only supreme governor*" in "*all* spiritual or ecclesiastical things." The whole legislation of England, from the Toleration Act to the present day, has established this. Thus this Article refers to a different constitution from that which we now live under, and binds us to nothing but the supremacy as supposed to be existing with the constitution of A.D. 1562; for the Church does not suppose others to be exempt from the royal supremacy, and *herself alone* subject to it. She does not say that the Crown is supreme over the "Church of England," but supreme over "this realm."

It is of the highest importance for us to understand distinctly, and to be prepared to show, that we are not tied to the supre-

macy of the Crown, as at present existing, by any declarations of
the Church of England. When this is fully understood (and
every means should be taken for making the world understand it)
one great obstacle to the liberation of the Church will have been
removed.   The existing supremacy will no longer be able to
appeal in argument to the authority of the Church of England in
its support ; and those who may seek to obtain the modification
or even removal of the supremacy in the case of the Church of
England, as it has already been removed in the case of all other
denominations of Christians, will not appear inconsistent with the
doctrines of their own Church.   It is in truth a remarkable
instance of retribution, that the State, in throwing off its creed,
has been by that very fact, deprived of all the benefit which its
pretensions over the Church gained from the Church's own declarations and authority.

As far as matters of mere *principle* are concerned, we think
the Church is now *wholly free;* she is not fettered by any of her
declarations on the subject of the Royal Supremacy.   The State
has, by its own proceedings, rendered those declarations and definitions no longer applicable to the existing state of things.   We
are here regarding the question in a moral and religious point of
view, not in a mere legal and technical way.   We have little
doubt that in the Courts of Law the supremacy is still held to be
in full force : but for this we care little ; for the only really important point is the question of principle—what is the real view
of the Church of England to which we subscribe ; and are we, as
members of that Church, bound to recognize the supremacy of
1850 as lawful?

We think that whenever the doctrine of the supremacy of the
Crown is recognized by Churchmen, the acknowledgment should
be restricted and guarded, so as not to let it be supposed that we
admit the *present* supremacy to be authorized or recognized by
the Articles and formularies of the Church.   But there is another
question which we have not yet considered, and which is of very
great moment.   It is the question, What power does or *did* the
Church of England ascribe to a " Church of England" or "orthodox" sovereign ?   The answer to this is comprised in the answer
to the question, "What powers were exercised by the Christian
emperors in the *Primitive Church?*"   For the Church of England acknowledges this in her Canons, as she does the example of
the pious and godly kings of the Jews in her Articles, as the only
rule by which her opinions on this subject are guided and limited.
The Church of England never acknowledged, even in the "orthodox" and " Christian" state, *more* than the primitive Church and
the Scripture allowed to godly princes.   As to the sentiments of

lawyers and of Acts of Parliament, we absolutely disclaim all authority in them; they have *nothing* to do with our belief as Churchmen, we are not in the slightest degree bound by them, we are only bound to obey laws; we are not bound, as Churchmen, to admit principles, or statements, or arguments, or assertions of legislators or of jurists.

We are indebted to Dr. Pusey for a learned and seasonable publication on this subject, the title of which we have placed at the commencement of these pages, and which brings a great body of facts to bear upon the solution of a question in which the character of the Church of England is greatly involved. There is, perhaps, nothing which has been found to work more injuriously against us than the doctrine on the Royal Supremacy, supposed to be upheld by the Church. Men have been too ready to make the Church responsible for all that has been said and done in former times, and in the present, by the State; and the effect has been, that many impatient spirits have fallen into the hands of Dissent and Romanism, whose most popular argument against the Church has always been founded on her admission of the Royal Supremacy.

From what has been said above, it will be seen that we are of opinion, that the time for advocating, *as churchmen*, the Royal Supremacy, has passed by. We have nothing to do with the actual Royal Supremacy; we only possess the *theoretical* or ideal supremacy, which was once a reality. We give up the actual supremacy as a matter that the Church has never approved of, and can never approve of. The formularies of the Church know nothing of the existing supremacy. So that the discussion in Dr. Pusey's volume might seem to have less immediate bearing on the questions at present most urgent than might be supposed. But this is not the case, for it is of the highest importance at the present time, to have clear views as to what the Church of England really did admit, when she recognized the supremacy of a godly prince; and such a discussion, too, supplies various instructive facts, which will be of great value even now, when the State is no longer one in faith with the Church.

The earlier part of Dr. Pusey's volume is directed to meet the difficulty which was felt by such persons as Messrs. Maskell and Dodsworth, in reference to the Gorham case—their opinions being, that the decision of the Committee of Council was virtually that of the Church of England, and that the Church's doctrine was at once altered thereby. In the general purport of Dr. Pusey's remarks on this subject, we feel that there must be a cordial concurrence on the part of all true churchmen. We were inclined to doubt whether he had sufficiently clearly stated the

practical evils to doctrine, likely to arise from a legal sanction
being given to persons of erroneous views to hold ecclesiastical
benefices ; but in the latter part of his volume, those dangers are
distinctly pointed out, while, at the same time, great indulgence is
shown towards many persons who may be supposed to be imperfectly
instructed.   The great evils which may possibly arise from discussions on the inspiration of Scripture, or other fundamental
doctrines, and the dangers of wrong decisions by a Court constituted like that of the Committee of Privy Council, and the
necessity of an alteration in the tribunal for the decision of causes
of doctrine, are clearly stated.   And the conclusion is then
drawn, that " the fundamental defect is, that the doctrines of the
Church should, for any purpose, be authoritatively determined by
any other than the Church herself."   This opens the question to
which the volume is an answer.

" Is then this state of things one to which the Church intended to
commit herself? or one to which we, by our acknowledgment of the
royal supremacy, are bound?
" For myself, I am satisfied that the Church never intended to
concede any thing of this sort, nor do I believe that Queen Elizabeth,
from whom the present Act of Supremacy dates, meant to claim it.
I say, Queen Elizabeth, because what such an one as King Henry VIII.,
who knew no law of God or man, but his own passions, secretly meant,
does not concern us.   He meant, doubtless, to remove any restraint
from his own will, and circumvented the Clergy to accomplish it.   We
have to consider principles, to which the Church has expressed her
assent, not the acts of a lawless king."—pp. 14, 15.

The object of the work, then, is to show what the Christian
emperors in the primitive Church did, and did not claim ; theirs
being the authority recognized by the Church of England, as
annexed to the Crown.   Dr. Pusey proves that they did not
claim authority in controversies of faith, but limited themselves
to convening the Bishops in synod, or appointing episcopal
judges ; that ordinary synods were usually independent of the
civil power, but that the emperors could urge obedience to the
canons.   There are many such points mentioned for which we
must refer the reader to the volume, contenting ourselves with
the following passage as bearing on one of the two great practical questions now before the Church, and which include every
other question—we allude to *free synods,* and *free elections* of
bishops.   With reference to synods of the British Churches, Dr.
Pusey speaks as follows :—

" Without going into questions as to the genuineness of this or that
very early British synod, it will strike every one, looking into our early

history, how all great public acts were done in synods. We have two synods of St. Patrick; Dubritius, A.D. 512, was made archbishop, his successor, bishop of Llandaff, in a synod, according to the ancient rule. St. David and others, A.D. 516; the Pelagians are refuted in a synod, A.D. 519; the British bishops meet St. Augustine in synods; repeated synods are held about the way of keeping Easter, about the variance between Archbishop Theodore and St. Wilfred, and, in later times, about the replacing of secular canons by regular. A synod of Mercia, A.D. 705, gives in charge to Bishop Aldhelm, when a presbyter, to write against the British way of keeping Easter; in A.D. 707 a new bishopric was formed by a decree of a synod, royal donations to a monastery or a cathedral church were given in a synod, a dispute about land between a bishop of Worcester and the monks of Berkeley is settled in a synod, A.D. 824 . . ."

It was afterwards the regular law of the Church that synods should be held every year (pp. 101, 102, 103. 105, 106). The series of authorities extend from A.D. 673 to A.D. 978. In the tenth century, however, the bishops began to sit in the secular courts, and some confusion of jurisdiction arose in consequence, which was put an end to by William the Conqueror.

Annual synods continued after the Conquest (p. 109), and the suspension of them for thirteen years is spoken of as a great evil. They were more rarely held by degrees. Archbishop Stratford held a provincial synod, A.D. 1341, after a lapse of eight years (p. 110).

" It seems probable that, in later times, the regular meeting of convocation superseded the provincial councils, as consisting of the same persons, though not acting altogether in the same way. The penalties annexed for quitting convocation without leave, are the same as those appointed by the canons for so quitting the annual synods. It sat always when Parliament sat; often when Parliament did not. Kings had occasion for it, because it granted them revenues; and these being often triennial grants, their meeting, at least, every third year, was the rather secured. The writs for summoning them ran, ' Convene them as usual.' The same language was used by Cranmer, Philpot, and Pole. But even as late as the first year of Henry VIII., Archbishop Warham summoned convocation to consider the state of the Church, independently of the Crown, by his own authority as Primate."—pp. 111, 112.

The mind of the Church is now thoroughly awakened to the necessity of putting an end to the thraldom, in which the Crown has now for 130 years held her, by the unconstitutional and illegal suppression of her synods, and which has deprived the Crown of all moral claim to possess the power of controlling her synods any further. The demand for the royal license for convo-

cation to resume its sittings, is, however, the first step in the
movement for the recovery of the Church's rights. But we have
no expectation that this petition will be acceded to. The Government, and the heads of the Church under its influence, will not
accede to a proposal which would give the Church a voice in its
own behalf. The Government will not give way to any such
desire for freedom. They are jealous of the Church, and they
seek to place it even more under the control of the State than
it is.

Now, then, it may be asked, What course should be pursued,
if the Crown and the archbishops refuse to permit the assembling
of convocation? We will enter into this question when we have
made some further remarks on the position in which we actually
find ourselves placed.

The dangers of the nineteenth century are widely different
from those of the seventeenth, the sixteenth, the fifth, fourth, or
third. We are in no danger of being compelled to worship false
gods. Heresy is not the evil of this age. Schism has lost its
vigour. Romanism deals only in arguments, addressed to the
reason or the senses, and evinces no wish to restore the stake and
the inquisition. All these sources of danger to the Church in
former times, are not the dangers of the present age. We do
not mean to dispute the activity of some of these agencies, or the
positive harm they are doing; but we say that, looking at the
subject as a whole, we do not think that our great danger is
from Dissent, or Methodism, or Socinianism, or Romanism. They
will never gain ground on the Church, which is fully a match for
them all. She will hold on her own way, acting on her own
belief, and leaving them to follow theirs.

But the real danger in the present day is INFIDELITY. We
are not now speaking of any open denial of Christianity, because
that is not the form which the infidelity of the ·present day
assumes. The days of Voltaire, and Diderot, and D'Alembert,
and Tom Paine have passed by; and no one now declares himself an unbeliever—in *England*, at least. There are now no
avowed *enemies* of Jesus Christ: on the contrary, the infidelity of
the nineteenth century is willing, if it recognizes his existence at
all, to admit Him to the same degree of respect which it pays to
Pythagoras or Confucius, to Socrates or to Schleiermacher.
Christianity is recognized as a beneficial system—a system from
which the world has largely profited—an important stage in the
development of the human mind. The purity of its moral system is acknowledged, and its doctrinal system is held to comprise
a larger infusion of truth than some other religions. The various
stages in the progress of Christianity itself, are regarded with

philosophical approbation. The papacy is held to have been a great blessing to the Church during the Middle Ages. The Reformation is upheld as another great step in advance. It is viewed as the era of the development of those principles of free speculation unshackled by authority, which are to lead ultimately to the regeneration of the world.

Thus, then, all is apparently respectful and friendly in the view which the infidelity of the present day takes of religion in general, and of Christianity in particular. Christianity is rather patronized than otherwise. But, notwithstanding this, there is an absolute want of faith—as *total* an absence of faith as if Christ were openly denied. For Christianity is considered as one out of many religions, exhibiting equal claims and credentials, and as holding no more right to the character of a Divine Revelation than they do. All religions, including Christianity, are believed to contain some truth and some falsehood; and the belief of Christians in the Divinity of our Lord Jesus Christ, the Divine Commission of the Apostles, the inspiration of Holy Scripture, or *the necessity of belief in any of the Articles of Christian faith*, is regarded as an antiquated absurdity, which is only deserving of pity and contempt.

But there are many degrees of progress in the development of opinions of this kind. It is not every one who has proceeded so far as to set all religions on an equality, and mentally to see no difference in truth between Christianity and Buddhism. Many men profess, and perhaps feel, a preference for Christianity, but they employ the powers of their mind to criticise its tenets, with a view to eliminate from them whatsoever does not meet the requirements of their reason. Hence we find all the external evidences of Christianity rejected—every thing denied which can give it *authority* over reason The inspiration of Scripture is systematically assailed : its interpretation is thrown open to the wildest license—its text is tampered with, and invested with doubt—its genuineness is involved in suspicion. All the authority of the belief of former ages, however universal or however ancient, is rejected with contempt. The practical conclusion aimed at is, that all sects of Christians are equally in the wrong ; that disputes about any of the doctrines or duties of Christianity are an absurdity, because there can be no such thing as certainty on any point ; that all disputes amongst Christians turn on points which are only matters of opinion, and on which every man has a right to his own opinion. Some, perhaps, are willing to acknowledge some doctrine or tenet to be true, but they argue that it is most absurd to affirm that the contrary opinion is false, or that it may not be held with perfect propriety. They look therefore on all creeds, formularies, and articles of faith, and on all judgments of the Church, in matters of controversy, as objectionable, inasmuch as they tend to impair that perfect liberty of opinion which they claim for all persons, on the assumption that *all* doctrines and tenets are matters of opinion, and therefore mere human speculations. They endeavour to excite prejudice against creeds and formularies in general, sapping and undermining their authority by all means in their power. They are favourable to all measures which tend to lower and break down the authority of the Church as a body holding certain specific doctrines and tenets, and requiring them to be held. They will support those from whom they differ most widely, in the assertion of their opinions, with a view to establish the utmost freedom for the expression of opinions of all kinds.

The legislation of the age is wholly imbued with this spirit; the literature of the day is increasingly so; the State in England has for many years thoroughly *represented* it, and is engaged in steadily carrying it out *in all directions*. It has even infected the Church itself in some degree: there are various advocates of such views, in a greater or less degree, amongst the Clergy—some amongst the Bishops, several amongst the other Dignitaries. The influence of the State on the Church, in the way of patronage, is sufficient to account for this in some considerable degree; and that patronage is likely to be increasingly exercised in the same direction. The " Evangelical" party in the Church, though firm in its own belief of the inspiration of Scripture and in the Divine origin of Christian doctrines, has been for years deceived as to the real character of the movement to be most apprehended ; has entered into terms of alliance with its most bitter enemies, and has placed itself unreservedly in the hands of the State, to carry out its policy in religious matters. It has been led into this false position by its dread of principles of a more orthodox character than its own, and which it identifies with Romanism ; but, deceived as it has been, it is apparently involved inextricably in the toils which have been laid for it, and, it is to be feared, that it will act henceforward as the ally and the tool of those who are thoroughly imbued with the infidelity of *this* age.

Such is the aspect of things around us. In every direction— within and without—are signs of the same plague of unbelief which has desolated Christianity in many parts of the Continent. Each day makes the nature of the case more and more plain, and writes before the Church, in more unmistakeable characters, the real perils we have to confront. Their progress is slow and stealthy, but ever advancing. Sometimes beaten back for a time, then spreading in another direction. Checked more or less by public opinion, then becoming bolder : always, however, spreading and gaining force. They are unpopular with the people, rejected by the mass of the bishops and of the clergy, and yet possessed of formidable vantage-ground in their entire possession of the State, and the support which they receive from all enemies of the Church—all sectarians—most liberals in politics—and the tacit co-operation of one believing party in the Church.

And at what immense disadvantage is the opposite principle of *firm hereditary faith* to be maintained ! It is to be maintained in opposition, too frequently, to authority. Those who see distinctly the real character of the questions before the Church, and who act accordingly, are liable to discouragements, opposition, condemnation, in even those quarters where their fidelity should obtain for them the most affectionate support and the most earnest co-operation. They are liable to be denounced sometimes as disturbers of the peace of the Church ; at other times, as disloyal to their sovereign ; and always as uncharitable to their neighbours. They are regarded as turbulent and factious men ; and the duty of sitting still and occupying themselves with the ordinary duties of their calling, and leaving higher matters to God and to those in authority, is pressed on them by earnest but mistaken men— by men who do not discern " the signs of the times."

The object of the heads of the Church is, for the most part, to maintain " peace" in the Church. Far be it from us to question the duty of endeavouring to preserve and restore peace. But there are times in which peace itself becomes a secondary object —nay, more, when it becomes treason.—And when all faith is endangered, it is the office of the Church to look, in the first place, to the preservation of *faith*—to take such steps as shall be necessary for placing the deposit of faith in security, and to do so without fear of consequences. There have been times when Christians were called, by the voice of conscience and by the sense of responsibility to their Maker and their Saviour, to disturb the world and the Church ; when they had to resist prevalent beliefs, and to disobey prevalent laws. And where should we now be, had the early Christians, and the orthodox in the time of Arius, and the English Reformers, listened to those who would have spoken to them of " peace, when there was no peace ?" When the *real* question at stake is, whether infidelity or faith is to have the ascendancy in the Church of England, we can know nothing of " peace." Far be it from us to doubt that the truth of this is felt where we should wish it to be felt. We have had some encouraging signs to persuade us that it *is* so ; and we feel hopeful that events will disclose more distinctly the course of 'duty, which at present appears to be entangled by complex considera-

tions, leading (with some noble exceptions) to an apparently ⸻
and uncertain course of action.

But we have this alarming fact, that the State, which is thoroughly imbued with the spirit of which we have been speaking,
exercises, in various ways, immense and most dangerous power
over our episcopate. The power of selection, *without the slightest
power of check or control* on the part of the Church, is, in the
present state of things, the most formidable danger we know of.
It is in this way that the most deadly blows may be struck at
faith. The State must be *expected* to place its own agents and
instruments in authority—men who will be prepared to carry out
its views, whatever they may be—men chosen for their principles.
This danger becomes imminent in proportion as the Church manifests its resolution to act on principles opposed to those of the
State. The immediate remedy of the State is, to exercise its
patronage, in order to break down opposition : it is already acting
thus in Ireland and in England. But, besides this, the fact that
all bishops owe their appointment to the Crown exclusively, *must*
exercise a powerful influence on their conduct, in binding them
to the leaders of one or other of the political parties ; all of
whom are connected, more or less, with the natural policy of a
creedless State in religious questions. Seats in Parliament,
connexion with ministers and ex-ministers, attendance on the
Court, association with the political and great world,—all tend
to form a pliant, an easily-managed episcopate—an episcopate
that will discourage all movements of which the State does not
approve.

Of the dignitaries of the Church, the deans are the nominees of Government, and therefore naturally reflect its views,
and are its advocates, for the most part : independently of
which, the Government has the power of advancing them.
The archdeacons are the nominees of the bishops, and are
therefore less directly under the influence of the State ; yet
they show, in too many instances, that the State has too
great an influence with them. The State nominates to 1200
parochial benefices out of 12,000, besides more than half the
canonries. By its occasional distribution of bishoprics and
deaneries it maintains its influence over the universities, the
rulers of which are unwilling to do any thing to impair their prospects. Generally speaking, there is a great temptation to all
men in leading positions in the Church to pursue such a line of
conduct as shall not exclude them from the favour of Government ; so that, at any crisis, they may very frequently be observed to be extremely timid, cautious, and rather an impediment
than otherwise.

Besides all this, the deliberative action of the Church in synod is wholly suppressed. In some instances, rural deans are permitted to hold meetings of the clergy; but the practice is very limited, and an isolated rural deanery, without the power of communicating with other similar bodies, can do little more than an isolated clergyman: for, fifteen or twenty clergy, even if met together, can do nothing. Archdeaconry synods there are none; it is wholly optional with an archdeacon to call a meeting of the clergy to petition, and in many cases it is refused. Diocesan synods there are none; the bishops apparently considering their assembly illegal or unadvisable, as they are never held. Convocation can only be held by consent of the State, and the State has exercised its power, and silenced it for a hundred and thirty years. Thus, amidst the dangers surrounding the faith of the Church, there is actually no regular mode recognized by the law for the members of the Church even to take counsel together, and to devise means for preserving the faith which they have received from their forefathers, and which they see to be endangered. This recapitulation of the perils to which faith is exposed, will show that the contest for the maintenance of that faith without any infusion of the principles of the present day, is indeed an arduous task. The question is, however, whether, by a series of concessions on one side, and of quiet and stealthy aggression on the other, those principles shall gain influence and ultimate ascendancy in the Church; or whether, by a course of proceeding adequate to the evil, the further influx of evil shall be checked, and the faith of the Church stand in security against alien influences.

Let us now briefly survey the circumstances which afford to us a reasonable ground for hope amidst the struggle which is unquestionably before us.

In the first place we must speak of the *spirit* of the Church itself—we mean the great body of the inferior clergy and the intelligent laity, who are wholly independent of Government. We believe that the Church in general is better prepared for the crisis than she has ever yet been. Her faith has been sorely tried for many years by doctrines and errors of various kinds, and in various directions, and the result has been, we think, to form a great mass of men in firm and robust principles, not likely to be easily shaken—men who have not the remotest inkling of an idea of leaving the Church of England for Rome, or for any other communion whatever—men who thoroughly understand their position, and will maintain it at all hazard—men who are determined that, as far as in them lies, not one point shall be conceded to the infidel spirit of the day, and not an effort shall be spared to obtain reasonable and satisfactory securities for the faith.

They have learned, at length, how to collect their forces, though by an imperfect organization, with leaders chosen, not for their official rank, but for their fidelity; and they have begun to make head against the foe, and already they have struck some lusty blows for the good cause, and stand prepared for more, and with increasing forces. Now we do say this, that the recognition of the principle of the *right of voluntary association*, a principle so reluctantly adopted, and still, in many quarters, regarded with so much jealousy, is the greatest step that the Church of England has ever yet taken towards self-protection. It gives to her members that which they have never had before—the power of conference and deliberation, and of combined and *continuous* action. This is an immense step gained. We are no longer a rope of sand, or a multitude of units without cohesion, or a body raised into momentary life and action by some attack, and then sinking back again into torpor and despondency; we are no longer without the power of conference and of action;—the necessities of the times have at length given us freedom so far, without seeking for the State's consent.

It is a well-known principle of the Universal Church, that in times of heresy, when the faith is endangered, all ordinary rules are suspended by necessity. In such times, steps become permissible without seeking the consent of superiors, which would not, in different times, be fitting. Another ground of hope arises from our episcopate. The conduct of a considerable number of bishops in the Hampden case, and the step which the whole episcopate has recently taken in agreeing to the measure which the Bishop of London has embodied in his Bill respecting appeals, must, we think, be felt by every one as steps in a course of policy which is very remote indeed from a spirit of subserviency to the State, and in both instances these steps were taken *in accordance* with the feeling of the Church. The State has not given way to the wishes of the bishops, they have thrown out the Bill; and it will be felt, that those prelates who are in favour of it will not be in favour with the Government. If so, the Government will have less influence in future over those prelates, and the cause of the Church will gain. On the other hand, had the Government offered no opposition to such a Bill, the bishops would have been encouraged, perhaps, to try to pass some *other* measure sought by the Church; therefore there is good in either case. And we have a further ground of hope in the unsatisfactory and bad appointments to bishoprics and deaneries which are taking place, and which will point out to orthodox bishops still more distinctly their duties towards the faith. We may also trust, that in proportion as the Church at large manifests its wishes in such a mode as to command attention from the State, and puts forward objects unexceptionable in themselves, the episcopate will be encouraged to take a more independent tone, and will feel themselves, in proportion as they do, supported by the Church in a manner which they have not hitherto experienced.

But there is another ground of hope, which we have not hitherto adverted to. The Church holds, in one important respect, a very different place from what she did a century ago. The episcopate was then limited to England and Ireland: it was wholly under the control of the State. No bishop in communion with the Church of England could be consecrated without the royal mandate or license. Every bishop was bound by oaths of allegiance to the English Crown; every bishop was bound to acknowledge the royal supremacy. No synods of bishops could assemble without the royal license; or make regulations, or exercise acts of high jurisdiction, or interfere with authority in Church questions, without the confirmation of King, Lords, and Commons. *That state of things has come to an end!* We now see in Scotland a Church which is thoroughly independent of the State, a Church regularly organized, in full communion with our own, and capable of interfering powerfully in the concerns of the Church of England in any case of necessity. We see in America a powerful and flourishing Church, animated, too, with the spirit of *freedom;* a Church which may be expected to sympathize deeply in all efforts made by the mother Church to obtain a measure of the same freedom which the daughter has acquired. And in the Colonies we see numerous Churches, not tied and fettered, as our own have been; but remote from Government influence, unaided by Government favour, despoiled by Government of their rights, and yet free (as we have heard from the Attorney-general) from the terrors of *præmunire!* In the Colonies the Government has been labouring to teach the Church, that it is not established by the State in preference to any others; and thus the colonial Churches are more at liberty, and may be expected to show that they are so.

Now all this appears to us to have a most important bearing on the Church of England herself. We are no longer an *isolated* Church. The advocates of our religious freedom will no longer be left alone to struggle with a creedless State. If *we* are under the yoke of laws which were adapted for a different age from ours, many of our brethren and our fathers are at liberty. The *majority of the episcopate* is either altogether free, or free to a great extent. And that episcopate possesses *universal* jurisdiction in times of

heresy or infidelity. The decree of a synod in matters of faith or
of essential discipline, has authority in every part of the world.
Were the whole English episcopate to fail utterly in faith, the
episcopate throughout the world could stand in the breach, and
create fresh leaders for the cause of Faith. In times of extraordinary peril to faith, there have been many instances of extraordinary exercise of power. Patriarchs have been deposed by synods
or bishops of remote provinces; decrees have been made in
condemnation of imperial laws and regulations; ordinations and
consecrations have been performed by bishops of other provinces;
common forms and ordinances have been dispensed with in case
of necessity;—in short, the inherent powers of an independent
episcopate are very great; and there *is* such an independent
episcopate.

There is yet another ground of hope. The State itself, having
no positive principles of its own, is subject to be swayed and guided
by external influences. In the contest for power, or for advantage of any kind, the victory is sure to remain with whatever
party is so strong and so pertinacious, that its claims become
troublesome. If the Church becomes troublesome to the State
in the *right* way,—that is, not by any such direct opposition as
would enable the State to strike a blow and weaken its petitioner,
but by such a course of steady complaint, petition, remonstrance,
censure, argument, and appeal to popular, fair, legal, and intelligible rights, claims, and securities; and so firm a resolution to
have them granted, and to disregard all threats, intimidations,
inducements, or bribes that may be held out; that it is evident
the petitioner cannot be cajoled, or induced to defer the petition;
—if this should be the case, we think the eventual success of the
Church morally certain, when we look at the *usual* course of
legislation under such circumstances. A measure is proposed;
it is rejected by Government and a large party; this is repeated
several times; at length Government becomes its advocate, to get
rid of an annoyance, and then it is passed. The Church has only
to seek for her rights, and they will be obtained. Let her bring
any large amount of force to bear continually and perseveringly
on the question, and she may get any thing she wishes. She
may gain free synods, and she may gain free elections of bishops.
She cannot have either one or the other at present; but she can
have them both in a few years, if she acts wisely.

In entering on the contest, however, for the restoration of the
Church's rights, with a view to the security of religion, it is difficult to foresee exactly what course the contest may take, as
regards the temporalities of the Church. We see no ground on
which the State could even threaten the temporalities of the

Church, if the course adopted by Churchmen, in pursuit of her liberties, were strictly legal, or such as, at all events, is practically so, from its general adoption by others. We do not think that, in the present day, the mere seeking for rights, which have been illegally suppressed (such as the meeting of convocation), or for free elections of bishops and deans, could be made a pretext for any intimidation; or that public feeling would bear out any government in any attack, either on property or on personal liberty. Every part of the law or constitution is open to revision; and as long as the law is not directly opposed, there can be no means of assailing the Church. Besides this, the great patronage enjoyed by the Crown, independently of the bishoprics and deaneries, and the patronage enjoyed by private individuals, and which no one proposes to touch, would be another guarantee. And, in fine, if the Church had sufficient power to carry her own liberation, she would have power enough to retain her property.

Such appears to us to be the most probable side of the question; but, at the same time, we think that the Church ought deliberately to make up her mind for whatever may happen, and to be ready to persevere in her demands, even if the result should be the confiscation of her whole temporalities. Grievous as such a blow would be, it would be a cause of *thankfulness*, if it saved us from the formation and perpetuation of a latitudinarian and infidel Church; a Church like that of Germany, having the name of Christianity, without its belief; a Church which admitted freely within its bosom Rationalists and Mystics, the Pantheist and the Materialist. There could be but one element to add horror to such a mixture,—the voluntary union of Christians with such a mass of corruption.

We would a thousand times prefer seeing all the temporalities of the Church destroyed, than see an established Infidelity like that of Germany.

In this view we should esteem it a calamity, if the minds of those who are firm in faith were brought to the adoption of such a course, as should lead to their exclusion from the possession of the benefices and positions which they hold in the Church at present; because the result would be, that their places would be filled by men of different principles, and the Church would receive an impulse in the very direction which is most perilous to her. To suppose the existence of a state of things analogous to what occurred in the time of the Non-jurors; to suppose the endowments of the Church, and all its advantages, and, above all, its *connexion with the people,* to remain in unsafe hands, would be, indeed, a deplorable view, and such a result the very clearest necessity alone could justify— such necessity as should be announced by the orthodox episcopate throughout the world.   No; if we are to lose our temporalities, let us all fall together, and all start fair again.   But do not let *our* fall be the means of giving the people into the hands of infidelity.

We trust that in any case in which the duty of Churchmen appeared doubtful, they would weigh well the evil, on one side, of being amalgamated with infidelity; and, on the other, the evil of giving over the people into the hands of infidelity; and we have no doubt that their course would be guided aright.   But we see no prospect of any such conjuncture of circumstances.   The faith of the Church is firm and unwavering, notwithstanding the failure, feebleness, timidity, and indifference of many amongst us.   All that possesses energy is firm in its faith.   And we think that there is reason to expect the increase of this firm and stedfast faith, instead of its diminution.

We now come to the steps which are being actually taken for the recovery of the Church's liberties.   The great object immediately before the Church at present, is the revival of her convocations, as the form of synod recognized by the latest precedents.

The State has for 130 years virtually suppressed these assemblies, by refusing its license for their deliberations, and exercising its influence over the archbishops, so as to prevent them from meeting except as matter of form.   That the State will alter the unjust policy which it has so long persisted in, in this respect, without the application of very strong influence, is not to be expected.   The Archbishop of Canterbury at present leaves the question, as he has informed some of the clergy, entirely to the discretion of the Government.   We must expect, therefore, that for some time, the applications made to revive convocation will be unsuccessful.   The prayers of the Church will be refused by the State, and the archbishops: but, supposing the State and the archbishops to refuse to permit convocation to act, their objections will doubtless be founded on the apprehensions of the one, lest the Church should interfere with its legislation on Church subjects; and the fear of the others, lest it should increase divisions in the Church, and endanger her temporalities.

Now, it is the judgment of those who are favourable to a restoration of the constitutional liberties of the Church in respect of synods, that either such apprehensions are altogether groundless, or else that they are not cause of alarm, or else that they must be disregarded in comparison with still greater perils. The great majority of the Church are, beyond question, favourable to the restoration of the synodal action of the Church in some form.

Differing, then, as we should in the supposed case, from the advisers of the Crown, (and yet those advisers being invested by law with the absolute power of preventing the meeting of convocation,) what is our course to be! We think it may be thus, in general, described.

The object of the Crown advisers in the supposed case, being to keep matters in a certain state, which they think would be disturbed by the meeting of convocation, it should be the policy of the Church, we think, to show that, notwithstanding the illegal and unconstitutional suppression of the regular assemblies of the Church, the *very same disturbance* which Government apprehends from convocations or synods, may exist and become permanent, notwithstanding the suppression of synods; and then, possibly, the assembling of synods may, after a time, be looked to rather as a *remedy*, than as an evil.

With this view, the organization of the Church by means of voluntary associations of clergy and laity, should be made as perfect as possible, so that no ecclesiastical division should be left without the means of prompt co-operation with the whole body, on any given point. The little which has been done as yet in this direction, proves the power which arises from such union and co-operation; and the movements of the Government, and certain indications in Parliament, show that the rise and increase of this power is felt with uneasiness. This is exactly as it should be. We shall never gain any thing, until far greater uneasiness is felt. Nothing will ever be gained, unless the agitation of the mind of the Church be such as to create considerable alarm, irritation, and disturbance " elsewhere" for several years. The Church must be prepared for intimidation, threats, insults, and possibly hostile legislation, with a view to bind her down more firmly, before she can look for relief. A steady continuance in the course which has been already adopted in part, but with increased vigour, will eventually obtain the restitution of Church liberties from the State.

But in order to obtain this, largely increased exertions must be made. The organization of the Church must be completed. No opportunity of resisting bad legislation must be lost. Nothing must be permitted to proceed either in Church or State with respect to Church questions, without a vigilant scrutiny, and a vigorous *action* either for or against it. The press must be kept at work in every way. In proportion to the vigour with which this course is taken, combined with such reasonable discretion as shall evade *all transgression of the laws* of Church and State, will be the success of the undertaking.

It will thus be seen, that if the object of the ministers in the unconstitutional repression of the Church's synodal action be to obtain

a body which shall be subservient and accommodating—a body
which shall exercise no will or judgment of its own, but be led
and guided exactly as the State pleases, they will be wholly disappointed.   They will be able to influence a certain portion of the
Church by their corrupt exercise of patronage, but they will not
be able to keep the Church, as a body, from being extremely
troublesome to them in every direction.   They will have to deal
with a body which is smarting under a sense of continued wrong,
and a body which will not be disposed to look with a friendly
eye on any of the movements of Government while this wrong
continues—a jealous, alienated, active, and powerful body—a
body which is continually gaining strength, and which will soon
be no subject for contempt to any Government.

Such, in general, is the line of policy which, judging by the
course of events passing before our eyes, we may reasonably expect to be effectual in wringing from a reluctant State the
restitution of the Church's rights.   We have no strength to
compel the surrender of the citadel by main force, but we
may beleaguer it, and leave it no rest or peace until it makes
terms.

It is, of course, advisable, in the first instance, to seek from
the *Crown* the restoration of the synod, which has been suspended, by an arbitrary and unconstitutional exercise of the royal
prerogative, in violation of the coronation oath, for 130 years.
This will be sought by various bodies of Churchmen.   It has
been so already.   It is being sought by a great assembly of
the clergy and laity from all parts of the kingdom.   But it
appears to us desirable that some additional agency should be
brought into play for giving a more formal and authoritative
character to the movement for freedom.   At present, if the
aggregate clergy and laity of England meet for any purpose, they
assemble, once for all, in a great meeting, bearing no directly representative character, and having no continuous existence.   There
may be some advantages in this; and yet we should wish, if possible, to give those proceedings something of a more formal, and
authoritative, and continuous character ; we shall be glad to see
some body of Churchmen which might act directly on the State
as the recognized organ of Church feeling, and might lead
the efforts of Churchmen for the attainment of Church objects.
The " Church Unions " have not this kind of *semi-authoritative*
character ; they are mere voluntary combinations of individuals,
and, admirably useful and effective as they are in their sphere of
operation, they yet can scarcely, at present, stand before the
world in such a position as to claim to be in themselves the representatives of the Church.   They are not so much *provisional*

bodies, acting merely until the regular synods are restored, and holding some *intermediate* authority, as the fortuitous combination of individuals associated under circumstances of extreme peril and necessity. Now we think that there is a want of some body possessing a *species* of authority, capable, in short, of filling the space left vacant by the synod, in some provisional and semi-authoritative mode, until the synod itself is replaced in the full exercise of its liberties. And such a want we conceive might be supplied by some such measure as the following.

It would be *illegal* to summon a convocation without the Queen's writ; therefore, a convocation, in the supposed case, we could not have. A national synod *might*, we believe, be summoned by the archbishops, for the submission of the clergy, and the consequent Act of Henry VIII. makes no mention of "synods;" but, of course, no archbishop *would* take such a step, even if he could. We see nothing, however, in the Acts of Parliament to prevent the assembling of a voluntary " convention of the clergy *and* people of the Church of England, Ireland, and the Colonies "—a " convention," not claiming the *legal* authority of a convocation or a synod; not claiming the right to "make rules, orders, or constitutions, in causes ecclesiastical, without the king's authority" (Canon XII.); but being, and assuming to be, the virtual and actual representation of the clergy and people of the Church; and as such, *authorized* to represent the wishes, and prayers, and grievances of the Church, and to interfere on behalf of the Church, and, to enter into treaties on her behalf, to issue recommendations and suggestions to the Church, and to receive petitions, and to enter into communications with the American, Scottish, and Colonial Churches. A body thus composed of laity, as well as of clergy, could not come under any "submission" made in the time of Henry VIII., because there were not any bodies of such mixed character then in being; and where the rights of any part of the nation to meet for purposes, consistent with obedience to the laws, are concerned, it is only fair, we think, that statutes should be taken in their strict and literal meaning, and not be stretched so as to restrain the liberty of the subject unnecessarily. As to any *moral* obligation on the clergy to adhere to the "submission" in the time of Henry VIII., the suppression of synods for 130 years by the Crown has annulled any such obligation. The "submission" would never have been made on any such terms.

Of whom should such a convention be composed? We should say, it should include (1) all archbishops, metropolitans, and bishops within the British dominions, whether at home or in the colonies, who were inclined to take part in its deliberations; (2)

all deans and archdeacons similarly disposed; (3) proctors for
the chapters; (4) proctors for the clergy of each diocese, in proportion to the archdeaconries, elected by beneficed clergy; (5)
proctors for the universities; and (6) deputies for the people of
each diocese, elected by communicants. In each of these instances
of election, many of the electors would not at first exercise their
right, being unfavourable to any such Convention; but this need
not prevent others from acting.

Whether any bishops or archbishops would, at first, take part
in the proceedings of such a convention would be doubtful. The
same may be said of the greater number of deans and archdeacons; probably very few of either would take part in the convention at first. The number would, however, increase after a
time, if the proceedings of the convention assumed a character of
importance, in consequence of their energy, discretion, moderation, and success. The recognition of the character of the convention by episcopal authority in Scotland, America, and the
Colonies would also give it weight; and the progress of events
might very probably induce some bishops and other dignitaries,
by degrees, to take part with the convention.

It would not be *necessary*, however, in any degree, to the success of the design, that the bishops should ostensibly take part
in it, and actually sit in the convention : business could be transacted in their absence; and as the object of the convention would
not be any authoritative enactments, but merely the recovery of
the rights of the Church, the presence of the episcopate would
not be requisite as a matter of principle. There would, however,
be this important consideration, that the bishops could, at any
moment that they thought fit, *confer* an authoritative character on the assembly by uniting themselves with it, in which
case the convention would be competent to any acts of spiritual
jurisdiction that might be requisite, *on any emergency.* Such a
body, composed of the episcopate and the representatives of the
clergy and people, might, *at any moment*, without an hour's delay,
declare itself a national synod, and act as such.

If this body were called into existence, it would be desirable to
give it such a character as should assimilate it in some degree to
the regular Convocations of the Church. Its proceedings should
commence with the Convocation prayers, if legally permissible : a
Prolocutor should be elected : its clerical members should appear
in their robes. Its proceedings should be of a grave and formal
character, like those of a Convocation or Parliament. It should
appoint its select and other committees, delegates, and deputa-
tions—issue its writs for elections, through its Prolocutor,—
nominate its civilians, and counsel, and consulting theologians;

its treasurers and secretaries, and other officers,—and raise funds to meet its expenses.

With reference to elections of proctors and deputies, we should imagine that some such course as this might be taken. The proctors for cathedral bodies might be chosen by such residentiaries, non-residentiaries, or honorary canons, as might be in favour of a Convention. The deputies for universities would be chosen at meetings of members of their convocation, or senate. The proctors for the clergy and laity might be chosen at meetings summoned for the purpose by the archdeacon, or some of the rural deans, or such other persons as might be commissioned; each of the clergy being requested also to convene the communicants of his parish, and cause them to elect a layman to represent them. Each of the clergy and laity so convened, and every member of the convention, should subscribe to a declaration of their wish to obtain the restoration of the liberties of the Church, throughout Great Britain and its dependencies, in reference to synods, and elections of bishops and other prelates; such declaration being subscribed and attested, the right of proxy might be permitted, and the elections be decided by the votes of those present; each having a number of votes in proportion to the proxies held by him from his own deanery.

And then the question arises,—Whence should the power to summon such a convention be derived? We think it might proceed from a general assembly of clergy and laity, which could appoint a committee authorized to carry out all the details of the proposal, and to regulate all the proceedings, prior to, and on the meeting of such a convention.

Such a body as this would, we conceive, in no degree supersede the action of " Church Unions;" but, in fact, become the authoritative organ of all that feeling which Church Unions represent, and which they have, and would continue to have, well-founded claims to direct. The Church Unions would necessarily be in very close union with any such body: they would continue all their present action; and the convention would give weight to all. The agencies then in operation for the recovery of the Church's rights would be (1) the Church Unions; (2) the ecclesiastical organization, under archdeacons and rural deans, as far as it can be made available; (3) the General Convention of the clergy and laity.

The benefit of the Church Unions, as it seems to us, is to set other machinery to work; to infuse the spirit of activity into the old organization of the Church; to aid in directing and advising the proceedings taken under that organization; and to act generally in making the existing machinery available. But when Church

Unions come before Parliament, or the Crown, or the Public, we think they have less weight, because they have no organization known to the public, and assume no character which gives authority to their representations. Such an assembly as we have described would have the highest claim to attention. We have no doubt that amongst its lay members might be found a large body of nobility, members of Parliament, jurists, and other distinguished and influential men.

The Convention should, we think, start into existence on the refusal of the Crown to grant Convocation, either directly, or by some evasion of the demand. It should then proceed to place itself in communication with the episcopate and churches throughout the world, and obtain their judgment on the position of the Church of England under the existing laws. It should seek for their alliance and aid. It should head the supplications of the Church of England for common justice, and for the relief of grievances. It should present to the nation an assembly scarcely less important, in its way, than the legislature itself: a body exercising influence independent of the Crown and of the Parliament, and far more active, united, and powerful than Convocation itself, as at present constituted, could be. Its voice should be heard in protest and remonstrance on all occasions when the security of the faith and discipline of the Church was invaded, or its temporal rights imperilled. Its missionaries should go forth to proselytize the whole people to the cause of Church freedom. In strict combination with the Church Unions, and with local organization of the Church in England, and with the sister churches in Scotland and in America, and the Colonies,—and with, at least, a portion of the English episcopate, which will assuredly adhere to the cause of GOD, even when it may be necessary to disregard the threats, ay, and the persecution, of "the powers that be,"— that Convention of the Church might bravely stem the torrent, and, at length, re-instate the Church of England in the full possession of her ancient Liberties and Rights.

Let us briefly indicate the course which might be pursued for the recovery of our rights.

The first appeal should be to the Crown. Ere these pages are before the public this appeal will have been made. It will consist in the moderate request—that Convocation may be permitted to deliberate on the questions now before the Church.

The next step, we conceive, might be, to summon a General Convention of the Church, in the mode suggested above.

After this, the appeal to the Crown might be renewed with more vigour ; requesting not merely that a Synod may be assembled, but that the Ministers be directed to introduce a Bill for restoring free elections of bishops and deans.

This appeal might be backed by any numerical force in the shape of petitions from clergy and laity, that might be deemed advisable.

The next step, in case of failure in the preceding, might be, to apply to the Legislature for the repeal of the Acts conferring on the Crown the powers which it holds at present, and for the restoration of the liberty of elections and free Synods, according to the ancient law of England.

In case of failure, an appeal might be made to the episcopate and Churches of the English communion throughout the world, to declare their judgment on the existing state of the law in England.

A final appeal might then be made to the English Legislature for justice.

In case of failure, it would then remain to appeal to the orthodox episcopate throughout the world, to enforce their judgment by spiritual censures—to exclude from their communion all who adhered to the existing law, or did not pronounce condemnation of it—to depose all archbishops and bishops who might adhere to it —and to consecrate bishops in their place.

In this event, the Church of England might be wholly deprived of its churches and endowments; but they would be enjoyed only by deposed and excommunicated sectaries, whose possession would probably be as short-lived as their faith was unsound. Either their property would be soon swept away by the revolutionary spirit of the times, or the Church of England would, after a time, re-enter on its possessions. Rationalism and Evangelicalism would soon break up the Parliamentary establishment; the Church of England would ultimately gain the adherence of all right-minded Evangelicals, against whom the door should never be closed; and a Rationalistic church would be unable to maintain its ground.

If, in any event, the Church of England and the State establishment should become two different bodies, we are anxious that it should be under such circumstances, that the Christian world may see that so great an evil has not taken place without sufficient warning and sufficient cause. Our sole anxiety is, that the course taken may be such as shall be justifiable by the imperative necessity of protecting the Christian faith; and that no hasty, impetuous, or impatient actions—no voluntary separations—no schisms unauthorized by the *orthodox* episcopate, and arising from our own individual sense of right—should mar, and impede, and disfigure our testimony for " the faith of JESUS CHRIST."

It is for this reason that we should regret to see any members of the Church at present attempt to forsake us, and to combine in a new communion. There is nothing in our present state that could warrant any such course, or exempt it from the imputation of schism. It may be said by them, that the supreme ecclesiastical court in England has pronounced against the faith of the Church concerning baptism. Be it so: yet it cannot be said that the Church has *acquiesced* in any such decision. Protests have been heard in many directions, and at this moment we are appellants to the decision of a Synod. Let the Synod meet, and we shall have all doubts put an end to. But while this appeal is pending, separation would be obviously without sufficient cause or justification. Let it be conceded that heresy has received encouragement by the recent decision, yet still the Church has to speak. It is at this moment gagged and bound by the Government: it will not long be so. Causeless divisions now would only have the effect of placing those who make them in a false position, and of precluding them from taking any part in the contest which the Church has commenced.

Let it not be supposed that, in offering this advice, we are insensible to the dangers of faith. We see those dangers distinctly. We see a deeper, larger, and more urgent danger, perhaps, than some of those do, who would forsake the Church on account of the recent decision. We are convinced that the *real* contest is between Christianity and Infidelity. But, in proportion to the magnitude of the question, is the anxiety we feel, that the advocates of the cause of *faith* in the Church of England should present an unbroken front; and that their proceedings should, throughout, be so plainly guided by reason; so evidently based in justice, faith, charity, and necessity, that there may be nothing for which the Church of England may hereafter have to blame her defenders; but that our cause may stand before the English nation, and before all Christendom, as a holy, and a righteous, and a just cause; that there may be no fundamental defects in our proceedings, which may hereafter be made the means of disturbing the faith, by assailing the ecclesiastical position of the Church of England.

Most fervently do we pray, that it may never be our lot to witness so lamentable a struggle for faith, though that struggle would be a glorious one. But the members of the Church have convictions and consciences too; and earnestly do we hope, that this may be discovered before it is too late; and that the timely concession of those liberties which have become essential to the preservation of religion, will prevent the fearful consequences to Church and State, which must otherwise ensue.

Art. V.—*The Guardian:* Wednesday, June 5, 1850.
The Morning Post: Tuesday, June 4, 1850.

THE introduction of the Bishop of London's Bill for a Reform of
the Tribunal for the decision of Doctrinal Causes, and the debate
in the House of Lords which ensued, are amongst the most important, and, in many respects, amongst the most cheering, of the
events which the Church has lately witnessed. In the Bill itself,
and in the debate, there was a healthy tone such as we have long
been strangers to; and although, as might have been anticipated,
the measure failed, in consequence of the opposition of Government, still we have reason to be most deeply grateful to the Right
Reverend author of the Bill, and to the prelates and nobles who
so worthily supported him: and it is with feelings which we are
unable to express that we recognize the guidance of the Divine
HEAD OF THE CHURCH in bringing about the unanimity which
on this occasion has so happily, and so wonderfully, been manifested by the Bishops of England.

While all Churchmen must honour the integrity, the ability,
and the perfect soundness of principle which the Bishop of London's advocacy of the measure evinced, we trust that the present
failure of this most righteous and healing Bill will not be found
to have the injurious effects which his Lordship anticipated.
Assuredly the failure of *any* measure in the present day which is
intended for the restitution of the Church's rights can afford but
little matter of surprise; nor can it, to any reasonable mind, produce any material difference in the view which he takes of his
duties to the Church. The State has retained—wrongfully and
unjustly retained—the powers which were given to it when it was
a Christian State, perfectly united in faith to the Church of
England. The State is obviously determined to retain those
powers as long as it can. It will offer a most obstinate resistance
to all attempts to eject it from the powers it unjustly holds; and
it has the law, the parliament, and the majority of the nation in
its favour, at present. Therefore it will, without scruple, resist
every attempt that the Church makes to get rid of its fetters.
Again and again we shall be frustrated; and it is only by perseverance that the claims of justice and of religion will make their
way. We should think, therefore, that the failure of this Bill, at

present, cannot produce any effect in causing persons to fall away from the Church, except in so far as every evidence of the State's actual power over the Church is to some minds a cause of doubt and of danger.

But we will say, with confidence, that we think the Bishop of London, and the archbishops and bishops of England, have done very much to reassure the minds of Churchmen generally, by the mere *fact* of agreeing to introduce such a Bill.

It is needless for us to enter into the details of the proposed Bill, as our readers must be familiar with them. Suffice it to say, that the important feature in the whole was, that all doctrinal questions were to be transferred by the Privy Council to the cognizance of a spiritual tribunal, consisting of the bishops of England ; and that the duty of the Privy Council was restricted to advising the Crown to carry the decision of the spiritual tribunal into effect. So that, substantially and really, while the theoretical supremacy of the Crown was upheld, just as it is now, with all the usual forms, the power of settling matters of doctrine was transferred, from a mere State tribunal without any creed, to a synod of bishops. The supremacy was, so far, practically transferred to the proper hands. The bishops were not to be called in merely as members of the Privy Council, or as mere advisers of the Privy Council, or of the Queen in Council ; but they were to act as bishops, in their separate court, and *practically* holding their independent and rightful sovereignty in spiritual matters by law. The Church was, through them, to protect her own faith. The religion of the Church of England was no longer to be left at the discretion of a set of lawyers and politicians who were thoroughly indifferent to religious truth, and who regarded all questions that might arise with the eyes of men of the world and statesmen, and with the policy of relaxing to the utmost degree the stringency of Church formularies. The Church itself was to look after its own faith. That very unenlightened body, still attached to the belief of the fourth and the sixteenth century, was to have the power of preventing Rationalists, Socinians, Infidels, Anabaptists, and all opponents of the faith, from becoming possessed of her benefices and ministering at her altars.

Now we do say, that the mere introduction of a Bill embodying such principles as these is a great benefit to the Church. It is an assertion of right and of principle. It is a declaration that the power of the State in reference to spiritual matters is too great—is dangerously great—and must be diminished. It is a recognition of the principle, that the royal supremacy, however excellent in theory, cannot practically be trusted—that it must be guarded against.

It is a recognition, too, of the justice of the apprehensions of those who regard the Judicial Committee of Privy Council as a dangerous and incompetent tribunal.

That such a Bill as this should have been introduced, and with the almost unanimous consent of the hierarchy, is, indeed, a subject of the highest gratification, and of some surprise also; for it was not supposed that the principles of reform had made so great a progress. And although we may readily believe that some of the supporters of that Bill have looked at it chiefly as a means for allaying the excitement which recent events have caused, yet still we do not suppose, that any of them can have failed to remark the real and substantial alteration and reform in essential points which it would make in the present relations of Church and State.

We cannot but marvel, however, that of all the bishops and archbishops of England in favour of the bill, two only, the Bishops of London and Oxford, spoke in its behalf. When we compare the interest excited by great questions in the House of Commons, and the anxiety of members to speak for or against measures of importance, we must certainly infer that, at present at least, ecclesiastical topics are not subjects of much interest in the House of Lords. To this indeed the Bishop of London seemed to allude at the commencement of his speech:—

" He had to submit to their earnest and serious consideration a measure far less interesting, he feared, than the ordinary topics which generally engaged the attention of the house."

Unless we are greatly deceived in " the signs of the times," we think this want of interest is not likely very long to continue. We expect to see Parliament as much excited on Church questions in a year or two, as they used to be on Catholic Emancipation. Up to the present time, however, it is evident that on Church subjects there is a great amount of indifference in the House of Lords as well as in the House of Commons. Church questions can only attract a slight interest. And yet this is our sole legislature for the Church! We are deprived by arbitrary power of our natural and constitutional legislature, and thrown for legislation on bodies which are indifferent to us, which feel no anxiety for our welfare. We cannot conceive that any thing but their knowledge of the temper of the house, and its unwillingness to hear lengthened discussions on Church subjects, could have withheld all our bishops, save three, from speaking on an occasion of such vital importance and unparalleled interest.

The Bishop of London, in the earlier part of his speech, drew attention to the benefits accruing to the State from the Church's possession of Christian liberty.

" He must attempt to induce their lordships to lay aside for a short season their thoughts and feelings as mere legislators, and to apply themselves to this question as members of that great spiritual body, the Church. It must not be supposed that he desired their lordships to put out of sight for a single moment, whilst legislating for the Church, the relation which the Church bore to the State, or the mutual claims and duties of the two. It was because he believed that it was *essential to the well-being of the State* that the Church should be enabled *to discharge its own peculiar functions without let or hindrance*, that he desired their lordships to direct their attention—perhaps somewhat more closely than they were wont to do—to the functions of the Church, as the keeper and teacher of God's truth."

A State like that of England does not understand what is most for its own interest, when it attempts to interfere with the internal concerns of any Church within its dominions. Whenever it has done so, disturbance has invariably been the result. Romanists would not tolerate its meddling in their affairs, nor Dissenters in theirs; because they are justly and reasonably jealous of the interference of a power which is alien in religion from themselves. The State has, for a long series of years, had very little difficulty in dealing with these various classes of sectarians. It takes care not to offend them by disturbing their internal arrangements, doctrines, &c. But what would be the state of things, if it were to put itself in the position of appointing their ministers, interfering with their endowments, prescribing rules for their education and worship, deciding questions of doctrine amongst them, and suppressing their synods and meetings in order to draw all power into its own hands! The answer is obvious : it would be most certainly, ignominiously repulsed. It does not possess power to carry out any such interference.

And now to look to the Church of England. We were long at peace with the State, because the State was of our own faith, and for the most part acted in such a way as to cause little jealousy or uneasiness to the Church. But twenty years ago it threw off the religion of the Church of England, and it has never since been at peace with the Church. There has been frequent collision between Church and State, and it is daily becoming more open and violent. And why so? Because the State does not maintain towards the Church the same distance as it does towards all the sects, contenting itself with mere protection of its endowments, and relinquishing interference in its internal affairs. Let it *reform* relations which were established for, and are only suited to a Church of England State, and let a creedless State acknowledge, in the case of the Church of England, the same religious liberties which it is *compelled* to yield to every other denomination of Christians. The State has never yielded religious liberty to any communion except on compulsion, and with the extremest reluctance. Let it now show that the examples of all enlightened governments are not lost on it, that the invariable issue of such contests is not forgotten, that its legislative intelligence is not limited by the precedents of the sixteenth century, and that it has, if no regard for justice—common justice, and fairness, yet at least some regard for its own quiet; and, as it has degenerated to the latitudinarianism of America and of France, let it imitate the conduct of either of those States in not interfering with the religious concerns of those who *have* a creed.

The Bishop of London discharged a most difficult task with singular address and good feeling, in pointing out the unfitness of the Judicial Committee of Privy Council for the decision of doctrinal questions.

"When they came to deal with ecclesiastical questions, it was seen that it was not a tribunal constituted according to the original principles of the Church, and—with respect be it spoken—he must say that the members were not competent judges of such questions. He apprehended that, in the constitution of an ecclesiastical tribunal, the State and Church could only have these objects in view ; and it was because there was a departure from these objects that he now called on their lordships, not to remodel the proceedings of that court, but to give some directions for its mode of procedure in certain cases. He said that it was the duty of the State, *looking at its compact with the Church,* to preserve inviolate that *compact,* and to preserve intact the doctrines and discipline of the Church, and to keep all ecclesiastical judges within the terms of that compact. On the other hand, he considered that it was the duty of the Church to preserve inviolate its doctrines and purely spiritual discipline, and to do this without the danger of coming into collision with the State. The whole course of his argument proceeded upon this assumption. He must say that *we were the only Church in Europe which was deprived of the freedom of synodical deliberation.* He thought the judicial committee was an incompetent tribunal for deciding questions of doctrine," &c.

Undoubtedly there was a *compact,* or an understanding and virtual engagement between the Church of England and the State. That is to say, in the reign of Henry VIII., the Church relinquished the power of assembling in convocation without the royal summons, and yielded up her right of free elections to the Crown, and recognized the Crown as supreme head of the Church, as far as was allowable by God's law—on the assumption, condition, and implied engagement of the Crown, that its power should always be employed for the maintenance of true religion, as held and taught by the Church of England. From that compact the Crown has departed, having consented to let its powers pass into the hands of a body which has no creed at all. Certainly the compact of the State with the Church involved, as the Bishop of London observed, the duty of "preserving intact the doctrines and discipline of the Church." Is the State doing this? Can it attempt to do so? It cannot, because it has no belief. Therefore it seems plain that the *compact* is at an end. The State having broken its part of the compact in the most essential point of all, the Church is no longer bound. A *new* compact must be formed. And how has it happened, that we are, as the bishop says, "the only Church in Europe deprived of the freedom of synodical deliberation?" It has been, simply, because the State has broken its compact with the Church—it has abused, for the destruction of the Church's liberties, a power which was only given for the honour of the Crown, on the supposition that it would be justly and righteously used. All compact on the subject of synods is clearly at an end now, at the end of one hundred and thirty years of its breach by the State.

The Bishop of London stated indeed a most striking and remarkable fact, in reference to the want of freedom of synodical deliberation in the Church of England. His lordship might have added that, while our synods are arbitrarily suppressed, no one has a right to blame those who associate for the restoration of the Church's liberties, or for the protection of her rights, in voluntary societies. Let the Church have the free exercise of those rights of synodical deliberation which the law gives her, and we shall have no more unions and meetings; but, when our legal rights are withheld, we must reclaim them as best we may, by those means and ways which the constitution still leaves to us for obtaining redress of grievances.

This brings us to Lord Lansdowne's speech in reply to the Bishop of London, in which the views of the Government on the Bill were fully and clearly stated. He objected to the Bill, first, because it would tend to damage the authority of the decision recently pronounced in the case of Gorham *v.* the Bishop of Exeter, which the Government intend to remain undisturbed as the legal and final decision on the subject, governing, of course, all similar and analogous cases; secondly, because the Bill would be an interference with the royal prerogative which "the Church of England herself" had repeatedly acknowledged; and thirdly, because there would be a risk of the minority of bishops in any decision being treated as heretics by the majority, and of the public looking to doctrinal qualifications in the appointment of bishops.

In short, the Government has plenty of reasons, such as they are, for refusing a bill they do not like. It would, we believe, be wasting breath to argue with them ; but the Church and country at large have not exactly the *same* kind of interest in the matter that the Government has, and are more open to reason. We shall offer therefore a few remarks on the line taken by the Government. In the first place, it is evident that they are *resolved* to maintain and carry out the principle contained in the decision in the Gorham case. They are determined to make it the law of the land, and to let nothing shake it. This is quite obvious, and it is well that it should be so. We see what is to be expected from Government. Nothing that can offer a prospect of reversing that decision will be assented to : therefore no *convocation* will be permitted to deliberate. Such is simply our position. The State is determined to *force* upon the Church that decision, with all that it contains—with all its perilous latitudinarianism—with its principle that our formularies are to be applied, *not* with a view to truth or falsehood, nor even with a view to their agreement or disagreement of doctrine with tenets under trial, but in the most loose, vague, and indefinite way that may be devised for the purpose of including the greatest possible number of different tenets in the Church. Such is the determination of the Government, which exercises the supremacy over the Church.

As regards the argument for the supremacy against the Bill, we really wonder that ministers have the face to talk of the "royal supremacy" as likely to suffer, when all the world knows that it is their *own* supremacy that is in question : but, putting this aside, we must offer one passing remark ; we warn those who are for ever throwing the "supremacy" in our teeth, that they are not serving the supremacy by this course. If they wish to preserve the supremacy, they would act most wisely in not drawing inquiry to the subject. As it is, the Church finds that, on every occasion when she seeks relief from grievance, or security for her faith, it is the "royal supremacy" that is in her way. The "royal supremacy" is invariably the bar to prevent our obtaining common justice, or even being treated with common courtesy. The "supremacy" is made to carry far too great a weight ; and it will infallibly break down under that burden, if this course is persisted in. If the Crown's "supremacy" is to withhold from us the enjoyment of those rights and liberties to which we are just as much entitled as any class of Her Majesty's subjects, we shall be obliged to petition for relief from a "supremacy," which has been *already abolished by law* in the case of every denomination but ourselves.

The appeal of Lord Lansdowne to the Church herself, in maintenance of the supremacy, is plausible, but valueless :—

" My lords, it is most important that your lordships should recollect, that the power of the Crown in governing the Church is one which, in all times before the Reformation, at the Reformation, and since the Reformation, was acknowledged *even by the Church itself*, and formed one of the most essential prerogatives of the Crown."

We grant that this power was acknowledged, and rightly acknowledged; but it was always conceived to reside in an orthodox sovereign exercising his royal powers for the maintenance of the faith, and the repression of heresy and schism. And this has nothing in common with a supremacy exercised by an oligarchy nominated by Parliament, neither one nor the other having, as such, any distinctive creed at all. We trust that men will soon be able to discern the hollowness of this appeal to the recognition of the supremacy in former times. As soon as the Government, and others who trade upon the " supremacy," have once been fairly met in argument on this subject in Parliament, they will find that silence, in regard to the supremacy, would be their safest policy. We have no wish to see the Crown deprived of any of its titles or honours; therefore we advise the ministers and others to leave the supremacy alone, and to refrain from introducing it as a means of preventing the Church from attaining securities for its faith. The Crown will assuredly suffer, if its prerogative is, on all occasions, made a pretext for disregarding the wishes and rejecting the petitions of the Church; if its very name becomes identified, in the Churchman's mind with all that is most offensive to his feelings, perilous to his faith, and injurious to his Church; if it is made the pretence for refusing him equal justice with persons of other denominations, and for treating him with arrogance and insult. If this is to be the effect of the royal supremacy, we fear it will come to be regarded as a badge of slavery, both bodily and mental, and its downfal will then be secured.

We are not contemplating an imaginary case. This has been regularly and systematically the course adopted for some time by the State towards the Church, whether in England, Ireland, or the colonies. We are every where treated as spiritual slaves; as the only race of men in the country who have no right to possess consciences, or to have any attention paid to their dictates. The Church *alone* is treated with imperious insolence.

Who can forget the tone and conduct of ministers in the

Hampden case; or the mode in which Lord Palmerston set at nought episcopal authority and Church rights in the question of the Madeira chaplaincy; or the insult offered to the Church in the appointment of individuals to deaneries and bishoprics, here and in Ireland, whose qualification consisted in their opposition to the Church's claim for liberty of instruction; or what has recently occurred—the mandate of Lord Dalhousie to the Church at Madras, to throw open our burial-grounds, and the tone of insolent authority adopted towards the archdeacon on his remonstrance?

Lord Lansdowne is very reluctant that a synod of bishops should decide on doctrinal questions, because the minority might be looked on as heretics, and there might be difficulties in the way of appointing new bishops. Awkward questions might be asked about doctrine. We do not doubt him. We are quite sure the ministry and the Parliament would wish the most ample scope to be given to various doctrines amongst the bishops and clergy. It is exactly what they are anxious to bring about. A creedless State, so closely allied to the Church, must naturally labour to make the Church creedless also. If it can obtain free entrance for doctrines of all kinds into the Church, the Church will be practically creedless, and it will eventually become wholly so by the removal of all subscriptions. This will be necessarily and inevitably the operation of a State without religion upon a Church over which it exercises the supremacy granted to religious sovereigns.

And now we come to Lord Lansdowne's remarks on Convocation. The noble lord is averse to Convocation; he thinks it would damage the Church. He "doubts much whether the revival of Convocation would not materially interfere with peace and tranquillity in the Church." We are really vastly obliged to the Government for their kind consideration for the Church; but would it not be as well, in the first place, to restore us our *rights*, when we ask for them? When the Government has given us back what belongs to us, we shall be more willing to listen to what they have to say; but we think that *restitution* of what has been wrongfully and unconstitutionally taken from us, should precede any advice to us from the actual spoilers.

We have now done with Lord Lansdowne and the Government; but it is curiously characteristic of the times to observe the Earl of Chichester, as a leader of the Evangelical section, coming forward in opposition to the Bishop of London's bill, and thoroughly taking part with Government, more especially on the point of the "supremacy." The Evangelical party is now wholly in the hands of Government, and supports all its most Erastian doctrines. It dreads the assembling of Convocation, or any free action of the Church, and takes refuge, along with the Rationalistic and Germanizing party, under the skirts of the Government. This is significant, and not without a measure of encouragement to the orthodox.

Then we had the Bishop of St. David's also opposed to the Bill. This prelate represents the "Germanizing" party, the combination of such thinkers as Sterling, Hare, Maurice, and all the other advocates of German theology and philosophical liberty of thought and free speculation on the inspiration of Scripture. Of course this able prelate would be opposed to any bill which tends to promote uniformity of belief. He has always been an advocate for the amplest measure of freedom of opinion. It is difficult indeed to say *where* the line might be drawn by such men.

There seems little calling for remark in the speeches of the other supporters of Government, such as Lords Brougham, Campbell, and Carlisle. On the other side the bill was ably advocated by Lords Lyttelton and Stanley; but the most remarkable speeches by far were those of Lord Redesdale and of the Bishop of Oxford, the tone of which was admirable, and precisely what is now wanted. To Lord Redesdale the warmest gratitude of the Church is due, for the vigour, firmness, and courage of his declarations; and of the Bishop of Oxford's speech we can only say— and we are saying much in speaking thus—that we think his conduct on this occasion is sufficient to redeem every fault that he has committed as a public man since his elevation to the episcopate, and to entitle him to the gratitude and the confidence of the Church.

The tone of Lord Redesdale is so remarkable in some parts of his speech, and the whole is so forcible, plain-spoken, and thoroughly honest, that we must transcribe it at length.

"Lord REDESDALE regretted the change of opinion avowed by the right reverend prelate [Bishop of St. David's]; because it was another instance of that want of courage in the bench of bishops which had led to so much of our present difficulties. What was wanted now was a clear and well-defined statement of the doctrine of the Church: and yet the right reverend prelate seemed to think that the Church might be left to go on, with its ministers holding every variety of opinion. Such a state of things was impossible. It was impossible at the present crisis in the Church that matters could be left to stand as they now were, without more serious evils and more undesirable effects being produced. The right reverend prelate said that the measure was viewed with doubtful satisfaction by both parties; that it was disliked by low churchmen, and regarded by high churchmen only as a step to some ulterior purpose.

He (Lord Redesdale) wished there was no such thing as party in the Church. It was the duty of their lordships, at all events, to disregard party, and to legislate for that 'body of the Church, that large and important body of men who accepted the Church as the Church, and were willing to be bound by her Articles, her liturgy, her formularies. The course now pursued was, to give a little temporary triumph to the one party or the other, and by that triumph to weaken the Church; for those who were most active in keeping up extreme parties were not the most numerous or the best members of the Church. In petty disputes, perhaps, the right reverend prelate's prescription of letting things take their chance might do no harm; but when the doctrines of the Church were assailed, her usefulness impeded, and her members discouraged and distressed, that was the time for the prelates of the Church to stand forward and pronounce fearlessly and boldly what her doctrines were. At the present moment no man doubted what those doctrines were. Not even the Committee of the Privy Council imagined for a moment that the doctrines held by Mr. Gorham were in accordance with the teaching of the Church. All that they decided was, that Mr. Gorham did not so clearly dissent from that which was laid down in the Articles, liturgy, and formularies, that he ought not to be allowed to hold a living. He begged their lordships to consider this point, for it was one which men did not often put to themselves,—too great liberty to the clergy was injury to the laity. Supposing he˙ (Lord Redesdale) lived in the parish to which Mr. Gorham was appointed, was it no injury to be placed under such a man as that? Not one of the right reverend prelates would say that they entertained the same opinions as Mr. Gorham on the doctrine in dispute: and, indeed, could any one say the doctrine could be held without variance with the Articles, liturgy, and formularies of the Church? By this decision he (Lord Redesdale) would be bound for his whole life under the teaching of a man of notoriously unsound doctrine, and would be bound, with his children and dependents, to submit to it. Were not all the laity who desired to give obedience to those doctrines laid down in the liturgy, articles, &c., in their pure, literal, and natural sense, without any non-natural interpretations, in that position? Their lordships ought to protect the laity against injury from all or any extreme. The right reverend prelate who had just come in (the Bishop of Worcester) very properly withdrew his licence, the other day, from a curate who entertained opinions of a tendency approaching to Rome, and thus protected the parish from teaching contrary to the Church. The right reverend prelate at the table (the Bishop of Exeter) was equally right in refusing to admit an individual who held opinions of another tendency, but equally dissonant from the pure and literal meaning of the Church's formularies, &c. He could tell their lordships, that the decision against the Bishop of Exeter was only looked upon with satisfaction by men of extreme parties; and by none so much as by the Roman Catholics and the most violent dissenters. They viewed it with satisfaction, because they saw that it lowered the Church in the eyes of the world, and enabled them to taunt those who remained in the Church with denying one of the Articles of the Christian faith. Was that a position in which they ought to be placed? And, being in that position, the bishops ought to come forward to their relief. The objections raised against the Bill, which placed such matters in the hands of the bishops, appeared to him to be unworthy of any great consideration. That which had been suggested, on the ground that the court might be nearly equally divided, thirteen against fourteen, or something like that, he did not believe to be possible. It certainly would not have occurred in regard to the question recently decided. Was a possible difference of opinion any argument against the establishment of a court? He could not conceive a court in which such a contingency was less likely to arise. It would be composed of learned men, all conscious of the sacred duty they would have to perform, and they were not likely to have great differences of opinion. He accepted the Bill, because it constituted the only Church tribunal there appeared to be any chance of getting at the present moment. He had never exhibited any violence of opinion on questions of this kind. No one had stronger objections to any violent change, and no person was more strongly impressed with the danger of continued agitation; and he should therefore have accepted also any alteration in the bill proposed by the Government in a fair manner, and with a disposition to afford relief to the Church. But when he saw the Government come forward to oppose this measure as a party question, he had very little hopes of any thing being done except by the Church bestirring itself in a manner which it had not hitherto done. The necessity for some change had come. Who then could doubt that there was a possibility, nay, that there was a probability that the next person appointed to a bishopric would be Mr. Gorham? That laugh would seem to say that such a thing was impossible; but by far the greater number of appointments recently made had been made with a view of showing the subserviency of the Church to the State. A bishop, not long ago, was appointed who laboured under the censure of his university for heresy; and, if Mr. Gorham was fit to hold a living, he was also fit to hold a bishopric. Every man who reflected upon the condition of the Church must see it could not last, and, with the Government of the day exhibiting such dispositions, he felt bound to avow himself a "reformer" with regard to the present question between Church and State. A large body of earnest men were now rapidly coming to the same conclusion. The relations of Church and State had been materially altered by changes in the latter, and common sense demanded a revision of the subject. He denied that it was any honour or advantage to the Crown, as the Queen, with the most awful responsibility upon her as head of the Church, to have forced upon her by the ministry a most heterodox person. The prosperity of the Church was the strength of the monarchy; and, so far from disloyalty being involved in an advocacy of an alteration in the supremacy, he contended that such a course would, on the contrary, strengthen the Crown. He should support the Bill.

It is seldom, indeed, that we hear this kind of speaking, this honest, independent, truth-telling tone. Lord Redesdale saw his ground distinctly, and with vigorous good sense and thorough sincerity went straight forward to his point, and, by the mere exhibition of plain and undeniable truth, was more effective than if his speech had been garnished with all the graces of rhetoric, and all the subtleties of a lengthened argument. His positions were throughout intelligible, reasonable, and practical. That such a man as Lord Redesdale should have been led to declare himself "a reformer with regard to the present question between Church and State," is a circumstance which shows, in the strongest way, the rapid progress which the cause of Church liberties is making; and which the events of every day are urging forward.

This is the species of reform we now require. We want an adaptation of the law to the altered relations of the State and the Church, in consequence of the State's relinquishment of the Church's creed. Our want is neither more nor less than such a reform as shall give us the power of self-legislation in a free synod, like all other Churches, and the power of choosing our own prelates. Both of those rights were for many ages recognized by the constitution of England; and though the one has been taken from us by the arbitrary abuse of the royal supremacy, and the other by the law, we feel confident that the extreme injustice and grievance of conscience, under which we are now suffering, cannot much longer be continued. We claim religious equality with all other denominations of Christians; and we are resolved to have it. If, for seeking religious liberty, we are liable to obloquy, insult, persecution, and confiscation itself, we are prepared to meet them.

Every one must feel, of course, that the Bishop of London's Bill, however excellent and judicious in itself, cannot relieve the Church from all apprehension as to the decisions of the proposed tribunal hereafter. It would be a perfectly satisfactory tribunal under existing circumstances. But, if Government are to continue to possess the power of naming bishops of their own choice, the Episcopal Bench will gradually become heterodox, or Rationalistic; and thus the judgments of that tribunal will be unsound. But this, of course, is only one branch of the danger resulting to the Church from the absolute power of an unbelieving State in the appointment of our chief pastors; and the possibility of such an event furnishes no objection to the Bill, because it is competent to the Church to seek for the free election of her own bishops. And, that right restored to her, the tribunal becomes as safe from all risk of heterodox or latitudinarian judgments in future, as we firmly believe it would be at this present moment.

Art. VI.—1. *Gorham* v. *the Bishop of Exeter.* " *The Judgment of the Judicial Committee of Privy Council, &c.*" London: Seeleys. 1850.

2. *A Letter to the Archbishop of Canterbury, from the Bishop of* Exeter. London: Murray. 1850.

3. *A Letter to the Bishop of Exeter, containing an Examination of his Letter to the Archbishop of Canterbury, from* Wm. Goode, *M.A., F.S.A.* London: Hatchard and Son. 1850.

4. *A Letter to the Rev. E. B. Pusey, D.D., on the Position which he has taken in the present Crisis. By* Wm. Dodsworth, *M.A.* London: Pickering. 1850.

5. *Reasons for not signing the proposed Address to the Right Rev. the Lord Bishop of Worcester, &c., in a Letter to the Rev. J. L. Claughton. By the Rev.* H. Hastings, *M.A.* London: Hatchard and Son. 1850.

6. *A Letter to the Hon. R. Cavendish, on the recent Judgment of the Court of Appeal as affecting the Doctrine of the Church. By* Julius Chas. Hare, *M.A., Archdeacon of Lewes.* London: Parker. 1850.

7. *A Letter to Archdeacon Hare on the Judgment of the Gorham Case, from the Hon.* R. Cavendish. London: Ollivier. 1850.

The world is going on, to all outward appearance, as usual. Our cities resound with the peaceful din of commerce; our villages and fields with the pleasant voice of labour. Business reigns, as erst, Supreme in the East, and Fashion in the West, of our Metropolis. No angry crowds collect in our thoroughfares. No ferment is visible among the great masses of our population. And yet the halls of our Courts of Justice, the naves of our Churches, and the walls of our Parliament are echoing with cries as thrilling—and only the less tumultuous because the Shibboleth of the Injured is Peace and Love—as ever rent the gates of Palace Yard in 1688, or woke the banks of Forth and Clyde in the spring of 1843.

How much longer even this external veil of things shall continue, who can say! Even now the more thoughtful among us descry signs of danger in the distance. The strongest minds stand shaken in their holiest convictions. Those distinguished above their fellows for learning and piety are wavering at their posts. Here are people distrusting the teaching of their spiritual pastors, which they had listened to undoubtingly for centuries ;—there ministers, for very fear for their souls, are fleeing from the flocks which were dearer to them than their own right hands, and hastening to an imaginary repose within the pale of a foreign communion. *Peaceful* men, who had never obtruded themselves to the world's gaze, though ever leavening its corruptions, are instant in remonstrances, and bestirring themselves to means of self-defence. *Loyal* men, the constant preachers of subjection to the " powers that be," are protesting against the decisions of the highest tribunal of the land. *Patient* men, from whom no amount of personal suffering would have wrung one word of murmuring, are clamorous in their demands for redress to the Church's wrongs. Fundamental Laws of the Church and State stand challenged. The Book of Common Prayer is handled with an avidity, and examined with a subtilty of reasoning, which contrasts strangely with the apathy with which it had previously been regarded. Old Statutes, that had been forgotten, or thought not to exist, are evoked from the slumber to which neglecting generations had consigned them. A controversy unparalleled in obstinacy has, now for years, been splitting the thinking portion of society into two opposite and contending parties, and still seems as far as ever removed from a solution. Where will all this end !

But besides, and sadder than all this, the natural difficulties of the contest have, as usual, been aggravated by the mutual recriminations, and personal prejudices, which have been interwoven with it. Preachers of righteousness and good-will among men have been hurling the firebrands of discord against each other, and cutting deep with the edge of sarcasm: he, whose indignation was just now fired, because an opponent had passed the bounds of Christian moderation in debate, is himself seen falling on him with the sword of a tenfold virulence. Alas ! why cannot the search after Wisdom be conducted by the process of a passionless argumentation. Alas ! why may we not discuss, and differ from one another, with the unruffled and unruffling energy of a calm Philosophy ! Alas ! that powerful penmen—whose influence for good or ill is so wide—do not or will not see, that every argument they rely on loses half its pungency by the very adjuncts with which they seek to enhance it. Personal invective may pour forth its venom: to bruise and sting it cannot fail. Does it speed on their way to the great goal of Truth its poison-pointed arrows !

The notorious case of Mr. Gorham, intricate as it ever must have been from the nature of its subject-matter, has been encumbered by collateral questions which, to our mind, never had any thing to do with the real point at issue. Had all the arguments been struck off from either side, which had reference only to the Baptism of adults—which never was a question under discussion[1];—and had it been clearly borne in mind, in all the stages of the controversy, that the essence of it was, not what Scripture, but what the Church of England, had laid down as Truth, that controversy would have ranged, in its legal aspect, within much narrower and more intelligible bounds. Within these bounds, and to that aspect, it is our purpose to confine our remarks, for as a legal question only did it come before the Ecclesiastical Courts at all; and it will then, we apprehend, stand reduced to the following, that is to say, " Whether, according to the Church of England, the grace of Regeneration, (whatever be the exact meaning of that word, of which more presently,) inseparably accompanies the administration of Baptism, in the case of every Infant?" Both parties set out with admitting themselves to be members of the Church of England; both appeal to her Formularies in support of their views; it is upon the footing therefore that she holds Scriptural Truth, that every argument in the case must be taken to proceed[2].

We are content to view the question through the same media, and to decide it by the same tests, as the Judges of the Judicial Committee have proposed. We agree with them, we take them upon their own terms, that " to ascertain the true meaning and effect of the Articles, Formularies, and Rubrics, we must by no means intentionally swerve from the old established rules of construction:" and, again, that " we must apply to the construction of those books the same rules which have been long established, and are by law applicable to the construction of all written instruments." From those " old established rules of construction " did the Judges, or did they not, in their late Judgment, swerve! Have they, or have they not, followed out their own undertaking! Now we find it laid down as a fundamental Common Law rule for the general interpretation of " all written instruments," that, " as often as there be no ambiguity in words, there no explanation is to be made contrary to those words[3]." Again: " When words are dubious "—*when*, observe, but *not until*—" then it may be

[1] See Sir H. J. Fust's Judgment, p. 30; and the Bishop of Exeter's Letter, p. 57.
[2] " Both sides are agreed in accepting the Prayer Book itself as sound and scriptural."—Mr. Goode's Letter, p. 82.
[3] " Quoties in verbis nulla ambiguitas, ibi nulla expositio contrà verba fienda est."—2 Saund. Rep. 251.

of singular use to compare a word or a sentence with the context, or to compare one law with other laws that are made by the same legislator[4]." Take the ordinary case of the construction of a will. Is not the primary document, by which we seek to determine the meaning of any particular bequest, the very will itself? Is it lawful to resort to any other document whatsoever for that purpose, until the will itself fail in supplying us with the required information? We fearlessly answer, No. So here: the question is— Does our Church leave a given doctrine an open one, or not? The Offices for Infant Baptism contain that doctrine[5]. Those Offices are complete, independent, substantive Services: they have as much claim to be dealt with as such, as the will has. They no more lose their individuality of character, because they have been incorporated into, and form part of, the entire Book of Common Prayer—than does each several Act of Parliament, because passed in the same Session, and bound up in one and the same volume, as other Statutes. And yet our Judges bid us look "dehors" those Services, (as the lawyers say,) and that, not to explain ambiguities in them—for there have been none alleged to exist—and if they did, who knows but that they might be reconciled by the context? And thus difficulties are imported into the Services, which did not appertain to them, by a comparison of them with other documents constructed under different circumstances, with different objects in view, and at different periods of time. Each several Service of our Church was impressed with a particular signification of its own, when it issued from the hands of its framers. That signification followed it through its various vicissitudes; and as long as it survives to speak the language of the Church *at all, so long it speaks it as it ever has spoken it.*

"Oh! but," it is said, "the question before the Court is an Article of Faith; and Articles of Faith are not to be looked for in forms of devotion; and the Baptismal Services are forms of devotion. They are, therefore, not the proper field to resort to for the settlement of a doctrinal point." But is the case really so? Are they forms of devotion *merely?* Not to mention here the Rubrics attached to them, (which are essentially connected with both doctrine and discipline,) the Exhortations which occur in them contain, as clearly as words can, instructions by the Priest as to what the People should *believe* and *do.* The sponsors, too, are specifically interrogated as to their belief in "all the Articles of the Christian Faith." It might as well be contended, therefore, that the opening Exhortation in the Order for Morning Prayer does not express the Church's mind upon the importance of

[4] 1 Blackst. Comm.   [5] 57 Canon. [1603 A.D.]

Public Worship; or that the Creeds themselves are not Summaries of Faith; as that the Baptismal Services do not contain her *doctrine* of Baptism, as well as her *devotions*.

Do we yet hesitate? The 57th Canon of our Church, which became a Law of the Church in 1603, *and is so still*, is decisive upon the point: "The doctrine both of Baptism and of the Lord's Supper is so sufficiently set down in the Book of Common Prayer to be used at the administration of the said Sacraments, as nothing can be added to it that is material or necessary." Why then did the Judges resort to the Thirty-nine Articles for an exponent of that doctrine? It is true, as Mr. Goode points out, that the above quotation is a portion only of the Canon, which had special reference to the refusal by the people of the Sacraments at the hands of unpreaching ministers. But we cannot see that the generality of the declaration is thereby restricted. May not an universal truth be enunciated in a resolution framed primarily to meet a particular case? Mr. Goode interprets it to mean, that "all which it is material and necessary to bring before the people when administering Baptism as to the nature of the rite, is contained in the appointed service[6]." *And so do we.* And we go on to engraft upon that interpretation this conclusion—that since "the nature of the rite" is therein "sufficiently set forth," we do not require, nay, it is against the plain rules of Law "applicable to the construction of all written instruments," (the Judge's own words,) to require, any other description, teaching, or evidence whatsoever, respecting it. Mr. Goode imputes to the Bishop of Exeter that he "wrested" the above quotation from its context, "concealed the true nature" [of the Canon,] and "managed to get" [only] "an appearance of an argument out of it[7]." Is it, then, "perversion" to quote only so much of an authority as is, or seems to be, material to prove one's case? Is it "concealment," not to fill one's pages with a description of all the surrounding circumstances of a passage, which was only referred to *at all* as containing the enunciation of a general truth? Is an authoritative declaration, that the doctrine of the Church on Baptism is sufficiently set down in her Baptismal Services, an "apparent," and not rather a most clenching and irresistible, argument?

Granting however, for the sake of argument, that the Judges were correct in referring to the Thirty-nine Articles in the first instance, to ascertain the Church's mind on Baptism,—see how they fail us!—fail us, in that they leave unsettled the very questions we consulted them on, namely, the meaning of a "worthy reception" of Baptism, and of the direction that "the Baptism of young children is any wise to be retained as most agreeable to the institution of Christ." See how they refer us, necessarily, back again to some other document for the elucidation of these points. And that document what other can it be, but those very Baptismal Services, which *we* contend should have been the first to be examined, but which *the Judges*, with one eminent exception, willingly and "intentionally" disregarded. We have as clear, categorical, ay as doctrinal a statement in the appointed Services, as the " wit of man could have devised :" we are forbidden to expound the Church's mind from that statement, and are referred, in lieu of it, to certain heads of doctrine, which treating *summarily* of Nine and Thirty distinct subject matters, it was obvious to see must necessarily be deficient in a *detailed* treatment of any one; and, to complete the Anomaly, we are compelled, by the very imperfections of the standard of appeal, to retrace our steps, for a final clue in the matter, to the original formulary which we had pronounced an incompetent guide. Who ever heard of the history of a whole nation being ransacked for the details of a single statesman's life, in preference to his own biography? Who ever heard of an Act of Parliament being construed by the marginal summary of its sections; of the less circumstantial being admitted, when the more circumstantial was within reach ; or of the abstract of a man's title being resorted to, instead of the title-deeds themselves? Yet this would be hardly more preposterous than the Law of Evidence which the Judicial Committee has sanctioned in the threshold of their enquiry.

Whether therefore first or last, mediately or immediately, it is to the Church's Services of Baptism that we must go for a consideration of her doctrine therein. Show us that any thing contained in them is at variance with any other of her doctrines contained in any other portion of the Book of Common Prayer ; show us even that there lurk in them any ambiguities, or equivocal, or intricate, reasoning, which of necessity require us to call in the assistance of extrinsic evidence for their interpretation— and we will at once abandon our position, and admit that the argument must be conducted on a different footing, *but till then* we assert the right to have it conducted on that footing, and on no other, just as is done every day of our lives, and with universal approbation, in Westminster Hall, in the interpretation of agreements, deeds, wills, and all other written instruments whatsoever.

In the spirit then of candid but reverent enquirers, let us now approach those Services. Should we seem to linger too long upon them, let us reflect that the legality or illegality of the recent Judgment *depends upon their construction*, and that it is impos-

sible to exaggerate the necessity of a close inspection of their
frame and context.   If it were the question of the meaning of a
deed, should we not examine carefully its details?   Were we
judging of the intentions of a testator, should we not scrutinize
narrowly the will?   And we are to proceed, say the Judges, in
this, as in any other case.   And here it is essential to ascertain
the Church's meaning of the word " Regeneration."   Eminent
writers have been called in to establish and describe the distinction between it and Renovation.   To us it seems unnecessary to
enter into that distinction at all.   The Church uses the word
" Regeneration."   It becomes incumbent therefore on us to
ascertain what she understands by it.   But to go into distinctions
between it and something else, seems as foreign to the purpose in
hand as it would be, when asked to define an acid, to propound a
disquisition on an alkali.   What is " Regeneration?"   The
Church herself supplies us with the answer.   In the Offices we
are considering she calls it " spiritual Regeneration."   She prays
too that water may be " sanctified," and when the child is
sprinkled with it, she *forthwith* pronounces him " regenerate."
Now water itself can't be made holy, except so far as it is the instrument of making the child so.   Again,—not to mention that
text (Tit. iii. 5) which Mr. Goode is so displeased with the
Bishop for " perverting⁸," (but his " perversion" of which is no
more " proven," than was his " wresting," and " concealment," of
the 57th Canon, inasmuch as the words of the original, grammatically considered⁹, support the Bishop's view of them, just as
much, *to say the least,* as Mr. Goode's)—Eph. v. 26 is strong
to show, that " Sanctification" is the " Regeneration" given by
Baptism; and to this agree the words of Hooker, " to our sanctification here [Baptism is] a step that hath not any before it¹⁰."
Yet Mr. Goode no where notices this important result of the
Sacrament, and in his silence of them *as cause and effect,* lies the
fallacy in his reasoning throughout.   He speaks of Regeneration,
but not as a spiritual operation.   He treats of it indeed as that
whereby the baptized becomes a " child of God," and a " member
of Christ," [Letter, p. 78,] but only in a formal sense, as a grant
" formally made over by Baptism " [ib. p. 63].   He compares it
again and again to the act of admittance to a human society.
Occasionally he *does* even speak of it as " spiritual Regeneration."

⁸ Letter, p. 12.
⁹ Whether the word ἀνακαινώσεως is governed by λουτροῦ, or by διά (understood), is surely a matter of opinion equally with the question, whether the phrase
" washing of regeneration " refers to Baptism at all.   How then can that be called,
in fairness, the " manufacturing of a statement," [see Letter, p. 12,] which is a
rendering that the context legitimately, though not solely, admits of?
¹⁰ Eccl. Pol. v. 60.

But then the context immediately discloses that he had in view a change only of the state, and not of the heart. Nay he expressly calls the grace of the Sacrament the "regenerate *state!*" Throughout, he studiously avoids committing himself to the assertion that it has any necessary connexion with inward Sanctification.

Nor is it immaterial to observe the mind of those who framed the first Liturgy of Edward VI. If much that was part of it was altered by the Liturgy of 1552, and has ceased to be the Law of the Church, much also has been left *unaltered*; and amongst the portions left *unaltered*, are the declarations, *still in use*, of the infants' "Spiritual Regeneration." That which was the meaning of the Reformers in 1549, as to that phrase, is the meaning of our Prayer Book now. To use the words of Archbishop Bancroft's chaplain, cited by Sir H. J. Fust, though for a different purpose, "the words be the same, and none other, than erst and first they were, and therefore the sense the same, the doctrines the same, and the purpose and intention of our Church still one and the same." What that sense was then, and that Sanctification was contemplated by the Church as often as she spoke of "Regeneration," is evident, from the repealed portions of the Liturgy of 1549; to which we have at least as much right to refer as our opponents have to search for the sense of the rubric of 1560 in that of a repealed one of 1536. Take, for example, the prayer of Exorcism before Baptism, and that striking act of putting the chrisom or white vest on the child after Baptism, with these words, "Take this white vesture for a token of the innocency which, by God's grace, *in this sacrament of Baptism is given* unto thee." What she meant by "Regeneration" *then*, she means *now*, for she still uses the word. Else, too, why was the Pentecostal anniversary for many ages of the Church one of the only two permitted festivals of the year for the administration of Baptism[11]? Else, too, what is the meaning and use of the prayers, immediately before the Priest names the child, "that the new man may be raised up in him;" "that all carnal affections may die in him;" "that he may triumph against the devil, the world, and the flesh;" "and that he may be endued with heavenly virtues?"—*prayers evidently fulfilled*, (according to the Church,) *immediately after water is poured on the child, because thanks are then returned for their fulfilment, and the language of supplication is exchanged for that of praise.*

Consider, finally, the language of the Church Catechism. Take,

---

[11] Wheatly on Common Prayer.

for instance, the Question, "What is the inward and spiritual grace of Baptism?" What says the Answer? "A death unto sin, and a new birth unto righteousness; for being by nature born in sin, and the children of wrath, we are hereby made the children of grace." What is this but to say, in so many words, "We are sanctified by Baptism?" But Faith and Repentance (the Catechism goes on to say) are required of persons to be baptized, and these shall be dispensed with, at least as to their present *performance*, in the case of infants, and a present *promise* of them, instead, shall be sufficient. Well, then, children who neither believe nor repent, but "promise both by their sureties," receive Baptism in the same way, that is, with the same benefits, as they who can and do both believe and repent. The inference is irresistible:—*The conclusion that all infants are infallibly regenerate by Baptism, is a logical and inevitable deduction from the Church's position respecting adults.* She cannot, without self-contradiction, lay down her rule of Faith as she does, with regard to the latter, and deny the invariable right reception of Baptism to the former.

Leaving the Catechism, however, the ingenuity of our objectors leaps to the Baptismal Service for Adults, and takes a different line of argument. "The Church," say they, "declares of adults, equally as of infants, that they 'are Regenerate by God's Holy Spirit.' The Regeneration, however, of adults is, you admit, contingent on their faith and repentance, and so must it be with infants, for the Church cannot be held to have used the word in the two Services in different senses. If the words are not to be taken in the *opus operatum* sense in both, they cannot in either." But to this objection there is an obvious answer. How can the later document be cited as affixing a meaning to the earlier, which was in use, and must have had an ascertained sense of its own, one hundred years before? Your argument, we reply, *might indeed be used the other way:* it might be contended that a dogmatic and unconditional sense is given to the term "Regeneration" in the Baptism of Adults, because it occurs in the Service for Infants; but it is impossible that the sense of the latter (whatever it was) was narrowed, or amplified, or, in fact, in any way affected, by the introduction of the same word into a subsequent Office applicable to a different class of recipients.

But to return: The Priest begins by beseeching the people to call on God, "to grant to this child" [at what time, save at Baptism?] "that thing which by nature he cannot have; that he may be baptized with water and the Holy Ghost." Here, then, is a presently future gift, and a presently future accomplishment, in view. And, after being reminded that Baptism was prefigured by the water which saved Noah[12], and the children of Israel, and was further sanctified by our Saviour in Jordan, the congregation prays God, to " wash and sanctify the child with the Holy Ghost, and that he may receive remission of sins by spiritual regeneration ; and that God will receive him, as he has promised, that he may enjoy the everlasting benediction of His Heavenly washing."

A yet clearer intimation of the Church's mind is next derived from the well-known passage from St. Mark : " Whosoever shall not receive the kingdom of God as a little child, shall in no-wise enter therein. And He took them up in his arms, laid his hands on them, and blessed them." She propounds the example of little children to all Christian men for their imitation. Were this the only passage in the whole Service which bore upon the point we are considering, it would be sufficient to prove that the inseparability of Grace from the Sacrament must have been present to the framers of it ; for, as the pious Bishop Taylor excellently well observes, " If all men, according to Christ's saying, must receive the kingdom of God as little children, *it is certain* little children do receive it ; *they receive it as men ought ;* that is, without any impediment or obstruction, without any thing that is contrary to that state[13]." Now this reception of the kingdom of God must mean something more than a mere passive or formal admission to Gospel Privileges ; otherwise no peculiar frame of mind would be enjoined. We should like to know how Messrs. Gorham and Goode get over this passage.

The Church next tells her people " to doubt not, but earnestly believe "—"to be persuaded"—"that our Saviour will receive and embrace the Infant, give him eternal life, and make him partaker of his everlasting kingdom :" nay, so persuaded is she of all this, that she proceeds to thank Him for it ; and further exhorting the sponsors, declares, that His promise to give all these things " He, for His part, WILL MOST SURELY keep and perform ;" praying, withal, that the child " now to be baptized may receive " [when—if not now ? by what—if not by Baptism ?] " the fulness of God's grace." Can words be stronger ! Can the precise time spoken of be more clearly pointed out ! Is this the

---

[12] It would be well if the full force of the passage, " who didst save Noah and his family in the ark from perishing by water," were more generally given by the Reader. The words " by water" depend grammatically on the word " save," and not on the word " perishing." Water was the cause of death to the world, but of salvation to Noah. Hence the ambiguity. A transposition of the words " by water " to their proper place, or a correct punctuation, would mark the sense.

[13] Works, vol. ii. p. 265.

language of hypothesis? Is it possible that the Most High
should condescend to promise and to bless—and the Church appropriate to herself that condescension—and yet no blessing be
left behind?—no fulfilment crown the promise? When on the
green grass, among five thousand—when at the Last Supper—
when at Emmaus—He blessed bread, did no inevitable efficacy
attach to it from the benediction? Does the water of Baptism,
which is blessed, remain thenceforth unsanctified? This we cannot hold. This did not the Reformers hold—Calvinists howsoever
they were—when, in 1549, they caused the Priest, anointing the
infant after Baptism to say, in the spirit of Apostolical authority,
" Almighty God, who *hath* regenerated thee by water and the
Holy Ghost, and *hath* given unto thee remission of all thy sins,
He vouchsafe to anoint thee with the unction of His Holy Spirit[14]."
For we must never forget, that what is left us of our mutilated
Baptismal Services for Infants was the creation of those very
Reformers; many of whose usages and much of whose discipline
our Church still upholds for Law; for " all ornaments of the
Church, and of the Ministers thereof at all times of their ministration, are to be retained and be in use, as were in the Church
of England by the authority of Parliament" [observe, not in the
fifth, but—] " in the second year of the reign of King Edward
the Sixth[15]." A pretty plain proof, one would have thought, that
the *animus* of those Reformers, notwithstanding the órdeals
through which the discipline and doctrine of our Church has
passed, has never been finally superseded or abandoned.

Hitherto the Church has assumed the attitude of an humble
supplicant, faithfully expecting, but without having received, an
answer to her petitions. But mark! The water is poured, the
name is named, the solemn words are said—thenceforth she takes
up the strain of joyous and exalting praise: " Let us give thanks,"
&c. " We yield Thee hearty thanks, that it hath pleased Thee to
Regenerate this Infant with thy Holy Spirit:" and then she proceeds to prayer—that he " being dead" [that is, having been just
made, by baptism, dead] " unto sin," according to the promises
before recited, (and of which the Church had "doubted not" the
fulfilment) that he should be " released from his sins," may " partake of Christ's resurrection."

But as though to put all doubt aside, and to condense the
Church's belief in a summary as purely doctrinal as any of the
Thirty-nine Articles themselves, a Rubric immediately follows in
these words, " It is certain, by God's word, that children, which
are baptized, dying before they commit actual sin, are undoubtedly

[14] See the First Prayer Book of Edward VI.
[15] See the beginning of the Order for Morning Prayer.

saved." One would have hoped that at least this proposition was categorical enough to have avoided all disputation, and satisfied a Bench of Law-Lords. But no. It is of it, that Lord Langdale declares, speaking the judgment of his Colleagues, that "it does not say such children are saved by baptism." (!) With reason indeed was it that the Bishop of Exeter wrote that he "could not argue such a matter." Nearly may we pardon even a Bishop's undissembled irony and "bitterness." Let us examine how far Lord Langdale was justified in such a declaration. Now we suppose that even in these our days of ingenious verbalities, and critical fastidiousness, words with less ambiguity *on the face of them,*—more strong to express what they signify according to their "true, plain, and literal" meaning, and less conditional or hypothetical, could not possibly have been chosen. But the difficulty which the Judges found, arose here also from their construing them by the side of another document, viz., the Rubric of 1536. To adopt such a mode of construction was subversive of the plainest rules of Law. Compare each part of the same Formulary together, to collect the meaning of the whole, or to explain the meaning of any part, unquestionably they might ; but to travel to a repealed Rubric, which for the purposes of the discussion ought to have been regarded as no longer, *and was in fact no longer, in esse,* to ascertain the effect of an existing one, is like interpreting a statute of Queen Victoria by an expired one of George III. According then to the Judges and to Mr. Goode, the sentence must be read as if there were another qualification, besides baptism, annexed as a condition to the infant's salvation —which there is not—and it will then run thus : " It is certain by God's word that infants which are baptized, [and which have received a prævenient grace], dying before they commit actual sin, are undoubtedly saved." But if this second qualification may be appended, why may not a third ; and if a third, why not a fourth ? and where will be the arithmetical limit of such introductions of new matter ?

It is difficult to calculate, it is alarming to contemplate, it is impossible to over-estimate, the danger of the precedent which the Judges have here laid down; it amounts to this, and nothing short of this, that let a sentence or clause of any written instrument whatsoever, no matter how solemn or important, be never so precisely, technically, guardedly worded by its author, it shall not be unlawful for any chance reader of it, nay, for any judicial expounder of it, to qualify, alter, narrow, or enlarge the same, by virtue of other words transported into it according to his own private judgment ; so that at last it will come to pass, that nothing will ever be allowed to mean what

it does really mean; no safeguard will exist in a man's title-deeds
—no certainty in the Gospels—no criteria in grammar, and no
tests in logic! According to the selfsame argument of the
Judges, even the awful teaching of the Church upon the doctrine
of the Trinity, as set forth in the Athanasian Creed, is not, or
perchance may not, be explicit or dogmatic. "This is the
Catholic Faith which except a man believe faithfully he cannot
be saved," "Whosoever will be saved, before all things it is
necessary that he hold the Catholic Faith," have no more reason
to be accounted the positive teaching of the Church, than has the
Rubric before us. Nay, Mr. Goode's own favourite oath of
Supremacy as administered in the Ordination Service will, when
tried by this rule, be found to dwindle into the mere shadow of an
obligation. The solemnity of all authoritative declarations consists in their positiveness. The terrors of the Decalogue lie in
this. Strip them of it, and invest them with an hypothetical
character, and you lay the first stone of heresy, and are rearing
an altar to misbelief. It is no answer to say there is a difference
between the doctrines of the Trinity and of Baptism, and that
they are not equally fundamental; for how are we to know which
doctrines the Church holds as fundamental, and which not, *except
by her language?* We must judge of the value she attaches to
any subject-matter by the phraseology which she employs with
respect to it. We have no right to hazard fanciful conjectures
as to her meaning; still less to interpolate words which she
never sanctioned.

But now let us grant, for a moment, that the Judges *were* justified in expounding the Rubric of 1560 by that of 1536. *Do the
two essentially differ?* Have they rightly interpreted the former
when they deny that it attributes, in terms, as much as the other,
the salvation of infants TO Baptism. Let us apply the terms of
the Rubric, *mutatis mutandis*, to a familiar instance or two from
daily life. "It is certain," we say, "that children which are
good will be happy?" Is this not equivalent to a predication of
goodness *as the cause* of their happiness? or suppose a person to
affirm, (no matter here what the truth of the affirmation be,) that
"it is certain that children which have been vaccinated will be safe
from the small-pox;" or that "ships which do not keep a good
look out on a dangerous coast will be undoubtedly lost." The
small-pox rages in a village, and carries off hundreds: the vaccinated children escape. Or a vessel is wrecked on the coast in
question. Will not the salvation of the children, and the loss of
the ship, be connected in the mind of the affirmant with the observance or neglect of the conditions which he attached to his
assertions, *as cause and effect?* To our unsophisticated understandings it is all one and the same thing to assert of children

" that those which are baptized will be saved," as to say "that those receiving baptism are saved thereby." The word " thereby " is mere surplusage.

We shall not dwell long, and that for the reason we are about to assign, on the question on which so much argument has been expended, what weight is due to the private opinions of the Reformers of the Church's Services. We confess we have never understood how, after passing in full review before them the writings of Jewell, Usher, Hooker, Taylor, Whitgift, Carleton, and Prideaux, the Judicial Committee could say that " they did not affirm their doctrines and opinions could be received as evidence of the doctrine of the Church of England." So, too, indeed, should we have said. But then the question leaps to our lips—Why quote those opinions at all? Why waste words on them? Why encumber the already encumbered question with them? They go for nothing, or next to nothing. They advance the controversy not a jot, according to the Judges' own admission, and yet we cannot help fearing that they have unconsciously gone for more than they ought. When once a document is inspected, which, according to the strict rules of evidence, ought not to be inspected, can we be sure our minds remain unaffected by the notice which it conveys?

Yet, stranger still—these very Judges who cite so willingly individual opinions, notwithstanding that they declare them " not receivable as evidence," have not attached the smallest weight, nay, have passed by altogether unnoticed, the clear and unanimous opinion of twelve contemporary Bishops, and eight contemporary Doctors of Divinity, who all declared their sentiments on this " open" question *just the other way!* Mr. Goode labours hard to prove that no value is due to those sentiments, as authoritative statements; but he can never disentitle them to at least as much deference, as he is anxious to procure for the citations from the Divines most favourable to his views. The Judges had no right to allow to Mr. Gorham the opinions of Hooker, Taylor, and the rest, and withhold from the Bishop those of the Divines, who were, most of them, members of that celebrated Convocation, from whose deliberations we have received our Prayer Book in its present shape. Moreover, the former class of authorities are, at the most, doubtful ones. For one passage which makes *for* Mr. Gorham, it is not difficult to produce from the same author another which tells *against* him. One unequivocal, as we had thought, and decided testimony is, a few pages further on, neutralized by others, which leave us in the dark what the real result of the writer's opinions was. Whereas the precise pinch of the Gorham controversy was presented pointedly to the notice of the Savoy Commissioners, and by them as pointedly answered. But if individual opinions are to be called in aid at all, as it can hardly be doubted they have been to an undue degree, notwithstanding Lord Langdale's disclaimer, why are those of living Churchmen entitled to no consideration; why, for example, should we disregard the fervid eloquence of a Wilberforce, the clear commanding logic of a Manning, the profound erudition of a Pusey, or the searching spiritual melodies of a Keble; leaders of a school as superior to the Evangelical in its depths of knowledge, as (to say the least) it is its equal in piety? Are living authors not to be cited on points of law? Does "Williams on Executors" cease to be an authority, because its eminent author still survives to adorn the Bench?

. The truth, however, seems to be, that the Church's doctrine on any particular question is to be learned, like any thing else, firstly, by an inspection and examination of those of her authorized Services, which relate exclusively to the controverted point; if ambiguity be discoverable therein, then, secondarily, by a comparison therewith of her other authorized Formularies; and that the private writings of Divines are valueless as criteria of her doctrine, unless, as was the case with the Savoy Commissioners, they concurred in any synodical compilation of her code; and then only to the extent of that concurrence.

Having dismissed the authority of individual opinions for one purpose, we shall not be expected to attach more weight to them when cited, as they have been, for another, to support the doctrine of "charitable presumptions." The Church, it is said, "presumes charitably" of infants, that they are worthy recipients of Baptism, and to substantiate that, several of the same Divines are referred to. This, we begin with saying, is fairly giving up the point. We had thought the argument had been throughout, that the Church *had laid down no doctrine* one way or the other, but had left it an "open" question to believe or not to believe, as each person chose. Now we are all at once told, that she *does* admit the doctrine, only, that she "presumes" it "charitably." If she presumes it, then she holds it. Presumption *is* belief. It *may* be strong belief. Nor need it be less a doctrine of the Church because it is a charitable one. Is it inconsistent with her dogmatic teaching that her dogmas should be based on that Charity, "which, believing all things," includes, and is "greater" than, Faith? She calls her "work," for instance, of bringing infants to Baptism, a "charitable" one [16]. Does she thereby intend to surrender one tittle of her conviction that that work is one of imperative duty also, enjoined to her by her great Head, and in no wise optional in her to disobey?

[16] See the Office for Infant Public Baptism.

And lastly, we are referred to the Burial Service. Because the Church uses the language of hope there, she does so here. Now this argument cannot hold good, unless those who advance it show further that the Church views the Burial of her dead as a rite equally important with the Baptism of her children. But the Burial of the dead is no Sacrament. She would violate no command, "ordained of Christ Himself," were she to refuse that rite. It would be reasonable therefore, *à priori*, to expect that in a ceremony which she only observes in charity, the language of charity only should find place. But that language can never be adduced to interpret another service framed *alio intuitu*, and for a much more solemn occasion. Must the Church have had one and the same view in all the matters included in the Book of Common Prayer? The parts of it are distinct, though united; and accordingly we find Dissenters agreeing with her in some, and parting company with her in others. *In one she may breathe the language of Hope, because she Hopes; in another the language of Belief, because she Believes. The question is, what is her language in each?*

And now to apply ourselves for a few moments, before we conclude, to the two principal letters which head our article. Mr. Goode has, we must say, been as unsuccessful in the legitimate stand-up warfare of logic with the Bishop, as he has been in that strategy of vituperation, which will, we fear, blemish indelibly his repute in the eyes of all those whose opinion is worth the having. Throughout full five-and-twenty pages of his letter he twits the Bishop for "intimating, that though he [the Bishop] had been the Primate's friend for nearly thirty years, he had been compelled to become now only his Grace's afflicted servant [17]." Did ever such an intimation fall from the Bishop? He had subscribed himself his "Grace's affectionate friend for nearly thirty years, *and* now afflicted servant;" but it is certainly the first time in our lives, that we have heard of the copulative "AND" being interpreted as the antithetical "BUT." There are legal cases, we believe, which have gone so far as to construe it synonymously with "or," but we stake our reputation on the assertion that it has no where been held to totally reverse the sense of a passage, as Mr. Goode would have it do. So he must not be surprised, if, when writing, in sorrow, to an old college friend, he shall sign himself his affectionate and now afflicted friend, his correspondent shall take it for granted that affliction has annihilated his affection, and that he has ceased to be his friend at all, because he has become a sorrowing one too. Truly,

[17] Mr. Goode's Letter, p. 3.

we have rather a pregnant hint, at the outset, how far Mr.
Goode is capable to conduct a controversy, or construe aright a
written instrument!

With the same inattention to facts, Mr. Goode charges his
superior with accusing the Archbishop that his change of views
was a "recent one"; although the Bishop had expressly stated,
when complaining of the change, that those "lower views" had
been "adopted" by the Archbishop "for some years". Nor is
he more happy in reminding the Bishop that he "stood aghast
at hearing such teaching from such a place fifteen years too late;
all this teaching, just concocted at Lambeth, having been before
the world all that time". Yes; but not before the world FROM
LAMBETH fifteen years; no, nor yet one; which was the gist of
the Bishop's lament. It was the teaching *from Lambeth* at
which he "stood aghast."

Again; the Bishop had objected to the Archbishop's wish for
more faith in the parents of the baptized, that it made "the first
moving of God towards them contingent on the will of man."
This objection Mr. Goode hurls back at the Bishop, rejoining,
that nothing could make that "first moving" more contingent
than the Bishop's own view; according to which, parents have
it in their power, by bringing or not bringing the children, to
"regulate the time when that moving shall take place". But
the same objection, if a good one, would apply to the other Sacrament. Priests, it might as well be said, have the power to keep
back the Eucharist from the people, by refusing to celebrate it.
The minister who only four times or thrice a year invites his flock
to the Lord's table, defeats, according to Mr. Goode, the grace of
that Sacrament. And yet we apprehend that he would not very
severely censure those who do not give the people the most frequent
opportunities possible of Communicating! The fact, however, is,
that the analogy instituted by Mr. Goode does not, strictly, hold
good. According to the Bishop, "it is *not* entirely in the parents'
power to prevent God's grace towards the child," any further, or
in any other sense, than this, that the parent has the power of
not bringing the child at all, *but when once brought, he cannot hinder
the grace;* whereas the Bishop's complaint of the Archbishop's
view is, that the parent *may* frustrate that grace, *after the very rite
itself is performed,* and thereby the ordinance of God be invalidated
by the will of man. The one does not derogate from the efficacy
of the Sacrament, *as a Sacrament:* the other obviously does.

Similarly, too, does Mr. Goode fail [22] in shaking the Bishop's

[18] Mr. Goode's Letter, p. 4.   [19] Bp. of Exeter's Letter, p. 4.
[20] Mr. Goode's Letter, pp. 6, 7.   [21] Mr. Goode's Letter, p. 8.
[22] Mr. Goode's Letter, p. 15.

assertion, that there is in Scripture no intimation of our Saviour's approval of the zeal of the Jewish parents, who brought their children to Him. When our Lord blamed those [that is, the disciples] that would have kept them [that is, the children] from Him, what allusion is made to the parents?

The Bishop and Mr. Goode are at issue about the African Code. It is true that Johnson does, in the passage referred to by the latter, refuse it a place in the Code of the Universal Church. But was he correct in excluding it? That is the question. It is to the Canon of the Council of Chalcedon that we must go, which runs thus: "We pronounce it to be fit and just that the Canons of the Holy Fathers, made in every Synod to this present time", be in full force." Johnson's note on it is this [24]: "By these words we are to understand only the Canons that have been already presented to the reader," [the African Code not being among that number,] "beginning with those of Nice, and which composed that Book of Canons so often cited in this Synod, as is agreed on all hands." Now, the African Code was settled by a great number of Bishops met in Synod at Carthage, more than thirty years before the Council of Chalcedon. Were not African Bishops Holy Fathers! Were not African Councils Synods! Why, then, is not that Code within the purview of the first Canon of Chalcedon! In truth it is not very clear what Johnson himself held to be the Code of the Universal Church, for in another passage [25] he states that the African Code *was* part of it. Thus after saying at the end of the 29th Canon of Chalcedon, "Here ends the Code of the Universal Church," he immediately adds, "'Tis true, if we take the Synod of Trullo for a General Council, AS IT REALLY WAS, AS MUCH AS ANY SYNOD WHATSO-EVER, then all the Canons contained in this volume" (the African code being of the number), "are part of that code, except the Papal decrees." He goes on indeed to say, that for several centuries, Rome had disallowed Trullo to be a General Council; but how can that neutralize the previous declaration of his own opinion! And if the Trullan were a General Council, the African was part of the Universal Code; for the 2nd Trullan Canon [A.D. 698] "confirmed all previous Canons of Councils and Fathers [26]." But be it so, that the African Code *was not* entitled so to rank. Mr. Goode ought at least to have told his readers, what Johnson says *in its praise* [27]." "It was always in the greatest repute in all Churches, next after that [the Universal] Code; it was of very great authority in the Old English Churches, for many of the

[23] i. e. A.D. 451.   [24] Clergyman's Vade-mecum, Part ii. p. 139.
[25] Part ii. p. 139.   [26] See the First Canon of the Trullan Council.
[27] Clergyman's Vade-mecum, Part ii. p. 171.

Excerptions of Egbert were transcribed from it." And what does its 110th Canon say, " He that denies original sin, or that infants are baptized for the remission of sins, be anathema." A stronger authority, if possible, in favour of the Bishop's views, than the 1st Canon of the 4th Council of Carthage would have been, if it had been an undisputed Canon of the Church.

The Archbishop in the body of his book on Apostolical Preaching, states it to be of " the positive doctrine of the Church, that renewal belongs to all who are baptized in the name of Christ :" in his new preface to that book he allows " that a Minister of that Church may justly maintain that the benefit of Baptism is limited to those cases only where an antecedent grace has taken place." Mr. Goode attempts no defence of this extraordinary contradiction between preface and context, further than by drawing off the reader's attention from it, by the *ad hominem* argument [28], that the Bishop had no right to challenge the Archbishop with it. Why not? Not because he had previously *approved* of his Grace's position—that would have been a good argument; but because, forsooth, he had previously quoted, *with disapproval*, passages of the same tendency as those he was then condemning !

We trust that his Grace will give or authorize to be given some explanation of the astounding phenomenon that in the self-same year in which he gives forth to the world his opinion, *as an author*, that a given doctrine *is* the positive doctrine of the Church, he, *sitting as an assessor to a Court of Justice*, declares that it is *not* the positive doctrine of the Church ! !

Then after four pages of personal invective, rendered doubly disagreeable to our ears by the zealous professions of regard for spiritual subordination which accompany it, and after several pages on adult baptism, which have nothing to do with the question, Mr. Goode accuses the Bishop of inconsistency [29], because in one place he had said that " all infants receive remission of their sins by Baptism because of their innocency ;" and in another, that the " guilt of original sin rested upon them until washed away in Baptism." Was Mr. Goode unable to perceive that when the Bishop mentioned infants as fit objects by reason of their innocency, he *of course* meant " innocency" from " actual" sin. May they not be guilty as to original, and yet innocent as to committed, sin?

The next charge is one [30] of ludicrous inconsistency, " in overstating the efficacy of Baptism in infants, and making it a nullity in the case of unbelieving adults." Because the Bishop had said that spiritual Regeneration was *the* effect of Baptism," ergo (Mr.

---

[28] Mr. Goode's Letter, p. 17.   [29] Ibid. p. 30.   [30] Ibid. p. 30.

Goode jumps to the conclusion) "if this is not given," in the opinion of the Bishop, "nothing is given." When we say, then, that "the effect" of inaccurate reasoning is to draw off men's minds from the truth, we are to be understood, according to the Rector of Allhallows, as limiting its ill effects to that one particular. Will he pardon us for asking him whether he himself could not suggest this other, that it damages the reputation of the inaccurate thinker? *Of course* the Bishop attributes to Baptism all its minor advantages, including, among them, the "sealing and confirming to us of the Gospel Covenant;" only he takes leave to add to them another and a greater one, which forms no part of Mr. Goode's Creed, and which he designates "the effect" of Baptism, because it is the *primary and principal one.*

Mr. Goode now passes in review those passages from our early Divines, which have been the subject of so much comment; but to which, as we have said, we ourselves attach very little importance in determining the present controversy. He may make what inference he chooses from them, (we cannot see how it will avail him, in this particular case,) *provided always that he does not misrepresent them.* For instance, we demur to his construction of the well-known passage from Bp. Taylor, cited at length in pp. 42, 43, of his "Letter;" two lines only of which, however, touch upon Infant Baptism. They are these: "In Infants it is not certain but that some [grace] is collated or infused; however, be it so or no, yet upon this account the administration of the Sacrament is not hindered." Is it possible, subjoins Mr. Goode, that words can be used more completely justifying Mr. Gorham's view? Now, we protest, that if the words above quoted are evidence one way or the other, they are rather a weak intimation of Bishop Taylor's opinion *against* Mr. Gorham than *in his favour.* "It is not certain, but," is, we take it, a qualified affirmative equivalent to "perhaps." At least, and viewed as favourably as possible to Mr. Goode's construction, (who lays stress on the phrase "be it so or no,") they leave the matter in pure uncertainty, and are tantamount to a declaration, that the point is an obscure one, upon which the Bishop does not like to hazard an explicit opinion one way or the other. He is like a witness who, when put into the witness-box, knows nothing at all about the *res gestæ* of the action [31].

[31] As a set-off to the above passage, even if we allow that it justifies Mr. Gorham's view, should be appended the following from the same eminent divine: "Since God hath given the Holy Spirit to them that are baptized, and rightly confirmed, and entered into covenant with Him, our bodies are made temples of the Holy Ghost, in which He dwells. It is St. Paul's argument, 'Know ye not that your body is the temple of the Holy Ghost?' and, 'He that defiles a temple, him will God destroy.'" Holy Living, p. 86. The bodies even of the unclean are holy Temples because of their Baptism, according to Bp. Taylor.

We next come to the Decades of Bullinger. Bullinger, it appears, wrote a volume containing fifty sermons; but of these four only treated of the Sacraments. From these four the Archbishop had culled certain passages, of which the Bishop thinks, that taken in their "real meaning, they contradict the very Articles and Formularies." In the main, however, he thinks the volume may have been an "useful manual." Out of this very plain and intelligible statement, however, Mr. Goode finds material for accusing the Bishop once more of self-contradiction. " Your endeavour to get over the fact of such a volume being set forth for the better exercise of learning in the inferior Clergy, merely because it was considered, in the main, an useful manual, though, in some most essential points, its statements contradict the very Articles and Formularies of our Church, I leave to the reader's reflection [33]." According, then, to Mr. Goode's logic, to say of a book, that a twelfth part of it contains objectionable matter, is as much as to say, that the remaining eleven-twelfths must contain objectionable matter likewise !

Again; after ridiculing the notion that any "order" in 1586, " ordering the Orders for the Discipline of the Church" to be observed, should be expected, Mr. Goode all at once stumbles upon such an order [33]. But unluckily this order, the existence of which vindicates the reasonableness of the Bishop's expectation, does not help the finder. The Bishop had doubted whether Bullinger's Decades had ever been authoritatively taught, on the ground, (though not " the " only ground) that no order, as far as he could find, was ever made *by the Upper House* of Convocation. To confute this, Mr. Goode produces an order made—by whom! not by the Upper House—that would have been *ad rem*—but *by the Lower!*

Again; the Bishop had said that no Canon or Act relating to Bullinger's book appeared in *the Acts of the Convocation* of 1586. Mr. Goode, whilst thinking to disprove this statement, unconsciously and remarkably confirms it, by quoting from Strype a circular letter of Archbishop Whitgift, in which he says, with reference to the "orders" in question, that " though it had seemed fit to himself and his brethren to put them in execution, such resolution *had not the effect of a Judicial Act*, or conclusion by the authority of Convocation [34]." Just what, and all that, the Bishop had asserted ! It is a rash thing to measure the sword of debate with so close and correct a reasoner as Dr. Philpotts.

Then, once more, Mr. Goode declares the Bishop has " with

[33] Letter, p. 47.   [33] Ibid. p. 48.
[34] Letter, pp. 50, 51. Strype's Whitgift, book iii. c. 20.

his own hands torn up his doctrine from the very roots, and made a most awkward slip[33]," because he could not imagine the Sacrament administered healthfully without God's grace and favour. This he considers an admission, that all infants *come to Baptism with grace*, and therefore must have had it before; and he eulogizes the judges for their acuteness in detecting that, if children come [to Baptism] under the weight of that original sin which deserves God's wrath and damnation, it is a contradiction to say they are in the possession of his grace. But can we argue at all upon such mysteries? Or, if it be allowable to do so, may we not reply, that there is nothing more abhorrent from the Divine œconomy in a sinful child becoming suddenly holy, than there is in an adult becoming suddenly converted, as we believe is not unfrequently the fact? Is there any thing more at variance with human reason in maintaining, with the Bishop, that children are made worthy from being unworthy recipients, by an instantaneous act of grace *at the time of* Baptism, than with Mr. Goode, that they become so *at some point of time anterior* to Baptism? Which ever be the exact moment when their Sanctification commences, up to that moment they must have been *aliens from*, and immediately therefrom and thenceforward have been *received into*, God's favour. Nor, again, is it more irreconcileable with the theory of the regenerating influence of a Sacrament (as has been objected by another class of disputants), that children should not grow up holier than we see they do, than that adults, of whom we do not hesitate to believe that they have received worthily the Lord's Supper, should not exhibit afterwards a life corresponding in all points to such a reception. Can we trace the mind of a child, and the first workings of its will? Can we tell how soon, or when first, or by what imperceptible degrees and ways and means it does despite to its Baptismal grace and purity?

Once more, and we have done for ever with Mr. Goode. He treats the Bishop as having denied the capability of infants *for God's favour*[34], when his only denial was that they were capable of the qualifications *of faith and repentance!* And the reader's attention is again led off to contemplate the absurdity of such a denial, which the Bishop not only never made, but could never have dreamed of making, because he had already said that they could not have the Sacrament administered *without* that favour, and had, according to Mr. Goode, torn up his doctrine from the very roots, by his own hands, *for saying so!*

We have neither space nor inclination to go through more of Mr. Goode's Letter. The above specimens may suffice as illustra-

---

[33] Letter, p. 60.   [34] Ibid. p. 65.

tions of the loose and inconclusive reasoning on which he has rested his own and his party's defence to the Letter of the Bishop of Exeter. But it is not for the sake of a mere intellectual treat as critics, nor yet as the moral censors of Mr. Goode, that we have thus dwelt upon our subject: we have a higher and more important object in view. There is a party among us, we lament to own, respectable in numbers, pre-eminent in piety, who regard the decision of the Judicial Committee as a righteous verdict. They believe that the Church *has* left the question of Baptismal Regeneration an open one. They begin to suspect she *has* forfeited her claim to be deemed the depositary of Catholic truth. They talk of consulting their own safety by flying to another communion. Is this an imaginary fear? We ourselves have conversed with those who, holding high preferment in our Universities, and having devoted the best years of their life with extraordinary zeal and fidelity to parochial labours, are now on the eve of parting for ever with the principles and precepts of their youth and manhood, and giving themselves over, temporally and spiritually, to a Church not our own. We would implore such, by all the persuasiveness we can command, to pause ere it be too late. We would beseech them to reflect on the temerity, we had nearly said, the common dishonesty, of such a course. Was it a thing unknown to you, we would ask, when you bound yourselves over to the service of the Church of England that she was in thraldom to the State? "*Qui sentit commodum debet sentire et onus*" is an old adage, and full of truth. You accepted her liabilities, when you availed yourselves of her privileges, *with your eyes open*. What were they? On the one hand, her high Apostolical descent; her unrivalled purity of doctrine; her great temporal advantages. On the other, her dependence on the State. What will you exchange her for? Will you abandon her for the untried regions of Papal autocracy, or hope for recognition by Scottish Episcopacy? You knew what she was when you did homage to her. Her constitution has not changed since then. Her Convocations were a dead letter—legal substances, but, like many other legal substances, literal shadows —long before you were born. Can you plead the non-revival of her ancient self-government as an excuse for your desertion of her ranks? Do you deplore her want of discipline? Look around you, and see how day after day is gradually and certainly restoring it. Surely, if ever, she has need *now* of her staunchest defenders. Is it comely to leave her in the battle-tide? Because a Court of Justice has declared her mind to be *what you at least must admit—since you think that declaration just—has ever been her mind,* can you in consistency cease to cleave unto her? Her laws are what they ever were. The Judges have interpreted, not made them. Remember, too, it is a solemn thing to trample under foot a vow. There was no mental reservation in your plighted troth to her. An oath is a conditionless and absolute thing. And by how much the more you deem her doctrines of Baptism fundamental Articles of Faith, in that exact proportion do you stand precluded from releasing yourselves from the self-devotion which you have pledged to her. If in politics, surely much more in Religion, is a change of opinions in fundamentals—TREASON!

To those who, with us, repudiate the Judgment of the Judicial Committee, let us, in conclusion, recapitulate the reasons why we venture to impugn it on legal grounds.

Firstly, we charge them with not having followed out their own undertaking, to apply to the case before them the same rules of construction "which are applicable to all written instruments;" for had they done so, they would have resorted, in the first instance, to the Church's language in her Baptismal Services as an exponent of her doctrines upon Baptism.

Secondly, we charge them with not observing, that the Baptismal Services contain Articles of Faith as well as forms of devotion; and particularly, with not heeding, though sitting as an Ecclesiastical tribunal, that Canon of the Church which, in ample terms, declares the all-sufficiency of those Services to determine a doctrinal question.

Thirdly, we charge them with inferring the Church's mind on Baptism from her mind as disclosed in the Burial of her dead; and with failing to perceive that, those respective Services not being in *pari materiâ*, it was to be expected that she would adopt, when speaking of a Sacrament, a more positive tone of teaching than when speaking of a non-sacramental rite.

Fourthly, we charge them with resorting to the extrinsic evidence of the other Formularies of the Church, though no ambiguity, or variance with the language of her other Formularies, was proved to exist in her Baptismal Services.

Fifthly, we charge them with having introduced an hypothetical principle of construction into the Church's Code, and into all other Codes, civil as well as ecclesiastical, which, once introduced, it is impossible henceforward to limit, and must tend to throw the interpretation of all written instruments into doubt and confusion.

Sixthly, we charge them with having unduly *regarded* the opinions of individual Divines, which, even if they were admissible evidence at all, do not always agree with those of one another, and sometimes are inconsistent with themselves, and are at least opposed to those of living Divines entitled to respect.

Seventhly, we charge them with having unduly *disregarded* the explicit unanimous declaration, *upon the exact controverted point*, of those Divines, most, if not all, of whom were members of the very Synod which finally settled the Book of Common Prayer, and whose opinions therefore it is invaluable to possess, not as being those of isolated individuals, but as those of a body exercising, simultaneously with what Mr. Goode calls the *unauthoritative* Conference at the Savoy, what he must allow to be at least the *authoritative* functions of a Convocation.

Lastly, and above all, we charge them with failing to perceive that the inseparability of the grace of Infant Baptism from its administration is the *strict necessary logical consequence* of the Church's doctrine on adult Baptism ; inasmuch as if she dispenses (as she declares she does) in the case of infants, with those conditions, which if fulfilled, she declares bring grace to adults, it follows *as a matter of course*, (if one may so speak,) that she cannot but accord to the former *without*, the benefits which she accords to the latter *with*, those same pre-requisites.

Nor let us be deemed presumptuous for arraigning the Justice of this Judgment. Lawyers, no more than Popes, are infallible. The Decree of a Judicial Committee no more forms the Code of the Catholic Church than did, of yore, those of Emperors. The mind of a Master of the Rolls may be less sagacious than that of a Vice-Chancellor. The theological lore of an Exchequer Baron is probably less profound than that of a Judge of the Court of Arches. One Bishop may equal two Archbishops. The Learned of the land are not unanimous. There has not been even any great preponderance of opinion among them. Nay, whilst we write, the foundations of this appellate tribunal are being shaken. The authority of laymen in Controversies of Faith may even yet be superseded. A little while, and who knows but the Judgment of this anomalous Judicature may be reversed, or at all events overruled ; and the Hierarchy of our land seen installed, in their proper place, as the legalized Interpreters of the mind of our Church!

ART. VII.—1. *The Book of Mormon; an Account written by the hand of Mormon, upon Plates taken from the Plates of Nephi. Translated by* JOSEPH SMITH, Jun., *Kirtland, Ohio.* Printed by O. Cowdery and Co., for P. P. Pratt and J. Goodson, 1837; (the second American edition, the first being published in 1830.) Second European edition, Liverpool, published by Orson Pratt, 1849.

2. *The Book of Doctrines and Covenants of the Church of Jesus Christ of Latter Day Saints; selected from the Revelations of God, by* JOSEPH SMITH, *President.* Second European edition (first in 1845), Liverpool: Orson Pratt. 1849.

3. *The History of the Saints, or an Exposé of Joe Smith and Mormonism. By* JOHN C. BENNETT, *General and Doctor of Medicine, Boston, and New York.* Leland and Whiting. 1842.

4. *The City of the Mormons, or Three Days at Nauvoo, in* 1842. *By the Rev.* H. CASWALL, *M.A., author of "America and the American Church."* Second edition, revised and enlarged. London: Rivingtons. 1843.

5. *The Prophet of the Nineteenth Century; or the Rise, Progress, and Present State of the Mormons, or Latter Day Saints: to which is appended, an Analysis of the Book of Mormon. By the Rev.* H. CASWALL, *M.A., Professor of Divinity, Kemper College, Missouri; and author of "America and the American Church," "City of the Mormons," &c.* London: Rivingtons. 1843.

6. *Letters exhibiting the most prominent Doctrines of the Church of Jesus Christ of Latter Day Saints. By* ORSON SPENCER, *A.B., President of the Church of Jesus Christ, of L. D. S. in Europe, in reply to the Rev. William Caswall, A.M., Boston, Massachusetts, U. S. A.* Liverpool: published by Orson Spencer, 1847, and collated in one volume, 1848.

THERE are few persons, probably, who have not, at one time or another, heard of the existence of a sect called the " Mormonites," or " Latter Day Saints," and of the crowds of deluded fanatics, who, under those names, have, from time to time, quitted the shores of this country, on their way to a new land of promise in the Far West. But among those under whose notice this one among the many religious phenomena of the present day has occasionally fallen, there are few, we apprehend, who have ever troubled themselves to inquire into the origin or peculiar tenets of the new sect,—few who have any conception of its numerical extent,—still fewer who have viewed it in its more important aspect as one of the "signs of the times." It is hard to say, how long this indifference of the more enlightened portion of the Christian public to the proceedings of the followers of Mormon might have continued, but for an attempt recently made to constrain a clergyman of our Church to desecrate the Burial Service at the grave of one of the members of the sect. While it appeared,—as in Mr. Caswall's two publications, Nos. 4 and 5, at the head of this article, and in a brief notice in a number of the *Church of England Quarterly*, some years ago, from the pen, we believe, of the Rev. Hartwell Horne,—simply as one of the extravagant phases of American religionism, it was not likely to excite any very lively interest in this country; but the case is altogether different when we find that the pestilence is spreading extensively in our parishes, as we fear it is, especially in the manufacturing districts; and that the spirit of ribaldry towards the Church, by which it has been characterized from the first, is changed into a spirit of persecution, endeavouring to expose her sacred offices to irreverent, and, if the profanation were acquiesced in, not altogether unmerited, scorn. The Church owes a debt of obligation of no ordinary kind to Mr. Sweet, for the firmness with which he resolved to withstand the nefarious demand made upon him by a family of Mormonites in his parish, for the manifest purpose of bringing the Church and her ministry into contempt among the people, and thus paving the way for a more ready reception of those misrepresentations of the Church's system, upon which those new sectarians rely to so great an extent for the recommendation of their own. In his own statement of the case[1] he has very properly taken a wider range, and considered the general state of the law as regards the obligation to use the Burial Office in cases for which it certainly never was intended. But the facts incidentally disclosed in his pamphlet, as to the pernicious tendency of the sect with which he has been brought into conflict, are such as are sure to excite very general attention, and we have therefore thought we should be doing good service to our readers, and especially to the clerical portion of them, if we put them in possession of the leading features of the Mormonite heresy, and of so much of its history as will enable them to appreciate the character of its founders and promoters.

With this view we have collected together a vast mass of documentary evidence, which we shall endeavour to present to our

[1] *The Defence of a Refusal to Profane the "Order for the Burial of the Dead;" with a Preface, dedicated to Members of Church Unions.* By James Bradby Sweet, M.A., Perpetual Curate of Woodville. London: Cleaver, 1850.

readers in a condensed and digested form. In doing so we hold ourselves wholly absolved from the necessity of dealing with the errors, the absurdities and blasphemies of the sect in the way of controversy. The imposture is too palpable, the heresy too manifest, to call for serious argument. The most efficient way to expose the imposture is to state the facts, as we find them set forth both by the Mormonite leaders themselves, and by certain parties who have broken off their former connexion with them,—the most powerful confutation of the heresy, to exhibit their doctrine as it is propounded by themselves, both originally in their doctrinal documents, and subsequently in their apologetic writings.

We shall begin our account by putting the Mormonite prophet himself into the witness-box. A History of the different American Sects—altogether forty-three in number—published at Philadelphia in the year 1844[2], contains, (pp. 404—410,) on the subject of the Mormonites, an article from the pen of Joseph Smith, under the title "Latter Day Saints, by Joseph Smith, Nauvoo, Illinois." The writer begins by stating that

"The Church of Jesus Christ of Latter Day Saints, was founded upon direct revelation, as the true Church of God has ever been, according to the Scriptures (Amos iii. 7, and Acts i. 2); and through the will and blessings of God, I have been an instrument in his hands, thus far, to move forward the cause of Zion."

He then proceeds to give a sketch of his own life. He was born, according to his own account, on the 23rd of December, 1805, at Sharon, Windsor County, in the State of Vermont, whence his parents removed, when he was about ten years old, to Palmyra, in the State of New York, and, after an interval of four years, to Manchester, in the same state, which was the scene of the first supernatural events in his life. At the age of fourteen, he states, he was much troubled in mind by observing the contradictions of the different religious denominations around him, and in his anxiety to be delivered from the confusion of mind thence ensuing, he was fervent in prayer for illumination from above. While thus engaged in a secret recess of a grove, he had a vision :

---

[2] The following is the title of this curious publication, in which the different sects are all permitted to tell their own tale :—HE PASA ECCLESIA. *An Original History of the Religious Denominations at present existing in the United States, containing authentic Accounts of their Rise, Progress, Statistics, and Doctrines. Written expressly for the Work by eminent Theological Professors, Ministers, and Lay Members of the respective Denominations.* Projected, compiled, and arranged by J. Daniel Rapp, of Lancaster Pa., Author of "Der Märtyrer Geschichte," &c. &c. Philadelphia: Humphreys. 1844.

" I was enwrapt in a heavenly vision, and saw two glorious personages, who exactly resembled each other in features and likeness, surrounded with a brilliant light, which eclipsed the sun at noon-day. They told me that all the religious denominations were believing in incorrect doctrines, and that none of them was acknowledged of God as his Church and kingdom. And I was expressly commanded to 'go not after them,' at the same time receiving a promise that the fulness of the gospel should at some future time be made known unto me."

This promise was fulfilled about three years after, when, on the 21st of September, 1823, being then near eighteen years old, he had in a room, three times repeated the same night, a vision of an angel who declared to him :

" That the preparatory work for the second coming of the Messiah was speedily to commence; that the time was at hand for the gospel in all its fulness to be preached in power, unto all nations, that a people might be prepared for the millennial reign. I was informed that I was chosen to be an instrument in the hands of God, to bring about some of his purposes in this glorious dispensation."

At the same time the Angel gave him " a brief sketch" of the origin and early history of the aboriginal inhabitants of America, and informed him that certain " plates of records," containing the details of which the Angel gave the epitome, were deposited in a certain place specified by the heavenly messenger. This was followed by many subsequent visits of Angels, till at last, on the morning of the 22nd of September, 1827, the Angel of the Lord delivered the records themselves into Joseph's hands.

" These records were engraven on plates which had the appearance of gold ; each plate was six inches wide and eight inches long, and not quite so thick as common tin. They were filled with engravings in Egyptian characters, and bound together in a volume, as the leaves of a book, with three rings running through the whole. The volume was something near six inches in thickness, a part of which was sealed. The characters on the unsealed part were small and beautifully engraved. The whole book exhibited many marks of antiquity in its construction, and much skill in the art of engraving. With the records was found a curious instrument, which the ancients called ' Urim and Thummim,' which consisted of two transparent stones set in the rim on a bow fastened to a breastplate. Through the medium of the Urim and Thummim, I translated the record, by the gift and power of God[3]."

[3] It is worth while to compare with this the account which Joseph Smith gave to one of his comrades, at the time when he first started the imposture, and before he had any idea himself of the extent to which the business might grow. An affidavit of Peter Ingersoll, one of Joseph Smith's acquaintances in early life, after giving a general account of the character of Smith, and of his occupations and practices as a money-digger, thus proceeds :—
" One day he came, and greeted me with a joyful countenance. Upon asking the

The translation, so made, is the celebrated Book of Mormon, (No. 1. at the head of this Article,) of which a brief abstract is inserted in the narrative. The prophet then proceeds to relate the origin of his Church :—

" On the 6th of April, 1830, the 'Church of Jesus Christ of Latter Day Saints,' was first organized in the town of Manchester, Ontario County, State of New York. Some few were called and ordained by the Spirit of revelation and prophecy, and began to preach as the Spirit gave them utterance, and though weak, yet were they strengthened by the power of God ; and many were brought to repentance, were immersed in the water, and were filled with the Holy Ghost by the laying on of hands. They saw visions and prophesied, devils were cast out, and the sick healed by the laying on of hands. From that time the work rolled forth with astonishing rapidity." . . . .

Next follows an enumeration of the various settlements succes-sively effected by his followers, in Jackson County, in Clay County, and in Caldwell and Davies Counties, in the State of Missouri, from all which they were ejected, from the latter in 1838, when they were, according to Smith's account, from 12,000 to 15,000 in number. On their expulsion from Caldwell and Davies Counties, they migrated to Hancock County, in the State of Illinois, where, in the " fall " of 1839, they commenced a city, which, in December, 1840, obtained an Act of Incorporation from the Legislature of Illinois, and received from its founder the name of " Nauvoo," signifying " beautiful." The city is described at the date of the account as containing 1500 houses, and upwards of 15,000 inhabitants. It was graced by an " University," and defended by a military body raised from the inhabitants them-selves, called the " Nauvoo Legion," commanded by a " Lieutenant-General" (a Mormonite), but subject to the superior authority of

cause of his unusual happiness, he replied in the following language :—' As I was passing yesterday across the woods, after a heavy shower of rain, I found, in a hollow, some beautiful white sand, that had been washed up by the water. I took off my frock, and tied up several quarts of it, and then went home. On my entering the house I found the family at the table, eating dinner. They were anxious to know the contents of my frock. At that moment, I happened to think of what I had heard about a history found in Canada, called the golden Bible ; so I very gravely told them it was the golden Bible. To my surprise, they were credulous enough to believe what I said. Accordingly, I told them that I had received a command-ment to let no one see it ; for, says I, no man can see it with the naked eye and live. However, I offered to take out the book and show it to them ; but they refused to see it, and left the room. Now,' said Joe, ' I have got the d—d fools fixed, and will carry out the fun.' Notwithstanding, he told me he had no such book, and believed there never was any such book ; yet, he told me that he actually went to Willard Chase, to get him to make a chest, in which he might deposit his golden Bible. But, as Chase would not do it, he made a box himself, of clapboards, and put it into a pillow-case, and allowed people only to lift it, and feel of it through the case."—*Bennett's History of the Saints,* pp. 63, 64.

the Governor of the State, and of the President of the United States. An eminence in this city was chosen for the site of the great Mormon temple, the building of which, at the date of the account, was still in progress :—

" The temple of God, now in the course of erection, being already raised one story, and which is 120 feet by 80 feet, of stone with polished pilasters, of an entire new order of architecture, will be a splendid house for the worship of God, as well as an unique wonder for the world, it being built by the direct revelation of Jesus Christ for the salvation of the living and the dead."

From this temple and city as its centre, Mormonism spread itself far and wide, not only through the United States, but beyond the Atlantic into Europe, and into other parts of the world. Such at least is the prophet's account :—

" Besides the United States, where nearly every place of notoriety has heard the glad tidings of the Gospel of the Son of God, England, Ireland, and Scotland have shared largely in the fulness of the everlasting gospel, and thousands been already gathered with their kindred saints to this the corner-stone of Zion. Missionaries of this Church have gone to the East Indies, to Australia, Germany, Constantinople, Egypt, Palestine, the Islands of the Pacific, and are now preparing to open the door in the extensive dominions of Russia.

" There are no correct data by which the exact number of members composing this now extensive, and still extending, Church of Jesus Christ of Latter Day Saints, can be known. Should it be supposed at 150,000, it might still be short of the truth."

So far the account given by Joseph Smith through the medium of "HE PASA ECCLESIA." We now turn to the history of the alleged revelations given to Joseph Smith from time to time, and recorded in the second of the Mormonite Standard Books. The first of these books is the Book of Mormon already referred to, which, containing what are alleged to be certain ancient records, answers in a manner to the Old Testament of the sacred volume, while the place of the New Testament is filled by " The Book of Doctrines and Covenants " (No. 2 at the head of this article). This volume, which was printed and published separately, consists of two parts ; viz. Seven " Lectures on Faith," or an abstract of Mormonite Doctrine in a homiletic form ; and a collection of " Covenants and Commandments," given by revelation, from time to time, divided into 111 Sections. They do not in the collection follow in the order in which they are alleged to have been received ; but as the date is generally attached to them, we shall be able to follow the history of the prophet as traced out by himself in this " canonical" book. The earliest of the revelations contained in it have reference to the translation of the " golden plates," and in particular to an untoward accident which happened at the very commencement of the work. Joseph Smith was employing an *amanuensis*, named Martin Harris, a farmer of some substance, and of an excitable temperament and unstable religious views, who from a Quaker had successively turned Methodist, Universalist, Baptist, and Presbyterian, and having grown tired of this last profession also, was at this time open to any religious novelty which might come in his way. On him Joseph Smith succeeded in palming off the story of the golden plates, and having embarked him in the enterprize, for which Harris was to find the money, he dictated to him from behind a curtain, from time to time, portions of what professed to be a translation of the golden Bible. While the work was thus progressing, Harris having taken home with him the first 116 pages of it, they were abstracted by an unfriendly hand, seemingly with the intention of embarrassing the prophet, and confuting him by the publication of them, if he should be unwary enough to attempt to reproduce them. To this circumstance allusion is made in a " revelation" dated July, 1828, in which it is said :

" Behold, thou art Joseph, and thou wast chosen to do the work of the Lord, but because of transgression, if thou art not aware thou wilt fall ; but remember God is merciful ; therefore, repent of that which thou hast done which is contrary to the commandment which I gave you, and thou art still chosen, and art again called to the work : except thou do this, thou shalt be delivered up and become as other men, and have no more gift.

" And when thou deliveredst up that which God had given thee sight and power to translate, thou deliveredst up that which was sacred into the hands of a wicked man, who has set at nought the counsels of God, and has broken the most sacred promises which were made before God, and has depended upon his own judgment, and boasted in his own wisdom, and this is the reason that *thou hast lost thy privileges for a season,* for thou hast suffered the counsel of thy director to be trampled upon from the beginning."—*Covenants and Commandments,* Sect. xxx. §§ 4, 5.

The work of translation was thus suspended, in the hope, no doubt, that the lost manuscript might be recovered ; but all endeavours to procure its restitution (Harris's wife was the thief) having proved fruitless, another revelation was given in May, 1829 :

" Now, behold, I say unto you, that because you delivered up those writings which you had power given unto you to translate, by the means of the Urim and Thummim, into the hands of a wicked man, you have lost them ; and *you also lost your gift at the same time, and your mind became darkened; nevertheless, it is now restored unto you again*, therefore see that you are faithful and continue on unto the finishing of the remainder of the work of translation as you have begun : do not run faster, or labour more than you have strength and means provided to enable you to translate; but be diligent unto the end : pray always, that you may come off conqueror ; yea, that you may conquer Satan, and that you may escape the hands of the servants of Satan that do uphold his work. Behold, they have sought to destroy you ; yea, even the man in whom you have trusted, has sought to destroy you. And for this cause I said that he is a wicked man, for he has sought to take away the things wherewith you have been intrusted; and he has also sought to destroy your gift ; and because you have delivered the writings into his hands, behold wicked men have taken them from you : therefore, you have delivered them up; yea, that which was sacred unto wickedness. And, behold, Satan has put it into their hearts to alter the words which you have caused to be written, or which you have translated, which have gone out of your hands: and, behold, I say unto you, that because they have altered the words, they read contrary from that which you translated and caused to be written ; and, on this wise, the devil has sought to lay a cunning plan, that he may destroy this work; for he has put into their hearts to do this, that by lying they may say they have caught you in the words which you have *pretended to translate.*

"Verily, I say unto you, that I will not suffer that Satan shall accomplish his evil design in this thing, for, behold, he has put it into their hearts to get thee to tempt the Lord thy God, in asking to translate it over again; and then, behold, they say and think in their hearts, we will see if God has given him power to translate; if so, He will also give him power again ; and if God giveth him power again, or if he translates again, or, in other words, if he bringeth forth the same words, behold, we have the same with us, and we have altered them : therefore, they will not agree, and we will say that he has lied in his words, and that he has no gift, and that he has no power : therefore, we will destroy him, and also the work, and we will do this that we may not be ashamed in the end, and that we may get glory of the world . .

"Now, behold, they have altered these words, because Satan saith unto them, *He hath deceived you :* and thus he flattereth them away to do iniquity, to get thee to tempt the Lord thy God.

"Behold, I say unto you, that you shall not translate again those words which have gone forth out of your hands; for, behold, they shall not accomplish their evil designs in lying against those words. For, behold, if you should bring forth the same words *they will say that you have lied ; that you have pretended to translate, but that you have contradicted yourself :* and, behold, they will publish this, and Satan will harden the hearts of the people to stir them up to anger against you, that they will not believe my words. Thus Satan thinketh to overpower your testimony in this generation, that the work may not come forth in this generation: but, behold, here is wisdom, and because I show unto you wisdom, and give you commandments concerning these things, what you shall do, show it not unto the world until you have accomplished the work of translation.

"Marvel not that I said unto you, here is wisdom, show it not unto the world, for I said show it not unto the world, that you may be preserved. Behold, I do not say that you shall not show it unto the righteous; but as you cannot always judge the righteous, or as you cannot always tell the wicked from the righteous, therefore, I say unto you, hold your peace until I shall see fit to make all things known unto the world concerning the matter.

"And now, verily I say unto you, that an account of those things that you have written, which have gone out of your hands, are engraven upon the plates of Nephi; yea, and you remember it was said in those writings that *a more particular account was given of these things upon the plates of Nephi.*

"And now, because the account which is engraven upon the plates of Nephi is more particular concerning the things which, in my wisdom, I would bring to the knowledge of the people in this account, therefore *you shall translate the engravings which are on the plates of Nephi, down even till you come to the reign of king Benjamin, or until you come to that which you have translated, which you have retained; and behold, you shall publish it as the record of Nephi,* and thus I will confound those who have altered my words. I will not suffer that they shall destroy my work; yea, I will show unto them that my wisdom is greater than the cunning of the devil.

"Behold, *they have only got a part, or an abridgment of the account of Nephi.* Behold, there are many things engraven on the plates of Nephi which do throw greater views upon my gospel; therefore, it is wisdom in me that you should translate this first part of the engravings of Nephi, and send forth in this work. And, behold, all the remainder of this work does contain all those parts of my gospel which my holy prophets, yea, and also my disciples, desired in their prayers should come forth unto this people. And I said unto them, that it should be granted unto them according to their faith in their prayers; yea, and this was their faith, that my gospel which I gave unto them, that they might preach in their days, might come unto their brethren the Lamanites, and also all that had become Lamanites because of their dissensions."—*Covenants and Commandments,* Sect. xxxvi. §§ 1, 2. 5—10.

The history of this *contre-temps,* which seriously perplexed the prophet for a time, is recounted with still greater plainness in the Preface to the first American edition of the Book of Mormon, published in 1830; but in the second American, and in both the European editions of the book, that preface has been suppressed. The passage in question is curious:

"As many false reports have been circulated respecting the follow-

ing work, and also many unlawful measures taken by evil designing
persons to destroy me, and also the work ; I would inform you that I
translated by the gift and power of God, and caused to be written one
hundred and sixteen pages, the which I took from the book of Lehi,
which was an account abridged from the plates of Lehi by the hand of
Mormon ; which said account some person or persons have stolen and
kept from me, notwithstanding *my utmost exertions to recover it again ;*
and being commanded of the Lord that I should not translate the same
over again, for Satan had put it into their hearts to tempt the Lord
their God, by altering the words, that they did read contrary from that
which I translated and caused to be written : and if I should bring
forth the same words again, or, in other words, if I should translate the
same over again, they would publish that which they had stolen, and
Satan would stir up the hearts of this generation, that they might not
receive this work ; but, behold! the Lord said unto me, I will not
suffer that Satan shall accomplish his evil design in this thing ; therefore thou shalt translate from the plates of Nephi, until ye come to
that which ye have translated, which ye have retained ; and behold, ye
shall publish it as the record of Nephi ; and thus I will confound
those who have altered my words. I will not suffer that they shall
destroy my work ; yea, I will show unto them that my wisdom is
greater than the cunning of the devil. Wherefore, to be obedient unto
the commandments of God, I have, through his grace and mercy, accomplished that which He hath commanded me respecting this thing. I
would also inform you that the plates of which hath been spoken, were
found in the township of Manchester, Ontario County, New York."

From the tone in which Harris the scribe—" the wicked man "
—is spoken of in the above revelation, it would appear that the
prophet was not without suspicion of his fidelity ; and Harris, on
his part, seems to have been uncomfortably pressing for a sight of
the golden plates from which the prophet was translating, or "pretending to translate." The curiosity of the scribe was accordingly
repressed, and his fears and his " faith" wrought upon to make him
an eye-witness of what he had *not* seen, by " revelation," in the
manner following.

" Behold, I say unto you, that as my servant Martin Harris *has de-*
sired a witness at my hand, that you, my servant Joseph Smith, jun.,
have got the plates of which you have testified and borne record that you
have received of me ; and now, behold, this shall you say unto him,—
he who spake unto you said unto you, I, the Lord, am God, and have
given these things unto you, my servant Joseph Smith, jun., and have
commanded you that you should stand as a witness of these things, and
I have caused you that you should enter into a covenant with me, that
you should not show them, except to those persons to whom I commanded
you; and you have no power over them, except I grant it unto you.
And you have a gift to translate the plates, and this is the first gift

that I bestowed upon you, and *I have commanded that you should* PRETEND *to no other gift until my purpose is fulfilled in this;* for I will grant unto you no other gift until it is finished.

"Verily, I say unto you, that *woe shall come unto the inhabitants of the earth if they will not hearken unto my words;* for hereafter you shall be ordained, and go forth and deliver my words unto the children of men. Behold, *if they will not believe my words, they would not believe you, my servant Joseph, if it were possible that you could show them all these things* which I have committed unto you. O! this unbelieving and stiffnecked generation! *mine anger is kindled against them.*

"Behold, verily I say unto you, I have reserved those things which I have entrusted unto you, my servant Joseph, for a wise purpose in me, and it shall be made known unto future generations; but *this generation shall have my word through you;* and in addition to your testimony, the testimony of *three of my servants, whom I shall call and ordain, unto whom I will show these things,* and they shall go forth with *my words that are given through you;* yea, they shall know of a surety that these things are true, for from heaven will I declare it unto them. *I will give them power that they may behold and view these things as they are;* and to none else will I grant this power to receive this same testimony among this generation, in this the beginning of the rising up and the coming forth of my church out of the wilderness, clear as the moon, and fair as the sun, and terrible as an army with banners. And *the testimony of three witnesses will I send forth of my word:* and behold, whosoever believeth on my words them will I visit with the manifestation of my Spirit, and they shall be born of me, even of water and of the Spirit. And you must *wait yet a little while,* for ye are not yet ordained; and their testimony shall also go forth unto the condemnation of this generation, if they harden their hearts against them; for a desolating scourge shall go forth among the inhabitants of the earth, and shall continue to be poured out from time to time, if they repent not, until the earth is empty, and the inhabitants thereof are consumed away and utterly destroyed by the brightness of my coming. Behold, I tell you these things, even as I also told the people of the destruction of Jerusalem; and my word shall be verified at this time, as it hath hitherto been verified.

"And now I command you, my servant Joseph, to repent and walk more uprightly before me, and *yield to the persuasions of men no more;* and that you be firm in keeping the commandments wherewith I have commanded you; and if you do this, behold I grant unto you eternal life, even if you should be slain.

"And now again I speak unto you, my servant Joseph, concerning the man that desires the witness. Behold, I say unto him, *he exalts himself, and does not humble himself sufficiently before me; but if he will bow down before me, and humble himself in mighty prayer and faith, in the sincerity of his heart, then will I grant unto him a view of the things which he desires to see.* And then he shall say unto the people of this generation, Behold, I have seen the things which the Lord has shown unto Joseph Smith, jun., and I know of a surety that they are true, for *I have seen them, for they have been shown unto me by the power of God, and not of man.* And I, the Lord, command him, my servant Martin Harris, that *he shall say no more unto them concerning these things, except he shall say, I have seen them, and they have been shown unto me by the power of God,* and these are the words which he shall say; but *if he deny this, he will break the covenant which he has before covenanted with me, and behold he is condemned.* And now, *except he humble himself, and acknowledge unto me the things that he has done which are wrong, and covenant with me that he will keep my commandments, and exercise faith in me, behold I say unto him, he shall have no such views,* for I will grant unto him no views of the things of which I have spoken. And if this be the case, I command you my servant Joseph, that you shall say unto him, that *he shall do no more, nor trouble me any more concerning this matter.*

"And *if this be the case,* behold, I say unto thee, Joseph, when thou hast translated a few more pages thou shalt *stop for a season,* even until I command thee again; then thou mayest translate again. And except thou do this, behold, thou shalt have no more gift, and I will take away the things which I have entrusted with thee. And now, because I foresee the lying in wait to destroy thee, yea, *I foresee that if my servant Martin Harris humbleth not himself, and receive a witness from my hand, that he will fall into transgression,* and there are many that lie in wait to destroy thee from off the face of the earth; and for this cause, that thy days may be prolonged, I have given unto thee these commandments; yea, for this cause I have said, Stop, and stand still until I command thee, and I will provide means whereby thou mayest accomplish the thing which I have commanded thee; and if thou art faithful in keeping my commandments, thou shalt be lifted up at the last day. Amen." —*Covenants and Commandments,* Sect. xxxii.

While this revelation, given in March, 1829, in the interval between the suspension of the work in July, 1828, and its resumption in May, 1829, was working in the mind of Martin Harris, another instrument was in training, in the person of one Oliver Cowdery, a school-teacher and Baptist preacher in the neighbourhood; to whom, in April, 1829, divers "revelations" were given, through Joseph Smith, from which the following are extracts.

"Behold thou hast a gift, and blessed art thou because of thy gift. Remember it is sacred, and cometh from above: and if thou wilt inquire, thou shalt know mysteries which are great and marvellous: therefore thou shalt exercise thy gift, that thou mayest find out mysteries, that thou mayest bring many to the knowledge of the truth; yea, convince them of the error of their ways. Make not thy gift known unto any, save it be those who are of thy faith. Trifle not with sacred things. If thou wilt do good, yea, and hold out faithful to the end, thou shalt be saved in the kingdom of God, which is the greatest of all the gifts of God; for there is no gift greater than the gift of salvation.

"Verily, verily, I say unto thee, blessed art thou for what thou hast done; for thou hast inquired of me, and, behold, as often as thou hast inquired, thou hast received instruction of my spirit. If it had not been so, thou wouldst not have come to the place where thou art at this time.

"Behold, thou knowest that thou hast inquired of me, and I did enlighten thy mind; and now I tell thee these things, that thou mayest know that thou hast been enlightened by the spirit of truth; yea, I tell thee, that thou mayest know that there is none else save God, that knowest thy thoughts and the intents of thy heart: I tell thee these things as a witness unto thee that the words or the work which thou hast been writing is true.

"Therefore be diligent, stand by my servant Joseph, faithfully, in whatsoever difficult circumstances he may be for the word's sake. Admonish him in his faults, and also receive admonition of him. Be patient; be sober; be temperate; have patience, faith, hope, and charity.

"Behold, thou art Oliver, and I have spoken unto thee because of thy desires; therefore treasure up these words in thy heart. Be faithful and diligent in keeping the commandments of God, and I will encircle thee in the arms of my love.

"Behold, I am Jesus Christ, the Son of God. I am the same that came unto my own, and my own received me not. I am the light which shineth in darkness, and the darkness comprehendeth it not.

"Verily, verily, I say unto you, if you desire a further witness, cast your mind upon the night that you cried unto me in your heart, that you might know concerning the truth of these things. Did I not speak peace to your mind concerning the matter? What greater witness can you have than from God? And now, behold, you have received a witness, for if I have told you things which no man knoweth, have you not received a witness? And, behold, I grant unto you a gift, if you desire of me, to translate even as my servant Joseph.

"Verily, verily, I say unto you, that there are records which contain much of my gospel, which have been kept back because of the wickedness of the people; and now I command you, that if you have good desires—a desire to lay up treasures for yourself in heaven—then shall you assist in bringing to light, with your gift, those parts of my scriptures which have been hidden because of iniquity.

"And now, behold, I give unto you, and also unto my servant Joseph, the keys of this gift, which shall bring to light this ministry; and in the mouth of two or three witnesses shall every word be established.

"Verily, verily, I say unto you, if they reject my words, and this part of my gospel and ministry, blessed are ye, for they can do no more unto you than unto me; and if they do unto you, even as they have done unto me, blessed are ye, for you shall dwell with me in glory; but if they reject not my words, which shall be established by the testimony which shall be given, blessed are they, and then shall ye have joy in the fruit of your labours."—*Covenants and Commandments*, Sect. viii. §§ 5—14.

In another revelation it is said :

" Oliver Cowdery, verily, verily I say unto you, that assuredly as the Lord liveth, who is your God and your Redeemer, even so surely shall you receive a knowledge of whatsoever things you shall ask in faith, with an honest heart, believing that you shall receive a knowledge concerning the engravings of old records, which are ancient, which contain those parts of my scripture of which have been spoken by the manifestation of my spirit ; yea, behold, I will tell you in your mind and in your heart, by the Holy Ghost, which shall come upon you and which shall dwell in your heart. . . . . .

" Doubt not, for it is the gift of God, and you shall hold it in your hands, and do marvellous works ; and no power shall be able to take it away out of your hands, for it is the work of God. And, therefore, whatsoever you shall ask me to tell you, by that means that will I grant unto you, and you shall have knowledge concerning it: remember that without faith you can do nothing, therefore, ask in faith. Trifle not with these things : do not ask for that which you ought not : ask that you may know the mysteries of God, and that you may translate and receive knowledge from all those ancient records which have been hid up, that are sacred, and according to your faith shall it be done unto you. Behold, it is I that have spoken it ; and I am the same who spake unto you from the beginning. Amen."—*Covenants and Commandments*, Sect. xxxiv.

Lastly, the hope of becoming himself a translator, which the preceding "revelations" had raised, is dashed to the ground by another "revelation," still in April, 1829, which reduces him to the simple condition of *amanuensis.*

"Behold, I say unto you, my son, that because you did not translate according to that which you desired of me, and did commence again to write for my servant, Joseph Smith, jun., even so I would that ye should continue until you have finished this record, which I have intrusted unto him : and then, behold, other records have I, that I will give unto you power that you may assist to translate.

" Be patient, my son, for it is wisdom in me, and it is not expedient that you should translate at this present time. Behold, the work which you are called to do, is to write for my servant Joseph ;. and, behold, it is because that you did not continue as you commenced, when you began to translate, that I have taken away this privilege from you. Do not murmur, my son, for it is wisdom in me that I have dealt with you after this manner.

"Behold, you have not understood ; you have supposed that I would give it unto you, when you took no thought, save it was to ask me; but, behold, I say unto you, that you must study it out in your mind; then you must ask me if it be right, and if it is right I will cause that your bosom shall burn within you; therefore, you shall feel that it is right; but if it be not right, you shall have no such feelings, but you shall have a stupor of thought, that shall cause you to forget the thing which is wrong: therefore you cannot write that which is sacred, save it be given you from me.

" Now if you had known this, you could have translated; nevertheless, it is not expedient that you should translate now. Behold, it was expedient when you commenced, but you feared and the time is past, and it is not expedient now: for, do ye not behold that I have given unto my servant Joseph sufficient strength, whereby it is made up; and neither of you have I condemned.

" Do this thing which I have commanded you, and you shall prosper. Be faithful, and yield to no temptation. Stand fast in the work wherewith I have called you, and a hair of your head shall not be lost, and you shall be lifted up at the last day. Amen."—*Covenants and Commandments*, Sect. xxxv.

The work was now resumed, Harris and Cowdery acting as assistants; and in the mean time " revelations " were given to various other parties, several of whom appear afterwards among the first founders and leaders of the sect. They are much of the same character, partly almost in the same words, consisting of announcements of the " great and marvellous work " about to come forth, and of promises of spiritual endowments to the persons addressed, if they have a desire to assist in " bringing forth and establishing " it, and faith to believe in the word of the Lord by his prophet. The following, " given to David Whitmer," who, with Martin Harris and Oliver Cowdery, was chosen to fill up the number of three witnesses mentioned in Section xxxii., above quoted, may serve as a specimen :—

" A great and marvellous work is about to come forth unto the children of men. Behold, I am God, and give heed to my word, which is quick and powerful, sharper than a two-edged sword, to the dividing asunder of both joints and marrow; therefore give heed unto my word.

" Behold, the field is white already to harvest, therefore, whoso desireth to reap let him thrust in his sickle with his might and reap while the day lasts, that he may treasure up for his soul everlasting salvation in the kingdom of God; yea, whosoever will thrust in his sickle and reap, the same is called of God; therefore, if you will ask of me you shall receive, if you will knock it shall be opened unto you.

" Seek to bring forth and establish my Zion. Keep my commandments in all things; and if you keep my commandments and endure to the end, you shall have eternal life, which gift is the greatest of all the gifts of God.

"And it shall come to pass, that if you shall ask the Father in my name, in faith believing, you shall receive the Holy Ghost, which giveth utterance, that you may stand as a witness of the things of which you shall both hear and see, and also that you may declare repentance unto this generation.

"Behold, I am Jesus Christ, the Son of the living God, who created the heavens and the earth; a light which cannot be hid in darkness; wherefore I must bring forth the fulness of my gospel from the Gentiles unto the house of Israel. And behold, thou art David, and thou art called to assist; which thing if ye do, and are faithful, ye shall be blessed both spiritually and temporally, and great shall be your reward. Amen."—*Covenants and Commandments*, Sect. xxxix.

Shortly after, in the same month of June, 1829, the minds of the three witnesses were judged to be ripe for the operation of attesting their sight of that which they had not seen, and a "revelation" was given to the three conjointly.

"Behold, I say unto you, that you must *rely upon my word*, which if you do, with full purpose of heart, you shall have a view of the plates, and also of the breastplate, the sword of Laban, the Urim and Thummim, which were given to the brother of Jared upon the mount, when he talked with the Lord face to face, and the miraculous directors which were given to Lehi while in the wilderness, on the borders of the Red Sea; and it is *by your faith that you shall obtain a view of them*, even by that faith which was had by the prophets of old.

"And after that you have obtained faith, and have seen them with your eyes, *you shall testify of them, by the power of God;* and this you shall do *that my servant Joseph Smith, jun., may not be destroyed*, that I may bring about my righteous purposes unto the children of men in this work. And ye *shall testify that you have seen them,* EVEN AS MY SERVANT JOSEPH SMITH, JUN., HAS SEEN THEM, *for it is by my power that he hath seen them, and it is because he had faith;* and he has translated the book, even that part which I have commanded him, and as your Lord and your God liveth it is true.

"Wherefore you have received the same power, and the same faith, and the same gift like unto him; and if you do these last commandments of mine, which I have given you, the gates of hell shall not prevail against you; for my grace is sufficient for you, and you shall be lifted up at the last day. And I Jesus Christ, your Lord and your God, have spoken it unto you, that I might bring about my righteous purposes unto the children of men. Amen."—*Covenants and Commandments*, Sect. xlii.

Upon the strength of this "revelation," the prophet obtained, as an endorsement of his work, the following "Testimony of three Witnesses," which is appended or prefixed to all the editions of the Book of Mormon.

"Be it known unto all nations, kindreds, tongues, and people unto whom this work shall come, that we, through the grace of God the Father, and our Lord Jesus Christ, have seen the plates which contain this record, which is a record of the people of Nephi, and also of the Lamanites, their brethren, and also of the people of Jared, who came from the tower of which hath been spoken ; and *we also know that they have been translated by the gift and power of God, for his voice* (i. e. through Joseph Smith) *hath declared it unto us;* wherefore we know of a surety that the work is true. And we also testify that we have seen the engravings which are upon the plates; and *they have been shown unto us by the power of God, and not of man.* And we declare with words of soberness, that an Angel of God came down from heaven, and he brought and laid before our eyes, that we beheld and saw the plates, and the engravings thereon; and we know that it is by the grace of God the Father, and our Lord Jesus Christ, that we beheld and bear record that these things are true; and it is marvellous in our eyes, nevertheless *the voice of the Lord commanded us that we should bear record of it ;* wherefore, to be obedient unto the commandments of God, we bear testimony of these things. And we know that if we are faithful in Christ, we shall rid our garments of the blood of all men, and be found spotless before the judgment-seat of Christ, and shall dwell with him eternally in the heavens. And the honour be to the Father, and to the Son, and to the Holy Ghost, which is one God. Amen.

"OLIVER COWDERY,
DAVID WHITMER,
MARTIN HARRIS."

To this testimony that of eight other witnesses is added, who profess to have handled the plates, and seen the engravings thereon ; but their declaration is brought in without any account of the circumstances under which they were admitted to the sight of a treasure so long and so mysteriously guarded, and they were one and all intimately connected with Joseph Smith, and embarked in his scheme, which they hoped would have been a lucrative one. Besides, though their names continue to appear in the successive editions of the Book of Mormon, of the eleven witnesses six apostatised from the faith in Joseph's lifetime ; while of the other five three died before him, and two were his own brothers. No weight whatever, therefore, can attach to this attestation of the existence of the golden plates ; on the contrary, it makes rather against the authority of the prophet, since, in his " revelations," the number of persons who should be permitted to see the plates, is expressly limited to three. As regards the value of Harris's testimony, in particular, the following anecdote is conclusive :—

"On one occasion a sensible and religious gentleman in Palmyra put the following question to Harris : 'Did you see those plates ?' Harris replied, that he did. 'But did you see the plates and the engravings on them with your bodily eyes ?' Harris replied, 'Yes, I saw them with my eyes; they were shown unto me by the power of God, and not of man.' 'But did you see them with your natural, your bodily eyes, just as you see this pencil-case in my hand ? Now say *no* or *yes* to this.' Harris replied, 'I did not see them as I do that pencil-case, yet I saw them with the eye of faith; I saw them just as distinctly as I see any thing around me, though at the time they were covered over with a cloth.' "

It appears, indeed, pretty p a n that Harris was all along suspended between " faith" and ddubt, for it was not without difficulty that he was prevailed upon, when the translation was completed, to supply the necessary funds for defraying the printing expenses. To stimulate his flagging zeal, he was favoured, in March, 1830, with an alarming " revelation," which throws a singular light upon the footing on which Harris, the prophet, and, it would seem, the prophet's wife, were with each other at this time. We give the more important passages :—

"Behold, the mystery of Godliness, how great is it ? for, behold, I am endless, and the punishment which is given from my hand, is endless punishment, for endless is my name : wherefore—
        Eternal punishment is God's punishment.
        Endless punishment is God's punishment.
Wherefore I command you to repent, and keep the commandments which you have received by the hand of my servant Joseph Smith, jun., in my name; and it is by my Almighty power that you have received them ; therefore I command you to repent—repent, lest I smite you by the rod of my mouth, and by my wrath, and by my anger, and your sufferings be sore—how sore you know not ! how exquisite you know not ! yea, how hard to bear you know not ! . . . .

"And again, I command thee that *thou shalt not covet thy neighbour's wife; nor seek thy neighbour's life.* And again, I command thee that *thou shalt not covet thine own property, but impart it freely to the printing of the Book of Mormon,* which contains the truth and the word of God, which is my word to the Gentile, that soon it may go to the Jew, of whom the Lamanites are a remnant, that they may believe the gospel, and look not for a Messiah to come who has already come. . .

"Behold, this is a great and the last commandment which I shall give unto you concerning this matter ; for this shall suffice for thy daily walk, even unto the end of thy life. And misery thou shalt receive if thou wilt slight these counsels ; yea, even the destruction of thyself and property. *Impart a portion of thy property ; yea, even part of thy lands, and all save the support of thy family. Pay the debt thou hast contracted with the printer.* Release thyself from bondage. Leave thy house and home, except when thou shalt desire to see thy family ; and speak freely to all : yea, preach, exhort, declare the truth, even with a loud voice, with a sound of rejoicing, crying, Hosanna, hosanna! blessed be the name of the Lord God."—*Covenants and Commandments*, Sect. xliv. §§ 2, 3. 5.

This admonition produced the desired effect. Harris became both paymaster and witness for the Book of Mormon, and an elder of the Church. This, however, was only a beginning of what awaited him; for in August, 1831, when the settlement in Missouri had been determined on, and community of goods was made the law of the "Church," we have the following revelation concerning him :—

"It is wisdom in me that my servant Martin Harris should be an example unto the Church, in laying his monies before the bishop of the Church. And also, this is a law unto every man that cometh unto this land, to receive an inheritance; and he shall do with his monies according as the law directs. And it is wisdom also, that there should be lands purchased in Independence, for the place of the store-house, and also for the house of the printing.

"And other directions concerning my servant Martin Harris shall be given him of the spirit, that he may receive his inheritance as seemeth him good. And let him repent of his sins for he seeketh the praise of the world."—*Covenants and Commandments*, Sect. xviii. §§ 7, 8.

So great was the ascendancy which Joseph possessed over the mind of Harris, that in spite of all his misgivings, and of all his losses and disappointments, he continued with him until the year 1837, when the failure of the "Safety Society Bank," established by the prophet at Kirtland in Ohio, having swallowed up the remainder of his property, he returned in great disgust to Palmyra, and openly denounced Joseph as "a complete wretch[3]." But we must not anticipate.

Before we proceed with our history, it will be proper here to give a short account of the contents of the book which has made so much noise in the world, and of its probable origin. As regards its contents, it professes to be the history of the descendants of one Lehi of the tribe of Joseph, who emigrated from Jerusalem in the days of Zedekiah, with his four sons, one of whom, Nephi, was a great prophet. After many perils by land and by sea, they reached the continent of America, where they divided into two great families, the Nephites or white men, and the Lamanites or red men. Besides the history of these tribes of the ancient stock of Israel,—including an alleged descent of Christ upon the American Continent, after his ascension from Mount Olivet,—the

[3] Caswall's Prophet of the Nineteenth Century, p. 129.

book contains a variety of prophetical matter. Nephi foretells,
with astonishing minuteness, not only the coming of the Messiah,
but the history of the Christian Church during the first four centuries.   Another great prophet, Mormon by name, nearly a
thousand years after Nephi, and four hundred years after Christ,
acts the part of Ezra, by collecting the plates on which the records
and documents of his race are engraved, and completing the
golden Bible ; which is deposited after his death by his son Moroni
under the hill, where, 1427 years after, by direction of the Angel,
it is found by Joseph Smith, in fulfilment of the Scripture prophecy, that " truth shall spring out of the earth⁴."
      With regard to the real origin of this book, we cannot do
better than transcribe from the " Boston Weekly Messenger" of
May 1st, 1839, the following document which, with remarkable
simplicity and manifest truthfulness, tells its own tale :—

ORIGIN OF THE "BOOK OF MORMON," OR "GOLDEN BIBLE."

      " As this book has excited much attention, and has been put by a
certain new sect, in the place of the Sacred Scriptures, I deem it a duty
which I owe to the public, to state what I know touching its origin.
That its claims to a Divine origin are wholly unfounded, needs no proof
to a mind unperverted by the grossest delusions.   That any sane person
should rank it higher than any other merely human composition, is a
matter of the greatest astonishment ; yet it is received as Divine by
some who dwell in enlightened New England, and even by those who
have sustained the character of devoted Christians.   Learning recently
that Mormonism has found its way into a church in Massachusetts, and
has impregnated some of its members with its gross delusions, so that
excommunication has become necessary, I am determined to delay no
longer doing what I can to strip the mask from this monster of sin, and
to lay open this pit of abominations.
      " Rev. Solomon Spaulding, to whom I was united in marriage in
early life, was a graduate of Dartmouth College, and was distinguished
for a lively imagination and a great fondness for history.   At the time
of our marriage, he resided in Cherry Valley, New York.   From this
place we removed to New Salem, Ashtabula county, Ohio ; sometimes
called Conneaut, as it is situated upon Conneaut Creek.   Shortly after
our removal to this place, his health sunk, and he was laid aside from
active labours.   In the town of New Salem, there are numerous mounds,
and forts, supposed by many to be the dilapidated dwellings and forti-
fications of a race now extinct.   These ancient relics arrest the attention
of the new settlers, and become objects of research for the curious.
Numerous implements were found, and other articles evincing great
skill in the arts.   Mr. Spaulding being an educated man, and pas-

---

⁴ For fuller particulars we refer our readers to Caswall's Prophet of the
Nineteenth Century, which, in an " Appendix," contains a copious epitome of the
Book of Mormon.

sionately fond of history, took a lively interest in these developments of antiquity; and in order to beguile the hours of retirement, and furnish employment for his lively imagination, he conceived the idea of giving *an historical sketch of this long lost race.* Their extreme antiquity of course would lead him to write in *the most ancient style,* and as the Old Testament is the most ancient book in the world, he imitated its style as nearly as possible. His sole object in writing this *historical romance* was to amuse himself and his neighbours. This was about the year 1812. Hull's surrender at Detroit occurred near the same time, and I recollect the date well from that circumstance. As he progressed in his narrative, the neighbours would come in from time to time to hear portions read, and a great interest in the work was excited among them. It claimed to have been written by *one of the lost nation,* and to have b. en *recovered from the earth,* and assumed the title of ' Manuscript Found.' The neighbours would often inquire how Mr. S. progressed in deciphering ' the manuscript,' and when he had a sufficient portion prepared he would inform them, and they would assemble to hear it read. He was enabled, from his acquaintance with the classics and ancient history, to introduce *many singular names,* which were particularly noticed by the people, and could be easily recognized by them. Mr. Solomon Spaulding had a brother, Mr. John Spaulding, residing in the place at the time, who was perfectly familiar with this work, and repeatedly heard the whole of it read.

"From New Salem we removed to Pittsburgh, Pa. Here Mr. S. found an acquaintance and friend, in the person of Mr. Patterson, an editor of a newspaper. He exhibited his manuscript to Mr. P., who was very much pleased with it, and borrowed it for perusal. He retained it a long time, and informed Mr. S. that, if he would make out a title-page and preface, he would publish it, and it might be a source of profit. This Mr. S. refused to do, for reasons which I cannot now state. Sidney Rigdon, who has figured so largely in the history of the Mormons, was at this time connected with the printing-office of Mr. Patterson, as is well known in that region, and as Rigdon himself has frequently stated. Here he had ample opportunity to become acquainted with Mr. Spaulding's manuscript, and to copy it if he chose. It was a matter of notoriety and interest to all who were connected with the printing establishment. At length the manuscript was returned to its author, and soon after we removed to Amity, Washington county, Pa., where Mr. S. deceased in 1816. The manuscript then fell into my hands, and was carefully preserved. It has frequently been examined by my daughter, Mrs. Mc Kenstry, of Monson, Massachusetts, with whom I now reside, and by other friends. After the 'Book of Mormon' came out, a copy of it was taken to New Salem, the place of Mr. Spaulding's former residence, and the very place where the 'Manuscript Found' was written. A woman preacher appointed a meeting there, and in the meeting read and repeated copious extracts from the 'Book of Mormon.' The historical part was immediately recognized by all the older inhabitants, as the identical work of Mr. S., in which they had been so deeply interested years before. Mr. John Spaulding was present, who is an eminently pious man, and *recognised perfectly* the work of his brother. He was amazed and afflicted, that it should have been perverted to so wicked a purpose. His grief found vent in a flood of tears, and he arose on the spot and expressed in the meeting his deep sorrow and regret that the writings of his sainted brother should be used for a purpose so vile and shocking. The excitement in New Salem became so great, that the inhabitants had a meeting, and deputed Dr. Philastus Hurlbut, one of their number, to repair to this place, and to obtain from me the original manuscript of Mr. Spaulding, for the purpose of comparing it with the Mormon Bible, to satisfy their own minds and to prevent their friends from embracing an error so delusive. This was in the year 1834. Dr. Hurlbut brought with him an introduction and request for the manuscript, signed by Messrs. Henry Lake, Aaron Wright, and others, with all whom I was acquainted, as they were my neighbours when I resided in New Salem.

"I am sure that nothing could grieve my husband more, were he living, than the use which has been made of his work. The air of antiquity which was thrown about the composition, doubtless suggested the idea of converting it to purposes of delusion. Thus an historical romance, with the addition of a few pious expressions and extracts from the Sacred Scriptures, has been construed into a new Bible, and palmed off upon a company of poor deluded fanatics, as Divine. I have given the previous brief narration, that this work of deep deception and wickedness may be searched to the foundation, and its author exposed to the contempt and execration he so justly deserves.

"MATILDA DAVISON.

"Rev. Solomon Spaulding was the first husband of the narrator of the above history. Since his decease, she has been married to a second husband by the name of Davison. She is now residing in this place; is a woman of irreproachable character, and an humble Christian, and her testimony is worthy of implicit confidence.

"A. ELY, D.D., Pastor Cong. Church in Monson.
"D. R. AUSTIN, Principal of Monson Academy.
"*Monson, Mass.*, April 1st, 1839."

· The story told by Mrs. Davison has since been the subject of careful investigation by other parties interested in unmasking the Mormonite imposture, and has not only been found correct, but has been confirmed by many circumstantial details, which those of our readers who may feel curious on the subject, will find briefly recorded in the second chapter of Mr. Caswall's "Prophet of the Nineteenth Century." For our present purpose it suffices to have authenticated the quarter from which Joseph Smith derived the materials of a work, which he was by no means qualified by his education to compose. Nor can there be much doubt left as to the medium through which the book found its way out of the printing-office at Pittsburg into the hands of Joseph Smith. There is a name mentioned in Mrs. Davison's narrative, which figures conspicuously, as we shall presently see, in the history of Mormonism; and the fact that the party in question, Sidney Rigdon, did not himself advance the forgery, but employed for this purpose Joseph Smith, a loose vagabond, whom his habits and occupation as a money-digger pointed out as a proper person for so audacious an attempt to impose upon the public, only proves the deep cunning with which the scheme was contrived. The pretended translation from behind the curtain, of which Martin Harris was made the dupe, was nothing more than a dictation of Spaulding's romance, with such alterations and embellishments as would suit the particular purpose which the two confederates—for such Sidney Rigdon and Joseph Smith doubtless were at this early period—had in view. The fact that the prediction of the discovery of the " golden plates," by a prophet in the latter days occurs in the " books of Nephi," substituted for the 116 pages which had been abstracted, is a critical circumstance. Joseph having interlarded Spaulding's manuscript with his predictions of himself in the character of a great prophet, could not venture to reproduce the same matter, as the least discrepancy between his first and second " translation" would have proved fatal to his whole device. Hence the delay of ten months, during which, in all probability, Smith was not only engaged in endeavouring to recover the lost manuscript, but in secret communication with Rigdon, as to the best way of extricating himself from the dilemma in which he found himself so unexpectedly placed.

The prophecy, itself, which points to Joseph Smith, jun., the Son of Joseph Smith, sen., the head of the Mormonite Sect, is to be found in the 2nd chapter of the 2nd Book of Nephi, and consists of a prediction said to have been uttered by Joseph, the Son of Israel, and recounted by Nephi to his youngest son, whose name was also Joseph. It runs thus:—

" Joseph truly testified, saying : A seer shall the Lord my God raise up, who shall be a choice seer unto the fruit of my loins. Yea, Joseph truly said, thus saith the Lord unto me : A choice seer will I raise up out of the fruit of thy loins; and he shall be esteemed highly among the fruit of thy loins. And unto him will I give commandment, that he shall do a work for the fruit of thy loins, his brethren, which shall be of great worth unto them, even to the bringing of them to the knowledge of the covenants which I have made with thy fathers. And I will give unto him a commandment, that he shall do none other work, save the work which I shall command him. And I will make him great in mine eyes; for he shall do my work. And he shall be great like unto Moses, whom I have said I would raise up unto you, to deliver my people, O house of Israel. And Moses will I raise up, to deliver thy people out of the land of Egypt. But a seer will I raise up out of the fruit of thy loins; and unto him will I give power to bring forth my word unto the seed of thy loins; and not to the bringing forth my word only, saith the Lord, but to the convincing them of my word, which shall have already gone forth among them. Wherefore, the fruit of thy loins shall write; and the fruit of the loins of Judah shall write; and that which shall be written by the fruit of thy loins, and also that which shall be written by the fruit of the loins of Judah, shall grow together, unto the confounding of false doctrines, and laying down of contentions, and establishing peace among the fruit of thy loins, and bringing them to the knowledge of their fathers in the latter days; and also to the knowledge of my covenants, saith the Lord. And out of weakness he shall be made strong, in that day when my work shall commence among all my people, unto the restoring thee, O house of Israel, saith the Lord. And thus prophesied Joseph, saying: Behold, that seer will the Lord bless; and they that seek to destroy him, shall be confounded; for this promise, of which I have obtained of the Lord, of the fruit of my loins, shall be fulfilled. Behold, I am sure of the fulfilling of this promise. And his name shall be called after me; and it shall be after the name of his father. And he shall be like unto me; for the thing which the Lord shall bring forth by his hand, by the power of the Lord shall bring my people unto salvation; yea, thus prophesied Joseph, I am sure of this thing, even as I am sure of the promise of Moses; for the Lord hath said unto me, I will preserve thy seed for ever. And the Lord hath said, I will raise up a Moses; and I will give power unto him in a rod; and I will give judgment unto him in writing. Yet I will not loose his tongue, that he shall speak much; for I will not make him mighty in speaking. But I will write unto him my law, by the finger of mine own hand; and I will make a spokesman for him. And the Lord said unto me also, I will raise up unto the fruit of thy loins; and I will make for him a spokesman. And I, behold, I will give unto him, that he shall write the writing of the fruit of thy loins, unto the fruit of thy loins; and the spokesman of thy loins shall declare it. And the words which he shall write, shall be the words which are expedient in my wisdom should go forth unto the fruit of thy loins. And it shall be as if the fruit of thy loins had cried unto them from the dust; for I know their faith. And they shall cry from the dust; yea, even repentance unto thy brethren, even after many generations have gone by them. And it shall come to pass that their cry shall go, even according to the simpleness of their words. Because of their faith, their words shall proceed forth out of my mouth unto their brethren, who are the fruit of thy loins; and the weakness of their words will I make strong in their faith, unto the remembering of my covenant which I made unto thy fathers."

The latter part of this "prophecy" seems to point to Sidney Rigdon, the position assigned to him in it tallying exactly with that which he occupied afterwards by "revelation" in the Church of Latter Day Saints. Further on, in the eleventh chapter of the same book, another prophecy is introduced, which bears directly upon the discovery and translation of the "Golden Bible" by the prophet Joseph :—

"But behold, I prophesy unto you concerning the last days ; concerning the days when the Lord God shall bring these things forth unto the children of men. After my seed and the seed of my brethren shall have dwindled in unbelief, and shall have been smitten by the Gentiles ; yea, after the Lord God shall have camped against them round about, and shall have laid siege against them with a mount, and raised forts against them ; and after they shall have been brought down low in the dust, even that they are not, yet the words of the righteous shall be written, and the prayers of the faithful shall be heard, and all those who have dwindled in unbelief, shall not be forgotten ; for those who shall be destroyed shall speak unto them out of the ground, and their speech shall be low out of the dust, and their voice shall be as one that hath a familiar spirit ; for the Lord God will give unto him power, that he may whisper concerning them, even as it were out of the ground ; and their speech shall whisper out of the dust. For thus saith the Lord God : They shall write the things which shall be done among them, and they shall be written and sealed up in a book, and those who have dwindled in unbelief, shall not have them, for they seek to destroy the things of God : wherefore, as those who have been destroyed, have been destroyed speedily ; and the multitude of their terrible ones, shall be as chaff that passeth away. Yea, thus saith the Lord God : It shall be at an instant, suddenly."

The people upon whom this destruction fell, were the builders of the ancient cities, the ruins of which put the first idea of the old romance into the head of Spaulding ; they are the "Nephites" of the fiction, whose records are upon the golden plates. After a sally against all the sects of Christendom, (among which the Church is of course not forgotten,) the "prophecy" thus proceeds :—

"And it shall come to pass, that the Lord God shall bring forth unto you the words of a book, and they shall be the words of them which have slumbered. And behold the book shall be sealed : and in the book shall be a revelation from God, from the beginning of the world to the ending thereof. Wherefore, because of the things which are sealed up, the things which are sealed shall not be delivered in the day of the wickedness and abominations of the people. Wherefore the book shall be kept from them. But the book shall be delivered unto a man, and he shall deliver the words of the book, which are the words of those who have slumbered in the dust ; and he shall deliver these

words unto another; but the words which are sealed he shall not
deliver, neither shall he deliver the book.   For the book shall
be sealed by the power of God, and the revelation which was sealed
shall be kept in the book until the own due time of the Lord, that
they may come forth : for behold, they reveal all things from the foundation of the world unto the end thereof.   And the day cometh that
the words of the book which were sealed shall be read upon the house-
tops ; and they shall be read by the power of Christ : and all things
shall be revealed unto the children of men which ever have been among
the children of men, and which ever will be, even unto the end of the
earth.   Wherefore, at that day when the book shall be delivered unto
the man of whom I have spoken, the book shall be hid from the eyes of
the world, that the eyes of none shall behold it, save it be that three
witnesses shall behold it, by the power of God, besides him to whom
the book shall be delivered; and they shall testify to the truth of the
book and the things therein.   And there is none other which shall view
it, save it be a few, according to the will of God, to bear testimony of
his word unto the children of men : for the Lord God hath said, that
the words of the faithful should speak as if it were from the dead.
Wherefore, the Lord God will proceed to bring forth the words of the
book ; and in the mouth of as many witnesses as seemeth him good,
will he establish his word ; and wo be unto him that rejecteth the word
of God."

A similar prophecy is placed on record by Moroni, the son of
Mormon, in the fourth chapter of that portion of the whole col-
lection called the " Book of Mormon," to which the title " The
Book of Mormon " specially belongs.

"I am the son of Mormon, and my father was a descendant of
Nephi ; and I am the same who hideth up this record unto the Lord;
the plates thereof are of no worth, because of the commandment of the
Lord.   For he truly saith, that no one shall have them to get gain ;
but the record thereof is of great worth ; and whoso shall bring it to
light, him will the Lord bless, For none can have power to bring it to
light, save it be given him of God ; for God will that it shall be done
with an eye single to his glory, or the welfare of the ancient and long
dispersed covenant people of the Lord.   And blessed be him that shall
bring this thing to light; for it shall be brought out of darkness unto
light, according to the word of God ; yea, it shall be brought out of the
earth, and it shall shine forth out of darkness, and come unto the knowledge of the people ; and it shall be done by the power of God ; and if
there be faults, they be the faults of a man.   But behold, we know no
fault.   Nevertheless, God knoweth all things ; therefore he that con-
demneth, let him be aware lest he shall be in danger of hell-fire.
And he that sayeth, show unto me, or ye shall be smitten, let him
beware lest he commandeth that which is forbidden of the Lord."

To these " prophecies " we shall add one more extract from

the twelfth chapter of the second book of Nephi, which defines
the position assigned to the "Book of Mormon" relative to the
Holy Scriptures.

"Behold, there shall be many at that day, when I shall proceed to do
a marvellous work among them, that I may remember my covenants
which I have made unto the children of men, that I may set my hand
again the second time to recover my people, which are of the house of
Israel; and also, that I may remember the promises which I have
made unto thee, Nephi, and also unto thy father, that I would remember your seed; and that the words of your seed should proceed
forth out of my mouth unto your seed. And my words shall hiss forth
unto the ends of the earth, for a standard unto my people, which are
of the house of Israel. And because my words shall hiss forth, many
of the Gentiles shall say, a Bible, a Bible, we have got a Bible, and
there cannot be any more Bible. But, thus saith the Lord God: O
fools, they shall have a Bible; and it shall proceed forth from the Jews,
mine ancient covenant people. And what thank they the Jews for the
Bible which they receive from them? Yea, what do the Gentiles
mean? Do they remember the travels, and the labours, and the pains
of the Jews, and their diligence unto me, in bringing forth salvation
unto the Gentiles?

"O ye Gentiles, have ye remembered the Jews, mine ancient covenant
people? nay, but ye have cursed them, and have hated them, and have
not sought to recover them. But behold, I will return all these things
upon your own heads: for I the Lord, hath not forgotten my people.
Thou fool, that shall say, a Bible, we have got a Bible, and we need no
more Bible. Have ye obtained a Bible, save it were by the Jews?
Know ye not that there are more nations than one? Know ye not
that I the Lord your God, have created all men, and that I remember
those who are upon the isles of the sea; and that I rule in the heavens
above, and in the earth beneath; and I bring forth my word unto the
children of men, yea, even upon all the nations of the earth? Wherefore murmur ye, because that ye shall receive more of my word?
Know ye not that the testimony of two nations is a witness unto you
that I am God, that I remember one nation like unto another?
Wherefore, I speak the same words unto one nation like unto another.
And when the two nations shall run together, the testimony of the two
nations shall run together also. And I do this that I may prove unto
many, that I am the same yesterday, to-day, and for ever; and that I
speak forth my words according to mine own pleasure. And because
that I have spoken one word, ye need not suppose that I cannot speak
another; for my work is not yet finished; neither shall it be, until the
end of man; neither from that time henceforth and for ever.

"Wherefore, because that ye have a Bible, ye need not suppose that it
contains all my words; neither need ye suppose that I have not caused
more to be written: for I command all men, both in the east, and in
the west, and in the north, and in the south, and in the islands of the

sea, that they shall write the words which I speak unto them: for out of the books which shall be written, I will judge the world, every man according to their works, according to that which is written. For, behold, I shall speak unto the Jews, and they shall write it; and I shall also speak unto the Nephites, and they shall write it; and I shall also speak unto the other tribes of the house of Israel, which I have led away, and they shall write it; and I shall also speak unto all nations of the earth, and they shall write it.

" And it shall come to pass that the Jews shall have the words of the Nephites, and the Nephites shall have the words of the Jews; and the Nephites and the Jews shall have the words of the lost tribes of Israel; and the lost tribes of Israel shall have the words of the Nephites and the Jews.

" And it shall come to pass that my people which are of the house of Israel, shall be gathered home unto the lands of their possessions; and my word also shall be gathered in one [s]. And I will show unto them that fight against my word and against my people, who are of the house of Israel, that I am God, and that I covenanted with Abraham that I would remember his seed for ever."

We now resume the thread of our history. The translation from the " Golden Plates," or the " Book of Mormon," being at last completed, and printed at the expense of Martin Harris, the prophet deemed that the time was now come for organizing a " Church." As far back as June, 1829, a " revelation " had been " given to Joseph Smith, jun., Oliver Cowdery, and David Whitmer," directing them to look out twelve men fit to be chosen as apostles, and announcing other measures preparatory to the " building up the Church of Christ, according to the fulness of the gospel." Another " revelation " to the same purpose, followed in April of the following year:

" The rise of the Church of Christ in these last days, being one thousand eight hundred and thirty years since the coming of our Lord and Saviour Jesus Christ in the flesh, it being regularly organized and established *agreeably to the laws of our country*, by the will and commandments of God, in the fourth month, and on the sixth day of the month which is called April; which commandments were given to Joseph Smith, jun., who was called of God, and ordained an apostle of Jesus Christ, to be the first elder of this church: and to Oliver Cowdery, who was also called of God, an apostle of Jesus Christ, to be the second elder of this church, and ordained under his hand; and this according to the grace of our Lord and Saviour Jesus Christ, to whom be all glory, both now and for ever. Amen.

[s] In like manner Christ is made to say, in the Book of Doctrine and Covenants, " The Book of Mormon and the Holy Scriptures are given of me for your instruction."—Sect. lv. § 3.

"After it was truly manifested unto this first elder that he had received a remission of his sins, he was entangled again in the vanities of the world; but after repenting, and humbling himself sincerely, through faith, God ministered unto him by an holy angel, whose countenance was as lightning, and whose garments were pure and white above all other whiteness; and gave unto him commandments which inspired him; and gave him power from on high, by the means which were before prepared, to translate the Book of Mormon, which contains a record of a fallen people, and the fulness of the Gospel of Jesus Christ to the Gentiles and to the Jews also, which was given by inspiration, and is confirmed to others by the ministering of angels, and is declared unto the world by them, proving to the world that the Holy Scriptures are true, and that God does inspire men and call them to his holy work in this age and generation, as well as in generations of old, thereby showing that he is the same God yesterday, to-day, and for ever. Amen.

"Therefore, having so great witnesses, by them shall the world be judged, even as many as shall hereafter come to a knowledge of this work; and those who receive it in faith, and work righteousness, shall receive a crown of eternal life; but those who harden their hearts in unbelief, and reject it, it shall turn to their own condemnation, for the Lord God has spoken it; and we, the elders of the church, have heard and bear witness to the words of the glorious Majesty on high, to whom be glory for ever and ever. Amen."—*Covenants and Commandments*, Sect. ii. §§ 1—3.

Then follows a short account, after Joseph's own manner, of the creation, the fall, the Old Testament, the coming of Christ, and the Christian dispensation, ending with the appointment of baptism, as the means of entrance into the Mormon "Church." After this, we have an outline of the constitution of the "Church," of the functions of her several ministers and members, and of the sacraments and ordinances. Baptism is to be ministered by immersion, but only to those who have reached the age of "accountability," which is fixed at eight years[*]. A difficulty having arisen from the wish of some persons to join the Church, who were, nevertheless, unwilling to be rebaptized, the question was settled by a special "revelation," which declared that

"Although a man should be baptized a hundred times, it availeth him nothing, for you cannot enter in at the strait gate by the law of Moses, neither by your dead works,"

and commanded them to—

"Enter in at the gate, as I have commanded, and seek not to counsel your god."—*Covenants and Commandments*, Sect. xlvii.

[*] Covenants and Commandments, Sect. xxii. § 4.

A special form is given for the administration of the Lord's Supper, but this is subsequently modified by a "revelation" which declares the use of the proper elements of the sacrament to be immaterial :

"Behold, I say unto you, that *it mattereth not what ye shall eat, or what ye shall drink, when ye partake of the sacrament,* if it so be that ye do it with an eye single to my glory; remembering unto the Father my body which was laid down for you, and my blood which was shed for the remission of your sins : wherefore, a commandment I give unto you, that you shall not purchase wine, neither strong drink of your enemies : wherefore, you shall partake of none, except it is made new among you; yea, in this my Father's kingdom which shall be built upon the earth."—*Covenants and Commandments,* Sect. 1. § 1.

The Church being constituted—at Manchester, State of New York—the prophet next had a "revelation," appointing himself to the prophetic office, and providing for his own ordination by one of the three witnesses :

"Behold there shall be a record kept among you, and in it *thou shalt be called a seer, a translator, a prophet, an apostle of Jesus Christ, an elder of the church through the will of God the Father, and the grace of your Lord Jesus Christ, being inspired of the Holy Ghost to lay the foundation thereof, and to build it up unto the most holy faith,* which church was organized and established in the year of your Lord eighteen hundred and thirty, in the fourth month, and on the sixth day of the month, which is called April.

"Wherefore, *meaning the church, thou shalt give heed unto all his words and commandments, which he shall give unto you as he receiveth them,* walking in all holiness before me ; for *his word ye shall receive, as if from mine own mouth,* in all patience and faith ; for by doing these things the gates of hell shall not prevail against you ; yea, and the Lord God will disperse the powers of darkness from before you, and cause the heavens to shake for your good, and his name's glory. For thus saith the Lord God, him have I inspired to move the cause of Zion in mighty power for good, and his diligence I know, and his prayers I have heard, yea, his weeping for Zion I have seen, and I will cause that he shall mourn for her no longer, for his days of rejoicing are come unto the remission of his sins, and the manifestations of my blessings upon his works.

"For, behold, I will bless all those who labour in my vineyard with a mighty blessing, and *they shall believe on his words, which are given him through me by the Comforter,* which manifesteth that Jesus was crucified by sinful men for the sins of the world, yea, for the remission of sins unto the contrite heart. Wherefore, *it behoveth me that he should be ordained by you, Oliver Cowdery, mine apostle :* this being an ordinance unto you, that *you are an elder under his hand, he being the first unto you,* that you might be an elder unto this church of Christ, bearing my name, and the first preacher of this church unto the church, and before the world, yea, before the Gentiles; yea, and thus saith the Lord God, lo, lo! to the Jews also. Amen."—*Covenants and Commandments,* Sect. xlvi.

Another "revelation" shortly after made provision for the temporal necessities of the prophet, while confirming his alleged inspiration:—

"Magnify thine office; and after thou hast sowed thy fields and secured them, go speedily unto the church which is in Colesville, Fayette, and Manchester, and *they shall support thee;* and I will bless them both spiritually and temporally; but if they receive thee not, I will send upon them a cursing instead of a blessing.

"And thou shalt continue in calling upon God in my name, and writing the things which shall be given thee by the Comforter, and expounding all scriptures unto the church; and it shall be given thee in the very moment what thou shalt speak and write, and they shall hear it, or I will send unto them a cursing instead of a blessing."—*Covenants and Commandments,* Sect. ix. § 2, 3.

And in September of the same year, 1830, a special "revelation" became necessary to repress rival claims to prophetic gifts. One Hiram Page, one of the eight witnesses, was instructed that "those things which he had written from that stone," were not of God, but that "Satan was deceiving him;" and to apostle Oliver himself, the wide distinction between himself and the prophet had to be pointed out:—

"Behold, verily, verily, I say unto thee, no one shall be appointed to receive commandments and revelations in this Church, excepting my servant Joseph Smith, jun., for he receiveth them even as Moses; and thou shalt be obedient unto the things which I shall give unto him, even as Aaron, to declare faithfully the commandments and the revelations, with power and authority unto the Church. And if thou art led at any time by the Comforter, to speak or teach, or at all times by the way of commandment unto the Church, thou mayest do it. But thou shalt not write by way of commandment, but by wisdom: and thou shalt not command him who is at thy head, and at the head of the Church, for I have given him the keys of the mysteries, and the revelations which are sealed, until I shall appoint unto them another in his stead."—*Covenants and Commandments,* Sect. li. § 2.

It would be an endless task to adduce the various "revelations" which now succeeded each other, all having for their object to enforce the prophet's behests in the Church, to consolidate his authority, to repress the claims of his accomplices in the fraud to a share of his power, and to dispose of intractable Church-officers by sending them forth on missionary excursions.

While the " Church" continued in Manchester and its vicinity, under the sole control of Joseph, he contrived to maintain his authority tolerably well. But a mighty change took place when, at the end of 1830, Sidney Rigdon's joint-authority was brought into play. His introduction to the Church was most skilfully managed by means of a mission to Kirtland, Ohio, where Rigdon was presiding over a congregation of Campbellite Baptists. On the new doctrine of the Book of Mormon being preached to them, a number of the Campbellites, and among them Rigdon himself, were converted, and received baptism at the hands of Joseph's emissaries. This was followed by a visit from Rigdon to the " Church" at Manchester, when this " revelation" was " given to Joseph Smith and Sidney Rigdon," in December, 1830 :—

" Behold, verily, verily, I say unto my servant Sidney, I have looked upon thee and thy works. I have heard thy prayers, and prepared thee for a greater work. Thou art blessed, for thou shalt do great things. Behold thou wast sent forth, even as John, to prepare the way before me, and before Elijah which should come, and thou knewest it not. Thou didst baptize by water unto repentance, but they received not the Holy Ghost; but now I give unto thee a commandment, that thou shalt baptize by water, and they shall receive the Holy Ghost by the laying on of thy hands, even as the apostles of old."
—*Covenants and Commandments,* Sect. xi. § 2.

Soon after this, at the beginning of the year 1831, the head-quarters of the " Church" were removed to Kirtland, and from this time forward the " revelations" assume a fuller and more ambitious character, which evidently bespeaks the influence of a thorough man of business, more highly educated, and more deeply versed in the Scriptures than Joseph. One Edward Partridge, a creature of Rigdon's, who had come with him from Kirtland to Manchester, and returned thither in his and Joseph's company, was by " revelation" appointed " Bishop;" an office which had regard rather to the ecclesiastical government of the " Church," and the management of her temporalities, than to spiritual oversight, and which rendered him at times very obnoxious to Smith, as several of the " revelations" testify. With Rigdon, too, there appears to have been sharp conflicts, which were composed on one occasion by a " revelation," dividing the blame between them[7]. Rigdon, however, soon attained to an equality of power with the prophet, and one of the visions, which sets forth the three states, the celestial, terrestrial, and telestial, runs in their joint names[8]. At one time Joseph Smith and

[7] Covenants and Commandments, Sect. lxxxiii. §§ 7, 8.
[8] Ibid. Sect. xcii. § 3.

Sidney Rigdon saw fit to send away all the elders from the "Church," on different missions, "two and two," that they should "teach the principles of the gospel, which are in the Bible and in the Book of Mormon, in the which is the fulness of the gospel," with a special injunction to "observe the covenants and church articles to do them." And all this they are bidden to

"Observe to do as I have commanded concerning your teaching, until the fulness of my scriptures are (*sic!*) given[9]."

The expression, the "fulness of my scriptures," has reference to a new translation of the Bible which had been taken in hand, probably as the suggestion of Rigdon, but the execution of which, except the publication of a few fragments, was apparently prevented by subsequent occurrences and by the want of funds.

On the 17th of February, 1834, the "Church" which had been going on increasing was finally "organized by revelation," when Joseph Smith, Sidney Rigdon, and R. G. Williams were acknowledged presidents. A council was appointed to assist them in the administration of its affairs, and a regular staff of resident and travelling officers, whose respective duties and relative positions were accurately defined[1]. A costly temple was erected, as well as private residences for Smith and Rigdon, who having possessed themselves of the surplus wealth of their converts, launched out into a multiplicity of enterprises, and among others established a "Safety Society Bank," which proved eventually the ruin of the Mormon cause in the State of Ohio. Of these transactions few traces are to be found in the "revelations" given at this period; the history of them is chiefly derived from the opponents of the Mormons; and as it lies out of the way of our more immediate object, we shall refer our readers once more to Mr. Caswall's book for information[2].

Long, however, before the removal of the "Saints" from Kirtland became a matter of necessity, in consequence of the failure of the bank, under circumstances of great disgrace, a scheme had been formed for the establishment of a much larger settlement than any this sect had as yet had, Farther West. As early as June, 1831, a "revelation" was given, pointing to certain land in Missouri, as land "to be consecrated to the Lord's people."

"If ye are faithful, ye shall assemble yourselves together to rejoice upon the land of Missouri, which is *the land of your inheritance*, which

---

[9] Covenants and Commandments, Sect. xiii. § 2, 5.
[1] Ibid. Sect. v.
[2] Prophet of the Nineteenth Century, chap. vii. viii.

is near the land of your enemies. But, behold, I the Lord will hasten the city in its time, and will crown the faithful with joy and with rejoicings."—*Covenants and Commandments*, Sect. lxvi. § 9.

An assembly of elders was convened, on the ground which it was intended hereafter to occupy, and which was now declared to be the proper location for the city of Zion, and the great temple that should be built [2]. At this time,—August 1831,—the idea of acquiring the land otherwise than by purchase, though probably broached, received no countenance :—

" Behold, this is the will of the Lord your God concerning his Saints, that they should assemble themselves together unto the land of Zion, not in haste, lest there should be confusion, which bringeth pestilence. Behold, the land of Zion, I, the Lord, holdeth it in mine own hands; nevertheless, I the Lord, rendereth unto Cæsar the things which are Cæsar's : wherefore, I, the Lord, willeth that you should purchase the lands that you may have advantage of the world, that you may have claim on the world, that they may not be stirred up unto anger; for Satan putteth it into their hearts to anger against you, and to the shedding of blood; wherefore the land of Zion shall not be obtained but by purchase or by blood, otherwise there is none inheritance for you. And if by purchase, behold you are blessed; and if by blood, as you are forbidden to shed blood, lo, your enemies are upon you, and ye shall be scourged from city to city, and from synagogue to synagogue, and but few shall stand to receive an inheritance."—*Covenants and Commandments*, Sect. xx. § 8.

In the following year, 1832, a formal promise of the restoration of Zion, the erection of the New Jerusalem in Missouri, was given by " revelation :"—

" A revelation of Jesus Christ unto his servant Joseph Smith, jun., and six elders, as they united their hearts and lifted their voices on high ; yea, the word of the Lord concerning his Church, established in the last days for the restoration of his people, as He has spoken by the mouth of his prophets, and for the gathering of his saints to stand upon mount Zion, which shall be the city New Jerusalem, which city shall be built, beginning at the temple lot, which is appointed by the finger of the Lord, in the western boundaries of the state of Missouri, and dedicated by the hand of Joseph Smith, jun., and others with whom the Lord was well pleased.
" Verily this is the word of the Lord, that the city New Jerusalem shall be built by the gathering of the saints beginning at this place, even the place of the temple, which temple shall be reared in this generation ; for verily, this generation shall not all pass away until an house shall be built unto the Lord, and a cloud shall rest upon it,

---

[2] Covenants and Commandments, Sect. xxvii. § 1.

which cloud shall be even the glory of the Lord, which shall fill the house."—*Covenants and Commandments,* Sect. iv. § 1, 2.

And in the month of December, 1833, a commandment went forth for a general gathering in all the churches in every part of the world, in order to collect funds for " the redemption of Zion [4]."

How far the investments in Missouri may have helped to embarrass the finances of the " Church" at Kirtland, it is impossible to say. The probability, however, is, that they had no small share in the catastrophe which eventually accelerated the transfer of the centre of Mormonism to the spot prophetically pointed out as the place in which the New Jerusalem should be erected. And certain it is that the most stringent measures were taken to levy contributions upon the members of the Church, by a system of enforced donations, which had much more the character of confiscation than of taxation. The principle of complete surrender of private property was laid down broadly, soon after the removal to Kirtland, in the first instance under the guise of securing support for the poor, but in reality for enriching the Church, and placing all the property of the members at the disposal of the leaders.

" If thou lovest me, thou shalt serve me and keep all my commandments. And behold, thou wilt remember the poor, and consecrate of thy properties for their support that which thou hast to impart unto them *with a covenant and a deed which cannot be broken;* and inasmuch as ye impart of your substance unto the poor, ye will do it unto me, and they shall be laid before the bishop of my church and his counsellors, two of the elders, or high priests, such as he shall or has appointed and set apart for that purpose.

" And it shall come to pass, that *after they are laid before the bishop of my church, and after that he has received these testimonies concerning the consecration of the properties of my church, that they cannot be taken from the church agreeably to my commandments;* every man shall be made accountable unto me, a steward over his own property, or that which he has received by consecration, inasmuch as is sufficient for himself and family.

" And again, *if there shall be properties in the hands of the church, or any individuals of it, more than is necessary for their support, after this first consecration, which is a residue to be consecrated unto the bishop, it shall be kept to administer to those who have not,* from time to time, that every man who has need may be amply supplied, and receive according to his wants. Therefore, *the residue shall be kept in my store-house,* to administer to the poor and the needy, *as shall be appointed by the high council of the church,* and the bishop and his council, and for the purpose of *purchasing lands for the public benefit of the church,* and build-

[4] Covenants and Commandments, Sect. xcv. §§ 9, 10.

ing houses of worship, and building up of the New Jerusalem which is hereafter to be revealed, that my covenant people may be gathered in one in that day when I shall come to my temple. And this I do for the salvation of my people.

" And it shall come to pass, that he that sinneth and repenteth not, shall be *cast out of the church*, and shall *not receive again that which he has consecrated unto the poor and the needy of my church; or in other words, unto me;* for inasmuch as ye do it unto the least of these, ye do it unto me; for it shall come to pass, that which I spake by the mouths of my prophets, shall be fulfilled; for I will consecrate of the riches of those who embrace my gospel among the Gentiles, unto the poor of my people who are of the house of Israel. . . ."—*Covenants and Commandments*, Sect. xiii. §§ 8—11.

However unpalatable this system might prove, and undoubtedly did prove, to many of the members, and especially the new comers, it was constantly enforced by "revelations," and carried out with greater rigour than ever, after the removal from Kirtland, as appears from a "revelation" given at Far West, Missouri, July 8, 1838, in answer to the question, "O Lord, show unto Thy servants how much thou requirest of the properties of thy people for a tithing." The answer is as follows:—

"Verily, thus saith the Lord, I require all their surplus property to put into the hands of the bishop of my church of Zion, for the building of mine house, and for the laying the foundation of Zion and for the priesthood, and for the debts of the presidency of my church; and this shall be the beginning of the tithing of my people; and after that, those who have thus been tithed, shall pay one-tenth of all their interest annually, and this shall be a standing law unto them for ever, for my holy priesthood, saith the Lord.

"Verily I say unto you, it shall come to pass, that all those who gather unto the land of Zion shall be tithed of their surplus properties, and shall observe this law, or they shall not be found worthy to abide among you. And I say unto you, if my people observe not this law, to keep it holy, and by this law sanctify the land of Zion unto me, that my statutes and my judgments may be kept thereon, that it may be most holy; behold, verily I say unto you, it shall not be a land of Zion unto you; and this shall be an ensample unto all the stakes of Zion. Even so. Amen."—*Covenants and Commandments*, Sect. cvii.

The settlement of Zion, however, notwithstanding the most confident predictions, and the most positive and explicit "revelations," proved an utter failure. One short year was sufficient to provoke the Missourians to a war of extermination against the sect, which ended in its expulsion from the State[*], and its

---

[*] For an account of the wars between the Missourians and the Mormonites, see Caswall, *The Prophet of the Nineteenth Century*, ch. ix. x.

removal to the State of Illinois, where, on the banks of the Mississippi, the foundations of the famous city of Nauvoo were laid in 1839. To avoid the confession of failure, the prophet boldly asserted, that notwithstanding all that had passed, Independence in Jackson County, Missouri, was the place where Zion should be built; but in the mean time, Nauvoo, "the beautiful city," was to be their principal "stake," until "the time of the Gentiles should be fulfilled." No one could suspect the straits to which the sect had been reduced, the sufferings which its members had undergone, or the damage which the character of the prophet had sustained, from the tone of gratulation and of triumph, and of arrogated supremacy over all the nations and kingdoms of the earth, which pervades the "revelation" given at Nauvoo in January, 1841:—

" I say unto you, that you are now called immediately to make a solemn proclamation of my gospel, and of this stake which I have planted to be a corner-stone of Zion, which shall be polished with that refinement which is after the similitude of a palace. This proclamation shall be made to all the kings of the world—to the four corners thereof —to the honourable president elect, and the high-minded governors of the nation in which you live, and to all' the nations of the earth scattered abroad. Let it be written in the spirit of meekness, and by the power of the Holy Ghost which shall be in you at the time of the writing of the same; for it shall be given you by the Holy Ghost to know my will concerning those kings and authorities, even what shall befall them in a time to come. For, behold, I am about to call upon them to give heed to the light and glory of Zion, for the set time has come to favour her."—*Covenants and Commandments*, Sect. ciii. § 1.

At Nauvoo the wickedness of the Mormon system reached its climax. Flushed by his success, after the most fearful reverses, the prophet now overleapt all the bonds of self-restraint, and in more than one sense carried himself as the Mahomet of the West. A full, and to all appearance authentic, account of the state of affairs at Nauvoo', and of the private as well as public conduct of Joseph Smith at this period, is given by one whose testimony it is hardly possible for a follower of the prophet to repudiate, considering the reception which was given him, the estimation in which he was for a long time held by the prophet, and the position which he occupied at Nauvoo, where he continued to live as a Mormonite, for the space of eighteen months, holding, during the greater part of that time, a high station in the sect, which gave him admission to all its mysteries, and a knowledge of all its secrets;—we allude to General J. C. Bennett, whose "*Exposé* of Joe Smith and of Mormonism" is quoted

(No. 3) at the head of this article. According to John Bennett's own account he never was a believer in Mormonism, but having reasons to suspect the Mormon leader of "a daring and colossal scheme of rebellion and usurpation throughout the North-western States," having in fact documents to show a scheme for conquering Ohio, Indiana, Illinois, Iowa, and Missouri, and creating a despotic military and religious empire, with Joe Smith at the head, he determined to spy out the land, and for this purpose feigned himself a convert to Mormonism. However questionable the morality of this proceeding may be[7], certain it is that the inspiration of Joseph did not serve him to discern the traitor in the camp. So far from discovering Bennett's real intentions, Joseph distinguished him by "revelation," as a valuable accession to the staff of the Church.

" Let my servant, John C. Bennett, help you in your labour in sending my word to the kings of the people of the earth, and stand by you, even you my servant Joseph Smith, in the hour of affliction, and his reward shall not fail if he receive counsel; and for his love he shall be great, for he shall be mine if he do this, saith the Lord. I have seen the work which he hath done, which I accept, if he continue, and will crown him with blessings and great glory."—*Covenants and Commandments*, Sect. ciii. § 6.

Such a " revelation" in the standard book of the sect, the record of the prophet's " inspired" utterance, bestowed upon a man who himself openly declares that he never was any thing but a spy and a traitor among the "saints," is the most conclusive evidence, if any were needed, that Joseph Smith has no pretensions whatever to be accounted a prophet. The mistake which he made in pronouncing Mr. Caswall's manuscript of the Greek Testament a dictionary of Egyptian hieroglyphics[8], is a mere trifle compared with the moral mistake of his reposing, and that professedly while under the influence of inspiration, the greatest confidence in an individual who was in fact at that very moment planning his destruction. Nor was this want of discernment confined to the one instance of the " revelation" quoted above; Bennett had not been much more than six months in Nauvoo, where Smith was then omnipotent, before he combined, in his person, the offices of Mayor of the City, Major-General of the Nauvoo Legion, and

[7] Bennett himself offers a kind of apology for it. " Persons unacquainted," he says, " with the subject can scarcely imagine the baseness and turpitude of Mormon principles, or the horrid practices to which these principles gave rise. When they learn how habitually the Mormons sacrifice to their brutal propensities the virtue and happiness of young and innocent females; how they cruelly persecute those who refuse to join them, and how they murder those who attempt to expose them; they will look with indulgence upon almost any means employed to thwart their villanous designs, and detect and disclose their infamy."

[8] Caswall's History of the Mormons, pp. 35—37.

First President of the Church of the Latter Day Saints; and it is worthy of remark, that when he determined to leave Nauvoo, he withdrew with the full knowledge and consent of Joseph, and received a vote of thanks from the City Council. All these circumstances, as well as his standing in society, which is attested by a number of testimonials of the first respectability, impart a degree of credibility, and an air of authenticity, to the report of General Bennett, to which few of the other opponents of Mormonism can lay claim.

Having, then, made our readers acquainted with the history aud character of our witness, we now proceed briefly to sum up the most important points of his evidence. According to General Bennett's statement, the whole community at Nauvoo was nothing more than a huge organization for the gratification of the rapacity, the lust and lawless ambition of Joseph Smith and his associates. While these were accommodated with comfortable quarters at the public expense, and lived in ease and comparative luxury, their deluded followers were exposed to every species of privation. This Bennett states, both upon his own authority, and upon that of others whose evidence he quotes; and, in illustration of the spirit in which the prophet acted, he adduces the following anecdote:

" At the very time that the elders of this Church, and indeed the poorer class, were suffering from the want of the common necessaries of life, Smith demanded, at the hands of the people, 1200 dollars per year, in order to aggrandize himself and enable him to live in luxury. And when some complained that this would be a violation of the rules of the Church, he remarked, that if he could not obtain his demand, his people might go to h—, and he would go to the Rocky Mountains." —*Bennett's History of the Saints,* p. 60.

While the general multitude of believers in Mormonism were thus left to toil and to starve, being deprived of their property by " revelations," under the plea of its being devoted to the service of the Most High, there was an extensive organization, under the name of the Order Lodge, to which those who were thought worthy of it, were initiated by the most ridiculous, profane, and indecent mysteries [9]. Among the ceremonies which took place at these secret rites, was a blasphemous personation of the Holy Trinity, in which, in General Bennett's time, God the Father was represented by Joseph, God the Son by his brother Hyrum Smith,

---

[9] The account given by Bennett of this Order Lodge is confirmed by a curious Tract, republished by Arthur Hall (London), entitled, "Sketch of the Rise, Progress, and Dispersion of the Mormons. By John Thomas, M.D., Author of ' Elpin Israel,' Virginia, U. S. of America: to which is added, *An Account of the Nauvoo Temple Mysteries, and other Abominations, practised by the Mormons previous to their Emigration for California.* By Increase M'Gee Van Dusen, formerly one of the Initiated."

and God the Holy Ghost by one George Miller. One of the most
horrible features of this secret organization was the spiritual
seraglio, formed for the gratification of the profligate propensities
of the prophet, and of the other leaders of the sect. We
cannot pollute our pages with any of the details given by General
Bennett ; suffice it to say, that a regular course of initiation
took place, of both married and unmarried females, through three
degrees, or orders, that of the " Cyprian Saints," or the " Saints
of the White Veil,"—that of " Chambered Sisters of Charity,"
or " Saints of the Green Veil,"—and, lastly, that of " Cloistered
Saints," " Consecratees of the Cloister," or " Saints of the Black
Veil ;" the adepts of the last and highest degree in this ascending
scale of corruption, being exempted from any restraint, and
living in the indulgence of the grossest debauchery with the
leaders of the sect, and especially with the prophet himself, who
in this select circle assumed the familiar *sobriquet* of the " Old
White Hat."

Another and most frightful part of this secret organization was
the body of desperadoes, incorporated originally at Zion, in Missouri, under the mysterious name of the "daughter of Zion," otherwise called the " Danites ;" men who were solemnly bound under
a fearful oath, and under the penalty of instant and certain death,
to execute the decrees of the leaders, and especially of the prophet
himself, whatever they might be : robbery, perjury, murder, or
whatever other crime it was desirable to commit, in furtherance
of the interests of the ruling body, these " Danites" were ready
to execute. At the time of General Bennett's sojourn at Nauvoo,
their number was 1200, and out of them the twelve most desperate characters were selected, and distinguished by the appellation, the " destroying angels," or, less obviously to the uninitiated,
the " flying angels." Most daring assassinations, at great distances, as well as at the Mormon city itself, were planned and
carried into effect ; among them that of Governor Boggs of
Missouri, whose violent death Smith had the audacity to predict.
Bennett himself was in no small danger from these emissaries of
death, after his separation from the sect ; but being thoroughly
aware of the system, he was on his guard and managed to
escape :—

"Nine hundred and ninety-nine thousandths of all the *faithful*,"
says General Bennett, " of the Mormon Church, regard Joe Smith as
God's vicegerent on earth, and obey him accordingly ; and all the
Danites of that Church (and, by the bye, they compose no very inconsiderable proportion of their mighty hosts), are sworn to receive him as
the supreme lord of the Church, and to obey him as the supreme God.
If, therefore, any state officer, in the administration of public justice,
happens to give offence to his Holiness the Prophet, it becomes the

will of God, *as spoken by the mouth of his prophet*, that that functionary should DIE; and his followers, *the faithful saints*, immediately set about the work of assassination, in obedience, as they suppose, to their Divine master; and for which NOBLE DEED they expect to receive an excellent and superior glory in the celestial kingdom . . . . ."

"The standard of morality and Christian excellence with them is quite unstable. Joe Smith has but to give the *word*, and it becomes the LAW *which they delight to obey*—BECAUSE IT COMES FROM GOD ! ! ! Acts, therefore, which but yesterday were considered the most immoral, wicked, and devilish—to-day are the most moral, righteous, and God-like; because God, who makes right, has so declared it *by the mouth of his anointed prophet.*"—*Bennett's History of the Saints*, pp. 148, 149.

Although, after all that has been stated respecting the character and career of the founder of Mormonism, it is impossible that he should be regarded in any other light than that of a daring impostor, yet the following anecdotes are not without interest, as showing the tone of his mind.

"One day, Joe, the prophet, was gravely dictating to George Robinson a revelation which he had just received from the Lord. Robinson, according to custom, wrote down the very words the Lord spake to Joe, and in the exact order in which the latter heard them. He had written for some considerable time, when Smith's inspiration began to flag; and to gain breath, he requested Robinson to read over what he had written. He did so, until he came to a particular passage, when Smith interrupted him, and desired to have that read again. Robinson complied; and Smith, shaking his head, knitting his brows, and looking very much perplexed, said—'That will never do! you must alter that, George.' Robinson, though not a little surprised at "*the Lord's blunder,*" did as he was directed, and changed the offensive passage into one more fit for the inspection of the Gentiles."—*Bennett's History of the Saints*, p. 176.

Upon another occasion:

"As General Bennett and Smith were walking together on the banks of the Mississippi, Smith suddenly said to him, in a peculiarly inquiring manner: 'General, Harris says that you have no faith, and that you do not believe we shall ever obtain our inheritances in Jackson County, Missouri.' Though somewhat perplexed by the prophet's remark, and still more by his manner, Bennett coldly replied: 'What does Harris know about my belief, or the real state of my mind? I like to tease him now and then about it, as he is so firm in the faith, and takes it all in such good part.' 'Well,' said Joe, laughing heartily, 'I guess you have got about as much faith as I have. Ha! ha! ha!' 'I should judge about as much,' was Bennett's reply."—*Bennett's History of the Saints*, p. 176.

It is no wonder that a community governed upon a system of such daring iniquity should have been torn by internal dissensions, and regarded with suspicion and hostility by all around. Many of those whom the prophet associated with himself in the government of Nauvoo, separated from him ; among them some of his early accomplices, and even Sidney Rigdon himself, the partner of his fraud from the beginning,—the feelings of the father overcoming every other consideration, on his making the discovery that Smith had attempted to add his daughter to the number of his " spiritual wives." The depredations of the Mormonites, and their lawless conduct, soon rendered them as obnoxious in Illinois as they had been in Missouri, and after another Mormon war, in the course of which Joseph himself, with his brother Hyrum, lost his life, being shot by an armed mob, in Carthage gaol, the remnant of the Nauvooans migrated still further west, and effected a settlement in California, where they cut a conspicuous figure, in that entertaining and instructive work, recently published ; Life in the Far West, by G. F. Ruxton.

But what is truly surprising, is that, notwithstanding all the reverses which the leaders of the sect suffered, their dissensions among one another, and the exposure of the fraud and imposture of the prophet himself, thousands should still be found who regard Joseph in the light of a martyr ; who receive the "Book of Mormon" and the "Doctrine and Covenants" as inspired writings ; and who look for the fulfilment of the promises given to the " Latter Day Saints" by the vilest religious impostor which the world has seen since the days of Mahomet. At this present moment we have reason to believe that the number of Mormonites in England is not much under 30,000. In London and the suburbs alone they have near upon twenty different meeting-houses, though all of very moderate dimensions. With fanatical expectations of worldly prosperity and temporal glory, the professors of Mormonism combine the most bitter hostility against every existing religious system, and especially against the true Catholic and Apostolic Church, whose commission they deny, and whose ordinances they revile in the grossest and most offensive terms. Their creed is a tissue of ignorance and profaneness, founded upon the most palpable perversions of Holy Scripture, and characterized by the most carnal conceptions of things spiritual. We had intended to have given an outline of the doctrines of the sect as they are set forth at the present time by the preachers of Mormonism in Europe and in America; but we have already so far exceeded our limits, that we must adjourn this part of our proposed labours to a future opportunity, if, indeed we shall ever be able to afford leisure and space to revert to a subject which would be altogether unworthy of serious attention, but for the extensive spread among our benighted populations of so fearful a spiritual pestilence.

NOTICES OF RECENT PUBLICATIONS,

ETC.

1.—*Wanderings of a Pilgrim in search of the Picturesque, during Four-and-Twenty Years in the East, with Revelations of Life in the Zenana. By* فاني پُرکس. *Illustrated with Sketches from Nature.* 2 vols. London: Richardson.

THE tone of bold and careless frankness in which this interesting and instructive work is written, is singularly attractive. " Les Indoos peints par eux mêmes" might be its title; for the " Pilgrim" appears to possess such thorough sympathy with, and knowledge of, the people described, as almost to be identified with them; and to enter so completely as the author has done

into the character of a people so difficult, and, in most cases,
so impossible to appreciate and understand, evinces no ordinary
power of observation, memory, and combination. The personal
adventures, which are very interesting, are agreeably told, and
possess all the freshness arising from their having been written
down at the moment, instead of being reserved for the stiffness of
a narrative intended for publication. The descriptions of customs
and manners appear to evince a thorough knowledge of the subject: indeed we are not acquainted with any work which conveys
so much minute information in matters of the every-day life of
India, both amongst the native and the European population;
and, judging from the survey which we have been enabled to take
of this publication, we think it can scarcely fail to be popular
with all who take an interest in India, and indeed with all who
happen to meet with it; for the amount of anecdote, and gossip,
and detail, extending to the most minute points, and especially
such points as ladies are peculiarly interested in, is such as quite
to take this work out of the ordinary class of books of travels;
and we can assure our readers, that this very ponderous work, in
two stupendous octavos, contains as much amusing and light
reading as if it were split into half a hundred pretty little manuals,
better adapted to the hands of young ladies than the magnificent
tomes before us.   In this publication we revel in all the luxury of
beautiful type and paper, and a gorgeousness of illustration, which
appears to have been the result of Oriental ideas rather than of
our more sober father-land. Plate after plate of engravings, glowing in the bright colours of India, and in many cases with gold,
place before the eye that strange state of society where men live
on rice and dress in cloth of gold; and where a bride would be
overwhelmed with despair if her fortune were placed at her
banker's instead of being expended in her wedding feast.
     In truth it is a strange and curious state of society, which
we can scarcely form a notion of without the aid of a work like
this. In glancing through its amusing pages, our eye is caught in
one place with an estimate of the expense of maintaining an
establishment of *fifty-seven* servants,—such, apparently, being the
allowance for a family of moderate pretensions!   This retinue is
maintained, it seems, for the small outlay of 290*l.* per annum!
The wonder is, how these unfortunates contrive to exist; but
apparently their *duties* are far from arduous: in one instance, the
authoress describes the whole employment of one servant in a house
as consisting in the duty of rubbing the master's eyebrows when
his head ached; and this servant was highly affronted at being
asked to rub any other part of the frame!
     There is a long account of a wedding between a young lady,

who was half Hindoo and half European, with a Prince of the Royal House of Delhi. The young couple were *without fortune*; but, nevertheless, the wedding was conducted on such a scale of grandeur, that all our European weddings sink into very tame affairs indeed in comparison. Endless ceremonies; processions of people carrying hundreds of trays filled with all sorts of presents; the bride and bridegroom anointed with a singular and very disagreeable unguent, and kept without motion (or asleep, we believe,) for several days; the slaves and all the company pelting each other with fruit, vegetables, &c.; the bride and bridegroom's neat little attentions to each other in the shape of lumps of sugar eaten off the person in some cases, and even, in one instance, off the *shoe*; powdering the face with gold and silver dust; and hanging all kinds of fruits about the body; all accompanied by music, dancing, feasting, scrambling, and mock fighting; in the midst of which the bridegroom gallantly carries off the bride in his arms, amidst the simulated grief of all the company; and wound up by the departure, in which the newly-married pair are attended by an enormous procession of plates, dishes, furniture, and wearing apparel;—is altogether about the most amusing piece of extravagance we have ever perused.

We cannot say that we like every thing in the volume. In fact, the description of a state of society, in which the gross and voluptuous systems of Hindoo and Mahomedan superstition are so universally prevalent, and in which Christianity is so often disgraced by the conduct of its nominal professors, must, if faithfully described, present features revolting to every right-minded person. It is a difficult and a painful subject for a female writer; and our authoress accordingly passes over much that she must have witnessed, and touches but briefly on the darker parts of the picture. The work, however, even as it is, discloses but too plainly the fearful moral atmosphere of India, and the evil effects which the continual presence of vice is calculated to produce, on those who are not guarded against it by the highest religious principles.

II.—*The Acts of the Apostles: with a Commentary, and Practical and Devotional Suggestions, for Readers and Students of the English Bible. By the Rev.* F. C. COOK, *M.A., one of Her Majesty's Inspectors of Schools.* London: Longmans.

THE author of this volume has executed a work for which the student of the English Bible has reason to feel gratitude. He will now be able to peruse the Acts of the Apostles with the aid of a Commentary exacting from him no knowledge of the original language, and no skill in Biblical criticism, but bringing to his aid a judicious selection and abridgment of those comments which critics of all ages have accumulated for the illustration of the Acts. In the present day, the history of the Apostles and of the earliest Church become continually more important to us, as we are thrown back more and more upon the first principles of Christian communion, by the gradual severing of those bonds which for many ages connected the Church and the State. In this study, Mr. Cook's really valuable work will be a safe companion and guide. We observe that he refers freely to German commentators; but we can attest, with thankfulness, his own exemption from tendencies in the direction of those systems of speculation which have gained for Germany an unhappy celebrity. His pages are characterized by the simplicity and sobriety of faith, while enriched by the stores of criticism; and we have been much edified by the tone of practical piety which pervades the devotional reflections at the end of each chapter.

The text of the Acts is printed with the Commentary, so that the student has before him the whole apparatus for the study of this important book.

Unlike the majority of our modern comments on Scripture, Mr. Cook's volume is adapted for the use of intelligent persons in general, even if they should be unacquainted with the learned languages. To those engaged in the instruction of classes in Sunday Schools, and to the teachers of National Schools, it will be eminently useful; and we feel assured that they will, in following Mr. Cook's Commentary, teach sound principles, both in doctrine and discipline, to the children entrusted to their care.

We shall select a passage from the Comment, with a view to show Mr. Cook's mode of treating his subject.

"Acts ii. 1.—And when the day of Pentecost was fully come, they were all, with one accord, in one place.

"1.—'*The day of Pentecost.*' Pentecost means fiftieth, and is used as a substantive. In the Old Testament it is called 'the Feast of Weeks,' and was kept at the end of seven weeks, or fifty days—including the day of the festival—after the Passover. As the Hebrew festival was instituted as a season of rejoicing and thanksgiving for the harvest, it was also called 'the Feast of In-gathering and First-fruits,' or, 'of Harvest.' Two loaves, made of new meal, were then offered in the temple as first-fruits.—Levit. xxiii. 17—20; Numb. xxviii. 27—29. So the Christian festival, which we term 'Whitsuntide,' commemorates the in-gathering of the first converts, whom God 'begat, of his own will, with the word of truth, that we should be a kind of first-fruits of his creatures.'—James i. 18. The Hebrews also celebrated the giving of the Law on Mount Sinai, on the last day of the seven weeks: and, latterly, they called the festival, 'the rejoicing of the Law.' We have to commemorate the complete and effectual revelation of that Law, which was henceforth written by the Holy Ghost, 'not on tables of stone, but on the fleshly tablets ' of regenerate hearts.

"'*Was fully come.*' According to the Law (Levit. xxiii. 15) the fifty days were reckoned from the end of the first day of Easter, or the sixteenth of Nisan, on which the paschal lamb was slain. In the year of our Lord's passion the sixteenth of Nisan began on Thursday evening at six o'clock, and lasted until the same hour on Friday. This day of Pentecost, therefore, began at six o'clock on the Saturday of the seventh week, and was fully come on the Sunday morning ; so that ' this day which the Lord hath made' is consecrated by the two most important events in the history of the world—the resurrection of Christ, and the coming of the Holy Ghost.

" '*All.*' All the Christians ; viz. the 120 mentioned in the first chapter.

" '*In one place.*' The place where the disciples were assembled must have been the temple. In the first place ; it was ' the third hour of the day,' (ver. 15,) *i. e.* nine o'clock in the morning, the hour of the morning sacrifice, when none of them were likely to be absent from the temple, even on a common day, (see ver. 46,) and certainly not on the great day of the festival. This reason appears to me to be conclusive. In the next place : it is not probable that the 'multitude of devout persons' mentioned, (ver. 9,) would have assembled in any other part of Jerusalem. The early Fathers are unanimous in this opinion. ' The house in which they were sitting' (ver. 2) was, probably, one of the large rooms, of which, as we learn from Josephus, there were thirty adjoining the great court of the temple ; and which appear to have been open to any worshippers who might wish to assemble for devotional purposes. Thus the solemn inauguration of the Church of Christ took place in the sanctuary of the ancient covenant."

The " Practical and Devotional Suggestion " on this is as follows : —

" 1—4. When Christians meet with one accord in places consecrated to the Lord's service, He will surely fulfil his promise to ' be in the midst of them,' and will vouchsafe proofs of his presence, which, though they may be imperceptible to the senses, will be recognized by the eye of faith, and produce results equally unmistakeable with the miraculous gifts which attested the descent of his Holy Spirit at Pentecost."

III.—*Three Letters to Sir George Grey, Bart., &c., on the Baptismal and Educational Questions. By the Rev.* WILLIAM H. HOARE, *M.A., late Fellow of St. John's College, Cambridge.* London : Rivingtons.

IF political questions were determined in the present day by considerations founded on justice, religion, and common sense, the Letters before us ought to exercise a material influence on the

important subjects to which they refer; and while we must lament
to feel that the rulers of the State in these times are, in their
official capacity, likely to give little heed to reasoning, however
forcible, if it is based on the religious peculiarities (as they would
call them) of the Church of England, we must yet feel, that every
writer who, like Mr. Hoare, states truth, and states it clearly,
forcibly, and in such a tone as to render it attractive to the
intellectual and cultivated classes of society, is a real benefactor
to truth.   In the Letters before us, Mr. Hoare enters on an
examination of the leading principles on which the Bill introduced
this session by Mr. Fox depends.   He proves very satisfactorily
that, to meet the present exigencies of the country, an education
is required which shall be not merely of a secular character, but
chiefly of a religious character.   And we doubt not, that the
earnest, and in some places eloquent, expostulations of the writer,
may have touched a responsive chord in the hearts of some of
those who aided in throwing out Mr. Fox's Bill.   Many men
adhere to religion for some time, when they have cast from them
the truths on which it reposes.   The State of England has, for
many years, ceased to possess a creed, and it includes Unitarians
and unbelievers of all kinds, and, without doubt, will, ere long,
include Jews and Mohammedans; yet, religion will still be recognised in some degree.   And, accordingly, we may remark, that
Lord John Russell objected to Mr. Fox's Bill, because it did not
include any provision for religious education.   The necessity of a
religious education, nay, of a Christian education, is, indeed, conceded by the great majority of intelligent men at present; nor
will there be any objection to admit the corollary which Mr.
Hoare annexes to it—that it is the duty of the Government to
assist in providing such an education for the people.   The large
grants made to the Committee of Council for Education, and the
mode of their employment, indicate sufficiently the recognition
of the general principle; but we fear that all community of principle parts at this point.   Mr. Hoare argues in his "Second
Letter" with great propriety, that the State is bound either to
support the teaching of the Church of England exclusively in the
schools, or else to aid her schools in common with those of other
religious communions, leaving to her, as well as to others, freedom to inculcate her own principles.   The chief part of his argument is concerned with a refutation of the notion, that morality
can be taught without religion, and that religion can be taught
without the admission of particular forms.   This last notion is
only one branch of that insidious system which meets us at every
turn,—that religion is independent of all dogmas,—that, in other
words, it is not inseparable from a belief in revelation.   Such is

the shape in which infidelity appears in the present age ; and the great divisions so long existing in England, having, in the event, led to a compromise and a combination of all sects in the State, the way is opened for such propositions as Mr. Fox's. Mr. Hoare argues with great force and eloquence against such false principles, and urges the duty of the State to uphold the truth of the Gospel.   He is one of those who are able still to see in the State and the Church merely different aspects of the same community, according to the view stated by Hooker, and so perfectly applicable in his days. To us, we confess, it seems, that the alteration in the religion of the State, by its rejecting the creed of the Church of England in 1828 and 1829, is so great, that we do not see how it is possible any longer to regard it as a State which we can look upon as holding a common faith with ourselves. We think that when men begin to consider the actual state of things, as distinguished from theories, and from the *former* state of things, they will be obliged to come, however reluctantly, to the same conclusion as that to which we have ourselves arrived. With the exception of this point of difference, there is scarcely any thing in which we cannot agree with Mr. Hoare; and we tender to him our thanks for the gratification which we have derived from the perusal of his able and excellent Letters.

iv.—*Sermons.   By* Joseph Sortain, *A.B., of Trinity College, Dublin ; Minister of North Street Chapel, Brighton.* London : Longmans.

The author of the volume of discourses before us is a dissenting minister; but his Sermons give evidence of no ordinary mental power and cultivation. If narrow views and prejudices have been sometimes supposed to characterize dissent, they are certainly not to be found in Mr. Sortain's pages: nor will we say that he is one of those advocates of a vague and unlimited speculation in religion, whose perilous theories have been substituted for the dogmatism which used to distinguish sectarianism. On the contrary, while Mr. Sortain advocates the rights of conscience in a tone which is as firm as it is charitable, he maintains most of the leading doctrines of Christianity with decision and boldness : the doctrine of baptismal regeneration alone being rejected.

As mere literary productions these Sermons possess high merit. Their language and style are forcible and eloquent; adapted rather to a highly-cultivated audience, than to what we should imagine to be the style of congregations that collect in a dissenting meeting-house. Indeed, were we to point out a fault in these discourses, we should say that they are rather too ambitious—

that there is a want of Christian simplicity. This is, however, a defect which they share with the discourses of Chalmers and Robert Hall; and we think the writer of the Sermons before us may very fairly be considered to hold an intellectual position on a level with either of the distinguished individuals whom we have named.

We extract the following passage, as affording a specimen of Mr. Sortain's style :—

" Our last practical consideration of the immutableness of Jesus Christ is, its influence upon

" 2.—*Our constancy and consistency in Christian doctrine.* We rest our authority for this reference on the immediate transition of the Apostle to the command, ' Be not carried about with divers and strange doctrines.' . . . As if he had said—In the infinite scheme of the Gospel there is one central, and at the same time universal, element; one with which all the innumerable constituents of that scheme—reach though it does from eternity to eternity—are homogenous; one which is its Sun of Righteousness—the Sun, not of a single system, but of all the systems of the spiritual universe, with which as they move, though in the remotest fields of lights, they ever harmonize. Beware, therefore, of aught that is alien from its inviolable simplicity. ' Be not carried about with divers and strange doctrines.'

" How much this must regulate into consistency our religious opinions, will appear from the untiring eagerness with which philosophy, in all time, has sought after primal truths. Even in its infancy it so intensely felt the want of these, that, in the impatience of its poverty, it grasped at fictions. And now that, taught in sorrow the follies of its fancy, it can content itself with nothing but the real, see it, as it ascends, step by step; never satisfied with its classifications, however severally consistent, until it attains the law which combines and unifies them all. ' Jesus Christ, the same yesterday, to-day, and for ever '—is *that* to the Gospel—nay, to all moral truth—which *that* would be to the science of the heavens if we could find some luminary, the focus of all worlds, whence all light, and heat, and attraction have been made by the Creator to irradiate. Yet, no! this, like all analogies, falls infinitely below Him and his relation. For He, Creator and Redeemer, is, *as Jesus Christ*, that Being ' whose centre is every where, whose circumference is no where.'—pp. 114—116.

We lament that so much ability and piety as these Sermons evince should not be employed in a more appropr ate sphere than that to which they are at present restricted.   i

v.—*A Chronological Catena of Ancient Fathers and Councils, together with the Teaching of the Reformers, and more recent Divines of our Church, on the Doctrine of Spiritual Regeneration in Holy Baptism.* Oxford and London: John Henry Parker. 1850.

In the present state of that great and vital question, which forms the subject of this work, the latter will naturally be regarded with deep interest. At all times that doctrine, which is to the Christian life what that of the Trinity is to the Catholic faith—the root, foundation, germ, and source of the whole—must be viewed with love and reverence and grateful loyalty: every thing which tends to support or illustrate it must be received with thankfulness; every thing which in any way assails or impugns it should be treated as an outrage on the Written Word, as well as a rebellion against the Church. At present, under the painful circumstances in which a lay tribunal has decided on the meaning of a priest's ordination vows, a peculiar value attaches to the volume under review. Such Catenæ are of importance, not because, as our opponents ignorantly assert, and also many of our own friends ignorantly admit, they state the views of this or that particular man—but because they prove that the Written Word of GOD was understood in the beginning as we expound it now, in its plain, literal, and grammatical sense, and show that the doctrine in question was always considered as an integral portion of the faith once for all delivered to the saints.

This "Catena" has also other merits, of a secondary but still high order, in the holy and edifying nature of many of the extracts.

What can be more beautiful than the following passage from Gregory Nazianzen?—

" Seest thou one naked? Clothe him, reverencing *thine own garment of immortality*, and that is Christ. 'For as many as have been baptized into Christ, have put on Christ.' "—p. 31.

What can be more magnificent than the following from Sulpicius Severus, Bishop of Bituricum in Gaul, who flourished A.D. 418?—

" Why, foolish woman, dost thou soothe and flatter thyself? In the beginning GOD made two of mankind, from whom the whole host of the human race sprung forth. Natural equality gives not earthly nobility, but the ambition of covetousness; and there can be no difference betwixt those *whom the second birth* hath brought forth, *by which* both rich and poor, free and slave, noble and ignoble, *is made the son of GOD*, and earthly nobility is eclipsed by the splendour of *heavenly glory*."—p. 37.

Alas! if we dwelt rather more on the doctrine of baptismal fraternity—that blazing beacon of the early Church—we should have far less difficulty in maintaining that of baptismal regeneration. It is because we have basely forgotten the one, that we find ourselves now compelled to do battle for the other.

VI.—*A Help to Prayer : in Six Tracts.* By the Rev. W. GRES-LEY, *M. A., Prebendary of Lichfield.* Oxford and London: Parker. 1850.

A VALUABLE and excellent little work; full of that strict common sense, for which the author is so well known, and at the same time truly spiritual. We heartily recommend it.

VII.—*The Ecclesiastical and Architectural Topography of England.* *(Published under the sanction of the Central Committee of the Archæological Institute of Great Britain and Ireland.)* *Diocese of Oxford.* Oxford and London : John Henry Parker. 1850.

A VALUABLE work as a book of reference, and interesting to the student of architectural antiquities; carefully done, and well got up.

VIII.—*"Bear ye one another's Burdens."* A Sermon, preached in the Chapel of the Magdalen Hospital, London, April 28, 1850. *By* ALFRED POTT, *M.A.* Oxford and London: John H. Parker. 1850.

WE have never met with any discourse which more truly, fully, and holily proclaims the duty of Christian love—a duty which men have well-nigh forgotten in their contests after those things which, however high and holy they be, are only its instruments; for, "the end of the commandment is love." We wish that all, but especially men who glory in their orthodoxy, would read this truly beautiful Sermon. It can scarcely fail of benefiting any one who has a mind to understand, or a heart to feel, or a conscience to upbraid them.

IX.—*Remarks on the Judgment of the Judicial Committee of Privy Council in the Case of " Gorham v. The Lord Bishop of Exeter."* *By a* SOLICITOR. J. H. Parker. 1850.

THIS is a very valuable pamphlet, and such as will amply repay the reading; which is more than can be said of the generality of such publications. In fact, no sooner does a question arise in Church or State, than every man with more leisure than zeal, who has the misfortune to possess a good pen and ink that runs easily, sets to work and defiles his portion of letter-paper—for we fear that the more appropriate foolscap is getting out of fashion.

We are happy to see that an excellently drawn up petition is now lying for signature at Mr. Parker's, and that it has been numerously signed, praying "That your Majesty will be pleased to give your royal assent, that all questions touching the doctrine of the Church of England, arising in appeal from your Majesty's Temporal Courts, shall hereafter, (as suggested to your Majesty's predecessor, King Edward VI.,) be referred to a Synod.—That your Majesty will be pleased to give your royal sanction to a Bill for enacting that the Judgment of such Synod shall be binding upon the Temporal Courts of these Realms."

We deem it expedient that all those who have signed, or shall hereafter sign, this petition, should be invited to enter into an engagement not to vote for a representative in Parliament of the University of Oxford, unless he will pledge himself to bring in such a Bill, and to do his uttermost to get it made the law of the land.

Why minds should be perplexed by the Gorham case, we know not: to us it seems but a warning voice, crying "Up and be doing." We do not read that either Ezra or Nehemiah were *perplexed* by the malice and power of the Ammonites, Moabites, and Samaritans, and their friends in high places: they prayed to the GOD of their fathers, and then acquitted themselves like men. Ours is a like trial, ours is a like duty; let us only manfully set about it, labouring with one hand and with our weapons in the other, and we shall have a like success.

THE LORD OF HOSTS IS WITH US: THE GOD OF JACOB IS OUR REFUGE.

x.—*The Cross and the Serpent. By the Rev.* W. HASLAM. Oxford and London: John Henry Parker. 1850.

THIS is a very curious and interesting work, and will amply repay a careful perusal. It has, indeed, its faults, both of manner and matter; and the author does not, to our mind, prove that the Cross was revealed to Adam in connexion with the triumph of the Seed of the woman over the serpent. He does, however, satisfactorily prove that much of the history of our Lord, and many of the doctrines of Christianity, were known by the immediate descendants of Noah, and must consequently have been revealed by GOD, either to that patriarch or our first parents. He entirely demolishes the very absurd and unscriptural notion, that man was left by his Creator to emerge from natural barbarism into civilization. He traces up many of the arts and sciences to the diluvian æra, and leads us to the conclusion, that GOD gave man, in the beginning, the use of letters and the rudiments of

science and art, as well as the power of language; so that barbarism, instead of being the natural state of man, is a retrocession
from nature.

XI.—*The Character of Pilate and the Spirit of the Age. A Course
of Sermons preached at the Chapel Royal, Whitehall.* By WIL-
LIAM SEWELL, *B.D.* Oxford and London: J. H. Parker,
1850.

THIS is one of those bold and single-minded expressions of deep
conviction, which so strikingly characterize Mr. Sewell. When
a future age shall have to inscribe its epitaph on this author, we
doubt whether even the stores of his learning, the riches of his
fancy, the treasures of his intellect, or the charm and energy of
his eloquence, great and incontestable though all of them be, will
leave such an impression behind them, as that simple-hearted
love of truth, and that courage and eagerness in proclaiming that
which he believes to be true, which so peculiarly distinguish him
in an age which is so overrun with scepticism, sophistry, and
special pleading. We must have Convocation the first moment
that we can obtain it; but we heartily recommend these stirring
and beautiful Sermons to all those who take an interest in the
prospects or the spirit of the age.

XII.—*The Singers of the Sanctuary and The Missionary. Two
Tales. By the Author of "Angels' Work."* London: John
Henry Parker. 1850.

THOSE who have read that exquisite tale entitled "Angels' Work,"
will need no further reason for reading a work by the same author;
and those who have not done so, cannot better employ the first
spare cash and spare time that fall to their lot, than by purchasing
and perusing that truly holy book. The Tales before us entirely
justify the high estimation which his former volume had led us to
entertain of the writer, and possess features which render them
peculiarly adapted for the members of our Church. The holy
married priest and his sweet helpful wife are exquisitely delineated,
and yet pourtrayed with those little faults and foibles, without
which no picture of humanity can be either true or harmless.
To paint perfection, except in the Sinless One, is a lie, and, as
such, is wrong as well as foolish. We earnestly wish this little
volume a large circulation, and trust that the author will be
spared to give us many more such treasures of wisdom and
goodness.

XIII.—*A New Elucidation of the Principles of Speech and Elocution; a full theoretical development, with numerous practical exercises, for the correction of imperfect, or the relief of impeded utterance, and for the general improvement of reading and speaking; the whole forming a complete Directory for articulation, and expressive oral delivery.* By ALEXANDER MELVILLE BELL, *Professor of Elocution, &c.* Edinburgh: Kennedy, &c. 1849.

So runs the lengthy title-page of an octavo volume of 311 closely printed pages. And, turning from this to the very *puzzling*-looking interior, we were tempted to reverse the old proverb, and say—in reference to the author's *object*—" Here is much wool, and little cry." However, though we still think that there is more than needful of the "wool" (in the sense in which we have used the word), patience has shown us that there is also some " cry."

The author is " Professor of Elocution" in the capital of that portion of the Queen's dominions which is not famous for the elegance or correctness with which they pronounce Her Majesty's native tongue: and seeing that his father professes in London, and his brother in Dublin, it may be hoped that these counteracting forces (to speak statically) result in a pleasant equilibrium, and render the Professor's labours of some service " for the general improvement of reading and speaking." We are informed in the " Preface," that " in his professional practice, the author daily felt the want of *collected material* to exemplify principles, and to furnish pupils with the means of private exercise upon them. . . . . It became, therefore, necessary that a text-book of principles and exercises should be in his hand." And, truly, he has collected material enough. Not that we undervalue the importance of the subject, or entertain an opinion one whit more favourable than the Professor's as to the reading and speaking of ninety-nine hundredths of Her Majesty's subjects. We wish the Messieurs Bell all success in their undertaking; and, could we have our own will, every school and college in the three kingdoms should ring with the teachings of some elocutionary *bell.* But we venture to think that—however intelligible and excellent our author's oral instructions may be—it will require a person to be uncommonly in earnest before he will be at the pains to wade through, so as really to profit by them, the hopeless-looking strings of homœo-phonetic words (if we may compound one for the occasion) which occupy the Second Part of the volume, or the still more puzzling numbers and hieroglyphics by which, respectively, he would denote the vowel articulations and the inflexions of the voice.

A work of this kind, to be really of use, should, we apprehend, be such as would teach a foreigner (always supposing he had patience to study it) the correct pronunciation of our language. We doubt whether that before us could accomplish this. No question, but it is a most difficult matter to represent sounds, especially diphthongal sounds, to the eye; but we are not now speaking of its practicability, or of the right way of effecting it. Mr. Bell has attempted it, and all we say is—that we question the entire success of his plan. For instance, he gives "a Table of the English Vowels numbered from 1 to 13," in which we observe,

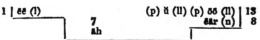

And he continues :—

"There are, besides, three combinations of simple sounds contained in the above table, forming the

DIPHTHONGS.

7-1, as in *i* (ale) | 7-13, as in *ow* (l)
10-1, as in *oi* (l)."

Now we must demur to the pronunciation of the accented vowel in the word *isle*, or any word into which *i* similarly enters, being properly represented by his "7-1," that is, by the combination of *a* pronounced as in the interjection *ah*, with that of *e* as in *eel*. Nor does he appear to us more happy in the mode adopted of expressing *ow* in owl, by combining the open *a* with the *u* of *pull*. That our readers may understand better the mode which Mr. Bell employs, we will present them with one stanza taken at random from several pages of benumbered words :—

10   7-1   5   5   1   8   2   11
" God might have bade the earth bring forth
1   9   10   3   5   10
Enough for great and small ;
1   12   1   5   2   1   7   1
The oak tree and the cedar tree,
2   7-13   6   7-13-8   5   10
Without a flower at all."

Upon which specimen it may be further observed, that the vowels in *have* and *bade* are designated by the same number ; which number, on referring to his table gives ă (n). Now this we deem calculated to mislead. These two words in juxta-position supply an instance of one of the multitudinous anomalies of our language : we have *a* before a consonant with *e mute* suffixed, taking—according to the pronunciation of them universally received in polite society—a different sound in the two words. In this, then, we say, Mr. Bell's numbering is faulty. Of course, if he chooses to publish "a New and Consistent Mode of Pronouncing the English Tongue," he is welcome to do so; and he may get men to follow it if he can. But so long as he aspires to no higher office than teaching us to speak our own language *as it is*, it must mislead to be told that both "have" and "bade" are to be pronounced in the same way. Does he mean to pronounce "have" like "bade," or "bade" like "have?" If the former, then his ear has become vitiated by the northern accent; if the latter (and it just occurs to us that he intended this), then we tell him that he is guilty of a vulgarism. So again we must object to his marking of *flower*. We are informed in a previous note, that "a *hyphen* between two numbers indicates that the sounds are diphthongally blended." Hence, if the sound of the diphthong *ow* is represented by 7-13, and that of *e* by 8,—then, since this "diphthongally blended" with the former combination, we argue that the student can derive no other impression than that the entire word is to be pronounced as a single syllable. But *e* cannot form a diphthong with *ow* (except with a totally different effect). Therefore this word can only be pronounced as a monosyllable, by the *elision* of the *e*. That the writer of these verses meant to use the word monosyllabically, we do not dispute; but then a professor who sets up to "correct imperfect utterance," ought to express this by the presence of the eliding comma; or, at all events, by some other process than that of giving a distinct pronunciation to the *e*, and yet appearing to "blend it diphthongally" with the previous syllable. Flower is a dissyllable—flow'r is a monosyllable. Let them not be confounded in the student's mind.

But we are likely to be at issue with the Professor on this point; for we perceive that, at p. 55, he lays it down that "*R* is not an articulation except when before a vowel." We differ from him herein (unless, indeed, we misunderstand his meaning). We hold that it is quite possible to pronounce the *r* in such words as *gorge, discern, warm, convert, flow'r;* and that the pronouncing or non-pronouncing it is just one of the *differentia* of good and bad reading.

The Professor is evidently *au fait* with his subject; and with much that he says we cordially agree. The following passage commands our ready assent:—

"To be able to read well at sight is not the work of a day; nor is it a power ever to be gained by the indolent or unthinking, or by those who neglect the study of reading as a science and an art. There is a vocal logic, a rhetoric of inflexion, a poetry of modulation, a commentator's explanatoriness of tone—and these are combined in effective reading. The musician's consummate skill, the delicacy of execution, in keeping the simple *air* running with a wavy current in the midst of a river of variations, has its counterpart in the reader's vocal adaptation of sound to sense. The painter's artistic excellence in selecting objects to be struck out with varied effects, or covered down for contrast, is emulated by the skilful reader, in the due subordination and prominence of every thought and circumstance, according to its relative importance. A master of ceremonies is not more punctilious in his arrangements, than the voice of a tasteful and judicious reader. . . . No man who felt his failings, and knew what might be done by the reader, would ever open his mouth in public to deteriorate the taste of an audience by such gross incompetency as is but too often manifested by public readers.

" To become a good reader requires long practice and deep study. It requires more than rules can teach, or art principle [1]; yet it demands nothing which the mind may not discover for itself, when it has become accustomed to fix its attention, and concentrate its powers in reading. The voice will soon learn expressive obedience, when it habitually watches for, and can recognize the mental promptings."—p. 242.

All this is sensible and true; and the want of this study and training of the voice, and of that which directs the voice—the understanding, is lamentably felt. Reading, like theology, would appear in the opinion of mankind to come to us naturally. And the consequence is, that in ninety-nine cases out of a hundred, when a person of education is called on in society to read something aloud, or a clergyman gets into the reading-desk, we are pained with an exhibition such as ought not to be suffered in the upper class of a national school. Really, without the slightest exaggeration or metaphor, we do not ourselves know above three or four *good* readers in the whole circle of our acquaintance. We cannot call merely *fluent* reading *good* reading, among educated men. The ear must be able to discriminate, and the obedient voice distinctly to utter the various minute gradations of vowel sound which belong to our own, perhaps, more than to almost any European language. Expression, emphasis, inflexion and modulation of voice, these all have their place among the *conditions* of good reading and speaking.

Now to speak of one of these—Emphasis; Why do we so constantly hear it wrongly or ineffectively laid? Chiefly from two causes, which may be thus stated,—*Ignorance of the principle by*

---

[1] We would beg to ask where Mr. Bell found this *verb?* He seems to be fond of ringing newly-coined changes upon the root, for he elsewhere uses the word *principiate.*

which it is to be made, and *Ignorance of the principle on which it should be made.* Under the latter, we include what the Professor calls "error in the management of adjectives and qualifying phrases," and we would add more particularly, of pronouns and pronominal adjectives;—the "*I* pray and beseech *you*, to accompany *me* with a pure heart," &c., of the General Confession. Under the former, we will exemplify our meaning in our author's words. He says:—

"Emphasis is commonly considered to be merely an increased *stress* of voice or articulation; but there is an emphasis of *time*, produced by a slower or quicker rate of utterance; an emphasis of *modulation*, by a change, as it were, of the key-note to a higher or lower pitch; an emphasis of *inflexion*, by a sweep of the voice upwards or downwards; an emphasis of *monotone*, by a solemn, little-varying movement of the voice; an emphasis of *aspiration*, by a sighing, husky, or choking expression of the voice; an emphasis of *whisper* even; and, combined with nearly all these modes of giving prominence to words, the emphasis of *pause*,—besides the emphasis of *force* or *stress*, which is vulgarly considered the type of all emphasis."—p. 255.

The *pause* we hold to be, perhaps, the most generally effective instrument of emphasis, and the least understood.

Much, too, depends upon *rhythm*, and what the Professor calls *grouping;* but we have not space to enter into this. We may say in one word, "the power of oratory has its foundations in the principles of our nature."

But we would ask, by way of conclusion to these remarks, how we can expect persons who do not pretend to be wiser than their neighbours in such matters, to pronounce correctly, when we find blunders like the following in the mouths of professors of elocution. Our author, at p. 214, "takes occasion to point out what he conceives to be the defects" of some of Mr. Pitman's *Manual of Phonography;* the same writer whom he had quoted (not, however, with approbation) at p. 29, for the following extraordinary assertion—viz., that *u* in *nut* is the short sound of *o* in *note;* sounds, which "Mr. P. declares to be *identical in quality*, and *different only in quantity or duration!*" We may add, that we have ourselves, within the last day or two, met with a parallel. We were looking over some sheets of Progressive Reading Lessons for Infant Schools (we forget the precise title), with the name of Mr. Varty attached to them—of the famous educational firm of Roake and Varty in the Strand; and in one of them we observed, and called to it the attention of a friend and the shopman (for we feared to state such a thing unsupported by witnesses), we observed one of the lessons on vowels headed thus:—

"*a* as in *cur;*"

and the examples given were *liar, vicar, tankard,* and a dozen or two more equally apposite ! Professor Bell, with all his faults, has not, we rejoice to say, been guilty of any blunder so untrue and so vulgar as this.

xiv.—*The Churchman's Companion, at Home, and in Distant Lands. By the Rev.* Thomas Dowell., *B.A., Incumbent of Christ Church, Wellington Heath, Herefordshire.* London: Longmans.

This is a work which, on the whole, we can highly recommend. How much of its matter is original we cannot undertake to say, but it professes to be mainly a compilation from Ambrose Serle, Bishop Mant, Hooker, Wogan, Hole, &c. It consists of a Series of Sermons, thirty-four in number, extending from the First Sunday in Advent to Trinity Sunday, the purport of each of which is, to draw, as it were, the services of each day to a special focus, combining in one view, the Collect, Epistle, and Gospel, and First Lessons for Morning and Evening Service. Much of the work is admirably done, and that, after a fashion likely to prove very acceptable to the emigrants, for whom it was in the first instance designed. Nothing that could be construed by malevolence into a sign of partizanship will be found in these pages, yet, strict Church principles seem to be maintained. Thus, the duty and efficacy of fasting is placed in a very clear point of view, especially in the Sermon for Ash-Wednesday ; and, again, Baptismal Regeneration is strongly insisted on in the Sermon for the First Sunday after Easter. We make two short extracts in confirmation of these facts : the first from page 202.

" The first and most obvious meaning of fasting, is to deny ourselves the full enjoyment of our daily food. Not that we are to suppose of God, that He has bestowed on us so many things convenient for us, without design that we should partake of them with thankfulness and joy. Certainly not :—but there is a time for all things,—as for enjoyment, so also for restraint. The practice of self-denial, moreover, tends to give a man more command over his appetites, more power over himself, more authority over those perverse and corrupt lusts in which many of his temptations begin."

Our second quotation is of a yet more decisive character.

" Let us, then, believe with holy confidence, that the Spirit of God doth indeed move upon the waters of Baptism, rendering them effacious to the purging away the guilt of original sin, to the renewing our natures, and planting within us the seeds of spiritual life."—p. 281.

Those clergymen will not make a bad selection who choose this

volume for a present to parishioners about to emigrate to
"foreign parts:" and, indeed, it may be found useful in England
also, conveying, as it does, much sound and instructive matter in a popular and unpretending form. We wish it success.

xv.—*Memoir of the Rev. Thomas Dikes, LL.B., Incumbent of St.
John's Church, Hull, with copious extracts from his Correspondence. By the Rev.* JOHN KING, *M.A., Incumbent of Christ
Church, Hull, &c.* London: Seeleys.

THE subject of this memoir was a very pious and excellent clergyman, of the Evangelical school, who died in 1847, after a ministerial career of about sixty years. We have been gratified and
edified by the general tone of character here presented, though
we feel that on some points we are unable to concur with the
opinions advanced. Such of the sermons as we have perused,
appear to combine a moderate view of those doctrines which are
sometimes called "Calvinistic," with the enforcement of practical
piety and morality. The discussion of such points as final perseverance and free-will before a congregation, is perhaps of rather
questionable expediency as a general rule ; but we are bound to say
that what we have seen of Mr. Dikes' exposition of those and
similar tenets, impress us with the conviction that he was more
under the guidance of Scripture than of mere theory.

Mr. Dikes was the friend and associate of Bickersteth, Scott,
Farish, and others of their school. He erected at his own expense a church at Hull, at a time when it was rare indeed to hear
of such ventures in the cause of religion. He opposed himself
with remarkable energy to the prevalent licentiousness and immorality, and he appears to have been charitable and tolerant in
his feelings towards persons of a different class of opinions. He
was strongly opposed to the concession of the Romish emancipation in 1829. We have the following remarks on this subject by the editor :—

"The storm which for some time had been gathering in reference to
the Roman Catholic claims, now reached its height. It was soon known
that the Government, with Wellington and Peel at its head, were inclined to surrender the great Protestant principles on which the constitution had been based at the commencement of the reign of William the
Third. It was rumoured that his Majesty had (with reluctance)
acquiesced in the wish of his ministers. At length Parliament assembled ; the King's speech announced the projected change ; and Sir
Robert Peel stood up to deal, as best he might, with the arguments
which he had himself so often advanced on the side which he had so
suddenly deserted."—p. 131.

Mr. Dikes, on this occasion, did his duty manfully in attending a public meeting at Hull, and speaking strongly against the ministerial measure. We find him thus writing in 1845,—

" I suppose you have felt deeply interested at Leeds, in the Maynooth question. It seems to me that some advantage may arise from manifesting a bold front of opposition to the measure; for though it can avail nothing under present circumstances, yet it may prevent the adoption of further and more offensive measures. I have no doubt it was the intention of Sir Robert Peel and his friends to pay the Roman Catholic clergy; but perhaps they will be afraid to hazard the attempt under present circumstances."—p. 221.

The editor of this Life has appended certain remarks on Baptismal Regeneration, putting forth the same interpretation of our formularies which is contended for by Mr. Gorham.

XVI.—*Scriptural Communion with God; or the Pentateuch and the Book of Job; arranged in Historical and Chronological Order, &c. By the Rev.* GEORGE TOWNSEND, *D.D., Canon of Durham, &c.* In Two Vols. London: Rivingtons.

THE author of these volumes has been long known and respected as amongst the most consistent and eloquent of our writers. His " Historical and Chronological Arrangement of the Holy Bible" has occupied a high place in public estimation, and in former years his publication, in controversy with Charles Butler, was of eminent service. That controversy has gone by, but it must at least be a melancholy satisfaction to have taken share in it. Such men as Dr. Townsend can tell the sincerity and the integrity of attachment to the Church of England which influenced the majority of her members in resisting the efforts of Romanism to gain political power. And they survive to feel that experience has proved they were *right* in believing the Church to be endangered by the grant of political power to its adversaries. It was easy to ridicule such apprehensions *then;* but now they have changed into realities. Dr. Townsend represents the school of the last generation; but we must do him the justice to say, that he is an assiduous student of the literature of the present day; and of this, the work before us offers indisputable proof.

It consists of the five books of Moses, arranged in chronological order, and includes also the Book of Job, inserted at the proper point in the sacred history, according to the chronology of Dr. Hales, viz. before the call of Abraham. The whole is divided into short sections for family reading, each of which is preceded by an exposition, followed by a prayer, and accompanied by annotations of various kinds. Prefixed to the work, and interspersed in it, are dedications to various exalted personages, one to the Pope, another to the Archbishop of Canterbury, urging for the most part the subject of Christian union. We confess that here we must look on our author as rather visionary and unpractical ; for what use there can be in exhorting the Archbishop of Canterbury to seek for union with foreign churches, we know not ; when we remember how much fettered the Church is at present, and how entirely the Archbishops are always under the influence of the temporal Government, and selected with a special view to the maintenance of that influence.

Dr. Townsend's expositions and prayers are, of course, intended chiefly for persons possessing some degree of education. The prayers are rather long, we think. The annotations are replete with valuable and important matter, and abound in defences of various principles and points against Infidels, Rationalists, Romanists, Romanizers, Dissenters, Unitarians, &c. &c. Altogether, Dr. Townsend's work is one of no ordinary character, and deserves a far more lengthened notice than it is now in our power to afford.

XVII.—*Footprints of the Creator ; or " The Asterolepsis of Stromness."* By HUGH MILLER, *Author of " The Old Red Sandstone,"* &c. London : Johnston & Hunter.

THE author of this work has acquired a high reputation by his previous researches into the structure of the earth. On the present occasion he appears before the world as the opponent of the "Vestiges of Creation," which, as our readers doubtless recollect, reduced creation to a nonentity, by advocating the Development theory. Mr. Miller, in the volume before us, addresses himself to the task of overthrowing this theory by the aid of *fact.* His researches in the more ancient geological formations have brought to light remains which exhibit a high degree of development as existing exactly at the period when the development theory would require the very reverse. Of course this is a very good argument. Mr. Miller plies it well ; though the thread of his discourse is somewhat interrupted by the multitude of geological details into which he enters, and which are of inferior interest, except to a professed geologist.

XVIII.—*Nine Sermons, preached, for the most part, in the Chapel of Harrow School.* By CHARLES JOHN VAUGHAN, *D.D., Head Master of Harrow School, &c.* London : Murray.

WE have been most favourably impressed by the tone and the substance of all that we have read of this volume of discourses.

There is a reality about them, and an affectionate solicitude for the highest interests of the young persons to whom they were addressed, which fills us with respect for the author. His observations on party spirit and its evils are peculiarly appropriate, and his warnings on the subject of scepticism are not less so. Violent and overstrained disputes on philosophical and religious questions generally lead to the rise of a sceptical and latitudinarian party. The reaction from puritanism led to infidelity in the seventeenth and eighteenth centuries.

XIX.—*Scripture Biography. By the Rev.* ROBERT WILSON EVANS, *B.D., Vicar of Heversham, &c. Third Series.* London: Rivingtons.

A MORE pleasing work than this for perusal in devout families cannot well be imagined. It combines so much of the biographical form, with the inculcation of sound moral and religious teaching that the attention is kept alive, and both pleasure and improvement will be reaped by the student. Much illustration is derived from the author's knowledge on cognate topics, and we need not recommend to our readers the tone of the work as delightful—for it is sufficient to remind them of the " Rectory of Valehead."

XX.—*Pilgrimages to St. Mary of Walsingham and St. Thomas of Canterbury. By* DESIDERIUS ERASMUS. *Newly translated, with the Colloquy of Rash Vows, by the same Author, &c. By* JOHN GOUGH NICHOLS, *F.S.A.* Westminster: J. B. Nichols & Son.

THIS volume possesses more than an antiquarian interest. It brings before the English readers the superstitions which were customary in this country before the Reformation, and which are still continued in Italy and in other countries under the dominion of Romanism. The superstitions practised at the shrine of St. Mary of Walsingham, or of St. Thomas à Becket, are exactly parallel to those which Mr. Seymour has ably described in his " Pilgrimage to Rome." Mr. Nichols has added copious annotations, exhibiting extensive research and antiquarian knowledge, and the volume is, on the whole, not only a curious, but a valuable and useful one.

XXI.—*The Diaconate and the Poor. The Duty of the Laity of England briefly considered, with reference to the above Two Objects. By a* PARISH PRIEST. London: Ollivier.

THE object of this publication is to urge the revival of the office of Deacon, in connexion with the Offertory, for the purpose of relieving the poor and afflicted. The notion is a noble one, and we heartily wish it were taken up in such quarters as might lead to a hope of its being realized. There is one difficulty that strikes us—the hard-hearted and covetous who form so large a portion of the community, and who possess the greatest portion of its wealth, would be exempt from contributing to the relief of the poor.—This would be, in our view, a decided evil. We extract the following passages from this publication, as illustration of its design :—

"Before the middle of the sixteenth century there had never been a Poor Law in England. Nearly 1000 years had passed since S. Augustine planted our Church, and, during the whole of that time, a compulsory maintenance of the poor had never been needed or required. Through the dynasty of Saxon and Norman, though the most salutary and excellent laws that now govern us had been passed, the principle had been maintained and acted on, that to the Church, and not to the State, belonged the care and guardianship of the poor. For nearly 1000 years our Church possessed this *visible* mark of belonging to Christ. Cannot then the early Christian Church, as the guardian of the poor, be taken as a model for a large and flourishing nation ? For 1000 years the poor in England lived, and were hospitably kept, on the tithes, alms, and offerings of the Church.

"By the 14 Eliz. the compulsory maintenance of the poor *first* came into existence.

"Nor did the government willingly take the poor under its charge subsequently to the Reformation. The State rulers had taken indeed the Church's property, but they denied its responsibilities. They left the poor to starve and die. The vital principle of Christian charity had declined before the Reformation: that event, and the frightful religious strife that arose upon it, well-nigh extinguished what was left. The old funds were gone ; the eternal imperishable doctrine was gone too ; what was to become of the poor ? They wandered about till they perished from hunger ; in their desperation they took up arms for bread : they were then hanged and shot. At length, in Elizabeth's time, the government were forced to grant the expediency—infidel—Poor Law.

"Thus, in the sixteenth century, our Church lost her property and her poor ; but before that, she had lost the vital living doctrine, and this loss led to the other. A long sore bondage have we since served to mammon. When shall our *visibility* be again manifested, and our lost jewels be recovered ? *Then*, when the lay members of the Church shall honestly endeavour to recover unto the Church her poor ; *to substitute in the place of mere secular enactments, the law of the Christian Church.*

The author thus remarks on the practical disuse of the office of Deacon, though the form of Ordination to that office is still preserved :—

" By a singular providence the form has been diligently used. Year after year, season after season, the ceremony has been performed in our cathedrals, but from that holy consecrating service there have come forth no ministers for the bodily wants of Christ's poor. The Church has continued nominally to appoint the officer, but the only deacons who have all the time walked our land have been the relieving officers and workhouse guardians of the State-expediency Poor Law.

" A few words will demonstrate these positions. In the preface to the form for making deacons the qualification for the candidate is stated, that he ' be a man of virtuous conversation and without crime ; learned in the Latin tongue ; and sufficiently instructed in Holy Scripture.' Then in the first rubric there is ordered ' a sermon, or exhortation, declaring the *duty and office* of such as come to be made deacons ; how necessary that order is to the Church of Christ : and how the people ought to esteem them in their office.'

" I am not aware that this sermon on *the duty and office of Deacons* as such is ever preached ; and, indeed, at present it is better let alone ; there is great good sense in omitting it. But that the reformers intended a temporal rather than a spiritual office the whole service makes most manifest. The collect, after mentioning ' divers orders of ministers in the Church,' speaks by name of S. Stephen and the others whom Apostles, under Divine influence, ordained Deacons, and then prays that ' God will mercifully behold those His servants who were then called to the *like* office and administration ; ' and that there might be no possible mistake about the nature of that office, one of the Epistles, which follows, is taken from the sixth chapter of the Acts of the Apostles, in which we are told that the *express* object, nay the *only* object, for which the order was created was ' to serve tables.'

" And, again, in the Bishop's charge to the Deacons, after he has spoken of their spiritual office, which is merely to *assist* the Priest, as a kind of Nethinim, in divine service, to read homilies and holy scriptures, and to teach the catechism ; but *not* to baptize except by necessity, or to preach except by license ; he adds, ' furthermore it is his office (where provision is so made) to search for the sick, poor, and impotent people of the parish, to intimate their estates, names, and places where they dwell unto the curate, that by his exhortation they may be relieved with the alms of the parishioners or others.'

" Not now to mention the other places in the office, in which the duty of the Deacon is clearly shown in the intention of the Church to be rather a temporal than a spiritual function, the last rubric is especially worthy of attention, from which it will be observed that the calling of the Deacons to the office of Priest at the end of one year is by no means a matter of necessary Church arrangement.

" From these observations it will be seen that in the *theory* of our Church, the diaconate is something very distinct from the priesthood.

As the *first* duties of the *priesthood* are *spiritual;* so the *first* duties of the *diaconate* are *temporal.* But is it so in reality and practice? The ordination sermon never alludes to the peculiar and *distinctive* duties of the Deacons. The same educational qualifications, as University degrees, &c. are required by the bishops for the deacons as for the priests, as if none were to be admitted into the former order who might be allowed to continue it. Men are *called* to the like office and administration with Stephen and the others whom the Apostles ordained; but it is impossible they can *go* to it, where no provision for 'serving tables' is ever made. Moreover, Deacons newly-ordained are even allowed to take the entire spiritual charge of large and important parishes, where the Priest is either absent, or so infirm as to be unable to discharge his duties; and in many cases our services are ministered without the absolution.

" The Deacons themselves, as is most natural, where no effort has been made to teach them their duties, or to assign a special administration, confound their functions with the *priesthood;* and few indeed, if any, are they who continue voluntarily in the diaconate beyond the shortest time allowed by ecclesiastical law; so entirely is the order regarded not as a distinct and honourable office in itself, but as a sort of probationary priesthood. Practically, we repeat, there is no order of Deacons in our Church. Is it because we have no Christian charity left? It cannot be because we have no poor.

" Ten thousand Deacons, one for every parish, would not cost any thing like so much as 10,000 relieving officers. To make Christ's Church again visible, would be a saving to the nation, looking upon it in this low mercantile view; of thousands, if not hundreds of thousands, compared with the maintenance of the present Poor Law. And surely our Church and nation could find 10,000 amongst her laymen who, without the qualifications for the higher order of the priesthood are, or could easily be made, fit for the Order of Deacons."

The following interesting facts, in regard to the Offertory, are mentioned in the Appendix :—

" The Isle of Man, with a population, in 1841, of 47,986 is not degraded and unchristianized by a poor law. There is a weekly offertory in every church in the island, and the poor are principally supported by the funds thus raised : this, too, in a place where, in other respects, Church doctrine is less distinctly recognized, and the Church itself is far less efficient than with us, and where, moreover, pecuniary means are less in ratio with the population.

" A plan exemplifying the principles advocated in this tract is also being carried out, with every prospect of complete and ultimate success, at W——— in ———shire ; a very poor, and until the last two years entirely neglected and heathen place. The weekly offertory there, in the present year, has amounted to 40*l.*, and out of this a regular payment is made to the poor and sick amongst the communicants and children unconfirmed, who attend the Church school. The population is composed (one family excepted) of colliers, hand-loom weavers, and small farmers."

XXII.—1. *Sister's Care. By the Author of "Michael the Chorister," "Rachel Ashburn." A Story of Real Life.*

2. *Harry and Archie ; or, First and Last Communion. By the Rev.* E. MONRO, *M.A.*

3. *Self-Devotion ; or, the Prussians at Hochkirch : a free translation from the German of Frederica Schwann.* London : Masters.

MANY little works of this nature does Mr. Masters send forth to the Christian world, and we are under no slight obligations to him for so doing. Mr. Monro's bold, and sometimes almost awful, allegories, are well known : they have, perhaps, more depth of meaning, and display more power of conception, than the very sweet creations of our departed brother, that faithful follower of Christ, the Rev. William Adams. "Harry and Archie" is very beautiful, and will no doubt command a large circulation. More touching, perhaps, is "Sister's Care ;" a charming little tale, which we can heartily recommend as a school gift for the children of the poor. "Rachel Ashburn" we like less : it is needlessly rendered complicated and intricate, if not confused, by a very singular whim of its author, who has chosen to make the real tale a mere retrospective episode in history, though it occupies just thirty-four out of forty-four pages. This is obviously absurd, and would alone suffice to prevent our recommending the story for general circulation. We must add, that it seems rather void of purpose, and could be of no use in any case to children, and yet it is pretty in its way. The tale from the German is also by no means devoid of merit.

XXIII.—*Letters on the Development of Christian Doctrine, in Reply to Mr. Newman's Essay. By the Rev.* WILLIAM ARCHER BUTLER, *M.A.*, &c. *Edited by the Rev.* THOMAS WOODWARD, *M.A.*, &c. Dublin : Hodges and Smith.

"DEVELOPMENT" has developed itself into oblivion, for no one ever hears of the doctrine or its author now. In fact, a doctrine which was very well in 1845, may, on the principle of development, be an obsolete one in 1850. It is certainly a very remarkable fact, how utterly the theory has sunk out of notice in the Church of England. Mr. Archer Butler's work, however, well merits a perusal for its literary and theological merit; and we

must again lament the early death of one of the brightest ornaments of the Irish Church.

xxiv.—*Sermons. By the Rev.* HENRY HUGHES, *M.A., Perpetual
Curate of All Saints, Gordon Square,* &c. London : Rivingtons.

THIS volume of Sermons which is dedicated to Sir Robert Inglis,
a relative of the author, is vigorously and forcibly written, with
much plainness of speech, and in a tone of manly and fervent
piety.   The Sermons are rather of the Evangelical school, but by
no means an extreme specimen ; and while earnest in their
denunciation of formality in every shape, are affectionate in their
tone as regards the Church, and the forms sanctioned by her.
There is much in these discourses which must command general
assent : they are decidedly practical.

xxv.—*A Manual of the British Marine Algæ : containing generic
and specific Descriptions of all the known British Species of Sea-
weeds.   With Plates to illustrate all the Genera.   By* WILLIAM
HENRY HARVEY, &c.   London: Van Voorst.

THIS is the second edition of a work on the same subject, published some time since by Professor Harvey, whose very able and
interesting volume, " The Sea-side Book," we had occasion to
notice in a former number. Dr. Harvey, in the volume before us,
gives a descriptive catalogue of all the marine algæ to be found
on the British shores, stating the characteristics of each plant,
and the localities in which it has been found.   The letter-press is
followed by a series of very well executed engravings in illustration of the different genera ; and the volume will be of course
indispensable to all who wish to study the branch of science to
which it relates, and which has but recently acquired the notice
which it deserves and repays.

xxvi.—*The Jamaica Movement for the Promoting the Enforcement
of the Slave Trade Treaties, &c.*   London: Gilpin.

EVERY one who has any feeling of justice must sympathize with
the efforts of the oppressed West Indians to obtain common
justice from the Imperial Parliament.   Their case is a cruel one ;
their property has been confiscated for the benefit of slave-holding
states by the policy of a country which maintains an enormously
expensive squadron on the coast of Africa to suppress slavery.
But justice and consistency are not to be expected from a democracy, and therefore the unfortunate planters of Jamaica and the

West Indies, like the landlords of Ireland and the farmers of
England, will be exterminated.   Ere long we suppose the West
Indies will fall into the hands of the United States, as they will
not be worth this country's keeping, and they may then flourish
once more.

XXVII.—*Westminster: Memorials of the City, St. Peter's College,
the Parish Churches, Palaces, Streets, and Worthies. By the
Rev.* M. S. C. WALCOTT, *M.A.*, &c.   Westminster: Masters.

THIS is one of those books that it is difficult to lay down, and
which you may open at any part, and your attention is arrested.
It is one of the most amusing topographical books we have seen,
and does great credit to the research and industry of the writer.
   The history of the Abbey is not included; but the antiquities
of the churches, palaces, parliament houses, college, and all the
various localities, are collected and told in a most interesting
way, and we should presume that the accuracy of the work may
be calculated on, as the author seems to have spared no pains or
labour in its compilation.   There are a few engravings of Westminster and its buildings in olden time.

XXVIII.—*The Resurrection of the Flesh.—Seven Lectures on the
Fifteenth Chapter of the former Epistle to the Corinthians. By*
HENRY BOND BOWLBY, *M.A.*, *Fellow of Wadham College,
Oxford*, &c.   London: Rivingtons.

WE have been pleased with all we have read of this series of discourses on the lesson read at the Burial Service.   They are explanatory and practical, and extremely well adapted to edify and
instruct a congregation.

XXIX.—*Meditations on the suffering Life on Earth of our Lord
and only Saviour. From the French of* PINART.   London:
Masters.

THIS work appears to be very carefully edited, so as to contain
nothing except what may with pleasure and edification be perused
by Churchmen.   It is impossible to open the volume without
being impressed by the tone of earnest and natural devotion in
which it is written.   The principal truths connected with our
Lord's incarnation, and the series of events included in his passion, furnish subjects for the chapters, each of which is followed
by a " Practical Resolution."

xxx.—*The Pilgrim's Hand-book; or Counsel and Comfort for the Wayfarers of Zion. Set forth by a* PILGRIM. London: Wertheim and Macintosh.

THE volume before us consists of a great variety of extracts from religious writers of different connexions, and of ancient and modern times, and while written with much piety and sincerity, is adapted for the use of persons of any religious denomination, no peculiarities being discernible. The author is one of those good persons who do not trouble themselves about controversies amongst Christians, but act on the principle of trusting to the " indwelling of the spirit in the heart."

xxxi.—*The Mercy Seat : Thoughts suggested by the Lord's Prayer. By* GARDINER SPRING, *D.D., Pastor of Brick Presbyterian Church, in the City of New York.* Edinburgh: J. and T. Clark.

WE are always glad to recognize and to sympathize with religious earnestness in different communions from our own ; and Dr. Spring is a writer to whom such praise is especially due. It is lamentable to think, in perusing volumes such as this, how much causeless division exists in the nominally Christian world ; for we really often peruse sermons and other writings by Presbyterians and Dissenters, which harmonize far better with the Church of England, than do those of some of her actual members ; and we should not be at all sorry to exchange the one against the other, if the transfer were possible. In the case of Dr. Spring, however, we regret that there is one material obstacle : he objects to all set forms of prayers, and argues stoutly against them.

xxxii.—*Sermons for the Sundays and principal Holy-days throughout the Year. By the Rev. Lord* ARTHUR HERVEY, *A.M., Rector of Ickworth, &c.* 2 vols. London : Hatchards.

THESE are really good, plain, practical discourses, preached to, and well adapted for country congregations. They are composed in a fluent and easy style, and avoid controverted questions, dealing as much as possible in the general doctrines received by all Churchmen.

xxxiii.—*The Church Schoolmaster. By the Rev.* SANDERSON ROBINS, *M.A.* London : Rivingtons.

THE object of this excellent work is to supply hints to schoolmasters on the leading points of their duties, and the course of

conduct which they should pursue in order to accomplish the
great objects of their office. There is much practical wisdom in
the suggestions offered in these pages, which we commend to the
especial attention of all who are interested in National Schools.

xxxiv.—*An Historico-Critical Introduction to the Pentateuch.* By
H. A. Ch. Hävernick, *Doctor and Professor of Theology in
the University of Königsberg.* Translated *by* Alex. Thomson,
A.M., *Professor of Biblical Literature, Glasgow Theological
Academy.* Edinburgh: Clark.

It is, without doubt, very laudable and commendable, in men like
Dr. Hävernick, to undertake the defence of the genuineness of
the Pentateuch, a point which, as the translator remarks, has
been "so much debated of late in Germany." We are glad to
find that there are some persons still remaining in Germany who
are willing to uphold the truth of the Mosaic records. But how
fearful a state of things it is, when such questions can be freely
discussed at all. Is nothing to be settled? Are men to be at
liberty to discuss every thing—even to the existence of God? It
is so in the Evangelical Church in Germany, and the State is
endeavouring to make it so in the Church of England; and such
will certainly be the event in England, if the State is not compelled to keep aloof from the Church. Dr. Hävernick appears to
have executed his melancholy work with fidelity and learning.
But who can make men believe, if they do not wish to submit
their reason to any authority!

xxxv.—*Occasional Sermons, preached in Westminster Abbey.* By
Chr. Wordsworth, D.D., *Canon of Westminster.* London:
Rivingtons.

The author of this volume is ever ready to engage in the cause of
the Church of England; and the learning, ability, and courage
which he brings to the aid of any cause which he undertakes, are
too well known to require any remarks from us. The object of
the Sermons before us (which were published separately) was, to
supply an antidote to the danger of secession from the Church,
arising from the recent decision of the Privy Council in the Gorham case. With this view, Dr. Wordsworth urges that the
doctrine of the Church of England is unchanged by that decision,
as we have ourselves urged; and he shows how plainly and distinctly our formularies teach the doctrine of Regeneration in Baptism, and how vain are all pretences to the contrary. In addition
to this, he shows how the inherent efficacy of our formularies

brought about the suppression of the Arian heresy in the early part of the last century. Dr. Wordsworth does not appear to look to the assembling of Convocation with any confidence as a means of settling our present controversies ; but he does not express any adverse opinion. On the whole, the impression conveyed by his Sermons is, that we should remain satisfied with our present position, and that no efforts are requisite to effect an alteration in the existing relations of Church and State. Condemning the decision, he holds that it will not materially affect the Church. We cannot concur in this view, because the case of Evangelicalism and Neologianism now is not parallel to that of Arianism in 1711, in our opinion ; and because the State, and the temper of the times, have widely altered in 140 years. The evil now is, that men of heretical, and even infidel, opinions will gain legal footing in the Church, and that the State will appoint them Bishops and Deans.

XXXVI.—1. *A Plea for Peace. A Charge delivered at his Primary Visitation.* By R. B. HONE, *M.A., Archdeacon of Worcester.* London : Parker.

2. *Dangers to Truth from Controversy and Agitation. A Visitation Sermon.* By the Hon. and Rev. W. H. LYTTELTON, *Rector of Hagley, &c.* London : Parker.

3. *A Sermon on* John iii. 5, *in reference to the case of Gorham* v. *The Bishop of Exeter.* By E. A. LITTON, *M.A., &c.* London : Hatchards.

SOME parties in the diocese of Worcester appear to have been rather annoyed at the success of what they call " agitation," in obtaining from the clergy of the diocese an expression of opinion on the Baptismal controversy. We are aware, from the public journals, that the Bishop of Worcester was adverse to any such movement ; and Archdeacon Hone, in his Charge, regrets that he himself had not had an opportunity of denouncing it. Mr. Lyttelton, too, is in great tribulation. We can feel for these excellent men. It is, indeed, most distressing to observe that the clergy of Worcester are inclined to think for themselves ; and that if they are of opinion that faith is in danger, they have actually the audacity to say so—though their Bishop and Archdeacon would wish them to be silent ! We live in *strange* times, indeed, when the clergy appear to have consciences, and to *act* on them ! Archdeacon Hone's suggestion, that the laity, in their " giant-power," should come forward, will not mend the matter ; it will only add to the agitation which he is so anxious to see at an end.

For no one can oblige men to cease from expressing their opinion. if they hold faith to be endangered; and those who think so will not dread *any* power on earth.   Mr. Litton's Sermon is a well-written defence of the decision of the Committee of Council.

xxxvii.—*Sermons on the New Birth of Man's Nature.   By* Robert Isaac Wilberforce, *A. M., Archdeacon of the East Riding.*   London: Murray.

These discourses deserve a far more lengthened survey and notice than we can at this moment afford to them.   To say that they are replete with sound and deep theology—that they are worthy of the author's reputation as one of our most distinguished divines—would convey an imperfect, though not untrue impression of their merits.   Though it might, perhaps, be supposed, from the title, that the volume was written with express reference to the controversy now pending, such a notion would be a mistaken one, the expressions employed in the title being used in the largest sense, though the privileges of Christian baptism are continually kept in view.   It is, in fact, a volume of discourses on subjects connected with the exaltation of humanity through the Incarnation, and amongst the rest, on the principal Festivals of the Church, and the mysteries thus commemorated.

xxxviii.—*Eruvin; or, Miscellaneous Essays on Subjects connected with the Nature, History, and Destiny of Man.   By the Rev.* S. R. Maitland, *D.D., &c.*   Second Edition.   London: Rivingtons.

Every one who is acquainted with this ingenious work of Dr. Maitland will be glad to see a reprint of it in the neat volume before us.

xxxix.—*Sermons, University and Parochial.   By* Edward Thomas Vaughan, *M.A., Vicar of St. Martin's, Leicester, &c.* London: Rivingtons.

A better style of sermon-writing appears to us to be growing up of late.   We have less of the mere religious-essay style than formerly; and Mr. Vaughan's discourses are good specimens of this improvement.   They are thoughtful, and yet practical; and quite sufficiently animated and interesting.   Our attention has been attracted more particularly to two discourses on Baptism, in which great truths are maintained, while all who hold those truths may not entirely concur in the views which accompany them.   We have read them with pleasure.

XL.—*The Age: being a Letter to a Society for the Improvement of Sacred Architecture, &c.* *By a* LAYMAN. London: Hatchards.

THIS " Layman" is evidently a very worthy and well-meaning man, but is a sadly long-winded one. His book is nominally to give some advice to Ecclesiastical Antiquarians, but after a few words to them, he runs off into endless talkification about every matter under the sun, going on steadily, without so much as the break or intermission of a fresh chapter, in one dreary outpouring of twaddle and truism. We should be sorry to have a button within reach of this " Layman," for we should never get away from him.

XLI.—*In Memoriam.* London: Moxon.

THIS little volume contains a series of poems in the same measure, which make up a whole, and they are in memory of a departed object of affection. There is a tone of melancholy music throughout, and a calm, sad reflection, which speaks of reality, and engages the sympathy of the reader. It is the tribute of a wife to her husband. We extract the following passage, not as the best in the volume, but as showing the kind of subjects on which it dwells.

> " Thy converse drew as with delight
>   The men of rathe and riper years:
>   The feeble soul, a haunt of fears,
> Forgot his weakness in thy sight.
>
> " On thee the loyal-hearted hung,
>   The proud were half disarm'd of pride,
>   Nor cared the serpent at thy side
> To flicker with his treble tongue.
>
> " The stern were mild when thou wert by,
>   The flippant put himself to school
>   And heard thee, and the brazen fool
> Was softened, and he knew not why;
>
> " While I, thy dearest, sat apart,
>   And felt thy triumph was as mine;
>   And loved them more, that they were thine,
> The graceful tact, the Christian art;
>
> " Not mine the sweetness or the skill,
>   But mine the love that will not tire,
>   And, born of love, the vague desire
> That spurs an imitative will."

There is a truthfulness about this volume that renders it extremely touching.

XLII.—*A Result of Meditation on the Bible, or an Inquiry into Truth.* By a LAYMAN. Brighton: Henry S. King.

THERE is much in this volume which we have read with pleasure. The writer is a very serious, sober-minded inquirer, quite of the old school, and valuing piety wherever he may meet it. His authorities, however, are to a considerable extent evangelical, where they indicate any particular religious views. There is nothing calling for very particular remark in this work. We have no doubt that where it is read, it will be valued.

XLIII. — *Letters in Vindication of the Church of Ireland; addressed to an English Member of Parliament.* By the Rev. J. M. MAGUIRE, B.A., *Vicar of Boyle, &c.* London: Rivingtons.

THE volume before us is one of the most valuable, as bearing on the case of the Church of Ireland, that we have ever seen. We have perused with pain the records of the injustice of the State to the Irish Church, and with pleasure the vindication of that Church's position. In Ireland the State policy had full play for a long series of years. The Sovereign appointed to bishoprics, without even the intervention of a nominal election, and it gradually destroyed the Church. Bishoprics were the bribes of political services. Even now, the patronage of the State in Ireland is unblushingly and openly employed for the purpose of breaking down the principles of the Church. The latitudinarian system of education established by the State, was condemned by the whole Church of Ireland, with scarcely a dissentient voice. Government appoints no one to bishoprics or other benefices, who will not declare himself in opposition to the sentiments of his Church! The conduct of the State to the Church in Ireland, is characterized by the same obstinate determination to carry out its latitudinarianism, as it has shown in England; and it must be confronted with equal obstinacy. We will only add, that the Church of Ireland will never gain any thing by meekness and submissiveness. They have to deal with a foe who only contemns them for obedience and quietness, and rejoices to think that they are tied down by their connexion with the State, and can only complain. We would advise the Church of Ireland to show something of the energy of the Church of England in seeking for their *liberties*, and then they will perhaps have less reason to complain of want of sympathy at this side of the Channel.

XLIV.—*Deeds of Faith: Stories for Children from Church History. By the Rev.* J. M. NEALE, *M.A.* London: Mozley.

A VERY pleasing collection of tales, some of them of rather a legendary description, relating remarkable instances of the powers of Christian faith in various ages. Mr. Neale excels in compositions of this kind.

XLV.—*Holy Men of Old: being short notices of such as are named in the Calendar of the English Church.* London: Mozley.

THE notices are very short certainly, but perhaps they are not the worse for that, for in very many cases there are not many authentic details recorded in history. On the whole it is a well written and interesting volume.

XLVI.—*Sketches of Character; and other pieces in Verse. By* ANNA H. POTTS. Cambridge: University Press.

WE are afraid we cannot speak very highly of these poems, though there is some cleverness in them. We extract part of the first as a specimen.

> " Husbands indeed ! Nay urge not again,
>   Not always may friendship's bright fancies expand ;
> But few can we sketch of this large class of men,
>   Who from woman, love, honour, obedience demand !
> The first is a clever but very vain man,
>   The envied young lady he takes for his bride,
> Though she loves him too truly his follies to fan,
>   Will quietly learn her own talents to hide ;
> For he thinks in her sex, the bright gifts of the mind,
>   Are best to the depths of oblivion consign'd."

And to those " depths of oblivion " we much fear Anna H. Potts' poems will be " consigned " likewise.

XLVII.—*Letters and Memoir of the late Walter Augustus Shirley, D.D., Lord Bishop of Sodor and Man. Edited by* THOMAS HILL, *B.D., Archdeacon of Derby.* London: Hatchards.

DR. SHIRLEY appears to have been a very good and earnest clergyman, and his parochial labours were highly successful; he was also a useful and efficient archdeacon; and thus possessed more qualifications for the office of bishop than can always be shown. His views were rather evangelical. He had only just been consecrated when he was carried off by a sudden attack of illness, to

the great grief of his friends.   Dr. Shirley would have been a
blessing to the Diocese of Sodor and Man, if his life had been
spared, for such sincerity and earnestness as his, and so much
substantial and real piety, even though tinged in some degree
with prejudices, could not have failed to draw down a blessing on
his labours.

xlviii.—*Liber Precum Publicarum, etc.*   Londini :   J. W.
   Parker.

A very neat and well printed edition of the Latin Prayer
Book, apparently well edited.

xlix.—*Sermons,   By the late Rev.* James Cowles Prichard,
   Vicar of Mitcham, Surrey, &c., with a Memoir.   London:
   Masters.

The lamented author of these discourses was a very earnest and
promising young clergyman, who was taken from us less than
two years ago.   His " Life and Times of Hincmar " has been
already noticed in this Review as a work of unusual merit, and
the pious and thoughtful sermons before us, prove the efficacy
of his pulpit ministrations.   They are quite those of a Churchman.

l.—*The Parson's Home: a Poem.   By an* English Vicar.
   London : Rivingtons.

This poem contains many pleasing descriptions of rural life and
feelings, and exhibits a degree of poetical power much like that
of the generality of prize poems.   The versification is good, the
imagery unexceptionable, and the classical allusions frequent.   It
is altogether a very readable volume, without any extraordinary
amount of poetical power.

li.—*The Judgments on Baptismal Regeneration, &c.   By* W.
   J. Irons, *B.D., Vicar of Brompton.*   London : Masters.

An able and thoughtful publication, comprising the various documents of importance which have recently appeared in connexion
with the Gorham case, and evincing a full appreciation of the
depth of peril now surrounding the faith of the Church, and the
imperative necessity of *action* in consequence.

lii.—*An Exposition of the Creed by John Pearson, D.D.,
   Bishop of Chester.   Revised and Corrected by the Rev.* Temple
   Chevallier, *B.D.*   Cambridge: University Press ; London :
   J. W. Parker.

An accurate and beautiful edition of Pearson on the Creed.   All the references have been carefully collated, and the work is here, we suppose, presented in the most perfect form it is capable of.

LIII.—*An Arctic Voyage to Baffin's Bay and Lancaster Sound, in Search of Friends, with Sir John Franklin. By* ROBERT ANSTRUTHER GOODSIR, *late President of the Royal Medical Society of Edinburgh.* London: Van Voorst.

THE author of this little volume is one of those whose relatives have taken part in the expedition under Sir John Franklin ; and, in the hope of hearing some tidings of a brother who had embarked in that expedition in 1845, he joined, as a medical man, a whaler, commanded by Mr. William Penney, and in March, 1849, sailed from Stromness for the Arctic Regions ; from whence he returned, after a voyage of eight months, and has since, as we learn from the Preface, joined in one of the expeditions recently dispatched in pursuit of the missing ships of Sir J. Franklin. The little volume before us is written with a freedom and a *bonhommie* peculiarly pleasing.. We are not aware that it throws any new light on the subjects of which it treats, but the descriptions of scenery, of the habits of the natives, and of the whale fishery, are extremely good and spirited. The last mentioned subject affords considerable scope for the pen, and is generally the most exciting we find in works descriptive of Northern voyages ; but in this volume the descriptions of perils on the ice, including the crushing and destruction of ships, divide the interest. We do not remember any where to have read more vigorous and graphic description of the " sport" of killing whales, in which there is certainly adventure enough to satisfy any amount of craving. We have no doubt that those descriptions will afford the highest gratification to all persons who are fond of such diversions ; and the evident feelings of triumph with which the author details the success of the warfare waged against the whales, are precisely those of a sportsman. We confess that the whole process appears to us something like butchery ; and we should be sorry to be one of those who could make up their minds to harpoon a whale which left itself exposed to danger and death, from maternal affection to its " calf," or young one ; of which we have an instance recorded in this volume. We suppose such feelings are very unreasonable, but we should think that many of our readers must have experienced them ere now in perusing accounts of the whale fishery, even while they may have admired the courage and dexterity of the harpooners and others engaged.

LIV.—*An Elementary Course of Geology, Mineralogy, and Physical Geography. By* DAVID T. ANSTED, *M.A., F.R.S., &c., Professor of Geology in King's College, London.* London: Van Voorst.

MR. ANSTED is already so well known to the public as one of our most eminent scientific men, and more especially for his admirable work on Geology—the best, we believe, on the subject—that his name is a sufficient recommendation to any thing that may proceed from his pen.

The work before us is one of the most comprehensive nature: it comprises an elementary course of instruction in Physical Geography, Mineralogy, and Geology, extensively illustrated by wood-cuts. The first part of this work comprises a Treatise on Physical Geography; in which the author considers the subject of Matter generally, and especially the mechanical condition and properties of the substances found near the surface of the earth; the focus of attraction and repulsion; light, heat, and electricity; the form and density of the earth; distribution of waters, rivers, mountains; currents in the atmosphere and sea; changes in the earth's crust, by alterations in temperature, and by the reaction of the interior of the earth through volcanoes, earthquakes, &c.; change of level; elevation of some parts of the earth, and depression of others.

He next proceeds to Mineralogy, arranged under the heads of crystallography; characteristics of simple minerals, of non-metallic simple minerals, and of metals and ores.

" Descriptive Geology " commences with an examination of the different species of rocks, and their formation; then proceeds to stratification and mechanical displacement of rocks, their classification, and the distribution of organic remains, together with their value in determining the relative ages of rocks. The rocks and fossils of the tertiary period, and of the secondary epoch, and those of the palæozoic period, are successively examined; after which, the connexion of geology with agriculture, engineering, and architecture is traced; and the Appendix contains a series of examination papers in mineralogy and geology, some description of the geology of India, with an excellent Index.

That so great an amount of scientific discussion should be included within 600 small pages, is a proof of the condensation to which Mr. Ansted has subjected his matter throughout. To students his work will be invaluable; and we can have no doubt that it will obtain the extensive circulation which it so well deserves.

LV.—*A Treatise on the Climate and Meteorology of Madeira. By the late* J. H. MASON, *M.D., Inventor of Mason's Hygrometer. Edited by* J. S. KNOWLES. London: Churchill.

THE great value of this work will be its utility as a guide to those whose health obliges them to seek a warmer climate. It comprises a series of observations by a medical man, and by others, on the climate, temperature, &c., of Madeira; in short, all that kind of information which is most important to patients and to physicians to acquire. It would appear that the persons who visit Madeira for health, are led to undertake excursions for the purpose of viewing the very remarkable scenery of the island, which frequently have the effect of preventing them from deriving the benefit they might otherwise have experienced from a residence there; and they do not seem to be aware that there are changes of temperature at Madeira as well as in England, and that it is requisite to act accordingly. To the general reader the greater part of this work, comprising observations and tables, will not be very interesting; but there is a very curious chapter by Dr. Peacock, Dean of Ely, on the tenure of land in Madeira, and the tenant right there established, which virtually amounts to giving tenants perpetual possession on paying a certain portion of the produce to the landlord. The working of this system appears to hold out no stimulus to industry, and the lands at Madeira appear to be wretchedly cultivated, and the landlords bankrupt. There is a well written and amusing tour of Madeira in the latter part of the volume, by Mr. Driver, making an excellent guide book.

LVI.—*Plain Parish Sermons, preached at Rotherhithe. By the Rev.* PHILIP BLAND, *B.A., Curate of St. Mary's Church.* London: Wertheim and Mackintosh.

THERE is a great temptation to young men in the ministry to gain attention by startling modes of expression. We are afraid Mr. Bland has yielded to this temptation. His Sermons are *plain* enough, but they lack propriety: for instance, at p. 178, he speaks rather contemptuously of the three Creeds, where he says of a certain text, "I do not hesitate to say, though composed two hundred years before Christ, it is a very *much better*, a much more Christian Creed than any of the three in our Prayer Book, which was written after Christ had been upon earth; but of which several parts are written in a sadly hostile and invidious spirit towards other parties; many of whom, there is no doubt, were much better Christians than their self-styled orthodox opponents. This, however, is not the place, neither is this the time, to compare the early creed in the text with the later ones, which we find in our Prayer Book ; which yet, of course, are quite open to have their merits discussed, *and their faults exposed*, as being human compositions, and therefore, at best, very much inferior to the simple word of God." This is something like "speaking out." Mr. Bland is evidently a candidate for a Bishopric, and such are the men who are now being appointed Bishops and Deans. To attack the Creeds, and sneer at *orthodoxy* is now the certain and infallible mode of gaining favourable notice from the State.

LVII.—*Letters to my Children on Moral Subjects. By the Rev.* W. J. E. BENNETT, *M.A., Perpetual Curate of St. Paul's, Knightsbridge.* London: Cleaver.

AN excellent series of moral instructions, entering into all those details which comprise the great difficulties of most minds in youth.

LVIII.—*Common Sense versus Common Law. By* WILLIAM MASSEY, *Esq., Barrister-at-Law.* London: Longmans.

EVERY one has heard of the "glorious uncertainty" of the law, even if he has not experienced it. Mr. Massey takes the law to pieces, and shows the cause of its uncertainty, and not unfrequent injustice ; and he appears to understand his subject perfectly well.

LIX.—*A Plea for the faithful Restoration of our ancient Churches, &c. By* GEORGE GILBERT SCOTT, *Architect.* London: J. H. Parker.

MR. SCOTT speaks with right feeling and right principle on the faithful restoration of our old Churches ; and yet there is nothing overstrained or absurd in his recommendations. Novelty should, as far as possible, be eschewed in Church restorations ; we mean, such novelty as amounts to material alterations in the character and style of the building, or the removal of ancient characteristics, as a general rule.

LX.—*Three Advent Sermons ; and a Pastor's Address on the Twentieth Anniversary of his Incumbency. By* EDWARD B. RAMSAY, *M.A., Dean of Edinburgh.* London: Rivingtons.

A VOLUME containing much sound and sober-minded teaching, in which the author appears anxious to trace his way between extremes in all directions, to which he is evidently very averse.

LXI.—*The Influence of the Hebrew and Christian Revelations on Ancient Heathen Writers.* (*Hulsean Prize Essay for* 1849.) *By* SAMUEL TOMKINS, *of St. Catharine's Hall.* Cambridge: Deighton.

A VERY able and well written work, affording indications of much promise. We are glad to see in the writer another advocate of Christianity in opposition to the speculations of German Infidelity.

LXII.—*Prayers and Rules for the Ordering and Use of a Church Guild. With Remarks on Ancient Guilds.* London: Masters.

MANY persons, on perusing this little book, might be disposed to regard the proposal of establishing Church Guilds as a matter undeserving of consideration. We do not concur in such a view; and although it may be possible that every part of the scheme here proposed would not be found beneficial, we should be glad to hear how such institutions work; for it is very easy to put forward plans, but not always easy to carry them into execution.

LXIII.—*Guardian Angels. A sacred Allegory. By* MARY N. LESTER. London: Masters.

A VERY pleasingly written allegory. The "Guardian Angels" are Faith, Hope, and Charity, who conduct a band of baptized Christians towards heaven.

LXIV.—*Phases of Faith; or, Passages from the History of my Creed. By* FRANCIS WILLIAM NEWMAN, *formerly Fellow of Balliol College, Oxford.* London: Chapman.

THAT such books as this should be published with impunity,—that gross and direct blasphemy, equal to that of any of the Encyclopedists, should be obtruded on the public, is a sufficient sign of the spread of infidelity; and a warning to Christians of the necessity of taking measures for the security of the Faith. Unbelievers like Mr. Newman may well hate the creeds and formularies of the Church. He calls for the abolition of creeds. So do all the Rationalists and heretics of the day; and this is what the State will do ere long, if the Church does not resolutely assert her liberty, and shake off the bondage of an unbelieving State.

LXV.—*God in Christ. Three Discourses, delivered at New Haven, Cambridge, and Andover, &c. By* HORACE BUSHNELL. London: Chapman.

MR. HORACE BUSHNELL is one of those persons who are very much grieved at the dogmatism of Christians, and particularly in

America, where Puritanism has given birth to all kinds of monstrosities in religion. He suggests to his brethren the expediency of relaxing adherence to their creeds and confessions of faith, in order to promote unity, So that Puritanism has come to this—that although it would not relax in such matters as a surplice or a Prayer Book, it is now called on, after two hundred and fifty years of trial, to relax its *faith!* Surely the judgment of God on causeless divisions is evident here. Mr. Bushnell is a believer in some of the chief doctrines of Christianity; but his system is that of letting any one deny them that pleases, and yet recognizing him as a Christian brother.

LXVI.—*Evening Thoughts.* By a PHYSICIAN. London: Van Voorst.

FROM all we have seen of this work, we have reason to express a very favourable opinion of it. In these days we must look with some degree of anxiety on philosophical views of religion; but in the volume before us, we are happy to see that philosophy is made, as it ought to be, " the handmaid of Theology." This physician has happily not reasoned himself out of the Christian faith.

LXVII.—*A Critical History of the Language and Situation of Ancient Greece.* By WILLIAM MURE, *of Caldwell.* London: Longmans.

THREE volumes of this learned and elaborate work are now before us, but the mass of criticism which they comprise, renders it hopeless for us to attempt at present to do more than state, that they form a portion of a complete literary history of Greece; the first two volumes being devoted to the early history of the language, and to Homer and Hesiod chiefly; the third to the lyric poets, and the early history of writing. Mr. Mure must contemplate an extensive work, when it is remembered what portion of Greek literature still remains to be criticized.

LXVIII.—*Apocalyptic Sketches or Lectures on the Seven Churches of Asia Minor.* By the Rev. J. CUMMING, *D.D., &c.* London: Hall, Virtue, and Co.

THIS series of Discourses is just suited for delivery in London, to a congregation made up partly of professing members of other communions, attracted by curiosity, or Dr. Cumming's power as a preacher. They are doctrinal, practical, and latitudinarian: the object before such preachers always being, to lay down such principles as may enable persons of all denominations to attend their ministry, without feeling that they are doing wrong in leaving their own Churches.

LXIX.—*Sermons. By* HENRY ALFORD, *B.D., Vicar of Wymeswold, &c.* London: Rivingtons.

A THOUGHTFUL and excellent volume of Sermons.

LXX.—*An Apology for the Septuagint, in which its Claims to Biblical and Canonical Authority are briefly stated and vindicated. By* E. W. GRINFIELD, *M.A., &c.* London: Pickering.

MR. GRINFIELD in this work argues that a species of inspiration must have guided the translators of the Septuagint. His position is maintained with much learning and speciousness, but we confess ourselves not convinced.

LXXI.—*Essays: Political, Historical, and Miscellaneous. By* ARCHIBALD ALISON, *LL.D., &c.* Edinburgh: Blackwoods, Vol. I.

FEW men in the present day have beheld the fate and prospects of the country with a more firm and vigorous grasp of intellect than the eminent author of the "History of Europe." These Essays evince the forethought of their writer. The nation however, or its rulers, have held a different view, and will adhere obstinately to it, according to all appearances. We can therefore only look for gradual ruin.

LXXII.—*Translation of Herman Venema's inedited Institutes of Theology. By the Rev.* ALEX. W. BROWN, *Minister of Free St. Bernard's Church, Edinburgh.* Edinburgh: Clark.

WHO "*Free* St. Bernard" was, we know not; but the Incumbent of his Church has translated a very sound book, quite in the old orthodox style, *i. e.* as much so as could be expected from a Dutchman, as we imagine Venema to have been.

LXXIII.—*The Gospel Narrative of our Lord's Ministry (the Third Year), Harmonized: with Reflections. By the Rev.* ISAAC WILLIAMS, *B.D., &c.* London: Rivingtons.

THIS is the conclusion of Mr. Williams's Harmony of the Gospel Narrative, and is characterized by the same excellencies as the preceding volumes. It is rich in illustration from the writings of the Fathers and other eminent Commentators.

LXXIV.—*Jesus the Giver and the Fulfiller of the New Law. A Course of Eight Sermons on the Beatitudes, &c. By the Rev.* ALEX. WATSON, *M.A., &c.* London: Masters.

WE have to thank Mr. Watson for this eloquent and able series of Discourses, setting forth the great doctrines of the Gospel, without fear or compromise.

MISCELLANEOUS.

WE have to acknowledge the receipt of many publications which it is impossible to notice as they deserve at this moment. Mr. Neale's " History of the Holy Eastern Church," in 2 vols., is replete with matter of the highest interest, but we must reserve a notice of it for our next publication. Amongst architectural publications we have to speak in high terms of commendation of Mr. Sharpe's " Decorative Window Tracery," (Van Voorst,) as amongst the most valuable and useful publications we have seen, and very beautifully illustrated. Mr. Freeman, in his " Essay on the Origin and Development of Window Tracery in England," (Oxford : J. H. Parker,) has broken ground on the same subject, and with great success. His design is larger than that of Mr. Sharpe.

We must now turn to the shoal of minor publications bearing on the present controversy, and the subjects connected with it. Amongst these we must first mention Dr. Mill's Sermon before the University of Cambridge (Deighton), as an able vindication of sound principle in opposition to the latitudinarianism of the Privy Council. " Contending for the Faith," a Sermon by Mr. Anderdon, (Masters,) and excellent in its way. " A Voice from the North," Nos. I. and II., (Masters,) a vigorous protest against laxity, and the production of a writer who is quite alive to the exigencies of the times, and equal to them. Two Sermons on Baptism, by the Rev. C. C. Bartholomew, of St. David's, Exeter, (Masters,) exactly in the right spirit. " Failing in the Faith," by Mr. Case, of Margaret Chapel, a title unfortunately applicable to the writer. " A Plea for the Church of England," by Mr. Worgan, (Rivingtons,) most excellent, asserting the rights of the Church in the right way. " The Controversy of Faith— Advice to Candidates for Holy Orders,". by Mr. Dodgson (Murray); a sound and orthodox view of the Gorham case, rather disinclined, however, to any synodical action of the Church at present, as scarcely fitted for it. We see difficulties and perils as Mr. Dodgson does, but we think there is no alternative; for it is impossible to let things remain as they are. " Church and State," reprinted from the last number of the " Christian Remembrancer " (Mozley); a very well-timed publication, distinctly pointing out the altered position of the Church through the transfer of the supremacy to a body of men without creed. " Stand fast in the Faith," a Sermon by the Curate of Stoke Damerel (Masters); very faithful to the Church, and in all respects worthy of praise. " Our Present Duties in regard to Holy Baptism," a Sermon by the Rev: T. L. Claughton (Rivingtons); an able, honest, and eloquent discourse. " A

Letter to all Members of the Church of England," &c., by
Mr. Watson, of Cheltenham, (Masters,) is a plain and forcible
tract addressed to the people, and pointing out the doctrine
of the Church in opposition to the Gorham heresy. "A Third
Letter to the Right Hon. Sir George Grey," by the Rev. W. H.
Hoare, (Rivingtons,) in continuation of the Letters noticed elsewhere in this number, and treating of the Baptismal Controversy
in a very pleasing tone. We agree with Mr. Hoare that the
two parties, to a great extent, hold views which might be harmonized; but this ought to be done by authority of the Church, and
extravagant assertions and heresies forbidden. All will be confusion till this is done. "A Brief Vindication of Jewel, Hooker,"
&c., by a Fellow of a College, (Rivingtons,) is a clear and
thorough exposure of the false quotations in the judgment in
re Gorham. "The Scottish Magazine," No. xxviii., contains
some remarks on the Gorham case, urging the imperative necessity of the Church of England's immediate exertion to reverse the
judgment of the Privy Council.

On the other side of the question we have "The Present Crisis
of the Church," by Dr. Hook, (Murray,) rather in favour of the
decision of the Committee of Council, and only apprehensive of
Romanism, which, indeed, appears to have been for some years
the only error on which Dr. Hook looks with alarm. "The
Trials of the Church, a quickening of her Zeal and Love," two
Sermons by the Rev. J. S. M. Anderson, &c. (Rivingtons.)
These discourses are intended for the purpose of retaining
persons in the Church, but they amount to a justification of the
Privy Council. "The Duty of Christian Subjection," by the
Rev. James Brogden, M.A., (Hatchards,) is, in fact, an
assertion of the highest claims ever made for State supremacy
when the State was orthodox, on behalf of the present un-
believing State. "A House divided against itself," by Mr.
Dodsworth (Masters); "The Royal Supremacy," by T. W.
Allies (Pickering); "Letters on the Present Position of the
High Church Party," by Mr. Maskell, (Pickering,) are all in the
same spirit. They are the publications of men who have been
driven into alienation from the Church by the tyranny of the
State, and who appear to despair of the cause of the Church.
We think that real loyalty to the Church and to her Divine
Head would rather lead men to co-operate for the removal, at all
hazards, of the evils now seen to be oppressing us, than to relinquish the struggle at the very beginning of it. Let us hope
better and nobler things from all who really *do* love the English
Church. Let them not desert the good cause, but urge it on
with all their hearts, and without permitting doubts and fears

to influence them. "A Few Words on the Spirit in which Men are meeting the present Crisis of the Church," by the Rev. E. Monro, (J. H. Parker,) is a well-meant publication, but one which is calculated to do harm, in persuading men to abstain from the only methods of action by which the Church can now be protected. There are many disadvantages and evils in voluntary combinations, but nothing else will *work ;* and in times like the present, the defence of the faith by every available means left us by the law, is the primary object to be put before us. In times of war, many of the blessings of peace must be sacrificed. We will give Mr. Monro one hint with reference to his proposal to leave all our Church affairs to certain lawyers. The difference between lawyers and clergy is, that the former *talk* on Church questions, while the latter *act* in them. Mr. Monro will live, we hope, to see his mistake. "The Judicial Committee of Privy Council and the Petition for a Church Tribunal," by an Anglican Layman, (Pickering,) is by one of those opinionated persons who will not take any part in a general movement, if it does not go exactly to the length they think advisable. He thinks the supremacy ought to be abolished, and therefore he will not ask for any lesser liberty for the Church. Men like these are perfectly impracticable, and are always in the way, with their pertinacious folly.

As long as bishoprics and deaneries are dispensed in reward of labours in defence of the Government system of education in England and Ireland, we shall have occasional pamphlets like that of Mr. Girdlestone, "The Committee of Council on Education; an Imaginary Enemy a Real Friend." (Hatchards.) The Government's possession of patronage will always raise up friends for it amongst the clergy. The Rev. E. W. Grinfield's very curious and learned work, "An Apology for the Septuagint," (Pickering,) which maintains the inspiration of that translation, is very well deserving of attention, as well as his "Letter to Dr. Wiseman" on an "interpolated" passage in the Vatican Septuagint. (Pickering.) The interpolation referred to is a curious one. We are glad to see a publication by Chancellor Harington, on "The Reconsecration, Reconciliation, &c. of Churches" (Rivingtons) : it abounds in learning and original documents. Archdeacon Hale's "Duties of Deacons and Priests compared," (Rivingtons,) contains most excellent suggestions for the revival of the diaconate; but we shall never be able to have such plans carried into effect till we get our synods. We shall then have a Legislature that looks to the spiritual welfare of the Church in the first place, instead of thrusting it aside amongst the lumber and rubbish which burden temporal legislation.

Foreign and Colonial Intelligence.

AUSTRIA.—*Emancipation of the Romish Church.*—An Imperial decree, of the 18th of April last, abrogates the restrictions imposed upon the Romish Bishops by the laws which have been in force in the Austrian Empire ever since the reign of Joseph II. both as regards their communication with the Pope, and their intercourse with their own dioceses ; with the only proviso, that, of documents intended for publication, copies shall be furnished to the civil authorities. The internal discipline of the Church is left entirely to the spiritual power, without any interference on the part of the State, which is bound to assist in carrying into effect sentences of the spiritual courts, on proof of the regularity of the proceedings. The Emperor still reserves to himself the nomination to vacant bishoprics, but promises to be guided by the advice of the bishops, especially of those of the province in which the vacancy occurs. The regulations of the Synods recently held at Olmütz and Salzburg, with regard to the exercise of ecclesiastical patronage, are confirmed by the Emperor. Other and minor points are left for adjustment hereafter, upon conference with the bishops, or negotiation, if necessary, with the Pope. The tendency of the whole decree is, to restore in its plenitude, and with hardly a limitation upon it, the power of the Romish hierarchy in the Austrian dominions.

BELGIUM.—*Legal Status of Romish Priests.*—The question whether the civil law should recognise the indelibility of the orders, and, by consequence, the irrevocable obligation of the vows of celibacy, of the Romish priesthood, has recently been brought before the legal tribunals of Belgium, under the following circumstances. M. Poulet, priest at Florée, suddenly renounced celibacy, and solicited the hand of a young girl. The father having refused his consent, his opposition brought the case before the tribunal of Ghent, whose decision rejects as unfounded this opposition ; the priest not having taken the engagement of celibacy towards the State, but solely towards his spiritual Head, and being entitled, on renouncing the advantages and immunities of his ministry, to all the privileges of a Belgian and a citizen. In France, the Court of Cassation has pronounced three judgments of a contrary nature.

CANADA.—*Toronto Diocese. The University Question.*—The sensation produced in the Diocese of Toronto by the recent secularization of the University, is deep and general ; and the suggestion of the Bishop for the establishment of a Church University, is meeting with the most active and liberal support. A General Board has been formed in Toronto City, for the purpose of promoting this important object, and has placed itself in immediate communication with the local

Committees throughout the Diocese. An instalment of twenty per cent. on all sums subscribed for the New University, has been declared due on the 1st of September, and measures have been taken for the conveyance of gifts of land to Trustees, who are to transfer such lands to the University upon its obtaining a Charter. The subscriptions announced up to the 11th of April last, amounted already to 23,363*l*., in money, land, and stock, besides 2840 acres and two town lots of land not valued. The *Church* Newspaper, too, is doing excellent service by republishing a series of documents connected with the history of the old University.

On the Bishop taking his departure for Europe, on the morning of the 10th of April, he was met on the wharf by a large concourse of the *élite* of Toronto, who remained to bid him farewell. Addresses from the different congregations of the city had previously been presented to his lordship. The following forms of prayer, ordered to be used throughout the Diocese, during the absence of the Bishop, will be read with interest.

Immediately on his lordship's departure it was ordered, that at Morning Prayer, when the Litany is used, after the words, "That it may please Thee to preserve all that travel by land or by water," should be added, "especially Thy servant, the Bishop of this Diocese." And at Evening Service, after the Prayer "For all conditions of men," the following Prayer was directed to be used :—"O eternal Lord, who alone spreadest out the heavens, and rulest the raging of the sea ; who hast compassed the waters with bounds until day and night come to an end ; Be pleased to receive into Thy almighty and most gracious protection the Bishop of this Diocese, that he may be preserved from the dangers of the sea, and may return in safety to enjoy the blessings of the land, and the fruits of his labours, and with a thankful remembrance of Thy mercies, to praise and glorify Thy holy name ; through Jesus Christ our Lord. Amen."

On the intelligence of the Bishop's safe arrival in England being received, the following prayer was substituted, to be used at Morning Service before the "General Thanksgiving," and at Evening Service, before the Prayer "For all conditions of men :"—"O Lord God, who by the guidance of a star didst direct the wise men to the birth-place of Thy blessed Son ; Prosper, we beseech Thee, Thy servant the Bishop of this Diocese in the work which he has undertaken ; protect him by Thy Providence ; and grant that, in Thy good time, he may return amongst us in health and safety, with the fruit of his labours, to Thine honour and glory, and to the benefit of this Church and people, through the merits of the same Thy Son Jesus Christ our Lord. Amen."

We readily give insertion to the following appeal, addressed by the Bishop to the Churchmen in this country, in furtherance of the object which, at his advanced period of life, has induced his lordship to cross the Atlantic :—

"Beloved Brethren,—Under the pressure of what I feel to be a very great necessity, I have ceased for a short time from my pastoral labours in the Diocese of Toronto, and have come to England to appeal, I hope not in vain, to the sympathy of the members of the Church of England in behalf of their brethren in Upper Canada.

" When, in the year 1799, I made that distant portion of the British empire my home, it contained not more than 20,000 inhabitants. Even in 1824, the population had only risen to 150,000; but since that period the increase has been astonishing, being now (1850) 800,000, or more than fivefold in twenty-six years, and according to its present rapid rate of increase, so much accelerated by steam navigation, and by the circumstances which compel emigration from Great Britain and Ireland, there is no doubt that many who are now living will see its population far greater than that of Scotland.

" Of its present inhabitants I may venture to say, that 200,000, at least, are members of the Church of England, and the greater part of them either emigrants from the United Kingdom, or the children of such emigrants. Hence the Diocese of Toronto promises to be the principal seat of our Church in British North America.

" The present policy of the mother country, whether it be wise or unwise, is to confer upon her great colonial possessions almost uncontrolled powers of government, so that their subordination to Imperial authority is in fact rather nominal than real. Being left to model their civil institutions as they please, their moral condition and social happiness are dependent on the chance of their forming a right judgment of their best interests. And this, where suffrage is almost universal, as it is in Upper Canada, leaves all dependent on the virtue and intelligence of the people.

" For the education of the great mass of the people in common schools, liberal provision has been made by the Legislature, under a system which is conducted with ability and zeal, but which, nevertheless, labours under the vital defect of excluding all doctrinal instruction in religion, or, in other words, all practical teaching of religious truth.

" To secure an adequate provision for education of that higher order which is necessary to prepare youth for the liberal professions and for the important duties of legislation, had been, for fifty years, the self-imposed labour of my life.

" In 1827, before which time the Province was scarcely qualified to receive it, we had the happiness to see in Upper Canada a University founded by Royal Charter, and liberally endowed by the Crown with a grant of land. So little exclusive was it in its character, that its advantages were open to all; no tests were required from professors or students, with the exception of the professor of divinity and of graduates in that faculty.

" But it was avowedly a College in connexion with the National Church, and provision was made in the Charter for insuring unity and consistency in its discipline and government.

" If it had been otherwise, the Charter would have been such as had never before issued under the Great Seal of England for the foundation of a University to be endowed by the Crown in any part of the British dominions. Yet, because it was complained of as unreasonable and unjust that a University should be founded by the sovereign in connexion with the Established Church of the empire, it was thought expedient to allow the Royal Charter to be so altered by a Colonial statute, as to leave no trace in it of a connexion with the National Church.

" This change was made in 1837 ; and, as was foreseen by many, it half accomplished the ruin of the University. For though neither religious instruction nor Divine worship was excluded, and though in deference to the express wish of the Sovereign, King William IV., a Professorship of Divinity according to the doctrines of the Church of England, and the daily use of her admirable Liturgy, were tolerated for a time, during which the University was flourishing, and rapidly rising in public estimation and confidence, yet the Colonial legislature, having been once allowed to mutilate the Royal Charter, has not stopped short in the work of destruction.

" In the last session an Act was passed, which came into force on the first day of January, 1850, expressly excluding from the College religious instruction according to any form of doctrine whatever ; prohibiting any form of prayer, or any act of public worship, and disqualifying any Graduate of the University, who may have taken holy orders, from having a voice in the Senate.

" By this measure, which I think I do not too harshly describe when I speak of it as impious, the munificent gift of His Majesty King George IV., (a gift the present value of which is estimated at 270,000*l.*, and yields a revenue, that is yearly increasing, of about 11,000*l.*), is at last worse than thrown away ; for, deprived of the respect and confidence of the sound and intelligent portion of the community, to whatever denomination of Christians they may belong, the University cannot flourish ; or if by any exertion it can be sustained for a time, it must be at the sacrifice of the highest and most sacred interests.

" A deep conviction of this forces itself upon the mind of every religious man ; but the members of the Church of England, utterly despairing of, and rejecting as they do what was once King's College, but is now the antichristian " University of Toronto," do yet not despair of their Church, or of their cause. Relying on the blessings of God, and using their own best exertions, they hope soon to succeed in establishing a University strictly and unreservedly in connexion with their Church ; a University not confining itself to instruction in human science, but a University of which the religious character shall be known and acknowledged, in which the doctrines of the Church of England shall be taught in their integrity, and in which her pure and 'reasonable service' shall elevate and sanctify the labours of the teacher and the scholar.

" We hope to succeed in establishing for ourselves, without pecuniary aid from any public source, a University clearly and avowedly in connexion with our Church, receiving only from our gracious Sovereign what other religious denominations in the province have received, a

Charter of Incorporation, providing for the government of the Institution, and conferring on it the privilege of conferring Degrees.

" I am labouring, at an advanced age, to lay the foundation of a work which I believe will, at no distant day, be of inestimable value to that rising country.—The efforts which I made in the province, just before my departure, have been nobly seconded. Within a few weeks, the contributions in money and land amounted to more than twenty-five thousand pounds. Yet this effort, astonishing as it is, considering the state of the contributors, struggling for subsistence in the wilderness, far from the land of their fathers, is scarcely sufficient to erect the necessary buildings. But does it not constitute a claim all but irresistible upon the members of the Church in this country, to supply the deficiency as to endowment? Hence, having done our utmost, my people as well as myself feel ourselves justified in relying with filial confidence upon the enlightened patriotism, the religious zeal, the generous sympathy of our brethren at home, for enabling us to establish, in this populous and important Colony, upon a sound foundation and on a liberal scale, a seat of learning with which political agitation shall have no pretence to meddle, and which will assuredly prove an invaluable blessing to the country, and to many thousands in it who were inhabitants of the United Kingdom ; and not a blessing to those only who belong to the Church of England, but to all who may desire to avail themselves of the means of education which such an Institution will offer.

" I trust God will put it into the hearts of those of our fellow-churchmen in this country to whom He has entrusted wealth, to give us liberally of their abundance ; and that those who can only by the exercise of a prudent economy have any thing to spare, may still spare us a little ; for what we have undertaken can only be accomplished on an adequate scale, by the co-operation of many.

" It is not long since an English gentleman, Mr. Smithson, bequeathed a princely sum of money for the promotion of science by means of an institution to be founded in the capital of the United States of America, to which country I am not aware that he was bound by any particular tie. If, happily, some other English gentleman, of equal means and equal philanthropy, should so far combine patriotism with benevolence as to make Upper Canada the recipient of so large a bounty, he would be laying the foundation of infinite good to a country rapidly rising into importance, and would be doing more than it seems can be done, in present times, by legislatures and governments for the best interests of the people.

" I am, beloved brethren,

" Your faithful and affectionate brother,

" J. Toronto."

" 19, *Bury-Street, St. James's, May* 4, 1850."

Repudiation of the University by the Presbyterians.—The Commission of the Synod of the Presbyterian Church at Kingston have resolved to carry on their own institution of Queen's College in conformity with its royal Charter, irrespectively of the University Act passed last session of the Provincial Parliament. Among the reasons assigned for this determination, the first is as follows:—

" The irreligious character of the Act referred to. Not only is the teaching of .Theology prohibited in the University of Toronto, but all forms of Divine Worship, all public prayer, every thing that can remind either professors or students of God, and the duties we owe to Him,— of our responsibilities and obligations, is rigidly and peremptorily excluded. . And as no test whatever is required of the professors, not even belief in the existence of God, there is nothing in the Act to prevent infidels, atheists, or persons holding the most dangerous and pernicious principles, from being entrusted with the instruction of youth at that time of life when evil impressions are most likely to be made upon their minds."

Building Society in connexion with the Church.—A Building Society in connexion with the Church has been formed in Upper Canada, with the approbation of the Bishop, who has recommended it to the clergy and laity of his diocese in a Pastoral Letter, in which his Lordship explains the manner in which such a Society may be useful to the Church, as well as to the projected Church University : —

" Persons of small means, who are anxious to do something for the Church, or University, frequently find it inconvenient to advance at once what they desire to give. Now, to such, the Building Society offers the advantage of profitable investment by receiving such dona-tions in small payments, monthly, quarterly, or half-yearly. This pro-cess may be beneficially applied to building Churches, Parsonages— Parochial Endowments—as well as to the University.

" I think it right to submit these suggestions to the members of the Church, lay and clerical, as meeting in the most easy way such efforts as our poor and scattered population are able to make, and which, if prudently carried out, seem to promise great advantage to the progress and stability of the Church. For details, I would respectfully refer to Thomas Champion, Esq., who is familiar with the working of Building Societies, and will give with pleasure ample information on the subject to any who require it.

" By following some such plan, we may soon have a fertile glebe, a parsonage-house, and a University lot, in every township."

Church Statistics.—The following tabular statement of the result of the Bishop's Visitations in the Diocese of Toronto at the periods named, presents, except as to the number of Clergy, a satisfactory view of the progress of the Church :—

	1840.	1842-3.	1845-6.	1848-9.
Parishes	96	102	197	210
Clergy	71	103	118	131
Persons Confirmed..	1791	3699	4358	5213

Colonial Church Emancipation.—A Bill is about to be, and probably by this time has been, introduced into the Legislature of Canada, by the Hon. P. De Blacquiere, for the better government of the Church in Upper Canada. The Bill proposes to divide the present Diocese of Toronto into three, viz. Toronto, Kingston, and London; the Bishops to be elected by a Convocation of Clergy and Laity of the province, and the election to be subject to the Queen's approbation. The alterations in the constitution of the Church, contemplated by M. De Blacquiere, are mainly borrowed from the regulations of the American Church.

Quebec Diocese.—The Bishop of Montreal has been engaged in February and March last on a Visitation tour through a portion of his Diocese, in the course of which he inspected Bishop's College, at Lennoxville, where he held an Ordination on the second Sunday in Lent, and admitted five Candidates to Deacons' Orders, and one Deacon to Priests' Orders. The number of Students still remaining at the College, in training for the Ministry, is twelve. He also held four Confirmations, at which 171 persons received that holy rite.

CAPE.—*Mission to Kaffraria.*—The Bishop of Cape Town has determined to make an attempt to christianise the Kaffirs, and with this view proposes the establishment of a Mission in British Kaffraria. The following is the plan on which the Bishop proposes to proceed:—" To endeavour to engage in the first instance, as a commencement of the work, the services of a Priest and Deacon, who shall proceed at once to the field of their future labour, and commence the work with the aid of a Kaffir interpreter, already provided. We do not contemplate going to any great expense in the erection of a Mission station and premises. We hope that the Clergy who may feel disposed to offer themselves for this work, will be prepared to lead a simple, self-denying life; engaging to some extent in manual labour, and willing to live with but few more comforts about them than those possessed by the people to whom they will be sent. We do not propose, therefore, to offer any stipend, but only to undertake to provide for the actual wants of our brethren."

FRANCE.—*The Educational Question.*—The new law of education, of which we gave an abstract in our last number [1], has given rise to so much difference of opinion among the French Bishops, as to the course which it was incumbent on them to pursue, that the Pope has been induced to interpose his authority, by means of a letter of instructions, addressed to them by the Apostolic Nuncio at Paris. The principal points of difficulty are, the right of inspection over the *petits séminaires* claimed by the State, the association of the Bishops with Protestant Ministers and Jewish Rabbis in the "Superior Council of Public Instruction," and the establishment of mixed schools by the State. The Pope, having taken the advice of a special congregation of Cardinals, convened for the occasion, points out to the Bishops the necessity of occasional compromise, in order to avoid more serious injuries to the cause of religion, and with a view to the maintenance and restoration of the

[1] See this volume, pp. 237—241.

" Catholic faith," as well as the importance of united action on the part of the Church. Acting upon this principle he gives his sanction to such of the Bishops as may be elected, taking their seats at the board of the "Superior Council of Public Instruction," in the hope that, "by their zeal and authority, by their doctrine and prudence, they will be enabled, under all circumstances, boldly to defend the law of God, and of the Church." In case, however, that adverse decisions should prevail in the Council, they are advised to make the matter the subject of communication to their flocks, so as to enlighten the public mind on the state of the question. The State Inspection over the *petits séminaires* is passed over in silence ; but, in reference to the establishment of mixed schools, the Pope urgently recommends, that, whenever in any diocese mixed schools shall be established, the Bishops should use the most unwearied efforts to procure for the "Catholic" children the benefit of a separate school. "For," says the writer, "the Holy Father, bitterly lamenting the progress which *religious indifferentism* has made in France, as well as in other countries, and the frightful effects which it has produced in corrupting the faith of the people, is most anxiously desirous, that, on this important point, the pastors should never cease, as occasion may serve, to lift up their voices, and carefully to instruct the faithful committed to their charge, on the necessity of having but one faith, and one religion,—truth itself being one ; and often to call to their remembrance, and to explain to them, the fundamental dogma, that " out of the Catholic Church there is no salvation."

ITALY.—*Return of the Pope to Rome.*—Pius IX. has at length returned to Rome. After much hesitation and repeated delays, he at last made up his mind to the journey, and arrived in his capital, in perfect safety, under the protection of French bayonets and the roll of French drums, on the 12th of April, after an exile of seventeen months. The measures of the police were so efficiently taken, that, with the exception of a small infernal machine, the explosion of which broke a few windows, and of several fruitless attempts to fire the city, in the quarter of the Quirinal, no symptoms of disorder appeared. Whatever could be done by state ceremonial and military pomp to give a striking character to the event, was done ; but the popular enthusiasm which had ushered in the reign of Pius IX., was visibly wanting on his restoration.

The course of the Papal Government since his return has been characterized by a manifest tendency to fall back as much as possible into the system which prevailed before the accession of the present Pontiff ; and while the occupation of the French arms continues, the population has no choice but to submit in silence.

On the 20th of May the Pope held a secret consistory, and delivered himself of an Allocution, which is the only official document of any importance connected with his restoration. After describing the late revolution as the work of the " Prince of darkness, who seemed to vomit forth all his rage against the Church, and against the Apostolic

See, and to disport himself in that very city, the centre of Catholic truth," the Allocution expresses gratitude to Heaven for having put an end to that state of things, and brought the Pope back to Rome. It then proceeds to mention in terms of eulogy and of grateful acknowledgment, the services rendered to the Pope by the King of the Two Sicilies, by the French Republic and its illustrious President, by the Emperor of Austria, and by the Queen of Spain, and even by Princes who are not in communion with the Roman See. The diplomatic body and the college of Cardinals come in next for a complimentary notice ; after which, the first part of the Allocution winds up with another thanksgiving to the God of mercy, and to "the most Holy Mother of God, the Immaculate Virgin Mary, to whose most powerful patronage we refer the deliverance which we have received."

The Allocution next glances at the present state of Christendom, and at the "terrible and internecine war carried on between light and darkness, between truth and error, between vice and virtue, between Belial and Christ," and exhorts the Bishops to do all that lies in their power to stir up their flocks, and especially their clergy, to strenuous exertions for the restoration of the truth, and of general religion. The document then adverts, with great satisfaction, to the concessions made to the Romish Church in Austria ; and, in the very opposite tone, that of severe censure to the recent proceedings of the Sardinian government. The conduct of the Belgian government on the Education question, is alluded to as a ground of uneasiness; and the whole winds up with pious wishes for the prosperity of the Church, that is, of Rome.

The Sardinian Government and the Papacy.—A dispute has arisen between the Sardinian Government and Legislature and the Romish Hierarchy in the Sardinian States, supported by the Pope himself, which is likely to lead to a complete rupture between them, and which is highly instructive, as it shows that the claims of the Papacy to a supreme jurisdiction over the subjects of independent States, supposed by a certain school of politicians to have been long extinct, are to this day maintained in their fullest extent, and, when occasion serves, with the utmost vigour.

Early in the present year a project of law was introduced into the Sardinian Chamber to abolish the jurisdiction of ecclesiastical tribunals in civil matters, to abrogate the immunities of the Clergy, to do away with the right of asylum in Churches and Monasteries, and to diminish, and regulate for the future, the number of Church festivals, on the ground of their interfering with the ordinary business of life. To this law, which, from having been adopted by the Minister, Count Siccardi, goes by the name of the Law Siccardi, the strongest opposition was offered by the Papal party in the Chamber, and by the Romish hierarchy; but the Chamber and the Government took no notice of this opposition, but proceeded with the measure.

During the early stages of its discussion, protests against the project were presented by the Bishops of the different provinces. The law was declared,—as, for instance, in the protest of the Bishops of Savoy, which is lying before us,—to be contrary to the fundamental Statute of the kingdom, which recognises the "Catholic, Apostolic, and Roman religion" as the only religion of the State. By this Article, the Bishops contend, "the Government of Sardinia stands pledged before the face of Europe and of the whole world, to acknowledge the Sovereign Pontiff as Head of the Church, and as Vicar of Jesus Christ upon earth," and to treat questions arising from time to time between the Church and the State "with suitable regard and deference." To abrogate the ecclesiastical jurisdiction in civil matters, without obtaining the Pope's permission to do so, is in this view a breach of the respect due to the Papacy, and absolutely unlawful. Mutual consent is necessary by the law of nations, for altering matters regulated by solemn treaties between different Governments; and surely, say the Bishops, the "august Sovereign of 200,000,000 of Catholic subjects, has a right to be treated at least on the same footing as the temporal Sovereigns of Europe." Sardinia, which has for ages admitted the jurisdiction now proposed to be abrogated, and which for more than a century has been bound in these matters by special Concordats,—the last of which was concluded in 1841 between Gregory XVI. and Charles Albert—is therefore incompetent to deal with this question by the act of its Government or its Legislature; to do so without the consent of the Sovereign Pontiff, is "a formal act of contempt, an open rupture, an incipient Schism." If this jurisdiction involves a concession on the part of the temporal power, concessions have also been made by the Papacy, *e. g.* the right of nomination to the Episcopate, which may be taken away again; and this particular concession it might be at this time expedient to revoke, and so to remove the selection of Bishops from the influence of political consideration.

As regards the reduction of the number of festivals, the Bishops declare that they do not object to the principle, but they think the law carries it too far; and above all, they complain of any thing being determined in this matter without a previous understanding with the Church. But especially they urge, that if the State by its law shall permit work to be done on certain days (which is all the law proposes to do), while the Church in the name of the Pope prohibits such work under pain of mortal sin, "the performance of work authorized by the law, and protected by the police, will be virtually a public profession of Protestantism."

The Bishops of Piedmont in their protest declare that to make the proposed changes without the intervention of the Sovereign Pontiff, is to overturn the divine constitution of the Church, to attack the rights of the Holy See, to violate all the Concordats, to trouble the consciences, and to wound and afflict all who desire to live and die in the obedience of the Catholic Church. They warn the king (to whom one of their protests is addressed) of the probable consequences, if Pius IX. should be forced to have recourse to an exercise of his Apostolic powers for the protection of his rights; they remind him that the laws of the Church threaten with excommunication all who shall violate the ecclesiastical immunities, or do violence to the ministers of the Sanctuary.

· On the festival question, they observe that the right to enjoin the observance of particular days is undoubtedly inherent in the ecclesiastical authority; and that the attempt made by the minister of a temporal Sovereign to reduce the number of festivals, is a violation of the most essential rights of the spiritual power.

These protests of the Episcopate were backed by a diplomatic note from Cardinal Antonelli, in which he expresses the Pope's determination to uphold the afflicted Church of Piedmont, and the rights of the Holy See ; and not only objects to the project of law itself, but complains of the insinuation, (contained in a communication on the subject, addressed to the Cardinal by the Sardinian Ambassador at Portici), that "the Holy See had refused to treat with the Sardinian Government." The Cardinal represents it as a great act of condescension, on the part of the Pope, that when, in 1848, the Count Siccardi was sent to him for the purpose of negotiating a fresh Concordat, he consented to entertain the proposal, instead of simply insisting, as he might have done, upon the observance of the existing Concordats ; adding, that if the negotiations had no practical result, this must be attributed to the force of events, in consequence of which Count Siccardi was recalled. Besides, he contends, that on the particular points contemplated by the project of law, the Count never made any communication whatever to the Holy See during his stay ; and that the communication, since received, transmitting the project of law, cannot be considered as an invitation to treat, as it was accompanied by a declaration that the mind of the Sardinian Government was made up upon the subject. Under these circumstances, while praying that Piedmont may be preserved from "the chastisements sent upon all other nations who thought to promote their prosperity by humbling the Clergy, and depressing the authority of Holy Church," the Pope, mindful of his duty, "protests loudly before God and man against the wounds about to be inflicted on the authority of the Church, against any innovation contrary to his rights, and those of the Holy See, and against any infringement of existing treaties, on the observance of which he insists."

In spite of all these protests, Episcopal and Papal, the Sardinian Legislature pursued its course, and while abandoning the question of the number of festivals, enacted a law on ecclesiastical jurisdiction and immunities, which was promulgated on the 9th of April, having received the Royal Assent, and of which the principal provisions are as follow :

Art. 1. Declares all civil causes whatsoever, whether between ecclesiastics and laymen, or between ecclesiastics only, to be cognizable by the civil tribunals.

Art. 2. Claims for the civil tribunals jurisdiction over all causes touching the right of nomination to ecclesiastical benefices, or the property belonging to those benefices, or to other ecclesiastical institutions.

Art. 3. Subjects the persons of ecclesiastics to the penal laws of the State.

Art. 4. Prohibits the infliction by ecclesiastical tribunals, of the penalties decreed by the laws of the State, restricting their power to the infliction of spiritual penalties.

Art. 5. Declares the general rules of competency to be applicable to the state of the law as altered by the four preceding Articles.

Art. 6. Provides that warrants for personal arrests, or search-warrants and executions, shall be carried into effect in churches and other places hitherto regarded as places of refuge ; taking care, however, not to cause any disturbance of public worship, and giving notice thereof immediately after to the proper ecclesiastical authority.

Art. 7. Charges the King's government with the preparation of a project of law for regulating the marriage contract in its civil character.

Immediately after the promulgation of this law, the Papal Nuncio took his departure, and the Archbishop of Turin issued the following Circular to his Clergy :—

" Turin, April 18, 1850.

" Sir and Brother,—As the civil law cannot absolve the Clergy from the spiritual obligations imposed upon them by the laws of the Church, and by the Concordats which regulate their application, I charge you to intimate to the ecclesiastics of your parish,—

" 1. That if they are summoned as witnesses before a lay-judge, they must apply as heretofore to the archiepiscopal authority, for the purpose of obtaining the necessary authorization.

" 2. That if they are cited before a lay-tribunal for causes which, according to the Concordats, are cognizable only by the episcopal courts, they must seek for proper directions from their Ordinary.

" 3. That if the lay-tribunal should take criminal proceedings against them, in other cases than those mentioned by the Convention of the 27th of March, 1841, they must likewise apply to the Ordinary ; and if, for want of time, or the necessary means, they cannot do this, or if they apprehend that their refusal to reply to the interrogatories may be attended by some great inconvenience, they must plead the incompetency of the tribunal, and protest that they intend no prejudice to the right of personal immunity, but are only yielding to necessity. After which their making answer will not be imputed to them as a fault.

" 4. The curate or rector of a Church must enter a similar protest as often as any act shall be committed, in contravention of local immunity.

" 5. If an ecclesiastical person or establishment has cause of action against any other ecclesiastical person or establishment, the Ordinary must be applied to for instructions as to the course of proceeding.

" 6. These directions must be considered as provisional, until the Holy See shall have transmitted the further instructions which have been applied for.

" I have no manner of doubt that, comprehending the importance of this subject, you will display your utmost zeal in an exact compliance with these directions, and think it, therefore, unnecessary to add special recommendations. I shall only add that, if any one should fail to observe them, I desire that I may be immediately informed of the fact.

"As the happy return of the Pope into his States must cause among all Catholics, and especially among the Clergy, the most sincere joy, and the most profound thankfulness to Divine Providence, the prayers *pro gratiarum actione et pro Papa*, will have to be added, provided the rite admits of it, both at mass, and at the benediction of the Holy Sacrament, during eight days from the receipt of these presents.

"I am, with sentiments of the most perfect esteem, your most affectionate brother,

"Luigi, Archbishop."

The appearance of this circular greatly exasperated the Government, which immediately caused every copy of it to be seized at the printer's, and even in the Archbishop's own palace. The Journal *L'Armonia*, which had given insertion to the document, with a few words of favourable comment, was likewise seized, both at the office of the Journal, and at the Post-office. The Archbishop himself was cited to appear before the *juge d'instruction*, with a view to legal proceedings against him. To this citation the Archbishop replied, that however willing he might be to act himself upon the rules laid down by him for the guidance of his clergy, it was impossible for him to do so, because, in criminal causes, the Bishops are exclusively subject to the Sovereign Pontiff, and any appearance of an Archbishop or Bishop before any lay authority, even in the character of a witness, without an express authorization from the Pope, is absolutely prohibited. He therefore prayed for time to enable him to procure such authorization, after which he expressed himself willing to comply with the requirements of the law. This demand involving the very principle at issue was, of course, refused ; and the Archbishop signified his determination to obey " God rather than men," and to abide the consequences. The result was that, on the 4th of May the Archbishop was arrested, and imprisoned in the citadel ; but with little effect, so far as the progress of the suit against him was concerned, as he still persisted in his refusal to answer any questions. Before however proceeding to this extremity, the Minister of the Interior wrote to the Archbishop to apprise him of his intention, at the same time making him responsible for whatever disorder might ensue, and suggesting the propriety of his avoiding arrest by quitting the town ; but the Archbishop repudiated the responsibility, and declared his intention to remain. No sooner had the intelligence of the arrest of the Archbishop reached the provinces, than adhesions of bishops and clergy to the course taken by him poured in from all sides, and the Government were obliged, for the sake of their own consistency, to deal a similar measure to the Archbishop of Sassari, who was likewise arrested on the ground of his disobedience to the new law; in fact, to have been perfectly consistent, the Government ought to have imprisoned the Episcopate of the entire kingdom. On the 23rd of May, the trial of the Archbishop of Turin came on. The principle for which he contended throughout prevented him from pleading before the Court, and as he intimated his resolution not to answer any questions put to him, if dragged into Court by force, his presence was dispensed with, the Court appointing counsel to defend him in his absence. The counsel for the prosecution pleaded simply disobedience to the civil law; the counsel for the defence pleaded the recognition of the ecclesiastical law by the State, and the legal validity of the Concordats, and contended that in a conflict between the ecclesiastical law and the new enactment of the civil legislature, the Archbishop had done no more than his duty, in issuing directions for the guidance of the Clergy under his jurisdiction; and that he was the less obnoxious to the civil law, because, so far from enjoining disobedience to it, he had in fact directed compliance with it, under protest, which was a legitimate course of action, and the only one possible under the circumstances, without a violation of the ecclesiastical law. The jury, however, found a verdict for the Crown, and the Archbishop was sentenced to one month imprisonment, to commence from the date of his arrest, and to a fine of 500 francs; a sentence which only provoked a fresh manifestation of feeling on the part of the united episcopate, in addresses of sympathy which declare that the course pursued by the Archbishop was the only course open to him in the conscientious discharge of his duty.

Meanwhile, the Pope himself was not a silent spectator of these transactions. Though the Papal Nuncio had been recalled from the court of Turin, the Sardinian Government had still an envoy at Rome, and to him Cardinal Antonelli addressed, on the 14th of May, a note, in which, on the part of the Pope, he protests, as formerly against the new enactment, so now against the imprisonment of the Archbishop, and demands his instant liberation, by way of reparation. Whether this note had reached the Sardinian Government before the trial of the Archbishop, does not appear; at all events, in the temper in which that Government is at present, it was not likely to be affected by it, being determined, it seems, to risk a rupture with the Papacy, rather than acknowledge the claims of supreme ecclesiastical jurisdiction, which to maintain in its integrity, is the object of the passive resistance of the Archbishop, and of the protests of his colleagues in the episcopate.

The following extract from the note of Cardinal Antonelli, embodies the principles upon which this claim of the Papacy is founded:

"Whatever reforms it may be thought desirable to introduce into the civil administration of the Sardinian states, the venerable laws of the Church will ever be superior to them, and entitled to be respected in a Catholic kingdom. And whatever right those states may have to constitute themselves under new forms of civil administration, that right can in no wise diminish the validity of the canonical sanctions, and of the solemn stipulations previously existing between the Holy See and Piedmont, sanctions and stipulations which bear in a great measure upon the very matters to which these legislative reforms are directed. The Government of the Holy See, strictly observant of these treaties, had a right to expect that the other contracting party, having entered into a formal engagement to do so, would likewise respect them. Such reciprocity was the more to be expected, as the aforesaid Convention was guaranteed by an express reservation in the fundamental statute of the kingdom.

" Having regard to the laws of the Church to which I have referred, and to the existing special treaties, your lordship and your royal government will, in their wisdom, have no difficulty to comprehend the gravity of the outrage committed by the civil tribunal against the person of the illustrious Archbishop.

" It is distressing to have to add, that the injurious treatment to which the prelate in question has been subjected, has resulted from no other cause than the care with which he has prescribed to his clergy for the guidance of their consciences, the rules which they were to follow amidst the innovations made in the civil laws of the state, innovations which violate the rights of the ecclesiastical authority, and which have been put in force, notwithstanding the just protests of the Supreme Head of the Church, whose directions the holy pastors, commissioned by the Holy Ghost to assist him in the universal government of the mystical vine of òur Divine Lord, are bound to follow without the least deviation."

Whatever may be the termination of this affair, and whatever the intrinsic unsoundness of the Papal theory, it is clear that according to that theory the Archbishop of Turin is perfectly justified in the course which he has taken, and is to be regarded in the light of a martyr; while, on the contrary, the conduct pursued by the Sardinian government is palpably inconsistent with the profession of the Romish faith, and with the relations in which it has hitherto stood to the Papacy.

Another Lying Wonder.—Among the means resorted to by the Romish Church for the recovery of her waning influence, is the revival of the lying wonders of the worst periods of mediæval superstition. At the present moment the Popish prints are full of wondrous tales of a picture of the Virgin at Rimini, which is reported to move its eyes in a miraculous manner. We borrow from the *John Bull* the following account of the alleged miracle, abridged from the letter of a correspondent of the *Ami de la Religion :*—" On Saturday, the 11th of May, it was observed that a picture of the Virgin Mary, which is worshipped in the small Church of Santa Clara, at Rimini, under the title ' Mother of Mercy,' and which is painted on canvas, framed and glazed, had moved its eyes. On the following day, being Sunday, the miracle was again observed, when a great crowd collected in the Chapel of the Madonna, and the most violent excitement of devotion ensued in the spectators. To convince the unbelievers, the picture was taken out of the frame, the glass removed, and the bare canvas exposed, and still the picture went on moving its eyes, and continued to do so several times on its way from Santa Clara to the great Church of St. Augustine, to which it was carried in procession. A number of miraculous cures were effected; among them, blind persons received their sight. The Bishop of Rimini proceeded to examine into the case, and certified the miracle, which is attested by other Bishops and Dignitaries of the Romish Church, and, moreover, by the Commandant of the Austrian garrison, who, and with him two officers, came in a scoffing mood, but—such was the effect of the miracle upon them—left their decorations with the Virgin as votive offerings." A subsequent account states that the Bishop of Cesena, after sending two of his Canons, and not being satisfied with their report, came himself, and after having been prostrated in prayer before the image for a few instants, he saw " the eyes of the miraculous Madonna opening, and fixed upon himself, and during five minutes he was enabled to contemplate the seven wonders of paradise, till he was obliged to turn away his eyes, being unable to endure the brilliancy of what he saw."

New Canonizations.—The Pope has added two new saints to the Calendar; Peter Claver, a Jesuit, who died nearly 200 years ago, and Germana Cousin, a shepherd girl, born in the neighbourhood of Toulouse in 1579.

The General of the Jesuits.—Father Roothan, the General of the Jesuits, has rejoined Pius IX. at Rome.

MADEIRA.—*Episcopal Countenance of Schism.*—It is with sincere regret that we place on record one of those unhappy facts which tend so greatly to the injury of our beloved Church by exposing the want of union and consistency within her pale. Our readers no doubt remember that there are in the island of Madeira two chaplains, and two congregations, both professedly belonging to the Church of England, but in direct opposition to each other: one of the Chaplains, the Rev. Mr. Lowe, officiating under the licence of his ecclesiastical superior, the Lord Bishop of London; the other, the Rev. Mr. Browne, under favour of the Secretary of State for Foreign Affairs. Such being the relative position of the two clergymen and of their congregations, we grieve to say, that the Bishop of Bombay, while a temporary resident in the island, has thought fit to attend Divine Service at Mr. Browne's chapel. A strong protest has been signed by several of the clergy resident in the island, against this proceeding on the part of his Lordship, as implying a sanction given by a Bishop of our Church to " the principle that there can be in the Church of England a so-called Episcopal body, not recognised by, or living in communion with, a Bishop."

MALTA.—*Aggressive Proceedings of the Romish Church.*—The spirit by which the Romish Church is animated, has recently been displayed in a most remarkable manner at Malta. In a new code of criminal laws proposed to be introduced in the island, which was framed by the Council of Government, certain articles were inserted intended to make

the Romish Church the *dominant* Church in Malta, and to extend to
her superstitions a protection exceeding that given to true religion.
The articles in question are to the following effect :—

46. Whosoever shall disturb with violence, or with the design of
profanation, the sacred functions or ceremonies of the Roman Catholic
religion, *dominant in Malta and its dependencies,* during their celebration, whether within the places destined for worship or without, shall be
punished with imprisonment from nine months to three years.

If the offence be committed without violence or design of profanation,
the punishment shall be imprisonment from one to three months, or
fine.

46 (A). Whosoever shall disturb with violence, or with the design of
profanation, the functions or ceremonies of any other worship dissentient
from that of the dominant Church, shall be punished with imprisonment
from six months to two years.

If the offence be committed without violence or design of profanation,
the punishment shall be imprisonment from one to three months, or
fine.

47. Whosoever shall insult the ministers of the Catholic religion, or
those of any other worship dissentient from *the dominant religion*, in
their functions, shall be punished with imprisonment from one to three
months, or from four to six months.

48. Whosoever shall in public blaspheme or impiously execrate the
name of God, or of any of the persons of the most Holy Trinity, or of
the Blessed Virgin, or of the Saints, or shall revile or put to ridicule by
words, gestures, or exhibition, any article of the Catholic religion, or
shall otherwise insult an essential article of the Christian religion as it is
received by the generality of Christians, shall be punished with imprisonment from four to six months, or from one to three months, or with
fine.

But in slight cases there may be applied any of the penalties established for contraventions.

49. Whosoever shall outrage the objects of worship of the Catholic
religion, whether within or without the places destined for worship, shall
be punished with imprisonment from one to three months.

When the outrage is a grave one, it shall be in the power of the Court
to apply the punishment of imprisonment from four to six months.

The same penalty established in the two preceding paragraphs, shall
be applied to whosoever shall outrage the objects of worship of any religious society dissentient from *the dominant religion*, in places destined
for worship.

49 (A). Whosoever shall steal from a church of the Catholic religion
or the premises adjacent, or any place destined for the worship of any
dissentient communion, sacred vessels or sacred furniture, or other objects dedicated to Divine worship, shall be punished, with forced labour,
from eighteen months to three years.

When the object stolen shall be the most holy Eucharist, the punishment shall be forced labour from three to five years, and there may be added solitary confinement for not more than six periods.

In consequence of this enactment, the Bishop of Gibraltar has addressed to the Governor of the island the following Protest:

" We, the undersigned, George, by Divine permission, Bishop of Gibraltar, being by virtue of our office, and by the authority of Her Majesty's letters patent, invested with the power of exercising episcopal jurisdiction according to the ecclesiastical laws of England, in all places belonging to the Church of England within the island of Malta, and being ordinarily resident within the said island, have considered it to be our duty to examine those articles of the proposed code of criminal laws for the said island, which are entitled, " Concerning Offences against the Respect due to Religion," as amended by the Council of Government, and having found that it is therein proposed to make the Church of Rome the dominant Church in Malta; to declare it to be exclusively the Catholic Church; to class the Church of England and other religious bodies of Her Majesty's subjects as dissentients from the Church of Rome as it at present exists in the said island; and to enact heavier penalties for offences against the Roman Catholic worship than for offences against others : therefore we, the Bishop aforesaid, do hereby protest in the strongest manner against the adoption of the said articles, for the following reasons :

" 1. Because, whatever may be the privileges granted to the Maltese, the supremacy of the English Crown carries with it of necessity the supremacy of the religion of the Queen and of the people of England, and establishes it by the law of the land in every colony and dependency of the empire, Malta included.

" 2. Because this proceeding of the majority of the Council in attempting to make the Church of Rome dominant in Malta, and to declare the religion of the said Church to be exclusively the Catholic religion, is an attack upon the supremacy of the Crown and the fundamental laws of the empire, and an invasion of the rights and privileges of the Catholic and Apostolic Church of England.

" 3. Because the attempt to class the Church of England and other bodies of Her Majesty's subjects together as being merely dissenters or dissentient from the Church of Rome as it at present exists in Malta, is an insult to the religion of the Queen and of the people of England.

" 4. Because the enactment of greater penalties for offences against the Roman Catholic worship than for offences against the worship of other Christian Churches, is a violation of the principle of equal protection for all classes of Her Majesty's subjects, and of the rights and liberties of Englishmen.

" 5. Because neither the clergy nor the people of the Church of England in Malta have given the least occasion for any such proceedings, they having been careful on all occasions to avoid giving offence to their Maltese fellow-subjects in all things connected with their religion.

"Given at Gibraltar Palace, in the city of Valetta, this twentieth day of March, in the year of our Lord one thousand eight hundred and fifty.   G. GIBRALTAR.

"To His Excellency the Honourable Richard More O'Ferrall,
                    "Governor of Malta, &c."

It appears from what passed in the House of Commons, on the intelligence of this proceeding on the part of the Romanists of Malta reaching this country, that the sanction of the Home Government is not likely to be given to the enactment protested against by the Bishop. Meanwhile, the spirit which has given rise to it, reigns supreme in the island, under the auspices of the Roman Catholic Governor, and has vented itself in outrages against the Protestant part of the community, on the occasion of the festivities held at Malta, to celebrate the return of the Pope to Rome. The following is the account of the circumstances given by the *John Bull*, on the authority of the *Malta Mail :—*

"A grand illumination to celebrate the event of the return of His Holiness Pio IX. to his dominions, took place, very generally, on the night of Saturday last (May the 4th), and partially on Sunday. On Sunday, High Mass was said in all the Churches, and a *Te Deum* sung. His Excellency the Governor and the Consular body, in full uniform, were present, by special invitation, at St. John's, in the morning, and, in the evening, at the Carmelitan Church. The first thing that engaged our attention before the illumination, was an address to the Maltese, in which this passage occurs :—' We, sons of a Father so dear ; SUBJECTS OF A SOVEREIGN SO LIBERAL.' The circulation of the address was illimited. The next was an innocent attempt to raise the character of the Jesuits, and consisted of a number of small envelopes, containing a piece of cotton. An inscription printed in Italian bore the words of which the following is a translation :—' Cotton, in which the bones of S. Francesco de Girolamo, of the Society of Jesus, were enclosed.' Another circumstance not less striking, is found in the fact of a lot of young people, evidently urged on by designing persons, ' running like mad,' waving flags, and shouting—Long live the Pope—Long live the *dominant* religion—Down with the press, &c. The police very properly stopped the dangerous proceeding, and, we believe, seized the flags. In the transparencies, several were ominously expressive of the feelings of the people, to lower the character of all faiths, in exalting their own.

"In our Church, at the dockyard, on Sunday morning, the Service was disturbed by the shouts of certain bearers of flags, which were beaten against the window—and in the evening by music. In the morning the aggressors were driven away by Mr. Napier ; but in the evening, the Rev. Mr. Hare was scarce enabled to continue Divine Service. Yesterday (the Ascension), during the performance of Divine Service in the Protestant Church of St. Paul, a stone was thrown through the window, to the alarm of the congregation.

"Another occurrence has caused much comment. As *Governor*, the Right Hon. R. M. O'Ferrall was invited to the Carmelitan Church, to take part in the ritual there performed—where, too, the foreign Consuls were invited to *meet him.* The notes of invitation gave the first place to the Right Rev. the Bishop of Malta, and the second to the Governor—and the programme was carried out to the letter. All respect to the Governor, as Her Majesty's *locum tenens*, was lost, by the Right Rev. Prelate having *first* left the Church, with his followers, leaving the Governor to follow, as he thought fit."

The following is a copy of the address as translated by the *Malta Mail :—*

" MALTESE !—The Common Father of the believers, the Supreme Hierarch of the Church, the Grand Pio IX., has returned to his Throne at the Vatican, amidst the exultations of the whole Catholic world.

" His ingress into the capital of the Christian world is a new triumph for our most holy religion, for that faith of which the Apostolic chair holds the keys, and the power which St. Peter received from Jesus Christ, and transmits to all his successors.

" The tempest has now passed : the heads of the Satanic family have fled from the city of the Cæsars ; the predictions of the pseudo-prophets have failed ; and the republicans of disorder and of battle are no more.

" The miserable and disgraceful unions of shouting insects tremble, horrified on reading the inscription, in large letters, sculptured on the portals of the Eternal City—THE GATES OF HELL SHALL NOT PREVAIL AGAINST THEE.

" We also, sons of so tender a Father, *subjects of so kind a Sovereign,* let us also celebrate a day of such fortunate advent, for which our most beloved Bishop, in his pastoral letter, has destined the evening of Saturday next, for the illumination, and the following Sunday, the 5th, for a solemn mass and thanksgiving, with a solemn *Te Deum*, in all the churches of this our island.

" May you, oh Maltese, eminently Catholic, who ever give indubitable proofs of your attachment to the Holy Chair, co-operate in giving, in the face of the whole world, demonstrations of joy, by making a spontaneous illumination, not on Saturday only, but also on the morrow, which will be the Sunday following, so that impiety and irreligion, in the presence of your joy, may remain humbled, confused, annihilated. This day on which the four Catholic powers have replaced on his throne the immortal Pio IX., the great High Priest, has already been written, in letters of gold, in the annals of the world.

" Let us then rejoice, with songs and with hymns, giving an echo of the joy of the people of the Eternal City, and of the whole Catholic world."

NEWFOUNDLAND.—*Education.*—A public meeting of members of the Church has been held at St. John's, in January last, to consider the state of Church education in Newfoundland. It appears that the Legislative Council grants from the colonial chest an annual allowance of about 5000l. for education; but this sum is divided among Roman Catholics and dissenters of all denominations according to their numbers, and the very small proportion which falls to the lot of the Church, has hitherto been administered either by the *Newfoundland School Society*, or by a mixed board of commissioners, in which clergymen, dissenting teachers, and laymen of all denominations are united. Under these circumstances, aggravated by the opposition offered to the Bishop by the *Newfoundland School Society*, it is cheering to find that a move is being made for a better state of things. The principal resolution passed at the meeting was to the following effect :—" That it is consistent with the principle already recognised by the legislature, and essential to the due promotion of Education in this Colony, that a proportionate part of any grant for the support of education, according to population, be awarded for the maintenance of schools, to be placed under the direction of the Bishop, Clergy, and other members of the Church of England only." Petitions in accordance with this resolution are to be presented to the legislature.

UNITED STATES.—*Diocese of Mississippi.—Pastoral Letter.*—Dr. Greene, who was consecrated Bishop of Mississippi on the second Sunday in Lent, at Jackson, the capital of the State, has issued the following Pastoral Letter to the members and friends of the Protestant Episcopal Church scattered abroad throughout the remoter parts of the Diocese of Mississippi.

" Dear Brethren,—It having pleased the great Head of the Church to put me in trust with the pastoral care of this Diocese, it becomes me, without delay, to set about the work which He has given me to do. Among the many duties pertaining to my office, there is none which demands more immediate attention than that of looking after the dispersed members of Christ's flock who have come to us from other dioceses, and are widely scattered throughout the several parts of this State, at a distance from the teachings and ministrations of the Church. It is in performance of this duty that I now address you, sending to each one of you my cordial greeting, and begging to be informed how I may best promote your spiritual good.

" Most of you, I fear, have suffered much from the want of those ministrations to which you were accustomed in the homes from which you came. Knowing this, therefore, and trusting that many of you are sincerely desirous of coming again under the instruction of the Church, and of worshipping at her altar, I now beg to be made acquainted with your wants, in order that, as God shall enable me, I may supply them.

" The labourers in this portion of the Lord's vineyard, though true to their trust, are as yet few in number. But, however faithful and diligent they may have been, they have been prevented, by the necessities of their position, from extending their labours beyond the immediate bounds in which they were employed. The same may be said of the labours of your late Provisional Bishop, and of the Bishops of Louisiana and Texas and Alabama, to whose nursing care this Diocese is so much indebted. Though desirous of imparting the full benefit of their ministrations to each and all of you, the pressing demands of their own respective charges have rendered it impossible for them to visit the remoter parts of the State. Through the want, therefore, of more missionary help, and of a full and permanent organization of the Diocese, many portions of the interior have been unavoidably neglected. And it is feared, therefore, that a number of the sons and daughters of the Church have either been led by the spirit of the world to forget her teachings, or been driven by a sense of spiritual destitution into strange pastures. To search out those who remain, to gather them and their little ones into the fold of Christ, and to lead them to the waters of salvation, will ever be one of the most grateful, as it is assuredly one of the bounden duties of my charge.

"With a view, then, to the accomplishment of this object, I now write to you, requesting that each member and friend of the Church to whom this may come will, without delay, furnish me with the information which I ask for.

"The points on which I particularly desire to be informed are these:

"In what county do you reside? How far from the county-town? and in what direction?

"Are any of your neighbours acquainted with the Church, or desirous of knowing her?

"Is there any house or public room in your neighbourhood, in which our services could be occasionally held?

"Do you need any Bibles, Prayer Books, or Tracts? If so, inform me how many, and by what conveyance I may send them to you.

"An answer to these inquiries, and any other information calculated to promote the object of this communication, I will be thankful to receive, at an early date. You may address me directly at Natchez, or else make known your wishes to any Clergyman of the Church who may be most convenient to you.

"Commending you, dear Brethren, to the good Providence and Grace of our Heavenly Father, and praying that his best blessing may descend upon you, I subscribe myself your loving brother and servant in the Lord, "WM. M. GREENE,

"Bishop of the Protestant Episcopal Church, in the Diocese of Mississippi.

"*Jackson, Feb.* 28, 1850."

Canon for the Excommunication of immoral and unsound Members.—The Convention of Pennsylvania has been engaged in the consideration of the following Canon which was laid over from the last Convention: —"*Offenders to be admonished or repelled from the Lord's Table.*—"Any member of the Church, being a communicant thereof, conducting himself or herself in a manner unworthy of a Christian, ought to be admonished or repelled from the Lord's Table, by the minister of the Parish or Church, according to the Rubric; and gaming, attendance on horse-racing, and theatrical amusements, witnessing immodest and licentious exhibitions or shows, attending public balls, the habitual neglect of public worship, *or denial of the doctrines of the Gospel, as generally set forth in the authorized Standards of the Church,* are offences for which discipline should be exercised. This enumeration, however, shall not be construed to include all the subjects of discipline in the Church; and in cases where it may be deemed expedient by the minister, or may be requested by the accused, the Churchwardens, or either of them, if communicants, shall be summoned to assist the minister in ascertaining the facts of the case: provided, that, if such warden or wardens shall fail to refuse to act within ten days, the minister shall proceed to act under the rubrics of this Church." The discussion occupied the morning and afternoon sessions of an entire day, and ultimately the Canon was passed by the following vote of the Clergy and Laity; voting by orders :—Clergy: Ayes, 50; noes, 14.—Laity: Ayes, 44; noes 14.

Proposed new Bishopric of Florida.—At the Twelfth Annual Convention of the Diocese of Florida, held in January last, at Tallahasse, the report of the Committee, appointed at the last Convention, to devise ways and means for the support of a Bishop, was brought under consideration. The report recommended that an assessment should be laid on each parish in proportion to its ability, to commence from the election of a Bishop; and a Committee be appointed to solicit contributions in different portions of the Diocese; also that the Bishop should hold the Rectorship of one of the principal churches in the Diocese. In accordance with these recommendations, a resolution was unanimously adopted, urging the full attendance of the Clergy at the next Convention, with a view to proceed to the election of a Bishop. In the mean time the Standing Committee were directed to invite the Right Rev. Bishop Southgate to perform Episcopal functions in the Diocese, and to request the Board of Missions to extend him a support while so acting.

Dr. Jarvis.—The following resolution has been adopted by the Convention of Pennsylvania:—"That as the House of Bishops, and that of the Clerical and Lay Deputies, in the Convention of the year 1847, passed a resolution to this effect, ' that it be, and hereby· is earnestly recommended to the members of the Church in the several dioceses to aid in carrying on the important work in which the rev. historiographer has been long engaged (while serving the Church without any stipend whatever, at a great expense of time and money on his part, to its great credit and advantage,) by giving to him or his agents their subscriptions, as well for the introductory volume, which has already appeared, as for the forthcoming volume or volumes of his history '—this Convention entreats the members of the Church in this diocese to comply with this earnest recommendation of our highest ecclesiastical council, and that the more especially as Dr. Jarvis has recently made an appeal to the Church for aid to publish the first volume of his history, which is now ready for the press."

Wisconsin Diocese.—Appeal of the Bishop for support.—The following passage from the address of Bishop Kemper to the late Convention of the Diocese of Wisconsin, throws a painful light upon the crippled state of the Church in that part of the world:—" The future prospects and present position of the Church in this diocese, are subjects to my mind of the deepest interest and anxiety. A people comparatively poor, and necessarily occupied with the various duties of new settlers, are anxious for the ministrations of the Gospel. Congregation after congregation can be organised and built up. But whom shall we send to proclaim to them the riches of the grace that is in Christ Jesus; and how shall they be supported? The experience of the few past years must satisfy us that our reliance upon the Board of Missions should be as slight as possible. Two clergymen have left us because they could not be sustained, and others feel as if they ought to follow their example for the same cause. And others, I know, are struggling with poverty, and almost with want. Under these circumstances, I must appeal to the laity, and I trust I can appeal to them in confidence. Cannot, dear brethren, cannot efforts, cannot even sacrifices be made for the glorious cause, in which the present peace and everlasting consolation of yourselves and children are deeply and permanently interested? I beseech you make it a subject of serious deliberation with your Christian friends, and of earnest private prayer. *Let each parish try if it cannot at once support its minister.* Who gives the tenth of his income to the cause of God and of his Church? And is it not a duty so to do? Are we not expected to give as freely as we have received? And will not even a cup of cold water, given from holy motives, be remembered and rewarded? ' The earth is the Lord's and the fulness thereof.' Let us return to Him, for his worship and service, a portion of his gifts. There is that scattereth and yet increaseth. Many a parish can afford as much again as it now pours into the treasury of the Lord. But not only is the worship of your own sanctuary to be sustained; you should delight in the privilege of sending heralds of the cross to our distant and waste places.

" Now is the time, brethren, for strenuous and successful exertions. We learn, from the daily papers, that two hundred and two congregations have been organized in this State by a highly respectable association of professing Christians. At the present moment we want eighteen clergymen or missionaries, besides one or two itinerants. I would that all the members of the Church now in the Diocese, be ascertained and found out, and the Gospel be brought to their doors, with all its vivifying truths and sanctifying tendencies, at least four times a year.

" May then every parish that is organized, endeavour to become self-supporting. May all the missionary collections required by our canons, be punctually, faithfully, and generously made. And let us often ask ourselves: what do we with all our high privileges, and, I fear, frequent boasting,—what do we more than others? There is much land to be possessed; it is fertile and full of promise. And brethren, it is in fact our duty, a duty of the most imperative nature, for which we must at a future day account,—it is our duty to ' do good, especially unto those who are of the household of faith.' "

INDEX

LONDON:
GILBERT & RIVINGTON, PRINTERS,
ST. JOHN'S SQUARE.

ENGLISH REVIEW.

VOL. XIV.

JUNE—DECEMBER.

LONDON:

FRANCIS & JOHN RIVINGTON,

ST. PAUL'S CHURCH YARD, & WATERLOO PLACE.

1850.

LONDON:
GILBERT & RIVINGTON, PRINTERS,
ST. JOHN'S SQUARE.

INDEX

OF

BOOKS REVIEWED.

*** For remarkable Passages in the Criticisms, Extracts, Notices, and Intelligence, see the Index at the end of the Volume.

a

ART. I.—1. *Memoirs of the War of Independence in Hungary.* *By* GENERAL KLAPKA, *late Secretary-at-War to the Hungarian Commonwealth, and Commandant of the Fortress of Komorn. Translated from the original manuscript by* OTTO WENCK-STERN. In 2 vols. London: Charles Gilpin. 1850.

2. *Hungary and the Hungarian Struggle: Three Lectures delivered before the Edinburgh Philosophical Institution, &c. &c. By* THOMAS GRIEVE CLARK (*Twenty months resident in Hungary during* 1847, 1848, *and* 1849). Edinburgh: James Hogg. London: R. Groombridge and Sons. 1850.

AT any other moment than that of the late apparently imminent triumph of democracy throughout Europe, and overthrow of all thrones and time-honoured institutions; when Vienna's self lay, or had but just lain, at the mercy of a triumphant mob; when red republicans were trumpeting far and wide the inauguration of the new era of Equality; at any other moment, we say, the fall of the gallant Hungarian nation beneath the arms of invading Russia would have called forth a burst of indignant execration from the whole of the civilized world; an execration, which would probably not have exhausted itself in cries and groans, but have demanded, and *enforced*, arms in hand, the just liberties of Hungary, driving back the interloping vassals of the Czar to the boundless steppes of their barbaric territory.

There can be no doubt whatever, that in the main question at issue betwixt the house of Hapsburg and the Hungarian nation, or let us say the Magyars, the latter had right on their side; and that despotic power alone has crushed Hungary, as it once did Poland, almost without a semblance of law or of reason.

We repeat that England, more especially, and the English nation, were prevented from protesting against Russian interven-tion, and enforcing that protest by arms, mainly, by the almost universal dread of democratic violence, which prevailed throughout the educated classes of this country; and which, for the time being, was even a stronger feeling than our national hatred of despotism and sympathy with freedom: sympathy, let us say, with a bold and gallant nation, defending its hereditary liberties, secured to it by as honoured and as time-worn a charter as our own. We believe, that at a calmer era, England would not have *suffered* this oppression of Hungary, one of the oldest constitutional monarchies in Europe, with political institutions bearing the strongest affinity to our own. But the whole "situation" was so complicated and peculiar, that our national sympathies were weakened, nay, well-nigh annihilated for the time; so that the nation, upon the whole, was best content to be a passive looker on, and not to interfere in any of the foreign quarrels betwixt kings and people.

And who that remembers the alarming prospects of that hour can feel surprise at this circumstance? In France, republicanism was triumphant; *red* republicanism seemed near the goal of victory; in Italy almost every ruler, save the King of Naples, had for the time been virtually, or formally, deposed and banished; in Germany most of the minor princes in a body had resolved to abandon their hereditary dominions; Dresden and Berlin had been saved from republican sway only after many days' fighting in the streets, and in the latter city the king had been compelled to throw himself upon the mercy of the mob; even in the capital of civilized autocracy, (for Russia is "hors de ligne,") even in Vienna, the old system was overthrown; the revolutionists, arms in their hands, had obtained possession of the city, from which its emperor had fled; in fact, throughout Europe the total overthrow of order appeared imminent, and the supremacy of red republicanism—anarchy of the most fearful nature—appeared to be *the* danger of the time.

Upon the whole, therefore, the educated classes of this country, though they knew that much of oppression was implied in autocratic sway, *desired* to see the democratic movement stayed throughout the world at whatever cost; to have these billows of popular emotion cast back for a while from the rock of authority; and they made up their minds to the infliction of wrong in some particular cases, rather than that all the monarchies of Europe should be crushed by the impending storm.

And *thus* it came to pass, that the Hungarians and the Romans were alike treated with the grossest injustice, and suffered to be thus treated, without any effectual protest from our nation. It was difficult, it seemed impossible, to isolate these cases amidst the general whirl of events, when the first principles of all law and government lay at stake, when crowns were shattering, mobs yelling, blood flowing in streams from fiercest civil strife. At such an hour, what could the Goddess of Freedom do but blush, and stand, her face averted, listing unwillingly to the echoes of such a strife? And perhaps, this attitude best befitted England, as freedom's representative, at that stern hour.

In politics, especially in foreign politics, we rarely seem able to do that which is positively *best*; there is no such *best* to find; we must be contented to choose the lesser of two evils!

The issue of that great struggle was the temporary restoration of order, coupled, almost of necessity, with many minor acts of injustice, the very worst of which, perhaps, was the robbery of those rights and liberties of the Hungarian nation, which they had enjoyed for the last four centuries; not undisturbed, indeed, but still recognized, on the whole, even by the House of Hapsburg, and gloried in by the Magyar race. Yet we are bound to admit, that the question as between Hungary and Austria was one of a somewhat complicated nature; and we may as well add, that *our* views upon the subject are *not* derived from the study of the works we have placed at the head of this article, which are productions of an essentially partisan character, and only show one side of every question at issue.

So much, however, is certain: Hungary has enjoyed a free constitution for at least four centuries; for the last three of which the princes of the House of Hapsburg have been its constitutional sovereigns, much after the fashion in which the Electors of Hanover, despotic in their own hereditary dominions, were the constitutional rulers of this country. The difference betwixt the two cases lay mainly in this: that while Hanover was a petty territory,—insignificant, when compared with the British empire,—the hereditary possessions of the House of Hapsburg, on the other hand, surpassed Hungary in extent and importance. This they could scarcely be said to do in 1549, when Ferdinand of Austria first mounted the Hungarian throne, by virtue of a false and a surreptitious election, not recognized by the nation; for Hungary had formally chosen another sovereign, John Zapolya, but finally acceded to Ferdinand's election from the dread of a Turkish invasion, which necessarily combined all arms against the infidel.

Gradually the House of Austria prospered, and spread their "stakes" abroad: Austria became a mighty empire; Hungary, though still an important monarchy, was scarcely competent singly to cope with that empire, though the spirit of its people was never damped; and her national parliaments continued to meet and make laws, though at somewhat lengthy intervals. It was natural, it was unavoidable, that the House of Hapsburg, reigning in Austria with autocratic sway, should not *willingly* accept the "rôle" of constitutional sovereigns in the neighbour land: they would naturally regard with animosity those institutions which were so utterly opposed to their own Austrian course of procedure; and their efforts were *sure* to be directed towards the gradual, not overthrow, but rather the desuetude and disuse of those more liberal institutions.

Aristocratic these institutions were, in the highest degree. The Magyars were a conquering race in Hungary; say, some three millions in number: three or four millions more of Wendes or Sclaves lived around them, who were regarded and treated as serfs, as conquered races. Again, out of the three millions of Hungarians, only those of noble, or rather, as we should express it, of *gentle blood*, were competent to be electors; but then there were districts in which the whole male population, peasants and all, were counted noble in this sense, so that there were several hundreds of thousands of these citizen-nobles in the country.

There were many abuses *connected with* this order of things, but so far we recognize no abuse; on the contrary, we pronounce this a most admirable form of polity. It is necessary for the liberties of any country that a portion of its citizens only should be entrusted with the suffrage; and that portion should, *if possible*, include representatives of all classes of society, as it did in Hungary. We have omitted to mention, that the chamber of Magnates corresponded precisely with our Upper House, and was formed of exactly similar materials, many of the noblest families in Hungary not possessing what we call the Peerage. The two great evils then existing were, that the class of electors or so-called nobles, though several hundred thousands in number, paid no taxes; and that serfage was allowed to exist almost under its mediæval aspect. The consequence of these institutions however, taken for all in all, was the existence of a free-spirited, noble-hearted aristocracy; not a limited oligarchy, like that of Venice; not a betitled and bedizened class, corresponding to the mock nobility of Germany, with its endless counts and barons; but a large and numerous body of freemen in all classes of society, from the Esterhazics and their fellows downwards; the noblest aristocracy indeed in the world, save that of England's gentry and nobility, and fit to challenge admiration by the latter's side.

They who have lived for years in Austria's capital, as we have done, could not but be struck by the enormous contrast (generally speaking) betwixt the Hungarian gentleman, and the Austrian or German noble. The latter was, at least, in too many cases, a serf in soul, despite his titles and his titular dignities: the former was a freeman! You saw it in his eyes, in his erect head, his bold and easy gait, his frank, manly, pleasant manner of speech. An Englishman's heart must always warm to a true Hungarian: he recognizes his fellow in an instant. We have stood on the race-course at Vienna, among the leaders of Viennese fashion (almost invariably Hungarians), both male and female; and, could we have closed our eyes, we might have supposed ourselves on the grand stand at the Derby: so thoroughly English, in the best sense, was *the style and manner* of the company there assembled. The Hungarian lady cannot be mistaken for any other than a daughter of the free. Compare her with the languishing Russian "grande dame," or the comparatively heavy and plebeian German fair: and oh, the difference! Those high and free and open foreheads, those dark and sparkling eyes, that graceful majesty of motion, all proclaim the children of a free-born race; and the consequence is, that the Englishman, even the stiffest, feels himself comparatively at his ease with them; he is, as it were, *at home again!* And this, which is true of Hungary's daughters, holds, as we have indicated, yet more distinctively perhaps of her sons; the difference is still more marked between these, and the men, the noblemen, of Austria; for the women of a country generally suffer the least from the servile political institutions which may therein prevail; these do not come home to *them*; they feel the chain far less! A Hungarian gentleman was and is *a gentleman;* and this says much! We scarcely know where you will find another such upon the continent. The French marquis of the old school has delightful manners in his way, we grant; grace, and seeming "bonhommie," and smiling courtesy; and again, the Italian noble may be impulsive and interesting, and the Spanish grandee magnificent (though we fancy that race has well-nigh passed away), and the German of the higher classes may be polished, well informed, decidedly agreeable; the German of the far north even bluff and hearty; but the thorough *gentleman* in tone and manners, as we understand that term, can or could be found, in perfection at least, out of England in Hungary alone.

Of course, there was bitter and continuous warfare betwixt this aristocracy and the House of Hapsburg. Despotism or autocracy always hates aristocracy, and it has ever been its policy to unite, if needful, with the mob against their betters in the social scale. Thus the House of Hapsburg in Hungary has played a partly despotic, and partly democratic game: it has striven to inflame the Wendes and Sclaves, the conquered races, against the Magyars; and again, the peasantry against the nobles; and finally, "by hook or by crook," as we may say, it has succeeded in its aims;—it has overthrown the aristocracy of Hungary, and established its own real dominion under partially democratic forms.

From the little we have said, however, it must be abundantly evident to our readers, supposing them to have been previously acquainted with the subject, that this question of internecine warfare betwixt Austria and Hungary was one of an exceedingly complicated character; nor have we yet mentioned those more peculiar circumstances which enhance the difficulty of arriving at a really distinct conclusion on this subject. Let us, as briefly as possible, with the omission of all needless dates and details, recount the leading events of the last few years.

As the demand for more liberal institutions in Germany became more and more alarming, the Austrian government became, as of necessity, more and more hostile to the Hungarian constitution, with its parliaments, double houses, open elections, free right of speech, &c.; it strove, but of course in a great measure, ineffectually to draw the " cordon " tighter betwixt Hungary and Austria, and prevent national intercommunication of thought and action. Thus it was absolutely forbidden to report the Hungarian debates ; and the sale of any MS., or printed document purporting to contain such debates, was punishable, and punished with several years' imprisonment. A " précis " or summary of these debates was forwarded however to the Austrian ministers ; and of this we for some time obtained the perusal at Vienna, and were exceedingly struck with the high tone and spirit of the speakers, both ministerial and opposition : for there were two parties there, as there are in all constitutional states ; one of which was disposed to condemn every measure of the Austrian government, and the other to palliate or defend them. The *liberal* party in that country desired to extend the right of suffrage to the Sclaves and Wendes, Croatians, &c., a step to which the government party, from widely varying motives, was opposed. Those who were officially connected with Austria, and were in fact its creatures (comparatively few), had received their orders from Vienna, and acted accordingly ; for, of course, nothing could be more fatal to the hopes of the Austrian government that they might ultimately overthrow the Hungarian polity, than to see the national breaches of Hungary all soldered up, and the Sclavonian and Magyar races at one. But this *Austrian* party, alone and unsupported, would have been powerless indeed in the free Hungarian chamber of magnates. Many "old Tory" magnates supported and voted with them from natural hereditary aversion to the conquered races : from the love of the past and of the present : they were afraid of the partly despotic and partly democratic tendencies of the " Sclave " race ; they feared that the democratic party, comparatively small, among the free Magyars, would be immensely strengthened by this extension of the suffrage to those who were in their eyes unworthy of it.

Perhaps this Tory party was wrong, but, at all events, there was a great deal to be advanced in favour of their views : the different Sclavonic races combined would numerically outnumber the Magyars, and would, as they believed, be ready, almost at any moment, to surrender up the long cherished liberties of their country to despotism; especially to the empire of the Czar, the natural head of all the Sclavonic races, a monarch under whom they might hope to become in their turn the conquerors of Europe. Let none of our readers therefore hastily condemn the *obstruction* party in Hungary under the old "régime," though they *were* thus induced to fight under the same banner with Austrian officials, whom they hated. We incline to think that they were wrong, and that Count Szecheny, then the leader of the liberal aristocratic opposition, was in the right; that amidst the whirl of events around them, the constitution of Hungary *could* not remain "in statu quo;" that it was needful for its lovers and admirers to extend its privileges to others, or to lose all themselves. The risk was no doubt great of entrusting the hostile "Sclaves" with power; but it had become needful, as it seems to us, to run this risk, to avoid a civil war betwixt races, from which Austria and despotism could alone have profited.

Accordingly, by degrees, after long and angry debates extended throughout several years, the liberal party triumphed, despite the "Tories" at home and Austrian influence. Croatia received a constitution; the Croatians became electors; other real abuses were swept away; the Magyar nobles even consented to be taxed; and all seemed to promise fair for Hungary. In time, perhaps, the animosities of races might have died out, and Hungary might have then become one of the noblest kingdoms upon earth.

But now fell the thunderbolt! Paris gave the signal: the greater part of Europe followed it. Vienna even was in the hands of the mob. At that hour Hungary stood firm to the House of Hapsburg: all its hereditary Tory loyalty burst forth in a clear flame; it entreated the Emperor to take up his abode at Pesth, where he already reigned in the hearts of his faithful subjects. But Austrian despotism, driven from Vienna, would not seek a dwelling in hated Pesth: Ferdinand fled with his court to the Tyrol. And now began the exhibition of the most hateful system of duplicity to be met with perhaps throughout the annals of history: Stephen, son of the former Archduke Palatine, who for forty years had swayed Hungary as the Austrian viceroy, to the satisfaction of all men, started for Hungary, ostensibly to place himself at the head of the gallant Magyars, and secure order throughout the land, really and truly to strike a death-blow, if possible, *at that very moment*, at the Hungarian constitution; a constitution almost identified in the thoughts and feelings of the Austrian ministry with their own "red republicans" at home.

Accordingly, secretly, with ever-to-be-execrated perfidy,

Austrian gold was lavishly employed to induce the Croatians to rise against the Magyars, though there was not the slightest shadow of a plea for such injury, the Sclavonic races having been at last intrusted with all the constitutional rights and privileges so long withheld from them.   Naturally enough, the events of the last two years could not be supposed to have eradicated a hatred of races which had subsisted for centuries: on this the Austrians calculated ; a civil war in Hungary, on whatever pretext, was what they aimed at, which might give them an excuse for *intervening* and extinguishing the liberties of that country. This was an audacious policy on their part, adopted when their · tenure of power at home was in the highest degree endangered, likely indeed to be taken from them from hour to hour.   But the extreme of danger prompts audacity. Where every thing was to be lost, all also, they thought, might be gained ; and so it has been for a while ! They knew that bewildered Europe, especially France and England, not understanding Hungarian politics, might suppose the question was simply one betwixt monarchy and democracy, and so would stand on one side as spectators, which they actually did.   Accordingly, as we have said, they sent spies and emissaries among the Croatians, to stir them to civil warfare, and they found a fitting tool for their vile purposes in a popular idol called Jellachich, a sensual vulgar roysterer, and fool into the bargain, capable of being deluded into the idea that the Magyars were at that moment the Croatians' direst enemies : for, though vanity may have greatly influenced this man, we do not suppose him to have been the mere creature of Austrian titles and Austrian gold. This Jellachich then, Baron Joseph Jellachich (may his name survive for everlasting infamy !), was appointed by the Austrian government, unexpectedly, to the utter surprise of all the world, the Ban of Croatia, a kind of viceroy : they had no right whatever to make this appointment, without the consent of Hungary ; but, when it was made, the Hungarian parliament and ministry, with the most unsuspecting confidence, being cajoled by the youthful Stephen, recognized Jellachich at once as Ban. The next step of this Austrian "employé" was to absorb all power in himself, to arrest all opposing magistrates, to talk loudly of liberty and equality, and to proclaim martial law against all men who held any friendly communion with the Magyars.   Not satisfied with this, he convoked a so-called "parliament" of his creatures, and actually commenced a civil war, as we have said, without the slightest tangible shadow of a pretext.

And how acted the Austrian government ! how the youthful Stephen ? Loudly and indignantly they repudiated all the acts of Jellachich : nay, they went further ; they declared that he had forfeited his viceroyalty ; they summoned him to lay down arms ; they pronounced him a traitor ! Secretly, all this while, they were in close communion with him : he was acting throughout, solely and exclusively, by their directions ! Will such perfidy be credited by an English reader ? But the farce was carried further yet. The Archduke Stephen placed himself at the head of the Hungarian or Magyar army to oppose the invading Jellachich. He departed from Pesth amidst the enthusiastic acclamations of a confiding nation, the most loyal-hearted race on earth. Within a week he had secretly deserted his army, and fled to Vienna, leaving it without a leader, hoping it might then fall an easy prey.

Now at last the eyes of the Magyars were opened : the Austrian creatures, whom they had suffered to head them in the first conflicts, and who had invariably betrayed them, were dismissed, and a Magyar general Moga took their place. A battle ensued, in which Jellachich and his Croatians were utterly defeated : he fled, ignominiously deserting his van-guard, ten thousand of whom fell into the hands of the Magyars. However, with his remaining forces, he joined Windischgrätz, and appearing before revolutionized Vienna, reconquered it for the Austrian sway *and the old "régime;"* for as to the bother about constitutional forms, which was then persisted in by the government, we have since learnt to know that this was only "words," and that the House of Hapsburg will stand or fall by autocracy. Meanwhile, will it be believed that the Austrian government, throwing off the mask, had the audacity at this crisis formally to condemn the Magyars for daring to defend themselves against Jellachich; that they commissioned Count Lamberg, an Austrian officer, to dissolve the Hungarian parliament, and further appointed him to the post of commander-in-chief of the Hungarian army? One scarcely knows how to credit such monstrosities.

Then it was that Magyar indignation burst all bounds. Lamberg was torn to pieces on the bridge at Pesth by the mob, he presuming to make a public entrance for the avowed purpose of disarming the nation, and laying them at the feet of their enemies, and this act of popular fury was the signal for the war betwixt Austria and Hungary.

What were the fortunes of this war our readers no doubt already know : we cannot undertake to follow them. For a little while Austria appeared victorious, but then the Magyar nation arose in its strength,—those noble four millions of men ; all internal feuds and dissensions were forgotten for a while : under the valorous leaders and generals, who have earned themselves such bloody laurels in this war,—Klapka, Georgey, Bem, Dembinsky, Guyon,—the Hungarians were every where victorious, and their far more numerous adversaries were actually driven from the field of conflict. The Austrians altogether evacuated Hungary. Then, at that crisis, an advance on Vienna might have given a totally different termination to the war. But it was not to be: wisely, perhaps, it was ordained, that despotism should triumph rather than democratic anarchy. For, unfortunately, the internal politics of Hungary, under Kossuth's direction, (an enthusiast, but not a practical man,) had assumed more and more of a democratic aspect. A republic—even a democratic republic—was madly proclaimed, owing in no small measure to Polish influence, but mainly, we fear, to the folly of Kossuth. The aristocracy was thereby in a great measure alienated from this popular conflict for life or death: many Hungarians were afraid to fight for their country, when the presumed issue was to be the triumph of the mob, or the dictatorship of the dreamer Kossuth. Thus, too, and thus only, a fair excuse was given to the Austrian government for the calling in of Russian assistance against a democratic and republican, an essentially anti-monarchical movement! That assistance was not refused. How should it be under such circumstances? Austria and Russia's steel-clad legions advanced simultaneously from various quarters on a land torn with internal divisions, with its best and wisest, its *proper* leaders driven from the national councils, and a Kossuth elevated in their stead!

Kossuth seems at this time to have monopolized all power as dictator; as far, that is, as the various generals would obey his orders, which was not often. There was little concerted action among them. Georgey felt an aversion to Kossuth, which he scarcely concealed; perhaps aimed at being himself dictator one day. At all events, all went wrong thenceforth. The Hungarians fought gallantly indeed, perhaps more gallantly than ever: they won one or two more pitched battles; but they were fighting on the retreat, and every day their position grew more difficult. Georgey, from what motives it is difficult to ascertain, unless the mere love of counteracting Kossuth influenced him, (for we do not suspect him, we cannot and will not, of being a predetermined traitor,) placed himself and his "corps d'armée" in the most dangerous position, risking all upon one desperate battle, which he lost; and then he surrendered at discretion, the remaining generals being all, with the exception of Klapka, simultaneously defeated in various quarters. Thus the war was virtually at an end. Klapka still held the fortress of Komorn gallantly, and succeeded, through his moral courage and resolution, in making good terms for himself and his garrison,—and

Hungary lay at Austria's mercy. Many of her best and bravest, including a wise and gallant Batthyani, were mercilessly murdered : and then a calm ensued. The free and ancient monarchy had become a mere province of the Austrian empire : her aristocracy had lost their prerogatives, and almost their existence : the noblest nationality of Europe was to all appearance sacrificed, and despotism was triumphant.

Will Hungary, will the Magyar race, ever arise from the dead ? Have they really sacrificed their existence to this phantom of a democracy and democratic republic ? Time will show. Our fear is, that this great cause, the cause of national freedom, espoused and represented by one of the noblest aristocracies on earth, has been trampled down for ever and a day by the combined forces of despotism and democracy, by a Kossuth and an Austrian government ; and we suspect that the home enemy was the direr foe of the twain ! Has not the nation lost all confidence in its *natural leaders ?* Are not those who are unwilling to be the serfs of Austria too willing now to hoist the red of democracy ? If it prove *not* so,—if the ancient institutions and liberties of the nation *can* revive,—we shall rejoice indeed : for, of all our natural allies, the Magyar race is by far the most conspicuous. Constitutional liberty and loyalty have been at once their glory. They were a free and a gallant people, among whom wisdom held sway ; not the voice of a single tyrant majority, that direst foe to reason and to right. Not omnipotent amongst them were " the sweet voices" of " the tagrag and bobtail," which certain politicians regard as the sure dispensers of a millennium. Carlyle, who amidst his wordy nonsense sometimes stumbles upon a truth, may read such men a lesson :—" Do you expect, my friends, that your indispensable aristocracy of talent is to be enlisted straightway by some sort of recruitment aforethought, out of the general population, arranged in supreme regimental order, and set to rule over us ? That it will be got sifted, like wheat out of chaff, from the twenty-seven million British subjects, that any ballot-box, reform bill, or other political machine, with force of public opinion never so active on it, is likely to perform the said process of sifting ? Would to Heaven that we had a sieve, that we could so much as fancy any kind of sieve, wind-fanners, or ne-plus-ultra of machinery, desirable by man, that would do it !" And again : " Liberty ! The true liberty of a man, you would say, consisted in his finding out, or being forced to find out, the right path, and to walk therein. To learn, or to be taught, what work he actually was for ; and then by permission, persuasion, and even compulsion, to set about doing of the same. That is his true blessedness, honour, ' liberty,' and maximum of well-being : if liberty be not that, I for one have small care about liberty. You do not allow a palpable madman to leap over precipices; you violate his liberty you that are wiser; and keep him, were it in strait-waistcoats, away from the precipices. Every stupid, every cowardly and foolish man is but a less palpable madman: his true liberty were, that a wiser man, that any and every wiser man could, by brass collars, or in whatever milder or sharper way, lay hold of him when he was going wrong, and order and compel him to go a little righter." Bene dixisti, Carlyle amice! Meanwhile, for lack of a little of such government of the wise, the foolish have ruined poor Hungary, at least for a while: let us trust and pray, not for ever!

We have been led to trace this rapid summary of the internal politics and the late progress of events in Hungary by the perusal of the two works, the titles of which we have placed at the head of our article. Each has its value in its way, though one is dry, and the other somewhat inflated. Mr. Clark's style is ambitious, but his matter is deficient in sound sense, and he is deficient himself in correctness of perception: he sees nothing but what is on the surface, and even that he sees not over well. And yet his little book is animated, and in a measure picturesque; he certainly loves the Hungarian people, well, if not wisely; he has a clever chapter on the past history of Hungary, and he describes amusingly enough what he has witnessed himself. We must only guard our readers against drawing any conclusion from the assertions of so evident a partisan. The gallant Klapka is scarcely as ready with the pen as with the sword. The opening retrospective chapters in his work are exceedingly well written, though they are of course one-sided, and fail to give much needful information; but the rest of the matter is unfortunately dull and dry. And yet, the theme is truly a stirring one, and of course many valuable facts and documents will be discovered in these volumes, from which the future historian must draw his materials in no small part. Indeed, few good libraries should be without these memorials of the hero of Komorn.

And so, we bid adieu for a while to Hungary. Gallant Magyar race, down-trodden and oppressed, our hearts are with thee still! thy time may come, and if it does come, old England will hope and pray, that Hungary may do her duty!

ART. II.—*The Expedition for the Survey of the Rivers Euphrates and Tigris, carried on by Order of the British Government, preceded by Geographical and Historical Notices of the
Regions situated between the Rivers Nile and Indus; in four
volumes, with fourteen Maps and Charts, embellished with ninety-
seven Plates and numerous Woodcuts.* By Lieutenant-Colonel
CHESNEY, *R.A., Commander of the Expedition.* (*Published by
Authority.*)   London: Longman and Co. 1850.

SINCE the commencement of the present century, when the Marquis Wellesley, then Governor-General of India, anxiously complained to Mr. Pitt that he was *six months* at a time without
intelligence from England, the means by which our communication with the vast Anglo-Eastern Empire could be facilitated,
have rightly engaged the serious attention of our most eminent
Statesmen, and have on several occasions been the subject of Parliamentary discussion and inquiry.

Indeed it is scarcely possible to overrate the importance of this
matter, whether it be viewed in relation to the maintenance of
British dominion in the East; to the good government of one
hundred millions of British subjects; to the extension of mercantile
operations, amongst at least four hundred millions of people, in the
richest quarter of the globe; and, above all, as affording a means
of facilitating the inculcation of the truths of that Divine
Revelation, which first illumining the East, thence shed its
bright beams over the Western world, and, by the blessing of
God, may now be reflected back on myriads of the human race,
who, deprived of its holy radiance, are sunk in idolatry, or bar-
barized by a pernicious Deism.

For every class of readers, excepting only those whose reading is restricted to the ephemeral literature of the day, these
volumes contain a rich fund of instruction, conveyed without
pedantry, yet bearing unquestionable evidence of laborious research: the annals of the past have been diligently examined;
and the history of the bygone glories of the vast countries
between the Indus and the Nile, adds to the deep interest which
the graphic account of their present condition is calculated to
produce. To enter at length into the merits and convey an
adequate idea of the contents of a work in which personal, politi-
tical, geographical, historical, and commercial considerations are
so intimately blended, is scarcely possible within the limits of a

review. Our efforts must, therefore, be restricted to a notice of a few of the leading points of interest, the more especially as the two volumes containing the narrative and proceedings of the author between the years 1829 and 1837 are not yet published.

It is, however, but right to notice the peculiar fitness of the writer for the onerous task he has undertaken. The author belongs to that branch of the military service which has been long distinguished alike by its valour in the field and skill in the pursuits of science. With a well-deserved classical and mathematical reputation, Colonel Chesney naturally sought some sphere for the development of an active mind, other than the monotonous routine of regimental duty at Woolwich; and, while still a junior artillery officer, he availed himself of opportunities of examining the armies of several European Sovereigns, inquiring more especially into the details of that powerful arm—the artillery—on which the decision of all great battles so materially depends. The experience thus derived has been found very valuable, and to some extent it has formed the basis of improvements in our own Ordnance Department.

Colonel Chesney was about to return to England at the termination of hostilities in 1829, after having visited the Russian and Turkish armies in Roumelia, towards the close of that year, when the British ambassador at the Porte, the late Sir Robert Gordon, suggested that a tour, similar to that which had been just made, should be undertaken, for the purpose of ascertaining the state of the other Turkish provinces.

At this period the comparative merits of the proposed lines of communication between Europe and India, viz. by the Euphrates and by the Red Sea, became a question with His Majesty's Government, and Mr. Peacock, then Assistant-Examiner at the India House,—whose far-seeing mind early noted the advantages to be derived from an "overland route,"—recommended an examination of the river Euphrates, for which purpose a list of queries was sent by the Earl of Aberdeen to Mr. Barker, then our Consul-General in Egypt. On arriving at Alexandria, Colonel Chesney was furnished with those queries. The Red Sea was then comparatively little known, and facilities for travelling in Egypt very different from what they are at present. Colonel Chesney devoted every energy to the advancement of the great national objects which His Majesty's Government had in view, and to him belongs the merit of being the pioneer of what is now familiarly known as the "Overland Route to India."

After examining the Isthmus of Suez, he passed down the Red Sea to the port of Kossier; there he debarked, and crossed the Desert to the Nile, which he descended to its embouchure in the

Mediterranean. On arriving there he embarked for Jaffa, proceeded through Palestine, Syria, &c., and, on reaching the Euphrates, descended that mighty stream on a raft made of hurdles, from El-Káyém to its estuary in the Persian Gulf, and prepared a map on a scale of two inches to a mile, showing the depth, current, &c. of the stream, throughout a distance of 701 miles. This was an extraordinary effort, and one requiring no ordinary amount of courage, skill, and persevering exertion, which we hope to find detailed in the volumes yet to be published. An examination of the ruins of Susiana followed the survey of the Lower Euphrates; and the author then journeyed through Persia and Asia Minor, carefully investigating the upper part of the Euphrates, as well as the country lying between its banks and the ports of the Mediterranean. He subsequently prepared a statement of the relative advantages of the routes to India by the Red Sea and by the Euphrates, which was transmitted to His Majesty's Government by Sir Robert Gordon and Sir Stratford Canning, the late and present British Ambassadors at the Porte.

Few but those who have visited the East, and travelled through regions infested by hordes of wandering Arabs, ready to plunder and slay any man, whether Christian, Moslem, or Infidel, can appreciate the value of the services thus rendered, and of the numerous dangers encountered by Colonel Chesney, who travelled with no official authority, and had to rely solely on his scanty pay as a junior artillery officer. He has added to the list of able officers of the army and navy, by whose patriotic zeal glorious services have been conferred on their country, and who have too frequently been left without honour or reward for their meritorious deeds.

The reports of Colonel Chesney led in 1834 to the appointment of a select committee of the House of Commons, to inquire into the means of promoting communication with India by steam. The Earl of Ripon, then Lord Goderich, and Lord Glenelg, then Mr. Chas. Grant, both cabinet ministers, took an active part in the matter; but the chief promoter of this truly national investigation was the late king, who was ever foremost in advancing any cause which had for its object the welfare of his people. And here it may be remarked that His Majesty did not restrict himself to giving merely a general acquiescence to any useful measure; he was pleased in this, as in other instances, to send for the person by whose efforts a matter of vital interest was brought into active discussion; to assure him of the support of His Majesty's Government and of the approbation of the Crown; and like all men of generous minds, to confide full powers to the head which planned and to the hand which was to execute the required or intended public service. King William the Fourth commanded the attendance of Colonel Chesney at St. James' Palace, and expressed the Royal desire that the route by the Euphrates river and the Persian Gulf should be practically put to the test, more particularly, as His Majesty observed, on account of the manifest advantages which it presented of involving little more than one-half of the length of sea voyage, compared with that of the route by the Red Sea.

The wishes of the king were carried into effect : the committee, after hearing very full evidence respecting the Euphrates, recommended that a grant of 20,000*l.* should be authorized by Parliament to defray the expense of trying the experiment by this route with the least possible delay. The money was immediately voted : two flat-bottomed steamers were constructed by Messrs. Laird of Liverpool, in such a manner as to permit their being taken in pieces on the coast of the Mediterranean, and conveyed, with their boilers, engines, cannon, and stores, on the backs of camels, to the Euphrates, and there re-constructed for the navigation of the river. The author, then Captain Chesney, was appointed under the Royal Sign-Manual, commander of the expedition, with the rank of Colonel " on a particular service ;" full instructions were issued by the Duke of Wellington to the Earl of Ellenborough, then President of the Board of Control; naval and military officers, of scientific attainments and repute, and a detachment of skilful workmen from the Royal Artillery and Sappers and Miners were ordered to be attached to the expedition ; the permission of the Government of the Sublime Porte was obtained, and His Majesty's ambassador at Constantinople was instructed to afford all possible assistance in the way of representation to the Turkish Government on any occasion where the intervention of that Government with its authority might be required. The King took a warm interest in the preparations for the expedition ; every step of the progress was made known to His Majesty through the excellent and lamented Sir Herbert Taylor; and His Majesty was pleased to direct letters to be written to the Ordnance, to the Admiralty, and to other depôts with a view to their hearty furtherance of the objects of the expedition. A week previous to the departure of Colonel Chesney, he was honoured with a private audience of the King, when His Majesty was pleased to issue his royal command in the following encouraging and expressive words :—

" Remember, sir, that the success of England mainly depends upon commerce, and that yours is a peaceable undertaking, provided with the means of opening trade : I do not desire war; but if you should be molested, due support shall not be wanting. You are to write from time to time, through Sir Herbert Taylor, for my information."

The orders given by the Duke of Wellington were precise and full, and his Grace stated that it was His Majesty's pleasure that instructions be issued to the following effect :—

" As the object of the House of Commons in appropriating a large sum of money to be employed by His Majesty for the purposes of this expedition was the promotion of the commerce and general interests of His Majesty's subjects, it will be Colonel Chesney's first duty to use every exertion to secure the success of the expedition in the shortest possible time, and always to bear in mind the necessity of making his arrangements in such a manner as that their utility may be permanent in the event of his success.

" Colonel Chesney will further be careful to maintain the most perfect discipline and subordination among the persons who compose the expedition.   He will explain to them that His Majesty will view with the severest displeasure any conduct on their part calculated to defeat the objects of the expedition, whether arising from disagreement among themselves, or from an indifference to the habits and prejudices of the inhabitants of the country in which they are employed.

" It will be the duty of Colonel Chesney, and of every other individual, to conciliate to the utmost of his power the friendship and good will not only of the authorities of the Grand Seignior, but of the different communities and tribes with whom he may have intercourse ; to abstain from all acts calculated to rouse the prejudices of the inhabitants ; to take no part in any disturbances or quarrels which may exist among adverse tribes ; and to avoid all acts of violence, unless in the last extremity, for the preservation of the lives of His Majesty's subjects.

" In short, Colonel Chesney is always to bear in mind that the character of the expedition is one of peace ; that it is undertaken with the permission of a friendly power, without whose countenance and cooperation success cannot reasonably be expected ; and that having for its object peaceful and beneficial interests, it is only to be conducted by peaceful means."

The expedition quitted England in February, 1835, and after various unforeseen delays and much sickness, of which eight men died, the two steamers, named the *Euphrates* and *Tigris*, were fairly launched on the Euphrates, and commenced the descent of the river from Bir 16th March, 1836. The objects contemplated were fairly and fully accomplished, as shown in the records of Parliament, and as we hope to have the satisfaction of stating when the two ensuing volumes appear.

It may be necessary to say a few words in explanation of the delay which has taken place in the publication of the work. When Sir John Hobhouse proposed to Colonel Chesney the preparation of a work which would furnish the British nation with a narrative of the events connected with the mission, and

which almost unavoidably involved a geographical and historical
sketch of the countries with which the *Euphrates* and *Tigris* have
been intimately connected from the earliest times, the author felt
that, irrespective of impaired health, (resulting from his long-continued and excessive labours,) his acquirements as a soldier were
not exactly calculated to qualify him for so serious a task; but
the President having observed that the task most naturally
devolved on the commander of the expedition, he expressed his
willingness to comply with the wishes of His Majesty's Government to the best of his ability.   Literary ambition or personal
vanity have had no share in the production of this great work, on
which the labour must have been immense.   The illustrations,
which are numerous and beautiful, were delayed by the artists
entrusted with their execution for nearly five years, and only then
obtained by the verdict of a court of law; and when this was
obtained Colonel Chesney was ordered out to China in command
of the Royal Artillery stationed at Hong-Kong.   On his return to
England on the completion of this service he was ordered to take
the command of the Artillery stationed in the South of Ireland,
where, notwithstanding his military duties during the recent
incipient rebellion, he has completed the geographical and historical account of countries which, to use the language of the
author, in the Dedication of his work to the Queen, "were the
cradle of the human race, and the theatre of the most important
events in the Jewish, Pagan, and early Christian histories."
    The subject has lost nothing of its interest by the time which
has elapsed.   Since the Expedition, which satisfactorily proved
the navigability of the Euphrates and Tigris, and the consequent
means of communication afforded by these rivers for rapid transit
between India and Europe, nothing has been done to render this
remarkable region the highway to the East.   The Red Sea, it is
true, is traversed, fortnightly throughout the whole year, by steam
vessels, and the mails and passengers are regularly conveyed in
thirty-five to forty-five days, between London and British India.
We have not, however, found any new marts for commerce.   The
entire line from Suez to Ceylon presents no means of extending
our trade; and the long sea voyage and heavy monsoons from
Egypt to Calcutta, forbid the possibility of this route being made
available for the transit of merchandise.   But the case is far
otherwise with the route by Syria, Mesopotamia, Armenia, Persia,
and the Indus.   If those regions were visited monthly by passengers to and from India, commerce must inevitably ensue: the
rocks in the bed of the Euphrates would be blasted, as has been
done so successfully on the Shannon river in Ireland; a canal
might be readily cut to avoid the Lamlún marshes below Babylon;

or the ancient canal that still exists between the rivers Tigris and Euphrates be widened to admit the passage of flat-bottomed tug-steamers with tow-boats, such as are now in use on the Ganges, each of which would convey nearly an entire regiment. Bagdad, the city of the Caliphs, would again become the great mercantile emporium of Western Asia. Persia, with its vast resources, would be awakened from lethargy; the rich regions and fertile soil of the territories around Mount Ararat would be an attraction for the exercise of British skill, capital, and industry; and the beautiful valleys of the Lebanon, and the neglected coasts of Tyre and Sidon might ere long become the scenes of a peaceful industry and a thriving commerce, which would spread a civilizing influence over myriads of the human race, now sunk in poverty and indolence.

But we must leave these glowing anticipations, and inform the reader of the contents of the two volumes before us; and this cannot be better done than in the concise language of their author.

" In the first, second, and third chapters of the first, or descriptive volume, the reader will find ample details of the four principal rivers of Western Asia; the soundings, bearings, &c. of two of them, the Euphrates and Tigris, laid down on charts, which, in the case of the former river, extend from Sumeïsat to the sea; and in that of the latter, from Mósul to the Persian Gulf. The charts in question, though only on a scale of a quarter of an inch to a mile, will, it is hoped, be sufficient for the purposes of navigation; since it cannot be supposed that, when full information is before the public, two such noble rivers will be allowed to continue to expend their waters without being rendered every year more and more serviceable to mankind.

" I'rán, [Persia,] in its largest sense, and its several provinces, are described in the succeeding chapters from IV to XII. In the last will be found various circumstances which tend to ascertain the primeval seat of the human race.

" Chapters XIII to XVI are devoted to the geography and the social state of Asia Minor. Besides the results of the author's own travels, he has availed himself of the journeys of others, together with the narratives and descriptions of ancient writers; and the mountain chains have been carefully laid down on the general, or index map.

" Chapters XVII to XXI, inclusive, treat of the climate and productions of Syria, Phœnicia, Palestine, &c.; and, in the same way, those from XXII to XXV describe Arabia, from every available source of information, as well as from personal observations.

" Besides objects of natural history, the Appendix contains a list of the ancient and modern Arab tribes, as far as they could be ascertained; and a copious index will enable the reader to find the various subjects contained in the first volume.

"The author cannot but feel some anxiety about the second volume of the work, the subjects of which deserve to have been placed in more able hands. His first journeys during upwards of three years in the East, opened to him a wide field of inquiry; and on his return, he availed himself of the vast stores of information contained in the British Museum. The extracts there made were found highly useful to the Expedition, when navigating the rivers which flow through lands memorable as the theatre of the great events recorded in sacred and profane history, and traversed by Cyrus, Alexander, Trajan, and Julian, as well as by the most renowned of the Muslim leaders.

"The stirring events which, in ancient and modern times, are more frequently connected with the Euphrates than, perhaps, with any other part of the world, seem to be the first which require attention. In attempting this task, the author had the assistance of Mr. Rassam, the principal interpreter of the Expedition, for Arabic researches; and afterwards that of the very learned and industrious Aloys Sprenger, M.D., who, being both an oriental and a classical scholar, was of the greatest service. During these researches, the resources of the British Museum, of the Bodleian at Oxford, and of the vast library at Paris, were turned to account; and the fifteen chapters, beginning with the dispersion of mankind and ending with the establishment of the Turkish power in Europe, have been the result.

"In Chapters XVI and XVII the author has endeavoured to show the connexion at different periods between Asia and Europe, with respect to literature and science. The eighteenth chapter is devoted to ancient and modern commerce. The nineteenth describes the architecture, sculpture, &c. of I'rán; and the twentieth, the boats and hydraulic works of the East.

"In the volumes now introduced to public notice, authorities will be found for every statement which has been made; and in some instances, circumstances have been confirmed by quotations from other writers, even though they have come within the author's knowledge."

Whatever may have been the labours of other geographers, there can be no doubt that we owe to Colonel Chesney a most finished and elaborate survey[1] of the greater part of the plateau of Central Asia, and of the numerous streams which flow from the mountain chains of Armenia, Kurdestân, and Asia Minor—countries which have long been a sealed book to European inquir-

[1] The numerous and extensive maps which accompany these volumes are—like every thing else undertaken by this accurate writer—complete; and the public are now in possession of a more perfect delineation of the Euphrates, and of its adjacent shores, than that of any other river of equal magnitude. The map of Arabia is very valuable in conjunction with the list of Arab tribes, and their military strength of horse and foot. The expense attending the preparation of these maps must have been very great; indeed, we hear that the work has already cost upwards of 5000*l.*, and of this but a small part has been defrayed by Her Majesty's Government. It is to be hoped, however, that the author will at least be indemnified against any pecuniary loss by his meritorious labours.

ers, although their history presents the most remarkable facts to be found in the wide field of ethnological science.

To the biblical student engaged in tracing in the history of past nations, the fulfilment of the prophecies of Holy Writ, the investigations of the learned and religiously-minded author, will be found fraught with interest. The researches in these volumes concerning the position of the Garden of Eden; the condition of the land in which the fathers of the human race sojourned; the dispersion of mankind on the plain of Shinar; the state of Arabia in the time of Lot and Abraham; the Jewish, Assyrian, and Egyptian histories; the fall of Babylon, and the site of Nineveh—are highly instructive, and calculated to strengthen and enlighten any mind alive to the importance of these subjects. True it is that the inspired volume was written to teach us things of deeper and more enduring value, than the geography or history of the countries or the nations therein mentioned; but it does, nevertheless, impart to us knowledge even on those points of which, without its testimony, we should have been utterly ignorant. We know, indeed, and blessed be God for the knowledge, that the saving truths of our religion are so plain, that " he who runs may read;" yet are we not the less sure that it has pleased God that the highest intellectual faculties given to man, should find healthy and invigorating exercise in tracing the history of his race, and striving, with humble zeal, to establish, by documentary and positive evidence, the accuracy of biblical narrative. The extraordinary success with which such efforts have been crowned, especially in the present day, afford indisputable evidence that in the moral, as well as in the material world, our Creator hath not left Himself without a witness; the marvellous prescience traced in the latter by such men as Ray and Paley, is but the counterpart of that which in the former, through the researches of Keith, Chesney, Layard, and others, has been so wonderfully permitted to be manifested:—and as surely as the heavens declare the glory of God, and the firmament showeth His handy work, so surely does the all-seeing Governor of the Universe, in His dealings with His responsible creatures, mark with indelible traces the retributive justice which it has pleased Him to award to those nations who, despising His commands, have suffered the inevitable penalty of their crimes.

Our space will not permit us to do justice to the merits of the really extraordinary work before us, but we must attempt to place before the reader a few extracts, with a view rather to afford a specimen of the nature of its contents, than to select the more remarkable and interesting details, for which we must refer to the work itself.

The introductory part of the work which is comprised in the two volumes now published, was undertaken by the author under the direction of persons in authority. He engaged to "execute the work in accordance with the outline then approved of; which was, that the account of the voyage should be preceded by a geographical and historical sketch of the countries with which the rivers Euphrates and Tigris have been intimately connected from the earliest times."

Different notions will be entertained as to the meaning of the word "sketch," and we should conceive it possible that there may not have been any original intention of so elaborate and so extensive a survey, as that for which we are indebted to Colonel Chesney. And while we are bound to testify our admiration of the labour and research which have been bestowed on these portions of his work, and our sense of the great value of their results, we must add an expression of apprehension, that to the general reader the great length to which the work is extended may, in some degree, operate as an impediment. To ourselves, we confess that the notion of a "sketch" would have conveyed a different notion from that which it seems to have done to Colonel Chesney; yet we must admit, that taking into account the great variety of objects touched on—the details of ancient and modern geography of the most interesting half of Asia, including almost every subject in connexion with the politics, commerce, manners, scenery, and remains of antiquity, the work *is*, after all, only an outline or sketch.

Although this be the case, Colonel Chesney has executed his work in no superficial way. Every page bears ample evidence of research in its margin, which teems with reference to all works, both ancient and modern, bearing on his subject. And, in truth, while we turn over his learned and yet unpretending pages, and the many interesting and well-executed illustrations which adorn them, we are forcibly arrested at each step of our progress, by reminiscences and associations, such as we have seldom experienced from the perusal of a work dedicated to such purposes as that before us. Not only is the field over which we are taken of the highest interest in reference to its present state and condition, but at each page, even of the geographical volume, is dropped some word which recals forcibly to the mind the glories and the ruin of ancient empires; or the fortunes of the Christian Church in her most illustrious period:—" Antioch," " Babylon," " Nineveh," " Prusa," " Smyrna," " Ecbatana," " Mecca," " Trebizond," " Seleucia," " Palmyra," " Cæsarea," " Susa," " Jerusalem "— are words of power, evoking the shades of buried ages, and peopling those desert lands with the pomp and pride of mighty

empire, the arts of civilization, the busy toils of commerce and
agriculture, the intellectual strivings of the learned and the wise,
and the progress and reverses of religion ; and, above all, revealing
the awful purposes and dealings of God with man. But inde
pendently of the historical interest of these lands, the monuments
of ancient art and civilization still remaining, promise to present
an inexhaustible fund of interest to the antiquarian and the chro-
nologer. The remarkable discoveries at Nineveh may probably
lead to still more interesting results as they are continued ; and
how many other buried cities still remain to reward the toil and
perseverance of their excavators !

Nor are these countries, though impoverished and degraded
beneath the sway of unenlightened governments, without interest
even in their present state to the politician, and the merchant,
more especially if the object of Colonel Chesney's Expedition
should be ultimately carried out.

The geographical part of this work commences with a general
account of the extensive basins forming the principal water-courses
of Western Asia. These are four in number, and are described
in the following terms :—

" The elevated plateau which extends from the base of Mount
Ararat into Northern Armenia, Kurdistan, and part of Asia Minor,
contains the sources of four noble rivers, having their estuaries in
three different seas ; and thus from Armenia, as from the centre of a
great continent, giving an easy communication to the several nations
of Europe and Asia. A reference to the index map will show that by
following the Kizil-Irmak through Asia Minor we reach the Black Sea ;
from whence there are inlets to Russia, Austria, Turkey, &c. In the
same way the Aras, by terminating in the Caspian, opens several routes
towards Great Tartary, as well as towards the rest of Central Asia and
China ; while the Tigris and Euphrates, with their numerous ramifica-
tions, afford abundant means of communicating with Persia, India,
Arabia, and the continent of Africa. An extensive mercantile intercourse is also maintained with the same regions by means of numerous
caravans, which since the time of Abraham, at least, have traversed the
countries watered by these four rivers."—i. 3.

It appears, however, that the Kizil-Irmak, which debouches
into the Black Sea, is not likely to be as useful in aiding communication. " It is not available," says Colonel Chesney, " for
the purposes of navigation, in consequence of the rapids which
occur in passing through the several chains of mountains, the
Kirk Delim, Kush Tagh, Al Goz, and Ada Teppeh ; as well as
from the existence of volcanic rocks in its bed at certain places."
It appears also that the Aras, or Araxes, which rises in the
same central plateau, and after a course of 830 miles enters the

Caspian, is like the Kizil-Irmak, interrupted by rapids, and even cataracts. These two rivers appear to afford no means of water carriage to any extent.

As regards the Tigris, the third of these rivers, we are informed by Colonel Chesney, that it still bears the scriptural appellation of "Hiddekel" amongst a large proportion of the people living on its banks; and it appears to be comparatively free from obstacles to navigation. We here become acquainted with the ancient contrivances for irrigation—the dykes or bunds, several of which are still in existence, more or less perfect, and are of profound antiquity. They were a kind of dam across the river for the purpose of raising the water so far as to fill certain canals and cuts made for the purpose of irrigation. These have, through the neglect of the government, been permitted to fall to decay; but in one instance, Colonel Chesney mentions the effect produced by irrigation, where the ancient system has been in some degree kept up.

" Just below Sammara, on the opposite bank, is the bed of the Dujeil, or Little Tigris. This cut, according to Abu-l-feda, went from thence and watered the land near Baghdad. It was met with in several places during the examinations of Dr. Ross; but owing to the neglect, so prevalent under Moslem governments in the present day, the dike, or bund of the entrance, has fallen into a state of decay; therefore, instead of constituting an abundant supply, the water carried along this channel only occupies a small part of the ancient bed, and this to a moderate depth. This cut takes a south-east direction through culti-vated lands, where its effects, even in its present diminished state, are most striking in fertilizing the grounds and fruit gardens surrounding the villages; this is particularly the case near the prosperous village of Sumeichah, situated about seventeen miles south-east from the com-mencement of the canal. Here irrigation has changed a tract which was previously barren, into one possessing the fertility ascribed to this region by Herodotus, whose account has too often been placed amongst the legends of fiction, by those who make the produce of ordinary countries a standard for estimating that of Mesopotamia."—i. 28, 29.

The Tigris is navigable even now by rafts at certain seasons from Diyar-Bekr to Mosul, close to the site of Nineveh, a distance of about 300 miles. Below Mosul it is so more or less throughout the whole year, and the passage to Baghdad is so easy and so rapid, that the river is known by the name of "the cheap camelier." The ordinary mode of transit appears to be by means of rafts, supported by inflated skins. A raft of this description is mentioned by Colonel Chesney, which was constructed in 1781, to convey the Right Hon. John Sullivan from Mosul to Baghdad, and which was supported by 200 skins, and had on it a small cabin. These inflated skins of animals are also used by the natives to cross the river, and Colonel Chesney has given us an amusing representation of two of these turbaned and bearded personages, each bestriding a pig-skin, and beginning the passage.

Amongst other still more ancient remains, the Tigris passes near the ruins of those once famous and imperial cities, Seleucia and Ctesiphon, the capitals of the Seleucidæ, and subsequently of the Parthian and Persian monarchs, whose power so severely tasked the energies of Rome in the height of their vigour, and in their decline. These now desolate ruins were on more than one occasion the scene of triumphant procession and rejoicings at the defeat of the Romans, and more especially after the destruction of the army of Crassus. A majestic building of great dimensions, called the "Arch of Chosroes," marks the site of Ctesiphon; and judging from the drawing in Colonel Chesney's work, we should suppose it must have formed a portion of an imperial palace rather than of a triumphal arch. It appears to be something of the dimensions of a good-sized cathedral, and, in point of fact, might be taken for a portion of one. We should suppose that in this vicinity excavations might bring to light many objects of interest.

The Tigris becomes considerably swollen during the rains in the month of November; it subsequently decreases and swells at intervals, until the different tributaries are bound up by the frost of January in the mountains of Kurdistan. It rises again about the middle of March, and is highest about May, when its velocity is 7.33 feet per second. It then falls more or less regularly till the middle of June.

"The large boats are not, however, obliged to diminish their cargoes till the month of August; between which time and the month of November, when the river is again at the lowest, they should not draw more than four feet of water. There is an active commerce along the Tigris, between Basrah and Baghdad, by means of the large country boats which go in fleets; and above the latter city it takes place chiefly by means of rafts to Mosul."—i. 39.

The fourth great river which rises in Armenia is the Euphrates, which forms the chief subject in the work before us. Its source is at no great distance from the Euxine, and in its course to the Indian Ocean it approaches very near to the Mediterranean—at one point to within 120 miles, so that a land journey of that moderate amount, and a subsequent river navigation of about 1100 miles, would take the traveller from the Mediterranean to the Persian Gulf. The fall from Bir to the mouth of the river (1117 miles) is very trifling, being only at the rate of six inches per mile; the Danube, between Ulm and Passau, having an average fall of two or three feet per mile. At the ruins of

Balis, the Barbalissus of the ancient Romans, and once the port of the ancient Beroe, the distance to the mouth of the Euphrates is only about 1030 miles, while the shore of the Mediterranean is distant only 123 miles in the direction through Aleppo to Suweidiyeh, and 118 through Aleppo to Iskanderun, being not much more than *half* the distance of the land carriage between Alexandria and Suez by Cairo.

In speaking of one of the tributaries of the Euphrates, Colonel Chesney gives the following interesting account of the remains of Al-Kadhr, on the authority of Dr. Ross:—

" The ruins are a mile in diameter, and are inclosed by a circular wall of very massive construction, with towers at intervals; the whole is surrounded by a deep ditch, and there are the remains of a mound, also circular, beyond it. In the centre of the town stands the principal object of curiosity; a range of buildings inclosed by a strong wall, square in the plan, and similar in construction to that of the city; the faces are opposite the four cardinal points, and each measures 300 paces in length inside. The buildings consist of spacious halls and chambers, covered by semicircular vaults, some of which rise to the height of sixty feet from the ground; and on the pilasters there are figures in relief, apparently Greek or Roman. The whole city is built of a brownish grey limestone, the blocks of which are so closely fitted that no cement is visible."—i. 50, 51.

When one reads of cities standing thus perfect after the lapse of 2000 years, the thought occurs, how few of our modern architectural efforts seem destined to a similar endurance. There seems to be much beautiful scenery on some parts of the Euphrates: at Karablah, where the river is obstructed by a ledge of rocks, which constitute the greatest difficulty experienced by boats from Bir to Basrah, the picturesque beauty of the scene appears to be considerable, the hills at one side being crowned by a walled town, while a little lower the houses of another town open to view among thick date groves, the river itself bearing a series of islands, and the ruins of the ancient Anatho appearing in the distance. Below this spot the course of the river lies amongst partially wooded hills, affording good pasture. Villages appear occasionally surrounded by cultivation; and numerous ancient aqueducts, in different directions, prove that in former times a wealthy and a civilized people inhabited this portion of the country. The famous bituminous fountains of Hit are in this neighbourhood, and boats coated with bitumen are still in use.

Having thus partially followed Colonel Chesney in his account of the four great rivers which take their rise in Armenia, we are led to direct attention to the views which he connects with them in attempting to fix the site of the Garden of Eden. That there are difficulties connected with Colonel Chesney's exposition of the

well-known passage in Genesis we feel, but we must say that his
view appears to us far more probable than the ordinary one,
which supposes Eden to have been in Babylonia. Colonel Chesney
supposes it to have been in Armenia, in the elevated plateau to
the north of Kurdistan. He observes that there is but little to
guide the inquirer in his investigations, except the very brief
description contained in the book of Genesis; and the difficulty is
increased by the probability that the designations of locality
given in Scripture must be traced amongst languages different
from that of the Pentateuch, and amongst nations who took possession of the tracts about the Black and the Caspian Seas after
those tracts had ceased to be called by their original names.
Under such difficulties, it might at first sight appear almost hopeless to determine the site of Eden; but many indications connected with the character and natural productions of the country,
which presented themselves in the course of Colonel Chesney's
extensive researches in that part of the world, led to the formation of an opinion which he thus states:—

"From these, and from the fact that the sources of the Euphrates
and Tigris, and of two other great rivers, exist within a very circum-
scribed place in Armenia, I have been led to infer that the rivers known
by the comparatively modern names of Halys and Araxes, are those
which, in the book of Genesis, have the names of Pison and Gihon; and
that the country within the former is the land of Havilah, whilst that
which borders upon the latter is the still more remarkable territory of
Cush."—i. 267.

It is a fact of some weight, that there is a tradition firmly
believed in the valleys of Central Armenia, that the tract allotted
to our first parents, or "as the Hebrew expresses it, the Paradise in Eden towards the East" (Gen. ii. 8), included the
northern portion of the Pachalik of Mosul, extending from this
part of Assyria to a little to the north of Erz-Rum; the western
border being in the vicinity of Tokat, in the direction of the
Halys; and the eastern including some portion of the district
beyond Lake Van. Within the limits of this extensive and
fertile tract of country are the mountain ranges of Ararat and
Nimrud, forming parts of the vast chain of the Taurus; and it is
certainly a remarkable fact, that in the great plateau round
Mount Ararat, within ninety miles from a common centre, there
are the sources of four noble rivers, of which two at least clearly
bear the names given to the rivers of Paradise in the Bible. We
must quote the whole passage.

" And the Lord God planted a garden eastward in Eden; and
there he put the man whom he had formed.

" And out of the ground made the Lord God to grow every
tree that is pleasant to the sight, and good for food; the tree of

life also in the midst of the garden, and the tree of knowledge of good and evil.

"And a river went out of Eden to water the garden; and from thence it was parted, and became into four heads.

"The name of the first is Pison: that is it which compasseth the whole land of Havilah, where there is gold; and the gold of that land is good: there is bdellium and the onyx-stone.

"And the name of the second river is Gihon: the same is it that compasseth the whole land of Ethiopia.

"And the name of the third river is Hiddekel: that is it which goeth toward the east of Assyria. And the fourth river is Euphrates."—Gen. ii. 8—14.

On this passage we have the following remarks:—

"We are told," says Colonel Chesney," that a river (or rivers, for the original word has both a singular and a plural signification) went out of Eden to water the garden, and from thence it was parted, and became into four heads. The name of the first is Pison, and the name of the second is Gihon."—i. 268.

Of the passage referred to, the following is given as a litera translation: "And a river (or rivers) went out from Eden, to water the garden: thence it (or they) spread out; that is, had four heads;" and it is observed that the words "went out" must be equivalent to "rose in;" for as the garden was planted in Eden (Gen. ii. 8), the river need not flow out from Eden in order to water it: the words signify to spread or dissipate, but not divide; and it is argued that the succeeding verses show that there were four distinct rivers corresponding with the four heads, as their names are given.

After these preliminary criticisms, the author enters on his task, which as regards the Tigris and Euphrates is an easy one. As for the Tigris, it still bears in many places the name of Hiddekel, Dekel, Dijel, or Diglath. The word "Tigris" in the Median tongue signifies "arrow," and is given to the river where it becomes rapid. The great difficulty regards the Pison and Gihon, and the lands of Havilah and Ethiopia, those names being now unknown. The Pison is supposed by Colonel Chesney to be the same as the Halys or Alys, the Eksios of the Armenians, which under the appellation of the Kizil-Irmak encompasses a large part of Asia Minor. The Pison is said in the Bible to "compass" the land of "Havilah." So that we have to make out that the part of Asia Minor thus compassed by the Alys answers the description given by Moses.

Now with respect to "the land of Havilah, more correctly Chavilah, Reland, after much pains and research, concludes that it coincides with the Colchis of the ancients." *If* this be a correct conclusion, it identifies the Havilah of Scripture with the country included by the Halys; but we are not furnished with the data on which it is based. But a more valuable fact is, that in this district, westward of the Euphrates and towards the Halys, there exists at this present day a town or village called *Haivali*, very much like "Havilah" in sound, and that "gold is found" here (i. 276). There is also a district in that neighbourhood called Chalva or Chalvata, which is very like "Chavilah" or "Havilah;" and it is ingeniously argued, that the fable of the "Golden fleece" in Colchis, is an indication of the abundance of the precious metals in that district in early times. It is also capable of proof from history, that gold abounded in that region in after-ages. As to the "bdellium" mentioned by Moses, there are considerable differences of interpretation amongst commentators, some supposing it to mean a kind of gum, others, a precious stone. In either case, however, it appears that the natural productions of this country meet the description; "emeralds," and "pearls," which are understood by some writers to be designated by "bdellium," being found in Colchis and the neighbouring district; and the gum supposed to be indicated, being also found in quantities, as well as turquois, beryl, and *the onyx.*—i. 279, 280.

We now come to the "Gihon," and the land of "Ethiopia;" or, more properly, "Cush," compassed by it. The Gihon is supposed by Colonel Chesney to be the same as the Araxes or Aras, which flows into the Caspian, and encompasses a land which he identifies with the "Cush" of Scripture. It is stated, but we do not see on what authority, that the descendants of Ham occupied this country (i. 275). The country, however, appears to be sufficiently identified in the following passage, which seems to us to make out the point sufficiently :—

"This territory, which was bounded on the north by the Araxes or Gihon, and which constituted the Cossea of the Greek and Latin writers, was the abode of the posterity of Nimrod up to the time of the Jewish historian, who says of the sons of Ham, 'time has not at all affected the name of Chus; for the Ethiopians over whom he reigned are to this day, both by themselves and by all the men in Asia, called Chushites.' . . . On the Nahr-Madcha, a little way north of Babel, are the ruins of the Kush of Abu-l-feda; a name which seems to be quite as ancient as the former city, and from whence and its neighbourhood the inhabitants were transported by Shalmanazar to Samaria. The word Chus remains almost unchanged in Kush, Shus, Sus, and Kushasdan, the land of the sun, and the land of the magi. It is also repeatedly mentioned in close connexion with the territory lying northward and north-eastward of Babylonia . . . . That Asiatic Cush has been rightly placed in the territory adjoining Colchis, seems tolerably clear from some of the old writers. Hieronymus says, that

Andrew, brother of Simon Peter, preached near the rivers Apsanes and Phasis, where are the inner Ethiopians . . . . Moses Choronensis is even more explicit; for he not only indicates the early locality of the sons of Cush, but likewise their possessions eastward of Persia proper, the latter being known as Kusdi Khorasan, whilst the former kingdom was called Kusdi Nimrud. Moreover, the Armenians call the Persians, and all the Hunnish tribes within the Caspian gates, Kushanians; and the whole tract eastward of the sources of the Araxes or Gihon, is expressly called Ethiopia by a remarkable Hebrew traveller; the well-known Benjamin of Tudela, who visited this part of the world in the twelfth century, and not only took notice of the territory of Cush, but likewise of the river Gihon."—i. 281, 282.

The evidence as to the river Aras having been called "Gihon" is, it must be confessed, rather feeble. Reland and others suppose this word to be derived from roots either in Hebrew or Armenian which signify impetuous speed, a description which well accords with the nature of the stream. This perhaps is not a very strong argument. An Armenian historian also is quoted, who states expressly that the name of the river Gihon was changed to Araxes by a king of Armenia, after his son. This may possibly be so; but as Colonel Chesney does not inform us when this author lived, or how far we may depend on his testimony, the argument appears defective. On the whole, however, we think there is a very high degree of probability that the view taken by Colonel Chesney is correct, and the facts he has collected are valuable, though we cannot say that they are arranged in very lucid order.

The country through which the expedition passed, is wonderfully rich in remains of antiquity of various ages. Take the following description of Halebi near the Euphrates, a ruined town once connected with Palmyra:—

"Twenty-six miles short of the eastern limits of the Pashalik, which are at the town of Deci, and on the slope of a hill rising abruptly from the right bank of the river, is Halebi or Zelebi. This striking place is fortified with walls and towers, which, as well as the public and private buildings, are constructed of fine gypsum. The town has the form of an acute triangle, whose base rests upon the river, whilst its sides ascend the steep acclivity of a conical hill, and terminate on its summit with a small acropolis. As the whole is completely seen from the exterior, the necessity of an increased number of flanking towers became very apparent: twelve of these works defend the southern side, and eight the northern or shorter side; whilst on that of the river, which is not commanded, they are further apart. In the town are the remains of a temple, and an extensive palace containing many ornamental apartments; also numerous well-constructed private dwellings, supported by arches; and in general the buildings are so well preserved, that the mind can scarcely be brought to feel that all have been so long unoccupied. The city of Zenobia (Halebi) was probably built by the queen of that name, and resorted to by her at certain seasons, in order that she might enjoy the refreshing breezes which are felt along the valley of the Euphrates. It also appears to have been the principal passage leading from Palmyra into Assyria; for a little below the walls, and opposite the ruined castles of Halebi on the left side, are the remains of an embankment, partly arched with bricks fifteen or sixteen inches square, but chiefly of solid stone.

"Like the great city on which it was dependent, the necropolis occupies a prominent situation in the valley and along the declivity of the hill westward of the town, and it is remarkable for a number of square towers, precisely of the same construction as those near Palmyra. The monuments of mortality usually consist of three stories, the lowest and middle appear to have been tenements of the dead, whilst the upper story served as a place of defence, and terminated either with a flat or a pyramidal roof, surrounded by battlements. In one of these tombs Captain Lynch recently discovered a female mummy, whose face was covered with a thin mask of the finest gold, which is to be seen at the India House; and in another tomb is an inscription which was copied by Mr. Ainsworth."—i. 418, 419.

The remains at Antioch are in some respects among the most interesting in the East. Colonel Chesney gives the following details of their present state:—

"Scarcely a vestige remains of that portion of ancient Antioch which, according to Pliny, must have occupied the northern banks of the Orontes. Walls and square towers of surprising solidity encircled the residence of the Syrian monarchs, the seat of pleasure, the centre of extensive commerce, and the third city of the habitable earth. The southern portion of Riblatha or Hamath the Great, occupied a singular and most striking position. This part of the city was bounded on the south-east by a high range of rocky hills, and on the opposite or north-western side, by the valley of the Orontes; whilst deep precipitous valleys formed its north-western and south-eastern limits. The walls have a circumference of nearly seven miles, and form an irregular parallelogram, with one of its longer sides touching the Orontes, and the other crowning the summits of the heights above-mentioned . . . .

"Near the western extremity of the city a portion of the walls has been razed to build the barracks and serai of Ibrahim Pasha; but from thence along the Orontes to St. Paul's gate, as well as on the rest of the circumference (about seven miles), the limestone walls and towers are remarkable for their superior construction."

In the lower part of the city no particular skill was requisite to provide the requisite defences, but in the higher and precipitous parts, great skill in construction has been shown. Walls have been carried sometimes up almost perpendicular cliffs, and in many places up acclivities so steep, that the wall becomes a

series of steep steps, defended at intervals by castles which ascend
above it, so as to protect its defenders from assailants; the wall
itself being throughout from fifty to sixty feet high, and eight to
ten feet wide at the top.   These castles remain so far perfect,
that their staircases, and vaulted and loop-holed chambers and
cisterns, are still apparently in much the same state as when they
were occupied by a Roman garrison.

The second volume of Colonel Chesney's work is chiefly historical; and it comprises a condensed account of the eastern world
from the Flood to the present day, including a survey of the spread
of the human race after the dispersion.   We fear Colonel Chesney
has been led to attach too much weight to the opinions of
the late Mr. Bellamy in this part of his work.   He appears to
refer to Mr. Bellamy's translation of the Bible as of authority.
Now we apprehend that this writer was a Unitarian; and under
such guidance an event which is usually and rightly considered
miraculous—the confusion of tongues at Babel—becomes merely
the arrival of another nation speaking a different language.   The
translation here propounded by Mr. Bellamy, in opposition to that
which is universally received as the real meaning, appears to us
most absurd in several respects, and we regret that Colonel Chesney   •
should have been led to depend on so untrustworthy a guide.
We regret to observe the same author followed elsewhere, as, *e.g.*
ii. 69, where the sin of Lot's daughters is explained away.   But in
saying this, we must add, that Colonel Chesney's tone of mind is
not to be inferred from such accidental mistakes.   On the contrary, it is eminently believing, and he refers for the most part
to the authorized translation, and without any attempt to explain
away the miraculous and other facts recorded in it.

It would be impossible to follow Colonel Chesney through the
wide range of his subjects in this volume, in which he writes on
the history, religion, philosophy, commerce, and arts of the ancient
world.   From all that we have seen he appears to have bestowed
extraordinary and most exemplary pains in accumulating materials
from all quarters, and condensing them into a connected narrative.   We must however find space for a few more extracts.

The following remarks on the architectural remains of Mesopotamia and Assyria are interesting :—

"Since architectural remains are justly considered good criterions of
the social state of the people by whom the works were constructed,
those of Mesopotamia and Assyria, which go back to the period of the
Noachian deluge, must possess considerable interest.   On approaching
the site of one of the primeval cities, the attention is attracted by what
at first appears to be a natural conical hill of considerable size, which
however proves to be the mouldering remnant of a vast building.   Such
a mound could not fail to be remarkable in any situation; but, rising

out of an apparently boundless plain, in a transparent atmosphere, the effect which it produces in the mind is most striking. The celebrated plains of Dura offer few other remains of antiquity ; and none which can be compared, in magnitude or in extent, to these gigantic masses, which have been formed by the ruins of some of the greatest works ever executed by man, and which now serve only to guide the traveller on his way.

" The alluvial district of Babylonia being without stone, it was necessary to resort to other materials for the construction of public and private works ; and, as clay existed in abundance, bricks were the materials chiefly employed by the builders of that country. But it is owing to the pyramidal shape of the edifices, rather than to any peculiar qualities of the materials, that these monuments of early art still exist.

" The Babylonian bricks were of two kinds : one kind consisted of such as are burnt in a kiln ; the other, and by much the larger proportion, being simply dried by being exposed to the sun. The former vary in size from 11 inches to $13\frac{1}{2}$ inches square, and they are $3\frac{1}{2}$ inches deep ; they are sometimes, however, much smaller, and they are of various colours : the bricks are chiefly cemented with common clay, but in the quays the foundation, and exterior parts of the structures that once adorned this mighty city, bitumen appears to have been extensively used. One face of each brick had on it an inscription, and sometimes a figure, and in some instances it is also glazed and vitrified ; and this face was placed downwards ; the cement is usually found adhering to the upper surface.

" The second, which is an inferior kind, is rather larger than those which had been kiln-dried, being nearly $4\frac{1}{4}$ inches deep, and from $11\frac{1}{4}$ to 14 inches square ; the larger ones weigh 38 pounds 11 ounces avoirdupois, and were formed of the pure clay of the country, rendered more tenacious by being mixed with a little sand, and some coarse straw or fine reeds. Those bricks when dried by exposure to a powerful sun, soon became sufficiently hard, and gave the means of rapidly raising a large structure which in so dry a climate was exceedingly durable."— pp. 604, 605.

We have the following remarkable account of ruins to the north of Persepolis :—

" On an eminence in the plain of Nungh'-áb, about fifty miles northeast of Persepolis, numerous remains mark the site of a very extensive city ; on which it is evident that much skill and art had been bestowed in order to render it worthy of being the seat of empire. The most remarkable portion of these ruins, the Mesjid-i-Maderi-Suleimán (the Mother of Solomon), has a grand pedestal, composed of immense blocks of white marble, on a base 43 feet long and 39 feet broad, and rising in six tiers or gigantic steps to the platform of the monument, which is at the height of 26 feet 9 inches from the ground. The walls of this Sarcophagus itself consist of four layers of large stones ; and the exterior dimensions of this structure are 20 feet 6 inches long, by 17 feet 2 inches wide, and 11 feet high to the cornice ; it is covered with a solid roof, whose exterior is arched. This entrance is in the north-western end; and above it are the marks of a tablet. The chamber is 10 feet 10 inches long, by 6 feet 10½ inches wide, and 6 feet 10½ inches high; it has a flat roof, and a stone floor, each composed of two great slabs of marble joined in the middle. On the wall facing the south-west, has been cut in later times an ornamental window, with an Arabic inscription. The pedestals of 24 columns placed around at 14 feet apart, with scattered fragments of their shafts, mark an area of 400 square feet; which at one time enclosed what is now ascertained to have been the tomb of Cyrus. The plain of Nungh'-âb is moreover strewed with ruins, some of which have arrow-headed inscriptions; but, as a whole, these remains are far inferior to those which constitute the ruins of Persepolis."

We have the following remarks on the ruins of Persepolis :—

" In glancing over these elaborate specimens of early art at Persepolis, the first place must be given to the excavations : a spacious niche, sculptured in the face of the rock, 130 feet high, and 72 feet wide, forms the façade of the principal tomb, which is in two portions, both highly finished. The upper compartment represents a kind of chest, having numerous figures sculptured on it ; also a fine altar, with a figure standing in the act of adoration, and an attendant spirit hovering above. A false door forms part of the sculpture of this second division, and through its lower part a passage has been broken into the tomb itself.

" The other objects of antiquity are in front of the tomb; and a general idea of these remains may be conveyed to the reader by observing that they occupy different parts of a grand terrace, which forms a very irregular parallelogram at the foot of a stupendous range of rocks. On the eastern side, the terrace is nearly 1600 feet long, and three of the sides are surrounded by massive walls, having in each a number of breaks or indentions forming right angles; but the direct distances from side to side are respectively, 1540 feet for the western face, 893 feet for the northern, and for the southern face 703 feet.

"This terrace is approached near the northern extremity of its western side, by means of the double flights of steps, which are separated by a landing-place 37 feet long by 24 feet wide ; and so gradual is the ascent, that it is suited for horsemen. It is constructed with such pondrous blocks of marble, that each piece contains several steps 17 feet long by 18 inches broad, and 3 inches deep, and the pieces are so neatly formed, that the whole has the appearance of having been cut out of the solid rock. A little way from the top of this grand approach, the road leads through two gigantic portals ; and there are yet standing two of the four great columns, which once occupied the space between the two entrances : their heights are 39 feet and 28 feet respectively. The front and interior sides of the first portal are supported by two huge unicorns, 14½ feet high ; and those of the second, by two winged animals, each having the head of a man, which is covered with a kind of cap: the unicorns are in front of the grand staircase, and the other animals are towards the mountains."—pp. 618—620.

On the subject of the navigation of the Euphrates—a subject perhaps now of less urgent importance than when the Expedition under Colonel Chesney was sent out—but still an important and interesting subject, the author writes as follows :—

" Previously to transferring the Euphrates steamer to the Bombay Government, in accordance with the original plan of the Expedition, reports stating the practicability of navigating the river Euphrates were sent to the Home Government from the late Commander Cleveland, R.N., from Mr. now Commander Charlewood, R.N., and Mr. now Captain Fitzjames, R.N. ; also from Captain, now Lieutenant-Colonel Estcourt, M.P., and Mr. Ainsworth ; and the opinions expressed in these reports were speedily confirmed by the ascent of Lieutenant, now Commander, Charles D. Campbell, I.N. (one of the officers serving under Commander Lynch) to Beles, the port of Aleppo, which, by the air-line, is only an hundred miles from Iskenderún. The rivers of Mesopotamia also had been thoroughly explored, and every thing promised the permanency of an establishment in those regions when the services of the steamers, Assyria, Nimrúd, and Nitocris, were required to assist in the operations on the Indus.

" It is to be hoped that the inopportune check thus given to the progress of steam navigation in Mesopotamia will be removed ; and that the day is not very far distant when other and more suitable vessels will be employed. A cheap and rapid communication with India may then be maintained by this route, and at the same time a considerable increase would accrue to the commerce of Great Britain.

" Without entering upon the subject at length, it may be sufficient to observe that small vessels of light draught, such as can now be constructed, will not experience any serious difficulties in carrying the Indian mail from the Persian Gulf to Beles, whence they could be transported through Aleppo, Iskenderún, Trieste, &c., to England. The transit would be accomplished in twenty-five days from the Gulf, or thirty-one days from Bombay. The mails from India might be brought by this route alternately with the Red Sea Line, according to the original intention."—pp. 600, 601.

We have said that the subject of the Euphrates navigation is of somewhat less importance than it was in 1835, fifteen years ago, when the Euphrates expedition was carried into effect, because the facilities for the overland journey by Suez have been much increased in the course of that time. By that route the journey from and to India is now accomplished, on an average, in about six weeks, or forty days. According to the foregoing statement of Colonel Chesney, the passage from Bombay to Beles on the Euphrates (about 100 miles from the Mediterranean) would occupy thirty-one days. In this we may add two or three for the land journey, unless a railroad were constructed ; and then we apprehend the sea voyage would be rather longer

than from Alexandria. So that, on the whole, we apprehend
there would be no gain in point of time by the Euphrates route,
except, perhaps, in going out to India, when the passage, in consequence of descending the Euphrates, would be somewhat less

Judging from the reports of the Officers in the Appendix of
the second volume, it would seem that there are actually difficulties
of no trifling description in the navigation of the Euphrates. We
refer to the Karablah rocks, over which there is only three feet
water in the low season, with a stream running seven miles an
hour, and where a vessel would require to be warped up the
stream. The Lamlum marshes also present a serious difficulty,
the river being, for a space of twenty-five miles, so much lost in
these marshes and in various branches, that the main stream in
the dry season has not above thirty inches water in some places,
besides being extremely difficult to navigate, in consequence of the
abrupt and sudden windings of its course. The practical inconvenience resulting from this would be, that goods and passengers
would have to be transferred to three different steamers on their
passage from Bombay to Beles on the Upper Euphrates; a large
steamer taking them from Bombay to Basrah, a very small one
through the marshes, and a larger again on to Beles. Of course
this difficulty could be got over by blasting the rocks at Karablah,
(which probably could be easily done,) and by cutting a canal for
twenty-three miles through the marshes. This latter operation
would be attended, we presume, with no inconsiderable expense;
but if the design were carried out, we should think the best course
would be to accept the offer made by the Pasha of Baghdad,
(if it should be repeated,) to dig a canal connecting the Euphrates
and Tigris, and thus avoid the Lamlum marshes: were this done,
the only great difficulty of the navigation would be got over.

We confess, however, that our nerves are rather shaken by the
kind of preparation which Captain Fitzjames recommends in his
communication; for we peaceful civilians do not exactly relish
the kind of reception we should be likely to meet amongst a
people who, we are told, " would certainly take advantage of the
vessels, and attack them if they imagined they were in a defence-
less state" (p. 693); and when Captain Fitzjames seriously recommends, that the steamers employed in the passage down the
Euphrates should have " *at least* one swivel gun forward or aft,
as *convenient*, to fire grape and canister, with four one-pounder
swivels, and two wall-pieces; a good portion of muskets or carbines, pistols, swords, &c. for the crew, and if *Congreve rockets*
could be kept from spoiling by the carriage or heat, a supply
would be *invaluable*" (p. 693); we own, that with all the anxiety
we feel to visit Mesopotamia, we cannot help shrugging our

shoulders, and feeling just as well pleased that we are not in one of the Euphrates steamers at this moment. We should beg leave to send Colonel Chesney, and his gallant associates, to *clear the way* for us in the first instance, and we have no doubt that were the "swivel" and the "Congreve rockets" brought actively into play for about half a dozen voyages or so, back and forwards, not forgetting the "wall-pieces," "carbines," &c., a considerable alteration would take place in the views and practices of the "bad set" of Lamlum and its neighbourhood; and of other persons of predatory habits. But under existing circumstances, as the steamers would have to "lie to" *every night*, we should not exactly relish the chance of finding some night our throats being cut by a party of Bedouins, or Mesopotamians. We protest, therefore, that nothing shall induce us to take our passage in the Euphrates steamer until Colonel Chesney shall have executed a *razzia* or two on the natives, with the energy of which we are sure he is capable; and shall have taught them to know the meaning of the word "Congreve" by experimental application. In the language of his friend Captain Fitzjames, we have no doubt the rockets would be "invaluable!"

We are sure Colonel Chesney will pardon us for joking a little over this matter. We must take leave of him with a smile, tendering to him our best thanks for the really noble work he has produced—for the extensive research which constitutes it a perfect Encyclopædia on all subjects connected with Oriental geography and history, and certainly a work full of more varied interest than any book treating on Oriental subjects that we remember to have perused

We are, seriously speaking, of opinion, that the Euphrates navigation *ought* to be tried again, notwithstanding the "swivels" and "Congreve rockets;" and that there are no insurmountable difficulties in the way. We would urge it especially on the ground of the great advantages to British trade and commerce, which are likely to ensue from throwing open the whole of Western Asia to our mercantile enterprize; and in concluding our remarks, we would only add the expression of our surprise in finding that promises of brevet rank, and of payment of expenses, were held out to Colonel Chesney when going out on his expedition which have never been realized. We think such a fact most discreditable to the various governments of the last fifteen years; and trust, most earnestly, that so great and long-continued an injustice will be at once remedied. It may be that the country has not derived from the expedition the practical benefit which was anticipated; but this is surely no reason for withholding from an excellent and most meritorious officer, the promised reward of services which he has faithfully performed.

Art. III.—1. *The Life of Anselm, Archbishop of Canterbury. Translated and abridged from the German of* F. R. Hasse, *Professor of Evangelical Theology in the University of Berlin. By the Rev.* William Turner, *M.A., Vicar of Boxgrove.* London: Rivingtons.

2. *The Life and Pontificate of Gregory the Seventh. By* John William Bowden, *M.A.* In 2 vols. London: Rivingtons.

Seven centuries have passed over the English Church since the great struggle in the days of Anselm and Becket; and now, in the mysterious cycle of Divine providence, we are again involved in much the same questions, and surrounded by many of the same circumstances, which, at that remote period, so keenly exercised the faculties, and aroused the passions, of our forefathers. The question of the nineteenth century is, like that of the twelfth, Whether the spirit of the world—the spirit of the age, is, or is not, to convert the Christian Church into one of its instruments; to imbue it wholly with its own earthly spirit, and tendencies, and objects; to extinguish its witnessing in behalf of Christ against the world, and the flesh, and the devil.—It may not be unprofitable in the present times, to review the course of events, in many respects so strangely similar, in which the Church found herself involved seven or eight centuries ago, inasmuch as it may tend to show, that as great dangers and difficulties as those we have to contend with have been the lot of our predecessors in times when the spirit of the age was untainted by the presence of speculative infidelity; and may also supply various practical lessons and suggestions in reference to the mode in which the contest between the world and the Church should be conducted in the present age.

In the eleventh and twelfth centuries, then, the Western Church generally found itself in the closest possible union with the State; a union which had existed for centuries, and which gave to the temporal sovereigns a control over ecclesiastical affairs scarcely inferior to that which was established in England in the time of Henry VIII., and which still in theory subsists amongst us. For three hundred years or more, *i. e.* from the time of Charlemagne, the bishops of the West had been possessed of princely and baronial power and rank; the synods of the Church had become parliaments, in which ecclesiastical and temporal affairs were discussed and regulated by the king and nobles as well as by the bishops and clergy; the popes, metropolitans, bishops, abbots, and other prelates, were, either directly or virtually, appointed by the temporal sovereigns. In every direction, the emperors and princes were in full possession of a supremacy in ecclesiastical affairs, guaranteed by ancient precedent, recognized by the Church and its highest authorities in former ages, and established by temporal law.

Had the State employed this supremacy with a due regard to the welfare of the Church, its rights would never have been disputed. The emperors would have continued to nominate the popes and the rest of the hierarchy. The fearful wars which for ages ravaged Europe, dethroned so many sovereigns, and ended in exalting the papacy above all the sovereigns of the West, would never have taken place. The sovereigns of England, in particular, would not have been involved in an unsuccessful struggle with the leaders of the Church party in their own dominions, nor been deprived, as they were for ages, by law, of all their higher ecclesiastical patronage. Every thing would have gone on smoothly and in perfect harmony between Church and State, if the State would have honestly and fairly fulfilled the duties which it assumed in taking on itself the ecclesiastical supremacy.

But this course, unhappily, was not pursued by the emperors and other sovereigns of Europe. They treated the Church as if it had been a department of the State. Its bishoprics became the rewards of royal favourites, or were abandoned to the principal vassals of the crown, in the hopes of strengthening the throne by thus subsidizing them out of Church property. The spiritual interests of the Church were wholly neglected. Piety, learning, orthodoxy, were set aside, to make room for birth, influence, or wealth. The State acted on merely secular and worldly principles in its dealings with the Church, making it subservient to the promotion of its temporal objects. And this went on for centuries, during which a general darkness overspread the Church. Its discipline sank into desuetude; its religion became either worldly or superstitious; its prelates became secular lords, the servants of the State, and not of the Church; theological learning became extinct.

Such were the results arising from the influence of the State upon the Church in those ages: the Church property alone was left, and the traditions of the faith; but that great body lay as it were without a soul for many years.

In the middle of the eleventh century, at length, a reforming party arose in the Church,—not amongst the rulers of the Church, or amongst the laity, but amongst the inferior clergy; which, though small in number at first, and of little power, was supported in its opposition to the gross tyranny and wickedness of the State by the weight of undeniable facts, and plain and palpable justice. It brought against the established abuses of the State's ecclesiastical supremacy the principle of religious obligation. And although the State was supported by an obsequious hierarchy, a proud and jealous peerage, and a vast body of other adherents; and the Church party had to contend with adverse laws, adverse precedents, a hostile episcopate, most awe-stricken by the temporal power, and deeply tainted by simony; yet, nevertheless, such was the force of truth, and the effect of the State's ungodliness in all Church matters, that this little party found leaders, whose stern and high-souled energies lifted the see of Rome, round which they rallied, above all the monarchs of the West; and the State not only lost, through its own corruption, the power which it had so long exercised in ecclesiastical affairs, but was obliged to yield to the temporal dominion of the Church.

At the era of the Reformation, the Crown of England, after various preparatory efforts in preceding ages, shook off the jurisdiction of the papacy, which was half spiritual and half temporal, and resumed the powers which the Christian emperors and princes formerly possessed. Henry VIII. obtained the same ample powers in ecclesiastical matters which Charlemagne and his successors held: nor did the Church offer any opposition to the exercise of these powers by Henry and his successors. Amidst various anomalies, and actions in themselves questionable,—as regarded strict regularity,—amidst various excesses of the Royal power in ecclesiastical matters, the Church felt that this great object of her existence was looked to by the State. She saw an anxiety to promote her spiritual welfare; her bishoprics sedulously filled by learned, pious, and zealous divines; her synods in full action; her discipline enforced; her opponents discouraged and repressed. Time passed on, and a change came over the State: the Church had become a tool in its hands for the promotion of its temporal objects. It ran precisely the same career which the temporal power in the West pursued for two hundred and fifty years before the time of Hildebrand. At length the proceedings of the State have been gradually becoming intolerable. A party has arisen in the Church which is at present in the minority, but which is strong in argument against the gross and unchristian abuses of the State's power over the Church. As before, the State has law on its side, old possession, precedents, patronage, a compliant and timid episcopate, a baronage jealous of Church liberties, and a host of adherents of all kinds. As before, those who oppose State corruptions, and assert the inalienable rights of the kingdom of God, are regarded as seditious and dangerous men, are discountenanced by the episcopate, and are in bad odour with the world.

Nevertheless it is plain that their movements will have results : whether they move or not, there are certainly great events and changes before us. Circumstances will raise up more powerful leaders than they now possess. Their cause will gain ground as discussion goes on, for they have a mass of monstrous and indefensible corruptions to expose, and their claims are founded in plain and palpable justice. They must, therefore, become each year increasingly formidable; they can appeal to the deepest-seated religious principle, to the sense of common justice and fairness implanted in our nature, to the breach of compacts and pledges, to the natural desire for liberty. The State is endeavouring to suppress this awakened spirit, but it will not succeed. What will be the course of events it is impossible to foretel with any certainty : but, in any event, the State will be severely punished for its unprincipled conduct. It will probably, eventually, lose all control over the Church ; and thus the present fears of statesmen may be realized through their own mistaken policy. This may happen, even if the State should have in the mean time confiscated the Church's property : for any such proceeding might not diminish the strength of the Church ; it might, under certain circumstances, largely augment it. If Parliament were to take away all Church property now, we are inclined to think the Church of England would soon be far the most powerful political body in the country, and would be able to do pretty much what she liked in politics.

The State might have prevented any such movement on behalf of the Church's liberties, by abstaining from acts which are really injurious to the Church, and by a right use of its ecclesiastical patronage. It might still, we believe, arrest the current of events, by doing its duty to the Church, even at the eleventh hour. But the temper of statesmen and their adherents is evidently very far from any wish to remove opposition by concession or conciliation. They persuade themselves that all opposition will speedily die away of itself, or else they are resolved to act unflinchingly, on a policy of repression and discouragement, in the vain hope of putting down a party which they regard with aversion. Such appears to be their fixed course of policy ; and therefore we think that the contest must go on continually increasing in strength, with every fresh opportunity of collision afforded by the progress of events. The Hampden controversy was one point in this contest. The Gorham case has afforded

another field. Such cases will arise frequently. The two which
have arisen have wrought an immense change in the Church's
mind towards the State, and have created an organized movement. A few more steps of the same kind will increase that
movement's power to an incalculable extent.

We must now revert to the history of the Western Church
from the time of Charlemagne.

According to Gieseler (ii. 21), the sovereigns of the Carlovingian dynasty " retained the general superintendence of the
Church," which they exercised by means of royal visitors or
envoys, who, under the title of " Missi Dominici," held regular
visitations of the bishops, clergy, and monks, and inquired into
their moral conduct and the discharge of their duties. These
sovereigns also possessed " the right of arbitration in Church
matters," and directed appeals to be made to themselves from
the decisions of the metropolitans. They assembled synods at
pleasure, and possessed " the direction and confirmation of all
ecclesiastical decrees." The decisions and canons of councils were
required to be confirmed by them before they could be put in force.
" Though Charlemagne wished to introduce again the election of
bishops by the clergy, they still continued for the most part to be
appointed by the king." The royal envoys attended at elections,
and their nomination was equivalent to a " Letter Missive " in
the present day. These sovereigns " allowed no interference" to
the pope " in the affairs of their own Church, but by argument
or persuasion."

Mosheim remarks, (Cent. viii. part ii. ch. 2,) that at this time,

" The supreme dominion over the Church and its possessions was
vested in the emperors and kings, both in the Eastern and Western
world. The sovereignty of the Grecian Emperors in this respect has
never been contested ; and though the partizans of the Roman pontiffs
endeavoured to render dubious the supremacy of the Latin monarchs
over the Church, yet this supremacy is too manifest to be disputed by
such as have considered the matter attentively ; and it is acknowledged
by the wisest and most candid writers even of the Romish communion.
Adrian I., in a council of Bishops assembled at Rome, conferred upon
Charlemagne and his successors the right of election to the see of
Rome; and though neither Charlemagne nor his son Louis, were
willing to exercise this power in all its extent, by naming and
creating the pontiff at every vacancy, yet they reserved the right
of approving and confirming the person that was elected to that
high dignity by the priests and people ; nor was the consecration of
the elected pontiff of the least validity, unless performed in the
presence of the emperor's ambassadors. The Roman pontiffs obeyed
the laws of the emperors, received their judicial decisions as of indis-

pensable obligation, and executed them with the utmost punctuality and submission. The kings of the Franks appointed extraordinary judges, whom they called envoys, to inspect into the lives and manners of the clergy, superior and inferior, to take cognizance of their contests, to terminate their disputes, to enact laws concerning the public worship, and to punish the crimes of the sacred order, as well as those of the other citizens."

Mosheim remarks, in addition :

"It is further to be observed, that the power of convening councils and the right of presiding in them, were the prerogatives of the emperors and sovereign princes, in whose dominions these assemblies were held ; and that no decrees of any council obtained the force of laws until they were approved and confirmed by the supreme magistrate."

The above statements represent to us a union of Church and State quite as intimate as any that has ever existed in England. This was the system which existed for ages in the West, and which might have continued without interruption had it not been extremely abused. We must adduce one more testimony, from the well written life of Anselm, by Professor Hasse, of Berlin, for a translation of which we are indebted to the Rev. W. Turner.

"Since all the political relations of the Germans rested on territorial possessions, the Church, by her richness in these possessions, early acquired an important authority in the State. And as she was chiefly indebted to the kings for these possessions, and relied on their protection for their preservation, they became the patrons of the Churches ; and the bishops, as stewards of ecclesiastical property, stood in a corresponding relation to the kings, as the vassals and functionaries, the 'people' of the same, whose temporal possessions originated with them, and to whom they formed a kind of spiritual nobility. . . . . The kings sought in them a counterpoise against the temporal peers, and in order to gain their attachment, conferred on them the highest political privileges, the so-called regalia, and made over to them whole counties in imperial fee, so that, subsequently, they were able to exercise sovereign sway in Germany. Thus the Church obtained an influence in public life which she never before possessed ; for she not only exercised temporal authority over a great part of the country, and in her own territories, but gave her concurrence, in all general questions of government, even to the possession of the throne. She maintained her seat and voice in the Imperial Diet, and besides, enjoyed all the rights which remained to her from the time of the Romans,—a right of inspection over morals and discipline, a peculiar administration of justice, the guardianship of orphans, &c. But, on the other hand, this worldly position brought her into greater dependence on the State than before ; for whilst her dignitaries were persons of such importance in the State, and in whose conduct kings were deeply interested, the latter strove to ensure their devotion to their service, and *for this end, above all endeavoured to acquire the power of distributing ecclesiastical honours.* The Church willingly acknowledged that such important offices should not be conferred without consent of the king, and expressly subjected the legality of episcopal elections to his approval, so that he had the right of recommendation to every see which he founded. Thus the old canonical form of election ' by Clergy and people' fell into desuetude, although in theory its freedom was supposed to exist, and it was even legally restored by the kings from time to time; but in practice the right of recommendation and confirmation had passed into a formal right of nomination. On the notice of the vacancy of an episcopal see, the king expressly ordered who should fill it, and merely allowed the form of an election, or, without regard to it, wrote at once to the metropolitan to consecrate the person whom he had designated. And since this nomination was at the same time an induction into the possession and privileges of the see, it gradually assumed the character of an investiture, especially when the bishops acquired temporal fiefs of the empire; and although this investiture referred to the property and rights, and not to the duties of the see, yet there was so little distinction between them that the act of investiture was at the same time a delivery of the signs of office, of spiritual office—the ring and the crosier; so that the power of the Church actually appeared to flow from that of the State, and the more so, as consecration followed investiture."—pp. 50—53.

In the foregoing description of the union of Church and State previously to, and subsequent to, the time of Charlemagne, many features will recal to the reader's mind the power of the Crown over the Church of England since the Reformation, and as we see it in the present day. Here is the very same system of State supremacy. In both cases it was introduced with the consent or submission of the Church. In both cases it was enforced by law; was one of the most highly prized branches of the royal prerogative, and existed for centuries.

Now, then, we proceed to trace the state of things in the Church under this royal supremacy of the Carlovingian, and other sovereigns in those ages.

Mosheim remarks on the ninth century :—

" In the Western provinces the bishops were become voluptuous and effeminate to a very high degree. They passed their lives amidst the splendour of courts and the pleasures of a luxurious indolence, which corrupted their taste, extinguished their zeal, and rendered them incapable of performing the solemn duties of their function ; while the inferior clergy were sunk in licentiousness. . . . . Besides, the ignorance of the sacred order was, in many places, so deplorable, that few of them could either read or write."—(Cent. IX. p. ii. c. 2.)

Of the state of the Church in the tenth century, Mosheim speaks in the following terms :—

" Besides the reproach of the grossest ignorance which the Latin Clergy in this century so justly deserved, they were also chargeable in a very heinous degree with two other odious and enormous vices, even concubinage and simony, which the greatest part of the writers of these unhappy times acknowledge and deplore. As to the first of these vices, it was practised too openly to admit of any doubt. . . . . The other vice above-mentioned reigned with an equal degree of impudence and licentiousness. The *election of bishops and abbots was no longer made according to the laws of the Church;* but *kings and princes, or their ministers and favourites, either conferred these ecclesiastical dignities upon their friends and creatures, or sold them, without shame, to the highest bidder*. Thus it happened, that the most stupid and flagitious wretches were frequently advanced to the most important stations in the Church ; and that, upon several occasions, even soldiers, civil magistrates, counts, and such like persons,· were, by a strange metamorphosis, converted into bishops and abbots."—(Cent. x. p. ii. c. 2.)

Of course, under such a system of appointment to the higher ecclesiastical offices, the most fearful evils must have become prevalent in the Church. We need not wonder, therefore, at the almost universal ignorance and immorality. But who was to blame for these evils? The State only. The Church had yielded up to the sovereigns of Europe the general superintendence of the ecclesiastical matters, and especially the appointment of bishops. The sovereigns, instead of regarding that patronage as a sacred trust for the benefit of religion, set aside all religious considerations, and dealt with ecclesiastical patronage as if it were merely secular.

The corruption of the Church, and especially of the episcopal order, in those ages, is also represented by Gieseler (ii. 98) ; and amongst other results of the general secularization of the Church was the virtual cessation of synods, which gradually merged in parliaments.

" Since," says Hasse, " the bishops had been attracted to the Imperial Diets, they were accustomed to discuss these ecclesiastical concerns ; consequently synods were more unfrequently held, and, when they did take place, they had an entirely juridical aspect, *i. e.* the temporal peers attended, and the approbation of the king was not only required for the assembly, but also for the measures under consideration, and the conclusions received their validity from his sanction. Yet *the nobles felt too little interest in spiritual affairs to attempt to influence the decisions concerning them.* Doctrine, worship, &c., were not interfered with. Their worst influence referred to the persons who had the administration of these things ; for *in the appointment of Church dignitaries, their attention was chiefly directed to their own political or local interests;* nor did they so much regard the spiritual qualifications of the candidates, as *the family, name, or party to which they belonged;* and if these points came not into consideration, the decision turned upon the sum which was offered to supply the pecuniary wants of the nobleman or his adviser. The most disgraceful simony was practised, to the increasing degradation of the Clergy ; for the prelates, in order to remunerate themselves for the price of their own dignities, made the disposal of the lowest offices in the Church a continual source of profit to themselves."—*Life of Anselm*, p. 54.

We might easily multiply references to works of authority in further proof of the prejudicial influence exercised on the Church by the State in those ages ; but it seems needless to supply additional evidence.

Now these sovereigns who thus inflicted the most fearful evils on Christianity, without doubt considered themselves perfectly authorized in the use they made of their powers over the Church. They held themselves responsible to no human power for the right discharge of their duties. They looked on the Church just as statesmen now do,—as an engine of State policy. The bishoprics and abbacies were spiritual lordships, which they dispensed on the same principles as they granted investiture of temporal lordships. They set aside altogether the question of spiritual qualifications : the only qualification they recognized was interest or money. Simony, in the gross form of giving and receiving money for the sale of spiritual offices, was a vice adapted to a coarse age ; and open profligacy, and military enterprises, were the shapes which worldliness assumed in those days. In a more refined age, the worldly spirit would have manifested itself in a different way. A baron in the nineteenth century is a very different person from a baron of the tenth century, though he may be under the influence of exactly the same passions. The spirit of the world is now a polite and civilized spirit.

We look back now with disgust on the descriptions we have of the episcopate in the tenth and eleventh centuries, but we forget that their vices were only those of the age. They merely followed the world in their days. They were "men of the world." The world was on very good terms with them. We do not hear that the sovereigns and barons thought the worse of the bishops for their simony and their concubinage. There seems to have been a cordial alliance between the Church and the State, between the Church and the world. The world had no troublesome monitor, no preacher of soberness, and righteousness, and judgment to come. The Church's witness was at an end : it was joined with the world in the service of the god of this world.

No doctrine, it is true, was touched : the Church remained in possession of its traditionary religion; but it was a cold and lifeless system, borne down beneath the weight of moral corruption and practical infidelity. The world had for ages been in possession of all the strong places of the Church, and, there seated, held in subjugation the greater part of its members.

The condition of the Church under the royal supremacy of the successors of Charlemagne and their contemporary sovereigns, will have reminded the reader in many ways of the state of the English Church for the last century and a half. We live, of course, under a different social system, and therefore our evils have been all connected with refinement, civilization, and policy. But nevertheless there are the same great features and principles in both cases : a State possessing itself of authority over the Church; exercising that authority wisely and well in the first instance, then treating the Church as a mere State engine; ignoring its spiritual character and objects; subjecting it to the legislation of worldly men; placing worldly men in its most important positions and offices; suppressing, as far as possible, all reformation emanating from purely Church sources; and, in fine, succeeding in imposing, to a great degree, its own character of worldliness on the Church. Hence, in both cases, the discipline of the Church became relaxed, theological studies were neglected, the prelates of the Church became courtiers and politicians, servants of sovereigns and ministers; and forgot their peculiar and first duty,—the ministry of the Sacraments and of God's Word, and the guardianship of the Faith; a general secularity invaded all classes, and the world and the Church were joined together in firm alliance. The Church learned to depend wholly on the protection and guidance of a State which showed, by all its acts, that it had no religious principle.—Such was the fallen condition of the Church in the tenth and eleventh centuries; nevertheless there were not wanting witnesses against this prevalent corruption, and they discerned at length the real cause of the evil, and set themselves to remedy it.

" The entire secularization of the Church," says Hasse, "stood at an alarming height, and the necessity for a combination of power was the more stringent, in order to extricate herself from this disgraceful dependence on feudal dominion. Since the time of her sinking into this state of subserviency, voices had not been wanting, which loudly complained and zealously resisted these abuses. But they were not listened to, because the whole system must acquire a certain influence before it could be felt in its crying opposition to the true notion of a Church. This period occurred in the middle of the eleventh century, when these commotions originated, which aimed at the release of the Church from her bondage, and finally led to the ' Investiture war ' with which the great struggle between Church and State more especially began, and which continued during the whole of the middle ages."— *Anselm*, pp. 54, 55.

When the power of the State over the Church has been for a long series of years established by law and with the original consent of the Church itself, it possesses a hold over men's minds which cannot be shaken by almost any amount of abuse. Without doubt there were many men in those ages who secretly lamented the fallen condition of the Church, and who, on fitting occasions, expressed their disapprobation of the principles on which ecclesiastical preferments were disposed of by the State; but they submitted to the abuses of the system, consoling themselves, without doubt, with the hope that God would dispose the hearts of rulers to act more justly towards the Church, and that it was their duty to remain in quietness and obedience to those laws, and that constitution in Church and State under which they had been placed by Divine Providence. They felt, we may suppose, that the removal of the corruptions and abuses of the Church was the duty of their bishops; and that to the hierarchy and to the rulers of the State all such high questions should be left. They, probably, persuaded themselves that their duty lay in the care of their own parishes, and the souls immediately entrusted to them; and that they had no call or claim to enter on the reformation of the Church. They may have mistrusted their own judgments perhaps, and may have supposed that they might have been misinformed as to the amount of the evils of their times, when they saw that the hierarchy were perfectly silent and acquiescent, and that no steps were taken to protect the episcopal office from the abuses of patronage which had occurred. It did not seem to them that there was any remedy, except in an improved moral and religious tone amongst rulers. Very probably they may have never imagined it possible that the Church could recover the power of electing her own bishops; they may not have been able to conceive the notion of a bishop appointed by the Church instead of the State, or, if they did, they probably shrank with affright from the notion, as involving the separation of Church and State, the confiscation of Church property, and renewed persecution. And there would not be wanting arguments gathered from Scripture, and from ecclesiastical history, to show how lawful and right the supremacy of Christian kings is. The fathers, the councils, and the popes of former ages, could be quoted in abundance in proof of the lawfulness of the power exercised by the emperors and kings over the Church. Then, there was the old established law of the land; the practice of past ages; the respect and obedience due to the sovereign; the fear of his displeasure; the consent of the barons, and nobles, and spiritual peers to the existing system. Any one who was dissatisfied with that system, and expressed his dissatisfaction, was, without doubt, regarded as a dangerous man ; and must make up his mind to be frowned upon by the great, and excluded from promotion, as an enthusiast, or as a factious, seditious, and designing person.

It is such arguments as these which generally weigh with the mass of well-disposed and conscientious persons. They are averse from agitation of any kind, and they look to their superiors for guidance ; they are disposed to trust in those superiors, and to believe that God's blessing will attend on this trusting submission to the powers that be. It was this view and feeling which probably protracted for centuries the evils of the Western Church ; for neither princes nor prelates attempted any reformation. Princes were but temporal rulers, and judged every thing by the rules and principles of temporal policy ; and the prelates were all *thoroughly mixed up with the transactions of the State.* They had purchased their bishoprics, they sold their parochial benefices, or they had been advanced without the slightest regard to qualifications or to the Church's spiritual good, possessing no claims except nobility of birth, or high interest, or services to sovereigns, or nobles, or ministers. They were in habits of intercourse with archbishops and bishops who had been appointed in the same way. They took part in ordaining such bishops. They sat with them in Diet or Parliament, which had superseded the synod of the Church. They were always about the court, high in favour with princes and ministers, invested with lofty titles, and extensive political power and jurisdiction ; and they thought that this was indeed a "good" system, which thus placed the heads of the Church high in the courts of princes. They loved that system, and they wished for no alteration in it. They were very lenient to its abuses ; and, without doubt, their advice to the clergy who complained of those abuses was always, " Be quiet." They, probably, charged their clergy on all occasions to attend to their parochial duties, and to let the Church remain *at peace.* " Peace," peace with this world, with the powers of this world, with the system of this world's rulers, was, without doubt, their perpetual admonition.—And it was to such spiritual rulers, to men who were completely identified with the system of Church and State union then existing, that the Church looked up for aid !

Certainly nothing seemed more hopeless, humanly speaking. The episcopate, as a body, was in favour of a system which had nearly eaten out the life of the Church ; and what could be done without the episcopate ?

The evil was apparently irremediable, and yet, the Church found a way to shake off the incubus that pressed upon her, though the struggle was a desperate one.

The first indication of what was coming was seen in the revival of learning. Any great movement in the Church is generally preceded by this sign. It was remarkably instanced at the Reformation, in the sixteenth century. From A. D. 1000 there was a general movement of intellect in the Church; theological studies revived, and schools were established. The time for change was come.

A party or school in the Church now began to grow up, which was at first very weak, but which gradually gained influence. This was the reforming party, which sought an alteration in the relations of Church and State, and which ultimately carried its point.

The see of Rome itself had fallen into deeper degradation than almost any other see in the West, and it was here that the struggle commenced. We must briefly touch on the antecedent circumstances.

It has been already observed, that the appointment of the pope was in the hands of Charlemagne and his successors. In course of time, in consequence of the temporary dissolution of the empire, the Roman States became independent for some years, and the appointment of the popes was usurped by the lawless and licentious nobles around Rome. After several most disgraceful appointments, usurpations, and schisms, pope John XII., one of the most licentious and reprobate of the series, was obliged to seek the protection of Otho, king of Germany, against the tyrants of Italy, and, in acknowledgment of the services rendered by that monarch, crowned him, in A.D. 962, as the successor of Charlemagne.

Invested with the empire, Otho became possessed of the ecclesiastical authority attached to it by law and ancient custom, and he put it in exercise by summoning a council at Rome for the trial of pope John, who was deposed for immorality; and another was elected in his stead under the virtual nomination of the emperor. An attempt was made by a party to maintain pope John's cause, and on his death a successor was elected; but the imperial authority prevailed by force of arms.

From this time, except for a short period, during which, on account of political disturbances, the papacy fell again under the power of the petty princes of the vicinity, the emperors exercised the power of appointing the bishops of Rome. One of these, Benedict IX., being desirous of contracting marriage, which involved his resignation of the papal see, entered into communication with the archpriest of Rome, named John Gratianus, and, on receiving from the latter a sum of money, resigned in his favour, and, on his election by the clergy and people of Rome, consecrated him with his own hands as his successor, by the name of Gregory VI., A.D. 1044.

The object of Gregory VI., in this very irregular proceeding, was to assert, in opposition to the aristocracy, the long-dormant right of the Roman clergy and people to the free election of their spiritual pastor.   He was amongst the most religious of the Roman clergy ; and on this occasion we first discern the existence of a reforming party in the Church.

" Unlettered as he was," says Mr. Bowden, " and unworthy as had been the mode of his exaltation, Gregory VI. seems to have been supported against his rivals by whatever of high feeling or Catholic principles yet existed in the papal city.   A school was now growing up, at Rome and elsewhere, of men, who, disgusted with the outrageous corruptions of the Church, pined for her reformation ; and who at the same time felt, that such reformation, to be essential and permanent, must be connected with her liberation from the thraldom in which she had long been held, to secular aristocratical power.   The supreme functions of her internal government having become—as though by the general consent of the collective episcopacy of the West—entrusted to the pope, they saw that the vigour of her administration must be crippled throughout, if the pontiff continued either the dependent nominee of a German monarch, or the creature of a Tusculan court.   They beheld the spirit of feudalism gradually drawing the hierarchies of the different nations of Europe more and more into its system, and confounding the spiritual character with the secularities around them."—*Bowden,* i. 113.

This first attempt of the anti-secular party at Rome proved a failure : for the emperor Henry had his own notions of ecclesiastical reform ; he was a reformer in his own way ; and his remedy for the evils of the Roman Church was to convene a synod of his bishops, and by their aid to cause the various claimants of the papal throne to resign or be deposed, and then to nominate a new pope himself.

Amongst those who resigned was Gregory, the pope of the anti-secular, or Church party of that day.   His resignation, which they considered with some reason to be a forced one, caused a strong feeling of discontent in their minds.   They had established in his case, as they had hoped, the principle of free election by the Church, and they saw in that principle the only instrument which might avail to save the Church from the impending danger of an increased thraldom to the temporal power, which had so grossly and so long abused its privileges.

" These, however, to whom thoughts like these suggested themselves, were but few ; and the cause with which they connected themselves was disgraced by too many foul stains, to permit them to hope for any general sympathy. Nor, however universal their feelings might have been, did there exist, in their long corrupted and degraded city, sufficient strength for any demonstration in opposition to the German sovereign's power."—*Bowden*, i. 120.

The result of the movement, then, was in the first instance very unfortunate. Like the opposition in the Hampden case, it placed the Church in a worse position than before, and consolidated the power of the sovereign. The pope was directly nominated by the emperor; and he left in triumph, carrying along with him into banishment the deprived pope of the Church party, and some of his more active supporters.

" This party, if we may so style them who were yet scarcely beginning to feel their union in the maintenance of the same great principles, seems now to have had its representatives spread over Western Europe; embracing in its fellowship several of the most learned, the most devoted, the most pure, among the Churchmen of the day. But its apparent force, as a party, even in its centre, the papal city, was as yet but small. The great majority of well-disposed men, naturally delighted at their liberation from such scenes as those which they had recently witnessed, and from the tyranny of such factions as those of Benedict and Sylvester, were disposed to hail with acclamations every step of the reforming monarch's career; he saw in that career the assertion of every principle fraught with danger to the future welfare of either Church or State. And Henry himself, it is probable, did no more than concur in opinion with these, in regarding the men whom he might perceive to be thus discontented, as theoretic speculators, better acquainted with books than with men, and vainly aiming, in human things, at a state of ideal perfection. The monarch could not understand the ties of sympathy which united those learned, pure, and thoughtful men, with those whom similar studies, similar contemplations, and similar purity of life, were leading in other countries to the adoption of similar sentiments. And still less could he appreciate the power which those principles, when appealed to in hours of trial, might excite over the hearts and affections of mankind."—*Bowden*, i. 124.

Amongst the members of this " Church" party was Hildebrand, a young monk, a native of Tuscany, who had passed his earlier years at Rome, and, being disgusted with the degeneracy of the Church there, had sought for a more fervent religion in the monastery of Cluni, in Burgundy. On his return to Rome, the zeal and strictness of principles which distinguished him, rendered him unpopular among the lax and worldly Churchmen of that day: but he took part with the unfortunate Gregory VI. in the struggle for the liberty of elections; and, on the failure of that enterprise, was obliged to leave Rome, and return again to the monastery of Cluni, where his eminent qualifications raised him speedily to the office of prior.

The " Church" party of that day was now apparently defeated. The emperor had nominated his pope, and appeared as a sturdy reformer of abuses, thus enlisting the public sympathies on behalf of the royal supremacy. The pope died in a year or two, and the emperor *again* nominated a pope. Scarcely had the latter ascended the pontifical throne when he died, and Henry had to nominate a third pope within the space of three years.

On this occasion, Bruno, bishop of Toul, was nominated by the emperor. Bruno was a pious, zealous, and unambitious man, and this was just the most dangerous person who could have been chosen under the circumstances. He had a high opinion of Hildebrand, and invited him to accompany him to Rome, where, on his arrival, his first step was to seek for the election of the Clergy and people of Rome, thus acknowledging that the emperor's appointment was *insufficient.*

This was a step, the importance of which was not seen at the time, but it involved principles which were carried out steadily from this time. The Church had now at its head a bishop who had the power and the will to reform abuses; and the emperor, who was equally zealous in the cause of reform, was delighted to see the zeal with which pope Leo held synods throughout Italy, Germany, and France, and deposed bishops and archbishops who had obtained their sees by simony, and condemned those who were guilty of immorality. From this moment the Church party began to gain the ascendancy: the popes were elected regularly by the Clergy and the people of Rome, and ere long the celebrated decree made by ecclesiastical authority investing the cardinals with the power of electing the pope, laid the foundation of a system which has endured for ages. The emperors attempted to maintain their right of nomination, and they were deprived of it only because the empire was so divided that they were unable to give their whole attention to the Church of Rome. It was soon seen that there were incurable vices in the system of royal nomination, and public opinion throughout Europe supported the Church in its struggle. On the accession of Hildebrand, the leader of the Church party, to the papal throne, the struggle came to an issue; and we shall here use the language of Professor Hasse which briefly states its issue.

" The great Reformation advanced, and when Hildebrand himself mounted the papal throne in 1073, he carried the contest to a most decisive pitch ; whilst at a Roman Council, 1075, he prohibited ' Lay investiture,' and threatened with excommunication, not only the Clergy who received investiture from a temporal hand, but the princes and nobles who claimed for themselves the right. . . . To force the emperor to an acknowledgment of the prohibition, and the surrender of his right of investiture, was the main point at issue; and it is well known what gigantic efforts were required to reach this aim. Gregory himself and Henry IV. died in the struggle; the one in exile, the other under excommunication. Anti-popes and anti-kings entered the field: Italy and Germany blazed with the fiercest wars. Almost half a century passed before the settlement of the protracted struggle. By the concordat of Worms (1122) the emperor gave back to God, the Apostles Peter and Paul, and the Holy Catholic Church, all investiture with ring and crosier, and conceded that *in all Churches, the election and consecration should take place free, according to ecclesiastical laws, without restraint and simony:* on the other hand, the pope approved that the elected should receive from the emperor through the sceptre the regalia, and thereupon rendered to ' Cæsar the things that were Cæsar's.' Although the investiture struggle in the last instance only could be decided in Germany, yet it was fought out in all other countries."— *Anselm*, pp. 58, 59.

Thus the issue of the whole was, that the State, in consequence of its gross and long continued abuse of the right of ecclesiastical patronage, lost its ancient rights, and had the discomfort of seeing the papacy possess itself of all the powers, patronage, and influence over the Church which had once been its own.

Scandalous abuses persisted in with obstinacy work their own cure. The most powerful sovereigns have experienced the truth of this: injustice and corruption are sure to be punished in the long run. It was so in the twelfth century, and it will be so in the nineteenth.

The sovereigns of England, in the eleventh and twelfth centuries, were amongst the most powerful princes of the West. William the Conqueror inherited from preceding kings of England great powers in ecclesiastical matters, and he exercised them vigorously. Lanfranc was appointed archbishop of Canterbury, royal chaplains were appointed to other sees, and every opportunity was taken to appoint Normans to the government of the Church and monasteries.

" All these nominations proceeded immediately from the king, in which he rather followed the counsel of his barons than that of his Clergy, and so zealously insisted on his right of investiture, that when Lanfranc once asked him for the appointment to an abbey which for ages had belonged to the see of Canterbury, he replied that ' he would not suffer a single crozier in England to be out of his hands.' He abstained, indeed, from enriching his treasury on the appointment of bishops (although he not unfrequently sold abbeys), so that only a single case of simony occurred. But according to Eadmer he only chose for prelates 'people in whom it would have been accounted dishonourable not to have been subservient to the king's will in every respect; and every one knew under what circumstances and for what purpose they were appointed.' For 'all things, divine and human, must be directed according to his will;' even the primate of his kingdom, at the assembly of a General Council, could adopt no measure without his approval and previous consultation. And in like manner, no bishop dared to summon before him any of his barons and friends, although guilty of the most open incest or adultery, without his permission; or to pass sentence of excommunication, or impose any other ecclesiastical penalty. Yet, under William I. things always went on tolerably well, for the king had the highest opinion of Lanfranc, who made use of his interest as far as he could for the good of the Church, although we frequently hear him bitterly complaining how little he was able to effect."—*Anselm*, pp. 64, 65.

The Church remained satisfied under the administration of William the Conqueror, even at the time when the Church and State in other parts of Europe were in violent collision; for there was no such gross and palpable abuse of royal power as could have afforded any pretext for disturbing the alliance of Church and State. But on the accession of William Rufus, the inherent vices of the system of royal supremacy became manifest. Rufus had inherited from his predecessors the right of enjoying the revenues of vacant sees, "jus spolii et regaliæ." This power had been conceded to the Crown together with investiture, on the assumption that it would be justly used; but in the hands of Rufus it became a dreadful evil, for he permitted the bishoprics to remain vacant, as their incumbents died, in order that he might possess their revenues, and when in possession, he injured in all ways the property of the Church.

The archbishopric of Canterbury was thus kept vacant for several years, and it was the expressed intention of the king to appoint no archbishop during his lifetime; at length, however, it was filled up under the following circumstances.

When the see of Canterbury had been vacant for nearly four years, the most respectable amongst the nobles of England, assembled at court at Christmas, 1092, agreed to address a petition to the king, "that they might at least be permitted to call upon God for the restoration of the archbishopric;" that the king would permit that prayers should be offered up in all the churches for this end. The king was embarrassed by this request, but he felt that he was not strong enough to refuse it, and accordingly Anselm, abbot of Bec, who was then in England, and was highly esteemed by every one, was directed to prepare a "form of prayer," which was used in the churches; the Crown exercising, apparently, the power of directing the composition of special forms, at that time as it does now.

This was the first step, and it did not seem what was next to be done, or whether any thing more could be done. However, the next step *was* taken, and it proved a *failure*. One of the nobles ventured to mention the name of Anselm in the course of confidential conversation with the king, observing that " in truth he lived only for God, his desires rested on nothing else." " Indeed !" said the king, " not even on the archbishopric of Canterbury ?" The king took occasion to express his resolution that " no one should be archbishop but himself ! "

It is a curious fact, that the *bishops* of England appear to have kept in the back-ground : they were apparently afraid to move lest they should incur the king's displeasure. They were generally men who had been appointed by William the Conqueror with the express object of maintaining the royal power. They were, in fact, more under the influence of the Crown than of the Church. The sequel will show this more plainly.

Apparently matters would have rested here, had not the king been seized with illness which threatened his life. In the immediate prospect of death, barons and prelates took courage to tell him the truth, and exhort him to think of his soul.

" Anselm by chance was in the neighbourhood of Gloucester when this occurrence took place. He was at once sent for, and requested to administer consolation to the king in his last moments. The first thing, he declared, must be a sincere confession, and the king must acknowledge his sins, and promise reformation. If there was yet time, he might then do what his nobles had advised him. In the agony of death the king consented to all. He confessed to Anselm, and called the bishops present as witnesses, that he at the same time vowed in future to exercise righteousness and mercy. On the high altar at Gloucester, they must lay their vows in his stead ; and an edict, furnished with the king's seal, was thereupon published, which ordered the liberation of all prisoners ; released debtors from outstanding sums, and offered pardon to all offences against his person. Good, holy laws, as in the time of king Edward, were to be re-established, justice impartially administered, and every violation of it strictly punished. The people received with joy this royal declaration, and flocked to the churches, in order to thank God, and pray for the king's recovery. The nobles now more urgently renewed their request for the nomination of an archbishop of Canterbury. The king was ready to comply, and, under the most excited expectation of those around him, *none of whom ventured to recommend any one*, nominated the abbot Anselm as the most worthy to fill that honourable station. An universal cry of exultation followed, whilst Anselm turned pale ; and when the bishops wished to introduce him to the king, in order to receive the crozier from his hand, he offered the most violent resistance. The astonished bishops took him aside, and with the most urgent entreaties, besought him to take charge of the oppressed Church."—*Anselm*, pp. 74, 75.

It is needless to occupy space by going further into details. Suffice it to say, that Anselm was at length compelled by force to receive investiture, and to assume the archiepiscopal office.

Here was the grand step gained which opened the way to the reform of the Church, and the restoration of its liberties. The Church party at once gained a *leader* who was in the highest position in the Church. Anselm went to work steadily, to remove the plague of simony, and to obtain the restoration of the synods which had been suspended by royal authority ; he also insisted on the recognition of one of the contending popes, in order to place the Church of England under his protection, and thereby to counterbalance the royal supremacy. Rufus, offended with the archbishop for declining to pay him a large sum on his appointment to the see, recognized the pope in the hope of obtaining his aid in the attempt to expel Anselm ; but in this design he failed, and Anselm had the support of the papacy in the struggle which ensued.

We must here introduce some sketches of the episcopate at that period.

William was bishop of Durham at this time :—a note, in the " Life of Anselm," gives us this information about him.

" William, as friend of Odo, bishop of Bayeux, the brother of the Conqueror, obtained the bishopric of Durham ; 'a man who attained his ecclesiastical dignity, not for his spiritual endowments, but, like the other Norman ecclesiastics, on account of his abilities as a courtier, man of business, and warrior.' He conspired with bishop Odo for the sake of establishing Robert on the English throne, and must leave England. He was restored to his see after the peace of Caen, 1091. He was, consequently, a firm adherent of the king's."— p. 82.

Ralph Flambard, a royal chaplain, was the king's justiciary, and appearing at Canterbury on the archbishop's enthronement, summoned the archbishop before his court, and commenced a legal process against the Church of Canterbury. Of him we read as follows :—

" He was surnamed 'Flambard,' or ' passe Flambard,' on account of his ability in discovering hidden treasures, according to William of Malmesbury. According to Anselm, 'propter crudelitatem similem flammæ comburenti.' Under William the Conqueror he had been made royal chaplain, and continued so under his successor, until his appointment to the see of Durham, in 1099. He also served the king

as ' summus regiarum opum procurator et justiciarius,' and was his
' exactor crudelissimus et consiliarius præcipuus,' *his chief instru-*
ment in enriching the royal treasury with the possessions of the
Church."

It is a curious illustration of the relations of Church and State
at that time, that this person, who was the chief agent of the
crown in plundering the Church, was rewarded for his unscrupulous conduct with the bishopric of Durham! The dignities of
the Church actually became the incentives to disloyalty towards
the Church, whenever the State was hostile to the Church. It is
consolatory to find that the nineteenth and eighteenth centuries
are not without parallel in former ages, in exhibiting instances
of Clergy who have taken part with the State against the
Church, and gained their reward.

The bishops of England had been most vehement in pressing
Anselm to accept the archbishopric, as soon as they learnt that it
was the will of the king to offer it to him ; their subsequent conduct exhibits them in the character of consistent courtiers. A
council was called at Rockingham, at Anselm's request, to consider the lawfulness of recognizing the pope, which Anselm pressed,
and the king objected to. Anselm explained the points in dispute before the council, and then directing his words to the
bishops, said to them, that the time had now arrived for them to
fulfil the promise they had made on his elevation to the see of
Canterbury, to support him with counsel and aid when his office
might oppress him. We must continue the narrative in Hasse's
words, which are really curious as illustrating a tone of mind in
the bishops of those days, of which we have had many instances
in our own times.

" The bishops answered, that they *were unable to suggest counsel*
in such a difficult emergency, and must leave the decision to his own
judgment. What they most desired *was his unconditional* (sine omni
aliâ conditione) *submission to the king,* and then they would be able
to restore things into their proper channel. . . . . When the bishops and
the barons had again assembled in the church, Anselm repeated his
request that they would assist him with their advice. They replied,
' that they knew of no other means of issue than that he would simply
submit himself to the king; but if he relied on spiritual counsel
(secundum Deum), then they must be silent."

How perfectly this was the language of courtiers and politicians,
unwilling to enter on the discussion of the question of religious
principle and duty, and resolved to look at the case and decide it
only on grounds of worldly policy ; and that policy involving implicit and absolute submission to the will of the temporal ruler !

Without doubt these servile prelates were of the opinion of Robert Count of Meulant, one of the king's counsellors, who said, " that the true majesty is only of God, and the *crimen læsæ majestatis* was therefore so called, because the king was the image of God upon earth."—p. 82.

In short, Anselm was left completely alone by the prelacy of England in his contest with the king, and he even found amongst them his chief opponents. The spokesman of the king's party, the bishop of Durham, pledged himself to compel Anselm either to renounce the pope or to resign his see, and, having collected a great number of bishops and barons, went to Anselm, and declared that the king would proceed against him for high treason, if he did not at once renounce the pope. After further discussion, the result was, that *all the bishops* (except one or two) *and abbots withdrew their obedience from Anselm,* and refused to acknowledge him as archbishop any longer, *in obedience to the king's command.*

A temporary reconciliation having taken place between Anselm and the king, the bishops hastened to apologize to the archbishop, and to renew their promise of canonical obedience; but the moment the contest began again, on occasion of Anselm's wish to visit the pope, the prelates, true to their principles, were again on the king's side ; and, on this occasion, their principles were expressed in the most undisguised manner. When Anselm had explained to a deputation of barons and bishops who came to him from the king, that he considered himself bound, for the sake of his own salvation, and that of the flock entrusted to him, to persist in his request to visit the pope, their reply was, " Abstain, for the king will never concede it."

" He then proceeded to explain to the bishops the reasons for his journey, and asked their opinion as to the validity of them. They replied, ' that they all really acknowledged the piety of Anselm ; but that as to themselves, they had too many earthly regards, too many relatives to provide for, &c., and were unable so entirely to turn their backs upon the world.' Anselm's aims were too exalted for them. If he would lower himself to their standard, they professed their readiness to support him ; but if he relied upon God alone, then they must leave him to himself, for on no account could they detach themselves from the king."—*Anselm,* pp. 108, 109.

Such illustrations of the spirit of the episcopate at that time show, that the tendency of the royal supremacy, as exercised in the nomination of bishops, is much the same in all ages,—that in the twelfth, just as much as in the eighteenth century, it created a worldly episcopate. If we see any thing of this spirit in our own times, it is evident, at least, that the reformation of the Church has not caused it, but the influence of the temporal power.

The controversy was at length terminated, after a long struggle, by king Henry's being obliged to relinquish the right of investiture, and the possession of episcopal revenues, during the vacancy of sees.

In the reign of Henry II. the Crown endeavoured to restore the great powers in ecclesiastical matters which it had formerly possessed, and especially to make the Church tribunals wholly subordinate to the State. In the contest which ensued between Becket and the king, we find again the episcopate of England, for the most part, adherents of the Crown.

But in these contests, and in that which ensued under king John, in which the Crown of England was obliged at length to relinquish all interference with elections of bishops and deans, and to restore the liberties of the Church in the amplest manner, there were two great advantages on the side of the Church,—the advantage of a leader in the person of the archbishop of Canterbury, and the advantage of a connexion with, and dependence on, a spiritual power abroad, which was independent of the Crown of England. This latter power balanced the power of the Crown, and protected the Church in its contest for liberty; though we know that it took advantage of these circumstances to extend its own dominion, and, in fact, to enslave the Church, just as much as the Crown had done.

And this leads us to compare the position now occupied by the Church of England with that which she occupied in the twelfth century, and to consider what prospects there may be of deliverance.

In the first place, the temporal power is now possessed of ecclesiastical prerogatives and powers quite as great as those of the kings in the twelfth century. It has also the advantage of having wholly got rid of the papacy as an opponent; the Church cannot derive any aid from that quarter; on the contrary, the Romish party would be the first to make the State power over the Church more absolute than it is, in the hope of degrading the Church and destroying it. Besides this, the State acts on a most jealous and cautious policy in its appointments to the archiepiscopal office. There is not the slightest chance of a second Becket, or Anselm, or Laud; it makes sure of its man. It holds by law the absolute power of appointing bishops and deans, and of compelling their election and consecration. It holds the power of preventing our synods from meeting, either by law, or by its influence over the archbishops. It has acquired the power of legislating for the Church. It is supported by a great body of adherents—by all the sectarians, by the evangelical party in the Church, by the rationalistic party, by statesmen of all parties in general, by radicals and liberals for the most part, and by a great many Churchmen who apply the principles of the sixteenth century to the nineteenth, without considering the change of circumstances.

But, on the other hand, the State now is a very different thing from what it was in the eleventh century. It is no longer a monarchy, the head of which concentrates the power of the State in his own hands, and whose will is for the most part paramount to all other considerations; a sovereign personally jealous of his own power and prerogative, and able to enforce it by stringent and arbitrary measures. The State is not this any longer; it is a democracy, retaining only the ceremonial of monarchy. The sovereign is powerless. All power has passed ultimately to the heterogeneous assembly in the House of Commons, and to the people. The government is consequently weak, vacillating, liable to be influenced by agitation, and unable to repress movements for liberty. It dare not take the course which a Rufus or a Henry would have taken to suppress agitation. All agitation which has the slightest appearance of reason on its side prevails over the government in spite of its resistance, sooner or later. The divisions of political parties may, in almost any important question, paralyze the movements of a government. In the present day, the tendency of every thing is, to remove restrictions on liberty generally; and if a case of grievance and oppression can be established, and if arbitrary and absolute power can be proved to have been abused, there is nothing that may not be accomplished, provided there be a sufficient amount of perseverance in bringing grievances before the public. The sovereignty has *in fact* devolved on *the people*, and if any large portion of the people are resolved on carrying any point, it is certain to be carried. Let any measure become a measure of *reform*, and it is at once put in the way of being carried. We live in an age of reform, and it will be impossible to resist the reform of abuses, if the public mind can be to any extent roused.

And now to come to the condition of the Church.

The Church, then, no longer includes the whole population of the country, but is opposed by many sects, and she is also weakened by parties within her own communion. She is no longer supported by the papacy, which in former ages was her great helper in her struggles with the State. She is in communion with churches beyond the limits of England, and with churches which are independent of the English State; but there is practically little intercourse with them; nor are they looked to, as yet, for support. Our archbishops are always certain to be partisans of the State, and our bishops are generally so to a considerable extent, though we are thankful, in comparing the conduct of our episcopate at present with that of their predecessors in the twelfth century, to see so much more of Christian courage and faith in the present day.

Nevertheless, though the Church has been much weakened by these various causes, we believe that the State has been still more weakened in proportion; and this debility of the State will, we think, make up for all the advantages and powers which the Church has been deprived of, so that she will be able, we trust, without any actual resistance to the law, to obtain the gradual removal of the grievances which oppress her, and a modification of that arbitrary legislation of the sixteenth century which represses her energies, and places her at a disadvantage as compared with all other communions of professing Christians within the British dominions.

It is true that the Church is *divided*. Of her bishops some are evangelical, some are rationalistic, several are partisans of the State, and care perhaps for little but the temporal advantages of the Church. Considerable parties are adherents of the State, and are able to throw various imputations on the motives of those who seek the reform of our laws on Church matters. Nevertheless, we do not think that any of these difficulties are insurmountable. These parties are all on the defensive, and if they get on the offensive, they will only weaken themselves, and strengthen the cause they dread. The country is not prepared for evangelical or rationalistic reforms in the Prayer Book, any more than for reforms in the opposite direction; nor will it enable the government to turn out of the Church all who seek for its liberty. If the State party get up counter addresses, petitions, &c., they will produce no effect ultimately in resisting the demands of those who have right on their side. They will only add to the agitation, protract the contest, and create additional embarrassment to government and to those bishops who wish the law to remain exactly as it is, and no disturbance to be made. Their best course is that which they have been pursuing hitherto,—silence and quiet; but that course is evidently a losing one in the long-run. The movement for Church rights arises from no transient or evanescent feeling; it is not the result of excitement, though circumstances have greatly added to its power. It arises from evils which all the world perceives, and which are continually thrown in our teeth by all the enemies of the Church. If we seek to know the abuses of the State supremacy over the Church, we can be at no loss; they are the grand popular arguments against the Church of England, which sectarians of all kinds are continually plying. We feel a state of the law which leaves us open to such attacks to be a grievance. It comes home to the Clergy and laity

in many other ways, that the interests of religion are compromised
by the operation of existing laws. And when all this is so, it is
not to be expected that men will remain quiet, and abstain from
seeking what they deem requisite for the welfare of their Church
and the security of their religion.

There are men in the Church to whom such considerations are
of *primary* importance, and who disregard all other considerations
in comparison with them; and to such men it is perfectly vain
to talk of " Peace, peace," and to urge them to abstain from
agitating their claims. Those who do so mistake the views of
the persons they address. They do not understand that it is
nothing but a principle of " duty to God and to His Church,"
which has induced others to undertake responsibility and labour;
and such men cannot, therefore, attend to exhortations to be at
" peace," and to abstain from " agitation," since they would be,
in their own opinion, relinquishing their duty to God by attending
to that advice. Without doubt such recommendations come
very well from those who think their duty consists in sitting still;
but they can have no weight with those who think it their duty
to press forward. More than one of the bishops has felt it
his duty to advise their Clergy against taking any share in
Church unions, or other organization for Church purposes. If
these prelates feel that the interests of the Church are likely to
be compromised by any such system of combination, they are
quite right to express their opinion; but, at the same time, we
must add, that it appears to us that any bishop would be going
beyond the limits of his duty and of his authority in condemning
such combinations, and requiring their dissolution; because
there is nothing, that we are aware of, either in the canons of
the Church, or in the law of the land, to prevent the establishment of Church unions, or any other organization, having for its
object the restoration of the Church's rights.

Under the English constitution, it is the recognized right
of any class in the community who think themselves aggrieved,
to combine for the purpose of seeking legislative relief from laws
which they consider oppressive, or for any other object consistent
with obedience to the laws. This is distinctly a legal and constitutional right, which all Englishmen, whether Clergy or laity,
are possessed of; and which they can be deprived of only by the
law itself. With the highest deference and respect for the
episcopal office, (especially when it is legally and canonically
exercised,) we conceive that its powers do not necessarily extend
to the suppression of the civil rights enjoyed by the Clergy and
laity. The same may be said with regard to the canons. If the
canons do not forbid Churchmen to adopt measures, in combina-

tion, for the restoration of the Church's rights, and for the enforcement of the canons themselves, no bishop is authorized to use his authority for the suppression of such efforts. He may express his opinion, and discourage them; but, to go further than this, would seem to be an infringement on the Christian liberties of Churchmen. If their conduct is violent, if their language is unchristian, they may indeed be deserving of censure in these respects.

When, therefore, bishops are heard expressing their fears or dissatisfaction at Church movements, directed either to the protection of the faith against State liberalism, or to the restoration of Church rights, or the removal of grievances caused by the present operation of the laws, it must be remembered that those prelates are merely giving expression to their own individual opinions, and are not authorized, either by the Church or the State, to enforce those opinions on others. It must also be remembered, that bishops who are nominated by the State, and who owe to it, and *not to the Church,* the possession of their emoluments and dignities, are not necessarily the best and most impartial judges in questions between the Church and the State; and that they will be regarded as inclining so much towards the interests of the State, that their *opinions* on any such question will have less weight than they could themselves wish. If, indeed, any prelate should have proved by his personal conduct, that he is able to act independently, and that he is prepared to make the cause of religious truth, and of the Church's well-being, his first object, and to regard the interests of ministers and political parties as of inferior moment, his opinion on any question must have great weight, and will of course receive all the deference due to it, while, in a matter of opinion, men must act in the mode they deliberately believe to be necessary for the security of the Church.

It is evident, however, that there are prelates who are wholly devoted to the temporal power, as might indeed be expected under the present system of appointment to bishoprics; and their sentiments will of course have little weight with those who are on the other side of the question. It is impossible to conceal from ourselves that on the episcopal bench are Evangelicals and Rationalists who are unsound in the faith, and Erastians who would sacrifice the Church's most cherished rights at the bidding of the temporal power. And, on the other hand, we are thankful to see many orthodox and religious prelates; and although we have to lament the presence of evil in some of the high places in the Church, we may comfort ourselves by the assurance that our case is not worse than that of our forefathers in the twelfth century.

Art. IV.—1. *In Memoriam.* London: Moxon. 1850.

2. *Christmas-Eve and Easter-Day. A Poem.* By Robert Browning. London: Chapman and Hall. 1850.

3. *The Virgin Widow. A Play.* By Henry Taylor, *Author of "Philip von Artevelde."* Longmans. 1850.

Amidst the existing trials and troubles of Christ's Church, the progress of poetry, however important in itself to the welfare of a people, may appear at least of minor consequence; among the stirring war-notes of the trump of controversy, the voice of the nightingale may well-nigh be hushed. However, two of the works before us, at least, possess such eminent merit in their respective spheres, that they have won our attention, even at this present crisis. Indeed, we cannot allow such passing troubles, however grievous, to engross our critical attention, or our individual minds: we are convinced that our Anglican branch of the Church Catholic is firmly built upon the One Rock, and that no tempest can uprear her from her strong foundations; and this conviction we are anxious to show forth, by devoting at least our usual amount of space to the literary and other questions of the day. We are not only convinced that "all things work together for good to God's elect," but also, that our English Church, despite her sins and short-comings, is in possession of the especial presence of her God, and is destined to be the great champion of Christianity in the approaching warfare with the spirit of Antichrist throughout the civilized world: and, in this persuasion, whatever foes assail or friends desert us, we may grieve indeed for the perversity of man, but our cheeks shall not blanch, neither shall our hearts be troubled. We mourn over existing divisions, but are intimately convinced that they subserve some high purpose in God's providence; we work indeed towards the goal of unity; but, *until* this goal is attained, we are content to abide in patience and in hope: "Heaviness may endure for a night, but joy cometh in the morning!"

And now, enough of this. Turn we from such solemn themes to the more pleasant task before us,—the critical acknowledgment of merits of the highest order. And here let us pause to say that though the name of Taylor stands with those of Tennyson

and Browning at the head of this article, we are very far from
ranking the first of these three authors (as our readers may
already know from earlier numbers of our "Review") with the two
latter bards, whom we have recognized, and do recognize, as
"facile principes," the undoubted chiefs of their poetic era.   We
have already dwelt with love on the exquisite grace and pathos
of a Tennyson, on the passion and power of a Browning; and
we have further acknowledged that they, with Mrs. Browning,
(late Miss Barrett) may fitly be regarded as the founders of *a
new school*, which, though it combines some of the elements of
Wordsworth's and of Shelley's poetry, the former's simplicity and
the latter's brilliancy, have yet produced effects which are altogether distinct from those of the bards just named; more substantial than Shelley, more concentrated and powerful than
Wordsworth.   A special mannerism, no doubt, does characterize
these living exponents of the beautiful; they are addicted to the
use of a certain half-German phraseology, which is not highly
to be commended; they are more or less mystical in their utterances, and they very frequently barely suggest where other
writers would express; they have sometimes the air of being
laboured and artificial just where they have most striven to be
plain and natural; they all require to be read more than once
before they can be appreciated; their philosophy and religion are
somewhat *dubious*.   Their feelings indeed are eminently reverential, and their love for Christianity appears sincere; but their
opinions would seem by no means formed, and they are more or
less wanting in that moral courage, which boldly proclaims its
own perception of the truth, without the remotest fear of man's
censure or the age's ridicule.

     We mean not to accuse these authors of a vulgar dread of
the critic; we doubt not that they hold the anonymous assumption of infallibility, which is now in vogue, in just as much contempt as we do ourselves, and that they would just as little
allow themselves to be guided by it.   They would scorn themselves, no doubt, if they were *consciously* influenced by one anti-
cipation of what the "small scribes" might say, who indite
critical judgments for "Athenæum" or "Examiner."   Indeed,
it is more than questionable, whether *any* author has yet availed
himself of a single hint given by an anonymous critic, *unless that
critic was not anonymous to him!*   And this, for various reasons.
In the first place, there is something so monstrous in that individual assumption of infallibility and omniscience, which seems to
be the invariable accompaniment of anonymous criticism, that the
true poet is necessarily disgusted at starting, and irritated at
every second word, yes, even by praise.   Who is this anybody

or nobody, who, perhaps without a single qualification for his task, sits down to deliver a judgment which professes to be final and without appeal, on my merits,—or on the merits or de-merits of a new work of "Tennyson's?" We repeat, that this assumption of superiority, and further of infallibility, on the part of the critic, is such an insult to the understanding, such an affront to common sense, that no poet, no author of genius, would be likely to profit by the delivery, even of the wisest sentence, from such a bodiless and viewless "voice." The fact is, that anonymous criticism, *literary* criticism that is, is altogether *a mistake*, and cannot be abandoned too soon: its only effect is to forward and realize that millennium of dulness and mediocrity, so long ago hailed by Pope and Dryden from afar: the true poet is slighted, the false is exalted, and "the public is led by the nose, as asses are."

Why then do we *ourselves* lend our countenance and assistance to such a system? Truly, for want of a better! Since this is the appointed medium of defending truth, we must avail ourselves of it, and not let the dunces have things all their own way. Nevertheless, we wish it to be distinctly understood, that we by no means profess ourselves to be infallible; that when we differ from the authors under our consideration, and pronounce their treatment of their themes defective, it is very probable that they may have considered the subject more deeply than we, and have arrived at far juster conclusions; and further, (though this at first sight may sound almost like blasphemy,) that a poet may actually be far more *sensible*, as well as far more genial, than a Quarterly Reviewer!

We must be by no means understood to declare war to "the Anonymous," altogether: we admit, that both in the political and theological arena of controversy, it may sometimes have its great uses; but never, we contend, in the literary.—In its general views, political or theological, any organ of the public press *may* assert for itself a quasi-infallibility: *we*, for instance, hold as an undoubted truth the essential orthodoxy of our English branch of the Church Catholic; and anonymous essays may very well be written on the assumption of such an infallibility as can be claimed for itself by any particular school of thought. But there is no such "quasi-infallibility" even, in matters of *taste;* there are no such well-defined parties there; "high church or low," tory or whig: and Heaven be praised, that so it is! Faction has not yet divided our literary world into any two hostile armies,—such as "romanticists and classicists." Each individual critic writes for himself, and gives his own perceptions; and what we complain of is, that in so doing he should be well-nigh *compelled* by the pre-

F 2

sent cruel system, and further, almost invariably induced, to affirm his own infallibility ; and treat the author under his consideration, however superior to himself, entirely " de haut en bas ;" positively condemning, it may be, the most beautiful creations of the mind, or lauding the worst of pinchbecks as true metal ; (perhaps a more frequent case ;) and thereby imposing on the general public ; leading them to purchase works which afterwards disappoint, and so contributing powerfully to bring about a general distaste for the higher branches of literature, or possibly sealing their sight to true merit, where, trusting their own eyes and hearts, that public would not have gone astray.

These are only a tithe of the evils resulting from anonymous literary criticism : the vast temptations to *dishonesty* which it affords need only be hinted at ; but its great effect is to advance and to establish the empire of *dull Conventionalism*. Under this anonymous system no man quite writes what he feels; each yields something of his own individuality of thought ; nay, in nine cases out of ten, he *has* no such individuality ; (few educated men have ;) he judges by the current standard of the hour, and reports the result as though it were a genuine and immediate, and further, an infallible perception of his own. The final effect is, a vague uniformity of judgment, without truth, or honesty, or reality, and the consequent promotion of any one artificial mannerism, which happens to be fashionable with the writers of the hour, to exclusive empire. At the present moment, for instance, " Tennyson " is " the rage," and justly so : that is, he is the rage in literary circles at least. The consequence is, that every poet is expected to write more or less like Tennyson, and that the small critics of the day discern no merit where they do not find this Tennysonian mannerism ; and where they do, are at once satisfied, however wretched may be the imitation, and so lose no time in proclaiming the advent of a new great poet. Take the instance of the self-dubbed " Sidney Gedings," whose " Roman," one of the most verbose and intolerably tedious "make-believes" we have ever striven to wade through, has been proclaimed one of the noblest productions of the century, a wonderful and glorious poem, &c.; or look at the almost equal success of the dull but well-meaning " Mackay," whose "Voices from the Crowd," and " Voices from the Mountains," and other " Voices," have elicited the most enthusiastic greetings from these said anonymous gentry. This writer, like poor " Swain," whom we dealt with briefly in our last, " apropos " of his " Reverberations," has possessed himself of certain catchwords of the present day ; a species of cant which is to us intolerably tedious, but which Tennyson nevertheless deigns sometimes to employ; respecting "the absolute perfectibility of man" in this world,—"the God in man,"—"the glorious heroic virtues of the workers and working classes," &c., and, of course, this political and moral transcendentalist (*i. e.* Mackay), who, with the best intentions, will never write poetry as long as he lives, has been proclaimed a great poet; quite Tennysonian in style and genius, &c. &c. By the bye, his very close imitations of Tennyson in his last production, "Egeria and other Poems," are absolutely comical: such harmless travesties, however, would never excite our wrath, were they not belauded by anonymous infallibility, which has succeeded and does succeed, in no small measure, in *gulling* the innocent public.

Yet the general effect of all this is, that the said public, finding itself so often taken in, gives up poetry altogether, as something no doubt fine, but unfortunately beyond the sphere of its comprehension; and thus even Tennyson himself loses three-fourths of his due readers and buyers. Poetic literature seems to be growing more and more the property of a *literary class*, and to have less and less to do with the life and heart of the nation.

No doubt, the very nature of Tennyson's genius in some measure accounts for this fact: he is not calculated, it may be, to be *popular:* and in so far as that is the case, he is *defective* as a poet: for the greatest poets, a Homer, a Shakspeare, a Schiller, a Goethe, are, as it were, the heritage of all! Still we would scarcely call Tennyson's occasional obscurity a defect; for it is ofttimes a great beauty: but, at all events, it is not to be commended as his chiefest excellence, or recommended as a fitting model for imitation. We believe and are convinced, that England,—that the human race, in fact,—has the same faculties for the love and appreciation of poetry it ever has possessed, and that a really popular poet might to-morrow find his way to the hearts of the million; might,—and yet *would not*, without *fighting* his way first, in the face of critical coldness, and the assumption on the part of the public, that he must be either nearly unintelligible,—too high for it,—or else, good for nothing!

Tennyson and Browning are great poets, and yet neither of these are really "household names," as Byron, and Scott, and others have been: one reason is, that they are in some respects superior to Byron or Scott as poets; that they do not descend, as *they* did, to the common level; that their merits are often higher and deeper: (for generally the *highest* genius cannot be recognised at once; we like Strauss's Waltzes on the very first time of hearing, but Beethoven's Symphonies may require more than one audience; Moore's "Melodies" please a child, but

Southey's " Roderick" will only be *duly* appreciated by one who
possesses a good heart and a cultivated understanding :) Tennyson and Browning have neither the merits nor the demerits of
Scott and Byron,—who, however, should only be classed together, as being both in the highest degree *popular ;* for Scott was
as superior in artistic unity and sound sense, as he was inferior
in power and passion. Our two modern bards have a language
and a philosophy of their own, and display, both of them, an
hitherto almost unparalleled combination of grace and pathos,—
almost unparalleled we say,—for Shakspeare has shown it us
before them, (he who has done all things,) in " Romeo and
Juliet," in the last wonderful scene of " A Winter's Tale," in
Desdemona's last conference with Emilia, in Lear and Cordelia,
&c.   They are, together with Mrs. Browning, pre-eminently
aristocratic and refined : theirs is indeed the aristocracy of poetic
genius, bordering sometimes on affectation, but rarely reaching it.
No poets understand better to draw tears,—" tears," as Southey
himself, a master of pathos, expresses it, " of pleasurable pain."
Their colouring is rich and deep, their language is passionate, and
their thoughts and feelings are pre-eminently *real*, even when
exaggerated in expression.   Indeed, no bards have carried
farther, or so far, the combination of the simplest every-day life
with the highest order of ideal poetry.

They possess, therefore, the very loftiest merits ; but these are
scarcely calculated to render them *popular ;* and criticism, to
speak generally, has done its utmost to retard their progress,
whether intentionally or no.   In the first place, it was right long
before it discovered their respective merits at all, especially those
of Tennyson and Browning.   The " Quarterly," which was ready
at once to laud a mediocre " Philip von Artevelde" to the skies;
the " Edinburgh," which could scarcely find language to express
its, if possible, still more glowing admiration for " Edwin the
Fair," by the same author, and which has recently bestowed
some fifty or sixty pages of laborious comment on that unfortunate abortion, Bulwer's " King Arthur," *had only scorn and ridicule, or total silence, for Tennyson for ten or twelve years.*   No
doubt his mannerisms did deserve reprehension, but still this
lamentable incapacity to discern true poetic merit was the perfectly natural characteristic of both our *presumed* chief literary
organs : now, at last, that they *have* learnt to admire, they err
just as widely in the opposite direction, praising indiscriminately,
and losing themselves in those vague common places, in which
mediocrity always takes refuge to conceal its real deficiency of
taste and judgment.

And here we may pause to observe, that after what we have

said of anonymous infallibility, this strong apparent assumption of it on *our* own part may seem "vastly entertaining;" but if we write anonymously, that is not our fault. We do not dispute besides, that a critic *may* assume the correctness of his own taste and views : all we desiderate is, that he should give his *name* at the same time to the public, as a testimony of honesty, and an unreserved confession, that, after all, what he says is only his own individual judgment. The public *will* attach a false importance to the *we*, as we said before; this *we* appears to involve omniscience and infallibility; but let an individual write ever so authoritatively with his name—after all, every body knows that *he* has just as good a right to judge for him or her self. The reader will then say,—"Well, that is the opinion of Mr. So-and-so : there seems to be something in the book he praises; at all events it is worth looking at, and I can judge for myself." Or, if the individual critic has been severe, the reader will be apt to hum— "Indeed! but, after all, Mr. So-and-so, though he is a sensible man, is not quite infallible; so, without despising his comments, I shall read the book for myself." Or, again he may say, " Mr. So-and-so is a fool, and I don't care one straw for his judgment : how fortunate it is that he cannot impose on me with his high-sounding *we!* He has a plentiful vocabulary at command, and my carelessness might have allowed itself to be beguiled by his anonymous *wisdom.*" We may remark, however, that under such a system as we wish for, and *expect soon* to see,—"fools" would cease to write criticisms ere long : they would be *found out*, and would therefore creep in silence to their holes,—Grub-street orators would be hushed for ever; mediocrity would no longer dare to lay its unhallowed paw upon the crown of genius! There would be far less criticism we suspect, but, what there was, would be *definite*, and not devoid of reason. Bad works would frequently escape notice altogether; but only the good would be commended, and rising genius would be sure to be welcomed by sympathetic spirits. For there cannot be a grosser error than to imagine, that the man of genius must be envious of a brother's greatness : true genius and envy will rarely dwell together. No doubt, false glare and glitter will often assail merit : Byron felt that his artificial tinsel could not be great poetry unless Southey's strains were very vile indeed : two men writing on such different systems could not both be right.

But we are eminently discursive. Waiving all further introduction, let us at once approach the works before us. The first, " In Memoriam," is a very singular production,—one continuous monody, we may say,—divided into a hundred and thirty separate strains. It is published without an author's name, but every line, every word bears the Tennysonian impress : the whole con-

Southey'?
possesse
son and
Scott
ther, /
as so
in [
and
hi'
a'

...... virtues, and powers,
...... of "A. H. H." (we believe,
...... the historian), a great friend
...... Pylades," or "Orestes," which you
...... the higher spirit!), his college-
...... his sister, the sharer in all his hopes
...... projects. Never has friendship been
...... ideal point of view: we have no doubt,
...... of rhymers will begin to discover from
...... that they are all possessed of the dearest
...... the world! It might be presumed, that such
...... to pages 210, upon the same simple theme,
...... ous: but this is scarcely the case. At least,
...... monotony here, the monotony of sorrow, it is so
...... that we could not wish it other than it is : but,
...... hopes and fears of the poet, as to a Providence and
...... the grave, and his general views of human life, are
...... embodied in this most exquisite collection; an heirloom be-
...... to our nation, and to be treasured by it, as long as the
English tongue endures. This, we say, speaking generally, and
recording our broad impression ; but by no means implying that
we imagine this work to be free from faults. Even literary
faults, we think, can be discovered in it; philosophical and religious deficiencies are, alas ! only too patent.

The poet commences in the dedication (written *last year*, and,
therefore, some sixteen springs after the commencement of the
series), by addressing himself (to all appearance, at least,) to our
Blessed Lord, and imploring His forgiveness for his short-
comings. He commences (it will be observed, that he uses small
letters where capitals are now *customary*) :—

> "Strong Son of God, immortal Love,
>   Whom we, that have not seen thy face,
>   By faith, and faith alone, embrace,
>   Believing where we cannot prove :"

And he continues :—

> "Thou seemest human and divine,
>   The highest, holiest manhood, thou :
>   Our wills are ours, we know not how ;
>   Our wills are ours, to make them thine.

Ending :—

> "Forgive my grief for one removed,
>   Thy creature, whom I found so fair,
>   I trust he lives in thee, and there
>   I find him worthier to be loved.

> " Forgive these wild and wandering cries,
>   Confusions of a wasted youth ;
>   Forgive them where they fail in truth,
> And in thy wisdom make me wise."

Is this Mr. Tennyson's deliberate faith? or are we rather to regard this prayer as the result of a poetic imagination? We know not: certain it is, that if Mr. Tennyson has mustered courage to believe at last (for courage was what was mainly wanting to him!), if he has received revelation as satisfying the highest reason, he has *then* much to answer for in publishing some of the stanzas in this collection, such a poem, for instance, as that on p. 52, commencing—

> " O thou, that after toil and storm,"

in which it is most falsely, and, we may add, offensively assumed, that the unbeliever in Christianity can possess a faith of his own, quite as real and as stable as that of the believer !

We do not mean to deny that there are not common-place men of the world by thousands,—we know many such,—who can neither be said to believe nor disbelieve ; who stand toward Christianity very much in the attitude of Mr. Taylor, whom we shall notice by and by ; whose prevailing characteristic is a mild and dull indifferentism. These good folks, if we may so call them, derive a general sense of God's existence and His goodness from that Revelation which they nevertheless ignore, they hold these things because they have been taught them, and because it is pleasant to hold them ; and as for the rest, they simply " let it go." But there is no logical self-consistency, and no high wisdom in this course ; there is merely a mild and self-sufficient selfishness ; so characteristic, for instance, of the ordinary statesman of the day. Genius has nothing, or should have nothing, in common with this obtuseness of perception. To set such a " Gallio," even the *least harmful*, intellectually above an ardent Christian, is not only an absurdity, but also a sin ; and to this fact we beseech Mr. Tennyson to open his eyes. We can scarcely conceive more dangerous language than *this* of his,—more flattering to the small vanity of a very numerous class already existing among us, and more calculated to lead thousands more astray :—

> " O thou, that after toil and storm,
>   Mayst *seem* to have reach'd a purer air,

(" *Seem* " indeed !—but let us go on !)—

> " Whose *faith has centre every where,*

(that is, *no where*,)—

>"Nor *cares to fix itself to form*,—

>"Leave thou thy sister, when she prays
>　Her early heaven, her happy views :

(How condescending !)—

>　Nor thou *with shadow'd hint* confuse
>　A life that leads melodious days."

Really, we could find it in our hearts to whip this self-conceited rhymester.　But we will give the last two mischievous verses without any comment :—

>"Her faith thro' form is pure *as thine*,
>　Her hands are quicker unto good.
>　Oh, sacred be the flesh and blood
>　To which *she* links a truth divine !

>"See, thou that countest *reason ripe*
>　In holding by the *truth within*,
>　Thou fail not in a world of sin,
>　And even for want of such a type."

Rather ten thousand-fold give us the insolent denunciations and open assaults of a Froude, than such insulting commiseration as this !　Honestly, Mr. Tennyson, what is it justifies *you* in employing such language?　Is it your own firm possession of "faith —void of form?"　*This*, at all events, does not look very much like it ! (p. 77) :—

>"*So runs my dream : but what am I ?*—
>　*An infant crying in the night ;*
>　*An infant crying for the light :*
>　*And with no language but a cry !*"

This does not *seem* the plenitude of self-contented faith and reason !

We are sorry to appear cruel, but "we are only cruel to be kind ;" and we are bound to consider the interests of many thousands of the poet's readers.　*Has Mr. Tennyson any perception of truth at all?　Does he care for truth?　Is he not an exclusive worshipper of the beautiful?*　We very much suspect it !　He appears to us to have faith or no faith, according to the poetic effect such quality, or the absence of such quality, may have upon his poetry ; not consciously perhaps, (we do not charge him with baseness,) but *really*, and as a matter of fact.　Sometimes he questions there being any life beyond the grave; *questions only*, but obviously with a doubt, as on p. 80 :—

" And he, shall he,

" Man, his last work, who seem'd so fair,
Such splendid purpose in his eyes,
Who roll'd the psalm to wintry skies,
. Who built him fanes of fruitless prayer,

" Who trusted God was love indeed,
And love creation's final law,—
*Tho' nature, red in tooth and claw
With ravine, shriek'd against his creed—*

" Who loved, who suffer'd countless ills,
Who battled for the True, the Just,—
Be blown about the desert dust,
Or seal'd within the iron hills?

" No more?   A monster then, a dream,
A discord.   Dragons of the prime,
That tare each other in their slime,
Were mellow music match'd with him.

" O life, as futile, then, as frail!
O for *thy* voice to soothe and bless!
What hope of answer or redress?
—Behind the veil, behind the veil."

And is it for such helpless ignorance as this, to assume airs of inflated *superiority?*   Ignorance, of which our author says (p. 78) :—

" I falter where I firmly trod;
*And, falling with my weight of cares
Upon the great world's altar-stairs
That slope thro' darkness up to God,*

" *I stretch lame hands*," &c.

And which can make such a pitiable confession (p. 185, very near the end) as *this :*—

" I *trust* I have not wasted breath:
I *think* we are not *wholly brain,*
Magnetic mockeries; not in vain,
Like Paul with beasts, I fought with death;

" Not *only* cunning casts in clay ;—
Let science prove we are, and then,
What *matters* science unto men,
At least to *me?*—I would not stay.

> " Let him, *the wiser man*, who springs
>   Hereafter, up from childhood shape
>   His action like the greater ape,—
>   But I was born to other things."

Is it this faint instinctive hope, trembling on the verge of despair, which is calculated to address faith after the following fashion? The poet speaks, say, to a sister (p. 142) :—

> " You say, but with no touch of scorn,
>   Sweet-hearted, *you*, whose light-blue eyes
>   Are tender over drowning flies,
>   You tell me, doubt is devil-born.

> " I know not : *one* indeed I knew,
>   In many a subtle question versed,
>   Who touch'd a jarring lyre at first,
>   But ever strove to make it true :

> " Perplext in faith, but pure in deeds;
>   At last he beat his music out,
>   *There lives more faith in honest doubt,*
> *Believe me, than in half the creeds.*"

Now, we repeat, that such language as this is infinitely mischievous. Such things are caught up as the catchwords of unbelievers, and go very far towards justifying them in their own esteem in their vanity and folly. No doubt there *may* be honest doubters, and there *are* hypocritical believers; but the assumption here seems to be, that doubt is almost of necessity a more honest thing than faith! Another very mischievous poem is that on p. 56, commencing,—

> " Tho' truths in manhood darkly join,
>   Deep-seated in our mystic frame,
>   We yield all blessing to the name
>   Of him that made them current coin."

That is, of course, of Christ our Lord. This is simply and purely blasphemy! This is the tone of " Emerson" and his "confrères;" the tone which Browning, in the admirable poem we shall deal with anon, alludes to, and dismisses so contemptuously. We might quote more to the same effect, but refrain. In other passages the dreams of the author of " Vestiges of Creation" seem to be realized and accepted by the poet, who says, addressing humanity, with reference to its earliest age :—

> "Arise and fly
> The reeling fawn, the sensual feast:
> Move upward, *working out the beast,*
> *And let the ape and tiger die.*"

But now let us leave this painful theme. We remain undecided as to Mr. Tennyson's faith, though we opine, that, strictly speaking, *he has none*, whether negative or affirmative, and advise him, for his soul's good, to try to get one! Let us now deal with the exquisite *poetical* beauties of the volume before us.

Mr. Tennyson is not a showy, not a gaudy, poet: he does not carry you by storm; his strain rather creeps gently into the heart, and awakens there a low and long resounding echo. We are rarely dazzled by him at first sight; he has few tulips to exhibit (though, if he likes, he can be gorgeous also), but his violets are wonderfully blue and sweet, and breathe forth such a delicious, though somewhat lingering, fragrance, that they seem to the beholder the very quintessence of all flowers. Here is a *theme*, which, treated by any other poet, would have been mawkish, nay, insupportable: but, treated by Tennyson, we are captivated, we are enchanted, almost against our wills: we think it at last the most natural of occurrences to write a hundred and thirty poems to the memory of one youthful friend.

Perhaps, the very unpassionateness of friendship, in a sense, may make this a subject well adapted for elegiac poetry: the friend seems to have leisure and ability to sound the depths of his loss, to measure the value of the lost one. The blindness and excess of mere passion are not here: the grief felt is real and deep; but it is not so violent and unutterable as *some* griefs, which would scarcely suffer such poetic contemplation. However this may be, we wish to moralize no longer, but to treat, for some little space, of the exquisite beauties before us.

To begin *seriatim*, the opening poems appear to us at present a little mystic and hard of comprehension: we may instance especially, No. III.; but V. is very natural and striking. We will quote it, though it is not precisely one of our favourites. We fear this language may seem very *hard-hearted* to the poet, dealing after this literary fashion with his heart's emotions; we cannot help it; we respect, we most sincerely respect, his feelings; but *we* have to deal with the poet, rather than with the man, and must act accordingly :—

V.

> " I sometimes hold it half a sin
>   To put in words the grief I feel;
>   For words, like nature, half reveal
> And half conceal the mind within.

> " But, for the unquiet heart and brain,
>   A use in measured language lies;
>   *The sad mechanic exercise*
> *Like dull narcotics, numbing pain.*

> " In words, like weeds, I'll wrap me o'er
>   Like coarsest clothes against the cold ;
>   But that large grief which these enfold
> Is given in outline, and no more."

(The italics throughout, we may observe, will be ours, as indicating what *we* consider "beauties.") The next, No. VI., is
exceedingly beautiful, on the common topics of consolation, and
their vanity. There is no bereaved one who has not felt the
truth of the poet's comment. No. VIII. is also admirable. We
quote only the last two verses, for lack of space:—

> " So seems it in my deep regret,
>   O my forsaken heart, with thee,
>   And this poor flower of *poesy*,
> Which, little cared for, fades not yet.

> " But, since it pleased a vanish'd eye,
>   I go to plant it on his tomb,
>   That, if it can, it there may bloom ;
> Or, dying there, at least may die !"

Then follow several very poetical addresses to " the ship,"
bearing young " Arthur's " remains from a foreign strand,—as
we afterwards learn, " Vienna,"—to be buried in his native soil.
Most admirable in its keen truthfulness is No. XIV., where the
poet declares, that if the report were brought him that the ship
had touched the land, if he went down to the harbour, and saw
his dead friend stepping from the vessel, striking " a sudden
hand " in his, asking " a thousand things of home,"—he " should
not feel it to be strange !" It is long, indeed, before the heart
realizes the loss of one who has perished at a distance and unexpectedly. He is brought to England. He is buried near the
Severn and the Wye. The cold white monument is raised to his
memory. Then, finally, the poet sings :—

> " I sing to him that rests below,
>   And, since the grasses round me wave,
>   I take the grasses of the grave,
> And make them pipes whereon to blow.

> " The traveller hears me now and then,
>   And sometimes harshly will he speak ;
>   ' This fellow would make weakness weak,
> And melt the waxen hearts of men.'

> " Another answers, ' Let him be,
>   He loves to make parade of pain,
>   That with his piping he may gain
> The praise that comes to constancy.'

" A third is wroth, ' Is this an hour
    For private sorrow's barren song,
    When more and more the people throng
The chairs and thrones of civil power ?

" A time to sicken and to swoon,
    When conscience reaches forth her arms,
    To feel from world to world, and charms
Her secret from the latest moon ?'——

" Behold, ye speak an idle thing :
    Ye never knew the sacred dust :
    I do but sing because I must,
And pipe but as the linnets sing :

" And unto one her note is gay,
    For now her little ones have ranged ;
    And unto one her note has changed,
Because her brood is stolen away."

We have given this at full, not so much for its poetic merit,
(though it has much,) as because it is the poet's apology for his
series ; and it was fitting we should let him speak for himself :
but we must be more cautious with our citations in future.
Nevertheless the next poem, XXII., tempts us so much, that
we must needs extract it.

" The path by which we twain did go,
    Which led by tracts that pleased us well,
    Thro' four sweet years arose and fell
From flower to flower, from snow to snow :

" And we with singing cheer'd the way ;
    And, crown'd with all the season lent,
    From April on to April went,
And glad at heart from May to May :

" But where the path we walk'd began
    To slant the fifth autumnal slope,
    As we descended, following hope,
There sat the shadow fear'd of man ;

" Who broke our fair companionship,
    And spread his mantle dark and cold :
    And wrapt thee formless in the fold,
    And dull'd the murmur on thy lip,

" And bore thee where I could not see,
    Nor follow, tho' I walk in haste ;
    And think that, somewhere in the waste,
The shadow sits, and waits for me."

The sad horror of this has rarely been surpassed. Beautiful are
the various "Christmas" poems: the three of the first year
are exquisite,—the first beginning "The time draws near the
birth of Christ,"—together with XXIX. and XXX.; especially
the latter, anent the Christmas songs and games. Then follow
two beautiful sections or tablets, (whatever they may be called,)
on Lazarus and his sister: the second of these is most exquisite
and *pious:* but, as if afraid of what he has written, the poet
hastens in the obnoxious XXXIII. already quoted at full, beginning—

> "O thou, that after toil and storm,"

to undo whatever good he may have thus accomplished. Then
follow several melancholy doubting sonnets, the tone of which has
been already condemned: the poet at last appears conscience-
stricken, and at last arraigns himself under the form of a repri-
mand, addressed by "Urania" to his "Melpomene" in XXXVII.,
where we learn accidentally that these were the views of his departed friend, who would appear to have been rather characterized by a delightfully genial temperament than by any genius of
a high order. Most exquisite is No. XXXIX., though too long
for quotation, replete with that sweet quiet pathos, in which
Tennyson is perhaps without an equal. Some compartments of
the poem follow in which the bard dwells on the mental superiority of his friend to himself, a superiority in which we cannot
very thoroughly believe.

> "I vex my heart with fancies dim :
> He still outstript me in the race," &c. (p. 64.)

Very fine is LIII. :—

> "Oh yet we trust that some how good,"

ending with a verse we have already cited, proclaiming the poet's
helplessness. Many of the work's sections hereabouts are bitter,
and dark with doubt. LVIII. is very sweet and touching. Still
more so, perhaps, is LXII., which we shall quote accordingly.
The poet addresses his friend's spirit :—

> "Dost thou look back on what hath been,—
>   As some divinely-gifted man,
>   Whose life in low estate began,
> And on a simple village green ;
>
> "Who breaks his birth's invidious bar,
>   And grasps the skirts of happy chance,
>   And breasts the blows of circumstance,
> And grapples with his evil star ;

" Who makes by force his merit known,
    And lives to clutch the golden keys,
    To mould a mighty state's decrees,
    And shape the whisper of the throne ;

"And moving up from high to higher,
    Becomes on fortune's crowning slope
    The pillar of a people's hope,
    ·   The centre of a world's desire,

" Yet feels, as in a pensive dream,
    When all his active powers are still,
    A distant dearness in the hill,
    A secret sweetness in the stream,

" The limit of his narrower fate,—
    While yet beside its vocal springs
    He play'd at counsellors and kings,
    With one that was his earliest mate :—

" *Who* ploughs with pain his native lea,
    And reaps the labours of his hands,
    Or in the furrow musing stands,
    ' *Does my old friend remember me ?*'"

This is exceedingly beautiful, though we cannot but think the poet rates himself too low, and his friend too high : however, to true affection this may easily be forgiven. A very singular strain is that headed LXVII., commencing,—

    " I dream'd there would be spring no more,"

wherein is a species of allegory : the poet describes himself as wreathing a crown of thorns around his brow, by which he types, we presume, this series of sad and sorrowful pipings ; the world calls him " the fool that wears a crown of thorns ;" but an angel touches it into leaf, and breathes a mystic blessing. This is very admirable of its kind, and will, it is to be hoped, operate as a warning voice to the vulgar, especially the vulgar *critic,* not to meddle with what he does not understand ! Very beautiful is LXXIII., beginning,—

    " I leave thy praises unexpress'd,"

an assertion, however, with regard to his lost, and, no doubt, much-loved friend, which our poet is scarcely justified in making. This poem concludes most nobly :—

    " Thy leaf has perish'd in the green ;
        And, while we breathe beneath the sun,
        The world, which credits what is done,
        Is cold to all that might have been !

> " So here shall silence guard thy fame ;
> *But somewhere, out of human view,*
> *Whate'er thy hands are set to do*
> *Is wrought with tumult of acclaim."*

Our poet's friend would seem to have been pre-eminently destined for a *worker:* he is described (p. 174) as likely to become,—

> " A life in civic action warm,
>   A soul on highest mission sent,
>   *A potent voice of Parliament,*
>   A pillar stedfast in the storm."

Another sweet Christmas memory follows on p. 106. The next, No. LXXVII., is a very graceful and tender apology to a brother, for an expression dropped before, " More than my brothers are to me;" concluding,—

> " At one dear knee we proffer'd vows,
>   One lesson from one book we learn'd,
>   Ere childhood's flaxen ringlet turn'd
> To black and brown on kindred brows.

> " And so my wealth *resembles* thine ;
>   But *he* was rich where *I* was poor,
>   And he supplied my want the more
> As his unlikeness fitted mine."

But truly, we must close our citations : we have exquisite reminiscences of past happiness in the family circle when the lost one was present ; one charming memory of college, LXXXV.; another touching series on the departure of the poet and his family from their native home or dwelling ; and one most lovely and pathetic poem on a learned and talented husband and his admiring wife, (pp. 144, 145,) perhaps, poetically, the most perfect thing in the book, but it is too long for extraction. One exquisite portraiture of the lost " Arthur" we must however add to our citations.   It forms the No. CVIII.:—

> " Thy converse drew us with delight,
>   The men of rathe and riper years ;
>   *The feeble soul, a haunt of fears,*
> Forgot his weakness in thy sight.

> " On thee the loyal-hearted hung,
>   *The proud was half disarm'd of pride,*
>   Nor cared the serpent at thy side
> To flicker with his treble tongue.

" *The stern were mild when thou wert by,*
   The flippant put himself to school
   And heard thee ; and the brazen fool
Was soften'd, and he knew not why.

" While I, thy dearest, sat apart,
   And felt thy triumph was as mine ;
   And loved them more, that they were thine,
The graceful tact, the Christian art ;

" Not mine the sweetness or the skill,
   But mine the love that will not tire ;
   And, born of love, the vague desire
That spurs an imitative will."

And now let us quote no more, though several of the remaining poems are also most beautiful. The epilogue, respecting the marriage of a younger sister of the poet, a child at the period of his friend's decease, is very exquisite, and will be felt by many, perhaps, as much if not more than any thing else in the volume: it is full of a happy, and we might almost say, a holy pathos, which melts on the heart like dew. And so we bid this work farewell. Much, much, remains to say concerning it; but we have no space for further comments. We must add, however, that it is scarcely possible not to think, that the existence of "Shakspeare's Sonnets" in some measure prompted the poet to the composition of his work: he has furnished them with a full worthy counterpart. One magnificent strain we have omitted to notice, on the bells ringing *out* the old, and *in* the new year: we are sorry to find it conclude with an expression, which *may* be interpreted as an endeavour to swell the cry of Carlyle, and Emerson, and "George Sand," and so many others for the future Antichrist; namely, "Ring in *the Christ that is to be ;*" but one verse should be cited for the sake of its mournful modesty :—

"Ring out the want, the care, the sin,
   The faithless coldness of the times :
   Ring out, ring out, my mournful rhymes,
But ring the fuller minstrel in."

He may long delay his coming: yet such a minstrel there no doubt *may be ;* for, as we observed before, despite the really exquisite beauty of much of his writing, Mr. Tennyson will always be a *class poet ;* he will never be *very generally popular.* Then, too, he *teaches* us nothing; he needs teaching himself; he is rather an exponent of this age's wants, than one who can in any measure undertake to satisfy them. And yet, with all this, we repeat, he is a great poet; and great he for ever will remain.

Turn we now to Robert Browning and his new creation. This is a wildly fantastic composition, powerful, earnest, in part devotional, yet audacious, and Hudibrastically satirical. In "Christmas-Eve and Easter-Day" Mr. Browning is understood to have expressed his religious convictions, and to have yielded on the whole his adherence to dogmatic Christianity as "the truth." That his manner of expression is strangely grotesque cannot be questioned; that his speculations are bold in the extreme nobody will deny. Nevertheless, he indicates in the first division of this poem his faith in Christianity *as a fact*, and in the second he expresses his sense of the necessity for loving God in Christ better than this world. The whole poem may be said to consist of two visions and their introductions; in the one of which the poet follows our LORD alternately to St. Peter's at Rome, and the lecture-room of a German Professor; he accepting literally the promise, " When two or three are gathered together," &c.; while in the other he witnesses the last judgment, and is condemned himself to enjoy this world, with no hope of any thing beyond it for ever and ever, for having preferred it to his God. This groundwork is certainly most *bizarre*, and the poem contains some even wilder things than these, which we can scarcely pause to indicate; but how much of deep thought and genuine feeling, what quiet yet earnest scorn for the mythical school of unbelievers, what concentrated power, and originality of execution shall we find here!

At the commencement the poet finds himself in a dissenting chapel, having been driven thither by a storm of wind and rain on the great Easter-Eve; there he falls asleep, under the infliction of a pulpit Boanerges, and imagines in his dream that he leaves the chapel, sees our Lord issuing from it, and follows Him, first to St. Peter's, then elsewhere, as has been already indicated. The description of the meeting-house, "Mount Zion Chapel," is most admirable; the arrival, or dropping in of the congregation, one by one, is touched with a master-hand. How graphic is this—

> " Well,—from the road, the lanes or the common,
> In came the flock :—*the fat weary woman,*
> *Panting and bewilder'd, down-clapping*
> *Her umbrella with a mighty report,*
> *Grounded it by me, wry and flapping,*
> *A wreck of whalebones.*"

This in its way can scarcely be surpassed. Then the arrival of this poor child of sin :—

> " A female something past me flitted,
> • • • •
> And it seem'd the very door-hinge pitied
> All that was left of a woman once,
> Holding, at least, its tongue for the nonce."

The poet's own resolve to step in at last—he is all this time waiting outside in the vestibule for the storm—is most characteristically indicated. The flock gives him angry supercilious glances in passing, or he imagines as much :—

> " There was no standing it much longer,—
> ‘ Good folks,' said I, as resolve grew stronger,—
> ‘ This way you perform the grand inquisitor
> When the weather sends you a chance visitor ?—
> You are the men, and wisdom shall die with you,
> And none of the old seven churches vie with you.'

But he goes in at last, and graphically does he describe the preacher's style, and the delight of the congregation :—

> "The flock sat on, *divinely fluster'd.*"

This passage is, we think, inimitable :—

> " My old fat woman *purr'd with pleasure,*
> And thumb round thumb went twirling faster,
> While she, to his periods keeping measure,
> *Maternally devour'd* the pastor."

Well, he imagines he leaves the chapel, emerging on the heath or common some where near London. Much admirable matter follows of a reflective order, though strangely expressed. The power of man to grieve or glorify God,

> " As a mere machine could never do,"

is asserted: his consequent *separation* from God, and yet the need of God's love in him to accomplish any thing. Then, after a fanciful account of a gigantic lunar rainbow, which attracts the poet's attention, our Lord is seen by him as coming from the chapel.

> "All at once I look'd up with terror.
> He was there.
> He Himself with His human air
> On the narrow pathway, just before ;
> I saw the back of Him, no more—
> He had left the chapel, then, as I !
> • • •
> My mind fill'd with the cataract,
> At one bound, of the mighty fact."

How finely said! The poet describes himself as pressing to "the salvation of His vest," striving to touch the border of His garment, and being hurried after Him in a rapid mystical flight, across land and ocean, to the gate of St. Peter's at Rome; all which is strangely but grandly told. Graphically pourtrayed is St. Peter's, where our Lord enters in this vision, but the poet does not: he fears to be confused by the idolatry within: he tells us, Deity might transcend all minor errors, where faith and love were present; but he, "a mere man," could not, must fear to quit the clue God had given him. Yet, on consideration, he half doubts whether he ought not to enter; whether for *him*, too, love should not obscure the presence of error :—

> " I see the error ; but, above
>   The scope of error, see the love."

Here follows a fine passage commencing,—

> " Oh, love of those first Christian days !"

on the apparent contempt shown by the early Christians for Pagan art and Pagan beauty ; over which we know not whether to rejoice or mourn.

> " Love, with Greece and Rome in ken,
>   Bade her scribes abhor the trick
>   Of poetry and rhetoric,
>   And exult, with hearts set free,
>   In blessed imbecility
>   Scrawl'd, perchance, on some torn sheet,
>   Leaving Livy incomplete."
>   *   *   *   *
> " Love was the startling thing, the new ;
>   Love was the all-sufficient too."

At last our Lord re-issues ; and now He wends His course, followed by our poet, to some "tall, old, quaint, irregular town," a university town of Germany ;—

> " It may be Göttingen,—most likely."

And there, to a lecture-hall, where a body of students are assembled on this same Easter-Eve, to listen to a mythical rationalistic lecture on our Lord and Christianity. The professor is described most graphically : his lecture, or what is given of it, is a perfect epitome of the common-places of the now fashionable transcendental infidelity, which Browning deals with unsparingly. *The myth* of Christ and its origin is dilated on ; how His word and tradition,—

> " Though it meant
> Something entirely different
> From all, *that those who only heard it*
> *In their simplicity thought and averr'd it,*
> Had yet a meaning quite as respectable !"

Rather a home-thrust this, O transcendentalists! Then the professor comes to the main upshot of this twaddle : " Was he," that is, CHRIST,—

> " *Was He not surely the first to insist on*
> *The natural sovereignty of our race ?*"

which detested cant wears out at last our poet's patience, and drives him from the lecture-hall to ruminate on what he has listened to. The mingled contempt and pity of the ensuing passage make it one of the most *telling* imaginable against the follies of infidelity. Clearly the poet shows, that if Christ's divinity be rejected, nothing virtually is left; for as to mere morality, that is admitted and proclaimed on other hands without the addition, that—

> " He, the sage and humble,
> *Was also one with the Creator !*"

Powerfully and unanswerably the poet proceeds :—

> " You urge Christ's followers' simplicity :
> But how does shifting blame evade it ?
> Have wisdom's words no more felicity ?
> The stumbling-block, His speech—who laid it ?
> How comes it, that for one found able
> To sift the truth of it from fable,
> Millions believe it to the letter ?"

Ay, *how*, indeed ? How were the Evangelists deluded, the Apostles blinded, and the whole world *taken in* by such a gigantic unreality ! There is but one answer. *They never were !* Browning goes on to tell us, that if Christ our Lord were man only, he should protest against all Socinian worship of Him : honoured He then might be as the Shakspeare of theology, but nothing more.

> " I would call such a Christ our Saint,
> As I declare our poet, him
> Whose insight makes all others dim."

But it is not new moral truths of which man needed or needs the communication, so much as—

> " *A motive and injunction,*
> For practising what we know already ;" .

And this the poet concludes accordingly was "the real God-function!" Finely he continues,—

> "And such an injunction and such a motive
> As the God in Christ, do you waive, and ' heady,
> High-minded,' hang your tablet-votive
> Outside the fane on a finger-post ?"

Again :—

> "What is the point where Himself lays stress ?
> Does the precept run, ' Believe in good,
> In justice, truth, now understood
> For the first time ?—or, ' Believe in ME,
> Who lived and died, yet essentially .
> Am Lord of life ?' "

This again is, we need not say, unanswerable. But the poet's scorn rises yet higher at the pretended admiration with which the rationalist or mythical misinterpreter *calls on us to take back our faith*, when he has made dust and ashes of it, and honour it as much as ever !

> " ' Go home, and venerate the myth
> I thus have experimented with—
> This Man, continue to adore him,
> Rather than all who went before him,
> And all who ever followed after ?'—
> *Surely for this I may praise you, my brother !*
> *Will you take the praise in tears or laughter ?*"

And further on :—

> " But still, when you rub the brow meticulous,
> And ponder the profit of turning holy,
> If not for God's, for your own sake solely,—
> *God forbid, I should find you ridiculous ! !*"

Certainly, the force of scornful pity can no further go. After some very far-reaching reflections on the apparent benefits of toleration and the need for some real creed, the poet follows our Lord again, as he imagines, back to the chapel from which he started, when his waking is well described. Strange to say, Browning has here thought fit to intimate his preference of some or any form of dissent to the teaching of the Church of England, or of any *Church:* thus we presume that we are to understand him, where he says :—

> "My heart does best to receive in meekness
> This mode of worship, as most to His mind,
> Where earthly aids being cast behind,

His all in all appears serene
With the thinnest human veil between !''

And yet we believe, we almost know, that our author has been throughout life a member of our Church Communion. Is this a mere freak of genius, or how are we to understand it? Some of the concluding reflections of the first part are very striking, as, for instance, where the poet says of the poor German Professor, whom he has described as apparently dying of a slow consumption :—

> "When thicker and thicker, the darkness fills
> The world through his misty spectacles,
> And he gropes *for something more substantial*
> Than a fable, myth, or personification,—
> May Christ do for him what no mere *man* shall,
> And stand confess'd as the God of salvation !"

Finally the poet says, vindicating the style and method of this poem,

> " If any blames me,
> Thinking that merely to touch in brevity
> The topics I dwell on were unlawful,—
> Or, worse, that I trench with undue levity
> On the bounds of the holy and the awful,—
> *I praise the heart, and pity the head of him,*
> *And refer myself to Thee instead of him;*
> Who head and heart alike discernest,
> Looking below light speech we utter,
> *When the frothy spume and frequent sputter*
> *Prove that the soul's depths boil in earnest !"*

And now we have allowed Mr. Browning to speak much for himself; and, we think, to some effect. Of the second part, " Easter-Day," we can only say that it is wilder again than the first, more poetic it may be, and grander ; the description of the final conflagration in the vision of the last day is truly magnificent and awful,—and that it deals with a most difficult subject, the degree to which asceticism should enter into the life of the true Christian. Our poet almost seems to imagine that he should give up the use of this world altogether, and to condemn himself because he cannot consent to do this. He states the ascetic argument derived from the death of Christ our Lord, as strongly as it *can* be stated, in the passage commencing :—

> " Enough ! you know
> The all-stupendous tale,—that birth,
> That life, that death !"

and appears to imagine the said argument incontrovertible; on which point we differ from him. We think, and know, that the use of this world *is* permitted to the Christian, yes, even to him who aims at perfection; after which all indeed are bound to strive, and not an isolated class. But, as a whole, this second part is far less satisfactory to us than the first: we think it founded, to a great degree, on a mistake. This is not the place, however, at the fag-end of a long literary article, in which we could enter into such a controversy. Much there is, no doubt, that is very admirable here, too, in this second part of the poems: and powerfully does the poet demonstrate, that earth without the hope of heaven would only be a wilderness.

On the whole, however, this contribution of Browning's to our poetic literature is a great work, and is gladly hailed by us as such. Essentially different as it is in all respects from "In Memoriam," they are both destined to an earthly immortality.

And now turn we to the Lepidus of this triumvirate, the unhappy Taylor: how sadly does he halt after his giant-brethren! But it is our fault for placing him in a false position. "The words of Mercury are harsh after the songs of Apollo." But, decidedly "the Virgin Widow" is no word of Mercury's even: it is a weak, colourless, poverty-stricken imitation of the inferior class of Elizabethan dramas; a kind of tragi-comedy; but the tragedy has no pathos, and the comedy no mirth. It bears in fact about the same relation to a true drama, which a stalking-horse does to a battle-courser. In the opening acts there is a certain amount of mellifluous gentle dulness, which is not displeasing; but as the play advances the total absence of creative power or dramatic sympathy becomes only too evident. The hero, as is usual with Mr. Taylor, is one of the dullest of the dull: his quiet indifference when deprived of his worshipped lady-love, where his quixotic friend offers to speak in his behalf, is positively comic. There is no true movement, no internal development of characters from first to last, not a spark of dramatic life, or even of *intention.*

We speak so gravely and severely, because some of the leading critical organs of this country go on to shout an "Io Pœan," after each fresh failure on the part of Mr. Taylor to realize his ideal; not that we believe he *has* an ideal strictly speaking. Isolated passages in "the Virgin Widow," are not altogether devoid of poetic merit; dramatic, as aforesaid, they have none: one or two little songs introduced, though they are only echoes of Elizabethan ditties, are rather pleasing in their way: the opening scenes are more bearable than Mr. Taylor's tragedies generally, because less pretentious; but, as a whole, "the Virgin Widow" is as weak as possible.

We confess that we have a grudge against this writer, moral as well as literary: we could pass over his absurdly exaggerated praises of Wordsworth in the "Quarterly:" we can appreciate the ethical and common-sense value of some of his reflections: but we can never forgive the composition of the "Statesman;" a work which we believe to have done more harm to rising politicians, to the statesmen of the age generally, than any other contribution to literature which could be named; to have done more harm therefore indirectly to our Church and country. Therein Mr. Taylor, under all manner of specious pretences, does not scruple to justify *dissimulation* and *falsehood*, necessity being of course the tyrant plea; he warns young statesmen not to form any connexions which cannot be *useful* to them, and not to express opinions strongly, lest they should be *hampered* in official life, and not enabled to follow the courses of expediency; he advises them to make a habit of speaking at debating societies *against their real convictions*, that they may so acquire a habit for future use in Parliament; he declares generally, that a great statesman should have few strong convictions, and should rather be the exponent and representative, than the guide of the public mind: in fact, all the philosophy of worldly false expediency, and of conventional mediocrity, is condensed under the most fair-seeming exterior in this mischievous little work, to which we probably owe more of moral and political evil than can easily be estimated; so great an authority has Mr. Taylor become, more especially with our *moderate Conservatives!* Christianity he ignores, lays altogether on one side, and so provides us with a wretched ethical substitute of lax morality. In nothing great or good does he believe! His work is essentially of the "Taper" and "Tadpole" order, and we believe it to be only too fair an embodiment of the man and of the school.

How then should such a thinker be a poet? Nay, the greatest poet and dramatist of the day, as "Quarterly" and "Edinburgh" inform us! For our part, we like better even the bold wickedness of a Byron, against which Mr Taylor declaims so loudly, than this washed-out, colourless, official prose and poetry, void of sense or of soul, a vague Wordsworthian philosophising, taking the place of religion, the very cant of respectability, the sublime of dulness. Ten thousand-fold rather would we deal with an open foe than with such half-and-half friends as these: we wish for no such allies: we protest against the *Christianity* of such writers as the vaguest of unrealities; and we maintain, that such a school could no more produce *a great poet*, than Thuggism could rear a blessed saint. Its nature, at best, is to be flat, dull, level, *essentially prosaic.*

We have no space for extracts from " the Virgin Widow " to prove the justice of our charges: where uniform dulness and deadness is the characteristic, single flagrant errors need not be sought for: it seems better to abstain from citations; and, besides, we have exhausted our space. " Quarterly" and " Edinburgh " may, and probably will, devote a long article each to " the Virgin Widow," but it is destined to speedy and certain oblivion: they may neglect Tennyson's " In Memoriam ;" (though this is not probable *now!* even dulness has acknowledged *him!*) they will certainly pass by Browning's new creation disregardingly; yet these two works will live, when a much-belauded " Philip von Artevelde " (not to speak of " the Virgin Widow ") is buried in " the tomb of all the Capulets." Pretentious mediocrity may run, or seem to run, cheek by jowl with genius for a while, nay, may altogether outrun it; but there is a quagmire on its path, into which, sooner or later, it must sink: may it rest in peace !

Art. V.—*An Appeal to the Clergy and Laity of the Church of England, to combine for the Defence of the Church, and for the Recovery of her Rights and Liberties.* By George Anthony Denison, *M.A., Vicar of East Brent.* London: Rivingtons. 1850.

That the Church of England requires liberty in order to execute her work, is a truth to which considerable numbers of her more intelligent members are beginning to be alive. It is true that as yet there is no movement on a large scale for the restoration of Church liberties: for Churchmen are as yet very imperfectly organized, and they have no recognized leader, and they are for the most part timid and uncertain in their movements, not feeling their course traced out with sufficient distinctness for them; and, not least, they are still, to a very considerable extent, subject to impressions, notions, and influences derived from the system under which the Church has been enslaved, and all of which tend to prolong the reign of that system. Nevertheless, there is light breaking in on all sides: men are investigating things as they are, and have been; they are learning to think for themselves, and to act with those who agree with them; they are learning how to associate for the redress of grievances, and how to proceed without the aid and countenance of persons of rank and station, and even when such persons discourage and condemn them.

All this affords satisfactory evidence of the preparation which is being made for the great struggle for liberty. The Hampden controversy and the Gorham controversy have shown Churchmen how powerless they are, under the existing laws, to check the inroads of heresy. These two cases have shown the State to be at once without religious belief, and without toleration for the consciences of Churchmen. They have set before us the claims of a temporal power, which believes no doctrine, to dictate on matters of doctrine to the Church; and they have shown that the law supports these claims through its ministers. Great as are the evils arising from such cases, we are yet indebted to them for a clearer view of our actual condition. Many Churchmen had been under the persuasion that the laws of the land protected the faith of the English Church, while they granted toleration to other religious communions; and that the State did not possess legally the power of imposing on the Church a bishop who did not hold her creed, or of intruding men of unsound faith into her parochial benefices. These points are now no longer doubtful: a bishop censured for unsound doctrine, contrary to that of the English Church, has been forced into one of her sees ; a priest has similarly been intruded into a parochial benefice ; and the State has asserted throughout its absolute and irresponsible power, —the power of nominating whomsoever it pleases, without reference to his belief or other qualifications.

Without doubt the statesmen and jurists who have of late claimed such absolute powers for the State and the Legislature in all respects, are, to a certain extent, in the right.   Every one must admit the *legal* omnipotence of the supreme legislative body, consisting of Queen, Lords, and Commons. As far as the law is concerned, as far as civil rights are concerned, there is nothing that Parliament cannot do. It may confiscate all estates, may abolish the national debt, may close all churches, chapels, and meeting-houses in the empire, and throw their ministers into prison, or cut off their heads. It may legalize incest, adultery, fornication, blasphemy, and irreligion, and may award prizes to the best proficients in any given vice. It may, in the same way, create bishops and priests, directing them to be ordained by the Secretary of State, or not to be ordained at all. It may place such bishops in possession of Church property, and recognize their ecclesiastical jurisdiction as the only jurisdiction sanctioned by law. It may require the license and ordination of such bishops as essential pre-requisites to the possession of benefices in the Church. It may abolish subscriptions to creeds and articles of faith, and enact penalties against any clergyman who should refuse to administer the sacrament to Dissenters, Jews, Mahommedans, or Pagans. All this the Legislature may do. It may even go beyond this, and require from every member of the community the worship of the reigning sovereign as a deity, or the adoration of Juggernaut, if it pleases.

All this the Legislature might do in its absolute sovereignty. States have before now enacted laws exactly of this description, and most rigorously enforced them. And, again, no one will deny the power of the Legislature to set aside the law of nations, as it is called. The Legislature might, if it chose so to do, decapitate all the foreign ambassadors in England, and might annex to the British dominions by force any of the neighbouring possessions of other powers, without their consent.—And could these acts be carried into effect, they would, if the British Legislature willed it, be perfectly *legal.*

Thus there is, in one sense, perfect truth in the statesman's and the barrister's principle, of the omnipotence of the law. The State *can* do as it pleases in theory. But there is another point of view in which legislation may be considered; there is such a thing as *unjust* legislation, there is such a thing as tyrannical and oppressive law. The law may be opposed to the revealed will of God, to the injunctions of conscience. When Christians were required by law, and on penalty of death, to sacrifice to false gods, the law was unjust and tyrannical. It was equally so, in the opinion of many persons, when penal enactments were in force against Romanists and Dissenters. It was perfectly legal to burn heretics till the reign of Charles II., yet those who acted on the law in that respect are now regarded as monsters of cruelty. In short, the Legislature, though perfectly absolute in theory, can enact laws, which are as unjust, cruel, and unrighteous, as any acts of individuals can possibly be.

And now to apply what has been said to a particular case. The Church of England is, at this time, labouring under oppressive and unjust laws in many respects. In the first place it is a most unjust law, however it may have originated, which gives to bodies and persons alien from the faith of the Church of England the power of regulating her doctrine and discipline, her worship and her endowments, at pleasure. The Church of England is not, like other religious communities, subject strictly to the regulation and guidance of her own members: she is subject to be interfered with by bodies and persons who do not agree with her in faith, but whose object is to injure her in all ways and to destroy her. She is subject to the legislation of Dissenters, Roman Catholics, and Infidels, or persons of no creed. We do not stop to inquire how this has been brought about: it was not *always* so. All we mean to say is, that this state of things is a crying and monstrous injustice. We care not by what theories statesmen or divines may seek to justify it. There can be no excuse for so gross a violation of the commonest principles of justice and religious liberty. Is it possible to justify such a state of the law as gives to persons of one creed the power of acting as rulers and directors of a creed to which they are opposed? Romanists and Dissenters do not believe the system of the Church of England to be true: they are bound by their own principles to seek the destruction of that system; and yet the law of the land invests them with the power of legislating for it!

On the other hand, the State has exempted all Dissenters and Roman Catholics from interference with their religious concerns by persons of other religious denominations. The Romanists can hold their synods without any admixture of other religionists, and arrange all their own doctrine and discipline. Dissenters are equally exempt from interference in their affairs. Parliament, and the Crown, leave them to act as they judge advisable. The Church of England, alone, is deprived, by the arbitrary power of the executive, of her constitutional right of settling her own affairs in her synods; and the temporal Legislature, composed in part of Romanists, Dissenters, Infidels, and persons of no creed, has usurped the right of being the sole legislature in Church matters. We say it has "usurped" the power, because it has assumed it without the consent of the Church, and in consequence of the arbitrary suspension of the Church's true legislature. The case is strictly parallel to that of Charles I. in attempting to dispense with Parliament. In the seventeenth century the Crown usurped the powers of both Houses of Parliament, and in the nineteenth the Temporal Legislature usurps the powers of the Church Legislature.

In fact, it would be just as reasonable and fair for the law to compel Churchmen to listen in their churches to Roman Catholic or Dissenting preachers, as to give to persons of a different creed the power of interfering in legislation for the Church, as under the present system.

It is a great injustice to give persons of a different creed the power of interfering in the concerns of the Church, when the members of the Church are excluded from all interference in the religious concerns of the creed professed by such persons. It is, in fact, to give the preference to other denominations above the Church—to give them rights and immunities which are refused to the Church. On what principle of justice and fairness is it possible to justify such inequality in the mode of dealing with the Church and with other religious bodies?

It may be said in answer to this, as it often is said, that the sects have not been endowed by the State, but the Church *has* been; and therefore the State has a right, in return, to regulate all the affairs of the Church. But this proceeds on an assumption which is untrue; because the State never *did* endow the Church, the property of the Church taking its origin from its own regulations, and from the gifts of its members, and the State having done nothing more than confirm what it found already in force, or protected the conveyance of property for religious purposes, as it does also in the case of Dissenters and Roman Catholics to a certain extent. So that the right of interference in Church matters, founded on this, is without sufficient grounds. The State did not take the property of the Church from Roman Catholics, and give it to the Church of England;—to say so, infers a gross ignorance of historical facts. The Church was reformed, and retained her property. But even supposing, for the sake of argument, that the case was as is asserted, and that the Church *had* been endowed by the State,—still this does not bring the advocates of State interference to the conclusion they want to arrive at; for, in the first place, it does not follow, that because the

State endows a particular religious community, it has therefore the right of regulating all the spiritual concerns of that community. The community itself must *consent* to this arrangement, or else the assumption of such power is unjust. It must be a matter of compact and agreement. To give a piece of land to provide for the support of the minister of a congregation, gives no necessary *right* to interfere with the doctrine or discipline of that congregation. So that the claim of right fails altogether in this point of view. And again; supposing that we were to *concede* the existence of such a right founded on endowment, still this would not justify the State in giving the exercise of that right to persons of a *different religion* from the Church. Supposing the Church had been endowed by the State, and had agreed that the State should regulate all her affairs, and had never possessed a convocation, or legislated for herself, yet still she never could have consented that persons *alien from her faith* should be her legislators.—This is the grand evil and injustice of the present state of things, which was never contemplated as possible by any party until recently.

Another crying injustice, which is perpetrated under the sanction of the existing law, is the appointment of the chief rulers of the Church by persons who are either indifferent to the spiritual welfare of the Church, or are actually hostile to her. The appointment of bishops and deans is notoriously influenced by considerations of a political description, by interest, or by other merely worldly inducements. It is placed in the hands of those who may be of no creed, or of some creed different from that of the Church of England. It is exercised by persons who are under the influence of others, who are aliens from the faith of the English Church, and seek for her destruction. The position of the Church is thus that of an army, whose generals are appointed by the enemy; or of a country, whose commanding positions are all in the hands of a hostile force. The enemies of the Church have the power, under the existing law, of appointing her bishops and deans. They may choose men especially for the purpose of bringing discredit on her, ruining her character, exciting and promoting divisions, or subverting her faith and discipline. All this is in their *power*, according to the existing law. And here a question arises, not only whether such a state of things is reconcilable with common justice and fairness, but whether it is consistent with the law of God! The Church of England is undoubtedly not responsible for the present state of things; for it has arisen wholly out of the changes in the constitution of the State. But it is a state of things in which the Church could not *acquiesce*, without serious sin. There is now no longer any sort of security for the soundness of faith of newly-appointed bishops. They may be advanced by disbelievers in the Church's creed; they may be selected in order to subvert the Creeds and Articles and Liturgy of the Church. However suspected their faith may be, however irreligious in life, immoral in conduct, heretical in doctrine, however unfitted they may be in all respects; yet the chapters can be compelled, on pain of imprisonment and confiscation, to elect them. The archbishops may be obliged, under the same penalties, to confirm them; and the bishops selected to consecrate may be compelled, under the same penalties, to join in the act. This is not " religious liberty:" it is absolute tyranny, and a gross infringement on the rights of conscience. Chapters, archbishops, and bishops are compellable by law to commit a most fearful sin, in sending forth those whom they may believe and know to be unfitted for their office. Chapters and bishops may be convinced that a person nominated for the office of bishop *has none of the qualifications required by Scripture in a bishop;* and yet they are made liable to premunire if they hesitate to elect and ordain! They are entrusted by God with the responsibility of sending forth faithful labourers into God's vineyard, and they are forced by law to disregard the responsibilities they owe to God !

Under these circumstances, we cannot avoid expressing the opinion, that the offices of deans and other members of chapters, and the offices of bishops and archbishops, are at present full of snares for souls; and that no man can with a safe conscience accept any of those offices, except with a resolution to discharge his duty in it with a single eye to the responsibility which he owes to God, and with a determination to submit to any legal penalties that may befal him, rather than consent to the election and consecration of a bishop whom he believes or suspects to be unworthy. We believe that those who, through fear of any temporal losses or penalties, take any part in betraying the flock of Jesus Christ to wolves and anti-christs, are guilty of most deadly sin. No pretence of obedience to most unrighteous laws of man, will avail them in the last day, when they are accused of having betrayed the trust confided to them by their God.

The present state of the law in this respect is really so monstrous, that it cannot possibly stand the test of examination. It only exists, because it is left unnoticed. Bring it to the light, and it is at once convicted. The dean and chapter are convened, and proceed under the usual forms to hold an election of a bishop, invoking the Divine aid to guide their choice, and having been duly authorized by the Crown to choose a godly and faithful pastor. The whole of this proceeding is converted into a solemn mockery by the provision of the law which gives the Crown the

power of nominating the person to be elected, and compelling the
chapter to elect him under penalty of premunire. As long as
the State was a thoroughly Church of England State, and the
Sovereigns in all their actions showed themselves resolved to
maintain and defend and advance the religion of the Church,
there was a reasonable ground for believing, that none but fit and
proper persons would be nominated for election by the chapters ;
but now all is changed. The nomination has passed away from
the Crown to the ministers. Those ministers are virtually appointed by the House of Commons, which is perfectly indifferent
towards the religious interests of the Church, being composed of
religionists of all kinds. The ministers reflect this indifference,
and, therefore, there is no kind of security that proper bishops
will be nominated ; and yet, the law continues to compel deans
and chapters to go through the form of praying to God for His
blessing on an election which they may have every reason to believe in their consciences to be injurious to religion ! Now,
such a state of things is really intolerable. It is a disgrace to
this age of liberty to continue regulations which are completely
imbued with the spirit of persecution. Men are compelled by
law to act against their consciences, on penalty of imprisonment
and confiscation ; archbishops and bishops are liable to the same
penalties, if they act on their consciences and refuse to confirm
and consecrate a bishop whom they know to be unsound in faith
or unholy in life.

But, it is argued, the ministers must have the absolute power
of appointing whom they please to be bishops, because the
bishops have seats in the House of Lords, and are thus mixed up
with politics, and it is therefore requisite that the political leaders
should be enabled to place partisans of their own in episcopal
sees. This view is one that, without doubt, exercises great influence over politicians, but it will not exercise any influence over
the minds of Churchmen. Are the interests of religion to be
subordinated to those of political parties ? The argument, in
fact, goes to show that the appointment of bishops should altogether cease to be made by the political ministry. Were it removed from the ministers altogether, and made unpolitical, all
political parties would equally lose the prospect of putting their
friends on the episcopal bench, and no one would be strengthened
at the expense of any other. What is most to be desired for the
welfare of religion is, that the Church should stand aloof from
mere party politics as much as possible. It is the general wish
of the country, that bishops should not be politicians : they lower
their influence and position by being so, and they seldom add
much weight to any party, because they are always divided in

politics. However, we have not the slightest expectation of convincing politicians and the heads of political parties that they would do well to relinquish this patronage : all we mean to say is, that the convenience of politicians does not in any degree diminish the *injustice* of giving to parties alien to the Church and hostile to her, the power of directly or indirectly nominating her bishops and leading dignitaries.

And now to pass on to another of the grievances arising out of the present state of the law. What can be more monstrous than that state of things under which the decision of cases directly affecting the doctrine of the Church of England, is placed in the hands of a court without any distinctive creed! Persons holding belief opposed to that of the English Church—Presbyterians, Roman Catholics, Infidels—may, under the present state of the law, be supreme judges in Her Majesty's Privy Council, of all causes affecting the faith of members of the English Church. A clergyman accused of denying the divinity of our Lord, may have his cause tried in this court by a Unitarian. Another, who shall dispute the inspiration of Scripture, and the fact of a Divine Revelation, may be tried by a judge who equally disbelieves in revelation. Now this is, we maintain, a perfect mockery of justice, if the court is supposed to be constituted for the purpose of upholding the doctrine of the Church of England. To permit persons who disbelieve her doctrines and are hostile to them, to determine whether this or that tenet is in accordance with those doctrines, is to give them the power of injuring her to the greatest extent, either by sanctioning tenets virtually contrary to her belief, or by obtruding on her, clergy who do not believe her doctrines, and who are labouring to subvert them. It is an extreme injustice to place any Church in such a position as this ; nor would it be tolerated for a moment, in the case of any other communion except that of the Church of England. It is no answer to this to say, that the Church of England has admitted the supremacy of the State, and therefore must take whatever the State pleases to ordain ; because the Church never *did*, in fact, admit the supremacy of a State without a creed, or including all sects of religionists. The State which the Church of England recognized as having more or less authority in ecclesiastical matters, was a strictly Church of England state, which was opposed to every other system, and tolerated no dissent. Give us such a state again, and we would let things remain as they were ; but to substitute Dissenters and Romanists for sincere members of the Church of England, and to give them the same authority over the Church, makes just all the difference between justice and injustice, between friendship and enmity, between toleration and persecution.

Another great injustice arising out of the present state of the law is, the impossibility of developing the system and discipline of the Church of England, without opposition and interference on the part of her enemies. The Church has, for a series of years, been earnestly desirous of an increase in the number of bishops, in order to promote her own spiritual efficiency. This is a point on which all Churchmen are agreed. The whole episcopate have expressed themselves favourable to it. So strong was the feeling, that the Government made its proposal to the bishops to add four to their number, and introduced a bill accordingly. The infidel and sectarian party in the House of Commons bitterly opposed this bill, and succeeded in preventing this development of the Church. The ministers have relinquished a measure which they do not deny to be a good measure in itself, because it is unpalatable to the enemies of the Church in Parliament. Here, then, is an instance of the unjust way in which the Church is treated under the present system. Her expansion in the mode which she herself desires, and which is admitted to be right and reasonable, is entrusted to a legislature which includes a large number of persons of hostile creeds, or of no creed at all. Her opponents are given the power of stopping any measures for her benefit. This is an extreme injustice and hardship to the Church of England, which no other communion in the empire experiences. The law does not prevent *them* from establishing new congregations, churches, synods, bishops, and ecclesiastical organizations. Why, then, should it interfere with the Church of England, and prevent it from exercising its own discretion as to what is advisable for the advancement of its spiritual welfare? It is a very great injustice, and a positive act of intolerance, to restrain a religious communion from making such regulations on points of this kind as it deems necessary for the welfare of religion; and more especially, when persons of a different faith are entrusted with this power of restraint. Of course, Dissenters, and Roman Catholics, and unbelievers, must be *expected* to oppose themselves to any measure which they conscientiously believe would be for the benefit of the Church of England. They would do very wrong, with *their* views, if they did not, to the utmost of their power, prevent any such measure from being passed; but then, on the other hand, it is a great hardship to the Church to be subject to their interference; and the State which has done them justice in relieving them from penal laws, is equally bound to do justice to the Church of England, by relieving her from their interference, which has been the result of the acts which gave religious liberty to them. In point of fact, the same legislation which gave religious liberty to Romanists and Dissenters, deprived the Church of her religious liberty, in placing her under the dominion of persons of a different creed from her own. Previously to that time, the State had been substantially a Church of England State: it then wholly ceased to be so. The moment that Dissenters and Romanists were granted freedom from all political disabilities, the Church became directly subject to them, while they are perfectly protected from any interference on her part. This is an extreme injustice, which ought to be removed. If the Legislature chose to relinquish its Church of England character, it ought, in common justice and fairness, at the same time to have ceased to be the Church's legislature on matters of doctrine, discipline, and revenues. As it is, the alteration of the law has placed the Church under disabilities which she never previously suffered from. Her wishes are now liable to be thwarted in Parliament, not merely on grounds of State policy, but by sectarian animosity. She has to do with a legislature, a portion of which is hostile to her on religious grounds, and therefore a positive wrong and injury has been done to her. We do not in the least complain that Dissenters and Romanists are exempted from our interference as Churchmen in their religious concerns; but it is a gross injustice that we should not be equally exempted from their interference in our affairs. We cannot have bishops without their consent; we cannot effect reforms of any kind in our system without their intermeddling; if our Ecclesiastical Courts require alteration—if our chapters are to be made more efficient—if regulations are to be made for the trial of offences against faith or morality—if any thing at all is to be reformed or improved in our ecclesiastical or spiritual system, infidels, Dissenters, and Romanists, aid in determining every question, and of course do their best to determine it against the Church, or in the mode most injurious to her.

Now we think it is sufficiently evident, from all that has been said, that Churchmen are greatly aggrieved by the present law—that they are not treated with the same justice, fairness, and toleration which is extended to every other denomination. Their religious system stands in a most precarious and dangerous position, in consequence of the powers over the Church possessed by the ministers of the Crown, and by the two Houses of the Legislature. And then the question comes, How can this evil be remedied? It is plain that it cannot be remedied by returning back to the old system, and removing Romanists and Dissenters from the Houses of Parliament. This is altogether out of the question: nor have Churchmen any right to call for the infliction of disabilities on others, if they can release themselves in some other way.

The only remaining course, therefore, for Churchmen to take is, to demand that they shall be placed on an equality with Dissenters, and other denominations; that they shall have the same immunity from the interference of all except their own members, which is enjoyed by all other denominations. We think that this demand is grounded in simple justice. Why should the Church alone be subject to the interference of persons who are not of her own communion? Churchmen are just as competent as Dissenters to manage their own affairs. They can be trusted with equal propriety by the State to arrange the concerns of their own religious system. They do not require the guidance or direction of the State more than Dissenters or Roman Catholics do. They are not to be treated as children, and held in leading-strings, while others are let go free. What possible reason or excuse can be given for so degrading a distinction? Are not Churchmen as well educated as Dissenters or Roman Catholics? Are they so much more quarrelsome than persons of other denominations, that they cannot be entrusted with the same liberties that every one else has gained? Have they alone no consciences? And are they to be expected to submit to the dictation and interference of persons of a different denomination from themselves, when no one else in the country is expected to submit to such an interference?

Politicians object to give the Church freedom, because they object to establish an *imperium in imperio*. But they have no scruple of this kind in dealing with Roman Catholics and Dissenters. They recognize the freedom of these communions in the fullest way. The Dissenters are an *imperium in imperio*, and so are the Roman Catholics, and so, therefore, may be the Church of England. If the one be right in principle, the other is equally right in principle; and if the power of self-legislation is recognized in the case of the Dissenters and Romanists, it is the grossest injustice to refuse it to the Church of England.

" Well but," it is replied, "you must not interfere with the royal supremacy. Every one admits the royal supremacy in religious matters. If you make the Church free, you destroy the royal supremacy." Now to this we reply by asking the meaning of those who argue thus. Do they mean that the royal supremacy is something necessarily inherent in the Crown, and extending to all the subjects of the Crown? Do they mean that the Queen, in virtue of her royal power, is supreme in religious causes over the nation? Because if they do, they mean that Dissenters and Roman Catholics are subject to the royal supremacy just as much as Churchmen are. If *this* be their meaning, they cannot pretend that to claim for the Church the same liberty which is possessed by Roman Catholics and Dissenters is to deny the royal supremacy. Of course, if the Crown is supreme over *them*, notwithstanding their freedom, the Church might be equally free, consistently with the supremacy. If, however, it is asserted that the Crown has not, in virtue of its royal power, any supremacy over Roman Catholics and Dissenters, it must be equally without inherent supremacy over the Church. The essential rights of the Crown must affect all classes of subjects equally. If any such right does not exist in relation to Dissenters, it exists in relation to no other class.

It is absurd to pretend that the dignity of the Crown would be diminished if the Church were possessed of the same liberty as is enjoyed by other denominations. It would be nothing more than carrying out the principle which has been already extended by the Legislature to every communion in England, except to the Church. If the dignity of the Crown is impaired by acknowledging the freedom of religious denominations, — that has been done already,—the Crown has lost its dignity, for half the people of the empire are in the possession of religious liberty. It would be a poor excuse to avoid doing an act of justice, to pretend that the Crown would lose its dignity by acknowledging the rights of conscience, when it has done so for all other religious denominations.

Another objection against allowing freedom to the Church of England is, that it would lead to quarrelling and disputes amongst her members. The persons who make this objection seem to think, that the members of the English Church require to be chained up, like bull-dogs, for fear they should tear each other in pieces. Is this the case? Surely it would be a libel on the character of Churchmen to affirm it. It is very true that there are parties in the Church; and from what cause have they arisen? They have arisen entirely from the suppression of the Church's liberties by the State. Had not the Church been gagged and tied, so as to prevent her from exercising her own free choice, there never would have been any parties of any magnitude within our communion. The Church would have interfered with authority at an early stage, and settled the matters in dispute. As it is, the State has arbitrarily interfered, and taken these matters out of the Church's hands. It has determined, for the last 130 years, that *no controversies shall be settled.* Of course the result is, that they go on smouldering at one time, and blazing at another, and party-feelings are engendered. The Evangelicals have constituted a Church within the Church. The blame rests wholly on the State. We are certainly divided; but the only possible way to heal divisions is to give the Church freedom. When it is free to act, different parties will make some terms with each other; there will be a way open to make some arrangement which shall not offend the consciences of any one; or if it be found that differences are irreconcilable, there will no longer be an attempt to keep compressed in the same communion elements which are mutually repulsive ; and peace will be the result. It is the clumsy and ill-contrived attempts of states to enforce external communion without making any provision for settling disputes on essential points, or silencing those in non-essentials, which invariably leads to the greatest disturbance in the Church. The State knows its own incompetence to deal with theological subjects : it will not trust the Church to settle its own affairs ; and so its only remedy is, to tell Churchmen that their communion must be made wide enough to accept, without dispute, any doctrine or tenet that may find its way into it. The State "recipe" for healing Church controversies is to force Churchmen to recognize as brethren and members of the Church those who, in their opinion, deny the essential doctrines of Christianity. Such a policy is sure to fail eventually, and it always largely increases the amount of irritation and the intensity of controversy. We believe that the differences between parties in the Church are perfectly capable of reconciliation to a great extent, if there was any way or means of reconciliation. But what can be done, when the State *will not permit any adjustment of differences to be made*,—when its only hope is, that those differences will die away? The effects of this policy is to aggravate differences to the extremest degree. If the State does not like existing divisions in the Church, it has no one but itself to blame for them.

We must say a few words more on the supremacy of the Crown, in order to place our argument in a clearer light. The Church of England, then, acknowledges, and we with her acknowledge, in the fullest and most ample terms, the supremacy of the Crown in ecclesiastical matters. With the Thirty-seventh Article, we assert the Queen to have the chief government of *all estates* of this realm, whether they be *ecclesiastical or civil*, in all causes. We maintain, with the same Article, that godly princes are authorized by God's word to rule *all estates and degrees* committed to their charge by God, whether they be *ecclesiastical or temporal*, and to restrain with the civil sword the stubborn and evil doers. According to the tenor of the old oath of supremacy prescribed by Stat. 1 Elizabeth, c. 1, we hold that "the Queen's Highness is the only supreme governor *of this realm*, and of all other Her Highness's dominions and countries, *as well in all spiritual or ecclesiastical things or causes* as temporal." With the Thirty-sixth Canon we declare, that "the King's Majesty, under God, is the only supreme governor of this *realm*, and of *all other His Highness's dominions and countries*, as well in *all spiritual or ecclesiastical things or causes* as temporal."

All this we cordially and earnestly acknowledge and assert.

But will our opponents assert as much? Will they go to the length which the Church of England goes in asserting the royal supremacy over all "persons," all "estates," all "things," and all "causes ecclesiastical and spiritual" within "this realm, and all other Her Majesty's dominions?" Will they assert that the Crown is, or ought to be, supreme in the "things and causes ecclesiastical and spiritual," of the Roman Catholics, for instance, or of the Wesleyan Methodists, or of the Independents, or the Baptists? All these "causes and things" are within "this realm:" the ecclesiastical "estates and degrees" of the Roman Catholics, Methodists, Baptists, Independents, Presbyterians, and Socinians, are "within this realm." Has the Crown *de jure* the supremacy over all these people? We maintain that it *has*. The Church of England declares that it has; and the law of the land, as embodied in the Act of Supremacy passed under Elizabeth, declares that it has. We assert the supremacy of the Crown over this *realm:* not over a part of the realm, but over the whole; not over a section of the population, but over the whole population. Will any of the advocates of the royal supremacy in Parliament or elsewhere, will the Ministers of State, will the Evangelicals, will the Liberals, will the Rationalists, and, above all, will the Romanists and the Dissenters, go as far as we do in asserting the royal supremacy? They will not. The Evangelicals, perhaps, may go to this extent; but the rest will in most cases deny that the royal supremacy ought to extend to all classes of men, and to all causes and things in this realm. We therefore claim to be the firmest upholders of the principle of the royal supremacy. We uphold it strictly, according to the declarations of the State itself, and of the Church in harmony therewith.

However, supposing that the various parties opposed to the Church of England do go as far as we do, and assert that the royal supremacy extends over all the people of this realm in ecclesiastical matters, we have nothing further to add, than to express our entire assent to the principle, and to explain that the utmost we seek is, that the royal supremacy shall be applied *equally* to all classes of the community, as the Church declares it ought to be. We are perfectly willing to admit that the supremacy ought to be exercised over the Church of England, just as it is over all the rest of the realm. We have not the slightest objection to the supremacy of a Christian sovereign over the English Church; but we think it is only fair to expect, that when the sovereigns have consented to transfer the exercise of their supremacy to persons who may be either themselves alien from the religion of the English Church, or under the influence of sectarians, the supremacy should be exercised towards the Church just as it is towards all other denominations,—that is, the Church should be, practically, free. If we admit the principle of the Articles and the Thirty-sixth Canon, and the Act of Supremacy, that the Queen's Majesty is supreme over all persons, things, and causes within this realm, and her other dominions, one point is very distinctly established,—that the appointment of bishops, and the summoning of synods, and the confirmation of their canons are *no part of the royal supremacy.* This may sound startling, and yet it is demonstrably true. For, observe the actual state of the case : bishops are appointed by the Roman Catholics in England, Ireland, and Scotland, and in Canada, Malta, and all the English colonies—" other Her Majesty's dominions"—without any claim, on the part of the Crown, to interfere in their appointment. The State—the law—*recognize* these persons, so appointed, *as bishops.* The law acknowledges their episcopal rank and jurisdiction over a portion of the people of the realm. Therefore, assuming that the law considers the Queen to be supreme over all her subjects, it is plain that the appointment to bishoprics is not a part of her supremacy. The law also recognizes the episcopal character of the bishops of Scotland,—it admits them to be bishops—and yet the Crown does not appoint them.

And now to consider the case of synods. The Roman Catholics in Ireland have lately held a national synod without asking the license of the Crown to meet, or seeking any confirmation from the Crown for their canons or regulations. The Wesleyan Methodists and Dissenters hold synods without being obliged to ask the Crown's leave or sanction. If, then, we hold that the royal supremacy extends to the whole realm and to all causes, and things, and degrees, it is evident that we cannot admit the summoning and confirming of synods to be amongst the essentials of the royal supremacy, because the law sanctions the people of this realm in holding synods without reference to the Crown.

We are aware that such inferences may not be palatable to some persons, but they have only one alternative—either they must hold with the Church of England and the act of supremacy, that the Crown has supremacy in ecclesiastical things or causes over the whole realm, in which case they must admit that the appointment of bishops and the summoning of synods are no part of the supremacy ; or else they must hold in contradiction to the Church of England, and of the whole theory of the constitution, and the whole body of the old statutes, that the Queen is *not* supreme in ecclesiastical things or causes over the whole realm, but only over a part of it—or over some portion of the people. If they maintain this latter principle, they undermine the supremacy, for they separate it from the royal power, in pronouncing that it is not universal. They make it a privilege, an advantage, a possession of the Crown—just as the Crown lands are a portion of the rights of the Crown, and yet are not inalienable. If the supremacy relates merely to the Church of England, it is a prerogative of the Crown, but it is not an inalienable prerogative : it is not an essential of the Crown's rights, which cannot be parted with. If others are exempted from the supremacy, the question occurs at once, why should not the Church of England be also ? It becomes then at once a question of expediency ; Whether it be or be not advisable to extend the same rule which applies to Dissenters to the Church of England also ? On this view it is quite impossible to defend the continuance of the supremacy over the English Church alone, as a matter of *principle*. Those who take this ground, must be contented to argue on grounds of expediency only.

We sincerely hope that these questions will be fully and freely discussed. In the present day all that is wanted is full inquiry. The Church of England will largely profit by the fullest investigation. We have seen a species of declaration put forth by some distinguished members of the Church of England on the subject of the royal supremacy, and the sense in which they understand it. We do not wish to express any opinion on this document further than this, that we trust it will lead to further inquiry, and to full discussion. We are at present living amidst a curious jumble of the institutions and principles of the sixteenth and the nineteenth century, which are diametrically opposed to each other. Inquiry and attention will dissipate the absurdities by which we are surrounded, and make " civil and religious liberty" as it should be— not merely the privilege of the Dissenters, but of *all* the people of England.

We have entitled this paper " Church Emancipation." We may as well explain what we mean by this term. We do not mean by it the liberation of the Church from the royal supremacy, or from the influence of Parliament. We mean by " Church Emancipation" nothing more or less than the liberty of Churchmen to settle the affairs of their own Church, without any interference, direct or indirect, by persons of any other religion, or of no religion at all. This is the point we contend for. It may and will involve the repeal of laws and the modification of the relations of the English Church with the imperial power ; but this is not the principle for which we contend. That principle is, that Churchmen shall, like all other Englishmen, be exempt from the interference in their religious concerns of persons who are not of their own communion. If this principle can be carried out without materially altering the laws, or depriving the Crown of any privilege it exercises, so much the better ; if not, we still claim what is nothing but plain and common justice. Churchmen alone are not to be left without freedom in religious matters, and obliged to submit to the interference of persons alien from their creed. They are not to be made the only exception to the general rule. Their claim for emancipation from the rule of persons not of their own creed, is one that only requires to be heard, in order to convince every fair-minded man of its justice and its moderation. That claim may be opposed for a time by clamour and misrepresentation; but if it is steadily persisted in, it must, in the end, be heard and conceded.

We therefore think that it is the duty of Churchmen to go forward firmly and unflinchingly in their course, seeking on all occasions the restitution of their religious liberties; and with a full confidence that they will eventually be attained. They must not be discouraged, or turned away from their purpose, by the attacks or the devices of their opponents. We have long foreseen the probability that the Evangelical party will not continue in its state of quiescence. They were kept quiet, evidently by Government and by the archbishops, for some time after the decision on the Gorham case. This was in accordance with the policy of the Government and the Privy Council party, who declared that the judgment had given general satisfaction, and who were extremely anxious that no movements should take place, but that the judgment should be allowed to pass at once as an undisputed law. When the opponents of the judgment began to make themselves heard, there was still evidently an *enjoined* silence maintained by the other party: it was curious to observe how anxiously their journals avoided notice of the subject, lest they should increase the excitement. *Then*, the feeling of the country began to show itself so very decidedly *against* the judgment, that there was equal discretion manifested in avoiding an attempt to elicit approbation of the judgment, which would probably have proved a failure. So that the Privy Council party had the great discomfort of seeing the whole display of public feeling against them. They had to sit by, and hear the most open confession of the truth by large masses of clergy and laity in every part of the country; to be condemned by bishops, and to witness great public meetings of laity and clergy against their views. All this was, of course, most trying to the tempers of the more violent partisans, who were thus curbed by orders from their superiors, on the wisdom of which they have probably had many a misgiving.

The Government having now succeeded in defeating any attempt which might have led to the immediate reversal of the decision of the Privy Council, are probably indifferent as to what course matters take; and hence there will, doubtless, be no opposition on their part, and that of the archbishops, to an organization of the Evangelical party for the purpose of counteracting the movements of the Church party. We shall probably see, ere long, the Evangelicals, who have hitherto been declaring on all occasions in the course of this controversy, that their whole wish is, that different parties and principles may live in affectionate fraternity in the same Church, as they have "always" done,—we shall see them now, most probably, adopting some course of directly aggressive policy, with a view of driving out of the Church those brethren to whom they are so much attached. It will probably be seen, ere long, that their notions of *toleration* are meant only to apply to persons of their own opinions. Their object will, probably, be to strike up a firm alliance with the State, in the expectation that the whole patronage of the Church will fall into their hands; and to endeavour to thwart the objects of Churchmen by directing against them a series of attacks, with the object of withdrawing their attention from the objects before them to their own defence. They will endeavour to carry the war into the enemy's territories, to compel him to act on the defensive. We have little doubt that this will be the course of policy pursued; Churchmen should be on their guard against being diverted by it from their objects. They must pursue their objects and defend themselves at the same time. We recommend great caution in dealing with the movements of any organization of Evangelicals; it will be conducted with much craft; and the Union movement must not be ready to take the course to which it may be provoked by its opponents.

Without doubt the great weapon employed in future against the Emancipationists will be, as it *has* been, misrepresentation of their objects and principles. There is but one way of meeting this. The objects and principles of the friends of Church liberty must be made as clear as the day *by themselves*, so that misrepresentation may only recoil on its authors. There must be no lurking suspicion left; but Churchmen must come forward so manfully and so openly with an account of their purposes, that it will be IMPOSSIBLE to slander them. When this is done, the whole strength of the opposition to them will be at an end. They will go on without any material let or impediment. But, let them pursue any policy of concealment, let them refrain from making their principles and objects unequivocally manifest, let there be any opportunity for the enemy to calumniate them, and represent them as *Romanists*,—and they will certainly fail.

On this account, as well as for other reasons of equal urgency, we would strongly recommend, that the greatest possible care and discrimination should be exercised in future in the choice of persons who are to hold any official or leading position in the Church movement. No man should be selected to fill such offices unless he possess the *first grand requisite of a firm faith in the English Church*, as she stands distinguished from Romanism and from other systems of religion. Without this essential qualification, no amount of rank, virtue, ability, or learning, should recommend any man to a prominent and leading position. If he does not stand forth and give clear and satisfactory evidence of the staunchness of his principles—if he refuses to give satisfaction to inquiries, but permits some mystery to hang over his sentiments on the fundamental point of adhesion *ex animo* to the creed and communion of the English Church in preference to the Roman, and to all others, he should be at once set aside as ineligible. It will not any longer do in these times to have doubtful, wavering, undecided men as leaders, who may shortly fall away from the Church, and who will always be sure to favour a weak, timid, tortuous, and unpopular course of policy. None but firm and open adherents of the English Church should be trusted to lead the cause of that Church. No cold and doubtful men will be a gain to that cause. We must have a bold, open, undisguised course of policy. We must plainly say what we want, and be prepared to prove that it is necessary for the security of the Church of England ; and if we act thus, no power can avail to crush our claims. If Evangelicals, and Rationalists, and Erastians, and Infidels misrepresent us, and oppose us, their misrepresentations will be only injurious to themselves if we are thoroughly honest, and thoroughly open and bold. If we merely seek for liberty—for the national rights of freedom which the constitution extends to all but ourselves ; and if we merely seek what we sincerely conceive and believe to be essential to the security of our own religion ; it will be impossible to raise any permanent feeling against us. If our opponents succeed in creating an opposition for a time, the people will fall away from them when they have ascertained the facts of the case ; and we shall then succeed.

To the Church, then, our advice is, to set aside all political parties—none of whom can be trusted :—to follow no political leaders :—to let Whigs and Conservatives, Free Traders and Protectionists—men in office and men out of office—settle their disputes as best they may. Let the Church—we mean the Church element within the Church—have nothing to do with party politics of any kind—because no parties can be trusted. Instead of thus depending on statesmen, let them throw themselves on the people—the sovereign people !—Let them engage the people on their side, and their work is done.

In applying to the people, the Church would apply to the real sovereign of the country. The supreme power is vested in their hands by the recent changes in the constitution. **England is a republic** with monarchical and aristocratical forms; but the people have a power before which all others in the State bend. Hitherto the Church of England has been altogether a royalist and an aristocratic Church: it is now bound to become a popular Church also. It is of much more importance to her to stand well with the people than with the other parts of the State. She is bound on principle to please the people, because they have been virtually invested with sovereignty by law. If the Church gains the support of the people, she will have the support of the Sovereign and the aristocracy.

Now on what principles must the cause of the Church be brought before the people? We can tell our learned theologians, and our subtle reasoners, that all their systems must be unlearned again, if they are to make any impression on the people. They may do well enough for educated, refined, thoughtful people; but they are simply unintelligible to the great mass of the population, *i. e.* to ninety-nine out of every hundred of our people. They cannot enter into discussions on Baptism and its effects. They cannot discriminate between "High Church" and "Low Church." Convocations and synods they know nothing about. They do not care a single farthing about the spiritual rights of the Church, or its liberties, &c. They, perhaps, know very little about any particular doctrines; and they see no danger in Evangelicalism, or any other "ism"—*except* Romanism. Now then, it is plain, that in applying to the people, "learning" and "eloquence," and so forth, will not be of the slightest use:—they will be rather a hinderance.

How, then, are the people to be influenced? There is but one way of moving them.—In the first place, they must be taught their duty to *obey* the law of the land, even if it should be an unjust law. They may then be led to see in what condition the law places them. They must be taught that they are a *degraded* and *enslaved* set of men; that they have not the religious liberties which Dissenters and Romanists possess; that Romanists and Dissenters regulate the affairs of the Church, though they will not let Churchmen interfere in their affairs; that we are suffering under a gross injustice, and are liable to continual insults from persons of different denominations. Put before the people the insulting language of Romanists and Dissenters charging the Church with being the slave of the State. Teach them to feel themselves insulted and degraded, and treated with injustice; and then "the Sovereign power" will begin to move in our favour. We think that if this course is pursued, eventual success is certain. Let the people of the Church once be brought to feel that they are injured, and that they have grievances to complain of; and nothing can or will prevent them from obtaining a remedy. Ministers may oppose, and Evangelicals may unite with them; but the sense of *wrong* once well-rooted will, in the end, prevail over all opposition; and those who are on the side of slavery will go to the wall. In order, however, to bring forward the cause of the Church with any reasonable prospect of success, the ordinary machinery must be provided for the purpose of setting the members of the Church to work in the right direction. Amongst the publications which have appeared in various ways, bearing on this subject, we have not seen any which appears to be equal in ability of conception and healthiness of tone to that which bears the name of Mr. Denison—the leader of the Church movement on the Education question. The gratitude which is due to Mr. Denison for his untiring advocacy of the Church's cause, and which is, we are assured, most widely and deeply felt, will at once ensure an attentive hearing to him on any subject bearing on the general interests of the Church. No man has more fully established his right to be heard on such questions. Mr. Denison apologizes in his advertisement for asking public attention at the present crisis; but none of his readers will feel that such an apology was requisite from him.

We are very glad to see that Mr. Denison is of opinion that the time has come to get beyond the Gorham case. We cannot go on eternally disputing on this case. It is now an established *fact*. The results and tendencies of that fact constitute a large item in the perils affecting the Church. Still, like the Hampden case, it is virtually settled, as far as the present law is concerned, and it would be unwise to go on attempting to found further agitation on that special case: it must now take its place in the general list of grievances. We entirely concur therefore in the following remarks of Mr. Denison :—

" It is no part of the writer's purpose to review any particulars of the Gorham case—all this has been already done—thoroughly and effectually done. The many fallacies of the judgment of the Supreme Court have been dragged to light—the claim of that judgment either to ability or truthfulness has been set aside—the sin of betraying the FAITH in the matter of Mr. Gorham's institution needs no further proof. It is time now for Churchmen to take off their minds, so far as may be, from this special case, as from a *detail*, and to fix them upon the *principle*, or rather upon the *negation of principle*, which has enabled Mr. Gorham to obtain an unworthy triumph over his diocesan, over the CHURCH and the FAITH. This negation of principle, including, first, the denial of objective truth, and, secondly, the absolute ignoring of the primitive and Catholic position of the Church of England—this negation of principle, upon which *alone* the judgment of the Supreme Court can be maintained, is the very spirit of anti-christ, tricked out in the garb of a more enlightened reason, and a more enlarged charity."

Mr. Denison remarks, with great feeling, on the painful position of Churchmen in these days, in finding themselves obliged to defend the faith of the Church against a State which had been for so many ages united to her in the closest alliance. It is our only consolation under this painful alienation, to feel that it has not been the work of the Church; that we have not to reproach ourselves for those alterations which have impressed a Latitudinarian and creedless character on the State, and have rendered it a perilous ally to us. There has been a continual protest against the various acts of legislation and policy by which the State has been so widely severed in faith from the Church. And yet it must be admitted, as Mr. Denison remarks, that the Church has not in fact resisted, as she ought to have done, the encroachments of the State on her spiritualities. She has not been alive, as she ought to have been, to the dangers thence arising. And why is this? We must ascribe it in great measure to her habitual dependence on the Government, and on the Hierarchy. That dependence, connected with the highest and best principles, and justified to some extent by the experience of former times, long prevented the Church at large from viewing her real position, and protecting herself. In depending on the State, or political parties in it, all freedom and energy was lost. Men were taught still to look solely to a temporal power, which was gradually ceasing to possess any religious principle. And the Episcopate has always been, for the most part, under the influence of the State to so great an extent, that it has never dared to move for the liberties of the Church. It has been divided in opinion, and has been unable to act together. Of course, the Church, in depending on the Episcopate to be led, has virtually relinquished all action on such questions. We are not quite prepared to agree with all that Mr. Denison says, in reference to the silence of so many of the bishops on the recent theological question. We have no doubt that several prelates, who have not spoken so openly as might have been wished, have not been restrained by any doubt on the question itself. Yet the expression of opinion ought to have been stronger and more unanimous on such an occasion; and it is lamentable to observe some prelates preaching "peace" in such a matter, or declaring that the faith is not in any way endangered.—But such things must be, while the Episcopate is nominated by the heads of political parties.

But there are other internal dangers besides these; and to one of them Mr. Denison draws attention in these words:—

" There are other Churchmen again ; men in one sense sound in the faith themselves, *i. e.* who profess the faith, but profess it as matter of their own subjective belief, not as matter of the objective belief of THE CHURCH CATHOLIC; who are very dangerous to THE CHURCH; men who hold contradictory positions ; men who hold the Scriptural doctrine of Regeneration in Baptism, and yet approve of the judgment of the judicial committee ; men who tell us to cease from contention about the doctrine of sacramental grace, and to unite with them in stemming the flood of infidelity, which is *about to assail*—they might say, which *has already* assailed—even the inspiration of the Scriptures. Do these not see, then, that the only ground upon which the battle of the judgment can be fought, is the very ground upon which are planted the outposts of the infidel ? Do they not see that the *denial* of *all* truth is aptly preceded by the *indifference* to any *specific form of it ;* and that the judgment of the judicial committee has but re-echoed the memorable question asked on the day of our redemption in the judgment-hall of doomed Jerusalem ; " What is truth ?" Or do they really think it possible that those who are content that the judgment should be such as it is, can ever be united for any good purpose with those whose daily prayer it is that they may have grace even to lay down their lives, so that one step might thereby be made towards blotting it out for ever from the records of the Church of England, and effectually preventing the recurrence of so perilous an experiment for the time to come ? "

After some further remarks on the possible rupture of the alliance between Church and State, in consequence of the proceedings of the latter power, Mr. Denison thus states the alternatives now before the Church :—

" 1. Submission to the claim of the State to create bishops, without regard being had to the judgment of the spiritualty as to their fitness for ' the office and work of a Bishop in THE CHURCH OF GOD.' Submission to the claim of the State to insist upon the institution of priests to benefices with cure of souls, without regard being had to the judgment of the spiritualty as to their fitness, at the time of institution, for ' the office and work of a priest in THE CHURCH OF GOD.' Submission to the claim of the State to insist upon any profanation of the offices of THE CHURCH, which may result from the application of those offices indiscriminately to all persons, whether in communion with THE CHURCH or not. Submission to the claim of the State to exercise that interference with the matter and the manner of the education of the people, which it is utterly impossible the State can exercise in any degree, consistently with the due discharge of the responsible office of the ministry of THE CHURCH.

" This is the first of the three things presented to the choice of the Church of England. It is the *existing* state of things,—a state of things in which the civil power does in effect claim, however it may disavow such a claim, to be supreme judge both of doctrine and discipline; to exercise a virtual control over the whole matter and manner of the education of the people. The claim is, indeed, protested against here and there, and some demands are made for redress, and *so far as this is done,* individual Churchmen are free from the guilt of acquiescence.

" But there is no *redress,* nor any *prospect of redress,* that I know of.

" 2. The second thing is to allow the existing submission to become *absolute, i. e.* to cease from protesting and demanding redress. In short, to submit, not, as now, in the hope of the dawn of better times, but because it has become the general opinion that, after all, it is as well to submit. In other words, to continue to be THE ESTABLISHMENT, but to cease absolutely to be THE CHURCH : because the sacred trust committed by the great HEAD OF THE CHURCH into the hands of the spiritualty, will have been abandoned and betrayed.

" 3. The third thing is to combine, as under a sense of the most imminent danger, and as warned of GOD, for the defence and assertion of the rights and liberties of THE CHURCH, and of her claim to be allowed duly to discharge those special functions, the due discharge of which is the very essence and principle of her original constitution by our BLESSED LORD.

" I believe I have fairly stated the case,—neither overstated it, nor understated it."

Those who are advising us to " be quiet," and to let " peace" return to the Church, are of course acting on their own view of what is best for the Church ; and it is quite right that they should be listened to with respect and good feeling. But they take so different a view of the state of things from others, that they cannot expect to have any influence with them. Those who wish us to be " at peace," and to let the State in general, and the Privy Council in particular, regulate our religious and educational affairs as they please, will not be able to enter into the principles and views which influence men like Mr. Denison. His view is this, and we believe it to be the only sensible view :

" Whatever may have been the case hitherto, THE CHURCH *cannot* any longer rest satisfied with protests and demands for redress from individuals or private bodies of her members : she *cannot,* because if she does, *she will die ;* that she *will not,* the last few years have served to indicate. The time is come now when the indication must be converted into a certainty, and THE CHURCH must set her own seal upon a great system of agitation, because it is plainly written upon the wall, that *if she do not she must shortly die."*

Some good men think, that by refraining from " agitation," and permitting the events to take their course, the Church will act most for her own security. All they want is " peace," and they persuade themselves that if " agitation " could be suppressed, there would be an end of dangers. They cannot endûre the barking and growling of the guardian of the fold. They would silence him, and trust to the mercy of the wolves who are prowling outside. They would disband the military retainers who walk about the towers of Zion, and leave themselves defence-less. They imagine that their deeds of benevolence and of charity—their obedience to the "powers that be"—their in-offensiveness and blamelessness, would save them from enemies to whom the very existence of those virtues and good works is the sorest of reproofs and the cause of the bitterest enmity and hatred. They trust in a State which has shown in all its acts that it is open to no considerations whatever but those of earthly policy, and temporary expediency—to a State which has given power to the hereditary enemies of the Church to legislate for her, and in all ways to interfere with her. With every possible respect for the good intentions of those who recommend a course of submission to this state of things, we must express our convic-tion that their policy is simply suicidal; and that the only safe policy is a bold, a resolute, and an open one. In the words of Mr. Denison :—

" *Churchmen must combine throughout the length and breadth of the land.* There has been such a thing *without* the pale of THE CHURCH, as 'a solemn league and covenant.' I am not afraid to say that there must be an analogous combination now *within* the pale of THE CHURCH. The great object of THE CHURCH's league and covenant must be the immediate restoration of her synodal action. So soon as this is attained and placed upon sure ground, let all irregular action and combination at once cease and determine. Till it is attained and placed upon sure ground, *let the whole land be filled with both ;* let it be a reproach to a parish that it does not agitate; that it does not contribute something, at least, of its means and its energies, towards the effective support and encouragement of those whose immediate business it will be to superin-tend and to conduct; pressing THE CHURCH's claim in every way which is open to men in free England, upon the public mind, upon Parliament, and upon the Crown. Does any one suppose that such entire freedom to agitate and combine in THE CHURCH's cause will be denied by the civil power ; that the liberty, conceded to the Corn Law League of our days, and to the schism of an hundred years, will be denied to THE CHURCH ? I have no belief that any statesman, however liberal, will be found to attempt so direct an infringement of popular rights : the attempt itself would not simply be ridiculous; it would not simply be an egregious failure ; it would tend very power-fully to encourage the entire movement and combination, which it was its object to defeat.

" It will be obvious at once that I am contemplating a very different thing indeed from the existing action and extent of Church unions.

The resistance offered, through their organization, to the encroachments of the civil power, has been hitherto desultory, and growing out of daily circumstances. It must henceforth be systematic and concentrated, and directed, as its *final* object, to the one great end of the restoration of the synodal action of THE CHURCH, as the legitimate remedy for all her difficulties. To say that Church Unions have not been without their use,—to say this, and no more than this,—would be thankless and unjust. But no one surely can suppose that their present extent and mode of action can suffice to meet the dangers and the requirements of THE CHURCH. Without them, indeed, THE CHURCH would have been powerless, and naked of all means of combined defence against the many aggressions of the civil power during the last five years. But as these aggressions multiply, and become more aggravated and more afflicting, more full of warning and of peril to the very life of THE CHURCH, so must the means of defence be multiplied, and extended, and developed also, and brought to such state of completeness, as any irregular action of THE CHURCH will permit.

" We have at present some twenty Church Unions ; they should be reckoned by hundreds."

This is the right spirit. Churchmen must put from them all timidity, and be ready to advance their cause boldly, in the face of the world, " before rulers and kings." They must put on the energies of primitive Christianity, fearing the face of no man on earth, and girded up for the contest in firm faith in the rectitude and justice of their cause. They must put from them the retiring, modest, and unassuming virtues, which have hitherto distinguished them, and come forth as soldiers of the Cross, prepared to do and to suffer in the cause of Christian faith. Such must be their spirit and their resolution, in case circumstances should call on them to make sacrifices for Christ. They will be met by opposition, contempt, ridicule, and persecution ; they must be prepared to bear it all, and even to glory in their tribulations.

For the details of the organization proposed by Mr. Denison we must refer to his pamphlet. It includes the design of a general meeting of members of Church Unions—a certain number from each—to be held periodically. This, and the other details of the plan, appear to be perfectly practicable ; and we hope the suggestion will be in some way acted on without delay.

On the financial branch of the subject, one of the highest practical importance, Mr. Denison offers the following remarks, which contain much matter for serious thought, as involving principles of deep importance, and which we never remember to have seen stated before.

" Is it too much to ask that, when the life of THE CHURCH is at stake, we should, each of us, carefully review our position and our means, and all the arrangements of our life, set apart the utmost we can give for Church Union purposes, *and make a great point of punctual payment?*

"But the exigencies and the nature of the case demand that we should go much further even than this. And I have two suggestions to offer,—the second of which is, I know, very little likely to be received favourably; but I offer it, nevertheless, because I know of nothing which represents so powerfully my own sense of the extent and the magnitude of the evil that has come upon us.

"First, then, I would suggest, that collections be made every year in our Churches, in aid of a fund, to be applied, at the discretion of the central consulting body, for promoting the restoration of the synodal action of THE CHURCH. There can be no just exception taken against making collections in our Churches for such a purpose. The restoration of the synodal action of THE CHURCH is, undoubtedly, a great and legitimate Church object,—I should say, especially under present circumstances, the greatest and the most legitimate.

"The second suggestion I have to offer—and which I entreat Churchmen to believe, that nothing but a deep conviction of our imminent peril would have persuaded me to offer at all—is this—that, if it be found impossible to give money for *all* Church purposes, that purpose, *which is the first and most pressing of them all*, and the present frustration of which is at the bottom of much of our present distress— I mean the restoration of the synodal action of THE CHURCH—should hold the *first* place, and that, if need be, all other purposes—whether these be *even* the support of the Church Societies—or such purposes again as the restoration and decoration of churches—or any other of those many ways in which Churchmen are denying themselves for THE CHURCH's sake—should give place to it, and that the money bestowed upon such purposes now should be given—until we get our synodal action fully and freely restored—in aid of this same fund. Now, as respects the Church Societies, a feeling of indignation, by no means an unnatural one, will doubtless arise in many minds, that any one should be found to make a proposal like this. Others again, who may have no strong feeling upon the matter, may say that it is like proposing to cut off the limbs to enable the body to move more freely. My reply to the first is, that it is not because I do not wish the Church Societies to flourish, but because I wish them to flourish *healthily* under the shelter of THE CHURCH herself, that I have made my suggestion; and my reply to the second is of the same kind,—that the body is diseased, and the limbs more or less infected thereby, and that before the limbs can do their office well, and before the discharge of that office can be a true sign of the body's vigorous life, that life and vigour must be found within the body itself. Till we get our synodal action, I doubt whether the working of the Church Societies can be really healthy; and what, after all, is the real " *bond fide*" use of Church Societies, if we cannot save THE CHURCH herself? Convocation, or Synod, is the one great

object before us—the one great point of safety : no support of Church
Societies will bring us nearer to Convocation ; once get Convocation,
and Church Societies will be placed on a far more satisfactory footing
than they are now.   If, however, Churchmen shrink from withdrawing
their contributions, of whatever kind, from the Church Societies, for
the above purpose, they will, I think, hardly refuse to place the Church
Emancipation Fund side by side with the funds of the societies, and to
make the same exertions for the one as for the other."

Without doubt there is much in this that is in a great degree
novel to us.   We have been so much accustomed to look to certain machinery for ordinary Church institutions, as the great object
which demands our sacrifices and our exertions, that the notion
of putting the demands of the Church Emancipation cause on a
level with them, or even above them, appears to us, at first sight,
somewhat startling ; yet we think that the more the point is examined, the sounder will appear the principles of the above passage.   If the very essence of the Church is endangered by the
present system, nothing can be of so much importance as to
correct that system and obtain security for the Church.   In times
of war the institutions of peace languish : in times of extraordinary peril, resources must be gained, if necessary, by severe
sacrifices.   Every thing may be dispensed with, save the great
duty of standing by the faith of the Church.

This sacred cause is not to be worthily defended by any men
who are themselves of ambiguous faith.   He who leads the host
of the Lord must not shrink from declaring himself solemnly to
be on the Lord's side, lest in the midst of the contest he should
be found a recreant and a deserter.   These are times in which
men must "speak out," in more senses than one.   They must
not permit their intentions to remain doubtful in reference to the
great point of adhesion to the faith and communion of the Church
of England.   They must make their choice between the Church
of England and Rome, and not shrink from declaring whose they
are.   If, from any cause whatever, they shrink from this, they
are not fitted to be leaders of the Church's cause.   We cannot afford to have leaders who cannot be depended on.   For the
following noble declaration of his adhesion to the Church, we are
deeply grateful to Mr. Denison.   We have always felt that
nothing less than the firm faith which the following declaration
breathes throughout, could have carried its author through his
exertions in the Education cause :—

"In coming forward, as I have now done, with an appeal to Churchmen to combine for the defence of THE CHURCH, and for the recovery
of her rights and liberties, and to make exertions, not in degree only,

but in kind also, such as have not been made hitherto, I feel that it would be inexcusable if I were to leave any room for a doubt as to what I mean when I use the words 'the defence of THE CHURCH,' and that I may be allowed, under the peculiar and pressing evils of these times, to make here a PROFESSION OF FAITH.

"I mean, then, the defence of the doctrine and the discipline of the Church of England, as distinguished, on the one hand, from the corruptions of Rome, and her. additions to the Faith; and, on the other, from the miserable results of the abuse of private judgment, and from the licence of those religious bodies who have, from whatever cause, departed from Apostolical order, and have devised 'Churches' without 'the Succession.' I mean the defence of the doctrine and the discipline of the Church of England as restored, after the model of primitive Christianity, in the sixteenth century.

"I am not concerned to defend the manner in which this was done, or all the agents in it, or all the parts of the act itself. But, if I rightly understand the true position of an English Churchman, it is this: that, looking back upon the events of the sixteenth century, and setting on one side the evils of severance of communion in which those events involved the Church of England, and, over and above these, the manifold evils of the abuse of private judgment; and, on the other side, the good which the same events produced in clearing away corruptions of the Faith, and in restoring amongst us primitive Christianity, he acknowledges, thankfully, and in strict accordance with true Church principles, that the good very far overbalances and outweighs the evils, great as these undoubtedly are, and blesses God that his lot has been cast in the Church of England. I have never been able to understand, I cannot understand now, in this, the darkest, hour of the Church of England, what it is that has power to prevail with our brethren to desert her Communion."

We must now bring our remarks to a close. We rejoice to believe and to know that such principles as Mr. Denison here so manfully avows, are deep-rooted in the hearts of the Clergy and Laity of England; and in this, under God, is our hope that the Church will gain what she requires. To that deep-rooted faith— to that firm and unswerving devotion to the English Church, we look with confidence—nay, with certainty—for the maintenance of those principles in which we have been nurtured. Come what may, the true sons of the Church will stand firmly arrayed beneath their banner; and though many should fall away—though they should be assailed on all sides—though even their Spiritual Rulers should depart from the faith, or yield to the pressure of an unbelieving State—the CHURCH OF ENGLAND can never fail, while even a few are found faithful to their principles and to each other.

Art. VI.—1. *The Testimony. To the Patriarchs, Archbishops, Bishops, and others in places of Chief Rule in the Church of Christ throughout the Earth, and to the Emperors, Kings, Sovereign Princes, and Chief Governors over the Nations of the Baptized.* 4to Edition. Printed by C. Morgan, Henry-street, Pentonville. 8vo Edition. Printed by Moyes & Barclay, Castle-street, Leicester-square.

2. *Narrative of Events affecting the Position and Prospects of the whole Christian Church.* Printed for Private Circulation, by George Barclay, Castle-street, Leicester-square. 1847.

3. *Proclamation of the Twelve Apostles of the Church of Jesus Christ of Latter Day Saints, to all the Kings of the World, to the President of the United States of America, to the Governors of the several States, and to the Rulers and People of all Nations.* Liverpool: Woodruff. 1845.

4. *Letters exhibiting the most Prominent Doctrines of the Church of Jesus Christ of Latter Day Saints. By* Orson Spencer, *A.B., President of the Church of Jesus Christ, of L. D. S. in Europe. In reply to the Rev. William Crowell, A. M., Boston, Massachusetts, U. S. A.* Liverpool: Orson Spencer. 1848.

5. *Divine Authority; or, the Question, Was Joseph Smith sent of God? No. I. The Kingdom of God. Nos. II. and III. By* Orson Pratt, *one of the Twelve Apostles of the Church of Jesus Christ of Latter Day Saints.* Liverpool. 1848.

6. *A Dialogue between Joseph Smith and the Devil.* No date.

7. *Absurdities of Immaterialism; or, a Reply to T. W. P. Taylder's Pamphlet, entitled, " The Materialism of the Mormons, or Latter Day Saints, Examined and Exposed." By* Orson Pratt, *one of the Twelve Apostles of the Church of Jesus Christ of Latter Day Saints.* Liverpool. 1849.

8. *Friendly Warnings on the Subject of Mormonism. Addressed to his Parishioners by a Country Clergyman.* London: Rivingtons. 1850.

Multiform as error is in its very nature, as the Protean counterfeit of unchanging truth, there are certain types and categories of error which re-appear from time to time, under different circumstances and under different aspects, yet with a certain kind of family likeness by which their kindred origin may be discerned. We drew attention to this fact when, some time ago, we gave an account of the Irvingite delusion [1]. We then pointed out the resemblance between the rise of the Irvingite sect in our own times, and that of the Montanists in the early Church, and of the French Prophets at the beginning of the eighteenth century. Since then our researches into the history of religious aberrations have brought us acquainted with another modern delusion, which, by a singular coincidence, started in the Transatlantic world, contemporaneously with Irvingism in this country. The coincidence in the time of the origin, as well as in the manner of announcement of, the two sects, respectively, is so striking, that we cannot forbear placing side by side their own records of the fact. The register of the birth of Mormonism, the American counterpart of Irvingism, we have already placed before our readers [2] in the words of the Mormon prophet, Joseph Smith, himself, and we here transcribe it :—

"On the 6th of April, 1830, the 'Church of Jesus Christ of Latter Day Saints,' was first organized in the town of Manchester, Ontario County, State of New York. Some few were called and ordained by the Spirit of revelation and prophecy, and began to preach as the Spirit gave them utterance, and though weak, yet they were strengthened by the power of God ; and many were brought to repentance, were immersed in the water, and were filled with the Holy Ghost by the laying on of hands. They saw visions and prophesied, devils were cast out, and the sick healed by the laying on of hands. From that time the work rolled forth with astonishing rapidity." . . . .

The autobiographic notice of Irvingism is contained in the " *Narrative of Events*," (No. 2, at the head of this article,) and is to the following effect :—

"In 1830, certain members of the Church of Scotland, who had been instructed to look for and expect a revival in the Church of Christ, and to hope and desire the restoration of the gifts of the Holy Ghost for the refreshment of the weary and disheartened children of God, were visited with spiritual power, and yielding to the movement of the Spirit within them, gave utterance to the voice of the Comforter, who thus ' with stammering lips and another tongue,' according to the words of the prophet (Isaiah xxviii. 2), put to shame the spiritual pride and intellectual drunkenness of the age, and in tongues and prophesying offered rest and refreshing to the simple and childlike, to those weaned from

[1] English Review, vol. ix. pp. 13—50.
[2] Ibid. vol. xiii. p. 403.

the milk and drawn from the breast. Some persons in London, members of the Church of England, who were partakers of the like faith, received also the like answer from God ; the Holy Ghost vouchsafing to them also to speak with tongues and prophesying."—*Narrative of Events,* pp. 6, 7.

Before we proceed further, it may be well to state, that since our article on Irvingism was written, a fortunate chance has thrown in our way two of the secret documents of the sect,—the " *Testimony* [3]," and the " *Narrative of Events.*" This circumstance, coupled with the fact that we were compelled by want of space to break off our account of the Mormonite sect without giving an outline of its doctrines, has determined us to devote another paper to the development of those twin-delusions ; thus performing a half-promise which we gave to our readers at the close of our last article on the Mormonites, and at the same time putting them in possession of some curious documentary matter, to which it is, under ordinary circumstances, impossible for the uninitiated to obtain access. We could have wished to have extended our store of materials in the last-named direction ; more particularly we were desirous to get hold of two Irvingite books, which play a conspicuous part in the proceedings of the sect, viz. a manual of esoteric liturgical offices, used mainly, we believe, in the visitation of the sick ; and the book of " *Records,*" *i. e.* the written record of the prophetic "utterances" given forth from time to time. Neither of these is, as far as we have been able to learn, suffered to fall into the hands of the Irvingite "laity," being strictly confined to the angels, priests, and other office-bearers of the sect, who—with a discretion second only to that of the Romish priesthood in hiding away the Bible from their flocks— read portions of the " *Records*" in the course of the public services, taking care, withal, not to read any thing to the people which might have the effect of " stumbling them," as it is appropriately termed. In this respect, it must be confessed, the Mormonites have the advantage of their European brethren. Not only is the " *Book of Mormon*" published to the world, but that which answers to the " *Records*" of the Irvingites, the " *Book of Doctrines and Covenants,*" is circulated freely within the sect itself, and sold to the public at large. Why should not the Irvingites follow this example? The mystery in which the principal documents of their faith are enveloped, has but an ill look,

---

[3] Of the " *Testimony* " there are, as we have indicated, two editions. The large one, in 4to, appears to be the earlier one ; the small one, in 8vo, being accompanied by notes, in which various points, especially those connected with the " fourfold ministry," and the organization of the sect generally, are more fully expounded. The date of the document itself is 1837.

and says as little for the genuineness of the pretended revelations as it does for the confidence of the sectarians in the character of their contents.   There can be no good reason why such documents should be kept secret, especially in a Christian country; the inference is, that their authors themselves feel that they are unable to endure the ordeal of criticism.   If they would avoid the suspicion that the foundations of their faith will not bear the light of day, let the Irvingites openly declare " those things which are most surely believed among them."   We hereby challenge them to do so; to cast off the veil of darkness in which they have enveloped themselves, and to " come to the light." Meanwhile we will do for them, as far as it lies in our power, what they seem unwilling to do for themselves.

The characteristic feature of both Irvingism and Mormonism is the pretension to a new revelation, rendered necessary by the alleged insufficiency of the Gospel as revealed by Christ and his Apostles.   In their view of the matter, there has not been, for many ages past, any true Church of Christ upon earth.   The existing Churches of Christendom, confounded in one common condemnation with all the sects, are denounced as being altogether carnal, destitute of the spiritual endowments, and lacking the spiritual offices, which are essential to the very being of a Church.   In the midst of this spiritual desolation the two sects, respectively, profess to have been raised up as the nucleus of the restored Church, at the close of the Christian dispensation, on the eve of the second Advent.   It is upon this view of Christendom that the " *Testimony* " is founded.   After a description of the Church as she should be,—bearing the " characteristics of oneness, holiness, catholicity, and apostolicity,"—it thus portrays the " failure of the baptized :"—

" We pause from the contemplation of this mighty mystery revealed unto the holy Apostles and prophets by the Spirit, and manifested in the Church, to this intent, that unto the principalities and powers in heavenly places might be known by the Church the manifold wisdom of God; and we look abroad to behold, in the baptized, the antitype of this vision of beauty, and blessedness, and glory,—a glory which depends not on the gorgeousness of earthly splendour, but which consists in righteousness, and peace, and joy in the Holy Ghost.   We look for an united body, the saints of God, manifesting his holiness—the purity and truth which becomes his children.   We look for that ministration of the Spirit, more glorious than that of the law, through the various channels ordained in the beginning, in the completeness whereof God is revealed; for by the gifts which He hath given, He dwells in his Church.   We look for an united people, as a body, bearing witness to God in the eyes of all men, that He is their Father, and they his children—and to

whom He giveth witness before all men by the mighty works of the
Holy Ghost. We look for these things; but where can we discover
them? The goodly order framed by God for an end not yet accomplished, hath been maimed of its noblest parts, and disfigured in
its fairest proportions; instead of going on unto perfection, the body of
the baptized hath retrograded; they have cast aside or carelessly let
slip the means which God had vouchsafed for their perfecting. Had
they used the means aright, the end should have been attained. 'Their
line should have gone through all the earth, and their words unto the
end of the world.' That witness should have been the means of
gathering the good seed into the garner, and the chaff unto the un-
quenchable fire; but the very first office in the Church, Apostleship, is
men Apostles,—that fan in the hand of the Lord whereby He purges
his floor,—that ordinance whereby He baptizes with the Holy Ghost
and with fire, hath departed (whatever partial apostolic ministry may
have survived), although the end of the gift of Apostles remains yet
unattained; the voice of the Lord in prophecy, through men, given to
that end, having been despised or dreaded, hath long ceased to be
uttered, and the people of God have been left to the silence of death;
the Spirit being quenched, hath refrained to manifest Himself as in the
days of old; the Comforter hath ceased to remind concerning Jesus, those
who in heart imagined that they had need of nothing; and the powers of
the world to come, the healing of the sick, the casting out of devils, and
every other demonstration that Jesus is Lord; and that the kingdom is at
hand, have all but disappeared, for men have sought to make this world
their rest, and no longer desired the kingdom of heaven. Oh, for the
awakening of the baptized from the long lethargy in which they have
been buried! for a ceasing from the petty controversies and divisions, the
heart-burnings and oppositions, the Eastern Church against the Western,
the Roman Catholics against the Protestants, wherewith Satan hath distracted their attention, that they may look around and survey the fearful
ruins of many generations! What section of the baptized beareth in
its outward lineaments or in its inward spirit the character of the one
holy Catholic Apostolic Church? Who can look at the glories of the
beginning and measure themselves thereby, without shrinking from the
comparison? But, though man may deceive himself, God is not
mocked. In vain He searcheth the face of Christendom for the *marks*
of the Christian Church. The churches, called by divers names, furnish
them not. Unity, the foundation of all the rest, is utterly destroyed.
Without this, the others cannot be possessed. The holiness described
in Scripture, is that of a body united and visible, complete in all its
parts, each part in its own measure manifesting holiness, and all in the
measure of every part growing up in holiness. Again; without unity
and holiness, catholicity cannot exist;—an united Church, an holy people, can alone preach the Gospel to every creature, or teach all nations
to observe all things which the Lord hath commanded, can cause all
men to believe and know that God sent his Son to be the Saviour of
the world. And, lastly, the one holy Catholic Church, can alone be

apostolic, for it is in such a body alone that God hath set 'first Apostles,' and such alone can send forth Apostles, or other ministers by Apostles ordained, to bear that witness and communicate that life, for which the Church was constituted. The Christian body as it is, can send forth only the missionaries of a sect, or of many sects, to the nations of the heathen. It cannot furnish Apostles, prophets, evangelists, pastors, and teachers, to minister from the body the one Faith, and the one Spirit. Tried by the line of judgment and the plummet of righteousness, it cannot be justified. As truly as the angels left their first estate, as certainly as the nations before the flood apostatized and quenched the light given unto them from God through Adam, as surely as the Jews who crucified the Lord rejected the counsel of God against themselves, so truly the baptized have fallen from the glorious standing wherein God placed the Church at the beginning."—*Testimony*, § 52.

This "failure," or "falling away" of the baptized, began, according to the "Testimony," in the days of the Apostles themselves, so that from the apostolic age downwards, the true Church has become extinct :—

"While St. Paul continued to labour among the Churches, he was compelled to complain that they had fallen from their first love into coldness, and from their grace and liberty into bondage. The Corinthian Church, filled with spiritual gifts, the earnest of the kingdom, and the preparation of the coming of the Lord (so that, as he saith, 'ye come behind in no gift, waiting for the coming of our Lord Jesus Christ') is at the same time described in his epistles to them, as polluted with scandalous sins ; idolatry of men, and partisanship, envying and strife, disorder and rebellion. And very speedily, after but a few years of active ministry, he was delivered up bound unto the Romans ; and then we find him complaining of those even at Rome, 'who preached Christ of contention, supposing to add affliction to his bonds.' And as the last scene of martyrdom approached, and the hour of his departure was at hand, in the midst of prophecies and forebodings concerning the evil days which were coming on the Church, we find that 'all they in Asia had turned away ;' Demas had forsaken him ; 'Alexander did him much mischief,' at his first answer 'no man stood with him, but all men forsook him.' While the memory of the Apostles has been loaded by posterity with honours all but divine, they were yet in their lifetime many times despised and set at nought, both by Churches and by individuals ; and God suffered the will of man to prevail, and withdrew, but only for a time, the authority which was resisted, and the holy rule and discipline which the unholy could not endure.

"Thus does Scripture indicate the existence of sins naturally leading to the withdrawal of the apostolic function as exercised in men set apart for that purpose ; but the fact that the gift of Apostleship hath been suspended in its actual manifestation in men, Apostles, God's ordinance for its manifestation, while God's gifts are without repentance, and the purpose remains unaccomplished for which that gift was given, is of itself

the overwhelming evidence of apostasy.   The suggestion of modes
wherein God hath or might have provided for the continuance of unity
of doctrine or administration in the Church, is beside the purpose: these
substituted means can never fulfil the work to which the original instrument ordained in the wisdom of God was adapted. . . . .

"We have shown that God's ordinance for unity of spirit, of faith,
and of rule, is the Apostle ; that the law of the universal Church can
flow only from those who, under Christ, have a permanent jurisdiction
and episcopate over the whole Church throughout the world ; and that
to Apostles alone hath that authority been committed,—nor by any
other, patriarchs, bishops, or presbyters, whose power of action is practically confined to their own province, diocese, or parochial district, can
universal control be exercised, or catholic reformation be introduced.
And, therefore, the duty of all bishops, from the beginning unto this
day, yea and of all who long for the peace and welfare of Jerusalem,
should have been to cry unto God, day and night, in the first instance
to preserve, subsequently to restore, the ministry of Apostles to the
Church.

"It is true that, when and as in consequence of that unbelief
and indifference which hindered the cry from ascending to God for the
continuation of his gifts, the Apostles ceased from the Church, the
bishops, by a necessary devolution and preference, succeeded to the
chief place of authority ; but it is equally true that *in that act,
and by that necessity,* God's way of unity in his Church was
violated : and the whole experience of the Church since that period
down to the present times, when a new and more monstrous form
of wickedness has come in, has been but a perpetual struggle for
an unity to be brought about by *unlawful means*—by appeals to the
strong arm of power (the first instance whereof was to a pagan emperor, Aurelian, and so early as the middle of the third century), or by
the usurpation of one bishop over his brethren.   Such was the sin, and
such has been the punishment of the baptized as a body : the sin—that
they were content, and their rulers interestedly content, in the cessation
of the Apostleship : the punishment—the cruel tearings and rendings of
the body of Christ ; the schisms, and distractions, and divergencies in
faith and discipline ; the tyranny of the power of the State, or the
usurpation of an universal bishop.   And yet it is never to be questioned, that God, the merciful and gracious one, has always from age to
age used and honoured in his Church the best He could find in it, and
so his saints and true children have never been altogether destitute, nor
hath He ever failed to be faithful to whatever of his name and ordinances
still survived under the load of human inventions." — *Testimony,*
§ 53—55.

The reservation made in the concluding paragraph, which
allows the continuance of the Church, and of the work of salvation in some sense, and in a limited degree, is further worked out,
and the failure of the Church described as consisting in the cessa-

tion of the apostolic and prophetic offices, and in the lowering of the measure of grace given unto men :—

"This is not a question of Church government alone; we have already shown the connexion between the ministers of the Church and the ordinances for spiritual life. It is true these have been still administered, not indeed by men ordained by Apostles, and on whom the word of prophecy had gone before, but by men ordained by those who had succeeded to Apostles, in whom did rest, and by whom was dispensed, a blessing of grace indeed, but a blessing curtailed in a measure proportioned to the curtailment of the office, and to the contraction of the Church in its principal members, and consequently in the whole economy of its existence. We may not deny that a measure of the Holy Ghost has been given by the laying on of bishop's hands, or that grace has been bestowed in the sacraments, administered by those whom they ordain; for that would be contrary to the verity of the continued existence of the Church as the body of Christ, and would imply that the Church had failed altogether; but it would be equally contrary to God's truth and the verity of the Church, to assert that a bishop is God's ordinance for bestowing the Holy Ghost, according to his own perfect way, revealed in his word, or that it is a matter of indifference whether the medium be a bishop or an apostle. For as we have said in respect of the pastoral, so we say of this function. An apostle is given of God, to rule over the universal Church, to confer the Holy Ghost by imposition of hands, and to minister the Spirit in all his fulness to bishops and all others. A bishop is a *bishop*, and not an apostle; with his own ministry to fulfil, however, and with a limited grace to confer, in the confines of a limited jurisdiction.

"It is true, that, although apostles and prophets had ceased, the Church was still, and hath ever been, complete in her head in the heavens. He was still the Apostle and Prophet to his people, and the Church was still *the body*, capable of receiving the ministrations of those offices in men, and of containing those manifested members (although not as it ought ever to have been, visibly complete in those memberships on the earth). And, therefore, it hath ever been possible that, as his wisdom might determine, those ministries should again be put forth in men, apostles and prophets. He could provide, and He hath provided, that his Church should never fail. But there hath been no change of plan, no secondary instrumentality for effecting his purpose, the first having failed, and been set aside as useless. The first, indeed, hath hitherto failed through the sin of his people, and He hath used what instruments He could, until He might again bring forth his first ordained means among a people who should have faith to receive them. But they have not been withdrawn, nor has their office been supplied without miserable loss. The full instrumentality by which the Holy Ghost ministereth grace to the baptized is not in operation, and, therefore, the full grace is not ministered; the gifts, by means whereof the Lord God might dwell among men, have not been retained; and the abiding presence of God hath been exchanged for a condition wherein the glory of th: God of Israel hath seemed to be obscured—hath, as it were, removed from off the holy resting-place, and hath been fain to linger on the threshold. The ordinances expressly provided of God for conveying life unto the Church, and the principal ordinances for circulating it from member to member, have been stayed; and the stream of life hath flowed scantily, and circulated feebly; the growth of the Church hath been hindered, all things have retrograded, and God's purpose in the Church hath rested in abeyance.

"The sacraments, therefore, being now administered by men who received their commission through inferior means, and unto a people who, as a body, could not be receiving the full ministry of the Holy Ghost—seeing that the ordained channel for that end was lacking,—have ceased to be the living realities they were intended to be,—the faith which in its wane could not retain the principal ministries of the Church, was insufficient to apprehend the full blessing in the sacraments. The disputes and controversies concerning sacraments are the standing evidence of apostasy and unholiness. If the baptized had continued in the enjoyment of the inward grace, there could have been no room for disputation as to the outward means. If the life of Jesus were manifested in their mortal bodies, and the mighty powers of the world to come exercised; if the Church were revealed as the true abode of the Lord Jesus Christ—by the Holy Ghost, and his real presence demonstrated by the changing of the faithful into his image from glory to glory—there could be no dispute whether initiatory ordinances were merely outward marks of Christian profession and an admission into outward privileges, or whether they impressed a spiritual and indelible character on the souls of the recipients, whether grace be conferred in sacraments, or merely faith be assured. But when faith ceases to realize, and to educe in the life and conduct, that the baptized are dead with Christ, and, through faith, freed from sin,—'dead unto sin, but alive unto God, through Jesus Christ our Lord,'—they cease to bear witness to God that He is faithful to his ordinances, and their unholiness is the practical denial that baptism is any thing else than a mere passport for admission to the outward privileges of the Church. And when the glorious mystery of the true sacramental presence of the Lord Jesus Christ in the Holy Communion, and of the true partaking of his most holy flesh and blood, has lost its spiritual and genuine demonstration in a people *consciously* and *manifestly* dwelling in the Lord, and He in them, through the Holy Ghost, they, conscious of their loss, have sought, by means which must infallibly lead to deeper evils,—by pageantry presented to the eye, or by ingenious arguments addressed to the understanding,—to set forth a truth which can only be apprehended in the Spirit."—*Testimony,* § 62—64.

The same view is taken of the subject in the "*Narrative of Events*," where it is set forth as the result of an immediate revelation :—

" At the time of the setting up of the Church in London, the APOSTLE was made to direct that the 2nd and 3rd chapters of the first book of Samuel should be read; and during the reading of these chapters words of prophecy were spoken, applying them to the present state of the priesthood throughout Christendom. Eli, grown old and blind, showed the present want of discernment and discipline in the Church, the true priestly dignity and authority nearly gone. The two sons of Eli, fulfilling the priestly office, showed the division between the episcopal and presbyterian forms of Church government; the conduct of the young men described the abuse of the priestly authority; the Churches defiled, treated, not as the holy Bride of Christ, but as harlots; the priests using the offerings of the Lord to their own advantage, and not for the glory of God. Samuel's call was applied to the work of God calling and appointing, in an extraordinary way, those who recognized his voice, and were willing to serve Him, to be priests in his house, instead of taking and using the established priesthood, who, as a body, had refused to recognize Him, and had departed from his way. 'For in those days the word of the Lord was precious, and there was no open vision.' Samuel, not knowing God's voice, but going to Eli, and learning from him that God had called him, was applied to the state in which those were among whom his voice was heard, who only recognized his purpose to use them by slow degrees, and after many private intimations; and only discerned that the call was of God from its accordance with what is found written in the ancient fathers and primitive documents of the Church. Other words were added as to the rejection of the present degenerate priesthood, and the bringing in of the true priesthood ' after the order of Melchizedec'—the priesthood in the power of an endless life. And the judgment upon the present priesthood was declared to be pronounced, though the full carrying of it out should only be seen when Solomon, the king of peace, should reign."—*Narrative of Events*, pp. 24, 25.

And in another place we have the following lamentation over the present condition of Christendom : —

" Alas! alas! for the blindness of eyes and hardness of heart of this generation. Speak to the most orthodox among them of the ministry of apostles, prophets, evangelists, and pastors, as the means of the perfecting of the Church, they do not understand what is meant; speak of the need of prophecy, they are their own prophets; speak of the unity of the Church, they say they have it, or they deny they want it ; speak of the first ' principles of the doctrine of Christ,' they are contending, might and main, for *their own views* on these subjects; but there is no unity—no standard—no certainty regarding them. They are contending, and contending in vain ; for false doctrines and wicked principles gain the upper hand daily. They are contending, and contending in vain; for without the four ministries in men, commissioned of the Lord, the Church must ever be blown about by every wind of doctrine. They are contending, and contending in vain ; for they contend against Goliath, with the unproved armour of Saul ; they meet and try to combat the attacks of the Philistines, the arguments of infidelity, by an appeal to human reason. There is no smith in all the land of Israel; the men of war go down to the Philistines to sharpen their weapons there ; the sword and the spear are wanting in the day of battle. (1 Sam. xiii. 19—22.) The glory of the Lord is departed ; the ark of God is taken. The Lord wept over Jerusalem of old, and Jerusalem now knoweth not the time of her visitation."—*Narrative of Events*, p. 50.

From these Irvingite denunciations of the existing state of Christendom, we now turn to the Mormonite view of the same subject : it is in substance the same, with this difference, however, that the condemnation of Christendom is more sweeping, and expressed in coarser and more offensive language. Orson Pratt, one of " the twelve Apostles," in his "*Kingdom of God*," says :—

" Among the vast number of national governments now upon the earth, where is there one that even professes to be the kingdom of God, or that its officers were called of God as was Aaron ? Human authority and human calling are the only powers which any nation professes to have. But there are certain petty governments, called churches, organized within these national governments, which claim Divine authority, and consider their officers authorized to act in the name of the Lord. But the great question is, Have any of them been called as Aaron was ? By *new revelation* Aaron was called. By *new revelation* the duties of his calling were made known. Have any of the Roman Catholic or Protestant officers been called by *new revelation?* Has God said one word to any of them? Do they not, with very few exceptions, declare that ' there is no later revelation than the *New Testament?*" If the revelations contained in the New Testament are the last ones given, then the persons to whom they were given, were the last ones called of God. When *new revelation* ceases to be given, officers cease to be called of God. When the calling of officers ceases, the kingdom of God ceases to be perpetuated upon the earth. Nothing is more certain, than that the church of God ceased to exist on the earth when new revelation ceased to be given. All the modern Christian churches, who deny new revelation, have no more authority to preach, baptize, or administer any other ordinance of the Gospel than the idolatrous Hindoos have; indeed, all their administrations are worse than in vain—they are a solemn mockery in the sight of God. It is a grievous sin in the sight of God, for any man to presume to baptize, unless God has authorized him by new revelation to baptize in his name. Saul, the king of Israel, lost his kingdom because he assumed the authority that did not belong to him. (1 Sam. xiii. 8—15.) Another king of Israel was smote with leprosy until the day of his death, because he attempted to administer an ordinance without being called and authorized. (2 Chron. xxvi. 16—22.) So all the baptisms and sacraments administered by modern Christian churches, who have done away new revelation, are an abomination in the sight of God. All persons who shall suffer themselves to be baptized, or partake of these ordinances through the administration of these illegal unauthorized persons, after having been duly warned of the evil thereof, will bring themselves under great condemnation before God, and unless they repent of that sin, they can in nowise be saved."—*Orson Pratt's Kingdom of God*, Part I., pp. 5, 6.

And again, in another place:—

" Since the Apostles fell asleep, the simplicity and purity of the ancient Gospel has been awfully perverted; its ordinances have been changed, especially the ordinance of baptism ; while the ordinance of the laying on of the hands for the gift of the Holy Ghost, has been almost universally done away. No churches, either among the Papists or Protestants, have taught all the first principles of the Gospel in their proper order. By this we know they are not the Church of God. God is not with them. Their sins are not forgiven them. The Holy Ghost is not given to them. And they cannot be saved in the fulness of the glory of the Father's kingdom—neither they nor their fathers for many generations past. All have gone astray, far astray, from the ancient Gospel. The Church of Christ never existed on the earth without inspired apostles and prophets in it, who administered all the laws and ordinances of the Gospel without any variation from the true and perfect pattern. But the apostate churches now on the earth, have neither inspired apostles, nor prophets, nor any other inspired officers among them, neither do they consider them necessary; and yet without inspiration or revelation—without immersion for remission of sins, or the ordinance for the gift of the Spirit,—they have the bold impudence to call themselves Christian Churches. But they have nothing to do with Christ, neither has Christ any thing to do with them, only to pour out upon them the plagues written. He has not spoken to any of them for many centuries, neither will He speak to them, only in his wrath, and the fierceness of his anger, when He riseth up to overthrow, to root up, and to destroy them utterly from the earth."—*Orson Pratt's Kingdom of God*, Part II., p. 8.

Similar is the language held by Orson Spencer, the " President of the Church in Europe:"—

" Now, Sir, what has become of this miraculous and almighty spirit? Has he ceased wholly from the earth? If so, then the WATER and the BLOOD are the only witnesses now left on the earth. But, perhaps, you will say, that the same spirit still remains, without exercising his miraculous gifts and powers (seeing they are not now necessary). Shall we then understand that this Almighty Spirit is still on the earth, and in the diversified and conflicting churches, and comparatively silent and inefficient, withholding from these churches (which are by supposition the BODY of Christ), his majestic displays of supernatural power in prophecies, healings, tongues; causing the dumb ass to speak with man's voice, causing powerful armies to flee before the pursuit of one man; and yet the world is perishing for lack of knowledge, and Christianity losing ground every day? Might we not as soon think the spirit has grown old to dotage, or lost his first love, or been beguiled into other pursuits of less importance? Surely, He never wrought so lazily, or in such imbecility and indifference in any other age, when true believers or prophets were on the earth? Strange, indeed, Sir, that he should drop off so suddenly his royal robes of prophetic, miraculous grandeur and power, to become the silent and inefficient inmate of more than six hundred clashing, contentious churches, that are yearly subdividing into minute fragments, to the confusion of all common sense throughout boasting Christendom! What a falling off of the spirit's power, and of the spirit's light and unity! Will the Holy and Eternal Spirit of God endorse such a powerless distracted state of things, as being in any way connected with his presence on the earth, or in any way the result of his doings? No, Sir, by no means. For the honour of this illustrious personage, let us never ascribe to HIM such a powerless distracted organization of heterogeneous ignorance and imbecility, as modern Christianity presents in contrast with ancient Christianity. The heavens may well blush with shame at this modern picture, purporting to be the kingdom of God on the earth. If it is the kingdom of God, how shorn of its miraculous strength! How are the prophets and seers covered!! How dim that fine gold that once shone resplendent with the celestial lustre of prophetic visions!!! Then men spoke as they were moved by the Holy Ghost, and the sick were healed, and he that lied to them was paralyzed in instantaneous death, at times.

"Orators 'boast,' as it is written of them in these 'perilous times,' of the spread of Christianity. Christianity spreading! Where is the evidence of its increase of power or knowledge? Where the least signs of approximation to 'unity of faith,' and the 'full stature measure of Christ' in 'manifold wisdom and power?' Where the ornamental beauty and symmetry of the Bride that is preparing for the marriage-feast of the Lamb? How many ten thousand years must elapse before it can be said of Christianity, 'the Bride hath made herself ready!' 'clear as the sun, fair as the moon, and terrible as an army with banners.' Surely, since her prophets have lost their power 'to quench the violence of fire, and subdue kingdoms, and stop the mouths of lions,' and her servants and handmaids to see visions, &c., the beauty of the Bride has failed—her breasts have diminished—her face is wrinkled—her eyes are dim and cannot see afar off; she is no longer a chaste virgin espoused to one husband—but she has as many husbands as sects, and yet none of those with whom she is now living can be called her husband.

"Now, Sir, will the Spirit join with such a *Bride*, and say to Jesus the Great Bridegroom, 'Come!' the Bride hath made herself ready! No, Sir, the Spirit of God will say, I never knew you; depart from me, you pusillanimous, benighted, powerless, contentious Christianity. ' Thou Aholibah and Aholibamah, thy lewdness is in all high places ;' ' thou hast played the harlot with many lovers—yea, thou hast even hired lovers' (with human inventions), instead of commanding admira‑ tion by the grace of thy ' seers,' and the ' visions of thy handmaids,' and the ' healing power of thine elders.' Thou shalt be burned with fire."—*Orson Spencer's Letters*, pp. 69—72.

The blasphemous extent to which these revilings of all Christendom are carried, in appeals to the popular mind, may be collected from the following extract, the only one we shall make from the vile publication, the title of which we have quoted under No. 6, at the head of this article :—

" *Smith*—Really, Mr. Devil, your Majesty has of late become very pious ; I think some of your Christian brethren have greatly misrepre‑ sented you. It is generally reported by them that you are opposed to religion. But—

" *Devil*—It is false ; there is not a more religious and pious being in the world than myself, nor a being more liberal-minded. I am decidedly in favour of all creeds, systems, and forms of Christianity, of whatever name or nature, so long as they leave out that abominable doctrine which caused me so much trouble in former times, and which, after slumbering for ages, you have again revived ; I mean the doctrine of direct communion with God, by new revelation. This is hateful, it is impious, it is directly opposed to all the divisions and branches of the Christian Church. I never could bear it. And for this very cause, I helped to bring to condign punishment all the prophets and apostles of old ; for while they were suffered to live with this gift of revelation, they were always exposing and slandering me, and all other good pious men, in exposing our deeds and purposes, which they call wicked, but which we consider as the height of zeal and piety : and when we killed them for these crimes of dreaming, prophesying, and vision-seeing, they raised the cry of persecution, and so with you miserable and deluded Mormons.

" *Smith*—Then, your most Christian Majesty is in favour of all other religions but this one, are you ?

" *Devil*—Certainly. I am fond of praying, singing, church building, bell ringing, going to meeting, preaching, and withal, I have quite a missionary zeal. I like also long faces, long prayers, long robes, and learned sermons ; nothing suits me better than to see people who have been for a whole week oppressing their neighbour, grinding the face of the poor, walking in pride and folly, and serving me with all their heart ; I say nothing suits me better, Mr. Smith, than to see these people go to meeting on Sunday, with a long religious face on, and to see them pay a portion of their ill-gotten gains for the support of a priest, while he and his hearers pray with doleful groans and awful faces, saying, ' Lord, we have left undone the things we ought to have

done, and done the things we ought not;' and then, when service is
ended, see them turn again to their wickedness, and pursue it greedily
all the week, and the next Sabbath repeat the same things.   Now, be
candid, Mr. Smith; do you not see that these, and all others, who have
a form and deny the power, are my good Christian children, and that
their religion is a help to my cause?

"*Smith*—Certainly, your reasoning is clear and obvious as to these
hypocrites, but you would not be pleased with people getting converted,
either at camp meeting or some where else, and then putting their
trust in that conversion, and in free grace to save them—would you not
be opposed to this?

"*Devil*—Why should I have any objection to that kind of religion,
Mr. Smith?   I care not how much they get converted, nor how much
they cry Lord, Lord, nor how much they trust to free grace to save
them, so long as they do not do the works that their God has commanded them; I am sure of them at last, for you know all men are to
be judged according to their deeds.   What does their good Bible say?
Does it not say, 'not every one that saith Lord, Lord, shall enter into
my kingdom; but he that doeth the will of my Father which is in
heaven.'   No, no, Mr. Smith, I am not an enemy to religion, and
especially to the modern forms of Christianity; so long as they deny
the power, they are a help to my cause.   See how much discord,
division, hatred, envy, strife, lying, contention, blindness, and even
error and bloodshed, has been produced as the effect of these very
systems.   By these means I gain millions to my dominion, while at
the same time we enjoy the credit of being pious Christians; but you,
Mr. Smith, you are my enemy, my open and avowed enemy; you have
even dared, in a sacrilegious manner, to tear the veil from all these fine
systems, and to commence an open attack upon my kingdom, and this
even when I had almost all Christendom, together with the clergy and
gentlemen of the press, in my favour."—*Dialogue between Joseph
Smith and the Devil*, pp. 4, 5.

It cannot have escaped the reader, while perusing the foregoing extracts, how adroitly the enemy takes advantage of all the
infirmities and defilements which, through the lapse of ages, and in
consequence of her intercourse with the world, the Church of Christ
has contracted; and of the countless schisms by which large portions as well as small sections of Christendom have been rent away
from the body of Christ.   We notice this particularly, because,
while we examine and expose the awful delusions of the two sects
which in our day lay claim to an extraordinary revelation, constituting them—respectively, according to their own pretensions,—
the predestinated restorers of Israel, we are desirous of turning
their errors to account for the edification of the Church, by
drawing attention to those points in the condition of the Church,
and of Christendom generally, which have given the propagators

of these sectarian and fanatical notions occasion to blaspheme the ordinance of God.

Two points, as far as we have proceeded, are clearly obvious. In the first place, the absence of a clear separation from the world is necessarily a stumbling-block in men's way, and forms a strong ground of impeachment against the Church. By a clear separation from the world, we do not mean an actual separation between Church and State,—which, until the Lord of the Church shall Himself force it upon her in the order of His providential dealings with her, it would be unlawful to bring about, or even to contemplate as an object of desire,—but so broad and distinct a line of demarcation between the spiritual character of the Church, with all things that appertain thereunto, and the temporal position of the Church in polities which adopt, or, at least, recognize her faith, as shall leave no room for the imputation and the taunt, that the Church has renounced her allegiance to Christ, and has become the bondslave of the secular power. It requires but little reflection upon the character of recent events to perceive how imperatively necessary it is,—unless we wish to play into the hands not only of the Romanist Communion, but of the Irvingite and Mormonite sects,—that we should jealously guard the Church's spiritual independence of all worldly rule, and, at whatever cost, vindicate that independence from the latitudinarian encroachments of the State.

The next duty which devolves upon us, if we would deprive the two sects in question of one of the most plausible arguments upon which their system of fallacy and delusion is built, is a firm, deliberate, and decisive stand against the sin of schism. So long as the infidel or the fanatic can point to the endless divisions of Christendom, as proofs that nothing certain is known touching the Church and the truth of Christ, he has a powerful argument at his command. To cut away this argument from under him, there is but one method. It cannot be done by compromise of the truth ; by creating, as the promoters of that abortive scheme, the Evangelical Alliance, attempted to do, an artificial unity comprehending within itself all the most incompatible diversities of opinion. It can only be done by drawing a sharp line of distinction between Catholicity and Schism ; by showing where the Church ends, and where Schism begins. Concessions on this point are, at all times, positively sinful ; but they become so especially when a pretext is afforded thereby to the gainsayers to deny the possibility of arriving at any certain and definite truth, or to call in question altogether the very existence of the Catholic Church. We would urge this consideration, more especially at this time, upon those who feel a difficulty and a hesitation in affirming the schismatical character of the Church of Rome, which, by enacting uncatholic terms of communion at the Council of Trent, has committed schism against the Church Catholic, and by intruding her bishops and priests into our dioceses, has placed herself in a position of twofold schism towards the English, as well as the Scottish and Irish Churches. So long as we do not make good the ground of our own Church, as being Catholic in position as well as in doctrine, antagonistically against Rome, we are unable to silence the Irvingite or the Mormonite, when he adduces the actual separation of the branches of the Church from each other, as an evidence of the failure of the Church. The existence of divisions, heresies, and schisms, is no argument against the truth of the Church, because their rise and progress is clearly predicted in the Word of God ; but the existence of separate Churches, all having an equal right to assert their character as Churches, and yet irreconcilably divided from each other, is wholly at variance with what Holy Scripture leads us to expect ; and furnishes, therefore, a plausible ground for the assertion, that the Church of Christ, as she was founded by Him, no longer exists in the world. And, from this view, there is but one step to the admission of the necessity of a new dispensation for the purpose of restoring the Church, preparatory to the Advent of her Lord.

This, as we have already stated, is the position assumed both by the Irvingites and the Mormonites. They announce to the world severally, that the Lord is at hand, and that previous to his coming He has visited his people, and raised up for Himself a Church of witnesses of his truth, and of his impending Advent. By the Irvingites this position was assumed as early as the close of the year 1835 :—

"Among the many words of prophecy spoken from time to time, which at first were but little understood, were words calling for ' the testimony, the testimony against Babylon.' . . . . The Holy Ghost, through the prophets, declared that the Churches in all Christendom had become corrupt, and that the rulers in the state had departed from God, and that the time of judgment was at hand ; that those words, *Mene, Mene, Tekel, Peres,* were written upon the institutions of Christendom ; and that the Lord would have a testimony borne to the rulers in Church and State ; and that it belonged to the apostles to bear this testimony. While the many words spoken on this subject were being considered, it was declared that the burden of the land rested upon the apostles, and they were directed, each one, to write down the burden of his heart respecting the sin of the land, and of its rulers in Church and State, and of Christendom generally ; and that all these papers should be delivered into the hands of one, the Senior Apostle[4] ; and

____

[4] The "SENIOR APOSTLE" is none other than the honourable member for West Sur-

that he should combine them into one ; and that the document so prepared should be delivered to the heads of the Church by one of the apostles. In like manner, and about the same time, one of the apostles, who had been also named the prophet to England, was bidden to write down and deliver to the Privy Councillors his testimony as to the state of the nation, and the work which the Lord was doing. . . . .

"According to the light of prophecy thus given, a testimony was prepared to the Archbishops, Bishops, and Clergy of the Church of rey, who every now and then relieves the dulness of the House of Commons by the fireworks of his racy eloquence, and who takes his place by the side of Colonel Sibthorp, among the Parliamentary celebrities. In the Legislature, where he is in a position of co-ordination, he cultivates the amusing line, but among "the Churches" his words are serious, and carry greater weight ; for it appears from the "*Narrative*" that he is something very like a Pope, having been, ever since Mr. Irving's death, the life and soul, and chief stay, of the sect. The following extracts will show the nature and extent of his authority :—

"The ministers of the Churches in London, and all the angels of the churches out of London, came together on the 7th of July, 1835, being summoned by the Senior Apostle, according to the light of prophecy ; and they were bidden to abide together for a week, and at the end of that time the Lord would fulfil his promise (of choosing the new apostles). During this period the Council in London assembled daily, and opportunity was given to the several angels to bring up any matters about which they required counsel. During these seven days, not only were all matters thus brought up settled, but the general order of the Council of the Seven Churches was shown, through light of prophecy, answering to the types contained in the several parts of the tabernacle ; and the Council was set in order by the apostles, according to the light thus given. In the Council so arranged, whenever any matter concerning the order and regulations of any of the Churches is brought forward, the question so proposed is submitted to the Council, the principles bearing upon the question are laid down by some of the apostles appointed for this end ; counsel is given by the elders of the Seven Churches, who sit as counsellors, and the seven angels gather up in a digested form the substance of the counsel thus given by their elders, adding their own views upon the matter. Seven ordained prophets, who have their places in the Council, have time and opportunity afforded them to speak any word from the Lord which may be given to them to speak. The apostles then retire to deliberate upon the whole matter, and subsequently their judgment is given by the Senior Apostle ; and thus the matter is settled."—*Narrative of Events*, p. 38.

"The apostles, as a body corporate or college, as an unity, are the lawgivers and rulers in the Church, through whom the Lord fulfils his office, as the antitype of Moses speaking from heaven (Acts vii. 35—39. Heb. xii. 25). In the Council of the Seven Churches, wherein the whole Church is represented, and in all cases where the apostles are officially present as a body, the Senior Apostle, speaking and acting for and in the name of the apostles, is *the only exponent of the mind of the Lord ;* while in each particular Church or division of Christendom, the apostle having charge over or visiting the same is, so far as all laws, orders, or regulations are concerned, the exponent of the mind of the Lord ; and wherever an apostle acts officially, he speaks and acts, not from himself or in his own name, but as expressing the mind of the Lord, which is only found in the Apostolic College, and to the Apostolic College he is responsible for that which he does."—*Narrative of Events*, p. 41.

We trust that honourable members, who have hitherto taken the liberty of deriving various measures of entertainment from the speeches of Mr. Drummond, will, after this disclosure of his real character, show a becoming sense of the reverence due to him who, in the only true Church upon the face of the earth, is "the only exponent of the mind of the Lord." The honourable gentleman is certainly cut out for his part, and, if we mistake not, his part for him.

England, which testimony was read in the Council of the Seven Churches in London, on Christmas-Day, 1835; and the testimony, and those who should bear it, were commended to the Lord at the same time.   In the beginning of January, 1836, the apostle to whom the duty of delivering the testimony to the bishops had been committed, and who was bidden to take another apostle with him as companion, proceeded to deliver the testimony to the Archbishops and Bishops of England, and to the four representative bishops of Ireland ; and at the same time the apostle who had prepared the document, he (*sic*) was commissioned to make ready for the Privy Council, proceeded to deliver the same in company with another apostle as a companion, he having obtained an audience of the King, to whom he gave a copy of the same document."—*Narrative of Events*, pp. 53—55.

This, however, was only a beginning; the horizon of the "apostles and prophets" shortly became more enlarged, and they embraced all Europe,—which, singularly enough, is, in their vocabulary, synonymous with all Christendom,—in their operations.   The manner in which this was done, technically termed " the Division of the Tribes," is too curious not to find a place among our extracts :—

" During the meeting of the thirteenth council, in June 1836, the second called apostle, speaking in the power of the Holy Ghost, was made to declare, that the Lord would divide Christendom among the apostles, the princes of the tribes of Israel.   And the whole of the continent of Europe was accordingly distributed into ten portions, to each of which an apostle was assigned ; while the two senior apostles respectively were shown that England and Scotland, with Switzerland, formed their tribes ; thus bringing out the twelvefold character of the spiritual Israel, answering to the twelve tribes in the Revelation, from among whom the sealed ones, the twelve thousand out of each tribe, should be gathered, who should be the first-fruits to God and the Lamb.   The apostles were further shown, that while the senior apostle remained in England visiting and strengthening the Churches, the others, according to their opportunities, should go forth into the different parts of Christendom."—*Narrative of Events*, pp. 55, 56.

After this partition of Christendom, or rather of Europe, the " *Testimony*" (No. 1. at the head of this article) was prepared :—

" Not only were the apostles bidden to consider Christendom as the object of their care, but they were also directed to prepare a testimony, to be delivered to the heads of Christendom, similar in character .to the former testimony, though more enlarged in its scope than that which had already been delivered to the bishops of the Church of England. And they were also shown, that it was the Lord's way to deal with the heads, through the heads ; and though this testimony was a testimony to an unfaithful people who had departed from his ways, and to rulers who had misused the authority he had entrusted to them, yet that He would not pass by his own ordinances. This testimony was accordingly prepared as the other, and was addressed to all ecclesiastical and civil authorities in Christendom."—*Narrative of Events*, pp. 58, 59.

The document so prepared was both to serve as a guide and text-book to the apostles in their proceedings, and to be delivered in writing to the various sovereigns and rulers, civil and ecclesiastical :—

" Generally the testimony was to form the rule according to which those who were sent forth should speak. The true end and purpose of God in the testimony was not the abolition or destruction of the proper dignity and authority of kings and priests, but on the contrary, the establishing them in the legitimate use of their authority, which they hold from and for the Lord, until He come again and claim his own. Nor were the people passed by therein, but the Lord was seeking to approach them in the true way of blessing, by turning the hearts of their rulers to the Lord, that through them, when subject to Him, the blessing should descend, like the holy oil of anointing, from the head even to the skirts of the raiment. Neither do the apostles, in that document, call upon the priests to resign their priesthood, nor to the kings to lay down their crowns, but they remind all in authority of their several liabilities, and that the Lord will require his people at their hands, holy and perfect; and they invite all, with one heart and voice, to join in prayer to God, that as He has thus far helped the apostles to bring this message, so He will also, in his own time, send them forth in the fulness of the blessing of the Gospel of Christ. The testimony was for healing, not for destroying. God alone, who knoweth the hearts of all men, can tell how far such witness has been received or rejected—not outwardly but inwardly. So far as outward circumstances are concerned, there has been but little wish or desire shown, on the part of the rulers, to fall in with the invitation thus given ; for of this generation it can be truly said, ' It is a people that do err in their hearts, that they should not know my ways.' Little as the called apostles were prepared for the work now set before them, yet trusting in the help of Him who had called them, they proceeded generally on their missions, and Russia, Sweden, North and South Germany, Greece, Italy[5], Spain and Portugal, Holland, Denmark, France, and Switzer-

[5] Among the " rulers " to whom the " Testimony" was delivered, was the Pope ; and it is curious, as an illustration of the character and the views of the sect, to see in what light he is regarded by them.

" The apostles were further shown, that, while the testimony was addressed to all in authority, yet that it should be first delivered to those who, in their official standing, represent the threefold character of our Lord's authority as the Melchizedec, King, and Priest, and who in their actual position show the threefold perversion of that authority. The Pope, as the representative of the Lord Jesus, the only King and Priest, the priest upon his throne—in which character he stands, officially at least, as the usurper and forestaller of the dignity and glory of the

land, were visited by the apostles, each one taking with him, as his companion, an ordained minister. And according to the word of the Lord to them, that they should return at the end of 1260 days, they met at Christmas, 1838, on which day the 1260 days from the separation of the apostles terminated."—*Narrative of Events,* pp. 62, 63.

Of this document we shall now—since we cannot refer our readers to the original—give a short abstract. It begins, more like a book of Euclid than like a message from Heaven, with definitions. We transcribe the whole of the opening paragraphs :—

"To the patriarchs, archbishops, bishops, and others in places of chief rule over the Church of Christ throughout the earth, and to the emperors, kings, sovereign princes, and chief governors over the nations of the baptized.

"In the name of the Father, and of the Son, and of the Holy Ghost, One God. Amen. The Church of Christ is the company of all who are baptized in the name of the Father, and of the Son, and of the Holy Ghost, without distinctions of age or country, and separated by their baptism from all other men. One body. The pillar and ground of the truth. The dwelling-place of God. The temple of the Holy Ghost. The declarer unto all men of God's will. The teacher unto all men of God's ways. The depository of God's word and ordinances, wherein is offered up all the true worship which God receives from his creatures of mankind ; through whom have been conveyed all those blessings, in civil and domestic life, which have distinguished Christendom ; wherein are contained the only hope for man, and the only means of accomplishing that purpose for which God waits, and which all creation earnestly expects.

"As the Church is the aggregate of the baptized, so Christendom is the community of those nations which, as national bodies, profess the faith of Christ's Church ; whose heads and rulers not only recognize that all their power is derived from God, but, being consecrated over their people in God's church, have acknowledged themselves to be occupiers of their thrones for Christ, until He come and take the kingdom ; have, by receiving anointing from the hands of God's priests, also acknowledged that their ability to rule is by the grace of his Spirit ministered unto them by his Church ; and, in that same holy act, have submitted, or professed to submit themselves and their people to be instructed in God's ways from the lips of those, from whose hands they have received their anointing. Christendom is one corporate body ; separated from all other nations of the earth, in that they recognize the doctrines of Jesus Christ as the basis of their international law, and of their dealings one with another ; distinguishable from all other nations in that, by their legitimate organs, they have been brought as nations into cove-

kingdom of Christ, for in his kingdom alone can the kingly and priestly offices be united in one person—was to receive the testimony first, and to him it was delivered by the apostle, second in his call to that office, in company with the apostle who had been designated for Italy."—*Narrative of Events,* p. 59.

nant with God; thus entitled to all the blessings, responsible for all the duties, and exposed to all the judgments attendant on, and involved in such covenant; and yet, as nations, distinguishable one from another, each governed by their legitimate rulers, whose authority is neither diminished nor increased, but sanctified by their profession of the true faith, and by the anointing which they have received at the hands of the ministers of God.

"It is to this Church we address ourselves through her bishops, on whom, with their clergy under them, has devolved the ministry of that priestly office which was constituted on the day of Pentecost; and to whom, as trustees thereof, in their several places, and parochial jurisdictions and dioceses, the souls of the baptized are committed by our Lord Jesus Christ, the Great Shepherd of the sheep.

"To this Christendom, also, the nations in covenant with God, through *their* anointed heads, their kings, and all their chief governors, whose acknowledged duty is to rule by God's laws, and to hear his Word from his Church, we address ourselves. And we beseech your patient audience, Holy Fathers of the Church, and royal potentates and dignities, imploring you for Christ's sake and in his name that you will not cast aside our word unheard, or, rashly and before consideration, account it our presumption; for we claim to have received His commission, who is your Head and ours; whom we may not dare to disobey; who will judge us if we have proudly and presumptuously taken on ourselves to do this thing; and will judge you, if ye reject those to whom He hath given commission to address you."—*Testimony*, § 1—4.

This is followed by a brief recapitulation of the history of the world from Adam and Noah downwards, and a dissertation, somewhat lengthy and verbose, on the disorganized state of Christendom, through the operation of revolutionary principles in Church and State. The picture is, on the whole, strikingly correct; but there is this curious inconsistency, that while indifference to schism and latitudinarianism is severely blamed, a censure hardly less severe is pronounced against all who maintain that they, to the exclusion of heretical and schismatic bodies, constitute the true Catholic Church and hold the true Catholic faith; a claim which, by whomsoever preferred, is condemned as a narrow-minded forgetfulness of "the brotherly covenant." The whole dissertation, which constitutes Part I. of the "*Testimony*," thus concludes:—

"Wherefore, with the respectful entreaty due to your sacred offices, we beseech you most reverend Fathers, who are charged with the souls of all God's children; you sovereign princes, whose authority from God is supreme over all your subjects, ecclesiastical or lay, and whose thrones we approach with the homage due to God's anointed; that ye will listen to the message which we bring to your ears, if haply ye may find that God has indeed visited his people as in the days of old. And though we must open the secret springs and sources of the evils wherein Christendom is involved, and of the far more fearful evils which are impending, by tracing the sins of kings and priests during many generations, and the failure and apostasy of the baptized; yet shall ye find that God hath not forsaken, nor our God forgotten us. And may his grace be with you that ye may hear and understand."—*Testimony,* § 17.

The second part of the "*Testimony*" consists of a second dissertation of similar tendency, in which the history of the Church, more especially, is passed under review; and the divisions of Christendom, the abuses and corruptions which have crept into the Church, and the evils which have resulted from the connexion between Church and State, are all painted in the darkest colours, with a view to bring out in striking relief the remedy provided, as it is alleged, by Christ, in the raising up of the Irvingite sect. That a portraiture of this description, drawn by the clever pen of Mr. Henry Drummond, should contain many striking passages, and many views to which the most orthodox Churchman cannot but yield a sorrowing assent, is no more than might be expected, however strongly we may feel ourselves constrained, however clearly justified, to repudiate the conclusion which they are intended to support, that the spiritual life of the Church has all but entirely departed from her, and that in the Irvingite sect that life is rekindled, and the Church restored in the fulness and perfection of her divine ordinances. In evidence of this revival and restoration, the "*Testimony*" adduces the re-establishment of the fourfold ministry,—of which more hereafter—while the spiritual desolation of the Church is asserted in a succession of tirades against all existing forms of Christianity, some of which we have already transcribed[6]. The wholesale condemnation of the Church, in common with all the uncatholic and heterodox communions which have grown up around her, is succeeded by an exhortation to repentance, addressed to all bishops, and to all temporal rulers, and by an assurance of comfort given to those who "mourn over the low estate of Christ's Church," that assurance being founded on the following announcement:—

" Already He hath arisen to rebuild his sanctuary, ' the tabernacle of David which hath fallen down,' his dwelling-place in Zion; and from whence his testimony proceeds unto all baptized men; and it comes by the hand of *twelve men, called to be apostles by the Holy Ghost,* separated from the lands which gave them birth unto the service of Christ for all lands, for Christ's sake; whose office it shall be, through the faith and diligent prayer of God's people, to convey unto all the baptized in every land the blessings which Jesus, the Apostle, would bestow on his Church through apostles."—*Testimony,* § 104.

<hr/>

[6] See pp. 125—130.

The revival in question is represented as an answer to "the secret prayer, the expression of the desires which his prevenient spirit hath stirred in the hearts of the hidden ones," as well as of "the prayers which in every age of the Church, by the dispensation of his Providence, have been offered in the ministrations of the separate communities of the baptized;" in illustration of which, the petition *Domine, afflictionem populi tui* &c., in the Paris "*Paroissien,*" and the Collect for the Fourth Sunday in Advent, in the English Prayer Book, are quoted. The first rise of Irvingism is then described:—

" During the course of this century especially, many who had a zeal for God in various places, but chiefly in Britain, appointed to unite in prayer for the special outpouring of the Holy Ghost. In the year 1830, in the west of Scotland, these prayers of God's people, this cry of the Holy Ghost, was answered by Himself, and the form of the manifestation in these days of spiritual drunkenness and disorder was, as Isaiah prophesied in his vision of the judgments coming on the drunkards of Ephraim and Jerusalem, ' with stammering lips and another tongue.' The members of the Church of Scotland, among whom the Spirit of the Lord lifted up his long silent and forgotten voice, were a simple and unlearned people, and as much unacquainted with any practical and literal meaning of the fourteenth chapter of Corinthians as the rest of the Church ; but they had been instructed, and were looking with expectant faith that the Church should be, as in the days of old, filled with spiritual gifts, to the end they might be established. Some persons in London also, members of the Church of England, and others who were partakers of the like faith, received the like seal and answer ; and when none of the clergy of the Established Church of that land stretched forth a cherishing hand to protect and shield the vessels of the Lord thus used, the Lord Himself found shelter for them, in the congregation of a minister of the Church of Scotland in London, who had stood as a witness that the Lord was at hand, and who waited for the consolation of Israel, in the restoration of the manifested gifts of the Comforter : to him, among all the good deeds for which his praise should be in all the Churches, belongs this peculiar honour, that he first recognized and permitted the voice of God to be heard in the assembly of those who professed to be his servants, and the disciples of Jesus Christ.

" It was a strange and fearful work which God then wrought, when He lifted up his voice in the midst of his assembled people once more. There was joy in heaven ; the angels sung and gave glory—the angels rejoiced in heaven when the voice of Jesus was heard in the midst of his people. That voice shall not be silent any more, but shall go forth to the uttermost parts of the earth.

" And what has been the fruit of that voice, which came into the midst of the Church, and which the Church rejected ; which came into the midst of the watchmen, and they knew not the sound of the trumpet and warned not the land ; which came into the midst of the people, and they scorned and heeded it not. The voice cried, ' all flesh is grass;' and it withered the flesh, its might and power, its glory and beauty. The walk of the most circumspect has been proved to be contrary ; the ways of the most upright have been shown to be very wickedness ; the wisdom of the wise, and the counsel of the prudent have been confounded ; the thoughts and intents of man's heart have been uncovered ; and his imaginations, which are evil continually, have been laid bare ; the light hath shined in a dark place ; the living commentary of the spirit on the Scriptures has been given, and the law and the testimony have been bound into one."—*Testimony*, § 106—108.

The constitution of the sect as a distinct body is next accounted for :—

" From the first moment that the voice of the Holy Ghost was heard in Scotland, the cry was raised ' for a body.' The meaning of this was little understood by any, and least of all by those prophets through whom it was uttered ; but now it has been clearly seen that the gift of prophecy can be usefully and safely exercised only within the borders of the Church, which is the body of Christ. But, though ill understood, the word was received in faith ; and in answer to the prayer of those who believed, and in despite of the sin and ignorance of his unworthy instruments, God has prevailed to raise up more than a hundred persons speaking in prophecy, by the Holy Ghost ; to separate, by solemn act of the Church, twelve men, with the name of apostle named upon them by the Word of Jesus, spoken in the Holy Ghost ; to bring out a pattern, a shadow of what his Universal Church should be, in Seven Churches in London ; and to set up Churches in most of the great cities in England, Scotland, and Ireland, and in some places on the continent of Europe, and in America,—Churches rebuilded on the foundation of apostles and prophets,—each under the rule of an angel or chief minister, and elders, not exceeding six in each Church, who with the angel form the sevenfold eldership, God's ordinance for spiritual light ; other elders, as the need of the flock demands, and God bestows them, serving as helps in the eldership, equal in office, but subject in rule and in place to the elders, deacons, and under-deacons. And to the poor the Gospel has been preached by Evangelists, as the ordinance for that special work of gathering into the Church."—*Testimony*, § 111.

From a consciousness, seemingly, that this formation of distinct and separate "Churches" has a remarkably sectarian aspect, the " *Testimony*" anticipates the objection by an express disclaimer of schism, and by a glowing picture of the revived " Church" in contrast with the rest of Christendom :—

" This is not a new sect ; it is God's work for imparting his blessing to the whole of Christendom, the baptized world. God casts none away; He will receive and set in their places all who in heart turn unto Him. It is God's witness; a Church in the midst of a disobedient and gainsaying generation, walking in obedience to all who have the rule over them. Through Christendom lawlessness prevails; here, submission to authority. Without are divisions and sects: here is a body, one in faith, its teachers speaking the same things. Without, synagogues of antichrist, presided over by heads chosen of the people: here, a body ruled by ordinances, not constituted by the people, but given of God. Abroad, the daily services of the Church falling into desuetude, or unfrequented by the laity: here, the daily worship, morning and evening, enjoined upon the faithful by the command of. God spoken in the Holy Ghost in the midst of the Church. Without, an infidel world, rising up against and rejecting kings, bishops, and titles, and all the institutions in Church and State; wives and children not honouring their husbands or their parents, and servants rising up against their masters: here, God's Church, reverencing the king and all in authority, parents, pastors, and masters, giving honour to all orders and degrees in Christ's Church, whether those continued by succession from the first apostles, or those now bestowed upon a spiritual people by that ordinance again reviving; paying all dues to the former, but also, rich and poor, at the command of the Lord, given unto them in these last days,—a command addressed to the conscience of a faithful people, and needing no human laws to enforce,—bringing the tithes of the whole of their income to the altar which He hath again rebuilded."— *Testimony*, § 113.

Somewhat inconsistently with this antithetical rhetoric — " look on this picture and on that "—a more conciliatory tone is presently assumed :—

" Men, brethren, and fathers, hearken ! We come not as judges and dividers over you, we come not to praise or to censure, we come not to justify or to condemn ; we come not to arbitrate between those who are disputing about the division of the inheritance of the Lord ; we come not to take up or to take part in the differences which, in many cases, from small beginnings have grown wider and wider until they have caused a fatal and incurable rent in the body of Christ,—we come as ambassadors from the Lord of Hosts, and beseeching you, as though God did beseech you by us, we pray you to be reconciled to God. We come to proclaim glory to God in the highest, on earth, peace, goodwill and favour to the children of men. We come to recall you back to the old ways, to bring you back from fleshly confederacies to the unity of the Spirit, and the bond of peace ; to bring to your remembrance that which ye have heard from the beginning ; to revive that which hath ever been the prayer, and the hope, and the strong consolation of the Church of God ; to show you the way of holiness, the way of glory ; to proclaim the acceptable year of the Lord ; that it is come, and the day of vengeance of our God, that it hasteth greatly.

We know you not as Roman Catholic, or Greek, or Protestant, nor by the other names which men assume to themselves or give to their brethren; these are not the names of unity, they are the signs of disunion. We know not, nor can we acknowledge, even as Jesus Christ, your Lord and ours, will not know, nor acknowledge the names of distinction by which the members of the ONE HOLY, CATHOLIC, APOSTOLIC CHURCH have been divided into many sects. We judge you not for what is past, that we may not be judged by ourselves; for he shall have judgment without mercy who showeth no mercy, and mercy triumphs over judgment. We judge nothing before the time ; but we tell you that the time of judgment is at hand; that the Judge is at the door, who both will bring to light the hidden things of darkness, and will make manifest the counsels of the heart, and then shall every man have praise of God."—*Testimony,* § 117.

The whole is wound up by an appeal, of which the following is the most material part :—

" All the faithful must be gathered into one, and by visible separation from the faithless be shown to be one. As the servants of the Lord go forth into the lands of Christendom, and raise up his standard, so doth Satan muster his host and proceed with *his* work. And if this be the true work of God, and verily it is his own most holy and pure work, what must be the inevitable consequences of rejecting or despising it? If God draw near to his anointed, vouchsafing to them the *only* means of reformation and deliverance, if He pour out his spirit and stretch forth his hands unto them, and they reject, what can hinder that their fear should come as desolation, and their destruction as a whirlwind? The preparation of the baptized to receive the Lord when He cometh, is the fulness of the Holy Ghost. If they abide in the flesh, when He calls on them, and brings near the means that they should be filled with the Spirit, what can hinder that they should be filled with the spirit of strong delusion, and delivered up to the man of sin? If the Lord be again sending forth apostles and prophets to his Church, and the baptized reject and persecute them, they thereby proclaim themselves apostate: and thus the light shall make manifest the darkness; the coming of the Lord in the Holy Ghost to his Church shall discover who they are who fear Him, and who are those who fear Him not: the spiritual word of truth shall try all those who profess, and who are bound to know the truth, whether they be spiritual indeed ; and like the water of jealousy, shall judge as faithless those who receive it not with joy.

" And now ye ministers of God, the bishops and pastors of his Church, first in blessing, and foremost in responsibility—as Fathers of the Church, as pastors of the Lord, we beseech you reject not this our Testimony. We offer to faith an help and power of God, which the upright must desire, the godly and well-instructed in the word will believe, and the faithful will seek of God. The prejudices of ages, the sins of many generations, the false steps, yea, even the endeavours to reform the evils under which the Church hath laboured, have involved you in difficulties which, if you receive our word, must press upon you with almost overwhelming power, and from which ye cannot deliver yourselves. We call upon you not to take any step in your own strength, nor to seek to free yourselves from the obligations wherein ye are involved to superiors, to equals, or to inferiors; but this God requires of you, to stand in the places where you are, acknowledging the hand of God in his present work; confessing the sins which, like a thick cloud, have hid the face of heaven, and obscured the Light of Life: to cease from all idolatry, to stand apart from every act, or word, or thought which in themselves are evil; but to wait, with your people under you, watching day and night for the salvation of Israel, more than they that watch for the morning; continuing instant in prayer, but joyful through hope, because of the approaching deliverance of yourselves and of your people, through the power of God in the Holy Ghost. Above all, praying for us, that like as now we have been used of the Lord to bring the word of these good tidings unto you, so also we may be made the instruments of his promised deliverance, and the channels of all the blessings which the Lord Jesus Christ longeth, and hath ever longed, to pour into the bosom of the Church.

" And you, ye monarchs and rulers of Christendom, be assured that in the returning glory of the Holy Ghost ministered unto the Church of God, is your true strength, and sure and only safety in the midst of these times of perplexity; and therefore we beseech you, in the name of our God, that ye will be bold as good soldiers for his truth, and for his Church. Stand ye faithfully in the fulfilment of your duties, discountenancing the immoral and profane; purging your courts of vice and corruption; calling into your service honest and faithful, and God-fearing men. Be ministers of good to those who are good, but of evil to the froward, not bearing the sword in vain; but above all, ye are pledged to shield and to sustain the Church of Christ; and we beseech you, leave it not to be a prey to the wicked attempts of men, nor, under whatever pretence of reformation, suffer them to dismember or destroy it: but acknowledge and uphold it in its due privileges and place, and submit yourselves in spiritual things to those who are over you, as over all others of the baptized in the Lord. And now that He raiseth up his primitive ordinances for spiritual rule and authority, fear not to acknowledge *them.* And as far as your lawful power, influence, and example extend, be helpful, that God's work may be fulfilled, and his blessing find undisturbed passage to his Church—for this is the only way of escape for you or your people. There is no refuge in any human defences from that storm which is ready to burst upon you. The only escape is in being taken from the evil to come, in ascending to the hill of God in seeking for, and hasting unto the coming of the Lord, for which this work of God is the only preparation,"—*Testimony,* § 120—122.

[*To be continued.*]

ART. VII.—*God and Man, being Outlines of Religious and Moral Truth according to Scripture and the Church. By the Rev.* ROBERT MONTGOMERY, *M.A., Oxon.* London: Longmans. 1850.

Is it because men bow with veiled eyes and faltering tongue before the omnipotence and omnipresence of Him who alone is Lord of lords and King of kings, who, correctly speaking, alone is, since in Him we live and move and have our being, since He is not only our Creator, but also our Sustainer, since He is not only the first source, but also the everflowing fountain of existence; is it because we find the utterance of such truths too much for our full hearts, and yearning souls, that we never mention His name, seldom refer to His existence, rarely appeal to His authority, and scarcely ever speak of the personal agency, or personal being of either the Father, the Son, or the Holy Ghost?

If so, we are certainly the most reverential as well as the most devout of mankind, and our pre-eminence in both respects such as must silence at once, and for ever, the reproaches of those who have hinted at our shortcomings in these points. But, alas! the proudest nationality, the warmest patriotism, the sincerest attachment to our Church, and the deepest devotion to our country, cannot venture to hazard such a charitable hope—it would indeed be hypotheticizing with a vengeance, and putting a non-natural sense on the plainest practical proofs to the contrary. Well does Mr. Montgomery represent the question in its true light, when he says:—

"A popular tendency to resolve the personal character of the revealed Jehovah into abstract terms and impersonal properties, serves to keep man from God's real nature, while it seems to connect him with His sacred name. But, as long as God is thus believed, He is nothing more than an Almighty Sentiment, an Infinite Notion, or Stupendous Idea, enthroned far away in some region of mist and mystery, where, indeed, speculation may soar and science dream, but from whence the intellect can derive no saving truth, and the heart acquire no sustaining motive. It is not enough, then, that we simply believe that God is, but that He so reigns, as to preserve, and possess, and empower, and control, and guide, and govern all things, from the minutest atom to the immensest world. For the correction of this popular theism, the Judaic theology is wonderfully calculated. There we find the personal agency and legislative will of the presiding God every where present, supreme, and active : the veil of visible instrumentality is withdrawn, and behind the palpable drapery of human means and material instruments, we are able to perceive the secret movements of the Divine hand, and to trace the inaudible motions of the Divine ways. Thus a cold system of philosophic causation is never allowed to usurp the place of the Triune Jehovah, as unveiling His personal glories in natural, providential, and spiritual manifestations."—pp. 215, 216.

It would seem, indeed, that we had reversed the course of error pursued by the philosophic idolaters of the Valley of the Nile. They personified divine attributes, and then resolved their impersonation into actual personalities, thus substituting the worship of many false deities for that of the One true God. We have, on the contrary, resolved the Godhead into His attributes— deprived the Eternal of His throne, the Almighty of His power, and so far proceeded in our course of virtual atheism, as to look upon creation, salvation, and sanctification, not as the personal acts of a voluntary agent, but as the mere modes of operation of an impersonal cause. Appalling as this statement is, it is strictly true ; and, what is more appalling still, there is scarcely one man amongst ten thousand whose mind and heart, whose faith and love, whose inward being and outward conduct, have not been, and are not, at the present moment, influenced, we should rather say, clouded and polluted, by the all-penetrating poison of this subtle miasma.

If we examine the matter carefully, and carry our investigation into all the schools of thought and feeling which possess any wide-spread influence, whether they be religious, political, or philosophical ; we shall find amongst the most striking characteristics of the day, a tendency *to finalize second causes, viewing those as the sources which are only the channels of power, and to actualize impressions, æsthetic, moral, or intellectual, thus substituting subjective shadows for objective realities.*

And both of these fatal misapprehensions, as to the real nature, order, and relation of things, arise from the absence on our parts, of a vivid and practical consciousness of the being and the nature of GOD, and from its natural result a desuetude and an actual inability to contemplate Him as He is.

The only chance for the moral regeneration of our country lies in a resuscitated consciousness of an indwelling and encircling God. The life of all that is living, the truth of all that is true, the Being of all that *is*, the only Lawgiver, the only Ruler, the only Source of all power, capacity, or capability, material or immaterial, physical or spiritual, moral or intellectual. Until we realize all this in our feelings, as well as our thoughts, in the spontaneous ebullitions of emotion and intelligence, which arise unbidden from our hearts and minds, and indicate the actual state of our inward being, we cannot cope with any of the multifarious forms of error and heresy which assault or threaten us. When we have done so, we are in a condition not only to defend ourselves, but also to rescue others.

I. God is the source of all truth; nay, He is the Truth Himself. In Him from all eternity have dwelt the forms of everlasting reality, moral and intellectual, the reflected images of which pervade His creation. There is no moral virtue, there is no mathematical certainty, there is no human obligation, there is no rule of ratiocination, which may not be referred directly to Him, who is the same yesterday, to-day, and for ever. All is true which accords with the truth; all is false which does not.

It was a strange infatuation of Horne Tooke's to argue from a fanciful derivation, that Truth had no substantive existence. It is a pity that that ingenious sophist had not investigated with equal pains and greater success the derivation of ΑΛΗΘΕΙΑ, which clearly is compounded of the *alpha privativa*, and the verb ΛΑΝΘΑΝΩ, and signifies, therefore, that which does not, or rather which cannot, lie hid,—in other words, that which is self-evident, that concerning which there is neither doubt nor obscurity.

What a noble train of thought does this open, when we refer such expressions to the Truth, considered as the name of God, who manifests Himself every where, and in every thing, to the eyes which are not blinded by ignorance or error!

But to return to our late subject.—God, and God only, is the truth. In His substance He is substantive truth; in the unity of the Trinity He is personal truth. Objective truth is but a partial vision of God, more or less modified by the medium, spiritual, moral, intellectual, or physical, through which He manifests Himself to us. Subjective truth is but the impression of God upon the soul, the last stage in the manifestation of God to man passing through the medium, or using the instrumentality of objects intellectually, morally, or æsthetically discernible.

All idea, therefore, of separating truth from God, of setting up any standard of truth except God, of looking upon subjective sensations or convictions, as of any value, save in proportion as they are faithful impressions of the Eternal *Sigillum Domini Nostri*, faithful images of the heavenly things, of which they claim to be the representatives, is manifestly absurd, nay more, impious. And hence we perceive the gross folly and wickedness of receiving human opinion as the standard of truth.

II. Again, God is the only Lawgiver. Not that He rules the universe, as some have profanely imagined, according to arbitrary caprice,—not that right is a mere emanation of power, and the Divine law a mere creature of the Divine will,—but that every perfection of truth, and goodness, and justice, and purity, and love, and beauty, and power are inherently and co-essentially eternal in the substance of the everlasting GODHEAD. God is His own law,—eternally, necessarily the same, from everlasting to everlasting! Inherently, essentially, He is the law Himself: relatively to His creatures, He is the Lawgiver by revealing Himself to them.

How monstrously profane, how utterly destitute of the semblance of a foundation, then, is that system, which would erect a standard of right and wrong *on* earth and *from* earth, *in* man and *of* man—instead of simply referring every moral dispute at once to Him who is in Himself the standard as well as the giver of all law!

Yet, if we look around us, we shall see that it is the general tendency of the present generation to appeal to public opinion instead of absolute truth, and to consider expediency as a profitable and laudable substitute for right. Yes, instead of seeking for the true and the right as inherent in, reflected from, or revealed by the One God, the philosopher of the nineteenth century points to the golden calves of public opinion and general expediency, and cries, in the fulness of sincere misbelief, These be thy gods, O Israel!

But is it only the philosopher, the politician, the heathen moralist, the material reformer, who appeals to these idols? Alas, no: the preachers of the Gospel, the Priests of the Church, the divines of this generation, and the teachers of that which is springing into life, are deeply impregnated with this enervating, misdirecting, and most accursed heresy.

But let us proceed to other points before we attempt to apply what we have said.

III. God is the source of all power—He *is* Power; the mainspring of all motion, and the life of all life. All the powers, and qualities, and tendencies, which we see in the material universe, are merely the outward signs of the one work carried on by the One Worker. It is, for example, no more necessary or, *per se*, likely, that fire should burn, or water quench, or air ascend, or lead descend, or that food should support life, or that eyes should see, or ears hear, or that herbs should grow, or flowers bloom,—than that the very opposite of all these laws should prevail: neither are these things regulations issued at some remote period from the throne of heaven; but they are merely universal rules, by which, in each individual case, in each single, separate instance, God works His constant work according to His good pleasure. Strictly speaking, the qualities, and capacities, and tendencies of material nature, and of each element, and each atom, are only the manifestations of such and such stages in the process of causation carried on entirely and only by the power of Him who hath and who is power.

IV. Thus, too, in the economy of grace, though each created spirit is endowed with the awful gift of a monadic individualism, though each human being is made in the image of God, and consequently endued with freedom of will, so that he may either subject himself to the Divine influence, or reject it; still, all the means by which God works, are only second causes veiling the action of the first cause. Men indeed become, in a certain sense, individually speaking, independent agents in the spiritual struggle continually carried on; in that they are called fellow-workers with Christ in the work of the salvation of their brethren; but even here their sufficiency is of God. He is their strength; and, in other cases, those we mean which do not involve the individual volition of external and responsible agents, the case is clearer, simpler; all the means of grace, written or oral, visible or invisible, individual or general, internal or external,—in fact, all those ways, or courses, or objects, or subjects, or channels, or instruments, or circumstances, or influences by which God works in us or around us,—are only effective through His power, only operative through His will. It is He, and He only, who works in and by them, according to His good pleasure, selecting, according to His absolute purpose and creative choice, those vehicles of grace which He deigns to employ.

V. Again: God, as we have before observed in the language of the Divine Oracles, is alone King of kings and Lord of lords: all legitimate authority exists only with reference to Him; all *absolute* authority is centred in Him; all *relative* authority is delegated by Him; all dignity and pre-eminence of every sort or kind flows from the simple fountain of His ineffable will.

It is clear, then, that any assumption of authority or jurisdiction, dignity or pre-eminence, on the part of any human being, or collection of human beings, except as being the possessor or possessors of a *specific office* committed to him or them by God, and accompanied by a certain limited amount of delegated authority, jurisdiction, dignity, or pre-eminence, is an act of rebellion against the majesty of God, and one which partakes more or less of the nature of blasphemy. And it is also clear that every recognition or admission of such an assumption is more or less idolatrous in itself, and has a further tendency to separate the soul from God.

VI. In Scripture, God is revealed to us not only as Truth and Law, as Power and Life, as King of kings and Lord of lords, but also as the Providential Governor and Director of all human events. "*A man's heart deviseth his way*," says the Divine philosopher, "*but the Lord directeth his steps.*" Nor does this doctrine, as is ignorantly supposed, interfere with the free will or the free agency of man. It actually asserts the one, and practically enforces the other: it actually asserts the one by stating that " a man's heart deviseth his way;" and it practically enforces the other, inasmuch as it leaves us at perfect liberty to frame our actions according to our sense of duty, trusting solely to God for the event. Instead of binding us down to the wheels of expediency, and inviting us to the practice of mean arts and unworthy methods, the word of God, in its simple theocracy, allows us, invites us, commands us, urges us to do our duty as it plainly lies before us; cheering us when dejected, and checking us when over confident, and warning us when we are tempted to do evil, that good may abound, to follow expediency rather than right, by the constantly repeated admonition, that however men may labour at the *means*, the end rests with GOD.

VII. After preferring such charges as these against the spirit of the present age as developed in all the schools of theology and philosophy with which we are acquainted, and as exemplified in the individual mind and character of almost every man around us, it may seem almost superfluous to bring forward yet another accusation of the same class. We feel, however, bound to advance it: the age we live in, and the individuals who compose it, ignore even when they do not deny, the omnipresence of God.

Take any ten men at random, and ask them what they mean by the Divine Omnipresence, and you will find that they entertain some vague notion of the *omniscience* of God, and confound or substitute this for His *omnipresence*. How far does this come short of the Truth! God is every where! The air we breathe, the ground we tread on, the sun that lights our path by day, the moon that dispenses her light by night, are instinct with Deity: not, as the Pantheist would have us believe, in their own nature or essence or being, but as the shreds of the raiment of HIM who clotheth Himself with light as with a garment. Nor is this all: God is absolutely, actually, PERSONALLY present every where: and—yet more stupendous thought—the whole of the universe which we inhabit, with all its myriad systems of matter, and millions of spiritual monads, does not fill even the hollow of His hand, Whose Personal Being is as infinite as the eternity which HE inhabiteth.

We have gone into some detail on these few points, because we feel, that however true and indubitable in themselves, men are fast losing sight of them; and we proceed now to exemplify some of our general statements, illustrating them, for the most part, from the able work before us; a work for which Mr. Montgomery deserves the admiration and the gratitude of all those, who, in contradistinction to the scoff of the hostile few, or the silence of the abject many, attempt to repair the ruined altar of the Lord of Hosts; and boldly trust, that however many knees have bowed, or however many mouths may have kissed the idol of this world's adoration, still, if we are only true to our God, faithful to His Church, we may yet live to hear the vast multitude of our fellow-countrymen proclaim, as with one heart so with one mouth : *The Lord He is the God, the Lord He is the God.*

We regret that a work of such intense power and intrinsic excellence should be disfigured—as the volume before us so frequently is—by extraordinary phrases, ungainly expressions, outlandish words, and startling cacaphonies. Mr. Montgomery's delight in the termination *ism* is very unpleasing, and at times really mars the sense as well as the beauty of some of the finest passages of this truly valuable work. We earnestly intreat him to alter these things in the next edition, and also to correct one or two cases of carelessness and misprint, which will not fail to arrest the attention of his readers. Thus he twice speaks of the Tower of Babel as ANTE *deluvian*, having evidently substituted one preposition for another in the MS., and neglected to correct it in the proof.

But let us to our subject, and exhibit some of the errors of the age inconsistent with a due realization of the Divine truths which we have enunciated.

I. By failing to realize the fact, that not only is truth an attribute, or, if we may be allowed the expression, a condition, of the Godhead, but that God is actually Truth, we arrive at a most inadequate notion of the reality, the supremacy, the eternity, the divinity of truth. In fact, we virtually lose sight of its real nature, and consider that which is the very substance of all substance as a mere shadow.

How strikingly this is the case in almost every religious, or moral school, or circle, or dissertation, or discussion of the present day, will appear to any one who impartially examines the subject.

Men seldom argue with the conviction before their eyes, that the truth which they are contending about is an eternal reality, is in fact their God. If such were their conviction, they would feel that they were on the holiest ground, they would feel the awfulness, the responsibility of what they were doing and saying; they would not be anxious either to convince others or themselves, so much as to obtain a clear vision of the truth, they would not use casuistic chicanery or rhetorical flourish, or ridicule, or invective;—they would, on the contrary, feel that all such words, and phrases, and arguments, belonged to that class of which men shall give an account on the day of judgment.

Again, how could latitudinarianism prevail, either formally or virtually, together with the conviction of the real substantive nature, and eternal, and Divine dignity of truth?—the thing is impossible.

Again, how could those who profess a zeal for God's truth, enounce the monstrous absurdity, that every man has a right to interpret the Bible as he pleases, and that he will be judged not by that Holy Volume, *rightly* interpreted, but by any interpretation which he chooses to put upon it, if they really believed in the substantive existence, the Divine nature of truth?

"The Word of God must not be considered merely as a magical power, a spiritual influence, or moral instrument, but rather as an inspired medium of divine language, through which the Trinity in covenant accord the faculties of man, when duly conditioned for hearing and understanding their august appeal.

"'He that is of God heareth God's words.' (John viii. 47.) Let it be remembered, then, that the bare perusal of the oracles of God will never, as such, render the reader 'wise unto salvation.' To understand this in a practical light, Scripture must be distinguished as to its own nature, absolutely regarded, and as to its relative influence when humanly applied. Touching the former, the perfect glories of revelation cannot be really modified by the imperfect faculties which they accost. They have their primal root in the Almighty, and their perfect result in eternity; and whether we scorn their claims or submit to their appeal, they remain in themselves the very counterpart of that Divine wisdom which they infallibly image forth, and express. This unalterable sublimity of the Bible cannot be too seriously, or too frequently, maintained. It is the very mouth of God, the mind of the Holy Ghost; and, albeit it comes to man clothed with mortal condescensions, derived from earth, and sense, and time, it still bears in every feature the heavenly trace of its true original,—even that Everlasting Reason who is 'the only wise God.'

"But as regards the relative influence of the Bible, just as beams of pure and perfect light, in passing through some coloured medium, appear to be modified by their passage, so do the revealings of Scripture, in their transit through the consciousness of man, seem to be hued by the moral condition and intellectual bias of the individual faculties through which they have to shine. How solemnly, then,

ought we to approach the 'lively oracles!' They will not really be
known unless truly loved; and never can they be truly loved without
that hidden preparation of the heart which descends from the intercession of our great High Priest above. We must draw nigh to this
mental shrine of the Almighty, this temple of words, where the majesty
of infinite reason dwells and speaks, with reverence and awe, with
humility, faith, modesty, and prayer. Moreover, we must keep a most
jealous watch on the peculiar temperament of our hearts, and the prevailing tone of our minds, lest, after all, we virtually communicate
ourselves unto Scripture instead of permitting Scripture to impart its
spirit unto us. We are all by nature radically corrupt; and this corruption itself does not cease to realize its abiding character, because we
place our hearts and minds in outward connexion with the grammatical
meaning of Scripture. On the part, too, of many who profess to
venerate the word of God, is to be found an excess of morbid egotism,
an intensity of intellectual and religious self, which causes the Bible
not so much to reflect the Divine ideas, as to become the troubled
mirror of a man's own individualism. This popular and prevailing
confusion between Scripture, regarded as the objective representation of
eternal wisdom and truth, and the same volume considered in the subjective interpretation of man's personal understanding, will explain
some of the leading fallacies which belong to the controversies of the
Church in all ages. As respects, for instance, the grand question,
'What is the rule of faith?' a stern and staunch Protestant accuses the
Romanist of reducing Scripture to a nullity or mere name, by adding
thereto a vague and vast tradition which can never be determined, and
by imposing the authority of an elastic convenience, a personified
abstraction, a formless and indefinite reality, called 'his Church!' On
the other hand, how seldom does the unwise glorifier of private judgment, in the pride of his protest, and in the passion of his zeal, remember, that mistaken liberty in reading Scripture often leads a sectarian
disposition to Papal tyranny in the interpretation of the same! In
short, what by theory ecclesiastical infallibility is to an implicit
Romanist, intellectual confidence becomes to an undisciplined Protestant when personal reason is exalted into a virtual Pope.

"Again: this confusion between a rule of faith objectively revealed
by God to man, and the same rule subjectively interpreted among mankind, throws light on the baseless argument, whereby heresy and
schism have often sought to protect their cause and justify their existence. Every reader is competent to prove this by recalling to his mind
certain eras of the Church, when passion, pride, and prejudice, political
anarchy, and social disorganization clothed their crimes with the very
language of Scripture—with the mental and moral drapery of the Holy
Ghost. . . . . Let us, then, beware of what 'manner of spirit
we are of,' and how far or not we dictate mind and meaning to the
Scriptures, instead of allowing them to dictate saving truth unto us.
Venerate the Bible by all means; it is a volume so infinitely precious,
pure, and important, that He who inspired it is alone competent to

appreciate it. . . . . But while this, and far more than finite eloquence could express, may be attributed to the Bible, the distinction is
again to be remembered between what it is in itself as a clear and
unclouded radiance in which God has mirrored His own mind,—and
what it becomes to us, when interpreted and applied through the dim
medium of our individuality."—pp. 5—8.

Again, if men had been taught to appreciate and accustomed
to contemplate the substantive existence, the immutable eternity,
the Divine personality of truth, they would never have produced
or listened to the doctrine of Development—its infidel and atheistic tendency would have revolted them—they would have seen,
that he who denied the immutability of Divine Truth, denied, by
implication, the immutability of God—they would have perceived
at once, that truth is not truth unless it be eternal; and that
if there be no truth, there is no God. The doctrine, the
system, the feelings which dictated it, the arguments which
supported it, would at once have been scouted as intrinsically
impious.

The same condemnation applies, though in a less degree, to all
paltering or dallying with error—particularly the errors of Rome.
If those who, having been taught the truth, had really believed it
to be true—had really thought every thing inconsistent with it to
be false—they would never have learnt first to palliate, then to
tolerate, and finally embrace that or any other system of falsehood. We are not speaking of those who have been brought
over by simple conviction, *if such there be*, but of those who,
though knowing and believing certain doctrines and practices to
be erroneous, gradually accustomed themselves to the contemplation of them, till by consuetude they embraced them. In all such
cases we say, that these men did not really believe the truth which
they abandoned—never had duly received the truth which they
renounced.

Another line of reasoning adopted, another argument listened
to by those who have either wavered in or deserted their allegiance to the Church, has shown an equal misapprehension, mis-
appreciation of the nature of truth—we allude to the plea, so
often advanced in favour of medieval corruptions on the ground
of their *prevalence*,—they *are*, and *therefore* they ought to be—
this is the naked argument; or the majority of Christendom believes them, therefore they must be true—a very logical application
of Horne Tooke's reasoning: Truth is what one troweth; the
majority of Christians troweth that creatures should be adored,
idols worshipped, &c.,—therefore these things are true !

Such an argument, we repeat, could find no reception, could
produce no effect, could be considered as nothing but an auda-

cious act of impious rebellion with any one who duly estimated the *nature*, much more the PERSON of truth.

We will touch briefly on the political questions connected with this view: suffice it to say, that they who believed in the inviolable nature of truth;—they, in fact, who believed really and honestly in any thing at all, however they might differ as to the civil or political privileges or immunities to be conferred on recusants from the national Church; could have no possible doubt whatever, that it was the solemn duty of the State to uphold the truth; that it was bound by the most stringent obligations to propagate what was true, and with equal stringency forbidden from propagating that which was false.

II. But we proceed to another point—the reality, the immutability, the eternity, the DEITY of Right. The opinion, alas! of the Epicurean sensualist — "utilitas prope et mater æqui"—is so generally admitted, that it is held to be a treason against the spirit of the age, to make any appeal from the tribunal of *Expediency*, except to that of *Public Opinion:* and yet the devotion given to these two idols is utterly inconsistent with a due appreciation of JEHOVAH, as the LAW or the Lawgiver. We cannot imagine any man, really believing God to be the Law of the Universe, by which, that is by Himself manifested to His creatures, He will judge them, ever, for one moment, losing sight of so awful so tremendous a fact, much less attempting to erect any other standard or rule of action.

We could also add, that the notion of expediency involves a misapprehension of the relative position and value of inferior causes, and a neglect of the one only cause. It ignores the fact, so nobly expressed by the Psalmist: "Except the Lord build the house, their labour is but lost that build it; except the Lord keep the city, the watchman waketh but in vain."

They who make *expediency* their *end*, finalize second causes, and consequently labour under a mistake, which, fatal in this world, will be doubly so hereafter.

The reference, too, constantly made, the deference constantly vaunted, to *public opinion* [1], is another proof of the absence in men's minds of a living consciousness of God as personal truth and personal law. How would men dare to appeal to the

---

[1] In America this has been carried out to its fullest extent. We quote the words of Fennimore Cooper, in one of his latest works :—

"So much are the Americans accustomed to refer the decision of nearly all questions to numbers, it scarcely exaggerates the truth to say that, on the stand, the opinion of half-a-dozen country surveyors touching a problem in geometry, would be very apt to overshadow that of a professor from West Point or Old Yale. Majorities are the *primum mobile* of the common mind, and he who can get the greatest number on his side is very apt to be considered right, and to reap the benefit of being so."—*The Ways of the Hour*, vol. i. p. 101.

temporary and fugitive decisions of public opinion, if they really believed in the substantive, much more the personal existence of truth and right?—it is monstrous :—

" What, then, shall we say to that mawkish and miserable philosophy of the age, which brands with the epithets 'bigoted,' 'assuming,' and ' audacious,' all brave-hearted and deep-toned assertions of a religious creed and a moral science, in opposition to the reigning Pyrrhonism around us? Men are sent into our world to fight *against* the world, the flesh, and the devil; and whenever the first sanctions practice, the second indulgences, and the third tendencies, which are contrary to revealed truth, and Christ's Church, no pusillanimous alarms about ' bigotry and intolerance' should tempt us to a vile neutrality, and a villanous indifference. Truth can only be uncharitable to falsehood, and principle intolerant only unto expediency ; and, therefore, in denouncing what Christ and His Church have condemned, and in upholding what the Divine Word hath proclaimed, there can be no real uncharitableness towards man. On the contrary, the truly uncharitable are those who leave men to perish in their sins, rather than risk offending their pride ; and the really illiberal are those dastardly minds, who would sacrifice ' the truth as it is in Jesus,' for any popular lie, or fashionable maxim, which antinomianism of politics, literature, or society, may choose to promulgate or adopt. Against this hardened and heartless compromise of truth and principle, for the sake of a false charity, and a fictitious liberalism, God and nature, reason and revelation, loudly and perpetually exclaim. Nature herself is, as it were, Athanasian in the nicety and exactness of her distinctions and exclusions. All her works and ways are those of decidedness : there is no indifference about her laws; and if you dare to infringe her institutes, or to violate her canons, a recoil will be felt, which makes both mind and body perceive that decision and definitiveness belong to her constitution. Providence also declares there is no middle path between virtue and vice, truth and falsehood, right and wrong ; and as for the doctrines of revelation, they pronounce a cold neutrality and a dead indifference to be rebellion towards Christ, and treason to His cause. But the prevailing sentiment of the times is at variance with this. A mock idol, a miserable impostor, a heartless cheat, under the soothing name of ' liberality,' is doing all it can to dishonour God, confound distinctions, annihilate moral certainties, and so to deal with Christianity and the Church, as if the former of these were an historical problem, and the latter the mere creation of the subjective conscience and will. The object of this revolting tendency is obvious enough,—to expel ' *the* truth ' from the world, and leave every individual mind to discover its *own* truth, declare its own God, imagine its own Christ, construct its own creed, fabricate its own Church, and thus introduce a pandemonium of human selfishness at last ! Against this lying spirit and infidel abomination the heroic disciple of the Cross will set his face ' like a flint,' and rather die at his post, than be

morally indifferent, or spiritually dead towards any one essential truth, principle, or practice, concerning which the God of the universe hath spoken out. Heaven's decisions are earth's certainties; and he who by faith knows the one, can never, in fact, dispute the other."
—pp. 166, 167.

III. But not alone on these points, vital though they be, has our age, in its general tone of thought and feeling, departed from that pure and simple and all-embracing and all-satisfying theocracy, which is the essence of all true religion, whether revealed in nature or in Scripture.

" If we avert our eyes from Scripture, we perceive that, since the close of the eighteenth century, a peculiar style of allusion to Divine agency in the world has been introduced into physical science and natural theology. The divines unto whom we refer were scholastic defenders of Christian evidences, and, we doubt not, did no small service to the outworks of the faith. But, it must be admitted, their cold, dry, and technical division of the Divine Nature into an orderly analysis of abstract properties, introduced a style of thought and speech touching the Supreme Being, which has led thousands to confound philosophical theism with the ' God and Father of Jesus Christ.' And thus there have been since their time, and *are* in this present era, here-sies propounded, which virtually untenant creation of its over-watching God, and leave its inhabitants to be the victims of a fatherless and forgotten world. According to this doctrine, our human system is little more than a stupendous masterpiece of material and moral mecha-nism; a vast machine, as it were, compounded of matter and mind, which, having been originally constructed for certain purposes, and endowed with corresponding attributes for self-conduct and self-expan-sion, is now left by its Almighty Architect to work out and work on as long as the mechanism can contrive to last. How men who profess to be guided by mere reason can allow themselves to be cheated by such profane Deism as this, surpasses our comprehension. Never has the Christless imposture of scientific terms and abstract personifications been more successful than when it tempts us to believe that passive causation will alone explain active effect. Why cannot these victims of philosophy admit, that 'gravitation,' 'attraction,' 'electricity,' 'course of nature,' 'laws of matter,' &c. &c. &c., are mere words, that serve to personify human ignorance, but which leave unexplained the real nature, course, and action of a single phenomenon in materialism, that science detects, or the senses can discern? The writers and lecturers to whom we chiefly allude speak of attributes, properties, and laws as vicarious agencies, unto which God hath so committed the operations of matter, that He Himself can personally recede into His eternity, and reign in awful indifference on His invisible throne. Thus it is that, while a living, personal, and omnipresent God in the Bible is ever represented as the grand explanation, origin, and cause of all that is

absolutely good, the leading systems of the age describe the world as
merely regulated by abstract laws and impersonal attributes. But, in
fact, this style of nomenclature is little more than a respectable way of
excluding God's ruling law and personal will from the active doings
and daily conduct of mankind. Sinful as men are, they have still a
feeling for the Infinite, the Eternal, the Vast, and the Invisible ; and
all the instinctive poetry of human nature responds to visions of ideal
glory and abstract magnificence. Moreover, curiosity is keenly excited,
intellect gratified, and the imagination profoundly overawed by a display of material wonders and physical mysteries. Nor do they dislike
to hear a scientific orator eloquently declaim on the 'Presiding Mind,'
'Infinite Wisdom,' 'Creative Power and Goodness,' &c, &c. And why
is this ? Because wisdom, power, and goodness are mere impersonal
things,—ideal properties, about which the intellect can occupy itself,
and the reasoning powers be interested, without the faintest demand
being thereby made on the conscience, will, and character of man. In
short, while in Scripture what we term 'Nature' is God in personal
action, and 'Providence' God in personal legislation, Nature and Providence, in the leading systems of the times, are philosophic refuges,
which are conveniently adopted to keep God's personal will and word
from actual interference with man's deeds and designs. In Scripture
the perfections of Deity are ever described in vital connexion with His
Infinite Personality, and hence they stand in direct relation to our
duties and destinies. But, in the fashionable science of the day, while
the attributes of the Divine Being are paraded before us with much seeming reverence and wonder, they exist apart from all responsibility ; they
reach not to our conscience, they appeal not to our responsibilities, and
apply to no point in our moral character. Thus, the God of science is
quite distinct from the God of Scripture : as the former, He is a mere
collective unity of impersonal attributes, which may interest our contemplation ; but as the latter, He is a Personal Being, holy, awful,
ever-present, and ever-active, whose will and word reveal themselves
through His ministers, and declare what is our responsible connexion
with His Perfections, both now and hereafter. In science, we learn to
speculate and admire ; but in revelation, we are commanded to adore,
believe, and obey."—pp. 152—155.

Such is a painful but a true picture of the line of thought and
tone of feeling universally prevalent. We talk of elements as if
necessarily existing; of the qualities of matter as if essentially
inherent ; of events, as if the undirected results of human agency ;
of means, as if they were the causes of those ends which, in the
Divine economy, they happen to subserve or precede.

The material universe, however, ought not to be looked upon
only as the ever-moving work of God ; it is also the ever-speaking
voice of God. The forms of material existence are cast in the
moulds of spiritual truth ; the visible creation is but the outward
manifestation of the invisible God.

M 2

" Matter as well as mind, body, and spirit, contemplated in their pure essence or absolute products, have both emanated from the creative wisdom of the Almighty. Moreover He who came to die on earth, that His redeemed Church might be incorporated with Him in heaven by spiritual life for ever, has put a mysterious glory on materialism, by assuming unto His incarnate person as God-Man, a portion of that very dust out of which our own corporeal frames are organised and made. There seems, then, to be one of those deep harmonies which characterize all methods of divine self-manifestation, in the fact, that our Saviour, both in His parables and homilies, caused the forms of visible nature to adumbrate and expound the faculties and feelings of the invisible soul. Doubtless, too, the highest functions of what science calls ' nature,' are alone fulfilled, when this material phenomena are enlisted into the service of spiritual mystery and moral truth. And let us add another thought before the subject closes. The popular criticism on the style in which the Holy Ghost hath been pleased to apparel His written mind in Scripture, is perhaps somewhat defective in reverence of tone when it touches on the figurative language of the Bible. The general impression which it is calculated to produce amounts to this,—that the inspired organs of the Spirit sought to illustrate abstract truths according to the poetic idealism, or oriental richness of their own suggestive fancies.

" But surely it hath a deeper view, and breathes a diviner philosophy to say that, inasmuch as God created all things ' for' Christ (see Col. i. 16), the law of analogy which enables matter to illustrate mind, is a predestined result of the Divine will. In other words, the outward system of material things which accosts the senses in the natural world, is a vast and varied parable, through which the Holy Spirit instructs man's embodied soul concerning the hidden secrets of the spiritual world."—p. 33.

IV. Strange and senseless as it is that men should lose sight of the living presence, the effective energy of God in the world of matter, it is yet more so that they should do this in the world of grace ; and yet, a very little examination of the subject, casting aside all party bias, will show us how general such a habit of thought has become. How many, alas ! are there who look upon the Church or the Sacraments, or the Bible, or faith, as the *efficient* instead of the *instrumental* causes of man's salvation ! How many are there who look on justification as the causeless operation of an impersonal law ; on the atonement as a fact existing independent of an agent ; on sanctification as the involuntary effect of a mere influence ! God the Father is too frequently looked on merely as an atheistic first cause ; God the Son, as the combination of certain qualities and conditions without an individual will ; God the Holy Ghost, as a spiritual emanation from the fountain of Deity, devoid of inherent power, volition, or personality.

If men could be induced to look through the means of grace on the God of whose grace they are the means simply of and by His will, there would be much less both of formalism and of rationalism than there now is ; much less of formalism, because men would not obscure the vision of the Godhead by those means which are ordained to communicate His presence ; much less of rationalism, because men would feel that there could not be any thing incongruous in His selecting any of the works of His hands as the channels of His mercy, or the tokens of His power.

" All objections to a regenerating process, derived from rationalistic views concerning the element of water and the agency of the minister are untenable. For instance, it appears an impious irreverence, and almost a profane treatment of divine mysteries, when men reason thus : ' What ! do you believe that a little water sprinkled by the hand of an ordained sinner can regenerate the infant ? ' This is not only irreverence, but untruth. No Churchman asserts that water regenerates, as an efficient means or elemental cause ; but what he maintains is, that the Spirit of God, in Baptism, consecrates water to be an ' outward sign,' which veils the mysterious process of an ' inward grace.'

" The humility of an earthly element cannot be safely objected to as an argument against the majesty of an heavenly operation. Nature itself is one immense symbolism, that is to say, it is the palpable clothing of certain almighty ideas in material forms, and which, as visible tokens, accost the senses, and through such sensitive medium appeal finally to the inner reason and central soul of man. Let it, above all, be remembered, that materialism has been everlastingly consecrated unto some ineffable functions, by being adopted into corporate union with the glorious person of the Incarnated God. He did ' not abhor the Virgin's womb' (*Te Deum*). Moreover, man's body was originally moulded out of materialism ; and perchance the mysterious combination of his own spiritual principle—a mind, with a body of organized flesh, —is almost as inexplicable as the conjunction of sacramental grace with an element of water. Again, when rationalistic scepticism sneers at the idea of water being instrumentally consecrated into the service of the Spirit, it is forgotten that the converting agency of a preached Gospel works through the medium of air, before the syllables of life come into contact with the soul."—p. 300.

V. It is not wonderful that an age, which has ceased to look upon God as Truth and Law, as Power and Life, should go on to ignore His character as sole Monarch of the universe : it is however equally true, that unless we do realize the fact, that the universe is a kingdom, and that Jehovah is its king, we fall below the level of pure theism. It is the preservation of this great truth in all its vital energy which gives to the Mohammedan apostasy that living power over the acts and thoughts of its votaries, which so constantly arrests the attention of Christian travellers. It is the gradual abandonment of this doctrine, its practical abandonment we mean, by the great majority of Christian nations, that assists, as much as any thing else, the instability of purpose and unreality of principle which meet us on every side. Without this crowning article of the theocratic creed, this corner-stone of the theocratic system, the social and political existence of mankind is so much practical atheism embodied in the forms of life and institutions of society. He who believes that he has a right to authority or dignity of any sort, except in virtue of an office specifically delegated to him from on high by the only King, believes what is both impious and absurd ; and he who recognises any final authority in man, he who contemplates any human authority without referring it to its Divine source, and obeys or reverences it as a final tribunal ; or, again, he who pays deference to any power which is not delegated from on high, is guilty more or less of sin, of the sin of giving to the creature that honour which belongs alone to the Creator, who is over all God blessed for ever.

This Kingship of God has been more or less maintained or denied in various ages—and various causes have led to its prevalence or retrocession. In the early days of Christianity, it had such a power over the language, as well as the lives of the brethren, that they were falsely accused of insubordination to their earthly rulers. It was strongly maintained, in after-times, and sincerely embraced by the first Teuton converts : but the oligarchical system of the Middle Ages, together with the usurpations of Rome, had well-nigh swept this vital doctrine from the face of the earth ; for the irresponsible authority and segregative tyranny of the nobles, on the one hand, and the blasphemous assumption of absolute spiritual and moral jurisdiction, on the other, interposed impassable barriers between the creature and its Creator, the sinner and its Saviour, the subject and its Sovereign, the soul and its God.

In this age of thick darkness—we are speaking now of England —and thinking of the centuries immediately preceding the Reformation, when the causes above referred to had had time and opportunity to bear fruit—the royal power became the last refuge, the only surviving witness for the Sovereignty of God ; for our kings claimed a power officially delegated from on high to them as the responsible viceroys of their heavenly Master. They did not claim to be the substitutes, but the inferior officers of heaven ; and thus the kingly power and kingly claim kept alive in the minds of men a recognition of a mighty truth which they were fast losing.

This great fact of the theocratic nature and claims of the

English monarchy, accounts to our minds, most satisfactorily, for the sympathy and co-operation which was so strong and so successful between our monarchs and our Reformers, and likewise for the cordial union which so long subsisted between our Church and our State. The principles, the doctrines of the English Church were, and are, purely theocratic in contradistinction to the various systems of error which asserted the finality, or denied the delegation of the Divine authority. The principles of our Constitution, and those too of our great statesmen, were absolutely theocratic, for a long time after the Reformation.

It was loyalty to the throne of heaven, which led Cranmer, Ridley, Latimer, to the stake; it was loyalty to the throne of heaven, which rallied the people of England, under Elizabeth and James the First, against their popish enemies.

It was loyalty to the throne of heaven, a conviction that he held a power entrusted from on high—a conviction of delegated authority and individual responsibility—which enabled Charles the Martyr to die—he went to the block not as an earthly king, but as a heavenly subject—not as a stubborn master of men, but as a faithful servant of God.

Nor did his enemies ignore the fundamental article for which we are contending. They maintained most earnestly and most sincerely the Sovereignty of God—the sole majesty, the sole dignity, the sole Kingship of Jehovah. They maintained that all authority must be referable to, and derivable from, the Lord of Hosts, though they declined to recognize that authority in either the Lord's Church or the Lord's anointed. In fact, they admitted the major, whilst denying the minor premiss of the royalist syllogism.

That such principles, or feelings, or notions, are now prevalent, or even *tolerated*, in an age which boasts of its tolerance, and which, to do it justice, *does* tolerate every conceivable system, or opinion, or creed—except that of theocracy—no one will presume to assert.

Take, for instance, the origin, nature, and extent of political power—though this is only one branch of the subject. One man tells you, that the people is the only legitimate source of power; another speaks of the "enlightened few," or the "educated classes," or the "higher orders," as the legitimate rulers of the land, adopting a kind of social angelolatry or political polytheism; a third treats political institutions as mere matters of chance, the result—as the more plain-spoken and therefore more honest atheist would say—of a fortuitous concatenation of atoms.

So much for the origin of power. As to its nature and extent, we hear much of the omnipotence of Parliament. Does this mean that our legislators are free to act like gods, according to their unbiassed judgment and unrestrained will, so that their decrees are the simple expression of the uninfluenced decision of the majority ? No ; the operation of this omnipotence is limited, or rather, we should say, directed, by internal influences of numberless and conflicting kinds. There is, in fact, *nothing* which may not legitimately be brought to bear upon any supposable question, and rightly and naturally exfluence any or every member of either house in giving his vote,—except the will of God ; for whilst abjectly cringing to the opinion of the creature, the legislator ignores the law of the Creator. Man may be allowed to encroach on that collective omnipotence, which must be stringently maintained only in reference to the Almighty. Every voice may be listened to, every word allowed its due weight, except the voice of the Church, and the Word of God.

It is strange to us that professing Christians, decent, respectable men, such as the late member for Tamworth, should legislate without any reference to the day of reckoning. It is clear that they cannot admit the doctrine for which we are pleading,—the sole sovereignty, the universal monarchy of God; otherwise, they would feel that political power is an official trust, delegated by THE KING, and that to use it without constant reference to Him, is *treasonable*, as well as impious.

We are told that principles are nothing, that results are every thing,—a doctrine as materially pernicious, as it is morally unsound. Yet let us look back to the time when every other throne was humbled, every other land deluged with blood. What was it which, *humanly speaking*,—for we are wishing to argue the point materially, and not providentially,—saved the English people from ruin, and the English Crown from humiliation ?—It was that he, who ruled that people, and wore that crown, " the good old king," believed in the creed, and acted on the system of theocracy. We do not assert that all his views were sound, or all his actions good; but we do assert that it was a constant, living, guiding, ruling consciousness of his own true position, as the divinely-appointed possessor of a delegated and responsible power, *as the officer of a theocracy*, which enabled him to stem the torrent, and repel the surge, before which the oldest and proudest trees of the forest were but as the stubble scattered by the wind.

Nobly has our author expressed himself upon this subject :—

" God is as truly the Almighty Head of a commonwealth, as He is the Creator and Governor of individual souls, whose united aggregate composes what we term a polity, or the corporate unity of a state.

Hence, on the hypothesis that it has pleased the Divine Being to make a formal revelation of His will unto mankind, it might be concluded beforehand, such revelation will address itself not exclusively unto the subjective consciousness of individual men, but unto the personality and responsibility of nations. To adopt another creed, and affirm the religion of Christ to be limited unto the sanctuary of a man's own spirit, and that as a member of a polity, a citizen in the commonwealth, his creed has no legitimate realm for unfolding its principles, is indeed to assert an individual ought to be religious, but society atheistical! To this heartless falsehood does the watchword of creedless democracy and parliamentary deism lead at last,—that motto, we mean, whose doctrine is,—' Politics and religion have nothing to do with each other.' Translate that paradox into a true and ultimate principle, and it amounts unto this revolting conclusion,—' Society and God have no moral relation unto each other!' And such is the impious dislike certain men feel towards the character of an ordered Church, the claims of an Apostolic priesthood, and the obligations of a definite creed, that, rather than submit their secular policy unto the test of spiritual wisdom, they are prepared to exclude the Almighty from all Scriptural interference with national duties and public responsibilities. According to their dreadful theory, in political life the more we approximate unto pure atheism, the nearer we approach unto the perfect ideal of a modern philanthropist, and liberal statesman !"— pp. 176, 177.

Let it not be supposed that in putting forward the dignity of the regal office, we advocate either despotism or absolutism. Despotism, *i. e.* the government of one or more according to his or their own will, without established law, is a practical denegation of more than one essential principle of theocracy. And though an absolute monarchy, or the rule of one according to fixed laws, is far preferable to either autocratic or democratic despotism; still the most perfect government, and that most consonant both essentially and actually with a practical theocracy, is one where the sovereign, representing individually the dignity of God, shares with her subjects that power of which he or she is the supreme head.

Again, the present age is peculiarly neglectful of the duties of children to their parents. The thing is so plain, the fact is so general, that we need bring no proof to show how this fault, both in principle and practice, pervades all orders of the community. Nor is it only that children fail to see in their parents God's special officers, appointed by Him even before their birth, as their rulers as well as guardians; but parents also for the most part have forgotten the responsibility of their office—have forgotten that their duties to their children are as clearly official

duties as those of a clerk in a public office to his under-clerks.
Even in those cases where authority, or respect, or any other
portion of the claims resulting *by Divine appointment* from the
parental and filial relation, are claimed or exercised, admitted or
practised—the Divine source, the purely theocratic nature of
these duties, is in most cases altogether ignored.   The parent
too often exercises authority from self-will, the child yields obedience from necessity or habit ; or where, as is, of course, very
frequently the case, affection has its share, and perhaps the
greater share in these results, the claims and rights of the
All-father are forgotten.   Nay, even in those cases where a sense
of duty has its effect on the children, it is too often a blind instead
of enlightened sense—one which views in the parent the final seat
instead of the delegated abode of authority.   In fact, parents and
children, whatever be their feelings or conduct towards each
other, seldom contemplate, and still less frequently realize the fact
that they are the officers and subordinates of a pure theocracy.

Again, in the economic relations of life, how very rarely does
it occur, that the employer and the employed recognize in the
least degree the official and theocratic nature of the connexion in
which they are placed !   How seldom, for instance, does the
master of a household, or the occupier of a farm, consider himself as the officer of a theocracy, as appointed by his MASTER to
superintend those subjected to his authority ; an authority officially and directly delegated by the ALMIGHTY in his Pantocratic
capacity, as possessed of a certain jurisdiction, forming part of
the government of the universe, to be exercised according to the
laws, and in furtherance of the principles, of the Universal King !
How seldom does he consider that he will have to give an account
of the way in which he has administered this office, as a sacred
trust committed to him for the moral and material well-being, for
the eternal felicity and the temporal happiness of those allotted
to his charge !

How seldom is this, the true view of the case, taken by the
subordinate !   how seldom does the inferior recognize in the economic ruler a minister of God !—Yet such views as these are true,
for they are taught by the Bible, and enforced by the Church.

Again, in matters ecclesiastical : how very little reverence or
deference is pa d, generally speaking, to the Bishop, *as Bishop!*
Men may, indeed, obey a Bishop from love, or fear, or interest, or
admiration of his talent, or accordance with his views : but how
very few are there who look upon the Bishop in his official capacity as

ΧΡΙΣΤΟΣ ΑΝΤΙ ΤΟΥ ΧΡΙΣΤΟΥ·

Anointed instead of The Anointed, and reverence him for his

office' sake without reference to himself! But, that it is our duty to do this as far as possible cannot for an instant be denied by any consistent Churchman.

Again, let us consider the relation in which the Clergy stand to their flocks, and we shall see how frequently both pastor and people ignore the theocratic nature of that relation. Too frequently the laity refuse to recognize in God's ordained minister the possessor of any spiritual office or divine jurisdiction,—a habit of thought and feeling which is encouraged by the loose and inadequate views entertained by many of the priesthood themselves. Too often, again, is deference given on the one hand, and received on the other, not as the result of a spiritual relation, but of a temporal difference ; not because the clergyman is the overseer of his flock, but because he is superior to them in some of the advantages or ornaments of this present world; so that frequently the very respect which is apparently given to God's minister is only a tribute to the "pride of life." And even in those cases where the nature of the pastoral relation is recognized as being of a spiritual character, the priest or the preacher is elevated into an idol,—the authority is recognized, but the AUTHOR is practically forgotten, and the creature is worshipped in conjunction with, and not unfrequently to the exclusion of, the Creator.

And before leaving this point, on which we have already dilated to a greater length than we had intended, let us again refer to the sad course of those who have deserted the fold of our Holy mother.

We do not believe that any one who had been duly instructed, and had duly learnt to realize this doctrine of the sole sovereignty of God, could by any possibility be induced to go over to a Church, which both invades that sovereignty in her own person by claiming a final instead of a responsible authority, an absolute instead of a conditional obedience, and also clearly and unmistakeably gives to another a portion of that honour which God has explicitly declared that He will not share with another.

We need scarcely add, that they who have left our pale for any of the many self-sown sects which surround us, can never have acknowledged the fact that God has delegated His Sovereignty in matters spiritual to His Church, and to Her alone ; that they who deny her authority are guilty of disobedience, and that they who claim such for themselves are guilty of rebellion,—such disobedience or rebellion being committed against *Her* and *their* LORD.

VI. On the sixth point at issue between us and the present age, we could easily establish our case were we necessitated to do so. The case is, however, too plain to need substantiation. Men do undoubtedly believe, not professed atheists, but professing

Christians, that events are the *creations* of actions,—not merely
the permitted result, but the necessary effect. On the fatal error,
the God-denying tendency, of this the popular view, we will not
enlarge at present; for there are still, we believe, and we thank
God for the conviction, many men who still sincerely maintain
the truth on this point; and yet how few are there of the Church's
champions—(is there *one* among the state's rulers? one po tical
leader? one man in public life?)—who really believes it! although
without believing it, none believes rightly in God. No; men
would never worship expediency if they had not previously deified
second cause. The age must choose,—the sooner the better,—
between theocracy and atheism.

VII. Denying, as it does, the theocratic principles which we
have already brought forward, it is natural that the present age
should reject altogether that which even further humbles the
creature, and exalts the Creator—the doctrine of the Divine
omnipresence, the belief that God is every where, not virtually,
not potentially, not providentially, not only in His might, His
power, His knowledge, or His will, but actually and absolutely,
essentially and personally. Yet such is the truth.—We are but
powerless atoms floating in the infinite ocean of personal Deity.

Let us sum up and once more declare those theocratic principles for which we are contending:—

I. God is Truth,—eternal, immutable, substantive, personal
truth. All forms around us are but the creations of His will, the
shadows of His reality—all opinions, and systems, and thoughts,
and convictions are proportionally true as they reflected Him,
proportionally false as they fail to do so.

II. God is Law,—in the enduring and unchangeable, beginning-
less and endless Now, which knows not time and embraces eternity, one and the same, without succession or growth, or progress, or mutation, uncreated and imperishable. Right is accordance with Him, wrong is discordance from Him.

III. God is power,—Life is His energy, growth His volition,
capacity His gift, operation His command. The elements of
matter, the powers of nature, are in themselves nothing; at first
the creatures of His will, they are still the vehicles of His free
pleasure.

IV. God is the Personal life of the soul. As He imparts Himself or refrains, the soul lives or dies. Man is free to seek, and
he who seeketh findeth; man is free to reject and to fall back to
perdition: but whether called for, or uncalled; whether from
without, or from within; whether by His Bible or His Church,
His servants or His Sacraments; whether by the works of
nature, or the machinery of Providence; whether by grief or by

joy, by friend or by foe, by example or by warning ;—it is God who worketh in us both to will and to do of His good pleasure.

V. God is KING. We are all merely monads in the countless catalogue of creation—subjects of one Almighty Lord. All lawful power, or authority, or supremacy, must be and is officially delegated by Him to those whom, directly or indirectly, He appoints as the superior or inferior officers in that vast theocracy of which He is the only ruler. All assumption, therefore, of final jurisdiction is blasphemy, whether by prince or people, Church or State ; all denial of the legitimate rights of official authority, civil or ecclesiastical, is impiety as well as rebellion. All claim to power or authority, except as the delegated official of God, is groundless and profane.—Nay, further, all pride or self-complacency in our own worldly advantages, all delight in making others humble themselves in any way or any degree to us as the possessors of any such advantages, all glorying in our own capacities, or capabilities, or gifts, natural or artificial, spiritual or temporal, *as though they were our own*, are actual sins in the sight of Him who alone possesseth all power, dominion, might, and majesty.

VI. God is alone the disposer of all events. Every attempt, therefore, to compass future good at the expense of present evil, and obtain that which *seems* desirable by the sacrifice of that which *is* right, is not only a gross mistake as regards man, but a gross outrage as regards God ; for it denies His power, and invades His prerogative ; it mentally unseats Him from His throne, and places man on it instead of His Maker.

VII. God is around and about us, within and without, above and beneath us. We float in a circumfluent eternity and infinity of personal being. It is not only that God sees us, hears us, knows us, searches and watches over the work of His hands, the visible and invisible creation with which we are surrounded, but that in the boundlessness of His divinity, He actually *is* every where. And hence we learn, that nature is not only an unwritten bible, a material parable, but that it is actually the visible, though only faint and partial manifestation of His truth, and law, and power, and life, and reign, and rule, and love, and wrath, the vastness of whose everlasting and omnipresent personality transcends the united conception of all the minds which He has created, fills all eternity, and overflows all space.

Such is the theocracy which Scripture teaches us from the first chapter of Genesis to the last of Revelations. Why is it, that we have deserted, rejected, denied, forgotten these truths ? Our Lord Himself has furnished us with the answer— *Ye cannot serve God and Mammon.*

This impossible achievement we have endeavoured to accomplish, these incompatible services we have attempted to fulfil; and the result has been that which was of old predicted—*We have held to the one and despised the other,*

"Commercial prosperity, manufacturing pursuits, scientific discoveries, luxury, wealth, and whatever tends to increase the several comforts and conveniences of ' the life that now is,' may and ought to have their due proportion of our regard. But at present they are pursued with idolatrous enthusiasm: religion, art, science, literature, taste,—all are touched by their low contagion: profit and loss are the two talismanic words which cause the social pulse of the empire to rise and fall; The Exchange is fast becoming our national temple, and the medium of market and money the only aspect through which we desire to interpret the true character of the nineteenth century!"—p, 170.

Wealth is the subject of our deepest studies, wealth the end of our most careful legislation, wealth the condition of political power, wealth the test of moral excellence, wealth the standard of social intercourse, wealth is the object of our constant endeavours, wealth is the God of our idolatry.

Political economy, a science good and useful in its proper place, has usurped the position of political philosophy; though to confound the two together is in reality an error analogous to that of identifying a mere druggist with an experienced physician.

Our politicians no longer believe that, in a temporal point of view, wealth is only desirable so far as it conduces to the enjoyment of mankind. They seek for prosperity not as the *handmaid*, but as the *substitute* for happiness. Any spiritual view by which wealth might be regarded as the bounty of God, entrusted to man for the honour of the OWNER and the good of HIS creatures, is universally ignored both by public men and private individuals. Does our Heavenly Father, or our Holy Mother require at our hands any portion of the goods that pertaineth to us?—The world is ready with some plausible excuse for our niggardly and undutiful selfishness—and suffers us not to do any thing for the honour of HIM who begat, or the service of Her who bare us. If a brother or a sister be naked, and destitute of daily food, theoretic philanthropy declares in the soft tones of fantastic sentimentalism: *Depart in peace, be ye warmed and filled ;*—but Mammon declines on philosophic grounds to *give them those things which are needful for the body:* or, if his sway be not yet undisputed in the heart, suffers them only *to be fed with the crumbs which fall from the rich man's table.*

Does Scripture declare, in no equivocal terms, " *Thou shalt worship the Lord thy God, and Him only shalt thou serve?*"—

Mammon points to all the kingdoms of the world, and the glory of them, and replies by the mouth of the political economist, " *All these things will I give thee, if thou wilt fall down and worship me.*"

Does one of Christ's poor demand from his richer brother that love which the Redeemer appointed as the distinctive mark of the redeemed, the sign by which His followers should be known, the test of their reality, and the pledge of their success? And does he strengthen his appeal for sympathy and kindness, by referring to the Apostle's words? *If ye fulfil the royal law of liberty, according to the Scripture, Thou shalt love thy neighbour as thyself, ye do well: but if ye have respect of persons, ye commit sin, and are convinced of the law as transgressors,*—Mammon is near at hand to suggest the reply, *Stand by thyself! Come not near unto me, for I am* WEALTHIER *than thou!*

So prevalent, so all-pervading, so all-polluting is this Mammon Worship,—commenced in defiance of our Lord's warning, and carried out to the denial of His truth, the neglect of His law, the dishonour of His throne, the disgrace of His Church, the disbelief in His power, and the disregard of His word.

Once more, notwithstanding its minor faults of style and arrangement, we commend Mr. Montgomery's work to the study of an age which is pre-eminently in want of the instruction which it contains, which has well-nigh forgotten those theocratic principles so ably and eloquently advocated in the volume before us,

In conclusion, we would urge upon our contemporaries, whether as individuals or members of the community, to abandon the vain endeavour to serve God and Mammon, and devote all their energies to the service of GOD AND MAN,

NOTICES OF RECENT PUBLICATIONS,

ETC.

.. A Physician's Holiday. By Rev. J. Forbes. 2. A Second Letter to Rev. W. Maskell. By Rev. M. W. Mayow. 3. The Church Apostolic, Primitive, and Anglican. By Rev. J. Collingwood. 4. Rev. C. Marriott's Sermons. Vol. II. 5. Rev. C. A. Heurtley's Parochial Sermons. 6. The Midnight Sun. 7. Rev. E. Cust's Family Reading. 8. Rev. J. A. Wickham's Synopsis of the Doctrine of Baptism, &c. 9. An Introduction to Conchology. By G. Johnston. 10. ΗΘΙΚΩΝ ΑΡΕΤΩΝ ΥΠΟΤΥΠΩΣΙΣ. A Selection from the Nichomachean Ethics of Aristotle. By Rev. W. Fitzgerald. 11. The Life, Letters, and Opinions of W. Roberts, Esq. By Rev. A. Roberts. 12. Hudleston's Sermons. 13. Fides Laici. 14. Monsell's Parish Musings in Verse. 15. Sir A. Edmonstone's Letter to the Bishop of Glasgow and Galloway on Church Affairs. 16. Fortescue's Tudor Supremacy in Jurisdiction unlimited. 17. Homer's Iliad, Books I.—IV., with Critical Introduction, &c. By Rev. T. K. Arnold. 18. Rev. G. Crabbe's Posthumous Sermons. 19. St. George for England! 20. Mrs. Jamieson's Legends of the Monastic Orders. 21. Hostius's Paradise of the Christian Soul. 22. Alison's Essays. Vol. III. 23. Eastern Churches. By Author of "Proposals for Christian Union." 24. Regeneration. A Poem. By George Marsland. 25. Dr. O'Brien's Visitation Charge in 1848. 26. Rig-Veda-Sanhita. Translated from the original Sanskrit. By Rev. H. H. Wilson. 27. Neale's Letter to Archdeacon Hare on the Gorham Question. 28. Emperors of Rome. By Mrs. H. Gray. 29. The Poor Artist. 30. Record of the College of Christ Church, in Brecon. By Rev. J. Pratt. 31. An Inquiry into the Catholic Truths hidden under certain Articles of the Creed of the Church of Rome. Part II. By Rev. C. Smith. 32. Stretton's Compilation of Church Hymns. 33. Canterbury Papers. 34. Jones's Tracts on the Church. 35. Sickness, its Trials and Blessings. 36. "One Lord, one Faith." 37. The Christian Gentleman's Daily Walk. By Sir A. Edmonstone. 38. Miller's Safe Path for Humble Churchmen. 39. A Brief Analysis of the Doctrine and Argument in the Gorham Case. By Lord Lindsay. 40. Tomlins' Sermons. 41. Sacra Privata. 42. The Changes of our Times. 43. The Child's Preacher. By the Hon. and Rev. L. Barrington.

I.—*A Physician's Holiday; or, a Month in Switzerland in the Summer of* 1848. *By* JOHN FORBES, *M.D., F.R.S., Physician to Her Majesty's Household.* London: Murray.

DR. FORBES writes for a very large class of the English community; for the love of travelling is almost a distinctive national characteristic in Englishmen of the higher classes. It would seem as if some sense of oppression weighed them down, in contemplating the limits of their sea-girt dwelling, and that they were compelled, ever and anon, for relief, to seek for the liberty of roaming over the Continent. We scarcely know to what else to attribute the inveterate habit of "travelling," which has become second nature to so many Englishmen. We often meet men who seem to spend their whole life in locomotion, and have no sooner returned to England, but they are preparing for the road again. What swarms of travellers crowd our sea-ports in

August and September on the summer migration! Statesmen and schoolmasters—clergy and stockbrokers—students and soap-boilers—all make a simultaneous rush for the Continent; and a prodigious relief must the said Continent experience when the inundation has fairly drained off, and left them time to look about them, and to eat their dinners in quiet.

Physicians are like other men: they have bodily necessities and ailments themselves; and when the golden stream of which they have been drinking fails, usually about the breaking up of Parliament, they feel themselves at liberty to follow the example of the rest of the world, and migrate. Dr. Forbes gives us an insight into the doings of this class of the community amusingly enough:—

"They who are fortunate enough to possess country-houses of their own, go to them, and there indulge in farming, gardening, tree-felling, walk-making, or any other of the well-known rural contrivances for letting the brain lie fallow, and killing time in an easy way.

"Sporting doctors fix the day of their departure from town either on the 12th of August, the 1st of September, or the 1st of October, according as their love is, respectively, for grouse, partridge, or pheasant; and their destination is determined accordingly, to the hills of Scotland, to the northern moors, or to the stubble-fields nearer home. The salmon-fisher retires to the river-side inns of Wales or Scotland. The lover of trout, if he cannot make his holiday terminate early in September, must be content to postpone his amusement to the spring, unless he knows where the grayling haunt in the streams of Hampshire, Lancashire, or Yorkshire. The patient and philosophic men of the Punt, whose sport is 'bottom-fishing,' and whose delight is in roach, dace, perch, chub, barbel, gudgeon, or bream, betake themselves to the localities where their prey lurk, east, west, north, or south, wherever streams flow, or ponds stagnate. But woe to the doctor who only exchanges the chair in the study for the chair in the punt. His holidays will hardly be more profitable to his body, whatever they may be to his soul, than if he had taken them in Hyde Park or on Primrose Hill.

"Some physicians join their yachting friends in a trip to Jersey, Lisbon, Malta, or the Azores; some make a voyage in a trading ship to Hamburg or Drontheim; while others of this class, but of humbler aims, appease their thirst for water by making the periplus of our own islands in the common steamboats. A few revive the associations of their youthful days in quietly traversing some of the northern *links* from breakfast to dinner-time, in philosophical pursuit of the golf-ball.

"Others whose love of art is too potent to allow them to go quite beyond the sphere of patients, transport themselves to Brighton, Ramsgate, Matlock, or other places of water, maritime or inland, where they may take a fee now and then, as well as fresh air and a walk in the country, and may return to town at a moment's warning, or once a week at least, to see one or two very old friends, or two or three very urgent cases, and then go back to their oppidorural retreat, in better spirits, and with renovated relish for both work and play. Some individuals of this class, of more vigorous frames or more active habits than their neighbours, have, since the epoch of railways, adopted a yet more efficacious method of combining the enjoyment of country air and country scenes with the ordinary labours of their vocation. They take a house near a railway station, ten, fifteen, or even twenty miles from town, possess themselves of a season-ticket for three months, and go backwards and forwards—to their work and their play—every morning and afternoon, except on Sunday, which they always allow to ' shine complete holiday' for them.

" Many busier juniors and less-endowed seniors must content themselves with doings of a humbler sort than this ; such as a residence for a few weeks in some similar locality, whence their hospital or dispensary can be visited twice or thrice a week. Some must even be content with a hebdomadal trip by the express-train of Saturday afternoon, to visit their distant friends in the country, under solemn protest that they must return on Monday morning.

" A philosophical friend, whose active brain will not allow him to desert his books and his apparatus, even for the woods and fields which he loves so much, takes his holiday sometimes in quite a different style ; he sends his horses to grass, shuts up his front-windows, retires to his library in the rear, and leaves strict injunctions with the footman to inform all inquirers, patients especially, that he has gone on his annual holiday. But he sins, and he knows it, worse than the punt-fisher.

" A travelling trip to Wales, to Scotland, or to the Continent, is one of the commonest forms of holiday-making for the London physician, and assuredly one of the best. This takes him thoroughly away from his business and books, changes every thing without and within him, climate, air, exercise, habits, studies, ideas ; and generally, within the period of five or six weeks, works such a thorough revolution in soul and body, that he returns to his home a new man, sunburnt and buoyant and keener and defter in his vocation than ever."

Dr. Forbes hopes to "allure " some of his professional brethren into continental travelling, by the publication of his adventures on the road. We must really remonstrate with the doctor on this course of proceeding. Can he doubt that almost every physician, surgeon, apothecary, and chemist, who can provide the necessary funds, is at this moment on the Continent, or as often as he *can?* We have no doubt on the subject; and then how cruelly tantalizing is it of the doctor to invite to forbidden pleasures those less fortunate members of the profession, whose circumstances oblige them to indulge in a suburban retreat for Sunday, and no more. Nay, the evil is not confined to *that* class either. Every Englishman who reads this book, and is chained by business to his own home, will be driven half wild at the description which Dr. Forbes with so much gusto gives of the progress of his tour. When this worthy "sexagenarian" straps his knapsack on his back, and clutches his Alpine staff; or as he whirls along in the desperate career of the railroad, or on the more sober-minded " char," he should bestow some thought in commiseration on that portion of his countrymen who are pining to follow his example. We speak strongly on the point, because we have experienced sensations ourselves in perusing Dr. Forbes' truth-telling and life-like descriptions, which others will without doubt share in; and though we can endure the monotony of old England, we confess to a sort of vague and half-formed resolution to start for Dover, and tempt the horrors of the passage to Ostend. The doctor may depend upon it that his exhortations to " travel " fall on very inflammable materials, when he addresses himself to an English population. We should like to be the proprietors of Murray's Handbooks, —those indispensable accompaniments of the portmanteau and the knapsack ; and Dr. Forbes' work will henceforth take its place regularly along with them in the hands of the tourist of the Rhine, and of Switzerland.

Dr. Forbes recommends the tour on *medical* grounds also. This is really too bad ; but still we cannot refuse to state what the doctor alleges, as it may be of use to some of our readers, whose good health we sincerely desire :—

" A journey of this kind, properly conducted according to the circumstances of the particular case, will be still more beneficial to that numerous—I had almost said that innumerable—class of invalids who, although unaffected by any fatal or even dangerous disease, are yet so disordered and distressed by chronic functional derangements of various kinds, and by consequent debility, that their condition is much more to be pitied than that of the victims of the severest diseases of an acute kind. To these unhappy persons, whether their malady be, in popular or learned phrase, ' bile,' ' liver,' ' stomach,' ' dyspepsy,' ' indigestion,' ' mucous membrane,' ' suppressed gout,' ' dumb gout,' ' nerves,' ' nervousness,' ' hypochondriasis,' ' low spirits,' &c. &c., I will venture to recommend such a tour as that described in this little book—*mutatis mutandis*—as more effectual in restoring health than any course of medicines, taken under the most skilful supervision, *at home*. And, to say truth, such a journey may be made to fulfil almost every indication of cure applicable to such cases, which, however varied in appearance, are, in reality, extremely similar in their more essential characters.

" A Course of Travelling of this sort—to speak medically—carried out in the fine season, in one of the healthiest localities of Europe, in a pure and bracing air, under a bright sky, amid some of the most attractive and most impressive scenes in nature, in cheerful company, with a mind freed from the toils and cares of business, or the equally oppressive pursuits, or rather no-pursuits of mere fashionable life,—will do all that the best medicines can do in such cases, and much that they never can accomplish.

" It is now well known to all experienced and scientific physicians, that chronic functional diseases of long standing, can only be thoroughly cured by such general and comprehensive means as act on the whole system, and for a certain period of time, influencing the nutrition in its source, not merely by the supply of wholesome elements, but by keeping the nutrient function active and vigorous over the entire fabric, by an equable distribution of blood and nervous influence, and consequent energetic action of all the secreting organs. When drugs are useful in such cases, they are so only as subsidiary means calculated to fulfil some special, local, or partial indication. It need therefore excite no surprise that a COURSE OF TRAVELLING, calculated as it is, or at least may be made, to fulfil all the foregoing requisites, should be held forth as one of the most important methods of curing many chronic diseases. But as I am not now addressing the sick, but the well, or at most those who, though classed as invalids, can, without hazard, comport themselves as healthy travellers, I shall, in the few remarks I am about to set down, make no reference as to what should be the proper proceedings of persons labouring under formal disease. They must consult their physicians. I address those only who have not and need not physicians."

The dietary of the tourist is no unimportant item in the whole affair. The keen air of the mountain regions of Switzerland, and the length of way to which the pedestrian in that favoured land is tempted and enabled to extend his walks, creates a demand for food, which is in danger of becoming at times voracious, and thereby inflicting serious injury on the animal economy. To the dyspeptic and pill-taking, again, the change in the habits of life is one of much practical importance. The daily pill and the potion are inconvenient inside passengers in long pedestrian excursions; and yet how are they to be dispensed with? This difficult problem is solved by the medical sagacity of our author. He makes the following useful remarks on the subject:—

" As invalids and, among the rest, dyspeptic or bilious invalids con-stitute an important section in the list of those whom I have recom-mended to travel, it may be expected that I should have something spe-cial to say respecting *their* diet and general mode of living. This, however, is not the case ; or if I would lay down any rules, they would all be comprised in the single word MODERATION—moderation in strong food, and still more in strong drink. So far from recommending rigid adherence to a precise and peculiar diet, I do not hesitate to say that one of the great advantages of travelling, in cases of this kind, is that it affords a most favourable opportunity for breaking through the trammels of such a system. Nothing is so easy as to coddle and pamper the stomach into intolerance of all the more common kinds of food, by adherence to certain rigid formulæ of diet ; and when this exclusiveness is once thoroughly established, it is hardly possible to break through it in the patient's usual sphere, although, while it exists, firm or stable health can never be attained. The institution of such a system of diet may be very proper in the first instance, in order to give relief to urgent symptoms, to correct still greater errors in the mode of living, or to give room for a rational system of cure ; but when it is made a permanent regulation, and when it and its universal accompaniment, the daily pill and potion, are relied on as the exclusive means of health and strength, nothing can be more delusive or more injurious. Instead of enjoying real, vigorous, independent health, the votaries and victims of such a system can only be said to live a sort of negative, artificial life, as if by nature's sufferance, not her sanction—and, for a man's life, one surely both afflicting and degrading. Out of such a thraldom it is barely possible for an invalid to escape *at home ;* but it is far from impracticable, if the case is not of very long standing, to do so abroad—that is, during an active tour.

"Almost the only way of breaking such a chain, is the way in which the analogous chains and circles of the magicians used to be broken— namely, by simply willing and daring to do so. What was felt to be impossible in London, and what, if attempted, would have really been unsuccessful in accustomed air and haunts, amid habitual occupation, or no-occupations, will be found perfectly practicable to a traveller amid the mountain valleys and breezy passes of Switzerland. The bracing air, the brilliant sky, the animating scenes, the society of cheerful and emulous companions, and, above all, the increased corporeal exercise, will soon produce such a fundamental alteration in mind and body, in spirits and stomach, that what would have been felt like poison, will be here not only harmless but wholesome. Therefore it is, that I advise invalid travellers—those at least of the bilious, dyspeptic, hypochondriac, pill-taking class,—to follow no special regimen, but to eat the food that others eat—with the sole provisoes, that they seek for and see the sights as others do, take all the exercise their strength will admit of, and remember the golden rule of *moderation* at all times, but more especially in the commencement of their emancipation.

"Those who have had opportunities of observing what coarse fare becomes perfectly digestible by the most pampered stomachs, under the rough treatment of the hydropathists, amid the bracing breezes of Graefenberg or Malvern, and with the accompaniments of cheerful society, encouraging promises, no wine, and plenty of walking, will not be much surprised at the recommendation just made; any more than the invalid patrons of the Alpenstock need be surprised to hear of the wonderful cures effected by the water-doctors. Both systems substitute action for inaction ; the toil of muscle for the toil of brain ; exposure for coddling ; the roughness of the ruder times and humbler classes for the luxuries and over-refinements of an advanced civilization; and the return to a natural condition of the system, that is, to Health, is the consequence."

" Sight-seeing " in Switzerland is not exactly the sort of thing that it is elsewhere. It possesses the dignity of " danger " for those who are willing to venture on the experiment. The following spirited description of the *Mer de Glace,* will recal to the reader's mind the sensations which he experienced in first looking down into its unfathomable chasms :—

" We had a fine view of the glacier below us, all the way as we advanced ; and looking back along its course to the green valley beyond, it presented a striking appearance. Through the greater part of its descent, its surface exhibits a sort of ice-forest—a continuous series of sharp icy pinnacles, set close to one another, and many of them of considerable height. This is the form that glaciers in certain positions constantly assume, in the process of melting, and it is a very picturesque one. These pinnacles are also very beautiful when the sun shines bright upon them, exhibiting something of translucency and blueness in their finer points and angles. We saw something of this on the present occasion, as the weather remained clear and fine during the two hours which it took us to reach the Mer de Glace.

" We attained the object of our walk just above the point where the two mountain bases retreat backwards, and open out a wider space for the main body of the glacier to spread itself. On getting upon this we found our progress much more difficult and slow than I had anticipated ; and we soon discovered that we had need of the aid and guidance of both our attendants. Although we had here none of the pinnacles which mark the glacier lower down, we had a good deal of the kind of surface which forms the base on which they stand, namely, a constant succession of round hummocks or narrow ridges of ice, with sides more or less steep and slippery, and separated from one another by pretty deep hollows or huge ruts, twisting about in all directions, with deep wells and chasms of every shape and size, some with water, some without, traversing and obstructing the path on every side. But for the aid of our Alpenstocks to steady our footing on the slippery slopes and narrow ridges, and to enable us to leap across the cracks and hollows, we could have hardly advanced at all ; and without the personal assistance of our guides, in the more difficult spots, even our Alpenstocks would have occasionally proved insufficient. Not that there were any extreme difficulties or imminent dangers encountered or overcome by us, nor even any obstacles sufficiently formidable to hinder a man of ordinary resolution from encountering them by himself; I mean simply to state, without exaggeration, that the route was not merely troublesome but difficult, and such as should, on no account, be attempted by a stranger, however active, without an experienced guide.

" The first part of our course lay nearly across the glacier ; and about its middle we encountered the grand chasm or crevasse which constitutes the channel of its main glacier-stream (Gletscherstrom). This channel was in some places open at top for a considerable space, at other times it was vaulted over and quite concealed by the solid ice. Where open, it twisted about through the mass of the glacier, exactly like the channel of the Rhine in the rocks of the Via Mala, or of the Tamina at Pfeffers, or the Weissenbach seen by us the day before. It resembled them also very remarkably in its size, depth, and configuration—being quite narrow, and the sides occasionally overlapping one another, so as to hide the stream from view, though its channel was quite open at top. When exposed, the stream, of considerable size, was seen at a great depth, rushing along its bed of ice with a tremendous noise and at an amazing rate, and shooting in beneath that portion of the mass which was yet unbroken. In no place, that we saw, had the stream sawn the ice quite through so as to have the solid earth or rock for its bed, which appears to me rather singular, considering the effect of such streams in cutting asunder the solid rock itself; an effect, by the way, which is admirably explained and illustrated by the phenomena of these rivers in the ice. Where the chasms were the deepest, our guides favoured us with the usual exhibition of tumbling huge masses of stone into them, in order that we might see them darting from side to side in their descent, and hear the prolonged echoes they occasioned. Even on the middle of the glacier there was no difficulty of meeting with plenty of materials for such an experiment, as the whole of its surface was strewed with large stones and fragments of rock, fallen from the mountains far beyond us on either hand, and now in progress towards its sides or end to supply fresh matter to the moraine.

"It was into this main channel that M. Monson, a Lutheran clergyman of Iverdun, fell, and was of course killed, in the year 1821. Our guides pointed out the very spot where he fell. It appears that the way in which this gentleman lost his life was this: fixing the point of his Alpenstock on the opposite side of the chasm to that where he was standing, he leant forwards upon it in order that he might obtain a better view of the chasm. While in this position the point of his staff slid from its hold, and he was of course precipitated into the gulf head foremost. After twelve days, the body was recovered by a guide and a friend of the deceased, who were let down by means of ropes to a depth of 130 feet. Owing to the conservative influence of the cold, the body, though broken and bruised, was found quite *fresh* when brought to the surface.

"An accident of a somewhat similar kind which once took place lower down on this glacier, had a more fortunate issue. An innkeeper of Grindelwald, of the name of Bohren, fell into a fissure upwards of sixty feet in depth; but though his arm was broken in the fall, he contrived to make his escape, by crawling along the downward course of the subglacial river, until it reached the open air. Luckily, the distance was not more than threescore feet."

The following description of an avalanche is very well executed :—

"We were all suddenly roused and startled by a tremendous noise behind us, like a continuous peal of distant thunder, which made us instantly stop; and while we were in the act of turning round, our guides, shouting ' An avalanche!' pointed to the mountain behind us. We looked, and from beneath the lower border of the mist which covered it, and out of which the hoarse loud roar which still continued evidently came, we saw a vast and tumultuous mass of snow rushing down and shooting over the edge of the sheer cliff into the air beyond. At first this had a pointed triangular or conical shape, with the small end foremost ; but as the fall continued, it assumed the appearance of a cascade of equal width throughout.   In this form it continued until its upper extremity had parted from the cliff, and the whole mass had fallen to the earth; renewing, as its parts successively reached the ground, and with still louder and sharper reports, the sound which had momentarily ceased while it was falling through the air.   The whole of the process, which has taken so long to describe, was the work of a few seconds, half a minute at most ; and all was over and gone, and every thing silent and motionless as before, ere we could recover from our almost breathless wonder and delight. The excitement was then great; every one, as if suddenly freed from a spell suddenly cast upon him, talking, and exclaiming, and expressing his agitation in his own particular manner.   What we had just witnessed—what we had seen, and heard, and almost felt—was, in relation to our perceptions, not a mere passive phenomenon, but *a work*, an active operation or performance, begun and ended in our presence ; and it affected the mind as if it were really a result of voluntary power, an action in which the beholder could feel a sort of reflected sympathy, and take a personal interest. Hence the agitation and excitement, so different from the tranquil, solemn, and almost melancholy feelings with which we had just before been contemplating the 'motionless torrent' of the glacier, and the unveiling of the silent Schreckhorn.

" The avalanche seemed to us to come down exactly in the line of our upward path on first crossing the glacier ; and we had, therefore, mingled with our other emotions, a sense of danger narrowly and happily escaped.   On examining the spot more closely, however, on our return, we found that the nearest part of our former path was probably half a furlong or more from the spot where the avalanche fell; and I believe we should have sustained no damage had it taken place when our position was the nearest to it. Our guides, however, thought otherwise, and persisted in maintaining, that if we had been there, or even on our path on the cliff at the opposite side of the glacier, we should have been destroyed by what they call the *dust* and *wind* of the avalanche. I was utterly sceptical on this point at the time ; and, much to the horror of the guides, could not help expressing my regret that it had not descended when we were close to it. I still think my opinion correct; but I own that it was somewhat shaken by what I afterwards learnt of the effects of an avalanche which fell from the Weisshorn in the year 1821, and which I shall have occasion to notice in a subsequent part of our journey.

" The avalanche which we had witnessed was admitted by our guides to be of extraordinary size to fall so late in the year; and the old goatherd whose chalet we were approaching when it occurred, said that it was absolutely the largest that had fallen from the mountain during the last twelve years. Our good fortune in witnessing it was therefore doubly great. On viewing, from the opposite side of the gorge, on our way home, the mass of fresh snow which had fallen, we calculated its longitudinal extent to be more than a furlong; and its depth may be guessed by the fact that it filled up the whole angle between the base of the precipice and the ridge of the glacier adjoining, whose crevices it completely obliterated to some distance from its border, covering it with a uniform sheet of snow. The impetus with which so great a mass must have fallen from such a height, would necessarily occasion a great compression and commotion of the air; but whether it would have been sufficient to operate at the distance believed by our guides, is still to me very doubtful; it is certain that, where we stood when it fell, no movement whatever, perceptible by the touch, was sustained by the air."—pp. 157—159.

The following remarks on the recent ecclesiastical reforms and regulations in Piedmont are interesting :—

" The two great practical boons the common people seemed best to understand and most to prize were, the relief from clerical oppression and taxation, and the liberty of the press. If I may trust to the fidelity and accuracy of my informants—and I obtained like statements from various quarters—it was indeed high time that the rule of the priests should receive a check in Piedmont: as it seems to have gone beyond all bounds of decency and moderation. The clerical fees seem to have been truly enormous, when the poverty of the people and the high value of money in that country are considered. I was assured that under the old regime, no less a sum than sixty francs had to be paid on the occurrence of a death in any family possessing the means to pay it, and this over and above the ordinary expenses for the coffin, &c. Out of the sixty francs some portion, as from five to eight francs, might go to cover a positive or ostensible outlay by the church, as for candles, mortcloth, &c., but all the rest went into the pocket of the priest of the commune. Sums proportionally great were paid for other offices of the church, as five francs for christening and twenty for marriage. These fines, to be sure, were the main source of the incomes of the clergy; but whether the resulting sums-total to the individual priests were little or much, it is self-evident that they were an intolerable burthen to the people. By the new constitution, the priests are to be paid directly by the state, out of the general taxes; and it is not doubted that their incomes will be much less than before.

" The general ecclesiastical rule, also, seemed to be of like arbitrary severity. Indeed, until the recent change, the priests appear to have here preserved all the power and authority of the old times. One of my informants, at Cormayeur, an apparently mild and moderate man, and with all the signs of an honest man in his behaviour, assured me that one instance occurred within his own knowledge, where a man underwent nine months' imprisonment, by the award of the bishop on the representation of the parish priest, for the sole crime of contumacy in refusing to attend confession.

" But all this abuse of power, and indeed almost all power whatever, of the clergy, is now at an end; and there is too much reason to fear that, for a time at least, religion itself will suffer in the correction of the misdoings of its ministers; it is certain that some of the dogmas and practices of the Roman Catholic church will from henceforth lose their influence and respect. I myself had sufficient proof of this. Many of the men of the lower ranks spoke with ridicule of confession, and still more of the power of the priest to forgive sins; the women, however, were still unshaken in their faith. Every one with whom I conversed seemed to be of opinion that the priests to a man desire the permanence of the old tyranny in the state as well as church, and, with this view, do all they can to prevent the instruction of the people. The Scriptures in their complete state are not forbidden in Piedmont, but they are not readily procurable, partly from their high price, and partly from want of facility of purchase: abridgments alone are in common use."

We must now take our leave of Dr. Forbes and his work. We have seldom perused a more interesting Tour, and we commend it with confidence to all who are about to visit the regions which he has so well described.

II.—*A Second Letter to the Rev. W. Maskell, M.A. By the Rev.* MAYOW WYNELL MAYOW, *M.A., Vicar of Market Lavington, Rural Dean, &c.* London: Pickering.

IT is a great satisfaction to find, that when men like Mr. Maskell assail the Church, they are not left without an answer. It was our impression on reading Mr. Maskell's first letter that his connexion with the English Church was virtually at an end. It was a kind of step from which a man cannot recede without indelible disgrace. Several of his previous publications had exhibited so strong a leaning towards Romanism, that the course he finally adopted ought not, we think, to have excited any surprise. The same may be said of Mr. Allies indeed; and it is not to be denied that there are others who may be expected to follow their examples. The truth is, the only cause for wonder is, that there have not been *more* secessions; for the influence exercised over some members of the Church by others of note, who seceded from us some time since, was so great, that it seemed very surprising that they had not yielded at once to the example of their friends. We had hoped that this Romanizing influence had died out; but recent events prove plainly that it is still in existence ; and it is a very noxious influence. We have not the slightest doubt, however, that the genuine Church feeling of the great mass of Churchmen will take such shapes as will soon detach it from any influence of the kind, and permit those who are inclined to Rome, to take their own course of proceeding. Mr. Mayow's pamphlet was written, in a great degree, before Mr. Maskell's secession, a fact which he notices in his Preface as explanatory of some part of his work. Its tone is that of a friend remonstrating with a friend, and while opposed to his views, yet doing justice to his motives and intentions. The earlier part of this pamphlet discusses various statements of Mr. Maskell's with reference to the assumed ambiguity of the doctrines of the Church of England, and the want of dogmatic teaching. After this Mr. Mayow discusses the judgment of the Privy Council, and proves its impropriety on various grounds. We extract the following passages, containing matter of great importance :—

"In the first place then, we find the following declaration of the judges, presenting their own view of their powers. 'The Court,' they tell us, 'has no jurisdiction or authority to settle matters of faith :' that is, they give us to understand it was by no means its province, and as little its desire, to invade the precincts of the Church's sanctuary, and 'determine what ought in any particular to be the doctrine of the Church of England.' Of course, the latter part of this sentence is true. Their duty was to declare, (so far as any jurisdiction they had might enable them to declare,) not what *ought* to be, but what *was* the doctrine of the English Church. If they only meant therefore to say, it was not their business or their wish to enact any new canon on baptism, one is almost tempted to smile at their simplicity in thinking it necessary so solemnly to enunciate such a truism, or thus to magnify themselves upon such moderation and forbearance ; but if they thought or meant to disclaim settling any thing concerning doctrine by the powers of interpretation, which they could not avoid exercising, one is tempted again to smile, only more bitterly, to think of any persons, and especially judges in so solemn a cause, entertaining so chimerical a notion as this disclaimer evinces. What! did they imagine they could escape 'settling doctrine' by the judgment they gave, merely by leaving every man to teach what he pleased? Did they forget that interpretation itself *is* a power that settles what it interprets? Did they suppose a translator assigns no sense to the book which he translates ? Did they, or could they, for a single moment lose sight of the fact, that

they *must* 'settle' whether Mr. Gorham were to be instituted to the
living of Brampford-Speke or not : and in so doing must determine that
' the doctrine held by him' was, or 'was not, contrary or repugnant to
the declared doctrine of the Church of England?' One can hardly
believe they could lose sight of or misunderstand such a point, and
therefore we seem driven rather to let them take refuge in the truism,
than chase them into the paradox, however the latter may be the more
natural suggestion of their words. But even so, it must, I think, be
allowed, that the diction of what ought to have been a most carefully
considered document is very clumsily obscure ; as is evident from the
number of persons since its publication who keep continually quoting
upon us those words of the judgment, and assuring us that by the
showing and declaration of the Committee of Privy Council itself,
' doctrine is not affected.'   And this obscurity is darkened even more
by the aid of the published comment upon, or perhaps I should say
reiteration of, the same view, given since by an eminent member of the
court.   Lord Campbell, in one of his letters to Miss Sellon, says, ' I
assure you we have given no opinion contrary to your's upon the doctrine of baptismal regeneration. *We had no jurisdiction to decide any
doctrinal question,* and we studiously abstained from doing so. We
were *only called upon to construe the articles and formularies of the
Church,* (!) and to say whether they be so framed as to condemn certain
opinions expressed by Mr. Gorham.' If Lord Campbell individually,
or the judges generally, mean merely that their own personal faith
being in agreement or disagreement with Mr. Gorham's opinions, is not
a point decided by their sentence, I most entirely allow this ; but if
they mean, as certainly a large portion of the world has understood
them to mean, that to admit Mr. Gorham to a benefice with cure of
souls, and to say the doctrine held and published by him is ' not contrary or repugnant to the declared doctrine of the Church of England,'
does not ' settle doctrine,' so far as that Church's teaching is concerned,
(and so far as they have authority,) this certainly strikes me as a most
marvellous inaccuracy, bespeaking any thing rather than ability or
judicial clearness.   Yet if they did not mean this, (though to speak of
a matter of personal faith might be in point, as far merely as regarded
Lord Campbell's clearing himself with Miss Sellon,) how should their
judgment tend, as they seem to have hoped it would, to peace :—' to
heal,' as Lord Campbell expresses it, ' the wounds from which the
Church of England has lately suffered?' ' What hast thou to do with
peace,' surely we may demand of the judgment itself, unless something
real is to be made of this profession of not settling doctrine ?   By such
a mode of writing, the judges appear to have thought peace could be
preserved ; nothing being settled, but the latitude of interpretation
which might, as they supposed, include all, and let every man do ' that
which was right in his own eyes :'—a scheme that might possibly
have answered if the points in question had been mere matters of human
opinion, or if there had been none in the Church who believed them to
be God's truth, which they had no right to give away : none also who

were sharp-sighted enough to see that to make any doctrine an open question, *is* to rule that there is no dogmatic teaching upon it at all. Not to have observed these things more distinctly, and not more distinctly to have expressed themselves as to what they really thought their office was, appears to me, in the very outset, to be *not* indicative of ability or acuteness in the Court."

After fully discussing the authority of the judgment of the Privy Council's judgment, Mr. Mayow proceeds to the question of the dogmatic teaching of the English Church; and he proves from Mr. Maskell's own statements, and also from the principles of the Church of England, that there is a body of dogmatic teaching in the Church.

" Let me ask you to examine with attention the evidence I am about to adduce. I would arrange it under the following heads :—

" I. Common sense, and the nature of things.

" II. Appeals of our Church to antiquity, and the teaching of the Church universal, as well as to her own previous constitutions and canons.

" III. Recognition of such previous teaching by the civil power; if not proving the same point positively, yet at least showing negatively that it is not contradicted.

" IV. Some confirmation of the above view·from considerations of what the Church of England would deprive herself of, (which no one has ever supposed her to have done,) if the principle were to be carried out that her existence is to be dated from the sixteenth century only; and nothing to belong to her rule of faith but what was then determined, and in words set down.

" I. Surely it is most certain, on grounds of abstract reason and common sense, that things will stand as they are, if they neither fall to decay of themselves, nor are altered by any external power. No one pretends that the dogmatic teaching of a Church will fall to decay of itself. The other alternative, therefore, is all we have here to consider. I say, then, that of any building, what you do not destroy remains. You find such or such a fabric standing. It is, in your opinion, out of repair, or deformed with unnatural or unsightly excrescences, which in process of time have overgrown, or been engrafted upon it. Additions you may conceive them to be to the original structure, and now, injurious or inconvenient. You resolve that these, whether accidental or evilly contrived, shall be removed, and you address yourself to the task.

" But further, we are not without an abundance of external proof, if I may so call it, besides this common-sense reasoning, showing that the Church of England at the reformation, if we gather her intentions not from opinions of individual reformers, but from her own authoritative acts, did not mean to adopt a wide and indiscriminate destruction of her previous teaching, and did mean to keep all that she did not mark to be destroyed. This point was the foundation of a large part of the most learned and able argument of Mr. Badeley before the Committee of Privy Council, by which he asserted, and as it seems to me, proved (although the Court appears to have taken absolutely no notice at all of this part of his speech) the certain and positive connexion of the Church of England with the previous Church in this country, and with the Church universal, and this, not only by the links of the same apostolical succession, but in the maintenance of a connected doctrine. And the general principle as to antiquity, and the sense of the Church precedent to the reformation, which Mr. Badeley laid down expressly with a view to the matter of the suit in which he was engaged, and in order to apply it immediately to baptism ; that same principle, be it observed, is applicable in exactly the same way, and the same fulness to every other article of the faith, unless any where it can be shown that the Church of England at the reformation did ' plainly, openly, and dogmatically contradict it.' It would therefore be very much to my present purpose to cite here nearly the whole of this part of Mr. Badeley's speech, but as you know it well, and can easily refer to it, I shall but extract a few of the more important passages, where the proofs of this principle being the rule of the English Church are given.

" ' I shall next appeal,' Mr. Badeley says, ' to antiquity in order to show more fully that this doctrine for which I contend,' (of course the immediate doctrine which Mr. Badeley had in view, was baptismal regeneration : but his argument reaches, as I have just said, to the full purpose for which I cite it;) ' has always been, and must necessarily still be, the doctrine of the Church of England. . . . , If there can be any doubt at all about the sense and meaning of our Church, if it can be supposed by any criticism or minute construction, that these articles and formularies do leave any question open—do omit in any degree to declare with certainty the doctrine of the Church, resort must be had not to the writings of the reformers, not to the opinions of any individuals, however respectable they may have been ; the only appeal can be to the early Church, and the doctrines which that Church professed. That is indisputably the standard to which we are referred, not only by our Prayer Book and our Homilies, but by those who took the most prominent part in the reformation in this country, and it is natural that this should be so, because what was in fact the reformation, and what its object? My friend, Mr. Turner, the other day, spoke of the Church of England in 1552, as being then in its infancy : but according to my understanding, it was then at least more than 1200 years old, for we have evidence of British Bishops having attended some of the earliest councils. Some are supposed to have been present at the Council of Nicæa, and it is positively stated that three attended the Council of Arles, which was prior to that of Nicæa. The Church of England, therefore, is an ancient and an apostolic Church, deriving its succession from the primitive Church, and one and the same through all ages. The reformation was no *new formation*, not a creation of a *new* Church, but the correction and restoration of an old one ; it professed only to repair and reform, not to found or create—and it assumed to do this, according to the doctrine and usages of the primitive Church. The reformers well knew, that if they did not stand upon that ground, they had no resting-place for the soles of their feet; they were fully conscious that if they attempted to alter the Church any otherwise than according to its ancient model, it would crumble to pieces altogether, and probably bury them in its ruins. All they professed was, to strengthen it where it was decayed, and to strip off those additions which have encrusted or grown upon it in the lapse of time, without the authority of the Scripture, or of primitive tradition; but to this they declared that they adhered; they bound themselves down by this rule, and appealed to antiquity for all they did.'

"Then having quoted a passage from 'Bishop Jewell's Apology,' appealing to antiquity as our Church's guide, and showing (to use Mr. Badeley's words) ' that the intention of our reformers in departing from the Church of Rome, was not at all to depart from the doctrine of the Catholic Church,' he goes on to cite confirmatory authority to the same point in even more weighty documents.

" ' In the preface to the Prayer Book, as well as in the Articles, we have frequent references to the Fathers and the primitive Church. We have the same in the Homilies; in almost every page they teem with quotations from the Fathers, and support themselves upon the ancient doctrine and the Catholic tradition; and therefore, in inquiring into what was the doctrine of the early Church upon the question now in issue, we are following precisely that course of inquiry, and appealing to that tribunal, which was marked out for us by the reformers themselves. They referred to the primitive doctrine as an indication of their meaning; and of course, if they had departed from that, they would have departed from the Church itself, because the Church, and the faith of the Church, can be but one.' . . .

" ' I can show, that at the time of the Reformation there certainly was no intention to depart, and was no real departure in any respect from the doctrine of the early Church, on this or any other matter, certainly not on the Sacrament of Baptism, or upon the Sacraments generally; AND WHATEVER WAS NOT ALTERED AT THE PERIOD OF THE REFORMATION, REMAINS, AND CONTINUES TO BE THE DOCTRINE AND LAW OF THE CHURCH TO THIS DAY.' "

The latter part of Mr. Mayow's pamphlet expresses sentiments with reference to the course which might, under certain contingencies, be the duty of Churchmen. He points out the possibility, in case of any attempt to enforce heretical teaching in the English Church, that a great secession may take place to Rome, or a free Church be established. We do not quite like the notion of dread of a secession to *Rome* on a large scale being contemplated, as an inducement to adopt any particular course; or, indeed, secession of any kind; and, indeed, we have no doubt, that Mr. Mayow would be the last person to recommend any such course. He contemplates, as every one must do, the *possibility* of the Church being a different body from the establishment. It may not be always in the power of Churchmen to remain in possession of the endowments of the Church, because the State may expel them by law, or their opponents may gain the ascendancy, and deprive them of their temporalities; but their spiritualities they may retain notwithstanding, and in retaining them, they would constitute the Church of England without any secession. We say this merely on the supposition of extreme cases, which, we trust, are not likely to be realized. For instance, were the plan of refusing communion formally to the Archbishop of Canterbury universally carried out, an Act of Parliament might be passed compelling such communion, and then men might be deprived in numbers of their benefices. We should not think it advisable to bring matters to such a crisis at present, or to any crisis of the kind, inasmuch as we think more evil than good would result to the cause of truth, in the present state of the public mind: therefore we should think it unadvisable to provoke any crisis; though Churchmen must always henceforward be ready for it, if it is forced upon them. We have been greatly interested by the perusal of this able and courageous publication.

III.—*The Church Apostolic, Primitive, and Anglican. A Series of Sermons. By the Rev.* JOHN COLLINGWOOD, *M.A., Minister of Duke-street Episcopal Chapel, Westminster: one of the Masters of Christ's Hospital, &c.* London: Rivingtons.

WE have perused much of this volume with sincere gratification at its healthy tone of Churchmanship. Mr. Collingwood is a faithful and an able advocate of the Church of England, as it stands distinguished from Romanism on the one hand, and from dissent and latitudinarianism on the other. In his preface, Mr. Collingwood notices the objection which some may advance to his work as being too decidedly anti-Roman, and as coming under the imputation of " throwing stones" unnecessarily. He observes in reply, that while composing the work, he had been excited to indignation by the arrogant and insolent denunciation of the English Church by Dr. Wiseman, in a Lent pastoral. " But," he continues,

" To throw aside the plea of special provocation, surely there is very much higher ground to be taken on this subject. Is it not a fact that from an amiable but mistaken feeling, the *suppressio veri*, with regard to Rome, has been too long tried? Is it not a fact that a delusive notion of *charity*, a desire of ' winning by gentle love,' have had too much weight with many, who are yet amongst the staunchest and soundest ministers of the English Church? Is it not true, not that our CATHOLICISM has been brought too prominently forward, for that can never be, but that our PROTESTANTISM has been too much kept in the back ground? And what has been the result? Let the ' Lenten Indult' and the 'Final Appeal' of Dr. Wiseman,—let the perversions to Rome, which ever and anon shows us too plainly that men holding 'all Roman doctrine,' alas, that it should be again said! have long been ministering at England's altars,—supply an answer to this question."

The fact is, that the reconciliation of the Church of England and that of Rome under existing circumstances, may be compared to that system of free-trade which has been so well described as "reciprocity all on one side." *We* are to give up every thing, and Rome is to give up nothing. That is the "plain English" of the transaction. We agree with Mr. Collingwood in recalcitrating most stubbornly against such a bargain. Our view of the question is rather different. We think the English Church might safely permit to the Church of Rome the use of the tonsure, of unleavened bread, and of lights on the altar, if Rome would undertake, on her part, to give up the Papal supremacy, transubstantiation, purgatory, and the worship of saints and images; but until she has done this, we would not move a step towards her. To do so only exposes ourselves to insult.

Mr. Collingwood first considers the Church, as a visible society, then proceeds to its government, including a discussion on the value of primitive testimony. The subjects of Christian unity, primitive Christianity, the Church of England before the Reformation, the Supremacy of St. Peter, the causes of the Reformation, the English Reformation, with its principles and results, the Supremacy of the Crown, and the responsibilities of Churchmen, form the chief topics of discussion : and in all we have perused of the volume, we have found sound principle and good sense. With reference to the supreme Court of Appeal in Ecclesiastical cases, Mr. Collingwood—and in our opinion justly—observes that the chief grievance is, that the members of this Court need not even be Christians. On the Royal Supremacy he has the following judicious remarks :—

" It is important also to remind you, that while on the one hand the English Churchman is bound to pay, and is ever ready to pay, all dutiful obedience to the sovereign of this country ; still, on the other hand, the circumstances bearing on the relations between the Crown and the Church, or rather, we should say, between the State and the Church, have so materially altered since the Reformation, that it is necessary to watch very narrowly the course of events at the present day, to take

care that the alliance between Church and State does not degenerate
on the one part, into unworthy submission; does not grow, on the
other, into an unjust usurpation. At the time the royal supremacy
was more distinctly than before asserted in the canons and formularies
of the Church, the sovereign of this country was the only ruling power
in it; and moreover, the Church herself was able to speak, in her own
name, and on her own behalf, through her own representative body, the
convocation of this realm. Whereas now, the power formerly inherent
in the Crown, is in a great measure vested, by the constitution of this
country, in the Legislature; and that, too, a Legislature composed not
simply of Churchmen, but not even necessarily of Christians; while
the representative voice of the Church is altogether silenced by her
convocation not being allowed to assemble to deliberate on spiritual
matters."

We beg to tender Mr. Collingwood our thanks for the gratification we have derived from the perusal of his excellent and able
work. Such men as this can do good service to the Church.

IV. — *Sermons preached in Bradfield Church, Berks, Oriel
College Chapel, and other Places. By the Rev.* C. MARRIOTT,
B.D., &c. Vol. II. Littlemore: Mason. London and
Oxford: Parker. 1850.

THESE are very beautiful sermons, and well suited for private
devotion or family reading. There is a depth of thought and
simplicity of heart about them which quite charms us. The
volume is not however free from oversights. In the sermon
" *Vengeance is for God*," we find the following :—

" And observe, that this is more especially the case in the Gospel.
For although there were saints under the law who forbore to avenge
themselves,—as David, when he might have slain Saul,—yet it was then
said, 'An eye for an eye, and a tooth for a tooth.' And our blessed
Lord expressly changed this law."

The mistake here is twofold. In the first place, David spared
Saul not as an act of mercy, but because he refused to lift his
hand against the LORD's anointed. In the second place, the *lex
talionis*, established by Moses, promulgated a penalty to be
enforced by the magistrate, not by private vengeance; though
the Jews wrested the enactment so as to make it a justification
of vindictiveness.

The twenty-first sermon has been written much too hastily; it
should be written over again, and the last paragraph of the
thirtieth sermon requires revision.

We cannot leave this book without giving one or two extracts.
The following on Baptismal Regeneration is very good :—

" . . . When a soul is dedicated to God in Holy Baptism, either with its own good will, or in the passive state of infancy, through the 'charitable works' of others, He takes that soul to Himself, and remits the penalty of Adam's sin, which denies the Heavenly gift of His Presence to man till ransomed by the Blood of Christ. And coming to dwell in that soul, He begins to work in it after His own manner, mightily, though invisibly, and though not so as to control and overpower the human will. He is ready to aid the first efforts of good will, to enlighten the first dawn of spiritual understanding, to give a meaning to those truths which the natural man cannot see, 'because they are spiritually discerned;' and as the inward man advances in growth, He is ready to aid the efforts of the enlightened soul to mould itself anew to the perfect likeness of its Creator, and to perform all its actions according to His holy will. Who shall venture, indeed, to say, that He may not implant in the unconscious infant the germs of graces that shall hereafter expand into glories, any more than we can venture to deny that the child that knows not its right hand from its left, ay, even the child unborn, has in it the first elements of a future character?"—pp. 22, 23.

The following passage strikes us as very beautiful:—

" It is grievous to think of; but so it is, that there are many people who wonder what is the use of having these things always sounded in their ears. What is the use of hearing every day of the same things, when we know them? What is the use of saying the same prayers again and again, when we perhaps know them by heart, and when God knows what we want before we ask Him? Asking such questions shows that people do not love God as His little children ought to do. We know that 'as a father pitieth his own children, even so the Lord pitieth them that fear Him.' Now a father is not tired of hearing his little child say the same words from day to day; nay, he is not tired his infant cannot yet speak, but only utter sounds which a parent's love only can understand. The babe in arms can show by such sounds, repeated again and again, that he knows and loves his father and mother: he loves to cry to them, though he cannot say any thing but show that he loves them, and is glad to be with them; and they love to hear his voice, and see him stretch out his hands. No one asks why. It is because God has made them so. And He made us to be born of earthly parents, that we might have something like His own love to remember and think of all our lives: He loves to hear us cry to Him; He loves to see us lift up our hands in prayer to Him; He loves to see us fix our eyes upon Him, by attending to all that is made known to us about Him, not only that we may know more, but that we may think of what we know."—pp. 204, 205.

The sermon on the Pharisee and the Publican is very striking —take, for example, the following:—

" He [the Pharisee] was not a Dives who fared sumptuously every day, nor one of those who made the temple a 'den of thieves' with their traffic, instead of a 'house of prayer;' nor was he one of those 'who devour widows' houses, and for a pretence make long prayers.' He went up into the temple really to pray. And in so doing he puts all those to shame, and leaves them behind, who go to church only for fashion's sake, and to be seen of men, and thought respectable; so far, his worship is better than theirs."—p. 325.

We would also point out the five last sermons as full of beauty and excellence.

v.—*Parochial Sermons, preached in a Village Church. Second Series. By the Rev.* CHARLES A. HEURTLEY, *B.D., &c.* Oxford and London: John Henry Parker. 1850.

THESE are excellent discourses, sound, manly, argumentative, and persuasive, with that clearness, both of conception and execution, which so strikingly characterize their author. It is really refreshing to see so much doctrinal orthodoxy, so much practical sense, and so much earnest piety combined together. We heartily recommend them to all those who wish either to *read* or to *preach* the sermons of others. There is a healthfulness about the volume which is quite invigorating.

vi.— *The Midnight Sun: a Pilgrimage. By* FREDERICA BREMER, *&c. Translated by* MARY HOWETT. One Vol. London: Colburn. 1849.

THE introduction, consisting of twenty-five pages of rubbish, we advise our readers to skip, and proceed at once to the story, which is one well worth the reading. The characters are graphically drawn, and all of them pleasing: the tale is pretty, the plot well managed, and the *denouement* striking; in fact, this is one of the most successful of Miss Bremer's shorter works; and though here and there there are little bits of nonsense, sentimental or transcendental, as the case may be, the general tone, tenor, and tendency of the volume is Christian in the fullest extent, and cannot fail, we should think, to do good to any one who enters into it.

vii.— *Family Reading. The New Testament Narrative Harmonized and Explained by the Bishops and Doctors of the Anglican Church. Compiled from Various Authors. By the Hon.* SIR EDWARD CUST. London: Rivingtons.

THIS work is intended for family reading, and will, we have no doubt, be an acceptable gift to the higher classes of society. Its price will restrict its use to those classes, which is to be regretted, for we should think it would be comprehensible to the middling classes; and its practical and uncontroversial tone renders it both pleasing and profitable. The author lays claim to little of the matter as original, having collected his materials from our eminent bishops and divines.

" The custom of family reading," says the author, " has become so universal, that an explanation of Scripture from the highest authorities appears to be still a desideratum for ordinary use; for, although our Biblical literature is rich in this branch of learning, there is still a deficiency of works popular enough for that object. I have endeavoured to avoid all polemical or doctrinal disquisitions, so that I do not apprehend that any reader need fear lest his prejudices should be shocked by the perusal of my work, if his object be only an unaffected sincere desire to understand the New Testament. At the same time I would not mislead him by showing any false colours. I am not solicitous to dilute the 'sincere milk of the word' to suit the religious palates of others. I write without any disguise as an episcopalian, and for the Church of my affections—the Church of England, alike removed from either extreme."

The above may afford some notice of the plain and unaffected style of the volume.

VIII.—*A Synopsis of the Doctrine of Baptism, Regeneration, Conversion, &c., and kindred subjects, by the Fathers and other Writers, from the time of Our Saviour to the end of the Fourth Century. By* J. A. WICKHAM, *Esq., of Frome, Somerset. With a Preface by the Rev.* D. WICKHAM, *M.A., late of Exeter College, Oxford.* London: Bell.

THE work, of which the volume before us forms a portion, was the result of sixteen years of literary research bestowed by its author on the examination of the opinions held in different ages on the subject of Baptism. The object of the writer, in the portion now given to the public, is to examine every vestige of the writings of Christian antiquity, and to extract all passages bearing on the subject of Baptism. The following passage from the preface by the editor, will speak for itself:—

" The investigation of the solemn truth so positively enunciated, that 'except a man be born again, he cannot see the kingdom of God,' was congenial to one who longed to be re-united to a spirit which he believed already a tenant of that better land. A small but well-selected library of old divines, inherited from cleric ancestors, among whom Squire and Stillingfleet might be mentioned, had long before acquainted my father with the various opinions which theologians entertained on the words of our Lord to Nicodemus, and on the efficacy of baptism generally ; and, without anticipating the labour he was about to impose on himself, he commenced with the books of divinity he possessed, to collect the opinions of many authors on this question. Feeling increased interest in the subject, and deriving great mental benefit from it, he soon had to look for authorities beyond those in his own possession. The extensive collection of divinity to be found in Mr. Darling's Circulating Library, and the shelves of the British Museum, were now explored, and many other available sources resorted to, in order to obtain a view which might claim catholicity. Thus sixteen years had passed away on the same undeviating and uninterrupted employment, the manuscript gradually increasing, volume by volume, till his friends wondered at the perseverance and unflagging interest which a single subject of a metaphysical nature had inspired."

The portion of the work now published, and extending to the end of the fourth century, will be found a very valuable acquisition to the library of the theologian. The extracts are given in their original languages, as well as in English.

IX.—*An Introduction to Conchology ; or, Elements of the Natural History of Molluscous Animals. By* GEORGE JOHNSTON, *M.D., LL.D., Fellow of the Royal College of Surgeons of Edinburgh.* London : Van Voorst.

THIS elaborate work is intended to present a view to the conchologist of the economical, physiological, and systematical relations of Molluscous Animals to each other, and to other created beings ; and it is believed that it is the only work in the English language in which this attempt has been made. The author acknowledges his obligations to J. E. Gray, Esq., keeper of the Zoological Collection in the British Museum, for many valuable contributions to the work. It is thrown into the form of Letters, and is written in a pleasing style. As some of our readers may need some explanation of the term MOLLUSCA, the author shall explain himself :—

" It was Cuvier, who first of all gathered together these animals, hitherto scattered among many classes, and assigned to the group, or sub-kingdom, the denomination of MOLLUSCA, a term in previous use, but which had been very vaguely defined and applied. They are so named, because they have soft fleshy bodies, devoid of bones. They are readily distinguished from all above them in the animal kingdom, by the want of an interior skeleton, and by the colourless condition of their blood ; and from insects and worms, they are distinguished with equal facility ; for the body of the Mollusca is never divided, like that of insects and worms, into rings, nor invested with a hard crust or skin, fitted like a coat of mail to the junctures, nor even furnished with jointed limbs and organs of progression. On the contrary, the Mollusca have a soft undivided body, covered with an irritable mucous skin, moistened with a viscous liquor, which exudes from it; this skin, in very many instances, is ample enough to be formed into membranes and fleshy folds," &c. &c.

It appears that there are no less than 15,000 species of these " viscous " animals in the world. We should not exactly like to be obliged to follow this study certainly, as far as the animals themselves are concerned, though we admire the Conchifera, for the endless beauty and variety of their shells. Notwithstanding our prejudices, however, against many of the tribes whose history is narrated in this work by Mr. Johnston, we are bound to say, that his book is full of amusement, as well as of general information and scientific research; and to all who are interested in the habits, dwellings, and organization of this sub-kingdom of the creation, we commend the work before us, in the fullest confidence that they will derive advantage of all kinds from its perusal. We should add, that it is copiously illustrated by well-executed wood-cuts.

x.—HΘIKΩN APETΩN YΠOTYΠΩΣIΣ. *A Selection from the Nichomachean Ethics of Aristotle, containing a Delineation of the Moral Virtues, with Notes, and an Introductory Discourse.* By William Fitzgerald, *M.A., Professor of Moral Philosophy in the University of Dublin, &c.* Dublin: Hodges and Smith.

A very neatly executed and well got up publication. It is intended for the use of senior sophisters in the University of Dublin. Mr. Fitzgerald's notes and preface evince much familiarity with his subject.

xi.—*The Life, Letters, and Opinions of William Roberts, Esq. Edited by his Son,* Arthur Roberts, *M.A., Rector of Woodrising, Norfolk, &c.* Seeleys: London.

The subject of this biography, who is chiefly known to us as the writer of Mrs. Hannah More's Life, was one of those good old staunch Tories, and Church and State men, who flourished in the days of Pitt and Eldon, and other worthies of those times. He was a vigorous opponent of liberalism in religion and politics, an antagonist of Whiggery, the *Edinburgh Review,* tractarianism, popery, &c.; and in the latter part of his life became imbued with evangelical views. He edited for some time the *British*

Review, a staunch Tory and anti-popish journal, and was in consequence noticed by some leaders of the Tory party, who obtained for him some posts under Government, of which he was deprived by the Whigs.   There are not many materials for biography here ; the chief interest being from the occasional introduction of greater personages on the scene.   Mr. Roberts was a good and highly-respectable man ; but we scarcely think he was of that class whose biographies the world will feel much interest about.

XII.—*Sermons. By the Rev.* ANDREW HUDLESTON, *D.D., Rector of Bowness, &c.*   London: Whittaker.

THESE sermons appear to be adapted for a country congregation, dealing as they do in explanation of elementary truths, and in homely and simple illustrations.   As a specimen of the style, we must quote the following passage from a sermon on Christmas-day, in which the preacher, in speaking of the office of our Lord, speaks thus :—

" In this respect, then, He was a Saviour, in the most eminent and emphatical sense of that expression; inasmuch as He came into the world, not to save us from the common evils of life, which are permitted as trials to exercise and improve our virtue, but to save us, in a spiritual sense, from the greater and worst of all possible evils,—the dominion, the drudgery, the guilt, and the punishment of our sins. The appellation of Saviour had indeed been anticipated before our Lord's birth, by an angel of God, who in a dream is made thus to expostulate with Joseph, the husband of Mary, the mother of Jesus: ' Joseph, thou son of David, fear not to take unto thee Mary thy wife ; for that which is conceived in her is of the Holy Ghost, and she shall bring forth a Son, and thou shalt call His name Jesus ; for He shall save His people from their sins.'   This name of Saviour had, we know, been given to characters of a very opposite description; to those mighty heroes and conquerors of antiquity who had preserved the safety of their respective countries by defensive, or had enlarged the boundaries of them by aggressive warfare, and sometimes to those great and wise legislators who had provided for their internal peace and security by wholesome laws and salutary municipal regulations ; but the name of Saviour will not apply to our blessed Lord in any of these senses."

We quite concur in the truth of this ; indeed, we presume it will be so generally admitted, that it would scarcely have occurred to us as necessary to state the fact ; and we must add, in candour, that there are occasionally statements of the same kind, which wear, at first sight, *rather* the character of what are called " truisms."   Still we are bound to say that the author exhibits no deficiency in the reasoning powers.   His sermons are in many places closely and argumentatively written; and his views are strictly orthodox. Infidelity, Methodism, and Calvinism are met and refuted. There is a highly complimentary dedication to the Earl of Lonsdale, who, we suppose, is a sort of sovereign in that part of England.

XIII.—*Fides Laici.* London : ♣ W. Parker.

THIS little poem is designed chiefly for the purpose of censuring certain proceedings of some members of the Church, opposed to the Evangelical section, whom the author considers to be Romish, or otherwise objectionable. He appears to be attached to the English Church; but there is not much ability in his verses.

XIV.—*Parish Musings in Verse.* By JOHN S. B. MONSELL, *Chancellor of Connor, &c.* London : Rivingtons.

THE author of this little volume modestly disclaims any merit in his poems, except their practical nature. They do not exhibit, in our opinion, any indications of very high poetical genius; but they are not unpleasingly written : and to very many persons their simple piety combined with tolerable versification, will render them very acceptable.

XV.—*A Letter to the Lord Bishop of Glasgow and Galloway on the present aspect of Church Affairs.* By *Sir* ARCHIBALD EDMONSTONE, *Bart.* London : Masters.

AMONGST the pamphlets which have appeared in reference to the present state of the Church, we have not perused any with more satisfaction than that of Sir Archibald Edmonstone. It is full of good sense and good principle,—two things which are not always combined. Sir Archibald Edmonstone sees distinctly the dangers of the Church, and points them out; but his remedy consists in vigorous actions, for the purpose of removing these dangers. He meets the common objections against Convocation very satisfactorily; and he is confident that our cause will be extensively supported, if it is rightly put forward. On this point we must extract one passage, in which we are happy to find our own opinion confirmed by Sir Archibald Edmonstone :—

" Not only is unity of purpose, but heartiness in the cause requisite. No one who doubts the Church's position can effectively fight her battles. And here I cannot but notice an impression, which more

perhaps than any thing, tends to impede our efforts. Many men who
have come forward as ardent champions of the Church, have ended in
desertion. Hence the fault is laid at the door of the principles they
advocate as having a natural tendency towards Rome."

XVI.—*The Tudor Supremacy in Jurisdiction unlimited. A
Sermon preached in the Parish Church of Kingsbridge, at the
Ordinary Visitation of the Venerable the Archdeacon of Totnes.
By* ROBERT HENRY FORTESCUE, M.A., *Curate of Bigbury,
Devon, &c.* London: Masters.

In the discourse before us, the author shows, and very sufficiently,
that the Tudor princes claimed and exercised a supremacy in
spiritual matters over the Church of England, which was extreme
in various points, and that the Clergy yielded to it more than
they might have done. We agree, with Mr. Fortescue, that
there is nothing to be gained by denying these facts; they are
palpable. The Clergy, however, who yielded to the aggressions of
the temporal power, did so when that temporal power was in the
strictest alliance with the Church; and when this has been the
case, encroachments of the State have been, in most cases,
submitted to very patiently. Mr. Fortescue, in the latter part
of his sermon, urges the claims of the Church to the right of her
spiritual jurisdiction unfettered by the Crown. The following
passage is of much interest and value :—

" In contending, then, for the recovery of the Church's just rights in
regard of jurisdiction, I would urge, as an essential point, that it is
useless to close our eyes upon, or to misrepresent our real position.
It is worse than useless to invite discomfiture by assuming a position
which cannot be defended,—by insisting, that, in the reigns of Henry
VIII., Edward VI., and Elizabeth, the doctrine of the Royal Supremacy did not invade the indefeasible rights of the Church. But since
that doctrine, as understood at the period of the Reformation, and as
exercised ever since, *has* involved the right of the Crown to appoint
any persons it sees fit, provided only they be ' natural born subjects,'
to constitute the court of ultimate appeal in suits involving doctrine, we
must take other ground for sustaining our most reasonable claims. We
must be bold to say to our rulers, that we think *too much* was then
conceded to the Crown, more than the Church had a right to concede,
or could alienate from itself. We must plead that no godly prince in
Holy Scripture is related to have ever intruded on the priest's office, so
far as to assume the judgment of leprosy; and in like manner, no
Christian prince should ever have arrogated to himself the judgment of
doctrine. We must contend that Henry VIII. professed to claim only
such powers as had been exercised by his progenitors; but (as we may
truly add) that he usurped more than he claimed. And to the objection,

that the concession for which we ask, would involve an encroachment on the royal prerogatives, we may reply, that such a difficulty has presented no obstacle to the enlargement of the liberties of the people; but that, in temporal matters, the prerogatives enjoyed by the Tudors have been so frittered away by repeated inroads, that now, instead of the strong absolute sway which those princes exercised, the Crown is virtually neutral, its will having been transferred to its responsible advisers; so that, at present, the supremacy of the Crown is, in point of fact, the supremacy of the *Ministers* of the Crown, who may be dissenters, or papists, or infidels. We must plead, also, the *injustice* of the State's still laying on the Church the full weight of its iron hand, to cripple its energies, to adulterate its doctrines, to fill its highest offices with suspected men, when that hand is no longer used to aid it in its work, to enforce its discipline, to coerce or to expel its adversaries, nor, as was promised, for the 'correction of errors, heresies, and schisms.'

"If we be told that our claims are inconsistent with our subscriptions, we may reply, that we think otherwise; that if all our claims were granted, there would still remain to the Crown a most ample supremacy; a supremacy, which the most potent Christian sovereign might be proud to exercise, and, at the same time, be thankful for the opportunities it afforded him of promoting the glory of God, the good of His Church, and the salvation of men. We fully admit, that Convocation may not legally meet, may not frame canons, may not enforce canons, without the royal licence; that, without the same licence, no bishop or ecclesiastical judge may perform one function of his office; that the permission of the secular power, and not that of the Pope, is requisite for the exercise of these rights within the imperial dominions; that, as Henry wrote to Cranmer, before he had fully thought out his theory of derived jurisdiction, they judge by the *licence* and *sufferance* of the Crown; that, further, as eight bishops acknowledged to the king, 'in case the bishops be negligent, it is the Christian prince's office to see them do their duty,'—to see that the laws and canons of the Church be enforced and obeyed; and, moreover, that every temporal penalty, of whatever kind, inflicted for ecclesiastical offences, results from the power, not of the Church, but of the State. We may reply that, in this sense, as we have taken, so we will take, and take conscientiously, the oath, and subscribe to the canon of supremacy; with no mental, but with an *express* reservation, that in this sense, and in this sense alone, we take and subscribe them; and we humbly hope that no bishop or commissary would object that this sense is insufficient. But we must add, that we deem it no rightful exercise of this supremacy,— we deem it tyranny,—absolutely to suppress the Church's power of legislation,—to make those canons which have been passed a dead letter,—to supersede the spiritual judge,—and, because it is found to be no longer politic to aid the discipline of the Church with the coercive influence of the temporal power, to forbid the exercise of all discipline whatever. To those, indeed, who would remind us of our oaths,

we might well reply, that they who imposed them have long since made
them inconsistent with facts, and obliged us in some sense to qualify
them ; inasmuch as, since the Act of Toleration, the dissenters have
been allowed to settle their own purely spiritual causes among themselves, and (as they thought fit) to sever members from their communion, and to deprive their ministers, without being subject to any
appeals to the civil power ; and that, more recently, in consequence of
concessions made to papists, the exercise of spiritual jurisdiction in this
realm, and the granting of dispensations by a foreign prelate, has been
connived at,—nay, more, has been permitted by the laws."

XVII.—*Homer's Iliad, Books* I.—IV., *with Critical Introduction
and Copious English Notes. By the Rev.* T. K. ARNOLD, *Rector
of Lyndon, &c.* London : Rivingtons.

WE are informed in the preface of this edition, that it is not
intended for the mere beginner, but for the pupil of more advanced
age, who is fitted by his general knowledge of the laws of Greek
construction, to commence the critical study of Homer.   The
work contains, besides the text, an Abridgment of Thiersch's
Treatise on the language of Homer, and very full Notes.

XVIII.—*Posthumous Sermons. By the Rev.* GEORGE CRABBE,
LL.B., *Author of* " *The Borough,*" *&c. Edited by* J. D. HAST-
INGS, *Rector of Trowbridge.* London : Hatchards.

THESE discourses are characterized by good sense and lucid
argument.   They are almost wholly practical, and are generally
sound ; but we do not like the tone of the author in speaking of
the Holy Communion, in reference to which, he explains away,
in a mode which appears to us very unsatisfactory, the language
of the Catechism ; and virtually removes all mystery from the
subject.

XIX.—*St. George for England ! An Address to, and Correspondence with, certain Persons disaffected to the Established Constitution. By a* MEMBER OF THE ENGLISH BAR.   London :
Rivingtons.

WE fear that the time for rallying men by the cry of " St. George
for England " is gone by.   Men in the present day care nothing
for the past ; have very little regard for established institutions,
except in so far as they are personally interested in them.   We
are speaking, of course, of the active and ruling spirit of the age.
The inactive and helpless majority think differently, and grumble
exceedingly at the innovations they see around them ; but they
have no spirit to join the " St. George for England " party,

because they have no leaders, and are as apathetic as they are amiable. We agree with this "Barrister" in admiring the old theory of the Union of Church and State, as represented by Hooker. It was a reality in the days of Hooker; but even the "Barrister" does not shut his eyes to the inroads which have been made on that theory by the course of legislation for the last thirty years. He sees that such facts as "Catholic Emancipation," the "Repeal of the Test and Corporation Acts," the "Godless Colleges," the "Maynooth Bill," &c., are all directly in the teeth of this theory. The "Barrister" imagines that the theory can go on very well notwithstanding, and that we are to regard the supremacy as exercised by ministers nominated by a creedless House of Commons, in just the same point of view as our forefathers did when it was exercised by an Elizabeth or a Charles. We are sorry that it must be our fate to differ from the "Barrister."

xx.—*Legends of the Monastic Orders, as represented in the Fine Arts. Forming the Second Series of Sacred and Legendary Art. By Mrs.* JAMIESON. London: Longmans.

THE many readers and admirers of Mrs. Jamieson's former work will look with interest to the appearance of a continuation, illustrated by the pencil of the gifted authoress. It is a compendious series of lives of the Romish saints, and as such, we should not put it into every one's hands in these days. To artists and connoisseurs, however, it will be found particularly useful.

xxi.—*The Paradise of the Christian Soul, delightful for its choicest pleasures of Piety of every kind. By* JAMES MERLO HORSTIUS, *of the Church of the Blessed Virgin Mary, &c.* London: Burns and Lambert.

THIS is a translation at full length of a work of Roman Catholic devotion, which has been already partially translated and modified by a member of the Church of England. It is, doubtless, extremely well adapted for the use of Romanists, and is neatly got up, though the illustrations are in a poor style of art. The species of devotion is this:

" Transfix the marrow of my soul, O lovely Jesus, with the sweetly penetrating arrow of Thy love, that my soul may be wounded and may languish with the inmost love of Thee and of Thy wounds; and then, being entirely dissolved into love of Thee, may melt away, and be wholly absorbed into Thee, and inseparably adhere to Thee. Amen. *Our Father, Hail Mary.*"

This style of address, combined with ardent prayer to Saints, and such other practices of Romish devotion, will no doubt render the little work before us highly popular in Romish circles. To others it is, of course, wholly unsuited.

XXII.—*Essays, Political, Historical, and Miscellaneous. By* ARCHIBALD ALISON, *LL.D., Author of the History of Europe, &c.* Vol. III. Edinburgh: Blackwood.

THE collected essays of Mr. Alison furnish one of the most valuable contributions to English literature made in our day. They consist of a series of articles contributed to " Blackwood's Magazine" during the last twenty years, and embrace a great variety of topics, historical, political, and literary. We can assure the reader that he will find a large fund of amusement and of information in these volumes. The last article but one in the volume before us contains an exposition of the political state of the empire, arising out of the Reform Bill, which is full of melancholy, and we fear, but too well-founded anticipations of the fall of England.

XXIII.—*Eastern Churches. Containing Sketches of the Nestorian, Armenian, Jacobite, Coptic, and Abyssinian Communities. By the Author of "Proposals for Christian Union."* Second Edition. London: Darling.

THIS little volume contains much interesting and curious information on the subject of the Eastern Churches, conveyed in a light and amusing style.

XXIV.—*Regeneration; or, Divine and Human Nature. A Poem, in Six Books. By* GEORGE MARSLAND. London: Pickering.

THE author of this work appears to be a Wesleyan Methodist, as it is dedicated to Dr. Dixon, late President of the Wesleyan Methodist Conference, as "one of the greatest and best of men." The author states, that he has written under the influence of inspiration: "I am conscious to myself that my mind has been, to a great extent, the passive instrument of the Great Spirit, who, through me, speaks to the world; and yet, whatever may be unworthy of God's glory I must take the blame of to myself. I have desired to produce a work that might be thought worthy to be offered up by the High Priest of Error as a propitiation to Satan." We should scarcely have supposed that Mr. Marsland could have expected such an issue of his labours, though he is pretty severe upon priests and Established Churches. We have no doubt that he will remain undisturbed by any persecution. His poem is a very respectable one ; rather more like an essay or a sermon than a poem. The author is a staunch Protestant.

> " No wonder that the Popes
> Forbid the reading of God's Word; for that
> Would show the cheat. Light has appeared on earth,
> But they have chosen darkness to prefer,
> Because their deeds are evil ; fearful lest
> They, by that light reproved, should be condemned.
> Were I to hold an order up to view
> Of universal execration, as
> Unfit to live, the serpents of our race,
> The Jesuits are the men ; no word can reach
> So low to meet their case, a libel on
> Our race, who scruple not to dress in garb
> Of deep sincerity, the wicked heart
> That has conspired with solemn vows to rob
> , The world of liberty."

This will convey some notion of the style in which this work is written.

xxv.—*A Charge delivered to the Clergy of the United Dioceses of Ossory, Ferns, and Leighlin, at his Ordinary Visitation in October,* 1848. *By* JAMES THOMAS O'BRIEN, *D.D., Bishop of Ossory, Ferns, and Leighlin.* London : Seeleys.

DR. O'BRIEN has favoured the Church, in his present Charge, with a lengthened exposition of his views of the Alliance of Church and State, and states many truths, which will be undisputed by Churchmen. Without doubt, Dr. O'Brien is perfectly right in pointing out what he conceives to be the State's duty towards the Church ; but his lordship appears to forget that the legislation in which he tells us that he himself and his friends concurred—the removal of all legal disabilities from Romanists and dissenters—has made them a part of the State, and that the State cannot therefore be expected to extend any peculiar favour to the Established Church, except as a mere State establishment.

" I am myself one of those who, regarding the removal of all *civil* disabilities connected with the profession of religion as essential to the perfect enfranchisement of conscience, earnestly desired this measure, and rejoiced when it was at last passed. The time, the mode, and all the circumstances under which it was carried, rendered it certain that the good results which might have been fairly expected from it, if it had been granted earlier, could be very partially, if at all, attained; and, indeed, made it likely that evils would follow from it which were no proper effect of the measure itself. But still I regarded it, upon the whole, as no mean good. And as to the security of the Church,—though I certainly did not hope that her conflict with her enemies would cease,—yet I desired to see her contending, if she must contend, for what it was a direct duty to maintain, and what therefore could be maintained with a clear conscience and upon intelligible principles, rather than for outworks which every one would feel it was her duty to give up, unless they were absolutely necessary to her preservation. While many regarded them as so far from having that claim to be upheld, that, on the contrary, they brought danger, not security, to her; not merely by stimulating the hostility of those upon whom they so severely pressed, but by dividing and arraying in hostile parties those who ought to be all united in her defence.

"It must be owned that the course of events since, seems to have justified the wisdom of those friends of the Church who so long and so strenuously contended for the maintenance of such distinctions, as essential to her security. I do not think that point so clear as many are not unnaturally disposed to regard it. But whether these friends of the Church judged rightly or not as to the securities which they desired to retain for her, they certainly did not, in their worst anticipations, overrate the bitterness and perseverance with which she has been assailed since they were surrendered.

" For obvious reasons connected with her position as the Church of the minority, the Church in Ireland had been the principal object of those fears. It was not unnaturally apprehended, that the Roman Catholics in this country looked with a jealous eye on the possessions of our Church, regarding them as of right belonging to their own. It was in vain that they averred that they did not covet any such provision for their Church. Few of those whom this renunciation was intended to satisfy believed it; and there were still fewer who doubted that, even if it were so far sincere that they had no desire to obtain them for their own Church, yet they were anxious to take them away from ours. They were now, it was said, pursuing another object, which not only gave them abundant occupation, but supplied very cogent reasons for not stirring claims or revealing designs which would excite alarm, and convert many of their best friends into enemies, and raise the most serious obstacles in the way of attaining their more immediate end. But it was confidently predicted, that if *it* were once obtained, all this reserve would disappear, and the Church—when she had divested herself of the most important of the means of defence with which the provident solicitude of earlier times had furnished her—would be seen, too late, to be the first object of their hostility.

" Such apprehensions of the consequences of removing Roman Catholic disabilities, were openly expressed by the friends of the Church. And the Roman Catholics were certainly not deficient in efforts to allay them. Their bishops and their political leaders testified, that the measure which they pressed on the Legislature would have the effect of taking away all grounds for such fears. If the position of the Established Church, as endowed and exalted, were looked upon with discontent by Roman Catholics, it was only because they themselves were suffering under the invidious and injurious civil disabilities which were connected with the profession of their religion. But, were these taken away, the Church might rest secure in its possessions ; and, at least, would be in no danger from the hostility of Roman Catholics.

" To set at rest, however, such fears more decisively, a special provision for the security of the Church was embodied in the Bill for the removal of Roman Catholic disabilities. It was argued : ' If any danger is to arise to the Established Church from throwing open to Roman Catholics seats in Parliament, and the various places of power and trust from which they have been excluded hitherto, it must be from some use which they are to make of the power thus acquired. But if, in every case, before such power is bestowed upon them, they are bound by an oath, man by man, never to use it to destroy or injure the Church, all such fears ought to be set at rest.'

" Accordingly, such an oath was framed and embodied in the Emancipation Act ; and, in conformity with the provisions of the Act, this oath is actually taken by every Roman Catholic member of both houses, before he takes his seat, and by every Roman Catholic appointed to any of the offices under the Crown which have been thrown open by that Act, before he enters upon his office.

" The amount of protection which this precautionary measure has extended to the Church, is well known. All the power acquired under the Bill, as well as all otherwise possessed by the Roman Catholics, very soon began to be exerted, and has been ever since exerted by them, (with a few most honourable exceptions,) in Parliament, and out of it, to overthrow the Protestant Church Establishment in this country. Of course they were not permitted to make such a use of the power entrusted to them, without being reminded of the oath which was intended to guard against it. But almost equally, of course, they loudly and indignantly denied that they were violating any obligations which it laid upon them !

" The oath does not appear to have been particularly well framed for its purpose ; but its purpose was, and is, universally known ; and its language, however deficient it may be in perfect exactness, is not so loose as to leave its meaning open to any reasonable doubt. But it has been subject to a process which language is not capable of resisting. And the statesman or lawyer who framed it, whoever he be, may be comforted under its failure, by the reflection, that the case in which his formula has failed, is one in which no other could have succeeded."

This is altogether a very poor comfort for those who took part in carrying " Catholic Emancipation." Any one, possessed of common sense, could have seen, that to give direct political power to the most bitter enemies of the Church, would do nothing but endanger that Church. Such persons as Dr. O'Brien had not the excuse of being unwarned. They persisted in their measure, in spite of the warnings and the most strenuous resistance of the really faithful part of the Church; and they have now the result before them. To such as Dr. O'Brien the impending ruin of the Irish Church is wholly and exclusively to be attributed. From open opponents of the Church we expect destructive measures; but it was only when a part of the garrison betrayed the fortress of the Constitution, that it fell into the hands of the foe. To reverse such steps is impossible. They are certain to conduct to ruin; and it is perfectly in vain for Dr. O'Brien, and such persons as him, to call upon the State to act now upon principles which he himself taught it to relinquish legislatively.

XXVI.—*Rig-Veda-Sanhita. A Collection of Ancient Hindu Hymns, constituting the first Ashtaka or Book of the Rig-Veda, the oldest authority for the Religious and Social Institutions of the Hindus. Translated from the original Sanskrit. By* H. H. WILSON, *M.A., F.R.S., &c.* London: Allen.

THE importance and value of this work to all who are engaged in studies bearing on the Hindu religion, cannot be too highly estimated. Mr. Wilson's eminent distinction as a Sanscrit scholar inspires perfect confidence in the accuracy of his version, and the annotations appended tend greatly to the elucidation of these extraordinary remains of heathenism. It is curious to mark their immense inferiority in all respects to the books of the Old Testament with which they may vie in antiquity. In the Rig-Veda, the usual address of the suppliant is to the Deity to accept and partake of his offering. The Deity is always supposed to drink the soma juice offered to him—a strong spirituous liquor.

XXVII.—*A Letter to Archdeacon Hare, with respect to his Pamphlets on the Gorham Question. By the Rev.* J. M. NEALE, *M.A., &c.* London: Masters.

IN this letter, Mr. Neale very satisfactorily exposes the latitudinarianism of Mr. Hare, and remarks on the violence of his language, and the attempt to stifle the expression of opinion on the part of the Clergy of his archdeaconry. Mr. Neale will find that there is no class of men so intolerant of differences of opinion, and so violent in their language, as those who object to party spirit, and advocate unbridled liberty of conscience.

XXVIII.—*Emperors of Rome, from Augustus to Constantine. Being a Continuation of the History of Rome.* By MRS. HAMILTON GRAY. London: Hatchards.

THE best written short history of the Roman Emperors we remember to have seen. The history of each reign is succeeded by collateral information of all kinds bearing on the subject, and this agreeably relieves the dryness of a compendious history.

XXIX.—*The Poor Artist ; or, Seven Eye-sights and One Object.* London: Van Voorst.

A VERY amusing extravaganza, in which flies, ants, spiders, &c., are made to hold conversations, in a very spirited style, with an artist.

XXX.—*Record of the College of Christ Church, in Brecon. By the Rev.* JERMYN PRATT. London: Masters.

THIS publication points out a very disgraceful state of things at the Collegiate Church of Brecon :—

" Having now given a description of the *ample* endowment of the College of Christ Church, Brecon, its charter, and archiepiscopal order for its rules and regulations to be strictly observed, it remains now only briefly to present the reader with an account of its present dilapidated condition.

" All that now exists of this collegiate fabric is the chancel, which is about sixty feet long by twenty-five wide, and contains stalls for the dean, treasurer, precentor, and prebendaries, in oak painted lead colour; with the names of the respective parishes annexed to their prebends, in gilt letters on the back of each. It has eleven narrow windows on the north side, and four on the east end of the south side. The two most to the westward on the south side are blocked up to receive a marble monument erected to the memory of Richard Lucy, Chancellor of St. David's. There are three sedilia and two piscinæ. The two most westward sedilia are blocked up by the above-mentioned monuments to Richard Lucy. The piscinæ and only sedile to be seen are given in a drawing with this record.

" Nothing can exceed the filthy state of this sacred edifice. The roof even now scarcely resists the rain, although subscriptions have, within the last three years, been raised by private individuals to repair it; and also to mend the windows, through which the boys of the town, previous to their being put in order, had free access. The dean and prebendaries were, at the time of raising the subscription, all applied to ; but almost all refused to lend their aid to so laudable an undertaking.

" The ceiling of this building is daily falling, and is allowed to remain as it falls, upon the pavement below,—no one being employed to clear the dust and mortar away.

" It appears that prayers were read, and a sermon preached, till about the year 1839 ; and the cause of the suspension of Divine service was, that the roof was considered too insecure to allow the usual duty to be performed with safety.

" The prebendaries used to reside in their turns, for a short time, in the memory of many persons living in Brecon ; but none have kept residence for the last twenty years.

" The school, however, was kept up till 1845 ; but from the inefficiency of the schoolmaster, (who nominally held the office of lecturer as well,) it dwindled away to a very few boys, and now there is none at all— *neither school, service, or lecture.* The small building set apart for the school-room is perfectly unfit for the purpose, and would, indeed, be a disgrace to the smallest population in any parish.

" The entrance to this collegiate church is through an archway of the old nave, by a miserable, rickety pair of old doors. They are merely fastened by a chain and padlock, which the person who has charge of the ruins, and who still retains his nominal office of clerk or sexton, is obliged to find at his *own cost.* He has received no salary since September, 1834. He was then paid by the register five pounds per annum for his services as clerk, and ten shillings for washing the surplice. The clerk also used to receive ten shillings and sixpence for every new prebendary installed.

" The piece of ground, containing about two and a half to three acres, which from its position was evidently the cemetery of the College, is a grass field to the north, adjoining the old fabric ; and even if its position did not accurately mark it out as the burial-place attached to the College, from time immemorial it has always been considered as such by the inhabitants of Brecon,—and such a supposition is fully established by the following circumstance. In 1845, while they were widening the road from Carmarthen to Brecon, which abuts on the piece of land just mentioned, four human skulls, together with some bones, were exhumed. In spite of this proof of the sanctity of this close, (as it is called,) it is now let as pasture by the Bishop of St. David's for sixteen pounds per annum ; and, moreover, a circus for horsemanship, almost every year, is allowed to be erected in the centre of this hallowed spot.

" The leases of several small parcels of land in the immediate vicinity of this College have lately fallen in, and the Bishop of St. David's does not intend to renew them.

" There is no doubt but that this record will be censured by many persons now enjoying emoluments from this sacred foundation. It is at once admitted that it may be (from the difficulty of acquiring facts) in some measure inaccurate ; but it is nevertheless sent into the world, in order to be the means of giving information to those in authority— of correcting, if possible, one of the grossest abuses of Church property, and in the earnest hope that this ancient College may yet be set apart for the purpose for which it was originally transferred and endowed, viz. to supply scriptural education to the poor—' *to improve the morals of the King's liege subjects*,' and advance the honour and glory of God."

XXXI.—*An Inquiry into the Catholic Truths hidden under certain Articles of the Creed of the Church of Rome.* Part II. *Original Sin and Justification.* By CHARLES SMITH, B.D., *Rector of Newton, &c.* London: J. W. Parker.

IN this work Mr. Smith examines, with much ingenuity and erudition, the Decrees of the Synod of Trent on Original Sin and Justification, connecting with them the various tenets and practices to which they lead, and commenting with much ability on the writings of modern controversialists in the Church of Rome. The work is rather discursive in its character, but it bears evidence of research and of ingenuity.

XXXII.—*Church Hymns; or, Hymns for the Sundays, Festivals, and other Seasons of the Ecclesiastical Year, as observed in the Church of England. Compiled, with an Introduction, by* HENRY STRETTON, *M.A., Perpetual Curate of Hixon.* London: Rivingtons.

THIS collection of Hymns appears to have been made with much judgment and care; and it seems to us, on the whole, more practically adapted to the use of the Church than any we have yet seen. Many of these Hymns are taken from ancient sources, and are very beautiful. We should be glad to see such a collection as this in general use.

XXXIII.—*Canterbury Papers. Information concerning the principles, &c., of the Founders of the Settlement of Canterbury, in New Zealand.* London: J. W. Parker.

THE Canterbury Settlement is a great experiment, to which we cordially wish success; but we presume that this colony, like others, will have its difficulties to contend with, notwithstanding the excellence of the soil, the fineness of the climate, and the other natural advantages, so temptingly placed before the colonist in the work before us. The founders of the Settlement have undoubtedly proceeded on right principles in their whole plan. There is one point, however, on which we feel obliged to make some observations at the present time. The endowment of the new See of Lyttelton is to be provided, we apprehend, by the colonists themselves, and in no degree by the State. On what ground, therefore, can the Crown justly claim the right of appointing the Bishop? We presume that the colonists do, in fact, appoint their own Bishop; but ought there not to be more than a secret understanding with the Government on this point? Ought it to be left in the power of future Governments to misunderstand the question, and to nominate without consulting the colonists?

xxxiv.—*Tracts on the Church. By the Rev.* WILLIAM JONES, *M.A., some time Rector of Nayland.* Oxford and London: J. H. Parker.

THIS very seasonable publication is one which ought to be extensively circulated amongst the middling and lower classes. It is precisely adapted to a parish lending library. The object is the defence of the Church of England against her various opponents. The author was a true and faithful Churchman, and, having lived in times long prior to our present controversies, his testimony is the more valuable.

xxxv.—*Sickness, its Trials and Blessings.* London: Rivingtons.

THIS work is from the pen of a Lady, who has herself experienced much sickness, and is therefore competent to advise others. With all that we have seen of it, we have been very much pleased. It is arranged under the following subjects:—The Manner of Looking upon Sickness; Trials and Temptations of Sickness; Duties and Responsibilities; Blessings of Sickness; Convalescence; Death. There is also a special chapter on reading the Scriptures, Sunday, the Holy Communion, and prayers for recovery. The work contains a preface by the Rev. F. C. Massingberd, vouching for its orthodoxy. We can recommend this work with confidence to the attention of invalids.

xxxvi.—*"One Lord, one Faith." Discourses Doctrinal and Occasional. By* JOHN BESLY, *D.C.L., Vicar of Long Benton, &c.* London: Rivingtons.

THE author of this volume of discourses explains in his preface, that they are enlarged or combined from parochial sermons preached at distant intervals, and without any design of forming a connected series. They do not seem to be very much connected in fact, except by harmony of doctrine. Amongst these sermons we have been particularly gratified by the perusal of Sermon xix. "The Old Paths of Discipline and Doctrine," in which the author bears testimony to the truth of the English Church, and urges stedfast adherence to it in all respects. These discourses are very well and carefully written.

xxxvii.—*The Christian Gentleman's Daily Walk. By Sir Ar-*
chibald Edmonstone, *Bart.* Third Edition. London:
Masters.

Our readers are doubtless familiar with the former editions of this truly excellent work. Would that the author's portraiture of a Christian Gentleman were more generally realized! but we have no doubt that his testimony has been extensively received, and that it will continue to be so.

xxxviii.—*A Safe Path for Humble Churchmen; in Six Sermons on*
the Church Catechism, adapted to the complexion of the Times.
By John Miller, *M.A., of Worcester College, Oxford.* London: Rivingtons.

Mr. Miller could not have selected a better subject for comment than the Church Catechism, which is familiar to all Churchmen, and which possesses so many excellencies. The following testimony from Mr. Miller in his preface will be perused with interest :—

" Any long dissertation here would be at once superfluous and weari-some. Let it be therefore only said, that the great power of the Cate-chism, as a sound Christian manual, lies in the fulness of its matter brought so simply into so small a compass. Its language could not well be otherwise than *positive* to a certain extent; but nothing can be less *offensively* dogmatic than its tone, while it is equally distinct and un-equivocal in its foundations laid, motives supplied, and principles enforced. There is no rashness in it, and no unworthy compromise. Though some perhaps might wish it *less* distinct *here*, and others some what *more* explicit *there*, it is a course of *early Christian teaching*, which no sincere and conscientiously-attached member of our own com-munion would be content to part with as a whole; even without regard to the consideration that, this once lost or laid aside, no other cor-responding general ' instruction' would ever be agreed to and accepted in its stead. And probably this wide-spread liking for the Catechism arises greatly from its having been composed without partiality, and with an eye continually kept upon the genuine ' simplicity' of *Gospel truths* alone."

The first sermon is on the " Evil of Unsettledness in Religious Persuasions "—a most weighty subject. Mr. Miller points out the Christian duty of a firm and fixed belief; and then describes the uncertainties and differences unhappily existing amongst men in the present day. Herein he takes occasion to point out to them the Catechism as a form of sound words in which all may agree. In his next discourse he proceeds to illustrate practically the first baptismal promise, and in the third explains the "three things" which the Apostles' Creed chiefly teaches; and which concludes thus:—

> "He that believes in God aright, will be found diligent in rendering to Him the things that are peculiarly His. He will reverence God's holy name, His house, His day, and all things specially belonging to Him. He who believes in a like way, in Jesus Christ, will not forget that our profession is to follow this example, and to be made like unto Him. He who has proper faith in God the Holy Ghost, will care for all those things which specially concern the soul and spirit. He who has due belief in the existence of the *Holy Catholic Church*, will take good care to cleave with stedfastness unto its doctrine and fellowship. If we receive into the heart a fit persuasion of the 'communion of saints,' we shall feel care and love for all our Christian brethren, and honour for the memories of those departed hence in God's true faith and fear. He who believes on solid ground—not merely for the saying of the words—that *sins will be forgiven*, will not forget that they must be *forsaken;* and he who rightly looks for *resurrection and the life to come*, will follow the example of St. Paul and exercise himself because of that belief, always to have a conscience void of offence, toward God, and toward men."

The remaining sermons are on the Identity of the Ten Commandments with the Gospel Two; the Lord's Prayer, as bearing on the Ten Commandments; the Two Sacraments, as implying continuity and stedfastness. These subjects alone will indicate in some degree the interest which even this brief and general treatment of the subject acquires in Mr. Miller's hands. We feel thankful for this valuable testimony to the duty of stedfastness in the faith.

XXXIX.—*A Brief Analysis of the Doctrine and Argument in the Case of Gorham v. the Bishop of Exeter, with Observations on the present position of the Church of England, with reference to the recent decision.* By LORD LINDSAY. London: Murray.

THE arguments and proceedings on the Gorham case have proceeded to such a length, that such a work as Lord Lindsay has here effected is extremely necessary for those who would have a distinct understanding of the course and mutual bearing of events and arguments. It must be admitted that the battle has been well fought. Though defeated at law, the cause of the Church has gained immensely on the public mind; and a vigorous protest and appeal to the spiritual authority from the temporal has been made. Lord Lindsay thus concludes his remarks on the proceedings which have taken place :—

" So far from being detrimental, the co-existence and antagonism of these two parties, the High Church and Low Church, have been most advantageous and beneficial to the Church of England. Each party has alternately asserted the great truths which more peculiarly animate its existence—each has alternately prevailed—and every struggle has left the Church on a higher vantage-ground than before, and nearer the recognition of Universal Truth—the Church (as comprehensive of both the parties in question) recognizing impartially and adopting as her own whatever wisdom or clearer perception of Truth has been contributed by either side or elicited in the collision. The experience of the last few years justifies this assertion. The Church, after a long struggle with Puritanism and Romanism, ending with the seventeenth century, had vindicated her position, rooted herself in the land, and impregnated the people with reverence for her authority. But, while defending her outworks, with but champions too few for the duty, it had been impossible adequately to tend the moral soil—the effort had been too great, and after the enemy had retired, she sat languid and exhausted till the middle of last century. By that time she had recovered herself, and, with God's blessing and obeying His impulse, she arose and girded herself to the work of evangelizing the nation—and from that moment till the present all has been renewed and continued progress. First came the Subjective, or, as it is popularly styled, the Evangelical movement—awakening the sense of Individual Guilt, Redemption, and Responsibility ; and then, in necessary sequence and relation to it, the Objective, or, as it is similarly styled, the Puseyite—restoring the true idea of the Church, as the Mystical Body of our Saviour,—the former converting us individually from sin as ' children of God,' the latter expanding our sympathies and duties as ' members of Christ,' and both unitedly preparing us for Eternity as ' inheritors of the kingdom of heaven :'—

" That, as might be expected from this comprehensive character of the Church of England, she confines her dogmatical teaching to such points as are absolutely ruled by direct Revelation and the judgment of Catholic Antiquity as tests of salvation ; and, even in these, makes allowance, so far as permissible, for the diversity of Objective and Subjective vision incidental to the present constitution of Human Nature—demanding only in such cases that neither view be held so absolutely as to exclude the other :—

" That, applying the preceding principles and considerations to the question now at issue, it would appear—That the High Church dwell so earnestly on the Sacramental virtue of Baptism as conferring grace on the recipient infant, and incorporating it with the Church, the Body of Christ, as comparatively to under-estimate the condition of faith and repentance required from him, and on the redemption of which, on attainment to the age of responsibility, the preservation of the grace in

question depends :—And that the Low Church, on the contrary, dwell
so earnestly on the condition on which grace is given, as comparatively
to under-estimate the Sacramental virtue of Baptism, and the benefit
of incorporation above stated as thereby conferred :—Whereas, the
doctrine of the Church, as comprehensive both of High Church and
Low Church—the doctrine expressed in her recognized formularies
and authorities, and stated in the preceding summary of the Bishop of
Exeter's argument, though perhaps more fully than the Bishop or his
advocates have thought it necessary to enunciate it—lays EQUAL stress
on the grace conferred, and on the condition upon which it is conferred,
and by non-redemption of which it is forfeited :—

 "That individual members of the High Church and Low Church
parties, who through their peculiar Objective or Subjective idiosyncrasy
attach inordinate importance either to the one or the other view of the
question, are not guilty of heresy, so long as they do not assert either
view to the exclusion of the other :—

 "That Mr. Gorham, individually, has asserted Subjective to the
utter and absolute exclusion of Objective Truth as regards the grace of
Baptism, and in so doing has diverged into heresy,—but that in this he
differs, as it is believed, from the majority of the Low Church party,—
who ought, if such be the case, to vindicate their orthodoxy by expressing their dissent, not from his opinions in general, but from his special
error :—

 "That the Judicial Committee of the Privy Council have, as it is
conceived, overlooked this heresy, but they have not sanctioned it.
They have merely sanctioned certain opinions which they attribute to
Mr. Gorham, and which, though they separate Baptism and Grace in
point of time, still connect them substantially with each other, but
which opinions are not Mr. Gorham's opinions in their full extent—do
not, as his do, absolutely separate Baptism and Grace—do not therefore
deny the Nicene Creed—and do not consequently amount to heresy. The
Judicial Committee do not moreover assert, that the opinions which they
attribute to Mr. Gorham are the doctrine held and intended to be
taught by the Church, but rather the contrary,—their sanction therefore
amounts to nothing more than a grant of legal toleration to such
opinions. But even had the sanction thus given included the whole of
Mr. Gorham's doctrines and affirmed heresy, such sanction, weighed
against the Creeds and Catholic consent inherited by the Church from
the Apostolic ages—fallibility, in a word, weighed against infallibility—
could not blot out the Truth, thus binding upon her, nor compromise
her Catholicity, so long as she did not, by a formal, conscious, deliberate act, of her own free will, rescind and repudiate what she at present
professes to hold :—

 "That Churchmen ought not to be discouraged by the failure of the
measure recently introduced by the Bishop of London, inasmuch as the
perils to which the Church is exposed by the present system of appeals,
and the necessity of such a measure, are as yet but very imperfectly
known or appreciated. The principle is in the meanwhile conceded,

that the present system is objectionable, and this is of itself an instalment of justice. 'Endure' ought therefore to be the motto of the Church at the present moment,—Time and Truth will work together in her cause, and failure may be followed up by success.—The Bill itself, supported by a very large majority of the Bishops, is likewise, in the interim, a protest of the Church, repudiating the interpretation supposed to be affixed by the Privy Council to her formularies and articles—a protest, to be followed, it is to be hoped, by a manifesto of the Bishops declaring and re-affirming the faith of the Church—which, though not perhaps strictly necessary, is most desirable in order to calm the public mind.—But under any circumstances it must be insisted upon, that neither the sanction given by the Privy Council to the teaching of one whom it is sad to be compelled to term a heretic, nor the defeat of the Bishop of London's Bill, nor any conceivable (or rather, inconceivable) accumulation of oppression, can furnish either cause or excuse to any one for quitting the Church for another communion. The duty of her chivalry is to stand by her, to defend her to the death :—

"That, finally, if any persist in quitting the communion of the Church of England in consequence of the recent decision, Rome can afford them but slender consolation, inasmuch as she is more grievously and hopelessly compromised on the question of Baptism than such persons suppose the Church of England to be,—to say nothing of her mutilation of the Eucharist in denying the cup to the laity, and other points of difference with ourselves. Whereas, on the other hand, if our friends must leave us, they may find refuge in the communion of the Episcopal Church of Scotland, a daughter of their mother Church, holding the same doctrine, and possessing the same comprehensive character, but untrammeled by State influence, and in no wise affected by the recent decision."

We trust no one will *leave* the Church of England in order to find refuge in the Church of Scotland, notwithstanding our cordial adhesion to that Church. In the English Church they were born to God, and to it they should adhere with inviolable fidelity, whatever may happen, that there may never be wanting men to uphold its cause, and carry on the succession of its faith and discipline. No; let them never leave the English Church for the Scottish, but let them look to the Scottish as a sister Church which possesses the power of restoring the Catholic succession of Bishops in England, if the clergy and laity should ever be compelled, through the apostasy of their Bishops, to elect faithful men in their stead. In *this* way the Scottish Church may yet save the Church of England; but there is no indication of any such necessity being likely to occur; still less could there be any reason for leaving the English Church, and thus flying like cowards from the contest for England's faith.

XL.—*Sermons. By the Rev.* RICHARD TOMLINS, *M.A., formerly
    Curate of Uttoxeter.* London : Masters.

MR. TOMLINS has a better right to publish his discourses than
nine men out of ten of the writers we meet with. His sermons
are excellent, intelligible, vigorous, well-reasoned, and orthodox.

XLI.—*Sacra Privata. The Private Meditations, Devotions, and
    Prayers of the Right Rev.* T. WILSON, *D.D., late Bishop of
    Sodor and Man. Adapted to general use.* Oxford : John
    Henry Parker.

IN this edition no additions or alterations of language have been
permitted, but those parts which refer exclusively to the Clergy
have been omitted. It is delightful to return to the simple and
elevated devotion of Wilson, after contemplating the exaggerated
ecstasies and familiarities of Romish and Wesleyan devotion.

XLII.—*The Changes of our Times ; or, the History of John Gray
    of Willoughby.* London : Hatchard.

A VERY interesting little tale, describing the changes in the
position of farmers effected by legislative measures, and connecting with these an account of alterations in Church matters, especially the evil effects of novelties in the performance of Divine
Service. The author is pretty sharp upon them, but he explains
in his preface that he only means to blame those with whom
external forms degenerate into a substitute for spirituality.

XLIII.—*The Child's Preacher ; or, the Gospel taught to Children in
    very Simple Language. By the Hon. and Rev.* L. BARRINGTON,
    M.A., Rector of West Tytherley, Hants. London : Wertheim
    and Macintosh.

THESE are a series of little sermons to children, delivered at a
separate service instituted for them. They are, in our opinion,
quite perfect in their way : we can hardly lay down the volume.
Let all mothers by all means get this little tome, and read it to
their children.

———————————

A great number of minor publications, single sermons, and
pamphlets, are before us, which we are unable on this occasion
to notice, through press of other matter.

Foreign and Colonial Intelligence.

AUSTRALIA.—*Meeting of the Bishops of Melbourne and Sydney.*— The Melbourne " Church of England Messenger " gives an interesting account of a meeting between the Bishops of Melbourne and Sydney, at Albury, on the Murray. " If ever that little township attain such eminence as to be noticed by the historian, the fact may be considered worthy of record, that it was the first village in the Bush of Australia that witnessed the meeting of two Bishops of our Church. There was a congregation, both morning and evening, of upwards of 100 persons. It so happened that all the ordinances of the Church were administered; for there were not only several children whose parents were desirous they should be baptized, but four young women, and one young man, wished to avail themselves of the opportunity for receiving Confirmation. In the morning the latter ordinance was administered, and the Bishop of Sydney delivered a short but very impressive address to the parties. The sacrament of the Lord's Supper was also celebrated; and all those who had just been confirmed partook of it. The Bishop of Melbourne preached in the afternoon. On the Monday, a meeting of the settlers on both sides the river, as well as of the town's-people, was held; and an arrangement was made for immediately proceeding to build a residence for a Clergyman, who should divide his ministrations between the township and the stations on the two sides of the Murray; and whose stipend should be raised, partly by local contributions, and partly by a grant, which the Bishop of Sydney undertook to procure for at least one year."

Romish Missions.—A large body of Romish ecclesiastics, to the number of thirty-nine, and artisans, headed by Bishop Serra, were landed at Perth, West Australia, from a Spanish ship-of-war, on December 29, 1849. It is reported that the Romish Bishop Salvando is about to remove from North Australia to Albany, in consequence of the abandonment of the former settlement by the British Government.

AUSTRIA.—*German Catholics.*—The " German Catholics," or " Free-Christians," in Lower Austria, having been refused recognition by the Government, on the ground of their having no definite creed, have remonstrated against this decision, and handed in the following as the summary of their faith: " I believe in God, and in the existence of the soul after death, and I endeavour deliberately to attain my destiny, the perfection of humanity, through a free development of my reason in the way of love which the sublimest of men, Jesus Christ, has pointed out as a duty in the words: 'Love God above all, and thy neighbour as thyself.'"

BRITISH NORTH AMERICA.—*Synodal Organization of the Church in Canada.*—We mentioned in our last, that a Bill was about to be introduced into the Canadian Legislature by the Honourable P. B. De Blaquiere, for the better government of the Church in Upper Canada, and the establishment of a Provincial Synod. The question was subsequently postponed in consequence of the Bishop's absence, as will be seen from the following correspondence between the Honourable Member and the Clergy of the Diocese :—

" To the Honourable P. B. De Blaquiere, Member of the Honourable the Legislative Council, &c. &c.

" Sir,—Having understood that it is your intention to bring a Bill into the Legislature during the present Session, on the subject of constituting new Bishoprics in this Diocese, and on other matters connected with its temporal and spiritual interests, we beg respectfully to suggest it as our opinion that it would not be advisable to introduce such a measure until the sentiments of the Bishop and Clergy of the Diocese could be officially had upon the subject. In the absence of the Bishop, we should not regard it as proper in itself, or respectful to his Lordship, to recommend to the Clergy the adoption of any action upon this subject,—much less that steps should be taken by them by which to ascertain the sentiments upon the same subject of the Laity of our communion within their respective parishes.

" We are persuaded that if, upon the Bishop's return, any considerable number of the Clergy and Laity should address his Lordship upon the subject to which your proposed Bill refers, and request him to adopt such steps as would most effectually call forth the opinions of the Church generally in this Diocese upon that subject, his Lordship would readily assent, and take the action petitioned for.

" Until, however, some movement is made in the matter by the Church collectively, and her voice in this Diocese ascertained in a regular and legitimate manner, it would, in our judgment, be premature, and defeat, perhaps, the end proposed, to press any measure referring to it upon the consideration of the Legislature.

" We trust, therefore, that, upon these grounds, you will be willing to postpone the introduction of your contemplated Bill until the opinions of the Bishop and Clergy of this Diocese, together with the flocks committed to their charge, can, with his Lordship's sanction and authority, be satisfactorily ascertained.

" We have the honour to be, Sir,
" Your obedient humble servants,
" GEO. O'KILL STUART, LL.D., D.D.,
                              Archdeacon of Kingston.
" A. N. BETHUNE, D.D.,
" *May* 27, 1850."   Archdeacon of York."

To this, Mr. De Blaquiere replied :—

"To the Rev. and Ven. the Archdeacons of Kingston and York.

"*Toronto, June* 4, 1850.

"Reverend and Venerable Sirs,—I have the honour to acknowledge the receipt of your letter of the 27th ult., and in doing so, I beg of you to believe that in any step which I may take on the subject to which that letter refers, it will be not only my earnest desire to promote the welfare of the Church in Canada, but also my anxious wish to secure the active co-operation of every member of the Church, whether clerical or lay.

"Agreeing in the views already advocated by his Lordship the Bishop, when Archdeacon of York, and by yourselves, together with a large number of the Clergy, in the year 1836 ; and believing that the true interests of religion are deeply involved in the speedy assembling of a Convocation, I am willing for the present to postpone the application to the Legislature in behalf of the Church to which I stand pledged, in the hope that by doing so I may hasten this important preliminary step.

"I am, therefore, induced, on my own responsibility, and in behalf of those of the Clergy and Laity, whose views on this important subject accord with my own, to request that you will convey to the Lord Bishop of the Diocese, our anxious and earnest hope that he will at once, while in England, take the necessary steps for obtaining the sanction of Her Majesty the Queen, for the assembling of a Convocation, either for the Diocese of Toronto, or for the Province of Canada in co-operation with the Lord Bishop of Montreal.

"As my address respecting the present state of the Church was made known through the press, I deem it necessary, in justice to myself, that your letter and this my reply should obtain equal publicity.

"I have the honour to be,
"Reverend and Venerable Sirs,
"Your faithful humble servant,

"P. B. DE BLAQUIERE."

Mr. De Blaquiere has since been induced to publish, in a further letter to the Archdeacons, the following additional explanation :—

"The object of any legislative enactment I could be induced to support, would not interfere with the rights of the Church, but simply place her, in her '*corporate capacity, in a position to exercise those rights.*' I hold with yourselves the object of a Convocation to be— '*To deliberate on, and to adopt measures for the general interests and more permanent establishment of the Church in this Province ; for the more efficient maintenance of discipline and order ; for the supply of Ministers where wanted ; for the support of those already employed ; and for securing unity of design and action in all.*' And I subscribe, *ex animo,* to the proposition that, '*In matters purely doctrinal, the Laity shall have no voice.*' May I not then reasonably anticipate the support of the whole Provincial Church, in my efforts to establish a Convocation? The necessity for such a measure is too generally felt and acknowledged to be called for a moment in question. It is, therefore, my settled purpose to introduce into this Legislature a Bill for the establishment of a Convocation, on the broad principles above stated; and I confidently rely upon the acknowledged judgment and experience of the Bishop of Toronto for assistance in framing such a Bill, and upon the general co-operation of the Clergy and Laity in perfecting it."

In connexion with the present movement for synodal organization, an account, of which the following is an abstract, is given by the Toronto *Church*, of a former attempt to obtain a Provincial synod. A society, called the "Western Clerical Society," was formed at the Rectory, Woodstock, on the 19th of November, 1834, seven Clergymen being present. The proceedings were transmitted to the Bishop of Quebec, who not only gave to the Society his unqualified approbation, but recommended all the Clergy in the West to join it. The fundamental rule of the Society was "to confer on the measures best calculated to advance the interests of the Redeemer's kingdom, and to afford such mutual aid as the circumstances of the Church or of each individual member of this Society may require." In carrying out this object, the attention of the Society was especially directed to the division of the Diocese, and to the establishment of a "Convocation." Frequent conferences were had, and various plans suggested, on which Archdeacon Strachan was generally consulted. On the 4th of November, 1835, the Society (twelve Clergymen being present) resolved,—"That we consider it of essential and vital importance to the welfare of the Church, that a general meeting of the Clergy of this Province be held at as early a period as possible, to confer on the general interests of the Church in the present critical posture of her affairs, especially with regard to the Division of the Diocese,—the provision for a Bishop, and the induction of the Clergy."

By the unwearied exertions of the Society, a meeting was brought about of all the Clergy of the Archdeaconries of Kingston and York, to the number of thirty-two, including the two Archdeacons, who assembled at St. James' Church, on the 5th October, 1836. Full service was celebrated, and the Holy Communion administered on the occasion, and the meeting afterwards proceeded to the consideration of a plan for the formation of a "Convocation," or "Convention." The following was unanimously adopted :—

"Whereas the Ecclesiastical Law of the United Church of England and Ireland has never been introduced into this Province, by reason of which much inconvenience has arisen in matters of order and discipline; and whereas from the increasing number of Clergy, and the great distances which separate them from one another, there is great want of mutual communication and unity of action in the regulation of Church affairs, and much hindrance is experienced by the Bishop in the exercise of his holy and important functions, it is deemed expedient that

Diocesan Convocations be held in this Province from time to time for the purpose of 'adopting such rules and regulations of discipline, and taking such measures for the good of the Church, as her particular situation in this Diocese may require, provided the same be not repugnant to the constitution of the United Church of England and Ireland, the laws of the Province, and the prerogative of the Crown. The following resolutions were unanimously adopted at a meeting of the Clergy of Upper Canada, and respectfully submitted to the Lord Bishop of Quebec for his sanction.

" 1. That there shall be an annual Convocation or meeting of the Clergy of that portion of the Diocese of Quebec, which is comprehended within the Province of Upper Canada, alternately at Toronto and Kingston, on such day as the Lord Bishop shall consider the most expedient.

" 2. That the Convocation shall be composed of such canonically ordained Clergymen as are resident in Upper Canada, and have the cure of souls, whether settled in parishes, or acting as Missionaries; as also of such Clergymen as are employed as professors or instructors of youth in public seminaries; and of not more than two lay-delegates for each rector or stated minister, to be chosen by the members of the Vestry being communicants, from amongst members of the Vestry (being also regular communicants) at the usual Easter Meetings.

" 3. That the Convocation shall be opened in Church—the Clergy attending in their robes—with public prayer, a sermon, and the Lord's Supper ;—the Bishop appointing the preacher.

" 4. That the Bishop, or, in his absence, the Senior Archdeacon, shall preside. In their absence, the President shall be chosen by the Clergy present.

" 5. That one or more Secretaries shall be chosen by the Convocation at its annual meeting, whose duty it shall be to keep a record of the proceedings, and to give due notice to each minister and vestry of the time and place of the next meeting.

" 6. That in all matters which shall come before the Convocation, the Clergy and Laity shall deliberate in one body ; but, in voting, the Clergy shall vote by individuals, and the Laity by congregations. Unless there shall be a majority of both orders, the measure shall be considered as lost. In matters purely doctrinal, the Laity to have no voice.

" 7. Special Convocations shall be summoned by the Bishop when he deems it necessary for the good of the Church, or when a requisition to that effect shall be made to him by seven or more Clergymen who have been at least five years in priest's orders.

" 8. That the following be the object of the Convocation :—To deliberate on and to adopt measures for the general interests and more permanent establishment of the Church in this province,—for the more efficient maintenance of discipline and order, for the supply of ministers where wanted, for the support of those already employed, and for securing unity of design and action in all.

" 9. That no discussion on any measure be had before leave of Convocation be obtained for its introduction.

" 10. That every measure adopted in Convocation shall be submitted to the Bishop for his approval, and if so approved, shall become a standing rule for the government of the Church.

" 11. That it shall be the duty of every Clergyman to attend the Convocation, that no excuse shall be valid except that of ill-health, extraordinary duty, or permission from the Bishop.

" 12. That these fundamental rules be not changed, unless the proposed alteration be submitted at one meeting of the Convocation, for the consideration of the next,—adopted by at least two-thirds of the members of each order present, and sanctioned by the Bishop."

At the suggestion of the Archdeacon of York, the resolutions were sent home for the advice and approval of the Archbishop of Canterbury ; and, subsequently, the Bishop of Toronto, in his first charge, gave the substance of the Archbishop's answer, which was to the effect that such a convention could not be allowed, and giving his reasons for such determination. Since then, the subject has been in abeyance until recently, when it has again been revived.

Toronto Church Society.—The anniversary meeting of this Society was held,—for the first time in the Bishop's absence,—on the 5th of June last. From the financial statement, it appears that the Society's income during the past year amounted to 3062*l*. 15*s*. 8½*d*., being an increase of 269*l*. upon the previous year. The report makes particular mention of the extension of parochial organization throughout the province :—" Increased attention has been given to the parochial subdivision of labour, in the formation of parochial committees. The organization of these committees in Toronto was noticed in last year's report, and in this city the most beneficial results have accrued from them. Since that time the same course has been pursued in various parishes in the home district and elsewhere. This we must regard as a most judicious movement towards fully carrying out the constitution of the Society, and it is hoped that no long period will elapse before a parochial committee has been similarly established in every parish or mission within the Diocese. The wisdom of the Church's parochial system has been proved by the experience of centuries, and it is certain that there is nothing on which we could depend for doing the work of the Church with the same regularity,—the same even, steady, and constantly-growing efficiency. We wish, therefore, to enlist the full vigour of this admirable system in behalf of the Church Society to the greatest possible extent of which the circumstances of the Diocese will admit. It is not saying too much to affirm, that the Church, except in a position purely and entirely missionary, could not prosper without it ; and every one must feel that the Societies of the Church will thrive just in proportion as they contain those integral elements of spiritual life and power which are essential to the Church itself." The parochial system has, it appears, even reached the Red men of the Forest, for " in the Mohawk Mission," the report says, " the annual meeting was numerously attended, and was rendered particularly interesting by addresses and remarks delivered by the catechist and one of the churchwardens, in their own language."

Romish Synod at Montreal.—A Synod of Romish Bishops has met at Montreal, and issued a circular to the Clergy and a pastoral to the Faithful. The latter prohibits the reading of the Bible in any but the Romish version, and without Romish annotations, as well as the perusal of tracts, pamphlets, or any other writings contrary to religion and morals, and enjoins in doubtful cases recurrence to the diocesan authorities—under pain of excommunication.

Clergy Reserves in Canada.—In consequence of the adoption by the Provincial Legislature of a Petition to the Queen, for the appropriation of the Clergy Reserves to secular purposes, meetings have been held in various parts of the Province, in opposition to that measure of confiscation. The following resolutions passed at a meeting at Toronto, the Archdeacon of York in the chair, will best explain the state of the case :—

" 1. That whereas an address to Her Majesty the Queen has passed the Legislative Assembly of this Province, praying that the lands therein appropriated for the maintenance of religion should be alienated from that object and applied to secular purposes, it is the duty of all sound Christians to protest against the sacrilegious spoliation contemplated in that measure.

" 2. That whereas by the act 3 and 4 Victoria, chap. 78, a definite settlement of the question touching the lands called Clergy Reserves was made, according to which the Church of England was secured in a limited share of the revenue derivable from those lands, it is the bounden and solemn duty of Churchmen to resist, by every constitutional means, the breach of faith, the gross injustice, and the great moral injury they would sustain by the success of any measure that would overturn that enactment.

" 3. That the Endowments and Reserves secured by that Imperial Act to the Church of England are wholly insufficient for her becoming maintenance in this province ; and that the effect of this intended measure of spoliation, should it be successful, will be altogether to deprive the more remote and poor settlements of the regular ministrations of the Church, and that every form of religious error, and even infidelity in its worst shape, must at no distant period be the consequence.

" 4. That this meeting views with indignation as well as regret the unjustifiable interference of members of the Legislative Assembly of the Romish communion in this aggression upon the property and privileges of Protestants, and laments the religious animosity and other evil consequences which must ultimately be the result of this ill-advised interference.

" 5. That the measure just sanctioned by a majority of the House of Assembly, characterized as it is by want of principle, injustice, and the spirit of infidelity, destroys totally the confidence of Churchmen in that body, and that this meeting do pledge themselves to use their best influence and exertions at the next general election to prevent the return to the Legislative Assembly of any person who will not pledge himself to respect the endowments of religion and the vested rights of the Church.

"6. That it is the bounden duty of Churchmen in this province to petition the Queen, and the House of Lords and Commons, without delay, and to express in the strongest terms their reprobation of this contemplated measure of spoliation, and to pray that the late decision of the Provincial Assembly upon the Clergy Reserves be disallowed by the Crown.

"7. That the petition recommended by the Archdeacons of Kingston and York in their circular address to the Clergy, subject to such correction as the authorities of the Church may hereafter recommend, be adopted."

Bishop's College, Lennoxville.—The Corporation of Bishop's College, Lennoxville, have addressed a petition to the Provincial Legislature, praying for the power of granting degrees in Arts and in Divinity, and for such an increase of the public grant for its support, as shall place it on an equality with other similar institutions.

Visitation of the Diocese of Fredericton.—The second triennial visitation of the Diocese of Fredericton took place on the 11th and 12th of June last. In the course of the proceedings various subjects were discussed by the Clergy under the presidency of the Bishop. His Lordship presented to each Clergyman "A form of Induction to a Benefice in the Diocese of Fredericton," which he had prepared, together with "A form of preparation for the Consecration of a Church, Chapel, or Burial Ground." The Bishop further presented each Clergyman with a Catalogue of the Cathedral Library, the gift of the University of Oxford, and other friends, amounting to seven hundred volumes; the rules drawn up by him having been unanimously adopted by the Clergy; and with a copy of "Prayers for a Church Choir," which he had composed. In his charge, the Bishop observed, in allusion to recent events at home:

"I cannot but earnestly protest against the doctrine that our Church speaks with the stammering lips of ambiguous and uncertain formularies. I desire before God, and as I shall give account hereafter, to receive the words of our Liturgy in their literal and natural sense, and to receive *in its fulness* the great Gospel truth that there is 'one baptism for the remission of sins!' I pray God that in this matter we may stand fast in the same mind, and in the same judgment."

FRANCE.—*Synods.*—The pages of the *Ami de la Religion* are filled with accounts of the Synods taking place in the different dioceses of France. The details of the proceedings are without interest, but the fact of the revival of the regular Synodal action of the Romish Church throughout France, as well as in other countries, is worthy of notice.

The Archbishop of Paris and the Press.—The Archbishop of Paris has published a long *mandement* promulgating the decrees of the Council of Paris relative to the religious press. The decree prohibits all discussion of controverted points in the public prints, and requires them to be referred at once to the ecclesiastical authority. A supplementary document singles out the *Univers* in particular as an offender. The *Univers*, promising to conform in the interim to the Archbishop's sentence, has declared its intention to appeal direct to the Pope.

The Education Question.—A society has been formed by the Romish Bishops and Clergy in France, for the promotion of schools of all grades, and of educational publications, on the principles of the Romish Church, under the name of *" Comité de l'Enseignement libre.*" The Archbishops of Rheims and Tours, and the Bishops of Langres and Orléans, as well as Counts Molé and Montalembert, and M. de Vatismenil and others, are on the list of its supporters and managers.

Decline of Protestantism.—The *Semeur*, one of the principal organs of the French Protestants, has ceased to appear.

GERMANY.—*Re-organization of the Prussian Church.*—A new constitution has, with the Royal sanction, been promulgated for the Evangelic Church of Prussia. It recognizes the writings of the Old and New Testament as the Word of God, and the three principal symbols of the Reformation as the rule of faith. The government of the Church established by this constitution is of the most democratic character.

Death of Dr. Neander.—The celebtated Prussian divine, Dr. Augustus Neander, well known in this country through the translations of his Church history and other works, died at Berlin on the 14th instant, in his 62nd year. He was Upper Consistorial Councillor, and since 1813 Professor of Divinity at the University of Berlin, and one of the chief promoters of the changes operated in the Protestant Establishment of Prussia, and of the compromise of the Lutheran and Calvinistic confessions in the so-called United Church. Though opposed to the offensive rationalism of the " Friends of Light," he was himself one of the luminaries of the unsound school of theology which has superseded the ancient traditions of the Protestant communions of Germany.

Progress of Rationalism.—A United Synod of German Catholics and Free Congregationalists has recently been held at Leipzig,—and on being expelled thence, at Cöthen, where the police likewise interfered, —which, as far as the proceedings could be carried, ended in a fusion of those two rationalistic off-shoots of the Romish and Protestant communions of Germany into a "General religious Association of free Congregations." Several of the German Catholic congregations have, however, repudiated the acts of the late " Council."

Scarcity of Priests.—There is considerable difficulty experienced in Prussia, in recruiting the Popish Priesthood. At the beginning of this year no less than 862 cures were vacant, for want of Clergy to undertake them.

INDIA.—*The Church planted in Borneo.*—A Missionary Church, dedicated to St. Thomas, has been erected, with the consent of the entire population, at Sarâwak. The mission-house has likewise been finished, and the school is in active operation. A home school has been formed, in which a number of orphan children, after receiving the holy rite of baptism, are educated as Christians, apart from native influence. A translation of the Church Catechism and of some of the prayers of our Liturgy has been made. The most encouraging view is given of the missionary prospects among the Dyaks by Mr. M'Dougall, an active missionary: "Our prospects of being able to lay the foundation of extensive missionary labours are increasing daily; nothing hinders now but want of labourers. Tribes upon tribes of Dyaks have asked me to send them teachers; some have even expressed their desire to become ' white men,'—meaning Christians,—at once, and wish me to baptize them at once; but until I have missionaries to place among them, and prepare them better, I do not dare to do so; for while I am alone, it would only arouse Mahommedan jealousy and suspicion, and in my absence the Malays would counteract all I might have effected; whereas if I had European clergymen or catechists to place among the tribes, they would effectually prevent all Malay intrigue or opposition, for when a European is present, the Malay has little or no influence over the Dyak."

Increase of Romish Bishops.—The Pope has issued "Apostolic Briefs" for the division of the Popish diocese of Bengal into two Vicarates of Eastern and Western Bengal.

Character of Romish Missions.—The writer of a series of interesting papers on the "Missions of the Church in Tinnevelly," in the *Colonial Church Chronicle,* makes the following statements respecting the character of Romish Missions, as the result of his own experience —

"During the many years that I have been acquainted with the missions in India, I have never heard of the Romanists doing any thing directly with a view to the conversion of the heathen. I believe it is many years since such conversions have taken place,—in the south, at least. They are ever eager to attack us and our people; and they compass sea and land to make one such proselyte; they watch around our missions, eager to weaken and counteract us, but of their labours among the heathen I know nothing.

"Those who are connected with them are suffered to remain—as far as my observation extended—in hopeless and helpless ignorance; and in the south, they have established scarcely a single school; they very seldom either preach or catechise, or use any other means for the instruction of their people. There are very few books in circulation among their congregations, except some against Protestantism. I never met a Romanist who had ever possessed any portion of the Holy Scriptures, except, indeed, he had obtained it from one of our missionaries.

"The worst features of Romanism are there the most prominently exhibited. Their churches are called, as far as I have observed, universally, by Christian and heathen, (without any idea of reproach,) "Máthá-Covil," *i. e.* "Mother-temples," and never Christian temples. It is understood universally among the heathen, that the Romanists worship images just as they do themselves. They appear to assimilate themselves to the heathen as far as possible. The heathen, in fact, do not usually speak of them as Christians; and, in several tracts which they have published against Christianity, they have taken especial care to state that they wrote only against Protestants, since they only were the uncompromising opponents of idolatry and caste."

The writer adds:—" I have said all this unwillingly. I am not fond of attacking any 'who profess and call themselves Christians;' but when invidious comparisons are made between Romish and Anglican missions, by Romanist writers, I feel it my duty to bear testimony, as abundant opportunities of personal acquaintance with the subject enable me to do, to the far greater reality, earnestness, sobriety, and spirituality, in my opinion, of the work as conducted by the English Church in Southern India."

ITALY.—*Jubilee on the Pope's Restoration.*—The Pope has ordered the celebration of an universal jubilee, in commemoration of his restoration to his dominions. The time is to be fixed by the bishops themselves in different parts of the world. It is to last fifteen days, and to carry plenary indulgence of one hundred years for each separate accomplishment of the set of devotional exercises to be prescribed by the bishops in their several dioceses.

Mariolatry.—It is officially announced that " the sovereign pontiff, being desirous of giving to the most holy Virgin Mary a mark of his gratitude for the deliverance of Rome, rescued last year by the French troops from the enemies of the Church, on the day of the Visitation, has elevated that festival to the double rite of the second class."

The Pope and the Dominicans.—The Dominicans having assembled for the election of a general, the Pope put a stop to their proceedings, and nominated a general, Father Jeandel, a French Dominican. A general remodelling of the constitution of the monastic orders is expected, the Pope considering them too democratic.

The Sardinian Government and the Pope.—The Sardinian government is afresh, and as it would seem hopelessly, embroiled with the Pope. Whilst the government was following up its measures, in pursuance of the law Siccardi,—among others, the execution of a sentence against the Archbishop of Sassari, on account of the Pastoral issued by him, for which he was condemned to one month's imprisonment and 500f. fine,—an event occurred which caused the flame of discord between the Archbishop of Turin and the government to break out anew. The archbishop had completed his term of imprisonment, and was again at liberty, when M. De Santa Rosa, one of the members of the cabinet, was attacked by a mortal illness. On its being intimated by the medical attendant of M. De Santa Rosa that his dissolution was approaching, the family sent to the priest of San Carlo, to request the administration of the last sacraments. After considerable delay and evasion, the priest confessed that he was prohibited by the archbishop from affording to the minister the last consolations of religion, except on condition of his disavowing all participation in the obnoxious law Siccardi, or else expressing his regret for it; neither of which M. De Santa Rosa was willing to do. The king, on learning the circumstance, sent the minister of war to remonstrate with the archbishop. The reply was, that not only the last offices of the Church, but the rites of Christian burial, should be denied to the minister, for his participation in the recent measures of the Sardinian government. The latter menace was subsequently withdrawn, but the denial of the dying offices was persisted in, and M. De Santa Rosa expired, protesting that if he had erred, his error was one of judgment. The religious obsequies took place on the 7th. The archbishop was arrested by order of the government, and consigned to the fortress of Fenestrelles. The archbishop had, previous to his arrest, the option proposed him of resigning his see, which he refused. The papers found in his palace were seized, and are said to be of the most compromising character. It is a curious coincidence, that on the day preceding his arrest, the subscription cross, that worn by Mgr. Affre on the day of his death on the barricades, was presented to the archbishop by one of the editors of the journal (the *Univers*) with which the subscription originated. The occurrence created a great sensation at Turin, and the priests were the objects of insult and violence at the hands of the mob. So great was the exasperation of the people, that it became necessary to remove the monks of the order of *Servi*, who had the charge of the parish of San Carlo, and to supply their places by secular priests. The monks surrendered all their property, excepting portable values, which they took with them, under protest, and were marched off under an escort, for their own safety, of national guards. Meanwhile the Sardinian government thought it prudent, after the arrest of the archbishop, who has ever since been kept in close confinement, to send a special envoy to Rome, to explain the circumstances of the case. The envoy, Signor Pinelli, lost no time, on his arrival, in soliciting the favour of an interview with the Pope, upon which Cardinal Antonelli sent him a note to the following effect :—

" The Holy Father will gladly receive Commander Pinelli as a private individual, as he indistinctly receives all the faithful; but as an Envoy from the Sardinian Government he cannot receive him, until the Venerable Archbishop of Turin shall have been set at liberty."

Immediately on receiving this communication, Signor Pinelli despatched a courier to Turin, and was on the point of quitting Rome, when, according to a letter published by the *Constitutionnel*, he was informed that the Pope consented to grant him an audience, without, however, recognizing him in his official capacity. The following account is given by the writer of the reception which took place in presence of witnesses :—

" M. Pinelli developed and advocated before the Holy Father the principle invoked by M. d'Azeglio in all his diplomatic notes; that is, the right of Piedmont to change her own laws, which, as Sardinian subjects, the members of the clergy were bound to obey. The Pontifical Government placed the question on another ground. It demanded the execution of treaties concluded by Piedmont with the Holy See, and contended that the Sardinian Cabinet should have commenced by applying to the Court of Rome, and made the suppression of the ecclesiastical immunities the object of a negotiation tending to modify the Concordat signed in April, and which guaranteed those immunities. The Pope then told M. Pinelli, that when Piedmont should have liberated the Archbishop of Turin, and re-established the *status quo* existing previously to the promulgation of the Siccardi law; its Government might then, if it thought proper, open negotiations with the Court of Rome to obtain modifications in that Concordat."

While the Sardinian envoy was thus endeavouring in vain to bring about an accommodation of the difficulties arising out of the case of the Archbishop of Turin, another *imbroglio* supervened, in the form of a quarrel between the Piedmontese Government and the Archbishop of Cagliari, which is likely to render a reconciliation with Rome more difficult than ever. Some time ago the Piedmontese Government named a commission to inquire into the revenues of the dioceses and Churches of the kingdom. The commission having addressed a circular to all the Prelates of the island of Sardinia, inviting them to send in statements of their revenues, all the Bishops complied with the request, with the exception of the Archbishop of Cagliari, who refused, on the ground that the King's Government had no right to institute such an inquiry, and published a monitory circular, dated Nov. 13, 1849, threatening with the penalty of excommunication those who should aid in compelling him to furnish the required information. The Siccardi law not being in existence at that time, the authorities were unable to take any steps against the archbishop on that occasion. Meanwhile, however, a religious institution, *La Contadoria*, had not yet been examined, and the commission again addressed a letter to the archbishop, desiring him to give information. On his refusal, the tribunal ordered the papers and books of *La Contadoria* to be sealed up; but when, on the 5th inst., the Judge proceeded to the door of *La Contadoria*, which is situated within the precincts of the Archiepiscopal palace, he found there an excommunication against the authors and abettors of the "usurpation," writen in the Archbishop's own hand, and ending thus:—"Given from our violated domicile, Sept. 4, 1850. Emmanuel, Archbishop." The Judge immediately caused this document to be taken down and transmitted to the public prosecutor, who commenced legal proceedings against the Prelate without delay. Here the matter rests for the present.

A false Christ.—A priest, named Don Grignaschi, has been passing himself off in Piedmont as Jesus Christ, or some Great One, and by the evidence of false miracles beguiled many persons. He has been tried and sentenced to ten years' exile, and five other priests and several lay accomplices besides him have been condemned to various punishments.

New See in Tuscany.—A new Bishopric has been created, by a Papal Bull, in Tuscany, with Modigliana for its see.

Return of the Jesuits.—A decree of the Duke of Modena recalls the

Jesuits, and confides to them the schools of Modena, Reggio, and Mazza.

An Italo-Catholic Schism.—A schismatic communion, professing the principles of Ronge, has been formed at Verona under t of a mercantile clerk.

MADEIRA.—*The Bishop of Bombay and the Rev. R. T. Lowe.*—The Rev. R. T. Lowe having transmitted to his diocesan, the Bishop of London, an account of the circumstances connected with the visit of the Bishop of Bombay to the island, of which we gave an account in our last number, together with the documents which passed on the occasion, his lordship has, in reply, addressed to Mr. Lowe the following letter :

" London, June 13, 1850.

" My dear Sir,—I have received your letter with its enclosures, and also one from the Bishop of Bombay, containing a copy of the correspondence which has passed between his lordship and you, together with a statement of facts.

" I cannot say how much pain has been occasioned to me by the perusal of these documents, nor how deeply I regret what has taken place. With every wish to uphold your just authority, and making every allowance for the peculiar circumstances in which you are placed, I can by no means approve of the line of conduct you have pursued towards that excellent and much respected prelate. I had entertained a hope that, under his kind and judicious advice, some step might be taken towards healing the unhappy difference in Church matters which prevails at Madeira.

" In a conversation I had with the Bishop just before he left England, I expressed this hope to him. I stated that, as you continued to hold my licence, the revocation of which you had done nothing to justify, I could not require any other clergyman, as authorized by me, to officiate in Madeira ; but I certainly did not speak of Mr. Brown, nor of his congregation, as being in a state of schism ; nor do I consider them to be so. I have no *legal* jurisdiction over them. It has long been held that English Clergymen in our colonies and in foreign parts, not being under the jurisdiction of any local diocesan, were under that of the Bishop of London ; but I am not prepared to assent that the non-recognition of that jurisdiction amounts to an act of schism. There are, or have been, not a few clergymen ministering to English congregations on the Continent, who have never acknowledged my episcopal authority over them, nor received my licence ; but, although I think they are acting inconsistently with true Church principles, I never held them to be schismatics, nor have I made any difficulty about admitting their catechumens to confirmation. If, therefore, you had made the same charge of schismatical conduct against a private member of the Church as you have made against the Bishop of Bombay, and had threatened on that ground to repel him from the Holy Communion, I should have felt myself bound, if appealed to, to express my disapproval of such a proceeding; but it is, as it appears to me, a much more serious matter to treat a Bishop of our own Church as an abettor of schism, and to admonish him as such not to present himself as a communicant. It was known to you that the Bishop of Bombay had been commissioned by me to administer the rite of confirmation to such young persons at Madeira as might be desirous of receiving it. Surely, then, it was your duty, if you felt any doubt as to the propriety of admitting him to the Holy Communion, to refer the matter to me; and, in the mean time, to treat him as your spiritual superior on the spot with respect and deference.

"I most earnestly press upon you the duty of making a proper apology to the Bishop on this account; and you cannot, I think, be surprised if I feel that I, too, have been placed in a painful and embarrassing position by this stretch of ecclesiastical authority on your part, while acting under my licence.

"The publicity which has been given to the proceeding in question makes it my duty to send a copy of this letter to the Bishop of Bombay, to be made such use of as he may think proper.

"I remain, Sir, your faithful servant,

"C. J. LONDON.

"The Rev. R. T. Lowe."

NEW ZEALAND.—*Visitation of the islands of New Caledonia.*—The *Colonial Church Chronicle* has an account of the recent movements of the Bishop of New Zealand. On the 1st of October his lordship returned in the "Undine," schooner, from a short cruise amongst the islands in the neighbourhood of New Caledonia. The Bishop visited ten of these interesting islands, and was every where received by the natives in the most friendly manner. He brought with him five young lads to spend the summer in New Zealand, and then return to their own country. Of these, one is a native of Lifu, another of New Caledonia, and the other three come from the island of Mare. In each of these places an entirely different language is spoken, and this, notwithstanding the fact that Lifu and Mare are within sight of each other, and are islands of very small size. The lads are now residing at St. John's College, and each of their three languages being committed to the charge of separate members of the college, a copious vocabulary will, it is hoped, be formed of all of them during the ensuing summer.

SWITZERLAND.—*M. Marilley.*—M. Marilley, the Bishop of Lausanne and Geneva, has addressed, from his exile, a letter to the clergy of his diocese, in which he warns them against the encroachments of the secular power, and prohibits them from acting in ecclesiastical matters without the express authority of their ecclesiastical superior, and from accepting any mission for the performance of their sacerdotal functions from the State.

UNITED STATES.—*Diocesan Convocations.*—The following is an account of the more interesting transactions of the Conventions of the American Church, recently held :

Diocese of Maryland.—The Convention had to deal with the following singular case of Church discipline. It appears that, in March last, the Bishop sent a letter to the Rector of Christ Church, Dr. Johns, setting forth that he (the Bishop) had not received any invitation from the Rector to visit his church, and as three years had elapsed since his last episcopal visit, in accordance with the canons of the Church, he notified the Rector that he would, on a certain Sunday, visit Christ Church, for the purpose of examining into the affairs of the same, performing Divine Service, preaching, and confirming such persons as might be presented ; and farther, that he should expect to administer the Holy Communion—the collection at the offertory to be for the Diocesan Board of Missions. To this letter the Rector of Christ Church sent one in reply, saying, that while he would be happy to have the Bishop visit his church, and administer the rite of Confirmation, he felt bound to deny his right to administer the Communion, and appropriate the offertory to the funds of the Diocesan Board of Missions, on the ground that the Bishop had no warrant for so doing, either by the general canons or in the rubrics of the Church, and that such an exercise of power would be in conflict with his rights as a presbyter of the Church. With regard to that portion of the Bishop's letter complaining that he had not been invited to visit Christ Church, Dr. Johns replied that, inasmuch as one of the canons made it the duty of the Bishop to visit every church in his diocese at least once in three years, he had deemed it his duty to await the pleasure of the Bishop. The Bishop, in answer to this letter, notified the Rev. Dr. Johns, that, inasmuch as his right to administer the Communion had been denied, he therefore revoked his notice to visit Christ Church. A letter was also read from the vestry of Christ Church, informing the Bishop of their intention to lay the whole matter before three Bishops of the Church for investigation, according to the canons of the Church. The letter in question was also put in. It was addressed to the Bishops of Massachusetts, Delaware, and Pennsylvania, and set forth the circumstances of the case, charging the Bishop of Maryland with having expressly violated the general canon of 1832, in not visiting Christ Church for a period of three years, to the great detriment of the congregation, depriving a large number of candidates for confirmation of an opportunity to receive that holy rite. To this letter no answer had been received from the Bishops to whom it was addressed. Dr. Johns deprecated the impression which had gone abroad, that his action had been somewhat discourteous to the Bishop. This was not so. The Bishop, from his sense of duty, pursued a course which he (Dr. Johns), also from a sense of duty, had felt constrained to oppose ; all that had been done was with the simple view of having the matter settled, so that all difficulty might in future be avoided. The matter was finally decided by the

Convention adopting the following three resolutions :—" 1. That a Bishop, in order to the exercise of his episcopal functions, possesses the right on occasions of canonical visitations to control the services, and to take to himself portions of them as he may think proper. 2. That this principle was recognized and settled as the law of the diocese of Maryland by the decision of the tribunal which the law of the diocese had constituted for the decision of ecclesiastical questions, and from the decisions of which tribunal no law of the Church recognized any appeal. 3. That the course of the Bishop of this diocese, in revoking his notice of a visitation to Christ Church, Baltimore, was the wise and judicious exercise of a discretion canonically vested in him, in a spirit of Christian prudence and forbearance which does him honour."

Diocese of Mississippi.—Among the most important matters transacted at this Convention was the organization of a society, in subordination to the Church, for the diffusion of Christian knowledge in the Diocese, embracing a well-digested plan of domestic missionary operations, together with the distribution of Bibles, Prayer Books, tracts, and other approved religious publications ; a system of convocations or meetings of the Bishop and a portion of his clergy in different parts of the Diocese several times in each year ; and the foundation for the establishment of a permanent interest-bearing fund for the support of the Bishop.

Diocese of North Carolina.—More than usual interest attached to the proceedings of this Convention, owing to reports which had been widely disseminated, that the Bishop was tainted with unsound doctrine. On the evening before the day appointed for the meeting of the Convention, the greater part of the Presbyters of the Diocese, in accordance with a previous call received from him, met their Bishop in Convocation, for the purpose of consulting on the means best adapted for restoring harmony and good will throughout the Diocese. At the conclusion of a long session, in which the greatest freedom of discussion was allowed, a committee of seven Presbyters was elected by ballot to confer with the Bishop on this most important subject. Upon the reassembling of the Convocation on the following day, this Committee reported that it was the intention of the Bishop, in pursuance of their advice, to make such statements in his usual annual address to the Convention, as would tend to remove the existing anxieties of the Diocese. Accordingly, in his address to the Convention on Thursday, the Bishop adverted to the causes of disquietude which had been brought to his notice, denying explicitly the false doctrines that had been imputed to him, and directly and distinctly declaring his adhesion to the truth of Christ's doctrine as laid down in the standards of the Church. The portion of the Bishop's address which related to this subject was to the following effect :—

" It remains to notice one of my official acts during the present year, which has been the occasion of a good deal of misapprehension, and which requires of me a few words by way of safeguard. I refer to the issuing of a Pastoral letter relating to the action of the last Convention

of this Diocese. Without going into a defence of the grounds which
seemed to me to make the publication of that letter necessary, I would
express my deep regret, that any of the statements should in any degree have admitted the idea of an intention on my part to question the
motives, the truthfulness, or faith of my Clergy. Notwithstanding the
circumstances which under Providence have given the appearance of
distrust between some of the most valued of them and myself for a
time, I desire now to assure them as a body, of my entire confidence
in their affection, their charity, and firm adherence to the faith, and
discipline of the Church. I have laboured among them for nearly
twenty years, I know very imperfectly, but with a sincere desire for
the good of my diocese, and I believe with unwavering fidelity to my
trust. Still I claim no infallibility beyond honesty of purpose and
diligence in duty, and no indulgence beyond that which is extended to
every man labouring under the infirmity of a human judgment, and the
oft recurring and sometimes prostrating diseases of a human body. For
myself as an individual, I have nothing to urge—nothing to say.—But
as your Bishop, responsible in some sort at least for the truth, I feel
bound to remove in terms of plain denial some misconceptions, which
are operating to hinder the due effects of that truth, as set forth in my
writings, and to keep up agitation and distrust in the Diocese. I neither teach nor hold, as some have thought, private auricular confession
and absolution in the Romish sense. The Romish Church holds them
to be a necessary sacrament in themselves, as is Baptism and the Lord's
Supper. I hold and teach that our branch of the Church denies this.
That Church makes them obligatory on all her members—I teach and
hold that our Church does not—but makes them an exception to a
general rule—which general rule is public confession and absolution
according to the forms in our Liturgy. That Church obliges the Priest
to see, that every communicant comes to them. I teach and hold that
our Church leaves it with the penitent to determine whether and how
far he need them, and does not permit the Priest to do more in bringing
the penitent to them, than to point out the dangers of self-trust and
self-delusion, and the benefits of unburdening the conscience and receiving the Godly counsel and service of God's ministers, according to the
direction of the exhortation to the Holy Communion in our Liturgy.
That Church holds to the necessity of confessing each mortal sin of
thought, word, and deed to the Priest. I teach and hold that our
Church regards it needful, that each communicant should so search and
examine his conscience according to the rule of God's commandments,
as to be able to confess all heinous offences 'in will, word, and deed,'
to Almighty God ; and that if he cannot by this means quiet his conscience, and come to the Holy Communion ' with a full trust in God's
mercy,' he shall open his grief to some minister of God's word, that he
may obtain his counsel and aid, to the removing of all scruple and
doubtfulness.

  " In regard to Christ's real presence in the Holy Eucharist, I neither
teach nor hold it, in the sense of *transubstantiation ;* neither do I teach

nor hold, as I do not understand how Christ is there present—further than that, He is not there in a material but spiritual manner—'but because *spiritual*, not the less *real*.' I do not hold or teach that 'the creatures of bread and wine' in the Holy Eucharist are to be in the meaning of the Twenty-eighth Article, 'reserved, carried about, lifted up, or even worshipped.'

"I do not teach or hold, that our Church allows any addresses, by way of prayer and invocation to the blessed Virgin, or to any Saint or Angel; while I regard the Romish doctrine of invocation to Saints, implying meritorious mediation and condemned by Article XXXII., as clearly derogatory to Christ, and opposed to God's word.

"Finally, I do not teach nor hold that our branch of the Catholic Church is from any cause either in heresy or schism, or that she is destitute of the true Sacramental system. This much have I thought it best to say *negatively*, to guard my affirmative teaching from misconstruction and misapprehension. That teaching is before you, in my published writings, with such explanations as I have felt myself called upon to give. Whatever may be the imperfections of the teacher (and he feels that they are many), for the returns made to him for his sincere, and he believes greatly needed efforts, he has the satisfaction of a firm conviction, and the privilege of constant prayer, that Almighty God will so overrule those efforts, as to make them redound to his glory and the good of his Church."

This explanation was received with great satisfaction by the great body of the Convention; but as it was feared that some further action would be necessary to a perfect restoration of peace, the Bishop on the following morning addressed the Convention as follows :—

"Brethren of this Convention,—Aware that the difficulties in this Diocese, to which I have alluded in my address, still threaten the peace of the same, and being anxious to do all in my power to restore perfect harmony and good will, I hereby ask of you a committee of clergymen and laymen to investigate the whole circumstances connected therewith, and report to a future meeting of this body."

Upon this the Convention resolved to accede to the request of the Bishop, by the election of a committee for the purpose specified by him, to consist of three clergymen and three laymen, whose duty it should be to report the result of their labours to the next annual Convention of the Diocese, to be held in May, 1851. The Committee on the State of the Church, in the usual annual report, alluded to these proceedings in the following terms :—

"The Committee have heard and read with great satisfaction, that portion of the Bishop's address which contains the explanation of doctrines taught, in his published writings, stating that 'he feels bound to remove, in terms of denial, some misapprehensions, which are operating to hinder the due effects of that truth, as set forth in his writings;' and they trust that these explanations will tend to remove the agitation and distrust of which the Bishop speaks, and have the same effect upon the Church throughout the Diocese, which they have had upon the minds of the Committee, of inducing the hope, that the peace and harmony, for which this diocese was formerly distinguished, may be restored. The Committee must not omit to express the gratification with which they have received the expression contained in the Bishop's address, of his entire confidence in the affection of the Clergy, and their firm adherence to the faith and discipline of the Church."

Diocese of Kentucky.—The striking features of this Convention was the charge of the Bishop, which the *Episcopal Recorder* describes as "decided in its tone, Scriptural and Evangelical in its doctrine, and, in the opinion of several who heard it, by far the best that has yet been written against the prevailing error of the day." The effect which it produced upon the Convention may be inferred from the fact that when, in the regular course of business, the election of delegates to the General Convention was proposed, one of the Clergy moved the postponement of all elections until the morrow, inasmuch as too much excitement prevailed among the members of the Convention to allow of their acting coolly and dispassionately. After a warm and animated discussion, the motion was carried, and the Convention adjourned. The result of the election was considered favourable to the "friends of evangelical truth."

Diocese of Indiana.—At this Convention an instance of the exercise of Church discipline occurred. The Bishop informed the Convention that he had approved of the sentence of the Ecclesiastical Court, in the case of the Rev. G. Lamb Roberts, who had been found guilty of heresy, schism, slander, and a violation of his ordination vows. The sentence of the Court was, that he should be degraded from his office as a Deacon of the Church. And the Bishop further declared that he had, in the presence of the Clergy of the Diocese, pronounced the sentence of degradation, and the Rev. G. Lamb Roberts was no longer a Minister of this Church.

Diocese of Michigan.—In this diocese, which, in common with other western dioceses, most keenly feels the loss occasioned by the withdrawal of the larger part of the appropriation heretofore made by the Domestic Board of Missions, the Convention passed a resolution requiring every Clergyman having parochial charge within the Diocese, on the second Sunday of each month, to read the offertory to his congregation, and take up a collection for missions.

Diocese of Texas.—The present was the first Convention of this newly-formed Diocese. Six clergymen were present from the parishes of Galveston, Houston, Matagorda, Brazoria, Washington, and San Augustine; lay representatives arrived from three parishes, presented their certificates, and took their seats in the Convention. The attention of the Convention was chiefly engaged in the consideration of two suggestions submitted by the Bishop. One was the appointment of a general missionary, who should travel over the State at large, visiting those places which were not favoured with the service of the Church, gathering her scattered members into parishes, and comforting them by the assurance, that at the earliest opportunity they shall have the services of those who minister in holy things. The other topic, suggested by the Bishop, was the necessity of establishing some where within the bounds of the Diocese a Church Seminary, where the devoted members of the Church might send their children with the confidence that they would receive a thorough classic education, under the most competent teachers, and be properly instructed in the peculiar principles of the Church—those teachers being clergymen—but the grand object of the school to be the training of young men for the work of the ministry. Both these suggestions, particularly the last, met with the hearty concurrence of the Convention. A committee was appointed to carry the proposal for a school into effect at as early a period as practicable. Within the last two years, the number of the clergy in Texas has been nearly tripled, and the members of organized parishes has increased from *three* to *ten*. In every place where the Church has been established, the prospects are cheering and encouraging. Application for clergymen are received from all parts of the State ; and with a sufficient supply of clergy, the number of parishes might be doubled in less than twelve months.

Diocese of Wisconsin.—This diocese is yet in its infancy, this being the fourth Convention. The Bishop in his address urged the increase of the Diocesan Missionary Fund, so as to support two additional itinerants. He also announced a plan, not yet matured in detail, for the establishment of a College or Church School. A committee was appointed to organize a subscription to increase the episcopal fund of the diocese. The constitution of the Convention itself underwent some modifications. The first of them is, that "every clergyman canonically connected with the diocese, and having charge of some parish (or officiating as a Missionary within its bounds, or having spiritual charge, as president, professor, tutor, or instructor in some college, academy, or seminary of learning, constituted or countenanced by ecclesiastical authority, or being a Chaplain in the Navy or Army of the United States), shall be entitled to a seat in this Convention. In every case, however, where a clergyman is not able to hold a cure of souls, arising from bodily infirmity, or age, he shall not for such cause be excluded from a seat in this Convention." With regard to the qualification of the lay-members, it was proposed, but decided in the negative, that " the lay-members of the Convention shall be either communicants of the Protestant Episcopal Church, or shall have been baptized by the office and ministry of the same." A canon was adopted for insuring ritual uniformity. It provides that questions of ritual and liturgical practice, ecclesiastical arrangements, &c., left open by the statute law of the American Church, are to be decided for this diocese by the Bishop and his council, the clerical members of the standing committee, acting judicially, when occasions arise ; such judicial decision to be obeyed as the common law of the Church in this diocese, under liability to the usual penalties.

Diocese of Missouri.—A canon was adopted requiring the appointment of a committee to make an assessment upon the parishes for the support of the episcopate. Such assessment was made, and although it is not expected in the present infant state of most of the parishes to yield much more than is needful to defray the travelling expenses of the Bishop, it is nevertheless wisely adapted to secure a revenue commensurate with the growth of the diocese for the important object in view.

Diocese of Tennessee.—In the address of the Bishop, the following passage occurs :—"Some portions of the Church have been much disturbed by questions which have been raised about doctrine and discipline. This diocese has hitherto been most happily preserved from these agitations, and I gladly avail myself of this occasion to say that we shall, by God's blessing, be kept in peace among ourselves, if the clergy will, as heretofore they have done, with scarcely an exception, adhere faithfully to 'the form of sound words' set forth by the authority of the Church, for use in the public worship of our congregations, and in the administration of the sacraments and other rites of the Church. The great doctrines of religion, about which there is almost universal agreement among intelligent Christians, are therein set forth, with so much admirable simplicity and plainness, that it seems to me that the mind which raises questions about the teaching of the Church, must be obstinately bent upon making difficulties."

Diocese of Virginia.—A stringent canon on Church discipline was passed by this Convention, which enumerates " gaming, attendance on horse-racing, and theatrical amusements, witnessing immodest and licentious exhibitions or shows," and " attending public balls," among " offences for which discipline should be exercised," with a general clause against " conducting one's self in a manner unworthy of a Christian." The canon in question has excited much attention, and provoked much comment in the Union generally, as tending to confusion by the establishment of arbitrary terms of communion.

Foreign Missions of the American Churches.—The annual meeting of the Board of Missions of the Protestant Episcopal Church in the United States was held at Hartford, on the 19th of June. In their Report the Committee state, that " notwithstanding some trials, the Missions of the Church under their care are, in general, acquiring stability, and that they have been visited with the Divine blessing in their operations during the year." On the subject of finance, which has of late been so unsatisfactory, the report contains the pleasing assurance, that " although the receipts of the past year have not equalled those of the two preceding, in consequence of some extraordinary specific benefactions made during the latter, yet the contributions from usual sources have been sufficient to prevent embarrassment, and have enabled the Committee to make remittances to their Missionaries with a good measure of promptitude." The report complains, however, that to the appeal made, as usual, at the Epiphany season, by way of collection, " the response was less general and less liberal than on former occasions." The aggregate of the receipts for the year are stated at 34,800 dols. 79 c.: the expenditure at 32,404 dols. 17 c. A particularly interesting account is given of the African mission, which requires the speedy appointment of a Bishop to carry out the important designs of the missionaries. The China mission is reported as suffering chiefly for want of labourers, male and female. A native (Chae) has been ordained deacon. The subject which excites the deepest interest is a projected mission among the Chickasaw Indians, arising from a request of the Indians themselves, through the United States Government, for the establishment among them of schools, &c., under the charge of the Episcopal Church. At the close, an informal debate took place upon the Constantinople mission, during which Bishop Southgate himself addressed the Board. The meeting came, however, to no conclusion upon this subject, and was adjourned *sine die.*

The Theological College, New York.—The annual meeting of the Trustees of this College took place on the 26th of June, and the commencement on the 27th. The occasion derived more than ordinary interest by the retirement, on the ground of old age, of Dr. Wilson, Professor of Systematic Divinity, and Dr. Moore, Professor of Oriental and Greek literature, who had both grown grey in the service of the College. The students presented each of the professors with a splendid Bible and Prayer Book, in costly bindings : and in memorial of them they presented, for the use of the chapel of the seminary, a handsome silver chalice and patine, from which the Bishop of Vermont immediately after administered the Holy Eucharist to the clergy, professors, students, and visitors collected on the occasion. The scene was most affecting, and many of those present were moved to tears.

Church History Society.—A " Protestant Episcopal Historical Society" has been established at Hartford, in the diocese of Connecticut, for the purpose of collecting, preserving, and publishing documents which throw light on the progress of the American branch of the Church. Churchmen paying two dollars annually are to be entitled to all publications. But the scope and the mode of its operations are explained in the address of the " Executive Committee," in which they say—

" The importance of securing a complete collection of historical materials, relating to the Protestant Episcopal Church, is so generally felt, that the members of this Committee do not presume that they can suggest any thing new to their brethren of the clergy and laity upon that subject. But as a number of the bishops, other clergy, and laity have associated in a Church Historical Society, and laid upon this Committee the honour and labour of furthering its objects, they venture to propose some plans for that purpose, asking co-operation from all who are interested in the subject, or in other words, from every member of the Protestant Episcopal Church.

" Their first duty is to make a complete collection of the historical materials now in existence. In order to do this they earnestly desire every clergyman and layman in the Church to transmit to the Secretary *a duly-attested copy* of every curious, valuable, or interesting entry in parish books or private papers, to which they can obtain access, or where it is possible, the originals themselves ; and also note down and transmit any historical traditions which may come under their notice.

" If persons will prepare manuscript histories of parishes, or of any particular events, this Committee will be happy to take charge of them, subject to any directions respecting the time of opening which their contributors may see fit to make ; *all facts, however, to be duly attested as to the source from whence derived.* This Committee will also be glad to receive any publications, old or new, which contain historical matters of fact, opinion, or controversy, bearing upon ecclesiastical history in America.

" A fire-proof depository will be obtained as soon as possible, the plan and details of which will be made known, when special subscriptions are solicited for that purpose.

" So soon as the catalogue of members contains the names of five hundred persons who have paid their subscriptions, this Committee will prepare and put forth the first volume of the Society's publications, of which each member will receive a copy, and will continue to pub ish from time to time, as the means of the Society will permit. It is, however, their fixed determination, that no liabilities shall be incurred until the money to meet them is in the hands of the Treasurer.

" This Committee designs to keep a chronicle of passing events, and will therefore be obliged to the publishers of the Church periodicals, if they will regularly send their papers to the Secretary. To the same end they will appoint, as fast as practicable, corresponding members in every diocese, whose duty it will be to collect diocesan historical materials, past and current, and forward them to the Secretary."

Schism among the Romanists.—A meeting has recently been held at Philadelphia, composed chiefly of Germans, having for its object the establishment of a " Free Catholic Church " in the United States. The reasons assigned for the secession are :—" First, Freedom of conscience. Second, Because we and our children are deprived of the Holy Bible. Third, We cannot recognize the Pope as the infallible head of the Church, or Vicar of Christ. Fourth, We do reject, that the Priests through their ordination receive power to rule over God's inheritance, to traffic in souls, enslave conscience, and stupify the mind with superstition. Fifth, We reject celibacy. Sixth, We reject auricular confession as unrighteous and demoralizing. Seventh, We reject purgatory. Eighth, We reject calling on the saints, veneration of images and relics. Ninth, We reject indulgences and pilgrimages, and making merchandize of men's souls." One of the leading speakers was Mr. Gustiani, formerly a Roman Catholic Priest, who has been for some time a Minister of the Methodist Church, Philadelphia. It remains to be proved whether the American " Free Catholics " are identical or not with the followers of Ronge in Germany.

THE
ENGLISH REVIEW.

DECEMBER, 1850.

Art. I.—*Lives of the Queens of Scotland and English Princesses, connected with the Royal Succession of Great Britain.* By AGNES STRICKLAND. Vol. I. London and Edinburgh: Blackwood and Sons.

THE author of Waverley was the first writer who, in our own times, invested history with the many-coloured hues of romance, and gave to fiction the force of reality, by identifying it with the events and manners of past ages. And many a labourer in the same fruitful field has followed ;—so many, indeed, and with such various success, that we have become familiarized with almost every conceivable way and mode of connecting fiction with history. We are prepared for the descriptions of scenery, the costumes, and even the principal characters, before we open the new romance. The language, manners, and incidents of the tale may be guessed with tolerable accuracy. The cavalier and the roundhead—the crusader and the priest—the outlaw's den, and the rude hospitality of the hostelry—the mimic war of the tournament, and the deadly onslaught of pitched battles,—are all as familiar to us now as household words ; and we are unable to revive those sensations which were excited by the first efforts of that great writer who called up the imagery of the past, and gave to it life and action in his immortal pages.

Miss Strickland has, we think, learnt from Sir Walter Scott the charm by which he elevated romance to the dignity of history ; but she has reversed the process : she has given to history the interest of romance. This may partly be ascribed to the subjects she has chosen : but chiefly to her mode of treating them ; for, in her hands, the dry record of the chronicle, the long-forgotten ballad, or the rude song, the most petty detail of antiquarian curiosity, however apparently useless ; the local legend, the old proverb, or the family relic and its history ; the dusty and time-worn picture ; the tottering ruin, or the genealogy of an ancient family, — all furnish forth a mass of materials, which, when fashioned and arranged, and intermingled with a thousand thoughts and reasonings, linking them together in a strange harmony, come forth at length in the wonderfully brilliant and life-like portraitures which the biographies of Miss Strickland invariably produce—those rich mosaics of infinitely varied colours, the materials of which, each, in itself, are perhaps of comparatively little interest, but, in their combination, present a masterpiece of art.

It is this reality and vividness which constitutes the great value of Miss Strickland's writings. In a merely historical view, we think they are rendered less valuable by the very presence of the attributes which confer on them their highest interest. Miss Strickland is essentially a poetess; her imaginative faculties are extraordinary, and the commonest event or circumstance is sufficient, to set them to work; and, when she has formed her idea of a character, she follows it out without stop or stay. Having been once unfavourably impressed, she has no mercy on the characters of her unfortunate subjects. A strong Jacobite, she cannot see any worth or merit in the sovereigns or statesmen of the opposite party. Their actions are always interpreted in the worst possible sense, and she appears throughout as a strong and ardent partizan. We have no doubt that Miss Strickland is sincerely convinced of the truth of her views; but the force of her imagination, and the prejudices which she sometimes betrays in consequence, while they add greatly to—nay constitute the especial interest of her volumes—detract from their value and trustworthiness, considered simply as historical compositions. They are brilliant historical romances, approaching as near to fact as the imaginative faculties of their gifted authoress will permit.

In the volume before us, which constitutes the first of a series of Lives of the Queens of Scotland, Miss Strickland has not only been fortunate in the selection of her subject, but she has sustained to the full the high reputation for research which her previous writings have acquired. Her choice has indeed been evidently directed to that period when Scottish history assumes the highest interest, and connects itself most closely with the sympathies of the present day. Every one must be curious to peruse Miss Strickland's Life of Mary Stuart, while every one can anticipate the verdict she will pronounce; and, in fact, it appears, that the present work is all intended to converge on that unhappy queen as its central and leading point. The general design of the work is thus described in the Introductory Preface:

"The lives of the Queens of Scotland, in the modern series which I have the honour of introducing in the present volume, commence with Margaret Tudor, the consort of James IV. of Scotland, and daughter of Henry VII. of England and Elizabeth of York. Margaret Tudor, like her illustrious predecessor and ancestress, Margaret Atheling, was an English princess in the direct line of the regal succession of that realm, and a queen-consort of Scotland. Her posterity by James IV. united the blood of the elder line of the Anglo-Saxon kings and the Norman Conqueror, blended with that of Bruce-Stuart and Plantagenet-Tudor in one rich stream. James VI. of Scotland, doubly her great-grandson, inherited the realms of England and Ireland, as the representative of that princess, whose hereditary rights are now vested in her august descendant, Queen Victoria.

"The Life of Mary Stuart, which will occupy two successive volumes of this series, was in preparation long before the publication of that of Elizabeth Tudor, in our Lives of the Queens of England; when it was promised as a companion biography, but a separate work.

"Inexorably as the destiny of Mary Stuart was influenced by Elizabeth of England, no one could mix the personal annals of those rival Britannic sovereigns together, without producing, as Camden has done, great confusion, and impairing the interest attached to both, by violating the individual unity essential to biography; for they were stars shining in different orbits, and never visible in the same hemisphere. Their lives ought, however, to be read in succession, because they cast reflected lights upon each other, and are calculated, like the contemporary biographies in both series, to illustrate the comparative state of society in the sister realms.

"My pledge to the public, touching the Life of Mary Stuart, could not be redeemed till after the arduous undertaking in which my sister and myself were engaged was concluded. The accomplishment of that task occupied several years, in the course of which, fresh sources of information connected with the personal history of Mary have been opened both in France and England. So numerous, however, are the works on this subject, of ever fresh and undying interest, that although not one of them has been written since the publication of Prince Labanoff's seven volumes of his letters, and La Mothe Fénélon's despatches, we determined not to infringe on the pre-occupied ground and literary property of other authors, by bringing out a new Life of Mary Stuart in three volumes singly, but resolved, proceeding on our own original track, to introduce it into a new series of royal biographies on the same plan as *The Lives of the Queens of England.* The biography of Mary will, of course, be rendered more perspicuous and intelligible by being preceded by those of the three queens in the present volume, and followed by that of her aunt, Margaret, Countess of Lennox, the mother of the unfortunate Darnley, which is full of curious information, bearing on the much-contested point of the guilt or innocence of Mary.

"The selfish and short-sighted policy of Margaret Tudor, while exercising the functions of queen regent for her son James V., her intrigues with England, the interminable embroilments caused by her marriages and divorces, sowed, as will be shown, the perilous seeds of which her unfortunate descendants, Mary Stuart and Darnley, were destined to reap the bitter harvest.

"The life of James the Fifth's first consort, Magdalene of France, having important connexion with political relations, but no entanglement with political intrigues, comes like a refreshing interlude of sweet and pleasant things between the turmoils and agitations detailed in the more eventful histories of Margaret Tudor and Mary of Lorraine. It is, in sooth, a romantic but carefully verified love-tale of royal romance, blended with the splendid pageantry and costume of the brilliant courts of those chivalrous monarchs, Francis I. of France, and the Fifth James Stuart of Scotland."

The biographies in this volume commence with Margaret Tudor, daughter of King Henry VII. and sister of King Henry VIII. She was born princess royal of England, in the palace of Westminster, A.D. 1489, and, the day after her birth, was baptized with royal pomp and ceremony in the adjoining parish church of St. Margaret's. It is curious to compare the ceremonial on this occasion with the forms of the present day; and really, taking into account all the religious changes which have since occurred, there is no such very great dissimilarity between royal baptisms in 1850 and in 1490. We miss, however, "the sacred silver font brought from Canterbury cathedral," and the "golden salt-cellar," and the "wax tapers," which then played a conspicuous part; but, on the other hand, we have in the present day the water of the River Jordan itself employed in our royal baptisms, —a custom, if we mistake not, derived from France. Passing over the curious details which are given of the management of the Princess Margaret during her infancy and early childhood, we come to the designs and policy of which she was the subject even from the moment of her birth. It was the purpose of her father, King Henry VII., from an early period of his reign, to make James IV., king of Scotland, his friend and ally, by giving to him the hand of his eldest daughter; and the baptism of the infant princess on St. Andrew's Day was intended as a special compliment to this sovereign and to the Scottish people. Even in her early infancy overtures were made to the Scottish king for his betrothal with the English princess; and, although he had already attained to man's estate before she was born, the overtures were not rejected, inasmuch as they enabled him to meet the remonstrances of his own counsellors against an attachment which he had formed elsewhere, by encouraging them to hope that he should at some future time form a matrimonial alliance with the princess of England. It appears, that so early as A.D. 1500 a dispensation had been obtained for this marriage, when Margaret was but eleven years of age; and in the following year the death of Arthur, prince of Wales, the eldest son of Henry VII., in leaving only one remaining son to that monarch, rendered the alliance with his daughter a matter of still more importance. The possible consolidation of the whole Britannic empire by means of such an alliance began to occur to sagacious politicians; and at length, in 1502, a formal embassy arrived, consisting of the Earl of Bothwell and the Archbishop of Glasgow, and demanded the hand of the Princess Margaret.

" The proposition was thankfully accepted by Henry VII., and laid before his Privy Council, at which debate occurred the celebrated saying, often quoted from Lord Bacon, in proof of the foresighted wisdom of that sovereign. One of the English lords present having objected that ' the Princess Margaret, being next heir to her brother Henry, England might chance to become a province to Scotland ;' ' No,' replied King Henry, ' the smaller will ever follow the larger kingdom.' "

The parliament of England having proved refractory, and declining to give any marriage-portion to the princess, King Henry VII. was obliged to provide a dowry out of his own private purse ; and the sum of 10,000*l.*, to be paid by instalments in three years, was all that the King of England could then afford to give as a dowry, while the princess was secured a jointure of 2000*l.* on lands in Scotland ; and it was stipulated that she should have the attendance of twenty-four English servants, besides those Scottish attendants whom her lord the king might deem requisite for her dignity. All these preliminaries having been duly arranged, the marriage took place by proxy, the Earl of Bothwell acting for the king, his sovereign ; and the other procurators for the marriage being the Archbishop of Glasgow and the elect Bishop of Murray.

As soon as the vows of betrothal had been completed, Elizabeth of York, queen of Henry VII., rose, and, taking the princess by the hand, led her to a banquet set out in her private apartments, where she was placed at table as if she had been a queen visiting her, and both dined from one dish. Similar ceremonies took place at the king's table, and a splendid jousting followed in the afternoon.

" Then, by the advice of her ladies, the young Queen of Scots gave personal thanks to all the gentlemen and nobles who had jousted in her honour. After the prizes had been distributed among them with her royal hand, a goodly pageant entered the hall, curiously wrought with *fenestralis* (windows), having many lights burning in the same, in manner of a lantern, out of which *sorted* (issued in pairs) divers sorts of *morisks*. Also a very goodly disguising of six gentlemen and six gentlewomen, who danced divers dances ; then followed a wide, or banquet."

John Young, Somerset Herald, has been an invaluable friend to Miss Strickland in the earlier part of her account of the espousals of Margaret to the King of Scots. The minuteness with which this writer enters into all the details of costume, entertainments, manners, and habits, furnishes exactly the sort of information which is most essential to such a writer as Miss Strickland. The Somerset Herald accompanies the juvenile queen, then but thirteen years of age, in her magnificent progress through the midland and northern counties of England, to her new home. Curious incidents illustrative of the rude state of society at that period, occur; such, for instance, as the performing of the royal toilet in a litter by the road-side, when some grand procession was near at hand. In fine, after all kinds of rejoicings, processions, feasts, and goodly devices, the bridal party rest for a couple of days at Berwick, in order to appear in "all their bravery," on occasion of their entrance into the realm of Scotland; and then the queen is handed over in due form and ceremony to her loving subjects, of whom the veracious chronicler, John Young, notes with some disappointment, that instead of being bedight in gold and tinsel, they wore only "doublets of good cloth or camlet"—a fact which, to the Somerset Herald, was as distressing, apparently, as the omission, at Durham, to "shoot off" artillery or ordnance in honour of the princess.

How ably our authoress introduces the contrast between the ruder and sterner scenery, manners, and habits of the northern kingdom, with which the youthful princess was first made acquainted!

"In those days of semi-civilization, it was a breach of etiquette, as it is now among the Orientals and the South American Indians, for exalted persons to express surprise at any thing unusual which presented itself before their eyes; therefore, it cannot be expected that Margaret's herald chronicler should mention her natural astonishment at the romantic scene which now opened to her view. Yet, reared as she had been among the soft meads of Shene, and never accustomed to raise her eyes to higher ground than Richmond Hill, she must have been struck with her progress through the bold defile of Cockburn's-path, anciently Colbrand the giant's path,—for it is connected with the earliest superstitions of the island. Royal letters in those days were devoted to other purposes than recording impressions of the beauties of nature; no trace of any such feeling can be found in Margaret Tudor's innumerable epistles. Still her eyes must have rested, as ours have done, on the wild and wondrous scenery through which she was brought ' to bedward' that night.

"Fastcastle is no other than the veritable Wolf's-Crag Tower, celebrated in Scott's *Bride of Lammermoor* as the abode of the Master of Ravenswood. It is seated on a lofty promontory, which commands the lonely indented bay of which St. Abb's Head forms the extreme point to the right, with a wild array of rifted rocks terminating in the Wolf-Crag, which soars high in mid-air above the fortress—black, gloomy, and inaccessible. The way by which the southern bride and her company reached this rugged resting-place lay across the Lammermuir, several miles of wild heath and treacherous bog, which no stranger might traverse in safety without guides well acquainted with the track. Before they entered on this pass, they had to descend a hill so steep and precipitous, that even within the last century it was customary for the

passengers by the mail-coach between Berwick and Edinburgh to alight
and cross it on foot, while the carriage was taken off the wheels and
carried over by a relay of men, stationed on the spot for that purpose.
Of course the roads were not better in the beginning of the sixteenth
century. Fastcastle is approached by one or two descents and ascents
of this kind, and is separated from the main land by a cleft between the
rocks, which has to be crossed by a natural bridge, formed of a ledge
of rock, without rail or guard, with the vexed billows boiling and
thundering sixty feet below.

"When the young Tudor queen made her passage across this *Al
Arat* of the Caledonian coast, she had the German ocean before her,
which beats against the rocky battlements and defences with which the
basement of the castle is surrounded. One of these masses resembles
the upturned keel of a huge man-of-war stranded among other fragments, which, like the relics of a former world, lay scattered at the foot
of the precipice, with the wild breakers rushing through their clefts,
forming a grand *jet-d'eau*, and tossing the light feathery foam on high.
The larger rocks are the haunt of innumerable sea-birds. Fastcastle
had formerly been the stronghold of some of those ferocious feudal
pirates, who may be regarded as the buccaneers of the Caledonian
coast. Many a bloody deed had been perpetrated within its isolated
and inaccessible circuit; but the festive solemnities and ceremonials
that surrounded the royal bride allowed no leisure or opportunity for
whispers of the dark tales and romantic traditions connected with its
history. Thoroughly tired must she have been with her long journey,
and the onerous task of playing the queen, instead of tossing her ball
and joining in the loud laughter and jocund sports of the companions of
that gay and happy childhood from which she had suddenly been compelled to step into the more than womanly cares and responsibilities of
a crowned head in a land of strangers."

This rude stronghold must indeed have presented many
strange objects to the young princess, who was transferred at the
age of thirteen to a foreign land. She appears, however, to have
learnt, at least, the etiquette of her station, and to have borne
herself with all the dignity and gravity exacted by court ceremonial: and, judging from her general character, it is probable that
she relished, very highly, the attention of which she became the
object, and the display of equipage and dress which her station
justified and required. Her education appears to have been
cared for, as far as the mere externals of address and demeanour
were concerned, and she was a proficient in dancing and in music.
But in the more substantial and simpler requisites of an ordinary
education—writing and spelling—her performances appear to
have been wretched; and our authoress never omits an opportunity of betraying to us the sad short-comings of Queen Margaret, by italicizing her mistakes, which, to say the truth, are

perfectly monstrous, though not so intentional as the coarse pleasantry of her brother, "King Hal," who invariably wrote of one
of her husbands as "Lord *Muffin*," such being his version of the
graceful title of "Methven." Queen Margaret's education had
been neglected in still more important points. She appears never
to have been instructed in the important duties of self-control,
and of integrity and honourable dealing. Her life was a tissue
of mean jealousies, intrigues, and treacheries, invariably guided
by the most excessive selfishness : and a stranger contrast could
not be presented than between such a disposition and that of the
high-minded, and generous, but passionate prince, her consort,
with whose romantic character we have been made acquainted
in *Marmion* and the *Lady of the Lake*. Her father's policy, however, sacrificed any chance of happiness for her in life, by match-
ing her with a sovereign who was thirty-one years of age when
she was only thirteen at their marriage, and who excited her
jealousy by the attentions which he continually offered to ladies
who had passed the age of childhood, while the unfortunate Margaret, thus prematurely exposed to the cares and anxieties of married life, passed the earlier years of her marriage in continual
illness and despondency, without the consolation of feeling that
she possessed her consort's undivided affection, and without inward strength of mind to bear her up amidst the loneliness of
her foreign home. Some of her letters express very strongly the
desolation of her position.

After the marriage of the royal pair had been celebrated in
Scotland with great pomp and ceremony, of which we have many
amusing details, gathered from the records of the Somerset
Herald, King James took his bride on a wedding tour through
the south of Scotland, to show his subjects his English consort,
during which, as it was observed by Bishop Lesley, they were
nobly entertained at abbeys, and propitiated by rich purses of
gold, the queen being equally favoured with the king in the latter
respect, and probably accepting such gifts with no little satisfaction. Indeed she must have often reverted in thought to
those pleasurable moments in after-years, when her necessities or
her avarice induced her to assume the character of an importunate beggar in her correspondence with the English court.
We have the following curious accounts of the royal bounties to
minstrels shortly after Margaret's marriage :—

"Margaret was still a child, therefore notations of pleasure and
amusements constitute the sole records of her married life for a year or
two. The anniversary of her marriage in 1504 was spent in the fortress of Dunottar, of which the head of the noble family of Keith was
then Castellan. Here, in August, James IV. kept court with princely

cheer, and gave, in the course of the month, many donations to Margaret's musical band. 'Two English songstresses, who sang in the pavilion to the queen at Dunottar castle, had a donation of 27s. The king likewise ordered a benefaction of 18s. to the *chield* that played on the monochord.' Queen Margaret's luter had fees amounting to 56s.; likewise Pate Harper, who played the *clarcha*. The English boy Cuddy, and Souter the luter, got a share in a largess of 3l. 10s., given by the royal Stuart. The queen's luter was given a donation to get his lute out of pawn; four Italian minstrels had fees to clear them of the town; and Hog, the tale-teller or *diseur*, was given a benefaction of 13s."

Several years after her marriage, Margaret became the mother of a prince, to the extreme joy of her consort, who in order to testify his affection for her, undertook a pilgrimage on foot to the shrine of St. Ninian, in Galloway, in order to obtain the recovery of her health; and the good people of Scotland were greatly edified, not only by this act of devotion, but by the coincidence of Queen Margaret's recovery, at the moment when the king offered in her behalf at the shrine of St. Ninian's. Of course the queen herself could do no less than follow up the example by making a pilgrimage of thanksgiving to the same place; whither she was accompanied by seventeen pack horses of baggage, while the "chapel graith" or plate and furniture of her chapel, came in two coffers. King James's wardrobe was carried by three horses—no very great allowance after all, and scarcely as much as some gentlemen of our acquaintance travel with even now.

But the unfortunate young queen was destined to lose her eldest son shortly after his birth, and another, who survived to be two years of age; nor was it till the tenth year of her marriage, that a son was born who was christened James, and who afterwards succeeded to the throne of Scotland. In the following year she became a widow, by the unfortunate event of Flodden Field, in which the sovereign of Scotland fell, in the flower of his age, and with him all the leading aristocracy of the country. Queen Margaret had been urgent with her husband to declare war against her brother, King Henry, who had withheld from her certain jewels and other valuables, to which she was entitled, under the will of Prince Arthur, her elder brother. Her extreme urgency on this point, combined with the obligations of the old treaty existing between France and Scotland, and the correspondence of Anne of Brittany, queen of France, who chose King James for her knight, and urged him to do his devoir by marching three days with banners displayed over the borders, led at length to the declaration of war, which issued so fatally for Scotland. As soon as the king had resolved on this course, Margaret became extremely alarmed, and sought to dissuade her consort from his intentions. She endeavoured, according to Miss Strickland, to introduce the supernatural in aid of her other arguments; and it appears that her dreams, by which she sought to terrify the king, "were dreamed for the nonce, as preludes to the following incident, which was probably contrived (or at least connived at) by her :"—

"James IV. had passed a few days at the queen's palace at Linlithgow, before he called together his feudal muster. At the council held in the morning, it was observed he was out of spirits. In the evening he attended vespers at the stately abbey-church of St. Michael, adjoining to the queen's palace, for the purpose of praying for the success of the expedition. While praying in St. Catherine's Chapel, near the porch, 'there came ane man, clad in a blue gown or blouse, belted about him with a roll of white linen : he had brodikins or buskins on his feet. His head was bare, bald on the top, with yellow locks hanging on each side : his age about fifty. He came fast forwards among the lords, crying and speering specially for the king, saying, 'that he wanted to speak with him.' It seems that petitions were often presented by the people when the king was at his devotions. He made no due reverence to him, or salutations, but leaned him *gruffling* upon the desk (bent down to the desk), and spoke thus,—' Sir king, my mother has sent me to thee, charging thee not to go where thou art purposed; which, if thou do, thou shalt not fare well, nor none that is with thee. Further, she forbade thee not to seek nor follow the counsel of women ; which, if thou do, thou wilt be confounded and brought to shame.'

" By the time these words were spoken, even-song was nearly done. The king paused, studying to give him an answer. Meantime, before the king's eyes, and in presence of all the lords about him, ' like the blink of the sunbeam, or the whiff of the whirlwind, the man vanished away, and could no more be seen.' ' I heard,' continues Lindsay of Pitscottie, ' Sir David Lindsay and John Inglish, the marshal, (who were at that time both of them young men, and special servants to the king's grace,) thought to have taken this man, that they might have speered further tidings at him; but they could not touch him."

Tradition and general opinion connect this scene with Queen Margaret as its designer, or as privy to the plan. King James appears to have suspected something of the kind, for he made no inquiries into the circumstance, and evidently attributed it to no supernatural causes. He went on his preparations in spite of this warning, and also of another attempt to intimidate by the ghostly summons issued at the market cross of Edinburgh, where the nobles, gentry, and others were summoned to the infernal regions within forty days. Such means of arresting an impending war sound very absurd in our ears; but the mere notion that kings and nobles could be influenced by such visions is amongst the most striking proofs of the immense change which has passed over the mind of man since those times. It is plain, also, that although King James was not himself influenced by these appearances, there were not wanting those who regarded them as miraculous; and, after the unfortunate issue of the Battle of Flodden, such predictions would naturally gain an attention they did not deserve; and, without doubt, the circumstances attending them were exaggerated, and rendered still more strange and supernatural by popular tradition and superstitious feeling. Indeed, the story of the ghostly summons of the market cross appears to have rested only on the testimony of one individual. "It is most probable," says Miss Strickland, "that Richard Lawson was the very person who contrived the incident; as he was one of the civic authorities, he had particular opportunities of arranging aught that was done or acted at the market cross; he was the only witness of the matter; and he was evidently of the peace, or queen's party."

Previously to his departure for Scotland, King James constituted his queen guardian of the prince, in case of his own death, and at the same time he confided to her the place of his treasure, and authorized her to receive, in trust for his infant son, the last subsidy which Louis XII. had paid him, being eighteen thousand golden sols, or crowns of the sun : and also placed in her possession many other valuables belonging to the crown.

The avaricious disposition of Margaret was unable to resist the opportunity of appropriating to her own use this mass of treasure, and accordingly, when the Scottish parliament assembled in consequence of the death of King James, and proceeded to settle the affairs of the State, the strange discovery was made, that the royal exchequer was wholly exhausted. The queen, however, whom no one suspected, was made regent, pursuant to the will of her consort.

"The parliament of Scotland was convened by Queen Margaret to meet at Stirling Castle, December 21, 1513, there the will of James IV. was read : although his request that Margaret would take upon her the regency and personal care of the infant king, was against the ancient customs of Scotland, which always placed the executive power in the hands of the next male heir; yet, the hearts of all present, being full of tenderness to the memory of their loved and lost monarch, no one could bear to gainsay his last wishes. Queen Margaret was, therefore, unanimously recognised as their regent, and the young king was solemnly given into her care. The Lord Chancellor, James Beton, Archbishop of Glasgow, the Earls of Arran, Huntley, and Angus, were deputed to assist her. Stirling Castle, the great palatial fortress of Scotland, was appointed as the residence of the infant monarch, and of the prince or princess the queen was expected to produce. Queen Margaret was to have possession of Stirling Castle until her son James V. came of age. But all her power and grandeur as reigning sovereign of Scotland were to cease if she made a second marriage: on this head the testament of James IV. was stringent."

Thus was Margaret, at twenty-four years of age, invested with the sovereign rule of Scotland, and she might have probably continued to sway the northern sceptre for many long years, had she not become enamoured of the youthful Earl of Angus, then but eighteen years of age. The queen had already been connected by policy with the powerful house of Douglas, and her sudden passion for its head was encouraged by the artful representations of his grandfather, Lord Drummond of Stobahall, who represented how impossible it was for the English party in Scotland to stand against the French faction, if the Duke of Albany should arrive as governor, unless the queen strengthened herself by the aid of the mighty Douglas clan and their adherents, amongst which the Drummond family alone would outweigh all the objections that might be made by the rest of the nobility to a second marriage of the queen. These arguments of state, coinciding exactly with the queen's private wishes, she proceeded to lavish, with the headlong favouritism of the Tudors, all appointments in the gift of the crown on the Douglas family and their friends. Gavin Douglas, the uncle of the Earl of Angus, was made Bishop of Dunkeld, and destined to be Archbishop of St. Andrew's. And shortly afterwards, only a year after the death of King James IV. at Flodden, Margaret was privately married to the Earl of Angus. Her attempt, immediately afterwards, to force Gavin Douglas on the see of St. Andrew's by her own authority, without any regard to the rights of election inherent in the Church, and the contest on which she entered with the Church, excited public attention, and caused inquiry into her motives for this proceeding, when it was discovered that she had been privately married to Angus.

"Great was the commotion, violent the rage, and intense the indignation of all ranks and conditions of the Scottish people. At last it was remembered, that if the Church had submitted more than was her duty to the despotism of the monarchical authority, by admitting the two preceding archbishops of St. Andrew's, Queen Margaret had no right to the same complaisance, since she had forfeited her regal station from the moment she had given herself in second wedlock to the Earl of Angus."

The result of this untoward discovery was, that the council met and deposed the queen from the regency, and, in conjunction with Parliament, offered it to the Duke of Albany, the next heir to the throne, who had become naturalized in France. A scene of great confusion followed, each party endeavouring to gain the ascendancy ; but the queen's party was the weaker, and she was ultimately compelled to relinquish the persons of the princes, her sons, to the care of the Regent Albany. We have the following interesting account of the mode in which this was accomplished :

" A more difficult undertaking than the deprivation of her political power was to wrest her children from Queen Margaret. The regent evidently demurred on a proceeding in which the kindest measures taken could not fail of seeming cruel in the extreme. July had nearly passed away, yet Queen Margaret still held possession of her little sons at the castle of Edinburgh. Albany made his approaches with great caution, while the Parliament was sitting at the Tolbooth. Then the national council chose eight peers, and out of them Albany was to appoint four by lot ; and from the four Queen Margaret was to choose three to intrust with the care of her royal infants.

" The four peers went in solemn procession from the Tolbooth (where the Parliament sat) up to Edinburgh castle-gate. All the Guid Town followed them on foot, in immense concourse, to behold the exciting drama in which their queen and her little ones played the principal parts. The gates were unfolded, and the people beheld the queen standing within the entrance, holding the young king, with his hand clasped in hers ; behind her was the nurse, with the infant Duke of Ross in her arms ; near her stood her husband Angus, and her household made a half circle in the rearward.

" The queen had certainly drawn up her little force with great scenic skill, and it had its due effect on the good people of Edinburgh, who hailed the *tableaux vivans* before them with long and loud acclamations. When some degree of silence was restored, which was only when the populace had shouted themselves hoarse, Queen Margaret, seeing the approach of the delegates from the Tolbooth, gave the words with much majesty and command, of—' Stand ! Declare the cause of your coming before you draw nearer to your sovereigns.'

" The four Scottish peers replied, ' that they were deputed by the Parliament then sitting, to demand and receive their infant king and his brother.'

" All the answer Margaret vouchsafed was, ' Drop the portcullis !' To the consternation of the parliamentary deputies, the massive iron gate thundered down betwixt them and the royal group.

" The queen then addressed the lords commissioned to take her infants from her arms : ' This castle of Edinburgh is part of my infeoffment ! By the late king, my husband, I was made sole governess of it, nor to any mortal shall yield the command. But I require, out of respect to Parliament and the nation, six days to consider their mandate : for my charge is infinite in import ; and, alas ! my counsellors be few !' She then led away her little monarch from the gateway, followed by her train; and the peers retired in great admiration of her beauty and high spirit."

We must pass over the interesting adventures of Margaret, in her escape from Scotland, and her reception by King Henry VIII. with fraternal cordiality. Here her mendicancy both to Henry himself and to Cardinal Wolsey, his minister, becomes absurdly importunate. No Irish beggar-woman was ever more persevering and more varied in her contrivances to extort money. Whatever was the subject of her epistle, like many a piquant anecdote which we peruse unsuspectingly in the public journals until we are entrapped into some recommendation of spectacles or dress, she always concludes with a request for plate, jewels, or cash. King Henry ultimately got weary of this propensity of his sister's, but he yielded to it for a time, and Margaret, when permitted to return to Scotland, arrived in very different guise from that in which she had left it, without possessions, treasure, or even wardrobe.

"'The Queen of Scots,' says her contemporary Hall, 'who had been a whole year at court and at Baynard's Castle, at the king's charge, and was richly appointed of all things meet to her estate, both jewels, plate, tapestry, arras, coin, horses, and all things of her brother's gift, liberally, departed out of London to Scotland, May 18, with great riches, albeit she entered England in great poverty. All her charges, both going and returning, were made at our king's cost.' Thus the 'sort of things' Margaret had to do at Baynard's Castle was no ather than securing this vast store of goods she had to convey back to Scotland!"

But no sooner had Queen Margaret returned to Scotland, than she became discontented with the conduct of her husband, the Earl of Angus, and she commenced a process for obtaining a divorce from him. The history of her proceedings in this case, and in another (for the queen married husbands and repudiated them something in the style of her brother, Henry VIII.), will show the extreme laxity of the Papal See on the subject of divorce, at that time. The example, indeed, had been set in the case of Louis XII., who, after he had been married to the Princess Joanna of France for twenty years, was divorced from her by Alexander VI. in 1498, on the plea that the princess's father, Louis IX., had been *god-father* to the king, and that no dispensation had been obtained, with other pleas equally frivolous; the *real* inducement being the investiture, by Louis, of the Pope's son, Cæsar Borgia, with the duchy of Valentinois.

With so convenient an example of Papal complaisance within the preceding twenty years, Queen Margaret flattered herself that she should find some means of inducing the Pope to dissolve her marriage with the Earl of Angus ; and, having made her peace with the Regent Albany, she succeeded, through his interest, after about seven years' perseverance, in obtaining the divorce she sought for.   We extract the following account of the conclusion of the affair :—

" Margaret's present object was to arrive at some decision concerning her divorce : for this purpose she affected to be on very friendly terms with Angus, and even had some amicable consultations with him on the subject.   Finding the delays of Rome interminable, she contrived to enlist Beton, Archbishop of St. Andrew's, on her side, who summoned Angus to hear his divorce from the queen pronounced according to the laws of the Church.   He appeared on the day appointed at the consistorial court of St. Andrew's.   Then the queen alleged ' that he had been betrothed, and given his faith and promise of marriage to a noble lady (some say, a daughter of the Earl of Traquair, and others, of Earl Bothwell), before he had married her (the queen), and so, by reason of that pre-contract, he could not be her lawful husband.'   The earl confessed all : upon which the archbishop pronounced sentence of divorce, making a proviso, ' that the daughter born of the queen should not suffer loss or disadvantage' from the ignorance of her mother of her father's pre-engagement.

" The legality of this sentence was immediately disputed.   The flaw appears to have been, the uncertainty which of the two noble ladies, Janet Douglas, or Margaret Hepburn, was Angus's *fiancée* when he wedded the queen.   There is nothing definite, therefore, alleged in any of the sentences of divorce.   Another passed later in the same year, dated at Ancona, in which the Pope mentions the marriage as infirm and bad, but gives no specific reason why it was so."

Queen Margaret had already provided herself with a new husband before the divorce had been solemnly pronounced ; and, as soon as that sentence was made public, she announced Henry Stuart, captain of her guard, as her spouse.   It is a curious coincidence, that the proceedings for the divorce of Henry VIII. from Catharine of Aragon commenced in the same year which brought to a close his sister's divorce from Angus ; but, strangely enough, King Henry looked with great disfavour on proceedings so analogous to his own.

" So far from pleading the example of his sister's long-pending divorce, Henry was heartily ashamed of the false position in which he exhibited himself in the eyes of the courts of Europe, as if he aped Margaret's disreputable proceedings.   It is curious enough to find him urging Wolsey perpetually to delay his sister's divorce at the court of Rome, which was done with such success that, of course, he became furiously suspicious that similar means were used when his own turn came."

lowed t
beauty

W

her
wit
hi
t

...husband were compelled to yield to
the D   ouglas   faction, on her mar-
...ed to co... herself for some time;
...revolutions of which Scotland exhibited
...shortly afterwards recovered her position,
...created Lord Methven by James V., and was
...possessions and high offices.   In the course of
...ver, Methven contrived to displease his wife,
...divorce was set on foot.   Apparently, this divorce
...have been conceded, the Court of Rome having doubt-
...in the interval, from the result of Henry's divorce
...it was imprudent to restrict the wills of sovereigns;
but King James V. most undutifully " prevented the sentence from
being promulgated," though Queen Margaret " had provided her
judge with four-and-forty *famous* proofs, as cause of divorce between her and Lord Meffin !"   There were some persons malicious enough to suppose that she designed to re-marry her *second*
husband, the Earl of Douglas ; but her intended appears to have
been a person named " John Stuart."   The inconvenient interference, however, of her son caused the overthrow of these fine
plans, and subsequently, under the influence of his queen, Mary
of Lorraine, she even relinquished her design, and lived in harmony with " Lord Muffin" till her death.

The character which Miss Strickland has described in her life
of Margaret Tudor is altogether one of the most unpleasing we
have ever met with.   There is a cold selfishness, an utter absence
of all high, honourable, and natural feeling about it, which entirely precludes any sympathy with her in the numerous calamities in which her ambition and avarice involved her.   And this is
felt still more strongly when contrasted with the beautiful picture
of gentleness and love which immediately succeeds, in the brief,
but touching memoir of Magdalene of France.

The history of the happy marriage of James V. and Magdalene is one of those episodes on which the imagination loves to
rest ; one of those rare instances in which the policy of states
has been subordinated to the instincts of natural human feeling,
and in which the mind delights to dwell on virtuous love hallow-
ing the union of princes.

Magdalene of France was the daughter of Francis I., and
was at an early age destined to be united to the young King of
Scots.   This design was however broken off by political intrigues, and also in consequence of the failing health of the
princess, who manifested symptoms of the family tendency to
consumption, which had already cut off her two sisters.

Under these circumstances, Francis entreated the King of

Scots to transfer his addresses to the Lady Mary de Bourbon, eldest daughter of the Duke de Vendôme, the first prince of the blood royal of France. James acceded so far to the wishes of his royal ally as to despatch an embassy to the court of the Duko of Vendôme, to open a matrimonial treaty ; but the Scottish king was determined to judge for himself, and was not content to see his future queen through any eyes but his own. He accordingly set forth for France, with 100 of his nobles, knights, and gentlemen ; but keeping from them as a secret the destination and object of his voyage. Accident, however, made them acquainted with the truth ; and the result was, that they actually changed the course of the vessel, and King James found himself again on the coast of Scotland instead of approaching the coast of France. A second attempt proved more successful, and King James was soon seen walking, incognito, about the streets of Paris, and making sundry purchases for the decoration of his outward man, in contemplation of the resumption of his proper rank. An amusing account is given of his doings in this respect, and of the liberal payment which must have indicated the rank of the employer to the operatives of Paris. After some time spent in Paris, the royal adventurer, travelling as the servant of his keeper of the wardrobe, went to the ducal château of Vendôme on the Loire.

" King James, instead of declaring himself, took the opportunity, which one of the continental fêtes or public days afforded to him and his pretended master, John Tennent, of mingling with the spectators and guests of humble degree at the lower end of the hall, fancying he should be able to make his observation *perdue* on the young princess, to whom his hand was pledged. Nature had stamped the impress of nobility too legibly on the graceful and majestic lineaments of James Stuart for him to pass unnoticed in a crowd. The princess, whom he had come so far to look upon by stealth, having been inspired with scarcely less curiosity than his own to see what manner of mate she had promised to wed, had, it seems, procured his portrait ; and the moment she saw him, though in a serving man's array, among the menial train at the lower end of her father's hall, she recognized him by the likeness, and frankly advanced to greet him."

Notwithstanding this frankness, or "pertness," as old Lindsay of Pitscottie terms it, the fair lady of Vendôme did not succeed in winning the affections of the Scottish king, who retired from the engagement with far greater precipitation than he had entered it, to the infinite mortification and grief of the poor discarded princess.

We next find James visiting the court of France, where he was recognized by the dauphin, and introduced to Francis I.,

who, with all his family, was in deep grief at the recent death of
his eldest son.   The dauphin and King James found that Francis
had retired to repose himself on his bed for his afternoon nap.
The dauphin, however, knocked loudly and hastily at the door.
" Who is it knocks so fast to disquiet me in my rest!" asked
Francis from within.   " It is the King of Scotland come to see
your grace, and to give you comfort," said the dauphin.   Francis,
on this, sprang from his bed, opened the chamber-door, and
received his royal visitor in his arms.

  " The advent of a sovereign like James V. under such circumstances
created a wonderful sensation among the nobles and ladies of the
French court, more especially the latter.   They marvelled at his boldness in undertaking so perilous a voyage in stormy weather, considering the roughness of the seas and the danger of the coast; that he
should have ventured on such an expedition without asking for a safe
conduct from either the King of England or the King of France; and
that he should be travelling in a strange land, not only without a military escort for the protection of his person, but attended by so few
servants.   There was no court in Europe where the spirit of knight-
errantry was so highly appreciated as in that of the chivalric Francis I.;
no man better qualified, both by nature and inclination, to enact the
part of a royal hero of romance than the fifth James of Scotland.   Gay,
gallant, beautiful, and fascinating, he excited the most enthusiastic feelings
of admiration in every breast, but in none more ardently than in that of
the young delicate invalid, who had been accustomed to regard him,
from her earliest recollection, as her affianced husband.   There are
instances when sickness, instead of marring, adds a touching charm to
female beauty, especially in early youth, when the malady is of a con-
sumptive or hectic character.   This was the case with the Princess
Magdalene of France, who is described by contemporaries as a creature
too fair and exquisite for this week-day world, in which she was to
have but a brief continuance.   King James, beholding in her the realization of his *beau-idéal* of feminine loveliness and grace, determined to
break through all contracts, treaties, and entanglements that might
prevent their union, and to woo and win her for his Queen."

  The course of true love, however, according to the old proverb,
was not to run quite smooth; for the council of France and the
advisers of the King of Scotland raised abundance of difficulties;
and Francis even went so far as to offer his younger daughter to
King James in lieu of the elder, apprehending that the cold
climate of Scotland and the voyage there might shorten the days
of Magdalene, as he had been advised by the physicians.   All
engagements, treaties, reasons of state, and apprehensions, however, were compelled to give way before the ardour of the royal
lovers.

"King James would have no one but her, sick or well, strong or weak. The Lady Magdalene was the mistress of his heart; and, the more difficulties that were made, the more eager he was to call her his own. As for Magdalene, she was deaf to all warnings. She had made up her mind to be Queen of Scotland, were the clime more ungenial than Lapland, and the people greater barbarians than Muscovites. She would be content to leave her own vine-clad hills, and all the refinements and luxuries of her native land, to share the fortunes of King James. Love, and the happiness of finding herself the beloved of the object of that first sweet passion which prevailed in her young heart over every other feeling, did that for the fair invalid which the skill of the physicians had failed to do,—it recalled her apparently to life, and all the hopes and blissful expectations from which she had been previously cut off in the spring-tide of existence."

The marriage was celebrated at Nôtre Dame with extreme splendour, in the presence of the Kings and Queens of France and Navarre, the dauphin, the Duke of Orleans, seven cardinals, and all the nobility of France, and the loyal portion of that of Scotland. We have much interesting detail in Miss Strickland's pages, of the costume, ceremonial, banquetings, and rejoicings on this occasion; and this season of happiness was protracted for several months, during which James allowed his bride to remain at her father's court, in the hope that the voyage to Scotland might be undertaken at a more favourable season, and the health of the young queen be restored. At length, however, these few months of unmingled happiness came to an end, and the royal pair took their leave, loaded with presents, and accompanied by the good wishes and prayers of all France.

"The royal voyagers made the port of Leith, Saturday, May 19, being the fifth day from their embarkation, and Whitsun Eve. They landed at the pier amidst the acclamations of a mixed multitude of living lieges of all degrees, who came to welcome their sovereign home, and to see their new queen. Magdalene endeared herself for ever to the affections of the people by the sensibility she manifested on that occasion; for when 'she first stepped on Scottish ground she knelt, and, bowing herself down, kissed the moulds thereof for the love she bore the king, returned thanks to God for having brought the king and her safely through the seas, and prayed for the happiness of the country.' This was, indeed, entering upon her high vocation; not like the cold state puppet of a public pageant, but in the spirit of a queen who felt and understood the relation in which she stood both to the king and people of that realm. A touching sight it must have been to those who saw that young royal bride thus obey the warm impulse of a heart overflowing with gratitude to God, and love to all she then looked upon."

In six short weeks that fair and happy young queen had yielded up her pious and gentle spirit to her Maker! Consumption, checked for a while by the impulse given by her happiness, fastened again on its victim, and in that cold northern climate it speedily proved fatal.

With this melancholy history we must conclude. The second wife of King James, Mary of Lorraine, possessed many high qualities, and the abilities of her mighty house ; but James must often have dwelt on the image of his loved and lost Magdalene of France, and it was probably her early death which caused so deep a shock to his feelings and affections, that when, in a few years afterwards, the death of his children was followed by a reverse to the Scottish arms, he was unable to bear up longer, and died of a broken heart. The volume continues with unabated interest to its close, when Mary of Lorraine is left a widow, with an unborn babe, the eagerly desired heir of the ancient kingdom of Scotland.

ART. II.—1. *The Testimony. To the Patriarchs, Archbishops, Bishops, and others in places of Chief Rule in the Church of Christ throughout the Earth, and to the Emperors, Kings, Sovereign Princes, and Chief Governors over the Nations of the Baptized.* 4to Edition. Printed by C. Morgan, Henry-street, Pentonville. 8vo Edition. Printed by Moyes & Barclay, Castle-street, Leicester-square.

2. *Narrative of Events affecting the Position and Prospects of the whole Christian Church.* Printed for Private Circulation, by George Barclay, Castle-street, Leicester-square. 1847.

3. *Proclamation of the Twelve Apostles of the Church of Jesus Christ of Latter-Day Saints, to all the Kings of the World, to the President of the United States of America, to the Governors of the several States, and to the Rulers and People of all Nations.* Liverpool: Woodruff. 1845.

4. *Letters exhibiting the most Prominent Doctrines of the Church of Jesus Christ of Latter-Day Saints. By* ORSON SPENCER, *A.B., President of the Church of Jesus Christ, of L. D. S. in Europe. In reply to the Rev. William Crowell, A. M., Boston, Massachusetts, U. S. A.* Liverpool: Orson Spencer. 1848.

5. *Divine Authority; or, the Question, Was Joseph Smith sent of God? No. I. The Kingdom of God. Nos. II. and III. By* ORSON PRATT, *one of the Twelve Apostles of the Church of Jesus Christ of Latter-Day Saints.* Liverpool. 1848.

6. *A Dialogue between Joseph Smith and the Devil.* No date.

7. *Absurdities of Immaterialism; or, a Reply to T. W. P. Taylder's Pamphlet, entitled, " The Materialism of the Mormons, or Latter-Day Saints, Examined and Exposed." By* ORSON PRATT, *one of the Twelve Apostles of the Church of Jesus Christ of Latter-Day Saints.* Liverpool. 1849.

8. *Friendly Warnings on the Subject of Mormonism. Addressed to his Parishioners by a Country Clergyman.* London: Rivingtons. 1850.

HAVING in former numbers traced separately the origin of the two sects which have risen up in our day, one in this country, the other in America, with the pretension of being appointed by God to prepare the world for the Second Advent of Christ, we proceeded in our last number to point out the remarkable analogy which exists between them. We now proceed with the parallel; the length to which the subject necessarily extends having com-

pelled us to break off in the middle.   Our readers will remember
the singular coincidence, in point of time, of the first rise of the
two sects, and the similarity of the statements in which they record their origin ; and further, the striking resemblance between
the views which they respectively take of the existing state of
Christendom.   It is true that there is a great difference, likewise,
between the two, both in their doctrine and manner of living;
but this difference is not greater than might naturally be expected
from the fact that one of them rose in the highly cultivated and
strictly regulated state of society in England, in the face of a
Church which has preserved the primitive doctrine of the Gospel
in all its purity and integrity, and still commands the assent and the
respect of the great body of the nation,—while the other grows
up in the semi-barbarous and lawless state of society which prevails in the Far West of America, in a country the population of
which never had a Church, but is, in a religious point of view, a
mere Babel-like conglomeration of religionists] of every conceivable variety, among whom the sapling of the true catholic
Church planted in those parts, occupies, to the general apprehension, only the position of one among many sects, and has,
therefore, little or no influence in checking the general growth of
extravagance of doctrine and licentiousness of practice.   Due
weight being given to these considerations, it will probably appear,
that in spite of the enormity of their errors and the grossness of
their proceedings, Joseph Smith and his followers present no
greater contrast to the tone of society and the state of religious
knowledge in the Far West, than Mr. Henry Drummond and his
associates, with their more subdued and refined fanaticism, to
the social and religious aspect of the world by which they are surrounded.   This acknowledged difference in the development of
the two sects, so far from effacing the similitude between them,
on the contrary brings out in stronger relief, to the eye of the
thoughtful observer, the essential identity of the ground on which
they both proceed, and of the principles on which they found
their extraordinary, their analogous, and rival claims to be κατ'
ἐξοχήν the Kingdom of Christ.
   Depreciation of the existing Church and of her means of grace,
—a wilful overlooking of the distinction between the Church and
the heretical and schismatical communions by which she is surrounded,—the assumption, that since the apostolical age the
Church has become extinct, or, at least, has not existed in her
integrity,—and the pretension that they, the Irvingites or the
Mormonites respectively, are the true Church, restored in preparation for the Lord's coming,—these are the essential features
which characterize them both.   At the close of our last article,
we laid before our readers copious extracts from the document

entitled the "*Testimony*," in which the Irvingite sect propounded these extravagant notions and pretensions to the
rulers of Christendom both spiritual and temporal. We now
turn to a similar document issued by the Mormonites. This
also runs in the name of "the twelve Apostles" of the true
"Church." It is a much shorter and much less elaborate document, as well as much more recent, bearing date "New York,
April 6th, 1845." It differs from the other, moreover, in this,
that it is not addressed to any spiritual rulers, but only to temporal governors; and that, instead of being privately delivered to
those to whom it was addressed, and not suffered to transpire
beyond the pale of the sect, it has been published to the world.
It opens thus:—

"Proclamation of the Twelve Apostles of the Church of Jesus Christ
of Latter-day Saints. To all the Kings of the world, to the President
of the United States of America; to the Governors of the several States,
and to the rulers and people of all nations.

"Greeting,—Know ye that the kingdom of God has come, as has
been predicted by ancient prophets, and prayed for in all ages; even
that kingdom which shall fill the whole earth, and shall stand for ever.

"The great Elohim, Jehovah, has been pleased once more to speak
from the heavens, and also to commune with man upon the earth, by
means of open visions, and by the ministration of HOLY MESSENGERS.

"By this means the great and eternal High Priesthood, after the
order of his Son (even the Apostleship), has been restored or returned
to the earth.

This High Priesthood or Apostleship holds the keys of the kingdom
of God, with power to bind on earth that which shall be bound in heaven,
and to loose on earth that which shall be loosed in heaven; and, in fine,
to do and to administer in all things pertaining to the ordinances, organization, government, and direction of the kingdom of God.

"Being established in these last days for the restoration of all things
spoken by the prophets since the world began, and in order to prepare
the way for the coming of the Son of Man.

"And we now bear witness that his coming is near at hand; and
not many years hence, the nations and their kings shall see Him coming
in the clouds of heaven with power and great glory.

"In order to meet this great event, there must needs be a preparation.

"Therefore we send unto you, with authority from on high, and
command you all to repent and humble yourselves as little children
before the majesty of the Holy One; and come unto Jesus with a
broken heart and a contrite spirit, and be baptized in his name for the
remission of sins (that is, be buried in the water, in the likeness of his
burial, and rise again to newness of life in the likeness of his resurrection), and you shall receive the gift of the Holy Spirit, through the
laying on of the hands of the apostles and elders, of this great and last
dispensation of mercy to man.

" This Spirit shall bear witness to you of the truth of our testimony, and shall enlighten your minds, and be in you as the spirit of prophecy and revelation ; it shall bring things past to your understanding and remembrance, and shall show you things to come.

" It shall also impart unto you many great and glorious gifts ; such as the gift of healing the sick, and of being healed, by the laying on of hands in the name of Jesus ; and of expelling demons ; and even of seeing visions, and conversing with angels and spirits from the unseen world.

" By the light of this Spirit, received through the ministration of the ordinances—by the power and authority of the Holy Apostleship and Priesthood, you will be enabled to understand, and to be the children of light ; and thus be prepared to escape all the things that are coming on the earth, and so stand before the Son of Man.

" We testify that the foregoing doctrine is the doctrine or gospel of Jesus Christ in its fulness ; and that it is the only true, everlasting, and unchangeable gospel ; and the only plan revealed on earth whereby man can be saved."—*Proclamation,* pp. 1—3.

An account of the new revelation, given by the hand of Joseph Smith, and of the constitution of the Church of Latter-Day Saints, follows, with an exhortation to all the nations of the earth to take their part in this great and glorious work. In the event of their refusing to do so, they are warned that it will be impossible for them to remain neutral, and that theirs will be the loss, as they will be vanquished in a great victory by the personal interposition of the Lord Jesus Christ descending on the Mount of Olives.

" In short the kings, rulers, priests, and people of Europe, and of the old world, shall know this once that there is a God in Israel, who, as in days of old, can utter his voice, and it shall be obeyed.

" The courts of Rome, London, Paris, Constantinople, Petersburgh. and all others, will then have to yield the point and do homage, and all pay tribute to one great centre, and to one mighty Sovereign, or, THRONES WILL BE CAST DOWN, AND KINGDOMS WILL CEASE TO BE.

" Priests, bishops, and clergy, whether Catholic, Protestant, or Mahomedan, will then have to yield their pretended claims to the priesthood, together with titles, honours, creeds, and names, and reverence and obey the true and royal priesthood of the order of Melchizedek, and of Aaron ; restored to the rightful heirs—the nobility of Israel ; or, the dearth and famine will consume them, and the plague sweep them quickly down to the pit, as in the case of Korah, Dathan, and Abiram, who pretended to the priesthood, and rebelled against God's chosen priests and prophets in the days of Moses."—*Proclamation,* p. 8.

This is followed by a special appeal to the governments of the United States, exhorting them to promote the civilization of the Red Indians as "the descendants of Joseph," and to protect the saints and indemnify them for the losses which they have sustained through the measures taken against them by the governments of the different states where they have been settled. In the event of their responding to this appeal, a promise is given them that they shall " be prospered and enlarged, and spread their dominion wide and more wide over this vast country, till not only Texas and Oregon, but the whole vast dominion, from sea to sea, will be joined with them, and come under their protection as one great, powerful, and peaceful empire of liberty and union." But if not, " the great Messiah shall execute judgment for the saints, and give them the dominion." The idea of the "saints" being deterred from the prosecution of their design by the forces arrayed against them is repudiated with utter scorn :—

" It is in vain to suppose that the sword, the musket, the thunder of cannon, or the grating and rattle of chains, bolts and bars, will take away the faith, hope, or knowledge of a Latter-Day Saint. They *know* some *facts*—and these will continue to be *known facts* when death and war in their most horrid forms are raging around them. They cannot shut their eyes upon these facts to please either governors, rulers, or the raging multitude.

" We would now make a solemn appeal to our rulers, and other fellow citizens, whether it is treason to *know*, or even to publish what we *know?* If it is, then strike the murderous blow, but listen to what we say.

" We say, then, in life or in death, in bonds or free, that the great God has spoken in this age.—*And we know it.*

" He has given us the holy priesthood and apostleship, and the keys of the kingdom of God, to bring about the restoration of all things as promised by the holy prophets of old.—*And we know it.*

" He has revealed the origin and the records of the aboriginal tribes of America, and their future destiny.—*And we know it.*

" He has revealed the fulness of the Gospel, with its gifts, blessings, and ordinances.—*And we know it.*

" He has commanded *us* to bear witness of it, first to the Gentiles, and then to the remnants of Israel, and the Jews.—*And we know it.*

" He has commanded us to gather together his Saints, on this continent, and build up holy cities and sanctuaries.—*And we know it.*

" He has said, that the Gentiles should come into the same gospel and covenant, and be numbered with the house of Israel, and be a blessed people upon this good land for ever, if they would repent and embrace it.—*And we know it.*

" He has also said, that if they do not repent, and come to the knowledge of the truth, and cease to fight against Zion, and also put away all murder, lying, pride, priestcraft, whoredom, and secret abomination, they shall soon perish from the earth, and be cast down to hell.—*And we know it.*

" He has said, that the time is at hand for the Jews to be gathered to Jerusalem.—*And we know it.*

" He has said that the ten tribes of Israel should also be revealed in the north country, together with their oracles and records, preparatory to their return, and to their union with Judah, no more to be separated.—*And we know it.*

" He has said, that when these preparations were made, both in this country and in Jerusalem, and the gospel in all its fulness preached to all nations for a witness and testimony, He will come, and all the Saints with him, to reign on the earth one thousand years.—*And we know it.*

" He has said, that He will not come in his glory and destroy the wicked, till these warnings were given, and these preparations were made for his reception.—*And we know it.*

" Now, fellow-citizens, if this knowledge, or the publishing of it, is *treason* or *crime*, we refuse not to die.

" But be ye sure of this, that, whether we live or die, the words of the testimony of this proclamation, which we now send unto you, shall all be fulfilled.

" Heaven and earth shall pass away, but not one jot or tittle of his revealed word shall fail to be fulfilled.

" Therefore, again we say to all people, repent, and be baptized in the name of Jesus Christ, for remission of sins, and you shall receive the Holy Spirit, and shall know the truth, and be numbered with the house of Israel.

" And we once more invite all the kings, presidents, governors, rulers, judges, and people of the earth to aid us, the Latter-Day Saints, and also the Jews, and all the remnants of Israel, by your influence and protection, and by your silver and gold, that we may build the cities of Zion and Jerusalem, and the temples and sanctuaries of our God; and may accomplish the great restoration of all things, and bring in the latter-day glory."—*Proclamation*, pp. 12—14.

The concluding portion of the "*Proclamation*" is remarkably practical and businesslike:—

" In fulfilment of the work assigned them, let the Saints throughout the world, and all others who feel an interest in the work of God, forward their gifts, tithes, and offerings, for the building of the temple of the Lord, which is now in progress in the city of Nauvoo, in the state of Illinois.

" Let them also come on with their gold, and silver, and goods, and workmen, to establish manufactories and business of all kinds, for the building up of the city, and for the employment and support of the poor, and thus strengthen the hands of those who have borne the burden and heat of the day, and who have made great sacrifices in laying the foundation of the kingdom of God, and moving on the work thus far."—*Proclamation*, p. 14.

Then comes a "solemn and earnest request" to "all editors of newspapers," both in America and elsewhere, to publish the Proclamation, which "cannot fail to interest the reading public, especially those who have prayed every day of their lives for the Lord's kingdom to come, and for his will to be done on the earth as it is done in heaven." Requests to promote its circulation are also addressed to "President Wilford Woodruff, who superintends the publishing department of the Latter-Day Saints in Liverpool;" to "Elder Jones, our minister to Wales;" to the German and Norwegian elders, and to "Elder Adison Pratt, our missionary to the Sandwich Islands;" and "last, but not least, to the editors of the *Cherokee Advocate*, and others of the remnant of Joseph." On their part, the apostles promise to publish one hundred thousand copies, gratis, from "their office, No. 7, Spruce-street, New York;" in aid of which publication, contributions are solicited, to be sent to the said office, where "copies for distribution" may be obtained "at fifty cents per hundred." Lastly:—

" The world are also informed, that further information can be had by applying to the following general publishing offices of the Latter-Day Saints:—Mr. John Taylor, *Times and Seasons* office, Nauvoo, in the State of Illinois; Messrs. Pratt and Brannan, *Prophet* office, No. 7, Spruce-street, New York; Mr. Wilford Woodruff, *Millennial Star* office, Stanley-buildings, Bath-street, Liverpool; also of our travelling elders, and in our religious meetings throughout the world."—*Proclamation*, p. 16.

It is at once apparent, that in all the main features there is the most striking similarity betwen the pretensions of the two sects,—equally apparent that they mutually exclude and thereby neutralize each other. If the pretensions of the Mormonites are well founded, those of the Irvingites must be false, and *vice versâ:* the most obvious conclusion being that they are both false. The analogy of their rival claims does not, however, end here. If the question be asked, what is the characteristic mark by which this new and restored "Church"—whether it be the one, or the other—is distinguished? the answer is in both cases the same. It is the restoration of the fourfold ministry of apostles, prophets, evangelists, pastors and teachers, and along with it the revival of the miraculous gifts of the Spirit, the possession of which is, according to their theory, limited to the fourfold ministry; both the ministry and the miraculous gifts being essential to the integrity of the Church. The Mormonite idea on this point is fully set forth in the letters addressed by Orson Spencer, the president of the " Church" in Europe, to Mr. Crowell, a Baptist

minister at Boston (No. 4. at the head of this article).   In dila-
ting upon the spiritual destitution of Christendom, he says :—

" Where, Sir, are the splendid gifts of apostles and prophets, evangelists, pastors and teachers, that Christ gave to men and set in his
Church, for ever to continue in the ministry, edifying ' the BODY of
Christ till we all come to the unity of faith,' and to such a knowledge
of God, and fulness of power and wisdom as dwelt even in Jesus?
They are no where to be found in modern Christianity! Modern
Christianity has the effrontery and shamelessness even to say that she
does not need them ; consequently she says that she does not need ' to
come to unity of faith,' and to that full and potent knowledge of God
that Jesus in the flesh possessed, and had decreed that all Saints should
possess and be like their ' elder brother.'

" Not one of these great and precious gifts are retained. The bare
name of evangelists and pastors is retained in modern Christianity,
without the shadow of the power and prophetic knowledge of the Holy
Ghost, with which these officers were *obliged* to be endued in the
primitive church. She admits, indeed, the form of the office, ' denying
the power.' She says, indeed, that she can come to ' unity of faith,' &c.,
without apostles, and without the help of the good old-fashioned Almighty
Holy Ghost.

" But how long a time does she want to run for this prize of ' unity
of faith, &c. ?' She has been running for the stakes nearly EIGHTEEN
HUNDRED YEARS, and is further from the goal than when she
started. When she started, ' false apostles and deceitful workers' were
her champions. In order to win the prize, these shed the blood of true
apostles, and the blood of saints was found in their garments. And
when her followers found that she had only the form or name of apostles
and prophets without the power, she said, we have no further need of
apostles, they have done their work, and miracles have ceased. Oh,
thou blood-guilty, ' lying,' Gentile Christianity! thy lineage takes hold
of the mother of abominations, clothed in scarlet! How great will be
the severity of God's judgments upon all that are accessory to modern
Christianity, except they repent and obey the Gospel!"—*Orson Spencer's Letters*, pp. 77, 78.

And further on :—

" The Holy Ghost is the grand agent by which the different orders of
priesthood have all their authority, wisdom, and power, to teach and
administer the laws and ordinances of heaven to men on earth. The
' MANIFOLD WISDOM OF GOD' flows through these orders of
priesthood from heaven to earth. But modern Christianity has abolished
these orders of priesthood, as no longer necessary; consequently, the
communications from heaven to earth have been stopped for nearly
eighteen hundred years ; and from *this cause* our race has witnessed
the most appalling picture of the progress of crime and wretchedness,
that has ever pervaded the earth since the dawn of creation. No man

has sufficient knowledge of figures to enumerate THE MILLIONS that have been slain in war, since the Gentiles were cut off for unbelief. The pestilence has never slumbered since man rejected the healing ordinance of God, for the aid of physicians that are of no value. Famine has locked hands with pestilence, causing *rot*, and *blast*, and *mildew* to lead many to fear that God had repented himself of the ' promised seed-time and harvest.'

" The social virtues that ought to be and ever would be, under the reign of God, like salubrious breezes of heaven, have become like the antagonistic and forked teeth of a *picking cylinder*, that, turned ever so much, will still be *picking* either in the offensive or defensive. The number of the oppressed is becoming so fearfully great and vast, that the captors know not where to find either room or keepers for their prisoners. The yoke of intolerance must have fresh iron fastenings of unheard of tenacity and rigour. The oppressor feels the danger of an awful outbreak from desperation that can be smothered no longer. The elements of revolution and self-destruction are sown deep in every government, and in every religious and social system that has not for its basis *truth immediately and continually revealed from heaven!*

" Now, all this direful state of things is because that men have ' forsaken God, the fountain of living waters, and hewn them out cisterns that can hold no water.' ' From the crown of the head to the soles of the feet,' modern Christianity, whether Protestant or Catholic, ' is full of wounds and bruises, and putrifying sores.'

" The prophets and apostles foresaw the Gentile apostasy that would spread over the earth, under the plausible name of Christianity, obliterating the knowledge of God, and ' denying the power of God, and changing his laws and ordinances,' till ' gross darkness should cover the people.' They saw the ' mystery of iniquity' working, and boldly foretold the '*falling away*'—the exaltation of the man of sin,—the removal of the priesthood and light of truth from the seven churches of Asia,—the refusal to ' teach all things that Jesus commanded,'—the irresistible fact, that men would not ' *endure sound doctrines*,' but would multiply discrepant teachers to suit ' *itching ears*,'—the introduction of ' *damnable heresies*,' and the ' *doctrines of devils*,' and the Church becoming like a blood-guilty ' *harlot*,' that had exterminated the whole order of apostles, and prophets, and spiritual gifts, and even denied the need of any such order of gifts and ministry as existed in the primitive Church."—*Orson Spencer's Letters*, pp. 79—82.

And then, in reply to the question, " If the Apostolical Church is again re-established, where is it?" he makes answer:—

" It is in the mountains where the Lord's House is to be built in the last days; driven by the cruel hand of persecution to the very place where the Lord has declared He will ' *hide* them till the indignation be overpast.' Do you also ask what kind of organization this Church has? The answer is, the same as that of the Apostolic Church in the days of Peter, consisting of Apostles, Prophets, Evangelists, &c.; with

the gifts of healing, tongues, interpretation, casting out devils, prophesyings, &c. Do you ask who has seen any of these miraculous
fruits of this Church?   I answer *a hundred thousand* living witnesses
are ready to testify that the 'signs' which Christ said 'shall follow
them that believe,' *do*, in very deed, follow believers in *this Church.*
Do you say, are they credible witnesses?   They were generally accounted credible persons, until they believed and obeyed this Gospel.
Do their lives show that they do sincerely believe and love the apostolic Gospel which they profess?   Nothing as yet, has been able to
separate them from it ; neither home nor country, nor the inheritances
of their fathers, nor penury or reproach, or evil report, or cold, or
nakedness, and no certain dwelling-place for years!"—*Orson Spencer's
Letters*, pp. 96, 97.

Now let the reader compare with this the following passages
from the " *Testimony :*"—

" God is unchangeable ; and the character of the Church can no
more be changed than the character of Him who ordained it in all its
parts.   Its character is such as He himself describes in his word ; and
no assembly, confederacy, association, or body of any kind whatsoever,
or what name soever it may take, is the Church of God as it is in his
contemplation and purpose, unless it answer the description He has
given of it.

" Now the Apostle Paul, as in many passages of his epistles casually
and unconnectedly, so most fully and distinctly, in his first epistle to
the Corinthians and in his epistle to the Ephesians, declares what is the
constitution of the Church as framed of God, what are its principal
memberships and parts, and what is the end and purpose to be accomplished in the Church by the co-operation and mutual ministrations of
those several parts, from whence we extract the following passages :—
In his first epistle to the Corinthians, the twelfth chapter, after setting
forth the diversities of gifts in divers men, in the body of Christ (the
which he illustrates under the figure of the human body, and that body
he declares 'is not one member, but many members, yet but one
body,' whereof each hath need of all others), he saith, 'Now ye are the
body of Christ, and members in particular ; and God hath set some in
the Church ; first, apostles ; secondarily, prophets ; thirdly, teachers ;
after that miracles ; then gifts of healings, helps, governments, diversities of tongues.'   And in his epistle to the Ephesians, the fourth chapter, he saith, ' There is one body, and one spirit, even as ye are called
in one hope of your calling ; one Lord, one faith, one baptism ; one
God and Father of all, who is above all, and through all, and in you
all.   But unto every one of us is given grace, according to the measure
of the gift of Christ.   Wherefore He saith, when He ascended up on
high, He led captivity captive, and gave gifts unto men.'   'And He
gave some apostles, and some prophets, and some evangelists, and some
pastors and teachers, for the perfecting of the saints, for the work of the

ministry, for the edifying of the body of Christ; till.we all come in the unity of the faith, and of the knowledge of the Son of God, unto a perfect man, unto the measure of the stature of the fulness of Christ.' . . .

"The saints must be perfected, not only by the indirect, but by the direct ministration of each of these ministries, and so the work of the ministry, internally, as well as externally, be fulfilled. It is not through the instrumentality of any one or two, but by receiving the blessing of all, that the child shall grow up into a perfect man; forasmuch as it is God's law and ordinance in his Church, that by these four means, and neither by more nor by fewer, that growth shall be obtained: for these are each and altogether necessary to the revealing of God and the showing forth of his glory; they are the gifts in the giving and receiving whereof God the Lord vouchsafes to dwell among men, and to this very end they were given. In other words, they are the ordinances whereby the essential goodness and blessings which are in God are manifested to the world, and poured into the bosom of the Church. They are ordained of God, because exactly adapted to those very ends, or rather they are the necessary and so the eternally ordained channels, whereby that Divine goodness and those blessings find their spontaneous means of manifestation and conveyance to man: and so far forth as they are withdrawn, and are not all and each existing in full exercise, his goodness is obscured and his blessings intercepted in their passage to the Church, and the Church fails to be the dwelling-place of God, the abode of his glory, and the declarer of his manifold wisdom to the principalities and powers in heavenly places. . . . . . .

"The Church is not a phantom of the imagination, nor is it merely a figure of speech to call it the ' body of Christ,' or its several parts members of that body; the Church is a reality, visible, tangible, definite,—a community of men disposed in various relations one to the other, and to Himself their head, in so true and real a union, that the human body can only imperfectly represent, nay, is but an outward type and shadow of the Church, which is the great original and archetype in the mind and purpose of God. Nor are these gifts which He received for men, and gave to men, impersonal influences nor abstractions, but they are themselves living men, by whom the fulness which is in Himself is, by the operation of the Holy Ghost, dispensed unto the Church; therefore, saith the Apostle, ' When He ascended up on high He received gifts (δόματα) for men; and He gave some *men* (τοὺς μὲν, not τά) (*men*, not *gifts*) apostles, and some *men* prophets, and some *men* evangelists, and some *men* pastors and teachers. And again, they are not given for a time which hath already expired;—the object to be attained by them hath not yet been accomplished, and by them alone can it be accomplished; for the saints are not yet perfected, the work of the ministry hath not yet found its termination; the body of Christ is not yet edified; the whole people of God have not yet arrived in unity of faith unto the perfect man, the measure of the stature of Christ's fulness; the Church hath not as yet been prepared as a spotless virgin for the marriage of the Lamb. And until these ends be accomplished, and that which be perfect is come, the instruments of God's appointment, for effecting them, cannot be dispensed with, and ought not to be suspended in their operations.   This will appear more evident from a consideration of the distinct offices of these several ministries."—*Testimony*, §§ 30, 31, 32. 35.

The necessity of the fourfold ministry to the integrity of the Church being thus declared, the absence of that fourfold ministry is advanced as an argument to prove that there has been no perfect Church upon earth since the extinction, as is alleged, of the apostolic office,—the succession of bishops not being recognized in the Irvingite theory, otherwise than as a most inferior and imperfect substitute until the time of the Church's restoration—and then in reference to the approaching advent of Christ, the question is asked, " Who shall abide the day of His coming ?" to which the reply is :—

" ' It is only an holy people who can abide before Him walking as children of light and children of the day ; it is only a people filled with the Holy Ghost, the servants of God, whom He sealeth on their foreheads before the four winds of heaven let loose the elements of destruction on the earth and on the sea.'   And that ministry of the Holy Ghost cannot be given, that sealing cannot be affixed, the Church cannot be perfected, except through those ordinances which God gave at the first for that end.   But they shall be given ; all the promises contained in his word of the restoration of his Zion, in the hour of her greatest peril, shall be fulfilled ; and that purpose shall be accomplished according to his own counsel, and by his own instrumentality, and by no man's devices.   God will appear again in the mighty presence of his Spirit ; again shall his gifts, given without repentance at the ascension of his Son, be manifested—apostles sent forth not of man, neither by man.— prophets, evangelists, and pastors and teachers, apostolically ordained, shall work the work of God in his church, and minister to the edifying of the body, and the body shall be replenished with life ; the dead bones shall be brought together, framed again in their wonted order, and shall stand up a mighty army ; and the followers of the Lamb, the undefiled, in whose mouth shall be no guile, without fault, before the throne of God, shall stand with the Lamb on mount Zion, the manifested first fruits unto God and the Lamb, the earnest of that glorious harvest, when the Son of Man shall send forth his angels, and shall gather his elect from the four winds, from one end of heaven to the other."—*Testimony*, § 101.

The promise of the revival of the fourfold ministry here made is, however, further on in the " *Testimony* " declared to be already fulfilled :—

" To have poured out the Holy Ghost on any one of the various sects would have been to vindicate that one, when all had failed ; to have poured out the Holy Ghost on all, would have been to confirm each in its separateness and self-complacency. But God's purpose hath been to raise up apostles and prophets, laying again the ancient foundations ; to rebuild thereon his spiritual temple, from thence to send his messengers, thither to invite, and there to bless all his children.

" He that dwelleth between the cherubims hath thus shone forth and stirred up his strength; and in reviving his fourfold ministry of apostles, prophets, evangelists, pastors, and teachers, He hath manifested again the eternal form of the going forth of the power of his Spirit for the revelation of Himself unto man ; and by these proceeding into every land united, summed up and directed in his apostles, shall all the saints of God be gathered, cleansed, and builded into his temple, and all his people, all his churches, all his hierarchies be seen throughout the earth to be one."—*Testimony*, §§ 118, 119.

If the question be asked,—which most obviously suggests itself, especially considering the concurrent and mutually exclusive claims preferred by the two sects to the possession of this fourfold ministry, and of the gifts of the Spirit attached to it,—what proof there is of this revival of the fourfold ministry and of primitive apostolic gifts, we find both parties advancing pretensions to miracles wrought among them. It is a singular fact, however, and one which must strike the most superficial mind, that the miracles of the Irvingites and Mormonites differ from the miracles recorded in the New Testament, in this particular, that the latter miracles were wrought openly in the sight of all men, so openly and so manifestly, that the enemies of the Gospel could not gainsay them, but were forced to admit the reality of the miraculous facts ; on the contrary, the miracles of the Irvingites and Mormonites are known only within the pale of those bodies themselves, and have not in any properly attested instance been wrought under the eyes, or for the conviction, of unbelievers. In connexion with this, it deserves to be noted, that both sects, inconsistently enough with the high claim they make to be the Church of Christ, revived in the fulness of her ministrations and spiritual powers (of which miraculous gifts are an essential part), speak in a tone of depreciation of the evidence of miracles ; as if conscious of the untenable nature of their miraculous credentials. By the Irvingites, the absence of really miraculous evidence stands almost confessed. After the flattering picture drawn of the " Church " in contrast with the whole of Christendom,* and after an enumeration of all the points of superiority by which the Irvingite sect professes to excel all other communions, the " *Testimony* " thus continues :—

* See pp. 146, 147.

" These are *signs* of Apostleship thus again put forth, and are the sure pledges that, when the Lord shall please to send forth his Apostles, to lay hands upon his people, the seal also of their Apostleship shall then be in the Lord ; signs which have been wrought in all patience, indeed, if not hitherto as by St. Paul, in signs, and wonders, and mighty deeds, as men count wonders and might. And yet with signs and wonders ; for what so bears the impress of God as that, in the midst of a perverse and gainsaying people, a witness should be raised up against all the forms of sin which are hurrying men into the ranks of Antichrist; and in things evident to the senses, also, in multiplied instances of healing the sick, and in deliverance—manifest to the eyes of men—of those oppressed by the devil in body and in spirit.

" Miracles, in the ordinary sense of the term, are not of themselves the test of truth. The evidences of the divine mission of the Lord Jesus Christ adduced by Himself, in the days of his flesh, were, first of all, his words and the fruit of them ; then his miraculous works. By the former, his disciples ' knew certainly that He came from God,' that ' He and the Father were one ;' and whilst the multitudes who saw his miracles, and many even of his disciples, fell away from Him, ' seeing, and yet not believing,' those who had tasted his words that they were precious, clave to Him still, saying, ' To whom shall we go ? Thou hast the words of eternal life.'

" In the revival of his Church now, the Lord is bringing forth this twofold evidence, but chiefly the first. By the words of truth and life He is separating the spiritual remnant from the mass of profession throughout Christendom ; and, although he has confirmed his Church by many signs and wonders in these days, yet the chief evidence of his work is *truth*—the discovery of the foundations of his word. He is dealing with nations professedly spiritual, therefore his appeal to them is according to their standing toward Him. He appeals to the spiritual in them by setting forth the truth—the things new and old from the oracles of God. If they cannot discern Him pleading for truth and opening the Scriptures, they will not discern Him in casting out devils and raising the dead. It is because ' that in the last times they receive not *the love of the truth*, therefore God sends them strong delusion that they should believe a lie.' They will not believe the truth, because they have pleasure in unrighteousness. On the other hand, the mark of Antichrist in the last times is the working of signs and wonders; by his wonders he will deceive the world, but by his lie he shall be detected by the saints. Again, the mark of the Lord's work in the last times is not only that truth in word is brought forth from the Scriptures, but that the fruits of that truth should appear in living men ; that his Church is rising from its ruins, according to the pattern given in the beginning; that the spirit of Elias, who should come, restoreth all things, turning the hearts of the fathers to the children, and the hearts of the children to their fathers, the disobedient unto ' the wisdom of the just.' And the signs pre-eminently to be looked for in His Apostles, as in the Church, are those set forth in the Epistle to the Church in Philadelphia,—a little strength, the *keeping of His word,* the not denying of his name."—*Testimony,* §§ 114—116.

The absence of miraculous gifts, properly speaking, caused, as is well known to those acquainted with the history of Irvingism in its earlier stages, much dissatisfaction among the members, and even among the officers, of the new Church, and led to more than one secession. It helped, with other circumstances, to open the eyes of one who had himself been one of the prophets, and whose testimony, publicly borne, that the whole work was false, and, so far as it was supernatural, of the devil, we adduced on a former occasion[*]. Among those who doubted the work, was even Edward Irving himself, who died in a state of gloom and perplexity, and uttered many words of exhortation and warning on the subject to those in attendance on his death-bed. This fact stands recorded in certain manuscript letters, giving an account of the close of Irving's life, which were privately circulated at the time, and which we ourselves have seen and perused, but under a special reservation that no copy should be made of them. This very awkward fact is got rid of, in the "*Narrative of Events,*" by the following cunningly constructed statement :—

"Mr. Irving, from whom the whole of the congregations obtained, with a show of justice, their name of distinction, having been called, not only to be Angel of the Church in London, but also to be an Evangelist and Prophet to his own land, was constrained by ill health to leave his place ; and after visiting several parts of England and preaching, according to his powers, proceeded to Scotland, in consequence of words of prophecy spoken to him, to counsel his brethren the clergy of Scotland who should seek to him for counsel. In the fulfilment of this duty he died, expressing to one called to be an Apostle, who was with him *six weeks before* and *at* his death, his perfect conviction of the truth of all that work in which he had taken part. And thus, having done his work, he fell asleep in Jesus, and waits his reward in the day when his own faithful testimony shall be fulfilled, of the doom of *Babylon,* and of the speedy coming of the Lord."—*Narrative of Events,* p. 36.

Literally, this statement is not inconsistent with truth. The person called to be an apostle, may have been with Irving both *six weeks before,* and *at* his death, and may have heard from him, *six weeks before,* "his perfect conviction of the truth" of the work ; but that he heard a similar declaration from him *at* his death, we very much doubt ; as, in that case, the unhappy man must, upon his death-bed, have held two opposite kinds of language on

[*] See English Review, vol. ix. pp. 25—40.

the subject. This, except under an impaired state of his faculties, no one, who knew Irving's character, would impute to him; nor is it necessary to have recourse to such a supposition. The statement which we have quoted does not really affirm that he expressed his conviction of the truth of the work *at his death*, but only that the person to whom he is said to have expressed that conviction, was with him *at* his death, as well as *six weeks before* his death; leaving it open to the construction, that what is said of his testimony to the truth of the work refers to the last-named period, while the uninformed would naturally enough refer it to both periods, and conclude that Irving died, *which he did not*, unshaken in his belief in the work which goes by his name.

That doubts should arise was, indeed, most natural. The very promise of the restoration of the Apostolic office, given "by utterance" in London, was contradicted, on its being communicated to "the brethren" in Scotland, by the prophets there, likewise speaking "by utterance." The "utterance" in London, which continued to assert the approaching restoration, raised large expectations of a full display of Apostolic powers which never came. The evidence on which the beginning of the work rested was of the most questionable kind; the Apostles being "called" by the Prophets, and the Prophets "ordained" *ex post facto* by the Apostles. Even this was not achieved without considerable difficulty. A most important circumstance, which in the "*Narrative*" is altogether suppressed, is the fact, which we have good authority for stating, that the first two individuals nominated to the Apostleship,—Mr. Baxter, the "prophet" and author of the disclosures before referred to, and a Mr. D**** D**,— declined the call, and pronounced the whole work to be a delusion and a snare of the devil. But there were others less diffident and less scrupulous. Mr. Drummond, another of the prophets, proceeded to call Mr. John Cardale, who accepted the office, and who for the support which he thereby gave to the tottering cause of Irvingism, was rewarded with the expressive title "Pillar of the Apostles." Nor was Mr. Drummond left without his reward for the decision with which he acted at so critical a moment; for the next call, proceeding from Mr. Bayford, another of the prophets, raised Mr. Drummond himself to the apostolic office[*]. The cue having been once given, the

---

[*] We owe an apology to Mr. Henry Drummond for having represented him,—erroneously as we have since ascertained,—as holding the place of "Senior Apostle." The Honourable Member for West Surrey is only second in rank. He yields precedence to Mr. John Cardale, whose claim to the Universal Apostolate has been asserted in opposition to the recent Bull of his rival Pio Nino, in the following

calling of Apostles proceeded rather more rapidly than was quite agreeable to the chiefs of the movement. The prophets in the

document, which we borrow from the columns of the "*John Bull*," leaving to the Editor of that journal the responsibility of its authenticity :—

"JOHN I., PILLAR OF THE APOSTLES.

"*In Perpetuam Rei Memoriam.*

" The power of restoring the Universal Church, put forth in these last days in the persons of the Twelve Apostles chosen for that purpose, and endowed with miraculous gifts, of whom I, John, am Senior and the Pillar of them all, has from the beginning filled Our heart with a glorious solicitude for the re-establishment of the Fourfold Ministry, and the increase of its helps and governments, as in all parts of the world, so especially in that famous city in which a spurious Apostolate, which is not an Apostolate, has for ages been set up under colour of a pretended succession from St. Peter the Prince of the Apostles. The fruit of this Our solicitude has been already reaped, not only by other nations and kingdoms, but especially also by the Pontifical States, among whose inhabitants light has begun to take the place of darkness from the time that Evangelists sent forth by Us have visited the benighted countries of Christendom. Among other measures taken by Us with a view to give to the Pontifical States the full benefit of this new revelation and regeneration of the Church, is the 'Testimony' which was addressed by Us in the year 1836 to the then Pope Gregory XVI. to whom We gave due warning of the invalidity of his claim to be the Head of Christendom, bidding him at the same time to submit himself in all due humility to the true Apostolate newly manifested in Us ; which We doubt not he did in his heart, albeit he was withheld by the spirit of pride and disobedience from giving unto Us any open and direct token of his submission. And further, when, in the same year, 1836, We divided the Tribes of Christendom between the Apostles, the Princes of the Tribes of Israel, We committed unto one of Our Brethren and Fellow Apostles the care of that part of the world called Italy, including the city of Rome and the Pontifical States.

" And now, having further considered the aspect of religious affairs in those States, in consequence of the evident decay of that spurious system of religion which has been long upheld there under an imperfectly constituted Ministry, and the downfall of the power of the Pope, whose throne is maintained by no spiritual authority appertaining unto him, but simply by the bayonets of the infidel democracy of France, We have thought that the time was come when the true Apostolate and the fourfold Ministry might be formally established in the Pontifical States, in the same manner as has already been done in other countries where the preaching of Our Evangelists has prepared the way for the restoration of the Church in the full efficiency of Apostolic power. For which purpose We did call together Our brethren of the Apostolic College, as likewise the Angels of the Churches in this Our Metropolis, and, after due deliberation had, their decision being in perfect accordance with Our own desire, We have concluded to carry the same into effect.

" Wherefore, after having accurately weighed the whole matter, of Our own motion and certain knowledge, and in the fulness of Our Apostolic power, We order and decree, that in the Pontifical States shall be re-established, according to the primitive order of the Church, the Hierarchy of Apostles and Angels, of Prophets, Pastors, Teachers, and Evangelists ; and that the following shall be the Angels of the Churches with the jurisdictions annexed thereto, which by these Our Letters We constitute in the several provinces of the Pontifical States.

" The Throne of the Apostle of Italy, and Pillar of the Angels in that part of the world, shall take its name from the Basilic of St. Peter, the Prince of the Apostles ; and he shall bear rule over all that part of the city of Rome called Trastevere, together with the Delegation of Viterbo and Civita Vecchia, or the Patrimony of St. Peter.

different churches exercised their newly acquired patronage so freely, that it became necessary to revoke their acts. Several persons, called to be " Apostles," were shorn of their new dignity, by a declaration that they had not been called " according to the mind of the Lord ;" and none were suffered to retain the Apostolic office but Mr. Cardale and Mr. Drummond, whose position in the sect was such that no man might call in question " the mind of the Lord " concerning them. Spiritual discipline was even brought to bear upon the prophets for their " excesses." as appears from the following statement contained in a narrative published as far back as the year 1838, by one of the seceders from the sect [1] :—

" And he shall have under him in the Pontifical States twelve Angels with their Thrones, to wit :—

" The Angel of St. John of Lateran, over the Southern part of the city of Rome, East of the Tiber, with the Delegation of Frosinone and Ponte-corvo and the Delegation of Benevento.

" The Angel of Sta. Maria Maggiore, over the Northern part of the city of Rome, East of the Tiber, with the Comarca of Rome.

" The Angel of Rieti, over the Delegation of Spoleto and Rieti.

" The Angel of Assisi, over the Delegation of Perugia.

" The Angel of Ascoli, over the Delegation of Fermo and Ascoli.

" The Angel of Loreto, over the Delegation of Macerata and Camerino.

" The Angel of Osimo, over the Delegation of Ancona.

" The Angel of Sinigaglia, over the Delegation of Urbino and Pesaro.

" The Angel of Forlimpopoli, over the Legation of Forli.

" The Angel of Faenza, over the Legation of Ravenna.

" The Angel of Lugo, over the Legation of Ferrara.

" The Angel of Medicina, over the Legation of Bologna.

" Provided always, that We reserve to Ourselves full power to appoint as many more Angels as We shall from time to time see fit, and to settle their Thrones and jurisdictions in such wise as may appear to Us most expedient ; Our meaning and intention being that nothing contained in this Our present Bull shall in any way abridge, or derogate from, the fulness of Our Apostolic power to deal with the nations and kingdoms of the earth according to Our own will and pleasure. And further We do hereby abrogate and annul, in the plenitude of Our Apostolic authority, all such Archbishoprics, Bishoprics, and ecclesiastical jurisdictions, as well as all constitutions, privileges, customs, of whatever kind, which may at any time, however remote, and even from time immemorial, have obtained in the Pontifical States; and We hereby authorize the Angels of the Churches whom We have appointed by these presents, to order all things as to them in their wisdom may appear meet, in accordance with the constitution of the Restored Apostolic Church. And We command all the Churches of the Saints in the Pontifical States to give unto the said Angels by Us appointed, the tithe of all that they possess. And if any should, upon the plea of any pretended authority or jurisdiction formerly exercised in those parts, presume to interfere with the execution of this Our Apostolic Decree, or in any wise to let or obstruct the Angels of the Churches in the exercise of their office, We hereby declare null and void any thing which might be attempted, in regard to these matters, contrary to these presents, knowingly or ignorantly, by any authority whatsoever.

" Given at Our Metropolitan Church, in Newman-street, London, on the Feast of St. Crispin, in the eighteenth year of Our Apostolate."

[1] Narrative of Henry John Marks, formerly a Jew. With an introduction. By the Rev. Charles B. Tayler. Hatchard and Son, 1838.

" The acknowledged prophet amongst us was suspended from the prophetical office for the space of many months, and was not allowed to partake of the Lord's Supper, because he called one of the elders to the Apostleship ; and another was put down because he had called the other prophet to the Apostleship."

In order to avoid the inconvenience of such promiscuous calls to the Apostleship, it was authoritatively announced that the remaining ten should be called by the mouth of one individual, dignified with the title " Pillar of the Prophets." This " Pillar " appears, his title notwithstanding, to have been one of the most insecure supports of the whole edifice, having been over and over again found a false prophet. As an instance of this, we have been informed that upon one occasion he mistook an American swindler for " a mighty Angel," who was to do " a great work for the Lord " in that country. When Mr. Irving proceeded to Scotland on his last visit to that country, the same " Pillar of the Prophets " declared that he was going forth as " a mighty prophet " to do " a great work for the Lord " in his native land ; the result being, that Mr. Irving died there, dispirited and brokenhearted. By the same authority sixty " Evangelists " were called and sent to preach in the streets of London, whose mission was subsequently revoked, and the whole pronounced to have been a work of Satan. The flock were warned at one time not to receive any " word " from his mouth, because " the streams were polluted." One of the prophetesses in the Church in Newman-street, on one occasion, openly denounced him as one who " never had the love of God, and never knew it."

While the authority of the prophets was thus seriously shaken in the person of their " Pillar," that of the Apostles rested on no better or more secure foundation. The constant doctrine, promulgated by authority, at the outset, and for a long time after, was, that the calling of a prophet was not of itself sufficient to constitute a man a minister, but that the laying on of the hands of the Apostles was required, who, it was promised, should be endued with " the power of the Holy Ghost in mighty signs and wonders." These " mighty signs and wonders," however, never came, and the Church was compelled to content itself, by way of evidence of its divine origin and constitution, with the bare assertion of the originators and leaders themselves, that they were inspired of the Holy Ghost. We are told, it is true, that " the first and second called Apostles, by whom the Apostolic Ministry in conferring ordination was first exercised, always waited to be moved by a sensibly supernatural power of the Holy Ghost, in laying on hands, or performing any other ministerial acts ;" but immediately after we have the following curious statement :—

"The supernatural power by which the two senior Apostles were moved at the first in fulfilling Apostolic acts, was one of the many instances in which the Lord graciously *condescended, for a season*, to the weakness and ignorance of those whom He had taken as his instruments."—*Narrative of Events*, p. 34.

So manifest was the disappointment of the promise of the plenitude of miraculous apostolic powers, that, as we learn from the "*Narrative of Events*," one of the "Apostles" themselves had misgivings and doubts as to their right and competency to assume apostolic authority, until they were visited with Pentecostal effusions ; and at one time there appears to have been a complete mutiny in the camp.   The manner in which this was got over is related in the "*Narrative*," and affords the most striking, though indirect, evidence of the unreality of the whole work, which rests, by the showing of the Apostles themselves, not upon any power which they were enabled to put forth, and thereby to silence the gainsayers, but upon the acquiescence of the subordinate ministers in the position assumed by the Apostles, that acquiescence being enforced by a proceeding the most unapostolic that can well be conceived, the threat of a wholesale resignation ; —much after the manner in which Lord John Russell every now and then coerces the House of Commons.   This page in the history of the sect is too curious not to be transcribed :—

"While the Apostles were most of them out of England on their duties, the senior Apostle, who had charge of the churches in England, and to whom the discretion was given to summon again the Apostles to England, in case of any thing occurring which required the united acting of the whole Apostolic college, felt himself compelled, about the end of the year 1839, to request the Apostles to return.   The necessity for this arose from the mistaken notion of some among the angels of the Churches and ministers attached to the Apostles, as to the true meaning of the opening of the first chapter of Ezekiel, and as to the standing of the Apostles towards, and in connexion with, the other three classes of ministers ; the results of which misunderstanding would be a virtual denial of the authority of the Apostles to rule the Church, and its consequences, the undermining of all order and discipline. . . . .

"The Apostles returned, according to the summons, about Midsummer, 1840, being recalled from the utmost parts of Europe and from America, having had their preparatory work towards Christendom thus interrupted.   On their return, after hearing the report of those things which had taken place, they requested all the angels and the

---

² It was on this occasion that one of the Apostles, a Mr. M * * * * * * * *, seceded, on the ground that he could not reconcile to his conscience the exercise of Apostolic power, without any satisfactory evidence of his mission, and without any of the "signs of an Apostle," to support so high-sounding a claim.

ministers of the universal Church to state any matters which they wished to state, to bring up any burdens they had to bring up, and in the fullest and freest manner to lay out their views on the subject of the Apostles' place and standing, of their own relative position towards the Apostles and the Churches. These communications having been received, the Apostles considered them, and after mature deliberation, and with a view to setting at rest for the future all doubt and uncertainty regarding their true position, they proceeded to draw up a declaratory statement of the duties of the Apostleship in its bearing upon the other ministries and the churches. And in submitting this document to the ministers associated with them, and to the angels, they intimated that they were willing either to be set aside, or to continue guiding the churches as the Lord gave them ability; but that on no other terms, on no other principles than those laid down in this document, could they undertake the care and responsibility of the care and guidance of the Churches. During this period of trial, while men's minds were troubled, and discord gave such opportunity to the devil to work his own work and sow seeds of evil, the Apostles felt it necessary to discontinue the monthly meetings of the Council in London, which had been continued until this time, even though all the Apostles, save the senior Apostle, were absent. And it was also found necessary for the present to dispense with the services of the ministers attached to the Apostles, especially those through whom all communications between them and the Churches were made; and further to intimate, that until all erroneous notions in the minds of any of these ministers regarding the discernment and true meaning of the words which had been spoken through the Prophets should be removed, the Apostles could not repose full confidence in them, and that they should for the present refrain from making use of any words of prophecy which might be spoken. The adoption of these measures by the Apostles resulted from the conviction that in such a serious state of things they must act independently, and, by a firm adherence to those principles and doctrines of truth of which they were the only depositaries and declarers, must either save the Church and bring back those who had been led astray, or be themselves the sacrifice for the sake of that which they knew to be the truth. God gave grace to the ministers generally, to see and acknowledge the truth of these principles so laid down by the Apostles, and the ministers and angels of the Churches were gradually instructed more perfectly in the true bearing and duties of the apostolic office; and at length (not without much difficulty) were they fully delivered from the error which had prevailed among them, and which had well-nigh caused the breaking up of the work which had, with so much labour and pains, been thus far carried on. Words of prophecy were spoken, showing the analogy between Aaron's sin in making a calf when Moses was away, and the sin of setting up a subordinate ministry in the place of the Apostleship[3]."
—*Narrative of Events*, pp. 80—82.

---

[3] The reader should compare with this the statement from " Baxter's Narrative "

By way of accounting for the difficulty, the following " note " is appended :—

" By much experience, by light of prophecy, and by the instruction contained in the epistle to the Corinthians, the Apostles had learned, that in the prophetic ministry, as in all other forms of ministry, the purity of the word spoken depended upon the inward cleanness of the individual, and that those whom the Lord was using ought to put away all filthiness of flesh and spirit. And they were also shown, that when a prophet or other minister was in an unclean state, no use could be made of his word or ministry ; for, where the inside of the vessel is unclean, whatsoever is put into it is polluted. And ' who can cleanse dirty water ?' "—*Narrative of Events,* p. 81.

The manifest deficiency of evidence to support the claim of the Irvingite sect to a revival of " Apostolic powers" for the introduction of a new dispensation preparatory to the second Advent of Christ, has not escaped the rival " Apostles" of the Mormonites, one of whom, in urging "the presumptive evidences of Joseph Smith's divine mission," thus alludes to the point :—

" Did Irving's apostles—or did any other impostors during the long age of darkness—profess that the apostleship was conferred upon them by those who held it last—by any angel who held the office himself? No ; and therefore they are not apostles, but deceivers. If Mr. Smith had pretended that he received the apostleship by the revelation of the Holy Ghost, without an ordination under the hands of an apostle, we should at once know that his pretensions were vain, and that he was a deceiver. If an impostor, how came Mr. Smith to discover this? Why did he not, like the Irvingites, assume the apostleship without an apostle to ordain him ? How came he to possess so much more wisdom than Irving, as to discover that he could not be an apostle without being ordained under the hands of an apostle ? If Mr. Smith be a false apostle, it must be confessed that he has exhibited far more judgment than all the false apostles who have preceded him, learned and talented as they were."—*Orson Pratt's Divine Authority,* p. 5.

Leaving the " Apostles" of the Irvingite sect to establish their claim to the apostleship in the best way they can, to the satisfaction of their Mormonite brethren, we now turn to the examination of the evidence by which the latter support their apostleship. As far as the evidence boasted of in the above passage is concerned, we are at a loss to discover its superiority,—except in point of impudence,—over that adduced by the Irvingites, seeing that on examination it reduces itself to a simple asseveration on the part of the " Apostle" and " Prophet," Joseph Smith himself,

(pp. 85, 85), quoted in our former article on this subject, " English Review," vol. ix. p. 40.

whose testimony to his own commission and ordination is thus recounted by one of his " Apostles :"—

" In what manner does Joseph Smith declare that a dispensation of the gospel was committed unto him ? He testifies that an angel of God, whose name was Moroni, appeared unto him ; that this angel was formerly an ancient prophet among a remnant of the tribe of Joseph on the continent of America. He testifies that Moroni revealed unto him where he deposited the sacred records of his nation some fourteen hundred years ago ; that these records contained the " everlasting gospel" as it was anciently taught and recorded by this branch of Israel. He gave Mr. Smith power to reveal the contents of those records to the nations of the earth. Now how does this testimony of Joseph Smith agree with the book of John's prophecy given on the Isle of Patmos ? John testifies that, when the dispensation of the gospel is again committed to the nations, it shall be through the medium of an *angel* from heaven. J. Smith testifies that a dispensation of the gospel for all nations has been committed to him by an *angel.* The one uttered the prediction ; the other testifies its fulfilment." . . . .

"A revelation and restoration to the earth of the '*everlasting gospel*' through the angel Moroni would be of no benefit to the nations, unless some one should be ordained with authority to preach it and administer its ordinances. Moroni might reveal a book containing a beautiful and glorious system of salvation, but no one could obey even its first principles without a legally authorized administrator, ordained to preach, baptize, lay on hands for the gift of the Holy Ghost, &c. Did Moroni ordain Mr. Smith to the apostleship, and command him to administer ordinances ? No, he did not. But why not confer authority by ordination, as well as reveal the everlasting gospel ? Because in all probability he had not the right so to do. All angels have not the same authority—they do not all hold the same keys. Moroni was a prophet, but we have no account of his holding the office of an apostle ; and, if not, he had no right to ordain Mr. Smith to an office which he himself never possessed. He no doubt went as far as he was authorized, and that was to reveal the '*stick of Ephraim*'—the record of his fathers, containing the '*everlasting gospel.*' How then did Mr. Smith obtain the office of an apostle, if Moroni had no authority to ordain him to such office ? Mr. Smith testifies that Peter, James, and John came to him in the capacity of ministering angels, and by the laying on of hands ordained him an apostle, and commanded him to preach, baptize, lay on hands for the gift of the Holy Ghost, and administer all other ordinances of the gospel as they themselves did in ancient days."—*Orson Pratt's Divine Authority*, pp. 4, 5.

Here we have it plainly enough stated, by what evidence the " Apostolic powers" of the Mormon " Church" are attested ; and, provided we can put perfect faith in the word of Joseph Smith, there can be no mistake about the matter. There is, it is true,

according to " Apostle" Pratt's statement, the additional evidence
of numerous miracles, wrought both by Joseph Smith himself
and by his successors in the apostolic office :—

" The miracles wrought by Joseph Smith are evidences of no small
moment to establish his divine authority.   In the name of the Lord he
cast out devils, healed the sick, spoke with new tongues, interpreted
ancient languages, and predicted future events.   Many of these miracles were wrought before numerous multitudes of both believers and
unbelievers, and upon persons not connected with our church.   And,
again, the numerous miracles wrought through the instrumentality of
thousands of the officers and members of this church are additional
evidences that the man who was instrumental in founding the church
must have been sent of God.   The thousands of sick that have been
miraculously healed in all parts of the world where this gospel is
preached give forth a strong and almost irresistible testimony that Mr.
Smith's authority is '*from heaven.*' "—*Orson Pratt's Divine Authority,*
p. 14.

Unfortunately, however, for the conclusiveness of this evidence, there happens to be no record or attestation of these miracles extant beyond the allegations of the Mormonites themselves;
and even these consist merely of vague and general statements
like the present, carefully avoiding all mention of *names, dates,*
and *places,* on which issue might be joined.   Not that miracle-
mongery is not, when opportunity serves, practised by the sect,
and that to a very daring extent, if there is any truth in the
following story related by Joseph Smith's *quondam* coadjutor,
General Bennett, who gives as his authority the name of an
American minister, the Rev. M. Turner :—

" Towards the close of a fine summer's day, a farmer in one of the
States found a respectable-looking man at his gate, who requested
permission to pass the night under his roof.   The hospitable farmer
readily complied ; the stranger was invited into the house, and a warm
and substantial supper set before him.

" After he had eaten, the farmer, who appeared to be a jovial, contented, humorous, and, withal, shrewd old man, passed several hours
in pleasant conversation with his guest, who seemed to be very ill at
ease, both in body and mind ; yet, as if desirous of pleasing his enter-
tainer, replied continuously and agreeably to whatever was said to him.
Finally, he pleaded fatigue and illness, as an excuse for retiring to rest,
and was conducted by the farmer to an upper chamber, where he went
to bed.

" About the middle of the night, the farmer and his family were
aroused by the most dreadful groans, which they soon ascertained proceeded from the chamber of the traveller.   On going to investigate the
matter, they found that the stranger was dreadfully ill, suffering the
most acute pain, and uttering the most doleful cries, apparently without

any consciousness of what was passing around him. Every thing that kindness and experience could suggest was done to relieve the sick man ; but all efforts were in vain, and, to the consternation of the farmer and his family, their guest expired in the course of a few hours.

" In the midst of their trouble and anxiety, at an early hour in the evening, two travellers came to the gate, and requested entertainment. The farmer told them that he would willingly offer them hospitality, but that just now his household was in the greatest confusion, on account of the death of the stranger, the particulars of which he proceeded to relate to them. They appeared to be much surprised and grieved at the poor man's calamity, and politely requested permission to see the corpse. This, of course, the farmer readily granted, and conducted them to the chamber in which lay the dead body. They looked at it for a few minutes in silence, and then the oldest of the pair gravely told the farmer, that they were Elders of the Church of Jesus Christ of Latter-Day Saints, and were empowered by God to perform miracles, even to the extent of raising the dead ; and that they felt quite assured they could bring to life the dead man before them.

" The farmer was, of course, pretty considerably astonished by the quality and powers of the persons who addressed him, and rather incredulously asked, if they were quite sure that they could perform all they professed to do.

" ' Oh, certainly ! not a doubt of it. The Lord has commissioned us expressly to work miracles, in order to prove the truth of the Prophet Joseph Smith, and the inspiration of the books and doctrines revealed to him. Send for all your neighbours, that in the presence of a multitude we may bring the dead man to life, and that the Lord in his Church may be glorified to all men.'

" The farmer, after a little consideration, agreed to let the miracle-workers proceed, and, as they desired, sent his children to his neighbours, who, attracted by the expectation of a miracle, flocked to the house in considerable numbers.

" The Mormon elders commenced their task by kneeling and praying before the body with uplifted hands and eyes, and with most stentorian lungs. Before they had proceeded far into their prayer, a sudden idea struck the farmer, who quietly quitted the house for a few minutes, and then returned and waited patiently by the bed-side until the prayer was finished, and the elders ready to perform the miracle. Before they began, he respectfully said to them, that, with their permission, he wished to ask them a few questions upon the subject of their miracle. They replied that they had no objection. The farmer then asked, ' You are quite certain that you can bring this man to life again ?' ' We are.' ' How do you know that you can ?' ' We have just received a revelation from the Lord, informing us that we can.' ' Are you quite sure that the revelation was from the Lord ?' ' Yes : we cannot be mistaken about it.' ' Does your power to raise this man to life again depend upon the particular nature of his disease, or could you now bring any dead man to life ?' ' It makes no difference to us ;

we could bring any corpse to life.'   'Well, if this man had been killed,
and one of his arms cut off, could you bring him to life, and also restore
to him his arm ?'   'Certainly, there is no limit to the power given
us by the Lord.   It would make no difference, even if both his arms
and his legs were cut off.'   'Could you restore him, if his head had
been cut off ?'   'Certainly we could.'   'Well,' said the farmer, with a
quiet smile upon his features, ' I do not doubt the truth of what such
holy men assert ; but I am desirous that my neighbours here should
be fully converted by having the miracle performed in the completest
manner possible.   So, by your leave, if it makes no difference whatever, I will proceed to cut off the head of this corpse.'   Accordingly, he
produced a large and well-sharpened broad axe from beneath his coat,
which he swung above his head, and was apparently about to bring it
down upon the neck of the corpse, when, lo, and behold! to the
amazement of all present, the dead man started up in great agitation,
and swore he would not have his head cut off for any consideration
whatever !

"The company immediately seized the Mormons, and soon made
them confess that the pretended dead man was also a Mormon elder,
and that they had sent him to the farmer's house, with directions to
die there at a particular hour, when they would drop in, as if by accident, and perform a miracle that would astonish every body.   The
farmer, after giving the impostors a severe chastisement, let them
depart to practise their humbuggery in some other quarter."

Attempts at imposture of so daring a character are not, we
apprehend, of frequent occurrence ; but that tricks are resorted
to for the purpose of deceiving the ignorant, both in the " Far
West," and, we fear, in the darker districts of our own country,
is far from improbable ; and it would be little short of a miracle,
if they were not occasionally successful.   Generally speaking,
however, the emissaries of Mormonism are remarkably cautious
in feeling their ground, before they assert their possession of
miraculous powers ; and, on a recent occasion, when they were
encountered by a clergyman of the English Church, the author
of the " *Friendly Warnings* " (No. 8, at the head of this article),
they actually disclaimed the possession of any such power.   Being
asked, " Can you work miracles in proof of your commission from
God ! " they replied, " *We cannot work miracles* to prove that
we are commissioned by the Holy Ghost."

As we have in a former article on this subject [4] furnished our
readers with ample materials for testing the claim of Joseph
Smith and his followers to miraculous attestations of the divine
origin of their sect, we shall not dwell on this point any further,
but proceed to notice, as another point of coincidence between

[4] English Review, vol. xlii. pp. 399.

the delusion of the Irvingites and that of the Mormonites, the remarkable fact that the latter no less than the former, shrink from resting their claim to men's faith in their work on the evidence of miracles, and point to their doctrine as furnishing more conclusive proofs of the truth of their work. The very same " Apostle" who vaunts the miracles of Joseph Smith, and of " thousands of the officers and members of the Church," as proofs of their divine mission, takes exception to the conclusiveness of miraculous evidence :—

" Although the great majority of mankind consider miracles to be an *infallible* evidence in favour of the divine authority of the one who performs them, yet we do most distinctly dissent from this idea. If miracles be admitted as an *infallible* evidence, then all that have ever wrought miracles must have been sent of God. The magicians of Egypt wrought some splendid miracles before that nation; they created serpents and frogs, and turned rivers of water into blood. If miraculous evidence is *infallible*, the Egyptians were bound to receive the contradictory messages of both Moses and the magicians as of divine authority. According to this idea, the witch of Endor must have established her divine mission beyond all controversy by calling forth a dead man from the grave in the presence of Saul, king of Israel. A certain wicked power described by John (Rev. xiii. chap.) was to do ' great *wonders*' and '*miracles*,' and cause '*fire to come down from heaven on the earth in the sight of men.*' If miracles are infallible evidences, surely no one should reject the divine authority of John's beast. Again (in Rev. xvi. chap.) John ' *saw three unclean spirits like frogs*,' which he expressly says, ' *are the* SPIRITS OF DEVILS WORKING MIRACLES, which go forth unto the kings of the earth, and of the whole world to gather them to the battle of the great day of God Almighty.*' The learned divines and clergy of the nineteenth century boldly declare that ' *miracles are an* INFALLIBLE *evidence of the divine mission of the one who performs them.*' If so, who can blame ' *the kings of the earth,*' and these learned divines, and all their followers for embracing the message of these divinely inspired devils ? For, according to their arguments, they should in no wise reject them, for they prove their mission by evidences which they say are infallible. We shall expect, in a few years, to see an innumerable host of sectarian ministers, as well as kings, taking up their line of march for the great valley of ' Armageddon,' near Jerusalem, and thus prove by their works that they do really believe in the *infallibility of miraculous evidence.* Devils can work miracles as well as God, and as they have already persuaded the religious world that miracles are infallible evidences of divine authority, they will not have much difficulty among the followers of modern christianity in establishing the divinity of their mission. But the ' Latter-Day Saints' do not believe in the infallibility of miraculous evidence. We believe the miraculous gifts are absolutely necessary in the church of Christ, without which it cannot exist on the earth. Miracles, when taken in connexion with *a pure, holy, and perfect doctrine, reasonable and scriptural,* is a very strong collateral evidence in favour of that doctrine, and of the divine authority of those who preach it. But abstract miracles alone, unconnected with other evidences, instead of being *infallible* proofs are no proofs at all ; they are as likely to be *false* as true."—*Orson Pratt's Divine Authority,* pp. 14, 15.

The test here proposed, viz. the character of the doctrine, whether it be " pure, holy, perfect, reasonable, and scriptural," is undoubtedly one which cannot fail to commend itself to every Christian mind. Whether that test applied to the writings of " Apostle" Pratt himself, and of his brother " Apostles " and " Evangelists," tells in favour of the Mormonite doctrine, is another question ; one which a very few extracts from their writings will set at rest. We need not, for this purpose, enter into recondite questions of theology ; the language,—almost too horrible to transcribe,—which is held respecting the three persons of the Ever-blessed Trinity, is conclusive as to the character of the Mormonite doctrine. We shall begin by quoting part of one of Orson Spencer's letters, entitled " The true and living God :"—

" A very general conviction concerning the character of God now is, that He is a Being without body, or parts, or passions. A greater absurdity cannot be furnished in all the annals of heathenism. Even images of wood, and brass, and stone are scarcely more remote from the picture of the true God, than the theory of a passionless, matterless God—an inconceivable sort of chaotic being, that is without form, or void, (*sic !*) or dwelling-place ! a being whose circumference is every where, and his centre no where !

" Another theory concerning God, that is entertained by Jewish Rabbies, though of an opposite character, is not much more extravagant than the common orthodox theory, viz., the Rabbies suppose that God is a Being of some '*millions of miles in length.*'

" Again, the popular notion of modern Jews, as expressed in a recent number of the *Jewish Chronicle,* is, that the Almighty God is a Being of such infinite *dimension,* that He cannot *condense* Himself sufficiently to speak to men, or be tangible or visible by mortals. Accordingly, when He gives revelation to men, He creates a fictitious or imaginary messenger, through whom He communicates his will, and this messenger has no real existence in the eye of God, and *only* in the momentary perception of the person addressed.

" From the foregoing it may be seen how grossly ignorant both Jews and Christians are of the person of God, the Creator and Saviour of the world ! All this, too, in an age of the world boasting of blazing light ! of a millennial dawn ! of the unparalleled march of improvement ! but, alas ! the very God and Father of us all, who ought to be *truly* known in order to be rightly worshipped, is regarded as the most insensible (a God without '*passion*' must be insensible), and irrational, and unattractive as to form, of all beings that can be conceived of; and the most surprising feature in all modern theology in an age of sanity is, that this notion concerning the person of God, is deducible from the scriptures of the Old and New Testament.

" The New Testament tells us most unequivocally what kind of person God has, and whether He is a Being having both passion and physical form. It tells us whether He can be so '*condensed*' as to speak to men, and be seen of them, and talk to them face to face, as a man talks to his fellow man. The New Testament declares that in Jesus Christ dwelt the ' FULNESS OF THE GODHEAD BODILY.'

'' Now, if the Godhead dwelt in the body of Christ, then it is certain that God is not without a *body*. But He has a body; and what is his body like unto? The New Testament tells us what his body is like. It is so nearly and exactly like unto the body of Christ, that there is no difference. Paul says, that Christ was the '*express image of his person*.' It is then beyond all dispute that the body and person of Jesus Christ and the Father are alike. Language cannot express the similitude of the Father and the Son in plainer or stronger terms. Then, if we can show from the New Testament what kind of body or person Jesus Christ had, we can also tell what kind of body the Father has, because they are alike. ·One is the express image of the other. If one has a fleshy material body, the other has the same. If one resembles in stature the seed of the woman, the other also wears the same resemblance. If one can be so ' *condensed* ' as to speak and walk, and feel and act like a man, the other can do the same. If one wearing a body of flesh and bones, in all points like unto his brethren, is capable of holding all power in heaven and earth, and also of displaying the brightness of celestial glory, the other can do the same in a similar body of flesh and bones.

" Well, now, what kind of body or person had Jesus Christ, which looked so much like the Father's person ? Was it an airy, invisible, evanescent, mystical *nothing*, which some would denominate spirit ? No, by no means ; very much otherwise. Hearken now, my dear Sir, and all ye readers, that have an honest desire to *know* the living and true God, and Jesus Christ whom He hath sent, in order that men might know from the person of the Son what is the personal appearance of the Father. He, ' *the Word, was made flesh and dwelt among us (and we beheld his glory, the glory as of the only begotten of the Father) full of grace and truth*.' Jesus had a fleshly form like the seed of Abraham, and being begotten of the Father He partook of his likeness. Men beheld his glory in human form, and Paul says that his glory was the glory of the Father.

" It appears from the conduct of some of his disciples, that they, like sectarian churches now, were tinctured with the idea that Christ, after his death and resurrection, was purely and exclusively a *Spirit ;* but He tells them to handle Him and see that ' *a Spirit has not flesh and bones as ye see me have*.' And He eat and drank with them as aforetime with his resurrected body, and afterwards ascended up from their midst with the same bloodless body into heaven; and in like manner will He come again.

"Thus, Sir, the notion of a God that is exclusively *Spirit* without bodily form, was banished from the minds of the disciples that saw the bodily image of the Father in the person of the Son after his resurrection. From heaven He will come again in like manner, and every eye shall see Him, and they that have pierced Him. But the popular God of modern times, that has no body or parts, cannot be seen. But, Sir, this popular God that has sprung into fashion, since the age of revelation, has no resemblance to Jesus Christ, who has both body and parts, and is the exact image of his Father. Jesus Christ declared that He could exercise all power in heaven and earth while He was in the body. His Father could do the same, because they were alike. It required no extraordinary *condensation* of the infinity of Jesus in order to reveal Himself to men, or in order that men should behold his glory."—*Orson Spencer's Letters*, pp. 99—103.

The same writer, in another letter, entitled "The Gift of the Holy Ghost," thus speaks of the descent of the Spirit on the Day of Pentecost :—

"If you will honestly listen to my description of the office-work of the Holy Ghost, you will clearly perceive, that, since the time Jesus left the earth, it is more extensive and important than even the work of the other personages of the Godhead.

"The Holy Ghost performs the double office of a WITNESS on earth and a RECORDER in heaven. Being an unembodied personage, He can move among men without the danger of being mobbed and killed, as was not the case with Jesus Christ. He takes up the work of man's redemption, just where Jesus Christ left it, and has a distinct part to act until the second coming of Christ, that in due time He also may obtain glory with the Father, even as Jesus does—yea, a fulness of the Godhead by Himself.

"According to promise He came on the day of Pentecost, either with a retinue of sanctified spirits, or in the simple unity and grandeur of his own potent agency, and filled the house. He then disbursed among the disciples a variety of tongues—gifts for men which the Conqueror had promised. With the keys of revelation, peculiar to his office, He unlocked their understanding (with perfect impunity to Himself) and bore witness that Jesus was Christ."—*Orson Spencer's Letters*, pp. 64,65.

We next turn to a passage in Orson Pratt's "*Kingdom of God*," in which he accounts for the alleged extinction of the Christian Church, or, as he expresses it, for the fact that the people "have not heard one word" from the King of the Kingdom "for upwards of seventeen hundred years :"

"I will now tell you the reason why the King has kept silence so long. It is because he has had no subjects to converse with; all have turned away from him and advocated other governments, as being the rightful and legal authority. They killed off and utterly destroyed every true subject of His kingdom, and left not a vestige of it upon the earth; and, to add to their guilt and wickedness, they have introduced idolatry in its worst forms, and utterly turned away from the true and living God. They have introduced a " *God without* BODY or PASSIONS." They have had the audacity to call this newly-invented god by the same name as the God of the ancient saints, although there is not the least resemblance between them. Indeed, there could be no resemblance between them; for a bodiless god, without '*parts or passions,*' could resemble nothing in heaven, on earth, or in hell. This imaginary modern god has become exceedingly popular. It is to him that a vast number of churches have been erected. It is not to the true and living God that they send forth petitions, but it is to this imaginary being. No wonder that they have received no communication from him; no wonder that he has not honoured them with a visit. As he has no ' PARTS,' he could neither be felt nor seen if he should visit them. Such a being could not speak, for he has no ' parts ' to speak with.

" There have been various species of idolatry in different ages of the world. The sun, moon, stars, beasts, crocodiles, frightful serpents, images of wood, of stone, and of brass, have been erected into gods, and worshipped by innumerable multitudes. But the system of idolatry invented by modern Christianity far surpasses in absurdity any thing that we have ever heard of. One of the celebrated worshippers of this newly-discovered god, in his 'Physical Theory of another life,' says, ' A disembodied spirit, or, we should rather say, an unembodied spirit, or sheer mind, is NOWHERE. Place is a relation belonging to extension, and extension is a property of matter; but that which is wholly abstracted from matter, and, in speaking of which, we deny that it has any property in common therewith, can in itself be subject to none of its conditions; and we might as well say of a pure spirit that it is hard, heavy, or red, or that it is a cubic foot in dimensions, as say that it is *here* or *there*. It is only in a popular and improper sense that any such affirmation is made concerning the Infinite Spirit, or that we speak of God as *every where* present. God is in every place in a sense altogether incomprehensible by finite minds, inasmuch as his relation to space and extension is peculiar to infinitude. Using the terms as we use them of ourselves, God is not *here* or *there*, any more than he exists *now* and *then*.' This species of idolatry, according to the foregoing quotations, approaches so near to Atheism, that no one can tell the difference. Reader, can you see the difference? A god '*without* a *body !*' A god '*without parts !*' A god that cannot be '*here* or *there !*' A god that is ' NO WHERE !' A god that cannot exist ' NOW and THEN !' A god that exists in NO TIME ! A god that has no *extension*—no '*parts*'—no conceivable relation to *time* or *space !* O, blush for modern Christianity !—a pious name for Atheism ! Some, perhaps, may think that I have not sufficient charity. But why should I have charity for a god that has no '*parts*'—no relation to space? Let him first have charity for himself. But this would be impossible, for he is a god '*without passions.*' He can have no charity nor love for himself nor any one else. There is no danger of offending him, for a passionless god is not capable of anger. One of the persons of this imaginary god is said to have been crucified; but this must be a sad mistake, for it would be impossible to crucify a portion of something that had no '*parts.*' The reason, then, why the people have not received any word from the Great King, is because they have petitioned the wrong god. Would you expect her Majesty, the queen of England, to answer your petition if it was directed to some African prince? Would you expect the God of heaven to answer a petition that was addressed to a Hindoo god? If, then, your petitions are addressed to the bodiless, passionless god of modern Christianity, you must not be surprised if the true God does not pay any attention to them. You need not expect that the true God will make any reply to petitions offered to any other being.

"The true God exists both in time and in space, and has as much relation to them as man or any other being. He has extension, and form, and dimensions, as well as man. He occupies space; has a body, parts, and passions; can go from place to place: can eat, drink, and talk, as well as man. Man resembles Him in the features and form of his body; and He does not differ materially in size. When He has been seen among men, He has been pronounced, even by the wicked, as one of their own species. So much did He look like man, that some supposed Him to be the carpenter's son. Like man, He had a father; and He was the '*express image of the person of the Father.*' The two Persons were as much alike in form, in size, and in every other respect, as fathers and sons are of the human race; indeed, the human race are '*His offspring,*' made in His likeness and image; not after His moral image, but after the image of His person. There is no such thing as moral image; such an image cannot exist. Morality is a property of some being or substance. A property without a substance or being to which it appertains, is inconceivable. A property can never have figure, shape, or image of any kind. Hence a moral image never had an existence except in the brains of modern idolaters.

"The Godhead consists of the Father, the Son, and the Holy Spirit. The Father is a material being. The substance of which He is composed is wholly material. It is a substance widely different, in some respects, from the various substances with which we are more immediately acquainted. In other respects it is precisely like all other materials. The substance of His person occupies space, the same as other matter. It has solidity, length, breadth, and thickness, like all other matter. The elementary materials of His body are not susceptible of occupying, at the same time, the same identical space with other matter. The substance of His person, like other matter, cannot be in two places at the same instant. It also requires *time* for Him to transport Himself from place to place. It matters not how great the velocity of His movements, *time* is an essential ingredient to all motion, whether rapid or slow. It differs from other matter in the superiority of its powers, being intelligent, all-wise, and possessing the power of self-motion to a far greater extent than the coarser materials of nature. ' God is a *spirit.*' But that does not make Him an immaterial being — a being that has no properties in common with matter. The expression, '*an immaterial being,*' is a contradiction in terms. Immateriality is only another name for nothing ; it is the negative of all existence. A '*spirit*' is as much *matter* as oxygen or hydrogen. It has many properties in common with all other matter. Chemists have discovered between fifty and sixty kinds of matter ; and each kind has some properties in common with all other matter, and some properties peculiar to itself, which the others do not inherit. Now, no chemist, in classifying his substances, would presume to say, ' This substance is material, but that one is immaterial, because it differs in some respects from the first.' He would call them all material, though they in some respects differed widely. So the substance called spirit is material, though it differs in a remarkable degree from other substances. It is only the addition of another element of a more powerful nature than any yet discovered. He is not a being ' without *parts,*' as modern idolators teach ; for every whole is made up of parts. The whole person of the Father consists of innumerable parts ; and each part is so situated, as to bear certain relations of distance to every other part. There must also be, to a certain degree, a freedom of motion among these parts ; which is an essential condition to the movement of His limbs, without which He could only move as a whole.

" All the foregoing statements in relation to the person of the Father, are equally applicable to the person of the Son."—*Orson Pratt's Kingdom of God*, Part I., pp. 3, 4.

Concerning the Third Person of the Blessed Trinity, the same writer declares :—

" The Holy Spirit being one part of the Godhead, is also a material substance, of the same nature and properties in many respects, as the spirits of the Father and Son. It exists in vast immeasurable quantities in connexion with all material worlds. This is called God in the Scriptures, as well as the Father and Son. God the Father and God the Son cannot be every where present ; indeed they cannot be even in two places at the same instant : but God the Holy Spirit is omnipresent—it extends through all space, intermingling with all other matter, yet no one atom of the Holy Spirit can be in two places at the same instant, which in all cases is an absolute impossibility. It must exist in inexhaustible quantities, which is the only possible way for any substance to be omnipresent. All the innumerable phenomena of universal nature are produced in their origin by the actual presence of this intelligent, all-wise, and all-powerful material substance called the Holy Spirit. It is the most active matter in the universe, producing all its operations according to fixed and definite laws enacted by itself, in conjunction with the Father and Son. What are called the laws of nature are nothing more nor less than the fixed method by which this spiritual matter operates. Each atom of the Holy Spirit is intelligent, and like all other matter has solidity, form, and size, and occupies space. Two atoms of this Spirit cannot occupy the same space at the same time, neither can one atom, as before stated, occupy two separate spaces at the same time. In all these respects it does not differ in the least from all other matter. Its distinguishing characteristics from other matter are its almighty powers and infinite wisdom, and many other glorious attributes which other materials do not possess. If several of the atoms of this Spirit should unite themselves together into the form of a person, then this person of the Holy Spirit would be subject to the same necessity as the other two persons of the Godhead, that is, it could not be every where present. No finite number of atoms can be omnipresent. An infinite number of atoms is requisite to be *every where* in infinite space. Two persons receiving the gift of the Holy Spirit, do not each receive at the same time the same identical particles, though they each receive a substance exactly similar in kind. It would be as impossible for each to receive the same identical atoms at the same instant, as it would be for two men at the same time to drink the same identical pint of water."—*Orson Pratt's Kingdom of God.* Part I., pp. 4, 5.

And in his "*Absurdities of Immaterialism,*" he endeavours to prove, that "Immaterialists are Atheists," by the following train of reasoning, if reasoning it can be called :--

"There are two classes of Atheists in the world. One class denies the existence of God in the most positive language : the other denies his existence in duration or space. One says, 'There is no God;' the other says, ' God is not *here* or *there*, any more than he exists *now* and *then.*' The infidel says, God does not exist any where. The Immaterialist says, ' He exists *No where.*' The infidel says, There is no such substance as God. The Immaterialist says, There is such a substance as God, but it is '*without Parts.*' The Atheist says, There is no such substance as *Spirit.* The Immaterialist says, ' A spirit, though he lives and acts, occupies no room, and fills no space, in the same way and after the same manner as matter, not even so much as does the minutest grain of sand.' The Atheist does not seek to hide his infidelity ; but the Immaterialist, whose declared belief amounts to the same thing as the Atheist's, endeavours to hide his infidelity under the shallow covering of a few words.

"The 'thinking principle,' says Dr. Thomas Brown, 'is essentially one, not extended and divisible, but incapable by its very nature, of any subdivision into integral parts.' What is this but the rankest kind of infidelity couched in a blind, plausible form. That which is 'not extended and not divisible ' and 'without parts,' cannot be any thing else than nothing. Take away these qualities and conditions, and no power of language can give us the least idea of existence. The very idea conveyed by the term existence is something extended, divisible, and with parts. Take these away, and you take away existence itself. It cannot be so much as the negative of space, or, what is generally called, an indivisible point, for that has a relation to the surrounding spaces. It cannot be so much as the negative of duration, or, what is generally called, an indivisible instant, for that has a relation to the past and future. Therefore, it must be the negative of all existence, or, what is called absolutely NOTHING. Nothing, and nothing only, is a representative of that which has no relation to space or time—that is, unextended, indivisible, and without parts. Therefore, the Immaterialist is a religious Atheist; he only differs from the other class of Atheists, by clothing an indivisible unextended NOTHING with the powers of a god. One class believes in no God; the other class believes that NOTHING is God, and worships it as such. There is no twisting away from this. The most profound philosopher in all the ranks of modern Christianity, cannot extricate the Immaterialist from atheism. He cannot show the least difference between the idea represented by the word *nothing*, and the idea represented by that which is unextended, indivisible, and without parts, having no relation to space or time. All the philosophers of the universe could not give a better or more correct definition of *Nothing*. And yet this is the god worshipped by the Church of England—the Methodists—and millions of other atheistical idolators, according to their own definitions, as recorded in their respective articles of faith. An open Atheist is not so dangerous as the Atheist who couches his atheistical doctrines under the head of "ARTICLES OF RELIGION." The first stands out with open colours, and boldly avows his infidelity; the latter, under the sacred garb of religion, draws into his yawning vortex the unhappy millions who are persuaded to believe in and worship an unextended indivisible *nothing* without parts, deified into a god. A pious Atheist is much more serviceable in building up the kingdom of darkness than one who openly, and without any deception, avows his infidelity.

" No wonder that this modern god has wrought no miracles and given no revelations since his followers invented their ' Articles of Religion.' A being without parts must be entirely powerless, and can perform no miracles. Nothing can be communicated from such a being; for, if nothing give nothing, nothing will be received. If, at death, his followers are to be made like him, they will enjoy, with some of the modern Pagans, all the beauties of annihilation. To be made like him! Admirable thought! How transcendantly sublime to behold an innumerable multitude of unextended nothings, casting their crowns at the feet of the great, inextended, infinite Nothing, filling all space, and yet ' without parts!' There will be no danger of quarrelling for want of room : for the Rev. David James says, ' Ten thousand spirits might be brought together into the smallest compass imaginable, and there exist without any inconvenience for want of room. As materiality,' continues he, ' forms no property of a spirit, the space which is sufficient for one, must be amply sufficient for myriads, yea, for all that exist.' According to this, all the spirits that exist, ' could be brought together into the smallest compass imaginable,' or, in other words, into no compass at all ; for, he says, a spirit occupies ' no room, and fills no space.' What an admirable description of Nothing ! *Nothing* ' occupies no room, and fills no space !' If myriads of Nothings were ' brought together into the smallest compass imaginable,' they could ' there exist without any inconvenience for want of room.' Every thing which the Immaterialist says, of the existence of *spirit*, will apply, without any variation, to the existence of *Nothing*. If he says that his god cannot exist '*Here*' or ' *There*,' the same is true of *Nothing*. If he affirms that he cannot exist ' *Now*' and ' *Then*,' the same can, in all truth, be affirmed of *Nothing*. If, he declares, that he is ' *unextended*,' so is *Nothing*. If he asserts that he is '*indivisible*' and ' *without parts*,' so is *Nothing*. If he declares that a spirit ' occupies no room and fills no space,' neither does *Nothing*. If he says a spirit is ' *Nowhere*,' so is *Nothing*. All that he affirms of the one, can, in like manner, and, with equal truth, be affirmed of the other. Indeed, they are only two words, each of which express precisely the same idea. There is no more absurdity in calling *Nothing* a substance, and clothing it with Almighty powers, than there is in making a substance out of that which is precisely like nothing, and imagining it to have Almighty powers. Therefore, an immaterial god is a deified Nothing, and all his worshippers are atheistical idolators."—*Orson Pratt's Absurdities of Immaterialism*, pp. 11, 12.

Such are the horrible tenets of Mormonism. No argument is needed to show that they are not "pure, holy, perfect, reasonable, and scriptural." Upon the very face of them they are as false and blasphemous, as the claim of Joseph Smith to be a Prophet of the living God. We should have hesitated to pollute our pages with them, but for the knowledge which we have of the activity of the missionaries of the Mormon sect in various parts both of England and Wales, and the consequent necessity of arousing the attention of the clergy to its real character. It is with this view chiefly, that we determined to resume the subject ; and, with the same view, we cannot do better than recommend, both for perusal and for distribution in localities in which it may be needed, the excellent and able Tract, entitled "*Friendly Warnings on the subject of Mormonism*," which originated in the invasion of a country parish by emissaries of Mormonism. To put a stop to the mischief, the Clergyman of the parish resorted to the simple and straightforward course of obtaining an interview with the preachers, two Mormon priests, in the course of which he elicited from them, by a series of well-framed questions, a statement of their doctrines, which he took down in writing, and obtained their signatures to it, in attestation of its correctness. As it forms a compendious abstract of the leading errors of the sect, we give it insertion :—

" I. What do you think of the Baptism of Infants?

" We think it absurd, unlawful, and without proof from Scripture, but contrary to the Word of God.

" Do you consider all Infant Baptisms performed in the Church of England null and void? Do you say the same of the baptisms of Dissenters and of Roman Catholics?

" Yes, we do.

" III. What do you think of the Sacrament of the Lord's Supper?

" We use bread and water, and consider that we receive pardon of our sins.

" IV. Do you consider that the Lord's Supper, as administered in the Church of England, or among Dissenters, or Roman Catholics, is a Christian rite, and that it is lawful to partake of it? Is it a sin to do so?

" We consider the Lord's Supper administered in the Church of England, and amongst Dissenters, and amongst Roman Catholics, null and void, and that it is wrong to administer it.

" V. Do you consider that there is any right or power in the clergy of the Church to administer sacraments, or to teach? What do you say of the Dissenting and Roman Catholic ministers?

" We consider that they have no right or power to preach or administer the sacraments. We consider them to be antichrists, false teachers, and teachers of false religion.

" VI. Do you consider the Bible, as it is received in this country by the Church of England, to be the Word of God?

" Yes.

" VII. Do you consider the Bible to include the whole of revelation, so that all articles of the Christian faith are contained in it? Is it imperfect?

" The Bible does not contain the whole of revelation. All articles of the Christian faith are not contained in the Bible. It is an imperfect revelation; it does not contain all that God has revealed.

" VIII. Have you a Bible of your own besides our Bible?

" We have the Book of Mormon, records which were taken out of a mountain, about twenty-two years ago, by a man named Smith. We consider this book of the same authority as the Bible.

" IX. Do you consider yourselves bound by every thing that is taught in the Bible, and in your own bible; or do you consider that new revelations are sometimes made which you are to follow?

" We consider ourselves bound by all that is written in the Bible, and in the Book of Mormon. We hold that new revelations are continually made, and that they cannot contradict former revelations.

" X. Do you consider every one of your body to be inspired by the Holy Ghost? Or do you think that being inspired by the Holy Ghost is necessary in order to preach the Gospel?

" We do not consider every one of our members to be inspired by the Holy Ghost.   We think that every preacher of the Gospel must be inspired by the Holy Ghost.

" XI. What do you think as to future rewards and punishments? Will they be eternal or only temporary?

" The wicked will only suffer for a *time* in the next world; not always.   Hell sufferings will not be eternal; but hell fire will be eternal.

" XII. What do you think concerning the kingdom of God on earth? Do you consider emperors, kings, and temporal rulers, to have authority according to God's law?

" We hold the dominion and rule of all emperors, kings, queens, and state governments to be unlawful and contrary to God's law—contrary to Scripture.   We consider Prophet Smith, or whoever represents him, to be our sovereign and king, and we consider ourselves released from all obedience to other sovereigns and rulers as a matter of conscience, though we obey the laws because we are compelled to do so.

" XIII. Had the world been existing without true religion until your prophet began to teach?   How long has the true religion, according to you, existed?

" Yes, the world remained without true religion from the time of the death of the last of the apostles or thereabouts, till the days of Smith. True religion has existed only about twenty years.

" XIV. What is your opinion of God?   Is He a spirit without body, parts and passions, or has He a body like us?

" God the Father has a body like ours.

" XV. Do Churchmen, and Dissenters, and Roman Catholics, worship the true God or a false God?

" We all hold that Churchmen, Dissenters, and Roman Catholics worship a false God—a God that does not exist; and that we worship the true God.

" XVI. Is the worship of God as practised by all classes of Christians in the Church, Dissent, and Romanism, an idolatry?

" We consider the worship of God as practised by Churchmen, Dissenters, and Roman Catholics to be idolatry.

" XVII. Is it blasphemy and wickedness to worship the God worshipped by the Church of England, Dissenters, and Romanists?

" It is blasphemy and wickedness to offer up prayers or worship to the God who is worshipped by Christians generally.

" XVIII. Can the true God eat, and drink, and talk?   Is he like a man in form, feature, and size?

" God the Father can eat, drink, and talk like us.   He is like a man in form, feature, and size.

" XIX. May there be several such Gods—more than one?

" There may be several such gods, and true gods.   We read there are gods—there must be more than one God—there is only one Supreme God, but there are many gods under Him.

" XX. Can God the Father be in two places at once?

" God the Father cannot in person be in two places at one time ; so that He is not omnipresent.

" XXI. Are there three *persons* in one God or three *substances* ?

" There are three substances ?

" XXII. Is the Son of God omnipresent ?   Can the Father and the Son, if not omnipresent, attend in person to the affairs of government in God's kingdom ?

" He directs his kingdom by the influence of his Spirit upon the apostles and teachers.

" XXIII. Are those who worship a God who is believed to be without body, and to be omnipresent, in the way of salvation, or in the way of perdition ?

" Such persons are not in the way of salvation, but in the way of perdition.   All Churchmen, Dissenters, and Roman Catholics, are therefore in the way of perdition.

" XXIV. Are you yourselves inspired by God ?

" We are inspired by the Holy Ghost to preach the Gospel.   We speak with the same authority as the apostles did.   We cannot make a mistake.

" XXV. Can you work miracles in proof of your commission from God ?

" We cannot work miracles to prove that we are commissioned by the Holy Ghost.

" XXVI. Is the worship of the God worshipped by all Christians till your commnnion began, an idolatry, as absurd as the worship of a crocodile, or of a bottle of smoke ?

" We consider it absurd to worship the God worshipped by Christians generally till our Church arose.

" XXVII. What officers are there in your Church ?

" Apostles, elders or bishops, teachers, priests, deacons."

By means of this document [1], the author of " *Friendly Warnings*" was enabled, without fear of contradiction, to state from his pulpit the nature of the Mormon creed, which, we need not add, it was easy for him to refute by p a n arguments drawn from Holy Scripture. The remedy proved efficacious ; error fled before the face of truth, and the false teachers ceased to molest his flock.

---

[1] Let those who doubt the propriety of the assembling of Convocation for the revival of the discipline, and the revision of the Canons of the Church, ponder the contents of this document, and reflect that, in the present state of Church law, a clergyman is liable to suspension from his office, as an " offender," if he feels it impossible, consistently with his conscience, to express over the corpse of one who lived and died in this delusion, the hope that " this his brother " is " resting in Christ," as one of " those that are departed in the true faith of God's holy name." Where, in the whole range of grievances, political and religious, is there another grievance greater than this ! And yet there are men, Churchmen, clergymen, nay, bishops, who see no occasion for the revival of the legislative functions of the Church !

We should be wanting in our duty to the Church if we were
to conclude the present exposure of these two fearful, and, to
some extent, analogous delusions, without expressing our sorrowful conviction that they are to be regarded, not merely as aberrations of the human mind, under the wily influence of Satan, but
as punishments which the Church has brought upon herself by
the inadequacy of her own teaching,—would we were not compelled to add, the faintness of her faith,—upon the subject which
forms the central point, both of Irvingism and Mormonism, the
influence and operation in the Church, of God the Holy Ghost.
We cannot better express the sense which we entertain of the
short-comings of our Church on this essential point, vitally connected with her very existence as a branch of Christ's Holy
Catholic Church, than by transcribing the following questions
publicly asked by one of her Presbyters, on the occasion of the
sanction given by a large portion of the English Episcopate to
the establishment of a regular order of unordained Scripture
readers, that is, in Church language, of evangelists sent forth
with a human commission and in human strength, to do the work
for which Christ has given His commission and the power of
His Holy Spirit.

" Is it dealing faithfully with the ordinance of 'Consecration of
Bishops,' which is one of the ordinances of the Holy Ghost, and the
highest of them, to confer that consecration upon men who are, by a
fiction of law, elected by the Church, but in reality nominated, not by
the Head of the State, whose supremacy the Church recognizes,—that
too has passed into a fiction,—but by the heads of the political party
which at any time may chance to wield the powers of the Crown, and
which, whatever be its name, can, in the present state of the country,
neither be expected to sympathize cordially with the Church, nor
expect to possess her confidence? Since the advisers of the Crown are
confessedly dependent on the support of an assembly in which, along
with a small minority of sound Churchmen, and a large number
of unsound and merely nominal Churchmen, Romanists, Protestant
Dissenters of every denomination, Socinians, Deists, and, as we shall
soon have to add, last not least, the Jew, are severally entitled to sit
and vote, can it be right, is it decent, that the advisers *pro tempore* of
the Crown should have the power of placing whomsoever they may
select, in that position in which Churchmen are called upon, by their
principles, to recognise them as those whom 'the Holy Ghost hath
made overseers over the flock?'
" Is it dealing faithfully with the ordinance of ' Ordering of Priests,'
which is another ordinance of the Holy Ghost, to confer the order of
the Priesthood upon men who, it is notorious, do not believe in the doctrine, and are not prepared to minister according to the discipline, of
our Church ; who are known to be, if not abettors, yet excusers, of the

erroneous and strange doctrines which they are called upon to promise that they will with all faithful diligence banish and drive away; men whose unsoundness might be ascertained even by simply laying the finger upon certain passages in the office for the ministration of the initiatory Sacrament of the Christian Church, and asking them the plain question: ' Dost thou honestly believe this ? and wilt thou honestly teach and maintain it ?'

" Is it dealing faithfully with the Ordinance of ' Ordering of Deacons,' which . is another Ordinance of the Holy Ghost, to confer the order of the Diaconate only upon those who seek admission to it as to a probation and transition state to the Presbyterate; and to allow the order of Deacons, in the true sense of the word, to remain a dead letter?

" Is it dealing faithfully with the Ordinance of ' Confirmation,' which is another Ordinance of the Holy Ghost, to minister it, as it is ministered in nine cases out of ten, to those who are not even aware that they are, by this Ordinance, to seek, and, seeking, to receive, the gifts of the Holy Ghost; who consider it merely as a decent ceremony, as a renewal of their Baptismal vows, and as a passport to another Ordinance, the Sacrament of the Holy Eucharist, which, after all, again, in nine cases out of ten, they never approach? Is it dealing faithfully with that Ordinance to minister it after the instruction, and upon the certificate, of Ministers who do not themselves believe, and therefore cannot teach, that it is the Ordinance by which the lay members of the Church are personally brought under the operation of the gifts and graces of the Holy Ghost; yea, and to discountenance, as is too often the case, those Ministers who set that Ordinance before their people in all its awe-inspiring dignity as the Ordinance of the Holy Ghost?

Can we expect, that where there is such extensive unfaithfulness in dealing with the Ordinances of the Holy Ghost, there will be a powerful exhibition of the presence of the Holy Ghost in the Church, as a Spirit of Truth, of Sanctification, of Union, and of Peace? Can we wonder that error, worldliness, division, and strife, should abound?

"And is it surprising that another, and a most awful step in this downward progress of unfaithfulness, the formal superseding of the Holy Ghost altogether, by the introduction of *an order of Ministers, set apart, but without any Ordinance of the Holy Ghost*, should find such extensive favour and such high sanction in our Church?"

We will only add, that the same faintness of faith,—not to call it unbelief,—as regards the presence and operation of the Holy Ghost in the Church of God, lies at the root of the hesitation felt by too many in our day respecting the only measure to which Churchmen can look with confidence, for the remedying of the many grievous evils under which the Church is suffering, the revival of her Synodal functions. If men were in the habit of realizing the abiding presence of God the Holy Ghost, the giver of life to the Church as a body, as well as to all her members,—instead of looking with distrust and apprehension to the meeting of her Bishops and Clergy, they would put their trust in the guidance of God's Holy Spirit, specially invoked by and for the deliberative assemblies of the Church, in the firm faith that He will not fail, now as of old, to be her guide into all truth, and to gird her with spiritual strength in the day of battle.

ART. III. 1.—*The Reformers of the Anglican Church and Mr. Macaulay's History of England, second edition.* By CHANCEL-LOR HARINGTON. London: Rivingtons. 1850.

Now that the first buzz which welcomed Mr. Macaulay's History into the reading world is over, we have some hope of a hearing.' When the world bursts forth into a rapture of hasty admiration of " the last new work," the wise critic will wisely place his pen behind his ear, lean back in his easy chair, and learning the art of well-timed silence, patiently " bide his time."

Sometimes our variable and eccentric friend, " the public," as premature in its praise as in its censure, is determined to be pleased before the book is out: the very advertisement is read with glistening and approving eyes ; the verdict is on the lip before the trial has come on ; partiality outstrips the slow, dull feet of evidence, and the judgment is prospectively pronounced. The moment Mr. Macaulay's History came reeking from the press, it was evident that the thing was settled, the mind of the public was made up, the book was to be received with ready-made applause. A long avenue of new editions opened on Messrs. Longman's delighted eyes ; young ladies and grave men agreed in commendation, differing only in the texture of their compliments ; the " charming," " beautiful," " interesting,"— the pound of feathers of the one, balancing the " powerful," " brilliant," " able,"—the pound of lead of the other.

For ourselves,—it may be from an unamiable prospective dislike of what every body amiably and prospectively admires,— we admit that we felt considerable distrust the instant we were told that the sparkling Reviewer was about to take the sterner task of the Historian. We were not prepared to accept the tableauxism of the Edinburgh articles as a sample of historic powers.

We do not purpose to weary our readers with analyzing the book from the first page to the last; but we shall content ourselves with a few brief remarks on a small portion of it, viz., on that portion in which Mr. Macaulay speaks of the Reformers of the English Church.

And here, first of all, we protest against the Romanism of Mr. Macaulay. He starts with the old Romish assertion, that the Reformation was no Reformation at all ; that the English Church was at that period born into the world, not reformed ; that it was not, that it did not exist, that there was no such thing; for he speaks of "*the Founders* of the Anglican Church." It is important in these days to recall the views of one who is of that political party now raving against Romish aggression, now affecting a righteous indignation and surprise at the Pope in treating the English Church as if it did not exist. This historian, not in the hasty language of periodical literature, but in the cautious, well-considered words of deliberate history, speaks of the *foundation*, of the birth, of the commencement of the English Church, as taking place at that juncture which historians call the Reformation. Such an assertion, of course, goes to the very root of the Church. If we were not at that time, we are not now; if the Church began then, was then formed, it was—it is, no part of the Church of Christ. Continuance is the very law of the Church's existence. There may be expansion; there may be developement; there may be growth of new limbs in new countries : but if in an old Christian country, which has been for centuries a portion of the body of Christ, a Church is *founded*, whatever is then founded is no true part of the Church ; if the old body altogether ceases and dies, and simultaneously with its death a new body arises, not sent from any other land, not growing out of the old branch, nor connected with it, but self-originating—originating with any man or set of men,—then either that man or set of men must lay claim to some new revelation, some miraculous powers; or we must condemn their work as the work of man, as mere hay, straw, stubble.

Mr. Macaulay then, be it observed, takes this ground, this Romish ground, this ground of Cardinal Wiseman in his new schismatic hierarchy ; anticipating their assumption, he says that the English branch of Christ's Church is not a reformed branch, but is something altogether new, a new creation, not an improved, purified continuation of an old corrupt branch of Christ's Church, but something originating at that time, or originating with certain men, with "founders,"—a new race of Apostles. We ask our readers to weigh well the words of this abettor and advocate of Romish views,—this forerunner of the Cardinal Archbishop; for it is important to show the public what political parties or men have had to do with Romish aggression.

Very different is the language of Bishop Hall, whom the Romanizing historian so plainly contradicts. "We profess this Church of ours by God's grace reformed—reformed, I say, not new made, as some envious spirits allege. For my part, I am ready to sink into the earth with shame when I hear that hackneyed reproach, 'Where was your Church before Luther! Where was your Church?' Here, ye cavillers ! We desired the reformation of an old religion, not the formation of a new. The Church was reformed, not new wrought. It was the same Church that it was before, only purged from some superfluous and pernicious additaments. Is it a new face that was lately washed? a new garment that was mended? a new house that is repaired? Blush, if ye have any shame, who fondly cast this in our teeth."

Now after starting with an assertion so opposite to that of Bishop Hall, Mr. Macaulay, with unhistorical inaccuracy, fails to give us any account or list of these "founders of the Anglican Church." We are left to grope in the dark, or to discover for ourselves who they are, or whom he means. Taking the hint of Mr. Macaulay's able assailant, Chancellor Harington, we must venture on the conjecture, that he must mean the compilers of the Book of Common Prayer. We must look upon the Prayer Book as the authoritative declaration of the Reformers' opinions, as the index of their minds, as their new statute-book, as the exponent of their notions of Scriptural and Christian truth. Without, then, at first looking at the men, we will look at their *work*,—at the fruit of their labours,—at the result of their joint counsel. With this Prayer Book before us, we hear Mr. Macaulay, first of all, charging the founders of the Anglican Church with the denial of Episcopacy as a divine institution; with the Prayer Book before us, we turn at once to that part which treats of Episcopacy, to see whether it agrees with Mr. Macaulay's charge. We find, however, that those who are said to have denied that episcopacy is of divine institution expressly assert the contrary. "It is evident," is the language of the Ordinal, "unto all men diligently reading *the Holy Scripture* and the ancient authors, that from the Apostles' time there have been these three orders of ministers in Christ's Church,—bishops, priests, and deacons."

Now we say that the Ordinal is *the* proof, *the* evidence upon this point. If upon any matter men have talked, deliberated, thought, consulted, we look to the *result* of their meetings, deliberations, thoughts, consultations, as the true test of their fixed, real, deliberate opinions. Whatever may have been started, canvassed, considered in the course of deliberation, we make light of, and look to the *result*. It is the only fair way of discovering what men really hold, what is their conviction, their real judgment. In this way we should deal with the Council of Trent: we are not anxious to inquire what the several members, in the course of deliberation, suggested, asserted, thought, proposed, or weighed; we cannot fairly charge them, as a body, with the opinions expressed in the course of their work; we look to the result, to the decrees of the Council, to the "litera scripta," to the authorized, formal, well-weighed issue of the various opinions of the various minds engaged : so, likewise, Mr. Harington rightly draws us to the Ordinal ; he rightly puts the preface to the Ordinal side by side with Mr. Macaulay's assertion ; he rightly says, There is the opinion, the fixed, well-weighed, well-considered judgment of "the founders of the Anglican Church ;" there they assert that episcopacy is of divine institution.   Whatever points may have been raised, whatever debates, whatever questions of difficulty, whatever variety of opinions, we find at last that all their minds were moulded into one, that all at last agreed together; and in judging of them fairly, we must judge of them by their great corporate act, to which each put his hand ; we must go to the Ordinal, and by the Ordinal their opinions on Episcopacy must be discovered.   In a day of great agitation, when new views, new ideas, new doctrines were continually broached, we might expect to find occasional inconsistencies in individual "founders;" but on them no stress can fairly be laid after they have once given forth a final judgment in so formal and so solemn a way.   "This office," we must remember, "was drawn up in the year 1549, under the authority of King Edward VI., by the archbishop, six bishops, and six other eminent Reformers, Cranmer being the chief."   Let us see how the Preface runs : " It is evident unto all men diligently reading the Holy Scriptures and ancient authors, that from the Apostles' time, there have been three orders of ministers in Christ's Church, bishops, priests, and deacons."   And " the DIVINE appointment of the several orders is expressly declared in the first and subsequent Ordinals :—' Almighty God, Giver of all good things, who by Thy Holy Spirit, hast appointed divers orders in Thy Church ; mercifully behold this Thy servant, now called to the work or ministry of a bishop,' (or priest or deacon, as the case may be)" and the slight alterations adopted in the subsequent editions, including the last in 1662, " tend to develope more clearly the views of our Church in favour of episcopacy, and the doctrine of apostolical succession."

In speaking of the Prayer Book, we include both the Liturgy and the Ordinal, afterwards added, as the work of the same hands, that is of the Archbishop Cranmer, Bishops Ridley, Goodrich, Holbech, Thirlby, Skyp, and Day, and six other divines.   Here, then, we see the men who framed this work ; we see " the founders of the Anglican Church."   These are the men who, in Mr. Macaulay's language, " retained episcopacy ; but they did not declare it to be an institution essential to the welfare of a Christian society, or to the efficacy of the Sacraments : Cranmer, indeed, plainly avowed his conviction, that in the primitive times, there was no distinction between bishops and priests, and that the laying on of hands was altogether unnecessary." We must read English backwards, after reading the Ordinal, to believe Mr. Macaulay.

But as we have now considered the result of the collective deliberations of the compilers of the Liturgy and Ordinal—men whom Mr. Macaulay must mean to describe as " the Founders of the Anglican Church," let us see whether the component parts of this body of divines were in the habit of promulgating other opinions in private, whether they were suprised into the framing of such a service by any one master mind, contrary to their ordinary and accustomed view. We designedly use the words " in the *habit* of promulgating other opinions," because is is but fair thus to speak: all men have their inconsistencies; sometimes men express themselves ill, sometimes hastily, and afterwards retract what has been ill or hastily expressed; and we must not confuse occasional with habitual expressions.

First of all, then, we come to Cranmer. Did Cranmer ordinarily hold the opinion that episcopacy was "not essential to the welfare of a Christian society," and merely "retained it as an ancient, decent, and convenient ecclesiastical polity?" Cranmer has spoken many times upon the point, and his habitual view is just contrary to that which our imaginative historian has ascribed to him. Thus in the " Institution of a Christian Man," published 1537, in " the Declaration of the Functions and *Divine Institution* of Bishop and Priests, 1536-8; in the Erudition of a Christian Man, 1543; in his Catechism, 1548; in the Reformatio Legum Ecclesiasticarum, 1551; and in the Preface to the Ordinal, Cranmer over and over again, in many different ways and forms of speech, plainly, clearly ' derived,' in Dr. Hickes's language. the order of bishops and priests from Christ and his Apostles, and from them successively to others, unto the world's end." We would refer our readers to Mr. Harington's pamphlet, from page 47 to 57, if they wish to see the passages in the different works alluded to, either compiled or sanctioned by Cranmer, in which he asserts that there are both bishops and priests, that they derive their mission from Christ and his Apostles, and that imposition of hands is not " superfluous." If our readers examine the dates of these various publications, they will see how wide the range is, —1536, 1537, 1538, 1543, 1548, 1549 (the Ordinal), 1551.

There is, indeed, a gap in these dates, a gap between 1538 and 1543. And here we come at once to one of Cranmer's inconsistencies. The inconsistency, however, will not much help the historian; for he has led the public to believe that it was the rule, not the exception, in Cranmer to deny the Divine institution of episcopacy. Mr. Macaulay has forgotten logic, however wide or various his other acquirements may be; he has drawn a universal conclusion from a particular premise, and this particular not persisted in but withdrawn. It is true that in the year 1540, to quote Dr. Brett, " Archbishop Cranmer's notions which he had were not agreeable to the doctrine of the primitive Church." But if, with so many, so frequent assertions of episcopacy, as a Divine institution and as necessary to the Christian Church, and unto the efficacy of the Sacraments, there was a single occasion on which these views were not maintained, we ought fairly to look upon it as an inconsistency in the man ; it cannot otherwise be judged : and that writer who seizes upon that single occasion, and draws from it a general inference, and speaks of Cranmer generally as one who did not think episcopacy divinely ordained, or needful, makes an unfair, an unjust, an unwarrantable use of his historic materials: he is a partisan, not an historian. What writer, we ask, is there who has not his inconsistencies? What writer has not, in some single passage, either appeared to contradict his general opinions, or really contradicted them? Yet we judge such contradictions as of little value, even if they are suffered to remain in their works.

But while Cranmer, in certain answers given to the questions of certain commissioners appointed by Henry VIII, in 1540, did show a wavering mind, and did express lax opinions; yet we find that he actually *cancelled* those lax opinions, and reverted to his former habitual and more deliberate views. We will take Bishop Burnet as our witness. Speaking of Cranmer's answers, he says, " In Cranmer's paper some singular opinions of his about the nature of ecclesiastical offices will be found; but as they are delivered by him with all possible modesty, so they were not established as the doctrine of the Church, but laid aside as particular conceits of his own. And it seems that *afterwards he changed his opinion*, for he subscribed the book that was soon after set out, which is directly contrary to those opinions set down in this paper." Nay more, Mr. Harington " proves that Cranmer, probably before the publication of the ' Erudition' in 1543, had repudiated the Erastian views imputed to him, by *cancelling his replies* to the ' Questions concerning the Sacraments,' and *subscribing to the opinions of Dr. Leighton*, who replied to the ninth question, ' That the Apostles *made Bishops by authority given unto them of Christ.*' " " And therefore," says Dr. Brett " those who urge Dr. Cranmer's authority, as the author of ' the Rights,' and others, have done, to prove that there is no necessity of an episcopal commission for the valid administration of the Sacraments, would do well to consider that it was not that prelate's settled judgment; and howsoever he did once give it under his hand as his opinion, yet he did not continue in that mind, but subscribed the contrary doctrine soon after."

Nay, we go farther than this, and say that the very fact of Cranmer returning to his first opinions adds immense strength to their truth, and to the strength of his own conviction; for if, after holding certain opinions for many years, a man reconsiders the matter, and modifies them, and yet cannot rest content with that modification, but withdraws and cancels it, we have tremendous testimony of the reality and intensity of his former views. That these temporary and passing laxities of Cranmer were withdrawn, is evident from that "great fact," the publication of the Ordinal, in which he had a principal hand, in the year 1549. He here puts his seal to his recantation.

What then, we ask, as regards Cranmer, one of the "founders of the Anglican Church," is the value of Mr. Macaulay's assertion, that he retained episcopacy "as an ancient, decent, and convenient ecclesiastical polity," that he did not believe it to be an institution "essential to the welfare of a Christian society, or to the efficacy of the Sacraments," but that, in the primitive times, there was "no distinction between bishops and priests, and that the laying on of hands was altogether unnecessary?" What shall we say of Mr. Macaulay's charge of Erastianism, when he says, "The king, such was the opinion of Cranmer, given in the plainest words, might, in virtue of authority derived from God, make a priest; and the priest so made needed no ordination whatever?" The Preface to the Ordinal is the best, and strongest, and most formal answers to these accusations.

We may here, perhaps, pardon Mr. Macaulay, who is not a theologian, for getting into some confusion as regards theological expressions concerning bishops and priests, though we cannot pardon his rashness in writing without knowledge. It is among the views of a great body of early writers, that there are but two orders, the priesthood and the diaconate; and reckoning the priesthood as a genus, they divide it into two species, the episcopate and presbytery; and yet these divines do not make any confusion between bishops and presbyters, though they assert only a twofold instead of a threefold order; they assert that it *is* "necessary to the welfare of a Christian society" and "to the efficacy of the Sacraments," that there should be bishops, priests, and deacons. Indeed, these opinions, in real matter and substance, are similar to those expressed in the Ordinal, though the word "order" is used in a different sense.

It is true, also, that Mr. Macaulay, acted upon, as we may suppose, by Mr. Harington's pamphlet, has altered several expressions in the fourth and subsequent editions of his History: instead, for instance, of the passage referred to running thus, "Cranmer plainly avowed his conviction that there was no dis-. tinction between bishops and priests," it is said, "Cranmer, indeed, *on one important occasion, &c.*" This alteration is a gain, so far, though it is but a part of the truth, as it is not stated that these views were altered, and opposite views afterwards embodied in the Ordinal. Part of the sting remains, viz., that once these views were held: the full truth would require the plain assertion that Cranmer afterwards thought them wrong.

But while we have this proof that Mr. Macaulay requires some such assailants as Mr. Harington to make him cautious in his assertions, what shall we say, not of a reviewer writing, like ourselves, often in hot haste, but an historian, who has so soon to. modify his statements? who dashed off something about Cranmer, and has to come down from making a general assertion to the fact that so far from being a general view, it was maintained on one solitary occasion, and afterwards cancelled in the most formal way?

But to give the whole question fair consideration, we must state that previous to the publication of the Ordinal, Henry VIII. died; and it is true, that Cranmer and his suffragans took out fresh commissions, 1546, "empowering them," as Mr. Macaulay says, "to ordain and to perform other spiritual functions, till the new Sovereign should think fit to order otherwise." Mr. Macaulay supposes Cranmer by this act to look upon "his own spiritual functions, like the secular functions of the chancellor and treasurer," which "were at once determined by a demise of the Crown." Now, first of all, we are not prepared at once to allow that the commission is so to be interpreted. We cannot at once give way to Mr. Macaulay's reading of the passage. If the fact is of any value to our historian, it of course proves, according to his view, that "all the power of the keys" was handed over to this royal pope by the archbishop. But as many previous writers have taken an opposite view of the commission, and consider that Cranmer did not design to place the king in St. Peter's chair, even though he may have conceded too much on some occasions to royal power, we may venture to follow these our forerunners, who anticipated Mr. Macaulay, and have thus prevented us from being singular in our interpretation of the fact.

Now, there are two passages in this commission on which stress is laid, and the real question is whether the one at all. qualifies the other. First, the archbishop is authorised to ordain and to perform all other spiritual functions, "vice, nomine, et·

auctoritate nostris." This seems, at first sight, to make the king the fountain of episcopacy; but there is a clause in the same commission which runs thus : " præter et ultra ea quæ tibi ex sacris literis divinitus commissa esse dignoscuntur." This seems, in our judgment, to qualify the former assertion. So it was held by the writers we have alluded to. Thus, Mr. Harington, in his Appendix, quotes largely from Leslie's "Case of the Regale and Pontificate, stated," in which he gives—

" A short and clear state of the case lately discoursed (at a conference) concerning the regale, or power of the State over the Church, as to her purely spiritual character, First, It was agreed on all hands that the State cannot deprive bishops of their episcopal character, (Mr. Macaulay asserting that it is in the king's power ' to confer the episcopal character, or to take it away',) but that they remain bishops still.' One of the conference here asked how this was consonant with ' the commission that Archbishop Cranmer took out for his bishopric from Edward VI.' &c., and the like done by other bishops, whereby they held their bishoprics during the pleasure of the king, and owned to derive all their power, even ecclesiastical, from the crown, ' velut a supremo capite et omnium infra'regnum nostrum magistratuum fonte et scaturigine,' &c.—it was said, 1st. That all this is to be understood only of the civil power and authority, which by the laws of the land were annexed to the sacred office; as the civil jurisdiction that is granted to the bishop's courts, to the bishops themselves, as lords of Parliament, &c.; to the civil penalties which follow their excommunications, and *the legal protection to their ordinations, and other acts of their office;* and these are derived only and solely from the king. Nothing of this was granted to the Apostles, or the bishops, their successors, by Christ; and as the State granted these, they may recall them, if there be sufficient reason for it. That in the very commission before-mentioned, which was given to Cranmer for his bishopric, there is an exception: ' Præter et ultra ea quæ tibi ex sacris literis divinitus commissa esse dignoscuntur.' These the king did not take upon him to grant, but only what was over and above these, that is, the protection and civil privileges granted by the State, which were annexed to fortify and encourage these. And take notice, that of that of which the king is here called the *head and fountain,* is *omnium magistratuum,* of the magistracy within his dominions, as well ecclesiastical as temporal ; for, there is a civil magistracy annexed by the laws to the ecclesiastical jurisdiction; and *of this only ought these expressions to be meant; because* we see the other, the spiritual authority, which, in Holy Scripture, is granted to the Church, is expressly excepted; and that ecclesiastical authority which, in this commission, is said to flow from the king, is 'juris dicendi authoritas, et quæcumque ad forum ecclesiasticum pertinent;' that is, the episcopal jurisdiction considered as a forum—a court established by the secular power, and part of the laws of the land. That in the said History of the Reformation, part i. in the

Addenda, No. 5, p. 321, there is a declaration made of the function and *Divine Institution* of bishops and priests, subscribed by Lord Cromwell, then vicegerent to King Henry VIII. in ecclesiastical matters, by Archbishop Cranmer, with the archbishop of York, eleven other bishops, and twenty divines and canonists, declaring that *the power of the keys and other Church functions is formally* distinct from the civil power, &c. And ibid, Collect, Records, No. 10, p. 177, there is a judgment of eight bishops concerning the king's supremacy, whereof *Cranmer* is the first, asserting that the commission which Christ gave to his Church, had 'no respect to kings' and princes' power;' but that the Church had it by 'the word of God, to which Christian princes acknowledge themselves subject.' They then deny that the commission Christ gave to his Church did extend to civil power over kings and princes; and they own that the civil power was over bishops and priests, as well as other subjects; that is, in civil matters, which the Church of Rome did deny; but they assert that 'bishops and priests have the charge of souls, are the messengers of Christ, to teach the truth of the Gospel, and loose and bind sin, &c., as Christ was the Messenger of his Father;' which sure was independent of all kings and power upon earth. Here one desired it might not be forgot that Bonner took out the same commission for his bishopric from Henry VIII., as that before mentioned of Cranmer from Edward VI."

Such is the view taken of the commission by no mean judges of such matters. But, after all, while this commission might, in Mr. Macaulay's view, be supposed to express a strong Erastianism, it leaves the question of the Divine institution of episcopacy untouched; the whole matter that is raised is, not whether bishops derive their mission from Christ, but whether they derive it through the medium of kingly authority, or not. For ourselves, we cannot but regard the term, "vice regis," coupled as it is, in the same document, with "divinitus commissa," &c. to be a loose expression, by which the King authorized the legal *exercise* of episcopal power, and did not mean to give as from himself that episcopal power. We cannot believe that Cranmer meant to admit that he ceased to be a bishop, as the chancellor or the treasurer ceased to be chancellor or treasurer, by the death of the king,— that bishops by kings' deaths were un-bishoped, and needed to be re-bishoped by the new kings. There must be an abundant mass of evidence proving the frequent and formal repetition of such a view, before we have any right, as candid searchers of truth, to admit it. We challenge proof of any such accumulated evidence as would make the words "vice regis" go the whole length to which Mr. Macaulay would stretch it. All the evidence that we can obtain tells the other way. Take, for instance, the Ordinal framed in 1549 : where is there a trace of any such view !

where any assertion, however faint or indefinite, that the king was "vicar of God;" that the bishop or priest confirmed, or administered Sacraments, "vice regis," as a mere deputy or proxy; that the king, if he willed, could confirm, or administer Sacraments; or that such confirmation, or administration of Sacraments, were valid? The notion is preposterous.

We must refer our readers to the various works and documents to which we have already alluded, issued or sanctioned by Cranmer in 1536, 1537, 1538, 1543, 1548, 1551.

While we thus vindicate Cranmer's memory, we are not saying that he did not practically leave too much to the will of the king; and yet, though through the necessity of the times, through lack of moral courage, through intimacy with foreign Reformers, he may have sometimes expressed himself inconsistently, and have given way too largely to kingly power, yet we see plainly, amid all his inconsistencies and concessions, what his own mind really was: he did believe that "it is evident to those diligently *reading the Holy Scriptures* and ancient authors, that from the Apostles' time there have been these *orders of ministers in Christ's Church—bishops, priests, and deacons,* which offices were evermore had in such reverend estimation, that no man might presume to execute any of them, except he were first called, tried, examined, and known to have such qualities as are requisite for the same; and also by public prayer, *with imposition of hands,* were approved and admitted thereunto by lawful authority." Passing from the Preface, we see his judgment of this "lawful authority;" we see that bishops consecrated bishops, according to the service which he helped to frame, without one word of reference to a higher earthly fountain, without one word of "vice regis;" that bishops with the presbytery ordained presbyters, without any reference to spiritual power or commission derived from God through kings. We find these awful words, "Receive ye the Holy Ghost," the whole power of binding and loosing, without any reference to the kingly authority, whether as affecting the bishop who ordains, or the presbyter who receives ordination. In short, the whole service is at this moment used by the American Church, without alteration, where there is no prince or king, so little is the royal popery of Macaulay's imagination embodied in it.

But passing from Cranmer to "less courtly divines," to the other compilers of the Liturgy and the Ordinal, the other "founders of the Anglican Church," we will consider whether they privately and individually held fainter notions concerning the Divine institution of episcopacy, &c., than those they corporately and jointly expressed in the Ordinal. Besides Cranmer there were six bishops and six other divines. The bishops, as we have already said, were Ridley, Goodrich, Holbech, Thirlby, Skyp, and Day. Now, there was put forth a certain "declaration made of the functions and *Divine institution* of bishops and priests," signed by thirty-eight bishops, divines, and canonists; of those, seven were compilers of the Book of Common Prayer, viz. Cranmer, Skyp, Robertson, Redmayne, May, Cox, and Goodrich.   Then we have the "Reformatio Legum Ecclesiasticarum," which speaks distinctly of the threefold ministry, as being the true Scriptural and primitive form : and in this work Cranmer, Goodrich, Ridley, Cox, Taylor, and May, six compilers of the Prayer Book, took part.   Bishop Thirlby writes thus, "Making of bishops hath two parts, appointment and ordering.   Appointment, which the Apostles by necessity made by common election, and sometimes by their own several assignment, could not be done by Christian princes, because at that time they were not; and now at these days appertaineth to Christian princes and rulers.   *But in the ordering wherein grace is conferred,* (as afore,) *the Apostles did follow the rule taught them by the Holy Ghost,* per manuum impositionem, cum oratione et jejunio."   Bishop Day declares that "bishops have authority by Scripture to ordain bishops and priests."

We think we have said enough, without wearying our readers with further evidence, to prove that Mr. Macaulay has spoken rashly; and that all the deliberate, unbiassed acts or expressions of "the founders of the Anglican Church" assert or imply the Divine institution of episcopacy.   In times so unsettled, so full of new thoughts, it is not strange that hasty opinions fell even from divines; and it might be easy to prove a variety of contradictory opinions, if chance phrases or occasional assertions were picked up here and there, and cleverly patched together; but we should not judge such times in such a way; we should endeavour to trace the under-current of the more sober and settled mind of the Anglican divines; and if this be done we have no fear as to the general result of such inquiries.   That they had faults and inconsistencies is but to say in other words that they were men; that some of them were sometimes drawn, in their haste to escape papal rule, to hurry too eagerly for protection under royal wings, is but to describe a great temptation to which they were subject; and yet the most time-serving of their acts of concession to royal rule in spiritual things, is surrounded by other acts in which they only give that due measure of authority which may be given to Christian kings.

We may wish, indeed, at this present time, that there had been throughout, and on every occasion, a plainer, more consistent definition of the extent and limit of the kingly power.

If such a definition had been wisely made at every turn of affairs,
it would have saved us from many of those difficulties which
press so closely upon us at this present time, and from those
dangers which threaten to sweep us on to an ultra assertion of
royal supremacy, in our present recoil from the aggressions of
the Pope. At all times it is and will be hard rightly to settle
with precision the boundaries of regal power, to give neither too
much nor too little, as there are many questions of a mixed
character; and, with a continual series of re-actions, we rarely
reach the true "via media" upon the matter. However, more
difficult still, is it for the Romanist to define the supremacy of the
Pope, and the Church of Rome is wise in surrounding it by a
mist of vague and hazy expressions. But, we ask, is it reasonable to expect most accurate and most precise definitions of
regal authority in all writings, works, documents, at a period
when the Church was struggling into independence, being utterly
unused to independence? _If, on the whole,_ in such an age, we find
general assertions of the limited monarchy which the crown has
in spiritual matters, and of the powers which the true ministry
derive from Christ independently of kings, however kings may
be appealed to to allow the open exercise of their power, we have
all that we can fairly expect on such a subject. Great indeed is
the debt we owe to the Reformers; and if there be some flaws in
such men, we should not found arguments upon those flaws;
neither because they may occasionally have yielded too much to
kingly authority, should we exclaim, "_All_ is the king's."

However, to return to the chief point we have considered,
that is, the _Divine Institution of Episcopacy as maintained by the
Reformers_, we think enough has been said to weaken the assertions of Mr. Macaulay. It only remains to offer Mr. Harington
our hearty thanks for his able and successful publication on this
matter.

ART. IV.—1. *Poems.*   *By* ELIZABETH BARRETT BROWNING.
New edition.   In 2 vols.   London: Chapman and Hall. 1850.

2. *The Prophecy of Balaam, The Queen's Choice, and other Poems.*
By HELEN LOWE.   London: Murray.

3. *Zareefa, a Tale; and other Poems.*   *By the Author of "Cepha-*
lus and Procris," &c.   London: Pickering.

FEMALE Poetry! this scarcely seems to us, ungallant as we
are, a delightful theme, or a glorious memory; for is it not,
generally speaking, mawkish, lackadaisical, and tedious?   To
us, at least, it is.   Look at the "Literary Souvenir," or
"Book of Beauty," if you want to see the kind of thing we
mean: what people denominate poetry of the affections.   Soft,
mellifluous strains, in which some one generally religious thought
is kept for the last verse; this kind of climax being repeated a
thousand times, with a more than wearisome uniformity.   Think
of the endless twaddle perpetrated by L. E. L., with here and
there something like a fresh flower peeping forth from amongst
her sere and withered blossoms.   That unhappy woman inflicted
an almost irreparable injury on English literature, on English
poetry at least; one from which the latter has taken many years
to recover.   She succeeded, supported, encouraged, and puffed as
she was by silly and ignorant critics, in persuading the general
public to identify poetry and mawkishness as one and the same
thing; to regard the strains of the lyre as naturally and necessarily morbid, and frightfully sentimental; and, consequently,
only adapted to the taste of very young gentlemen and ladies, and
exceedingly mischievous for *them.*   We know her unhappy fate, and
have mourned over it, and have thereby been induced to keep silence
for a time; but the truth must be told at last.   She was one of
the most utter nuisances the literature of the nineteenth century has been afflicted with!   Here and there she really struck
out a poetic thought, though it was almost always marred in the
delivery; and some few of her shorter strains, for instance, the
illustrations of modern pictures (we may mention "the Combat,"
by Etty), have some real power and sweetness: but, O! the
ocean of morbid common-place in which swim these waifs:—the
wretched, intolerably wretched, versification, the bad rhymes, the
careless grammar, the unpardonable profanation of the good and
the beautiful!   Consider this one fact.—This woman undertook

for years to fill a large annual with nothing but her poetry, in illustration of certain prints to be furnished her, whatever they might be! Now this fact alone expresses far more than any condemnation of ours could do. What a vista of dreary, morbid, boundless common-place does this disclose to us! And contemporary criticism could applaud, could think this *annual* undertaking perfectly natural, and rather sublime.

We repeat, that poetry has suffered amongst us from nothing more than from this unhallowed desecration. It became for a long time a valueless drug in the market. The very fact that L. E. L. did possess natural powers only rendered their exertion the more fatal to our poetic literature. The existence of and the praise lavished on this wordy trash formed one great barrier to the rising fame of Tennyson; and has impressed the majority of those now living with a conviction, not to be shaken, that English poets of the present day are second-rate, and little worthy of attention.

Mrs. Hemans was less sickening; and yet, looking over her vague, dreamy, wordy compositions, we almost feel inclined to recal that more favourable verdict. Here is a tiresome, mellifluous sweetness, an almost total absence of thought, a superabundance of morbid feeling always welling forth. But we admit that there is gentleness, and sometimes fancy, and even poetry also, to set off against all these defects.

There are moods in which certain of Mrs. Hemans's strains are dear to us, as they are perhaps to many of our readers: only not too many at a time! Then there was another of this class, a Miss Jewsbury. To be sure she has passed away, and it may seem unkind to revive her memory: yet in all "Affection's Gifts," and " Friendship's Keepsakes," you will be sure to find one or two of her vague wandering—melodies we cannot call them, unless slow, dull, autumn breezes, whining through a keyhole, deserve that appellation. Always the same leafless gloom, amidst which, here and there, a little pale, frightened flower, colourless and marred, may perk its head up, and yield you a sickly smile, and smile itself to death again!

We do not wish to upbraid more of these doleful lady-singers, and truly their number is countless. "Breezes sigh," they may answer us, "why should not we? rain-drops weep, why are tears denied us? night mourns, why should we be gay! True, there is heaven above: when we go thither, we will sing more gladly with the angels!" Now, this is a very pretty lady-poetess's speech: only, unfortunately, she would have condemned us to listen to as many stanzas of eight lines each, as there are thoughts or rather fancies in our answer: any one of the class in question could do it, and their compositions would be as like as two T's; a little better or a little worse to be sure, as far as rhyme and language are concerned, but all "so very sweet," "so charming really." Well, is this a true count, or is it not? Do we exaggerate? Now, all poetesses are *not* of this order and calibre, witness the two names at the head of this article. Besides, there is Mrs. Southey, of whom we take shame to ourselves for knowing so little; but what we do know has seemed to us of sterling quality; and, again, there is Mary Howitt, some of whose sweet, fresh, cheerful strains are really pure, as the dewdrops of the morn, not like the tears of an autumn mist: and, no doubt, there are others who ought to be mentioned (we beg any lady poetess who reads this, and has published, to take for granted she is included amongst the number), and still one general verdict must stand against the lady-singers. We know not whether there is essentially or necessarily an absence of concentration in female thought: judging from many novels we have seen, and many letters also, we should say, No! The memory of Miss Edgeworth only forbids the thought. Women are not necessarily or usually thus morbid in their ordinary talk: were they so, they would by no means be the queens of creation we consider them. It is only *female poetry* which is thus deficient in healthfulness, cheerfulness, and sound sense. With regard to the latter quality, it is our mature opinion that women are usually more sensible than men: but you certainly would not guess it from their poetry, where they seem to think it *necessary* to be weak and foolish. Of course this dictum is to be taken with a due degree of allowance for its sweepingness.

Foreign poetesses are not a whit better than English; think of Madame Desbordes-Valmont (we think that is the way she spells her name), think of her pitiful wails and lamentations, "Mes Pleurs" and "Mes Larmes" innumerable, enough to fill an ocean. As for Germany's songstresses, though she has several, they are all unknown to fame, save "Betty Paoli," whom we admire greatly, and should rank upon a level with Mrs. Browning and Miss Lowe, for artistic power; that is, we recognise her's as a kindred spirit with those of Germany's greatest bards, one who may justly claim equality with them; but then we have always called her "the female Byron," so sad is she, so bitter, so painfully passionate; nevertheless, she is great. We recommend Betty Paoli's poems to the study of every lover of German poetry; they are pure and noble artistic creations, earnest-hearted and earnest-minded, and above all, *not diffuse* (wonderful to relate); her words rarely or never outrun the thoughts they represent.

Still, in every country, female poetry *is* doleful or morbid, and generally speaking it is weak and diffuse, and therefore, as we said at starting, it does not present a too delightful theme.

But it is far otherwise with the strains of Elizabeth Barrett Browning and Helen Lowe, who, though widely different, are both true poets; not *poetesses only*; each taking a high rank amongst her bardic peers, and one which, if we mistake not, she is destined long to keep. We cannot aver that either is wholly free from that shade or tinge of morbid sorrow from which no female poetess has ever yet escaped; but in neither of them is this the predominant feature: it rather forms the background in both instances (if we may consider their poetry as two great master-pieces by some illustrious artist), from which the main subject stands out in bold and bright relief, commanding our hearty admiration. As a lyric *poet*, Mrs. Browning takes high rank among the bards of England: there are few to surpass her; perhaps none in her especial beauties,—in the combination of romantic wildness with deep, true tenderness and most singular power. And so, again, Miss Lowe need not fear comparison with great dramatists: in her works there is little or no display of passion; all is calm, concentrated power, fixed energy of thought, a certain reserve of greatness. This latter lady has not yet been acknowledged, we believe, as she should and must be, though the "Quarterly" hymned her praises after its own fashion some years ago: and this is not wonderful, for her powers do not dazzle; there is little to startle or amaze, and, though there is much to thrill the thoughtful, there are few appeals to tears. "The Prophecy of Balaam" is, in our estimation—and we speak advisedly—one of the grandest dramatic poems in existence. Once read by one who is capable of reflection, it can never be forgotten: it is based on eternal truth, and its power is only deeper and more real from the total absence of effort. All is grand, stately, and yet beautiful, like some fixed marble statue: only *here* there is life in the veins; a heart throbs beneath the marble, —"it could arise and walk!" What wonder that contemporary criticism should neglect such a work? The old adage applies as ever:—the boys pick up the shining pebbles by the sea-shore, but they cast the pearls away. Then, for "The Queen's Choice," what sweet, calm, happy grace and plaintive mournfulness breathe from this drama! If we compare it with the successful plays of the day (and we are willing to acknowledge the occasional power and pathos of "Marston", despite his abominable taste, and the stage-cleverness of Lovel), we feel that we are passing at once from the world of false to that of true art,—from fiction to reality. Even on the stage, adequately represented, "The Queen's Choice" would excite a profound sensation ; but our voice cannot reach managers ; and if it could, wrapt in their comfortable mantle of stolidity, they would turn a deaf ear to our assertions.

But to our more general theme :—Mrs. Browning is not exclusively lyric, nor Miss Lowe dramatic ; for the former's " Drama of Exile" is an exquisite work of its kind, and some of Miss Lowe's poems, though we do not like them as well as her plays, have much real merit, merit of a quiet and somewhat sombre character, like the beauties of an autumn twilight, sinking down on a fair landscape, fringed with dark and leafy woods. We cannot hope to do justice to both of these ladies, or perhaps to either of them, on the present occasion : perhaps we have acted wrongly in stringing their names together.

Mrs. Browning may well feel that she had a right to an article for herself alone, as much as her great poet-husband, to whom we strove to do tardy justice but lately. He and she are kindred spirits ; and yet there is vast difference between them. His genius is essentially, we might almost say exclusively, dramatic. The simplest line that falls from him, no matter in what shape, is a strong dramatic utterance. He has an instinctive knowledge of the hearts of men, a power of identifying himself with the passions of others, and of realising them in their most fiery outbursts, making them his own. Thus far he is impulsive, *most* impulsive, *dramatically* so; but there his impulse, comparatively, ends : free lyric power is *not* his characteristic. A contemporary has said this but lately, and it is true : yet, it is not from lack of impulsive power that Browning fails here ; nay, he does not fail, for he never makes the attempt : he is too *exclusively* dramatic, as we have said. His earnestness of passion forbids all lyrical redundancies. It is utterly false that —as the same critic asserts, as it is not unfashionable to say,— he is devoid of *beauty.* He has the highest beauty, the highest grace : witness " Paracelsus," " Pippa Passes," " Colombe's Birthday." But he never seeks beauty for beauty's sake : his aim is the reality of passion, good or bad : if beauty is consistent with the truth, then it will be certain to be there : but the passion may so arrest your sight as to blind your eyes to the beauty ! your heart is too strongly appealed to, to allow of your stopping to admire !—A mere love of words for their own sake, this he does not seem to possess. Now a true lyric poet must ! He sings because he loves singing : true, he must have something to sing about, but this need not be much : the nightingale sings, no doubt, of the beauty of the early spring, but not over distinctly. Now Mrs. Browning is oftentimes possessed with the fine lyrical " afflatus," the *passion of song*, and pours herself forth in verse. This is what Browning seldom or never does, in the same sense or way; yet he is not a *made* poet, but a *born* one: it is his instinct to be dramatic, "voilà tout!" Both he and Mrs. Browning feel intensely: he thinks perhaps most deeply, yet she is a thinker too: both have a wild imagination and a potent fancy: he has a genuine vein of humour; she has a pleasant, genial, meditative lofty strain, such as inspired her "Wine of Cyprus." Upon the whole, we think Browning's the higher and the master spirit; her's the more tender, and the more musical also.

But to the volumes before us, which we must deal with, we fear, very summarily. "The Drama of Exile" is a fervid and yet a sacred strain. At the gate of Paradise, where Milton left our first parents, the spirit of the poetess has met them, has listened to their wails of fond regret, and recorded their first wandering out into the sterile earth, thenceforth to yield man bread by the sweat of his brow. It is a grand and a solemn composition; somewhat too diffuse perhaps, and shadowy, and mixing up ideal conceptions, abstract ideas personified, such as the Spirits of the Earth and of the Creatures, with real actual sentient beings, in a manner we can scarcely approve. This, unintentionally, gives an unreal effect to much that would be otherwise very beautiful, and even holy. And even if we admit of these twain impersonations of the powers of nature, what shall we say to those shadows of shadows, the signs of the Zodiac—vast spectral forms representing these signs being made to form a circle round the exile wanderers? We do not see the meaning of this; and we are sure that its effect is unhappy. Again, we must blame the almost ludicrous and hopeless pertinacity with which the chief of fallen angels is represented as troubling those with his presence who incessantly request him " to go." There is something even comic in this, and we beg Mrs. Browning to believe that we do not make the remark irreverently; the opening discourse between Gabriel and Lucifer is almost entirely, on the former's part, a series of first commands, and then entreaties, to the latter to retire: it is obvious that Gabriel should not be made to speak so forcibly at first, if he has no power to enforce his commands; and his entering into long reasonings afterwards, on the same theme, is a token of weakness we should not have expected from an angel. We almost fear we are waxing irreverent, which it is certainly far from our intention to be, firmly as we believe in angelic agency, and strongly as we desire to do honour to those blessed spirits which stand in the presence of our God around the throne. This first scene, very fine in parts, is followed by an exquisite chorus of Eden spirits, while Adam and Eve fly across the track traced for them by the glare of the sword of fire, self-moved, for many miles along the waste.   There are seven lines in this chorus which seem to us particularly beautiful, and which recur oftentimes in their mournful sweetness, with slight changes, adapting them to the various singers, from the Spirits of the trees, rivers, flowers, &c.   Take the second of these :—

> " Fare ye well, farewell !
> The river-sounds, no longer audible,
>   Expire at Eden's door !
>   Each footstep of your treading
> Treads out some murmur which ye heard before :
>   Farewell ! the streams of Eden
>   Ye shall hear nevermore."

Is not that melancholy music, recalling the sweet songs of our own early childhood? Mark the lingering sweetness of the last two lines, where the cadence falls and rests.   There is a plaintive tenderness in this, rarely surpassed. The song of the Bird-spirit should be quoted, but we have no space for it.   Then follows a beautiful colloquy between Adam and Eve, held on the verge of the sword-glare: both characters are nobly conceived. We find no trace of selfishness in what falls from either of them; only the love of God seems no longer to tenant their hearts; intense love of each other has taken its place.   We have not space to go through the drama *seriatim;* it is grand throughout.   To our mind it is very questionable whether Lucifer should be represented as fraught with love for any thing, even for his own morning-star. Scripture represents hate and scorn as his essence, and in these consist his enmity to God.   However, the song of the Morning-Star to Lucifer is exceedingly wild and glowing; we regret that we have not space to enrich our pages with it; all the lyrics introduced in this poem are noble; but most intense, perhaps, is the power displayed in that song of the Earth-spirits, when they curse our first parents for having brought the curse on them (p. 59).   Its wildness is great, but is exceeded by its power:—

> " And we scorn you ! There's no pardon
>   Which can lean to you aright.
> When your bodies take the guerdon
>   Of the death-curse in our sight,
> *Then the bee that hummeth lowest shall transcend you :*
>   *Then ye shall not move an eyelid,*
>   *Though the stars look down your eyes ;*
>   *And the earth, which ye defiled,*
>   *She shall show you to the skies,—*
> ' *Lo! these kings of ours—who sought to comprehend you!* '

" *First Spirit.*
" And the elements shall boldly
    All your dust to dust constrain ;
Unresistedly and coldly,
    I will smite you with my rain !
From the slowest of my frosts is no receding.

" *Second Spirit.*
" And my little worm, appointed
    To assume a royal part,
He shall reign, crowned and anointed,
    O'er the noble human heart !
Give him counsel against losing of that Eden ! "

What a magnificent rhythm for scorn and irony ! The final apparition of our Lord is calmly and grandly treated. Altogether, the " Drama of Exile" is a great, though somewhat sad, creation : it is like the eyrie of the eagle, built high and near the stars, but rather cold and lonely. We cannot speak as favourably of " The Seraphim," also dramatic in its form, and, upon the whole, only an ambitious failure : it should have been excluded from the volumes before us. Its " Part the First," is peculiarly meaningless ; in which all the myriads of the angel-host having departed to gaze on *the Crucifixion*, two only, the interlocutors, Ador and Zerah, remain at the gate of heaven, also intending to follow their brethren, but stopping in the first instance for the bare purpose of talk-talk-talk, as dreary as it is meaningless. We are sorry to speak thus harshly, but the theme of the Crucifixion is too awful and too blessed not to have forbidden such a desecration as this, however unintentional. The whole poem labours under a painful sense of unreality, and that in treating of the greatest of all realities. There is an irreverence to our feelings in the stage-directions, so to speak, respecting the shut heavenly gate, which shocked us even at starting. The everlasting gates, which rolled aside when He, our Lord, ascended to His glory, were not " a gate :" rather were they intervening spheres, or worlds of darkness and of majesty. Does not Mrs. Browning feel that the glories of heaven are too great for her earthly grasp ? that it far rather becomes her on such a subject to tremble and adore ? Let her pardon our frankness ; but we confess this poem (if so we must call it, where we see few poetic sparks from first to last) shocks us, and forms, in our judgment, a most unworthy sequel to her " Drama of Exile !" As critics, and as Christians, *we entreat* that " The Seraphim " may be removed from the next edition !

The translation of " Prometheus," which follows, has great merit ; but we do not wholly like it. It displays Mrs. Browning's

usual power, especially towards the close, as in the mad song of
" Io ;" but Prometheus's complaints are rather too rhetorically
rendered, without sufficient dramatic earnestness. Pass we to
to the lyrics. First come two long strains, both noble, yet not
amongst our favourites. "A Vision of Poets" reminds us of
Tennyson's "Two Voices;" but it is far less thoughtful and
more indistinct. It is emphatically a vision, and possesses only
visionary beauties ; and yet it is neither devoid of sublimity nor
tenderness of heart. We object to what *seems* suggested by
some expressions,—that every great poet must be unhappy ; that
he must be earnest, we believe. The portraits of the poets,
drawn with a few bold lines, are sometimes very striking. Take,
for instance,—

> " Here, Homer, with the broad suspense
> Of thunderous brows, and lips intense,
> *With garrulous god-innocence.*"

Or again,

> " Hesiod old,
> Who, somewhat blind and deaf and cold,
> *Cared most for gods and bulls.*"

Or,

> " And Ossian, dimly seen or guessed :
> *Once counted greater than the rest,*
> *When mountain-winds blew out his vest.*"

Or, once more,

> " And Goethe—with that reaching eye,
> His soul reached out from, far and high,
> *And fell from inner entity.*"

How true of that sublimest of egotists, who became so objective at last as to be no longer a human being ; who from very
selfishness lost self ! There is beauty and majesty in this long
poem, but we cannot moralise on its bearings. Pass we to the
companion " Poet's Vow," which we like not much. It is
poetically executed indeed, but sadly unreal. The hero gives up
earthly happiness and a loving bride from mere unnatural misanthropy. He will not be happy, since so many of his fellow-men
are not ; and so shuts himself up, and lives and dies, useless to
himself and others, a blot upon the face of nature. Such a song
as this is like a picture of the desert : the leagues on leagues of
weary sand may lie in the broiling sun before us, as white, as
sterile, and as hideous as on the desert's self, but where was the
good of painting them ? If there ever *were* such a misanthrope,
surely it would have been better to leave him " to perish in his
self-contempt." Now follows one of the wildest romances in
the English, or in any tongue, but it is also most beautiful.

The title is the " Romaunt of Margret." It is a weird tale of woe and spectral horror ; but how wonderfully told ! and the clinging faith of the heroine through her terrific trial endears the poem to our hearts. We shall not quote it, or quote from it, but refer our readers to the volume. This, however, we may say : it is like some wild forest-scene at midnight, with just one break in the dark round of trees, where the silvery moon shines through, sadly, palely, and sweetly, while a woodland-brooklet murmurs by. Had Mrs. Browning written this alone, she had earned our most earnest admiration. " Isabel's Child " is less perfect in its execution, we think ; but very beautiful in conception. A mother, by her earnest prayers, (such prayers have power !) has prevailed on God to spare her infant, assailed by deadly fever ; but as she is keeping watch over the reviving babe a strange apparition chances : it looks upon her with thoughtful eyes, through which gleams a spirit in maturity, and it finds a voice and speaks, imploring no longer to be stayed from the blessed joys of heaven. At morn the nurse finds the child dead on the mother's knee, and that mother blesses God for having taken away her darling.—Then come the Sonnets, which, generally speaking, are very fine. Let us be pardoned for suggesting that the first, " The Soul's Expression," is a little, a very little, too self-asserting ! But we pass that by. There is great power in these sonnets ; a concentration of thought and expression, of which ordinary lady-poetesses could form no conception in their dreams. Perhaps we should cite one.—

> " I tell you, hopeless grief is passionless.
> That only men, incredulous of despair,
> Half-taught in anguish, through the midnight air,
> Beat upward to God's throne in loud access
> Of shrieking and reproach. Full desertness
> In souls, as countries, lieth silent-bare
> Under the blenching vertical eye-glare
> Of the absolute heav'ns. Deep-hearted man, express
> Grief for thy dead in silence like to death ;
> Most like a monumental statue set
> In everlasting watch and moveless woe,
> Till itself crumble to the dust beneath.
> Touch it : the marble eyelids are not wet :
> If it could weep, it could arise and go."

We thought of naming the more singularly beautiful sonnets, but there are so many beautiful that we must refrain. We pass to the second volume. Here come all our prime favourites, which we are unable to dwell on now as we should wish. Here is " the Romaunt of the Page," sad and sweet : may not blue-

bells ring out such music to fairy ears when the summer-winds
pass over them! Yet, no; there is too much of gloom and sorrow here: rather may the elfs of the woods list such wild strains,
sung to them by autumn breezes rustling the green leaves of the
old oak-tree. Then comes the magnificent "Onora, or Lay
of the Brown Rosary," as it is entitled. We should like to
tell the story of this last; but we may not. A good and
gentle girl, who abandons heaven to keep her life! Her lover is
returning from the wars, yet she must die, unless she make her
unhallowed compact: and she makes it; and her little brother
suspects the terrible truth; and at the altar her lover——but no,
we will tell no more. Only let us say, never was wilder, sweeter
ballad sung or said! And for the second part, where Onora is
sleeping, and the angels dare not draw too nigh her, since she
has forsaken God, and the evil spirit bids her yield her good
dream, in which she wanders with her dead father through the
summer fields—What say you to this, reader our's!—

> "*Evil Spirit in a Nun's garb by the bed.*
>
> "Forbear that dream! forbear that dream! too near to heaven it
> leaned.
>
> > "*Onora in sleep.*
>
> "Nay, leave me this—but only this! 'tis but a dream, sweet fiend!
>
> > "*Evil Spirit.*
>
> "It is a *thought.*
>
> > "*Onora in sleep.*
>
> "A sleeping thought—most innocent of good—
> It doth the Devil no harm, sweet fiend! it cannot, if it would.
> I say in it no holy hymn,—I do no holy work,
> I scarcely hear the Sabbath-bell that chimeth from the kirk.
>
> > "*Evil Spirit.*
>
> "Forbear that dream—forbear that dream!
>
> > "*Onora in sleep.*
>
> "Nay, let me *dream* at least!
> That far-off bell, it may be took for viol at a feast—
> I only walk among the fields, beneath the autumn-sun,
> With my dead father, hand in hand, as I have often done.
>
>   *   *   *   *   *
>
> > "*Evil Spirit.*
>
> "Thou shalt do something harder still.—Stand up where thou dost
> stand,
> Among the fields of dream land, with thy father hand in hand,
> And clear and slow, repeat the vow,—declare its cause and kind,
> Which, not to break in sleep or wake, thou bearest on thy mind.
>
> > "*Onora in sleep.*
>
> "I bear a vow of wicked kind, a vow for mournful cause:
> vowed it deep, I vowed it strong—the spirits laughed applause:

The spirits trailed, along the pines, low laughter like a breeze,.
While, high atween their swinging tops, the stars appeared to freeze.

" Evil Spirit.

" More calm and free,—speak out to me, why such a vow was made.

" Onora in sleep.

" Because that God decreed my death, and I shrank back afraid.—
Have patience, O dead father mine ! I did not fear to die ;
I wish I were a young dead child, and had thy company !
I wish I lay beside thy feet, a buried three-year child,
And wearing only a kiss of thine, upon my lips that smiled !

We break off abruptly, where it seems sacrilege to abbreviate ;
every word is so beautiful. We shall not tell the issue. Then
follows the " Rhyme of the Duchess May," most exquisite and
withal most powerful ; " The Romance of the Swan's Nest," with
a kind of innocent infantine beauty ; " Bertha in the Lane," very
sad, but still sweeter ; " Lady Geraldine's Courtship," most noble,
with a mighty sweep of verse, and a corresponding grandeur of
feeling ; the wild passionate outcry of " the Runaway Slave ;" the
deeply-pathetic " Cry of the Children," never surpassed, and not
to be surpassed for lyrical freedom, and exceeding tenderness, and
still more exceeding power. We quote one verse ; it is the factory
children who are speaking : (we trust they are saved now:)—

" ' True,' say the young children, ' it may happen
      That we die before our time.
Little Alice died last year—the grave is shapen
      Like a snowball, in the rime.
We looked into the pit prepared to take her—
      Was no room for any work in the close clay :
From the sleep wherein she lieth none will wake her.
      Crying, ' Get up, little Alice ! it is day.'

If you listen by that grave, in sun and shower,
      With your ear down, little Alice never cries !—
Could we see her face, be sure we should not know her,
      For the smile has time for growing in her eyes,—
And merry go her moments, lulled and stilled in
      The shroud, by the kirk-chime !
' It is good when it happens,' say the children,
      ' That we die before our time.' "

Was there ever keener pathos ? And one more verse :—

" For, all day the wheels are droning, turning,—
      Their wind comes in our faces,—
Till our hearts turn,—our hand, with pulses burning,
      And the walls turn in their places—

> *Turns the sky in the high window blank and reeling—*
>   *Turns the long light that droppeth down the wall—*
> *Turn the black flies that crawl along the ceiling—*
>   *All are turning, all the day, and we with all.—*
> And all day, the iron wheels are droning;
>   And sometimes we could pray,
> 'O ye wheels,' (breaking out in a mad moaning,)
>   Stop! be silent for to-day!"

We have not even space to enumerate our favourites : " The Fourfold Aspect;" " The Virgin Mary to the Child Jesus;" " To Plush my Dog," sweet and tender, and cheerful-hearted; " The Cry of the Human," passionate and powerful; " The Sleep," mournfully holy; " Cowper's Grave," sublime in its deep tender pathos; " The Lady's Yes," " A Woman's Short-comings," " A Man's Requirement," all three happy strains; one of a higher order, " A Year's Spinning," rarely surpassed or equalled for its expression of deep grief; " Catarina to Camoens," most tender of canzonets; and " Sonnets from the Portuguese," the veil of which it behoves not us to rend away; suffice it to say, " they are beautiful exceedingly." And that is *all :* all we can at least find a space for, and enough, in our judgment, to crown a lady Queen of Song; and that *is* Mrs. Browning. Certainly she is not a faultless poet ; she deals too much in frequent double endings, some of which are strained and forced; she is apt to play Greek freaks with her English tongue; she is sometimes too weird; rarely too sentimental. And now, that we are about to leave her, we feel as if we had said nothing about her; nothing truly to the point. But necessity commands, and so we leave the theme.

Still more unjustly are we constrained to treat Miss Lowe; we had hoped to linger over some of her calm stately lyrics also; so self-possessed in their sadness. There is " Zareefa," which gives its name to one volume, thus characteristically opening :—

> "When I consider time's unfolded page,
>   Where man his soul hath graven on each line,
> And note his wrongs in every clime and age
>   To woman, *yet how evermore doth shine*
>   *Her spirit over his, almost divine,*
> When most reviled in goodness eminent;
> I marvel much, and grieve, yet rest content."

There is a slap in the face for male critics at starting! but we will not be rebuffed. The tale is a very graceful, though a sad one, most gracefully told. In strong contrast with Mrs. Browning, Miss Lowe is rarely outwardly impulsive; she gives you, mainly, results of past thoughts and emotions; does not fling her feelings forth in the very act of composition. Indeed, there is a peculiar reserve about Miss Lowe's poetry in this respect, which distinguishes it from almost all other poetry written by ladies; but we are already lingering. The song, "Peace, O peace!" is a peculiarly characteristic strain, and very beautiful; we must cite it:—

> "Peace, O peace! the air is still;
>   Sighs are spent, and sorrow dead:
> Look around and take thy fill
>   Of quiet joys around thee spread.—
> No! the past no power can break:
> Still its mournful memories wake,
>   Every care is vain.
> Not till throbs thy pulse no more,
> Till life's fever'd dream be o'er,—
>   Shalt thou rest from pain."

"The Burden of Britain," "Threnodia," "An Evening Ode," "The Vallisneria," "Milton," "The Departed," and other lyrics in this volume have a calm still beauty of their own.

But these lyrics are far inferior, in our judgment, to the two dramas we meant to have dilated on. First, that charming "Queen's Choice," so utterly void of all *aim* at power, and yet so full of the thing itself: the deepest seas are apt to be most still: but here this image is out of place, for this drama is sunny on the whole, and leaves a happy memory behind it. Yet more highly do we think of "the Prophecy of Balaam;" all the characters introduced are strongly individualized,—the mean and selfish, and yet strong-souled prophet, emblem of genius misapplied; the reckless warrior-youth, Zuriel; the wise and holy Thirza; the gentle Milcah; the fierce Prince of Midian; all are painted with a master-hand: all are truth itself. Here is power, and yielding tenderness, and subtle wisdom; strong sound sense being perhaps, after all, the most marked characteristic. We must conclude: some day or other, we trust yet, to do more justice to Miss Lowe; we cannot think the theme exhausted; indeed it has scarcely been touched.

One circumstance is very remarkable, connected with our subject; it is, that both these poetesses in their spheres, so far greater in the boldness and grandeur of their thoughts than their sister-singers,—are comparatively *learned!* both are good Greek scholars; Miss Lowe, we believe, is well read in Hebrew also:—has this aided to impart or sustain the grandeur which they do most undoubtedly possess? Can we draw an argument from this fact for making our young maidens classical adepts? We would not do that; but the fact, we think, should be recorded.

ART. V.—*The Works of* JOHN JEWEL, *D.D. Bishop of Salisbury.
Edited by* RICHARD WILLIAM JELF, *D.D., Canon of Christ
Church, and Principal of King's College, London ; formerly
Fellow of Oriel College.* In 8 vols.   8vo.   Oxford: at the
University Press.

> WAS never man yet surely at debate
> With Sapience, but that he did repent.
> Who that is ruled by her high estate
> Of his after witte, shall never be shent ;
> With walles sure she doth him fortifie
> When it is nede to resist a contrarie.

So spake one of our old poets—Stephen Hawes, to wit—in his
" Pastime of Pleasure ;" and the latter words especially might be
applied to the labours of Jewel against the Romanist, and those
of Hooker against the Puritan,—contraries which had to be resisted, but at the same time contraries, which have met more
than once " in the whirligig of time," as South showed in his
bitter but marvellous sermons, which are the standard of English
prose, and which will meet again—QUOD AVORTAT DEUS !

But of this elsewhere, and at another time, if necessary.   Meanwhile we have a word to say of John Jewel, sometime Bishop of
Salisbury, who has been as fortunate in his Editor, as his pupil,
Mr. Richard Hooker, the author (as honest Izaak Walton styles
him) of those learned books of the laws of Ecclesiastical Polity.
All readers of Jewel and Hooker have to thank Dr. Jelf and Mr.
Keble for their labours ; and it is fair to say, that the labour of
editing works like these is immense, known only to those who
have quarried in the same mines.   As relates to the work at the
head of this article, we have only to refer our readers to the " List
of Authors and Editions," at the commencement of the first
volume—from which and from the foot notes they may draw a
tolerably fair opinion of the quiet and patient research requisite
to put forth to the world works like to those of the author of the
" Apology for the Church of England," and the " Defence of it
against Harding."

In the remarks which follow, we purpose to lay before our

readers the contents of this edition, together with such particulars as are to be gleaned from the Editor's Preface, a sketch of Jewel's Life, and, lastly, a few observations (warnings, if others please to construe them as such) upon Roman Catholic aggressions, and upon that implicit faith of theirs in unscriptural articles, as Lord Brooke says,

" Binding men's minde with Earth's imposture line².'"

First, however, we beg to quote from a cotemporary,—as our researches have only tended to strengthen our own opinions—what is there said of this excellent Bishop by the divines of the seventeenth century—by those who " were honourable men in their generation," and fully competent to form an unbiassed judgment.

" One Father of our Church has been reserved, that he may be spoken of separately—spoken of, as these his brethren always spoke of him, turning aside whenever mention of him occurred, as if their pious humility would not allow them to pass without some token of gratitude and reverence, the recognized defender of the Church of England, Bishop Jewel. If one fault be enough to blot out a whole 'angelic life,' a life spent in the service of the Church, between his chapel and his study ; if some hasty words are to condemn as unworthy of confidence the man who set an example to all, that in treating of holy things he did not ' set abroad in print twenty lines, till he had studied twenty years'—then we may presume to speak lightly of Bishop Jewel. But not so the true and grateful and humble-minded sons of the Church of England. They will reverence him with Hooker, as ' the worthiest divine that Christendom hath bred for the space of some hundreds of years ;' with Bilson, as ' that learned Father ;' with Laud, as ' that painful, learned, and reverend prelate ;' with Usher, as 'ὁ Μακαρίτης Juellus, ille nunquam satis laudatus episcopus ;' with Bancroft, as ' a man to be accounted of as his name doth import, and so esteemed, not only in England, but with all the learned men beyond the seas, that ever knew him or saw his writings ;' with Morton, as ' that admirable doctor in God's Church,' ' that godly Bishop,' ' whose name we acknowledge to be most honourable in the Church of Christ ;' with Montagu, as ' that Jewel of England ;' with Cosen, as ' that worthy and reverend prelate ' (præstantissimus præsul) ;' with James, as ' one of the most precious and peerless Jewels of these later times, for learning, knowledge, judgment, honesty, and industry ;' with Bramhall, as ' that learned prelate ;' with Carlton, as ' Master Jewel, the reverend Bishop of Salisbury, for piety and learning, the mirror of his time ;' with Hall, as ' that precious

² Treatise of Human Learning.

Jewel of England,' ' whom moderate spirits may well hear,' ' who alone
with all judicious men will out-weigh ten thousand Separatists;' with
Field, as ' that worthy bishop;' with the Martyr Charles, as ' one whose
memory he much reverenced, though he never thought him infallible;'
with Heylin, as ' that most reverend and learned prelate, of whom I
would not have you think, but that I hold as reverend an opinion, as
you or any other, be he who he will;' with Godwin, as ' felicissimæ
memoriæ;' with Bishop Bull, as ' clarissimus;' with Sancroft, as ' our
reverend and learned Jewel;' with Stillingfleet, as ' that incomparable
Bishop, ' that great light and ornament of his Church, whose memory
is preserved to this day with due veneration in all Protestant Churches;'
and lastly, with Whitgift, as ' that so notable a Bishop, so learned a
man, so stout a champion of true religion, so painful a prelate;' ' pardon me,' he concluded, as we will conclude also, ' though I speak
somewhat earnestly; it is in behalf of a Jewel that is contemned and
defaced—he is at rest, and not here to answer for himself.　Thus have
I answered in this behalf, who, both in this and other like controversies,
might have been a great stay to this Church of England, if we had been
worthy of him.　But whilst he lived, and especially after his notable
and most profitable travails, he received the same reward of ungrateful
tongues, that other men be exercised with, and all must look for that
will do their duty[3].'"

So spake the men of renown, famous in the congregation; and
when Jewel's fair name has been lightly spoken of, we think it an
act of justice to record their testimony in our pages.　He whose
Lyrics cleared Thebes of the imputation of intellectual cloudiness,
said,—

> ὁ μέγας κίνδυ-
> νος ἄναλκιν οὐ φῶ-
> τα λαμβάνει—"

and such was Jewel, in a time of great need, and when the doctrines of the Papacy were paraded as " the truth that is in Jesus."
Great was the popularity of his writings then; nor, as Dr. Jelf
expresses himself in his Preface, " has the popularity of his writings been confined to a few readers in his own generation, or to
the solitary student of after times.　His works have been the
armoury from which polemical divines have borrowed their keenest
weapons against the errors and corruptions of the Church of
Rome: and much of that wholesome dread of Popery, which is so
deeply implanted in the English mind, might be traced perhaps
to the copy of Bishop Jewel's works, which the foresight of Archbishop Bancroft chained side by side with Erasmus's Commen-

---

[3] Quart. Rev. vol. lxix. pp. 476, 477.

taries, for the instruction of the people, on a reading-desk provided for that especial purpose, in the side-aisle of many a parish church." Long may this wholesome dread of Popery remain! May we be enabled still to baffle the attempts of subtle foes within our own boundaries, as well as the open attacks of the Romanist from without! Say what men may—reason as they like—the spirit of the Seven Hills is the same spirit still—not laid, not cast out, not exorcised! It is with Rome as with individuals, whether Romanists or others,

'Ανδρὸς χαρακτὴρ ἐκ λόγου γνωρίζεται.

But to turn to the Editor's Preface, wherein, after having informed us that he commenced his laborious work of correction "in conformity with a wish of the late Professor Burton"—(one out of many amongst the wise suggestions of that excellent man), —and after having dwelt upon the many imperfections of all preceding editions, which, in this instance, is most true; he proceeds to inform us of what are the contents and arrangement of the Edition before us. But, as this portion of the Preface is valuable, because it gives the real dates of what are called the *two controversies*, we propose laying it before our readers at length.

" The first six volumes of the present edition are equally divided between the two great controversies, in their natural order; the first division comprising the Challenge, the Short Reply to Cole, and the Replie to Mr. Harding's Answer; the second, the Apology of the Church of England, and the Defence of the Apology, The two last volumes contain the Commentary on the Thessalonians, the Sermons, the Treatises on the Scriptures and on the Sacraments, the Letters, and other miscellaneous writings. A copious general Index is subjoined," —the reader will find it most useful—instead of the two inconvenient and imperfect ones, which preceded the " Replie" and the " Defence," in former Editions.

" It must be borne in mind, that *two controversies*, or rather, phases of the same controversy, between Bishop Jewel and Harding, though begun at different periods, were going on simultaneously, and in such a manner as nearly to alternate with each other. The Sermon at Paul's Cross, embodying the Challenge, had been first delivered in 1559; it was answered by Harding in 1563, and defended by Bishop Jewel in 1565. In the interval between the Challenge and the Answer, 'The Apologie of the Church of England' appeared (1562); the 'Confutation' of which by Harding was published in 1565, four months earlier than the publication of the 'Replie.' The first edition of the 'Defence of the Apologie' came out in 1567, and was followed, in 1568, by Harding's 'Detection of sundry foul errors, &c.;' which produced Jewel's second and final edition of the Defence, as the close of the controversy, in 1569[4]. This necessarily complicated statement will be elucidated by the following table, in which the works on either side are detailed in chronological order, those appertaining to the Challenge being printed in Italics :—

1. *Challenge Sermon at Paul's Cross.*
   —————— first delivered, Nov. 26, 1559.
   —————— repeated at Court, March 17, 1560, N. S.
   —————— again at Court, March 31, 1560.
   —————— imprinted at London by John Day, May 18, 1560.
2. *Dr. Cole's first Letter.* March 18, 1560.
   Correspondence between Cole and Jewel, imprinted May 18, 1560.
3. Apologia Ecclesiæ Anglicanæ. 1562. (See note).
   First Translation (attributed to Abp. Parker). 1562.
4. *Harding's 'Answere to M. Iuelles Challenge.'* 1563.
5. Lady's Bacon's Translation of ' the Apologie.' 1564.
6. Harding's Confutation of a book entituled ' An Apologie of the Church of England.' 1565.
7. *Jewel's Replie to Harding's Answere.* Aug. 1565.
8. *Harding's ' Rejoindre to M. Jewel's Replie.'* Aug. 31, 1566.
9. *Another Rejoindre to M. Jewel's Replie against the Sacrifice of the Mass.* 1567.
10. Jewel's Defence of the Apologie. Oct. 27, 1567.
11. Harding's ' Detection of sundry foul errors uttered by M. Jewel in his Defence of the Apologie.' 1568.
12. Second and enlarged edition of the ' Defence,' exposing also ' the Detection.' Dec. 1569.

It is to the neglect of the foregoing chronological distribution, that the confusion is to be described, which has prevailed even amongst well-informed writers, respecting the different portions of Jewel's works. It is nothing uncommon to find the controversy on the Challenge confounded with that on the Apology; and this want of discrimination has been greatly encouraged in the editions hitherto most accessible, viz., those of 1609 and 1611, by the singular perversity of bookbinders in placing the Defence of the Apology next after the Reply to Cole and the Sermon at Paul's Cross; an arrangement so general, even in copies still appearing in their original bindings, as almost to lead to the conclusion that the works were printed in that order. It may be here stated, that these two impressions, although so closely resembling each other as to give rise to the suspicion of a re-issue with a new title-page, appear, on a closer inspection, to have been independent editions, as is indicated by the fact, that the headings and contents of the pages, and even the errors of the press, do not always correspond ; and that of the two editions the later is the less correct. It has been already intimated, that the first of these editions was issued by command of Archbishop

[4] " This is a sufficient answer to a writer under the name of Walsingham, who, amongst other gross and cunning falsehooods, has stated that the Detection was the last that passed between the two disputants."

Bancroft; and it is not unlikely that, the first impression being found insufficient for the supply of the parishes, the second was added in a form as nearly resembling it as possible. It must be owned that, considering the haste with which these reprints were prepared at a particular juncture, they represent correctly the text of the last edition revised by the author; and though of no value as critical editions, were yet sufficient to serve the immediate purpose which the Archbishop had in view—the general instruction of the people."—*Editor's Preface,* pp. xii.—xvi.

All readers of Jewel's works, we think, will thank us for this lengthy extract. On referring to the book itself, they will find the statements well supported by the foot-notes; and although, at first sight, we fancied we had reason for some hesitation, a cautious examination of the whole subject has led us to acquiesce entirely in the Editor's views. No reader of Jewel, with the old folios before him, but· must have been sorely puzzled, and have numbered himself, possibly, with the Dulhead and the Dulman family! But, as Bellanima says in Thomas Nabbe's Microcosmus, "All lets are now removed."

It did not fall in with the Editor's views, either to write a life of Jewel, or to enter into any detailed examination of undeserved aspersions which have been thrown out against him, whether in or near his own days, or since the Romanist has unguardedly taken up the stop-gap of Developement[s] in preference to the old Palladium of Christian antiquity, which he so long claimed as his

---

[s] It may be observed in a note, that "Developement" has been more than once hinted at in days gone by; but, the ground being dangerous, was given up as untenable. Verily, there is nothing new under the sun! The following passage occurs in *Doctor Cole's Answer to Certain Parcels of the Second Letters, &c.* 8 *Aprilis, anno* 1560. "The Church of Christ hath his childhood, his manhood, and his hoar hairs: and, as that that is meet for a man in one age, is unmeet in another, so were many things meet, requisite, and necessary in the Primitive Church, which in our days were like to do more harm than good." Vol. i. p. 64. To this Jewel makes answer in his reply, "Ye know that ye yourself, in your last answer, granted me that the examples of the Primitive Church are on our side, and therefore ye rest upon another point, that the Primitive Church in the Apostles' and old Doctors' time, *was but an infant and babe in comparison of your Church of Rome,*" &c. &c. Ibid. p. 85. In these and like instances, we see the germ, at least, of Developement, on which we had purposed saying something, had our limits admitted. Our readers are, no doubt, well aware, that the subject is taken up in America, and that the dangerous ground has been pointed out in "Brownson's Quarterly Review." We may refer to a former Number for some very well-timed and grave remarks on this head. We suspect that very many are already sorry that they took to hallooing before they were out of the wood!

Τὸ καυχᾶσθαι παρὰ καιρὸν
μανίαισιν ὑποκρέκει.

Pind. Olymp. ix. 58.

Something of this "Developement" may be observed in the works of Cardinal Cusanus. See the Defence, &c. pt. vi. c. 12. divis. 4. Of this Edition, vol. vi. p. 395—408.

own indefeasible right, in accordance with which all his faith was moulded, and the denial of which at Paul's Cross scared him almost from his propriety. " Imperfectly done," says Dr. Jelf, it " would be unjust to the author, and injurious to the cause of truth, to fulfil it adequately, even if it were in the Editor's power, would swell the present edition to an inconsistent size." One point, however, he has thought it right to dwell upon, and this we cannot do better than give in his own words.

"The only exception which demands notice, as taken against the tone and supposed tendency of some passages in Bishop Jewel's works, is not that of the open or secret adherent of the papacy—for to such an one the plain, straightforward, English strength of the author's polemics must ever be extremely distasteful—but that of some faithful and dutiful disciple of the Church of England, who, without intending to disparage one of her great lights, may be sensible of a difference between the theological school of Jewel, and that of others whose names are identified with the sober defence of Church government, in the succeeding generation. But even admitting such difference to exist, this were but another instance of the Divine protection extended over our Church, that it has pleased God, by raising up at sundry times special instruments for his service, to check at one period the innovations of Rome, at another the no less dangerous and uncatholic novelties of Geneva. And it is our wisdom, surely, no less than our duty, to accept and enjoy the different portion of our rich inheritance of theology. It may be that Bishop Jewel did not foresee the rise and fatal effects of Puritanism : he was engaged in defending one wing of the army of the faith, and he did not see clearly what was passing on the other ; yet none of his acts or of the principles of his warfare were inconsistent with its subsequent defence by such an one as his great successor, the author of the ' Ecclesiastical Polity.' Nor ought it to be forgotten, that if he spoke contemptuously of Rome, it was from a clear appreciation of the primitive model, which she had forgotten or debased, and out of a singlehearted zeal for God's glory, which she had dishonoured and profaned : that while his intimate relations with foreign reformers, who had been his benefactors in exile, inclined him to speak hopefully and respectfully of their churches, as then constituted, he was by no means blind to the superior blessings, in respect of government and apostolic order, as well as of worship, which Divine Providence had vouchsafed to England : that he desired nothing more or less than the general restoration of catholic faith and practice, such as the Reformation in England had been providentially designed to secure ; and finally, that, if in some matters, as, for instance, with respect to the habits, we may concede his argument to have been wrong, his conduct in his practical and official relations to the Church was dutiful and right."—*Editor's Preface,* pp. xxii.—xxiv.

Certainly, in the works of those two great theologians,—Jewel and Hooker,—we have the very best armoury wherefrom to draw our weapons against the Romanist and the Puritan; and as long as we refer to them wisely, and without taking needless exceptions, the Papacy must quail, and the grand Mufti of Geneva (as South pointedly calls the Calvinist) give way; — provided we do not forget "that there is an Anti-Calvinism which is as much at variance with the doctrines of the Church of England and with Scripture, as the decrees of the Synod of Dort can be [*]." The point to be remembered is, that neither Jewel nor Hooker are infallible; and, as regards individuals, SIMON PURE is not a whit the less cunning in his way than that august individual, POPE SELF. Had this been well considered, many a ponderous tome of polemics might have been comprised in an epitome. Who, on reading the conventional harshness of controversial language,—its angular points and its asperities,—whether Harding's or others', is not willing to exclaim, with the wise poet,—

"And in the best, where science multiplies,
Man multiplies with it his care of minde:
While in the worst, these swelling harmonies,
Like bellowes, fill unquiet hearts with winde,
To blow the flame of malice, question, strife,
Both into publicke states and private life?"

No doubt "wrangling Elenchs" will be necessary as long as the world lasts, and truths must be defended; but those things which make for peace leave no sting behind. And how, in the midst of controversy, must the amiable Jewel have longed for this peace! How did his heart burn within him when all was hubbub and confusion! "*Nur die Seele giebt den Masstab der Leiden!*" and, that he felt it, any one who reads his sermons will readily conclude. These the reader will find in the seventh volume of the present edition; and they are well worth a most careful perusal. All of them, it is true, are posthumous[7], but there is every external evidence of their genuineness. Such passages as the following, illustrative of what has been said relative to Jewel's desire for peaceful worship, are to be met with in the whole series;—little oases, as it were, when all around was tempestuous and sandy controversy and strife:—

Σὺν δ᾽Ἔρις, οὐρανόμηκες ἀναστήσασα κάρηνον.

"By how much the heavens are greater than the earth, and God is more excellent than a creature, so much doth the knowledge of God and his true worship pass all worldly blessing, and all other felicity that can be devised under the sun. For what knoweth he, which knoweth not

---

[*] Short's Sketch of the History of the Church of England, § 557.
[7] See Introductory Note, vol. vii. p. 434.

God? or what worshippeth he, which worshippeth not God? He that worshippeth not God, hath not the comfort of God : but he that hath God, and knoweth God, and serveth God, hath a sure help and defence in all assays. Let us therefore be glad and rejoice, let us witness our joy, and sing unto the Lord a new song. Let us kindle in our hearts the fire of the love of God, and of our neighbour, and let the flame thereof break out to the glory of God. Let us deck the altars of our hearts with the flourishing branches of virtue and good works : let us sacrifice and kill our lusts and affections. In this manner, if we shew our thankfulness towards God, we shall hinder the wretched purpose of them that wish the restoring of Jericho, we shall see the land of God's promise, and enter into his rest."—Vol. vii. p. 367.

It is in such passages as these, sparkling as they do—*Per quæstionum vincula, Per syllogismos plectiles* [*]—that we behold Jewel —as he would have been had he only had to visit from house to house, and to teach publicly in parochial ministration ;—even as he did, many times and oft, when the diocese of Sarum was as blessed with his presence, as was Mona with that of the sainted Wilson ;

" Good men,
Who long served Heaven with praise, the world with prayer [*]!"

It was the former who said that, " like as the errors of the clock be revealed by the constant course of the sun, even so the errors of the Church are revealed by the everlasting and infallible Word of God ;" the life and writings of the latter bore testimony to the same great truth. Indeed, the "*buccina Romæ*" never seems to have disturbed his quiet. In these his inestimable sermons when he touches upon Romish errors, he takes the high ground he knew was his own, and that of his Church, and he departs from it never. The parallel to Jewel's words occurs in his Maxims of Piety and of Christianity. " By the Holy Scriptures every man may see what he is, what he is not, and what he ought to be. Let us therefore meditate upon them, consult them as our rule, and make them evermore our pattern."

But, impressed with the great value of Bishop Wilson's writings, we are wandering from our subject. Having, then, expressed our sentiments clearly as to the importance of Dr. Jelf's labours on Bishop Jewel's Works, we will now attempt a sketch of that excellent Prelate's Life, whose name will be held in honour as long as there is " any virtue, and if there be any praise." It will be hardly necessary to say, that all the several Lives of Jewel are before us, in one shape or another ; and that we draw from each what seems to our purpose ; but we cannot avoid stating, that the one by

---

[*] Prudentius.   [*] Gondibert.

Mr. Le Bas is one to be put into the hands of all, being written in the kindliest spirit, and with the soundest Church views.

JOHN JEWEL, one of ten children, sons and daughters, was born at Buden, in the parish of Berinber, that is Berryn-arbor, or Barinarber, as Godwin writes it, in the county of Devon, the 22nd of May, 1522. His father, though not a rich man, was a man still of some means, and of an ancient family. His mother's maiden name, whose memory he so fondly cherished, was Bellamy; and it was from his uncle John Bellamy, the incumbent of Hampton, that he received his earliest instruction in the rudiments of grammar. From thence he was removed successively to Bramton, Southmolton, and Barnstaple, where he was placed under the care of Walter Bowen, a pious and excellent man, whose name he never ceased to hold in honour. From his earliest years, Jewel seems to have been a promising youth, and it was natural enough that the advantage of a university education should be sought for him. Hear what Master Featley, "now" (in Fuller's days) "at rest with God," says of him, in the Abel Redivivus: "If ever any was happy in the imposition of names in those whom they dedicate to God at the Font, certainly they were who christened this holy and learned man *John Jewel;* for his rare and admirable parts, and both natural and supernatural gifts, were every way corresponding to his gracious and precious name. According to his Christian name *John,* signifying *grace,* he was a *gracious* instrument of Christ, to reform the gold of the sanctuary, which through the negligence or impiety of later times became dim and drossy with superstition. And according to his surname he was a rich *Jewel,* consisting of many *gems,* shining as well in his life, as his incomparable writings extant, almost in all languages."

Almost all who wrote or spoke of him when his fame became great, were in the habit of alluding to this play on his name; and doubtless he was a jewel to his parents, who, as was customary in those days, contrived to get him admitted at Merton College, Oxford, before he had completed his thirteenth year. A century later we may recollect that Milton was only fifteen when he entered on his residence at Christ's College, Cambridge[10]. Jewel's

---

[10] It is well known that Milton is said to have been whipped at Cambridge. Without entering on the disputed point, we subjoin his own lines to his friend Charles Deodate.

> Jam nec arundiferum mihi cura revisere Camum,
> Nec dudum vetiti me laris angit amor,
> Nuda nec arva placent, umbrasque negantia molles,
> Quam male Phœbicolis convenit ille locus!
> *Nec duri libet usque minas perferre Magistri*
> *Cæteraque ingenio non subeunda meo.*
> ELEG. i. 114.

[Humphrey

first tutor was Master Peter Burrey, afterwards preferred to the vicarage of Croydon—one, it is said, who was neither a person of great learning, nor much addicted to the Reformation. Happily he did not remain his pupil for long, but was made over to Mr. John Parkhurst, then a Fellow of Merton, afterwards promoted to the Rectory of Cleve, in the Diocese of Gloucester, and eventually the excellent Bishop of Norwich. In Featley's Abridgment of Humphrey's Life, prefixed to the folio edition of Jewel's Works, the exchange of pupils and the well-known subsequent exclamation of Parkhurst, is thus alluded to:—" But because (Master Burrey of Merton) had a post-master before (Divine Providence so disposing), by him he was recommended to Master Parkhurst, who, wanting one, most willingly received him into his tuition, and the place which he had in his gift; and being desirous, together with all wholesome learning, to season his tender years with pure religion, took occasion often before him, to dispute with Master Burrey about controverted points, and, intending to compare the translations of Coverdale and Tindal, gave him Tindal's translation to read, himself overlooking Coverdale. In which collation of translation Jewel oft smiled, which Master Parkhurst observing, and marvelling that in those years he could note barbarisms in the Vulgate translation, brake into these words: SURELY, PAUL'S CROSS WILL ONE DAY RING OF THIS BOY ! prophesying, as it were, of that noble sermon of his at Paul's Cross, which gave such a blow to the superstitions of the Popish Mass, or rather to the whole mass of Popish superstition, that all the defenders of them have ever since staggered."

It was whilst he was a member of Merton College that he contracted that lameness which never left him, owing to a cold " he had caught him at Witney," or, as others say, " at a place called Croxham, in a lower chamber, where the College removed in the time of the plague in Oxford." Here, no doubt, as when in Oxford, he persevered in that intense study to which he had given himself up—from four in the morning till ten at night—and this, added to the damp of the chamber, is sufficient to account for his weakly constitution and his early death. None can overcharge the powers of the mind or the body with impunity, and those who will live two days in one, however goodly the intent, should bear in mind, that their days, which are but a span long, must, in the ordinary course of things, be contracted further still,—a point this which it were wise in parents to impress upon their sons, in these

---

Humphrey gives the story of " *Edvardus Annus*" (Edward Year's) whipping for his verses against the Superstition of the Mass. See Jewel's Life, p. 77, and Fuller's *Church Hist.* book viii. cent. xvi.

days when knowledge, after its sort, is increased. Ἄπονον ἔλαβον χάρμα παῦροί τινες—but there is a moderation in every thing, and the wise and the thoughtful will see to it !

Four years Jewel remained at Merton, and then, by the procurement of one Mr. Slater, and Master Burrey and Parkhurst, his two tutors, he migrated to Corpus, the 19th of August, 1539, in his seventeenth year. He would seem to have been a prodigy in attainments, young as he was; and at Corpus there was a better opening for him to distinguish himself, which, as it is very well known, he did, notwithstanding the envy of his equals, who often suppressed his ingenious exercises, and read others that were more like their own. The next year he proceeded to the degree of Bachelor of Arts, the 20th of October, 1540. And now commenced his excellent labours as Tutor of his College, in which office no one ever comported himself with greater exactitude, whether we look to the instruction of himself or others.

"Never," said that excellent man and prince of pædagogues, the late Bishop Butler, some time Master of Shrewsbury, but now with God, " do I presume to come in to instruct, without having carefully looked over the lesson on hand." And so thought Jewel, and first he taught himself, and then others. Like Erasmus and Bishop Sanderson, he was a devoted lover of Horace ; and every one who reads the Apologia Ecclesiæ Anglicanæ, will see at once how dear Cicero was to him, and how his style is imbued with the purest Latinity. " At the same time," adds Mr. Le Bas, " the practice of Demosthenes suggested to him the discipline by which he might best prepare himself for public speaking ; only that the woods of Shotover, instead of the ocean-beach, were the scenes of his solitary exercises in declamation. By labours and arts like these, he acquired the habit of expressing himself with facility and force when called upon by sudden occasions, and with copiousness and dignity when time for preparation was allowed. History and philosophy, logic and mathematics, all were concluded in his scheme of study ; and the whole of his vast acquisitions were made, eventually, subservient to the mistress of all sciences, Theology." In fact, even now, his thoughts were toward that great end and aim of his life; for, says Master Featley, "being but a Bachelor, he sifted much of the flour of St. Augustine with divine aphorisms." And his life was in accordance with his studies, so that even Master Moren, Dean of the College, and no friend to the Reformation, was constrained to say, " I should love thee, Jewel, if thou wert not a Zuinglian. In thy faith I hold thee a heretic, but surely in thy life thou art an angel. Thou art very good and honest, but a Lutheran !"

Meanwhile, though but a Bachelor, the Rhetoric Lecture was conferred upon him by his college, and both as private tutor and lecturer, he gained no common name. It is delightful to read the eulogium passed on him in the former capacity by Humphrey —his devotedness to his pupils—his entire love for them—his care of their morals and studies.

Such was his manner of teaching, such the persuasion with which he spoke, that even his own teachers became his hearers. Hear again what Master Featley says, in Humphrey's words and his own. The Rhetoric Lecture " he read with such facility and felicity, that all his auditors perceived that he spake *potius ex arte*, than *de arte Rhetoricâ*, rather from an excellent faculty that he had in that *flexanimous* art, than of the art itself. Neither were these his lectures only *strewed* as it were with flowers of rhetoric, but richly fraught with all variety of human learning; which drew many auditors to him from other colleges, and among them his tutor Master Parkhurst, afterwards Bishop of Norwich, who took great delight to behold the *sparkling* of that *diamond*, which himself had first *pointed;* and he could not contain his joy, but vented it on the sudden in this extempore disticon :—

> " Olim discipulus mihi, care Juelle, fuisti ;
> Nunc ero discipulus, te renuente, tuus."

It was during this period that, amongst others, Mr. Antony Parkhurst became his pupil, though the connection was almost immediately dissolved, owing to the influence of one Robert Serles, Vicar of St. Peter's. It is alluded to here, because the reason assigned was, Jewel's teaching of Greek, which shows that the words of Erasmus respecting Germany were still true, more or less, as regarded England, *Literas Græcas attigisse hæresis erat!* " It was worth notice (says Knight in his Life of Colet[1]) that Standish, who is a bitter enemy to Erasmus, in his declamation against him, styles him *Græculus iste;* which was a long time after the phrase for an heretic, or one falling under the suspicion of heretical pravity. And for this very reason, those very few who understood Greek were afraid to teach it, lest they should be thought to propagate heresy." The readers of that old morality " Lusty Juventus," will observe how the learning of the new Gospellers, as those were called who favoured the Reformation, was

---

[1] We would recommend to all students this Life, and his Life of Erasmus, together with that most interesting piece of biography, Churton's Life of Alexander Nowel, the " Piscator Hominum," and friend of learning.

every where spoken against. A well-known character there utters this complaint :—

> " Oh, oh, ful wel I know the cause
> That my estimacion doth thus decay ;
> The olde peple would beleve stil in my lawes,
> But the yonger sort lead them a contrary waye ;
> They will not beleve, they playnly saye
> In old traditions and made by men,
> But they wyll lyve as the Scripture teacheth them."

The 9th of February, 1544, Jewel commenced Master of Arts, the charges of his degree being borne by his old tutor and constant friend, Mr. John Parkhurst, of Cleve. Nor was this the only instance of his liberality, for it appears that he was in the habit of inviting him there twice or thrice in a year. "And one time above the rest," says the current story, " coming into his chamber in the morning, when he was to go back to the university, he seized upon his and his companion's purses, saying, ' What money, I wonder, have these miserable and beggarly Oxfordians?' and, finding them pitifully lean and empty, stuffed them with money, till they became both fat and weighty."

When Jewel entered into Holy Orders has not been ascertained, nor yet the time of his election to a fellowship at Corpus, where he spent the quietest period of his life. "Halcyonian days," as one of his biographers calls them. But, all this while, he was clearly looked upon as the friend of the Reformation ; and, his receipts as Fellow not being enough to help him to promote the great work he had in hand, he received sundry sums from the well-wishers of the cause, which, though now they may appear small, were at that time considerable. Amongst these benefactors were Mr. Curtop, formerly a Fellow of Corpus, but now Canon of Christ Church, who allowed him forty shillings per annum ; and Mr. Chambers, who put at his disposal six pounds yearly, out of the fund collected in London for "the benefit of indigent scholars, professing the doctrines of the Reformation." This allowance was a specific one, and such as received it were obliged to sign certain articles condemnatory of Romish tenets, such as the Supremacy of the Pope, the doctrine of Transubstantiation, the Sacrifice of the Mass, Justification by Works, Purgatory, Praying to the Saints, Worship of Images, Religious Service in a tongue unknown to the people, and, lastly, the refusal of the Sacramental Cup to the Laity. Jewel, of course, must have signed them. In fact, we know from the Life of Humphrey, that he was pitched upon by Mr. Chambers, to advocate the principles of the Reformed faith ; and the substance of his discourse is extant, and henceforward he becomes prominent as a leader, as well literary as theological.

And now it was that a turning point in his life is to be reckoned—his intimacy with Peter Martyr, who, within two years after the accession of Edward VI., was made Professor of Divinity at Oxford. Nothing could be more close than the intimacy that subsisted between these two earnest men, and it continued to the last. Meanwhile Jewel became one of his constant hearers;—"observed," says Master Featley, "his art, copied out his sermons and lectures, was his notary in that tumultuous disputation in the Divinity School, with Cheddey, Tresham, Morgan, and others about the Divine Presence." As is well known, he was skilled in short hand, and it was this same skill which enabled him to take down the famous debate of Cranmer and Ridley, which preceded their condemnation in 1554.

It appears from Wood's Fasti Oxon. that Jewel was admitted B.D. in 1551 ; and it was upon this occasion that he preached the celebrated Latin Sermon on 1 Pet. iv. 11, *Siquis loquitur, quasi sermones Dei, &c.*[1] His license for preaching was granted this year, as may be seen in Strype ; and he now accepted the living of Sunningwell, that he might labour in his vocation, and do the work of an Evangelist amid a country congregation. Here, notwithstanding his lameness, he went on foot at least once every fortnight to preach, continuing to do the same both privately in college and in the university pulpit. In the university and out of it, Jewel had now a name ; and shortly after, in 1552, on Dr. Morvent, the President of Corpus, being summoned to appear before the Privy Council, the government of the college was committed by their order to Jewel during the six weeks of his absence.

Meanwhile, "unseen, like mandrakes wedded under ground," dark days had been gathering. Edward the Sixth, whether, as one says, he went or was sent to his grave, was no more. July 6, 1553, Mary, surnamed the Bloody, began her reign ; and a sore time was it for those unto whom the title of Gospellers attached. And such was Jewel. Nay, more, his place was in the van. Accordingly, he had to stand the first shock ; and almost immediately we find him ejected from his college as the follower of Peter Martyr,—as a preacher of heresy,—as ordained uncanonically,—as a despiser of the Mass.

> " The secret grudge and malice will remain :
> The fire not quench'd, but kept in close restraint,
> Fed still within, breaks forth with double flame[2]."

[1] See vol. viii. p. 221, &c. of this edition.   [2] Gorboduc.

And so it was. The ornament of his College must quit. Yet, those who ejected him, through fear and interest combined, could not deny him the last opportunity of addressing those whom he had taught so faithfully; and most affecting is the address contained in the pages of his earliest biographer, and which, did our space admit, we should most willingly extract[4]; but we must content ourselves with the concluding words: *Valeant studia, valeant hæc tecta, valeat sedes cultissima literarum, valeat jucundissimus conspectus vestri, valete juvenes, valete socii, valete fratres, valete oculi mei, valete omnes, valete!* "Thus," says Master Featley, "he burst out of his speech, and his hearers burst out into tears."

It has been remarked as strange, that Jewel should not at once have perceived, that neither Oxford nor even England were now safe places for him. The probabilities are, that he was fully alive to the fact; but that, being told to depart, he put it off as long as possible. In the interim he was received within the walls of Bradgates Hall, since the chancellorship of the Earl of Pembroke better known by the name of Pembroke College, his own body bitterly repenting the course they had taken, and for which indeed they were twitted by Dr. Wright, Archdeacon of Oxford, who, upon their boasting that their College alone, among all the university, had kept their Church treasure and ornaments entire, closely laid up in their vestry, admitted indeed the fact, but added, "that they had thrown away wilfully one ornament and great treasure, more precious than any of them," obviously alluding to Jewel. The university likewise, even at such a conjuncture, was of the same opinion, for they deputed him, Gospeller as he was, to address a letter of congratulation to the Queen. There is no just cause to suppose, with Fuller (Book viii.), that this appointment was the work of his enemies. With some, no doubt, as hinted at before, secret grudge and malice had their resting-place, but the sense of the university at large was in his favour. Whether or not, Jewel acted wisely in penning the letter "warily, and in general terms." It might do good,—it could do no harm; and, as Fuller remarks, "all as yet were confident that the Queen would maintain the Protestant religion, according to her solemn promise to the gentry of Norfolk and Suffolk." We give the story of the great bell of Christ-Church in the old historian's words, which (although he draws all his statements from Humphrey) are quite characteristic.

"And because every one was accounted a truant in Popery who did

---

[4] The reader may see the substance of it in Wordsworth's Eccl. Biogr. vol. iii. p. 330, and in Le Bas, p. 21, 22.

not outrun the law, Dr. Tresham, an active Papist and a van-courier before authority, repaired the great bell in Christ-Church, which he new-named and baptized Mary ; and, whilst Mr. Jewel was reading the letter he had penned to Dr. Tresham for his approbation thereof, presently that bell tolled to Mass (a parenthesis which was not in the letter), and Tresham, breaking off his attention to what was written, exclaimed in a zealous ecstacy, ' Oh! sweet Mary, how musically, how melodiously doth she sound!' This bell then rung the knell for that time to the truth in Oxford, henceforward filled with Protestant tears and Popish triumphs."

We have before stated, that we believe Jewel to have been alive to the danger he was in ; and we need not wonder that he should have been, when the basilisk eye of Marshall, Dean of Christ Church, was upon him. Peter Martyr[5], it seems, had left, and the Dutch congregation in London had departed for Denmark. And so Jewel casts about for a friend ; and, in the midst of frost and snow, and crippled with lameness, he goes in search of his old benefactor and tutor, Dr. Parkhurst, of Cleve. Arrived there, he finds that he had fled. The Mass restored, there was no place of rest for him in Gloucestershire. And thus, weary and heart-sick, Jewel had to retrace his steps, and again we find him in Oxford. Subsequent to this visit, Jewel wrote two letters to his old friend, headed severally "*Juellus Parkhursto*," which are still extant, but without the date of the year[6], and expressing ignorance of his locality ; so that we have no means of knowing how they were transmitted, or how they came to hand. As Jewel acted with Gilbert Mounson as notary in behalf of Cranmer and Ridley during their Disputation at Oxford, the next sad incident in his life dates subsequently to April 1554. It scarcely needs to say that, what is here alluded to is, the joy of his enemies, THE JOY OF BACK-FRIENDS TO PROTESTANTISM, —his apostasy !

Without being able to give an explicit and definite date, it is enough to say, that no long time after this the Philistines were upon him, with the renegade Marshall at the head of them. Full sure, they had watched their time and opportunity, and when his body was weak and his mind harassed and distressed, like Cranmer's, there is sent by the inquisitors a bead-roll of Popish doc-

---

[5] Notwithstanding the virulency of Tresham, Peter Martyr contrived to find a place of refuge with Cranmer at Lambeth. As the public faith was pledged for his safety, even Gardiner hastened his departure, and he reached Strasburgh in safety on the 30th of October, 1553. Le Bas, p. 38. Wordsworth's Eccl. Biog. iii. p. 334.

[6] See vol. viii. pp. 108, 109, where they are reprinted from Strype. Dr. Jelf brackets the date as 1554, which we believe to be correct.

trines, to be subscribed by him upon pain of fire and fagot, and other grievous torture. Some taunt, it is likely, was uttered about his caligraphy, or this saddest of all playfully painful sentences had not been uttered : "*Have you a mind to see how well I can write ?*" Whereupon he took the pen and unwillingly and hastily wrote his name. Those who call to mind similar expressions, under different circumstances,—such as those of Anne Bullen, or Sir Thomas More—will know how to count the bitterness of sore distress with which they are uttered; and who recollects not how Hannibal's heart was wrung, after Zama's fight, and when he laughed aloud, and was reproved for it, how he made answer, —*Si, quemadmodum oris habitus cernitur oculis, sic et animus intus cerni posset, facile vobis adpareret, non læti, sed prope amentis malis cordis hunc, quem increpatis, risum esse* [f] *?*

> "Ah ! nought is pure. It cannot be denied
> That virtue still some tincture has of vice !"

Thus fell JOHN JEWEL, one of the tallest and most promising cedars in the infant reformed Church, and the Romanist rejoiced, and believed his retractation—not a whit ! And from that time to this the wolf in sheep's clothing has used his name as a by-word ! Even then scorn and derision, perhaps, overwhelmed the comfort of the pitiful ! At any rate, he must escape for his life; and, though we do not know exactly how long he remained in Oxford after his recantation, this we *do* know, that had he abided there one night more after the resolution to depart was taken, or had he gone the right way to London, the blood-hounds let slip by the turn-coat Marshall would have caught him. As it was, he was well-nigh lost, and, humanly speaking, owed his life to old Latimer's faithful servant, afterwards a minister of the Gospel,— Augustin Berner, a Switzer. By him he was found lying upon the ground, almost dead with vexation, weariness (for this lame man was forced to make his escape on foot), and cold ; and, setting him upon a horse, conveyed him to the Lady Ann Harcups, a widow, who entertained him for some time, and then sent him up to London, where he was in more safety. There, having been thrice obliged to change his lodgings, he remained, till, by the kindness of Sir Nicholas Throgmorton, a passage was procured for him across the seas. Further particulars are not at hand. It is enough to state that he arrived at Frankfort, the then refuge of the persecuted Reformers, in July or August 1555.

Reader ! art thou inclined to join in with the hunts-up (Shak-

[f] Liv. lib. xxx. c. 44.

speare, and Drayton in his Polyolbion, are our authority for the
term) that have endeavoured to cry down the name of this holy
man!   If so, we recommend thee, on thy knees, to offer up that
prayer of Cranmer's, which he devised for his own comfort, or ever
he was taken to the stake!   It will teach thee to be humble-
minded, and, when thou thinkest thou standest, to take heed of
falling!   Fuller's spirit, be sure, was rightly tempered when he
wrote : " Thus the most orient jewel on earth hath some flaws
therein.   To conceal this his fault had been partiality ; to excuse
it, flattery ; to defend it, impiety ; to insult over him, cruelty ; to
pity him, charity ; to admire God in permitting him, true devotion ; to be wary of ourselves in the like occasion, Christian discretion :" and that person of quality* who wrote Jewel's Life in
1685, and spoke of his works as being ' superannuated or neglected,' penned no better sentences than these : " It is an easy
thing for those that were never tried, to censure the frailty of those
that have truckled for some time under the shock of a mighty
temptation : but let such remember St. Paul's advice, ' *Let him
that standeth, take heed lest he fall*.'   This great man's fall shall
ever be my lesson, and, if this glittering jewel were thus clouded
and foiled, GOD BE MERCIFUL TO ME A SINNER !"
    To say, even though merely stating facts without imputing mo-
tives, that " Jewel was a staunch Protestant, when Protestantism
was in vogue ; in time of trial away went his Protestantism all
in a moment ; among kindred spirits, and in a calmer time, he
was a Protestant again ; and he died bishop of Salisbury*;" is but
nigri succus loliginis.   We estimate Jewel's character otherwise !

        " Non, siquid turbida Roma
    Elevet, accedas : examenve improbum in illâ
    Castiges trutinâ[1]."

    But it is time to follow Jewel to Frankfort—the refuge of the
Protestant fugitives.   And here the first thing we read of is, the
retractation of his subscription at St. Mary's, Oxford.   As he subscribed to the Articles publicly, so he renounced them publicly.
This, it is said, he did at the solicitation of Thomas Sampson, late
Dean of Chichester, and Mr. Chambers, whose name we have
referred to before ; and Humphrey, Strype, Le Bas, and others,
fall in with this view.   But Jewel himself, in his " Reply" to Cole,
who twitted him with the fact, says, " I have confessed it openly

---

    * This Life, from which we have drawn largely, is reprinted in Wordsworth,
Eccles. Biog. vol. iii. p. 307, &c. new ed.   The author is unknown.
    [9] The British Critic, No. lix. p. 14.
    [1] Pers. Sat. i. v.

and *unrequired* in the midst of the congregation[2]." The two statements are easily reconciled. Jewel might himself have *suggested* the course he took; and in this his friends would naturally back him. So or not,—on the very next Sunday after his arrival, as Master Featley abridges Humphrey, "he made an excellent sermon, and in the end of it openly confesses his fall, in these words : ' *It was my abject and cowardly mind and faint heart, that made my weake hand to commit this wickedness.*' Which, when he had brought forth with a gale of sighs from the bottom of the anguish of his soul, and had made humble supplication for pardon, first to Almighty God, whom he had offended, and afterwards to his Church, which he had scandalized ; no man was found in that great congregation who was not pricked with compunction, and wounded with compassion ; or who embraced him not ever after that sermon as a most dear brother, nay as an angel of God. So far was this saint of God from accounting sophistry any part of the science of salvation, or justifying any equivocating shifts, which are daily hatched in the school of Anti-christ." We give the words as they stand, not in the Abel Redivivus, but pre-fixed to the folio edition, 1611.

Jewel's abode at Frankfort was but for a little while. Peter Martyr, after his escape from England, had returned to his for-mer residence in Strasburg ; and no sooner did he learn that Jewel was safe, than he entreated him to come to him there. Jewel had, as we have seen, suffered for his intimacy with Peter Martyr ; and the latter had a grateful and a capacious heart, and the invitations " *to Argentine* " were pressing and frequent. The result was, that Jewel became his inmate, and the two friends were united once more in kindred pursuits. "There was at Strasburg," says Churton, " a college of English,"—(*in hoc lite-ralissimo Collegio*, are Humphrey's words)—" who had a common table, and devoted themselves to the pursuit of literature, with great harmony and great ardour. Jewel was here, and Nowel was here, and Poinet, Bishop of Rochester (afterwards of Win-chester), and Grindal and Sandys, afterwards successively Arch-bishops of York ; nor did the learned laymen, Sir John Cheke, Sir Richard Morison, Sir Peter Carew, Sir Thomas Worth, and others disdain to hear Peter Martyr expounding Aristotle's ethics and the Book of Judges[3]." Thus was passed the time of his sojourn at Frankfort ; and in Jewel we still behold the scribe who prepared Peter Martyr's Commentary on the book of Judges for the press.

[2] See vol. i. p. 99 of this edition. Strype's Eccl. Mem. vol. iii. pt. i. p. 231.
[3] Life of Nowel, p. 22, &c.

At this time a great man died at Zurich, Conrad Pellicanus, the Hebrew Professor there, next to Reuchlin considered the first Hebrew scholar in Germany Upon this the senate of the Ligurines sent for Peter Martyr to succeed him. The invitation was accepted, and he removed there, not without Jewel, the 13th of July, 1556. Here likewise, as at Strasburg, he was domesticated with his friend, and here also he found other sufferers. Tmongst them were John Parkhurst, Laurence Humfrey[4], his friend and earliest biographer, and James Pilkington, afterwards bishop of Durham. Humphrey extols the great hospitality and kindness of the magistrates of this town ; and it is well known that but for their liberality and the alms of the London merchants, through the procurement of Chambers, the exiles must have starved. Fitting is it that their names should be preserved as they have been ! But even this pittance was at length cut off through the intervention of Stephen Gardiner, who, on finding it out, declared that " he would in a short time make them eat their fingers' ends for hunger ! " Happily his power was not equal to his malice. Something, no doubt, still oozed out from England ; the *incredibilis humanitas* of the senate of the Ligurines supplied more ; and a friend was raised up in Christopher, Prince of Wittemberg, who invited many of them to him.

It has been supposed that Jewel made his journey to Padua during the period of his residence at Zurich. He alluded to his studying there at the commencement of the celebrated letter to Scipio, the Venetian senator, *de Concilio Tridentino*, in these words : " Scribis ad me familiariter pro eâ consuetudine, quæ inter nos semper summa fuit ex eo usque tempore, quo unà viximus Pataviæ, tu in Reipublicæ tuæ tractatione occupatus, ego in studiis literarum[5]." It seems most probable that the supposition is true ; but, if so, we must again suppose that Jewel had his purse replenished, whether by the generosity of the London merchants, or the Ligurines, or that of Peter Martyr. But it would not be consistent with the statement of Humphrey to consider his absence of long duration, as he states that Jewel remained with Peter Martyr at Zurich till the time of his return to England. We may observe here, that Dr. Jelf in his Preface decides in favour of the genuineness of the letter here alluded to, which leads him likewise to add :—

"The fact also of Jewel's sojourn at Padua has been called into question ; and an attempt has been made to show, from a comparison

---

[4] See Strype's Eccl. Mem. vol. iii. pt. i. 232. He was with the twelve original comers to Zurich. They lived " together in the house of Christopher Froscover's printer, and paid each for his ordinary."

[5] Vol. viii. p. 73 of this edition,

of dates, that there is no period during his exile which would admit of his visiting Italy at all. But the notices of his proceedings during those years are too scanty to justify any such conclusion; and it may well be believed that the 'good horse' which he gave to Richard Hooker,—the staff which had supported him in his wanderings through many parts of Germany,—would have carried him across the Alps, particularly when we consider that Padua was the university of his intimate friend and protector Peter Martyr."—p. xxviii.

Previous to Jewel's residence at Zurich, the exiles there had been addressed in consolatory letters both by Calvin and by Peter Martyr, which may be seen in Humphrey; but on his coming there he took upon himself to comfort and support them, by every means in his power. "And if," says Master Featley, "he heard any, more grievously than others, groaning under the burden of his affliction, and seeking to cast it off, he persuaded him to patience; admonishing him that he ought not to leap from the smoke into the fire, that we all ought to bear a part of Christ's cross, by whomsoever it be imposed, that now, when our brethren suffer extreme tortures in England, we must not look to live deliciously in banishment, shutting up all with that sweet close often repeated by him: *Hæc non durabunt ætatem: Bear a while, these things will not endure an age.*" These his words were listened to by the mourners then, and afterwards they looked upon them as "something like prophetic strain." The fact is, there was a general expectation that the revival of Popery in England, and its consequent cruelties, could not be of long duration; and, as we can see now clearly enough, its very supporters were bringing about that consummation so ardently desired by the exiles. The well-known story of Fox the Martyrologist's sermon told how earnestly they looked for the wish of their heart to be true! *Now was the time come,* said he, *for this their return into England, and he brought them that news by the commandment of God.* Rightly enough was he censured by the graver divines then present; but it so fell out, that Mary died the day before[*]!

Still, exiles though they were, they had their lives given them for a prey; and it might have been expected that their time would have been spent at least in religious peace, such as this world neither gives, nor taketh away. Alas! how little do we know the weakness of our nature! Let the time-honoured author of the Ecclesiastical Sketches speak of what was now to ensue.

> " Scattering, like birds escaped the fowler's net,
> Some seek with timely flight a foreign strand;
> Most happy, reassembled in a land

[*] The story occurs in John Fox's Life, by his son. It may be seen in the Eccl. Biog. vol. iii. p. 337. It was inserted on the authority of Bp. Aylmer, who heard it.

By dauntless Luther freed, could they forget
Their country's woes? But scarcely have they met,
Partners in faith, and brothers in distress,
Free to pour forth their common thankfulness,
Ere hope declines; their union is beset
With speculative notions rashly sown,
Whence thickly sprouting growth of poisonous weeds;
Their forms are broken staves; their passions steeds
That master them. How enviably blest
Is he who can, by help of grace, enthrone
The peace of God within his single breast!"

Differences, it is well known, now arose on the subject of ceremonies and Church discipline, which the exiles brought, not from
England, "but, like scattered seed, they received from the nature
of the place and soil where they were dispersed;" though it is
asserted by Heylin, that Wittingham, Williams, and Goodman,
the chief promoters of the movement at Frankfort, were Zwing-
lians before they left. Whether or not, from Frankfort the
epidemic spread to Zurich, and, in the stead of peace amongst
those whom sorrow should have bound the closer, there was dissension. The originator of this discord, which spread from
Geneva to Frankfort, and so onwards to other places, was that
great author of confusion, Mr. John Calvin, of whom Hooker,
whilst opposing him, declares: "for mine own part, I think him
incomparably the wisest man that ever the French church did
enjoy, since the hour it enjoyed him[']." Look where we will
amongst our great divines, and we shall find one and all admitting
his ability. South even, who saw the ruinous working out of his
principles, ending in Socinianism, and bringing in misrule, admits
it; coupling his name with Erasmus, Melanchthon, Politian, and
Budæus[*], names that stood out in the boldest relief as the mists
of ignorance and error gathered up. Admitting, however, his
great powers, and the value of his commentaries[*], where particular
doctrines do not interfere—it must be admitted that a greater
schismatic never rent the Church of Christ in latter days. To
which we may add, that wherever Low Church views, such as his,
are encouraged in high places or in low, there will be, as a necessary harvest, confusion and every evil work. Let those who wish
to see this fully propounded study the immortal Hooker!

['] Preface, c. ii. § 1. Origin of the New Discipline.
[*] See Sermons, vol. iii. p. 467. Of his anti-monarchical doctrine and assertions
he speaks at length in p. 544—546, dubbing him with the title of THE GRAND
MUFTI OF GENEVA, than which no happier one could have been devised.
[*] We have cautiously, and more than once over, examined the Archbishop of
Canterbury's "EXPOSITION" with Calvin's Harmony and Commentary, and none
would be more ready than his Grace to acknowledge his obligations.

Into this controversy our limits will not permit us to enter. Let it be enough to say that, as early as 1554, the exiles at Frankfort framed themselves a Liturgy and Order of Service, addressing likewise a letter to those scattered abroad in Strasburg, Zurich, Embden, and other places, and inviting them to come where "God's Providence had procured them a Church free from all *dregs of superstitious ceremonial.*" Their answer was, that they would adhere to "the order last taken in the Church of England" —and that they were "fully determined to admit and use no other." This reply, and others like, were of no avail; and the fray was only thickened by the evil counsel of John Knox, afterwards so well known as the "great incendiary of Scotland." Other letters now passed, and the men of Frankfort wrote to the men of Zurich an open defiance of the English formularies. Grindal and Chambers attempted in vain to rule the strife, sent from Strasburg for that purpose. Letters to that intent were equally unavailing, whilst Knox and Wittingham were at work in secret, and when the reply of Calvin, whom they had taken upon themselves to apply to, though it contained no virulence equal to theirs, yet described the Prayer Book as containing *multas tolerabiles ineptias.* Things continued pretty much in this state till the March of the following year, when Dr. Richard Cox entered Frankfort, drove Knox out, and re-settled the Liturgy there. All this, nevertheless, was of little avail, for although in the August following, "Fox, with some few others, went to Basil," the main body followed Knox and Goodman to Geneva, and chose them for their preachers ; under which ministry they rejected the whole frame and fabric of the Reformation made in England in King Edward's time, and conformed themselves wholly to the fashions of the Church of Geneva. *Hinc illæ lacrymæ!* Division of every sort and kind—lack of all charity and harmony—Socinianism, in its various phases—and, in due time, "THE GREAT REBELLION!" Those who sowed to the wind left the whirlwind to be reaped !

Meanwhile, as may be supposed, Jewel was no easy spectator of these sad divisions. His visit to Padua may have helped to divert his wearied spirit ; but, for the most part, his heart must have been rent to think how, every where, so to say, the exiles were devouring one another. That he made an open complaint against Knox we know, but few particulars have come down to us relative to the pains he took to still the storm. Residing with Peter Martyr, no doubt he had the best advice, and took the wisest course—allowance being made for his friend and benefactor's learning, to such alterations as he had probably[10] suggested in

---

[10] On this, perhaps, questionable point, see Dr. Cardwell's Preface to The Two Liturgies of Edw. VI. compared.

the Liturgy before he quitted England. " These small jarring
things," says Master Featley, "which have so much troubled the
sweet harmony of our Church, he then sought by all means to
put in tune, exhorting them, as brethren, to lay aside all strife and
emulation, especially about such small matters ; lest thereby they
should greatly offend the minds of all good men : which thing, he
said, they ought to have a principal care of." Sure we may be,
that such distraction ill suited Jewel's well-regulated mind.

> " His brest was hole withouten for to seen,
> But in his herte ay was the arwe kene!"

But happier and better days were now approaching, and the
exiles were to be free in body, though many a mental chain was
yet to warp their efficiency : " God," as Hooker writes, "whose
property is to strew his mercies then greatest when they are nearest to be utterly despaired of, caused, in the depth of discomfort and
darkness, a most glorious star to arise, and on her head settled
the crown, whom himself had kept as a lamb from the slaughter
of those bloody times ; that the experience of his goodness in her
own deliverance might cause her merciful disposition to take so
much the more delight in saving others whom the like necessity
should press[1]." Mary, in fact, was no more. On the 17th of
November, 1558, Elizabeth succeeded to the throne.

The news soon spread. In January, 1559, we find Jewel at
Strasburg, on his way to England ; for, in a letter addressed to
Peter Martyr, dated the 26th of that month, he tells him that
many had already reached him, and that " *reditum illorum reginæ
esse gratissimum, idque illam non obscurè præ se ferre*[2]." She had,
however, interdicted preaching, whether by Papist or Gospeller,
and, as we can see now, there was reason enough for her caution.
When Jewel arrived is not quite clear; but, as he dates his next letter
to Peter Martyr the 20th of March, it could not be long after; and
it was previous to that of his old friend and benefactor Parkhurst,
who, doubting the safety of Jewel's route, took another, and was
robbed by the way, thus giving Jewel the happy opportunity of
assisting him on his return. All, or nearly so, were in a bad
plight, as may be readily supposed, and more or less dependent

---

[1] See Eccl. Pol. book iv. xiv, 7. He is there taking a view of God's special providence over England since the Reformation. The praises lavished on Elizabeth
must be received *cum grano salis ;* but we are very far from being of the number of
those who take upon themselves to decry her. " The bright Occidental Star,"
to say the least, was a mighty Queen. Bp. Short throws out a wise hint, where he
says, " the first principles of toleration were then unknown, either in Church or
State ; but toleration is a plant of Protestant growth, and all true Christians may
join in the prayer, that her ' branches may cover the earth.'"—Short's Sketch, &c.
§ 443.

[2] See vol. vii. p. 109.

upon others. Jewel, we read, " was harboured, about three
months, with Nicholas Culverwel, a citizen, living (unless I mistake,
says Strype) in Thames-street: then, the Lord Williams of
Thame, being sick, sent for him, and with him he abode some
time[3]."

In the letter last alluded to, Jewel gives but a desponding account of the state of religion. The *Aposcopi*[4], i. e. the Romish
Bishops out of place, had not given way to the *Episcopi*, but were
throwing every impediment to the furtherance of the Reformation. The Queen, nevertheless, was proceeding cautiously and
wisely; not as Jewel saw then, but as we see now—and the great
fact in the letter is, that she had appointed a Disputation to be
held at Westminster, " with a view to the settlement of the main
points in debate between the Romanists and the Reformers." This
was to come off on the 1st of April; and on the 6th of that month
Jewel writes an account of it to his friend at Zurich. Those who
took part in it, and its results, are sufficiently well known, and
need not be recorded here. The reader will find an excellent extract in Le Bas' Life, who, on the recorded wish of Jewel, that
" once again (as the time would serve) there might be had a quiet
and sober Disputation," makes these very pertinent remarks: " In
expressing this opinion, Jewel must, surely, rather have consulted
the candour and integrity of his own nature, than his knowledge
of history, or his experience of mankind. For public disputations
on religious matters have seldom been found to terminate in any
thing but an aggravation of the embroilment."—We wish this
may be borne in mind, both as regards the Papistic and Puritanic
contest, whose dark forms are now looming in the offing[5]!

Jewel, meanwhile, kept up a constant correspondence with
Peter Martyr, hoping and desponding alternately. On the whole,
despite of massing, priests, and the little crucifix in the Queen's
chapel, the Reformation proceeded.

The next material incident in his life was, his appointment to
be a Commissioner in the general visitation of the dioceses, decided
upon in the Parliament which ended the 8th of May, 1559. His
commission bears date July 19th; and in his letter to Peter Martyr
of the 1st of August, he speaks like one just setting out: "*Alterum
jam pedem in terra habeo, alterum tunc sublatum in equum.*" His

[3] Strype's Annals, vol. i. pt. i. 192.
[4] See note by Dr. Jelf, vol. vii. p. 112. *Episcopi* is, however, used later in the same letter.
[5] " Unless we read amiss the signs of the times, that contest with the Church of Rome and with the Puritan, which has loomed in the offing these twenty years, is now taking a shape more definite, and day by day is drawing nigher and nigher." *Uncontroversial Preaching of the Parochial Clergy.* By JOHN WOOD WARTER, B.D. 1848.

destiny was to the West, through Reading, Abingdon, Gloucester, Bristol, Bath, Wells, Exeter, Cornwall, Dorset, and Salisbury: "and so it fell out very fitly," says Master Featley, "that he presented the first-born of these his labours in the Ministry, after his return, in Devonshire and parts adjacent, there first breaking the bread of life, where first he received the breath of life." It is in this letter that he speaks of the decided progress of the cause, though the Romanists, in their turn, were hoping that the present change *would not last an age*—as well as of the intent, on the Queen's part, of sending him as Bishop to Salisbury: "*Quod ego onus prorsus decrevi excutere.*" Speaking of himself, his words are, "*Ego minimus apostolorum.*" His having already preached at St. Paul's Cross, on the 18th of June, this year, was preparatory to his designation. On the 24th of that month, St. John Baptist's Day, the Latin Mass Book was abandoned, and the English Liturgy re-established.

> "St. John the Baptist's Day,
> Put the Pope away."

Three months of patient travel were consumed on his journey as Commissioner, and on the 2nd of November he again writes to Peter Martyr, informing him of his return—"*tandem tamen aliquando Londinum redii, confecto molestissimo itinere, confecto corpore.*" When we consider the lameness of Jewel, and that this was neither the age of roads, coaches, nor rails, we may be sure he wrote feelingly. The letter in question[6] contains a most interesting account of his labours, and of his success. Jewel was, in fact, just the man to fulfil his office well; for, like Dan Chaucer's "pour Persone of a toun,"

> "Christes love, and his apostels twelve,
> He taught, but first he folwed it himselve!"

But not only in the district apportioned out to him, but throughout the whole of England, the effect of this visitation was to forward the Reformation entirely. "And of the clergy," says Strype, "that is, bishops, abbotts, heads of colleges, prebendaries, and rectors, the commissioners brought in but one hundred and eighty-nine, throughout the whole nation, that refused compliance with the declaration which restored her Supremacy to the Queen, and admitted the Book of Divine Service to be according to the Word of God[7]." It is remarkable, by the way, in the letter above alluded to, that Harding, Jewel's after antagonist, declined

[6] See vol. viii. p. 128.
[7] See Strype's Annals, vol. i. p. 255. The form of subscription is also given, as he "found it in the MS. library at the Palace of Lambeth."

to acquiesce: "*Hardingus homo constans locum mutare maluit quam sententiam.*"

The matter which henceforward was the great impediment to peace, and so to the advancement of the Reformation, was, the question of habits and ceremonies—in short, the continuation of that dispute which had commenced at Frankfort. Into this controversy of pitiful scruples, unto which so much forbearance was long shown, we have no time to enter. Jewel, it is well known, like his friend Peter Martyr, was for some time more entangled in these cobwebs than might have been expected; and, with his abhorrence of the rags of Popery, he had communicated not only with him, but with Bullinger likewise. In his letter to Peter Martyr, dated 5th Nov. 1559, he thus expressed himself: "*Sunt quidem istæ, ut tu optimè scribis, reliquiæ Amorrhæorum; quis enim id neget? Atque utinam aliquando ab imis radicibus auferri atque exstirpari possint. Nostræ quidem nec vires ad eam rem, nec voces deerunt*[8]." Time however, and consideration, and experience, which teaches the teachable, taught Jewel the futility—not to say the imminent danger—of such controversies; and it is most satisfactory to read this under his own hand, in a letter to Archbishop Parker, wherein he speaks of the cap, and surplice, and tippet, and so forth, as "*this vain contention about apparel.*" The letter is dated from Sarum, 22nd Dec., 1565; and, curious enough, it had reference to the admission or refusal of his future biographer, Humphrey, to a benefice in his diocese. The turning point was Humphrey's well-known leaning to Puritanism, and with it to all vain disputations which at this time were rending the Church of England[9].

In passing on, we will only remark how near we were, two or three years ago, to the revival of this melancholy dispute; and how little many seemed to have profited by the documentary history of the past which lay ready to their hands. The diocese of Exeter, it will be at once recollected, was in a ferment; and how near the diocese of Chichester was to the cauldron of confusion will not be forgotten. Such powerfu agents are trivial disputes in disturbing public as well as private repose! Learned and judicious Hooker, best of counsellors, how many might take advice of thee! "What habit or attire doth beseem each order to use in the course of common life, both for the gravity of his place and for example's sake to other men, is a matter frivolous to be dis-

[8] Vol. viii. p. 134.
[9] The reader is referred for further and fuller information to Strype's Annals, vol. i. pt. i. p. 256, c. xiii.; to Burnet's History of the Reformation under v. Habits; to the authorities referred to by Keble on Hooker's Preface, c. ii.; to Churton's Life of Nowel, p. 113, &c.; and to the eminently just and wise views of the lamented Southey in his invaluable Book of the Church. Peter Martyr's views may be seen very well put by Mr. Le Bas' Life of Jewel, pp. 83. 85.

puted of. A small measure of wisdom may serve to teach them
how they should cut their coats. But seeing all well-ordered
politics have ever judged it meet and fit, by certain special distinct ornaments, to sever each sort of men from other when they
are in public, to the end that all may receive such compliments of
civil honour as are due to their rooms and callings, even when
their persons are not known; it argueth a disproportioned mind
in them whom so decent orders displease[10]."

But we must now turn to Jewel in a different capacity,—as a
Bishop of the Church. On his return from his visitation, the See
of Sarum was offered to him; and although he did not wish to
undertake the burden, he was unwilling to disobey the commands
of the Queen, and accordingly was consecrated by Archbishop
Parker the 21st of January, 1560. Even so soon after as the
4th of February the burden sat heavily upon him; for he writes
to Peter Martyr, saying, "*Nunc ardet lis illa circularia*," and presently adds, "*Eo jam res pervenit, ut aut cruces argenteæ et stanneæ,
quas nos ubique confregimus, restituendæ sint, aut episcopatus relin-
quendi*[1]." By degrees, however, these fears and scruples died out,
and we find him at his post. "And surely," says the abbreviator
of Humphrey, "if ever to any, then unto him, his bishoprick was
a continual work of ruling and governing, not only by the pastoral staff of his jurisdiction in his consistory, but also in the
course of men's conscience, by the golden sceptre of God's Word
preached. The memory of his assiduity in preaching, carefulness
in providing pastors, resoluteness in reforming abuses, bounty in
relieving the poor, wisdom in composing litigious strifes, equity in
judging spiritual causes, faithfulness in keeping, and sincerity in
bestowing church-goods,—is as an ointment poured out and blown
abroad through the diocese of Sarum, by the breath of every
man's commendation." Certainly, if at the first he held the
crozier with an unwilling, or even a timid, hand, it grew firmer
and well fitted to his grasp! And if he thought—

> " A verdict in the jury's breast
> Will be given up anon at least,
> And then 'tis fit we hope the best[2];"

he has the verdict of religious and good men in his favour. He
did his duty and has his praise, notwithstanding evil days or evil
tongues!

Those who succeeded to bishoprics now found them sadly impoverished. "Though the Church was replenished with Gospel
Bishops, yet not," says Strype, "had any cause to envy their

[10] Eccl. Pol. Book v. lxxix. 13.   [1] Vol. viii. p. 139.
[2] Ford. Epilogue to the Lady's Trial.

wealth or greatness." Their Popish predecessors went upon the principle, of making hay whilst the sun shone, and so contrived to alienate all they could, *per fas et nefas,* for present benefit. Nay, more, said Strype's informant, these Marian prelates "had so leased out their houses, lands, and parks, that some of the new Bishops had scarce a corner of a house to lie in, and divers not so much ground as to graze a goose or a sheep, so that some were compelled to tether their horses in their orchard[3]." And this it was which gave occasion to the outcry amongst the poor of " parsimonious Protestants;" whereas, in truth, so little was left them to give, that they were constrained to live in the simplest manner, and few were enabled to steer clear of debt.

Pretty much in this state was the diocese of Sarum. Jewel's predecessor in this see was one hight John Capon,—as it happened, an unlucky name. He had died some three years before, but had so contrived matters as that scarce a good living was left sufficient to support a learned man, which gave occasion for Jewel to say, *"Capon hath devoured all!"* Hence "the good Bishop was forced all his lifetime after to take extraordinary pains in travelling and preaching in all parts of his diocese, which brought him to his grave the sooner." Happy Jewel! happy Wilson! Who so happy, says the author of Gondibert,

" As those whose bodies wait upon their minds ?"

Would that many of our Bishops now were better acquainted with their dioceses ! Would that those who have the *will* had the *power!* It would be the means of defending the cause of the poor ; it would better the working of that most ill-regulated body —the Ecclesiastical Commission for England ; it might hinder a new Commission, which, once constituted under existing feelings, would cut Episcopal revenues to the quick. In short, it would hinder some truthful and plain-spoken Latimer from saying, " Meseems, it were more comely for my lord (if it were comely for me to say so) to be a preacher himself, having so great a cure as he hath, than to be a disquieter and a troubler of preachers, and to preach nothing at all himself[4]." Who reads old Latimer's

---

[3] Annals, vol. ii. pt. i. p. 233. What follows reminds us of the documents said to exist in Ireland : " And yet had these fathers provided that, if they should have been restored (which they looked for, as many thought), they should have all their commodities again."

[4] Latimer to Sir Edward Baynton, Knight, Works, vol. ii. p. 328, Park. Society's ed. We cannot avoid this opportunity of paying a passing tribute to the late Archbishop of Canterbury. Who so ready of access ! who so thoughtful for his Clergy ! We heard a story of a Bishop, not many years ago, who at his Triennial Visitation (the only time that some of his Clergy ever saw him) sipped and sipped, but was observed scarce to eat. The company soon broke up, and his lordship went to dine at the *great house,* hard by the provincial inn, where numbers had come from a

sermons, and does not see how much of them is applicable to the Episcopate even nowadays ?   Charles Borromeo set an example at Trent which may be acted up to in Protestant England ! " May God all amend !" quoth the motto to Master Rudyng's arms, sometime Archdeacon of Lincoln[5].

But to return to Jewel. It was in this year, March 31st, 1560, and on the second Sunday before Easter, that he delivered his celebrated sermon on 1 Cor. xi. 23.   The most celebrated of the exiles were naturally appointed to preach at Paul's Cross, and Jewel's name, of course, was amongst the chosen ones.   The sermon in question had evidently attracted great attention, for it is to be borne in mind that (in a less expanded form probably) it had been twice delivered before,—Nov. 26, 1559, at St. Paul's Cross, March 17, 1560, at Court[6].   There can be little doubt, we think, but that its contents were expected, and that it was looked upon as THE CHALLENGE repeated.   We have not space to insert the several articles protested against, but refer our readers to the sermon itself, giving only the conclusion :

" If any one of all our adversaries be able to avouch any one of all these Articles, by any such sufficient authority of Scriptures, Doctors, or Councils, as I have required, as I said before, so say I now again, I am content to yield unto him and to subscribe.   But I am well assured that they shall never be able truly to allege one sentence ; and because I know it, therefore I speak it, lest ye haply should be deceived."—Vol. i. p. 32.

The letters which followed with Dr. Cole, whose character and history are well known, and the thoroughly weighed " Reply of the Bishop of Sarum," may be considered as introductory to the great controversies which followed.   It was in this Reply that, on Dr. Cole's saying, " I see well ye write much and read little," Jewel acquainted him with the severe course of study he had pursued ; " *and yet*," he adds, " *until this day I never set abroad in print twenty lines*[7]."   What he wrote afterwards fully exemplified the poet's words :—

great distance, from personal respect to THE OFFICE.—Such things should not be, or, if they be, the MAN loses all respect !   We say, as Skelton said,

> Of no good bishop speak I,
> Nor good priest of the cleargy—
> *   *   *
> By my recountyng is
> Of them that do amiss

COLIN CLOUT.

[5] Letters from the Bodleian, vol. ii. p. 182.
[6] See note, vol. i. p. 3.   By this arrangement Cole's expression in his letter of March 18th (p. 42), " in your sermon yesterday at Court," is explained.
[7] Vol. i. p. 86.   In writing to Simler the next year, May 4, 1561, Jewel states

> "No man can attayn perfect cunnyng,
> But by long study, and diligent learnyng."

In September this year, a commission was issued by Arch-bishop Parker for the visitation of the cities and dioceses of Sarum and Bristol, dated September 8th. This was committed to Jewel; but the commission to visit the cathedral church of Sarum to Dr. John Cottrel, "that all occasion of contest between the Bishop and Dean and Chapter might be avoided." The next year Jewel seems to have been pretty much in residence, and employed in his arduous and well-comprehended duties as a Bishop; though we find that on the 13th of April he was pitched upon to preach at St. Paul's; and there is a letter of his to Simler, dated London, May 4th. "It was the wisdom," says Strype, "of the present governors, to put up from time to time able, learned, discreet, and aged men to be teachers of the people at these solemn and great assemblies, who did commonly make it their business in their sermons to prove and evince the present proceedings in religion; and, as occasion served, to lay open the errors and corruptions of that religion and worship that was now lately rejected[*]." In this same year we find a letter from Peter Martyr to him, dated Zurich, 15th August, on the subject of the Ubiquitarian controversy[8]; and it may be remarked in passing, —especially as the matter is again under debate, and many side with Pelican, Paullus, Fagius, and Lyra,—that he was likewise consulted on the subject of marriage with two sisters, which he expressed himself as opposed to. Bishop's Jewel's letter on the subject is extant, bearing date "From Sarum, Calend. Nov. 1561." It evidently arose, as Dr. Jelf remarks, "out of the case of the Earl of Westmoreland, who had married two sisters successively." For our own parts, without entering into particulars, we wish to state decidedly, that we agree with Jewel, and are not surprised to find that Elizabeth wrote to the Archbishop of York, express-ing her astonishment that the Earl should be permitted to keep the sister of his former wife as his wife, such being contrary to the law of God[1].

The ensuing year, 1562, might be called the " magnus annus" or " the climacteric" of Jewel's life, for in it he published his well-known work, the " Apologia Ecclesiæ Anglicanæ." In his letter to

---

that he is no penman, "Nos vero, qui ista non possumus," &c. How little, as Dr Jelf remarks, "did Jewel then think that he would have to conduct the most im-portant controversy of his time!" Vol. viii. p. 152.

[8] Strype's Annals, vol. i. pt. i. 369.

[9] On this question, then agitated in Germany, see Le Bas' Remarks, p. 127, &c.

[1] Dr. Jelf gives this from a curious letter in the State Paper Office from the Queen. See vol. viii. p. 160, note.

Peter Martyr, February 7th, this year, are these words: *Edidimus nuper Apologiam de mutatâ religione et discessione ab ecclesiâ Romanâ. Eum ego librum, etsi dignus non est, qui mittatur tam procul, tamen ad te mitto.* Internal evidence fixes this letter to the *New Style*, and so fixes the year in which the Apology was published. This point is canvassed in the notes to the Editor's Preface, p. xiv.

It has been the fashion amongst a party to decry this most valuable work. Indeed, the works of the English Reformers have been spoken of as "literary curiosities," rather than "valuable contributions to our theology[1]." We need not say how utterly opposed we are to such sweeping assertions; and as to the publication itself, nothing could be better timed, nothing is even now more profitable. We have just risen from reading it, and the racy translation of it by the Lady Bacon, (very properly inserted in the eighth volume of this edition, because adopted generally as the text book for Harding's Confutation, and Bishop Jewel's Defence,) with increased delight. To the young theological student, we say, LEGAT, RELEGAT. Yea, with Lawrence Humphrey, we could wish it—in the place of sundry unclassical works,—OMNIBUS SCHOLIS CHRISTIANÆ JUVENTUTI AD EDISCENDUM PROPONI. Were it duly and rightly studied, we should have fewer *amateurs* of Popery;—we can apply no worthier appellation to sundry λιποτάξεις of modern days! To the Jesuit, Protestant, or other, we offer the well-known lines in Wallenstein, for his consideration:

> " Nicht hoffe, wer des Drachen Zähne sä't
> Erfreuliches zu ärnten. Jede Unthat
> Trägt ihren eignen Rache-Engel schon,
> Die Böse Hoffnung, unter ihrem Hertzen!"
>
> Tod, i. vii.

But we are not called to do what has been done, and done well, by countless others—that is, to make an Apologia Apologiæ. Suffice it to say, that although it be not an authorized book, yet, in a sense, it is authorized by the Church of England; for, in Elizabeth's days, together with Fox's Book of Martyrs, and the Holy Bible, "it was enjoined to be set up in some convenient place in all parish churches, to be read at all suitable times by the people, before or after Service[2]." The general reader, provided he be a scholar, will admire the elegance of the Latinity,—the divine, the soundness of the position it maintains. The cry is still raised, as it was when Jewel wrote, " Nos ab Ecclesiâ Catholicâ tumultuosè defecisse, et nefario schismate orbem terrarum concussisse, et

---

[1] Brit. Critic, ut supra, p. 9.   [2] Strype's Annals, vol. iii. pt. i. p. 738.

pacem communem atque otium Ecclesiæ publicum conturbasse ;"
the answer he makes, is our answer too. In the Bishop of St.
Asaph's words, who, it is clear from his Sketch, &c., is not
bitterly opposed either to Papist or Puritan,—in some' points is
almost their apologist :—He there states, in a brief and oratorical
style, the grounds of the separation of our Church from that of
Rome ; showing that, in what she had done, England had rather
returned to the state of the Primitive Church, than occasioned a
schism in the Christian family, and that the innovation with which
we were charged was merely the rejection of the errors introduced
by the community from which we had separated." (VIII. § 411.)
Of its publication into sundry other tongues, Jewel himself speaks
in his Preface to the Defence of the Apology, or rather in an
Epistle to Queen Elizabeth ', prefixed to it. And few books probably
have been wider circulated. No wonder that Bullinger, and
Gualter, and Wolf thought so highly of it on the Continent—
no wonder that Peter Martyr, some three months before his death,
should thus write :—"*Ego verum plurimum lætor, quod illum
diem viderim, quo factus sis parens tam illustris et elegantis filii.*"
These words were written circa August, 1562. On the 12th of
the November following, he died.

In concluding our remarks on this celebrated work, we may
subjoin the words of Jewel himself, from the Defence of the Apology, Part i. c. 4. Divis. 2. " It was read," says he to Harding,
" and sharply considered, in your late convent at Trident, and
great threats made there that it should be answered, and the
matter by two notable learned Bishops taken in hand, the one a
Spaniard, and the other an Italian : which two, notwithstanding,
these five whole years, have yet done nothing, nor, I believe, intend
anything to do. Indeed, certain of your brethren have been often
gnawing at it : but such as care nothing, nor is cared, what they
write." As Master Featley says, " they are now not to answer
the 'Apologie,' but to apologize for their politick not answering it !"

On the question of the Second Book of our Homilies, we have
not space to enter ; nor on the controverted dates, ranging from
1560 to 1563. We refer our readers to Bishop Short's valuable
note (VIII. § 412) ; giving, at the same time, the extract following,
from Hey's Lectures on Article XXXV.: " Our *Second Book*
of Homilies, the titles of which are mentioned in our Article, was
published early in the reign of Queen Elizabeth, in 1560. They
had been prepared, or nearly so, before the death of King Edward ;
and they seem to be, in a manner, promised in his injunctions.—
They were composed, in a good measure, by Bishop Jewel, author

---

' See vol. viii. p. 170. This letter is usually prefixed to the Apologia.

of the famous 'Apology for the Reformation.'" Since Dr. Cardwell published Richard Taverner's Postils, two of them— the first Homily on the Passion, and that on the Resurrection, have found their right owner. These Postils, by the way, are a very remarkable composition. They were compiled and pub- lished in the year 1540.

We must not omit to state, that Dr. Jelf refers the celebrated Letter of Jewel to Seignor Scipio — supposed by the late Dr. Wordsworth to be Scipione Biondi, the son of Michel-Angiolo Biondi [5]—to this same year; and the internal evidence he points out is in favour of the supposition. It appears first in Brent's translation of Father Paul's " History of the Council of Trent;" —and, as we remarked before, Dr. Jelf concludes it to be, if an unfinished, yet a genuine work of Jewel. The drift of the letter is probably known to most of our readers :—those who may wish to refresh their memories, are referred to Fuller's Church His- tory (Book ix. Cent. xvi.), where they will find " the sum of Mr. Jewel's answer" set down. That Jewel contemplated an answer, as to why we did not send representatives to Trent, we collect from his letter to Peter Martyr, dated 7th of February, this same year. The words are these: " *Nos nunc cogitamus publicare causas, quibus inducti ad concilium non veniamus. Ego quidem sic statuo et sentio, istis congressionibus et colloquiis nihil posse promoveri hoc tempore, nec Deum velle uti istis mediis ad propagandum evangelium.*" The proceedings of this Cabal had caused Jewel to alter his opinions, expressed some years before.

Of Jewel's labours in the year 1563, we have scarcely any record at all; but we know well enough that every day brought its appointed task ; and his position was now such as to render him a counsellor upon all occasions. One date assigned would lead us to suppose that he was engaged upon the second Book of Homilies. Three letters only are given in the present edition for 1563—so memorable for the termination of the Council of Trent. One of them is to Bullinger,—the other two to Josias Simler, the successor of Peter Martyr in the theological chair at Zurich. In the former of these, in which reference is made to the Ubiqui- tarian Controversy before alluded to, occurs one of those painful passages, so properly referred to by Dr. Jelf, in his note, Vol. vi. p. 233, in which he hints, quoting the 22nd Book of Sleidam's History, that " unscrupulous and shocking pleasantry of this kind seems to have been the fashion of the day." Expressions such as these, are the only excuse for the no less intemperate remark of the late Mr. Froude,—as he ever appeared to us a very hasty,

---

[5] Eccl. Biog. iii. p. 308. See Dr. Jelf's note, vol. viii. p. 73

a very weak and ill-judging young man: "As to the Reformers, I think worse and worse of them. Jewel was what
you would, in these days, call an irreverent Dissenter. His
defence of his Apology disgusted me more than almost any
work I ever read[6]." How entirely wise are that noble poet's
words :

> " Farre more delightful than they fruitful be,
> Witty apparence, guile that is beguil'd ;
> Corrupting minds, much rather than directing
> The allay of duty, and our prides erecting[7] ! "

Of the two letters to Simler, one is a playful one, and the other
has reference to his departed friend Peter Martyr, in which he
acknowledged the receipt of an image of him wrought in silver,
and encourages the Professor to proceed in editing his Commentaries on Genesis, which Jewel had not seen, and a complete collection of his works. Strype[8] states that, on the present occasion,
these Commentaries accompanied Simler's oration of Martyr's
Life. If so, it must have been in MS. (which is unlikely), as
Jewel's words are,—" *tamen non dubito esse ejusmodi, ut,* SI EDAN-
TUR, *videri possint Petri Martyris.*" We must refer our readers
to the original letter for the affecting words relative to what he
missed in the *Effigies*, and must not omit to state that Peter
Martyr had dedicated to Jewel his treatise *De utrâque in Christo
Naturâ*, as may be seen in his Letter to him, August 15, 1561.

But, although the particulars relative to Jewel himself for this
year are few and scant, it is remarkable for Harding's " *Answere
to M. Juelles Challenge.*" For four years it had grated upon the
Romanists ; and, at last, Harding was put forth as their champion. Of others, and minor antagonists, we have no space to
speak ; and we refer our readers to Churton's 6th Section of the
Life of Nowel, where they will find the information they may
want. Of Harding, however, we must speak a word ; " for this
is that Master Harding," says Dr. Overal, in the Preface to the
folio edition[9], following the words of Humphrey, " which, in the
days of King Edward, publicly and frequently preached in defiance
of our religion ; and so earnestly in opposition against Popery,
and particularly the paper walls and painted fires of Purgatory,

---

[6] Froude's Remains, vol. i. pt. i. p. 379.
[7] Lord Brooke, Of Human Learning.
[8] See Annals, vol. i. pt. i. p. 430.
[9] See Fuller's Abel Redivivus, p. 313. He informs us that Dr. Overal wrote the
Preface, and that the Appendix was by Bishop Morton. Godwin, de Præsulibus
Angliæ, says of Harding, " Non defuit tamen Dares qui hunc Entellum provocaret,
Hardingus quidam," p. 354. He appears to have borrowed the expression from
Jewel himself. It occurs in a letter to Bullinger, vol. viii. p. 186.

that he wished his voice had been equal to the great bell of Os-
ney[1], that he might ring in the dull ears of the deaf Papists." The
annexed rapid sketch of his life is in the words of Mr. Le Bas.

" Thomas Harding, like Jewel, was a Devonshire man. He was
born at Comb-Martin, in 1512. His earliest education was at Barnstaple. From thence he was removed to Winchester, and afterwards to
New College, Oxford ; of which he became a Fellow in 1536. In 1542
he was appointed by Henry VIII. to the Hebrew Professorship. His
religious notions or professions must therefore have, at least, kept pace
with the proceedings of the King. When Edward came to the throne,
however, his Protestantism assumed a much more decided aspect. In time,
he was appointed chaplain to the Duke of Suffolk, father of Lady Jane
Grey ; and had the honour of instructing that ill-fated lady in the doctrines of the Reformation. The accession of Queen Mary in a moment
reconverted him to Popery ; and the chaplain of the Lady Jane now
became the chaplain and confessor to Bishop Gardiner ! His prompt
repentance was rewarded, first, by a stall at Westminster, and next, by
the Treasurership of the cathedral of Salisbury[2]. The death of Mary
and the accession of Elizabeth were fatal to his preferments, but effected
no change in his last religious profession. When the Romish cause
became desperate in England, he retired to Louvain in Flanders, where
his time was chiefly employed in his controversy with Bishop Jewel,
and where he died in the year 1572."—p. 139.

As it will not accord with our limits to speak particularly of
Harding, we may here remark, that the very fact of his being
pitched upon as the one most fitting to be answered by Jewel,
shows that he was the doughtiest antagonist of the Roman band.
Even Humphrey, whose philippic is so trenchant, admits, *In
multis pares sunt, et ambo doctrinæ et eloquentiæ gloriá præcel-
lentes.* Ourselves certainly do not think that they were *in multis
pares ;* but the powers of Harding must have been very considerable, or Leland the Antiquary would hardly have spoken of him
in the way he did in his Cycnea Cantio and in his Encomia. In
the first he says,

" Cultor præterea sacræ loquelæ
Hardingus numerum politus auget[3];"

and in the latter, addressed *Ad Tho. Hardingum Theologum*—in
somewhat rhetorical style, he compared his eloquence to that of
Cicero and Demosthenes. Of course, it is not meant to press

---

[1] Jewel himself refers to this story in the Defence of the Apology, pt. v. c. vi.
div. 1. vol. vi. p. 83. He there calls it "the bell of Frideswise" or "Frideswide."
[2] We lighted upon the following in Leland's Itinerary, a few days back. "Hardingus primus *Thesaurarius* Eccles. Sarum !" fol. 65. vol. iii. p. 80. ed. 1744.
[3] Itinerary, vol. ix. ut supra, vv. 639, 640. The Encom. is in the Collecteanea,
vol. v. 136.

such eulogistic strains beyond the mark, but the bare fact shows that his literary capacities must have been great. As the Collectanea are not in every one's hands, we transcribe the commencing lines:—

> " Talis nuper erat tua certè oratio felix,
>   Excoluit linguæ quæ decus omne sacræ,
> Qualis erat magni Demosthenis optima quondam,
>   Atticus effluxit cujus ex ore lepos.
> Qualis et eximii Ciceronis floruit illa,
>   Qua duce securus constitit ipse Milo!" &c. &c.

Thus much we thought it right to say of the man whom Wood calls in the Athenæ Oxon. " the target of Popery, and a zealous asserter of his religion."

But, whatever may have been the powers of Harding, his powers of abuse and his coarseness seem to have superseded his better capacities; and no friend to Jewel's memory says, that " as far as language goes, he is even mild in comparison with his Roman antagonist[4]." And not only so, but Ἁμέραι ἐπίλοιποι μάρτυρες σοφώτατοι, declare the ascendancy of Jewel in all and every argument he uses; his collections for his great controversial works being, it is to be noted, the result of his own industry, and, even at such a time, unprecedented reading; whereas, the replies of Harding, it seems pretty clear, as was intimated over and over again by Jewel, were the combined efforts of his College and of his Church. After-days, likewise, have ascertained that his authorities are often second-hand. This was noted by Churton in his Life of Nowel, and is now confirmed by Dr. Jelf. We give his own words, as we have above given all the credit to Harding which is his due: " Harding's style is wearisome and affected; his reasoning often ridiculously illogical, and most of his authorities borrowed at second hand: much of his work, as has been correctly remarked by Archdeacon Churton, in his Life of Dean Nowel, being a literal translation of Hosius[5]." For an account of Jewel's writings, and particularly the controversy with Harding, the reader is referred to the plain and straightforward account of Mr. Le Bas, in the ninth chapter of his work, in which he says, we believe justly, " I am unable to recollect a single passage in which he disgraces himself by an imitation of his enemy" (p. 248). We will only observe, in conclusion, that Mr. Hallam, in his " Literature of Europe[6]," gives no opinion on these controversies, stating that he is not competent; for ourselves, we have given the opinion of those whom we judge to be so.

---

[4] British Critic, ut supra.　　　[5] Editor's Preface, p. xxi. note.
[6] See vol. ii. p. 118.

For the year 1564, we have scarce any data at all. Jewel's Letter to Sir William Cecil, dated "*From my poor house in Sarum,* 30 *Januarii,*"—internal evidence gives to the next year. From the Table we gave at the commencement, it will be seen that the Translation of the Apology by that "learned and virtuous lady" —the Lady Anne Bacon—is assigned to 1564. Nothing can be more striking than the compliment paid her by Archbishop Parker; the more so, if, as Stype asserts, he had a great hand in the first, which came out in 1562. His words are these: "And now to the end both to acknowledge my good approbation, and to spread the benefit more largely, where your ladyship hath sent me your book written, I have with most hearty thanks returned it to you (as you see) printed; knowing that I have herein done the best, and in this point used a reasonable polity; that is, to prevent such excuses as your modesty would have made in stay of publishing it." Jewel, in adopting it, paid a like tribute to its "worth and hers." Like Margaret, the daughter of Sir Thomas More, and like Mrs. Godolphin, a century later, she must have been a most intelligent creature, and one worthy to be the mother of the great Lord Bacon. Reader! "because the heavens such grace did lend her[7]," thou wilt be well pleased to break a dull continuity with these exquisite stanzas from Davenant's Gondibert:

> "The court (where single patterns are disgraced;
>   Where glorious vice weak eyes admire;
> And virtue's plainness is by art outfaced,)
>   She makes a temple by her vestal fire.

> "Though there, vice sweetly dress'd, does tempt like bliss
>   Even cautious saints; and single virtue seem
> Fantastick, where brave vice in fashion is;—
>   Yet she has brought plain virtue in esteem[8]."

On the 30th of January, 1565, as hinted at above, Jewel wrote to Cecil, from Salisbury, most heartily desiring that he might not be called "to preach this Lent before the Queen's Majesty," stating, as a reason, that many were looking for his book greedily, and some wondered it was not abroad long sithence, and that if he

---

[7] We do not mean to compare the intellectual capacity of Mrs. Godolphin either with that of the Lady Anne Bacon, or with that of the saint-like Mrs. Roper, the married name of More's "dear Meg," as he styles her, whose praises Erasmus and Stapleton could not sufficiently enunciate. But of Mrs. Godolphin, "a virtuous woman, mild and beautiful," we can most truthfully say,
> "Holy, fair, and wise is she;
>   The heavens such grace did lend her,
> That she might admired be."
>   *Two Gentlemen of Verona,* iv. 2.

[8] Book iii. canto v.

were obliged to present himself, it would be unto him a great loss of time, and a great hindrance unto the matter, and so a great encouraging unto the adversary[9].　The book alluded to was the "*Replie to Harding's Answere,*" which appeared in August[1]; but, from the letter to Cecil, it is evident that either the MS. or the earlier sheets had been shown previously.　Why or wherefore Jewel's request was not acceded to is not known; but we find from Strype, that he was called upon to preach, and in May we find him at Paul's Cross.　Upon this occasion, he took upon him to make some observations upon some authorities in Harding's Book; " wherein were alleged, with much vaunt, spurious authors; and among the rest, Amphilochius, which author Jewel said in that audience,"—(he asserts the same in the Replie, vol. i. p. 314,) —that he had bound up in an old parchment book, with St. Thomas, the Popish martyr.　He mentioned also, it seems, out of that book, with some sport,—(we may suppose after Latimer's manner) —a tale of angels' singing pricksong to St. Basil's mass, &c. &c.[2]" The result of this was an angry letter from Harding, "to Maister John Juell," from Antwerp, dated 12th June, demanding the whole sermon, as yourself will stand to it, together with a Postscript "To the Reader," in which he is informed that "Mr. Juell's Replie is begonne to be in print," warning him at the same time of what " maner of pelfe must be the stuffing of his huge work now in the presse."　The reader will hardly need to be informed that henceforth Amphilochius, and other authorities of Harding, equally authentic, became a sort of by-word.　In a letter of the next year to Bullinger, he speaks of him as a " *vilis apostata—qui me ex Amphilochiis, Abdiis, Hippolytis, Clementibus, Victoribus, Athanasiis suppositiciis, Leontiis, Cletis, Anacletis, Epistolis Drecketalibus, somniis, fabulis, refutaret :*"—where, by the way, Dr. Jelf suggests that *Drecketalibus*[3] is a play on the word *Decretalibus, Dreck* in German signifying filth.　Possibly our word *dredge* and *dredging-net* may be as near kinsmen to it as to the usual acceptation of *drag.*

It was in this same year that Harding's Confutation of a Book

.

[9] Vol. viii. p. 181.

[1] The Preface " unto the Christian Reader " is dated *from London, the 6th of August,* 1565, so that Jewel must have been in London twice this year, unless we suppose he remained there from May to August.

[2] See Annals, vol. i. pt. ii. p. 176.　Harding's Letter, presently referred to, is printed at length in the Appendix, No. xxx. On the term " prick-song," see Nare's Gloss. in v.　Aubrey tells us, by the way, in his Life of Hobbes, that " he had always bookes of *prick-song* lying on his table," &c., and that " he did believe it did his lungs good, and conduced much to prolong his life."—Letters from the Bodleian, ii. p. 623.

[3] " Hoc est *stercoreis.*"　Strype, in margin, Annals, vol. i. pt. ii. 543.

entitled " An Apologie of the Church of England," was put forth
by him. This is alluded to by Jewel in his letter to Bullinger,
just now cited; and from this time, notwithstanding his care for
his diocese, which will be referred to by and by, we must look
upon him as plunged still deeper in the vortex of controversy. " *Vix
dum absolveram*"—he means his "Replie"—"*evolat extemplo Apologiæ nostræ Confutatio. Hic ego rursum petor*," &c., to which he
presently adds, "*Hæc idcirco visum est scribere prolixius, ut, si post-
hac literæ istuc à me infrequentius venerint, quam aut vos expectatis,
aut ego velim, id cuivis potius rei, quam aut oblivioni vestri, aut
ingratitudini tribuatis*[4]."

On reference to the Fasti Oxonienses, it will be seen that
Harpsfield, Harding, and Cole were admitted Doctors of Divinity
in 1554. From the same authority we learn, that on May 26,
1565, " it was granted by the Venerable Congregation that JOHN
JEWEL, bishop of Salisbury, should, tho' absent, be actually
created doc. of div. by a certain graduate to be assigned by the
commissary. This was accordingly done at London, but the day
when, appears not." Master Featley notes that "he was solemnly
created Doctor, and bare the part of a Moderator in those
famous acts, concluding with a divine speech, of our then, and
now more truly to be called *Urania, Elizabeth*,"—all from Humphrey.—We are afraid Miss Strickland and these writers would
be much at issue.

The letter to Archbishop Parker, relative to the " vain contention" about the habits, has been referred to before. It is
dated 22 Dec. 1565. Though we know a good deal both of
Sampson and Humphrey, it is curious that we do not know the
result of this debate, except by implication. Jewel, with his own
private scruples, attested in a letter written to Bullinger not two
months afterwards, continued firm, for the peace of the Church;
and, as it appears, declined instituting him. " Eventually"—we
use the words of Mr. Soames—" Cecil procured him the deanery
of Gloucester, strongly advising his conformity. Humphrey's
eye was now cooled by riper age, and it could rest complacently
even upon a vesture approved at Rome. He listened accordingly
to Cecil's advice, and wore, all his latter years, at least while
resident as Dean, the very dress that he had long denounced as an
intolerant remnant of exploded superstition[5]." How affecting is
it to find, that even all that had occurred marred not the friendship of Jewel and Humphrey! That he was sent for by the
Archbishop to preach his funeral sermon when he died; " but,

[4] Sarisberiæ, viii. Febr. 1566, vol. viii. p. 186.
[5] Elizabethan Religious History, p. 56.

this being a plague year, Humphrey was removed from the University, so that the messenger that came to Oxford could not find him to deliver the message[6]!" That he was pitched upon by the Archbishop and by the Bishop of London to write his life! That this HUMPHREY IS JEWEL'S FIRST AND EARLIEST BIOGRAPHER! What better illustration of the sacred text,—"*Many waters cannot quench love, neither can the floods drown it : if a man would give all the substance of his house for love, it would utterly be contemned[7]?*"

A matter is alluded to in the letter to Archbishop Parker which we must not omit to refer to,—we mean the destitution of the parochial pulpits. To obviate this evil, the archbishop had granted licences to certain preachers to preach throughout the kingdom. But those appointed swerved from their duties, and deceived the expectations of those who appointed them. "They went up and down," says Strype, "preaching where they pleased in any church ; and the curates allowed them, fearing to gainsay their licences[8]." Such was the origin of the words which follow : "Certain, having obtained your Grace's licence, pass up and down the country from church to church, preaching every where as if they were apostles, and, by virtue of your Grace's seal, require money for their labours. I will stay one or other of them if I can, that your Grace may know him better." The evil wrought its own cure, and the licences were eventually reversed. No doubt the adage *necessitas nullas habet leges* was acted upon, but, as it turned out, unluckily ; for the evils resulting from such a course were precisely similar to those which put down the Mendicant Friars. The readers of Piers Ploughman, of Skelton's[9] poems, and of old Latimer's Sermons will not need catechising in what these evils were. In referring to Latimer, by the by, we may not omit

---

[6] Strype's Parker, vol. ii. p. 49, 50.
[7] Canticles, ch. viii. ver. 7.
[8] Strype's Parker, vol. i. p. 376, &c.
[9] The story of " John and the Ten Commandments," in Latimer, is known to every one. Amongst other staves, Skelton sings thus :

> "Many a fryar, God wot,
> Preaches for his grote,
> Flatterynge for a new cote,
> And for to have his fees,—
> Some for to gather cheese.
> Lothe they are to leve
> Either corne or malte :
> Sometime meale and sault,
> Sometime a bacon flicke,
> That is three fingers thycke,
> Of larde and grese,
> Their covent to encrease."
> COLIN CLOUT.

to state, that the idle and thoughtless amongst the clergy contrived to turn these Friars to account. " Also vicars and par-
sons," quoth he, in the sixth sermon on the Lord's Prayer, " be
afraid when there cometh a sickness in the town ; therefore they
were wont commonly to get themselves out of the way, *and send
a friar thither, which did nothing else but lop and spoil them.*"
Who can ever forget the words which were uttered by the time-
honoured Wicklif—with countenance so beautiful—when, raising
his attenuated form on the bed, he exclaimed, " I shall not die,
but again declare the evil deeds of the Friars !" No improper application of Scripture was there here ; but words they were of one,
righteously applied, which will be remembered as long as mortal
words may[1] !

> " For thoughe his bodye be dead and mortall,
>   His fame shall endure, and be memoriall[2]."

During the year 1566, it does not appear that Jewel published
any thing ; but it may be noted that Harding's " Rejoindre
to Mr. Jewel's Replie" is dated the 31st of August. From this
time, in fact, to his death, the data, by way of annals, are few and
scanty. Of the two letters which refer to 1566, one has been
quoted before, and the other likewise addressed to Bullinger. It
may be here added, that in the first of these Jewel speaks of the
severities of the preceding winter, and the scarceness of corn in
consequence ; and that it was three years now since he had set
eyes on his friends Parkhurst, Sandys, and Pilkington—*ita procul
disjecti sumus.* He next adverts to the affairs of Scotland, France,
Denmark, and Sweden, and then thanks Bullinger for his Commentary on Daniel, and Lavater for his on Joshua, conveying at
the same time to them the sum of twenty crowns, his annual pen-
sion to Julius, the attendant of his never-to-be-forgotten friend
Peter Martyr, and twenty crowns more to Bullinger and Lavater
—*ut eos vel in cœnam publicam pro more vestro, vel in quemvis
alium usum pro vestro arbitrio consumatis.*—Such was the freedom
of those days ; such the intercourse of Jewel with those he loved.

The other letter above referred to, written hardly more than a
month after, shows how Jewel was engaged,—that is to say, in
preparation of the Defence of the Apology. With reference to
certain points, he there puts these questions to Bullinger, appealing to him remarkably—" *Tu enim solus jam superes, unicum prope*

---

[1] See the Life of Wicklif, by Mr. Le Bas, p. 196. Of this Life also we must
speak as we have done of the Life of Jewel. In these days they are good for
" all men's hands." Of the History of the Mendicants, and of their introduction
into England, 1221, he treats in the third chapter.

[2] Hawes's Past. of Pleasure.

oraculum Ecclesiarum." 1. Whether the Christians in Greece, Asia, Syria, and Armenia used private Masses, as the Papists did; and what kind of Masses, whether public or private, the Greeks at Venice then used. 2. Whereas there was one Camotensis, who had writ somewhat sharply against the lives and insolence of the Popes; who he was, and where he lived. 3. What he thought of the German Council, which they say met under Charles the Great, against the second Nicene Council, concerning images; because some said there was no such Council[2].—Our particular object in quoting these queries is, because of the word "*Camotensis*," which was fastened upon by Harding. Jewel quotes the word as he found it in Cornelius Agrippa. The real author is now well known to have been Joannes Sarisburiensis, sometimes called *Carnotensis*, from his see of *Chartres*. It may be satisfactory to the reader to refer to Dr. Jelf's note, which he will find in vol. ii. p. 217, and to what Jewel himself says in " A Preface to the Reader," vol. iv. p. 119. The question of the Eastern Church is dealt with in the Defence, Part v. chap. 15, div. 1, vol. vi. p. 183, &c.; that of the Council, held at Frankfort, A.D. 794, in Part vi. chap. 17, div. 1 and 2, vol. xi. p. 463, &c. No reply from Bullinger is extant; but, in a letter to him the year following, Jewel thanks him for his very learned and lengthened reply. This letter of Bullinger's may yet be found.

The year 1567, in which " Another Rejoindre to Mr. Jewel's Replie against the Sacrifice of the Mass" appeared, is notorious as the year in which Jewel's Defence of the Apology was published,—that book which drove Harding and the Papists to desperation,—which from that day to this (unpleasant as is the tone of controversy) has been the storehouse of authorities to be wielded against the pretensions of the Seven Hills—the Pope in conclave—abetted by his Cardinals, or standing alone in his all-sufficiency. We wish not our youths to be given up to disputation, but prepared they must be, if they are to hold their position as divines; and therefore do we call upon them to consider well the points on which the contest with the Church of Rome turns. As a help, and a great one, Jewel is never to be passed by; Barrow, also, on the Supremacy, should be at their right hand.

The letter from Jewel to Bullinger, dated 24th February, this year, alludes to his constant occupation on the Defence. "*Lovanienses nostri turbant, et clamant, quantum possunt, et habent fautores, non ita multos, plures tamen multo quam velim;*" to which he adds, that, as ill luck would have it, all their attacks made him their butt. The same letter contains reference to Eliza-

---

[2] This is from Strype. See Letter, vol. viii. p. 188.

beth's unwillingness to name her "successor '," and to the fearful
tragedy in Scotland. The death of his much-regarded Julius, he
says, has been reported to him; but he sends the annual pension
nevertheless, with a request that, if he be no more, it should be
expended *in epulum scholasticum.* The softened style in which
he speaks of the question of the habits shows how his opinions
on this head had become modified. The words are so striking,
that we subjoin the original: " *De religione, causa illa vestiaria
magnos hoc tempore motus concitavit. Reginam, certum est, nolle
flecti. Fratres autem nostri quidam ita eâ de re pugnant, ac si in
eâ omnis nostra religio versaretur. Itaque functiones abjicere—*
(we must not forget that this too was once Jewel's own resolution)—*et ecclesias inanes relinquere malunt, quam tantillum de sen-
tentiâ decedere. Neque aut tuis, aut D. Gualteri doctissimis scriptis,
aut aliorum piorum virorum monitis moveri volunt '."* It is with
individuals as with improveable lands, provided proper culture be
used.

> " Multa dies, variusque labor mutabilis ævi
>   Rettulit in melius ! "

   The letter to Cecil relative to the letter to the Queen,—" An
Epistle to Queen Elizabeth,"—is dated September 27, 1567.
The Preface to the Defence, October 17, 1567. It may be well
to quote these words near the conclusion :—" It may please your
Majesty graciously to weigh it, and to judge of it, not according
to the skill and ability of the writer, but according to the weight
and worthiness of the cause. The poor labours have been mine ;
the cause is God's. The goodness of the one will be always able
to countervail the simplicity of the other."—Vol. iv. p. 105.
   Reserving our remarks upon his episcopal and ministerial
labours for the present, we follow Jewel according to his correspondence, from which we learn, that at the commencement of 1568
he was entering into the visitation of his diocese. This drops out
accidentally in the first of his four letters to Archbishop Parker.
This no less faithful than munificent Prelate,—the friend of learning and of learned men,—had this year, by a commission dated
July 7th, received authority from the Council for searching after
antiquities. From Jewel's letter, *Sarum,* 18 *January,* in which
he thanks his Grace for " his great gentleness," and tells him
likewise " that he had ransacked the poor library of Salisburie,"
but that he "had found nothing worth finding, saving only one
book in the Saxon tongue,"—it is clear that Parker was occupied

---

⁴ The same thing is hinted at in Lord Buckhurst's Gorboduc,—or, as it is sometimes yet called, Ferrex and Porrex. Southey has somewhere noted this.
⁵ Vol. viii. p. 191.

in his search previous to the grant of the Commission. What literature and theology owe to his exertions, this is not the place to dwell upon; but neither Protestant nor Romanist will forget the publication of Elfric's famous Paschal Homily, which speaks things "plainly and evidently contrary to the novel doctrine of the Papal Transubstantiation." The extract following, from Strype, which calls to our minds the

"Virtus Scipiadæ et mitis sapientia Læli,"

we cannot prevail upon ourselves to omit: "The spare hours of his old age (which was pleasant and cheerful) he spent in searching into ancient authors, then not come to light, and in comparing the opinions of the modern Doctors with the opinions of the ancients. And especially he inquired into our British and Saxon monuments, which treated of this Church of Britain, whereby he saw evidently how much this our Church, by the encroachments of the Papacy, had deviated from its ancient doctrines and practices[6]."

The book found and forwarded by Jewel turned out to be Pope Gregory the Great's Tract, *De Curâ Pastorali,* turned paraphrastically into Saxon by King Alfred; also that King's Preface, with a poem, wherein the book speaks to the reader; turned out of Saxon into Latin by some modern person, supposed to be William Lamburd. The two letters here referred to are at the end of the volume in the public library, Cambridge.

Two more letters to Archbishop Parker relate to other matters, now without so much interest. He incidentally mentions again the ordering of ministers by M. Lancaster[7], "now Elect of Armach," adding that one had been admitted, whom, "for many good and just causes," Jewel had for eight years refused. In both letters, he refers to the purpose, by the printers, of again putting forth his Latin Apology, and he intreats the Archbishop to stop the publication till better revised. To errors and mistakes, he says, "these printers have small regard, as tendering only their private gain." 26 April, and again 7 Maii, 1568: "I am afraid of

---

[6] See Strype's Parker, vol. ii. p. 455. The account of the Saxon Homily is in vol. i. p. 472, &c. On this see Soame's Inquiry into the Doctrines of the Anglo-Saxon Church; and, for a just estimate of Parker's labours, his Elizabethan Religious History.

[7] "On account of the poverty of the see of Armagh," says Bp. Mant in his History of the Church of Ireland, "Thomas Lancaster, who succeeded to the primacy, on which occasion he preached his own consecration sermon, had a licence, a few days after his consecration, to hold *in commendam* several benefices both in England and Ireland, which at the time of his advancement he possessed, and to retain them during such time as he should continue primate; but under a proviso, that the said churches should not be defrauded of their usual service, but be supplied with a provision of vicars and curates."—Vol. i. p. 282. This passage is referred to in Dr. Jelf's note. Happily things are not quite so bad now!

printers. Their tyranny is terrible!" All readers of our old
Divines must be well aware, that these worthies did then print and
spell as it seemed good in their own eyes! Of the three other
letters to Cecil, from the original MS. in the State Paper Office,
we have no information, so as to throw light upon them, at hand.
They relate to certain poor Greeks and their books, whom Jewel
wished to serve. One of them, Nicolas de la Turre, he mentions
by name ; and their books, it appears, were purchased.

We must not omit to mention that it was in 1568 that Harding published his "Detection of Sundry foul Errors uttered by
Mr. Jewel, in his Defence of the Apology."

The year 1569 drew from Jèwel the second and enlarged
Edition of the "Defence," exposing also the "Detection." This
came out in December, and with it the controversy may be said
to have ended. The date is, (vol. iv. p. 131,) "*From Salisbury,*
11th Decemb. 1569." Dr. Jelf informs us that the Defence of
the Apology, in these volumes, has been collated with the Edition
of 1570 "imprinted by Henry Wyke," which contained the last
correction of the Author.

In the present Edition will be seen likewise a letter of Bishop
Jewel, found in his study "certain months after his forsaking his
earthly dwelling," and sent to John Garbrand, to whom he bequeathed all his papers and note books, dated 20th August, 1569.
It relates to the subject of "*usury*[a]," on which Jewel, like many
of our elder Divines, held very rigid opinions. His views may be
seen by the reader in his Exposition upon the First Epistle to the
Thessalonians, ch. iv. ver. 6. (vol. vii. p. 63, &c.), which appears to
have been delivered this year, in a Series of Discourses in his own
Cathedral. This and other posthumous works, were published by
the above-named J. Garbrand in 1582 and 1583. Not only this
Exposition, but the Treatise of the Sacraments (vol. viii.), and
the Treatise of the Holy Scriptures (vol. vii.), may be read with
the greatest benefit. We believe they have all been republished
separately, and we recollect how, many years ago, we were surprised to find in them such sound doctrine and unpresuming piety
—as Dr. Jelf says, "singleness of purpose,—and withal, plain
good sense, and pure English!"—*Editor's Preface*, p. xxvii. Brown,
in his "Britannia's Pastorals," speaks of Daniel as the "well-lan-

[a] Apb. Abbot, in his Fifth Lecture on the Book of Jonah, has some striking
remarks on this head. See pp. 89—91, ed. 4to, 1613. Dr. Jelf, in alluding to Jewel's
mistaken views on this point, has the following very just remark : "And yet in an
age, which is too much disposed to worship Mammon, the lesson need not be
entirely thrown away. Avarice, exorbitant interest, extortion, and taking advantage of the necessities of our neighbours, are even now amenable to Jewel's severest
rebuke."—Note, vol. vii. p. 63.

guaged Danyel." The same epithet—controversy apart—might be applied to Jewel.

The next year, 1570, we find the honest indignation of Jewel roused by Felton's posting up the Bull of Pope Pius V. on the Palace Gates of the Bishop of London. This Bull, it is well known, denounced Elizabeth as an heretic and a favourer of heretics, deprived her of her pretended title, and absolved her subjects from their oath of allegiance. Jewel was at this time engaged on his Lectures upon the Second Epistle to the Thessalonians (2. ii. 3); but such, it appears, was his earnestness, that he could not refrain, but at once declared its contents to his audience. Being a matter different from the Practical Exposition he was engaged upon, he entreats his hearers' pardon—" seeing the occasion is such, it driveth me to be plain and earnest. For she is the servant of God: she is my gracious lady and dread sovereign. I have sworn truth to her Majesty. If I knew there were in mine heart one drop of disloyal blood towards her, I would take my knife and let it out'." No doubt Jewel had found reason to be thus loyal, for the Bull itself bore date " the fifth of the Calend. of March, in the year past,"—that is, 25th February— and by this time leaven had worked. Besides the danger near at home, to it he attributes the rebellion of the Earls of Westmoreland and Northumberland, and the commotions in Scotland. "*Remember,*" says he, " *what ensued the summer following. The coals were kindled here, but the bellows which gave the wind lay at Rome, and there sat he which made the fire.*" Jewel asserts the same thing in his Letter to Bullinger, dated 7th Aug. 1570: " Omnes istas turbas nobis dedit sanctissimus pater! Is enim pro suâ sanctitate et sapientiâ submiserat in Angliam ad suos bullam (aureamne dicam et plumbeam?) magni ponderis. Ea menses aliquot inter paucos obscurè fruebatur," &c. &c. To which he adds, " *Mitto ad te exemplar illius putidissimæ atque inanissimæ bullæ,*" &c. which " unworthy Bull," says Strype, in his Life and Acts of Archbishop Grindal, " Bullinger took the pains to answer," and sent it to England about August this year (i. e. 1571), " as he had also sent copies of it to the Bishops of Ely and Sarum, who were his acquaintance formerly in their exiles [10]."

Men's minds were in a transition state; and thousands (with no evil intent, but with an unformed judgment) were oscillating be-

---

[9] See View of a Seditious Bull, vol. vii. p. 237. See the Bull translated in Fuller's Church History, book ix. cent. xvi.; and the original in Burnet, II. ii. p. 531; and Cardwell's Doc. Annals, vol. i. p. 328.

[10] Strype's Grindal, p. 253.

tween Romanism and the doctrines of the Reformation[1]. On the
whole,—even as admitted by Dr. Short,—the measures adopted
by Elizabeth towards Rome had been conciliatory,—"and they
were at first met by a corresponding return on the part of the
majority so treated,"—so that "the Roman Catholics did generally conform to the worship of our Church, to which, though
they might not have approved of all the alterations in it, they
could raise no sound objection" (§ 437). But, after the promulgation of this Bull,—solicited by the importunity of Dr. Harding,
Dr. Stapleton, Dr. Morton, and Dr. Webbe,—matters changed.
The Roman Catholics no more came to worship,—all was suspicion, jealousy, conspiracy, and cabal,—and the result was, the
enactment of those laws which, in one shape or another, pressed
heavily upon them, and preserved us from their machinations, till
the wisdom of the present century again gave free and open course
to the "land-louping Jesuit," thereby inflicting a wound on the
Church of England and Ireland, which the present generation
will not see healed! There's no weapon salve for it! Most certainly we concur in Jewel's indignation and earnestness; and,
although

> οὐ τοι ἅπασα κερδίων,
> φαίνοισα πρόσωπον ἀλάθει' ἀτρεκής,

we may confidently refer any reader to "A View of a Seditious
Bull" for truths which are not obsolete in 1850. The attacks of
the Papacy are never to be made light of; and, though the Pope
be not what he is represented,—

> "Proin vide, ne, quem tu esse hebetem deputes æque ac pecus
> In sapientiâ, munitum pectus egregium gerat,
> Teque regno expellat[2]."

At the same time, in making these remarks, and in expressing
our deep-rooted dislike to the doctrines of the Roman Catholic
Church, let the insidious attacks of POPE SELF be well borne in
mind; for time runs in a circle, and the same salient points are
ever and anon touched upon, which left a slur on the Reformation
in the days we are speaking of. Take what we allude to in Mr.
Le Bas' truthful words :—

"It must not be disguised, that the evils of that period were miserably aggravated by the apathy, or the perverseness which began to disgrace the followers of the Reformation. The zeal which had animated

[1] We particularly recommend to the reader's attention the very sensible remarks
of Mr. Le Bas on this head. Life of Jewel, p. 180, &c.
[2] Accius apud Cic. de Div. i. c. 23.

and united the Protestants, on the re-establishment of their faith at the accession of Elizabeth, was already waxing somewhat cold ; and they who professed to retain most of its original fervour, were unhappily wasting their energy in the agitation of questions which lay on the out-side of Christianity, instead of devoting it to the promotion of its vital and essential interests. And thus, strange as it may seem, while the Pope was labouring to empty our churches by denunciations from the Vatican, the Puritans were *virtually* aiding him by pouring contempt upon every thing which could remind the people of his authority, or even of his existence. And hence it was, that the enlightened friends of discipline and order were placed, as it were, between the upper and the nether mill-stone. They were assailed by enemies from abroad, and by false brethren at home. As the Puritanical controversy became more exasperated, the position of the Church of England became, of course, more critical and dangerous. That she has emerged in safety from the dangers which then environed her, and from the still more calamitous vicissitudes that followed, we gladly and thankfully ascribe to the protection of God's gracious providence."—p. 184.

We may note that, in the letter to Bullinger before quoted, he tells him that it is now six years full since he had seen Park-hurst, but that he was alive and well. It was written, it appears, on his visitation, the concluding words being, " Ex itinere : nunc enim obeo provinciam meam." Bullinger had written and com-plained of his silence, which accounts for it.

We arrive now at the last year of this great and good man's life—the year 1571, early in which (the 2nd of March) he writes to his friend Bullinger. This letter is, in part, a repetition of the last, under the idea that it might have been lost. Amongst the new matter, he refers to the silence of the Romanists. " Lova-nienses nostri," says he, "unum jam atque alterum annum nihil scribunt ;" and he states, in conclusion, that two years' pen-sion is due to " his Julius," to whom he had written that he might know to whom he might remit it, but had received no reply. But the most important point referred to is, the Parliament summoned for this year, with its Convocation, when he hoped once more to see the face of Parkhurst, whom he loved so well. The words run thus : " Elizabetha Regina nostra convocavit proceres, et indixit parliamentum in secundum diem Aprilis ; quod felix faus-tumque sit et ecclesiæ et reipublicæ. Ibi demum, spero, videbo Parkhurstum tuum meumque, quem septennim jam totum nunquam vidi[3]." This point we consider the most important, because Jewel, as is well known, was much concerned in the revision and re-publication of the Articles, as well as in that requisite sub-scription which was brought about by the opposition of the Puri-

[3] Vol. viii. p. 203.

tanical party to existing regulations, headed by the notorious
Thomas Cartwright. This, however, is another matter of great
import, on which we have not space to dwell; in fact, it runs onward
beyond the days of Jewel, and is to be coupled rather with those
of Whitgift and Hooker. Suffice it to say, as regards Jewel, that
on the 4th of May it was decided upon, "that when the Book of
Articles touching doctrine shall be fully agreed upon, that then
the same shall be put in print by the appointment of my Lord of
Sarum[4]," which was done accordingly. Minute corrections were
certainly made by Jewel, and he is justly said to have "put the
finishing hand to our present articles;" but we doubt very much
what is said by Mr. Soames, in his Elizabethan History, "that
Jewel, then near his end, might seem to have omitted the affirmative clause in the XXth Article, which Burton branded, in Archbishop Laud's time, as a prelatical forgery."

With regard to the prevailing troubles to the coming Puritanical storm, we have Jewel's own testimony to his earnest anxiety.
It was dwelt upon by him in his last sermon at Paul's Cross, and
in his conference about the ceremonies and state of the Church.
It was his earnest desire, that there should be peace; but when,
in the stead of peace, the contrary faction prepared themselves for
the battle, then he stood forward as the defender of existing institutions, and the Church as established in these realms. And
all this, to a certain extent, must have been drawn from him by
the pressure from without; for we know, from his residence at
Zurich, how tender he was upon such points—how much he would
have conceded. But now the hydra head of Puritanism was lifted
up, the fruits that proved so bitter were beginning to ripen, and
so one of the last acts of his valued life was the setting to paper
his "*Novitiorum Assertio*" for the use of Whitgift. What appertains to it will be found in Strype,—the history in vol. i. p. 76,—
the document itself in the Appendix, vol. iii. p. 21. As is well
known, this paper was afterwards brought forward by Whitgift in
his answer to the Admonition to Parliament.

Once more we find Jewel's name mentioned publicly, and that
is in Queen Elizabeth's Letter to Archbishop Parker for uniformity in Church matters, given at Hatfield, the 28th day of
August, 1571[5]. By this document the Archbishop was to asso-

---

[4] See the Acts and Proceedings in Convocation. Cardwell's Synodalia, vol. ii.
p. 531, and Dr. Lamb's Historical Account of the XXXIX Articles. The question of the Articles is carefully canvassed by Dr. Short in his Sketch. See Appendix c. to chap. x., and his remarks are well worth reading. For the general history,
see Strype's Parker; and, for the particular statement made by him, see vol. ii.
p. 54.

[5] See Strype's Parker, vol. ii. p. 76, or Cardwell's Doc. Annals, vol. i. p. 332.

ciate with him the Bishops of London and Sarum, communicating
these letters, and to charge them straitly to assist from time to
time, between this and the month of October, to do all manner of
things requisite to reform such abuses as afore are mentioned, in
whomsoever ye shall find the same." But, or ever October came,
good Jewel was released from toil and trouble, and from the sore
weariness of earthly travel. He had begun "the travel of eternity!" His release had come,—

> "For thoughe the day be never so long,
> At last the belles ringeth to even song[4]!"

Humphrey relates that he felt his end approaching, and that he
had a strange percept on of it some time before, as he declared by
letters to his friend Harkhurst, whom he looked forward to see at
that Parliament which he referred to likewise in his last letter to
Bullinger. But it was with Jewel according to that proverb of
the Germans,—*Geist kann man nicht verderben;* and so he
laboured the more, the nigher he found his end approaching. But
the account of his last days, so pathetically told, because so simply, we give in Master Featley's Abridgement of Humphrey,
prefixed to the folio edition of Jewel's works. Long as it is, we
question if any one will complain of its length[7]:

"The supernatural motions of God's Spirit within him in the end became, as it were natural, *in fine velociores,* and the last endeavours of
grace in him were most vehement; for, after his return from a conference
at London, he began a new and more severe visitation through his whole
diocese than ever before, correcting the vices of clergy and laity more
sharply, enjoining them in some places tasks of holy tracts to be learned
by heart, conferring orders more circumspectly, and preaching oftener.
By which restless labours and watchful cares he brought his feeble body
so low, that, as he rode to preach at Lacock in Wiltshire, a gentleman
friendly admonished him to return home for his health's sake, saying,
'that such straining his body in riding and preaching, being so exceeding weak and ill-affected, might bring him in danger of his life; assuring
him, that it was better the people should want one sermon, than be
altogether deprived of such a preacher.' To whom he replieth, 'It
becometh best a Bishop to die preaching in the pulpit;' alluding perad-
venture to the apophthegm of Vespasian,—*Oportet imperatorem stantem
mori*[8]; and seriously thinking upon the comfortable eulogy of his

---

[4] Hawes' Pastime of Pleasure, capit. xlii.

[7] We may add, in a note, that it was on this his last visitation, when 'he preached
at Abingdon, a religious town in Berkshire, not far from Oxford,' that the well-
known quotation was made by him from Gregory's Epistles, in which he gave the
MS. reading *exercitus* instead of *exitus.*—See the story at length, quoted in Wordsworth's Eccl. Biog. iii. 350 and note, from Dr. James's Treatise, &c. Jewel not
unfrequently quotes the passage, e. g. vol. ii. p. 142. vii. p. 174, and in Sermon on
Haggai. Ibid. p. 377.

[8] Cf. Sueton. in Vit. ad fin.

Master: *Happy art thou, my servant, if when I come I find thee so doing.* Wherefore, that he might not deceive the people's expectation, he ascendeth the pulpit; and now nothing but spirit (his flesh being pined away and exhausted) reads his text out of the fifth to the Galatians: *Walk in the Spirit,* &c., and with much pain makes an end of it.

"Presently after sermon, his disease growing more upon him, forced him to take his bed, and to think of his dissolution now not far off. In the beginning of his extreme fits he made his will, considering therein his brother J. Jewel[*], and his friends, with some kind remembrances, but bestowing the rest more liberally upon his servants, scholars, and the poor of Sarum. The Saturday following, nature, with all her forces (being able no longer to hold fight with the disease), shrinking and falling, he calleth all his household about him, and after an exposition of the Lord's prayer,— *Cantator cycnus funeris ipse sibi,*—thus he beginneth his sweet song :—

"' I see I am now to go the way of all flesh, and I feel the arrows of death already fastened in my body ; wherefore I am desirous in a few words, while yet my most merciful God vouchsafeth me the use of my tongue, to speak unto you all.—It was my prayer always unto Almighty God, since I had any understanding, that I might honour his name with the sacrifice of my flesh, and confirm his truth with the oblation of this my body unto death in the defence thereof; which seeing He hath not granted me in this, yet I somewhat rejoice and solace myself, that it is worn away and exhausted in the labours of my holy calling. For while I visit the people of God, God, my God, hath visited me with Mr. Harding, who provoked me first. I have contended in my writings not to detract from his credit and estimation, nor to patronize any error to my knowledge, nor to gain the vain applause of the world, but according to my poor ability to do my best service to God and his Church. My last Sermon at Paul's Cross, and Conference about the ceremonies and state of our Church, were not to please any man living, nor to grieve any of my brethren who are of a contrary opinion ; but only to this end, that neither part might prejudice the other, and that the love of God might be shed in the hearts of all the brethren, through the Spirit that is given us. And I beseech Almighty God of his infinite mercy to convert or confound the head of all these evils, and ringleader of all rebellions, disorders, and schisms, the Bishop of Rome, who, wheresoever he setteth foot, soweth seeds of strife and contentions. I beseech Him also long to preserve the Queen's Majesty, to direct and protect her Council, to maintain and increase godly pastors, and to grant to his whole Church unity and godly peace. Also, I beseech you all that are about me, and all other whom I ever offended, to forgive me. And now that my hour is at hand, and all my moisture

---

[*] It is remarkable that Jewel's brother's name should have been John, but so it appears. Strype says, " he had a brother John, to whom he made bequests," &c. Parker, vol. ii. p. 49.

dried up, I most earnestly desire of you all this last duty of love, to pray for me, and help me with the ardency of your affection, when you perceive me, through the infirmity of my flesh, to languish and wax cold in my prayers. Hitherto I have taught you and many other; now the time is come wherein I may, and desire to, be taught and strengthened by every one of you.' "

" Having thus spoken, and something more to the like purpose, with much pain and interruption, he desired them to sing the 71st Psalm [1] (which begins thus: *In thee, O Lord, I put my trust, let me never be confounded*), himself joining as well as he could with them: and when they recited those words, *Thou art my hope, O Lord God, my trust even from my youth,* he added, *Thou only wast my whole hope:*. and as they went forward, saying, *Cast me not off in the time of age, forsake me not when my strength faileth me; yea, even to mine old age and gray head, forsake me not, O God;* he made this application to himself, *He is an old man, he is truly gray-headed, and his strength faileth him, who lieth on his death-bed.* To which he added other thick and short prayers, as it were pulses, so moved by the power of God's Spirit, saying, *Lord, take from me my spirit; Lord, now let thy servant depart in peace; break off all delays; suffer thy servant to come unto thee; command him to be with thee; Lord, receive my spirit.*

" Here, when one of those that stood by prayed with tears, that (if it might stand with God's good pleasure) he would restore him to his former health, Jewel, over-hearing him, turned his eyes, as it were offended, and spake to him in the words of St. Ambrose [2]: *I have not lived so, that I am ashamed to live longer, neither do I fear to die, because we have a merciful Lord. A crown of righteousness is laid up for me. Christ is my righteousness. Father, let thy will be done, thy will, I say, and not my will which is imperfect and depraved. O Lord, confound me not, this my* TO-DAY. *This day quickly let me come unto thee: this day let me see the Lord Jesus.* With these words the door was shut by the base sound of the grinding, and the daughters of singing were abased, the silver cord lengthened no more, the golden ewer was crackt, and the pitcher broken at the well; yet the keepers, with much 'trembling, stood erect,' and they that looked out of the windows, though dark, were yet fixed toward heaven, till after a few fervent inward prayers of devotion, and sighs of longing desire, the soul returned to God that gave it. Master Ridley, the steward of his house, shut his

[1] John Garbrand's words are, in his Preface to A View of a Seditious Bull, " In the day and night before his departure out of this world, he expounded the Lord's Prayer, and gave short notes upon Psalm lxxi. to such as were by him." Vol. vii. p. 234.

The authorities for Humphrey's Life, it is well-known, were these, John Garbrand, Parkhurst, Bishop of Norwich, and his old tutor, Giles Laurence, who preached his funeral sermon, and his surviving brother. See Le Bas's Life, p. 237. The Dedication of Humphrey's Life is September 23, 1573, just two years after Jewel's death.

[2] Jewel presses the same words in his Treatise on the Sacraments. See vol. viii. p. 70.

eyes in the year of our Lord, 1571, Sept. 22 (*quære* 23d), about three
of the clock in the afternoon, *ann. æt.* almost 50.—Such was the life
and death of Bishop Jewel, a most worthy trumpet of Christ's glorious
Gospel."

Nothing simpler or more touching than such an account as
this! Like Richard Hooker, whom he patronized, like Barrow
and many others who wrought much in a shorter space of time,
and left a name behind not to be forgotten, Jewel, too, died
young, at least, comparatively. But, " he lived long in the short
scantling of his life ; " and his works, now so well edited, tell one
part of the labour of his days. We touch not upon the old saw,
Ὁν οἱ θεοὶ φιλοῦσιν ἀποθνήσκει νέος,—as it is in Britannia's Pastorals,

" Since what is best lives seldom to be old; "—

because truth lies on both sides, and such an impression is usually
dictated by feeling and affection ; but we hint in passing, that the
early death of the great and the good, who during life " kept the
vigils of their Sabbath-day in heaven," calls upon all to labour in
their vocation whilst their day lasts, and so to labour as that
their labour be not in vain. " Sincerity, and simplicity, and perseverance, and performance, bescem the child of God[*]." Happy
such in their life—happier in their death !

Εἰρηνικῶς θνῄσκουσιν εἰρήνης τέκνα.

None will visit fair Sarum's Cathedral without a thought of Jewel !
Buried in the midst of the choir, we leave his ashes to sleep in
quiet,—" *the pawn*," as old Fuller says, on another occasion, "*for
the return of his soul!*"

Time and space fail us to tell of the calumnious insinuations, as
well as of the open charges, made against him by the Romanist,
who attributed his learning to his familiar—a huge black cat, to
wit—declaring, at the same time, that he recanted on his death-
bed, and died in the odour of sanctity and in the arms of Rome !
confounded, nevertheless, at the errors of his life, and in the
agonies of remorse and despair at the thought of them ! After
the peaceful end we have quoted at length, we leave our readers
to reconcile such contradictions, referring only to the passage in
Bacon's " Observations on a Libel," given as an instance of the
height of impudency that these men are grown unto, in publishing
and avouching untruths, on the principle of *audacter calumniani,
semper aliquid hæret :*—" Mr. Jewel, the Bishop of Salisbury, who,
according to his life, died most godly and patiently, at the point
of death used the versicle of the hymn ' Te Deum, O Lord, in
Thee have I trusted, let me never be confounded,' whereupon,

[*] Abbot on Jonah, p. 169.

suppressing the rest, they published that the principal champion of the heretics in his very last words cried he was confounded[4]!"" More on these points must be sought for in the Life of Humphrey.

In the stead of dwelling on such matters, we will now turn to his general life and character, by way of summary, which was not so easily introduced into the annals of his public career;—and here, as before, we shall pretty closely follow Mr. Le Bas, whose selections, as usual, are pertinent and judicious.

As a scholar and a divine it must be admitted that JEWEL was amongst the first men of his time. A hard student from his earliest days till the day of his death, he was, as Eunapius says of Longinus, a Βιβλιοθήκη τις ἔμψυχος καὶ περιπατοῦν μουσεῖον, but without ostentation, and without the pride of learning. Knowledge puffed him not up, but humbled him, teaching him the extent of his own ignorance, and so turning every endowment of his mind to the service of God and his Church; for, as himself said, " he is over well-learned, that bendeth his learning against God." His memory, which Lord Brooke calls the

" Register of sense
And mould of arts, and mother of induction,"

was wonderful; neither was it such by nature only, but improved by art, for he used what has since been called a " *Memoria Technica*," and taught it, amongst others, to his old friend and tutor, Parkhurst. Strange feats are recorded by his biographers, —as strange as of Fuller, in after-days. But, as Bishop Morton said, " *no man's memory is omnipotent*," and Jewel accordingly had immense stores laid up in his Common-place Books[5], made ready to his hand by carefully digested indexes—"many in number, and great in quantity, being a vast treasure of learning, and a rich repository of knowledge, into which he had collected sacred, profane, poetic, philosophic, and divine notes, of all sorts;" but the indexes, it appears, were drawn up in characters for brevity, and thereby so obscured, that they were not of any use, after his death, to any other person. And, besides these, he ever kept

[4] See Works, vol. v. p. 469, 8vo.
[5] The immense stores of all sorts of information contained in the lamented Southey's Common-place Book will, in due time, be given to the world. We expected to have seen the first volume before this. Years ago we were delighted with the privilege of turning them over. He drew upon them in his *Vindiciæ*, &c., as Jewel did upon his in his controversy with Harding. Southey, by the way, to use the words of Marston in his " Scourge of Villany,"

" *Had made a common-place book out of plays.*"

We saw it many years ago, and regret to hear that it has been lost. Since this was written three series of these Common-place Books have been published, and the fourth is advertised as nearly ready. The mass of information they contain is wonderful,—and the labours of preparing them has been, as we have good occasion to know, immense.

diaries, in which he entered whatever he heard or saw that was
remarkable ; which once a year he perused, and out of them extracted whatever was more remarkable. To speak of Jewel's knowledge of Latin and Greek were superfluous ; but his love for
Horace and Cicero, for the Greek poets, orators, and historians
has been recorded. In these, it is said, he was especially well
versed, but above all, in the ecclesiastical historians. It is
mentioned, likewise, that Gregory Nazianzen was a particular
favourite with him, and that he quoted him on all occasions. We
all know Barrow's love for Chrysostom, and how he studied the
golden-mouthed Father in the imperial city where he preached.
We must not omit to add, that Erasmus stood very high also in
the estimation of Jewel.

And, thus prepared, he came to the work he had in hand, and
from these his immense collections he was enabled not only to
proclaim the Challenge from Paul's Cross, in the cool and positive
way he did, but likewise to confront the combined efforts of the
Romanists ; for, as we observed before, the controversy was not
so much with Harding, as with the whole consistory of the
Papistic doctors. We have not space to record how he used his
note-books in the contest ; but the reader may inform himself fully
by turning to the life of Jewel by a Person of Quality, in Wordsworth's Eccles. Biogr., vol. iii. p. 355.

But, if Jewel was a scholar and a divine, he was more also.
He was the most faithful in all his ministerial duties; and, although
many particulars are not handed down to us, yet, when Whitgift
numbered him among "the most notable and painful prelates" of
his time, we know that he gave utterance to the common testimony of all good men in his favour. So that if

"The gyse now-a-days
Of some jangling jayes
Is to discommend,
What they cannot amend[6],"

they have but to turn to Jewel's contemporaries, and to the
divines of the following generation ; and there they will find equal-
handed justice dealt out to "the bright and shining light," who did
as much as ever any man did to shoulder back the τρικυμία,—the
fluctus decumanus of the roaring Papacy[7]. "We saw the poppets,"
are his words, "but the juggler that drew the strings kept himself close[8]."

If we follow him to his diocese, there we find him, like Paul of

[6] Skelton's " Philip Sparowe."
[7] It is old Burton in his "Anatomie of Melancholie" that speaks of the " Bull
bellowing Pope" and the " Land-louping Jesuits."
[8] Vol. vii. p. 261. " View of a Seditious Bull."

old, in labours more abundant. Day and night he seems to have devoted to the exercise of his calling, "insomuch that it was a question whether his mental or his bodily labours were the more." And if he was, as a Bishop ought to be, διδακτικός, he was also φιλόξενος; and though, as he said on his arrival in his see, " Capon had devoured all," yet he found means by rigid economy to exercise, in no common degree, the virtues of hospitality and munificence. His doors were open,—without respect of persons, save and except any came from Zurich and from Peter Martyr, and then there might be,—to all who were his proper guests; and for the sick and needy none could say, with more truth than Old Sarum's Bishop,

> " The threshold of my door
> Is worn by the poor[*]."

Few readers of Bishop Latimer's Sermons will forget his indignant pleading for poor scholars,—as, for example, in that preached at Stamford :—"Every man scrapeth," says he, " and getteth together for his bodily house; but the soul's health is neglected. Schools are not maintained; scholars have not exhibition ; the preaching office decayeth ; men provide lands and riches for their children, but this most necessary office they for the most part neglect. *Very few there be that help poor scholars ; that* set their children to school to learn the Word of God, and to make a provision for the age to come [10]." So spake this thorough and most honest martyr to Christ. But no imputation of this sort clung to Jewel ; none knew the necessities of the times more than he, and none did more than he to stay the evil, yea, even beyond his power. Usually, we find, he had with him in his house half a dozen or more poor lads which he brought up in learning ; and took much delight to hear them dispute points of grammar, learning in Latin at his table when he was at his meal, improving them and pleasing himself at the same time. And besides these he maintained in the University several young students, allowing them yearly pensions, and, whenever they came to visit him, rarely dismissed them without liberal gratuities, following in this the solid example set him by his dear friend and tutor Parkhurst, when at Cleave. And never was example better followed, or more gloriously rewarded ; for it was by Jewel's bounty that Richard Hooker was trained in that scholarship which produced that most invalu-

[*] See Herrick's Hesperides. It is to be recollected, that it was in 1572 that provision was, what is called, legally made for the poor. We may refer to some very judicious remarks on this head by Bp. Short, in his Sketch, &c. § 436. Jones of Nayland observes the same, vol. iv. p. 160: and we are still searching for what Warburton says was not found in his day, that is, " the proper remedy." Vol. x. p. 257.
[10] Vol. i. p. 391. Park. ed.

able and never-to-be-dispraised work, THE ECCLESIASTICAL POLITY.

This beautiful episode in Jewel's history no reader of the "meek Walton"—meek, notwithstanding Lord Byron's flippant and indecent remark,—knoweth not. It appears that when Jewel was appo nted Commissioner for the West of England, as we have recorded i in its proper place, he then became acquainted with John Hooker, at that time Chamberlain of Exeter, Richard's uncle, who had been induced, on the representation of the boy's kind-hearted schoolmaster, to forward his nephew's education. For further particulars,—how the uncle, on Jewel's coming to his diocese, interceded with him for the lad,—how he had him brought to him, in company with his schoolmaster, the Easter following, — how he rewarded the schoolmaster, and* pensioned Richard's parents, and took upon himself his case for a future preferment,—for these and other points we must refer to those pages, of which Wordsworth says,

> " *The feather whence the pen*
> *Was shaped, that traced the lives of these good men,*
> *Dropt from an angel's wing ;"*—

but we cannot resist giving the conclusion [1] — (it was after Hooker's sore sickness)—in the simple words of that most touching of all biographers :—

" As soon as he was perfectly recovered from this sickness, he took a journey from Oxford to Exeter, to satisfy and see his good mother, being accompanied with a countryman, and companion of his own college, and both on foot: which was then either more in fashion, or want of money, or their humility made it so : but on foot they went, and took Salisbury in their way, purposely to see the good Bishop, who made Mr. Hooker and his companion dine with him at his own table:

---

[1] Thus alluded to in the same Poet's Ecclesiastical Sketches, under the head of "Eminent Reformers," part ii. xxxii.

> " Methinks that I could trip o'er heaviest soil,
> Light as a buoyant bark from wave to wave,
> Were mine the trusty staff that JEWEL gave
> To youthful HOOKER, in familiar style
> The gift exalting, and with playful smile :
> For thus equipped, and bearing on his head
> The Donor's farewell blessing, can he dread
> Tempest, or length of way, or weight of toil !
> More sweet than odours caught by him who sails
> Near spicy shores of Araby the blest,
> A thousand times more exquisitely sweet,
> The freight of holy feeling which we meet,
> In thoughtful moments, wafted by the gales
> From fields where good men walk, or bowers where they rest."

In the simile of " Araby the blest" it may be almost needless to say that Wordsworth, as well as Cowper (his lines are very beautiful), both follow Milton.

which Mr. Hooker boasted of with much joy and gratitude, when he saw his mother and friends : and at the Bishop's parting with him, the Bishop gave him good counsel, and his benediction, but forgot to give him money ; which, when the Bishop had considered, he sent a servant in all haste to call Richard back to him ; and at Richard's return the Bishop said to him, Richard, *I sent for you back to lend you a horse, which hath carried me many a mile, I thank God, with much ease;* and presently delivered into his hand a walking staff, with which he professed he had travelled through many parts of Germany. And he said, Richard, *I do not give, but lend you my horse ; be sure you be honest, and bring my horse back to me at your return this way to* Oxford. *And I do now give you ten groats, to bear your charges to* Exeter; *and here is ten groats more, which I charge you to deliver to your mother, and tell her I send her a Bishop's benediction with it, and beg the continuance of her prayers for me. And, if you bring my horse back to me, I will give you ten groats more, to carry you back to the College ; and so God bless you, good* Richard.

"And this, you may believe, was performed by both parties. But, alas ! the next news that followed Mr. Hooker to Oxford was, that his learned and charitable patron had changed this for a better life. Which happy change may be believed, for that as he lived, so he died, in devout meditation and prayer; and in both so zealously, that it became a religious question, *Whether his last ejaculations or his soul did first enter into heaven.*"

His munificence was further shown by the building a library for his Cathedral. Books, he knew, were to the divine what tools are to a carpenter, and he took care that there should be a proper depository for the after liberality of others. The original library, which belonged to Old Sarum, was founded by Bishop Osmund ; but of its contents little or nothing is known, save only as regards the book called the " Custom," composed by him. From his time Salisbury became, as we know from Caxton, the great authority on all such matters; and when the Archbishop of Canterbury celebrated the Liturgy in the presence of the Bishops of his province, the Bishop of Salisbury (probably in consequence of the general adoption [2] of the " Use" of Sarum) acted as Precentor of the College of Bishops, a title which he still retains. But this by the way, and because no Cathedral Church is so rich as Salisbury in what appertains to its ritual. Of more consequence is it to remark, that Jewel was not deceived in his anticipations ; for his very next successor, Edmund Gheast (Almoner to Queen Elizabeth, and of great use in settling the affairs of the Reforma-

---

[2] See Mr. Palmer's Dissertation on the Liturgy of Britain and Ireland *Orig. Liturg.,* vol. i. p. 187.

tion ') supplied it with a collection of books. Both their names
are perpetuated in the following inscription, which we transcribe
from Godwin's *De Præsulibus Angliæ* :—" Hæc Bibliotheca instructa est sumptibus R. P. ac D. D. Joannis Jewelli, instructa
vero libris à R. in Christo P. D. Edmundo Gheast, olim ejusdem Ecclesiæ Episcopo, quorum memoria in benedictione erit."
For the praise of those who build libraries,—second only to that
of those who build churches and hospitals,—we beg to refer our
readers to the " Oratio in obitum Thomæ Bodleii," by the ever-
memorable Mr. John Hales, of Eaton.

Elizabeth, it is well known in the present day, pillaged the
Church most unmercifully. As Bishop Short says', "she did
not begin the custom, but she ought to have put a stop to it."
Jewel, however, stepped forth on all occasions, as Latimer had
done aforetime, and endeavoured to stem the evil. He did what
he could, and his praise remains. Allowances are to be made for
what we will call the complimentary language of his day; but
courtier, in a bad sense, was he none. No prebend in his day,
and with his good will, could make a merchandize of the Church's
patrimony ; and when one layman came on such an errand, backed
by legal authority, his well-known reply still stands on record :—
".What your lawyers may answer, I know not. But this I know,
—that I will take care that my Church shall sustain no loss while I
live." Nor, in the presence of his Sovereign Lady the Queen
was his tongue tied. Nor love of place, nor forfeiture of favour,
would have influenced him. Witness his well-known sermon on
Psalm lxix. 19 : " *The zeal of thine house hath eaten me*'." We
wish we had space to extract the whole, as well as other passages
to the same extent ; a part we cannot refrain from giving, inasmuch as in our days the results of constant spoliation are so clear.
" *Solvat Ecclesia*" is still the cry which produces Tithe Commuta-
tions and Ecclesiastical Commissions ! Save the mark ! What
a pliant thing is a " cheveril conscience '!"

" All other labourers and artificers have their hire increased doubly
as much as it was wont to be, only the poor man that laboureth and
sweateth in the vineyard of the Lord of Hosts hath his hire abridged

---

' Parker, vol. ii. 459. The name is severally spelt, *Gest* or *Guest*. See Index
to Strype.
' See his very true remarks. Sketch, § 429.
' Vol. vii. p. 400. The passage referred to is in p. 413.
' Few people, nowadays, are conversant with old Quarles' " Divine Fancies ;"
but, if any chance to have the book, they will find some very plain remarks there,
under " ANANIAS," lib. iii. 82, and "On IMPROPRIATOR," lib. iv. 73, 74. He elsewhere says:
  " *They're two things to be worldly great and wise.*"

and abated. I speak not of the curates, but of parsonages and vicarages, that is, of the places which are the castles and towers of peace for the Lord's temple. They seldom pass nowadays from the patron, if he be no better than a gentleman, but either for the lease or for present money. Such merchants are broken into the Church of God, a great deal more intolerable than were they whom Christ chased and whipped out of the Temple. Thus they, that should be careful of God's Church, that should be patrons to provide for the consciences of the people, and to place among themselves her ministers, who might be able to preach the word unto them, out of season and in season, and to fulfil his ministry, seek their own and not that which is Jesus Christ's. They serve not Jesus Christ, but their belly. And this is done, not in one place, or in one country, but throughout England. A gentleman cannot keep his house, unless he have a parsonage or two in farm for its provision.

"O merciful God, whereto will this grow at last? If the misery which the plague worketh would reach but to one age, it were tolerable. But it will be a plague to the posterity, it will be the decay and desolation of God's Church. Young men, which are toward and learned, see this; they see that he which feedeth the flock hath least part of the milk: he which goeth a warfare hath not half his wages. Therefore they are weary and discouraged, they change their studies: some become prentices, some turn to physic, some to law: all shun and flee the ministry. And besides the hindrance that thus groweth by wicked dealing of patrons, by reason of the impropriations, the vicarages, in many places, and in the properest market towns, are so simple, that no man can live upon them, and therefore no man will take them. They were wont to say, '*Beneficia sine curâ,*' 'Benefices without charge:' but now may be said, '*Cura sine beneficio,*' 'Charge or cure without benefice.'"

All this, the reader must bear in mind, was preached in the ears of Elizabeth,—no common woman, and one who, when provoked, declared herself to be of the masculine, and the feminine, and the neuter gender too; one whose vanity was easily ruffled, and before whom a "*prudens simplicitas*" was advisable. But Jewel was a truth-teller, when truth was needed, and he spoke before her as honest old Latimer did in his first and sixth sermons before Edward VI.[7] At this day the back-wave of spoliation is

[7] In the first sermon he says, "There lieth a great matter by these appropriations, great reformation is to be had in them. I know where is a great market town, with divers hamlets and inhabitants, where do rise yearly of their labour to the value of fifty-pound, and the vicar that serveth (being so great a cure) hath not twelve or fourteen marks by year; so that of this pension he is not able to buy him books, nor to give his neighbour drink: all the great gain goeth another way." p. 100.—In the sixth he tells us, how the Devil "invented fee-farming of benefices, and all to decay this office of preaching; inasmuch that, when any man hereafter shall have a benefice, he may go where he will, for any house he shall have to dwell upon, or any glebe land to keep hospitality withal: but he must take up a chamber

still rolling in, and our poorer livings are quite inadequate to the decent maintenance of a clergyman; and "was it not," as one says, "for the piety of those who, through the possession of private property, are enabled to devote their talents to the service of God, by entering into the ministry, a great number of parishes in England would be destitute of an educated pastor."

Having referred to his sermons, we may state that, polemical as some are, they are still most scriptural; and if, as Luther said, a good textman be proof of a good divine, Jewel must have been eminently such. The Scriptures were at his fingers' ends and in all his writings he shows, practically, what he years before declared to Dr. Cole: "Like as the errors of the clock be revealed by the constant course of the sun, even so the errors of the Church are revealed by the everlasting and infallible word of God [1]." Of the style we said something before. We may here add, that he is plainness itself; and proper words (Swift's test of a good style) are always to be found in proper places. In the words of one of his biographers, "He affected ever rather to express himself fluently, neatly, and with great weight of argument and strength of reason, than in hunting after the flowers of rhetoric, and the cadence of words: though he understood them, no man better, and wrote a dialogue [2], in which he comprehended the sum of the art of rhetoric:" or, in the original words of Humphrey: "*Curiosam et affectatam eloquentiam in concionatoribus semper damnavit, et ipse devitavit. Rhetor esse quam haberi maluit.*" He that harangued in his younger days the woods of Shotover spake of the things of Christ sweetly and persuasively,—"*leni ac dulci voce, et idoneis verbis.*" But his own views on this head he had presented to the reader in his sermon on Joshua vi. 1—3, and they are well worth perusing. See vol. vii. pp. 362, 363.

---

in an ale-house, and there sit and play at the tables all the day. A goodly curate!" p. 203. Park. edit.—Who need wonder, after such instances, that Cock, Gammer Gurton's boy, should be sent by his master to seek Doctor Rat,

"at Hobfilchers shop; for as charde it reported
Ther's the best *ale* in all the town, and now is most resorted!"—ii. iii.

[1] Vol. i. p. 127.

[2] The academical prolusion, now printed for the first time by Dr. Jelf from a MS. in the British Museum, collated with two others in C. C. C., can hardly be here alluded to. It is quite worth reading. The title is *In Rhetoricæ Vituperium.* See vol. viii. p. 209. The following story is new to us, and may be so to some of our readers:—

"Muliercula quædam olim Cantiana, cum Lundini forte, in magnum numerum juvenum nobilium, qui tum juri publico operam de more dabant, incidisset; percontata quinam essent, aut quid vellent, cum eos legum studiosos et etiam brevi tempore jurisperitos et patronos fore accepisset: O res (inquit) perditas, o miseram atque infelicem rempub.! Rogata, cur ita se affligeret, mulier ignota et peregrina: Quoniam jurisperitus (inquit) apud nos unus jampridem omnium fortunas compilavit, et regionem totam exhausit."—p. 217.

The question as to whether Jewel saw the evils of Puritanism, was slightly touched upon before ; and we have not space to dwell upon that point now. Engaged with the Romanist, probably he did not. And, as for Calvin, he thought of him as did many of our great divines, that is to say, as a reverend father and worthy ornament of the Church of God[1]. The immediate danger was from Rome ; and Calvin, being altogether opposed to the Papacy, was naturally an ally of Protestants. But to say that Jewel brought back with him from the Continent nothing but the general spirit of Protestantism, and that he left behind him the peculiar spirit of the Church of England, is not the case, as Mr. Le Bas has well argued. Jewel was, in truth, on all occasions, a sober defender of ecclesiastical discipline ; and that the platform of Geneva was contrary to his views is evidently to be inferred from his opposition to Humphrey's institution before referred to. Acts speak stronger than words, and so did Jewel's. Tender upon these points, and very fearful of the Romish moss and lichen again creeping over the pillars of our sanctuary, which had been so lately scraped, no doubt he was ; but we warn all those who may be in the way of hearing Jewel's name traduced as an "irreverent dissenter," at once to rebut the charge, and to acknowledge him to be, as he was, a true and worthy member of the Holy Catholic Church. As for the term Roman Catholic, now so familiar, it is, as Dr. Overal says in his Preface to Jewel's Works, "either a *contradictio in adjecto,* using Catholic for the Universal Church (as it signifies properly), or, at least, a *terminus diminuens,* taking Catholic (as it is commonly used) for orthodoxal."

But we find that we cannot enter into more particulars. Suffice it to say, that he was the constant preacher, even in the meanest village of his diocese; on which occasions, as on all others, he dared not to speak without precedent meditation, and writing also the chief heads of his sermons. Extemporary his preaching might be, to a certain extent, as we collect from the sermon at Paul's Cross, but unprepared was it never. His notes probably were longer than any modern discourse. Reynolds, and Whitaker, and Bilson, and Abbot, all "tinded their candles" at his and Peter Martyr's torches, as Master Featley remarked ; and, notwithstanding all differences on points,—great differences, we are ready to admit,—they shone gloriously. No matter where we look for Jewel, whether on his visitations, or in his closet, or in his chancery, there he was always the same ; the mild and cheerful Bishop of the Church of God, the defender of the poor, the encourager of religious and useful learning, the friend and the beloved

---

[1] Defence of the Apol. pt. ii. chap. 7. div. 2. vol. iv. p. 517.

of all good men, an angel in his life, his enemies themselves being
judges. Sarum, says Featley, in the "Abel Redivivus," was his
golden candlestick, and there "he shined most brightly for eleven
years, and after his extinction by death left a most sweet smell
behind him, the savour of a good name, much more precious than
ointment, for his apostolic doctrine, and saintlike life, and prudent government, and incorrupt integrity, unspotted chastity,
and bountiful hospitality ³."

Thus, as the new edition of his works has given us fit and
proper occasion was it our wish to speak,—how imperfectly have
we spoke!—of reverend Jewel;—a man, like other men, of sins,
and weaknesses, and short-comings, and doubts, and misgivings;
but withal a mighty prelate of the Church of Christ, a humble
penitent, a saint, who, in the midst of all his troubles, had joy in
the Holy Ghost! Imperfectly, however, as we have spoken of a
name never to be forgotten by all good Protestants, we have
done it, not forgetful of the great moral truth conveyed in those
lines of William Browne, in that beautiful poem, "The Britannia's
Pastorals:"—

"FOR EVER WHERE TRUE WORTH FOR PRAISE DOTH CALL;
HE RIGHTLY NOTHING GIVES THAT GIVES NOT ALL!"

We ought to add, in conclusion, that no trace, up to the present time, remains of his Paraphrase and Interpretation of the
Epistles and Gospels throughout the whole year,—of his con-
tinuate Exposition of the Lord's Prayer, the Creed, and the Ten
Commandments,—of his Commentary upon the Epistle to the
Galatians, or of that on the First of Peter. John Garbrand, it
is well known, published the posthumous works we have; and the
other loose sheets and MSS. on his death fell into the hands of
Robert Chaloner and John Rainold, doctors of divinity, as we
are informed by Antony à Wood. "What became," says Dr.
Jelf, "of these MSS. subsequently we are not informed. It

---

³ We transcribe from the "Abel Redivivus" the concluding well-known verses,
"done by Master Quarles, father or son":—

> "Holy learning, sacred arts;
> Gifts of Nature, strength of parts;
> Fluent grace, an humble minde;
> Worth reform'd, and wit refinde;
> I witnesse both in tongue and pen;
> Insight both in Booke and men;
> Hopes in woe, and feares in weale;
> Humble knowledge, sprightly zeale;
> A liberal heart, and free from gall;
> Close to friends and true to all.
> Height of courage in truth's duell;
> Are the stones that made this Jewell.
>   Let him that would be truly blest,
>   Weare this Jewell in his breast."

seems probable, however, that Garbrand himself, who lived five years after he had published the posthumous works, purposely excluded the treatises in question from the number. Admitting, therefore, in general, that the dust of such a man is gold, we may perhaps console ourselves under the disappointment of a fruitless search, by the conjecture that the lost works, however useful in their generation, were not considered by the author's intimate friend and literary devisee of sufficient importance to warrant their publication."—*Editor's Preface*, p. xxx.

We promised to conclude with some few warnings suggested by the existing state of Romanism amongst us,—an aggressive rather than a spiritual power, which, constituted as it is, and as long as it abides by the creed of Pope Pius IV. it always must be, can never be encouraged with safety; for, once let the κύριαι δόξαι of the Papacy become naturalized, and they will eat as doth a canker, turning religion into rebellion, and faith into faction. We have not sufficient proofs at hand for a detailed analyzation of the matter, but we do sadly believe, from observation, that a good deal of present disturbance arises from that leaven of unruliness which is fostered in the uneducated breasts of wild Roman Catholics, turned loose upon society. Sufficient, and more than sufficient, blame attaches to ourselves, as a nation, for not looking to the spiritual improvement of our people. But we cannot forget that our huge mobs, as well in London as in the manufacturing districts, are swelled into "a tympany" by masses of Irish, and we much fear that the poor and ignorant amongst them, which constitute the multitude,—as, for example, in St. George's, Manchester,—are not held back by that implicit obedience which is a tenet of their Church. On the contrary, that implicit obedience must array them against the Protestant Church, and invidiously lead them on to acts of insubordination inconsistent with peace and quietness and good government. We wish we may be deceived in our surmises, and that the letter from the Vatican may be the means of repressing seditious priests in Ireland. Certainly, before its arrival we were asking, with Jewel in his Apology, "*An pontifex ista à suis dici nescit? aut tales se habere patronos non intelligit* *?*" We have enough of ungodliness—we had almost said atheism—to answer for ourselves. God in His mercy turn from us "sedition, privy conspiracy, and rebellion!"

But, at the tail of a long article, we find we have not room to enter upon this point—the back-wave of '29—as we ought to do. We will therefore advert to a few heads, which we think of material consequence, because there are many who suppose that the

* Vol. iv. p. 53.

Roman Catholics are not now what they were; and that, as Mr. Henry Drummond said in the House in the debate on the Roman Catholic Relief Bill, there is " a most essential difference between the dead Papists of books and the real live Roman Catholics;" while, as we ourselves know quite well, Rome *quâ* Rome admits of no change, though she may, as in the case of Developement, now and then take a false step [4].

I. And, firstly, let all who are harnessing themselves for the battle be prepared well on the subject of the Supremacy; for on this, after all, the whole matter will turn. " A man," says Bishop Croft in his Legacy, " would wonder to see them, like cats, knocked down and quite dead in all appearance, yet rise up again with this text in their mouths,—" *Thou art Peter*," &c. [5] Yet so it is, and the Supremacy and consequent Infallibility of the Church of Rome is a point which will ever be insisted upon by her followers. Happily, we have a work at hand from which every reader may draw sufficient proofs of the falsity of the position : we allude, of course, to " Barrow's Treatise on the Pope's Supremacy," and to this we may confidently refer, though, as Tillotson says in his Preface, it " wants the finish of his last hand." This point, we need not inform our readers, was a portion of Jewel's Challenge, and is dwelt upon at great length in the Reply to Harding (Vol. ii. pp. 130—318). Coupled with " Barrow's Treatise," it affords a perfect armoury for authorities, and we may assert, in its concluding words, " That albeit Mr. Harding have travailed painfully herein, both by himself, and also on conference with his friends, yet cannot he hitherto find, neither in the Scriptures, nor in old Councils, nor in any one of all the ancient Catholic Fathers, that the Bishop of Rome, within the space of the first six hundred years after Christ, was ever entitled, either the Universal Bishop, or the head of the Universal Church." The whole, in fact, is a figment, and no record exists; and we might say, as Donato did to Julius II., when that haughty pontiff asked him, what title Venice had to the sovereignty of the Adriatic ? " Your Holiness will find it on the back of the record of Constantine's donation of Rome to the Pope ! "

II. We must warn all those who have not studied the deep

[4] We may refer here to what Dr. C. Wordsworth says in his 9th Letter to M. Jules Gondon : " By the reception of the Author of this Essay of the Developement, with this unhappy book in his hands, and by proclaiming his *conversion* as a signal and glorious *triumph*, instead of censuring him and his work as promoting heresy and infidelity, the Church of Rome has publicly declared to the world, that there is no truth so sacred which may not ,be assailed in her communion, no error so destructive to Christianity, and derogatory to the Divine dignity, which may not be professed there, especially if the assault of truth and the profession of error be for the purpose of maintaining the Supremacy of the Pope."—p. 230.

[5] See pp. 57—59. 4to, 1679.

cunning of Rome to beware! We are not to be deceived by specious pretences. It is the character of the Church of Rome not to advance a jot. All must be concession upon the part of Protestants, and they must virtually confess themselves to be schismatics, if they will be at one with Romanists. And then comes the question, Can we as Protestants concede to Romish error once more? The answer is simply this:—

QUID ROMÆ FACIAM? MENTIRI NESCIO.

None more than ourselves wish for reconciliation; but, as long as the pretensions of the Papacy remain unchanged, the gulf is impassable. All recent discussion shows this, and we see at least the deep wisdom of Bishop Morton, who "dehorted the dishonest Spalatensis (*i. e.* M. Antonio de Dominis) "from his vagary into Italy, to accommodate truth and peace, for the Italians would never be persuaded to retract an error!" We all know the end of him, and of his broad motto of union and concord, Rome and England[6]. Later attempts have fared no better even in honest hands. We need scarce refer to the honoured name of Archbishop Wake, or defend him from the remarks in the Confessional; but our readers will quite understand, after what has here been said, the meaning of the words which follow: "*Ces liaisons étoient innocentes, et Mr. Du Pin ne les entretenoit que pour l'honneur et l'avantage de l'église.*" Lesley and Bull and Nelson were willing to do what they could, but all was fruitless.

III. As for our diplomatic relations with Rome, we shall be sorry to see the day when they are established *according to the wishes of the Romanists*[7].

"Hoc Ithacus velit, et magno mercentur Atridæ!"

Luckily, for the present, there seems to be a hitch, and "the common witte, the first of wittes all," that is to say, plain common sense, as yet stops the gap. "The last leger of the English nation to Rome, publicly avowed in that employment," says

---

[6] The Bishop of London, in his much-abused charge, has referred to this incident. It will be found in Hacket's Life of Archbishop Williams, p. 108. We may here thank Dr. Wordsworth for his reprint of R. Crakanthorp's "*Defensio Ecclesiæ Anglicanæ contra Archiepisc. Spalatens.*," which is before us. When we think of de Dominis, we cannot but call to mind the words of Mendoza in the Malcontent,

"A churchman once corrupted, O avoid;
A fellow that makes religion his stalking horse."

[7] We bear in mind those words, "*Statuimus, id est abrogamus.*" See Letters between Bishop of Sarum and Dr. Cole, vol i. p. 54. This would be the language of the Vatican, when likely to be received. Certainly, "*In novis rebus constituendis evidens debet esse utilitas.*" See p. 48.

Fuller[a], was Sir Edward Carne, who "pretended that, as the Queen would not suffer the Pope's nuncio to come into England, so the Pope would not permit him to depart Rome; whereas, indeed, the cunning old man was not detained, but detained himself, so well pleased was he with the place, and his office therein, where soon after he died." The mission of Roger, Earl of Castlemain, we make no account of, as he was sent by James II.; but it were ominous, were our Sovereign Lady the Queen to accredit an envoy there in 1850! Whom the Pope might send here is, possibly, since the Duke of Wellington's remark (very unpalatable, as is to be picked out from recent letters); but, as the Black Bishop's Pawn says on Middleton's Game at Chess,— (though a play, a play well worth reading on this head),—there are plenty of Jesuits ready, at the Pope's bidding, to gull John Bull, if he please to be gulled.

> " They're not idle,
> He finds them all true labourers in the work
> Of th' universal monarchy, which he
> And his disciples principally aim at:
> Those are maintained in many courts and palaces,
> And are induced by noble personages
> Into great princes' services, and prove
> Some councillors of state, some secretaries;
> All bring in notes of intelligence—
> As parish-clerks their mortuary bills—
> To the Father General: so are designs
> Oft-times prevented, and important secrets
> Of states discovered, yet no author found,
> But they suspected oft that are most sound."

When the Earl of Arundel and Surrey tells us that "the Jesuits are the most loyal subjects of any government under which they live, whether republican or despotic[b]," we must beg to demur, and call to his recollection their expulsion from the various countries of Europe no less than thirty-seven times between 1555 and 1773. Neither can we ourselves forget that Louis de Montalte, the author of the Lettres Provinciales, was no less a person than the celebrated Pascal, whose testimony is clean and quite on the other side the question. True are the words of Henry King (some time Bishop of Chichester)—

> —" Rebellion wants no Cad nor Elfe,
> But is a perfect witchcraft of itself."

[a] Church History, book ix. sect. xvi.
[b] Debate on the Roman Catholic Relief Bill, "Times," June 1, 1848.

IV. "But," saith the Romanist, "your Anglican Church is so full of differences and dissensions, that there is no rest for restless souls—no balm in such a Gilead. 'A quiet life doth pass an empery,' but quiet in such a schismatic Church there can be none!" And with suchlike words the weak are beguiled, and, as in the first Charles's time, so now, they are drawn into the Maelstrom, by visions of comfort, before they are aware. Now, in all this again, there is subtilty and delusion, and Jesuitic cunning; and the boasted successor of St. Peter seems forgetful of St. Paul's words (1 Cor. xi. 18, 19), who was not a whit behind the chiefest of the apostles. The real truth of the matter is (a mighty warning this!)—that in the Romish Church, with all its vaunted unity, there is perhaps more division than in any other. "Not to mention," says good old Adam Littleton, whose sermons will rise in price since the notice of them in the Doctor, &c.; not to mention "their other differences about doctrine, those different *Orders of Religion* amongst them are neither better nor worse than so many sects and several castes of religion; only they have that advantage in managing their divisions, which we have not, to pack up their fanatics in convents and cloisters, and so bring them under some kind of rule and government [1]."

To any who are in doubt, and who are tempted to leave their own Mother Church, this is a matter for most serious consideration, inasmuch as, the step once taken, few, like Chillingworth, have the honesty to confess their error, but lead a life of sadness and disappointment. Apart from profaneness,

> "*Pauci, quos æquus amavit*
> *Jupiter, aut ardens evexit ad sidera virtus*
> *Dis geniti potuere!*"

We need hardly call to our readers' minds how admirably Jewel has handled this point in the Apology,—

> "Like as a scholar who doth closely gather
> Many huge volumes into a narrow space [3]!"

"Verum, ô Deus bone," are his commencing words, "quinam isti tandem sunt, qui dissentiones in nobis reprehendunt? An vero omnes isti inter se consentiunt! An singuli satis habent consti-

---

[1] See Sermons, p. 105, pt. ii. 6.
[2] The history of Chillingworth is one to which, in a note, we beg to refer our readers. His Treatise, "The Religion of Protestants a Safe Way to Salvation," has very properly been reprinted.
[3] Phineas Fletcher's Purple Island.

tutum, quid sequantur? An inter illos nullæ unquam dissentiones, nullæ lites extiterunt! Cur ergo Scotistæ et Thomistæ, &c. &c." Turn to the passage, good reader, as well as to the Defence of the Apology, vol. iv. p. 31; vol. v. p. 288.

V. With respect to such men as Mr. Newman going over to the ranks of the Papacy, this we must look upon as a sad fall and a perversion of the right—unless, as in poor Blanco White's case, there be an over-raught and restless mind to contend with. But any how, in Henry Vth's words to the Lord Scroop,

> "Thy fall hath left a kind of blot
> To mark the full-fraught man, and but indued
> With some suspicion."

As respects many others, however, what Brevint says in the Preface to his Saul and Samuel at Endor, is pretty much the case. "The truth is," says he, "ignorant sinners run generally for shelter to Rome, as broken merchants do to the King's Bench, with hope of being there secured against the ordinary courses of justice." This, at least, will apply to such as do not seek mere notoriety, or are not intellectually weak. But our object in referring to this individual case is to express our opinion relative to fallers off. We do not now, and we did not at the first, suppose that Rome would gain many converts. A contest is at hand, and we must abide it, but we are hopeful as to the result. Take our opinion in the words of Bishop Croft's Legacy, before referred to: "No man is such a stranger in our Jerusalem as not to know what is daily discoursed in all places. Many timorous zealots cannot hold in their fears; many insulting Papists cannot hold in their hopes, that Popery will again bear rule in this nation. For my own part, weighing things according to reason, I mean such a reason as God hath given me, I cannot see any great probability of it[4]." Such surmises are not unfrequently to be traced to Papists themselves, whose "wish is father to the thought." The words of the great historian of the Peloponnesian war are most applicable to the Romanist's wishes, whilst they convey a caution to us. Τὸ δὲ πλέον βουλήσει κρίνοντες ἀσαφεῖ ἢ προνοίᾳ ἀσφαλεῖ, εἰωθότες οἱ ἄνθρωποι, οὗ μὲν ἐπιθυμοῦσιν, ἐλπίδι ἀπερισκέπτῳ διδόναι, ὃ δὲ μὴ προσίενται, λογισμῷ αὐτοκράτορι διωθεῖσθαι[5]. But, let us be upon our guard, and we need not fear.

VI. Once more, with respect to the trite objection as to the Errors of the Reformers and of the Reformation, we are not

---

[4] Ut supra, p. 68. [5] Thucyd. lib. iv. c. 108.

careful to answer otherwise than in the words of the much-traduced Laud—often erring, but constant unto death—in his Conference with Fisher: "As for any error which might fall into this (or any other reformations), if any such can be found, then I say, and it is most true, reformation, especially in cases of religion, is so difficult a work, and subject to so many pretensions, that it is almost impossible but that the reformers should step too far or fall too short in some smaller things or other, which, in regard of the far greater benefit coming by the Reformation itself, may well be passed over and borne withal. But, if there have been any wilful and gross errors, not so much in opinion as in fact (sacrilege too often pretending to reform superstitions[6]), that is the crime of the Reformers, not of the Reformation; and they are long since gone to God to answer for it: to Whom I leave them[7]."

VII. If any Irish Roman Catholics should do us the honour to read these pages, we request that they will peruse (at their leisure) the following four productions of that excellent man, George Berkeley, some time Bishop of Cloyne, in Ireland: "*A Word to the Wise; or, An Exhortation to the Roman Catholic Clergy of Ireland;*" "*A Letter to the Roman Catholics of the Diocese of Cloyne, published in the late Rebellion, A.D.* 1745;" "*Maxims concerning Patriotism;*" and, "*The Querist.*" We have wondered that the wisdom of this good man has not been called forth before this, and made public. The evils that beset Ireland in his day were just the same as those which beset it now; and for many of these he proposed antidotes, some of which have been tried, and the sooner others are tried the better for the people and the land. Without referring to his many anticipations[8] of improvements already made, we give the following Queries of his, for his countrymen to chew.

No. xix. *Whether the bulk of our Irish natives are not kept from*

---

[6] For the term Reformation misapplied, the reader will do well to consult South. Amongst other many passages, that in vol. iv. p. 220 of his Sermons is none of the least remarkable. On "*further reformation,*" may be added vol. i. p. 203. Speaking of the Puritans, he says, elsewhere, they knew very well that there was "a conversion of lands as well as a conversion of unbelievers." We have lost this reference. All will recollect the words of the Homilies, in the fourth part of the Sermon against wilful Rebellion: "Surely that which they falsely call *reformation* is indeed not only a defacing, or a *deformation,* but also an utter destruction of all commonwealth," &c.—p. 534.

[7] Sect. 24. v. p. 128. Ed. Cardwell.

[8] Those who shall refer to these remarkable documents will find how he encouraged and improved cultivation in all sorts of grain, as well as the growth of *hemp and flax,* so suited to the country. With many points we may not agree, but no one can read Berkeley without admiring his heart and his intellect. What Christ-Church man forgets,

"To Berkeley every virtue under heaven!"

thriving, by that cynical content in dirt and beggary, which they possess to a degree beyond any other people in Christendom?

No. cxix. *Whether it be possible the country should be well improved, while our beef is exported,* AND OUR LABOURERS LIVE UPON POTATOES!

No. cclxxi. *Whether there be any country in Christendom more capable of improvement than Ireland?*

No. dxcv. *Whose fault is it if poor Ireland still continues poor?*

Such and the like were his Queries, who thus addressed a Word to the Wise: "Raise your voices, Reverend Sirs, exert your influence, show your authority over the multitude, by engaging them to the practice of an honest industry, a duty necessary to all, and required in all, whether Protestants or Roman Catholics, whether Christians, Jews, or Pagans. Be so good, among other points, to find room for *this*, than which none is of more concern to the souls and bodies of your hearers, nor consequently deserves to be more amply or frequently insisted on." The concluding words are memorable: "*Fas est et ab hoste doceri.* But, in truth, I am no enemy to your persons, whatever I may think of your tracts. On the contrary, I am your sincere well-wisher. I consider you as my countrymen, as fellow-subjects, as professing belief in the same Christ. And I do most sincerely wish there was no other contest between us but, *who shall most completely practise the precepts of Him by whose name we are called, and whose disciples we all profess to be*[1]."

Imperfect hints, and links, and affinities, all these; but, if we mistake not, they will give rise to sober thought and searchings of heart. In one and all we have not disguised our own sentiments, and we shall rejoice—none more—to find that we are prophets of ill; but, at the same time, we cannot disguise to ourselves the danger likely to accrue from concessions which avail not, or from truths

> "Half told
> Like story of Cambuscan old."

Look where we will—press our inquiries where we may,—there is a general and a vivid impression—(it has even been hinted to exist in the Odd Fellows' Societies)—that the emissaries of the staid old soldier of Pampluna are at work—that the ashes of dulness are again blown off from the torch of Ignatius Loyola.

> "Who with a rabblement of his heretics
> Blinds Europe's eyes, and troubleth our estate[2]."

[1] The passages will be found in pp. 120. 131. vol. i. ed. 8vo, 1820.
[2] Marlowe, Massacre of Paris. By the by we must not forget that there is such a thing as an ANTIPAPIST JESUIT! Let the reader consult Antony Farindon's Sermons, vol. ii. 1108, folio.

And if we speak in accordance with our fears (even although, as we said, we do not anticipate any great falling off), yet we have a good hope of numbers of Roman Catholics; and, even if they despair of us as heretics [3], "Heaven's gates" (as Laud said) "were not so easily shut against multitudes, when St. Peter wore the keys at his own girdle." Individually, and speaking for ourselves, one of the very best men we. ever knew,—an Irish merchant in a northern capital,—was a Roman Catholic. Despite the sinfulness of our nature—"*nonnulli* (they are Cicero's words) *sive felicitate quâdam, sive bonitate naturæ, sive parentum disciplinâ rectam vitæ secuti sunt viam* [4];" and so was it with this good man,—still living to bless those around him. His heart was always open, and his purse was never shut. It is hardly likely that we shall meet again on this side the grave; but there is room enough beyond, and then we shall all find that there is but one real Purgatory,—that is, Christ's blood shed to wash all penitent sinners clean. In the words of the Third Part of the Homily concerning Prayer, in the second tome revised by Jewel, "the only Purgatory, wherein we must trust to be saved, is the death and blood of Christ, which, if we apprehend with a true and stedfast faith, it purgeth and cleanseth us from all our sins, even as well as if He were now hanging upon the cross."

But enough. And, lest it might seem that we have forgotten that Jewel's Works are before us, we conclude with the two extracts following, the one and the other from "A View of a Seditious Bull."

"As Pope Pius complaineth now of the councillors of England, so did the wolf some time make complaint to the shepherd against the dogs. 'Thou hast two vile ill-favoured curs, they jet up and down, they bark and howl, and trouble the flock, which cannot be quiet nor feed for them. Remove them away, tie them up, brain them, hang them, what do they here? The shepherd answered, 'Would you so? Nay, I may not spare my dogs, they do me good service. Spaniels and greyhounds are fair and dainty, yet they never do me so much good: these watch when I sleep, they ease me of much pain, and save my flock. If I should tie them up, thou wouldest be bold with me, and take thy pleasure.' I shall not need to apply this. The Queen's Majesty is our shepherd, we are left by God to her safe keeping. The faithful councillors are like the watchful mastiffs, they take pains, they ease our shepherd, they save the flock. Now you may soon judge

---

[3] See Donne's Serm. x. on the Purification, p. 101, folio.
[4] We willingly adopt the words of Abp. Sumner from the conclusion of his Exposition, which has just reached us, "Undoubtedly the inward belief of many of them is purer than the articles of their Creed, and their practice governed by the real law of God, uncorrupted in things essential by the traditions of men which render it of none effect." 2 Thess. ii. 1—4. p. 84, 8vo.

who is the wolf. If Pope Pius could place his pilot in our ship, he would make us arrive at what port he listed."—vol. vii p. 261.

" And Thou, O most merciful Father, be our defence in these dangerous times. The lion rangeth, and seeketh whom he may devour. Look down from Thy heavens upon us. Give Thy grace unto Elizabeth (VICTORIA) Thy servant. Thou hast placed her in the seat of her fathers : Thou hast made her to be a comfort unto the people : Thou hast endued her with manifold gifts : shadow her under the wings of Thy merciful protection : confound and bring to nothing the counsel of her enemies : direct the work of Thine own hand : establish that, O God, which Thou hast wrought in us : so we, which be Thy people, and the sheep of Thy pasture, shall give Thee honour and praise for ever and ever. Amen."—Ibid. p. 284.

POSTSCRIPT.—Since this Article was written, the fears and the warnings in it have, sooner than expected, become painful realities[5]. The Bull has gone forth, and England,{ Protestant England, is not acknowledged as among *the Faithful;* but, on the contrary, as heretical, and in need of conversion. Unchanged and unchangeable is the Church of Rome. Otherwise it cannot be, as long as it abides by its principles !

Meanwhile, if, as some even of their own selves confess, the mine has been sprung too soon, let us be none the less on our guard. As far as they go, and for as much as they are worth, we receive Lord Beaumont's, and we receive the Duke of Norfolk's letter ; but, cautiously worded as they are, they do not persuade us that ultramontane notions will not be broached and maintained wherever it is possible they may be. What a clever Jesuist said the other day,—irritated with the vanity and the blatant ambition of Cardinal Wiseman[6], and possibly not unaccompanied with some personal dislike,—only shows us which way the wind blows,—" HIS CONDUCT HAS THROWN US BACK A HUNDRED YEARS !" The hope and the intent are all one as they ever were, and Roman Catholic ascendancy is uppermost in their minds when they write or speak in terms the softest. Many forms, doubtless, there are of Antichrist[7]; and every man, as

---

[5] Will the Government now take any effectual step *retrogressive?*—not of the first grand error—the πρῶτον ψεῦδος—of Catholic Emancipation,—but of the confirmed series of dangerous concessions they have ever since been stringing to the KITE'S TAIL !

[6] It was an old received opinion, that the Pope *shut the mouth* of a new Cardinal. He forgot to shut Dr. Wiseman's !

[7] If our memory serves us right, the Pope is only once called Antichrist in our Homilies,—viz. in the *Third Part of the Sermon of Obedience.* " He ought, therefore, rather to be called Antichrist, and the successor of the Scribes and Pharisees, than Christ's Vicar, or St. Peter's successor ; seeing, that not only on this point, but also on other weighty matters of Christian religion, in matters of remission and forgiveness of sins, and of salvation, he teacheth so directly against St. Peter, and

Gauden says in the Hieraspistes, "hath cause to suspect *Anti-christ in his own bosom* "—but the pushing horn of the Vatican cannot but call to men's mind the insolence of the Seven Hills in former days, and, as they dwell upon these things, they are apt to draw a conclusion from proceedings before their eyes, and to think within themselves, " What has been may be again ! "

It only remains that we tender our best thanks to Dr. Jelf for his ready courtesy in offering us his corrections to the " List of Authors and Editors," provided we could wait till he could gather them together. Unluckily, it is too late to stay the press, and we are only able to insert the following. What it relates to, will be found in vol. vi. 295. Defence of Apol. part vi. chap. 7. divis. 2. " BEMB. CARDINAL. Epistles written in the name and by the authority of Leo X. Jewel's reference is to a Letter addressed to Charles V.—It should be ' ad Recanatenses.' [Epist. lib. viii. *Cal. Julias anno secundo.*] Jewel's statement as to the Virgin Mary being called Dea is quite correct."

We do not know at present that we can refer to any other sources where information is likely to be found on this head,— one only excepted, which is the "*Irish Literary Gazette* " for July and August, 1848, in which the Rev. R. Gibbings has supplied several desiderata.

against our Saviour Christ, who not only taught obedience to kings, but also practised obedience in their conversation and living."—p. 114. Ed. Clar. 8vo. 1822.

ART. VI.—1. *An Appeal to the Reason and Good Feeling of the English People on the Subject of the Catholic Hierarchy.* By CARDINAL WISEMAN. London: Thomas Richardson and Son.

2. *The Cardinal Archbishop of Westminster, and the New Hierarchy.* By GEORGE BOWYER, Esq., *D.C.L., Barrister at Law &c.* By Authority. London: Ridgway.

3. *Diotrephes and St. John; on the Claim set up by the Bishop of Rome to exercise Jurisdiction in England and Wales, by erecting therein Episcopal Sees. No. IX. of Occasional Sermons.* By CHR. WORDSWORTH, *D.D., Canon of Westminster.* London: Rivingtons.

4. *The Bull of Pope Pius the Ninth, and the Ancient British Church. A Letter.* By E. C. HARINGTON, *M.A., Chancellor of the Cathedral Church of Exeter.* London: Rivingtons.

WHEN Her Gracious Majesty was induced a year or two since to express Her sympathy with the Pope in his distresses, and when Her Majesty's Ministers lent the aid of the Crown to replace the Pontiff on his throne, and to crush the liberties of the Roman people, it was little anticipated that acts of such high favour—acts indicative of such very cordial and amicable feeling towards the see of Rome—would be so ill repaid as they have been within the last few months. The *first* return of the papacy for the support extended to it by the Crown of England, was the condemnation of that favourite plan of the Government and of the leading political parties—the royal colleges established in Ireland, and bearing the "Queen's" name. The *second* is the division of all England into archiepiscopal and episcopal sees, and the appointment of bishops by the Papal authority. What will the *third* be? We suppose it will be to absolve all Romish subjects of the British Crown from their allegiance to a heretical prince. But matters are not quite ripe for *that* step at present. What has occurred, however, was exactly what might have been expected by those who are acquainted with the spirit and policy of the papacy and of its adherents. It appears to have come quite by surprise on the Government, and yet the design of establishing a Romish hierarchy, and, in particular, an Archbishop of Westminster, had been publicly known for several years. We have ourselves called attention to the scheme, and have urged that changes should be made in our own hierarchy, in order to meet the coming evil. There was no attempt on the part of Romanists to conceal the design, as Dr. Wiseman has observed with perfect correctness in his Appeal. We can ourselves bear witness to the truth of his statements on this point.

In September, 1847, we spoke thus in reference to the intentions of Romanism in this country.

" It seems to us that the present crisis is of the highest importance to the Church, and that on the judicious and active management of her affairs at this time very great results are dependent. There are great questions affecting her, which are likely to engage the attention of the public ere long, and we earnestly trust that apathy, or fancied security, or a mistimed feeling of dignity, may not prevent the adoption of efforts commensurate to the occasion. The apparently divided state of the Church (we trust that division will not prevent the co-operation of Churchmen for the welfare of the Church generally); the attacks in Parliament on the Ecclesiastical Commission; the virulent radical opposition to the increase of the episcopate; the exertions of sectarians to extend their own system, and to prevent the extension of the Church; the important questions involved in the Bishopric of Manchester Bill; are charged with important results on the welfare of the Church herself.

" That the Church of England has possessed a vantage-ground over her opponents, in the possession of the episcopal sees of her ancient hierarchy, has long been felt by both friends and foes. It is something to have to contrast the succession of archbishops in the episcopal chairs of St. Augustine and St. Paulinus, with the strange and foreign titles of Romish " Vicars Apostolic ;' and what authority bishops of ' Debra,' or ' Chalcis,' or ' Melipotamus,' can claim in England, is not very evident. This is a contrast which has been long and keenly felt by many of the English Romanists; and many have been the ineffectual efforts which they have made to induce the see of Rome to substitute bishops and archbishops possessed of the titles of the English hierarchy, for the system of ' Vicars Apostolic,' who derive their jurisdiction so entirely from the Pope, that they might at any moment be deposed by simply withdrawing the Papal licence under which they act. But, though such attempts have hitherto been unsuccessful, for some secret reasons, we should think the time cannot be very far distant, in which we shall see a rival hierarchy in England, usurping the titles of English sees. The appointments of Romish archbishops and bishops in the colonies, with titles derived from the countries in which they are settled, seems an indication of what is likely to be effected in England itself before long. Of course, such a step will not in reality alter the position of the respective parties, and the very novelty of the Romish hierarchy will, for a long time, be successfully pleaded against its claims; but we must be prepared for the annoyances which would, in various ways, result from the usurpation of the titles of English

bishoprics by Romanists.   If report speaks true, very great efforts are
now being made, with the object of introducing this innovation."
English Review, No. xv. p. 146, 147.

On the same occasion we urged that the see of London should
be made an archbishopric, in order that the head of the Church
in the Metropolis might not be inferior in ecclesiastical rank to
his Romish opponent and rival.

" We would strongly urge, that in any plan for Church extension the
Crown should be given the power of raising bishoprics to the title and
rank of archbishoprics.   If this be not done, the effect will be, that in
a short time we shall find Romish ecclesiastics holding the title of *archbishop*, in positions where the head of our Church bears an *inferior
title*.   The effects of this will, we are convinced, be *most injurious* to
the Church.   We feel confident of the truth of this, from having
observed the effect of such apparent superiority in the colonies and in
Ireland.   The Bishops of London, Durham, and Winchester, who hold
the rank of *protothrones* (to speak ecclesiastically), ought, in our
opinion, at once to become archbishops, holding their present temporal
rank and precedence.   The same rank ought, without any loss of time,
to be given to the Bishops of Calcutta, Sydney, Jamaica, and Montreal.
Will it be for the the benefit of the Church to see a Romish ' *archbishop*' of London or Westminster, while the Bishop of London is
possessed of an inferior title?   We think that this inconvenience might
be obviated, by introducing a provision into any measure of Church
extension now to be brought forward.   In a few years hence it might
be unattainable, especially if proposed as a separate measure."—p. 174.

At the same time we directed attention to the means for
increasing episcopal superintendence, and suggested that sees
should be founded, amongst other places, at *Plymouth, Shrewsbury, Westminster, Birmingham, Liverpool, Hexham,* and *Beverley.*
So that we have seen with regret the Church of Rome taking
possession of these and other important titles of sees, which
ought long since to have been appropriated by the Church of
England.   We claim no credit for foresight in expecting that the
Church of Rome would soon place her hierarchy in a more imposing position in England.

The design of creating a Romish hierarchy was publicly
known in 1847.   It was, also, as it appears from Dr. Wiseman's statement, communicated to Lord Minto in 1848, when
that diplomatist was at Rome.   And, moreover, Her Majesty's
Government had witnessed with perfect equanimity, not merely
the continuance of the Romish hierarchy in Ireland, though
day by day assuming more and more openly the style and titles
attributed by law only to the archbishops and bishops of the
established Church; but even the conversion, throughout all the

colonies and dependencies of England, of vicars-apostolic into territorial bishops. Not a remonstrance was ever heard from the Government on the point; nay, these very archbishops and bishops, assuming territorial titles, were officially recognized in their respective ranks; and Romish archbishops nominated by the Pope were given precedence over bishops of the Church, nominated by the Queen. Lord Stanley offered no objection to the establishment of a Romish territorial hierarchy in North America when consulted by Dr. Wiseman in 1841. Lord Grey has followed up the same liberal policy. Now the Supremacy of the Crown is precisely the same in Ireland and in the colonies as it is in England. Whatever is an invasion of the ecclesiastical rights of the Crown in England is equally an invasion of those rights, if attempted in Ireland or in any of the dependencies of the British Crown. If a Romish territorial hierarchy in England be inconsistent with the rights of the Crown, it is exactly as much inconsistent in Ireland, and in North America, and in Australia, and in the West Indies, and elsewhere. If, then, the present aggression of Rome be a just cause for "indignation" to Her Majesty's Ministers, what are we to say of those ministers themselves who have permitted the royal prerogatives to be infringed in the same manner, or even in a more openly illegal way, for a series of years?

The fact is this—that successive Governments have been for a great length of time permitting the ecclesiastical supremacy of the Crown to be infringed on by the papacy. The Government takes offence at the last step, having virtually sanctioned every other. And what has led to this exhibition of zeal on the present occasion?

If we may be permitted to hazard a conjecture, we should say, that the tone of the English ministry would have been very different on this occasion, and consequently the tone of their party and of its press, had not the *Irish colleges* been formally condemned by the Romish Synod of Thurles, in obedience to the Pope's rescript, only a few weeks before. The moment that this decision was made known, the " Times," and all the ministerial and liberal press, altered their tone in regard to Romanism. The course taken by the Pope, and the Romish National Synod at Thurles, was indeed as offensive to the Government as it could possibly be. A plan carried through Parliament in open opposition to the wishes of the people of England, and put in operation at great cost, and with every circumstance which could give it dignity and weight—a system which was thus carefully, and anxiously, and perseveringly set up for the express purpose of gratifying the Romanists of Ireland—was destined to find the strongest opposition from the

very community it was intended to serve; and this, too, after the
Government had been instrumental in greatly augmenting the endowment for Maynooth, without attempting to shackle its grant
by any conditions, and in defiance of the universal and indignant
remonstrances of the English people. The Maynooth grant was
forced on by the Ministers of the Crown, in opposition to the people. The "godless" colleges were carried in the same way. But
as soon as ever the buildings were erected, and the long array of
presidents, and principals, and wardens, and professors, and other
officials were nominated, and in possession of their respective
emoluments, and these institutions had been opened with every
kind of pomp and ceremony, the Pope and the Romish bishops
came to the resolution, that no member of their communion should
enter these "irreligious" institutions; and that a "Catholic"
university should be established in opposition to them! Now
this was undoubtedly the severest provocation that could well be
offered to the Government. It was not merely to reject a proffered
favour, but it was to reject it under such circumstances as made
the proceeding of the Government look perfectly absurd and ridiculous. The Queen's name had been bestowed on stately buildings, where no pupils except Protestants were to be permitted
to enter; and these "liberal" colleges were finally destined to
dwindle from the lofty position of national establishments, for the
education of the whole people, into mere "Protestant" seminaries
—and this, too, when Trinity College, Dublin, and the Belfast
Institution, were amply sufficient for the instruction of all the
Churchmen and Presbyterians who required a collegiate education!
Nothing could be more absurd than the position in which the
Government was thus placed by the decrees of the papacy and of
the synod of Thurles; and though little has been said on this
painful subject, except by the Government press, we cannot but
suppose that the insult has been keenly felt, and bitterly resented
in secret; and certain it is, that the "liberal" mind was grievously discomposed by the conduct of the Pope in this matter,
when the bull founding English dioceses came to blow their discontent into a flame.

We do not remember that any portion of the public press,
however, took notice of the fact, that the whole circumstances
attending the Romish Synod of Thurles, were quite as palpable
an infringement of the Royal Supremacy, as the bull appointing
English sees. The Supremacy exists in Ireland just as much as
it does in England. How comes it then, that without the slightest remonstrance or expression of dissatisfaction, the Pope's bull
or rescript was published, authorizing the assembling of that
council, when it is a well-known branch of the Royal Supremacy

to summon synods ; and all persons assembling such synods, and making canons in them without the royal assent, are subject to the penalties of premunire? It is generally supposed that synods cannot be assembled without the royal licence ; but yet, in defiance of this law, a national synod was openly and ostentatiously celebrated, with the full knowledge of Government, and canons were enacted, and the persons attending it assumed in the most public way the rank of territorial archbishops and bishops, and were recognized as such, in opposition to the archbishops and bishops appointed by the Queen. In the whole of this transaction, the Queen's Supremacy was ignored, and the Papal Supremacy was substituted in its place. And yet, not a voice was raised by any one against this flagrant usurpation of the papacy—this insult to the Crown. We confess our satisfaction that a Government which has connived at so public a violation of the Royal Supremacy in Ireland, should in a few weeks afterwards object to its violation in England. If the ministers take steps to punish the erection of new bishoprics without the Queen's leave, they are certainly bound equally to punish those who have assembled and celebrated national synods without the Queen's leave.

A new light seems to have opened upon the whole subject of the Royal Supremacy just now. The ministers and the people of England have suddenly discovered that the appointment of territorial bishops of any communion, without the Queen's consent, is an infringement of the Supremacy of the Crown. Undoubtedly it is so, according to the views taken of the Supremacy of Henry VIII. and Elizabeth, and by all our sovereigns till within the last century. When the Oath of Supremacy was instituted by Henry VIII., and revived by Queen Elizabeth, the declaration that the sovereign was supreme in all spiritual and ecclesiastical things and causes, meant, unquestionably, that every subject of the British Crown was bound to submit to that Supremacy, and that no regulations on religious subjects could be made without the sovereign's consent. The declaration that no foreign prelate or potentate hath, or ought to have, any jurisdiction within this realm, was intended to exclude especially the Papal power, to deny its existence as an authority, to refuse to recognize it as in any way existing over the subjects of the English Crown, whether in England or in any of its dependencies. The sovereigns who imposed this oath did not intend to permit the existence of the Papal jurisdiction at all in this kingdom. And such undoubtedly was the intention even of the Parliament of King William, which omitted the positive part of the Oath of Supremacy, and only retained its declaration against foreign jurisdiction. Its intention was unquestionably the same as that of the Parliaments of Henry

VIII. and Elizabeth, to oblige those who took it to deny the existence of any Papal jurisdiction in England; to refuse to recognize it as a power holding authority over all or any of the subjects of the English Crown.

Such was the old and genuine view of the Royal Supremacy : it was a power which was supposed to be inherent in the Crown, to be co-extensive with the nation, to be based on Scripture, and to be supported by the practice of Christian emperors. It authorized the sovereign to convene synods, to repress all schisms and heresies, to keep every subject of the Crown in obedience to the true religion maintained and established by the Crown. All persons who refused to adhere to the national faith and worship were regarded and treated as criminals. The attempt to establish any jurisdiction, or worship, or religious organization, whether Romish or Puritan, was repressed by the strong arm of the law. Every one was liable to be called on to take the Oath of Supremacy; so that the Supremacy was held to extend to *every subject* of the English Crown. All this was perfectly consistent and intelligible.

And such clearly is, to a considerable extent, the view taken of the Royal Supremacy by the mass of the people at this moment, and in general by all the opponents of the recent measure of Pius IX. They all regard it as an invasion of the Royal Supremacy. From the Sovereign on her throne down to the poorest of her subjects, all concur in repudiating this attempt as an invasion of the Royal Supremacy. It has been in vain for dissenters to protest, as they have done at a few public meetings, that they could not join in asserting the Royal Supremacy in opposition to the Papal. They have been hooted down, or hustled; and the whole people have declared that the Royal Supremacy must be maintained against the Papal usurpation. Now what is the meaning of this? Its meaning is that Romanists are, in their capacity of British subjects, bound to submit to the Queen's Supremacy; that the Supremacy extends its jurisdiction over *all* her Majesty's subjects. Certainly there cannot be a sounder or more correct principle that this. If the ecclesiastical Supremacy be an attribute of the Crown, it extends wherever the authority of the Crown extends, and over all the subjects of the Crown. Whatever may be the religious tenets of any man, whether he be Romanist, or Churchman, or dissenter, or Presbyterian, he is equally subject to the ecclesiastical Supremacy of the Crown.

Mr. Bowyer and Dr. Wiseman argue, in their respective pamphlets, that the State, in granting emancipation to Romanists, intended to grant them full permission to deny the Supremacy of the Crown, and that they are accordingly wholly free from that Supremacy, and only subject to the Papal Supremacy. The Roman Catholic Oath in the Emancipation Act being so constructed as to require only a rejection of the doctrine that the Pope has any "temporal or civil" jurisdiction in this realm, Mr. Bowyer infers that it was intended to leave Roman Catholics at liberty to hold that the see of Rome has "spiritual" jurisdiction in the dominions of the British Crown. Dr. Wiseman adds, that by these Acts "Catholics" were freed from all obligation of acknowledging the Royal ecclesiastical Supremacy, and that the Supremacy is not admitted by any dissenters—that, in fact, the Supremacy is limited strictly to the Church of England—that any one can cease to be subject to the Royal Supremacy by merely separating from the Church. And he quotes Lord Lyndhurst to show that as "Catholics" may, without being liable to punishment by the common law, assert the Papal Supremacy, so they may equally deny the Royal Supremacy.

But Dr. Wiseman's own authority here fails him most sadly; for it so happens, that, in respect to the last point, Lord Lyndhurst, as quoted by Dr. Wiseman, says precisely the contrary; his words are these:—

"On the other hand, if any person improperly, wantonly, or seditiously, called in question the Supremacy of the Crown of England—and *that*, it was to be observed, included the temporal as well *as the spiritual power of the Crown*—if any, from any improper motive or purpose, or in any improper manner, questioned *that* Supremacy, then that person would be liable to a prosecution at the common law; and there could be no doubt, if the learned judges were consulted, they would so determine."—p. 12.

Here is exactly the highest authority for the assertion that the Queen's Supremacy *still* extends to every subject of the Crown. Lord Lyndhust admits indeed that a Romanist may hold the Papal Supremacy; but he must not dare to deny the *Queen's* Supremacy. He is left to reconcile the two Supremacies in the best way he can; but the Royal Supremacy over him in ecclesiastical matters is fully asserted, and if he pretends to *deny* that Supremacy on any account—even on account of his duty to the Pope—he is liable to punishment at common law, and all the judges would affirm that he is so!

And is it not obvious that it must be so? The Queen is supreme in ecclesiastical and spiritual matters by common and statute law. Certain classes of British subjects, holding peculiar religious views, were for a long time held to be traitors or evildoers, for disobedience to the Royal Supremacy. They were at length tolerated, relieved, and emancipated from the various pains, penalties, and disabilities inflicted on them by law. The oaths and declarations were modified to meet their case, and permit them to exercise the peculiar religions they had chosen. But *in no one instance* was the Royal Supremacy ever brought into question by any legislative act. It may have been practically compromised, by not being enforced, or being permitted to lie dormant; but in no act of relief, toleration, or emancipation has the Crown ever conceded to any body of men the right of denying its Supremacy. The law may not be so enforced as to require every one to profess that Supremacy; it may wink at much that is going on; it may reserve the assertion of rights for special occasions: but it is evident that at this moment the Crown holds in theory, and according to all the principles of the law and constitution, the same ecclesiastical Supremacy over every subject of the Crown that it did in the time of Queen Elizabeth. Dr. Wiseman must not suppose that every thing which is tolerated is legal. The Crown has as little relinquished its ecclesiastical Supremacy over Dr. Wiseman himself, as the Pope has relinquished his temporal Supremacy over the Queen of England. Neither power is enforced, and neither power is relinquished. Dr. Wiseman may deny, as much as he pleases, the ecclesiastical Supremacy of the Crown of England over himself and other Romanists within this empire; but his and their denial will not in the least change the state of the law, or divest the Crown of the powers which constitutionally belong to it.

To suppose, indeed, as he does, that any man who pleases to walk across the street from the parish church, to Salem or Ebenezer, or the popish chapel, can, by that easy and simple process, free himself, not merely from any necessity of professing belief in the Royal Supremacy, but from all *subjection to that Supremacy in the eye of the law*, is certainly a strange supposition; and, in order to reconcile us to the notion that the Supremacy is placed in so precarious, nay, so ridiculous a position by law, something more than mere logical inferences from certain Acts of Parliament ought to be forthcoming.

We beg leave, therefore, to assure Dr. Wiseman, and his co-religionists in England and Ireland, that they are at this moment in the eye of the law just as much subject to the Royal ecclesiastical Supremacy, whatever they may say, as members of the Church of England are. The only difference is, that toleration is extended, and liberty conceded to Romanists, which is not in the same way requisite for Churchmen, who are obedient to authority. Presbyterians, Independents, Baptists, Wesleyans, and dissenters of all kinds, are all equally by law subject to the Royal Supremacy. The Supremacy has never been relinquished

by law in the case of any sect.   Not a statute can be pointed out
which states that Romanists, or any other religious denomination,
are exempted from the Royal Supremacy.

This is not the view generally taken ; but we feel convinced,
by all we have lately seen and heard, that it is the true view.   Of
course, if the Queen's ecclesiastical Supremacy does not extend
over the whole nation, the recent appointment of Bishops by
the Pope is no violation of the Supremacy.   If the law exempts
Romanists from the Royal Supremacy, the Pope may do what he
likes with reference to their affairs.   But the whole nation is
convinced that there has been a direct infringement on the Royal
Supremacy.

The results of the step taken by Pius IX. cannot fail to be
of very great importance in various ways.   In the first place, the
Prime Minister of the Crown has expressed himself in such indignant terms, as to have held out to the people of England an
expectation that the temporal power will be employed to repress
the attempt which has been made by the Pope.   Every one
appears to expect that legislation will take place with a view to
such cases.   On the other hand, to attempt, either by enforcing
the laws, or by enacting new ones, to put down the recent proceedings of Pope Pius, would give mortal offence to the adherents
of the papacy.   Nor is the influence of that party to be despised
by the present Government.   Sixty or seventy Irish votes might
not be able to prevent the passing of measures against the
Romish hierarchy ; but they would be able to turn out the ministry, by siding with the Conservatives in the next division ; and
such will probably be their policy.   They will never permit an
insult to their hierarchy : they will tell the minister that their
votes depend on his conduct in this matter ; and he will succumb.
We can scarcely persuade ourselves that any legislation can take
place on this subject, or that the Government will take any
steps against the new Romish hierarchy.   To do so would be to
reverse the policy which for many years has influenced this
country.   It would be to maintain the ancient institutions of this
nation—to protect the Church of England—to uphold the Royal
Prerogative against Papal aggression—to run the risk of displeasing the Romanists of the United Kingdom.   We shall not
believe this possible, until we have been convinced by the evidence
of positive facts.   Whatever may be the excitement of the people,
we can scarcely expect that it will induce a " Liberal " House of
Commons to alter its policy.   That policy is no innovation : it
has presided in the councils of successive Governments for thirty
years.   From the moment that George IV. was advised by his
minister to receive the Romish hierarchy officially and publicly in

1821, on occasion of his visit to Ireland, an uninterrupted series of concessions has manifested the wish of each successive Government to gratify the Romanists in Ireland and in England. Political parties have for several years vied with each other in bidding for the good will of the Romish interest. Sir Robert Peel and his friends were as anxious as Lord John Russell and his to subsidize the Romish priesthood of Ireland, by granting them glebes, and houses, and payments from the Treasury; and that this has not been done has arisen solely from the obstinate refusal of the Romish priesthood and hierarchy. Dr. Wiseman has proved, and unanswerably, in his Appeal, that for a long series of years the Church of Rome has been encouraged by the Governments of England, in its successive movements and aggressions. We cannot conceive that this policy is now about to be reversed.

But, if it be not reversed—if the Romish hierarchy be left substantially in the occupation of the position it has taken—what will be the position of the Church of England? We put out of sight the mere denial of her character, and authority, and even existence, by the recent measures, but we look to their practical bearing. Will not the people, then, be confused and disturbed by finding a rival hierarchy claiming their adhesion? Nay, in places where none of our bishops are placed, will not the Romish bishop be recognized gradually as "the bishop" of the place? At Birmingham a Romish ecclesiastic will be the only "bishop" known in the place. So again at Liverpool, in Southwark, Plymouth, Northampton, and other important places where we have no bishops. Those places will virtually be handed over to the Church of Rome to assume there the position of the regular episcopate. Our people will, we fear, be greatly confused by all this.

And, moreover, the rank and station now assumed by Romish ecclesiastics will operate most injuriously in giving to them influence over weak-minded persons, who may be caught and attracted by high-sounding titles, and the show of a hierarchy surrounded with all those formalities which Romanism knows so well how to avail itself of. And this is but the first step. The next will be to summon a national synod with as much pomp as can be assigned to it, and to carry out the organization by nominating deans, archdeacons, canons, vicars-general, chancellors, precentors, and rectors and vicars. Every incumbent of a parish in England, in which there is a Romish priest, will very soon find himself confronted by a rival rector or vicar who will treat him as an usurper, and hold himself entitled by all the laws of God and of holy Church to the churches, and tithes, and lands of that benefice.

It is vain to conceal from ourselves that all this would place the bishops and clergy of England in a position they have never occupied before. At every turn they would be met by rivals.

Now all this will be positively and seriously injurious to the security of the Church of England. Every one sees the dangers arising from a Romish hierarchy in Ireland: dangers the same in kind, though not in degree, as yet, will follow from a similar proceeding in England. The rights of the Church will be endangered: and her position lowered; and advantages will have been conceded to her rivals to exert all their powers for her subversion. The Crown will, if it permit this invasion of the rights of the national Church, have consented to allow her opponents, without let or impediment, to take every step within their power, to adopt the most perfect and systematic organization, for the exact purpose of destroying the Church of England.

How it would be possible to reconcile such a course of proceeding as this with the engagements of the Crown, to protect the faith and the rights of the Church of England—engagements imposed by oath on the sovereign by the very same authority, which requires from the subject the oath of Supremacy; how the Crown can be considered to discharge its part of the compact, and can call on others to respect their part of the compact, if it permit the rights of the Church to be flagrantly violated, and the security of the Church and of its faith to be endangered as they are by the measure of Pius IX., we are unable to see. The Coronation oath is surely as binding on the sovereign, as the oath of Supremacy on the subject. That Coronation oath was, we think, really broken, when Roman Catholic emancipation was granted, notwithstanding the pretended securities by which it was accompanied. It has not been attended to, we fear, by successive ministers, who have advised the relinquishment of security after security for the Church, and the adoption of measure after measure in furtherance of the claims and objects of the Church's opponents, without even the pretence of further securities for the Church. But now a blow is aimed at the Church far more formidable than any that has yet taken effect; and if this blow is permitted to descend —if it is not warded off—if the Church of Rome is permitted to make its descent like a bird of prey upon us—we think the question must at once occur to every Churchman's mind: "Is the Crown of England keeping its engagements to the Church and the country?"

We can only see one way in which this question could be satisfactorily answered, supposing that the Crown were not prepared to recommend the repression—the effectual repression of this Romish outrage on the Church. If the Church of England, including bishops, clergy, and laity fairly represented in synod, and subject to the Royal Supremacy, were permitted to take counsel together for the purpose of developing the internal resources of the Church, and completing her organization in opposition to the rival which has now started up, we should feel that something at least had been done in the way of giving securities to the Church. But to feel, that while we are unable to get a single additional bishopric, and while the cause of that difficulty is chiefly the presence of Roman Catholics and dissenters in Parliament, the Church of Rome is to be allowed to multiply her episcopate *three-fold* in ten years, with prospect of further increase, and to usurp positions which ought years ago to have been occupied by the national Church, would certainly impress the mind with a strong sense of grievance and wrong.

We are not, however, disposed to think that any steps for the security of the Church of England are likely to be taken at present. The excitement of the public mind has been directed by Lord John Russell with considerable adroitness to the Tractarian doctrines and practices as the sole cause of the recent Papal aggression. The unpopularity of these tenets rendered it an easy task to effect this diversion of the popular fury, which might otherwise have burst upon the course of state policy to which the advocates of the Papal proceedings have appealed in their justification. The Evangelical party have eagerly taken the opportunity of assailing their opponents in every way. How far this course may be pursued when Parliament meets remains to be seen. There are parties in the legislature who will not be disposed to let the question be shifted from its true grounds. We may expect indeed that Tractarianism will be severely condemned in Parliament, nor shall we be much surprised even to see measures taken for its suppression, if such can be devised. But we can scarcely suppose that, even if such measures be introduced, the Parliament of England would be prepared to sweep every " High-Church" incumbent out of the Church, and to leave none remaining except those who adopt the Calvinistic view of regeneration.

There has been considerable dissatisfaction on the subject of the Royal Supremacy for some years past. Let the Supremacy, however, be fairly and *bonâ fide* exercised in the spirit of the engagements which it involves, and which the Sovereign undertakes by oath at his coronation, and all difficulties will be at an end. If the Supremacy be religiously exercised—if it be exercised in the spirit of the godly kings and Christian emperors of old, or of our own Edwards and Elizabeths, then it will be an unspeakable blessing to the country.

If the State should now honestly, consistently, and *bonâ fide* adopt the policy of protecting the Church and the Royal Supremacy in this empire, by repressing the recent attempt of the Papacy, and taking all steps within its power for withdrawing the recognition it has extended to the Papal jurisdiction at home and in the Colonies—if this should be the course adopted, our advice to all faithful Churchmen would be to co-operate cordially and earnestly with any Government which thus acted up to the responsibilities incumbent on it, and to refrain from the expression of any sentiments of distrust, or of opposition, which might have the effect of diminishing the unanimity of a movement possessing many and great claims on their approbation.

We are aware that there are some circumstances in the movement which we have seen which are calculated to cause uneasiness in the minds of good Churchmen. Principles have been not unfrequently broached at public meetings which would, if fairly carried into effect, amount to the overthrow of the Church of England. Men, in their indignation at the dangerous tenets of Rome, and the follies and apostasies of some among ourselves, have sometimes spoken in such terms as are not consistent with a knowledge of the principles of their own Church, or with faithfulness to her. But it must be observed, that in such public meetings persons of all creeds and denominations were present, and took part in the proceedings ; and this naturally led to the expression of sentiments, in many instances, inconsistent with the right tone and spirit of members of the Church of England.

These meetings have, however, been valuable in one respect. They have distinctly proved what the feeling amongst the overwhelming mass of the people of England is in reference to "Tractarianism." We think it is most highly desirable that the extent of this feeling should be fully and distinctly understood. That it has not been appreciated by those against whom this movement has been chiefly directed is quite certain. Had they understood it, they would not have entertained any hopes of introducing alterations in the laws relating to the alliance of Church and State, by any efforts which they themselves could make, or in which they were prominent leaders. The state of the public mind has now been so unequivocally manifested that there can be no longer any mistake on the subject. The general hostility to "Tractarianism" is extreme ; understanding chiefly by that name approximations to Romish ritual, and doctrine, and practice, exemplified in an attention to symbolism, mediæval arrangements, and decorations of chancels ; the use of lights, flowers, crucifixes, and rood-screens ; the practice of systematic confessions, penances, and absolutions ; of invocations of saints, and the use of rosaries and books of Romish devotion. And, through the strong, and not unfounded hostility to the system which is thus distinguished, a very great difficulty is placed in the way of all those clergy who are desirous of promoting decency and propriety in public worship; of observing the directions of the Church, and of urging on their people the duty of remaining in its communion, and not frequenting dissenting places of worship, or allowing their children to be brought up as Dissenters. The existing prejudice in the popular mind against " Puseyism," or " Tractarianism," leaves this very large portion of the Clergy, and even of the Episcopate, in a painful and disadvantageous position. It is in the power of any person to whom a faithful and conscientious clergyman may have given offence in the discharge of his duty, however unintentionally, to excite a prejudice against him by vague and unfounded charges of " Puseyism." It is in the power of Dissenters to set his flock against him by whisperings which perhaps never reach his ears, and which he has no means of effectually meeting and refuting. The Romanist will often insidiously claim him for his own, with the express purpose of sowing dissension in his flock. The present state of things, therefore, gives the enemies of the Church the most effectual means of undermining the usefulness of every man who is not remarkable for his association with dissenting teachers, or who does not occupy his hearers' time with pulpit denunciations of " Popery" and " Puseyism." A clergyman may exert himself in every way to guard his flock from Popish emissaries. He may refrain from every approximation to the Romish Ritual, and limit himself entirely to the directions of the Book of Common Prayer. He may deeply lament the practices which he hears of elsewhere, and may express his regret at the course which is being taken. He may be really opposed to "Tractarianism;" may have no intercourse with its leaders, or with any partizans; and yet this will not protect him from imputations as grossly unjust as they are painful and injurious. A clergyman may write and preach against the errors of Romanism, and yet even this will not exempt him from the suspicion of being a " Puseyite," and therefore a " Papist."

But the great evil arising from this is, that the ministerial usefulness of any clergyman is thus liable, without the slightest fault on his part, to be impaired, and the cause of the Church injured. It may be impossible for him conscientiously to accept the Calvinistic views which some of his brethren entertain, and perhaps, if he were to adopt them, his congregation would be highly dissatisfied. It may be impossible for him, acting on his view of duty, to introduce irregularities in the mode of performing Divine service, or to teach his people that it is a matter of indifference whether they go to church or to meeting-house. Yet surely a clergyman ought not to be placed in the position of being considered as a traitor to his Church merely because he tries to do his duty according to the best of his knowledge and conscience, and adopts the course which has been recommended by all our great Divines in former ages. That men who are devotedly attached to the Church of England, and who have not the slightest leaning towards Romanism, but are ready on all occasions to resist its inroads, should be liable, as they are, to the most unfounded imputations, is a severe trial and hardship in itself; and, if the popular feeling should lead to the expulsion of such men from the Church of England, that Church will be no gainer by the result.

It seems to us far from improbable that we are on the eve of measures directed to the professed removal of Romanizing practices and tenets from the Church. Our reasons for so thinking are these. The excitement of the popular mind is so profound, and so unusually protracted, that it has even brought forward numbers of members of both houses of Parliament, men of the most "liberal" views in politics, to denounce at public meetings the twofold peril of "Popery" and "Puseyism." Now this is quite a new feature in the times. The agitation in 1829, and in the time of the Maynooth Bill, was extensive, but it was not participated in by all classes of the community, and by persons of all shades of politics and religion, as this has been. The "liberal" party is thus committed, not only by the act of Lord John Russell, but by its own participation in the agitation, to do *something* in the next session of Parliament. The people who have been thus excited cannot be put aside with mere words: something must be *done*, if the popularity which Lord John Russell has attained is to be preserved; if the popular feeling is to be prevented from turning into one of exasperation and disappointment.

It is therefore evident that something must be done: but, considering the political influence exercised in the House of Commons by the Romish party, and a certain body of "liberals" in connexion with them, we think it impossible that any measures of real repression of the recent papal aggression can be urged or even attempted. The alternative then will be, to gratify the popular mind by measures for the purpose of purging all Romanizing practices, forms, and ceremonies out of the Church. To do any thing effectual it might, perhaps, be necessary to go to Parliament for powers. We may very possibly, ere long, have royal injunctions, and a visitation to carry them into effect, as was the case in the time of Edward VI.

Now, if any such course should be adopted, we would express in the first place our earnest hope, that Churchmen would not be too hasty to take offence at what they may justly consider in some respects an evil; for the interference of the temporal power in religious matters is not a novelty either in England or elsewhere; and, when the interference is directed to right and lawful objects, the Church has frequently tolerated irregularities, and even derived benefit from them. The great point, therefore, for consideration ought to be the *substance* and *nature* of the reforms or alterations contemplated. In the event of any such measures being adopted, it would, most probably, be managed and directed by persons of the Evangelical and Latitudinarian schools. It would, therefore, be possible, that a course might be taken which would not merely repress Romanizing innovations, but might go further, and alter in some material points the discipline or doctrine of the Church of England. Now, the result would be this. If measures were taken, *bonâ fide*, for the repression of Romish practices and ceremonies, we should suppose that no material difficulties would arise. The great mass of the clergy who hold the doctrine of Baptismal Regeneration, and are, therefore, unjustly called "Tractarians" and "Puseyites," have no wish to see any Romish practices or ceremonies introduced into the Church : they grieve to hear of such things being attempted; and they would not be found amongst the advocates of those who may have indiscreetly or improperly introduced them. The only ground on which they might be led to oppose themselves to such a process of reform as we have referred to would be unwillingness to recognise a power which might be capable of gross abuse, and might be hereafter employed for the subversion of the faith as held by the Church of England. This would be, probably, the ground also taken by the advocates of Romish practices and tenets, who would trust to it as a means of exciting feeling in their behalf, which would never be called forth by any mere defence of Romanizing practices. Such is the strong feeling of dislike of the interference of a State which includes persons of all religious creeds in the spiritual concerns of the Church, that we can well imagine that various persons might be led to identify themselves with the small Romanizing faction, in support of what they did not themselves approve. But we should not suppose, that any material number of persons would refuse submission to measures, even if somewhat irregular, provided those measures were simply and *bonâ fide* for the purpose of removing decidedly Romish or Romanizing practices, ceremonies, &c.

But on the other hand, if any thing *more* were attempted—if under cover of this removal of Romanism it were attempted to introduce peculiar views of the sacraments, or to limit the freedom of opinion which now exists on these points, or to lower the doctrine of the English Church as now settled, the result in the present state of men's minds might be fearful to contemplate. Let any step be taken, which, under the dictation of the temporal power, appeared to alter the doctrine of the Church of England, and left it out of the power of its advocates to say that doctrine remained unaltered; and a shock would be given to the Church of England, the effects of which might be most fearful. A schism would probably immediately take place, and the Established Church would lose thousands of clergy and hundreds of thousands of laity, and find a second rival episcopate established in the land.

The extreme difficulty and danger of any such attempt as we have referred to are sufficiently obvious: we do not, however, by any means intend to affirm that no attempt ought to be made to meet an evil which certainly exists—a strong tendency to Romanism in some quarters. There is danger evidently: the continued secessions prove that there is. If, then, it be requisite to take any steps for removing causes of distrust and division, let them be taken in the regular way. Let the Sovereign commend certain questions to the consideration of Convocation, with a view to provide a remedy for the evils complained of. Convocation would *undoubtedly* repress every thing that could be fairly considered as Romanism. It would require of every clergyman to renounce certain practices, and would give to ordinaries additional powers. Such a course would have this advantage, that the competency of Convocation has been fully recognised by all those who are usually liable to imputations of Romanizing. It would be impossible to oppose its decisions on the ground of standing up for the liberties of the Church.

If, however, there be insuperable objections to Convocation, then we would say, let any doctrinal questions be settled by the episcopate of the Church of England. We observe, that in the address of the laity to the Queen, adopted at the meeting in Freemasons' Hall, under the presidency of Lord Ashley, the authority of the heads of the Church is recognised. The passage to which we refer is as follows:—

"But we humbly entreat your Majesty, in the exercise of your Royal Prerogative, to direct the attention of the primates and bishops of the Church to the necessity of using all fit and lawful means to purify it from the infection of false doctrine, and as respects external and visible observances, in which many novelties have been introduced, to take care that measures may be promptly adopted for the repression of all such practices."

We think that all real danger would be avoided in the present crisis, if the spirit of this suggestion were acted on, and the discussion of all points of importance in reference to the questions which have been raised in the matter of "Tractarianism" were referred to the Primates and Bishops of the Church. We believe that the result of such a reference would be satisfactory to the infinite majority of all real friends of the Church. We believe that it would meet the wishes of the Evangelical body generally, and that it would not be unsatisfactory to the great mass of the High-Church Clergy, because we feel assured that the bishops, as a body, would not act on the principle of driving out of the Church those who only hold the doctrines of all our greatest and most learned divines and bishops, such as Beveridge, Taylor, Hall, Leslie, Bingham, Bull, Van Mildert, Jebb, and Howley, but would repress tenets and practices which are of a Romish complexion and tendency. We must frankly say, that if this were accomplished, we should regard it as a benefit to the Church of England, and we are confident that a great body of High-Churchmen would support such a decision, and would have reason to feel thankful that any means were afforded them of testifying openly their adhesion to the principles of the Church of England, and their rejection of all that tends towards Romanism.

We are too sensible of the momentous nature of the consequences of any such course to venture on expressing any definite wish on the subject. But at the same time, if any thing should be done, we trust that the object of those who have influence will be to execute their work in as moderate a spirit as possible, consistently with their sense of duty. It has pleased God to throw the chief influence and guidance of the affairs of His Church in England into the hands of a party with whom we should not have sought for correctness of Church principle. The want of common sense, and the extravagancies of another party, and the secessions of its members to Rome, have delivered the Church into the hands which now sway it, supported by the national voice. Although we are unable to subscribe to all the views of that dominant party, we still trust, that love for the Church of England —regard for its security—and a disposition to tolerate differences of opinion in points which are not absolutely vital, will induce the heads of the Church at least, to adopt such a course as shall not drive honest, learned, and sincere members and ministers of the English Church in thousands out of her communion; but to limit themselves to the expulsion of what is plainly inconsistent with fidelity and attachment to the cause and the religion of the Reformation as established in England.

The enemies of the Church will urge the adoption of the most sweeping measures—the establishment of levelling and latitudinarian principles, which would silence the mere claim of the Church of England to be a society founded by Christ and his Apostles. But we will indulge in the hope, that all persons of weight and influence, however they may be opposed to " Tractarianism," will hesitate before they consent to break down any of the system which has been handed down to us from past ages, and that the power they may exercise will be used with something of that " common sense" which we must admit them to possess, and the absence of which will prove the ruin of " Tractarianism." The leaders of the latter system have unfortunately always closed their eyes to the " signs of the times :" they have never known when to yield : they have ignored the people of England. We have now in consequence to see the inevitable triumph of a party which their imprudence alone has exalted. But, while we witness this result with regret, we still cherish the hope that God will watch over His Church amongst us, and not permit it to be further weakened by extensive secessions or expulsions, and that none may fall away except those who are either disloyal to the Church, or who will not permit their faults to be corrected by authority.

It is a matter of deep pain, that, as circumstances now stand, the Church is left a prey to the struggles of parties without any check or limit. In one direction, some men are permitted to declaim against the doctrine of Baptismal Regeneration in such terms as amount to positive dissent from the Church of England. In another direction, men introduce Romanism, and, when they have played with it for a time, apostatize from their Church. We strongly disapprove of all party organizations and proceedings ; but we regret to be obliged to admit, that the party which is more or less unsound on the point of Baptismal Regeneration is practically a less evil to the Church than another extreme party which is continually recruiting the Church of Rome with new converts. The apostasies which have taken place, and which are still in progress, are facts which are open to universal observation, and which absolutely close the mouths of those who wish to advocate Church principles. It is hopeless to argue that those principles do not lead to Romanism. We may ourselves see clearly that they ought not to do so, and may have arguments enough to prove that we are in the right ; but we can never answer the *fact* of apostasies, so as to satisfy the public mind. It is in vain to pretend that the apostates were all Latitudinarians or Low-Churchmen ; for they had subsequently adopted very different views.

The triumph which will be gained by the Evangelical party will, however, probably ere long be shared by another party, which they will have reason to dread, at least as much as they do the "Tractarian" party. They will have to contend with Rationalism. Perhaps, when that contest arises, those Church-men who have remained attached to their principles, though sobered and saddened by the reverses of their cause, will be enabled again to contend, without encountering suspicion and enmity, for the principles of the Christian faith. At present all sound Church principles—those principles which our great Divines in former ages have upheld, in their contests with the enemies of the Church of England—are exposed to undeserved obloquy and hatred; because they are identified with the exagge-rations and Romish tendencies which have unfortunately been adopted by some of their advocates. When, however, it shall have been seen, that certain principles have carried those who hold them, through the difficulties of the times; and that they stand at the last where they began, opposed to Romish error and to Latitudinarian laxity; public opinion will, at length, gradually repair the injustice it has done.

Art. VII.—1. *Game Birds and Wild Fowl: their Friends and their Foes. By* A. E. Knox, *M.A.*, *F.A.S.* London: Van Voorst, 1850.

We are not among the number of those who join in wholesale condemnation of the dog and gun. We cannot concur in the unmitigated abuse sometimes heaped upon field-sports by well-meaning people. True, indeed, destruction is the essence of sport, and the criterion of skill: true also, too true, that many an unoffending victim gasps out its little life in the secrets of the covert, while its mangled members add another witness to the wantonness of power in the self-styled "lord of the creation." All this is true, all this is humiliating, all this would damp our own enjoyment in the field: but we must not stop there. It would be unfair not to look at the other side. Restrained from excess, these sports afford opportunities for the exercise of many qualities, both of body and mind. They supply, in time of peace, a safety-valve for energies which cannot find a vent in graver deeds of arms; they offer, if not the most ennobling, at least an innocent amusement for idle hours. But, in making this admission, we have specially guarded ourselves on two points: first, they must be restrained from excess; secondly, they should be enjoyed strictly as a recreation. If carried to excess, they must degenerate into mere butchery; if pursued with too great avidity, amusement becomes occupation, and loses its innocence by handing over to trifles faculties and energies which were created for a nobler purpose. We are under no great apprehension in regard of the former point; while we cannot but regret that the foreign predilections of a high personage should have imported into this land the fashion of the *battue* (we could forgive him, if this were his *only* attempt to Germanise our mind and manners); we have too high an opinion of English generosity and love of fairness to fear that the old British mode of sport will ever give place to a system of carnage so abhorrent to one's better feelings. As to the undue devotion of our energies to a mere amusement, too much watchfulness cannot be observed That which is fascinating from the healthy manliness which attaches to it, or the skill which it requires, is more than likely to prove too attractive for many.

It is easy to see how "nights shivered behind a stanchion

gun," and "a great portion of the early period of life devoted to the noble craft," may be not merely the recollections of a mere lover of the field, but also the confessions of that, which were innocent in moderation, made guilty by excess.   And we must own that, to us, there is something approaching to the ludicrous in such a flourish as the following :—" the same energy and spirit which enabled him to overcome the numerous obstacles to a full enjoyment of this animating pastime in the British islands has at a later period, since serving with his regiment in the East, carried him "—whither! to the cannon's mouth, or the onslaught of the Affghan ?—merely, "into the swamps and jungles of Indostan, in spite of Thugs, tigers, and fever, and rewarded him with the acquisition of many a sporting trophy."

Under due restriction, then, we repeat, we see no reason, upon the whole, to condemn field-sports, but rather the contrary. They at least afford scope for energy and skill, if they do not elevate the feelings or improve the mind.   They are healthful and manly, though they fall far short of perfection.

But all this is irrespective of the means adopted to promote them. *Game-laws* and the *preservation* of game we hold in abhorrence : we have never heard a good argument in their favour ; we believe that they cannot stand the test of inquiry by Christian men.   If not *de facto* (for we know not the date of their first enactment), they are certainly in spirit the remnants of a former age ; they are the very caterers for crime ; *sibi ipsæ pabulum subministrant*—they create what they punish ; they spring from the selfishness of the rich, and, setting a fictitious value on the objects of their protection, they work upon the disposition of human nature to taste what is forbidden, and, so working, conduce to a multiplicity of wrong.   Erase the game-laws from the statute-book, divest pheasants, partridges, and hares, of their fictitious value, place them on a level with foxes and wild-fowl, by throwing open your coverts to any who can pull a trigger ; and our belief is, that in ten years' time no hypocritical John Bright will have to move for committees of investigation in the House of Commons, nor any sincere philanthropists have to deplore such fatal conflicts as have lately stained the noble woods at Bolsover.

The causes which lead to poaching will, doubtless, be differently assigned by different minds : for our own part, we are inclined to take a view of the matter which will not find favour in the eyes of some.   It is, no doubt, easy to get up an appeal *ad misericordiam ;* and we agree with the author of the work before us as to " the encouragement which the profession of poaching has received of late years from the misapplied sympathy of morbid humanity-mongers, and the verdict of many a magisterial bench." Looking at the statistics of crime, it is impossible to be deceived as to the condition of those who compose the great body of the poaching fraternity. *It is not want which drives them to this.* Here and there we may be told, and truly withal, a pitiful tale ; but, in the majority of cases, the men who figure so plentifully at the Petty Sessions at this season of the year are men who might be, if they would, far removed from the impulses of that stern mistress which " has no laws :" labourers and mechanics too often stand charged with the well-known " trespass in pursuit of game." We have no documents at hand to prove this point ; but it is the impression left upon our own minds by what we have ourselves read and learnt of such matters. Let the credulous consult any gaol-chaplain on the point. Englishmen—from the *sans-culottes* to those of gentler blood—do love the chase in whatever form it be offered. There is no denying this national characteristic. Hence the selfish preserve, and the unprincipled poach. *A fontibus derivantur amnes.* He who began with snigging a stray hare, more "to be even with the old squire" than for any graver cause, marches forth to his end with a miscreant gang, ready for the midnight fray with armed keepers. We deliberately repeat it : the landlord in a game-preserving district has a fearful question to ask himself. Legally, no doubt, he has a right to warn off the intruder from meddling with *any* part or species of his property. But why are hares, partridges, and pheasants to be differently treated in this respect from foxes, rats, or weasels ? The former must equally with the latter be ranged under the head of vermin. What better fun than a day with lurchers in an old barn ? yet who would dream of "preserving" rats ? who could, if he would, keep a fox-hunt to himself ? Once more, then, we feel that *the game-laws must be repealed.*

But to return from this digression, which is not exactly in our line ; or, at least, we suspect, not much in our readers' line.

Were we inclined to despise all lovers of field-sports, an exception must, in fairness, be made in favour of those who can turn them to account for better purposes than the mere excitement of a shot. Upon the *mere* sportsman we do not look with much greater complacency than Dr. Johnson on an angler. The having bagged a certain number of head of game per diem is, after all, but a poor account to give of a portion of our annual life. It is little more than the exercise of manual dexterity in no very noble cause. But he enlists our warmest sympathies who can make the pleasures of the chase minister to the pursuit of science. Such an one is Mr. Knox. He modestly disclaims, indeed, for his very pleasing little book all pretension to a scientific treatise. Yet, we must beg leave to say, that no man, who, as occasion serves, will " abandon both dog and gun for a couple of days, and relinquish for that time some of the best snipe-shooting in Ireland," and " pass many a cold and anxious hour in a well-concealed position," for the purpose of "improving his acquaintance with " the habits of a bird (in the case which we specially remember, it was a peregrine falcon in her winter quarters),—no man who will so wait upon nature with an effort and a sacrifice, not because he has no relish for sport, but because he relishes the higher pursuit more keenly still,—no man with such tastes and such perseverance can fail to add some grains to those little discoveries of nature, the aggregate of which we call knowledge.

Gentle reader! if thou art half as weary as ourselves of controversy, half as satiated of polemics, thou wilt thank us for turning thy thoughts to matters of a lighter mould and a more peaceful hue. For the rest, then, of the space allotted to us, we will eschew all argument, abstain from criticism, and pull from these "Game Birds and Wild Fowl" such feathers as may tickle thy fancy, and add their quota to thine enjoyment of happy Christmastide.

We have already referred to Mr. Knox's observations of the falcon. Our first few extracts shall relate to this interesting bird :—

" It has often been a question with ornithologists in what precise manner the falcon deals the fatal blow. Some authors have asserted that it is by means of the foot; others attribute it to the breast-bone, protected as it is by such strong pectoral muscles that the concussion which is supposed to deprive its victim of life can have no injurious effect upon the author of the momentum. My own opinion, which is fully corroborated by the more extensive experience of Colonel Bonham, is, that it is by means of the powerful hind talon that the deadly wound is inflicted. If a grouse, a duck, or a woodcock that has been thus suddenly killed by a peregrine be examined, it will generally be found that the loins and shoulders are deeply scored, the back of the neck much torn, and even the skull sometimes penetrated by this formidable weapon. Now, as the stroke is almost always delivered obliquely— that is, in a slanting, downward direction from behind—this laceration could not be effected by any of the talons of the front toes; nor could the severest possible blow from the breast of the falcon produce such an effect. Indeed, Colonel Bonham had several rare opportunities of witnessing the operation distinctly; and his testimony on this point ought to be conclusive. On one occasion in particular, when in Ireland, a woodcock, after a long chase over an adjoining moor, had taken refuge in a small cover, whither it was closely pursued by the hawk, the falconer and several assistants following. Colonel Bonham himself made for a nearer point of the coppice, and had just taken up his position under a tree at the side of a ride or alley, when he saw the woodcock flying towards him, and its enemy close upon it. As the former passed within a few yards of the spot where he stood, he perceived, by its laborious flight and open beak, that it was much exhausted. The next moment down came the falcon, and he could see distinctly that the blow was inflicted by the *hind* talons. The effect was instantaneously fatal, and precisely such as might have been expected from the nature of the weapons that were brought into play. The back of the woodcock was completely ripped up, and the lower part of its skull split open."—pp. 169—171.

There are few points, perhaps, upon which one may hear greater variety of opinion and discrepancy of assertion, on the part of those who pretend to be knowing, than on the rate and distance of the flight of birds. Beyond question, these must vary with the several species. The question is,—Do they vary in the same species, at least, in any considerable degree. The following anecdote deserves to be preserved. Mr. Knox was hawking in the county of Monaghan, Ireland, when

"a woodcock 'took the air,' closely pursued by the falcon, who had her bells and 'varvels' on, with the name and address of the owner engraved upon them. In a short time, both birds had attained such an elevation, that it was only by lying down on their backs, and placing their hands above their eyes, so as to screen them from the rays of the sun, and at the same time contract the field of vision, that the spectators could keep them within view. At last, just as they had become almost like specks in the sky, they were observed to pass rapidly towards the north-east, under the influence of a strong south-west wind, and were soon completely out of sight. Some days elapsed without any tidings of the truant falcon; but, before the week had expired, a parcel arrived, accompanied by a letter, bearing a Scotch post-mark. The first contained the dead body of the falcon; the latter the closing chapter of her history, from the hand of her destroyer, a farmer who resided within ten miles of Aberdeen. He was walking through his grounds, when his attention was attracted by the appearance of a large hawk which had just dashed among his pigeons, and was then in the act of carrying one of them off. Running into the house, he returned presently with a loaded gun, and found the robber coolly devouring her prey on the top of a wheat-stack. The next moment the poor falcon's wanderings were at an end; but it was not until he had seen the bells on her feet that he discovered the value of his victim, and, upon a more careful examination, perceived the name and address of her owner; and while affording him the only reparation in his power, by sending him her remains and the account of her fate, he unconsciously rendered the story worthy of record in a sporting and an ornithological point of view; for, on a subsequent comparison of dates, it was found that she had been shot near Aberdeen, on the eastern coast of Scotland, within forty-eight hours after she had been flown at

the woodcock in a central part of the province of Ulster, in Ireland."—
pp. 171—173.

That is, somewhere about 280 miles within eight-and-forty hours,
and therefore only six miles per hour, supposing its flight to have
been continuous; but then, rapidity of flight is not an accomplishment of which hawks in the nineteenth century can boast.
There is on record a notable instance of their swiftness of which
there is no reason, we believe, to doubt the accuracy. It is
related of a falcon, belonging to Henry IV., king of France,
that it traversed the distance between Malta and Fontainebleau,
not less than 1350 miles, in twenty-four hours. In this case,
supposing it to have been on the wing the whole time, its rate of
flight must have been nearly sixty miles an hour; but, as falcons
do not fly by night, it was probably not more than sixteen or
eighteen hours on the wing, and its rate must, therefore, have
been seventy or eighty miles an hour.

While upon the subject of the falcon we cannot resist transcribing the following anecdote, recounted by the author with a
view to rescuing the character of his favourite bird from the
imputation of insusceptibility of personal attachment. It is as
follows :—

"The late Colonel Johnson, of the Rifle Brigade, was ordered to
Canada with his battalion ; and, being very fond of falconry, he took
with him two of his favourite peregrines, as his companions across the
Atlantic.

"It was his constant habit during the voyage to allow them to fly
every day, after 'feeding them up,' that they might not be induced to
rake off after a passing seagull, or wander out of sight of the vessel.
Sometimes their rambles were very wide and protracted. At others,
they would ascend to such a height as to be almost lost to the view of
the passengers, who soon found them an effectual means of relieving
the tedium of a long sea-voyage, and naturally took a lively interest in
their welfare ; but, as they were in the habit of returning regularly to
the ship, no uneasiness was felt during their occasional absence. At
last, one evening, after a longer flight than usual, one of the falcons returned alone. The other—the prime favourite—was missing. Day
after day passed away ; and, however Captain Johnson may have continued to regret his loss, he had, at length, fully made up his mind that
it was irretrievable, and that he should never see her again. Soon
after the arrival of the regiment in America, on casting his eyes over a
Halifax newspaper, he was struck by a paragraph announcing that the
captain of an American schooner had at that moment in his possession
a fine hawk, which had suddenly made its appearance on board
his ship during his late passage from Liverpool. The idea at once
occurred to Captain Johnson, that this could be no other than his
much-prized falcon ; so, having obtained immediate leave of absence,

he set out for Halifax—a journey of some days. On arriving there, he lost no time in waiting on the commander of the schooner, announcing the object of his journey, and requesting that he might be allowed to see the bird. But Jonathan had no idea of relinquishing his prize so easily, and stoutly refused to admit of the interview, 'guessing' that it was very easy for an Englisher to lay claim to another man's property, but 'calculating' it was a 'tarnation sight' harder for him to get possession of it; and concluded by asserting in unqualified terms his entire disbelief in the whole story. Captain Johnson's object, however, being rather to recover his falcon than to pick a quarrel with the truculent Yankee, he had fortunately sufficient self-command to curb his indignation; and proposed that his claim to the ownership of the bird should be at once put to the test by an experiment, which several Americans, who were present, admitted to be perfectly reasonable, and in which their countryman was at last persuaded to acquiesce. It was this:—Captain Johnson was to be admitted to an interview with the hawk, who, by the way, had as yet shown no partiality for any person since her arrival in the New World, but, on the contrary, had rather repelled all attempts at familiarity, and if at this meeting she should not only exhibit such unequivocal signs of attachment and recognition as should induce the majority of the bystanders to believe that he really was her original master, but especially if she should play with the buttons of his coat, then the American was at once to waive all claim to her. The trial was immediately made. The Yankee went up stairs, and shortly returned with the falcon; but the door was hardly opened before she darted from his fist, and perched at once on the shoulder of her beloved and long-lost protector, evincing by every means in her power her delight and affection, rubbing her head against his cheek, and taking hold of the buttons of his coat, and champing them playfully between her mandibles, one after another. This was enough. The jury were unanimous. A verdict for the plaintiff was pronounced. Even the obdurate heart of the sea-captain was melted, and the falcon was at once restored to the arms of her rightful owner."—pp. 177—180.

But the Order *Raptores* is not the only one which has fallen under Mr. Knox's observation. The Rasorial and Natatorial families—as it were to be expected—come in for their share of the sportsman's attention. Two chapters are devoted to the Pheasant; and he favours the world with a series of remarks, the result of his own "considerable" experience on the "best mode of hatching, rearing, and breeding" them. Of these, different opinions will probably be formed, differing as his recommendations do, in some points, from established usage. For our own part, we have read them with so much interest, and have heard them so well spoken of by some qualified to form a judgment on the matter, that we purpose to lay some of his remarks before our readers; premising that he is not alluding to the system of bringing up young pheasants in aviaries, fowl-yards, and enclosures, but to rearing out of doors, and turning down in preserves, a number of healthy poults. He begins, by laying down as a safe principle, that, where possible, every thing should be left to nature. On this principle, he is of opinion that

" the eggs of pheasants, even when found in an outlying nest, should not be taken for the purpose of placing them under barn-door hens to be hatched. No foster-mother or nurse can compare with the natural parent; and it is surprising—indeed, almost incredible, except to those who have witnessed it—how frequently a hen-pheasant will succeed in bringing up her brood in safety, although the nest may be placed in the most exposed and dangerous situation, within a few inches of a foot-path traversed by hundreds of idle, bird-nesting boys, and in the immediate vicinity of a common or waste ground, where the authority of the landlord is a dead letter, and where, except for the safeguard which the quiet and unobtrusive colours of her plumage afford, the speedy detection of the bird would inevitably take place."

Still there are circumstances under which it may be desirable to remove the eggs. Should such arise, they ought, when removed, to be covered with several handfuls of soft, dry grass, placed in a handkerchief, and lodged as soon as possible in a cool cellar, unless there is a sufficient number for a sitting, and a domestic hen ready for immediate incubation. The author does not join in the recommendation of bantams for this purpose, owing to their diminutive size; neither in that of the large Dorking fowl, having "seen so many cases of unintentional infanticide committed by these huge, clumsy-legged, five-toed matrons." Nor, for the sake of the little members of a neighbouring clutch, does he approve of the truculent game-hen for a foster-mother. What he has generally found to answer best for the purpose is a cross between a common dunghill hen and the game fowl.

" As soon as the young birds are hatched they should be left with their mother for a day and a night; during which time they require no food, nature having provided nutriment for their immediate sustenance in the yolk of the egg, the residue of which has been recently drawn into the body of the chicken and absorbed; but the genial warmth of her body, under which they all nestle, is of the greatest importance to them. The first food that should be given them is ants' eggs. These are, strictly speaking, the cocoons of the large rufous ant (*formica rufa*), which are tolerably plentiful in most great woods during the summer. The nests are of considerable elevation, cone-shaped, and constructed generally of very small twigs and leaves of the Scotch fir. Some persons find it difficult to separate the eggs from the materials of the nest. The simplest mode is to place as much as may be required

—ants, eggs, and all—in a bag or light sack, the mouth of which should be tied up. On reaching home, a large white sheet should be spread on the grass, and a few green boughs placed round it on the inside, over which the outer edge of the sheet should be lightly turned ; this should be done during sunshine. The contents of the bag should then be emptied into the middle, and shaken out so as to expose the eggs to the light. In a moment, forgetting all considerations of personal safety, these interesting little insects set about removing their precious charge—the cocoons—from the injurious rays of the sun, and rapidly convey them under the shady cover afforded by the foliage of the boughs near the margin of the sheet. In less than ten minutes the work will be completed. It is only necessary then to remove the branches ; and the eggs, or cocoons, may be collected by handfuls, unincumbered with sticks, leaves, or any sort of rubbish.

" Many kinds of farinaceous and vegetable food have been recommended for young pheasants when they are a little older; such as green tops of barley, leaks, boiled rice, Embden groats, oatmeal, &c. They are all excellent; but I am satisfied that they are almost always given at too early a period. In a state of nature, their food for a long time would be almost wholly insectile. Now, as it is not in our power to procure the quantity and variety of small insects and larva which the mother so perseveringly and patiently finds for them, we are obliged to have recourse to ants' eggs, as easily accessible and furnishing a considerable supply of the necessary sort of aliment within a small compass. Ants' eggs, indeed, are the right hand of the keeper when bringing up young pheasants : without them he may almost despair of success ; and with a good stock of them his birds will thrive apace, and escape many diseases to which they would otherwise be continually liable."

We have extracted the foregoing passage *in extenso*, because we consider that it involves a principle, having a much wider range of application than that of pheasant-rearing—that of a close imitation of nature. The author next instructs us as to the construction of the coops, which he recommends to be moved morning and evening, as the hen ought to have a fresh piece of greensward underneath her twice every day. "Attention to this point" he declares to be " of the greatest importance." But we will conclude the subject with another extract relative to the food of the young ones :—

" When about a week or ten days old, Embden groats and coarse Scotch oatmeal may be mixed with the ants' eggs, and curds made from fresh milk with alum, are an excellent addition. If ants' eggs cannot be procured in sufficient quantities, gentles should be occasionally given, which may be procured in the following manner : An ox-liver, a sheep's head and pluck, or the leg of a horse, should be suspended from the bough of a tree in a warm, sheltered situation. Beneath this, a wide shallow tub, half filled with bran, should be placed. In a short time, the meat will be thoroughly fly-blown, and in a few more days, it will be covered with maggots, or gentles, which will continue to drop into the tub, where they soon become cleaned and purged in the bran. A large spoon or saucer may be used for removing them. Next to ants' eggs, these, perhaps, constitute the best ' standing-dish ' for young pheasants, and have, besides, the advantage of being within the reach of every breeder. Wasps' nests, containing the larvæ and pupæ, may be procured without difficulty at a later period of the season, and afford a most acceptable treat. If the supply of these should be too great for immediate use, or if it should be thought advisable to economize the stock, it will be necessary to bake them for a short time in an oven. This will prevent the larvæ and nymphs from coming to maturity—in fact, kill them—and the contents of the combs will keep for some weeks afterwards. Hempseed, crushed and mingled with oatmeal, should be given when about to wean them from an insect diet. Hard-boiled eggs also form a useful addition, and may be mixed for a long time with their ordinary farinaceous food. A supply of fresh water is important."

The following, which we select from another part of the volume, is amusing, as showing the maternal ingenuity of birds to evade discovery by one species of enemy, as contrasted with that of another enemy to outwit them :—

" The eggs [of the pheasant] are usually deposited in rank grass on the sides of hedges and ditches, in narrow plantations, or in meadows, clover, or corn-fields ; and very rarely in the heart of great woods or covers, to which localities the keeper is generally too apt to confine his attention. When suddenly disturbed, the hen will sometimes rise at once, as she would if leaving her nest voluntarily in search of food, and thus expose her treasure to the eyes of any wandering clown who may have unintentionally stumbled on the spot ; but more frequently she has recourse to artifice, and on the approach of danger, quietly slips off her eggs, and runs with a noiseless pace for a considerable distance before she takes wing. On returning to the nest, however, she adopts a different manœuvre, and if her only enemies were of that class usually denominated vermin, it would almost invariably be attended with success. She continues on the wing until she arrives immediately over the nest, and then drops at once upon it, thus leaving no beaten track through the long grass, by which the indefatigable stoat or the prowling cat could find a ready clue to her citadel, or which would at once catch the eye of the cunning magpie or the hungry crow while sailing over the field on a preying expedition. With the poacher, however, the case is different. He has only to secrete himself under a tree, or, it may be, to sit leisurely on a neighbouring stile, immediately after feeding time in the early morning or in the afternoon, and watch the female bird as she returns to the fields in the vicinity of the preserves. He fixes his eye on her as she comes skimming over the hedge, and marks the exact spot where she drops among the weeds, grass, or clover. If this should happen not to be in the middle of the field, or if anxious to secure his prize immediately, he walks round with apparent unconcern—keeping close to the hedge all the time, and never once taking his eyes from the spot—until he arrives at the spot nearest to the nest, and then stepping up quickly, bags the eggs as expeditiously as possible : but should he think that his tactics have been observed or his intentions suspected, he coolly 'takes an observation' by means of trees, or any other prominent objects, and accurately marking their relative bearing to the situation of the nest, he is then at leisure either to watch for a fresh arrival in the same quarter, or to pursue his avocation in a different direction until the shades of evening enable him to complete his work in security."

Mr. Knox is severe, but not more so than is deserving, in his remarks upon "egg stealers," who—"without a spark of the mere brute courage which animates the night-shooter, or the skill and talent for evading discovery which characterize the successful wirer or trapper,—possess not a single redeeming quality, and can have no claim whatever on the sympathies of even the most tender-hearted philanthropists."

A singular instance is recorded of intense cold, which may be introduced here as not uncongenial with the shivery day on which we are writing. The occurrence took place in the winter of 1838 --9, at which time Mr. Knox was living at Bognor. About the middle of January he set out on an excursion to Pagham Harbour, in quest of the wild fowl which congregate so thickly upon its muddy flats and calm waters. "On my way," he writes,—

" I met with a singular evidence of the extreme intensity of the cold. Several fish of different kinds lay scattered at intervals on the beach, some dead, others dying, but all in a perfectly fresh state, having been frozen in their lairs at the bottom of the sea, and cast up by the waves. Some of these were of a species entirely new to me, and which I have never since met with. Their colours were indescribably beautiful. Every hue of the rainbow seemed to have been transferred to their scales. My astonishment could hardly have been surpassed by that of the poor fisherman in the 'Arabian Nights,' when he drew forth the variegated fish from the enchanted lake. I could not help regarding this discovery as a lucky omen for myself; so, having selected half-a-dozen of the brightest, I concealed them under a heap of pebbles, and continued on my way to the harbour."

Mr. Knox adds in a note, that Mr. Yarrell, to whom he related the circumstance, " conjectures that these fish belonged to the Wrasse family (*labridæ*), some of the rarer species of which are remarkable for their beautiful iridescent colours." We have given this story as we find it ; but Mr. Knox will pardon us, if we confess ourselves a little sceptical as to the *place* in which he so unhesitatingly affirms these fish to have been frozen. Do not well ascertained facts, relative to the temperature of the sea at various depths, render it highly improbable that they should have been frozen " in their rocky lairs at the bottom of the sea!" The truth is, that the sea *never* freezes at the *bottom*, and therefore could not congeal the fish there: but it often freezes at the surface, and the growing ice having hemmed in some of its inhabitants, froze them. We apprehend that this is a more probable explanation of the phenomenon to which the author was witness.

We cannot resist the following description of an *Irish* woodcock battue. It is genuine:—

" The southern and western provinces are more celebrated than the northern and eastern, although I have had good sport in them all. When the party is numerous a great number of cocks are killed in the large woods; twenty-five, thirty, and even forty couple being frequently the result of one day's sport. It is usual on such occasions to employ a host of beaters, whose proceedings are conducted upon a very different plan from that generally observed by the steady-going assistants of the pheasant shooter in England. A heterogeneous army of men and boys —whose appearance might recall the description of Falstaff's ragged recruits at Coventry,—each furnished with a long pole, are drawn up at one side of the cover. The guns are either placed at intervals where a backward growth of the brushwood may afford them the chance of getting a shot as they work through its mazes—for rides or alleys are but little known in these wild, natural woods—or else station themselves in different parts of the coppice, or on some eminence that commands a wider range of view—and these are the most knowing ones of the party—until at last the word is given to advance, when each beater shouting ' Heigh cock!' at the very top of his voice, and laying his stick about him with all the energy of a thrasher, such an uninterrupted and discordant row ensues as might well startle every cock within hearing from his place of concealment, and, in fact, causes numbers of those birds to spring prematurely from distant parts of the wood. Here, however, those wary gunners who have previously taken up their position on favourable heights possess a great advantage, and bring down many woodcocks as they fly in various directions, sometimes towards the beaters, sometimes in the face of the shooter, each struggling to escape the danger, but not knowing from which quarter it proceeds. By this time all discipline is at an end. Some of ' the boys' having caught a glimpse of a falling woodcock in the distance, now fling away their poles, and rush to the spot, all anxious to be the first to pick up the bird, and to congratulate the successful shooter on his dexterity; who, by the way, receives their compliments with marked ingratitude, as they come rushing through the cover, insist on keeping close to his person, and so, effectually spoil his sport for the rest of the day. The same scene is probably enacting in ten different places at once. All order is at an end. Far

away in the distance the cry of ' Heigh cock! Heigh cock!' during the
intervals of the confusion from a solitary beater who as yet has listened
to nothing but the sound of his own voice, and instead of proceeding
in a straight line, has made a wide circuit, and now finds himself
unexpectedly at the very point from which he started; while another,
who has independently advanced all alone, and at least half an hour
too soon to the opposite end of the wood, is flashing the cocks by
dozens, without for a moment considering where the guns are, or which
way the affrighted birds take, but delighted all the time at his own
performance, while the distant sportsman inwardly curses him from his
heart.   Many a cunning old beater, too, who has been too long used to
the thing to feel any excitement in it, drops quietly into the rear, and
squatting quietly under a half-bush, lights his ' dudeen' with the utmost
sang froid, regardless of all that is passing around him.   At last, the
storm gradually subsides.   A few dropping shots alone proceed from
the intervals from the outskirts of the wood.   The shooters and beaters
emerge, one by one, at different sides, all eloquent on the subject of
their own performances, not excepting him of the dudeen, who exult-
ingly points to sundry recent scratches on his face and shins, and
swears that he ' never had such hard work in the whole course of his
life.'"

But it is time that we take leave of Mr. Knox—we hope, only
for the present: one, gifted with his keenness of pursuit and intelligence of observation, cannot fail, when he turns author, to be
both amusing and instructive in his peculiar line.   And we can
assure our rural readers that, in the work before us, they will find
several useful hints and interesting remarks, from the best mode
of breeding a retriever to a generous deprecation of the persecution of the harmless squirrel and the useful mole.

NOTICES OF RECENT PUBLICATIONS,

ETC.

1. Journal of a Tour in Italy. By Rev. Geo. Townsend. 2. Sermons for the Holy Days observed in the Church of England. By Rev. J. H. Pinder. 3. Inquiry into the Principles of the Distribution of Wealth most conducive to Human Happiness. By W. Thompson. 4. Light in the Dark Places. Translated from the German of the late Augustus Neander. 5. The Four Gospels Combined. 6. War ; religiously, morally, and historically considered. By P. T. Aiken, Advocate. 7. The Book of Common Prayer. By Rev. R. Mant. 8. A Catechism of the Holy Scriptures for the Use of Church Schools. By Rev. E. J. Phipps. 9. The Wedding Gift. By Rev. W. E. Heygate. 10. Daily Steps towards Heaven. 11. Brief Outline of the Study of Theology. By the late Dr. Friedrich Schleiermacher. 12. Reflections of the Past. By the Author of "Daniel the Prophet." 13. The Theory of Baptism. By the Rev. G. Croly, LL.D. 14. A History of the Holy Eastern Church. Part I. By the Rev. J. M. Neale. 15. Ordination, Matrimony, Vectigalia, and Extreme Unction, Theologically Considered. By the Rev. D. P. M. Hulbert. 16. Remarks on Architecture of Llandaff Cathedral. 17. Mrs. Jameson's Legends of the Monastic Orders. 18. The Church and the People. By Rev. Christopher Robinson. 19. Cornish's Selection of Psalms and Hymns. 20. The Philosophy of Spirits, &c. By C. M. Burnett, M. D. 21. Letters to Young People. 22. Robinson's Leisure Hours in a Country Parsonage. 23. A Score of Lyrics. 24. Readings for the Aged. By Rev. J. M. Neale. 25. "Is the Church of Rome the Babylon of the Book of Revelation ?" By Dr. Wordsworth. 26. Remains of the late Rev. H. F. Lyte. 27. The Churchman's Diary. 28. The Revelation of Jesus Christ explained agreeably to the Analogy of the Holy Scripture. 29. A Letter to Lord Ashley. By W. J. Edge. 30. Eidolon. By W. R. Cassels. 31. An Exposition of the Thirty-nine Articles. By Rev. E. H. Browne. 32. A Selection from the Sermons and Practical Remains of the Rev. G. J. Cornish. 33. The Life of James Davies. Written by Sir Thos. Phillips. 34. Archdeacon Bather's Sermons on Old Testament Histories. 35. Moody's Exposition of the New Testament. 36. The Danger and the Foe. By Rev. A. Gurney. 37. The Old Paths of the Church of England. By Rev. D. Butler. 38. Tales and Allegories. 39. Old Christians. 40. The Christian Year. 41. Rev. Jas. Beaven's Catechism on the Thirty-nine Articles. 42. Eastbury. By A. H. Drury.—Miscellaneous.

1.—*Journal of a Tour in Italy*, in 1850, *with an Account of an Interview with the Pope, at the Vatican. By the Rev.* George Townsend, *D.D., Canon of Durham, &c.* London : Rivingtons.

To those who have given much attention to the principles of the Church of Rome, it will at first sight appear almost inexplicable, how a person of the experience, and the attainments of Dr. Townsend, could have persuaded himself of the possibility that the Pope might be induced to consent to the summoning of a general council for the decision of the controversies existing amongst professing Christians, on the principle that dogmas already defined and recognized as articles of faith in the Romish Church, should be open to further discussion. Dr. Townsend appears to admit that his view of such a proceeding as possible, is peculiar to himself; but he has formed his opinion, as it seems, not so much from a contemplation of the apparent facilities or difficulties of the case, as from his view of what is predicted in Prophecy, his opinion being that the Church of Rome will ultimately relinquish its errors and embrace the truth.

There is much amusing matter in this Journal, and some very instructive matter. In the latter respect, we refer more especially to the strong evidence which is supplied in various places to the prevalent opinion of Romanists abroad, that England is gradually returning to its obedience to the See of Rome. This is especially stated in the following account of the conclusion of the author's interview with Cardinal Mai, at Rome:—

"Some English books were shown to me; and in making some remarks upon them, I observed that it could not be expected that the nation which had produced such works, would ever be again submissive to Rome. I shall never forget the expressive manner in which the Cardinal paused, and pronounced the word *Paulatim*, 'By degrees.' He was evidently, as I found from this, and from some other expressions uttered in the course of our remarks on the books before us, impressed with the conviction,—which seemed, indeed, to be general among his brethren,—that England was returning to the adoption of the Papal additions to the faith of Christ. I sighed at the mistake, and expressed again my conviction and my hope that this could never be: and he again said with emphasis, *Paulatim*."—pp. 112, 113.

Poor Dr. Townsehd appears to have found all parties agreed in assuring him that his designs were altogether visionary and unpractical. From the Pope down to the layman of the Romish communion, and from the Archbishop of Canterbury to the Free-Church Presbyterian, every one he conversed with regarded his plans as involving impossibilities; and the Doctor appears himself at length to have arrived reluctantly at the same conclusion. The account of the interview with the Pope has rather disappointed us. It was, to be sure, conducted under rather unfavourable circumstances, as neither Dr. Townsend nor the Pope appear to have understood each other except very imperfectly, in consequence of the difference between the Italian and the English mode of pronouncing Latin.

II.—*Sermons for the Holydays observed in the Church of England, throughout the Year. By the Rev.* JOHN H. PINDER, *M.A., Principal of the Wells Theological College, and Precentor of Wells Cathedral.* London: Rivingtons.

FROM all that we have perused of this volume, we are enabled to speak of it in terms of the highest commendation, as thoroughly sound in its general tone of doctrine, and as combining instruction, interest, and a sincere and fervent piety in a very unusual degree. The excellent writer is indeed one who appears "rightly to divide the word of truth," and who is able to provide "milk" and "strong meat" according to the capacities of his hearers. The volume before us will be found to supply abundant materials for profitable study in private, and to the clergy its utility will be very great. We should rejoice to see a course of Sunday sermons for the year from the same pen. We have never seen more admirable parochial sermons.

III. — *An Inquiry into the Principles of the Distribution of Wealth most conducive to Human Happiness.* By WILLIAM THOMPSON. *A new Edition by* WILLIAM PACE. London: Orr and Co.

THE first edition of this work was published about thirty years ago, but fell "still-born" from the press. It is now re-published in a cheaper and abridged form by Mr. Pace, who appears to be a Socialist, and ascribes the formation of his own opinions to the work which he has now edited. The principles here put forward are very much those of Owen, the founder of New Lanark. They amount to the equalization of all classes, the abolition of primogeniture, entails, religious establishments, universities, and every thing else which interferes with the equality of man. We observe one curious omission. The author holds that it is absurd and wrong to restrain or coerce in any way the gratification of the sensual appetites; and he supposes the people to have ample means of gratifying them by eating and drinking as much as they please. The difficulty, of course, would occur, that, if you give men drink *ad libitum*, the result will be habits of drunkenness, which would destroy all order and decency. Our author *does not deal with this question at all*; but limits himself to the easier question, how excess in *eating* is to be prevented. This one example is a sufficient indication that the writer does not look at the practical difficulties of the case.

IV. — *Light in the Dark Places; or, Memorials of Christian Life in the Middle Ages. Translated from the German of the late* AUGUSTUS NEANDER. London: Low.

THIS little volume comprises a series of short biographies of eminent missionaries and Christians during the dark ages, much on the same plan as that adopted in Mr. Palmer's compendious Ecclesiastical History, from which we are inclined to think the notion of the book was derived. The sketches of Christian life in this publication are very pleasing and instructive; and we have not observed any thing in its tone which could offend Churchmen, or, indeed, any one else.

v.—*The Four Gospels combined; or, the Life of our Lord and Saviour Jesus Christ, as narrated by the Four Evangelists,* &c. London: Simpkin, Marshall, and Co.

A VERY good idea is well carried out in this publication. It presents a continuous Narrative of the Life of Christ, without deviating from the words of Scripture. The compiler observes, that although the chain of the separate narratives has been broken and linked together again in upwards of 1800 places, the only additions that have been made have been these: The words *or, in, it, her, him,* and *them* have been introduced once only; *the* has been inserted twice—*they,* four times—*he,* six times—*and,* twenty-three times. One or two more trifling additions are made and specified. Nothing is omitted, except what is elsewhere as fully or more fully stated. The author adds, that the omission of repetitions reduces the combined length of the Gospels by only one eighth. These are curious facts, and the author has, on the whole, brought together a valuable English Harmony of the Gospels.

vi.—*War; Religiously, Morally, and Historically considered.* By P. T. AIKEN, *Advocate.* London: Hamilton and Adams.

THE author of this Essay is a man of sense, and while opposed to all unjust aggressive war, yet holds that it is necessary to protect ourselves. It appears that there are some advocates of peace who go to this length, and Mr. Aiken thus discusses the subject with them:—

" If some subjects resist their rulers wrongfully in open rebellion; if foreigners, on some unlawful pretext, threaten to invade our shores, shall no avenging arm be uplifted to prevent and to punish them, although both might and right are on our side? Shall robbers and murderers be made to suffer for their crimes against individuals, but when they conspire in multitudes and rebel against the whole nation, shall they be allowed to prosecute their nefarious designs unresisted, and to accomplish them with impunity? Shall an armed host of spoilers and manslayers from abroad, prepared for rapine, bloodshed, conflagration, and remorseless ruin, be tamely permitted to land on our coasts, slaughter the dismayed inhabitants, and devastate the country?

" Some amiable and very estimable men take this view of the unlawfulness even of defensive war. Rebels, it is said, or foreign invaders, may sack and burn our towns and villages; our mothers, wives, and daughters may be carried off by a licentious and brutal soldiery; our country may be ruined, its power broken, its glorious institutions perish, the abodes of domestic peace, comfort, and happiness be laid waste with fire and slaughter, and the remnant of the miserable inhabitants be enslaved,—but we must not fight. Our repugnance to battle is not from cowardice, but from principle ; our courage may be strong, but our consciences must be tender. Brave as lions, we must be gentle as doves.

" These pacific sentiments, when conscientious, are to be respected. If all mankind were to think and act thus, wars would cease. But as this is still a wicked and a warring world, we are compelled to believe, that the time has not yet come when it is possible to dispense with policemen and soldiers, or that we can safely turn our gaols into granaries and our swords into ploughshares.

" After the unusual interval of peace among the nations of Europe for more than thirty years, civil war broke forth in France, and spread from nation to nation ; Milan, Genoa, Messina, Naples, Venice, Berlin, Vienna, were successively a prey to revolutionary war. It overspread the plains of Lombardy, it travelled along the Rhine, it reached Denmark, it broke forth at Rome ; it raged so fiercely in Hungary, that Austria, divided against herself, was glad to owe her preservation to Russian armies. There have been tumults and bloody conflicts in the streets of many of the chief cities of Europe ; battles in the tented field, sieges, bombardments, burnings and massacres, desolation, and misery. The degree of peace and security which Europe enjoys, has been obtained in the various countries where those revolutions occurred, by the suppression of an organized conspiracy, extending from kingdom to kingdom, to overthrow the established governments, to dissolve existing institutions, and on the ruins of the old social system to erect a new one, in which public and private property were to be seized and distributed, and all things were to be enjoyed in common, until all things were consumed. From this happy consummation the continental nations have been preserved *by means of their armies.*"

The author proceeds to vindicate the character of soldiers from the imputations cast on them by the advocates of non-resistance.

" And are we to view in the odious light of transgressors our soldiers and sailors, who disregard blood and wounds, who bear the brunt of battle, risking their own lives in defence of our lives and liberties and happiness ? Were those victories, for which our best naval and military officers have received honours and rewards, only public wrongs ? Is Christian England—is Christendom in error for supposing that armies and navies are not necessarily bands of robbers and murderers ?

" The army of Gustavus Adolphus, the Protestant King of Sweden, used to assemble for worship. Munro, an officer who served in that army, describes them before the battle of Leipzig, by public and private prayers ' recommending ourselves, the success and event of the day, to God.' The soldiers flocked around their Swedish minister, and besought him to preach. Overpowered by his feelings, as he surveyed the field and the two armies, he said, ' My brethren, yonder is the enemy !' He pointed to the sky, ' There is God—Pray !' The minister and the soldiers fell on their knees in silent adoration. Many of Cromwell's Ironsides, notwithstanding their fanaticism, were really devout and moral men; and it was their moral and enthusiastic courage, under a skilful commander, which changed the fortune of the civil war, and the aspect of affairs in England. To maintain a good character in the condition of a soldier, is to maintain it under trying circumstances; as it is also peculiarly difficult to be virtuous amid the temptations which riches or extreme poverty supply. But there are officers who have made their companies, their regiments, and their ships, by proper attention to the religious and moral conduct of the men, patterns to the rest of the army and navy of what good soldiers and sailors ought to be, and might far more generally become. We are to remember that the Jews, a peculiar people, and to whom, at one time, alone was committed the true worship, were enjoined to keep strictly the moral law, and yet were a nation of warriors, and that sanctioned by the Divine government."

The authority of Scripture is then referred to, in proof of the lawfulness of bearing arms at the command of the civil magistrate, and generally for self-defence, according to the principle laid down in the Thirty-ninth Article of the Church of England.

The author in his second chapter gives a sketch of the vast European war in the time of Napoleon Buonaparte; and having pointed out the fact, that a peace of thirty-five years' duration has been purchased by military prowess, proceeds to meet an objection to the cost of standing armies.

" But armies and navies cost a great deal of money. It also costs money to insure warehouses against fire, vessels and their cargoes against shipwreck. Yet prudent men prefer to pay for insurance, rather than risk ruin; and a wise people will choose to be taxed for their defence, rather than dwell in perpetual insecurity. A rich and unwarlike kingdom is an irresistible temptation to poorer and more martial states; and if Great Britain, with her vast territorial and commercial wealth, and manufacturing industry, her colonies and settlements in every quarter of the globe, were to neglect the armaments necessary for her protection, a catastrophe might ensue, not only fatal to this country, but which would resound through the world, and be detrimental to the best and highest interests of the human race.

" It is true that in the year 1701, the national debt of Great Britain was only about 15,000,000*l.*, that in seventy-four years it had increased to 125,000,000*l.*, and after the lapse of another seventy-five years, in 1850, amounts to about 800,000,000*l.* Our ancestors fought for themselves and their posterity, not always wisely and justly, but, on the whole, we have not much cause to complain, considering the momentous interests involved in their wars, and the victories they obtained. Great reason have we for gratitude to Providence, that we, their successors, occupy so elevated and responsible a position, possess such vast influ-

ence for good or evil, and enjoy so many and so great blessings. We
may regret that those wars were carried on with such lavish expenditure,
especially in subsidies to foreign states, by which so heavy a debt was
contracted, and the burden of its repayment devolved on us and our
descendants. But the victory at Waterloo, having been the means of
procuring thirty-five years of peace, posterity may blame us who have
lived during that time, and the governments, who have courted popularity by taking off taxes, whenever there was a surplus revenue; thus
transmitting to the indefinite, and perhaps troubled future, the national
debt almost undiminished. By a wise economy we might adequately
provide for our country's defence, and also set apart a surplus revenue
in the sinking fund. But the lovers of peace may console themselves
with the reflection, that if they have to pay for past wars and present
security, the heavy incumbrances of European nations are among the
impediments to the renewal and continuance of hostilities."—pp. 59
—61.

It appears from the statements of this writer, that the suffering
and loss of life in wars now, are far less than in ancient times,
when the use of artillery was unknown. Various instances of
gallantry in battle are recorded in the following passages :—

"British soldiers and sailors never desert the national flag which
floats over their ship, and is borne into the thickest fight. In Lord
Howe's engagement with the French fleet, on the first of June, 1794,
the 'Marlborough' in breaking the enemy's line, was dismasted, and had
all her colours shot away. Appleford, an English sailor, called to his
messmates, 'The English colours shall never be doused where I am!'
He hoisted a marine's red jacket on a boarding pike, and the sailors
fought under that standard till the victory was won. Appleford, during
the same action, rivalled the heroism of Coriolanus. The dismasted
'Marlborough' had drifted under the bows of a French eighty-four, and
Appleford climbed the bowsprit and alone drove the Frenchmen from
the forecastle. Not being followed by any of the crew of the Marlborough, which began to drift away, he made good his retreat along the
bowsprit of the French man-of-war, just in time to leap down into his
own ship.

"At Waterloo, the standard-bearer of a Scottish regiment, when
mortally wounded, held the colours so firmly in his dying grasp, that a
serjeant of the regiment could only rescue them by carrying off on his
shoulders the dead soldier and the colours together, in the presence of
the enemy.

"During the civil wars in the reign of Charles I., there were many
examples of female heroism, as in the gallant defence of castles and
fortified houses by ladies, in the absence of their husbands. The wives
of British sailors have sometimes helped them to serve the guns.
During the assault of Zaragoza, when the French had killed or disabled
every Spanish soldier on the battery of Portillo, Augustina Zaragoza
rushed to the battery, fired a cannon, and, by her heroic conduct, ani-

mated her fellow citizens to renew the combat. She was pensioned by the government, and has a place in history. And there, also, the young and beautiful Countess of Burita was perhaps more appropriately employed with a company of women, who fearlessly carried refreshments and afforded help to the wounded soldiers, while shot and shells flew around them."—pp. 94—96.

On the whole we should think this little work an admirable antidote to the follies of the " Peace Societies," who denounce all war, however just, and would insist on our being disarmed, and left a prey to the French or any other nation that chose to attack us.

VII.—*The Book of Common Prayer and Administration of the Sacraments, &c., with Notes. By the Right Rev.* RICHARD MANT, *D.D., late Lord Bishop of Down, Connor, and Dromore, Sixth Edition.* London: Rivingtons.

THIS edition of Bishop Mant's Prayer Book is brought within a very moderate compass, and appears to be very well executed. We are glad to see the labours of this useful ritualist continue to be so justly appreciated. It should be, of course, in every clergyman's library.

VIII.—*A Catechism on the Holy Scriptures of the Old and New Testaments, for the Use of the Church Schools. By the Rev.* E. J. PHIPPS, *B.A., Rector of Devizes.* London: Masters.

THIS little work contains a series of questions for schoolchildren on all the books of the Bible; and appears to be well executed. We should think the plan suggested by Mr. Phipps calculated to promote an intelligent study of the sacred volume by children.

IX.—*The Wedding Gift; or, a Devotional Manual for the Married, or those Intending to Marry. By* WILLIAM EDWARD HEYGATE, *M.A.* London: Rivingtons.

A VERY excellent little Manual of advice and devotions on the subject of Marriage. It contains chapters on these subjects— Considerations before Marriage—Preparation for Marriage— Solemnization of Matrimony—Early Married Life—Married Life—and Devotions.

X.—*Daily Steps towards Heaven; or, Practical Thoughts on the Gospel History, and especially on the Life and Teaching of our Lord Jesus Christ. For Every Day in the Year, according to*

*the Christian Seasons. With Titles and Characters of Christ;
and a Harmony of the Four Gospels. Second Edition.* London: J. W. Parker.

A WORK of this kind supplies a want that has been long felt.
Within the compass of a very small volume the Christian will
here find pious thoughts for every day in the year, grounded on
Holy Scripture. A work of this kind is much preferable to
translations from books of Romish devotion, which almost always
retain some tinge of doctrine that is objectionable.

XI.—*Brief Outline of the Study of Theology, drawn up to serve
as the Basis of Introductory Lectures. By the late Dr.* FRIE-
DRICH SCHLEIERMACHER. *To which are prefixed Reminiscences
of Schleiermacher, by Dr.* F. LÜCKE. *Translated from the
German by* WILLIAM FARRER, *LL.B.* Edinburgh: Clark.

THE chief interest of this volume is the Reminiscences of Dr.
Lücke; for the Outline of the Study of Theology is so brief and
so obscure, that it is of very little value. Schleiermacher was
the originater of the design of uniting the Lutheran and Reformed in one communion, without any attempt to interfere with
their respective doctrines. Dr. Lücke thus relates the origin of
the design which was afterwards carried out by the king of
Prussia.

" His reformatory activity was directed at a very early period towards
the circumstances and the necessities of the Church's life as a whole.
His first publication in connexion with this subject consists of ' Two
Non-prejudicative Opinions in matters connected with the Interests of
the Protestant Church; with a more immediate reference to the Prussian State' (1804). This document was written about the time when
he had finished his profoundly thoughtful work on the Criticism of the
Doctrine of Morals. It appeared without his name; but it bore the
impress of his mind. In the first Opinion, which relates to the separation of the two Protestant Churches, the ecclesiastical life-question of
his mind, the Union, already makes its appearance, as clearly and
definitely as possible. He points out the mischiefs of the separation
hitherto existing: how, in relation to the religious interest, it nourishes
superstition on the one hand, and, on the other, indifference towards
even the essentials of religion; then, moreover, how it also operates
injuriously in relation to general morality and true culture; and again,
lastly, how, in relation to the State and the school, it also shows itself
as an evil which it is high time to remedy. All this is worked out in
a manner distinguished as much by the truthfulness of lively experience, as by genius and wit. But Schleiermacher did not content himself with complaining of the evil; even then, along with the necessity

of the Union, he also pointed out the proper manner of its *accomplishment:* he demanded that the *fellowship* of the Churches should be restored, without touching the differences in the system of *doctrine* or the variations in the *ritual,* and insisted that this restoration should be effected without circumscribing the liberty of faith and action of any individual. Even at that time, he called attention to the fact, that in the community of the United Brethren this idea of Union was realized in a satisfactory manner."

We have, further on, the following account of Schleiermacher's exertions and labours in the cause of the Union :—

" It was but for a short time that he was permitted to take part in the general government of the Church in one of the higher spiritual offices connected with the State. It was at that season of the regeneration of the Prussian State, when those ministers of powerful intellect, Von ·Stein and Wilhelm Von Humboldt, were seeking, in every department, to place the most able men at the head of affairs, and when, accordingly, Schleiermacher also could not fail of finding his place. I do not know in what manner, nor to what extent, he exercised an influence at that period in connexion with the reform of the Church. But this I know, that he willingly withdrew from the position, when, subsequently, the troublesome quickness and decision of his mind met with more of simple resistance than of positive effect. After this he confined himself to aiding, according to his ability, partly as a writer, and partly as the freely elected President of the Berlin Synod, in promoting the conduct, upon the right basis and in the right way, of the reform of public worship and the constitution of the Church (which had been agitated, especially since the year 1814, even in the *highest* quarter); and, along with this, of the Union. To this period belongs the series of his *occasional* publications relative to ecclesiastical affairs, —chiefly of a polemical character, and commencing with the celebrated " Letter of Congratulation to the Very Reverend the Members of the Commission appointed by his Majesty the King of Prussia for the purpose of preparing new Liturgical Forms" (1814). The anonymous guise of this work did not prevent the instant discovery of the author; so completely does it bear the impress of his mind. Rather a condolence and warning than a congratulation, and not wanting in a certain degree of irony, it was nevertheless received by the Commission with more than kindness. One might almost say that none of Schleiermacher's writings attained its end so immediately as this. The Commission, with noble self-denial, entered into the ideas of Schleiermacher; instead of precipitately constructing new liturgical forms, it proposed that a constitution should first be given to the Church, by means of which it should be possible to give to the needful reform, as proceeding from within outwardly, the character of a collective volition of the Church. It pertains to the imperishable renown of the King of Prussia, that he entered into this idea with all the interest of his Christian mind, and all the energy of his kingly will. It is true, the new Liturgy for the Court and Garrison Congregation at Potsdam and the Garrison Church at Berlin was little adapted, even by the manner in which it was introduced, to give rise to the hope of a true, comprehensive reform, brought about in a proper way. Schleiermacher, like a watchman on the battlements of the Church, observant of every appearance and movement in the ecclesiastical horizon, did not omit—this time with the avowal of his name—with frankness, yet in a tone of mildness, to subject the new Liturgy to criticism, in his pamphlet 'On the New Liturgy for the Court and Garrison Congregation at Potsdam (1816); and, at the close, to direct attention anew to this point,—'that a well-ordered Synodal Constitution affords the only means of securing for the Church a legitimate co-operation towards the reform of Divine worship,—so that neither the caprice of the individual shall be able wildly to wander at pleasure in the sacred concerns of public worship, nor a fruitful and acknowledged point of union be wanting to the like-minded, who would fain enter into a mutual connexion,—nor the man of experience and of eminence be destitute of that silent, direct influence which it is proper for him to exercise. When, then, upon the occurrence of the jubilee of the Reformation in 1817, the King, by his praiseworthy example and excellent arrangements, prepared the way for, nay, in very strictness founded, the Union of the two Protestant Churches, and, as early as the spring of 1817, the official notification with regard to the formation of Presbyteries, and the union of the Protestant clergy into district, provincial, and national synods, made its appearance as the result. Schleiermacher's rejoicing over the incipient success of his fairest and most cherished desires was equalled only by the zeal with which, by counsel and by deed, with love and diligence, he sought to promote and defend the new work. His ideas, in the mean time, had found entrance and patronage in more extended circles; a number of the clergy, especially the younger part of them, had come forward as follow-labourers and fellow-counsellors in the sacred enterprise. Schleiermacher, with thankfulness and modesty, cheerfully recognised this fact; devoid of envy, he rejoiced that he was neither the *only* labourer, nor, outwardly, the most important one. In order, however, that by the communication and discussion of his opinions and counsels with respect to certain particulars of the official notification just referred to, he might unite such as were like-minded to a deliberate and unanimous action at the Synods which were shortly to be held, he hastily stepped forth in advance, and wrote, as early as the summer of 1817, his 'Observations concerning the Synodal Constitution about to be established for the Protestant Church of the State of Prussia.'—When, soon after this, the Berlin Synod assembled, and as a mark of honour elected him to be its president, he fulfilled the duties of this office with such zeal, such aptness, patience, and love, that even those who had, until then, rather feared and mistrusted him, began to bestow upon him their affection and confidence; so that the labours of the Synod evidently prospered under his guidance, through the increasingly lively harmony which pre-

vailed amongst its members. The union, and the new constitution of
the Church, appeared at that time inseparable,—the one was the necessary auxiliary of the other. Thus, the first sign of life given by the
Synod was its ' Official Declaration respecting the Celebration of the
Lord's Supper, to be held by the Synod on the 30th of October.'
Schleiermacher was the author of this document. In it, he sets forth
the union, in a brief and popular, a gentle and earnest manner, as a
purely ecclesiastical pacification,—*unconnected* with any settlement of
dogmatical differences, which would be useless, nay, would lead to new
divisions,—and *testified* by means of a new and common ritual in the
celebration of the Lord's Supper."

The great object of Schleiermacher's Church policy was, to
obtain freedom of action for the Church, to exempt it from the
domination of the State. It is curious to find how men of the
most opposite principles alike perceive the evils which the Church
suffers from the suppression of its liberties by the temporal
powers. The Rationalist and Latitudinarian of Germany, and
the orthodox Churchman of England, equally feel it ; and the
State is every where jealous of the religious liberties of the people.
We have the following account of the discussions relative to the
Prussian Liturgy in Dr. Lücke's pages :—

" But this was not the last conflict which our valiant combatant in the
cause of the union and constitution of the Church had to sustain ; others,
incomparably more severe, were impending. No long time elapsed before the ecclesiastical horizon was enveloped in an exceedingly ominous
gloom. To the statesmen of the old school the development of a more
liberal constitution, and a more important position for the Church, was,
from the very first, a source of great annoyance. The suspicion of a
new *hierarchical* preponderance found utterance ; at first in secret, but
soon, also, aloud. Mistakes, exaggerations, remissness, and precipitation on the part of the theologians, gave a semblance of reason to the
objection that the age was neither peaceful enough nor mature enough
to allow of the Church's having a constitution of greater vitality [than
that to which it had been accustomed]. And as, in the department of
political life, especially from the year 1819, something of crime and
something of thoughtlessness, revolutionary giddiness, and the fantastic
tricks of a superficial liberalism, called forth a necessary reaction, and a
defensive solicitude and apprehensiveness with regard to every excitement of a free and lively character seemed almost to be but a part of
the duty of caution and circumspection, it could not but be that, by degrees, in the ecclesiastical department also, preference should be given
to the policy of stopping short and standing still, rather than to that of
following up the movement which had been begun. This is not the
place, nor is it possible for me, to set forth and to pass judgment upon
the individual *momenta* of the reaction in ecclesiastical affairs, as they
followed upon and in consequence of one another. Enough, the ap-

pearance of the new Prussian Liturgy and Agenda was the commencement and the signal of a new and, in part, opposite tendency, obstructive at once—at least in its immediate result—to the union and also to the constitution of the Church. Schleiermacher could not, in accordance with the principles of his practical theology, approve either the contents or the form of the new liturgical arrangements. He would have been untrue to his most inward and essential nature, if he had agreed to them ; and it was a consequence involved in the energetic character of his mind, as well as in the nature of the position he had previously occupied, that he became the leader of the opposition. His pseudonymous publication, ' On the Liturgical Right of Evangelical Sovereigns, a Theological Deliberation, by Pacificus Sincerus,' (1824,) struck at the root of the opposite tendency, and stirred up anew the controversy respecting the principles of law involved in the connexion between Church and State ; a controversy which, in the age of indifference, had almost been laid to sleep amongst the theologians, and had merely dragged along a wretched and spiritless existence in the schools of the jurists. The consequence has been, that since that time there has also arisen in this department, amongst theologians and jurists, a more lively intercourse and conflict of diverse tendencies and opinions. In appearance the noble hero was vanquished. The opposite tendency has, *practically*, obtained the upper hand. But that its supremacy is, I might say, merely *interimistic*, and that its theory, half out of fright at the consistent, logical development of itself in the writings of Augusti and others upon this subject, and half from a consciousness of the power of truth arrayed on the other side, becomes increasingly *modified*, relaxes, and concedes, until, perhaps, a point has been found in which the true medium is situated,—this is the work of the man who so long and so steadfastly maintained and led the opposition ; until so much had been conceded on the other part, that he thought he could not, without doing violence to the claims of truth and love, delay any longer at least a cessation of hostilities."—pp. 68—70.

Schleiermacher was one of that large class of thinkers in the present day who are of opinion that all religious opinions ought to be tolerated in the Christian Church ; and therefore, of course, that all creeds and confessions of faith, and all obligations of believing any distinctive doctrine, should be removed. This system has been realized in the so-called Prussian Evangelical Church, which Schleiermacher suggested ; and the result of this mixture of faith with unbelief is, that the mass of the community have no religion at all.

XII.—*Reflections of the Past, and Shadows of the Future. A Book for the New Year. By the Author of " Daniel the Prophet."* Dublin: Hodges and Smith.

A SERIES of pious meditations, which cannot fail to benefit the

reader. Their subjects are not connected by any chain of
thought, but appear to be the outpourings of a devotional and
contemplative mind.

xiii.—*The Theory of Baptism. The Regeneration of Infants in
Baptism Vindicated on the Testimony of Holy Scripture,
Christian Antiquity, and the Church of England. By the Rev.*
George Croly, *LL.D., Rector of the United Parishes of St.
Stephen, Walbrook, and St. Benet, London.* London:
Rivingtons.

Dr. Croly's abilities and learning are as well known as his uncompromising attachment to the principles of the Reformation.
The testimony of such a writer, therefore, in behalf of the true
doctrines of Baptism, is of very high importance, and deserves a
proportionate attention. In the preface to his work he states his
object to be that of furnishing an original treatise on Baptism,
comprised within a moderate compass, and avoiding the bitterness
of controversy. He remarks on the necessity of vigilance on the
part of the Church, in consequence of the sudden rise of dissension on this vitally important subject, and he remarks on the
evils attending such a mixed tribunal as the Privy Council
consists of:—

"Without denying," says Dr. Croly, " that it may have the due feeling for spiritual difficulties ; that it may acquire the due knowledge for
spiritual questions; that it may exhibit the due impartiality in the
midst of conflicting interests ; and may apply itself to its repulsive task
with a zeal which seems to turn law into a formality, and leave decisions
behind ; still the constitution of such a tribunal places the Church in
difficulty. Standing before that court, it loses a privilege conceded to
the lowest condition of defence—it cannot challenge its jury. The time
may thus come, in the possibilities of the future, when a mixed tribunal
may be the very last to which, with safety of conscience, or in the exercise
of a sound discretion, the Church would submit its cause ; when it
might see a Socinian deciding on a Trinitarian doctrine—a Presbyterian
on Episcopacy—an Independent on Church discipline—or an avowed
unbeliever on the whole system of Revelation.

"If we are told that this is but like a trial before the Bench in
Westminster Hall, an answer is, that the judges are more trained to
jurisprudence ; that they have a professional character to maintain, and
a professional penalty to fear ; that they cannot escape from the results
of error, or throw up their responsibility with their commission. The
inherent evil of all temporary judicatures is their intangible nature;
while retribution attempts to grasp them, they are gone : public opinion,
the Nemesis of our day, has no wings to follow a phantom."

Dr. Croly subsequently proceeds to criticise the judgment of

the Privy Council with his usual ability, and takes occasion to
observe that, if there are Clergy who omit in the Baptismal
service those parts in which infant regeneration is pronounced,
they ought to resign their charges ; and he is by no means
fearful of the effect if they should altogether leave us.

" If fears are felt that the withdrawal of all who are thus tainted
would weaken the Church, the fear is groundless. The strength of
the Church is in its sincerity. The relief of its incumbrance would be
only an increase of its vigour ; the amputation of the decayed limb
would give new health to the frame. What the establishment lost in
numbers, it would gain in the most important of all possessions—
character. Even those who withdrew would gain in character ; the
pardon which we must now refuse to their tergiversation, we might
then give to their independence."

We cordially concur with Dr. Croly in these sentiments.   Disloyal members of the Church, whatever may be their views, never
add to its strength. We are unhappily burdened with many such.
Dr. Croly thus points out the evils of the present times :—

" The true danger of our day is the restlessness of opinion. The
'right of private judgment' is the charter of Protestantism ; but the
truth of obscure petulance, the rashness of ignorance, or the mere vanity
of being notorious for the mischief which the meanest faculties have the
power to inflict on the community, have often created mighty evils,
even in the firm-set and guarded mind of England.
" The real object of dread ought to be the possibility of addition to the
mass of schism, which already overlays and corrupts so large a portion
of the spiritual fertility of England. Every sect finds a reception in our
day ; every dreamer can find an audience for his rhapsodies ; every
rambling performer on popular credulity can 'do great wonders, and
make fire come down from heaven on the earth,' in the sight of men."

Space does not permit us to enter on Dr. Croly's argument in
reference to Baptism ; but it is well worthy the attention of the
theological student.

xiv.—*A History of the Holy Eastern Church.   Part I., General
Introduction.   By the Rev.* J. M. Neale, *M.A., Warden of
Sackville College, East Grinstead.*   London : Masters.

The two large volumes before us constitute only the Introduction
of Mr. Neale's History of the Eastern Church.   We can very
well believe the author when he speaks of them as the result of
the more or less continuous labour of between five and six years.
Years very soon pass away in the composition of works like this.
The Introductory Part here presented to the public describes the
rites, offices, faith, and customs of the Eastern Church.

The first book of the Introduction refers to the Geography of the Eastern Church. In preparing this, Mr. Neale has experienced great difficulties, for the want of trustworthy information. He complains of the inaccuracy of the older writers, such as Carolus a Sancto Paulo, and the Notitiæ given by Leunclavius, Goar, and Bingham. He mentions the case of the Notitiæ of one province in Bingham, in which fourteen names out of thirty are more or less wrong. His chief authority is Le Quien's Oriens Christianus; but he has applied to more modern sources of information. Of the Patriarchates of Jerusalem, Antioch, Alexandria, and Russia, of Armenia, and the catholicate of Chaldea, his list is official and complete: that of Constantinople is not official, and is, therefore, imperfect, while he has been unable to obtain any account of the Jacobite Patriarchate of Antioch, and the Metranate of Ethiopia. The labour bestowed upon the details of this work must have been enormous. Those lists of bishoprics, which stand so neatly arranged in parallel columns, have cost an immensity of labour; and all kinds of information, ancient and modern, are collected for the benefit of the reader; and then the ecclesiology of the Oriental Church, which forms another portion of this work, is really most curious and interesting. We are here made acquainted with the oldest existing remains of Christian antiquity. The architectural style, too, is so very unlike any thing we have ever seen or read of in the West, and yet in some cases so rich and solemn. The work contains a number of plans of ancient Oriental Churches, and illustrations very beautifully executed. Minute details are given of the ecclesiastical vestments used in the East, with illustrations.

After this, Mr. Neale examines the Liturgies of the East, arranged under their great heads—Jerusalem, Alexandria, and Edessa. The latter head is one of Mr. Neale's own devising. He argues that the Nestorian Liturgy of the Apostles must have been an Apostolic liturgy, and he remarks that Mr. Palmer's opinion appears not to be sufficiently founded. There may not perhaps be any very conclusive force in Mr. Palmer's arguments on the subject; but we confess that we do not think Mr. Neale has established the point *he* contends for, because he has not adduced any direct evidence of quotations in ancient writers to show the ancient existence of this rite, but appears to depend upon the assumption, that one of the Liturgies of the Nestorians is older than another; and this appears to us by no means certain. We should be glad to see the subject further inquired into; but at present we do not feel convinced by Mr. Neale's reasoning.

After this the Liturgies themselves are given at great length, with copious and learned explanatory notes, and dissertations on different subjects related to the Liturgies. This takes up by far the greater portion of the Introduction. The Calendars of the Eastern Churches are treated of at great length ; and we know not where the information here given could be found, except in this book. An elaborate dissertation on the office-books of the East is appended ; and the various sacraments and rites are detailed at great length with much learning. On the whole, we must express our admiration of the research, and indefatigable industry of the author, and our high sense of the addition he has made to our theological literature in this very learned publication.

xv.—*Ordination, Matrimony, Vectigalia, and Extreme Unction, theologically considered. Dedicated to all who revere Supreme Authority in Church and State, as vested in our Most Gracious Sovereign the Queen, Defender of the Faith. By the 'Rev.* DANIEL P. M. HULBERT, *M.A., Priest in Holy Orders, and Member of the Senate of Cambridge.* London : Painter.

THE title of this publication is rather singularly drawn up ; and it may in some degree serve to indicate the principles of the author, who is a strong opponent of schism in all shapes, and denounces the Dissenter as having never had the succession, and the Romanist as having lost it by idolatry. The author is very far indeed from what is called "mock modesty," or an under estimate of his own powers and abilities. He appears to consider the publication of these papers, with the avowal of his name, long concealed, as an event of no inconsiderable importance.

"In obedience," he says, "to the wishes of friends, who have been aware of my having for many years (over six years) contributed anonymously to very many weekly (and other) publications for the wealth of the country, I have at last revealed my name ; conceiving, moreover, that reference to circumstances affecting some of my past ministrations, and departed associates and acquaintances, rather required a revelation of the author of the following four treatises. Yet, had I consulted my own inclination and comfort, ' as *unknown* yet well known ' would have far better suited my views. But if the author of the ' Epistle to the Hebrews,' or the ' Acts of the Apostles,' some man might say, thought fit to suppress his own name, might not these Essays have done as much good in their day as do those books in successive generations, although wise men have often fought about the respective authors," &c.

The author argues in reply, that it is evident from experience, how much discussion and inconvenience have arisen from suppressing the names of the authors of the Epistle to the Hebrews or the Acts; or, in later times, of the Poems of Ossian, and the Letters of Junius. So that he leaves us to infer, that he acts for the good of his brethren, in relieving them from the anxiety which they may hereafter be liable to suffer, if the authorship of certain articles in Periodicals were not made known. We are sure the public will thank the author for his kind intentions. The only thing that will occur to most men will be, how profound must be their ignorance, in never before having heard of these articles, or of their reverend author; and we are concerned to own, that we are ourselves in this distressing predicament. " Vectigalia" is made to take rather a wide range, as it includes a plan for paying off the National Debt.

xvi.—1. *Remarks on the Architecture of Llandaff Cathedral, with an Essay towards a History of the Fabric.* By EDWARD A. FREEMAN, *M.A.*, &c. London : Pickering.

2. *A Letter to the Lord Bishop of Llandaff on the peculiar Condition and Wants of the Diocese.* By THOMAS WILLIAMS, *M.A., Archdeacon of Llandaff.* London: J. W. Parker.

THE publications before us afford gratifying evidence of the exertions which are being made in the diocese of Llandaff to promote the efficiency of the Church. The cathedral of this diocese has, from a variety of causes, fallen into a very sad state of decay, the nave having been in the course of the last century unroofed, and the rest of the building disfigured by tasteless and injurious innovations. It is very cheering to find that the work of restoration, in good taste, has been commenced and is progressing ; for, although Llandaff itself appears to be a place of no importance, still it conveys a very unfavourable impression of the efficiency of a Church, to see its principal edifices in ruin ; and the residence of the bishop, the works now in progress at the cathedral, and the exertions making to extend the Church cause in the diocese, all afford proofs of improvement and of life, which will operate beneficially on every Churchman in South Wales, and lead him to feel more attachment to his Church. We do not like the tone of Mr. Freeman's remarks on subjects connected with the Reformation : they are more or less tinged with the views of those who look on the Reformation as an evil, and speak unfavourably of it on all occasions. We cannot avoid entering our protest against such views, and more especially when we remember the practical effects which this system of talking and insinuation has had.

The letter published by Archdeacon Williams discloses the fearful inadequacy of means in the hands of the Church to meet the spiritual wants of the people of South Wales. The increase of population in the diocese of Llandaff is enormous, and the numbers of clergy and churches wholly inadequate. The first step, however, to remedy these evils, is to ascertain their extent, and Archdeacon Williams has done this. We rejoice to hear that further efforts are making, to which every one must wish success.

XVII.—*Legends of the Monastic Orders, as represented in the Fine Arts. Forming the Second Series of Sacred and Legendary Art.* By Mrs. JAMESON. London: Longman and Co.

THE volume before us comprises short biographies of all the principal saints and founders of monastic orders, and of eminent personages connected with them, with a view to the illustration of paintings and other works of art referring to such subjects. It is richly illustrated by Mrs. Jameson, like her other works. Of course, we are not to look for strict accuracy of historical detail in a work like this, which is intended for popular use. We have been, on the whole, satisfied with what we have seen of the tone of the author, and the general treatment of the subject, while in some places we have observed slight inaccuracies in history.

XVIII.—*The Church and the People.* By the Rev. CHRISTOPHER ROBINSON, *B.A., Curate of Audenshaw.* London: Hamilton, Adams, and Co.

THIS little volume was written with the object of meeting all the popular objections against the Church of England raised by Dissenters in the manufacturing districts. It appears to us to be very well executed; and it is written in a tone of genuine loyalty to the Church. We should think it would be extremely useful for parochial lending libraries, and generally for circulation in parishes where dissent exists.

XIX.—*A Selection of Psalms and Hymns.* By the Rev. H. K. CORNISH, *Vicar of Bakewell.* London: Mozleys.

FROM all we have seen of this collection it appears to be well and carefully made; but we cannot help expressing regret at the present state of things, which gives to each clergyman the power of publishing a book of Psalms and Hymns for the use of his own church. The effect is, to prevent a stranger from joining in the psalmody, unless by chance some one should lend him a copy of the Psalter in use in that church. It is also very possible that a new clergyman may introduce a new collection of Psalms or

Hymns. All this is very inconvenient. It were much to be wished that a short collection of the best and most popular Hymns should be always printed with the new Version of the Psalms in our Prayer Book. Surely this might be easily managed by some arrangement between the Universities and the Christian Knowledge Society. It would be a very great benefit if such a collection were to be found in all Prayer Books, so that every one should be provided with the words of some, at least, of the hymns sung in any church he might attend.

xx.—*The Philosophy of Spirits in relation to Matter: showing the real Existence of two very different kinds of Entity, &c.* By C. M. BURNETT, *M.D.* London: Highley.

DR. BURNETT has bestowed deep thought and research on the mysterious and difficult subject to which he has directed his attention; and we have been interested and instructed by all we have read of his book. He assumes the authority of revelation as the basis of his inquiries; and we, therefore, need not add, that they are conducted in a reverential and a Christian spirit. The phenomena of Mesmerism he identifies with the ancient magic, and ascribes to the influence of the devil. He, of course, admits the reality.

xxi.—*Letters to Young People.* By the late WALTER AUGUSTUS SHIRLEY, *D.D., Lord Bishop of Sodor and Man.* London: Hatchards.

THIS little volume contains a selection of the letters of the late Bishop Shirley, addressed to members of his own family and other young people. They have, for the most part, been already published in the Memoirs of this pious and excellent man. Although the atmosphere of thought and opinion to which these letters introduce us is somewhat peculiar, we must yet admit the substantial excellence of much of what we find here; and all we have perused of the volume has instructed and edified us not a little. Bishop Shirley would, without doubt, have been a blessing to his diocese, had he been spared.

xxii.—*Leisure Hours in a Country Parsonage; or, Strictures on Men, Manners, and Books.* By the Rev. J. K. ROBINSON, *Prebendary of Whitechurch, Diocese of Ferns.* Dublin: M'Glashan.

THIS work comprises a series of Essays on a great many amusing and interesting subjects, such as, " The Petty Jealousies and Envyings of a Country Neighbourhood," " Female Dress," " The Theatre," " The Effects of Residence in France," &c. As far as we have been enabled to judge, these Essays are very well executed,—something in the style of the "Spectator" and "Rambler." They contain much good sense, and in point of principle are very "old-fashioned;" the author appearing to hold what were esteemed good, sound, Protestant, *i. e.* Church of England Protestant principles, forty or fifty years ago.

xxiii.—*A Score of Lyrics.* Cambridge: Macmillan. London: Pickering.

WE took up this little volume with an involuntary feeling of something like impatience at the remembrance of the innumerable disappointments we have experienced in perusing new volumes of poetry; but, as we read, our attention became arrested by much which really deserves the name of poetry—much which has really gratified us, and which proves the writer to be possessed of powers which afford promise of still higher excellence. We quote the following lines as a specimen from "Westward, ho!"—

> "But, alas! Old England's prime is flown,
> 'Tis merry now no more,
> Where the land is growing to one vast town,
> Where they fence the copse and mete the moor,
> And, spurned from all, save the prison-door,
> A man needs flee, for place there is none
> Where he might be free and poor.

> "Then, hey! for a life wild, uncontrolled,
> In prairies yet untrod!
> Where the hand that's strong, with a heart that's bold,
> Has nobler work than to delve the clod,
> Or cringe 'neath laws at rich men's nod,
> Repealing Nature's fiat old,
> And stinting the gifts of God."

After all, perhaps, notwithstanding the enclosure of commons, and the poor-law unions, there are some advantages still remaining in Old England. There are many disadvantages certainly; but is there nothing to be apprehended from the scalping-knife of the savage, or the rifle of the squatter? Every one to his taste, however.

xxiv.—*Readings for the Aged. By the Rev.* J. M. NEALE, *M.A.,* &c. London: Masters.

THIS work consists of a series of lectures for the various seasons of the Christian year, which the author prepared in the course of his duty as ministering to aged and infirm persons. He states that these lectures were understood by those to whom they were addressed. This is a great point. We have been pleased with all we have seen of the volume: it is interspersed with anecdotes, and, like all Mr. Neale's works, is extremely well written.

xxv.—*"Is the Church of Rome the Babylon of the Book of Revelation?"* *An Essay by* Christopher Wordsworth, *D.D.,* &c. London: Rivingtons.

This little volume contains a careful and learned survey of the very important question on which it treats. We have never seen the subject so clearly and ably treated, and in such a short compass, nor do we see how it is possible to resist the force of Dr. Wordsworth's argument.

xxvi.—*Remains of the late Rev.* Henry Francis Lyte, *M.A., Incumbent of Lower Brixham, Devon; with a Prefatory Memoir by the Editor.* London: Rivingtons.

How little does the world know of the virtues, and the high intellectual attainments, which in many a sequestered corner are employed in the service of the Church! We have here before us the biography of a man who was calculated to fill a far more distinguished sphere than that in which his lot was cast; yet it is now for the first time that the world gains any acquaintance with this admirable man. The memoir is beautifully written, and presents to us a most touching picture of ministerial faithfulness. The poems included in the volume show very high power and accomplishment of mind. We must quote the following beautiful lines :—

> "What strains are those, what sweet familiar numbers
> From old Ierne o'er the waters wind?
> How welcome wakening from its lengthen'd slumbers,
> Sounds the heart-music of my earliest friend!
> Well might that hand amid the chords have falter'd,
> That voice have lost the power to melt and move :
> How pleasant, then, to find them still unalter'd,
> That lyre in sweetness, and that heart in love!

> "Ah me! what thoughts those few bold notes awaken,—
> Bright recollections of life's morning hours;
> Haunts long remembered, and too soon forsaken;
> Days that fled by in sunshine, song, and flowers;
> Old Clogher's rocks, our own sequester'd valley;
> Wild walks by moonlight on the sounding shore,
> Hearts warm and free, light laugh, and playful sally,
> All that has been, and shall return no more.

"No more—no more—moods ever new and changing,
  Feelings that forth in song so freely gush'd,
Wing'd hopes, high fancies, thoughts unfetter'd ranging—
  Flowers which the world's cold plough-share since has crush'd.
Dear early visions of departed gladness,
  Ye rise, ye live a moment in that strain,
A gleam of sunshine on life's wintry sadness,
  Ah! why so bright, to flit so soon again?"

XXVII.—*The Churchman's Diary: an Almanack for the year of Grace*, 1851. London: Masters.

PERSONS who put forward almanacks of this kind are really incurring a heavy responsibility, in giving offence to many weak brethren, and in causing the way of truth to be evil spoken of. It commences with what is called a "Directory for the celebration of Divine Services," in which the following principles are laid down: 1. That, as the chancels are to "remain as in times past," the clergy and choir "shall have their places there and no one else;"—that "the whole service (unless portions are 'sung') should be 'said,' *i. e. intoned* or recited musically on a single note;"—that the sentences at the beginning should be regarded as antiphons, and that they should be arranged for the seasons; 'repent ye' and 'enter not' being for Advent, and so on;—that there are "*Ferial* days," as in the Roman ritual;—that "as there is one altar so there can be but one priest (acting in that capacity), whose place is to stand *at, i. e.* in front of the altar, at the north side, facing south-east;"—that, "in consecrating the elements, the priest should be careful *to lift them up,* so that the people may see;"—that the services for the state holidays "have not received the consent of Convocation; and should therefore *not be used.*" The calendar contains not only the usual English festivals and saints' days, but those which were "provided for the Church of Scotland by Archbishop Laud." In the calendar, we find in February 1, "the *flowers* should be removed from churches this morning;" March 5, "if any person be unable to keep the fast of Lent *strictly,* he should apply to his parish priest for *direction.*" April 20, "It is an ancient and pious custom, on this and other chief festivals, to decorate churches, and especially altars, with *flowers.*" June 26, "Remove Easter decorations." July 7, We find the festival of "the Translation of St. Thomas of Canterbury," and December 29, the feast of "St. Thomas of Canterbury, Archbishop and Martyr," re-inserted in the calendar, though it has never been authorized since the Reformation.

We have directions as to the size of the altar: "as a general rule, it should not be less than six feet in length and four feet high." If there are several sets of vestments, *white* is to be used at some seasons, *red* at others, *violet* on other occasions, *black* on special days, *green* on all other days; the colours and seasons being regulated, we apprehend, by the rubric of the Roman Missal.

Now, without meaning to express any strong condemnation of every particular detail noted above, we must express very deep regret at the whole, inasmuch as we have here a Directory introducing a number of rites, forms, and observances, which are unauthorized by the ritual of the English Church, and which approximate more or less to Romanism. From the mode in which directions are given, a reader, who was not on his guard, might suppose that the various observances here prescribed or recommended have the authority of the Church of England in their favour.

XXVIII.—*The Revelation of Jesus Christ, explained agreeably to the Analogy of the Holy Scripture. By a* CLERGYMAN. London: Masters.

As far as we can judge, the author of this interpretation does not vary essentially, *i. e.* in the *great* features of his system, from other Protestant expositors. At the same time we observe that he professes peculiar views, and views which will not be accepted generally, *e. g.* he supposes the Angel speaking to St. John to be one of the Prophets of the Church—a human being like St. John himself. He also inclines to expect, with the Mormonites and Irvingites, the restoration of a fourfold ministry, of which the Apostleship will be the first rank. The work appears to us to be rather obscure in point of style, and it presents less indications of research than we are accustomed to expect in commentaries on the Apocalypse in these days. It is really astonishing to observe the multiplicity of new publications on this subject, no one appearing to be satisfied with the explanations which have been hitherto given; and yet they are for the most part very much alike in material points. There is much peculiarity of thought in the fifth part of this book, in reference to the Reformation.

XXIX.—*A Letter to the Right Hon. Lord Ashley, M.P., on the Alleged Romish Tendency of the Younger Clergy. By* WILLIAM JOHN EDGE, *M.A., Perpetual Curate of Hartshill, Warwickshire.* London: John W. Parker, West Strand. 1850.

AMIDST the thousand and one waifs of the present hour, launched from as many sources, floating about on the billows of popular emotion, we have been especially struck with this one, which has a definite aim most happily embodied. It is designed to teach all good "evangelicals" (so called) charity and tenderness for their younger high-church brethren; and we venture most sincerely to recommend it for general circulation with this view. It is eloquently, indeed we might say, beautifully written; but it is the *spirit* of the pamphlet which most delights us, so thoroughly Catholic and Christian. It cannot fail to work extensive good, wherever known. We cite one passage, addressed, remember, to Lord Ashley :—

" Can you desire the return of that disgraceful negligence which rendered our national church a scandal to her true friends, and the scorn and laughing-stock of her enemies? Would you recall the age of deserted churches—deserted by the people, because forsaken by the priest, —when two services on the Lord's Day were, even in large towns, the exception rather than the rule, when the poor were virtually banished from the services of the Church, not by crowded congregations of their superiors, but by appropriated and dragon-guarded pews,—when our glorious Liturgy was degraded into a cold and lifeless dialogue between the officiating clergyman and a blundering clerk, for the edification of a few mute and scattered auditors, *moping* in their huge and dreary pews, like pelicans in the wilderness or owls in the desert? Would you recall the age of rare communions and rarer communicants, of private baptisms and domestic churchings, of careless pastors and neglected flocks,—that age, the monuments of which are visible in every parish, in those ungainly Temples of Dissent, to which the disgusted children of the Church were driven from a cold and deadening formalism? I anticipate your reply.—' God forbid,' I hear you say, ' that such simplicity should return.' From this scandalous laxity the Church was aroused by the fervent piety of the Herveys and Romaines, the Cecils, the Newtons, and the Scotts of the last century. I thank God, my Lord, for the ministrations of these holy men; nay, even for the zealous labours of Whitfield and Wesley; and I most heartily wish that their zeal had been directed (as it might easily have been) to the edification rather than the weakening of the Church of England! The ' Evangelical' movement of the last century was indeed an infusion of fresh life into the paralyzed and torpid Church. It aroused many sleeping souls into activity; its authors served God in their generation, and are now blessed for evermore! But it had its faults. Its prevalent Calvinism cramped it, and hung like an incubus about it, rendering its system exclusive and anomalous; *exclusive* in its virtual excommunication of the great body of the people, and *anomalous* in its contradiction to the comprehensive spirit and language of the Prayer Book. Its exclusiveness gives it the semblance of severity and bigotry, and thus rendered it repulsive to enlarged and generous minds."

Then, after an admirable passage on the workings of this system, we read :—

" There are, my Lord, many sincere and hearty Protestants, who see and lament the faults and deficiencies of that religious movement of the last age, who, nevertheless, love, and endeavour to develope, its virtues, and to leaven it with the spirit and doctrine of the Prayer Book. At the present juncture these men are, by the thoughtless and ill-informed, confounded with the Romanizers, because they happen to hold in common with them the distinctive doctrines of the Church, and agree with them, to a certain point, in wishing to give efficiency and solemnity to the public offices of religion. I lift my feeble voice in behalf of these men, as one who endeavours, and always has endeavoured, to be one of them ; and let me add my conviction, that they constitute the majority of the younger clergy of England."

A feeble voice you do not lift, Mr. Edge ; but a strong and a sweet one. Such writing, so truthful, so generous-hearted, so free from the slightest taint of party-spite or bitterness, we do not meet with every day. Mr. Edge's pamphlet, we repeat, must work extensive good. We would gladly cite the whole of it in our pages, but, as we cannot do this, must content ourselves with recommending it most strongly. We were acquainted with this author before. His baptismal tracts pleased us much ; and his " Vision of Peace" is decidedly a beautiful poem, and one that will *live*, though only published in the form of a pamphlet ; but this present Letter confers a real benefit on all sound Churchmen, far and near.

xxx.—*Eidolon, or the Course of a Soul ; and other Poems.* By Walter R. Cassels. London : Pickering.

A new and pretentious versifier. Mr. Cassels *aims* at great things, but he does not *perform*. He is vague and diffuse, almost wholly wanting in true beauty, and, what is worst of all, he almost always chirps a parrot-strain ! For instance, here we have Tennyson, and " the Lord of Burleigh :"—

> " She had suitors many, many,
> The fair Lady Annabel ;
> *But she loved him more than any,*
> *For she knew he loved her well.*"

This gentleman is always writing about aristocratic ladies falling in love with poetic young gentlemen of lowly origin : that is one of *the* themes of the day. Marston has written three or four tragedies about it, and Mrs. Browning one beautiful poem ; so of course Mr. Cassels must " say his say" too. Well, here again is Mrs. Browning at second hand,—we need not say an indifferent copy,—all the grace and beauty of the original departed :—

> " O, poor world! immersed in folly; O, dull world! that will not hearken
> To the music of a poet singing of the beautiful,
> Close your heart against its teaching, though it be so sweet, and darken
> All the sunshine of the spirit by the coldness of your rule!"

Here is weak moonshine aping sunlight; or would not even the image of a farthing candle seem more appropriate? We are severe, but not unjustly so. We cannot away with these mocking-birds' songs: they vex us past endurance: in themselves they are most wearisome; but it is their effect which is so utterly deplorable in disgusting the public with poetry, and causing the true bards, whom these bardlings imitate, to be confounded with them in popular estimation. Here lies the mischief! As the song says,—

> " Amidst the noisy cuckoo's cries
> The linnet hear but few;
> *And all these false realities*
> *Now nearly hide the true.*"

Then Mr. Cassels gives us a long production "à la Keats," entitled "Alceste," in which he tells over again, coarsely and badly, what Leigh Hunt has told so well before him in his charming "Legend of Florence." Here is originality for you, dear reader, who know and love Keats's "Isabella" ("Alceste," p. 109):—

> " The tresses rustling on her neck, and she
> A woman meek, and tender as a dove;
> Yet to her full heart stricken utterly;
> And, as she went, her moist eyes turn'd above,
> Sighing, ' Poor Julian, Heaven have care of thee,
> And grant thee mercy for thy hapless love!'
> She said no more, but 'twas a piteous thing
> To see a helpless maid so sorrowing."

Now we affirm that Mr. Cassels has no right to desecrate our memories in this manner. We must have forgotten "Alceste" before we can again enjoy with keen delight the plaintive "Isabella," and the matchless "Eve of St. Agnes." Then for "Eidolon," the great achievement, ninety-two pages of weary blank-verse, with here and there a pleasing image, but scarce a new *idea*, and the most wearisome iteration. Man or woman who has not the faculty of concentration has no right to versify! Conceive this kind of thing,—we take the first passage that comes to hand,—continued for several thousand lines! (p. 19):—

" Then, as an eagle flieth to his crag
High in the stillness of the dim cloud-land,
Fled I from man into the trackless woods
To sate my soul with quietude and song.
Then, too, ye saw me, ye pure orbs of heaven,
And sent your blessed radiance to my heart
In the still twilight of my calm content!
Then came an answer to the unseen voice—
' O holy calmness of the inner soul!
Treasure of treasures! sweetness of all sense!
Athwart the smoothness of whose liquid tide,' "
&c. &c. &c.

Does any body see a prospect of an end to all this! Might it not flow on for ever to remote oblivion? The same dreary boundlessness characterizes that young gentleman, Mr. Sidney Yendy's outpourings in his " Roman :" when our eyes have dwelt for some few minutes on such musings, we are summoned back in fancy to past hours of fever-weariness, when the hot fit was succeeded by a vague wretchedness. Such is the general character we should ascribe to " Eidolon." Yet Mr. Cassels has the trick of writing, and at a first glance you might conceive his musings exceedingly sublime. Unfortunately, they are hollow and barren —as vacancy. We can find no fitter image. Much such another is the American Lewel, whom we have recently laboured to digest. He, too, has given us a long " Legend " like Keats, which would not be so bad, really, if no Keats had ever written : but, before you have read two verses, you detect the copy, and, if you then get through twenty more, we think you possessed of most heroic fortitude. We don't deny that there may be some little poetry in both these men, " at second hand :" but where is the good of that? They have both felt a little, and thought a little, and are thoroughly imbued with what is called " the spirit of the age," retailing all the oracular utterances of their elder brethren as fresh and genuine inspirations. We will not positively undertake to say that nothing can be in them. Only let them fully understand they have done nothing yet! If they can conceive or execute for themselves, we will grant them " a clear stage and no disfavour." Both have certainly a great power of talk; but, as it is, even if more wonderful, we could only say with Dr. Johnson, pronouncing on a lady's musical performance to a sitter-by,— " Would it were *impossible*, Madam!" If these would-be bards are eagles indeed, they will soar upward despite the blast of our displeasure; if they are owls, kites, or mocking-birds, these too must have their day : " *Requiescant in pace!* "

XXXI.—*An Exposition of the Thirty-Nine Articles, Historical and Doctrinal. Being the substance of a Course of Lectures delivered to Candidates for Orders at St. David's College, Lampeter. By* EDW. HAROLD BROWNE, *M.A., Prebendary of Exeter, &c.* Vol. I. London: J. W. Parker.

FROM all we have seen of this work it appears to us amongst the most useful and the soundest publications of the day. The author proceeds to expound the Articles with a view to the contemporary errors against which they were directed,—a very necessary point, which has been too much overlooked in such expositions. His views are sound and moderate, his learning very extensive, and his references to works of English theology of standard merit copious. We have been highly gratified by all we have seen of this volume.

XXXII.—*A Selection from the Sermons and Poetical Remains of the Rev.* GEORGE JAMES CORNISH, *M.A., late Vicar of Kenwyn and Kea, &c.* London: Mozley.

THIS volume possesses a high interest as a memorial of a most excellent and revered clergyman, whose death appears to have been felt in the diocese of Exeter as a severe loss to the Church. The selection of Sermons and of Poems now before us proves sufficiently the high qualifications which he possessed as an able, eloquent, and edifying preacher; and the accomplishment of mind, refinement of taste, and poetical power, which must have shed a charm over his general character and conversation, are apparent in the beautiful pieces which adorn the volume. Of the Sermons we must say, that they are amongst the most interesting we have ever seen. Their style is peculiarly graceful and flowing, eminently the writing of one who viewed subjects under the mingled light of a poetic temperament and a mind deeply stored with scriptural thought and imagery. In doctrine they are most sound and orthodox, and we rise from their perusal with mingled feelings of regret that such a man should be no longer with us, and of thankfulness that he was so long permitted to be a blessing to the Church.

XXXIII.—*The Life of James Davies, a Village Schoolmaster. Written by Sir* THOMAS PHILLIPS. London: Parker.

A MOST striking piece of biography. This village schoolmaster's life ought to be in the hands of every member of the Church of England, high and low. We can recommend it as an invaluable book for a Parochial Lending Library. It is perfectly charming.

XXXIV.—*Sermons on Old Testament Histories. Selected from the*

Parish Discourses of the late Ven. Archdeacon BATHER. London: Society for Promoting Christian Knowledge.

WE are sure that the Christian Knowledge Society could not have taken a more desirable step than that of publishing, as they have done, a selection from Archdeacon Bather's Sermons. To that writer we owe one of our best works on Catechising; and his experience and success in parochial ministrations, the sound judgment and zeal which he always evinced, and the intimate terms on which he stood with all his people, render his addresses of peculiar value. They are just the sort of discourses which plain people can understand and relish; and we have no doubt that their circulation will be extensive, and will make the name of their venerable author as familiar to the poor of our Church as it is already to the clergy and to all persons of education.

xxxv.—*The New Testament, expounded and illustrated according to the usual marginal references in the very words of Holy Scripture. Together with the Notes and Translations, and a complete marginal Harmony of the Gospels. By* CLEMENT MOODY, *M.A., &c.* London: Longman and Co.

THE title-page of this book explains sufficiently its design. It comprises the marginal references arranged at the foot of the page at full length. We have no doubt that it will be found extremely convenient to the student of the Bible, and will tend to a more intelligent use of the sacred volume.

xxxvi.—1. *The Danger and the Foe. A Sermon, delivered in Trinity Church, Exeter. By the Rev.* ARCHER GURNEY. Exeter: Wallis. London: Masters.

2. *Union and Victory. A Sermon, by the same Author.*

AMONGST the various Discourses to which the late Papal aggression has given cause, these two Sermons by Mr. Gurney claim a distinguished place, from their assertion of strong Anti-papal principle, in combination with a manly effort to do justice to the clergy of Exeter who had been accused of Romanism by the enemies of the Church. These Discourses are the production of a generous and charitable spirit, which reserves its antagonism for the enemies of the faith. The facts referred to in these Sermons, as to the efforts made by the *Jesuits*, at the present time, to sow dissension between the clergy and laity of the Church of England, are most important.

xxxvii.—*The Old Paths of the Church of England. A Sermon preached in St. John's Chapel, St. Marylebone. By* DANIEL BUTLER, *M.A., Assistant Minister.* Rivingtons.

A VERY excellent discourse, pointing out the duty of Churchmen

in these days to adhere to a system which has antiquity and
truth on its side, in opposition to the innovations of Dissent on
the one side, and Romanism on the other.   Its tone is remarkably calm and argumentative.

xxxviii.—*Tales and Allegories.*   Oxford and London : J. H.
Parker. 1850.

This is one of the prettiest and most pleasing volumes that we
have seen for a long while.   The Tales and Allegories which it
contains are already known to most of our readers, having previously appeared in the Parochial Tracts.   We have never read
a more attractive as well as instructive tale than that entitled
" It might have been worse ;" in which the style of a well-known
and justly popular writer may easily be recognised, except that
he has here quite surpassed himself.   Amongst others that have
particularly pleased us are, " Edwin Forth ; or, the Emigrant in
Canada ;" " Harry Fulton ; or, the Merchant's Son ;" and "Thou
shalt not Steal ; or, the School Feast."

xxxix.—*Old Christmas.*   Oxford and London : J. H. Parker.
1850.

Just what its name imports : admirably suited for children of
eight or ten years old, and will be read with pleasure and profit
by their parents.

xl.—*The Christian Year.*   Thirty-eighth Edition.   Oxford and
London : J. H. Parker. 1850.

A pocket edition of this very popular work : very well got up,
and very cheap.

xli.—*A Catechism on the Thirty-nine Articles of the Church of
England.   By the Rev.* James Beaven, *D.D., &c.*   Oxford
and London : J. H. Parker.

Dr. Beaven's work, " A Help to Catechising," is probably well
known to all our readers as amongst the most useful manuals on
the subject of which it treats.   The little work before us is
written in the same style, and possesses in its way equal merit.
The Articles, however, are not likely to be so much studied in
schools as the Catechism ; and the explanation which Dr. Beaven
has here given is calculated for schools or for very young persons.   It may, however, be useful to students in the Universities : indeed, we think it *will* be so : and we trust it may obtain
the circulation which it certainly deserves.   We should scarcely
have said, as at page seventy, that the Romish doctrine concerning Purgatory, against which the Twenty-second Article is
directed, is not exactly known.

XLII.—*Eastbury : a Tale.* By ANNA HARRIET DRURY, *Authoress of Friends and Fortune.* London: Pickering.

WE have met with Miss Drury before: the placid grace of her poems surprised and delighted us, recalling Goldsmith, Crabbe, and Gray, yet marked with a peculiar feminine delicacy and refinement. Her poems did, indeed, greatly please us, and her tale of "Friends and Fortune" won from us a richly deserved encomium in the pages of this review. Therefore, late as is the hour and day on which we have received this, her last production, "Eastbury," we have hurriedly perused, in order to be able to say (as we honestly can), that it is worthy of its elder sisters or brothers. It is, take it for all in all, a very delightful story, though we are not sure that it is wholly equal to "Friends and Fortune." The subject is not, perhaps, as pleasing, and our attention is too much divided between two heroines, the least interesting of whom, to us most unexpectedly, obtains—but we must not tell any secrets, or mar the effect of *the surprise*—which, if most readers are as blind as we were, will prove great indeed. Miss Drury's style is peculiarly easy and agreeable ; upon the whole, we prefer the lighter passages, thinking some of the more serious a little too ornate, and also too determinately " good ;" but this is a fault on the right side, no doubt. Such a model of perfection in a young lady's eyes as the clerical hero surely never was realised on earth, such a combination of meekness and daring, of Fenelon and the admirable Crichton ; but it is all very delightful, at all events. We do think him, however, slightly addicted to speechifying— but he is a noble parish-priest, and we only wish there were a thousand such,—" if wishers were choosers," as the proverb says. One recommendation this tale has for us, it is a thorough Church of England book, free from all sentimental tamperings with Popery, and presenting us with an admirable model-bishop of our own. There is an interesting mystery connected with the more romantic heroine, Beatrice, and wild adventure is not wanting ; but still we think the plot might have been managed more effectively. We presume the general moral may be held to be the necessity for telling the whole truth at whatever sacrifice ; and better moral can be none. By the by, where did Miss Drury discover those very beautiful lines (pp. 216, 217), of which she speaks so slightingly ? To us they are unknown. " Eastbury " will bear reading more than once ; we scarcely know of a more fitting birth-day gift.

MISCELLANEOUS.

AMONGST the recent publications which have come under our notice are the following :—" Arctic Expeditions," a Lecture by Mr. Weld, Assistant Secretary of the Royal Society (Murray), giving a brief and well-written account of the various expeditions to the Arctic seas; " The Merits and Tendencies of Free Trade and Protection," by Dr. Calvert (Hearne), recommending the storing of corn in seasons of plenty; " An Inquiry into M. D'Abbadie's Journey to Kaffa," by Dr. Beke (Madden), in which the author proves that M. D'Abbadie's journey is an invention ; " The Church Review and Ecclesiastical Register" (Newhaven), a most admirably conducted American Theological Review, published quarterly ; " The Bible of Every Land" (Bagster), a very curious and interesting account of all the versions of the Bible, with specimens of each version. We trust this important and expensive undertaking meets support. " The Blank-paged Bible" (Bagster), an extremely beautiful and complete Bible, with maps, marginal references, interleaved pages, and every thing which adapts it for the use of clergymen or students. A Sermon, by Mr. Watson, of Cheltenham, " The Church's own Action" (Masters), refers to the recent aggression, and is ably written. We have also Sermons on the same subject by the Rev. Nugent Wade, and Rev. H. D. Hilton ; a strongly Anti-Tractarian Sermon, " Christian Liberty," by Mr. Benson, Canon of Worcester (J. W. Parker) ; " Education," a Sermon by Dr. Molesworth ; " Discourses on Colonization and Education," by Mr. Wynter (J. W. Parker) ; "Abuse of Oaths," by Mr. Beames (Skeffington and Southwell) ; a useful tract, entitled " Congregational Independents, an Inquiry into their Faith and Practice," by Rev. H. Wray (Masters) ; an interesting *brochure* on " Church Colonization ;" by Rev. J. Cecil Wynter (J. W. Parker) ; " Five Sermons, preached at Galby," &c., by Mr. Rawstorne (Hamilton and Adams), to aid in restoring the church, which was injured in a thunder-storm ; a Sermon on " Papal Aggression," by Mr. Eddrup, Camden Town ; " Plain Lectures on Romanism," by Rev. E. W. Relton (Wertheim) ; " Rome and her Claims," a well-written Sermon, by Mr. Jackson, St. James's ; " Stand Fast in the Faith," by Rev. Ernest Hawkins (Rivingtons), an excellent discourse ; " The Bull of Pope Pius IX., and the Ancient British Church," by Chancellor Harington (Rivingtons), written with the author's well-known research. Space forbids us to notice further at present these and other publications now before us.

Foreign and Colonial Intelligence.

UNITED STATES.—*General Convention of the Protestant Episcopal Church.*—At the present moment, when not only the revival of the active functions of the English Synods is becoming daily more probable, but when, moreover, the propriety of admitting the lay element into them is very generally canvassed, it will be interesting to our readers[1] to see a more extensive abstract of the proceedings of the triennial meeting of the American Church Convention, held at Cincinnati in the course of October last.

The opening of the Convention took place on Wednesday, October the 2nd, and its proceedings were brought to a close on Wednesday, October the 16th.

On the former day, a large number of Clergy, including twenty-three Bishops, and of lay deputies, assembled in Christ Church, Cincinnati, when, after a sermon preached by Bishop Smith, of Kentucky, on Ephesians iii. 10, the Holy Communion was administered.

The service being concluded, the Bishops retired to their own House, the proceedings of which are not regularly published, but become known only through the official result communicated to the House of Clerical and Lay-deputies, and sometimes by occasional revelations on particular questions. After the names of the deputies had been called over, and their testimonials produced, the Rev. Dr. Wyatt, of Baltimore, was unanimously elected President. After the election of a Secretary, and the transaction of other preliminary business, a resolution was passed, to the effect—

" That a committee be appointed to inform the House of Bishops that this house is now organized and ready for business."

Another resolution was passed—

" That the clergy of the Protestant Episcopal Church, students of the General Theological Seminary, candidates for orders, and members of the vestry of Christ Church, be invited to honorary seats in this convention."

THURSDAY, THE 3RD.—The Rev. Dr. Stevens, of Pennsylvania, moved :—

" That the House of Bishops be respectfully solicited to favour the house with their opinion as to the proper posture to be observed in the baptismal service."

This gave rise to an animated discussion.

---

[1] We hesitate the less to give precedence to this subject over every other, as there is no intelligence, either Colonial or Foreign, of great importance, excluded by the devotion of our pages to this record of the Convention of the American Church.

Against the motion it was urged that such motions were dangerous, as having a tendency to throw indirectly into the hands of one branch of the Convention the power of legislating in rubrical matters, which belonged to the whole Convention. If the meaning of the rubrics was uncertain, the legitimate mode was to alter them, as the constitution provided, by a concurrent vote of both houses. Besides, the proposed mode of settling the question would not really settle it, because the opinion of the House of Bishops was not authoritative and binding, and individuals who disagreed from it would therefore still be able to follow their own course. The same experiment had been tried with regard to the Sacrament of the Lord's Supper, and had failed; no uniformity of practice having been attained through the opinion of the House of Bishops pronounced in regard to it. The Bishops had no right to institute, alter, or abolish any rites or ceremonies. It was undesirable to attach so much importance to the subject; as there was a tendency to make buildings and their ornaments, attitudes and gestures, the signs of great and mysterious truths. There was great danger of the Bishops assuming too much power; the very deference which was paid to them was calculated to stimulate the lust of power which was natural to the human heart. The power of their Bishops had been increasing from the beginning. At first they were not a separate House. Then they had only a qualified veto on the proceedings of the deputies, which could be overcome by a certain vote of that house. Now they had an unqualified veto, and were a co-ordinate branch. Without contending that this was not right, it showed that there had been a progress. Want of uniformity was an evil no doubt, but they might run into other evils while seeking to avoid it. It had been so in reference to the opinion of the Bishops as to the Holy Communion. The men who did not follow it were denounced as non-conformists. Compliance or non-compliance became a party badge. And it had so far the power of law as to bring odium and denunciation upon all who did not comply with it. It was doubtful whether the Bishops themselves would like to have such an application made to them. They had been pleased that it was not done at the last Convention, and they would probably feel the same now.

In support of the motion it was said, that it contemplated no alteration of the rubric, but merely the solution of a doubt concerning a point on which the rubric was silent. In such cases it was provided that they should individually apply to the Bishop, and there was no reason why the same thing should not be done collectively. Uniformity of practice was desirable. If a man came to church in Ohio, and, as he had been accustomed, knelt in his pew, he found that all about him were standing. If he went to Virginia, and stood up, he would find all others kneeling. This was not only unpleasant but unseemly. In questions of indifference, such as this, deference to those placed in a position of superiority was the best and safest course. It was a fitter question for the Bishops to decide, than for a House partly composed of laymen. (This was urged by a layman, Judge Chambers.) There was no danger of the Bishops ever over-riding the authority of that House. The opinion of the House of Bishops relative to the posture at the Holy Communion had not been altogether ineffectual; there had been, since 1832, a growing uniformity both as to the form of words used and as to the posture. The opinion of the Bishops continued to have increasing effect. The Bishops being the Ordinaries; it was their proper province to decide such questions, and necessarily their collective opinion would have more weight than that of individual Bishops.

Among the supporters of the motion was the Rev. Dr. Mead of Connecticut, who pleaded precedent in support of the proposition. This would not be the first action of this kind in the history of the Church. In 1832, the opinion of the House of Bishops had been asked as to the proper posture to be observed in the Communion service. It had been given, and had gone far to produce uniformity, and to relieve them from many perplexing questions. In 1835, two similar questions had arisen. One was respecting the practice of repeating the Lord's Prayer and a collect in the pulpit, before the sermon. There was no rubric for it, but such had been in some parts the practice, and there had been a diversity. The opinion of the Bishops had been asked, an answer obtained, and the practice was now uniform. In 1835, also, a lay member from Pennsylvania had introduced a motion asking the opinion of the Bishops as to the proper method of repeating the Confession and the Creed. An answer had been obtained, and uniformity on this point was now almost, if not altogether, universal. As to the point before them, what brother had not been shocked at the irreverence often exhibited in receiving a member into Christ's visible Church? Other societies, masons, odd fellows, &c., showed more reverence for their initiatory services.

Mr. Patterson, of Mississippi, was afraid the resolution would tend to the abrogation of a custom of the early Church. The custom of the early Church was to have the font at the door. When Baptism was administered there, all, of course, must stand. But, out of special reverence for the Lord's Prayer, the rubric required that they should kneel when it was said. A custom had grown up to place the font in the chancel, and now they called upon the Bishops to sanction this custom, which they had no right to do.

The Rev. Dr. Seabury, of New York, opposed the resolution on a specific ground, the peculiar situation of the diocese of New York. Its effect would be to impose a law on the Church. And it would be hard on the diocese of New York, which would in this case have *no* voice in determining the practice she would have to follow.

Eventually it was agreed to let the motion lie on the table.

FRIDAY, THE 4TH.—The Standing Committees were appointed on the third day; they are the following: On the State of the Church; On the General Theological Seminary; On the Domestic and Foreign Missionary Board; On the Admission of New Dioceses; On the Consecration of Bishops; On Canons; On Elections; On the Prayer Book; On Expenses: On Unfinished Business. Of these the first is by far the most numerous, consisting of twenty-seven members, while the others mostly count only nine members.

The journals of the several dioceses since the last meeting of the General Convention were handed in, and referred to the Committee on the State of the Church.

A question arose, on the report of the Committee on Elections, as to the propriety of admitting to seats in the House of Deputies persons not elected directly by the Conventions of their respective dioceses, but indirectly by authority delegated from the Conventions, and by the nomination of substitutes by the Bishops in cases when the principals absented themselves. There were many conflicting opinions, and among them the subject was permitted to drop.

After some motions relative to the order of business, a resolution was adopted, on the report of the Committee on New Dioceses, for the incorporation of the newly organized diocese of Texas into the Protestant Episcopal Church in the United States, on its admission to representation in the General Convention.

It was notified that the House of Bishops had passed a resolution, that the alteration of article " First " of the Constitution, to wit, the substitution of the first Wednesday of September for October, as the time proposed at the last General Convention for holding the triennial meeting, be agreed to and ratified. This led to considerable discussion, which turned upon the inconvenience of members from the different states attending at certain seasons, and upon the unhealthiness of the South at the period proposed. On a vote being taken, the proposition was lost, and an intimation of the non-concurrence of the House of Deputies was ordered to be conveyed to the House of Bishops.

SATURDAY, THE 5TH.—The admission of the Diocese of Texas into union with the Convention by the House of Bishops was notified to the House. The delegates were subsequently introduced.

The General Theological Seminary became the subject of an animated discussion. An alteration was proposed by Judge Bullock, of Kentucky, in the constitution of the seminary, so as to provide that a meeting of the board of trustees shall always be held at the same time and place with the General Convention, and that special meetings of the board may be called by the presiding Bishop, at the request of a majority of the Bishops. According to the present constitution, all meetings of the board of trustees must be held in the diocese in which the seminary is situated, and, all special meetings of the board must be called by the Bishop of that diocese. It was desirable to have the seminary in reality what it was in name, a General Theological Seminary; which it was not, since the first of the provisions alluded to deprived other dioceses of their fair share of representation in the board. As to the other provision, the diocese of New York had no Bishop, and therefore, there could be no special meetings. It was desirable to have some officer empowered to call such meetings, and none could be more competent than the presiding Bishop.

Another member, Mr. Newton, of Massachusets, proposed an amendment to the 6th article of the constitution of the seminary, with a view to allow absent members of the board to vote by proxy. The whole government of the seminary was practically in the hands of the diocese of New York. The members from other dioceses present at the meetings never amounted altogether to a majority of the whole. So much was this the case, that South Carolina, which had taken more interest in, and done more for, the seminary than any other diocese, save New York, had found herself in such a dead minority, that she would no longer send her men or money to it. It would be morally impossible for trustees from distant dioceses to be present at the proposed meeting of the 2nd of November, when the election of a professor was to take place.

After a lengthened and warm discussion, it was agreed to let the further consideration of the subject stand over till the following Thursday.

A series of canons, in reference to the ordination of deacons and presbyters, the principal of which provided that candidates may be ordained deacons, without examination on any points, except fitness to discharge the duties of deacon specified in the ordinal, was referred to the Committee on Canons. The Canons were subsequently referred to the next Convention.

MONDAY, THE 7TH.—The question touching a revision of the German version of the Prayer Book was mooted by the Rev. Mr. Henderson, of New Jersey, the appointment of a joint Committee for the purpose by the last Convention having proved inoperative. He stated, that, among the 40,000 inhabitants of the city of Newark, there are 7000 or 8000 Germans; and in Cincinnati, which has 130,000 inhabitants, there are 30,000 or 40,000. The Bishop of Indiana took part in the discussion, and observed that there was no more interesting field of missionary labour than this open to the Church. The German population of the country was totally uncared for by the Protestants. The only religious influence which was exerted on them was that of Romanism, and they were fast sinking into downright infidelity. A fresh Committee was appointed to revise the German Prayer Book, and to report to the next Convention.

An important proposal was the introduction of a canon for systematizing the American canon law. Uniformity in the administration of law, the proposer argued, was a matter of great moment. It was hardly to be expected that the various Episcopal and Diocesan Courts would arrive at the same conclusions upon the various questions brought before them. An Appellate Court was, therefore, needed: and it was important to include in it that feature that had been found to work so well in the English Ecclesiastical Courts,—the introduction of laymen learned in the law. The proposition only gave jurisdiction in questions of law; it did not touch questions of fact. The canon, entitled "On Appeals," was read. Its first section provides that, in all cases decided by any diocese or court, involving questions of law, the party who considers himself aggrieved may have an appeal. He shall file a notice of it, specifying the points which he considers erroneous, and the reasons of his objections, and a declaration that he considers and believes himself to be wronged thereby. The appeal shall be heard by the three Bishops next in seniority to the presiding Bishop and to the Bishops, if any, who may have last served in this court, and by three laymen, to be chosen, one by the applicant, one by the presiding Bishop, and one by the ecclesiastical authority of the diocese where the trial has been held. Of these, none but the layman chosen by the presiding Bishop shall belong to the diocese whose court is appealed from. The second provides for staying all proceedings until this appeal is decided; that such decision shall be final and authoritative; that it shall be certified to the ecclesiastical authority of the diocese in question, and a record be kept and deposited with the Secretary of the House of Deputies, to be accessible to every member of the Church. The third provides that a majority of this court shall be a quorum; that it shall meet within three months of the period when the appeal is entered, at the time and place fixed by the presiding Bishop. The ecclesiastical authority of the diocese where the trial took place to furnish a copy of the papers to the presiding Bishop, within one month after the appeal is taken, otherwise the decision of the Diocesan Court to be void. The fourth provides, that, in case the presiding Bishop be appealed from, the next in seniority is to perform *his* duties. The fifth, that the expenses shall be paid by the diocese appealed from. The canon was referred to the Committee on Canons.

Another and most interesting discussion arose on the subject of evidence in ecclesiastical trials; in which, in reference to a canon proposed by Mr. Duncan of Louisiana, the Committee of Canons had reported that legislation was at the present time (i. e. with reference to the still pending case of Bishop Onderdork, of New York) inexpedient. Although no practical result was arrived at, the discussion possesses great interest, both on account of the intrinsic importance of the subject, and because it throws light upon the peculiar difficulties with which it is surrounded, in consequence of the state of the law generally in the United States. Judge Chambers observed,—"Our judiciary is differently situated from that of England. With us the laws of evidence vary in different States. It is intended that the law, as existing in each State, is to be observed by the Ecclesiastical Court, according as it meets in one or another of them. But the difficulty is to know what the law is. The Bishops cannot be supposed to know. And it is, in my judgment, unnecessary that they should. There are certain great principles of justice, which when faithfully applied are abundantly sufficient." Mr. Duncan said, these propositions had been submitted to several Bishops, and met their approbation. The question was, "whether, when the highest judiciary of the Church meets to determine questions under her general laws, it shall have rules of evidence to guide it. The dioceses have, in many cases, legislated for themselves in this matter. It is not intended to touch their provisions. The proposed canon refers only to the proceedings of the Court of Bishops. Now, is the law of evidence such, that that court can safely and wisely proceed under it? I would not allude to a case that may cause excitement, but

would refer to what lawyers call ' a case in the books,' in order to
show the necessity of some alteration. When that court was last in
session, its members felt and expressed the difficulty. They felt themselves governed by different rules of evidence. Is such a condition of
things right? Is it just to the defendant? I think not. In such a
case the defendant may be sacrificed to the conceptions of his judges.
We need a canon that may guide the court, obviate this difficulty, and
bring them to a conclusion, after having travelled the same course and
taken the same views of law. In order to show the confusion of the
law, and the injustice which may result from it, let me call the attention of the House to what one of the judges (the Bishop of Western
New York) said on the occasion alluded to. ' It must be admitted,' he
remarked, ' that the canon is defective—that it leaves unsettled, and
even untouched, many important points. It fixes no rule as to the
number of witnesses necessary to establish any point, no limitation of
time within which it is lawful to bring forward charges; it even leaves
it dubious whether the presenters may not be of the court, provides no
right of challenge, no penalty for witnesses who refuse to attend,
and we are left to grope our way in the dark.' Shall we leave them
thus to grope their way amid darkness, when we have it in our
power to shed light on their path? This is a favourable time when
there is no case in prospect. I trust there will never be another. I
hope the court may never be called together again till the resurrection
morn. But it may be. And therefore it is wise that we do not leave
them in the same perplexity and at liberty to legislate on the subject.
Bishops have been consulted, and they prefer that action on this matter
should emanate from this house. It might not be seemly for them to
originate the mode by which they may be themselves hereafter brought
to trial. There are several difficulties connected with the present canon,
The time in which it shall be lawful to hear accusations against an
individual after the criminal act has been committed is not fixed. It
ought to be. I have inserted three years. The Presbyterian Church
limits such time to one year. Without such a limitation a defendant
may be sacrificed. An accusation may be kept until the witnesses are
scattered or gone to their own final account, and then brought forward.
And especially is this needed in our country. We are a moving people,
and the witnesses to any transaction are scattered where it is impossible to collect them. Then, as to the rules of evidence, what could be
safer than to adopt that of the State? This may involve some disadvantage, but a disadvantage far inferior to that incurred by putting a
defendant on trial under rules of evidence different from the only ones
which he can be supposed to know, those adopted in the State where
he resides. Nor can there be any real difficulty arising from the diversity of those laws. The Supreme Court of the United States is in
such a category. It gives, and rightly gives, sometimes on the same
day, directly opposite opinions under the precisely same state of law
and fact. And why? Because they arise in different States where
different laws of evidence prevail. And they do right; because all

men are supposed to know the law 'which is in force in the State where
they reside.   The Court must, where the alleged crime has been committed, ascertain both the law and the facts.   In this is there any safer
guide than the law of the land ?   I think not ; but, if hat should not
be the general opinion it will be easy to fix upon some other rule."
Mr. Duncan concluded by reading his canon, entitled a " Canon Supplementary to Canon 3 of 1844, of the Trial of Bishops," and which
provides,—

" 1. That no alleged offence of longer date than three years' standing
shall be a subject for trial.

" 2. That the rules of evidence shall be observed by the court, which
are observed by the civil tribunals of the State in which the trial is
held.

" 3. That the name of any known person in the city where the trial is
held, or within twenty miles of it, who, being summoned as a witness,
shall refuse to appear, shall be reported by the Court to the Rector of
the parish to which he or she belongs, and, if the person be a communicant of the Church, the Rector shall proceed at once to strike his or her
name from the list of communicants."

After some further discussion the canon was laid on the table.

Another question connected with the case of Bishop Onderdonk was
brought on by Judge Chambers, who moved that it be referred to the
Committee on Canons to inquire into the expediency of so amending
Canon 2 of 1847, as to require that the call of a special meeting of
the House of Bishops therein provided for shall be made within a
reasonable time after the application by five Bishops to the Presiding
Bishop.   In the year 1847, he remarked, the General Convention
passed the canon referred to, for the purpose of admitting a modification by the House of Bishops of a sentence of suspension.   It provided
for a call of the House for this purpose, by the Presiding Bishop acting
at the suggestion of five other Bishops, and that the time shall be fixed
at a period not less than three months after the request shall be made.
A well-known principle of law ought to have put a limit on the other
side.   That principle was, that when a thing is commanded it must be
done in a reasonable time.   This, Judge Chambers complained, had
not been done in the case of the requisition addressed by Five Bishops
to the Presiding Bishop, for the reconsideration of the case of Bishop
Onderdonk of New York.   The Presiding Bishop had delayed the
matter for eight, some said for twelve months, till the meeting of the
General Convention, and thereby defeated the object of the requisition.

After a lengthy and occasionally warm discussion, the motion to lay
on the table was put and lost.

TUESDAY, THE 8TH. Judge Bullock presented a Memorial addressed
to the General Convention by clergymen and laymen of the diocese of
Maryland.   The memorialists understand the Bishop of the diocese
of Maryland to claim the right,—

" 1. Of administering the Lord's Supper by virtue of his office, and
without the invitation of the rector, in every parish and congregation of

his diocese, on occasions of canonical visitation, or at any other time, when, with due regard to circumstances, he may express the desire to do so.

" 2. The right of appropriating the offerings of the people collected on such occasions.

" 3. The right, when he may be present at public worship in any church of his diocese, to pronounce the declaration of absolution in the morning and evening prayer."

The memorialists then go on to discuss the "nature and extent of the claims of the episcopal authority asserted and maintained in the diocese of Maryland ; the reasons for believing them unfounded ; and the necessity of legislation upon the subject."

The memorial gave rise to a long and most animated discussion between those who take a high, and those who take a low view of episcopal prerogative ; which, however, is of slight interest, as it turned not so much upon the intrinsic merits of the point at issue, as upon the question whether the matter should be left to be dealt with in the ordinary way by the Committee on Canons, or referred to a special Committee. The House being unable to come to a conclusion, the question was adjourned to Thursday.

WEDNESDAY, THE 9TH.—The Committee on Canons reported a canon on clergymen who declare they will no longer be ministers of the Church, providing for a delay of three months in all cases, and an additional delay of three months at the discretion of the ecclesiastical authority of the diocese, between the receiving such a declaration from a minister and the pronouncing of his displacement. During this time it shall be lawful for the minister to reconsider and withdraw his declaration.

The Rev. Dr. Mason proposed an amendment to Canon 3 of 1844, on the trial of bishops. It provides that the court shall consist of the bishops of the five nearest dioceses, provided none of them be of the number of the presenting bishops, and gives the accused bishop the right of challenge for cause against any of the judges. The proposed amendment, together with the canon on the same subject, referred by the last General Convention to this, and the canon on the same subject, proposed by Mr. Duncan, were referred to the Committee on Canons.

On a message from the House of Bishops, a joint committee was appointed, on the report of the missionary bishops.

A resolution that, the House of Bishops concurring, a joint committee be appointed to prepare a table of the degrees of consanguinity and affinity within which it shall not be lawful to marry, and publish the same in the standard Bible, was laid on the table after a few remarks on the excitement which this question had caused in the Church of England, and among the Presbyterians.

The consideration of the Maryland memorial having been resumed, it was resolved, in the event of the House of Bishops concurring, to refer it, and the report of the Committee on Canons, relative to the existing canons bearing on the point, to a joint committee of both

Houses, including seven members of the House of Deputies. A difficulty then arose as to the selection of the Committee; the chairman declining the task, two members (one from each party) were appointed to nominate the seven members of the committee. They agreed on six, and being unable to agree on the seventh, proposed two names, of which the House selected one by ballot.

The consideration of the General Theological Society was resumed: The committee reported that it was inexpedient to hold the triennial meeting of the Board of Trustees at the same time and place as the General Convention, and recommended two Canons, to the following effect:—" 1. The board of trustees concurring, that hereafter special meetings of the Board may be called by a majority of the bishops, they designating who of their number shall act in calling it.

" 2. That absent members of the board of trustees may vote, in the election of professors, by proxy given to a co-trustee."

These two resolutions having been adopted, Mr. Newton, of Massachusetts, moved, that in the opinion of this House it is expedient that the triennial meeting of the board of trustees shall be held at the time and place of that of the General Convention, and that the report be recommitted to the committee, with instructions to report to that effect. The seminary was now under the control of the diocese of New York, and it would never be otherwise, unless there could be some such occasion of a general meeting of the board. This was important, both to the Church and the seminary. It had enormous property, understood to be worth about 350,000 dollars, to which had been added recently 100,000 dollars more ; and was doing, in proportion to its means, but little good. One reason was, that it had been under a partial and local influence.

Mr. Dobbin, of Maryland, a member of the committee, observed, that the seminary, as a literary institution, differed from all other Church institutions. As such it had buildings, libraries, professors,—in short a local habitation. Hence it seemed essential that its government should be carried on upon the ground where it is placed. The Convention was migratory. The trustees amounted to more than 200 in number—the members of this convention between 200 and 300. There would be a great inconvenience in bringing some 500 gentlemen a long distance from home, not for the transaction of business, but for review, terminating most usually in a mere formal report.

The Rev. Mr. Mead, of Connecticut.—Of the 200 members of the board, 135 lived within one easy day's journey of the city of New York. He would ask if there were any inconvenience where the large number were thus within a day's journey of the place of meeting, so as to demand that the whole body shall be dragged to any place, however distant, where the General Convention may meet? The great evil under which the seminary had laboured was, that it had been for some years an institution without a head, which had arisen from the fact that it had had a non-resident bishop at its head. There were great difficulties growing out of this, as to the police regulations of the institution. The trustees had laboured hard to correct this, and had once passed a code which they thought would do so. It was within a year of the meeting of the General Convention in New York. The triennial meeting of the board was held. They reviewed the proceedings and swept the whole away, disheartening those who had laboured, and leaving the whole work to be done over again. Ought this to occur? But, adopt this alteration, and the evil would be tenfold. It had been said that the seminary, with its large property, had done comparatively little good. Its property might be large, but it was unproductive. It was in real estate, which, however it might be estimated, did not yield a large revenue. It had increased and was increasing in value. But the trustees would not sell or encumber it. But it had done good. It had improved its real estate and erected two buildings sufficient for the accommodation of 140 students and the professors. See too what they had done in the way of theological education. More than twenty members of this House, and four of the right reverend members of the other House were among the alumni.

Mr. Williams, of Virginia, observed that at the last triennial meeting of the board there were only fifty-six members present. Of these thirty were from New York. And yet special efforts had been made to get a full attendance. Now, if this was a general seminary, let some plan be adopted by which it shall be no longer virtually a diocesan institution. He felt constrained to state that the confidence of the Church in the institution seemed impaired. This was evident from the diminished contributions. The question was, whether the interests of the Church would be best promoted by holding the meetings of the board where only a few could attend, or at the meeting of the General Convention, where more could be present.

Dr. Mead, in reply, accounted for the diminution of the contributions on the ground of the erroneous impression prevalent that the seminary was rich, and did not need money.

Judge Conygham was on the joint committee of the convention of 1844. There was then a general feeling that something ought to be done to secure to the more distant dioceses their proper influence. At that time the committee had thought and reported that the adoption of the proxy system would be all that was necessary. The case was plain. If the dioceses were to be represented in the board, their trustees ought to have a voice. But the difficulties in the way of their attendance were so great as to make it almost impossible. It was important to remove this difficulty. The proposition of the gentleman from Massachusetts did this. Of the 134 trustees who could conveniently attend the meetings of the board now, seventy belonged to the state of New York. This demonstrated how completely the seminary had become the property of New York. And, as all alterations of the constitution were to be the joint act of the trustees and the convention, it would be well to bring them near together.

The Rev. Mr. Patterson, of Mississippi, wanted to see justice done the Seminary. The Theological Seminary was born, endowed, built up in the diocese of New York, and then offered as a boon to the Church. This was the relation of the Church and the diocese to that institution. It was given on conditions, which the Church would violate if they passed this resolution. The reason why there were so many trustees in the diocese of New York was, that the Church had heretofore complied with those conditions. The non-attendance of the trustees who resided near New York was quoted as proving that the Seminary was regarded with suspicion. But there was another reason. They saw the good which it was doing. And they knew that this must be the result of good management. Who were those who spoke of suspicion? Had they ever given any thing to its funds? Not a dime. Were they the men who ought to speak? It was well to let well alone. The seminary had done well and needed no legislation, especially from those who were interested in rival institutions. Ought they to come and seek to break the compact under which this seminary had been established?

The Rev. Mr. Trapier rose to correct a mistake of the last speaker as to the history of the seminary, but was interrupted by a message from the House of Bishops, informing this House that they have concurred in referring the Maryland memorial and its accompanying documents to a joint committee, and had appointed on their part on said committee Bishops Brownell, Hopkins, Ives, McIlvaine, and Polk.

THURSDAY, THE 10th.—A message from the House of Bishops announced their concurrence in a resolution previously passed by the House of Deputies, designating New York as the place for the next meeting of the General Convention.

The Committee on Canons reported a canon " on Assistant Bishops," providing that, in case of any permanent cause of disability in a Bishop of a Diocese, an Assistant Bishop may be elected. In case the disability arise from a suspension of the Bishop, he shall not direct the services of the Assistant. But a suspended Bishop shall have power to give his assent to the election of an Assistant. The canon was ordered to be printed.

The adjourned debate on the General Theological Seminary having been resumed, the Rev. Mr. Trapier, of South Carolina, said the seminary was not, as had been alleged, a boon from the diocese of New York to the Church, but rather the reverse. It had existed in Connecticut as a general seminary before it was transferred to New York. That it had previously existed in New York, he would not deny. But this had nothing to do with the point in hand. In 1812 the subject of a General Theological Seminary had occurred to the mind of Bishop Dehon, of South Carolina. He spoke to several individuals, among whom was Bishop Hobart, then Assistant Bishop of New York. The prelate's view was, that it was desirable to have one; and his first proposal was, that it should be located in the diocese of New Jersey (where he had a country-seat which he was fond of visiting), and to be under the presidency of the Bishop of New York, and the vice-presidency of the Bishop of New Jersey. It was not, however, a general, but a diocesan seminary which he desired.

The Rev. Dr. Jarvis.—The time of the conversation was 1812. The proposal for a general seminary was brought forward at the general Convention of 1814, in the House of Bishops, by Bishop Dehon, and in the House of Delegates by Dr., now Bishop Gadsden. At that time the Bishop and Delegates of New York opposed it. In 1817 it was again brought up in the House of Bishops, and was favourably received.

The Rev. Mr. Trapier.—Bishop Hobart's views, then, were for a diocesan seminary ; Bishop Dehon was for a general one. Bishop Hobart consented finally to this, on condition that it should be located in New York. To this Bishop Dehon agreed, in order to secure his co-operation, and the General Convention, in 1817, adopted the provision. The whole object of the proceeding, however, was to harmonize the Church in the establishment and support of the institution. The efforts to establish it were not at first successful. Such was the report of the Committee to the Convention of 1820. That body recommended its transfer to New Haven, where it did next exist for a short time ; but, before the next General Convention, Mr. Sherred died, and it was ascertained that a considerable sum, say 60,000 dollars, might be secured by removing the seminary to New York. To consider this, the special Convention of 1821 was called, and they changed once more its location to New York.

The Rev. Dr. Van Ingen.—The will did not make the condition that the General Seminary should be removed to New York.

The Rev. Mr. Trapier.—The will was in substance this. Certain moneys were to be invested in stocks at compound interest, until such time as a general or diocesan Theological Seminary should be established within the diocese of New York, and then they should go to the trustees of the said seminary. There was, at the time, a diocesan seminary in New York, and a legal question arose, whether the general seminary, being first mentioned, or the diocesan, being already on the ground, had the first claim. An agreement was, however, arrived at which rendered a legal decision unnecessary. The General Seminary was transferred to New York. And a constitution was adopted which gave, as some thought, quite sufficient control to the diocese of New York. For not only was the institution located there, but the trustees met there, its Bishop called all special meetings, and no professor could be removed except at such special meeting. Such was the history, from which it was manifest that the seminary was not established in and by New York, and given as a boon to the Church, but, having been established, was finally located there to secure co-operation. There were some dioceses that had not as yet a pecuniary interest in it, but they had an equal spiritual interest in it, and it was their duty to do what they could to guide it aright. The South was not opposed to its interests. South Carolina was among its warmest friends until recently. This interest had been for several years declining. Their candidates for orders were, with only an occasional exception, sent elsewhere. Their trustees had ceased to attend the meetings. This change was not limited to South Carolina. In the Augustan age of that institution there were ninety students. Last year there were only forty-eight. Their clergy, meanwhile, had doubled in numbers; their candidates for orders increased. The difficulty arising from the present arrangements, which prevented the attendance of trustees from a distance, was one of the causes of the subsiding interest in the institution. At the last meeting thirty-one trustees present were from the diocese of New York, and only nineteen from elsewhere. This was on no less an occasion than the nomination of trustees. As to South Carolina, she had found herself in such a dead minority that her trustees had ceased to go, and their election was regarded as almost a mere form. He was glad of the concession of the proxy system as far as it had gone. But it did not satisfy him. It did not extend, for example, to the nomination of professors, but only to the election. But none could be elected who had not at a previous meeting been nominated. The proposed resolution was the only adequate remedy. As to what had been said about the injury arising from frequent changes in the government of the seminary, he would say, that either this seminary as a *general* one was impracticable, or these disadvantages must be risked. If the seminary continued as it was, *not*, in fact, a *general* one, the result would be, that, as the Church extended, the interest in it would diminish. If they wished well to this institution, they should adopt some such measure as this. The inconveniences connected with this were better than the greater evils which must exist while things remained as they were. Either let the seminary be in fact what it was in name, or make it in name what it was in fact.

The Rev. Mr. Corbyn, of Mobile, thought that the attendance of a greater number of trustees at a triennial meeting could not be secured by this resolution. Of this board, 156 members resided on the Atlantic coast, and could easily reach New York. But suppose the General Convention were to meet in St. Louis, only sixty-four of that number could come as delegates. The remaining ninety-two must come at an aggregate expense of some 9000 dollars. Was it in accordance with common sense to require this? Again. It would be the death-blow of this institution to have its affairs controlled by a deliberative body. It was the evil under which so many of their literary institutions suffered, to be controlled by legislative bodies who knew nothing of their wants. The number of students was not the question. The seminary might be doing a noble work, if it had only nine instead of ninety students. If it kept up the standard of theological learning, it was doing such a work. And the effect of their interfering with it would be to lay that standard in the dust.

The Rev. Mr. Patterson, of Mississippi, repeated that the seminary was a boon to the Church, and that it was established under a compact, which this resolution would violate. Out of 287,000 dollars the diocese of New York had given all but 58,000 dollars, and had a right to control it. New York had the means to erect a seminary, and she did so, and made it a general seminary, on the condition that she should control it. And no convention could violate this condition without radicalism.

The distant trustees, having institutions of their own, and their interests being naturally engaged for these, did not care for the General Seminary. And ought the majority of the board to be moved about from place to place to meet men who had no interest in the concerns of the institution under their care? In every period when the religious spirit was aroused, there was a tendency to extremes. It was so now. Some were disposed to think well of Rome and her errors,—some went so far into radicalism as to call the illegitimate brood of dissent sister Churches. Neither were men to legislate on the affairs of the Church. They did not represent the mass, who were as much unaffected by these extravagances as the depths of the ocean by the storms which vex the surface. If such men were permitted to meet in the board of trustees, would they be any wiser or less wedded to their peculiar opinions? And was the board to degrade itself, by permitting these strifes to be carried on in the midst of it?

Mr. Dobbin, of Maryland, agreed that the interest of the trustees of all the dioceses should be operative. He thought this secured by the action already had. There were two classes of duties belonging to this institution, teaching and police. The first was by far the most important to the Church, and over this the provision of voting by proxy in the election of professors gave all the trustees their due control. As to the other, interference and change was to be deprecated. Stability was essential, and if it could not be secured they had better give the institution up.

Mr. Williams, of Virginia, thought the distrust in the seminary arose from the fact that it was thought to be under the control of the diocese of New York. But he rose chiefly to remonstrate against what the gentleman had said of the radicalism of those who called the illegitimate brood of dissent sister Churches. If the gentleman had learnt this of his Alma Mater, it might help to account for the general distrust. But when they looked around, and saw God blessing the labours of other Christian bodies, he asked himself, " How shall I curse whom God hath not cursed?" When he found their Church in the preface to her book of Common Prayer, calling them Churches, why should he not do so with perfect consistency? He thought of our Saviour, when told that the disciples had forbid one to cast out devils because he followed not after them, and when He said, " forbid them not." He entered his solemn protest against such language.

After some further discussion, the resolution of amendment requiring that a meeting of the trustees shall be held at the time and place of the General Convention was carried. The vote was taken by dioceses and by orders, with the following result; twenty-nine dioceses were represented by the clergy, of which seventeen voted in the affirmative and ten in the negative, and two were divided; twenty-four dioceses were represented by the laity, of which fifteen were in the affirmative, seven in the negative, and two divided.

FRIDAY, THE 11TH.—The Committee on Canons reported that a section be added to Canon 4 of 1844, providing that, in case a suspended Bishop desire to resign, at any period not within six calendar months before the meeting of any General Convention, he shall make known such desire to the Presiding Bishop, who shall communicate the same to every Bishop in this Church having jurisdiction, and, in case a majority of said Bishops return to the Presiding Bishop their written assent to such resignation, the same shall be valid and final, and the Presiding Bishop shall make known such resignation to the Bishop and diocese concerned, and to each Bishop of this Church.

The Report of the Joint Committee on the Maryland memorial was presented. It recommended the adoption of the canon reported by the Committee on Canons of the House of Deputies, on Episcopal Visitations, somewhat amended, as follows :

"ON EPISCOPAL VISITATIONS.

"Sec. 1. Every Bishop in this Church shall visit the churches within his Diocese, for the purpose of examining the state of his Church, inspecting the behaviour of his Clergy, ministering the Word, and, if he see fit, the Lord's Supper, to the people committed to his charge, and administering the Apostolic Rite of Confirmation. And it is deemed proper that such visitation be made once in three years, at least, by every Bishop to every Church within his Diocese, which shall make provision for defraying the necessary expenses of the Bishop at such visitations. And it is hereby declared to be the duty of the Minister and Vestry of every Church, or Congregation, to make such provision accordingly.

"Sec. 2. But it is to be understood that, to enable the Bishop to make the aforesaid visitation, it shall be the duty of the Clergy, in such reasonable rotation as may be devised, to officiate for him in any parochial duties which may belong to him.

"Sec. 3. It shall be the duty of the Bishop to keep a Register of his proceedings at every visitation of his Diocese.

"Sec. 4. Canon 21 of 1832 is hereby repealed."

The report further stated, that, as no question occasioning difference of opinion remained unadjusted by the canon, they advise, that the canon reported as an amendment to Canon 26 of 1832 be withdrawn. The report was signed by Bishops Brownell, Hopkins, Ives, and Polk, Rev. Dr. Van Ingen, Rev. Mr. Tomes, and Messrs. Chambers and Wharton.

The minority of the committee presented a counter report, recommending the following resolutions :—

"1st. That it is inexpedient at present to legislate upon the subject of the canon proposed by the Committee on Canons.

"2nd. That the committee be discharged from further consideration of the subject."

This was signed by Bishop M'Ilvaine, Rev. Drs. Stevens and Neville, and Mr. Taylor.

. The whole subject was laid on the table, and made a special order for Saturday.

The canon on the journal of the last General Convention, giving to a suspended Bishop the power to resign was taken up, as reported by the Committee on Canons, and on the motion of the Rev. Dr. Mead, adopted. At the suggestion of the delegation from New York, the delegation of any diocese were empowered to have their dissent on this canon entered upon the minutes. The clerical delegation from New York, and the lay delegation from New Jersey, availed themselves of this privilege.

The canon on the last journal, on the certificates of bishops elect, requiring a majority of two-thirds of a diocese to elect a bishop, was indefinitely postponed.

A canon reported by the Committee on Canons, of candidates for orders who have been ministers or licentiates of other religious denominations, was then taken up for consideration. The canon requires such persons to remain candidates at least a year instead of six months as heretofore. The Rev. Dr. Van Ingen moved its adoption. The Rev. Dr. Atkinson opposed it. He thought it well to leave the discretion of the bishops untouched. Judge Chambers showed that the canon relates exclusively to candidates who had been ministers of other denominations, who were now admitted at half the time in which it was possible for those who had been bred in the Church to obtain orders. The question was, should this continue? The Rev. Mr. M'Coy said : " I am situated amid a population of some 40,000 souls, where I am the only minister of the Church. Within the sphere of my knowledge there are several who are, and have been for two or three years past, investigating the claims of our Church. They have studied its peculiarities, and, by the aid of all the helps they can get, are inquiring as to its conformity with Scripture. Now, after a man has spent years in this study, as I did, and is about sundering many ties dear to his heart, and when all the difficulties connected with that severance press upon him, will you compel him to provide for his family for this additional time? Will you throw this increased difficulty in his way ? I think such a course impracticable and injurious. I hope that the discretion heretofore confided in the bishop will be continued. We need a supply of ministers who, in the spirit of our Master, will do the Church's work. There is nothing I desire so much as to have ten such men near me to help me in the work which the Church has assigned me. And, if God is opening the eyes of men in other religious bodies to see the excellence of our Church, I hope we will allow them to come and help us." The canon was lost.

Another canon was reported by the Committee on Canons, of ministers removing from one diocese to another, in substitution of Canon 5 of 1844. This provides by an additional section that every minister removing from one diocese to another shall apply for letters dimissory. If he does not do so within three months, the ecclesiastical authority of the diocese which he has left may send them to the authority of the diocese to which he has removed ; and, if this latter refuse to receive him, he must return to the former diocese.

The Rev. Dr. Van Ingen said this new section was to enable the ecclesiastical authority of a diocese to reach clergymen who now by absenting themselves from their canonical home, and residing in distant dioceses, escaped discipline. Rev. Dr. Vinton.—This canon is not confined to such cases. It covers the whole subject of removals. It touches an original principle. It recognises the right of a bishop to refuse to receive a clergyman who comes to him with letters dimissory, and to send him back to the diocese whence he came. This had never before been conceded to a bishop. Rev. Dr. Jarvis.—It is implied in the canon already existing. Rev. Dr. Vinton.—I want to see the statute which confers it. The Church has no where sanctioned the principle, and will we now introduce it in a covert way? He thought the Church and the Convention were not prepared to assent to it. The Rev. Dr. Jarvis explained a principle of canon law which applied to this matter. A bishop may not ordain a presbyter without a title, that is, without the assurance that some parish will support him. If he does, he is bound to support him. Now he may ordain a man who is inefficient, and a burden on his hands. He may therefore be willing to send him away to trouble some other bishop. This canon is to enable him to protect himself, and it is a just and equitable provision. The discussion was further continued in favour of the canon, upon the ground of the necessity of some such action to meet the cases, such as occurred and might occur, in which clergymen, leaving their own dioceses without taking letters dimissory, and going to reside in distant parts of the country, were practically emancipated from discipline. And on the ground that the separate dioceses, which were distinct and perfect Churches, had not, in coming into the union of this Church, parted with the inherent right which belonged to every bishop to decide whether or not he would admit any minister among the number of his clergy.

It was urged in opposition to it, that it embodied a new principle which was contrary to their past and present legislation, by which they held a bishop bound to receive every minister coming with clean papers, and that it interfered with the rights of the laity to elect and have their own ministers. It was contended that the true remedy for the evils alleged was to provide by law for the trial of clergymen in the place where the crime was committed, and any method of determining what are the rights of a bishop from any source but the laws and canons of the Church was protested against. The discussion was adjourned.

A message was received from the House of Bishops, informing the House that they concurred in passing the canon of episcopal resignations.

The House then took up the order of the day, viz. the canon of Assistant Bishops, reported by the Committee on Canons, which is as follows :—

" OF ASSISTANT BISHOPS.

" SECT. 1. When the Bishop of any Diocese is unable, by reason of any permanent cause, to discharge his episcopal duties, an Assistant Bishop may, with his consent, be elected by, and for such Diocese, who shall in all cases succeed the Bishop, in case of surviving him. The Assistant Bishop shall perform such Episcopal duties, and exercise such Episcopal authority in the Diocese, as the Bishop shall assign to him ; and in case of the Bishop's inability to assign such duties, arising from the suspension of his jurisdiction, or declared by the Convention of the Diocese, the Assistant Bishop shall, during such inability, perform all the duties, and exercise all the authorities which appertain to the office of Bishop. No person shall be elected or consecrated a Suffragan Bishop, nor shall there be more than one Assistant Bishop at the same time.

"Sect. 2. If the Bishop of the Diocese shall be under sentence of suspension at the time at which it is proposed to elect an Assistant Bishop, he shall, notwithstanding such suspension, be competent to give his assent to the election of an Assistant Bishop.

"Sect. 3. Canon 6 of 1832 is hereby repealed."

Mr. Yerger, of Mississippi, proposed a substitute, providing that a sentence of suspension which has been, or may hereafter be, inflicted on a Bishop, shall be among the reasons for appointing an Assistant Bishop,—that where a Bishop is suspended, or shall be declared by his Convention incapable, the services of the Assistant shall not be under his direction, and in such case his assent shall not be necessary to the election. He referred to the case of the Diocese of New York, and her application for relief. He thought the Committee's canon would not give her the relief she required, because it did not specify suspension as a reason for electing an Assistant Bishop. But more than this, because it made the consent of the Bishop necessary even when he had been suspended. This principle he maintained to be contrary to the established law of the Church for twenty years back. And he thought that, although the proposed principle was sustained by the practice of the primitive Church, they were bound in a case like this, which involved nothing higher than human regulations, to follow the laws of their own Church. He thought, too, that it would be difficult, and in some cases impossible, to obtain the consent of a Bishop. He concluded by a touching appeal to the friends of the Bishop of New York, to acquiesce in some such arrangement as this.

Eventually the subject was recommitted to the Committee on Canons, with instructions to report a canon authorizing a diocese having a suspended bishop to elect an assistant bishop.

SATURDAY, THE 12TH.—The Committee on Canons reported a canon of the trial of Bishops, the same as that on the journal of the last Convention, with a few verbal alterations. They also reported, in pursuance with the instructions of the house, the following Canon of the election of an assistant Bishop by a diocese whose Bishop is indefinitely suspended. A diocese deprived of the services of its Bishop by a sentence of suspension heretofore pronounced, and not limited to a precise time, may proceed to the election of an assistant Bishop,

who, when duly consecrated, shall exercise all the powers and authority of the Bishop of the diocese during the suspension of the Bishop,
and who, in case of the remission of the sentence of the Bishop, and
his restoration to the exercise of his jurisdiction, shall perform the
duties prescribed by Canon 6 of 1832, and who in all cases shall
succeed to the Bishop, on his death or resignation. The Rev. Dr.
Higbee, in behalf of the delegation from New York, called for the vote
by dioceses and orders. The vote was then taken, and resulted as
follows :—Of the clergy twenty-seven dioceses voted aye, and one
(that of New York) in the negative. So the canon was adopted.

An amendment to the canon on appeals before offered, providing
that, in all questions of doctrine, a majority of the Bishops on the
Appellate Court shall be necessary to a decision, was referred to the
Committee on Canons.

On the order of the day on the reports of the majority and minority
of the Joint Committee on the Maryland memorial, the Rev. Dr.
Vinton moved that the report be recommitted, with instructions to report that it is inexpedient to legislate at this time, except in the way
of appointing an appellate tribunal.

Judge Chambers thought they were bound, by every consideration,
to act on the canon. Three years ago a proposition had been introduced, having reference to this subject, which was referred to the
Committee on Canons, who reported it as a matter proper for the action
of this Convention, to which it was referred. In consequence of this
delay, the subject became again a matter of discussion in Maryland.
And now they were asked to set aside the proposed action altogether,
for the reason that it may at some future day be determined by some
other body, or some judicial tribunal to be hereafter established. The
question of the propriety of such a court was one which should be
considered by itself, when the Church was absolutely unruffled by the
slightest breath of any exciting or personal question. This Convention
was not now prepared to act on it.

The Rev. Dr. Vinton said, by adopting the idea of an appellate
court, they should not be legislating for a special case, but on the broad
basis of general principles. They might with propriety defer the present
proposed action, since the attention of both Houses was turned to
the other question.

Mr. Newton of Massachusetts observed, that it was stated in the
report of the minority, "that it is not expedient to invest the Bishops
of this Church with the right of administering the Lord's Supper upon
occasions of canonical visitation." That had been placed on the record.
And, if they postponed the consideration of this subject, they would
affirm that proposition. And were they who believed in the apostolic
authority of the office of a Bishop going to affirm such a proposition as
this ? It would be a disgrace to the Church to do so.

Mr. Pendleton, of Ohio, did not think that the postponement would
affirm that proposition, but rather the contrary. It merely amounted to
a declaration that it was inexpedient at this time for the Convention to

act upon the subject. And he thought it was so. They could not legislate upon it without altering the rubrics. And he protested against that. He could not imagine any contingency that could exist to induce him to lay hands on the Prayer Book. The Constitution had thrown its safeguards around it. And with extreme solicitude it guarded the approach to any change in it. He would not discuss the question whether there be a conflict between this proposed canon and the rubric. But they would see the fitness of that article of the Constitution which regulates the whole matter of altering the Prayer Book. It was the arms of the Church thrown around that depository of her conservatism. This was the first case where such a collision had sprung up. And he could not agree that they were to meet it by altering the order of the Constitution.

After a lengthened discussion, the vote upon the motion indefinitely to postpone the whole subject of the Maryland memorial was taken by orders and dioceses, and the question decided in the negative.

MONDAY, THE 14TH.—A report of the Committee on Canons recommended the postponement, until the next General Convention, of the proposed amendment of the Constitution, requiring delegates to be communicants; of the canon of ministers officiating within the parochial cures of other clergymen ; and of the canon of appeals.

The report also recommended the adoption of the canon transmitted by the House of Bishops, making it the duty of the presiding Bishop to call a meeting of the House of Bishops within a period, not less than three, nor more than six, months from the time of his being requested so to do.

The Committee having reported that it is inexpedient to amend the Constitution, by striking out that clause of article 5th (the third), which requires 8000 square miles and thirty presbyters in each division of any existing diocese, before such division can be made, a discussion ensued, and eventually the subject was referred back to the Committee on Canons, with instructions to report a resolution recommending such an alteration of the Constitution.

Two messages were received from the House of Bishops.

The first informed the House that they had passed a canon, " of clergymen canonically resident in one diocese, chargeable with misdemeanors in another." The first section provides that, if a clergyman canonically resident in one diocese be chargeable with misdemeanor in another, the ecclesiastical authority of the latter shall inform that of the former. If this diocese do not act upon the information in three months, then the ecclesiastical authority of the diocese where the offence was committed may have him tried, as if under its jurisdiction. The second section provides, that if a clergyman who has come temporarily into a diocese, and not with intention to reside, be chargeable with any crime or misdemeanor, the ecclesiastical authority of the diocese, if satisfied thereof, may prohibit his ministering within its bounds ; of which prohibition due notice shall be given to the ecclesiastical authority of the diocese to which he belongs, and to the minister of every parish of the diocese in which the prohibition has been made. And this prohibition shall continue until the ecclesiastical authority which has inflicted it remove it. This was referred to the Committee on Canons.

The other message informed the House that the House of Bishops had resolved, this House concurring, that the Convention should adjourn *sine die*, on Wednesday, Oct. 16, which was agreed to.

The debate on the Maryland memorial was again resumed, and continued till the adjournment of the House.

During the discussion several messages were received from the House of Bishops :—

1. Transmitting a canon just passed by them on the removal of Ministers from one diocese to another.

2. Informing the House that they had amended and passed the canon of the election of assistant Bishops, passed by the House. The amendment consisted in striking out the word "*assistant*" in the title and body of the canon wherever it occurs, save in the last instance.

3. Informing the House that they concurred in the proposed alterations of the constitution of the General Theological Seminary, with the amendment, that, when a *vacancy* existed in the diocese of New York, the Bishops might call special meetings.

TUESDAY, THE 15TH.—The greater part of the day was again consumed by the debate on the Maryland memorial, and terminated in a vote giving the Bishop the right to administer the Communion during his visitation, which was carried by a large majority of both orders.

The House also determined to employ the New York Bible and Prayer Book Society to publish a standard edition of the Bible.

WEDNESDAY, THE 16TH.—The House was informed that Bishop Southgate's resignation of the mission to Constantinople had been accepted by the House of Bishops.

The canon on *Foreign Missionary Bishops* was, with the concurrence of the House of Bishops, amended, making them eligible to Diocesan Bishoprics by permission of *three-fourths* of the House of Bishops, and *three-fourths* of the House of Clerical and Lay Deputies or Standing Committee.

The canon relative to the election of a Provisional Bishop in a diocese whose Bishop is indefinitely suspended, as amended by the House of Bishops, passed by the following vote—Clergy, ayes, 26; noes 1. (New York.)—Laity, ayes, 20; noes 1. (New Jersey.)

The remaining business being disposed of, and the Bishops having entered the House, the whole Convention united in prayer, and adjourned.

The following proceedings are stated to have taken place in the House of Bishops, of whose deliberations there are no regular reports published. On the question touching the Maryland memorial, the Bishop of Virginia offered a resolution, "that it is inexpedient to take any legislative action on the subject referred to in these memorials," which obtained only three or four supporters, and was accordingly rejected. The Bishop of Pennsylvania then moved, "that further action on the subject, by the House, at this time, is not advisable." This was supported by twelve votes,—those of the Bishops of Illinois, Connecticut, Virginia, Kentucky, Ohio, Louisiana, Georgia, Delaware, Massachusetts, Pennsylvania, and Maine, and the Assistant Bishop of Virginia. The matter finally terminated by the adoption of the canon "on Episcopal Visitations" before reported, which passed by a vote of 17 to 10.

The Bishop of Western New York presented a series of resolutions, with a view to the institution of Provinces and Provincial Conventions, intermediate between the General and Diocesan Conventions.

On the motion of the Bishop of Pennsylvania, and with no dissenting voice but that of the Bishop of Kentucky, a committee was appointed to report, in 1853, whether some plan cannot be devised by which, consistently with the principles of our reformed faith, the services of intelligent and pious persons of both sexes may be secured in the education of the young, the relief of the sick and destitute, the care of orphans and friendless immigrants, and the reformation of the vicious. The committee is composed of the Bishops of Connecticut, Rhode Island, New Jersey, New Hampshire, and Pennsylvania.

The Rev. John Payne was elected missionary Bishop for Western Africa.

The House of Bishops have refused to remit the sentence of Bishop B. T. Onderdonk, of New York, and have rejected the petition of the diocese by a majority of about 2 to 1. They have also refused to restore Bishop H. U. Onderdonk, of Pennsylvania, by a vote of 17 to 9.

At the close of its Report the *New York Churchman* observes:—"We are happy to learn from various independent sources that the meeting was conducted with great dignity, suavity, and harmony on the whole, considering the great diversity of views existing among the members, and that the impressions produced upon those who witnessed it cannot but be favourable."

Special Convention of the Diocese of New York.—As soon as the decision of the General Convention had been duly notified to the Standing Committee of the diocese of New York, a notice was issued by that body, convening a Special Convention for Wednesday, the 27th of November, "To take into consideration the Canon passed in the late General Convention, entitled, ' Of the election of a Provisional Bishop in the case of a diocese whose Bishop is suspended, without a precise limitation of time ;' and to proceed to the election of a Provisional Bishop under the said Canon, should the Convention so determine."

On the Convention being assembled accordingly, a motion was proposed by the Hon. J. C. Spencer, to the effect: " That, as doubts were entertained of the power of the Standing Committee to call a Special Convention, this Convention will not proceed to any business."

On the question being put, the votes stood: Clergy, ayes, 17; noes, 94. Laity, ayes, 18; noes, 109.

The motion was therefore lost, and the election made the order of the day for the following day. On Thursday, after morning prayers, the business of the election was proceeded with. Seven ballots were had in succession, on Thursday and Friday, but without effect. In the first ballot Dr. Seabury had a majority both of Clerical and Lay votes, the names next to his being those of Dr. Whitehouse and Dr. Williams; but, Dr. Seabury's votes not amounting to a clear majority (above one-half of all the votes) of either order, there was no election. On the second ballot, Dr. Whitehouse having withdrawn his name, Dr. Williams had a majority in both orders, but not a clear majority of clerical votes. On the third ballot, Dr. Seabury's name having been withdrawn, and that of Bishop Southgate substituted, Bishop Southgate had a clear majority of clerical, and Dr. Williams a clear majority of lay votes, so that by reason of non-concurrence there was no election. The same result attended the fourth and fifth ballots. On Friday, Bishop Southgate having been withdrawn, and Dr. Creighton substituted, after a long conference between the two parties, two more ballots were taken, on both of which Dr. Creighton had the majority of the clerical, and Dr. Williams of the lay votes. After the seventh ballot it was acknowledged that an election was impossible, and a motion for adjournment, *sine die*, was proposed and carried by a majority of 119 clergy, and 103 laity, against 45 clergy, and 50 laity.

While the business of balloting was in progress, a motion was made, and after much discussion, and several unsuccessful amendments, carried, for the payment to the provisional bishop to be elected of the surplus of the Episcopal Fund over and above the 2500 dollars paid annually to Bishop Onderdonk.

An attempt to revive the claim of the coloured congregation of St. Philip's for admission into the Union was likewise unsuccessful.

INDEX

OF THE

REMARKABLE PASSAGES IN THE CRITICISMS, EXTRACTS, NOTICES, AND INTELLIGENCE.